Literature Criticism from 1400 to 1800

Guide to Gale Literary Criticism Series

For criticism on	Consult these Gale series
Authors now living or who died after December 31, 1959	*CONTEMPORARY LITERARY CRITICISM (CLC)*
Authors who died between 1900 and 1959	*TWENTIETH-CENTURY LITERARY CRITICISM (TCLC)*
Authors who died between 1800 and 1899	*NINETEENTH-CENTURY LITERATURE CRITICISM (NCLC)*
Authors who died between 1400 and 1799	*LITERATURE CRITICISM FROM 1400 TO 1800 (LC)* *SHAKESPEAREAN CRITICISM (SC)*
Authors who died before 1400	*CLASSICAL AND MEDIEVAL LITERATURE CRITICISM (CMLC)*
Black writers of the past two hundred years	*BLACK LITERATURE CRITICISM (BLC)*
Authors of books for children and young adults	*CHILDREN'S LITERATURE REVIEW (CLR)*
Dramatists	*DRAMA CRITICISM (DC)*
Hispanic writers of the late nineteenth and twentieth centuries	*HISPANIC LITERATURE CRITICISM (HLC)*
Native North American writers and orators of the eighteenth, nineteenth, and twentieth centuries	*NATIVE NORTH AMERICAN LITERATURE (NNAL)*
Poets	*POETRY CRITICISM (PC)*
Short story writers	*SHORT STORY CRITICISM (SSC)*
Major authors from the Renaissance to the present	*WORLD LITERATURE CRITICISM, 1500 TO THE PRESENT (WLC)*

ISSN 0740-2880

Volume 30

Literature Criticism from 1400 to 1800

Criticism of the Works
of Fifteenth, Sixteenth, Seventeenth, and
Eighteenth-Century Novelists, Poets, Playwrights,
Philosophers, and Other Creative Writers.

Jennifer Allison Brostrom, Editor

Dana Ramel Barnes
Jelena O. Krstović
Mary L. Onorato
Associate Editors

An ITP Information/Reference Group Company

Changing the Way the World Learns

NEW YORK • LONDON • BONN • BOSTON • DETROIT
MADRID • MELBOURNE • MEXICO CITY • PARIS
SINGAPORE • TOKYO • TORONTO • WASHINGTON
ALBANY NY • BELMONT CA • CINCINNATI OH

STAFF

Jennifer Allison Brostrom, *Editor*

Dana Ramel Barnes, Jelena O. Krstović, Mary L. Onorato, *Associate Editors*

Matthew C. Altman, Gerald R. Barterian, Ondine Le Blanc, *Assistant Editors*

Susan M. Trosky, *Managing Editor*

Marlene S. Hurst, *Permissions Manager*
Margaret A. Chamberlain, Maria Franklin, *Permissions Specialists*
Susan Brohman, Diane Cooper, Michele Lonoconus, Maureen Pul, Shalice Shah,
Kimberly F. Smilay, Barbara A. Wallace, *Permissions Associates*
Sarah Chesney, Edna M. Hedblad, Margaret McAvoy-Amato, Tyra Y. Phillips,
Lori Schoenenberger, Rita Velázquez, *Permissions Assistants*

Victoria B. Cariappa, *Research Manager*
Maria Bryson, Tammy Nott, Amy Steel, Tracie A. Richardson, *Research Associates*
Julia C. Daniel, Amy Beth Wieczorek, *Research Assistants*

Mary Beth Trimper, *Production Director*
Deborah Milliken, *Production Assistant*

Erin Martin, *Desktop Publisher*
Pamela A. Hayes, *Photography Coordinator*
Randy Bassett, *Image Database Supervisor*

™
∞ This book is printed on acid-free paper that meets the minimum requirements of American National Standard for Information Sciences—Permanence Paper for Printed Library Materials, ANSI Z39.48-1984.

Library of Congress Catalog Card Number 94-29718
ISBN 0-8103-9275-5
ISSN 0740-2880
Printed in the United States of America
Published simultaneously in the United Kingdom
by Gale Research International Limited
(An affiliated company of Gale Research)

I(T)P™   Gale Research, an International Thomson Publishing Company.
ITP logo is a trademark under license.

10 9 8 7 6 5 4 3 2 1

Contents

Preface   vii

Acknowledgments   xi

Preface

L iterature Criticism from 1400 to 1800 (LC) presents criticism of world authors of the fifteenth through eighteenth centuries. The literature of this period reflects a turbulent time of radical change that saw the rise of modern European drama, the birth of the novel and personal essay forms, the emergence of newspapers and periodicals, and major achievements in poetry and philosophy. Many of these historical forces continue to influence modern art and society. *LC,* therefore, provides valuable insight into the art, life, thought, and cultural transformations that took place during these centuries.

Scope of the Series

LC provides an introduction to the great poets, dramatists, novelists, essayists, and philosophers of the fifteenth through eighteenth centuries; and to the most significant interpretations of these authors' works. Because criticism of this literature spans nearly six hundred years, an overwhelming amount of scholarship confronts the student. *LC* therefore organizes this material into volumes addressing specific historical and cultural topics, for example, "Literature of the Spanish Golden Age," or "Literature and the New World." Every attempt is made to reprint the most noteworthy, relevant, and educationally valuable essays available.

Readers should note that there is a separate Gale reference series devoted exclusively to Shakespearean studies. Although belonging properly to the period covered in *LC,* William Shakespeare has inspired such a tremendous and ever-growing corpus of secondary material that the editors have deemed it best to give his works extensive coverage in a separate series, *Shakespearean Criticism.*

Each author entry in *LC* presents a survey of critical response to an author's oeuvre. Early criticism is offered to indicate initial responses, later selections document any rise or decline in literary reputations, and retrospective analyses provide students with modern views. The size of each author entry is a relative reflection of the scope of criticism available in English. Every attempt has been made to identify and include the seminal essays on each author's work and to include recent commentary providing modern perspectives.

The need for *LC* among students and teachers of literature and history was suggested by the proven usefulness of Gale's *Contemporary Literary Criticism (CLC), Twentieth-Century Literary Criticism (TCLC),* and *Nineteenth-Century Literature Criticism (NCLC),* which excerpt criticism of works by nineteenth- and twentieth-century authors. There is no duplication of critical material in any of these literary criticism series. Major authors may appear more than once in one or more of the series because of the great quantity of critical material available, and his or her relevance to a variety of thematic topics.

Thematic Approach

Beginning with Volume 12, all the authors in each volume of *LC* are organized around such themes as specific literary or philosophical movements, writings surrounding important political and historical events, the philosophy and art associated with eras of cultural transformation, and the literature of specific social or ethnic groups. Each volume contains a topic entry providing a historical and literary overview, and several author entries, which examine major representatives of the featured period.

Organization of the Book

Each entry consists of the following elements: author or thematic heading, introduction, list of principal works, annotated works of criticism (each preceded by a bibliographical citation), and a bibliography of further reading. Also, most author entries contain author portraits and other illustrations.

- The **Author Heading** consists of the author's full name, followed by birth and death dates. (If an author wrote consistently under a pseudonym, the pseudonym is used in the author heading, with the real name given in parentheses on the first line of the biographical and critical introduction.) Also located here are any name variations under which an author wrote, including transliterated forms for authors whose native languages use nonroman alphabets. Uncertain birth or death dates are indicated by question marks. Topic entries are preceded by a **Thematic Heading,** which simply states the subject of the entry.

- The **Introduction** to each entry provides social and historical background important to understanding the criticism, and an overview of the biography and career of the featured author.

- Most *LC* author entries include **Portraits** of the author. Many entries also contain illustrations of materials pertinent to an author's career, including author holographs, title pages, letters, or representations of important people, places, and events in an author's life.

- The **List of Principal Works** is ordered chronologically, by date of first book publication, identifying the genre of each work. In the case of foreign authors whose works have been translated into English, the title and date of the first English-language edition are given in brackets beneath the foreign-language listing. Unless otherwise indicated, dramas are dated by first performance, not first publication.

- **Criticism** is arranged chronologically in each author entry to provide a useful perspective on changes in critical evaluation over time. For the purpose of easy identification, the critic's name and the date of first composition or publication of the critical work are given at the beginning of each piece of criticism. Unsigned criticism is preceded by the title of the source in which it appeared. All titles by the author featured in the critical entry are printed in boldface type. Publication information (such as publisher names and book prices) and some parenthetical numerical references (such as footnotes or page and line references to specific editions of works) have been occasionally deleted to provide smoother reading of the text.

- Critical essays are prefaced by **Annotations** as an additional aid to students using *LC*. These explanatory notes may provide several types of useful information, including: the reputation of a critic, the importance of a work of criticism, the commentator's individual approach to literary criticism, the intent of the criticism, and the growth of critical controversy or changes in critical trends regarding an author's work. In some cases, these notes cross-reference the work of critics within the entry who agree or disagree with each other.

- A complete **Bibliographical Citation** of the original essay or book follows each piece of criticism.

- An annotated bibliography of **Further Reading** appears at the end of each entry and suggests resources for additional study. In some cases, significant essays for which the editors could not obtain reprint rights are included here.

Cumulative Indexes

Each volume of *LC* includes a cumulative **Author Index** listing all the authors that have appeared in the following sources published by Gale: *Contemporary Literary Criticism, Twentieth-Century Literary Criticism, Nineteenth-Century Literature Criticism, Literature Criticism from 1400 to 1800, and Classical and Medieval Literature Criticism,* along with cross-references to the Gale series *Short Story Criticism, Poetry Criticism, Children's Literature Review, Authors in the News, Contemporary Authors, Contemporary Authors Autobiography Series, Contemporary Authors Bibliographical Series, Dictionary of Literary Biography, Concise Dictionary of Literary Biography, Something about the Author, Something about the Author Autobiography Series, and Yesterday's Authors of Books for Children.* Readers will welcome this cumulative author index as a useful tool for locating an author within the various series. The index, which includes authors' birth and death dates, is particularly valuable for those authors who are identified with a certain period but whose death dates cause them to be placed in another, or for those authors whose careers span two periods. For example, F. Scott Fitzgerald is found in *TCLC,* yet a writer often associated with him, Ernest Hemingway, is found in *CLC.*

Beginning with Volume 12, *LC* includes a cumulative **Topic Index** that lists all literary themes and topics treated in *LC, NCLC, TCLC,* and the *CLC* Yearbook. Each volume of *LC* also includes a cumulative **Nationality Index** in which authors' names are arranged alphabetically under their respective nationalities and followed by the numbers of the volumes in which they appear.

Each volume of *LC* also includes a cumulative **Title Index,** an alphabetical listing of all literary works discussed in the series. Each title listing includes the corresponding volume and page numbers where criticism may be located. Foreign-language titles that have been translated followed by the tiles of the translation — for example, *El ingenioso hidalgo Don Quixote de la Mancha (Don Quixote).* Page numbers following these translated titles refers to all pages on which any form of the titles, either foreign-language or translated, appear. Title of novels, dramas, nonfiction books, and poetry, short story, or essays collections are printed in italics, while individual poems, short stories, and essays are printed in roman type within quotation marks.

A Note to the Reader

When writing papers, students who quote directly from any volume in the Literary Criticism Series may use the following general forms to footnote reprinted criticism. The first example pertains to material drawn from periodicals, the second to material reprinted from books.

T. S. Eliot, "John Donne," *The Nation and the Athenaeum,* 33 (9 June 1923), 321-32; excerpted and reprinted in *Literature Criticism from 1400 to 1800,* Vol. 10, ed. James E. Person, Jr. (Detroit: Gale Research, 1989), pp. 28-9.

Clara G. Stillman, *Samuel Butler: A Mid-Victorian Modern* (Viking Press, 1932); excerpted and reprinted in *Twentieth-Century Literary Criticism,* Vol. 33, ed. Paula Kepos (Detroit: Gale Research, 1989), pp. 43-5.

Suggestions Are Welcome

Since the series began, features have been added to *LC* in response to various suggestions, including a nationality index, a Literary Criticism Series topic index, and thematic organization of entries.

Readers who wish to suggest new features, themes or authors to appear in future volumes, or who have other suggestions, are cordially invited to write to the editor.

Acknowledgments

The editors wish to thank the copyright holders of the excerpted criticism included in this volume and the permissions managers of many book and magazine publishing companies for assisting us in securing reprint rights. We are also grateful to the staffs of the Detroit Public Library, the Library of Congress, the University of Detroit Library, Wayne State University Purdy/Kresge Library Complex, and the University of Michigan Libraries for making their resources available to us. Following is a list of the copyright holders who have granted us permission to reprint material in this volume of *LC*. Every effort has been made to trace copyright, but if omissions have been made, please let us know.

COPYRIGHTED EXCERPTS IN *LC*, VOLUME 30, WERE REPRINTED FROM THE FOLLOWING PERIODICALS:

Criticism, v. XXXV, Summer, 1993 for "Writing in Service: Sexual Politics and Class Position in the Poetry of Aemilia Lanyer and Ben Jonson" by Ann Baynes Coiro. Copyright, 1993, Wayne State University Press. Reprinted by permission of the publisher and the author.—*Early American Literature,* v. XVI, Spring, 1981 for "No Rhet'ric We Expect: Argumentation in Bradstreet's 'The Prologue'," by Jane Donahue Eberwein; v. XXIII, 1988 for "Gender, Genre, and Subjectivity in Anne Bradstreet's Early Elegies" by Timothy Sweet; v. XXIII, 1988 for "'To Finish What's Begun': Anne Bradstreet's Last Words" by Paula Kopacz; v. XXIV, 1989 for "'Then Have I . . . Said with David': Anne Bradstreet's Andover Manuscript Poems and the Influence of the Psalm Tradition" by Beth M. Doriani. Copyrighted, 1981, 1988, 1989 by the University of Massachusetts. All reprinted by permission of the publisher and the respective authors.—*English Literary Renaissance,* v. 14, Autumn, 1984; v. 19, Spring, 1989. Copyright © 1984, 1989 by English Literary Renaissance. Both reprinted by permission of the publisher.—*English Studies in Canada,* v. XV, March, 1989 for "'A Sydney, though un-named': Lady Mary Wroth and her Poetical Progenitors" by Janet H. MacArthur. Copyright © Association of Canadian University Teachers of English 1989. Reprinted by permission of the publisher and the author.—*Essays in Literature,* v. IV, Fall, 1977; v. XIV, Spring, 1987. Copyright © 1977, 1987 by Western Illinois University. Both reprinted by permission of the publisher.—*The Huntington Library Quarterly,* v. 47, Autumn, 1984; v. 56, Summer, 1993. Copyright © 1984, 1993 by The Henry E. Huntington Library and Art Gallery, San Marino, CA 91108. Both adapted by permission of The Henry E. Huntington Library.—*International Journal of Women's Studies,* v. 3, March/April, 1980 for "Female Writing Beside the Rhetorical Tradition: Seventeenth Century British Biography and a Female Tradition in Rhetoric" by Patricia A. Sullivan. Copyright © Eden Press, 1980. Reprinted by permission of the author.—*Modern Language Studies,* v. XXI, Fall, 1991 for "A New Woman of Romance" by Anne Shaver. Copyright, Northeast Modern Language Association, 1991. Reprinted by permission of the publisher and the author.—*The New England Quarterly,* v. XLIII, March, 1970 for "Anne Bradstreet's 'Contemplations': Patterns of Form and Meaning" by Alfred H. Rosenfeld. Copyright 1970 by The New England Quarterly. Reprinted by permission of the publisher and the author.—*Restoration: Studies in English Literary Culture, 1660-1700,* v. 14, Spring, 1990 for "Excusing the Breach of Nature's Laws: The Discourse of Denial and Disguise in Katherine Philips' Friendship Poetry" by Celia A. Easton. Copyright © 1990 The University of Tennessee, Knoxville. Reprinted by permission of the publisher and the author.—*Signs,* v. 15, Autumn, 1989. © 1989 by The University of Chicago. All rights reserved. Reprinted by permission of the publisher.—*South Atlantic Review,* v. 56, May, 1991. Copyright © 1991 by the South Atlantic Modern Language Association. Reprinted by permission of the publisher.—*Studies in English Literature,* v. 29, Winter, 1989 for "'Not much to be marked': Narrative of the Woman's Part in Lady Mary Wroth's 'Urania'," by Naomi J. Miller. © 1989 William Marsh Rice University. Reprinted by permission of the publisher and the author.—*Tulsa Studies in Women's Literature,* v. 11, Fall, 1992. © 1992, The University of Tulsa. Reprinted by permission of the publisher.—*Women's Studies: An Interdisciplinary Journal,* v. 7, 1980; v. 15, 1988. Copyright © 1980, 1988 Gordon and Breach Science Publishers. Reprinted by permission of the publisher.

COPYRIGHTED EXCERPTS IN *LC*, VOLUME 30, WERE REPRINTED FROM THE FOLLOWING BOOKS:

Blaydes, Sophia B. From *Man, God, and Nature in the Enlightenment*. Donald C. Mell, Jr., Theodore E. D. Braun, and Lucia M. Palmer, eds. Colleagues Press, 1988. Copyright © 1988 by Colleagues Press Inc. All rights reserved. Reprinted by permission of the publisher.—Caldwell, Patricia. From *An Annual of American Cultural Studies*. Edited

the author.—Smith, Sidonie. From *A Poetics of Women's Autobiography: Marginality and the Fictions of Self-Representation*. Indiana University Press, 1987. © 1987 by Sidonie Smith. All rights reserved. Reprinted by permission of the publisher.—Spencer, Jane. From *The Rise of the Woman Novelist from Aphra Behn to Jane Austen*. Basil Blackwell, 1986. Copyright © Jane Spencer, 1986. All rights reserved. Reprinted by permission of Basil Blackwell Limited.—Waller, Gary. From *The Sidney Family Romance: Mary Wroth, William Herbert, and the Early Modern Construction of Gender*. Wayne State University Press, 1993. Copyright © 1993 by Wayne State University Press, Detroit, Michigan 48202. All rights reserved. Reprinted by permission of the publisher and the author.—Wilson, Katharina M. and Frank J. Warnke. From *Women Writers of the Seventeenth Century*. Edited by Katharina M. Wilson and Frank J. Warnke. The University of Georgia Press, 1989. © 1989 by The University of Georgia Press, Athens, Georgia 30602. All rights reserved. Reprinted by permission of the publisher.—Wilson, Rob. From *American Sublime: The Genealogy of a Poetic Genre*. The University of Wisconsin Press, 1991. Copyright © 1991 The Board of Regents of the University of Wisconsin System. All rights reserved. Reprinted by permission of the publisher.—Woolf, Virginia. From *A Room of One's Own*. Harcourt, Brace and Company, 1929. Hogarth Press, 1929. Copyright 1929 by Harcourt, Brace and Company. Renewed 1957 by Leonard Woolf. Reprinted by permission of The Hogarth Press Ltd. In the U. S. by Harcourt Brace & Company.

PHOTOGRAPHS AND ILLUSTRATIONS APPEARING IN *LC*, VOLUME 30, WERE RECEIVED FROM THE FOLLOWING SOURCES:

Sutherland Collection, Ashmolean Museum, Oxford: **p. 156;** The British Library, 022445, Frontispiece of The World's Olio, 1671 edition, engraved by Abraham van Diepenbeke: **p. 210;** Viscount de L'Isle, Penshurst Place, Tonbridge, Kent, from his private collection: **p. 329.**

Women Writers of the Seventeenth Century

The following entry provides historical and critical commentary on English-language women's writing and feminist thought during the seventeenth century.

INTRODUCTION

Seventeenth-century England witnessed a surge in literary activity by women, despite the restrictive gender roles of the time. Unlike women's literature of the middle ages and renaissance, which is predominantly devotional, seventeenth-century writings by women treat a variety of secular subjects through such forms as drama, fiction, and autobiography. Modern feminist thought also finds its roots in seventeenth-century polemical writings and activities by women, many of which have only recently received significant scholarly attention.

The English Civil Wars contributed to the expansion of women's roles in many areas, including an increase of publishing activity; and many women began to perceive themselves for the first time as part of a larger social group, inherently equal to men, but subjected to discrimination that restricted their opportunities. Modern feminism stems from this philosophy, which was a significant departure from the traditional conception of women as isolated individuals whose fates were predetermined solely by their biological status as the "weaker sex." Critics view the seventeenth century as a time of increasing, although highly ambiguous, female social awareness. The exclusion of women from universities and academic societies, for example, was regarded by early feminists as an instrument of social repression, but protests most often hinged on the argument that equal education for women would enhance their abilities as wives and mothers, rather than as scholars or professionals. Restricted access to education undoubtedly thwarted the potential achievements of women writers, since the seventeenth-century education of girls focused largely on domestic skills in the service of religion, wifehood, and motherhood, rather than development of intellectual and artistic abilities. It was quite common, for example, for women to be taught to read the Bible, but not to write. In rare instances, girls received a more extensive private education from friends or relatives, but this was the exception.

In addition to barriers to education, women writers encountered the obstacle of public condemnation of their efforts. Only certain nonthreatening literary forms were considered socially appropriate for women, such as polite and pious verse, or translations, which were generally viewed as far removed from the "serious" literature dominated by men. Women who addressed original themes with an original voice risked being labelled as immoral, or even insane. Seventeenth-century women nevertheless played a significant role in the evolution of each of the literary genres. They contributed in particular to the development of the novel, partly because the relative newness of prose fiction meant that there were few rigid rules concerning form, allowing many literate women to attempt works with little or no artistic training. Domestic subjects, however, were not yet considered valid material for fiction, which posed a difficulty for women who were excluded from the types of experiences necessary to handle such popular forms as the picaresque novel or guild tale. The pastoral romance, therefore, became the chosen form of many early women writers of fiction, such as Mary Wroth. Biography was another viable and socially legitimate genre for women, with the most common biographies by women being records of their husband's lives or chronicles of family histories. Critics have observed that many of these biographical and autobiographical writings are characterized by a lack of realism associated with the restricted treatment of domestic subjects—in some cases, events that dominated the lives of authors, such as childbirth and motherhood, are given only brief, superficial references. Seventeenth-century women also made notable contributions to drama. Aphra Behn, for example, shocked some audiences with her candid treatment of arranged marriages and adulterous relationships in several successful plays. Generally viewed with more tolerance than fiction writers or dramatists, women poets expanded popular poetic forms and techniques to accommodate a feminine perspective. Mary Wroth, for example, transformed the traditional Petrarchan conceit of woman as love object into an expression of a woman's love for a man in her sonnet sequence *Pamphilia to Amphilanthus,* while Aemilia Lanyer created a feminine recasting of Christ's Passion in *Salve deus rex judaeorum.*

REPRESENTATIVE WORKS

Barker, Jane
    Poetical Recreations 1688
Behn, Aphra
    The Amorous Prince 1671
    The Forc'd Marriage 1671
    The Dutch Lover 1673
    Abdelazar 1677
    Poems upon several occasions 1684
    Oronooko 1688
    The Histories and Novels of Aphra Behn 1696
Bradstreet, Anne
    Several Poems by a Gentlewoman in New England 1678

Cary, Lady Elizabeth
    The Tragedie of Mariam, the Faire Queene of
        Jewry 1613
Killigrew, Anne
    Poems 1686
Lanyer, Aemilia
    Salve deus rex Iudaeorum. Containing, the
        passion of Christ 1611
Newcastle, Margaret Cavendish, Duchess of
    Philosophicall Fancies 1653
    The Worlds Olio 1655
    Description of a New World 1666
    Observations Upon Experimental
        Philosophy 1666
    The Life of William Cavendishe 1667
    Grounds of Natural Philosophy 1668
    Plays, Never Before Printed 1668
Pembroke, Mary Sidney, Countess of
    A Poetical Rapsody (contributor) 1602
    Six Excellent Treatises of Life and Death
        (translator) 1607
Philips, Katherine
    Poems 1664
Poole, Elizabeth
    A Prophecie Touching the Death of King Charles
        1649
Rowe, Elizabeth Singer
    Poems on Several Occasions 1696
Speght, Rachel
    Mortalities Memorandum, with a Dreame
        Prefixed 1621
Weamys, Anna
    A Continuation of Sir Philip Sydney's Arcadia
        1651
Wells, Mary
    A Divine Poem 1684
Wroth, Lady Mary
    The Countesse of Mountgomeries Urania 1621

OVERVIEW

B. G. MacCarthy (essay date 1944)

SOURCE: "Cogent Influences," in *Women Writers: Their Contribution to the English Novel, 1621-1744*, 1944. Reprint by Cork University Press, 1945, pp. 11-46.

[In the following excerpt, MacCarthy examines the treatment of several genres by women writers of the seventeenth century and considers how the experience of adversity and prejudice influenced women's writing during this time.]

Women's contribution to literature is no arbitrary or artificial distinction. However much the reformer may welcome, or the conservative lament, the growth of a harmonious sharing of ideals between men and women, that growth has been a hard-fought struggle. It has been an escape from a prison, which, when it did not entirely shut out the greater world, at least enclosed a little world of education meant for women, a literature adapted to the supposed limitations of their intellect, and a course of action prescribed by the other sex. . . .

When women at last began to seek after literary expression, it was inevitable that they should attempt to tell a story. There has always been, and there always will remain, deep-rooted in the human heart a desire to hear something told of the world without us and within. From these roots in varying forms and often strangely transmuted grew all education and the arts. For men it was a transition from telling to writing, and for women the transition was no less long, and like their opportunities for literacy, took place far later. Women as listeners influenced the art of story-telling long before they actually shared in it, and naturally the growth of the novel gained in variety and verisimilitude when women were given a place in the subject-matter. The novel is a very improbable development of the Odyssey, but it is an inevitable development of *Daphnis and Chloe*. Beowulf and his fire-drake are almost as far from the art of fiction as they are from probability, and such sagas could be of no interest to women. It is not the titanic figure, with his death-dealing sword, invincible in his destiny, that a woman loves, in fact or in fiction—or at any rate, not until he has shown himself vulnerable to human emotions. Victorious Perseus, flying through the clouds, does not win a woman's interest until he sees Andromeda and comes down to earth. This descent from free fancy to actuality is, in a word, the evolution of the novel.

Women make their entrance into fiction with the development of the short tale such as the *novella*, which had love-interest as its pivotal point. Marie de France, writing in England in the twelfth century, found in her episodic lays exactly the mould which suited her, and she used it with such ease that she had scope to develop her technique and to create from the oft-told tales of the minstrels works of art which not only endured, but served as an inspiration to later writers. Margaret of Navarre, writing in prose, found the short tale equally suited to her powers, and in her case also, ease in technique allowed her genius to express itself with a power perhaps not surpassed by Bandello or Boccaccio. These women excelled because they were, for the most part, retelling stories they had heard, but most of all because they had for subject-matter themes and events most familiar, if not in their own lives, then certainly in the lives of those about them.

But alas for the women writers! Daphnis and Chloe, neglected on their pastoral slope, were growing up and developing a stultifying artificiality. Their simple idyll was now to be complicated by rival lovers, perfidy, royalty incognito, shipwreck, and chivalrous emprises, into a superfluity of characters endlessly involved in a maze of tedious events. And where Sir Philip Sydney led, what could an ambitious niece do but follow? It could not be expected that Lady Mary Wroath would escape the quagmire of the Pastoral Romance, and in fact, she overpassed its pitfalls with far more success than might have been expected. If women were daring even in attempting to write, it is not to be expected, at that stage, that they would have the extreme audacity to become innovators as well. If only, instead of being satisfied with diligently copying the headline set by men, they could have bridged the great gap between romantic and domestic fiction, then not only would the development of the novel have been hastened by hundreds of years, but women would have been able to exert their talents on exactly the subject-matter which they knew best, and consequently there would have been far more women writers. It is obvious that creative imagination, no matter how individual and how varied its power of synthesis, must have material to synthesise, and this material may be real life, or some artistic reproduction of life, or, as is most usual, both. This does not mean that because women's actual experience of life was limited to only one aspect, therefore they could not exercise creative imagination. Certainly they could have done so, as did, for example, the two gifted women already mentioned, and if we wish to understand why women were not at that time actively creative, we must consider the education at their disposal, and we must remember that an ability to read and write is not education, though it may be a means thereto. Such education as women received was nominal, and creative imagination without education is not productive. One must either admit this fact, or else assert that women in bygone ages lacked the kind of imaginative power which later women most obviously possessed. Any view which claims variation in the mental capacity of women at various epochs is quite untenable. On the other hand, any view which explains the dearth of early women-writers by reference to their limited experience, does not need to be disproved. It simply collapses of itself, because it is illogical in theory, and its invalidity is proved by the evidence of the great women-writers who, despite a human sphere as circumscribed as that of their ancestresses, later achieved fame. We know that the material on which creative imagination may work can be found in daily life no matter how limited in extent. Experience need not be wide for human or literary fulfilment, but it must be deep, and, for literary purposes, it must be artistically realised, and it must be expressed. Depth of experience implies depth of character, but does not connote the power of artistic realisation or artistic expression, and it is precisely in this relation that the question of education arises. Creative imagination transforms experience into a work of art, but it can only give artistic form when it is familiar with such forms, and can manipulate the chosen form with ease. It requires training and familiarity with many aspects of one's art before one masters technique, or develops individuality in technique. Nor can one even say that we achieve a work of art merely by giving artistic form to experience, for the truth is that the artist apprehends experience in a fashion which is partly the result of his mental characteristics, but also the result of his artistic training. Perhaps we may say that art is experience realised in a special way and expressed in a corresponding medium. Emily Brontë's experience of actual human life was unusually limited, and yet she produced not only a work of art, but one of unusual power. If it were possible to analyse her genius, one might suggest that it consisted in intensity of

experience, in her case mainly imaginative experience, which she realised in literary terms, and embodied in the artistic form she knew best—the art of fiction. But it is worth noting that not only was Emily Brontë endowed with natural genius, but was, for that period, very well educated and very widely read. Yet despite these advantages, which enabled her to use language in a plastic, even in an intuitive way, *Wuthering Heights* is structurally clumsy, because, of course, a literary education is merely a way by which we recognise and evaluate literary technique, but only by literary experiment can we develop such technique in ourselves. *Wuthering Heights* also shows that imaginative experience is not in itself a sufficing material for realistic fiction, for it is clear that, though Emily Brontë knew hell and heaven, she did not know how farm-hands talk.

In judging the average woman's chance of success in the writing of fiction, it seems, perhaps, a digression to speak of Emily Brontë, whose genius must always entitle her to be judged apart, but we deliberately choose her, because we wish to show that even such genius cannot arrive at technique without an apprenticeship, and that even such genius cannot safely depend on imaginative intuition, cannot dispense with the necessity for everyday experience. Writing of the essential characteristics of a great novelist, Fielding states the necessity for *Genius, Learning, Conversation,* and "*a good heart.*" By *Genius* he means "that power or rather those powers of mind, which are capable of penetrating into all things within our reach and knowledge, and of distinguishing their essential differences." These powers he distinguishes as *Invention* and *Judgment* under the collective name of *Genius*. By *Invention* Fielding means, not the creative faculty, but quite literally the power of discovery—"a quick and sagacious penetration into the true essence of all the objects of our contemplation. This, I think, can rarely exist without the concomitancy of judgment; for how we can be said to have discovered the true essence of two things, without discerning their difference, seems to me hard to conceive. Now this last is the undisputed province of Judgment."

Of the necessity for learning, Fielding finely says: "Nature can only furnish us with capacity . . . or the tools of our profession; learning must fit them for use, must direct them in it, and lastly must contribute part at least of the materials. A competent knowledge of history and of the belles-lettres is here absolutely necessary; and without this share of knowledge at least, to affect the character of an historian (i.e., a novelist) is as vain as to endeavour at building a house without timber or mortar, or brick or stone. Homer and Milton, who though they added ornament of numbers to their works, were both historians of our order, were masters of all the learning of their times."

Conversation, by which Fielding meant experience of life, he held to be absolutely indispensable to a novelist: "However exquisitely human nature may have been described by writers, the true practical system can be learnt only in the world." People who write without experience of life are only making a "faint copy of a copy . . . which can have neither the justness nor spirit of an original. Now this conversation in our historian must be universal, that is with all the ranks and degrees of men, for the knowledge of what is called high life will not instruct him in low, nor, è converso . . . and though it may be thought that the knowledge of either may sufficiently enable him to describe at least that in which he hath been conversant, yet he will even here fall greatly short of perfection: for the follies of either rank do, in reality, illustrate each other."

But Genius, Learning, and Conversation do not dispense a great novelist from the necessity of having a *Good Heart,* by which Fielding means humanity.

Applying Fielding's words to women-novelists, their handicaps at once become only too apparent. Genius and a good heart they might have as natural endowment, but learning and "conversation" were beyond their reach long before and long after Fielding's time. These facts prepare us for the low standard very often observable in the novels written by women, but they do not prepare us for the inexplicable way in which women persisted in proving that they could rise above their limitations. It is not feminism, but the merest common-sense to insist that women's contribution to fiction can only be judged in relation to their opportunities. That this standard of judgment is not sufficiently remembered is, perhaps, because so much that women contributed, by its own merit claims equality with the best attainments of men-novelists, and appears to dispense with the special consideration which is actually its due.

That the writing of fiction becomes clumsy hackwork in the hands of the uneducated is proved in the works of large numbers of the women . . . but we must remember that the art of fiction evolved so slowly and with so many digressions of form and content that there was not, for a long time, any clearly defined standard of. what fiction ought to be. This was one reason why women were brave enough to attempt such writing. Women enjoyed stories (particularly love-stories which confirmed their personal view of the focal point of life) and, unlike poetry, unlike essays which called for a cultural mould and commerce in abstractions, a story could be told by anybody who had sufficient gumption to sandwich a middle between a beginning and an end. "To the composition of novels and romances," says Fielding, bitterly, "nothing is necessary but paper, pens, and ink, with the manual capacity of using them." George Eliot, passing judgment, after several centuries, on the large brood of incapable women-novelists of her day, gives the reason thus: "No educational restrictions can shut women out from the materials of fiction and there is no species of art which is so free from rigid requirements. Like crystalline masses, it may take any form and yet be beautiful, we have only to pour in the right elements—genuine observation, humour, and passion." But pour them into what? George Eliot does not discriminate between the lack of a cultural mould and the lack of the novelist's technique. However, she expresses very well the danger which lay for women in the very looseness of the fictional medium:

It is precisely this absence of rigid requirements which constitutes the fatal seduction of novel-writing to incompetent women. Ladies who are not wont to be very grossly deceived as to their power of playing on the piano; here certain positive difficulties of execution have to be conquered, and incompetence inevitably breaks down. Every art which has its absolute technique is, to a certain extent, guarded against the intrusions of mere left-handed imbecility. But in novel-writing there are no barriers for incapacity to stumble against, no external criteria to prevent a writer from mistaking foolish facility for mastery.

If this could be said in the middle of the nineteenth century, how much less formulated was the form of the novel, three centuries earlier! And yet one cannot fail to observe that, according as the art of fiction became (as it did) more exigent with advancing years, women continued not only to maintain the required standard, but often to surpass it, and even to contribute to the development of new genres.

It might have been imagined that when Elizabethan fiction developed along the lines of the Pastoral Romance, the picaresque novels, and the guild-tales, that women writers would have retired from the lists, despairing of ever achieving the pseudo-Greek note, the pot-house experience, or the tradesman's touch so necessary respectively to these three types of fiction. Of the three, the Pastoral Romance was the easiest, because though one might not progress with classic grace, one could, at any rate, undulate pleasantly through mazes sufficiently intricate to defy detection. Since pre-Restoration women writers were of the upper-classes, it was not likely that they would choose such plebeian realism as the guild-tales for their literary medium, even if they felt competent to portray that aspect of life, and it was not to be imagined that any female pen would then dare to follow, or could successfully follow a rogue, whether Spanish or English, into the unimagined dens of his villainy. The picaro's swashbuckling attitude to women could not be changed unless by reforming the picaro, and a reformed picaro is a contradiction in terms; therefore, with a delicate flutter, the female pens took refuge in gentle valleys, beside murmuring brooks, where shepherd and shepherdess anticipated the poses of Dresden. Thus Lady Mary Wroath and still later Anne Weamys, both with more success than might be expected in so artificial a type of fiction, and, in the case of the *Urania,* with realism staring out from the courtly inanities like a pair of honest eyes from a mask.

But although the Pastoral novel was moribund with the passing of the Elizabethan age, its mummied form obtruded itself for long upon the attention of the reading public, and its ghostly accents continued to echo in the style of subsequent prose fiction for a century and a half. The persistence of the Pastoral tradition and the delay in the development of realistic fiction is more easily understandable when we recall that people of the sixteenth and seventeenth centuries preferred to find life represented before the footlights than in the pages of a book. Women in Shakespeare's time did not write plays, because the blank-verse form called for a technique in language which they did not possess, but with the Restoration period came a spate of women-dramatists, most notably Aphra Behn, Mrs. Centlivre, Mrs. Manley, Mrs. Pix and Mrs. Trotter. These were highly successful in this new medium for story-telling, mainly because drama had taken a different turn, and instead of tragedies in conception too lofty and in form too difficult for women who lacked learning, now the learned sock was off, and the comfortable buskin which had only to find its way through domestic intrigue, fitted the women beyond any possibility of limping. Not only was the subject-matter more congenial, but the prose dialogue most generally used required only the power of brilliant verbal fencing which would be instinctive in a witty woman. Background and dialogue were rudimentary as yet in the novel, and characterisation was so rare as to be almost non-existent. Still, in a prose story it was necessary to sketch some sort of background, to describe the passage of events and to interpolate conversations, or at least to report them. It was necessary to indicate the passage of time, and in all this there was no very clear precedent for one's procedure. Such freedom was an advantage to the original, but the tendency of the more average person would naturally be to imitate a form which had clear rules for guidance. In drama women found such a form, because, though one could transcend certain of the unities, yet they always remained as a reliable framework of construction. These points, no doubt, served to encourage women, and partly account for the increase in women-writers at this period.

But there was another consideration which, from the beginning of women's literary adventuring had loomed large, and greatly affected their work and their status. This was the condemnatory attitude of the reading public towards women-writers. Masculine condemnation of women's quill-driving was "compounded of many simples" but chiefly of a double fear: fear that women's new occupation might change their attitude towards domestic and social duties, and fear that women's achievements might eclipse those of men. For countless ages women had been given the sort of education which fitted them to become wives and mothers in this world, and saints either here or hereafter. These activities were conducive towards man's happiness, and were no encroachment on the territory he was accustomed to consider as peculiarly his own. But if women were to realise themselves in some separate way, if they, like men, should have an intellectual life, which, of necessity, must be led alone and which, as man knew, was richly self-rewarding, might not women become intolerable from the man's point of view? That is to say, not merely preoccupied with other than domestic details, but no longer looking up to man as the arbiter of her fate. "While thou keepest always looking up at me, and I down at thee, what horrid obliquities of vision may we not contract?"—obliquities not to be quickly cured, capable of distorting all one's impressions, and very painful if readjusted too suddenly. "I imagine," says the Duchess of Newcastle, "that I shall be censured by my own Sex; and Men will cast a smile of Scorne upon my Book, because they think thereby, Women incroach too much upon their Prerogatives; for they hold Books as their Crowne, and the Sword as their Scepter, by which they rule and gov-

erne. And very like they will say to me, as to the Lady that wrote the Romancy,

> Work, Lady, Work, let writing books alone
> For surely wiser women nere wrote one.

And she continues:

> Spinning with the Fingers is more proper to our Sexe, than studying or writing Poetry, which is spinning with the Braine, but I, having no skill in the art of the first (and if I had, I had no hopes of gaining so much as to make me a garment to keep me from the cold) make me delight in the latter . . . which made me endeavour to Spin a Garment of Memory, to lapp up my Name, that it might grow to after Ages. I cannot say the web is strong, fine, or evenly spun, for it is a course piece; yet I had rather my Name should go meanly clad, than dye with cold.

Mean indeed was the reputation of women-writers, when they were so fortunate as to have any reputation at all. The reading public and the general public (those widening circles in the pool of opinion, obedient to the stones cast by the critics) divided women writers into three chief classes, each of which received a different judgment. First, there were the women-writers, who not only escaped condemnation, but were never even put on trial. These were the dilettante ladies, the literary dabblers, who wrote polite verse, translated plays and pious treatises, and kept their eyes well averted from the roaring pageant of life. Always they were of the privileged classes. Often they were the relatives of literary men, and won an amused tolerance or a degree of kindly commendation for their prococity. In the case of Sir Philip Sydney's sister and niece, they might have written the *Heptameron,* and not the slightest murmur of disapproval would have disturbed the pæans of loving praise which enveloped that illustrious family. Amongst its many virtues was a profound generosity in literary patronage, and so it was that the Countess of Pembroke was accounted a notable success in literature. Yet her works, so lavishly eulogised, consist of a play translated from the French, (never acted, and never even read by the critics who extolled it); a poem whose sole claim to recognition was that Spenser published it with his *Astrophel;* and a metrical version of the Psalms, in which she was helped by her brother and her chaplain. Nash, Spenser, Nicholas Breton, Whincop, Osborn, Langbaine and many others were loud in her praise, and her epitaph was written probably by Ben Jonson.

Let us compare the case of Marie de France, who made so notable a contribution to French literature:

> Tous, à l'exception de Denys Pyramus, qui en a dit peu de chose, ont gardé un profound silence sur cette femme fort supérieure à son siècle par ses lumières, par ses sentiments, et par le courage qu'elle eut de dire la vérité a des oreilles mal disposées ou peu accoutumées a l'entendre.

What is the explanation of this silence? It is, apparently, that Marie belonged to the great company of women-writers who were condemned by their own generation. They were condemned because they were suspected either of looseness or eccentricity. If they were suspect on moral grounds, absence of evidence did not acquit them and the best they could hope for was the grudging Scottish judgment of "Not Proven." The third class, those who were obviously above moral reproach but were still suspect of some abnormality, was labelled "Queer." For whatever cause, it is clear that Marie was attacked, for she says:

> Indeed, wherever there is a man or a woman of great fame, those who are envious of her good work often slander her, and with the intent to lessen her fame, play the part of a wretched cowardly dog, a cur that bites folk stealthily. But I will not leave off for this, even though backbiters and false flatterers work mischief against me—for to speak ill is their nature.

That the Duchess of Newcastle was considered queer is confirmed by all the criticisms of her own time. Queer she undoubtedly was, but she had sufficient genius to justify her eccentricity, a fact recognised by Disraeli. And though she showed a fine disregard for her critics, male and female, yet she was very conscious that current opinion was opposed to literary pursuits for a woman. She appeals endlessly for her right to be an author. Is it not better for her to occupy her time in writing than to behave loosely as so many Court ladies do? Is her occupation really less useful than painting and embroidery, or "the making of Flowers, Boxes, Baskets with Beads, Shells, Silke and Strawe?"

> I hope you will spare me [she says to her readers] for the Harthe is swept cleane, and a Bason of Water with a cleane Towell set by, and the Ashes rak'd up; wherefore let my book sleep quietly, and the Watch-light burning clearly . . . and let it be still from your noise, that the feminine Cat may not Mew, nor the masculine Curs bark nor howle out railings to disturb my harmless Booke's rest.

The feminine Cats, however, continued to mew, as they had done from the beginning of women's literary efforts. Again and again the women-writers comment on this feminine attack upon them. "Nay, even my own sex, which should assert our prerogative against such detractors, are often backward to encourage the female pen." And writing long afterwards (1791) another woman says: "You know how female writers are looked down upon. The women fear and hate, the men ridicule and dislike them."

Still, it must be allowed that, apart from the prejudice and even the possible envy with which the non-literary woman regarded her more gifted sisters, there was very often a legitimate reason for objecting on moral grounds to the women who wrote fiction, and to the kind of fiction which they wrote. Men had created the standard of literary taste, and if women were to write at all they had to compete with men on their own ground. It was not considered improper that men should write loosely for a reading public (or for an audience) composed of women as well as men,

nor even that they should write lewdly for women's particular instruction, as for example, did Jacques d'Amiens, whose *"L'Art d'Amors"* was merely one of many such works during the Middle Ages:

> Chez Jacques d'Amiens les femmes ne sont pas considerées que comme des joujoux qui sont là uniquement pour le plaisir des hommes: il ne considère jamais le côté moral des choses; il n'a pas de sens moral.

It seems surprising that women might consume such literary repasts in the privacy of their bowers, but emphatically might not cater for such tastes in others. There is indeed a moral distinction in culpability, but it was not this consideration which inspired the general condemnation of women-writers. It is not for us to determine whether women-writers should have wished or attempted to evangelise the reading public. In any case, they could not possibly have done so. The fact that they entered into literary competition meant that they accepted the code established by the majority of writers in accordance with popular demand. Literary fame and, later, financial success depended on playing the game at least as well as their masculine adversaries, and playing a game involves the acceptance of definite rules and the developing of a particular technique. Women who wrote according to a standard of their own would have had as much hope of success as if they decided to play hockey with a crochet-hook. Playing even in the accepted way, they had to take it for granted that the umpire-critics would always be prejudiced, and that the public would howl them down at every opportunity. They were like a visiting team in hostile country where their every effort would be adjudged offside. If they were ever to win approval, they needed to be not merely as good as, but better than their opponents, and the difficulty of this was evident, when one reflects that they were heavily handicapped from the beginning. That they did adapt themselves to the rigours of the contest, that they did score so early in the game was a triumph—unpopular, and not without its price. Wounded reputation was to be expected, and at one period was really deserved, although even then the public put the cart before the horse. The literary women of the Restoration were not loose because they were writers. They were writers because they were loose. They were adventuresses before they adventured into literature. In a word, they were driven by circumstances to drive a quill, and they had the only equipment by which a woman of that time could succeed in letters—a great intellectual vigour and an absence of scruples. It was nothing much to them that, as women-writers, they lost caste. They had lost caste already. Mrs. Behn, Mrs. Centlivre, Mrs. Manley, Mrs. Pix, Mrs. Haywood and the rest of the battered crew, came to the profession of writing with no illusions, almost no education, a wide though ill-balanced experience of life, and an immense vigour of mind and body. They asked, and they got, no quarter, and they stamped their names defiantly into the minds of their contemporaries and into literary history. It is no mean feat at any time to make a living by free-lance writing. In the sixteenth, seventeenth and eighteenth centuries it was incredibly difficult. It was easier to starve than to eat by the sweat of one's brow, as even men-writers, from the days of Nash, Dekker, Fox and Drayton knew to their cost. To be a genius was no guarantee against the gutter or imprisonment for debt. It was necessary to find patrons and to keep them from tiring; to cultivate anyone who might have influence; to ingratiate oneself with editors and booksellers; to flatter the critics; to be hail-fellow-well-met with all sorts of people, in all sorts of places; to be ready to turn one's hand to anything—play-patching, "ghosting," political propaganda, rudimentary newspaper work; to haunt the greenrooms, and "keep in with" the players; to write plays for a small circle of loose-livers at a time when no decent woman would go to a theatre, and even the courtesans went masked. It will be admitted that no conventional woman could do all this, and if a group of unconventional women did it, then we must evaluate the gain entirely from the literary point of view. Nobody can contest the literary contributions of Mrs. Behn, Mrs. Centlivre, Mrs. Haywood, and even of Mrs. Manley. With the exception of Mrs. Centlivre (who excelled exclusively as a dramatist), these women wrote not only plays (which had an indirect but definite influence on the growth of fiction) but notably aided the development of the novel, both by using accepted forms, and by helping to initiate other forms. In their own time (and even now) women-writers of that particular period were strongly censured for their loose writing. One might as well blame an Arctic fox for changing his colour in the winter. He lives by adaptation, and so did they. From amongst the innumerable evidences that a double standard of criticism was exercised on a single standard of writing, we may perhaps mention one example. Aphra Behn, as brilliant as any writer of her generation, was loaded with obloquy for plays which, compared to those of Dryden and Congreve, might almost be considered pure. Dryden, writing to Mrs. Elizabeth Thomas in 1699, expressed his certainty that she would avoid the license which Mrs. Behn allowed herself "of writing loosely, and giving, if I may have leave to say so, scandall to the modesty of her sex. I confess I am the last man who ought in justice to arraign her, who have been too much a libertine in most of my poems; which I should be well contented I had time either to purge, or to see fairly burn'd."

He was, indeed, the last man who should have attacked licentiousness in any writer, and he should have abstained from casting a stone at one of his few direct imitators. "I should be inclined," says Nicol, "to think that it is almost entirely the influence of Dryden which has led this authoress away from the comparatively pure plots to this of most immodest intrigue. 'Mr. Limberham' could contaminate a whole shoal of writers; and Dryden with his immodesty was showing to the playwrights of his time exactly what the audiences of the time desired." An interesting sidelight on the single standard of popular taste is given by Sir Walter Scott. He says that an aged lady, a relation of his, "assured him that in the polite society of her youth, in which she held a distinguished place, the plays and novels of Mrs. Aphra Behn were accounted proper reading"; and, "she added, with some humour, it was not until a long interval, when she looked into it at

the age of seventy that she was shocked with their indecorum"—shocked, that is, only in retrospect and when influenced by the more correct moral standards of a later age.

This anecdote to the contrary, there is no room for doubt that even in a grosser period the type of women-writers to which we have referred could not avoid ostracism. It is worth considering whether their equivocal position had any effect on their writing, apart from what we have already discussed. There is little question that it had, and there are gains and losses to be computed. It was a gain that declassed and plebeian as they were, they could not shelter behind a coat of arms, or a sermonising mediocrity, or a précieux classicism, nor lap themselves about with the facile and soothing adulation of a select coterie. They were in no danger of being praised for powers they did not possess. On the contrary, they had to fight for recognition, and the only compliment they received was that of being treated as responsible writers, able to take and to give blows, and with no privileges at all. The struggle to find and to retain a place for themselves, led them to realise and, so far as they could, to remedy their deficiencies. Sometimes, as in the case of Mrs. Manley, they made the mistake of endeavouring to achieve by slanderous salacity what they could not achieve by literary ability, but this recourse to mere licentiousness for a *tour de force* is rare. The chief women-writers of that period had enough real literary power to have succeeded in a happier age. That they had a wide though unfortunate experience of life meant something on the credit and on the debit side. In losing an idealised view of existence, they found a measure of reality, and they encountered a multiplicity of human types, reacting characteristically to a variety of circumstances—sufficient in number and diversity to enable them to see a pattern in the confusion and a unity in complexity. They could see that heroes and villains had much in common, and that characterisation deals with material far less easily recognisable than virtues and vices. It is better to see a courtesan as she really is, than to imagine a shepherdess as she never really was? One cannot doubt that for realism in literature it is better to write with one eye on the object. But an idealised representation of life is not more unreal than life depicted as entirely without ideals. Realism must take into account that ideals are actual forces intermingling with the stuff of events, sometimes shaping and sometimes merely interpreting them, but in either case by no means to be discounted. And this is exactly where the Restoration women writers, following the rules laid down by their stronger brethren of the pen, lost the authentic touch in interpreting and expressing human life. But their own experiences made it all the easier for them to concur in a view of life which mocked at ethical conventions, and it was natural that they should carry off their ostracism by laughing loudly at the unco' guid, whose prudery caused them to miss all the fun. It was easier to go a step further, and to believe self-justifyingly that all of life was as they knew it, and that virtue at best was merely a seductive perfume, an alluring patina; at worst a hypocritical veil for the subtle. In the writings of these women this added impetus of experience is often detectable:

Mrs. Behn, perhaps, as much as any one, condemned loose scenes and too warm descriptions; but something must be allowed to human frailty. She herself was of an amorous complexion; she felt the passions intimately which she describes, and this circumstance added to Necessity, might be the occasion of her plays being of that cast.

And sometimes added to the impetus of personal experience is the impetus of personal spite, a desire for vengeance on that society which drew its skirts aside. This is one reason why Mrs. Manley and Mrs. Haywood took to the histoire scandaleuse like a duck to water. In Mrs. Haywood's case, it was not lack of ability to do good work in a superior genre of fiction, as is proved in her authorship of *Miss Betsy Thoughtless* and *The History of Jemmy and Jenny Jessamy*. When Defoe and Mrs. Haywood both used the life of the deaf and dumb fortune-teller, Duncan Campbell, as material for fiction, their respective points of view are very evident. Defoe was interested in recounting the wonders of Campbell's powers, and specifically mentions that he omits tales of Mr. Campbell's women consultants, because they were so numerous that, if included, the work would be endless. Mrs. Haywood, however, "was evidently more interested in the phenomena of passion than in the theory of divination," and she also utilises the opportunity of revealing scandalous secrets, and opening old wounds. In fact, she makes her material serve the purpose of the histoire scandaleuse—an erotic arrow dipped in poison.

The point to be observed is that in the already ill-balanced literature of that period, any added impetus which further disturbed the balance, was artistically inadmissible. Measure, balance, symmetry—these are in life, and no matter how brilliant, vivid and witty the literature of a period may be, a fault in emphasis is a a fault in art, and must lead to the decay of that genre. In this case, the emphasis was on an aspect of life which allowed, after all, very little variety. Few things are less capable of variation, and therefore few things are more monotonous than the representation of vice. The conventions of immorality in drama and fiction are really more stultifying than the conventions of virtue.

But even at worst, such drama and such fiction were alive, and it was easy to see how they might develop when they had outgrown the excesses of youth. In its immature state, however, because it was, perhaps, of more mixed ancestry than the accepted forms of writing, and because it was, at that stage of its evolution, very lacking in art, fiction was regarded as a raggle-taggle sort of composition. Sir Philip Sydney claimed that the *Arcadia* was poetry, and later Fielding speaks of *Tom Jones* as "this heroic, historical, prosaic poem." Poetry had a high and ancient tradition, and its female devotees, thus chaperoned by the muses, were regarded with much indulgence. Such a one was Catherine Philips, and though she did not write fiction and therefore does not enter our field of consideration, she serves to show that, by adherence to a classical genre, a mediocre woman could win a literary reputation without sacrificing either her good name or her

reputation for good sense. Nothing could be more fantastic than the legend of the Matchless, the Incomparable Orinda. Speaking of the "celebrated scribbling women" of the 17th century, Sir Edmund Gosse says:

> Among all these the Matchless Orinda takes the foremost place—not exactly by merit, for Aphra Behn surpassed her in genius, Margaret, Duchess of Newcastle, in versatility, and Catherine Trotter in professional zeal; but by the moral eminence she attained through her elevated public career and which she sealed by her tragical death. When the seventeenth century thought of a poetess, it naturally thought of Orinda; her figure overtopped those of her literary sisters; she was more dignified, more regal, in her attitude to the public than they were, and in fine she presents us with the best type we possess of the woman of letters in the seventeenth century.

Even if "the best" meant simply the most moral, she could claim no prëeminence over Lucy Hutchinson or the Duchess of Newcastle. It is clear that "the best" does not mean the most gifted, versatile or zealous. "The best type" cannot mean the most typical of seventeenth century England, because Orinda is really not even representative, and would have claimed France as her spiritual country.

This incredible précieuse, born of honest, middle-class Cockney parents, is a fine example of what may be achieved when a facile talent is exploited by a pose so convincing that it is even self-hypnotic. Catherine Philips, née Fowler, used her pen as a vaulting-pole into society, and was never so happy as when, by her imagined poetical genius, she edged her way into a higher social stratum. She wrote a considerable quantity of artificial poetry, translated two of Corneille's plays (*Pompée* and *Horace*) into wooden verse, and carried on an epistolary correspondence with Sir Charles Cotterel (Poliarchus). These works are the apparent basis of her literary reputation, and her passport to the friendship of such men as Cowley and Jeremy Taylor. Her patrons and associates were such people as the Earls of Orrery and Roscommon, the Countess of Cork, and the Viscountess of Dungannon. When the Countess of Cork caused *Pompey* to be acted, the Earl of Roscommon spoke the prologue. Orinda was lauded to the skies, and critics like the sycophantic Langbaine said that she far surpassed Corneille. Her death left *Horace* unfinished and it was completed by Sir John Denham and acted at Court by "Persons of Quality" fourteen years later, the Duke of Monmouth speaking the prologue. What was the secret of that extraordinary furore which has not withstood the impartial judgment of posterity? It is, simply, that Catherine Philips's greatest creation was Orinda and she, alas! was subject to mortality. She was the first sentimental writer in the English language. She created a cult of sentiment and classicism, and loved to imagine that she was the leader of a salon which she called the Society of Friendship. Her house in Wales was a kind of Hotel de Rambouillet, or rather hers was a peripatetic salon, following her peregrinations among the houses of her patrons. Honest English names offended her sensibilities, and her friends were obliged to masquerade under such titles as Poliarchus, Palaemon, Lucasia, Valeria. She averred that she read English books with patience, but French ones with pleasure. She indulged in an endless series of sentimental friendships with young women, and was always mortally offended when they abandoned classicism for marriage. The patient and unassuming Mr. Philips (alias Antenor) quietly continued to eat roast beef and Yorkshire pudding, and to live his own life outside the Society of Friendship. One imagines him smiling in humorous resignation on reading his wife's poems, and discovering that she is "dying for a little love."

Writing eight years after Langbaine, Charles Gildon scornfully contradicts his statement that Orinda is a better writer than Aphra Behn, and accuses him of snobbish bias. He says "I must confess I cannot but prefer Mrs. Behn infinitely before her; she seems to be a very cold Writer, while you may find in Aphra both Fire and Easiness, which Mrs. Philips wanted." By 1747 the myth of Orinda, which needed the support of her living personality, had so far faded, that Whincop, under the blunt heading: "C. Philips," records all that remains: "She was commonly called the Matchless Orinda, on account of an Epistolary correspondence carried on between her and Sir Charles Cotterel, under the feign'd names of Orinda and Polyarchus." Then follow, without comment, the names of those plays which surpassed Corneille.

The case of Catherine Philips illustrates the fact that a woman of mediocre mind and a veneer of education could, by adherence to an accepted genre of writing, not only secure powerful patrons, and an immediate success, but also an immunity from that criticism which ever pursued the women who wrote fiction, and which persisted even in the days of Jane Austen and the Brontës. "Orinda" was a *nom de panache,* but "Ellis Bell" was a guilty expedient, and it is strange to reflect that though, with the lapse of centuries, the novel increasingly proved its claim to be recognised as a particular form of art, and the world became increasingly familiar with the ability of women-novelists, yet the old stigma remained, and drove even genius to conceal itself under a pseudonym.

But there was a kind of literary composition, other than poetry, which even in the sixteenth and seventeenth centuries was considered legitimate for female pens. This was the biography or autobiography, and it is interesting to note in how far it shaped towards fiction in the hands of those women who employed it. Anne Clifford, Countess of Pembroke, the Duchess of Newcastle, Mrs. Lucy Hutchinson, and Lady Fanshawe wrote their biographies, the first so as to clarify her daughter's claims in a legal dispute; the Duchess and Lucy Hutchinson, as it were, *en passant,* their particular interest being centred in writing their husband's biographies. Lady Fanshawe more evenly develops her own life-story with that of her husband.

Biography had for women the advantage of giving them a chance to write on a subject they really knew, but the necessity for authenticity which was the object, and to them the justification of their compositions, crippled their imaginative powers. Their very familiarity with the people and the events in these works made it difficult for them to realise the necessity for describing them fully for other people. Thus, with the exception of Lady Fanshawe (the most vivid and detailed of the female biographers), they do not essay descriptions of domestic events, nor attempt to sketch in, however roughly, the backgrounds they knew so well. One does not often find in the biographical writings of Anne Clifford, the Duchess of Newcastle, or Lucy Hutchinson a realistic and full presentation of such events as are described, though frequently one is conscious of emotion flowing, with awakened memory, into their narratives. Still, they do not recreate happenings by the illumination of subsequent experience. They do not show much perspective. There is no dramatic irony. There is an entire lack of humour, due, no doubt, to the fact that when these women wrote they were worn out by many griefs. Their unrelieved seriousness must also be ascribed to an excessive anxiety. They are determined to present their husbands, their families and themselves in the best possible light, and it is hard to smile with one's teeth clenched. With all four women there is a definite effort to achieve character-portraits, and not much notion of how to proceed. For the most part, they simply enumerate the ineffable virtues and bodily characteristics of those whom they wish to describe. Apart from the self-consciousness and difficulty in perspective which are obvious disadvantages in recording one's own life or that of a near relation, these women were also confronted with another serious handicap, namely, the necessity of showing the development of their family fortunes in relation to a complicated background of political events. Anne Clifford simply presumes such knowledge, as well she might, since she wrote only for her daughter. Lucy Hutchinson and the Duchess, forced to deal with the maze of the Civil War, and aware of their inability to do so, depend on others for their account of political and military events, the Duchess with her usual frankness, and Lucy Hutchinson without acknowledging her sources. As is only to be expected, both fail to control this extremely complicated mass of material, and they are very much at a loss as to how best it might be introduced into their narratives. The result is clumsy, and no wonder, seeing that the genre of the historical novel, shadowed faintly forth in their compositions, was yet almost a century and a half from its full evolution. When, about fifty-five years later, Defoe published, in 1722, the *Journal of the Plague Year* and *Colonel Jacques,* we see that despite the power and realism which characterised his works, he also failed to manage the historical background which his circumstantial method of composition forced him to introduce. Actually he should have experienced less difficulty in mastering his historical material, since, as his aim was really fiction, he had naturally no hesitation in juggling with historical data. In the *Journal of the Plague Year* this lack of technique is clearly evident. "Large parts of the book are cast into statistical form: they read more like a Blue Book than anything else." This goes to show that even the freedom of fiction in the hands of a genius could not yet give ease in the interweaving of historical and personal material, and gives us moreover a true idea of what might reasonably be expected from the Duchess and Lucy Hutchinson. Lady Fanshawe makes no attempt to sketch in a comprehensive background of the Civil War—a wise abstention on the whole, although it often leaves the causes of the great Fanshawe Odyssey too obscure. Whatever the short-comings of these biographers, it was a step in the right direction that they were endeavouring to tell a story which was part of their lives, and much of which came within their personal experience; but it is amusing to reflect that while these women, pen in hand, endeavoured to marshal troops, to take castles, to summon and dismiss Parliaments and to discuss treaties, Mr. Pepys was committing to an undreamed immortality the colour (and price) of his wife's dresses; the furnishings of their house; the sort of dinner one might expect on washing-day; the servant problem; the latest play; his outings with his wife, their friends, their quarrels, their reconciliations—in fact all the fabric of daily life, the fabric of domestic fiction, which had never yet been attempted by any writer, man or woman.

Katharina M. Wilson and Frank J. Warnke (essay date 1989)

SOURCE: An introduction to *Women Writers of the Seventeenth Century,* The University of Georgia Press, 1989, pp. xi-xxiii.

[*In the following excerpt, Wilson and Warnke discuss the surge of literary activity by women during the seventeenth century in the context of the rise of feminist thought, the inaccessibility of education for women, the influence of the Baroque sensibility, and the significance of religion and religious controversy during this time.*]

The seventeenth century witnessed a great surge of literary activity by women. It has been estimated that four hundred wrote between 1640 and 1700 in England alone and that their writings constituted approximately one percent of the texts published. A large portion of the works penned by women in the Early Modern era, as in the Middle Ages and the Renaissance, were devotional or religio-political in nature; but the ratio of religious to secular texts became a great deal more balanced as time progressed. Analogously, women scholars, while still considered oddities, did increase in number in the 1600s; the mid- and late seventeenth century therefore witnessed an unprecedented number of women who decided to write polemically and with a collective awareness of their gender in order to address the subject of women's condition and potential, thus partaking in the philosophic/theological debate concerning the spiritual equality of the sexes. Men, too, participated in the debate on both sides of the issue, and the numerous catalogs of good (or famous) women and essays in defense of (or attacking) the female sex proliferated during the period and bear witness to the fervor of the controversy. As Moira Ferguson remarks, "Fostered by the influence of Cartesian, Lockean, and spiritual egalitarian views of the world, . . . several sturdy defenses of women . . . launched forthright feminist essays on a surprised public." "The human animal is," Marie de Gournay wrote in 1622, "neither male nor female. . . . And if I am allowed to jest a little in passing, I have a joke that is not altogether irrelevant: nothing resembles a

male cat on a windowsill more than a female cat." And Rachel Speght argued similarly, though less wittily, in a 1621 poem:

> Both man and woman of three parts consist,
> Which Paul doth bodie, soule, and spirit call:
> And from the soule three faculties arise,
> The mind, the will, the power; then wherefore shall
> A woman have her intellect in vaine,
> Or not endeavour Knowledge to attaine.

Some women scholars of the period advanced the idea that the education of women is for the benefit of men as well. Bathsua Makin, for instance, suggests that women's education will act as an incentive to men to keep up their studies. Keeping women ignorant, she asserts, is simply a tool of domination: "Let women be fools, and then you may easily make them slaves."

The equation of learning with at least limited power made it politically wise, even essential, that Early Modern women scholars circumscribe the field of application as well as the extent and availability of education for women. Almost invariably they limited their advocacy of learning to women "of estate"; they pled for private (as opposed to public) instruction; they often reassured their audience that they did not wish to hinder "good housewifery"; and they usually linked the support of education to moral probity.

In the realm of belles lettres, the seventeenth century also saw a great flowering of women's art, giving us several women who—either by necessity or by choice—lived by their pen. Whether conforming to Baroque sensibilities or deliberately avoiding them, seventeenth-century women writers left us both with a legacy of feminist aesthetics (marginal in some cases, but surprisingly pronounced in others) and with a complex picture of female experience in the wide range of intellectual perspectives that they chose to provide. Perhaps the most important aspect of this legacy was the growing collective awareness of gender not only as a determining factor of individual identity but also as the parameter of most tenets of social, political, and intellectual endeavor. While during the Middle Ages and the Renaissance, as Merry E. Wiesner observes, women by and large succeeded in intellectual pursuits when they simultaneously rejected the world of women, several Early Modern women writers gave public expression to the recognition "that women as a group suffered discrimination and should be given rights and privileges because of, not despite, their femaleness." The rights and privileges which Early Modern women sought involved remedying the long tradition of patriarchal suppression; their goal was a degree of sexual egalitarianism. One should judge a person by his or her accomplishments, early feminists argued, not by gender. Leonora Christina, the Danish princess imprisoned for her husband's alleged crimes, remarks, for example: "The mind pays no heed to sex and is not changed through external form or figure. . . . often women acquit themselves heroically. How often does one not see effeminate hearts in men's bodies and, on the contrary, virile strength in weak vessels. It is unfair to measure the deed by the person and not to esteem the person by the deed." Her courageous conduct in and out of prison, one should add, bears ample testimony to the "virility" of her mind.

This new awareness that women can succeed *qua* women contrasts most clearly with the perception of medieval writers. Patristic theology and Church tradition predicated the notion of the baptismal equality of the sexes, an equality to which women could rise by embracing virginity and becoming, in St. Jerome's words, "like men." The female ideal as a male clone thus pervaded the consciousness of many medieval women writers. Not surprisingly, therefore, the large majority were single women either confessed in vows (like men) or widowed or abandoned by their husbands. Women writers of the Early Modern era, on the other hand, most typically were married and did not necessarily aspire to the male ideal in their creative efforts. Consequently, seventeenth-century women writers often succeeded in creating female heroes (not heroines who were appendages to men) in an effort to valorize the female experience and women's contributions to society.

The sense of gender-collectivity is also reflected in the modes and models of discourse women writers chose for expression. With some frequency, Early Modern women writers modeled their texts on their female predecessors: the Spaniard Marìa de Zayas y Sotomayor used Marguerite de Navarre's *Heptameron* as a source for her *novelas;* Polish author Elzbieta Druzbacka patterned her fantastic tale of a young prince's life in fairyland, the *Fabula o Ksiazeciv Adolfie, dziedzicu Roksolanii,* after Mme d'Aulnoy's *L'Histoire d'Hypolite, Comte de Duglas;* and Mme d'Aulnoy used Mme de LaFayette as her model for the *Histoire,* to mention a few examples. The works of women scholars of the Early Modern era also bear eloquent testimony to their awareness of shared, gender-specific experience and ideas. Many corresponded with one another, and most were aware of and built upon the works of their female contemporaries. Bathsua Makin and Marie de Gournay both corresponded with Anna Maria van Schurman; Makin incorporated some of Schurman's ideas into her own pedagogical manifesto; Mme de LaFayette's first published work was a literary portrait of her friend Mme de Sévigné; and Ana Caro composed a eulogy for the preface of Marìa de Zayas y Sotomayor's *Novelas.* Moreover, in many of the seventeenth-century women's texts, the same sense of collectivity is felt in the almost inevitable catalogs of famous virtuous/heroic women of the past and the present, whose examples are presented to support the view that women's suppression and supposed inferiority are by no means historic, philosophic, or ethical absolutes.

Yet this female self-consciousness among seventeenth-century authors is complex and at best ambiguous. Some of the women writers are outright misogynists when discussing public positions sought by women or public protests for reform voiced by women. Some deliberately embrace a class- rather than a gender-consciousness when faced with controversial issues. Even the passionately vocal defenders of women's right to education often hasten to provide assurances that female education is to be limited to the nonpublic, nonprofessional spheres and is only to be pursued if servants can discharge household duties.

The new self-consciousness about gender is most clearly pronounced in the writings of the polemicists (such as Makin, de Gournay, and Schurman) and in works of women *not* members of the aristocracy. Aristocratic women appear to view themselves as aristocrats first and women second; some, like the Duchess of Newcastle, deliberately distance themselves from their lower-class and militantly reformist sisters. The self-consciousness also appears to be more pronounced with successful writers: Aphra Behn, Marìa de Zayas y Sotomayor, and Ana Caro, for instance, repeatedly emphasize this awareness of a gender-bond, whereas Camilla Faà Gonzaga, who wrote furtively and produced only one work, does not.

Confessional allegiance does not seem to have been much of a conditioning factor in the literary creativity of seventeenth-century women. Catholic Spain and Poland produced their share of literary women, but so did Lutheran Denmark and Sweden. The most staunchly Calvinistic centers—Geneva or, early in the century, the Palatinate—may have stifled female artistic activity with more than customary vigor, but then one must consider predominantly Calvinistic Holland, where Maria Tesselschade and others flourished. Dutch Calvinism, however, was less hostile than the Genevan variety to belles lettres as a whole, because of the firm links between the burghers and the local aristocracy, the relative openness of a maritime commercial culture, and the degree of religious tolerance granted, albeit grudgingly. An atmosphere in which one is reminded of the existence of options may have played a role in fostering female artistic activity. England and Holland were *relatively* tolerant; Austria and Hungary, at least early in the century, had not forgotten religious diversity in the face of the Habsburg insistence on orthodoxy; and even in the repressively Catholic society of Louis XIV's France, some court intellectuals had not altogether forgotten the heritage of Henri IV or of Montaigne. . . .

The baroque is the dominant style of the literature and art of the seventeenth century. To most authorities, that great style—or complex of styles—manifested itself first in Italy and France in the 1580s, and later extended to termini in the various national cultures. It shaded into Neoclassicism in France and England during the 1660s; continued rather later in Spain, Latin America, and the German-speaking world; and lasted well into the eighteenth century in Russia and Eastern Europe. Some historians posit a period of Mannerism that intervened between the Renaissance and the Baroque and included such figures as Montaigne, Cervantes, and Donne. From the comparatist's point of view, however, it is perhaps wise to think of Mannerism as one of the many currents within the Baroque rather than as a separate period.

What then is the Baroque? In technique it is distinguished

by devices of extravagance, ingenuity, playfulness, and exaggeration. Sometimes relying heavily on sensuous effect, Baroque authors often go to the opposite extreme and favor forms of expression so intellectualized as to approach the abstract. When Baroque art is sensuous, however, it aims not at the careful mimesis typical of Renaissance art but rather at a kind of frankly artificial phantasmagoria. Whether sensuous or stern, Baroque literature characteristically derives its features from a strenuously active intellect—an intellect aware of the contradictions of experience (above all, the problem of appearance versus reality). Hence Baroque authors extensively use the figures of contradiction: irony, paradox, ambiguity, antithesis. Over their work hovers always the faculty of wit (Italian *ingegno,* Spanish *ingenio,* French *esprit*), which the seventeenth century defined as the ability to discern the similarities among apparently dissimilar phenomena.

Struck by the contradictions of life, Baroque authors thirst for the divine and transcendent unity that they believe must lie beyond those contradictions. Sometimes they seek it in sexual love, sometimes in religious devotion—themes often to be found in the work of the same author. The Baroque is one of the great ages of Western mysticism; at the same time, it is the age in which the scientific world view of Galileo, Kepler, Bacon, Descartes, and Newton definitively ousted the traditional world view—symbolic, poetic, ordered, and hierarchical—that had prevailed since classical antiquity. In an era of such intellectual ferment, it is not surprising that literature itself was keenly intellectual.

The Baroque literary imagination achieved its greatest triumphs in lyric poetry and drama, although one must not forget that it also produced *Don Quijote* and *Paradise Lost.* In both the lyric and the drama, one encounters notable contributions by women writers: Catharina von Greiffenberg, the Austrian mystic and religious poet who achieved remarkable heights of intellectual exaltation; Kata Szidónia Petr czi, the Hungarian lyric poet and translator of German pietistic writings whose passionately personal poems were not discovered until the nineteenth century; Sibylle Schwarz, the sensitive German lyric poet and dramatist who enjoyed great contemporary popularity; Ludamilia Elisabeth von Schwarzburg-Rudolstadt, whose devotional poems contributed to the formation of the religious vernacular in Germany; the Dutch poet Maria Tesselschade, learned, witty, and much respected by her contemporaries; Ana Caro, one of Golden Age Spain's outstanding playwrights; and Aphra Behn, lyric poet, productive and distinguished dramatist, and one of the founders of the English novel. Even though prose fiction is not one of the dominant genres of the Baroque, the seventeenth century did have its share of glorious novelistic triumphs; the century opened with the *Quijote* and closed with *La Princesse de Clèves* by Mme de LaFayette, perhaps the first true novel in French and certainly one of the greatest.

In whatever genre they chose to write, Baroque authors seem to have been obsessed by two venerable *topoi*—the

Illustrations from The English Gentlewoman *(1631), by Richard Brathwaite.*

world as theater, and life as a dream. The relevance to the general preoccupation with appearance versus reality is obvious, and that preoccupation itself may to some extent explain the great efflorescence of dramatic literature in the seventeenth century. In the novelistic genre, on the other hand, the appearance/reality question is frequently bonded with a strong didactic concern, as evidenced by the many "exemplary novels" popular in the seventeenth century. The masterful collections of María de Zayas y Sotomayor and Mariana de Carvajal employ the form to convey their essentially feminist aesthetics, clothed in the conventional topos of the dichotomy between illusion (delusion) and reality, a dichotomy that is frequently presented in a gender-specific manner. The fables of Mme d'Aulnoy, didactic and escapist at the same time, also formulate new and surprisingly feminist perspectives by assigning nontraditional roles to males and female—for example, the nurturing, passive role to man and the guarding, fighting, active role to woman.

The seventeenth century was also a great age of epistolary writings. Mme de Sévigné, perhaps the most prolific *epistolière* of the age (there are over fifteen hundred extant letters penned by her) gives us a lively account of the glorious reign of Louis XIV and provides us with her intimate personal views on subjects as diverse as religion, children, gambling, travel, syphilis, medicine, literature, court intrigues, and wars.

If the conflict between the traditional symbolic and the emerging scientific world views is one of the factors conditioning the Baroque mentality, another of equal significance is surely the religious controversy between Catholic and Protestant, Anglican and Puritan, and Lutheran and Calvinist that left so heavy and tragic a mark on the age. Catharina von Greiffenberg, an Austrian Protestant noblewoman reared a generation before the Habsburgs had effectively imposed Catholicism on all their realms, was obliged to flee her estate for the sanctuary of Lutheran Nuremberg (where she was warmly welcomed by her fellow poets). She planned a trip to Vienna to convert the emperor to Lutheranism but, fortunately for her, was dissuaded. On the other hand, in what must have been one of the best-publicized events of the century, Queen Christina of Lutheran Sweden renounced her crown, converted to Catholicism, and played a significant role in the Counter-Reformation. In Hungary the Lutheran noblewoman Kata Szidónia Petr czi heroically resisted the Catholicizing tendencies of the Habsburgs; Mary Ward fled England to escape the religious persecution of Catholics, only to occasion vituperative criticism by the Catholic clergy who attempted to suppress the schools for girls she founded throughout Europe; and the staunchly Calvinistic Anna Maria van Schurman, disillusioned by the doctrinal rigidities of the church, abandoned her intellectual and literary aspirations to join a persecuted pietistic sect.

Baroque society was not hospitable to the artistic and intellectual endeavors of women, its authoritarianism and increased centralization having tightened the grip of traditional conservative attitudes. Mary Ward faced constant criticism and persecution by the clergy; Anne Bradstreet was regarded as an oddity; and Margaret Cavendish, the Duchess of Newcastle, was widely viewed as mad. (In relatively tolerant Holland, Tesselschade had better fortune.) Neither Protestantism, with its hectic and neurotic concern for doctrinal purity, nor Counter-Reformation Catholicism, with its paranoid fear of heresy, could provide an ambience like that of the High Renaissance. In its sophistication and relative openness to the arts, the Renaissance permitted—and in some cases even fostered—the work of such women as Vittoria Colonna, Gaspara Stampa, Louise Labé, and Marguerite de Navarre, and it made possible the protests of the very same literate women whom it sought to oppress. Joan Kelly remarks: "Feminist theorizing arose in the fifteenth century, in intimate association with and in reaction to the new secular culture of the modern European state. It emerged as the voice of literate women who felt themselves maligned and newly oppressed by that culture, but who were empowered by it at the same time to speak out in their defense." Despite the hostile atmosphere, and in some instances in dialectical opposition to misogyny, seventeenth-century women wrote their works, displaying a marked flair for the great and difficult Baroque styles.

Not all seventeenth-century writers, male or female, can justly be classified as Baroque; an adversarial stance toward patriarchal authority induced in some an avoidance of what was, in effect, the style of the establishment. The Baroque was a current in the art of the period, albeit the most important one. One might argue that Aphra Behn flourished after the English sensibility had become Neoclassical rather than Baroque. *La Princesse de Clèves* is justly regarded as a masterpiece of Neoclassicism, although some scholars would contend that Mme de LaFayette, like her contemporary Jean Racine, epitomizes a *baroque dompté* (the term is Helmut Hatzfeld's) in which classical *bienséance* cannot conceal the turbulence of Baroque passion. The Danish countess Leonora Christina and the Italian Camilla Faà Gonzaga practice, in their gripping memoirs, a style that does not even attempt the fashionable devices of the Baroque; they write straightforward, highly personal prose guided by no principles apart from their own genius and firm convictions. Camilla Faà, indeed, sees the process of writing as the only path left to (re)establish her identity—to recollect, rectify, and justly preserve the story of her life which her husband, Duke Ferdinand, had misrepresented. Finally, the memoirs of Queen Christina of Sweden, while rhetorical and occasionally ebullient, preserve in an essentially personal prose a fascinating individual's struggle to achieve her ambitions.

Even when composing in the traditional genres and forms of Baroque letters, women writers were autodidacts by necessity and often stood outside the mainstream. Unable to attend universities and rarely permitted to join literary societies, they were forced to work in relative isolation—a phenomenon at least partially responsible for the noted independence and "modernity" of their thought, form, and style.

Scholarship and learning, as well as belles lettres, attracted many women during the seventeenth century. The learned lady, as Natalie Zemon Davis observes, "struggled to establish a role herself: the female schoolteacher became a familiar figure, whether as spinster or as an Ursuline." Frequently labeled "bluestockings," often distrusted or even ridiculed, women scholars voiced ardent concerns for the position, education, and educability of women; they advocated serious intellectual training and sustained study. "Not to find pleasure in serious reading," wrote Mme de Sévigné in 1689, "gives a pastel coloring to the mind," and her sentiments seem to have been shared by scores of seventeenth-century women.

While the fifteenth-century *querelle des femmes* never disappeared entirely from the literary scene (and was vigorously sustained by the women humanists of Renaissance Italy), it flared up again with renewed vigor after the publication of Jacques Olivier's *Alphabet of the Imperfection and Malice of Women* in 1615. Among the illustrious participants in the debate were Europe's leading women scholars: France's Marie de Gournay; Holland's Anna Maria van Schurman; Italy's Lucrezia Marinella; England's Bathsua Makin, Margaret Cavendish, and Aphra Behn; and Spain's María de Zayas y Sotomayor. More than their fifteenth- and sixteenth-century predecessors, these seventeenth-century women addressed many of the philosophical and theologial issues raised by misogyny: Is woman, indeed, an incomplete version of the male? Are men and women equally prone to sin? Are women capable of bettering their lot? Will women be resurrected in female form after the last day of judgment?

Early Modern women scholars advocate boldly and often uncompromisingly the spiritual and intellectual equality of the sexes in their early works. Anna Maria van Schurman, perhaps the most famous (though certainly not the most militant) among them, formulates her views in a syllogistic manner:

> 1) Nature has given every human being the principles or the potential to grasp the principles of all arts and sciences. Women, too, have been given their principles; therefore, women are capable of grasping the arts and sciences.

> 2) Whoever has a desire for pursuing the arts and the sciences (cf. Aristotle, Metaphysica I:2), can do so. Women as members of the human species do have this desire; therefore, women are capable of pursuing the arts and sciences.

Schurman's defense of education for women is firmly anchored in ethical concerns; it rejects the prevalent view of the dangers posed by women's learning—namely, the tendency to heresy, pride, and sexual infidelity. Within the Renaissance tradition of More and Vives, who advocated women's education as a means to moral improvement, Schurman insists that education, the study of letters, leads to "the true greatness of soul." She differs from her Renaissance predecessors in her unwillingness to ascribe intrinsic value to household activities and her firmly optimistic view of the inevitable social and intellectual results of the education of women. In her devaluation of exclusively domestic, ornamental occupations for women, Schurman is joined by her English contemporary, Bathsua Makin. Makin argues in her introductory remarks to *An Essay to Revive the Antient Education of Gentlewomen:*

> Before I mention the Objections, I shall state the Propositions I have endeavoured to prove; That which I intend is this, That Persons of competent natural parts, indifferently inclin'd and disposed to Learning, whom God hath blessed with Estates, that are not cumbred in the World, but have liberty and opportunity in their Childhood; and afterwards, being competently instructed in all things now useful that concern them as Women, may and ought to be improved in more Polite Learning, in Religion, Arts, and the knowledge of things, in Tongues also as subservient to these, rather than to spend the over-plus time of their youth, in making Points for Bravery, in dressing and trimming themselves like *Bartholomew*-Babies, in Painting and Dancing, in making Flowers of Coloured Straw, and building Houses of stained Paper, and such like vanities.

Unlike Lucretia Marinella and the more radical writers who advocated woman's superiority to man or delivered sweeping defenses of sexual egalitarianism, Schurman represents the more widespread view of seventeenth-century feminists writers: the potential equality of male and female, a potentiality which can be realized through equal education, social acceptance, and public opportunity.

While Schurman is deeply religious and cerebral in the logic of her defense of women, her French contemporary Marie de Gournay is polemical and delightfully irreverent. On the subject of the masculine identity of Christ (and therefore of priests), the Catholic de Gournay argues that Jesus' incarnation as a male is no special distinction bestowed upon the male sex, but simply a matter of historic convenience. "If men pride themselves," she says, "on the fact that Jesus Christ was born of their sex, the answer is that this was necessary for the sake of decency, for if he had been a woman, it would have been impossible for Jesus to go out at all hours of the day and the night and mingle with the crowds to convert them and to help and save mankind, without creating a scandal, especially in the face of the malice of the Jews." A correspondent and admirer of Schurman and a noted philological scholar herself, de Gournay presents her readers with a display of satiric pyrotechnics when faced with male scholars' disregard for female scholarship and art. Speaking of women collectively, de Gournay delivers a moving plea for equality. At the beginning of "The Ladies" Grievance," which she dedicated to the competent French regent Anne of Austria, de Gournay expresses her outrage at patriarchial prejudices by addressing the quintessential concern of women since time immemorial—freedom: "Happy are you, reader, if you do not belong to this sex to whom all good things are forbidden, since to us freedom is forbidden; and whom they [men] prevent from acquiring almost all virtues by keeping us away from power. . . . Happy are you, therefore, for whom it is no crime to be intelligent and learned, since the mere fact that you are a man allows you to think and do as you please and makes whatever you say right, and other people will believe you or at any rate listen to you."

Freedom, of course, is a protean term: ambiguous at best, constantly changing, and almost impossible to define in absolute as opposed to relative terms. Ever since Joan Kelly's pioneering work over a decade ago, scholars have believed that the freedom of Renaissance and Early Modern women declined in the context of an increasing disjunction between the public and private spheres of life through a restricting of female activity to the domestic sphere. More recently, Merry Wiesner has argued that, for Renaissance and seventeenth-century women, freedom specifically meant the ability to participate in public life. Margaret Cavendish, Duchess of Newcastle, for example, wrote in 1656: "Thus by an Opinion, which I hope is but an Erroneous one in Men, we are shut out of all Power and Authority, by reason we are never Imployed either in Civil or Martial Affairs, our Counsels are Despised, and Laught at, the best of our actions are Trodden down with Scorn; by the Over-weening conceit Men have of Themselves, and through a Despisement of us." Demanding equal education for women, Margaret Cavendish defines freedom as access to the means and tools of power, the opportunity of full participation in public and intellectual life. Her French contemporary Marie de Gournay addresses the question of freedom in broader and more psychological terms, a definition that seems to hold true for most seventeenth-century women writers. Freedom, she asserts, is the phenomenon of being taken seriously, of having the opportunity for intellectual and artistic fulfillment and success—aspirations not very different from recent efforts by women scholars to establish a policy of anonymous submissions for publication. In her advocacy of equal opportunities for men and women, de Gournay goes one step further by suggesting that the victims of patriarchal chauvinism are ultimately men as well as women. Concluding her tract, she warns of the dangers presented by the ignorance of prejudice: "Men will find out, moreover, that in order to pay them back, women are seeking to acquire that same fine habit they have of wanting to belittle our sex without even listening to us or reading our writings, for we have listened to them and read their works. They should also remember a dangerous expression of excellent origin: only the less able can live content with their own wisdom, looking over their shoulder at that of others, and ignorance is the mother of presumption."

WOMEN AND EDUCATION

Myrna Reynolds (essay date 1920)

SOURCE: "Learned Ladies in England Before 1650: Period from 1603 to 1650," in *The Learned Lady in England: 1650-1760,* Houghton Mifflin Company, 1920, pp. 23-37.

[*Below, Reynolds focuses on the nature of women's education in England during the first half of the seventeenth century, describing the intellectual background and training of several women writers of the period.*]

With the death of Elizabeth we come practically to the end of the favor accorded learned women. The changed tone of public opinion may be fairly indicated by a few scattered utterances from contemporary poems and essays.

Sir Thomas Overbury, in his *Characters* (1614), describes "A Good Woman" as one "whose husband's welfare is the business of her actions." Her chief virtue is that "Shee is Hee." In *A Wife* he says that "Books are a part of Man's Prerogative." He praises a "passive understanding" in women and deprecates learning since

> What it finds malleable it maketh frail
> And doth not add more ballast, but more sail.

Powell, in *Tom of All Trades* (1631), is emphatic in his plea for the domestic as against the learned lady: "Let

them learne plaine workes of all kinds, so they take heed of too open seaming. Instead of Song and Musicke, let them learn Cookerie and Laundrie. And instead of reading in *Sir Philip Sidney's Arcadia,* let them reade the grounds of good huswifery. I like not a female Poetresse at any hand." William Habington, in *Castara* (1634), a series of poems in honor of Lucy Herbert, his wife, gave a comprehensive description of the ideal wife's attitude towards her husband: "Shee is inquisitive onely of new wayes to please him, and her wit sayles by no other compass then that of his direction. Shee lookes upon him as Conjurers upon the Circle, beyond which there is nothing but Death and Hell; and in him shee beleeves Paradice circumscrib'd. His vertues are her wonder and imitation; and his errors, her credulitie thinkes no more frailtie, then makes him descend to the title of Man." Richard Brathwait, in *The English Gentleman,* comments with apparent approval on the ancient seclusion of women. He says, "*The Ægyptians,* by an especiall decree (as *Plutarch* reports) injoined their Women to weare no shooes, because they should abide at home. The *Grecians* accustomed to burne, before the doore of the new married, the axletree of that coach, wherein she was brought to her husbands house, letting her understand that she was ever after to dwell there."

Sir Ralph Verney said of his own daughter: "Pegg is very backward. . . . I doubt not but she will be schollar enough for a Woeman." With regard to little Nancy Denton he wrote: "Let not your girl learn Latin nor short hand: The difficulty of the first may keep her from that vice, for soe I must esteem it in a woeman; but the casinesse of the other may be a prejudice to her; for the pride of taking sermon noates hath made multitudes of women unfortunate." Miss Nancy was quite in advance of her godfather in her conception of the studies appropriate for her. She wrote to him: "I know you and my coussenes will out rech me in french, but i am a goeng whaar i hop i shal out rech you in ebri grek and laten." Sir Ralph answered: "I did not think you had been guilty of soe much learning as I see you are; and yet it seems you rest unsatisfied or else you would not threaten Lattin, Greeke, and Hebrew too. Good sweet harte bee not soe covitous; beleeve me a Bible (with yᵉ Common prayer) and a good plaine cattichisme in your mother tongue being well read and practised, is well worth all the rest and much more sutable to your sex; I know your Father thinks thise false doctrine, but be confident your husband will bee of my oppinion. In French you can not be too cunning for that language affords many admirable books fit for you as Romances, Plays, Poetry, Stories of illustrious (not learned) Woemen, receipts for preserving, makinge creames and all sorts of cookeryes, ordring your gardens and in Breif, all manner of good housewifery."

The general opinion was quite in accord with Luther when he said: "Women should remain at home, sit still, keep house, and bear and bring up children"; or, at the best, with Milton's "He for God only, she for God in him."

Mr. Baldwyn, it is true, in 1619, in his *New Help to Discourse,* praises England as the place where women had the greatest prerogatives. In England, he says, women "are not kept so severely submiss" as in France, nor so jealously guarded as in Italy. "England is termed by foreigners the Paradise of Women as it is by some accounted the Hell of horses and the Purgatory of Servants. And it is a common byword among the Italians that if there were a bridge built over the narrow seas all women in Europe would run into England." But this favorable opinion must be discounted as being a retrospective estimate based mainly on the attitude towards women in the sixteenth century; and further, as being an Englishman's attempt to exalt English as against continental customs.

Of more curious interest is the ingenious attempt of the Bishop of London to interpret the account of the creation of Eve from Adam's rib as an intention on the part of the Creator to teach the equality of woman with man. The Bishop says: "The species of this bone is exprest to be *costa,* a rib, a bone of the side, not of the head: a woman is not *domina,* the ruler; nor of any anterior part; she is not *prælata,* preferred before the man; nor a bone of the foote, she is not *serva,* a handmaid; nor of any hinder part; she is not *post-posita,* set behind the man; but a bone of the *side,* of a middle and indifferent part, to show that she is *socia,* a companion to her husband. For *qui jungunter lateribus, socii sunt,* they that walke side to side, cheeke to cheeke, walke as companions."

One book definitely in honor of the ladies came out rather late in the period. This was Charles Gerbier's *Elogium Heroinum. The Ladies' Vindication: or, The Praise of Worthy Women.* The threefold dedication to the Princess of Bohemia, "whose marvellous wisdom and profound knowledge in Arts, Sciences, and Languages, is admired by all men," to the Countess Dowager of Claire, "a Patroness of the Muses, a general Lover of the Languages, and Knowledge"; and to the "Vertuous Accomplisht Lady Anne Hudson," is justified by the three principles in natural philosophy, the three theological virtues, and the three graces. "Woman," says Mr. Gerbier, "is capable of as high improvement as man," an assertion which he proceeds to establish by the following arguments: "Does not *Sophia* signify wisdom? Are not Faith, Hope and Charity represented as Women? Are not the Seven Liberal Arts exprest in Women's Shapes? Are not the Nine Muses Daughters of Jupiter? Is not Wisdom called the Daughter of the Highest?" His list of worthy women begins with the Queen of Sheba who disputed with Solomon, goes enthusiastically through the famous dames of Greece and Rome, including the Muses and the Sibyls, and touches upon later learned women such as "Christine de Pisan, Margaret of Vallois, Lady Jane Grey, the Countess of Pembroke, the daughters of Sir Anthony Cooke," and a few other outstanding personages of Tudor times. Praise so heterogeneous and uncritical was perhaps of little value, but such as it is, it stands alone in England in the period between Elizabeth and Charles II as a defense of learned women. And no defense or protest comes from the pen of a woman.

It should, however, be noted that in European countries women were more vitally concerned in their own desti-

nies. Between 1600 and 1641 there appeared at least three significant books by women dealing with the intellectual emancipation of their sex. The earliest of these came from Italy in 1608 with a second edition in 1621. It was written by a young Venetian widow, Lucrecia Marinelli (1571-1653), and was entitled *Della notabilità e della eccellenza delle donne e dei difetti degli uomini.* A second and better known book was by Marie de Jars, the *fille d'alliance* of Montaigne, usually known as Mlle. de Gournay. Her book, entitled *L'Egalité des Hommes et des Femmes,* appeared in 1604 when "the Pride of Gournay," "the French Siren," as she was called, had become well known in the cultivated circles of Paris through her definitive edition of Montaigne's works in 1595. Mlle. de Gournay's thesis as to the dignity and capacity of women is established by divine authority and by citations from the church fathers and ancient philosophers. She follows up these expressions of opinion by a thorough résumé from sacred and profane history of the women who have worthily held high places. M. Feugère voices what must be the opinion of any modern reader [in *Les femmes poetes an XVI siècle*] when he says that *L'Egalité* would be *plus piquant* without the pedantic form in which it is cast, without *les citations fréquentes et les raisonnements scholastiques qui le surchargent.* But however cumbersome we may find her method, it apparently suited her public, for the book was enthusiastically received.

The third and by far the most important book on the position and desirable training of women was by Anna van Schurman of Utrecht. The extremes to which Mlle. de Gournay carried her doctrines were distasteful to Anna van Schurman, yet many of her ideas were doubtless based on the work of her French predecessor, *la mère du féminisme moderne.* Anna van Schurman's book was translated into English and had a direct influence on the progress of English educational ideals for women. It is taken up in detail later in this discussion.

The low estimate of learning, in the first half of the seventeenth century, as an appropriate pursuit for women, had as its natural outcome a great decrease in the number of women who devoted themselves to any form of scholarship. The names that remain to us from this period as in any way connected with literature or learning form a singularly inchoate list, interesting, for the most part, because of the oddities it represents rather than because of any solid achievements. Of considerable importance are several ladies in the early years of the Stuarts who followed in the footsteps of Lady Pembroke as patronesses of learning. The first of these was Lady Bedford, who held her "graceful and brilliant little court" at Twickenham Park between 1608 and 1618. Daniel, Drayton, Donne, and Jonson were among those who celebrated her munificence. Though Lady Bedford wrote verses she had no pronounced literary pursuits of her own. Her "considerable and varied learning" went preferably along antiquarian and horticultural lines. She collected medals and pictures, and she designed a garden highly praised by Sir William Temple. She is of importance chiefly because, in an age when learning lived only as it found patrons, she was magnificent in her hospitality to the poets. Lady Mary

Wroth was a niece of Lady Pembroke and carried on the traditional family attitude towards poets. Jonson's *Alchemist* (1610) was dedicated to her, and Chapman's *Iliad* (1614) had a prefatory sonnet addressed to her. She wrote *The Countess of Montgomerie's Urania* (1621), in four books, a work modeled on her uncle's *Arcadia*. A third patroness was Elizabeth Spencer, wife of Sir George Carey. She was a kinswoman of Edmund Spenser and he commemorated her for "the excellent favors" she had granted him.

One of the most notable young women of the time of James I was Elizabeth Jocelyn (1596-1622). She was brought up by her grandfather, William Chaderton, Bishop of Lincoln. He was a friend of Sir Anthony Coke and Lord Burleigh and naturally shared their ideas as to education. The quick wit and remarkable memory of this little granddaughter greatly pleased him and he took the utmost pains with her education, training her carefully in "languages, history, and some arts," but principally in "studies of piety." She died nine days after the birth of her first child to whom she left *The Mother's Legacie to her Unborne Childe*. The third edition came out in 1625, an incorrect impression in 1684, and a reprint of the 1625 edition in 1852. The little book contains a letter to her husband in which she indicates her wishes in case the child should be a girl:

> I desire her bringing up to bee learning the Bible, as my sisters doe, good housewifery, writing and good workes: other learning a woman needs not; though I admire it in those whom God hath blest with discretion, yet I desired not so much in my owne, having seene that sometimes women have greater portions of learning than wisdome, which is of no better use to them than a main saile to a flye-boat, which runs under water. But where learning and wisdom meet in a vertuous disposed woman, she is the fittest closet of all goodnesse. She is, indeed, I should but shame myself, if I should goe about to praise her more. But, my dear, though she have all this in her, she will hardly make a poore man's wife: Yet I leave it to thy will. If thou desirest a learned daughter, I pray God give her a wise and religious heart, that she may use it to his glory, thy comfort, and her owne salvation.

Nearly all of the book is given up to cautions and plans for a boy's education. And for boy or girl there is great emphasis on religion, on attending services, reading the Bible, and keeping up habits of daily devotion. Of the prayers definitely recommended, one for morning is one hundred and eighty lines, and one suitable for all times is three hundred and fifty-nine lines. In the brief portion addressed directly to the girl, "Devout Anna, Just Elizabeth, Religious Ester, and Chaste Susanna" are held up as exemplars. Self-effacement seems the chief duty enjoined on the girl: "If thou beest a Daughter, remember thou art a Maid, and such ought thy modesty to bee, that thou shouldst scarce speak, but when thou answerest." The book was deservedly popular because it was so genuine in its forecast of sorrow, so pathetically eager in plans and hopes for her husband and child. No other work so personal and human in its appeal comes to light in this period.

There are during the first half of the century a few books by women on practical subjects. They could hardly take rank as learned productions, but they are significant as early attempts on the part of women to put into some sort of readable form, and to print for the instruction of other women, the wisdom garnered through years of experience. One of these books appeared in 1628 and was entitled *The Countess of Lincoln's Nurserie*. The Countess was the mother of seven sons and nine daughters and wrote this little treatise particularly for the guidance of her daughter-in-law Bridget. It is described as "a well-wrote piece full of fine arguments, and capable of convincing anyone that is capable of conviction, of the necessity and advantages of mothers nursing their children." A second book transmitted information of another sort. Before 1651 Elizabeth Grey, Countess of Kent (1581-1651), the granddaughter of Bess of Hardwick, wrote or compiled *A Choice Manuall, or Rare and Select Receipts in Physick and Chyrurgery*. A second part, entitled *A True Gentlewoman's Delight Wherein is contained all manner of Cookery*, reached its nineteenth edition in 1687. *The Legacie*, the *Nurserie*, the *Choice Manuall*, were the direct outcome of interests considered appropriate for women, and such publicity as they involved would not be challenged.

Letter-writing is also a realm ascribed without question to women, and when chance has rescued from oblivion any group of their letters, social history has been thereby enriched. The earliest Englishwoman, any large number of whose letters have been preserved and published, is Lady Brilliana Harley (1600-43) who wrote to her son Edward while he was at Oxford in the years 1638-40. She was a woman of pronounced religious and political opinions, observant, domestic, and with a ready pen for picturesque detail, and her letters are of more interest than most of the contemporary published work.

A few women have more directly to do with learning than those already mentioned. Occasionally in some great family Tudor traditions were maintained. Margaret, Countess of Cumberland (1560-1616), for instance, held to the idea that maidens of noble houses must be nobly educated, and she induced the poet Daniel to live at Skipton Castle as tutor to Anne, her nine-year-old daughter. Bishop Rainbow, who knew the family well, gives the following account of Anne:

> She could discourse with virtuoso's, travellers, scholars, merchants, divines, statesmen, and with good housewives in any kind: insomuch that a prime and elegant wit, Dr. Donne, well seen in all human learning . . . is reported to have said of this lady, in her younger years to this effect; that she knew well how to discourse of all things from predestination to slea-silk. Meaning that although she was skilful in her housewifery, and such things in which women are conversant, yet her penetrating wit soared up to pry into the highest mysteries, looking at the highest example of female wisdom. Although she knew *Wool* and *Flax*, fine *Linen* and *Silk*, things appertaining to the spindle and the distaff: *yet she could open her mouth with wisdom*. . . . If she had sought fame rather than wisdom,

possibly she might have been ranked among those wise and learned of her sex, of whom *Pythagoras* or *Plutarch,* or any of the ancients have made such honourable mention.

A portrait of Anne at thirteen represents the books supposedly read by her under her tutor, Mr. Daniel, and her governess, Mrs. Ann Taylor, whose heads appear in the picture. The books are "Eusebius, St. Augustine, Sir Philip Sidney's Arcadia, Godfrey of Boulogne, The French Academy, Cambden, Ortelius, and Agrippa on the Vanity of Occult Sciences."

At nineteen Anne married the Earl of Dorset. Her second marriage, in middle life, was to Philip Herbert, Fourth Earl of Pembroke and Montgomery. In alliance with these noble houses she was extremely unhappy. In her Journal she says: "The marble pillars of Knowle in Kent and Wilton in Wiltshire, were to me often times but the gay arbor of anguish. A wise man, that knew the insides of my fortune, would often say, that I lived in both these my lords' great families as the river Roan runs through the lake of Geneva, without mingling its streams with the lake; for I gave myself up to retiredness as much as I could and made good books and virtuous thoughts my companions." A portrait, belonging to this period of middle life, indicates as the books then most favored, "the Bible, Charron on Wisdom and pious treatises." Lady Pembroke's pursuit of abstract and theological learning was, however, largely the outcome of her repressed and unhappy life. On her second widowhood, in 1650, she forsook learning and gave free reign to her "master-passion for bricks and mortar." But most of this energetic work, during which she rebuilt or restored her six castles and several churches, belongs after the Restoration. As a woman of affairs Lady Pembroke made a remarkable impression on her age. Bishop Rainbow, who says she had "a clear soul shining through a vivid body," emphasizes also "her great understanding and judgment." Pennant, in his *Tour,* said that she was regarded as "the most eminent character of her times, for intellectual accomplishments, for spirit, magnificence, and benevolence."

Another lady who carried over into this period the liberal training of Tudor days was Elizabeth Tanfield (1585-1639), who, at the age of fifteen, married Henry Carey, later Viscount Falkland. Our knowledge of her very interesting life and character is derived mainly from a *Life* written by one of her daughters. She was a lover of books from her childhood and learned languages—French, Latin, Greek, Hebrew, and Transylvanian—practically without a teacher. Her daughter said of her:

> When she was but four or five years old they put her

to learn French, which she did about five weeks, and not profiting at all gave it over; after, of herself, without a teacher, whilst she was a child she learned French, Spanish and Italian; . . . she learned Latin in the same manner. . . . Hebrew she likewise, about the same time, learned with very little teaching. . . . She then learned also of a Transylvanian his language, but never finding any use of it forgot it entirely. She read so

incessantly at night that her mother forbade the servants to give her candles. But she bought candles at half a crown apiece of the servants and at twelve was £100 in their debt, a debt which she paid on her wedding day.

Her work as an author began early, for her first play was written about the time of her marriage. It was dedicated to her husband. A second play, *The Tragedy of Mariam the Faire Queene of Jewry,* was written when she was eighteen or nineteen, though not printed till 1613. She was early recognized as one of the most intellectual women of her time. In 1612 she was one of the three "Glories of Women" to whom John Davies dedicated his *Muses Sacrifice.* Later, in 1633, the publisher of Marston's Works dedicated them "To the Right Honourable the Lady Elizabeth Carey, Viscountess Falkland," because she was so "well acquainted with the Muses." That Lady Falkland's appetite for learning never abated is apparent from her daughter's testimony:

> She had read very exceedingly much: poetry of all kinds ancient and modern in several languages, all that ever she could meet; history very universally, especially all ancient Greek and Roman histories; all chronicles whatsoever of her own country, and the French histories very thoroughly: of most other countries something, though not so universally, of the ecclesiastical very much, most especially concerning its chief pastors. Of books treating of moral virtue or wisdom (such as Seneca, Plutarch's *Morals,* and natural knowledge, as Pliny, and of late ones, such as French, Mountaine, and English, Bacon) she had read very many when she was young. Of the fathers and controversial writers on both sides a great deal even of Luther and Calvin.

Lady Falkland was converted to Catholicism in 1605 and she devoted all her learning to the service of the Church. She translated Cardinal Perron's *Works* and wrote lives of the saints in verse.

Lady Falkland's son Lucius married Letice Morrison, another "undue lover of books," who abridged herself of sleep that the hours of reading might be prolonged. This daughter-in-law of Lady Falkland was not only eager for learning, but she had independent views along social lines. One of her schemes was the foundation of houses "for the education of young gentlewomen and the retirement of widows with the belief that through such houses learning and religion might flourish more than heretofore in her own sex." Her early death in the time of the Civil War frustrated her plans, but they have an especial interest as forecasting the ideas set forth by Mary Astell later in the century.

Anna Hume, the daughter of David Hume, was carefully educated by her father at Godscroft, a property to which he retired that he might be unmolested in his devotion to literature. Anna joined in his pursuits with eagerness and intelligence, and after his death she did much to complete his work. In 1644 she superintended the publication of his *History of the House and Race of Douglas and Angus.* She translated Latin poems, and in 1644 she also published *The Triumph of Love, Chastity and Death,* translated from Petrarch. Drummond of Hawthornden speaks highly of her learning and of her "rare and pregnant wit."

Esther Kello (1571-1624) is often spoken of as one of the notable women of the Stuart period. Her works were counted worthy gifts for kings, and are preserved in royal libraries. Calligraphy was one of the fine arts in the seventeenth century. To write many different hands, to make flourishes, to decorate margins, to illuminate titles and capital letters, to make elaborate head or tail pieces to chapters, and to write the alphabets of many languages, were the elements of this art. No other accomplishment was so often advertised. It was in this art that Esther Kello excelled. *Les Proverbes de Salomon* (1599), written in forty hands, and with all possible ornamental detail, was one of her most famous books. It was preserved in "Bodley's Library." In exactness, fineness, and beauty her books are said to rival the old illuminated manuscripts.

There was published in 1630 a twelve-page tract entitled *A Chain of Pearl, or a Memorial of the Peerless Graces and heroic Virtues of Queen Elizabeth, of glorious memory, composed by the noble lady, Diana Primrose.* The Pearls of the Chain are Religion, Chastity, Prudence, Temperance, Clemency, Justice, Fortitude, Science, Patience, and Bounty. A preliminary address to the author by one Dorothy Berry greets Diana as "the *Prime-rose* of the Muses nine." The Pearls are in the style of exaggerated compliment always associated with the name of Queen Elizabeth, but they could not have been inspired by any interested motives, for Elizabeth had been dead nearly a generation when they came from the press. Save the date of publication I have no facts about either Diana Prim-rose or Dorothy Berry. Perhaps their youth was spent during the "blest and happy years" when the Heroine they praised was on the throne.

> She, she it was that gave us golden days,
> And did the English name to heaven raise.

If so, and if they wrote when trouble was brewing between the King and the people, we can well understand the ardor of Diana Primrose's eulogy of the days when the Prince and People agreed "in sacred concord and sweet sympathy."

A very curious book is by Mary Fage. It is entitled *Fame's Roule* and appeared in 1637. It is a collection of the most ingenious anagrams and acrostics on the names of four hundred and twenty persons of the "hopeful posterity" of Charles I. John Weymes, for instance, is anagrammed into "Show men joy" and John Hollis into "Oh! on my hills." The amplification of the anagram is mainly compliment with now and then a trace of exhortation. This was an age when playing with words gave undoubted pleasure, but four hundred and twenty anagrams on royal names would seem an undue tax on even the most agile manipulator of the alphabet.

Katherine Chidley wrote and spoke on questions of Church

and State. In 1641 she published a quarto volume entitled *The Justification of the Independent Churches of Christ,* in which she maintained that the congregations of the Saints should receive "no direction in worship from any other than Christ their head and lawgiver." She is described as "a most violent independent who talked with so much bitterness and with so clamorous a tongue as to vanquish opposing divines, and who wrote as furiously in behalf of her cause as if she were the Amazonian Queen in defence of the Trojans."

A literary oddity of the Cromwell period, a fertile writer whose half-mad and often unintelligible prophetic writings yet came true often enough to secure her a troublesome reputation as a "Cunning Woman," was Lady Eleanor Davies, the wife of Sir John Davies of Hereford. She was twice married and both husbands had burned her manuscripts, but finally, in 1651, there was printed a pamphlet, *The Restitution of Prophecy; that Buried Talent to be revived. By the Lady Eleanor.* The Lady Eleanor was as devoted to anagrams as was Mary Fage. The change of Eleanor Davies into "Reveal O Daniel" was her mystic authorization as a prophet, until some wit shattered her anagram by producing "Never so mad a lady."

WOMEN AUTOBIOGRAPHERS

Mary Beth Rose (essay date 1986)

SOURCE: "Gender, Genre, and History: Seventeenth-Century English Women and the Art of Autobiography," in *Women in the Middle Ages and the Renaissance: Literary and Historical Perspectives,* edited by Mary Beth Rose, Syracuse University Press, 1986, pp. 245-78.

[*In the following essay, Rose examines the early development of the autobiography, focusing on the memoirs of four women: Margaret Cavendish, Lady Ann Fanshawe, Alice Thornton, and Lady Anne Halkett.*]

In the late seventeenth century English women began to write secular autobiography. Largely excluded from the political arena and the professions, Early Modern women had not added to the accounts men wrote of their public lives and the development of their careers. When a woman wished to assert herself as a member of the community whose experience was worth recording, she was confined to the family history—her role as daughter, wife, and mother—or to the accounts of religious experience—the visions, trances, ecstasies, and conversions which often exempted her from traditional sexual arrangements, as well as from the social and moral taboos against female self-expression. But when, in the late seventeenth century, English autobiography began to depart from its diverse and complex origins in religious narrative and in accounts of the public actions of famous men, women who were neither saints, mystics, nor proselytizers, but traditional wives and mothers, began not simply to record the deeds of their male relatives, but to explore their own identities and experience in autobiographical form.

When the modern conventions of autobiography as a distinctively personal, secular, and introspective literary form began to coalesce during the British Restoration, then, traditional wives and mothers can at once be recognized among the liveliest, most imaginative contributors to the evolving genre. Viewed in terms of the early development of modern autobiography, the four women whose life accounts are the subject of this essay—Margaret Cavendish, the Duchess of Newcastle (1625-1674), Anne, Lady Halkett (1623-1699), Ann, Lady Fanshawe (1625-1680), and Alice Thornton (1626/7-1706/7)—immediately sensed the literary opportunity to assert themselves as social personalities. Rather than the articulation of their personal experience of the supernatural, or as passive recorders of genealogy and observers of men's deeds, what these women depict are their relations with other people and their actions within a social world of contemporary events. Although they are all pious, they do not seek to transcend what is experienced as the confinement of their bodies, but rather to embody and enact their spirituality in sexual relationships and social life.

Several reasons enabling these women to overcome the cultural injunction against female self-expression to the point of asserting the value of their individual secular experience in autobiographical form immediately suggest themselves. In general, the individual self and the private life, realms in which women could claim some authority, were beginning to be publicly valued in the seventeenth century. Secondly, cut off from continental influence and freed from the stylized requirements of the conversion narrative, the conventions of English secular autobiography had yet to be formed; as feminist criticism has shown, women writers often excel when generic boundaries are construed as fluid and flexible. Thirdly, as is the case with three out of the four texts under consideration, secular autobiographies by both women and men tended to remain unpublished before the eighteenth century, so that women autobiographers during the Restoration need not worry that they were asserting themselves scandalously in public. Finally, and as I will argue, most importantly, all four of these women lived through the English Civil War, a period of social chaos which liberated them from many of the ordinary constrictions of sexual ideology.

Yet even the fortuitous combination of gender, genre, and history which allowed these four women to make early contributions to secular autobiography did not mitigate their expression of their social identities as problematic. Indeed, it is precisely the felt conflict between self-effacement and self-assertion, between private and public life, and between individual personality and social role that gives shape to their narratives and which they seek to resolve through the art of autobiography. In this essay I am not attempting to establish the extent to which women may be credited with influencing the development of secular autobiography. Rather, by examining four texts in detail, I will explore the ways in which the early devel-opment of modern autobiography as a form of personal assessment was congenial to the expression of female sexual and social identity in late seventeenth-century England; and will demonstrate that the particular problems that women felt in constructing their identities were the very problems which the newly evolving genre was being designed to represent.

The critic Georges Gusdorf distinguishes helpfully between two types of autobiography. The first, which he calls "propaganda for posterity," comprises the attempts of the famous to commemorate and justify their public deeds; as we have seen, early modern English women were prevented from contributing to this type of life account. But as Gusdorf and many other scholars agree, autobiography finds its fertile artistic impulse and becomes a major literary genre "when the private face of existence assumes more importance" than the recording of official facts.

As Gusdorf explains [in his essay "Conditions and Limits of Autobiography"], the second type of autobiographer, who is the concern of this essay, seeks above all to gain self-knowledge and to confer meaning on his or her experience through the unifying structural techniques of narrative. The author of an autobiography "strains toward a complete and coherent expression of his entire destiny . . . to reconstitute himself in the focus of his special unity and identity across time" by regarding the narrative as "an avowal of values and a recognition of self by the self—a choice carried out at the level of essential being." According to Gusdorf, the autobiographer's attempt to narrate a coherent selfhood is characterized by the apparent contradiction that arises when the self becomes both subject and object, creating "a considerable gap between the avowed plan of autobiography, which is simply to retrace the history of a life, and its deepest intentions, which are directed toward a kind of apologetics or theodicy of individual being." Because the autobiographer must assume, for example, the reliability of memory, the "impartiality of the self to itself," and the ability successfully to merge the present with the past in a single narrative framework, he or she "take(s) for granted the very thing that is in question," a gap between public and private intention that explains the puzzlement and the ambivalence of the literary genre. The success of an autobiography therefore depends on the author's ability to reconcile these generic ambivalences by imposing on the material a narrative structure that comprises a coherent vision of him or herself as a unique, integrated human being.

Gusdorf's formulations allow us to approach autobiography as an individual's struggle to define his or her experience by the narrative creation of a unified personality, through which the author attempts to reconcile the public and private aspects of being, often represented as conflicting. Considered as the dilemma of merging apparently contradictory levels of being into a coherent identity, the autobiographer's particular task can be equated with that of the woman writer in any form. As many scholars have shown, the attempts of woman to define herself as an integrated individual in a male-dominated society are, at worst, self-contradictory and paralyzing, and, at best, problematic. In a recent essay Elaine Showalter argues that women's writing can be comprehensively assessed as a "double-voiced discourse," the product of a muted group within a dominant structure that participates both in its own unique reality and in the shared reality engendered by the more powerful elements of society: "Both muted and dominant groups generate beliefs or ordering ideas of social reality at the unconscious level, but dominant groups control the forms or structures in which consciousness can be articulated. Thus muted groups must mediate their beliefs through the allowable forms of dominant structures."

Showalter makes clear that this "female tradition can be a positive source of strength and solidarity as well as a negative source of powerlessness; it can generate its own experience and symbols which are not simply the obverse of the male tradition." As I will try to show, in female autobiography the dialogue between muted and dominant voices which Showalter describes is conjoined with the generic impulse to impose a coherent structure of self-hood on potentially contradictory aspects of identity. Because of this congeniality of impulse between gender and genre, the four texts I am about to consider become important not only as evidence of the ways in which four Early Modern women experienced the past, but also as four early, self-conscious female attempts to create the self in literary form by constituting personality as a unifying narrative principle. In each case, the success of the author's life account depends upon her ability to mediate between apparently conflicting realities by imagining herself as a socially and psychologically integrated individual.

Insofar as autobiography attempts to unite the potentially disparate materials of individual identity through the author's creation of a coherent narrative and personality structure, the Duchess of Newcastle's *A True Relation of My Birth, Breeding, and Life* (1656) is an interesting and most illustrative failure. Among the four female autobiographers considered here, the Duchess is in several important ways an exception. Like the other women, she is an upper-class Anglican and Royalist; the English Civil War ruptured the stable social and emotional world in which she was brought up, filling her life with chaos and a variety of experience that, in all likelihood, would otherwise have remained completely unavailable to her. Unlike the other three women, however, she never becomes a mother, nor is she a widow at the time she writes. *A True Relation* is composed while she is exiled in Antwerp with her husband, William Cavendish, the Marquis of Newcastle, who, in Virginia Woolf's words, "had led the King's forces to disaster with indomitable courage but little skill." The Duchess is also the only one among these women who writes with the conscious intent of publication and, indeed, her autobiography (along with other writings of hers) was published during her lifetime. Rather than composing as the others do, with her youth, her marriage, the Civil War, and the fear of indiscretion safely behind her, the Duchess abjures the organizing principle of hindsight, choosing instead to write, as it were,

from the eye of the storm. As a result, although the challenges and problems of female identity remain unresolved in her narrative, they are nevertheless articulated with an immediacy that is unusually poignant and clear.

Not surprisingly, the Duchess's unresolved narrative and personal dilemmas center on issues of independence, power, responsibility, and freedom of choice. As several critics have noted, she begins and ends her autobiography by defining herself in terms of her relations with others. Mary Mason has recently argued, for example, that the Duchess's narration presents a model of female autobiography, in which women consistently "record and dramatize self-realization . . . through the recognition of another"; and, according to Mason, the Duchess establishes a "pattern of alterity-equality" in her depiction of her relationship with her husband. But, as we will see, the Duchess's sense of attachment is in fact overwhelmed in her account by a more pressing sense of problematic uniqueness. It is true that her claim to attention as daughter and wife provides the rhetorical framework for her narrative; yet her descriptions of her relations with others emerge not as a central, but as a subordinate element in the more compelling representation of her singularity. As an alter ego William Cavendish cuts a feeble, shadowy figure in *A True Relation,* never coming alive as a personality and making only brief, unconvincing appearances as an idealized moral character and as a writer whose abilities supposedly exceed those of his wife. What does emerge from the account is not a personality who defines herself through relationship, but rather a troubled, complex, and indecisive shaping intelligence, whose narration can be characterized more usefully by the author's persistent attempts to subsume her individuality in her social role or her personal life.

At one point, in an erratic burst of candor, the Duchess announces both a competitive desire to excel and an independent wish to control her own destiny: "I think it no crime to wish myself the exactest of Nature's works, my thread of life the longest, my Chain of Destiny the strongest, my mind the peaceblest; my life the pleasantest, my death the easiest, and the greatest saint in heaven; also to do my endeavour, so far as honour and honesty doth allow of, to be the highest on Fortune's Wheele, and to hold the Wheel from turning, if I can. And if it be commendable to wish another's good, it were a sin not to wish my own."

But the natural self-regard and confident joy in singularity which this passage expresses is not sustained in *A True Relation.* Indeed the Duchess is incapable of asserting herself without beating an instant retreat. The narrative effect of her conflict between self-assertion and self-denial can best be disentangled by observing her repeated attempts to define herself not merely in terms of her personal attachments, but rather according to a Renaissance ideal of femininity, in which relations with others form a single element in a composite of prescribed character traits, including, along with subordination and obedience, modesty, chastity, shyness, gentleness, innocence, and silence. These traits permeate the Duchess's idealized portrait of her mother, whom she memorializes as exquisitely beautiful, retiring, and even-tempered, a woman who, in educating her daughters, stressed the importance of moral character not as conjoined with, but at the expense of, discipline and skill. Indeed the Duchess has internalized this cultural ideal of the feminine, and she goes on to represent herself as (with the exception of beauty) the embodiment of these qualities.

Yet the Duchess proves as unable to commit herself to the self-effacement required by socially defined female behavior as she is to the more fully human challenge of individualism. Attempting to seem modest, for example, she often assures us that she is bashful to the point of foolishness: "I durst neither look up with my eyes, nor speak, nor be any way sociable, insomuch as I was thought a natural fool," she explains, in a purportedly self-critical account of her behavior as a young lady at Court. But her girlish modesty turns out to be foolish wisdom: "Neither do I find my bashfulness riseth so often in blushes, as contracts my spirits to a chill paleness," she confides later, betraying a vain, rather disintegrated preoccupation with the advantages her shyness lends to her physical appearance; indeed it is this very shyness that wins the love of the Marquis. But the Duchess does not simply disguise self-idealization as self-deprecation. She also does the opposite, namely, subverting her own claims to achievement or ambition with denial and self-contempt. Shortly after the passage quoted above, in which she exults in her uniqueness, she confesses to the reader in a moving and forthright paragraph the actual intensity of her ambition for fame which, even "if it be a vanity," she nevertheless desires above all things. On the same page, clearly wishing to appear more "silent, chaste and obedient," she reassures us that her deepest instinct is actually to "willingly exclude myself, so as never to see the face of any creature but my Lord as long as I live, inclosing myself like an anchorite, wearing a frieze gown, tied with a cord about my waist." But she had elaborated earlier her love of dressing up in fashion designs of her own invention, "for I always took delight in a singularity." Furthermore, despite "being addicted from my childhood to contemplation rather than conversation," she not only likes going "abroad," but finds exposure to public life necessary in order to gather fresh material for her writing. In short, the Duchess's attempt to characterize herself in terms of the world's image of womanhood, to which she feels deeply attached, is nevertheless compromised everywhere by contradiction and hyperbole. Is she a moody, melancholy, contemplative genius, whose delicate modesty and innocence cannot bear the boisterous intrusion of the vulgar world? Or is she an intelligent, talented writer whose gregarious energy and productivity demand both company and fame? Is she a serious artist, whose overwhelming wealth of ideas requires nurture and expression? Or a foolish, shallow dilettante, inattentive and vain? She tells us all of these things, affirming them each with equal vehemence, denying them all with unyielding self-doubt. Are her thoughts and ideas really worth writing about? Does the world's opinion matter, or should she disregard it? Should she assert herself, taking responsibility for her desires? She cannot decide.

How does such profound ambivalence translate itself into action? When the Duchess recounts her failed attempt to save her husband's estate during the Protectorate, she reveals the paralysis inherent in her approach to the world. Exiled in Antwerp, she learns that the wives of Royalist owners of sequestered estates could receive allowances; "necessity"—the Duchess never admits to acting by choice—forces her to return to England with her brother-in-law, harboring "hopes I should receive a benefit thereby." We learn from her account of this episode neither the facts of her case, nor the details of her transactions. Instead she dwells on her lady-like "absolute refusal" either to plead in her own behalf or to plan an effective course of action because "I had a firm faith, or strong opinion, that the pains was more than the gains, and being unpractised in publick employments, unlearned in their uncouth ways, ignorant of the humours and dispositions of those persons to whom I was to address my suit, and not knowing where the power lay, and being not a good flatterer, *I did not trouble myself or petition my enemies; Besides I am naturally Bashful . . .*" (italics added).

Desperately needing the money, having made the dangerous, painful journey to obtain it, the Duchess then abdicates all responsibility for her property in order to consolidate the pose of female innocence so crucial to her self-conception. Boasting of her ineptitude, she clarifies the way in which female "success" becomes equivalent to male failure, making all action on her part futile. As we will see, the Duchess's self-defeating attitude toward her practical abilities stands in vivid contrast to the more constructive approaches taken by several of the other women autobiographers under consideration, all of whom are forced by political exigency to transcend the constrictions of sexual ideology in the effort to save their property.

But the Duchess cannot adjust to emergency: naturally she loses her cause. She ends the account of her failure in a burst of misogynist rage, castigating women who seek "pre-eminence of place" by words: "words rushing against words, thwarting and crossing each other . . . it is neither words nor place that can advance them, but worth and merit." The Duchess does not connect this wrath against other women's attempts to excel verbally with her own prodigious literary output and acknowledged desire for fame; therefore she misses, as she continually does, the opportunity for self-knowledge. It is this failure to merge, to make connections, which pointedly fractures her self-conception and her uneven run-on narrative. Her attempts at structure are repeatedly undetermined, for example, by her inability to settle on a point or commit herself to an idea. At the beginning of *A True Relation* she links the unfortunate disruption of her nuclear family with the disastrous disruption of the kingdom; but then we learn that she left home out of desire, actively wanting to go to Court where, although she describes herself as maladjusted in an attempt to seem meek, she in fact achieves a happy and brilliant marriage. So much for the connecting theme of unwanted personal and political change.

Often called incoherent, the Duchess's narrative actually

imitates the psychological logic of ambivalence. Gusdorf argues that an autobiography "does not show us the individual seen from outside in his visible actions but the person in his inner privacy, not as he was, not as he is, but as he believes and wishes himself to be and to have been." The Duchess's disjointed narrative makes clear that she cannot begin to formulate a desired identity: she simply cannot *decide* how she "wishes [herself] to have been." Insofar as *A True Relation* reveals the urgently problematic, ambiguous nature of feminine identity, it can be considered, as scholars have argued, a model of female autobiography.

Claims for viewing *A True Relation* as an influential forerunner in this genre should not, however, be exaggerated. The other three women under consideration confront the same problems of role and individuality that the Duchess of Newcastle does, but each manages to find more coherent personal and narrative strategies for resolving them. Unlike the Duchess's equivocal, urgent self-assertion, Ann, Lady Fanshawe's autobiography is written as a recollection during her widowhood and is cast in the socially conventional form of the family history. Addressing her *Memoirs* (1676) to her son, she explains that she writes to memorialize her excellent husband for her son's benefit; publication appears never to have been her goal. When we approach Lady Fanshawe's *Memoirs*, Mary Mason's argument that women define themselves in relation to others therefore becomes considerably more useful than in the case of the irrepressible narcissism of *A True Relation*. As I hope to show, Lady Fanshawe's text reveals the advantages as well as the price of such self-definition.

Unlike the Duchess of Newcastle, Ann Fanshawe succeeds remarkably in subsuming her individuality within her role. Characteristically, the cultural superego through which she defines herself is not the prescribed composite of individualized female character traits with which the Duchess struggles, but rather the seventeenth-century Protestant vision of the perfect wife. Since the British Reformation in the 1530's, the essentially Pauline conception of "holy matrimony," wherein "the husband is head of the wife, even as Christ is head of the Church" (Ephesians 5:23) had been refined and reiterated in Protestant moral and religious writing. At the very beginning of her narrative, Lady Fanshawe succinctly presents the image of her desired identity as a fortunate partner in such a union, the "great mystery" in which the husband and wife "shall be one flesh," the husband loving the wife as he loves himself, the wife submitting to the husband, reverencing him (Ephesians 5:21-33): "*Glory be to God* we never had but one mind through out our lives, our soules were wrapped up in each other, our aims and designs one, our loves one, and our resentments one . . . What ever was reall happiness God gave it me in him; but to commend my better half . . . methinks is to commend myself and so may bear a censure."

At no point in her narrative does Lady Fansawe deviate from her loyal, loving adherence to this idealized partnership of identical emotions and goals. Indeed she recounts the one moment of matrimonial conflict in her autobiog-

raphy only in order to reveal the ease with which she overcame her need for self-assertion. In this isolated instance she discusses her attempt during the height of the Civil War to extract secret information from her husband, Sir Richard, who was performing crucial services for the beleaguered King Charles: "I that was young, innocent, and to that day had never in my mouth 'What news,' begun to think there was more in inquiring into buseness of publick affaires than I thought off." She wheedles and cries, refuses to eat or sleep until he tells her what he knows; he condescends, kisses her, changes the subject, until finally compelled by her weeping and begging to declare that, though his life, fortune, and "every thought" are hers, yet "my honour is my own." It never occurs to Lady Ann to question either openly or deviously an arrangement in which her husband's knowledge and attachments are so much freer and more various than her own. Instead the unequal logic of patriarchal power relations is revealed to her through the glow of Sir Richard's undoubted affection and, as she watches him, the scales fall from her eyes: "So great was his reason and goodness, that upon consideration it made my folly appeare to me so vile that from that day until the day of his death I never thought fit to ask him any business, but that he communicated freely to me, in order to his estate or family."

The problem for this inquiry becomes: how does a self-defined silent partner manage to generate a narrative unified and enlivened by her integrated conception of her individuality? As Lady Fanshawe continually makes clear, her goal is not to act, as a subject, but to be loved, as an object of devotion. The lack of conflict with which she discards her girlish fondness for physical activity in order gladly to assume her dead mother's modest, subdued role as family caretaker indicates the potentially static quality of her life account. Yet most of her *Memoirs* tell a lively and engaging story.

Surprisingly, in telling her story, Lady Fanshawe eschews two rhetorical strategies that female autobiographers commonly employ when confronting the contradiction between culturally enjoined silence and the need for self-assertion, or between the peaceful, cyclical orderliness assumed to comprise feminine destiny and the linear, suspenseful quest motif required for the construction of conventionally masculine narrative. The first of these strategies, devious self-assertion, takes the form either of self-idealization disguised as self-deprecation or the overt denial of anger and hostility, prominent emotions that, because they cannot really be ignored, form a subversive subtext. The Duchess of Newcastle and, as we will see, Alice Thornton, are experts at this double-edged, often self-defeating technique. At times the violence and self-hatred implicit in Lady Fanshawe's complete identification with male superiority are starkly revealed, as in her account of her son Richard's death. "Both my eldest daughters had the smallpox att the same time," she explains, underscoring the virtue of her priorities, "and though I neglected them, and day and night tended my dear son, yet it pleased God they recovered and he dyed, the grief of which made me miscary and caused a sickness of 3 weeks." But the inhumanity in this passage is shocking precisely because it is exceptional; furthermore, no unacknowledged emotional conflicts surface to disturb the author's untroubled identification with the sexual status quo.

A second narrative strategy which female autobiographers commonly use involves the creation of a conventional linear quest motif out of the author's romantic adventures, which culminate in her destiny-as-marriage. Lady Anne Halkett uses this strategy with great success, a point to which I will return. But, despite her genuine love for her husband and her dramatic location of selfhood in marriage, Lady Ann Fanshawe alone among the four autobiographers under consideration fails to tell the saga of her courtship. For her, the story of self-creation begins, rather than ends, with marriage.

In Lady Fanshawe's case, it is clearly the Civil War that liberates her from the acquiescence and passivity required by the sexual ideology to which she is profoundly attached; it is therefore the War which gives her story a plot. Because Sir Richard is deeply involved in Royalist intrigue, Lady Ann must frequently act to protect him, along with their joint property interests. Unlike the Duchess of Newcastle, whose ambivalence about public self-assertion and individuality paralyzes her, Ann Fanshawe responds to the call to independent action as a challenge. In three daring episodes, for example, she not only makes dangerous, clandestine nightly trips to visit her husband in jail, but also intrigues resourcefully for his freedom; imitating romantic tradition, she disguises herself as a man and stands by her husband's side during a shipboard battle with Turkish pirates, inspiring Sir Richard to cry, "Good God, that love can make this change!"; she plots and successfully enacts a courageous escape from Britain, forging her passport in order to join her husband when he is exiled in France. Significantly, the perilous exigencies of Civil War in no way compel the boldly and publicly active Lady Ann to feel conflict about her feminine identity. On the contrary, the war simply lends wider meaning to her role as faithful, obedient, and loving wife. Unlike the Duchess's, her identification with her role is complete and untroubled, enabling her to perform effectively on her husband's behalf. Just as her duty as wife and mother later becomes the rationale for the act of writing her *Memoirs,* so her marriage provides her with a motive and cue for action during the Revolution without requiring her to question prevailing sexual assumptions, which she never does.

For Lady Ann Fanshawe, the female autobiographer's task of integrating potentially conflicting aspects of identity in the creation of a story and a self is thus considerably reduced in difficulty by the Civil War. The external chaos of the Revolution paradoxically releases her from internal conflict by allowing her to merge her private concerns with the larger political environment. Specifically, the exterior strangeness of the political scene enlarges the internal borders of the psychologically familiar, enabling her to act by rendering her vision of the ideal Protestant marriage more expansive and flexible. This point becomes clear when we examine the progress of her narration, which

divides neatly between accounts of the Revolution and the Restoration. In her retelling of Civil War experiences, Lady Ann structures her vision of her marriage with a coherent narrative pattern of death and resurrection, disaster and delivery. Replete with echoes from the Gospels and the Book of Acts, her story of holy matrimony plagued by war becomes a secular scripture recounting separation from and reunion with her husband who, going about "his master's business," becomes a type of Christ that she can follow, serve, and adore. This scheme works well to propel the narrative forward but, when the two are permanently reunited at the Restoration, the successful pattern inevitably dissolves.

During peacetime, when Sir Richard serves as ambassador to Portugal and Spain, the flamboyant public drama of war, resonant with the depth of emotional life, dwindles to a shallow catalogue of ceremonies and gifts that is enlivened only by Lady Ann's sensual love for exotic and colorful objects, along with her splendid eye for concrete physical detail. Indeed the depiction of her passionate attachment to money and property alters drastically as her experience shifts from war to peace. The pattern of separation from and reunion with Sir Richard, for example, allows her to unite money with love in a blissful epiphany of bourgeois marital goals: "He with all expressions of joy received me in his arms and gave me an hundred pieces of gold, saying, 'I know that thou that keeps my heart so well will keep my fortune.' . . . And now I thought myself a qween, and my husband so glorious a crown that I more valued myself to be call'd by his name than borne a princess . . . and his soule doted on me." In peacetime Spain, however, this ecstatic merger of affection and property is reduced to representing the once dynamic soldier Sir Richard as a colorful, although lifeless, diplomatic artifact: "His sute was trimed with scarlet taffeta ribbon, his stockings of white silk upon long scarlett silk ones, his shoes black with scarlett shoes' strings and garters, his linnen very fine laced with very rich Flanders lace, a black beavour button on the left side, with a jewell of 1200 lb."

Lady Fanshawe's capacity for reverence has given way to the related but less creative capacity to be dazzled. In the second part of her narrative, her need to be loved is represented in the reiterative rendition of public honors—the banquets, gifts, and canon salutes that celebrate her and her husband by diplomatic requirement. It is a static picture of power without desire: she has become absorbed in the institution, rather than the relationship of marriage. It is not surprising that her narrative trails off inconclusively after her husband's death, although she survived him by fourteen years.

Lady Fanshawe's *Memoirs* provide an excellent example of the way in which a chaotic period of history involves a woman whose conventionality and single-minded devotion to her husband would otherwise have restricted her to silence and passivity in an engaging and dramatic story. In Elaine Showalter's terms, the Revolution releases the muted female voice to achieve creative expression within the "allowable forms" of masculine adventure and narration. Yet to read the *Memoirs* is to become increasingly aware of an inhibited, repressed story. It is not simply that Lady Fanshawe's narration dwindles from war to peace, drama to stasis, ceasing entirely with the death of her husband and her role as his wife. Rather there is an essential tale that remains untold, namely, the saga of Lady Ann's body. During the twenty-two years of her marriage, Ann Fanshawe gives birth to fourteen children, nine of whom die, and this impressive statistic does not encompass the repeated trauma of miscarriages, including one of triplets. In short, while during both war and peace she is almost constantly pregnant, miscarrying, or giving birth, Lady Ann treats these experiences peripherally, merely mentioning rather than exploring them. This astonishing omission cannot be accounted for by attributing to her an anachronistic reticence about sexuality. It is rather that, in her selection of material and her choice of narrative strategies, she assigns a secondary value to this highly individualized aspect of her experience.

Was participation in endlessly similar diplomatic ceremonies really more compelling to this sensual, erotic woman than the precarious adventure of pregnancy and childbirth in the seventeenth century? Or was there simply no "allowable form" in which to tell such a story? The *Autobiography* (c. 1670) of Mrs. Alice Thornton proves that there was.

Alice Thornton (1626-1706/7) was an Anglican and Royalist from a distinguished upper gentry family, and her father, Christopher Wandesford, became Lord Deputy of Ireland before his death forced her mother to return with her family to England during the chaos of the Irish Rebellion in 1641. Mrs. Thornton's *Autobiography* is a long, bulky account of her childhood, the political upheavals she experienced in Ireland and England, her marriage and numerous pregnancies, her squabbles with relatives, friends, and neighbors, her many illnesses, and her efforts to retain her property.

Upon this variety of selected material Alice Thornton imposes the same narrative pattern that Ann Fanshawe uses to organize the first half of her *Memoirs:* the scriptural sequence of death and resurrection, affliction and delivery. As we have seen, Lady Fanshawe creates this structure to convey her love for her husband and to define herself by dramatizing her relationship with him, an imaginative feat made feasible by the intervention of the Civil War in her emotional life. Further, her location of meaning in her relationship to her husband causes her virtually to ignore her frequent pregnancies and childbearing, experiences which he could not directly share. In stark contrast, Alice Thornton uses the same narrative pattern precisely to convey her struggles with her body, and, in so doing, she seeks to dramatize herself not as a partner, a secondary ally, but as a hero, a primary object of God's love.

In Mrs. Thornton's *Autobiography,* her body becomes the symbol for the questing, surviving, even the competing self. Delivered from fire, revolution, smallpox, drowning, and rape, her body also endures the heroic adventure of

childbirth. Indeed Mrs. Thornton's narrative shows itself most vivid and interesting when, for example, she describes in full physical detail the sometimes delightful, often hazardous process of nursing one of her babies, the painful phenomenon of a breech birth, or the grotesque details of the illnesses she suffers as a result of childbirth: "The haire on my head came off, my nails of my fingers and toze came of, my teeth did shake, and ready to come out and grew blacke". In a characteristic passage worth quoting at length, she relates the death of her baby son, providing in the process an intimate and detailed account of the frequent experience of infant mortality in Early Modern life:

> . . . and my pretty babe was in good health, suckeing his poore mother, to whom my good God had given the blessing of the breast as well as the wombe, of that childe to whome it was no little satisfaction, while I injoyed his life; and the joy of it maked me recrute faster, for his sake, that I might doe my duty to him as a mother. But it so pleased God to shorten this joy, least I should be too much transported . . . for on the Friday senitt affter, he began to be very angery and froward . . . his face when he awaked was full of red round spotts like the smale pox, being of the compasse of a halfpeny, and all whealed white all over . . . and, about nine a'clocke on Satterday morning he sweetely departed this life, to the great discomfort of his weake mother, whoes only comfort is that the Lord, I hope, has receaved him . . . And that my soule may be bettered by all these chastisements He pleaseth to lay upon me, His vilde worme and unprofitable servant . . . Whereby He has corrected me, but not given me over to death and destruction, for which I humbly magnifie His glorious name for ever.

The above passage should help to clarify the way in which Mrs. Thornton's recognition of the importance of her body allows her to generate a coherent story and a self. But in presenting the components of her claim to attention as piety, humility, affliction, and rescue, this passage, like many others in the book, also reveals the extent to which her location of individuality and heroism in her body depends upon pain and loss. Again and again she falls ill or loses a loved relation, suffering outrageously; yet repeated sorrows only appear as further "signes of His love to me." In short, Mrs. Thornton's is the self-sacrificing heroism of the martyr, for whom endurance is the highest form of activity. In the spiritual pattern to which she adheres, affliction becomes a badge of moral prestige. Disaster and recovery illuminate the individuality of the sufferer by marking her as one of God's chosen, for whom He personally demonstrates both potential destruction and promised delivery from death. Dame Julian of Norwich "prayed for an illness that would both confirm and deepen her vocation," writes a recent critic, "that illness [was] the gift and sign of her grace." By choosing the state of prestigious affliction as a projection of her desired self, Mrs. Thornton thus adapts a conventional Early Modern form of piety which was available to both sexes. More interesting for these purposes, however, is the fact that, with repetitious intensity, she applies this religious configuration to her specifically secular, feminine experiences of marriage and childbirth. As a result, her *Autobiog-*

raphy very clearly dramatizes the morality of female self-sacrifice by revealing its spiritual and psychological dynamics at work in secular life.

Alice Thornton's narrative makes clear that the religious configuration of prestigious affliction, with its psychological purpose of self-sacrifice meeting a deferred reward, achieves only limited success as a pattern of adjusting to reality when transferred to the realm of female secular experience. I have suggested the ways in which Mrs. Thornton's conscious identification with her body endows her with individual integrity and provides a detailed and revealing account of the monumental physical hardships that a traditional wife and mother faced and surmounted in seventeenth-century England, all of which lends great conviction to her *Autobiography*. Like the Duchess of Newcastle's, Mrs. Thornton's internal drama centers on issues of independence, power, and choice. We can recall that the Duchess oscillates wildly between professions of inner weakness and inner strength, often confusing the two and creating as a result a bewildering, run-on narrative structure in which conflicting psychological claims exist side by side unmediated, demanding equally to be heard. Subtext is not subordinated to primary text: her ego cannot settle on a pose. Lacking the Duchess's undisciplined, aristocratic arrogance, as well as her sensitivity and grace, Alice Thornton also lacks her ambivalence. Consequently she achieves a more coherent identity by recognizing that her physical weakness *is* her moral strength and finding an appropriate narrative form for this paradoxical self-conception in the scriptural sequence of delivery from death. Despite the greater firmness and coherence of her narrative self-conception, however, Alice Thornton shares with the Duchess of Newcastle the unresolved problems of moral responsibility that result from attempting to quell the individual ego within a culturally defined, often internally conflicting conception of femininity. Much longer and more consistent than the Duchess's, Mrs. Thornton's narrative allows us to observe more closely the effects of these moral and psychological tensions on the author's own consciousness, her text, and her relations with others.

Like the texts of the Duchess and Ann Fanshawe, Mrs. Thornton's *Autobiography* contains an untold tale, a submerged story which, in Alice Thornton's case, calls into question the integrity of her account. Here "integrity" should not be confused with accuracy or literal truth. As Gusdorf makes clear, the significance of autobiography exists beyond truth and falsity: "the truth of facts is subordinate to the truth of the man . . . the narrative offers us the testimony of a man about himself, the contest of a being . . . seeking its innermost fidelity." To acquire reader sympathy, then, the autobiographer must meet the demands of unflinching self-scrutiny, in order faithfully to reproduce the image not of the "actual," but of the desired self. Yet throughout Mrs. Thornton's account it becomes clear that her introspection has not been heroic and is therefore not adequate to the autobiographer's task. A bitter subtext of egotism repressed and turned resentful distracts the reader with increasing frequency, revealing that the narrator has failed not only to express, but even

to recognize all of her wishes and hopes.

Mrs. Thornton's characteristic mode of self-presentation involves denying the claims of her ego while simultaneously asserting them in devious boasts of traditionally feminine virtue. Recounting her mother's generous legacy to her, for example, she concludes, "All which I confesse farre exceeding my merritt, but not her intire affection, for my constant beeing with her in her sorrowes and solitudes." Equally typical is her use of illness to compete with siblings, friends, and spouse: if her neighbor falls down the stairs, she falls faster and harder; if her husband becomes ill or melancholy, she gets sicker and more depressed. Determined to exceed all rivals in illness, accident, misfortune, or pain, Mrs. Thornton portrays herself as existing perpetually at death's door, a representation which, if understandable given the actual perils of her life, nevertheless jars oddly with the fact that she outlived not only her husband, but all nine of her children, lasting until what was for the seventeenth century the remarkably old age of 81. Anxious to create herself as weak, sick, and pitiful, Alice Thornton was in fact tough and enduring, a survivor.

Duplicitous humility, petty competition, subversive self-aggrandizement turning strength to weakness and weakness to strength: the disingenuousness that results when these qualities converge in Mrs. Thornton's subtext can be merely amusing or annoying. Yet more serious, negative moral implications to her drama of alleged self-sacrifice are revealed in her account of her marriage, where anger and aggression are only barely contained by the counter-mythology of female passivity and innocence that shapes the primary text.

It is when Mrs. Thornton gets married—her "great change" as she calls it—that the English Civil War plays a leading role in determining her personal destiny. Suddenly the victorious forces of Oliver Cromwell destroy the peace of her childhood by seizing on her brother's estate, "wherein my father's family was fairely designed for ruine." The Wandesford family's escape from financial disaster turns out to consist in offering the fifteen-year-old Alice in marriage, in return for which the designated groom's uncle promises to retrieve the sequestered Wandesford property: "Thus the bargain was strucke betwixt them before my deare mother and my selfe ever heard a silable of this mater." In other words, Alice Thornton's match was an openly loveless deal, struck for the financial advantage of interested relatives. Although such economic arrangements were the norm for marriages throughout the Middle Ages and the Renaissance, all known evidence indicates that, by the late seventeenth century, individual choice of a partner and, as a consequence, love marriages, were gaining in frequency as well as prestige among the upper classes. Yet, though several of her contemporaries are known to have done so successfully, Alice Thornton does not contest her fate. It is true that she registers open anger at the indignity of existing as an object, bartered and compelled: "Which manner of perswasion to a marriage, with a sword in one hand, and a complement in annother, I did not understand, when a free choyce was denyed me.

Tho' I did not resolve to change my happy estate for a misserable incombred one in the married; yett I was much afflicted to be threatened against my owne inclination (or my future happiness), which I injoyed under that sweete and deare society and comfort of my most deare parents' conduct."

Nevertheless she chooses to submerge her rage at this ruthless disregard of her individuality, piously surrendering her feelings and needs to a political and religious configuration of self-sacrifice: " . . . my marriage was laid in the skaile, to redeeme my deare brother's estate from the tiriny of our oppressor, by the sequestration of all that was a friend to loyalty or the Church of God then established in England. But since I was thus disposed, it became my duty to stand my ground in a strange place, and amongst strange people, and that I was resolved to doe, by God's grace and divine assistance."

This passage concisely delineates an unresolved conflict implicit throughout Alice Thornton's narrative. Does she regard her marriage as chosen or compelled, a tyranny forced upon her, or a duty cheerfully and willingly undertaken? Here—and in many other passages where she reminds the reader of the inadequacy of her husband's estate in order to protest that she doesn't care—Mrs. Thornton represents the sacrifice of her personal happiness as a deed that, if originally compelled by her family, has subsequently become a chosen act of political and domestic altruism, about which she feels both reconciled and proud. But her ego does not in fact consent to be merged so crudely with notions of the collective good, and unsuccessfully repressed anger finds an outlet in the revenge of domestic strife.

The nature of this process is clarified in her self-contradictory account of her relationship with her husband. When Alice Thornton eventually becomes a widow, she spares no pains embroidering her sorrow, mourning her late husband as "my cheifest comfort and suport," and punctuating her life account with lengthy, grieving odes and pious lamentations. Yet throughout her narrative Mrs. Thornton portrays her husband as a kindly bumbler, whose melancholia, obstinacy, naiveté, and financial ineptitude reach their apogee in his refusal to listen to her good advice. In Mrs. Thornton's portrayal of her husband's weakness, we can discern her peculiar, if inevitable, reaction to the collapse of Royalist male social superiority and political hegemony that so drastically affected the lives of the women writers under consideration. As we have seen, Ann Fanshawe, defining herself through relationship, views the social chaos of the Revolution as an emotional opportunity and makes creative use of disorder by expanding her wifely role as helpmate and companion. In contrast, Alice Thornton, defining herself as a victim of the males to whose power she has surrendered her fate, can only respond with rage and a bitter sense of betrayal to their loss of control over their status and property. Like her father, her brothers and, eventually, her brother-in-law, her husband becomes yet another man who has failed her. His badly timed death comprises an additional instance of his desertion; furthermore, his failure to make a will involves her in complicated, exhausting property struggles, extending the consequences of his fiscal inadequacy well beyond the grave and providing posthumous material for her anger and disgust.

Undeterred by the magnitude of her own revelations, Mrs. Thornton insists on describing her awful marriage to the incredulous reader as that of "a deare and loving couple." It is not that, like the Duchess of Newcastle, she bewilders us with the complex ambivalence of her feelings. Her contempt for her husband is dominating, consistent, and whole. It is rather that, in refusing to acknowledge her obvious personal rage at being forced to marry a man she does not respect, she never attempts to reconcile her anger with the cultural demand that she be a loving and devoted wife. This inability, or unwillingness, to perceive the roots of her own suffering constitutes a refusal, even an evasion, of self-knowledge. It becomes impossible to sympathize with her account. Whatever may have been his virtues and failings, Mr. Thornton appears to the reader not as a person, but as an object, the dehumanized target of his wife's wrath.

This detachment from the feelings and desires—in short, from the emotional reality—of others extends as well to Alice Thornton's treatment of her children. In an uncanny instance of the oppressed become oppressor, she arranges the marriage of her fourteen-year-old daughter to a much older man with the same economic pragmatism and thoughtless domination that determined the identical fate which she had confronted with reluctance and sorrow. But Mrs. Thornton displays neither memory of her own unhappiness nor awareness that she is bartering her daughter's destiny. In recounting her motives for arranging the match, she cites economics and—what else?—illness: "My owne great illness, and many weakness on myselfe . . . did pres much upon my spiritt, least we both should be snatched from our deare children, and they left in a forlorne condittion of both theire parents gon." In other words, Mrs. Thornton presents her carefully and explicitly calculated decision to marry off her daughter not as a chosen act for which she is responsible, but—to quote Carol Gilligan's study of female moral and psychological development—"as an act of sacrifice, a submission to necessity where the absence of choice precludes responsibility." Furthermore, we learn that Mrs. Thornton rushes this marriage, which was greatly disapproved of by her relatives, in order to quash scandalous rumors that she herself is romantically involved with her daughter's fiancé. Never in the lengthy account of this affair do we hear one word about her daughter's feelings or desires. But Mrs. Thornton expresses no doubts that she has behaved with the most scrupulous maternal benevolence since "God is on my side." The dubious logic inherent in such an unacknowledged assertion of personal power comprises an evasion of responsibility that is "critical to maintaining the innocence [the woman] considers necessary for self-respect," although it "contradicts the reality of her participation in the . . . decision."

Alice Thornton's account of her relations with her husband and children therefore reveals the psychological connection between the unacknowledged rage engendered by the ethic of female self-sacrifice and a profound lack of moral responsibility on the part of its protagonists. Turning her husband and daughter into objects without understanding that this is her goal, she follows the golden rule of revenge, doing unto others what, she makes clear, "has been done" unto her. The passive verbal construction here is relevant. Her acquiescence in the role of victim and object in an attempt to please others has, with irony, made her almost totally self-centered. Her barely suppressed rage corresponds directly to her disengagement from the feelings and needs of other people.

Whatever the obvious limitations of Alice Thornton's chosen identity, her conception of herself as heroic victim did encourage a resilience that, in contrast to Ann Fanshawe, allowed her to extend her narrative self-definition beyond her husband's death. In any event, it is not my purpose either to praise her as enduring and determined, or to discredit her as sentimental, manipulative, and self-deceived. My main interest in calling attention to the angry and subversive subtext in the autobiography of this virtuous widow is to illuminate the ways in which historical circumstance, gender, and genre converge in the literary creation of female personality. When the psychological dynamic of prestigious affliction is transferred from the religious realm and applied to secular female experience, we can recognize a feminine mode of negative self-assertion that is clearly identifiable from Alice Thornton to Alice James.

In the *Memoirs* (1677-8) of Anne, Lady Halkett (1623-99), self-assertion takes a uniformly positive shape. Among the four texts under consideration, Lady Halkett's stands out as the most interesting and successful, in which the author simultaneously confronts and resolves the woman autobiographer's task of narrating a coherent personal identity by merging potentially conflicting aspects of the self. As scholars already acquainted with this text agree, although Lady Halkett did not write for publication, her *Memoirs* deserve recognition as a literary achievement of high quality. A wife, mother, and—when she writes—a widow, she manages to construct a brilliant narrative and authentic self-definition without in any way foregoing her attachment to traditional female values and goals. In the process she displays the Duchess of Newcastle's grace, sensitivity, and loyalty without her paralyzing ambivalence; exhibits Ann Fanshawe's resourcefulness, affection, and courage without her dependency and naiveté; and demonstrates Alice Thornton's resilience and energy without her self-pity and unwillingness to accept moral responsibility for her actions and desires.

How can we account for the superiority of Lady Anne Halkett's autobiography to the texts of the Duchess of Newcastle, Ann Fanshawe, and Alice Thornton, women with whom she shares political affiliation, religious persuasion, and social position? Like these three women, Lady Anne is an upper-class Anglican and Royalist, who struggles to define herself within a culturally prescribed conception of femininity while, at the same time, her social and personal horizons are being drastically altered by the Civil War. Part of her ascendancy over her contemporaries must of course be attributed to the intangible factor of greater talent. Yet when Lady Halkett's circumstances and self-image are viewed in contrast to those of the other three women under discussion, a picture of significant differences in the factors affecting her accomplishment comes into view. It should be stressed that this emerging picture reflects differences of degree rather than kind; for this inquiry it has the advantage of illuminating the ways in which a range of subtle variations in psyche and circumstance can converge to affect self-conception and literary achievement in female autobiography.

The first significant difference in Lady Halkett's text is her depiction of her relationship with her mother. Among the four autobiographers discussed here, Anne Halkett alone refrains from idealizing her mother. All four writers recognize the significance of the mother-daughter bond in the formation of their identities. The Duchess of Newcastle presents her adòred mother as the perfect embodiment of the Renaissance cultural ideal of the feminine; Ann Fanshawe makes her claim to attention as the special object of her mother's love, gladly subduing her more active personality traits in order to assume with unbroken continuity her dead mother's passive domestic role; and Alice Thornton, angry with almost everyone else in her life, reserves a special respect and tenderness for her mother. In contrast, Anne Halkett's story as well as her independent self-conception begin with conflict between her widowed mother and herself. "In the year 1644 I confese I was guilty of an act of disobedience," she tells the reader, and, with this declaration, her narrative begins.

Lady Halkett's youthful disobedience involves a clandestine engagement to Thomas Howard, eldest son of Edward, Lord Howard of Escrick. As she relates it, this romance was explicitly forbidden by her mother, both for economic reasons and also, as Anne suggests, for motives of sheer intransigence on her mother's part. The drama of this episode unfolds as a counterpoint between Anne's audacious romantic strategems and secret encounters with Thomas Howard and her struggles with her "offended mother, who nothing could pacify." Telling Thomas she will never marry him without parental consent while telling her family she will never break her engagement unless Thomas marries another, she never admits to defying her mother's authority, although her actions clearly reveal that she remains unterrified by parental power. The battle of wills that ensues between mother and daughter takes revealing shape in the following dialogue:

> I said I could nott butt regrett what ever had occationed her displeasure . . . butt I was guilty of noe unhandsome action to make mee ashamed; and therfore, what ever were my presentt misfortune, I was confident to evidence before I died that noe child shee had had greater love and respect to her, or more obedience.

> To which she replied, 'Itt seemes you have a good opinion of your selfe.'

Thus Anne's independence and self-respect are interpreted by her mother as willfulness and conceit. Although she refuses to capitulate to parental tyranny, Anne nevertheless suffers painfully from her mother's disapproval. After Lord Howard finally sends his son to France to "secure" him from Anne, Anne's mother declines to speak to her daughter (except to reproach her) for fourteen months, commenting "with much bitternese shee did hate to see mee. That word I confese strucke deeply to my hart." Furthermore, maternal scorn continues even after Anne's troublesome romance is finished. When the young Thomas Howard eventually proves faithless, returning to England to marry an heiress, Anne, grieving sensibly, makes a rapid recovery, in which "nothing troubled mee more then my mother's laughing at mee." Faced with humiliation, defeat, and the double rejection of mother and lover, Anne's response is characteristic: rather than giving in to her grief, she struggles harder against it, finally outwitting her mother by asking a relative to find her a place in a Dutch nunnery for Protestants. The sympathetic relation then persuades Anne's mother to forgive her daughter, "and from that time shee receaved mee againe to her favor, and ever afffter used mee more like a friend then a child."

This last point reveals Anne's romance with Thomas Howard for what, in large part, it was: not only a spirited young woman's search for passionate adventure, but also—and perhaps more importantly—her struggle for freedom and equality. That she would choose to undertake, rather than to deny, ignore, or submerge this struggle with authority of course distinguishes Anne Halkett from the Duchess of Newcastle, Ann Fanshawe, and Alice Thornton. As her conduct and resolution of the struggle imply, Anne confronts, even instigates dramatic and psychic conflict, using it as a means of attaining independence and personal growth. After Anne wins recognition as an adult from her mother, that authority figure disappears from the autobiographical tale; we do not even hear about her death. Anne Halkett's life story has become truly her own.

Lady Halkett's early conflict with her mother therefore assumes importance both as a revelation of her character and as a means of understanding her narrative technique. As many scholars have argued, the achievement of self-definition through separation and conflict is characteristically masculine rather than feminine. In literature this mode of personal development often takes narrative form as a linear quest motif, in which the hero struggles to attain his destiny. As noted earlier, the conception of destiny as the result of personal evolution achieved through the surmounting of conflict runs counter to the common cultural expectation that women's lives will assume a unified, cyclical form in accordance with unbroken, recurring tradition. Yet an important exception enables the literary representation of female destiny to take the allowable, linear form usually preserved for masculine narration: that is, when marriage is construed as the destiny which the female hero struggles through romantic conflict to achieve. With its origins in religious and romantic story, this structure of course reaches its greatest secular expression in the novel. It is Anne Halkett's confident grasp of this

narrative strategy, which she uses to represent her conception of herself as a hero actively creating—rather than avoiding (the Duchess), adapting (Ann Fanshawe), or enduring (Alice Thornton)—her destiny that gives her *Memoirs* such interest and force.

Anne Halkett's penchant for conflict-engendering romance and her narrative skill combine with the Civil War to give scope to her creation of a story and a self. This fortuitous convergence can best be perceived in her account of her long, ambiguous connection with Colonel Joseph Bampfield (designated throughout her text as "C.B."), which comprises the bulk of the narrative. C.B. is a dashing, handsome cad, a non-fictional predecessor of Jane Austen's Willoughby and Wickham, whom Anne comes to know as a friend of her brother's. This exciting adventurous soldier operates at the center of Royalist intrigue, and he and Anne together engineer the daring, theatrical escape of the Duke of York from England, an episode Anne relates in full dramatic detail. In the highly charged atmosphere of the Revolution, love and politics inevitably unite. Although C.B. is married when Anne meets him, he convinces Anne that he has had news of his wife's death, and the two become secretly engaged.

Is C.B.'s wife dead or not? It seems astonishing, impossible, that Anne would not be able to determine this simple fact, yet, whatever measure of self-deception may have influenced her discernment, her account of the sheer difficulty of obtaining reliable information during the chaos of the Civil War, particularly when one is on the losing side, makes the obstacles to her knowing the truth entirely credible. Forced to leave London and hide in the north after her part in the Duke of York's escape, Anne is separated from C.B. and subjected to numerous conflicting accounts about his integrity. Relatives appear from distant parts of England, swearing his wife is alive and well; equally believable witnesses come forth to persuade her that he is indeed a widower. She receives ominous letters from disapproving siblings, one of whom challenges C.B. to a duel, where the latter vows when wounded that he believes his wife is dead and that he is eternally devoted to Anne Murray (later Halkett). Various reunions with her clandestine lover alternately reassure and torment her, and the reader enters sympathetically into her powerfully rendered wavering and frustration. Lady Halkett's skill at involving the reader in the suspense surrounding C.B.'s personal life not only draws the narrative forward; the story of one woman's war-time romance also gradually expands in significance to encompass the larger theme of the impossibility of knowing. In this late seventeenth-century saga of political intrigue and social disorder, the reliability of communications can finally be determined only by inner resolution. Despite recurring doubts, Anne keeps her faith in C.B.'s loyalty until Sir James Halkett comes along and convinces her that C.B.'s wife is still alive. That she believes James Halkett, whose information she has no more apparent reason to trust than anyone else's, simply means that she has overcome her conflict and achieved her destiny by finding her future husband.

Another way to say this is that Anne Halkett creates her

narrative self-conception according to the demands of her inner life. The amount of courage required for a single woman thus to view herself and act independently is clarified in the extent to which she both risks and successfully avoids ruinous social scandal. The episode that best makes this point is her account of her virtual expulsion from Naworth Castle where, having sought a purportedly secure hiding place with Sir Charles and Lady Anne Howard after her dangerous rescue of the Duke of York, she finds herself vulnerable to the sexual slander of a duplicitous minister, a Tartuffe in whom she unfortunately confides the details of her relationship to C.B. Although Lady Halkett fully acknowledges her vulnerability as a woman alone, involved in a questionable engagement and supported by neither wealth nor consistent family loyalty, she never succumbs to the temptation of portraying herself as a victim, a misunderstood and mistreated case of injured virtue. Instead she takes full moral and social responsibility for her actions and desires. For example, although recognizing the dubious wisdom of her clandestine relationship with C.B., she nevertheless refrains from blaming his faithlessness for her plight; while she acknowledges a distinction between social appearance and moral reality, she does so without bitterness, refusing to dwell on it as the major issue determining her conduct. Instead she assesses the difficult attachment forthrightly as her own choice, made according to her individual desire:

> I know I may bee condemned as one that was too easily prevailed with, butt this I must desire to bee considered: hee was one who I had beene conversantt with for severall years before; one that proffesed a great friendship to my beloved brother Will; hee was unquestionably loyall [i.e., politically], handsome, a good skollar . . . att least hee made itt appeare such to mee, and what ever misfortune hee brought upon mee I will doe him that right as to acknowledge I learnt from him many excellentt lessons of piety and vertue and to abhorre and detest all kind of vice. . . . From the prejudice which that opinion brought upon mee I shall advise all never to thinke a good intention can justify what may bee scandalous . . . And I confese I did justly suffer the scourge of the toung for exposing my selfe upon any consideration to what might make mee liable to itt, for which I condemne my selfe as much as my sevearest enemey.

Although Lady Halkett does manage to find essential protectors after leaving Naworth Castle, her text is also full of instances in which she acts effectively alone, not only in behalf of her property or her reputation, but also altruistically, as when she nurses wounded soldiers with such skill and tenacity that her performance is rewarded by Charles II. As she does in the remarks about scandal quoted above, Lady Anne demonstrates in all of these actions her respect for the social and political culture that, in her erotic life, she has defied. Her triumph as a determined, individualistic female is never to become marginal. Acknowledging and acting on her own often socially subversive desires, she avoids the role of the nonconformist, the sinner or saint, choosing neither to be punished by cultural convention nor to transcend it, but rather to struggle toward creating a desirable position for herself in the mainstream of society. This successful reconciliation makes it appropriate that Lady Halkett should end her story by dramatizing the wished-for institutional symbol of public and private life harmoniously conjoined: the marriage that is at once suitable and happy, encompassing stability as well as desire. As an autobiographer writing twenty years after the fact, depicting her long romance with one man ending in her marriage to another, she achieves in narrative form what Gusdorf believes is the goal of the genre: "a recognition of the self by the self—a choice carried out at the level of essential being."

With the partial exception of the religious narrative, female self-expression in late seventeenth-century England was regarded as neither moral nor suitable: Aphra Behn was considered a scandal; Anne Finch lived in bitter seclusion; the Duchess of Newcastle was laughed at as an exhibitionist and a fool. Despite this virtually unchallenged injunction to female silence, a number of women made important contributions to the early development of English secular autobiography during the Restoration. The women discussed here do not write in a prevailing spirit of challenge or defiance. Rather they identify themselves as well-established, often conservative voices within the mainstream culture: they are traditional wives and mothers of the Anglican upper classes, actively loyal to husband, country, and King.

Viewed from historical perspective, the traditionalism of these women—their attachment to established patriarchal values and goals—can be seen to have played a paradoxical role in freeing them to write. All four women are Royalists, confronting temporary social and political defeat in the English Civil War; and their active participation in wartime events suggests the way that social chaos, upsetting the conventional sexual arrangements to which they adhere, can generate female creativity. While all four autobiographers witness the loss of social superiority and political hegemony of the men who dominate their world, their consequent attempts to rectify and compensate for this loss of status, money, and power give their lives an added public dimension that drastically alters their horizons. Indeed they discover that the only way for a female effectively and openly to defend the status quo is to break its rules, by violating the culturally prescribed definition of women as modest, passive, silent, and obedient.

In their autobiographical responses to this quandary of conflicting demands, all four women under consideration share certain narrative and behavior patterns that, as scholars of women's literature have been pointing out, can be identified as characteristically female. This material illuminates the ongoing discussion of typically womanly modes of imaginative response. Yet examining women's autobiographies in some detail within their historical context also suggests the variety, the richness of possibility in female self-expression that can occur even among only four women of similar social standing, religious persuasion, and political affiliation writing about the same series of events.

Like their male counterparts, few female autobiographers in the late seventeenth century considered exposing themselves and their families through publication of their work. But the fact remains that, during the Restoration, traditional women assigned enough value to their individual secular experiences to find them worth recording and, in the process, attempted to create themselves in literary form. While the responses of each individual woman to the dilemma of negotiating conflicting aspects of the self vary impressively, their common effort to reconcile public and private identities into a coherent literary form can be recognized as the (often problematic) goal of secular autobiography. Whatever ultimately may be shown to have been the extent of women's influence in creating modern autobiography, the convergence of gender, genre, and history that occurred in late seventeenth-century England should be given full consideration both in relevant studies of the female imagination and in any study of the form.

WOMEN'S DIARIES

Sara Heller Mendelson (essay date 1985)

SOURCE: "Stuart Women's Diaries and Occasional Memoirs," in *Women in English Society, 1500-1800,* edited by Mary Prior, Methuen, 1985, pp. 181-210.

[*In the following essay, Mendelson discusses the historical and sociological significance of women's diaries during the seventeenth century.*]

Sources that offer a direct record of women's everyday experience for the Stuart period are neither abundant nor easy to find. To be sure, there is plenty of contemporary material *about* women. Sermons and conduct books, plays and pamphlets all claimed to delineate women's true nature and prescribe their ideal role. But, although these works tell us a good deal about contemporary attitudes towards the female sex, they rarely address themselves to women's own sensibilities or the *minutiae* of their daily lives. In order to learn about women from the female point of view, we must turn to the diaries and occasional memoirs that were written by women themselves.

The present study is based on the works of the twenty-three Stuart women who left diaries, occasional memoirs or other serial personal memoranda which it has been possible to locate. Although the number is small, it contains a surprisingly heterogeneous group of diarists and diaries. In age the women range from Lady Elizabeth Delaval, who first began to record her meditations when she was 14 years old, to Sarah Savage, who was still keeping a diary at over 80 years of age. Every matrimonial status is represented: unmarried women, wives and widows, once and twice married, with or without children. The diarists also differed greatly in temperament and in their motivation for keeping personal memoranda.

Celia Fiennes described her extensive travels, Joyce Jeffreys kept detailed business accounts, and other women chronicled local or national happenings in addition to their own spiritual and material concerns.

In their literary form, journals and memoirs varied as much as the women who composed them. Seventeenth-century memoirs had not yet crystallized into their modern-day forms, the diary and the autobiography. Instead, they represent a continuum from one genre to the other, ranging from the daily journal to a variety of sporadic memoranda. In part, this stylistic diversity can be attributed to the protean quality of feminine writing. Quite a number of women left a hodgepodge of miscellaneous manuscripts, including diaries, occasional meditations, instructions for their children, autobiographical reminiscences, extemporaneous prayers, rules for living, notes and commentaries on the Bible, and unclassifiable memoranda. Some women attempted to keep a daily journal and then gave it up in favour of the less taxing occasional memoir. Others began to record their spiritual meditations but found their egos intruding in the form of autobiographical asides. Several women appear to have reworked their original diaries into a more continuous narrative, sometimes providing a preface, a table of contents, or other products of hindsight.

For the purposes of this study, the self-conscious autobiography—that is, an entire life recollected from a particular point in time—has been ignored. The sources chosen consist of diaries and other personal memoirs written in serial form through a succession of moments in time. Hence some of the best-known female autobiographers, such as the Duchess of Newcastle and Mrs Hutchinson, have been excluded. Of course, this distinction cannot be maintained in its pristine purity. Most of the writings included here were subject to tampering after their original composition, whether by their own authors or by later editors. In any case, even an immediate record of the day's experience is always subject to selective processes. None the less, even if we cannot hope to find raw experience conveyed in neat daily bundles, there is much to be learned from these occasional memoranda about the *minutiae* of women's daily lives and their feelings about the events they set down.

A major disadvantage presented by this material is that it is not representative of women as a whole but only that élite minority who had learned to write. One undisputed attribute of the seventeenth-century female population is its overwhelming illiteracy with respect to writing skills. Although there was a considerable rise in female literacy in London towards the end of the seventeenth century, all the literacy tests indicate that, for most of the century, few women throughout England were able even to sign their names. This finding does not necessarily imply that the majority of women were unable to read. In fact it was a widespread practice to teach girls to read but not to write, and the actual extent of female illiteracy with respect to reading ability remains a matter of controversy among historians. In any case, it seems clear that most women were disqualified from the start from composing memoranda of their experiences.

Women of the lower ranks were rarely literate. No example has survived of a female diary below the level of the middle class. It should not be assumed, however, that all female authors were gentlewomen. Elizabeth Walker, for example, was described by her husband as a 'plain private Woman, and conversed only with obscure Persons of low Degree.' Anne Bathurst's journal of mystical visions reveals her to have been on the very edge of illiteracy. In all, six of the women can be ranked as middle class. Of the remainder, thirteen came from various degrees of the gentry, and four belonged to the aristocracy by birth or marriage.

Although female illiteracy accounts in part for the small number of diaries below the gentry level, there is reason to suspect that accidents of survival played a role as well. Several autobiographical fragments have been preserved which were written by women of the servant and labouring classes. Such autobiographical memoirs were printed verbatim by contemporaries and were consequently saved for posterity. Some women from the lower ranks of society even managed to break the literacy barrier by narrating their experiences to others who saw to their publication. Journals, in contrast, usually required a heroic editing job because of their sheer bulk and repetitive quality. As Samuel Bury commented on his wife's diary:

> It has been one of the greatest Difficulties to me . . . to leave out at least Nine Parts in Ten of what I thought was truly Valuable . . . yet . . . was absolute'ly necessary, or else the Volume must have swell'd to such a Bigness, as to have been Useless . . .

Moreover, there was a fundamental difference of intention between the autobiography and the diary. The autobiographical memoir was written with a public audience in mind, whether that audience included all posterity or was limited to the author's own children. Although some mixed motives are evident among female diarists, their journals were generally intended for their own private use, not for publication. In fact, most diarists took active steps to conceal their writings from all other eyes. A common and effective method was to employ a personal shorthand. Of course, Samuel Pepys is the most well-known exemplar of the practice, but women often acquired shorthand in order to take sermon notes, and there is no knowing how many female diaries are now lost to us because family members were unable to break the code. Elizabeth Bury kept her spiritual diary in shorthand for the first twenty or thirty years. As her husband lamented after her death, 'her accounts . . . cannot be recovered by me, nor, I believe, by any other, because of many peculiar characters and Abbreviations of her own.' Mrs Elizabeth Dunton took double measures to prevent the posthumous disclosure of her journal:

> Mrs. Dunton had . . . kept a Diary for near on Twenty Years, and made a great many Reflections, both on the state of her own soul, and on other things. . . . But she was so far from Vain-Glory, or Affectation of being talkt of after Death, that she desired that all those large Papers might be burnt, though . . . much of what she writ was in a short-hand of her own Invention.

Several of her contemporaries also destroyed their own manuscripts when the dangers of childbirth or a serious illness made them apprehensive of posthumous discovery.

Some women were apparently diffident about attempting a journal at all because they had no means of keeping it secret. Sarah Savage had been discouraged from beginning a diary for a long time partly for lack of 'the advantage of writing characters'. Finally she decided to use longhand but to 'endeavour to keep it private'. Katharine Austen, a widow at the time she began her miscellaneous diary, prefixed a warning to the casual reader:

> Who so ever shal look in these papers . . . wil easily discerne it concerned none but my self & was a private exercise directed to my self. . . . The singularity of these conceptions doth not advantage any.

Other women had to rely on the discretion of their husbands. When Elizabeth Walker was caught red-handed by her husband in the act of writing, she extracted a promise from him that he would never look at her papers so long as she lived, a vow he 'most faithfully made good'. Elizabeth Pepys was less prudent. During a quarrel, she read aloud to Samuel Pepys an unflattering memoir she had composed about her situation. As he remarked in his diary, it was

> so picquant, and wrote in English and most of it true, of the retirednesse of her life and how unpleasant it was, that being writ in English and so in danger of being met with and read by others, I was vexed at it and desired her and desired her and then commanded her to teare it . . .

No doubt many diaries and memoirs were lost, like other women's manuscripts, because family members or heirs who were able to decipher them at all were liable to find them either embarrassing or irrelevant.

It is impossible to estimate how many diaries and occasional memoirs were either saved or destroyed because of the nature of their subject matter. It is probably no accident that three-quarters of the works in the present sample contain considerable devotional content. Feminine piety always reflected well upon the family, and any tangible display of it might be considered sufficiently edifying to preserve or even print. Of course, to some extent this profusion of devotional literature reflects the real importance of religion in the lives of seventeenth-century women. Indeed, the female sex was thought to exceed the male in that particular virtue. 'The weaker sexe, to piety more prone', wrote the Earl of Stirling, voicing a common sentiment of the time. On the other hand, it is clear that a large number of women's diaries would never have been undertaken in the first place if their authors had not been goaded on by religious fervour. Over half the diaries and occasional memoirs included in this study appear to have been initiated for spiritual purposes of one sort or another. In fact, the need to enforce a devotional regime was the reason most commonly supplied by women for beginning a daily journal. Elizabeth Bury had

> often advised with herself and others, upon the properest and most effectual Means to promote and carry on her spiritual and pious Designs; and at last determin'd upon this one, *To keep a daily Memorial of what she did;* which should be a *Witness betwixt God and her own Soul.*

A similar motive impelled Sarah Savage, who hoped her diary might be 'a means to make me the more watchful of the frame of my heart when it must be kept on record.' Among the pious, successful diarists were likely to be drawn from the more fanatical end of the spectrum. In his guide to diary-keeping, *The Journal or Diary of a Thankful Christian* (1656), John Beadle admitted that the practice was regarded as an extraordinary duty rather than a normal one: '*But what needs this waste,* may some say, *of time and paines? it's too strict and precise a practice . . . a duty too legall for Gospel liberty.'*

Since religious discipline usually supplied the driving force behind spiritual journals, it is not surprising to find in many of these works the family likeness of a genre. It is not known exactly how or when the keeping a spiritual ledger in diary form became widespread. Lady Hoby began her journal in 1599, more than half a century before John Beadle published his manual for diary-keeping in 1656. In any case it is evident that the model behind these early works was the Puritan duty of pious self-examination. Richard Rogers, one of the earliest spiritual diarists, was also the author of a popular guide to the art of godly self-examination. Scores of such guides were published throughout the century, some of them directed specifically towards women. One of these, John Featley's *A Fountain of Tears* (1646), includes a list of thirty-eight questions for women to ask themselves each night before going to sleep, in order to scrutinize every aspect of the day's activities.

> 1. At what time . . . did I arise from my bed?
> 2. What first did I?
> 3. How devoutly prayed I?
> 4. What Scripture read I?

The catechism continues through the day's household business, dinner, company, recreation ('Was it not affected with too much delight?'), to the final evening prayers. When we look at actual female spiritual diaries, we can watch their authors ticking off these points one by one.

Thus the spiritual journal helped women to fit the day's activities into a godly straitjacket, and it is not surprising to find that a common trait displayed by female diarists was the urge to impose some comprehensible order upon the fortuitous incidents that made up their lives. Elizabeth Bury, for example, 'would often say, That were it not for her *diary,* she should neither know what she *was,* or what she *did.*' Indeed, this interpretative function of the diary

was one of its main *raisons d'être,* as John Beadle explained to his readers: 'Take great notice of the singular peculiar excellency of all Gods dispensations towards you above the world. . . . Every passage of providence towards you, if you be the Lords, hath something more speciall in it.'

The providential interpretation of life's accidents which moulded contemporary spiritual diaries offered a coherent and satisfying explanation of world-historical events. It could also transform an outwardly dull and unhappy life into scenes of high drama, punctuated by hairbreadth escapes from death or damnation. Perhaps more important, the habit of looking for patterns in chance circumstances helped women get through life from day to day. Writers often noted that they had read through old volumes of their diaries to give them insight into current problems. As Mrs Bury expressed it, 'the review of former experience was an Extraordinary Help to future Confidence.' Many of these daily balance sheets seem to have had a cathartic as well as an interpretative function. Elizabeth Mordaunt believed that by recording and then repudiating her sins she could 'Laye me dounc and rest in pece, with a full ashuranc, that they shall never more be layde to my charge.' Sometimes this confessional purpose of the diary could lead to exaggerated expressions of guilt for minute lapses, so that the author could be sure she had settled her spiritual account for the day.

The introspective purpose of spiritual diaries was apt to influence their mood as well as their contents. The Countess of Warwick's journal exhibits so many expressions of despairing self-reproach that we might infer she was continually depressed. Yet her chaplain described her cheerful temper as the 'sweetest . . . in the world'. Presumably her devotional exercises, which included the duty of reviling herself daily for her sins, imparted their peculiar tone to many of her diary entries. In other cases, this excessive rigour seems to have been associated with a special emotional make-up. One anonymous diarist voiced her suspicions that her own religious impulses were merely the product of her neurotic personality: 'I fere to[o] much of my zele was ockashoned by the naturall sadness and pevisness of my temper which is apt to ca[u]se a meltingness of hartt to[o] oft mistaken for zele.'

Another highly influential genre which helped to shape both form and content of female reminiscences was the narrative of God's mercies to the author. A typical example of the genre is found in the memoirs of Alice Thornton, who justified her occasional memoranda by prefacing them with the following observation:

> it is the dutie of every true Christian to remember and take notice of Allmighty God our Heavenly Father's gracious acts of Providence over them, and mercifull dealings with them, even from the wombe, untill the grave bury them in silence, as also to keepe perticuler remembrances of His favours, both spirituall and temporall, together with His remarkable

deliverances of theire soules and bodies . . .

The genre produced all sorts of sporadic memoirs: occasional meditations, intermittent chronicles, lists of providences, prayers and miscellaneous memoranda. These occasional reminiscences selected the high and low points of life and omitted the uneventful jog-trot of domesticity. Since they recorded notable happenings, whether good or bad, they tend to convey an atmosphere of crisis. Although there are grounds for suspecting that seventeenth-century life was considerably more crisis-ridden than its modern equivalent, we should allow for the influence of contemporary models in suggesting some of the contents of occasional memoirs. 'Put into your Journal all deliverances from dangers, vouchsafed to you or yours', John Beadle instructed his readers. This practice was certainly followed, sometimes with more enthusiasm than judgement. Among many remarkable escapes listed in her memoirs, Mrs Thornton expressed her indebtedness to God for a deliverance from a surfeit of lobster, Richmond, 1643. Dame Sarah Cowper noted in her diary that her husband had been thrown into the river during a coach ride without her, and added, 'I believe Providence directed me to avoid a fright and danger'. Such lists of nearly averted disasters found in most memoirs of the period seem to have served a practical purpose. Those who had been spared for the present could hope to ward off future harm by recording their gratitude that they were still alive and well. The petitionary prayers and occasional meditations that women produced in abundance at this time are another variation on the same theme. They tend to be selective in their subject matter, partly because women were apt to record their private prayers and meditations chiefly during periods of anxiety or despair. Entries describing the pleasures of everyday life are comparatively few, although they are not entirely absent from occasional memoirs.

Although spiritual memoirs account for a large proportion of the feminine manuscripts that have been preserved, it is impossible to estimate how much secular material failed to survive or was deleted by editors of manuscripts that were subsequently printed. There are reasons for suspecting that a substantial amount of non-devotional writing may have disappeared in this manner, because editors from the seventeenth to the nineteenth centuries exhibited a marked preference for female piety. This preference is evident in their editorial prefaces, which usually single out their subject's religious fervour as an especially praiseworthy attribute. It is also evident in their selection of diary passages best calculated to display the saintliness of their authoress. In many cases in which the original manuscript still exists, comparison with the printed version reveals that personal and secular matters or lapses from spiritual perfection were systematically omitted. To add to these selective effects, it should be noted that a high proportion of female diarists were the wives, daughters or patronesses of clergymen. Of the six middle-class women in the sample, three were wives of clergymen and a fourth was the daughter of a famous Nonconformist preacher. Clergymen's families, like clergymen themselves, were more literate than the average for their social class, and the wife's facility in self-expression was apt to be matched by her husband's ability to edit and publish her manuscripts. Clerical editorial principles placed a high priority on the spiritual edification of the reader.

Among the various types of personal writing, devotional diaries offer the most detailed picture of the domestic routine. Although incidents recorded in spiritual journals are apt to be distorted by the religious lens through which they are viewed, we can nevertheless glimpse women's daily round. Naturally, since their chief concern was spiritual, these diaries devote a good deal of space to recording the performance of religious duties. Most of those who noted their pious endeavours appear to have followed contemporary guides to devotion with few deviations into originality. These standard exercises, usually performed two or three times daily, included private prayer, reading a portion of Scripture and books of devotion, several hours of divine meditation, and the confession of sin. This was a time-consuming routine which in some women took on the dimensions of a career. In his devotional guide *The Heart's Ease* (1660), Simon Patrick admonished those who took an exaggerated view of their spiritual requirements, 'as those do, who think they must alwayes be at prayer, or hearing Sermons, or reading spiritual books.' But quite a number of women recorded slack or indifferent performance of their duties, and there are grounds for suspecting that they often found the practice of piety tedious. The diaries and meditations are filled with confessions of dullness and coldness in prayer and wandering thoughts in divine meditation, even from those women who were renowned in their day as paragons of piety.

Many diarists also recorded their domestic routine. It is noteworthy in this connection that early rising was reckoned as one of the spiritual graces. For example, Elizabeth Walker generally rose at four o'clock, winter and summer, and Elizabeth Delaval resolved to make do with only '6 houer's slepe in the 24' as part of her spiritual discipline. This spiritual impetus behind early rising helps explain how Stuart women managed to get through such a heavy load of secular responsibilities. After devotions and family prayers were finished, much of the day was devoted to housework, even among upper-class women. Although servants performed the menial and heavy work, their activities were subjected to continual supervision by the mistress of the household. The Countess of Warwick directed all the domestic affairs of her Essex manor, keeping a close eye on subsidiary concerns like the dairy and henhouse. She was also involved in the business side of estate management, for it was she who checked the annual accounts. Elizabeth Walker not only supervised the farm labourers and household servants in their tasks, but shared some of the work herself, especially in exacting enterprises such as dairying and brewing. Most women occupied their spare hours with needlework, the great feminine time-filler. Some also noted their reading. Although the spiritual journals indicate that contemporary devotional guides made up women's staple reading, some diarists lamented their wicked youth which had been wasted reading plays, poetry and romances. The most commonly recorded leisure activity was social visiting—the favourite diversion of both sexes, and of the middle as well as the upper classes. Women's immense enjoyment of social gatherings was the source of a great many confessions of guilt among the pious, often expressed in their diaries as a condemnation of their own 'vain and frothy discourse' on these occasions. Hospitality could lead to other sins as well. After friends from Whitchurch had visited Sarah Savage, she noted in her diary how 'the desire to entertain them handsomely easily degenerates into Pride'. In Stuart England, as in other pre-industrial cultures, hospitality was not only the expression of obligatory reciprocity, but also an opportunity for conspicuous display. The overall impression that emerges from the diaries is that women took an equal share and derived equal honour from the rites and exchanges entailed by hospitality.

It is interesting to note that the diaries reveal fewer class variations in women's daily round of activities than might have been expected. For example, the aristocratic Countess of Warwick and her middle-class neighbour Elizabeth Walker performed similar tasks and indulged in similar recreations. Both spent their day running the household, educating their children, supervising servants, sewing and reading, entertaining friends and relations, visiting the neighbouring poor, and performing a lengthy devotional routine. The differences appear to lie more in the scale of their responsibilities than in the essential nature of their duties. The most conspicuous variations found in female occupations arose not from social rank so much as from age and matrimonial status. No doubt a different picture would emerge if we were to include lower-class women, who do not appear directly in the diaries. But among those women who left personal memoirs, gender was apparently more important than class in shaping the basic pattern of their lives.

Contemporary modes of thought divided female life into three distinct stages: virginity, marriage and widowhood. The conduct books employed this tripartite scheme in their description of feminine duties and privileges, and women themselves appear to have been very self-conscious about passing through each condition in turn. For example, in beginning her narrative of 'the first yeare of my widowed condition', Mrs Thornton commented:

> I haveing now passed through the two stages of my life of my virgin estate, and that of the honrable estate of marriage as St. Paull tearmes it (tho' with much troubles in the flesh), the same has had its comforts alaied to me . . .

Nor was the concept an artificial one. Women's diaries and memoirs illustrate the notion of three modes of feminine existence, each with its appropriate deportment, duties and concerns.

Although unmarried young women comprise the smallest group of diarists, it seems clear that, despite continual subordination to parents or guardians, maidenhood represented the most carefree and enjoyable of the three female conditions. Indeed, most of the anxieties expressed

by the youngest writers in the group stemmed from their guilt at taking too much pleasure in life. In her earliest meditations Elizabeth Delaval noted her repentance for flirting shamelessly with suitors, running up debts at court, mounting a production of *Il Pastor Fido* with a cast of Lincolnshire yokels, and over-indulging in fruit. At the age of 23, Sarah Henry, who came from a deeply religious background, appears to have been extremely happy living in the bosom of her family. Her most serious worry before she became engaged to be married was her habit of sleeping through the sabbath service.

Once marriage was in prospect, however, young women often entered a tense and anxious period. Sarah Henry noted herself 'much perplexed with thoughts about the changing of my condic n.' Other diarists noted their unwillingness to abandon their liberty. Alice Thornton recalled, 'For my owne perticuler, I was not hastie to change my free estate without much consideration . . . wherein none could be more sattisfied.' Mary Boyle, although her father was besieged with offers for her hand, 'still continued to have an aversion to maridge, liveing so much at my ease that I was unwilling to change my condition.' Marriage could represent a major trauma for women, and various sources reveal that they regarded it as the crucial turning-point in life. Their hopes and fears about matrimony are symbolized by a common female superstition concerning the wedding-day—the belief that the state of the weather on that occasion would foretell their future happiness or unhappiness with their husbands. Obviously this was an unfortunate superstition to hold in England. Elizabeth Walker felt that she had good grounds for her optimism when providence caused the sun to shine literally as well as figuratively upon her nuptials. Elizabeth Freke's experience was less propitious. She noted in her diary: 'I was maryed 14 of November 1671, to Mr Percy Frek, withoutt my deer Fathers Consentt or knowledg, In a most dreadfull Raynie day, A presager of all my sorrows & Misfortuns to mee.'

Marriage initiated a number of significant changes in feminine behaviour, as social pressures combined with religious precepts to mould wives' deportment towards their husbands, their in-laws and the world at large. Soon after her marriage, Elizabeth Delaval noted that

> in every change off our life we have reason to set a new watch upon our selves; for the same actions are not alike inocent in every condition . . . the gayety of my humour and the harmelesse mirth in my conversation was pleaseing to those I formerly kept company withall, and what was estimed by them to be wit . . . is look'd upon to be a gidynesse unbecomeing a wife . . .

Newly married Mrs Mordaunt reproached herself in her diary for feuding with her mother-in-law, and for gazing at a former suitor 'when it might renue his pashon for me, which being marryed was unlafull'. Sarah Savage prayed on her wedding night for 'a new heart for my new condition, & help mee to discharge ye duties of it, as a wife, a Mother, & a daughter in law'.

As for the success or failure of these unions, the diaries vividly portray a diversity of connubial relations, from uxorious bliss to bitter enmity and desertion. Some women did not conceal the failure of their marriages. On the contrary, they appear to have derived a gloomy satisfaction from recording their husband's shortcomings and their own undeserved martyrdom. Elizabeth Freke's diary, suggestively titled 'Som few remembrances of my misfortuns which have atended me in my unhappy life since I were marryed', is a catalogue of personal and financial disasters which she attributed to Mr Freke and his relations. Lady Anne Clifford commended God for taking her side in her running battles with her husband. Dame Sarah Cowper filled her diary with rancorous complaints against her husband Sir William, whom she described as 'the most difficult humour to live at Ease with this world ever afforded'. Elsewhere she commented, 'since it is not possible for me to redress these Domestick greivances, I wou'd notice them to no other purpose, but to find by what means to sustain and bear them well.' On the other hand, a number of extremely happy unions were recorded. Sarah Savage wrote on her wedding anniversary, 'my greatest fear this last month . . . is lest our love to each other would exceed—tis hard to keep the mean'. Others left similar expressions of wedded bliss.

One anonymous female diarist agreed with certain modern historians that married love was 'a thing very rare', but evidence derived from such diaries and memoirs as survive does not bear out her opinion. By counting the number of successful and unsuccessful unions among the diarists, it is possible to give some precision to vague impressions about the distribution of matrimonial happiness. Of the twenty-three women, two remained spinsters. (Incidentally, to all appearances, both were perfectly happy in their maiden state.) Of the twenty-one women who married, four of them married twice, making a total of twenty-five unions. Four of these marriages do not offer sufficient information for our purposes. Among the twenty-one remaining ones, there were fifteen loving and companionable marriages, and six unsatisfactory marriages. Although it might appear that the numbers are biased in favour of happy unions because loving husbands would have preserved their wives' manuscripts, this tendency is sufficiently balanced by those disgruntled wives who wrote their memoirs in order to vilify their husbands. There does not seem to be an obvious explanation for the high proportion of happy unions. In thirteen of the twenty-one marriages, however, there is some information about the circumstances in which these unions were contracted. Eight happy marriages included the following patterns: two love matches in which parents were displeased but finally gave consent; three cases of free choice (two were second marriages); two arranged marriages with a clear veto allowed to the bride; one arranged marriage in which the bride was only 13. Five unhappy unions included the following circumstances: one elopement; two forced marriages; the two marriages of Lady Anne Clifford, of which the first was arranged, and the second her own choice. If any conclusion can be drawn from these examples, it is the importance that contemporaries attached to giving all parties the opportunity to consent to the union. In the two extremes of elopement and forced marriage in which parents or children withheld their consent, the union was more liable to founder. Arranged marriage did not necessarily lead to unhappy unions, so long as children were offered a reasonable chance to express their own inclinations.

One pattern exhibited in both happy and unhappy marriages is the role played by contemporary religious teaching in reinforcing wifely obedience. Those diarists who took their piety seriously felt obliged to confess and repudiate all manifestations of marital insubordination. Thus an anonymous diarist deplored 'some litell frowardness and unbecoming pevishnes to my Husband which tho I aproved not I did not strive enouf against'. The most exhaustive illustration of this pattern is found in the Countess of Warwick's mammoth diary. From 1666, when she first began to keep a journal, until the Earl of Warwick's death in 1673, there are frequent entries detailing her continual struggle to repress her own strong will in conformity with her biblical notions of wifely subjection. Occasionally the urge for self-expression got the better of her, as on one evening when she returned late from a visit:

> my lord fell, without any occasion given by me, into a great pasion with me, which troubled me so much that I fell into a dispute with him wherin I was very pationately affected, and wepte much, and spake unadvisedly . . .

Afterwards, ashamed of this lapse of self-control, she begged God's pardon 'for my shedding so many teares for anything but my sinnes, and for not being content with what his providence was pleased to order for me'.

If piety was apt to buttress traditional social roles in the married state, we can also see some women turning to the religious life to compensate for the inadequacies of wedlock. For a summary of contemporary thinking on this subject, we can turn to a little essay on marriage found among the Countess of Bridgewater's occasional meditations. She pointed out that, in the case of a truly intolerable union, the practice of piety offered the wife what amounted to an alternative spouse:

> if he [the husband] be fickle and various, not careing much to be with his wife at home, then thus may the wife make her own happiness, for then she may give her self up in prayer . . . and thus, in his absence, she is as much God's as a virgine . . .

This species of displacement to a heavenly object was strongly encouraged by the devotional literature of the time. In sermons and tracts, divines quoted the Song of Songs in advising women to take Christ as their spouse. But what we find in some women's diaries is an emotional involvement with God which goes far beyond the allegorical relationship that clerics presumably had in mind. Among certain women with no husband or an extremely unsatisfactory one, some sort of erotic transference seems to have taken place. During periods of her husband's most outrageous behaviour, the Countess of Warwick recorded numerous experiences of the passionate 'warmth' and 'fire' of God's love. She seems to have recognized an earthly tincture to her more rapturous expressions, since she crossed them all out at a later date. The widow Anne Bathurst recorded mystical visions which carried the notion of a heavenly spouse to the most extravagant lengths. On one occasion she 'desyred often in the day his return of Love, and hoped at night yt I might ly in his arms as I had done the night before'. A few days later, Christ seemed to her 'to kiss me with the kisses of his mouth'. Although admittedly an extreme case, she was not an isolated example.

One of the most significant features of women's private memoranda is their expressive portrayal of the biological cycle of married life. Most species of feminine writings tend to reiterate similar concerns, which were much the same as those that obsess demographers of the present day: marriage, conception, birth, illness and death. But, unlike demographers, seventeenth-century women were interested in the personal rather than the statistical application of these patterns. The more arduous aspects of married women's biological and social role were ably summarized by the Duchess of Newcastle, herself childless:

> all the time of their lives is ensnared with troubles, what in breeding and bearing children, what in taking and turning away servants, directing and ordering their family . . . and if they have children, what troubles and griefs do ensue? Troubled with their forwardnesse and untowardnesse, the care for their well being, the fear for their ill doing, their grief for their sicknesse, and their unsufferable sorrow for their death . . .

In diaries such as that of Sarah Savage we can follow every stage of this process. In the early years of marriage she recorded her anxiety each month that she would never become pregnant. Eventually she succeeded, but her first pregnancy ended in miscarriage, and she was soon apprehensive about the possibility of another. Having finally succeeded in bearing a son at full term, she watched him die when he was a few days old. By the end of her life she had borne nine children, of whom four were to survive her.

Women's anxieties about pregnancy and childbirth form a leitmotif which appears in various guises throughout their diaries and memoirs. They expressed their apprehensions about the pain of labour; the Countess of Bridgewater periodically beseeched the Lord to 'have compassion on me in the great paine I am to fele in the bringing forth of this my child . . . lay no more on me then thou wilt enable me to beare.' Many voiced their expectation of dying in childbirth. There was also concern about the child to come, especially the oft-expressed worry that it might be born misshapen. A deformed infant represented not only a physical but a moral reflection on the parents, since contemporary superstition held that an infant's malformation was a direct punishment for the sins of the parents. Thus Lady Bridgewater begged that her child

might be 'borne without any deformity, so that I and its father may not be punisht for our sinnes, in the deformity of our Babe'. Lady Mordaunt requested a similar favour during her pregnancy. She also asked, 'if it be thy blessed will let it be a boy', a common appeal by prospective parents of both sexes.

As for the lying-in itself, some women provided full obstetric details of their labours. Alice Thornton offered the following account of the breech birth of her fifth child. After three days in labour, she fell into 'exceeding sharp travill' so that the midwife thought she was ready to deliver.

> But loe! . . . the child staied in the birth, and came crosse with his feet first . . . at which time I was upon the racke in bearing my child with such exquisitt torment, as if each limbe weare divided from other, for the space of two houres; when . . . beeing speechless and breathlesse, I was . . . in great mercy delivered.

Unfortunately her labour was so prolonged that the child was 'half-strangled' and lived only half an hour. Mrs Thornton left similarly gruesome accounts of her other eight labours. Her descriptions convey not only the great terror she felt at the prospect of childbirth, but pride in her strength and fortitude in surviving the ordeal.

Women's diaries also illustrate the degree to which childbirth was a communal event rather than a purely individual trauma. Diarists often left accounts of those labours of relatives and friends whose lyings in they were duty bound to attend. The Countess of Warwick described her niece's ordeal:

> my Lady Barringtons being in labor . . . I went directly thither. . . . I stayde with her all night she haveing a most terable sharpe labor I was excidingly afraide of her and with much earnestnes and many teares begde a safe dealivery for her . . .

Sarah Savage offered a much lengthier narrative of her daughter's labour and subsequent illness. Not only did most women run the gauntlet themselves many times, but they were continually called upon to witness their friends' agonies in like circumstances. And so these sociable childbed gatherings—which were intended to provide maximum support for the woman in labour—became a means of equitably distributing her terror to the rest of her female acquaintance.

Once a woman had borne a child, it was no easy matter keeping it alive. Lady Isabella Twysden was exceptionally fortunate in bearing six children who each survived to adulthood. At the other extreme, Elizabeth Walker was the mother of eleven children, all of whom predeceased her. Most of the women diarists' experiences were somewhere in the middle, and their prayers and occasional meditations are filled with desperate appeals to heaven for the recovery of their sick children, and with moving elegies on their deaths. Usually these maternal laments represented an attempt to bear the loss with Christian fortitude. Women tried to assure themselves that their own sins were to blame and that in any case their innocent children had attained the joys of eternal life. One of Anne Bathurst's mystical visions was of her dead children rising to heaven:

> as they came up, I remembered Two little children, died one at fourteen weeks, the other at fourteen days end, and imediatly as soon as I began to desire it, they came like two Bright Sparks, one after another, and entred into this great Light and became one with it . . .

The Countess of Warwick kept the anniversary of her son's death as a fast day each year, noting in her diary the assurances she had obtained that he was in heaven, and reckoning up her own sins which had caused him to be taken from her.

Lady Warwick was heroically successful in her efforts to put a stoical face upon her grief. As her chaplain Anthony Walker recalled, 'her behaviour was so submiss, serene, and calm, I confess I cannot but judge it scarce imitable.' But many women betrayed an internal struggle between the irresistible urge to mourn their loss and the compulsion to behave in conformity with contemporary religious orthodoxy. When Mrs Thornton grieved excessively for the death of her baby son, she received a lecture from her 4-year-old daughter:

> My deare mother, why doe you morne and weepe soe much for my brother Willy? doe you not thinke he is gon to heaven . . . wher he has noe sickness, but lives in happines? . . . be patient, and God can give you annother son to live with you and my father . . .

At this speech Mrs Thornton did 'much condemne' herself and begged patience from the Lord, who 'had putt such words into the mouth of soe young a child to reprove my immoderate sorrow'. In one of the Countess of Bridgewater's occasional meditations entitled 'upon occasion of the death of my boy Henry', she struggled against 'heathenish' impulses:

> let me not fall to wish I never had borne it, rather than to part with it, Lose it I cannot say, if I be a christian . . . in the knowledge of all this, why should I wish my Babe had not beene, rather then to dye?

After the death of Elizabeth Walker's eleventh and last child, she fell into a prolonged atheistic depression.

While female meditations and prayers tend to be dominated by the crises of child-bearing and child-rearing, daily journals offer a glimpse of the rewarding side of the maternal role. Mary Woodforde proudly chronicled her family's comings and goings, noting her sons' progress at school and college. Lady Clifford's satisfaction in one of the lesser *rites de passage* of her little daughter is evident from her diary:

> May 1617. Upon the 1st I cut the Child's strings off

from her coats and made her use the togs alone, so as she had two or three falls at first but had no hurt with them.

Widowhood was the third 'estate' of womankind. Of the twenty-one diarists who married, thirteen are known to have been widowed at some point in life. Eleven of these composed some portion of their memoranda during widowhood. The diarists display a wide variety of reactions to their widowed estate, ranging from almost suicidal mourning to barely disguised relief. Out of this diversity of experience, two contrasting patterns are especially noteworthy. First, some women apparently came into their own when the toils of child-bearing and the rigours of wifely subordination were over. They had earned the independence and resources to do as they pleased, and they derived comfort and respect from a web of social relations centred on children and dependants. This matriarchal model is found particularly among aristocratic dowagers like the Countess of Pembroke and the Countess of Warwick, each of whom enjoyed the status of monarch in her own local world. Women of minor gentry status might also behave in this fashion, albeit on a smaller scale. Elizabeth Freke took pleasure in building a comfortable little fortune from her farming activities, once she had been freed from the burden of her feckless husband.

For other women, widowhood not only deprived them of a beloved companion but plunged them into a sea of economic difficulties. In her miscellaneous diary, Katherine Austen continually bemoaned the sad state of her financial affairs since her widowhood, railing at the treachery of friends and relations who took advantage of her naïve lack of business acumen. The widowed Mrs Thornton also found herself in a financial morass which she attributed to her husband's mismanagement during his lifetime. Attempting to salvage an estate heavily encumbered with debts, she was obliged to borrow from numerous friends and relations, and bitterly remarked:

> it was a very pinching consideration to me that I was forced to enter the first conserne of my widdowed condition with bonds, debts, and ingagements for others, whereas I brought soe considerable a fortune, and never knew what debt was . . . but what I had bin servicable to many in necessity to lend for charity . . .

The fact that women's diaries tend to illustrate sharply defined life stages—the periods before, during and after marriage and child-bearing—distinguishes them from contemporary male diaries, where the most obvious variations relate to class and occupation. There is also a discernible difference in atmosphere. Women's diaries are more apt to be centred around the household and its personnel. The prevailing picture of everyday life evoked in their writings is of women going about their domestic tasks, retreating to their closets to perform their devotions, entertaining and being entertained in each other's houses. Men's diaries exude more of the atmosphere of public life: occupations outside the home, social gatherings in alehouses, political gossip interwoven with narratives of local affairs. Of course, this divergence between male and female perspectives does not preclude a good deal of overlap. Men often wrote about their wives in their diaries; they also recorded the illnesses and deaths of children. In some memoirs men even narrated their wives' childbirth experiences. When diarists of either sex wrote of domestic life, they described the same world, although they looked at it from different angles. However, a number of works convey a sense of the separation of masculine and feminine realms, much as they were set forth in early seventeenth-century conduct books. Men were supposed to 'travel, seek a living . . . deal with many men . . . dispatch all things outdoor'. Their wives should 'keep the house . . . oversee and give order within'.

Nevertheless, some important exceptions to this generalization should be noted. First of all, the picture would be much altered if diaries existed for women from the lower ranks of society. We should be able to see them working in the fields, selling their wares at markets and from door to door, travelling long distances without their husbands to find work, and participating in an alehouse culture of their own. Secondly, exceptional circumstances might cause a middle- or upper-class woman to take on a 'male' role, whether permanently or on a temporary basis. The necessity to fight a lawsuit or serve as the executor of a will could force a widow to journey to London with newly acquired expertise in the masculine realms of legal stratagems, high finance and parliamentary procedure. Thirdly, certain periods of national crisis appear to have captured the imagination of female diarists, provoking them to take a consuming interest in political affairs. A good example is the Civil War diary of Lady Isabella Twysden, much of which is devoted to recording current events of national significance. Other major crises like the invasion of William of Orange were noted by many female diarists who ordinarily said little or nothing about current events.

Finally, it is possible to discern the vague outlines of a trend away from feminine domesticity from the late sixteenth to the late seventeenth centuries. In her Jacobean diary, Lady Anne Clifford noted her boredom and resentment at being marooned in the country while her husband enjoyed himself in the capital:

> All this time my Lord was in London where he had all and infinite great resort coming to him. He went much abroad to Cocking, to Bowling Alleys, to Plays and Horse Races. . . . I stayed in the country having many times a sorrowful and heavy heart . . . so as I may truly say, I am like an owl in the desert.

But, despite her exceptionally stubborn spirit, she was unable to move unless her husband sent for her. Writing almost a century later, Dame Sarah Cowper appears to exemplify a change in mores. Her diary combines the pious introspection of an earlier age with a lively commentary on the intellectual and political currents of the time. Like Lady Clifford, she was on bad terms with her husband; indeed, they rarely spoke to each other except

in order to quarrel. Yet when Sir William went to London for the season his wife assumed as a matter of course that she would accompany him. Perhaps the most suggestive symptom of a new outlook on female potentialities is not a memoir at all but the travel diary of Celia Fiennes. Having concluded her heroic series of journeys throughout the length and breadth of England, she prefaced her account of them with advice to the rest of her sex to expand their horizons in like manner:

> with a hearty wish and recommendation to all, but especially to my own Sex, the studdy of those things which tends to improve the mind and makes our lives pleasant and comfortable as well as proffitable in all Stages and Stations . . . and render Suffering and Age supportable and Death less formidable and a future State more happy.

Women's journals were ready to shift their attention from the inward contemplation of the soul to a lively appreciation of the world at large.

SEVENTEENTH-CENTURY FEMINISTS

Hilda L. Smith (essay date 1982)

SOURCE: "Feminism and Its Seventeenth-Century Adherents," in *Reason's Disciples: Seventeenth-Century English Feminists*, University of Illinois Press, 1982, pp. 3-17.

[*In the following essay, Smith examines the development of feminist thought during the seventeenth century, asserting that the movement was influenced by the rise of revolutionary political ideology and the weakening of women's social power and a sense of purpose during the late 1600s.*]

During the second half of the seventeenth century a group of English women began to write critically about their exclusion from educational institutions and positions of importance within English society and the restrictions placed upon women within the home. They also urged all financially able women to become serious scholars, to use their minds to their full potential, and to give up decorative, leisurely, and inconsequential existences. . . . [Seventeenth-century feminists included] Margaret Cavendish, Duchess of Newcastle; Bathsua Makin; Hannah Woolley; Jane Sharp; Elizabeth Cellier; Mary Astell; Elizabeth Elstob; Lady Mary Chudleigh; Anne Winchilsea; Elizabeth Singer Rowe; Sarah Fyge Egerton; and Margaret Fell Fox. . . .

Though all were educated, these feminists came from a rather wide spectrum of English society. One was a duchess, one was a servant who later advanced to the post of personal secretary, three were either governesses or teachers in girls' schools at periods in their lives. Most were part of the leisured upper or upper-middle classes. Of the ten about whose identity we are certain, eight were married and three had children. They were predominantly Anglican in their religious beliefs and Tories politically.

These seventeenth-century women fall into two groups. The first group presented their ideas in essays and in introductory materials to cookbooks, scientific works, and general literary efforts from 1655 to 1675. They wrote mostly on the subject of education, and their numbers included the duchess of Newcastle, Bathsua Makin, and Hannah Woolley. Only the duchess wrote about women's general position within society, while her contemporaries focused almost exclusively on the topic of education. The second group of writers, publishing between 1690 and 1710, raised more general questions about women's position within the family and how that position restricted the development of their talents. These later writers included Mary Astell, Elizabeth Elstob, and the anonymous author of *An Essay in Defence of the Female Sex.* Four feminist poets also wrote in this period, most extensively during the first decade of the eighteenth century: Anne Winchilsea, Lady Mary Chudleigh, Elizabeth Singer Rowe, and Sarah Fyge Egerton.

[These] women were the first group of modern "feminists"—that is, individuals who viewed women as a sociological group whose social and political position linked them together more surely than their physical or psychological natures. This view led them to favor a number of changes in the relationship between the sexes. First, because they believed that women were men's intellectual equals whose potential had been thwarted by exclusion from institutions of higher learning, they argued for the establishment of a women's college, advanced secondary schools for girls, and the furtherance of learning by women in their own homes. More important, they endeavored to change the attitudes of both women and men about female intellectual capacity and to challenge the popular belief that women should be educated only on less advanced philosophical, scientific, or theological subjects.

Their demands for change were not limited to the intellectual realm; they argued just as strongly against women's secondary role within the home. These feminists viewed marriage in general, and the relationship between husband and wife in particular, as an institution which operated for the benefit of men. They termed the wife an "upper servant" and argued that until the marriage relationship was more nearly equal women could not fulfill their potential as human beings. Wives led trying existences filled with repetitive chores and often irrational husbandly demands, with little escape from family duties. Further, husbands were legally political lords, with full control of finances during the marriage. Under these conditions there was a necessary conflict between a woman's personal and intellectual needs and her duties as wife and mother.

Seventeenth-century feminists fitted these two major points—intellectual restriction and domestic subordination—into a general system of protest against men's total control of the public and private institutions of English society. These women desired to change the sexual balance of power. They did not simply criticize women's position in society, but saw social change as necessary to restoring women's rightful opportunities.

This desire to change women's lives, rather than simply to recognize isolated injustices, separated the feminists from other sixteenth- and seventeenth-century critics of women's role in society. Humanist writers such as Juan Vives and Sir Thomas More, for example, urged stronger intellectual training for women, but rested this call for expanded education on the view that a mentally trained women would not merely modify but would improve the traditional sexual relationship by becoming a better companion for her husband and mother for her children. More warned his own daughter that her learning should never be made public but should be kept for the enjoyment of her husband and father. Vives's "expanded" education for women stressed piety, modesty, and obedience, and eschewed advanced learning as unsuitable to females. And for both writers, female education meant tutoring for the few who could afford to be trained privately. There were to be no institutions comparable to those available to males to bring the "new learning" to women.

Seventeenth-century French writers who dealt with the question of women's secondary status favored expanding women's education and increasing their role in the salon and the court, but held that women's public role was to be enhanced for the benefit of men and society more than for women. Although they decried women's inadequate education and the waste of théir talents within the home, these French writers believed in inherent sexual differences and in a different educational agenda for women. They wanted to retain the positive qualities of "femininity," while giving an opportunity for the intellectually talented and socially cultivated aristocratic woman to be free from the stifling controls of her family. Their program combined intellectual with social and sexual liberation, so that this special kind of woman could mingle freely with males of like interests and sophistication.

Seventeenth-century feminists, in moving beyond these "improvements" in a few women's lives, spoke not of the single or exceptional woman, but addressed all women of the educated classes. To be sure, they did not speak to the daughters of the poor, urging them to higher educational goals, but they did ask all women of their class to devote time and talent to advanced learning and to utilize their full intellectual capacities. They spoke of women, or of ladies, in their writings, but not of individual women, no matter how talented. And, although in reality these "women" referred only to a small minority of the female sex, feminist works were little different in this regard from the general works of social and political theory of the period, in which "men" meant only a minority of the male members of society.

The feminism of these women was rooted in the intellectual currents of their century. Seventeenth-century rationalism, particularly René Descartes's writings, provided the crucial ingredient for these feminists' proof of women's essential equality and gave incentive to work for a society where women could employ their powers to the fullest to understand truth, both godly and secular. By coming to the realization that women were thinking individuals and not a historical, unchanging species whose sexuality defined them as more emotional, weaker, and less intellectual than men, they rejected inherent sexual differences. Moreover, in looking for other answers to the question of why and how women were "inferior," these feminists developed a new understanding of women's basic identity as a sociological group.

An understanding of the feminist view of women as a sociological group is essential to grasping the thought processes of individual seventeenth-century feminists and to placing them into a continuum of feminist ideology reaching from that century to our own. A feminist ideology can incorporate a number of interests focusing on women and divergent viewpoints about women's position within a given time and place, but it must include some understanding of women as a group whose lives have differed from men's on account of their sex. The move toward such a group-centered understanding of women is especially important for an initial expression of feminist thought.

The thoughts and writings of individual seventeenth-century feminists reveal the budding and growth of such ideas. The imagery and the language used in sixteenth-century works on women did not concentrate on women's group identity. Rather, the writers argued that individually talented females should pursue intellectual interests, and they supported this view by examples of earlier great women who had revealed exceptional intellectual or moral character. From the various defenses of women's abilities in the sixteenth century, such as Agrippa's *Nobilitie and Excellencye of Woman Kynde* or Sir Thomas Elyot's *The Defence of Good Women,* to Thomas Heywood's mid-seventeenth-century history of women, defenders of the sex repeated similar lists of "women worthies" to demonstrate that individual women could rise above the general limitations of the sex. But the seventeenth-century feminists seldom supported their belief in women with evidence culled from the accomplishments of past exceptional (and often mythical) females; rather, they argued from the axiom that men and women were given equal rational abilities. By the late seventeenth century, they took this position as a given and then asked why the equal abilities of both sexes had led to such divergent results in intellectual accomplishment. In developing their explanation of this apparent paradox they came to argue that women's unity did not come from likenesses based on physiology, that women had to be seen not only as a biological but also as a sociological group.

Seventeenth-century feminism was important because it implicitly worked out a definition of feminism that was continuingly relevant. This sociological definition was an initial step crucial to the development of a feminist chain of thought. There are a number of ideas commonly connected to feminism: belief in the equality of the sexes,

desire to end arbitrary sex-role divisions, support for equal public and legal rights for both sexes, and understanding of the relation of women's inferior role in the family to general social restrictions placed upon them. These components of feminist thought imply not only recognizing unjust restrictions but acting upon them as well. They also rest on a basic premise which views women as a group whose status is subject to change. If women are only isolated individuals, there can be no theory about them as a whole. If they form a group only by reason of their sexual functions or supposed psychological peculiarities, such differences are either good, functional, or essentially unalterable. The assumption that women are a socially defined group is essential to a hope that their lives may be socially altered.

Coming to this realization was especially important for feminist ideology in its earliest stages. When the necessary assumptions become matter of course, particular groups may effectively focus more on action than on ideology, because fundamental feminist principles have already been formulated. Yet feminists could neither expand their efforts nor refine their arguments while constantly debating first principles: Are women truly oppressed? Is there a basic equality of the sexes? Is women's circumscribed social role the result of physiological necessity?

A number of corollaries flow from the feminist view of women as a sociological group. The view implies the existence of a group, namely men, with the means and desire to establish social and political controls over women's lives. Seventeenth-century feminists, and those who followed, were adamant in arguing that men excluded women from positions of power for their own ends, and that they instituted a "private tyranny" in the home. Men had stressed women's biological and psychological differences to exclude them from training so that females could not compete successfully for dominance within society and could be held to traditional roles of providing sexual and domestic services.

If women's inferior opportunities are socially derived, they are of course not necessarily permanent. Feminists during the 1600s established a pattern, followed by their later counterparts, of arguing that there was nothing sacred, or necessary about women's secondary role within the home or society generally. They insisted that women must better equip themselves, both intellectually and practically, to compete with men. Women must first come to a realization of their own worth and then demand that society alter its institutions to represent their needs and interests more fairly. These early feminists urged their sisters to use their minds to the fullest, while at the same time criticizing society for restricting women's chances in both school and home. And they stressed that men must change—that they must give up their position of domination and share society's rewards more equally with women.

Feminists have traditionally assumed the general sisterhood of all women. One seventeenth-century feminist,

Mary Astell, spoke of herself as being a "lover of my sex," and another Sarah Egerton, of "being too much a woman" to ignore the plight or wishes of other members of her sex. Despite recognition of class, racial, or national differences among women, feminist writers have always stressed the similarities rather than the differences in women's lives, noting a common core among all women based on shared experiences. The largest numbers of women marry into an institution that requires more time and commitment from the wife than from the husband; a large majority have children for which they provide the primary care; and all are raised in cultures in which masculine activities and achievements are more highly valued than feminine ones. To stress the unity of women is not to deny vast personal and social differences, but merely to stress the central importance of such shared realities.

Thus by seeing women as a sociological group and by using that vision to establish programs and viewpoints which work to end the inequalities in women's status as a group, feminists separate themselves from those who do not concern themselves with changing the lives of all women. It is the uniting of the experience of one woman, or a group of women, to a general understanding of women as a whole that is the beginning of a feminist chain of thought and action. Those seventeenth-century feminists, then, by linking their personal experiences to those of women generally and by speaking of women's past and present relationships with men in terms of one sex's treatment of the other, established that feminist construct which became the model for later feminist theorists.

Why these early feminists moved toward their views is, of course, a complex social and ideological question. The conditions of seventeenth-century England were obviously conducive to the attempt to develop new ideas about the relationships between the sexes. The general social and political turmoil of the English Civil War created a favorable setting for people questioning traditional relationships. Essayists and authors of tracts were continually debating the meaning of tyranny and the rights of free-born Englishmen. The Levellers criticized the domination of the large landowners in both the national and local political and social structure. Religious sectarians questioned the authority of the ministers and the religious orthodoxy of the Anglican and Presbyterian establishments. The Baconians attacked the universities' rigid academic curricula while expanding the purview of what was properly called learning. Educational reformers, drawing their program heavily from the ideas of Comenius, wanted to open up English education to those outside the triumvirate of grammar school, university, and the Inns of Court. In this time of profound social questioning, it is not surprising that a few women began contemplating aspects of sexual inequality.

It was a period of intellectual as well as political stirrings, and the feminists could draw upon a wide range of ideas to aid them in formulating a new explanation for women's current status within society. The literature of the mid-seventeenth century was commonly prescriptive, en-

couraging readers to think in terms of right and wrong and of desirable or possible social change. General essays calling for social or political reforms almost never addressed the status of women, but they obviously helped establish an intellectual milieu which encouraged the questioning of the fundamental principles which bind a society together. The ideas of the feminists were always outside the liberalism or radicalism of those advocating change during the 1640s and 1650s, but their political and religious conservatism perhaps made them especially aware of, and pleased to point out, how sexually circumscribed were the glowing definitions of liberty which emerged from that period.

The political and social writings of the left during the Civil War at once encouraged and restricted the efforts of feminists. The feminists, predominantly royalist and Anglican, were unsympathetic to the viewpoints of most of the country's diverse revolutionaries: Puritans, common lawyers, Levellers, sectarians, and communal groups. Each of these groups pointed out the threat to English liberties implied by the unjust restrictions placed upon constituencies such as soldiers, small and medium-sized landowners, sectarians, Puritans, lawyers, and freemen generally. Yet none of these reformers concerned themselves with the rights of women, though they deified the rights of individual Englishmen to govern their own families and their own property against the arbitrary power of the king. These Anglican and Tory women could justify their own political, religious, and feminist position by sharply asking why the likes of John Milton, concerned about English freedom, did not "cry up liberty to poor females slaves" in the home. Such rhetoric obviously drew on this revolutionary ideological tradition even while attacking its basic lacunae. Concern for the rights of Englishmen had obscured, not included, those of English women.

If the ideas of seventeenth-century political and social reformers did not address themselves to the needs of women, feminists found two things which they could use as a positive basis for their thought. Their observations on the lives of English women in their century, their own and their sisters', gave direction to feminist concerns. Furthermore, in seventeenth-century rationalism, most clearly represented in Cartesian thought and scientific ideas, they found intellectual principles on which to build their ideas.

Although our knowledge of the lives of English women is limited, we have some information about the conditions that angered the feminists. Contemporary historical accounts agree that women were losing some of the social roles they traditionally had held. Social changes decreased upper-class women's useful functions on family estates and encouraged their becoming social ornaments and gadabouts. This wasteful and empty existence was a major target of feminst ire. The same basic process went on at other social levels. With the beginnings of professionalization in medicine and the decline of women's status within the guilds, women who were trained as medical practitioners, midwives, or skilled artisans found it more difficult to get a fair wage for their skill or to function as independent workers. Feminists who were midwives or teachers made clear the financial and social plight of this group of women. Similarly, the growing specialization of agriculture in some regions lessened the woman's traditional role as a partner in the family enterprise. It was becoming more and more difficult, also, for women to receive a fair economic settlement upon marriage, especially at the highest social ranks, because of the larger numbers of suitable female partners for upper-class men. Feminists wrote much about the economic powerlessness of women in landholding families. Finally, women at all class levels were more poorly educated than their brothers, and their talents were seldom utilized to the fullest; the waste of women's intellectual talents was a central theme of feminist writings.

Only isolated facts about the lives of individual feminists remain, making it difficult to link their writings directly to what we know of the lives of seventeenth-century women. Yet their experiences as women with decreasing social power and, among the upper class, more leisure time, obviously encouraged them to raise basic issues about the general devaluation of women's usefulness during the late 1600s.

The development of rationalism as a complement to the use of faith in discovering truth provided the feminists with a significant method to analyze the relationships between the sexes. They spoke of reason in both general and specific Cartesian terms. Generally, they saw custom as an often irrational and unjust foundation for social relationships, though, like any number of seventeenth-century thinkers, they employed the term "right reason" loosely, as if it were a self-defined concept. When speaking of women, however, they were clear that custom, or any continuing action whose only justification was its historical precedence or longevity, was no guide. They would not accept the view that women's role in the family or society was justified because women had always held that position in England. Rather, they argued, women's role in the family and in society should be based on two premises: that God had created women as human beings with rational souls which he expected to be developed, and that men and women had equal rational abilities.

Seventeenth-century feminism expanded and deepened its feminist perspective over the course of the second half of the century. The earliest feminist writers—Newcastle, Makin, and Woolley—often wrote cautiously, and, in the case of the duchess, contradictorily. Later feminists, on the other hand, were more systematic and rigorous in their denunciation of women's subordinate role in society. Finally, the feminist poets, writing predominantly between 1700 and 1710, added an element less easily discernible in the earlier works—personal anger and frustration at the unlikelihood of change in either the attitudes of men or the lives of women.

The duchess of Newcastle was, in many ways, the most difficult to fathom of these feminists writing during the 1600s. Writing first, she often argued the most extreme case of women's familial and social subordination, and

she just as often drew back from the implications of her feminism. The idea of sex division as a means of ordering society dominated her works; she constantly reminded her readers that she was a woman and that this meant she was poorly educated, had little chance for lasting fame, and was subject to an inferior status within marriage and society. She also stressed women's frustrations in rearing children for men's glory. Newcastle realized that women were not citizens, and she pointed with bitterness to the subordinate wifely relationship as the only significant political role open to women.

Yet her own childless marriage was a happy one. It was true that she failed to gain for her writings the acclaim that she desired so strongly. But if she lived under a masculine despotism, it was surely a mild one, coming from a husband who gave her constant encouragement in her intellectual pursuits and who accepted her ineptitude in the management of a household. Perhaps even more puzzling was the lack of any obvious intellectual influences leading her to an understanding of the importance of sexual division in structuring society. She was very much the theorist moving in new directions, with little guidance from either her contemporaries or past writings. She often faltered on the route to a feminist analysis, veering from blaming women for their incompetence or weakness to arguing that men falsely denied women's strength and purposely would "hide them in their houses or beds as in a grave." Often she seemed unable to make up her mind about the reasons for women's lack of intellectual success. But as a true pioneer in feminist thought, she often expressed far-ranging and insightful analyses of women's position within society. Her works highlight the possibilities of an individual woman's coming to a feminist understanding of society with little personal or intellectual encouragement other than her own shrewd observations.

Her contemporaries, Bathsua Makin and Hannah Woolley, focused more narrowly on questions of education. Woolley's educational concerns were of a practical kind, geared generally to the needs of housewives of divergent social ranks. She provided, along with a feminist analysis of women's position, practical advice on medical needs, children's education, social etiquette, and cooking. Her work was directed as well toward servants and governesses who would perform a portion of such wifely duties. Her own background as a servant and a teacher often led her to sharper and more earthy expressions than those employed by Bathsua Makin, who had served as governess to the daughters of Charles I. Makin wanted women to pursue advanced training in their secondary schools, comparable although not identical to what boys were receiving at grammar schools. She lamented and deplored the decline in the prominence of the "learned lady" of the Elizabethan court and wanted women of her generation and later to return to the serious intellectual endeavors of the former century. Her work on the education of gentlewomen was sometimes daring, but more often it was a conservative document arguing the benefits to men of educated companions. She encouraged wifely obedience, as did Woolley, and simply wanted the wife's role to include adequate educational preparation before marriage and an opportunity to use her mind after she wed.

Makin's work was published in 1673; the next significant feminist work did not appear until 1694, in the form of Mary Astell's *Serious Proposal to the Ladies.* Astell continued the demand for quality education for women, even calling for the establishment of a women's college. However, her major contribution to seventeenth-century feminist thought was her systematic analysis of the reasons women lacked a proper education, the kinds of bad decisions this led them to make in terms of marriage, and the inequities that constricted a married woman's intellectual and personal growth. She wrote works on both marriage and education and revealed more clearly than had her predecessors how women's lack of serious intellectual interests was integrally linked to the kind of role they were expected to play as wives. An Anglican and Tory, her conservative political and religious views sometimes hampered her critique of women's place within the home and society generally, but she clearly provided the broadest intellectual bases for women's need and right to develop their minds and personal characters fully.

Astell's friend, Elizabeth Elstob, was a scholar and a feminist whose prefaces to her Anglo-Saxon translations lamented women's miserable education and pushed for its improvement on lines similar to those of Makin and Astell. Through her informal relationship with Oxford University, because of her brother's presence there, she was acutely aware of what she missed as a female scholar excluded from England's universities.

The four feminist poets of the early eighteenth century—Winchilsea, Chudleigh, Rowe, and Egerton—wrote personal and polemical verse hitting at women's unfair treatment in the England of their day. They seldom wrote poems to men, although Egerton and Rowe discussed the enticements of heterosexual relationships. Winchilsea and Chudleigh, on the other hand, spoke much about retreating from society and developing perfect, platonic friendships with other women. They actively argued with those they deemed to be women's enemies—insensitive playwrights, obtuse and arrogant scholars, and self-righteous and foolish clergy. Rowe and Egerton throughout their poems either toyed with or agonized over their relationships with men, but both rejected such relationships in the end. All of these poets developed their views of men and women from a basically feminist perspective. They continually revealed a high degree of anger at both the personal and public treatment of women by men and divided their literary efforts between outlining women's unjust oppression and suggesting their own solutions to this imbalance of sexual power. Often the most impatient of the feminists of their time, these poets revealed both feminist anger and a strong commitment to the interests of women.

These seventeenth-century feminists did not have a lasting impact on the lives of women in the following century or a direct influence on feminist writings in the future. Yet it is possible to measure their impact in a number of areas of late seventeenth-century and early eighteenth-century English society and culture. Women's periodicals were appearing in increasingly large numbers at the turn of the eighteenth century. From John Dunton's *Athenian Gazette* of the 1690s to Richard Steele's collection, *The Ladies Library,* in 1714 there were considerable numbers of publications aimed at the educated woman. Also, these learned females often revealed their interest in feminist topics through poems or letters to the editors submitted to the various publications. Further, although not built directly upon feminist principles, the charity schools of the 1690-1720 period took pride in educating poor girls along with their brothers.

The heroines of Restoration comedy sometimes expressed feminist ideas, and when these heroines did not speak directly in feminist language, they still displayed the independence of spirit that the feminists tried to instill in their sisters generally. There were too a number of male authors, including most significantly Daniel Defoe, who also developed ideas and plans with strong feminist overtones. Defoe's plan for a female academy was quite close to Mary Astell's serious proposal to her sex. William Walsh and Nahum Tate wrote tracts with strong prowoman sentiments, though with some gushy language and imagery that undercut their ideas.

This turn-of-the-century feminism was to fade when faced with eighteenth-century values that embraced sentimentality and feeling rather than reason. Serious feminist thought did not mesh well with the more subtle and less confrontational advances made by heroines in the early eighteenth-century novels. Nor would the seventeenth-century feminists have approved the bluestockings' intermingling with the literati of their day on an accepted but clearly inferior level. The salon allowed intellectual women to display their talents during the early eighteenth century, but it did not encourage them to raise such indelicate issues as the exclusion of women from educational institutions or the basic oppressiveness of the husband-wife relationship in contemporary marriages. The isolated, somewhat embittered, but principled feminist of the late seventeenth century would have felt sorely out of place in the polite society of the literary and educated elite of eighteenth-century London. Her feminism was too much a product of the political questioning and rationalism of the 1600s to move forward into a more sentimental setting, and such thoughts were seldom publicly urged again until Wollstonecraft's writings near the end of the 1700s.

Seventeenth-century feminism, then, evolved out of the experiences of a group of women who were aware of the conditions of their sisters' lives and who realized that the vision of seventeenth-century reformers did not include women. Upon a rationalist base they built a new understanding of women as a group, intellectually equal to men but socially and politically separate from them. In this sense they were the earliest individuals to develop a theory of women as a sociological group, capable of, and in need of, fundamental change in their lives. If their influence was historically truncated, still their ideas retain continuing relevance.

Elaine Hobby (essay date 1988)

SOURCE: "Prophets and Prophecies," in *Virtue of Necessity: English Women's Writing, 1646-1688,* Virago Press, 1988, pp. 26-53.

[*In the following essay, Hobby discusses the use of "divinely inspired" prophetic writings as vehicles for social commentary by seventeenth-century women, with specific reference to the activism of Quaker women.*]

Well over half the texts published by women between 1649 and 1688 were prophecies. These were written by women who present themselves as divinely inspired counterparts of the Old Testament prophets, whose role was to report and interpret God's messages to His people. They addressed the major issues of national politics of the day, such as the call for the abolition of tithes and establishment of true religious freedom, and engaged in disputes over specific elements of doctrine. This was especially common in the 1650s, when the various radical sects that had mushroomed into existence before and during the English revolution struggled to establish the new form of state that they had fought for in the war. These groups (their members were known as 'sectaries') emphasised the importance of direct divine inspiration as a source of authority that was not dependent on the hierarchies of the national church they had overthrown. Phyllis Mack has shown that women could be perceived as particularly suitable vessels for God's messages. Their lowly status, it was reasoned, would make them less predisposed to the sin of taking pride in their heavenly inspiration, and demonstrated that, with God's help, the last could indeed be made first. In addition, it was felt that women's irrational and emotional essence and lack of strong personal will could make them especially receptive to the external Voice of God. Women prophets were possessed by the Lord, burdened with the duty to speak.

After the Restoration, as persecution of radicals increased under the workings of the Clarendon Code, sectaries were gradually reduced to silence and inertia. During the 1670s, one of the most radical groups, the Quakers, instituted a major internal reorganisation which served to 'temper the Spirit' of its members. These changes included reassigning women to more feminine caring roles, and most of the prophecies published by female Friends in the latter part of the period are quieter, more 'rational' affairs than the enthusiastic *Warnings* and *Messages* of the era of revolutionary potential, more concerned with questions of internal discipline than matters of state.

In assessing the meaning and significance of these pamphlets, I will be questioning the assertions of two schools of thought about women sectaries. The first of these, represented in the work of Keith Thomas and Christopher Hill, presents female prophets as mere auxiliaries to their male counterparts, and fails to understand how the women's activities present a case for their right to be involved in matters of national government. A second interpretation appears in Hilda Smith's *Reason's Disciples*. She asserts that the prophets were not really woman-centred, or concerned with issues of family structure or male power, and so were not challenging patriarchal domination as their later, royalist sisters did. I believe that, on the contrary, they actively and deliberately transcended the bonds of true feminine self-effacement, using the ideas and structures of contemporary thought to negotiate some space and autonomy. The very terms of this rebellion, however—the women described themselves and perhaps perceived themselves as passive instruments of God's Will, mere channels for his Word—also made possible their eventual reconfinement to less noisy, more feminine concerns.

EARLY PROPHETS

During the 1640s and 1650s, more and more women refused to stay silent on the great religio-political questions of the day, and took to prophesying in churches, marketplaces and in the street. Some of them wrote down and published their messages. The most prolific of these early prophets was Lady Eleanor Davies (or Douglas), whose very high social status and knowledge of Latin actually make her atypical. She had risen to prominence in court circles during the 1620s and 1630s as a noted prophet, running into trouble in 1633 when she began to predict the death of Charles I. Her earlier forecasts of the death of her first husband as punishment for destroying her writings, and of the Duke of Buckingham, had proved disturbingly accurate, and she was sentenced to the first of several periods of imprisonment. She continued to publish her messages throughout the 1640s and after the king's execution became particularly prolific, her writings becoming ever more ecstatic and allusive. It would be a mistake, however, to dismiss her prophecies as the spontaneous outpourings of a rambling madwoman. In *From the Lady Eleanor, Her Blessing to her Beloved Daughter,* 1644, Lady Eleanor explains that time is short. This is the period predicted by Daniel, when prophecy would come into its own and be understood

> although penned somewhat hastily or unperfectly, etc., being like the honey: and like the honey gathered out of so many parts, I shall the less need to excuse it unto such as have full knowledge of the scriptures, that should it be written at large a chronicle or a book as ample as those tables of the maps of the world could I suppose not contain it.

> Not suitable to the little book, being but an epitome as it were, and so much for being not voluminous, especially when the time so short too.

An examination of several copies of *Elijah the Tishbite's Supplication,* 1650, reveals that identical meticulous corrections of the printed text have been made in Lady Eleanor's own hand: her prophecy, for all its obscurity, was an exact one. In *The Appearance or Presence of the Son of Man,* 1650, she interprets verse eleven of Revelation as referring to a female deity and creator, who will bring peace and an end of oppressive religion, a woman superior to 'man' who is associated with death and hell.

She whose throne heaven, earth her footstool from the uncreated, saying, I am A and O first and last, both beginning and ending, by whom all things were done: not without her anything done or made; Trinity in Unity, of manhood the head; who of death have the keys, and hell: than the Queen of the South a greater, born a greater not of woman: Malea, by interpretation, Queen of Peace, or She-Counsellor. And so much for this without contradiction, she his executioner, made like unto the Son of God, the Ancient of Days' likeness: owner of the title of tithes, to whom the patriarch offered a tenth.

This 'A' and 'O' (alpha and omega, the first and last letters of the Greek alphabet) become 'Da.' and 'Do.' in the course of the pamphlet, which are taken as abbreviations of Lady Eleanor's two married surnames, Davies and Douglas. She herself, with the voice of God in her, is the deity described: 'I am A and O'.

Other female radicals might not have claimed to be deities themselves, but their activities were still seen as dangerously subversive, and many attacks on them were published. *A List of Some of the Great Blasphemers,* for example, records that many women asserted they were pregnant with the new Christ of the Second Coming. David Brown's *The Naked Woman,* 1652, was written in outrage after a woman had stripped naked in Whitehall to mock a sermon delivered by Peter Sterry on the theme of Resurrection. Brown was furious that the minister had failed to reprimand the woman or have her arrested, believing that this kind of rebellious behaviour was symptomatic of a more general rejection of the new government's authority. She should have been closely questioned, he asserts, in a manner which would make her proper, submissive role clear to her.

> She ought to have been demanded . . . 4. With what company she walketh? 5. How long? 6. Whether or not she was sent by them? 7. If not, then by whom? 8. If by none at all, then did she not run unsent? 9. What her name was? 10. If she hath a husband? 11. If yea, what his name was? 12. Where he dwelleth? 13. And if he and she live together?

Although Lady Eleanor's pouring forth of God's word was a highly unusual occurrence when she began to prophesy in the 1620s, by the time of her death in 1652 many women were finding their voice. The popularity of the idea that women could serve as particularly direct funnels for the conveying of divine commands was evident in 1654 when the royalist Arise Evans edited and published *A Message from God (By a Dumb Woman).* The 'dumb woman' was Elinor Channel, who had been found wandering around the streets of London. She had walked to the city from her Surrey home, leaving behind her husband and many children, driven by the necessity to find someone to write down her prophecy for her. Her message appears to be concerned with one of the great issues of the day: the treatment of debtors. It is distorted by Evans in his marginal notes into a call for Cromwell to align himself with Charles II, and restore the monarchy. Evans seems to have hoped that his version of Channel's

prophecy could be used to offset the influence of another divinely inspired woman, the radical sectary Anna Trapnel. Some of Trapnel's hold over her audience had come from the fact that her prophecies, calling for the overthrow of residual monarchical structures in the nation, were spoken in a trance. This could be interpreted as a sure sign that the hand of God was upon her. Channel also exhibited bodily signs of direct divine intervention. When her husband had refused to allow her to travel all the way to London to deliver her message, Evans tells us, she had been struck dumb, and had remained speechless until her husband consented to the journey. Lest the reader should fail to notice the parallel with Trapnel, Evans points it out explicitly.

> And though it be but short, yet you shall find more truth and substance in it, than in all Hana Trampenel's songs or sayings, whom some account the Diana of the English, Acts 19.34, as may appear by this that was written for her.

Another woman whose pronouncements produced public controversy was Elizabeth Poole. In 1649 she was granted an audience with the General Council, where she prophesied against their intention to execute Charles I. Agreeing that the king had broken his agreement with the people and been justly overthrown, she nonetheless argued, using an extension of the popular metaphor which likened the nation to a large family, that the country stood in the same relation to the monarch as a wife does to her husband. It was God's will, she proclaimed, that the people not harm the king's body, just as a woman must submit to her husband's body.

> You never heard that a wife might put away her husband, as he is the head of her body, but for the Lord's sake suffereth his terror to her flesh, though she be free in the spirit of the Lord. (*A Vision,* 1648/9)

In her prophecy she drew on women's experience and elements of feminine duty to define the correct political response of the country in general. Her church (the Baptists led by William Kiffin) responded to this boldness by expelling her, and by publicising charges of immorality against her which would undermine her right to use women's conduct as a basis for ethical decisions. When Poole left London, a warning about her was circulated to various people including John Pendarves, the minister of Abingdon. This was intercepted by his wife Thomasina who, fearing that the accusations were endangering Poole's income—

> you cannot be ignorant that she hath no livelihood amongst men, but what she earns by her hands: and your defaming her in this manner cannot in an ordinary way but deprive her of that, and so at last bring her blood upon you

—demanded that Kiffin make a public retraction. 'I have not yet acquainted my husband with your letter' (Elizabeth Poole, *An Alarum,*), she adds, but explains that this action does not mean that she is a rebellious wife: she is merely God's passive instrument.

A woman prophet could claim a duty to publish, since her writings were not her own works, but God's. Mary Cary's image of her passivity in this arrangement is especially interesting.

> I am a very weak, and unworthy instrument, and have not done this work by any strength of my own, but have been often made sensible, that I could do no more herein (wherein any light, or truth could appear) of myself, than a pencil, or pen can do, when no hand guides it.

By using this particular analogy for her impotence, Cary also brings to mind a picture of her own hand guiding the pencil. Her role as writer of the text is actually accented, while she makes the requisite denial of her agency in the matter. Her identity as author is further enhanced when she explains to the reader that she had signed herself as 'Cary' because this is the name she was using when she last published, in 1648. She has since changed her name to Rande, but is publishing under her previous surname so that both texts will be identified as hers. Although there is no way of knowing whether Cary was being deliberately self-effacing to make her writing more acceptable to her audience, the image she chose certainly serves the double function of both confirming her feminine passivity and providing her with access to the status of author. Affirming her femininity might have been especially necessary. *The Little Horns Doom and Downfall* is followed by *A New and More Exact Mappe, or Description of New Jerusalems Glory*. This second part of the text includes a call to war, asserting that the Saints can justly use the 'material sword' to establish the New Jerusalem. Her prophecy thus directly opposes Elizabeth Poole's understanding of the people's duty.

Her vision of the Godly Commonwealth is an especially female one. She is particularly concerned to portray the new roles open to women in her utopia, where all will be prophets, unlike the contemporary situation where

> they are generally very unable to communicate to others, though they would do it many times in their families, among their children and servants: and when they would be communicating to others into whose company they come, though sometimes some sprinklings come from them, yet at other times they find themselves dry and barren.

To use the word 'barren' to refer to a woman's inability to speak confidently in the public world is a direct challenge to an orthodoxy which would see her only significant products as those of her body, her only 'barrenness' a failure to provide an heir for her husband. She also makes a more direct reference to the property relations between husbands and wives. She makes their legal identities as one person into a proof of a woman's right to property, 'for there is nothing that he possesses that she hath not a right unto'. In Cary's new world, 'no infant of

days shall die', and the laziness of the rich will cease: 'such idle and profane creatures shall then have no allowance or sufferance to live such lives as now they do'. Cary's commitment to a radical equality between people extends to her relationship with her readers. She says that her message will only be confirmed as the will of God if others recognise Christ's voice in it. God's will, as transmitted by Cary, is that a profoundly egalitarian society be established. In *Twelve Humble Proposals* she warns the government to see to the needs of the poor before worrying about other matters, and calls for an absolute ceiling of £200 a year to be placed on earnings. Lands confiscated from delinquent royalists, she adds, must not be resold into private hands, but kept in the common treasury for the good of all.

ANNA TRAPNEL AND THE FIFTH MONARCHY

Parliament paid no heed to Cary's prophecy, and more women began to speak out against the new government's decisions. If we look in a little more detail at the writings of one of them, we will understand more about how female prophecy was defined and understood. Anna Trapnel's name first appeared in print early in 1654, with the publication of *Strange and Wonderful Newes from Whitehall*. This short pamphlet describes her falling into a trance on 11 January that year, and prophesying for eleven days and twelve nights to the crowds who came to hear her. A detailed rendering of some of the verses followed in *The Cry of a Stone*, the text of which was apparently taken down as she was speaking, with a view to publication. She laments the state of the Commonwealth, referring to the present powers as the 'fourth horn' of Daniel's prophecy, which must be overthrown at the imminent arrival of the Fifth Monarchy, the time of Christ's personal reign. Her outpouring was provoked by recent events in the government. The Barebones Parliament (Parliament of Saints), a nominated assembly which had included twelve Fifth Monarchist leaders among its 144 members, had been dissolved on 12 December 1653. The arrests of certain Fifth Monarchists (Christopher Feake, John Simpson and Vavasor Powell) had swiftly followed, as they began to prophesy and preach against Cromwell. It was at Powell's trial in Whitehall that Trapnel first fell into her trance.

Shortly after her recovery, Trapnel was called on by God to visit Cornwall. In *Anna Trapnel's Report and Plea* she describes the conversation she had with the divinity on that occasion, and her attempts to talk him out of the idea. The Lord was adamant, however, and so she set off, despite her own misgivings and those of her friends (pp. 1-2). In Cornwall, she visited two Fifth Monarchist members of the Barebones Parliament, Francis Langden and John Bawden, travelling and preaching in the vicinity until she was arrested and imprisoned, first in Plymouth, then in Bridewell, London. While she was in prison, the congregation of her church, All-Hallows the Great, published her account of her conversion, *A Legacy for Saints*. This was followed by her narrative of her visit to Cornwall, and subsequent arrest, in her *Report and Plea*. These publications appear to have helped to bring her plight to public notice, and she was soon released from prison. In August 1657 she again fell into a trance, and her prophecies were recorded in *Voice for the King of Saints*. After August 1658, her prophetic voice fell silent. She does not appear to have written anything at the time of the failed Fifth Monarchist rising in 1661.

Although Trapnel did not actually *write* several of the texts published under her name—they were written down by someone else while she was in her trances—they bear her name on the title page, and we can assume that she approved their contents. *Voice for the King of Saints* even has a final sheet listing printer's errors, indicating that close attention has been paid to the details of the text.

If Anna Trapnel's travels and trances can be understood as a response to the imprisoning of male members of her movement, it is her relationships with women that dominate the writings themselves. The women might have had their own meetings and organisational structures. The Fifth Monarchist congregation led by Thomas Venner certainly did: the 'sisters that meet together' had the task of spreading the rebels' manifesto in preparation for the 1657 uprising. There is so little evidence about these women's meetings that it is difficult to know what to make of them. Certain references in Trapnel's works, however, suggest the existence of special bonds among female Saints. After her dispute with God over the necessity for her to travel to Cornwall, for instance, she discusses the plan with her 'sisters', and before she sets off ten of them sit up with her all night to pray for a successful outcome (*Report and Plea*). After her arrest, she is visited in Bridewell by women, and one of them, Ursula Adman, moves into the prison with her, staying for seven of the eight weeks of her imprisonment.

The possibility that these women were able to help one another establish some autonomy from their 'brothers' is increased by Trapnel's passing references to marriage. One of her utterances in *Voice of the King of Saints* is addressed to her unnamed 'companions'.

> Hallelujah, Hallelujah Lord,
> For companions I will sing,
> And praises shall be given here,
> Because they have not been
> Carried about, not yet enticed,
> From thee by any means,
> And they shall here meet with reproof,
> If on creatures they lean.
> Hallelujah, Hallelujah for
> Companions that do come,
> And are not wedded to anything,
> But to King Solomon.

In this instance, of course, her use of the term 'not wedded' can be interpreted metaphorically. During her questioning at her arrest in Cornwall, however, she explicitly equates marriage with a loss of freedom—something that she has been saved from.

> Lobb: I understand you are not married.

A.T.: Then having no hindrance, why may not I go where I please, if the Lord so will?

Trapnel was careful to make it explicit that God's message was addressed to women as well as men. Rejoicing in salvation, she reflects 'Oh to be in Christ! Who can tell out his or her estate, night and day? How pleasant it is?' (*Legacy*). She explicitly proposes that women are included in God's promises, and that their responsibility is directly to him, not to men.

> John thou wilt not offended be
> That handmaids here should sing,
> That they should meddle to declare
> The matters of the King.
> John will not be displeased that
> They sit about the throne,
> And go unto original
> And nothing else will own . . .
> And the handmaids were promised
> Much of that spirit choice,
> And it is, and it shall go forth
> In a rare singing voice.
>
> (*Voice*)

Her use of other biblical references is also selective. When describing Christ's resurrection, for example, she stresses that it was to women that He first appeared, and that men played a lesser role (*Voice*).

Trapnel's prophecies pour forth in verse. To the modern eye, this might make it hard to believe that such an avalanche could have happened spontaneously. To Trapnel, it was a sure sign that the hand of God was upon her. 'Inflamed with love' for her Creator, she could not help but sing. She sang hymns of praise in every conceivable circumstance, including when on the road to Cornwall, and while in prison in Bridewell. Once she is singing, she enters a state of oblivion, in which she is secure from the physical conditions which might oppress her (*Report and Plea*).

Her contemporaries might be uncertain whether to perceive her as God's handmaid, or as mad. John Evelyn mentions a sightseeing visit he made to Bedlam, London's insane asylum, where he saw 'nothing extraordinary, besides some miserable poor creatures in chains; one was mad with making verses'. Trapnel also met her share of doubters. Her preface to her *Report and Plea* explains that she had decided to print her account of her imprisonment because she had been adjudged as mad. In *The Cry of a Stone* she adds that this 'distraction' has been called a kind of 'immodesty', and appeals to God to prove that she acts at his bidding.

To be assessed as mad could have caused her to be confined to Bedlam, as Lady Eleanor was. Equally dangerous was the charge that she was a witch, the tool of the devil. *Anna Trapnel's Report and Plea* is centrally concerned with the problem of witchcraft, since this was in fact one of the accusations made against her. While she was in prison, people in Dartmouth reported that she had bewitched the winds, preventing their ships from setting sail. She was also threatened with a visit from a 'witch-tryer-woman', and thanked God that he preserved her from this, and 'her great pin which she used to thrust into witches, to try them'. Her description of her trial in Plymouth indeed reveals a great deal of the terror a woman accused of witchcraft was subjected to. When she came to give evidence in court, her ready control of language, which in other circumstances might have condemned her as unfeminine, became imperative. Should she have been too nervous to speak eloquently when publicly questioned, she would have been burnt as a witch.

> The report was, that I would discover myself to be a witch when I came before the justices, by having never a word to answer for myself; for it used to be so among the witches, they could not speak before the magistrates, and so they said, it would be with me; but the Lord quickly defeated them herein, and caused many to be of another mind.

The suspicion of evil magic was dropped once she had proved herself able to speak up for herself: 'And the rude multitude said, "Sure this woman is no witch, for she speaks many good words, which the witches could not"'. Even once this was apparently settled, her skill with words was put to further use. She describes how on another occasion her questioner tried to give his own interpretations to her replies, and she had to struggle to prevent this: 'The Lord kept me out of his ensnarements'. It is not surprising that she ascribes her survival to an act of God. Her life was in serious jeopardy, and she had already experienced her inspiration to versify as proof of His control over her. In general, women's command of language was a far more tenuous affair, as the quotations above from Mary Cary's prophecies indicate.

Although Trapnel describes in detail her persecutions, she unfailingly returns to interpret them as having a general, historical significance. It is because she is a Fifth Monarchist, propagating belief in Christ's imminent Second Coming, that she is suffering, not because she is Anna Trapnel. The prophecies she makes during her trances are unequivocal in the alliances she seeks to forge. In *The Cry of a Stone* she calls on Cromwell to abandon his title as Lord Protector, and acknowledge Christ as the only real Protector. She accuses him of having betrayed the revolution, remarking 'If he were not [speaking of the Lord Cromwell] backslidden, he would be ashamed of his great pomp and revenue, whilst the poor are ready to starve'. She exhorts the army sergeants to remember that their allegiance should be to the common people, and appeals to soldiers not to attack Saints, but hold fast to their original aims. She condemns tithing, and appeals to merchants not to betray the radical aims of the war. In her *Report and Plea* she also describes how she worked long hours to make money to help finance the parliamentary army.

Although the major modern study of the Fifth Monarchists, Bernard Capp's *Fifth Monarchy Men* (sic), portrays the movement as elitist, Trapnel's writings clearly show that the apocalypse she longs for will transform the lives of all, not just benefit a blessed few.

> Methinks I see not only foolish virgins slumbering and sleeping, but the wise virgins are also in a slumber, but when the bridegroom's appearance shall be manifested, shall they still lie in a slumber? I believe otherwise, that there shall be such an awaking of all things, the very foundation of all things shall be shaken by that foundation that shall stand for ever. (*Legacy*)

Anna Trapnel, like many of her sisters in the 1650s, was awake, and hurrying to awaken others to the 'true meaning' of God's promises.

RADICALISM AND RETREAT

The vast majority of extant women's prophecies were written by Quakers, which might reflect the particularly active role played by women in the Society of Friends. The large number of female Quaker writings is also no doubt due in part to the decision by the Society in 1672 to acquire and preserve two copies of every text published by Friends since the beginning of their movement. No such efficient collection was made of other prophetical writings, and it seems likely that many were lost. What is clear is that the activism of women sectaries was not originated by Quakerism. Women had played important parts in the development of the Familists and Anabaptists earlier in the century. It has often been observed that George Fox (the Quaker leader) made his first 'steeplehouse' interjection in defence of a woman who had asked a question of the church minister. Women, it is suggested, were drawn to the sexual egalitarianism that Quakerism offered. But presenting the origins of the sect in this manner is a distortion. In the early days, in the 1640s and 1650s, the Society of Friends was not a ready-formed body, with established policies and principles, to which women were attracted. Richard Vann has shown that the first Friends were not 'converts' as such. They recognised one another as like-minded individuals. When Sarah Blackborow recalls how she came to join the Quakers, for example, she describes how she found that their message was consistent with her own beliefs. Perhaps the first person to join Fox in those early days was a woman, Elizabeth Hooton. She was already an established preacher when she met Fox, and subsequently became the first Quaker to be imprisoned for preaching. Such a sequence of events can scarcely be interpreted as evidence of women being secondary in the establishment of Quakerism's ideas. We derive a more accurate impression of their role if we reflect that, while it is true that Fox supported a woman's right to speak in church, the initiative in the much-cited case was taken by the woman who asked the question.

In many respects, the ideas and activities of early Quakerism reveal women's part in its establishment. Quaker emphasis on Inner Light as a source of understanding and guide for action grew out of, and made possible women prophets' challenge to their restriction to the private sphere. Women's freedom to minister and to publish the opinions

God had revealed to them swiftly extended into a duty or right to 'witness against' specific men. They could criticise men's views because the equality of Spirit in women and men gave equal validity to their interpretations of God's will. In 1655, for example, Margret Braidley assured the minister John Shopp, 'Thou art no minister of Christ, but a minister of Antichrist.' This practice served as useful training for women like Mary Pennyman, Ann Mudd and Elizabeth Atkinson, who later left the Society of Friends and published attacks on their former allies' beliefs. These women felt confident to discuss in detail specific questions of religious doctrine and cite biblical texts in defence of their conclusions. Elizabeth Atkinson's first criticism of the Quakers, *A Breif and plain discovery of the Labourers in mistery,* was swiftly followed by a second and longer text, after Rebeckah Travers had dismissed her argument as 'so contradictive in itself' as not to be worthy of serious refutation, and Anne Travers and Elizabeth Coleman had suggested that she was not the true author of her work.

These early Quakers also instituted other practices which gave women access to activities that might have been proscribed as unwomanly. In her autobiography, Alice Curwen recollects how, on hearing of the suffering of Quakers in New England, she knew that God wanted her and her husband to travel to Boston and preach against persecution. Her husband was opposed to the idea, and finally she set off without him. Her description of this disagreement is noteworthy. It is not presented (nor, perhaps, perceived) as a clash of their individual, human wills. Her intention to travel is a result of God's bidding, and she is puzzled that God has not yet made this desire known to her husband.

> Then I having this testimony sealed in my heart, I laboured with my husband night and day to know his mind, because it was much with me, that we were to travel together; but he did not yet see it to be required of him at that time . . . but the Lord make me willing to leave all (that was near and dear to me) and I . . . made preparation to go to sea, and having got my bed and clothes on board ship, it pleased the Lord (in whom was and is my trust) to send my husband to go along with me.

Alice Curwen's call to travel with her husband was relatively unusual. More commonly, these women journeyed and preached with female Friends. When Joan Brooksop and Elizabeth Hooton went to Boston to warn the rulers to cease persecuting Quakers, Hooton, who was aged about sixty, was already a widow. Brooksop, however, had 'forsaken all my relations, husband, and children' to make the journey. Theophila Townsend's *Testimony* for Jane Whitehead recalls Whitehead's first companion, Frances Raunce, 'who is entered into rest with her, and was a fellow labourer with her in the same work and service'. After her marriage, Whitehead continued to minister, and on one occasion was imprisoned in Ilchester away 'from her husband, and four small children, and one tender child she carried in her arms'. Joan Vokins, who travelled ceaselessly in Ireland, the West Indies and New England de-

spite constant ill-health, also left behind her husband and children, noting in one of her letters home

> It is troublesome for me to write, the vessel doth so wave. I desire that Susan Dew, and Mary Elson may see this, or have a copy of it: and also my dear husband and children.

Perhaps the most remarkable travelling fellowship was that between Katherine Evans and Sarah Chevers, who in 1658 set off together for Alexandria, leaving behind their husbands and children. They only got as far as Malta, where they had already been kept in prison by the Inquisition for three years when another Quaker, Daniel Baker, visited them, and published their account of their sufferings. Their courage and determination, and confidence in one another's fortitude, even when kept in solitary confinement for months on end, are compelling. Their identity as prophets gave them a route out of the narrow confines of their families and dependence on their husbands. Their role as God's messengers might also have been the deciding factor in achieving their release. As the period of their incarceration lengthened, they took more and more to fasting and stripping naked to prophesy God's vengeance on their behalf. When a gunpowder store was struck by lightning, causing much damage in the city, Sarah Chevers was accused of witchcraft but was not executed (*A True Account*). Perhaps the Inquisitors were not quite confident of their diagnosis. As negotiations for the release continued, the Inquisition kept reducing its demands, until finally the women were granted their freedom in return for an undertaking that they would go away and not return. As Katherine Evans expressed it, 'We were very dreadful to them'. The likelihood that the women convinced the Inquisition of their divine inspiration is increased in the light of subsequent events. After they left Malta they stopped at Tangiers to prophesy. They were arrested, but this time not imprisoned: 'The Governor said, he did lovingly receive our good instructions and admonitions, and promised to follow our counsel'. In general, the achievements of all these women were made possible by the power they obtained through being identified as the weak recipients of God's word. Within the confines of femininity, they were able to negotiate a space that allowed for decidedly unfeminine activities.

Quaker writings pass through a series of changes in the period. Among the very first publications are texts written during imprisonment. The women appeal against prison conditions, or reaffirm their belief in the principles for which they were arrested. *The Lambs Defence against Lies,* 1656, contains Dorothy Waugh's description of what happened when she spoke out in Carlisle marketplace in 1655 'against all deceit and ungodly practices'. She was promptly hauled off to jail. When she was unrepentant, the mayor ordered the scold's bridle to be put on her head to make an example of her. This cruel contraption, which was also used against witches and 'nagging' wives, was a heavy iron mask with three bars across the face and a large piece which, crammed into the woman's mouth, caused her great pain and made her incapable of speech. Dorothy Waugh's jailer tried to make some money from the situation, charging people two pence a time to view her.

> And the people to see me so violently abused were broken into tears, but he [the mayor] cried out on them and said 'For foolish pity, one may spoil a whole city'.

Later, she was turned out into the street still wearing the bridle, and ordered to be whipped from city to city until she was home.

From about 1655 onwards, more prophecies were published calling on specific groups of people, such as priests and lawyers, or the inhabitants of particular towns, such as Plymouth, Oxford, Dartmouth or Dover, to repent. The writers dwell less on the specific circumstances of their own sufferings, emphasising the general judgement and overturning that is imminently expected. Some of these simply address 'all the world', explaining that their message is from God, and must be heeded before it is too late. The year 1659 also saw a mass Quaker women's petition, carrying seven thousand signatures, calling for the abolition of tithes and recommending other radical changes. These warnings reach a peak between 1659 and 1662, a period which, as Barry Reay and Alan Cole have shown, was a turning point for Quakerism. The millenarian optimism of early 1659, when Lambert restored the Rump, was swiftly replaced by the spectre of Charles's return and the Restoration. Before 1659, the Society of Friends was not a pacifist movement. Although Quakers firmly believed that the struggle to establish God's kingdom could not be won by the sword alone, they did not scorn its use. Many applied in 1659 to rejoin the armed forces from which they had been expelled. Grace Barwick's petition, carefully addressed *To all present Rulers, whether of Parliament, or whomsoever of England*, reminds General Lambert that her husband had once served as his cornet (cavalry officer). She exhorts the rulers to use force to carry through the long-promised reforms and abolish tithing, assuring them that

> Being once brought down, and the people eased from it: it can never be supposed, that reasonable men will be so foolish as ever to fight to set it up again, and the people loves liberty, and however that shall come to them, it will be thankfully received, whether by a law or contrary to a law.

As 1659 advanced, hostility towards Quakers grew as it was carefully orchestrated through the pulpit. After the restoration, official persecution intensified, despite the toleration promised in the Declaration of Breda. In 1662, Sarah Blackborow's *Oppressed Prisoners Complaint* reflected

> Is liberty of conscience now a sin,
> Though promised by the word of a king . . . ?
> Nine score prisoners in Newgate now doth lie
> For justice, justice, these aloud do cry.

The unsuccessful uprising of the Fifth Monarchists in 1661, and the concentrated persecution of all sectaries under the Clarendon Code, made it necessary for them carefully to bury their involvement in armed radicalism in order to survive. After that date, the character of women's writing slowly changes. Although some continue to rail against persecution, or undertake careful rebuttals of their opponents, by the 1670s many of their publications are concerned either with ending strife within the Society and calling on Friends to stand firm in the faith, or with describing the deathbed testimonies of dying Friends.

The prophecies of the 1650s are very radical texts. Through their relationship with the Spirit, Quaker, Baptist and other radical women can claim a freedom to publish, and they explode into print with rage and joy. This in itself would justify the description 'radical'. In addition, some of the pamphlets exhibit other unconventional or innovative features. The first texts are almost all collective enterprises, written by or on behalf of imprisoned prophets. Most characteristically, they are also jointly written. The most interesting in this respect is *The Saints Testimony Finishing Through Suffering*. The text is a compilation of accounts of the charges against a number of Quakers imprisoned in Banbury. It is prefaced by a description of their subsequent trial, which is written by a body of Friends from Bristol, Gloucester and Berkshire, who travelled to attend it. The pamphlet as a whole shows much evidence that its internal structure and arrangement were carefully discussed by its (mostly anonymous) authors, and the reader is frequently referred from one section to another for further elucidation of specific points. It is surely no conincidence that this work also includes one of the earliest extended Quaker justifications of women's preaching.

This tradition of shared enterprise is also the informing experience that produced Elizabeth Hincks's image of the Body of Christ in *The Poor Widows Mite*, 1671. To describe the church as a body was of course to use a highly conventional image. Hincks's particular vision of the interdependency of its parts, though, and their reliance on one another, is a portrait of collective working.

> And so the head it cannot say to the foot, I need
>   not thee;
> Nor eke the eye unto the ear, O be thou gone
>   from me:
> For that the body is but one, yet members hath
>   it many:
> Appear there would deformity, if lack there were
>   of any: . . .
> So what is wanting in each one, a supply others
>   have;
> To minister unto each wants, by it their souls to
>   save.

The radicalism of the texts extends beyond the circumstances of their actual writing. The world of interdependence and shared labour that the early prophets were heralding would be one without difference of 'degree' (social status). This was succinctly expressed by the Baptist Margaret Abbott, who delivered God's promise to his children that they shall build houses, and dwell in them; they shall not build, and another possess; they shall plant vineyards, and eat of the fruit of them; they shall not plant, and another eat. (*A Testimony*)

Three years later in 1662, Hester Biddle rebuked the new order for its neglect of God's commands.

> Oh you high and lofty ones! who spendeth God's creation upon your lusts, and doth not feed the hungry, nor clothe the naked, but they are ready to perish in the streets; both old and young, lame and blind lyeth in your streets, and at your masshouse doors, crying for bread, which even melteth my heart, and maketh the soul of the righteous to mourn: did not the Lord make all men and women upon the earth of one mould, why then should there be so much honour and respect unto some men and women, and not unto others, but they are almost naked for want of clothing, and almost starved for want of bread? (*The Trumpet*)

The desire to dispense with class differences also led Anne Clayton, in *A Letter to the King,* to address the returning sovereign as her 'dear Friend' and 'dear Heart'.

The overturning of traditional religious hierarchies and assertion of the Sainthood of all believers could also result in an authorial stance very different from the passive, self-deprecating attitude of Mary Cary quoted above. Hester Biddle's address to the city of Oxford, which was reprinted verbatim as an attack on its twin town of Cambridge, is written in a first-person voice which stands for both Biddle and God. The text opens:

> Woe to thee city of Oxford, thy wickedness surmounteth the wickedness of Sodom; therefore repent whilst thou has time, lest I consume thee with fire, as I have done it; therefore harden not your hearts, lest I consume you in my fierce anger, and so be brought to naught.

God's voice and the voice of Hester Biddle are one and the same. The prophecy concludes, 'Remember you are warned in your lifetime, and all left without excuse. Hester Biddle.' Margaret Killin's warning to the 'parish teachers' of Plymouth does not contain such an extended merging of the voice of God and that of his prophet, but it does use similar biblical allusions to dramatic effect.

> If ye had stood in my counsel, ye would have turned away from the evil of his doings, but because ye have departed out of my counsel, I will spread dung on your faces, yea I have cast dung on your faces already.

The language of these female prophets also explores in a more diffuse way their relationship with their Lord. God is frequently referred to as a 'nursing mother'. In itself, this phrase is a commonplace in the religious writings of the time. Its meaning when used by men or women differs, however. For the male prophet, it describes a relationship in which he receives care and nourishment, as he did in his relationship with his own mother. For a woman, it also describes an activity which she herself has per-

formed, or might one day perform, when giving suck to her own babies. The dominant, male reading of the image is contested and altered by the female experience. God has qualities that are specifically feminine, and women therefore have a privileged access to understanding those aspects of the divinity. Elizabeth Hincks explains the origin of the term 'nursing mother' by leading the (female) reader into the role of nursing a baby. She also adds a dimension to the arrangement: once the child has fed, the breast feels more comfortable. The relationship is one that provides mutual comfort and benefit.

> And us seeking thus unto God, is as a sucking child,
> That seeketh for its mother's breasts, that is tender and mild.
> And when the child has sucked its fill, the breast likewise is eased,
> The child then it is satisfied, and mother also pleased.
> This figure God made use of when to Israel he did say,
> Her child, can a mother forget, that sucks on her each day?

This can be contrasted with the use made of the image by male preachers in Massachusetts when describing themselves as the 'breasts of God'. Cotton Mather's bizarre expansion of this image—that the *lips* of the ministers are 'the breasts through which the sincere milk of the Word has passed unto you, for your nourishment'—is a purely symbolic use of the metaphor.

The research of present-day feminist linguists has shown that the use of 'man' and 'he' to refer to people of both genders has the effect of eclipsing women, invisibly excluding them from discourse. It is interesting to find, therefore, how frequently the phrases 'he and she' or 'women and men' occur in the visions of the prophets, even though there is no consistent use of such formulations. When they appear however—and they do so remarkably often, as some of the passages quoted above have already shown—they can disrupt the smooth progress of a sentence, drawing the reader's attention to the idea that God's promises were made to women as well as men. Sarah Blackborow, for instance, manages this interruption with the use of parentheses: 'Many there be (sons and daughters) who witness his death and resurrection, who hold forth a true testimony of Jesus to the world' (*Herein is held forth*).

The most frequent appearance of images of women in these texts, however, are derogatory descriptions of Popery or the established church as witches or the Whore of Babylon. These comparisons were contemporary commonplaces, and it would be difficult to imagine women condemning the theology of their opponents without using such expressions. Such metaphors were not innocent in their appearance in men's writings, of course. They grew out of, and helped to perpetuate, a perception of women as sexually threatening, and as inherently more sinful than men. The female prophets engage in this implicit debate on the nature of women in their condemnation of the 'harlot'. While agreeing that Popery is abhorrent, they strive to produce a desirable model of femininity which will allow women to escape identification with the Whore. Hester Biddle addresses the women of London, calling their attention to the plight of the poor. Women who ignore these social issues, she suggests, are no better than the Whore of Babylon. Another kind of behaviour is both commendable and attainable.

> Yet thou canst pass by them in thy gaudy apparel, and outstretched neck, with thy face decked with black spots, which are the marks of the Whore, the Beast and the False Prophet, which is not the attire of Sarah, Abraham's wife. (*A Warning*)

The Bible was a useful source of examples of the existence of earlier women prophets. (A comprehensive listing of them, with descriptions of their activities, was made by Elizabeth Bathurst in 1683, and published as *The Sayings of Women*.) It was also the authority for the injunction that women should not minister. The most frequently cited text is Paul's first Letter to the Corinthians, verses 34 and 35.

> Let your women keep silence in the churches: for it is not permitted unto them to speak; but they are commanded to be under obedience, as also saith the law. And if they will learn anything, let them ask their husbands at home: for it is a shame for women to speak in the church.

It has been suggested that the first published Quaker rebuttal of this text was made in George Fox's pamphlet *The Woman Learning in Silence* in 1656, and that this was later expanded by Margaret Fell in 1666 and 1667 in the two editions of *Women's Speaking Justified*. In fact, the argument predates Fox's contribution. Earlier extended discussions of the matter appear in Richard Farnworth's *A Woman Forbidden to Speak,* 1654, and in Priscilla Cotton's and Mary Cole's pamphlet *To the Priests and People of England* and the collectively written *The Saints Testimony,* both of which appeared in 1655. *The Saints Testimony* cites examples of biblical women prophets, which include some in Paul's own church. Cotton and Cole set out more boldly to turn the Bible against itself, quoting other texts which, they say, make it necessary to reinterpret Paul's message.

> Thou tellest the people, women must not speak in a church, whereas it is not spoke only of a female, for we are all one both male and female in Christ Jesus (Gal. 3.27, 28), but it's weakness that is the woman by the scriptures forbidden, for else thou puttest the scriptures at a difference from themselves, as still it's thy practice out of thy ignorance; for the scriptures do say, that all the church may prophesy one by one, and that women were in the church, as well as men.

They insist that the text be interpreted as having metaphorical significance only. 'Woman' is to be read as meaning 'weakness'—one of the qualities most commonly associated with womanliness in contemporary discourse. Since 'man in his best estate is altogether vanity, weakness, a lie', both men and women are forbidden to prophesy if what they speak is merely human, and not divinely inspired. With the help of the Light Within, however, anyone can speak, because their words are no longer 'weak'.

> Here mayst thou see from the scriptures, that the woman or weakness whether male or female, is forbidden to speak in the church . . . Indeed, you yourselves [the church ministers] are the women, that are forbidden to speak in the church, that are become women.

For a woman to minister she had to confront direct biblical prohibition, as Priscilla Cotton and Mary Cole had. Susannah Parr could not countenance such a change, and repeatedly refused to obey the orders of her church minister to speak her opinions in church. As time passed and she grew increasingly unhappy with the doctrinal path her church was pursuing, however, she began to argue with Mr Stucley during the services. Presumably he had not been prepared for the alteration in church practices to have such an effect. Susannah Parr was told that she must not speak for herself, but talk to one of the men, who would then preach for her. After this, she ceased to attend services there, transferring her allegiances to another church. Finally, when Mr Stucley and his congregation separated from the national church she severed all contact with them. When they excommunicated her three years later and published charges against her, she found herself forced into print in her own defence. The book she wrote is formed from the same contradiction as her earlier behaviour. Steadfastly opposed to women speaking in church or publishing their views, she does both while still asserting their immorality. In the dedicatory epistle to *Susanna's Apologie* she tells her reader

> Weakness is entailed upon my sex in general, and for myself in particular, I am a despised worm, a woman full of natural and sinful infirmities, the chiefest of sinners, and least of Saints.

She then proceeds to make a lengthy examination of the doctrines espoused by Mr Stucley, entering into close textual argument with him, in a book that extends to more than one hundred pages. Men like Mr Stucley were taken by surprise by the outcome of their insistence that correct female behaviour should include giving vent to God's word.

Susannah Parr's story demonstrates that a woman could be allowed or even encouraged to prophesy by men who had not considered the possibility that such behaviour would lead them to rebel against male authority. After the Restoration, as I shall demonstrate in more detail below, men's dominance was reasserted. In order to survive, the Society of Friends had to deny many aspects of its early radicalism. One of the most striking of these was the need gradually to abandon the more public roles open to women in the 1650s.

The earliest vindications of women's preaching were written from prison in the mid-1650s. These texts are visionary and extravagant in their use of scripture, turning St Paul's works against themselves to argue that the 'women' who are forbidden to speak are the male church ministers. Firm in their conviction of direct contact with God's meaning and purpose, they give a symbolic reading to biblical commands. Although Quakers continued to advocate women's right to prophesy, as time passed their official stance on the subject became ever more guarded. Margaret Fell's 1666 pamphlet, *Women's Speaking Justified,* which David Latt, its modern editor, wrongly describes as the first radical statement of a woman's right to speak in church, is in fact a far more careful and conservative presentation of the case than that practised and argued for a decade or more before. Her judicious, rational presentation of Bible verses which counter Paul's injunction to silence has none of the ecstatic fervour of Cotton and Cole. Indeed, Fell's pamphlets generally are more measured and 'rational' than those of her Quaker sisters. She addresses readers with a tone of clear authority which has none of the fervour of, for instance, Hester Biddle's early exhortations.

Fell was, however, far more supportive of women's right to prophesy, even though in a muted form, than was the influential Quaker George Keith in 1674. Addressing the question of female prophecy, he admits that such a thing exists, but seeks rigorously to control the circumstances in which it is permissible. Where Cotton and Cole had accused the priests of being 'women' who have no right to speak, George Keith would allow *any* man to ask questions in church or to minister, but only in extreme circumstances permit a sister to break her silence.

> If they [women] speak, they are not to do it by permission, but by commandment, whereas it is permitted unto men, at all times, to speak in the church . . . An unlearned man may be permitted to ask a question in the church, which is not permitted unto a woman, nor is it needful, for she may ask her husband at home.

When the special category of 'public ministers' was established by Friends in the 1670s, very few women were given official approval to travel and preach. Earlier, no such corporate licence had been necessary. Women who presumed to claim divine inspiration and defied the ban were dealt with sternly. Margery Clipsham's *The Spirit that works Abomination,* 1685, attacks the activities of Elizabeth Aldridge, who had dared to travel around the country to both men's and women's meetings testifying against Quaker doctrines. Rather than welcoming her as God's enlightened prophet, Clipsham presents her as mentally deranged (hysterical), due to problems experienced in giving birth.

> In the time of her lying in, being weak, and disordered in her head (a distemper which divers of her relations have been subject to, and her own mother died in, soon after the time of the birth, as we have been credibly informed), her mind was filled with strong

imaginations; and after she was up, she came forth again with a pretence of visions and revelations, wherewith Friends were greatly dissatisfied, and burthened.

The reduction of women's right to deliver the Word is also reflected in the epistles prefacing many of the texts they print in the late 1670s. Isabel Yeamans and Elizabeth Bathurst, for instance, both apologise for the length of their texts, and justify their publishing in more detail than their earlier Sisters had. In 1672, in fact, Quakers had established a censorship system, whereby only those texts approved by the Second Day Morning Meetings were allowed to be published. By this date, some of the more outrageous women—Martha Simmonds, Mary Howgill, Anne Gargill—had left the Society. Margaret Killin had died. When Hester Biddle was arrested in a Quaker meeting in 1662, the court claimed to be shocked to hear of a woman preaching, and the judge reproved her:

> 'She should ask of her husband at home.' She said, 'If her husband should be a drunkard, or a sot, what should she learn of him, to be as wicked as he was?' R. Brown [the judge] asked if her husband were so? She said no, but if he were so, what could she learn? 'But Christ is my husband, and I learn of Him,' said she. Alderman Brown said she had left her husband two years, and went with a young man into other lands. She told him that was not his business to judge at this time, nor was it fit for him to accuse her, but she went with three women as she was moved of the Lord.

Biddle responded to this attack on her virtue by reminding the judge of his own erstwhile involvement with the sectaries of 'Oliver's days'.

> Richard, dost thou not remember that thou prayedst in the camp by Abingdon, and was that an unlawful meeting? Was that not a good day with thee? I am afraid thou wilt never see such another.

After being imprisoned in Newgate in 1665 for speaking in the street, Hester Biddle seems to have fallen silent. Certainly she published no more after 1662, although she did not die until 1696.

The role of women within Quakerism changed radically, in fact, as the century passed. The female prophets retreated to Women's Meetings, the concerns of which were limited to more conventionally feminine tasks. These meetings were introduced as part of Quakerism's administrative structure during the 1670s, although some groups of Quakers, notably those in London, had organised separate women's meetings (which might not have been so restricted in their brief) since about 1657. The duties of the formally established meetings were described by Anne Whitehead in 1680. She uses biblical precedent not to justify women's preaching, but to show that women's task is to be helpmates to men,

> as the good women of old were helpers in the work of the gospel, in such things as are proper to us, as visiting and relieving the sick, the poor more especially and destitute amongst us . . . Again, we being met together,

the elder women to instruct the younger to all wholesome things (having their own husbands and children, to be discreet, chaste, sober, keeping at home), that the work of God we profess be not blasphemed, etc., with many other matters pertinent to us.

These 'other matters' included finding work for servant girls and apprenticing the sons of poor Friends, and the investigation and suppression of scandal. It seems unlikely that the women's meetings of the 1650s had such a limited brief. In 1672, the men's and women's meetings in London published jointly *An Exhortation and Admonition,* rebuking unmarried servant girls who had taken to leaving their jobs and living alone in lodgings, 'whence many inconveniences and evils have ensued'. Where early Quakers had suffered beatings and imprisonment for refusing to heed social rituals marking dominance and submission, in 1685 the Women's Meeting at the Bull and Mouth issued *A Tender and Christian Testimony to young People,* counselling them to show proper respect to their elders and betters. They especially reprove

> those servants that profess the truth, which will not be subject in their places, in those things that are wholesome, honest, and just, but take liberty as they will, being stubborn and perverse, not answering the blessed principle of truth, so becoming a stumbling to them without, an ill example to our children and families within, a sore disorder, and grievous burden.

With the Society of Friends undergoing fierce attack from outside, and with the millenarian optimism of the 1640s and 1650s long dead, prophets turned their attention to defensive tactics. By the 1680s, most of the pamphlets published by women consist of lamentations that established Friends are 'falling away', and exhortations to the young to follow faithfully parental guidance. The 'truth' that is being defended, however, changes in nature. Fortitude and gravity become virtues in themselves, and the larger social demands of Quakerism are abandoned. *A Tender and Christian Testimony* is particularly concerned to find Friends dressing with less formality than they earlier had. Mary Forster's *Some Seasonable Considerations to the Young Men and Women,* 1684, warns that 'if any of you indulge a loose careless spirit, such make void their suffering, invalidate their testimony, and fall short of the reward and comfort of the upright, and so will not hold out to the end'. Geertruyde Dirrecks advises Quakers to strengthen the Society by exercising strict discipline over their offspring, to control their 'stout and stubborn will' (*An Epistle,* 1677). Other pamphlets serve as didactic writings, presenting images of exemplary women as role-models for little girls. It is quietness of spirit, constancy and respect for orderliness in Anne Whitehead, Elizabeth Braywhaite, and Elizabeth Furly that are praised in the testimonials written about them. The power-structure of the patriarchal family, which had been severely strained by the activities of women prophets, was being reasserted.

The transformations that these writings undergo are a clear example of what it means to think of femininity as a negotiated construct. In the early years of the period, while other women were also petitioning parliament and calling for legal reforms, prophets asserted a right to preach and then to publish the fruits of their divine inspiration. These acts were not made possible through an outright rejection of the bonds of femininity. On the contrary, women's identification as 'weak vessels' particularly prone to irrational, hysterical acts, provided the framework which made such behaviour thinkable. Women might in general be enjoined to silence, but if their words could be interpreted, by themselves and others, as issuing from God, they could speak and would be listened to. The wariness of the Inquisition in its dealings with Katherine Evans and Sarah Chevers exemplifies this.

By the late 1660s, such behaviour had become unacceptable as a part of feminine identity. The development of the patriarchal nuclear family was closing off these options. At the same time, the increasing persecution suffered by the Society of Friends led to the growth of its bureaucratic structure, and stress on the importance of the family, as a means of self-protection. The female prophets were exiled to the feminine duties of Women's Meetings, which controlled women in new ways while they also provided a ground where they could regroup and develop other challenges to the limits of femininity. Anne Tobin's (unpublished) study of the minutes of the White Horse Vale Meeting of the early 1680s has revealed, for instance, that the Women's Meeting used its control over charitable funds to continue to support families which were being rebuked by the Men's Meeting. Such activities help to explain why some male Friends resisted so vehemently even the limited powers given to their Sisters' meetings, necessitating Joan Vokins's rapid return home to defend them in about 1680. God called her back to her native Berkshire from New England, she recalled, and blessed her mission with success:

> though Amalek lay in wait by the way, and the opposite spirit did strongly strive; yet our Good Shepherd did visit his handmaids, and (blessed be his name) filled us with his overcoming power, when the mothers in Israel were so dismayed, as we were likely to have lost our Women's Meetings.

The shift to an apparently more tranquil female role after the Restoration also markedly affected the writings. While it is true that Elizabeth Bathurst and Isabel Yeamans were far more apologetic about their works than earlier prophets had been, they still benefited from the tradition of writing which by that time had been established by their Sisters. The books they publish are more evidently crafted than those of their predecessors. Once 'inspired' behaviour was no longer desirable, writing God's words no longer had to appear to be an effortless outpouring. (It had never in fact been effortless, of course, as the careful emending described above of Lady Eleanor's text might illustrate.) A woman could, with apologies, order and structure her final product. Elizabeth Bathurst prefaces her book with a list of its contents, and with remarks which are self-effacing and yet which emphasise the care with which she has constructed her text.

The truth is, though I at first thought to have filled but one sheet of paper, when I set about it, I saw a field before me, which cost me some spiritual travel before I got through. And now, lest any should think the trace too long to follow, I have taken pains to prefix and page contents to every material point, that so they may readily turn to that which they are most desirous to be at.

When Rebeckah Travers, one of the most influential of women Quakers was asked in 1680 to promote the publication of Alice Curwen's autobiography, she refused, 'there not being much prophecy in it'. On reflection, however, she changed her mind. She says that the decision was caused by her belief that Curwen's cheerful acceptance of death as God's will and her refusal to be given medicine were a good example of commendable behaviour. Perhaps this image of Curwen as a truly holy woman was the factor that enabled her text to be published. The main body of the work, however, consists of her own account of her travel in New England and Barbados. If she had died less meekly, the tale of her earlier heroism might never have been made public. Quaker women were not silenced in their retreat, but the price they paid to continue being heard was a high one.

ANNE WENTWORTH: BABYLON AND MALE POWER

At first glance, therefore, it comes as a surprise to find the Baptist Anne Wentworth publishing ecstatic millenarian prophecies as late as 1679. Her *True Account*, *Vindication* and *Revelation* all look forward to an imminent judgement day, a 'great overturning' when her persecutors, and most specifically her husband, will receive their just punishment at God's hands. God will take care of her, and her husband's power over her will cease.

> And he has assured me, that the man of earth shall oppress me no more; no more shall I be under the hands of the hard-hearted persecutors, unless he become a new man, a changed man, a man sensible of the wrong he has done me, with his fierce looks, bitter words, sharp tongue and cruel usage. (*Vindication*)

Her other tormentors, named in *The Revelation* as Hickes, Dicks, Knowles and Philip Barder, are also assured of their specific punishment for orchestrating 'the flood of scorn, contempt, bitter railing, false accusations, scandalous papers, and lying pamphlets' (*The Revelation*) against her.

By the time *The Revelation* appeared in 1679 (as a preamble to the text by a woman friend explains), she had been ejected from the marital home by her furious husband, and he had withdrawn all financial support from her. It also seems likely that he was trying to divorce her, and she had been 'rejected by all her friends and relations, and left by them to shift for herself'. Husband, religious community and family had collaborated to try to silence her prophetic voice. What was the nature of her prophecy?

The title pages of her *Vindication* and *The Revelation* juxtapose the fates of 'Babylon' and 'Zion'. Earlier in the century, prophetic writings had used 'Zion' and 'Babylon' as symbols of good and evil: the longed-for triumph of the Saints would include the overthrow of 'Babylon', a state which could be variously interpreted as referring to King Charles, Cromwell or 'kingly power'. Anne Wentworth uses these same metaphors to describe her own situation. She is a 'daughter of Zion, newly delivered from the captivity of Babylon' (her husband and his allies) (*Vindication*). She explains how Christ revealed to her the truth which she must now pass on to people at large: this is no mere personal oppression of herself by her husband. The images of Zion and Babylon are appropriate because what is at issue is a far more general oppression of good by evil. She communicates to the reader the insight which freed her, making her able to understand male power as a general evil, supported by a legal system that must be resisted.

> The Lord showed me why the people did not understand me, nor my work; because they will not (saith the Lord) go to the root of the matter, but blind themselves with pouring so much upon a man and his wife, and will look no further: but continue writing all faults in thy forehead, as delusions and disobeying of thy husband, and see none in themselves: they are so stark blind that they can see nothing at all of what I the Lord am doing: they will not see, how I have placed the two spirits in a man and his wife, to figure out Zion and Babylon . . . And then the Lord spake thus in verses:
>
> Full eighteen years in sorrow I did lie,
> Then the Lord Jesus came to hear my cry;
> In one night's time, he did me heal,
> From head to foot he made me well.
> With ointment sweet he did me anoint,
> And this work he then did me appoint.
> A hand in Babylon's ashes I must have,
> For that end the Lord took me from the grave,
> And said, 'A new body I the Lord will give thee,
> To convince thy enemies . . .
> I the Lord will openly, and surely avenge thy cause,
> Upon all thy enemies, for their unjust laws'.
> (*Revelation*)

The term 'new body' refers in part to her 'resurrection' into the number of true believers. It also evokes the physical battering she has suffered at her husband's hands. In her *Vindication* she explains that she had fled her husband in literal fear for her life. The eighteen years of sorrow and oppression to which she repeatedly refers is the timespan of her marriage.

> He has in his barbarous actions towards me, a many times overdone such things as not only in the *spirit* of them will one day be judged a murdering of, but had long since *really* proved so, if God had not wonderfully supported, and preserved me.

The earlier prophets of revolution had claimed that they were not the originators of their works, but were being used as divine instruments. Anna Trapnel had even recorded her argument with God, asking him not to send her on his mission. Anne Wentworth also presents herself as a reluctant handmaid, who would rather have remained in ignorance, or at least stayed silent. The compulsion to communicate her truths, however, was too strong. She declares that she felt

> that I might rather die, than do it. That I was commanded of God to record them. That my own natural temper was so greatly averse to it, that for eleven months together I withstood the Lord, till by an angel from Heaven he threatened to *kill me,* and took away my sleep from me. (*Vindication*)

She must endeavour to present herself as properly feminine if she is to have any hope of acceptance. Perhaps, too, she found the burden of seeing the reality of male power very heavy to bear, and would have preferred to have been left in ignorance. But to a battered wife, well-versed in biblical imagery, the grim reality was too clear to be refused. The passage quoted above continues

> And indeed, the writings that man was so displeased with, were in themselves very warrantable, if I had not had any command of God, for I only wrote the way he led me in a wilderness of affliction for 18 years . . . And I do further declare, the things I have written are true, and no lie: and that what is so distasteful in them to man, are such things as I could not leave out, without prejudice to truth, and disobedience to God.

Her foes attempted to discredit her, she says, by describing her as an archetypally unfeminine woman taken over by the deplorable 'enthusiasm' that characterised the radical sectaries.

> I am reproached as a proud, wicked, deceived, deluded, lying woman, a mad, melancholy, crack-brained, self-willed, conceited fool, and black sinner, led by whimsies, notions and kinck-knacks of my own head; one that speaks blasphemy, not fit to take the name of God in her mouth; an heathen and publican, a fortune-teller, an enthusiast, and the like much more.
>
> (*Revelation*)

The re-establishment of order at the Restoration made such charges dangerous for anyone, and especially for a woman. Her fourth revelation contains an amazonian image of herself equipped for battle, which would have served as ammunition in these accusations. God has given her strength to stand

> Against all my enemies, with His battleaxe in
>   my hand,
> To wound, kill, amaze and put to flight, and cut
>   them down,
> And when they are in their graves, I shall wear
>   a crown.
>
> (*Revelation*)

In leaving her husband, she has also made herself vulnerable to the most damaging accusation: that she is a loose woman. Her publication of her *Revelation* comes partly from the need to deny 'that I keep men company, and have rogues come to me, and live a scandalous life in an almshouse'.

The suppression of women during the reign of Elizabeth I

That a society in which both life and art suppressed women so severely was ruled by a woman for close to fifty years is highly ironic. Yet, although many women did rule in Europe during the sixteenth and seventeenth centuries, there is no doubt that the woman ruler was incongruent with the mores of this period concerning woman's place. The adroitness and political genius of Elizabeth Tudor endeared her to her subjects, but her rule was not established easily or unshakily: broad, traditional questions concerning the rule of a woman, inflamed in England by the clumsiness and misgovernance of Mary Tudor and Mary Stuart, were aroused by her accession. . . . Even at the height of her power, Elizabeth could not exercise power as straightforwardly as her male counterparts, though, unlike the two Marys, she learned to develop sophisticated methods for circumventing invidious constraints. Still, it is widely recognized that Elizabeth's firm grasp of the power she wielded so effectively was accomplished only through her personal sacrifice of ordinary domestic life.

Betty S. Travitsky, in *The Renaissance Englishwoman in Print: Counterbalancing the Canon,* edited by Anne M. Haselkorn and Betty S. Travitsky, The University of Massachusetts Press, 1990.

Anne Wentworth's mission is to reveal to the world the true identity of 'Zion' and 'Babylon'. If her husband will agree to her doing this, she will return to him

> provided I may have my *just* and *necessary* liberty to attend a more than ordinary call and command of God to publish the things which concern the *peace of my own soul,* and *of the whole nation.* (*Vindication*)

This is scarcely a likely outcome, of course. She had discovered the same catch that, in the twentieth century, was to cause the creation of the slogan 'the personal is political'. Her revelation is not purely personal, but comes from and is part of the power structure of patriarchy. At one level, her husband might not be personally responsible for oppressing her, and in theory his help could be enlisted to overthrow 'Babylon'. (Though this might be an unnecessarily charitable interpretation of the behaviour of a man who had repeatedly beaten his wife. Such violence lies at the extreme edge of what patriarchy finds permissible.) In fact, he is the personification of male power, created by it. She will not abandon the hope that he might, somehow, be converted. But in the mean time, she is living alone, drawing strength from her God who has shown her the truth, and from her woman friend.

For the moment, she ends her text preparing to write more. She is an isolated woman, unsupported by a wider social movement as the earlier Quakers and Baptists had been. She cannot call on others to take up arms, as Trapnel and Cary had, or change the laws as Barwick had. Her only possible contribution to the great change she sees approaching is to save her own life, and record her message. It is unimaginable that women, divided in their homes, could unite to bring about the apocalypse. Her religion had provided the tools to analyse oppression, and it had also suggested only one solution. Women must be patient and wait for God to intervene.

> From Heaven will I the Lord come to appear,
> For to make them all my own voice to hear:
> And all those, that long to see this thing done,
> Must patiently wait till I the Lord do come.
>   (*Revelation*)

The earlier revolution of the Saints had failed to bring the New Jerusalem into being. Anne Wentworth had given a new identification to 'Babylon'. Alone in her newly privatised home, a single 'daughter of Zion' could not destroy it.

FURTHER READING

Bibliography

Hageman, Elizabeth H. "Recent Studies in Women Writers of the English Seventeenth Century (1604-1674)." *English Literary Renaissance* 18, No. 1 (Winter 1988): 138-67.

> Provides citations and descriptions of selected editions of works by seventeenth-century women writers, as well as critical studies and relevant historical studies.

Criticism

Beilin, Elaine V. *Redeeming Eve: Women Writers of the English Renaissance.* Princeton: Princeton University Press, 1987, 346 p.

> Examines the Renaissance tradition of women's writing and the cautious conservatism that characterized the attitudes of many women toward literary endeavors.

Haselkorn, Anne M., and Betty S. Travitsky, eds. *The Renaissance Englishwoman in Print: Counterbalancing the Canon.* Amherst: The University of Massachusetts Press, 1990, 363 p.

> Presents selected critical essays on the following topics: "The Outspoken Woman," "Woman on the Renaissance Stage," "The Woman Ruler," "The Private Woman," and "Women and the Sidneian Tradition." Correlates "writings by men that have traditionally been contained within the literary canon with writings by women that have traditionally been marginalized."

Lamb, Mary Ellen. *Gender and Authorship in the Sidney Circle.* Madison: University of Wisconsin Press, 1990, 297 p.

> Critical study including discussion of Mary Wroth, which "takes as its special province the various writings, ranging from translations to unpublished manuscript verse, produced by the male and female members of one extended family, the Sidneys."

Lewalski, Barbara Kiefer. *Writing Women in Jacobean England.* Cambridge: Harvard University Press, 1993, 431 p.

> Examines the female experience of Jacobean culture through analysis of texts by nine women writers.

Maclean, Ian. *The Renaissance Notion of Woman: A Study in the Fortunes of Scholasticism and Medical Science in European Intellectual Life.* Cambridge: Cambridge University Press, 1980, 119 p.

> Examines Renaissance texts with a view to understanding attitudes towards women during the seventeenth century.

Mason, Mary G. "The Other Voice: Autobiographies of Women Writers." In *Autobiography: Essays Theoretical and Critical,* edited by James Olney, Princeton: Princeton University Press, 1980, 360 p.

> Includes discussion of the autobiographical works of Margaret Cavendish, Margery Kempe, and Anne Bradstreet.

MacCarthy, B.G. *Women Writers: Their Contribution to the English Novel, 1621-1744.* Dublin: Cork University Press, 1945, 288 p.

> Discusses societal influences on women's literary production and examines the contributions of women to a variety of forms including pastoral romance, biography, and satire.

Mermin, Dorothy. "Women Becoming Poets: Katherine Philips, Aphra Behn, Anne Finch." In *ELH*: 57, No. 2 (Summer 1990): 335-55.

> Examines Katherine Philips, Aphra Behn, and Anne Finch as seventeenth-century women poets who managed to achieve fame and success during their lifetimes.

Nadelhaft, Jerome. "The Englishwoman's Sexual Civil War: Feminist Attitudes Towards Men, Women, and Marriage, 1650-1740." *Journal of the History of Ideas* XLIII, No. 4 (October-December 1982): 555-79.

> Examines how seventeenth-century women writers "developed a sweeping and powerful criticism of men's attitudes towards and treatment of women" and argues that "[modern historians] have not done the dissenters justice."

Schofield, Mary Anne and Cecilia Macheski, eds. *Fetter'd or Free?: British Women Novelists, 1670-1815.* Athens: Ohio University, 1986, 441 p.

> Presents discussion of women novelists by selected critics, organized in the following sections: "Gender

and Genre," "Feminine Iconography," "Love, Sex, and Marriage," "Moral and Political Revolution," "Fictional Strategies," and "The Novel and Beyond: Critical Assessments."

Singley, Carol J. and Susan Elizabeth Sweeney, eds. *Anxious Power: Reading, Writing, and Ambivalence in Narrative by Women.* Albany: State University of New York Press, 1993, 400 p.
     Presents selected essays informed by the theory that "reading and writing are by no means gender-free acts." Focuses "specifically on narrative representations of women's ambivalence toward language."

Wilson, Katharina M. and Frank J. Warnke, eds. *Women Writers of the Seventeenth Century.* Athens: The University of Georgia Press, 1989, 545 p.
     Presents an international overview of important seventeenth-century women writers.

Aphra Behn

1640(?)-1689

(Pseudonym of Aphra Johnson or Aphra Amis; also Aphara, Ayfara, and Afray; also wrote under pseudonyms of Astrea and Astraea) English novelist, dramatist, poet, essayist, and translator.

For further information on Behn's works and career, see *Literature Criticism from 1400 to 1800,* Vol. 1.

INTRODUCTION

Behn is best remembered as the first woman in England to earn her living solely by writing, and is credited with influencing the development of the English novel toward realism. Attributing her success to her "ability to write like a man," she competed professionally with the prominent "wits" of Restoration England, including George Etherege, William Wycherley, John Dryden, and William Congreve. Similar to the literary endeavors of her male contemporaries, Behn's writings catered to the libertine tastes of King Charles II and his supporters, and occasionally excelled as humorous satires recording the political and social events of the era. Behn's most enduring work is the novel *Oroonoko; or, The Royal Slave,* which is considered to be one of the earliest novels to use realistic technique and incorporate a title character often regarded as the first "noble savage" in English literature.

Biographical Information

Behn's birthplace and date of birth, as well as the identity of her parents, have never been conclusively established. However, it is generally agreed that she and her family sailed to Surinam in South America, most likely in 1663, and that her father, who had been appointed lieutenant-general there, died en route. Living in Surinam for several months before the Dutch takeover and her return to England, Behn accumulated colorful impressions of the country, which she later recorded in *Oroonoko.* It has been speculated that after returning to England in 1664 she married a man of Dutch descent. Behn seems to have been wealthy during this time, becoming popular at the court of Charles II and well known for her charm and wit. Her husband died shortly after their marriage and, for reasons unknown, Behn was left an impoverished widow. It is only after this point in her life that substantial information about Behn has been documented. In 1666, Charles II employed Behn, a staunch royalist, to spy on a disaffected English group in Antwerp. Although the mission provided the crown with valuable information, Behn was not renumerated for her espionage efforts. She returned to England in poverty and spent a brief time in debtors' prison before ultimately deciding, as she said, to "write for bread." Before Behn, women writers were primarily aristocrats who were regarded as dabblers, and their works were not taken seriously. Thus, Behn's decision to join London's Grub street hacks was both bold and unprecedented. Her first play, *The Forced Marriage; or, The Jealous Bridegroom,* demonstrates her familiarity with stage techniques, and the popularity of the work proved that a woman could successfully write the same bawdy material that the male playwrights of the era were producing. Eventually, however, Behn's work was attacked as immoral by many of her contemporaries. Undaunted by the criticism, she continued to write and spent most of her literary career defending her works against charges of indecency that were based primarily on the fact that the works were written by a woman. Behn's political commentaries were halted in 1682 when she was arrested for a written attack on the Duke of Monmouth; she produced no works for the next two years, and thereafter wrote only poetry and fiction. For the most part, Behn lived an impoverished life, and hardship contributed to a prolonged illness in her later years. After her death in 1689, she was honored with burial in Westminster Abbey.

Major Works

Behn's early dramas were written to satisfy her audience's taste, and most fall into the category of the romantic tragicomedy popularized by Francis Beaumont and John Fletcher during the Jacobean period. Although her plots were hardly original—many were freely borrowed from both English and foreign authors, a common practice of the time—Behn wrote with wit, vitality, and a dramatic sense for creative staging. *The Forced Marriage* comically introduces Behn's candid opinion regarding arranged marriages, while her second drama, *The Amorous Prince; or, The Curious Husband,* portrays the difficulties of friendship between lovers. These works explicitly depict adulterous bedroom scenes, and players appear in "night attire"—bold stage situation for Restoration drama. Both of these works were popular successes and encouraged Behn to produce *The Dutch Lover.* This third play weaves together a comic and a serious plot, as several sets of lovers cavort through episodes of mistaken identities, masquerades, and love trysts. *The Dutch Lover* was not a popular success, however, and Behn was attacked by Puritan critics who found her work lewd and immoral.

Behn's most productive and financially successful literary years were between 1676 and 1682. During this middle phase her works were more carefully constructed, and while they continued to convey her unconventional morality, their scope was expanded to satirically record the political climate of the period. Behn's best-known work of this time is the drama *The Rover; or, The Banished Cavaliers, Part I.* Like *The Dutch Lover, The Rover* combines farce and intrigue in a skillfully crafted format which again revolves around mistaken identities and masquerades. *Sir Patient Fancy* offers an interesting commentary on seventeenth-century customs and manners, satirizing arranged marriages, Puritanism, and pedantry. *The Roundheads; or, The Good Old Cause,* Behn's first attempt to fuse comedy and politics, displays her Tory sympathies by portraying Whig politicians as purely comic figures. Behn's second attempt at political satire, *The City Heiress; or, Sir Timothy Treat-all,* was well-received by audiences, and critics regard it as one of her best comedies. *The City Heiress* utilizes several sets of lovers to convey Behn's unconventional view of marriage, love, and sexual freedom, but in this work her political satire is more artfully integrated into the framework of the drama. Written during the last phase of Behn's literary career, *Oroonoko* is her most acclaimed work, and in the past three centuries it has received a significant amount of commentary much of which is concerned with the work's influence on the development of the novel. According to Behn, the story of the Coramantien prince Oroonoko and his beautiful West Indian lover Imoinda is based on her own "true," "eyewitness" accounts of events in Surinam. The first-person narrative gives verisimilitude to the novel, as does the vividly described local color, with the theme of the innate goodness of the "noble savage" skillfully juxtaposed against the barbarity of "civilized" English intruders.

Critical Reception

Critics continue to be intrigued by Behn's dramas and poetry, but *Oroonoko* has emerged as the chief focus of attention. Many commentators regard the work as an early attempt at realism in literature, and the novel is often discussed as a precursor to the works of Daniel Defoe, who thirty years later refined technical aspects of the first-person narrative and demonstrated that fiction could be made more life-like or realistic through careful selection of vivid detail. *Oroonoko* also holds an important place in English literature as one of the first social statements against slavery. Today Behn is acknowledged for her revolutionary influence on the novel form and serves as a pioneering example to female professional writers. A controversial and vital figure during her lifetime, she contributed to Restoration literature while boldly attempting to overcome the barriers of seventeenth-century prejudices and rigid gender roles.

PRINCIPAL WORKS

The Forced Marriage; or, The Jealous Bridegroom (drama) 1670

The Amorous Prince; or, The Curious Husband (drama) 1671

The Dutch Lover (drama) 1673

Abdelazer; or, The Moor's Revenge (drama) 1676

The Town Fop; or, Sir Timothy Tawdrey (drama) 1676

The Rover; or, The Banished Cavaliers, Part I (drama) 1677

Sir Patient Fancy (drama) 1678

The Feigned Courtesans; or, A Night's Intrigue (drama) 1679

The Roundheads; or, The Good Old Cause (drama) 1681

The Second Part of the Rover (drama) 1681

The City Heiress; or, Sir Timothy Treat-all (drama) 1682

The False Count; or, A New Way to Play an Old Game (drama) 1682

Love Letters between a Nobleman and His Sister (fictional letters) 1684

Poems upon Several Occasions, with a Voyage to the Island of Love (poetry) 1684

The Case for the Watch (poetry and prose) 1686

The Luckey Chance; or, An Alderman's Bargain (drama) 1686

La Montre; or, The Lover's Watch (poetry and prose) 1686

The Emperor of the Moon (drama) 1687

The Fair Jilt; or, The History of Prince Tarquin and Miranda (novel) 1688

The History of the Nun; or, The Fair Vow-Breaker (novel) 1688

Lycidus; or, The Lover in Fashion (poetry and prose) 1688

Oroonoko; or, The Royal Slave (novel) 1688

The Lucky Mistake (novel) 1689

The Widow Ranter; or, The History of Bacon in Virginia (drama) 1689

The Histories and Novels of the Late Ingenious Mrs. Behn (dramas and novels) 1696

Love Letters to a Gentleman (letters) 1696
The Lady's Looking-Glass, to Dress Herself By; or, The Art of Charming (poetry and prose) 1697
The Plays, Histories, and Novels of the Ingenious Mrs. Aphra Behn. 6 vols. (dramas and novels) 1871
The Works of Aphra Behn. 6 vols. (poetry, dramas, and novels) 1915
Selected Writings of the Ingenious Mrs. Aphra Behn (poetry, novels, dramas, and essays) 1950
The Novels of Mrs. Aphra Behn (novels) 1969
The Uncollected Verse of Aphra Behn (poetry) 1989

CRITICISM

Virginia Woolf (essay date 1929)

SOURCE: A chapter in *A Room of One's Own,* Harcourt, Brace and Company, 1929, pp. 100-36.

[*Woolf is one of the most prominent literary figures of twentieth-century English literature. Like her contemporary James Joyce, with whom she is often compared, Woolf is remembered as one of the most innovative of the stream-of-consciousness novelists. Concerned primarily with depicting the life of the mind, she revolted against traditional narrative techniques and developed her own highly individualized style. Her criticial essays, which cover almost the entire range of English literature, contain some of her finest prose and are praised for their insight. Here, Woolf comments on Behn's importance to the history of female writers in England.*]

[With] Mrs. Behn we turn a very important corner on the road [in the history of women writers]. We leave behind, shut up in their parks among their folios, those solitary great ladies who wrote without audience or criticism, for their own delight alone. We come to town and rub shoulders with ordinary people in the streets. Mrs. Behn was a middle-class woman with all the plebeian virtues of humour, vitality and courage; a woman forced by the death of her husband and some unfortunate adventures of her own to make her living by her wits. She had to work on equal terms with men. She made, by working very hard, enough to live on. The importance of that fact outweighs anything that she actually wrote, even the splendid **"A Thousand Martyrs I have made,"** or **"Love in Fantastic Triumph sat,"** for here begins the freedom of the mind, or rather the possibility that in the course of time the mind will be free to write what it likes. For now that Aphra Behn had done it, girls could go to their parents and say, You need not give me an allowance; I can make money by my pen. Of course the answer for many years to come was, Yes, by living the life of Aphra Behn! Death would be better! and the door was slammed faster than ever. . . .

Aphra Behn proved that money could be made by writing of the sacrifice, perhaps, of certain agreeable qualities; and so by degrees writing became not merely a sign of folly and a distracted mind, but was of practical importance. A husband might die, or some disaster overtake the family. Hundreds of women began as the eighteenth century drew on to add to their pin money, or to come to the rescue of their families by making translations or writing the innumerable bad novels which have ceased to be recorded even in text-books, but are to be picked up in the fourpenny boxes in the Charing Cross Road. The extreme activity of mind which showed itself in the later eighteenth century among women—the talking, and the meeting, the writing of essays on Shakespeare, the translating of the classics—was founded on the solid fact that women could make money by writing. Money dignifies what is frivolous if unpaid for. It might still be well to sneer at "blue stockings with an itch for scribbling," but it could not be denied that they could put money in their purses. Thus, towards the end of the eighteenth century a change came about which, if I were re-writing history, I should describe more fully and think of greater importance than the Crusades or the Wars of the Roses. The middle-class woman began to write. For if *Pride and Prejudice* matters, and *Middlemarch* and *Villette* and *Wuthering Heights* matter, then it matters far more than I can prove . . . that women generally, and not merely the lonely aristocrat shut up in her country house among her folios and her flatterers, took to writing. Without those forerunners, Jane Austen and the Brontës and George Eliot could no more have written than Shakespeare could have written without Marlowe, or Marlowe without Chaucer, or Chaucer without those forgotten poets who paved the ways and tamed the natural savagery of the tongue. For masterpieces are not single and solitary births; they are the outcome of many years of thinking in common, of thinking by the body of the people, so that the experience of the mass is behind the single voice. Jane Austen should have laid a wreath upon the grave of Fanny Burney, and George Eliot done homage to the robust shade of Eliza Carter—the valiant old woman who tied a bell to her bedstead in order that she might wake early and learn Greek. All women together ought to let flowers fall upon the tomb of Aphra Behn which is, most scandalously but rather appropriately, in Westminster Abbey, for it was she who earned them the right to speak their minds. It is she—shady and amorous as she was—who makes it not quite fantastic for me to say . . . : Earn five hundred a year by your wits. . . .

Martine Watson Brownley (essay date 1977)

SOURCE: "The Narrator in *Oroonoko*," in *Essays in Literature,* Vol. IV, No. 2, Fall, 1977, pp. 174-81.

[*In the following essay, Brownley discusses Behn's handling of the narrator in* Oroonoko, *asserting that the narrative persona is used "to unify and to add realism to disparate elements" in the novel.*]

In the past the narrator of **Oroonoko** has, with very few exceptions, been studied mainly in terms of the life and ideas of Aphra Behn. Since what little we know of Behn's life is just as exciting and romantic as any material in her writings, it is easy to see why the narrative *persona* of *Oroonoko* has taken second place to the woman who was traveler, spy, pioneer female author, and political intriguer. For the moment controversy over Behn's biography seems to have died down. Undoubtedly the lull is temporary, for many fascinating questions remain unanswered. Nevertheless, the pause offers a useful chance to consider the role of the narrator within the context of the novel itself. *Oroonoko*'s importance in early English prose fiction has long been established, and, as George Guffey points out [in his *Two English Novelists,* 1975] the "particularly well-defined narrator" is one important element which distinguishes the work from other fiction of the time. Functioning as a strongly felt presence throughout *Oroonoko,* the narrator unifies the novel, enhances the tenuous realism of the basically heroic story, and offers a viable standard of judgment for the readers.

Since in general what the narrator says is more important than anything she actually does in the context of the story of *Oroonoko,* narrative control of language emerges as one of her most important functions. Other than the character of Oroonoko himself, the voice of the narrator is the major unifying element in the novel. Behn carefully develops a distinctive voice for her narrative *persona;* in *Oroonoko* the contrast of realism and romanticism in the narrator's expression gives the style its unique quality. This contrast in style, of course, reflects the uneasy alliance in *Oroonoko* of romantic elements from the heroic play and realistic elements later prominent in the novel. The synthesis is not entirely successful, but Behn's manipulation of the narrator's romantic and realistic styles to control point of view accounts for some of the success that she managed to achieve in *Oroonoko.*

The romantic element is apparent in the narrator's eloquent style, found particularly in the elaborate rhetorical speeches which reflect Behn's dramatic background. The overstatement and hackneyed imagery typical of the heroic play also occur, as one would expect, whenever narrator or characters speak of love. When Oroonoko faces separation from Imoinda by military duty, "every Day seem'd a tedious Year till he saw his *Imoinda*"; after their reunion in Surinam, the lovers agree that "even Fetters and Slavery were soft and easy, and would be supported with Joy and Pleasure; while they cou'd be so happy to possess each other". The narrator pulls out all the stops in her heroic description of Oroonoko's appearance, which abounds in superlatives. His shape is "the most exact that can be fancy'd"; his mouth is "the finest shaped that could be seen"; he has "the best Grace in the World." She combines the best of nature and of art to depict him: "The most famous Statuary cou'd not form the Figure of a Man more admirably turn'd from head to foot," while "bating his Colour, there could be Nothing in Nature more beautiful, agreeable, and handsome" than his face. Having exhausted superlatives in describing Oroonoko, she can only do justice to Imoinda's charms by calling her a fit consort for Oroonoko, "the beautiful Black *Venus* to our young *Mars*". With one exception, the hyperbolic heroic style is always used in connection with Oroonoko and his activities. Only Oroonoko's execution, when he is finally

destroyed by men who cannot tolerate what he represents, is described in realistic terms. In this passage the straightforward language heightens Oroonoko's heroic actions by the narrator's grimly effective contrast of style and content. Through the rest of the novel, the heroic style sets him apart within the narrative just as his ideal love, truth, and honor separate him from the ordinary standards of those around him.

Oroonoko is at least partially the story of these ordinary people and their reaction to the extraordinary. Neither these people nor the narrator herself could be appropriately delineated in heroic terms, and so realistic colloquial elements are a part of the narrative style. This informal oral style suggests Behn's contemporary reputation as a witty and enjoyable conversationalist. The narrative is filled with conversational insertions: "I had forgot to tell you"; "as I said before"; "I must say thus much." Using this style, the narrator adds realism by infusing her own personality into the narrative, enhancing the story with her own experiences—"I have seen 'em [the Blacks] so frequently blush, and look pale"—and her personal opinions—"For my part, I took 'em for Hobgoblins, or Fiends, rather than Men." To modern tastes, this realistic element is the most familiar and pleasing aspect of the style in *Oroonoko.* Unfortunately, though the oral style adds realism and is most effective at times, the colloquial narrative is too often difficult to follow. Poorly structured sentences, the mixing of verb tenses, and especially pronouns with ambiguous references hinder the reader's understanding of the action. The clumsiness can be defended, just as Defoe's similar carelessness has been, by suggesting that the author intended the grammatical mistakes to characterize the narrator's mind and outlook. In both cases any gain in characterization would seem to be more than offset by the reader's confusion. The speed at which Behn and Defoe were known to produce also seems to indicate that authorial carelessness rather than deliberate artistry in characterization caused the stylistic problems. That Behn managed in any way to fuse the realistic and the romantic styles in *Oroonoko* is an achievement of sorts. The effectiveness of the narrative voice unifies the disparate elements and appropriately focuses point of view. But style cannot finally account either for Behn's success in *Oroonoko,* or for her purposes in delineating the narrator.

Despite its inadequacy, the fact that the realistic style is present at all in *Oroonoko* leads us to the major function of the narrator. It is she who grounds the improbable romantic story in at least a semblance of reality. Very view of the other elements in the novel provide realism. The action, with its fantastic coincidences, noble posturings, and terrible catastrophes, is straight from the pure romance of heroic drama. Behn had chosen backgrounds which would arouse interest; Coramentien provides the remote and glamorous setting typical of a heroic play, while Surinam combines similar exoticism with the topicality appealing to a public eager for information about the colonies in America. Horace Walpole, writing in the middle of the next century, indicates that because of the West Indian War, "I read nothing but American voyages, and histories of plantations and settlements," but even in times of peace Europeans enthusiastically devoured accounts of the new world. Although the African background is not portrayed realistically in any way, the descriptions of Surinam may well have seemed realistic enough to a public accustomed to paradisiacal accounts of the newly discovered hemisphere. Today, despite establishment of Behn's accuracy in describing parts of the background, the Edenic fantasy in too many of her descriptions makes the locale seem just as romantically unreal as the actions.

The characters of *Oroonoko* are in general no more realistic than the action and setting of the novel. Most of the characters in the story are described in exaggerated terms, emerging as excessively good or extraordinarily bad. Practically everyone in the novel is exceptional: Oroonoko and Imoinda are of course perfect; the Council "consisted of such notorious Villains as *Newgate* never transported"; Aboan is "not only one of the best Quality, but a man extremely well made and beautiful"; Banister is "a Fellow of Absolute Barbarity". Even the somewhat colorless Trefy is described as "a Man of Great Wit, and fine Learning," and "a Man of so excellent Wit and Parts". Only the narrator emerges as rather ordinary. Of her own characteristics, she heavily emphasizes only her credibility, obviously performing the standard obeisance to the antifictional bias of the age. She devotes the first two paragraphs of the story to establishing her reliability in the narrative role, assuring the reader of the literal truth of her tale and the trustworthiness of her sources. Astutely flattering her audience, she emphasizes her conscientiousness as a narrator; she is in complete control of her material and recognizes her obligations not to tell anything which "might prove tedious and heavy to my Reader, in a World where he finds Diversions for every Minute, new and strange". During the rest of the novel she establishes a pleasant enough narrative presence. Her most important trait is her fundamental decency and humanity, apparent in all of her actions and remarks. Critics note that she does try to emphasize her own importance whenever possible, but despite her insistence on her position, neither her remarks nor her actions establish her as an unusual person. No reader would characterize the narrator in the glowing terms she uses to describe the other characters in the story; she emerges as a character with whom the reader finds it easy enough to identify. Throughout the novel the narrator seems to be an ordinary woman in an extraordinary position, and she therefore adds a sense of realism lacking in the action, setting, and other characters in the story.

Thus in a strange and exotic world of romantic wonders, the narrator helps the reader to keep his bearings. She adds realism to the story, offering a standard of normalcy in an environment of extraordinary people and actions. As such, she can fulfill her other important narrative function, which is to provide an acceptable standard of judgment in ordinary terms for the events and characters in *Oroonoko*. Oroonoko himself of course provides the noblest example of human excellencies in the novel, but he is ideal rather than real. As Lore Metzger points out, Oroonoko's "heroic ideals cannot prevail in the real world [introduction to *Oroonoko,* 1973 ed.]. The novel requires

standards in ordinary as well as ideal terms, and the narrator, a decent, average woman, can focus the scale of values in the realistic terms required. As a participant in the story she several times serves as a link between Oroonoko and the European world, and in the novel she interprets him to this world. It is her standards which finally emerge as most interesting to the reader, because of their possible applicability to his own experience.

The narrator provides standards of judgment at several levels for her audience. At the lowest level, she seeks to make the unusual comprehensible to her English audience by comparisons with things familiar to them. The Amazon is "almost as broad as the River of Thames"; the Indian stools are painted "in a sort of Japan-work"; the grove of trees near her house spreads "about half the length of the *Mall*". But the narrator also has some advanced ideas to share with the audience. As Behn openly avowed, her main purpose in all of her writing was entertainment, but throughout *Oroonoko* she does not hesitate to include social, political, and moral observations in the narrator's commentary when opportunities arise. The narrator never interrupts the progress of the story by preaching; the remarks are brief, pithy, and usually pointed. Almost every commentator has pointed out that the ideas on civilization, religion, and morality expressed in *Oroonoko* presage those of the French thinkers of the Enlightenment. Although Oroonoko is clearly not a noble savage, Behn uses him in the way philosophers would later use the figure. As Haydn White points out [*New York Review of Books,* 25 November, 1976], the myth was generally used not to gain better treatment for native people, but to attack "the concept of 'nobility' in Europe." Metzger, Guffey, and other critics have shown that claims for *Oroonoko* as an early anti-slavery novel are unjustified, and the narrator definitely does not finally indict the entire institution of slavery. She fails entirely to exploit the ironic potential in such situations as Oroonoko's inciting the men he himself enslaved to rebel against their masters. Nevertheless, the narrator exposes through Oroonoko the mistreatment of slaves, and his speeches are a powerful condemnation of the entire system. If he is not radical, she at least shows substantial humanitarian concern and sympathy. Always concerned with substance over form, her anger flashes against injustice and hypocrisy throughout the novel; her condemnation of certain practices in "*Christian* Countries, where they prefer the bare Name of Religion; and, without Vertue or Morality, think that sufficient" typical.

Like all good stories, Behn's entertaining tale is an exploration of human nature, and in *Oroonoko* she knows what happens when the real confronts the ideal, with the narrator serving as a standard of judgment. Ostensibly the narrator is judging Oroonoko and the unprincipled inhabitants of Coramentien and Surinam, proving his unparalleled nobility and their irredeemable wickedness. In *Oroonoko* the weak are those who lack power as well as principles. The slaves in Surinam are of this class and their reaction to Oroonoko takes two extreme forms. They either worship him—he is, after all, described in divine metaphors throughout the novel—or they actively participate in destroying him. On the other side are those un-principled men who wield power. More threatened than the weak by the confrontation with the ideal, they rely on deceit. They either play on Oroonoko's noble nature to save themselves (Coramantien's old king) or abuse his honor and trust to destroy him (the slave trader and the colonial administrators). Whether weak or strong, those lacking principles cannot live with the ideal in their midst. Such judgments are too obvious to be particularly interesting, but in the process of making them, the narrator also makes one more judgment. Guffey points out that in her hero Behn emphasizes the type rather than the individual, and the same is true for the other characters. Between the base who totally lack humanity and the heroic who live and die only for honor is a third group, in which the majority of people always fall. One of the most interesting judgments Behn finally makes through the narrator is on the narrator herself and on the ordinary, decent, principled people like her. The judgment is made implicitly through the narrator's actions at the end of the novel rather than explicitly in direct commentary.

The narrator's absence from the events at the end of her story is disturbing, and at first glance it seems to indicate sloppy craftsmanship. Her removal is presented somewhat awkwardly, and the excuses she gives for her flights seem weak for one who has previously presented herself as one of Oroonoko's strongest partisans. Yet her flights are realistic and valid in psychological terms. Despite her protestations of support for Oroonoko, the narrator has long before the end of the novel revealed a divided spirit. Her position is portrayed as ambiguous. She truly admires Oroonoko, but as a representative of western civilization her commitment to him shows a certain shakiness. Scattered remarks made in the first person plural show that she identifies with the Europeans in Surinam, although never with the colonial administrators. She is Oroonoko's supporter, but even though he has shown his devotion to honoring his commitments, she does not finally trust him. When he promises her to wait with patience for a little longer for the Lord Governor and his freedom, she does not think it "convenient to trust him much out of our view."

Her distrust of him emerges even more clearly during the rebellion. Oroonoko has previously vowed that he would never under any circumstances harm her and those around her: "As for my self, and those upon that Plantation where he was, he would sooner forfeit his eternal Liberty, and Life it self, than lift his Hand against his greatest Enemy on that place." Yet when the women near of the revolt: "we were possess'd with extreme Fear, which no Persuasions could dissipate, that he would secure himself till night, and then, that he would come down and cut all our throats." She explains that this apprehension "made all the Females of us fly down the River, to be secured," and thus the narrator's first flight occurs. Her reactions perhaps suggest what social conditioning can do to the ordinary and decent individual; in a moment of fear, she falls back on stereotypical reactions, forgetting or distrusting all that she has learned of Oroonoko's honor and nobility. She finally is no more able than the wicked to live with

the extraordinary and the ideal, because she cannot believe enough in the reality of Oroonoko's goodness to trust him fully.

This first flight to the river shows her divided spirit, her ultimate lack of commitment to the ideal under adverse circumstances. She returns, only to leave again when Oroonoko is dying, and her second flight reflects more than simply a last failure of belief in the extraordinary by the ordinary. Her excuse for leaving seems no more valid than the first one: "The Sight was ghastly: His Discourse was sad; and the earthy Smell about him so strong, that I was persuaded to leave the place for some time, (being myself but sickly, and very apt to fall into Fits of dangerous Illness upon any extraordinary Melancholy)." Similar incapacities have often enough been attributed to women under such conditions. As Johnson in his *Life of Pope* tries to account for Martha Blount's neglect of the sick poet in his last days, his first speculation is that Pope perhaps "considered her unwillingness to approach the chamber of sickness as female weakness. . . . " But the narrator has not previously shown any traits which would suggest weakness. For example, she was among three out of eighteen who went up to the Indian town when "the Hearts of some of our Company fail'd, and they would not venture on Shore." At the end of the novel, the reader gets the impression that the narrator can no longer cope with the situation and is so overwhelmed by what has happened that she can only disengage herself personally and allow events to sweep to their natural culmination in violence. It is difficult to avoid the feeling that the narrator could and should have done more. In fact, she herself directly contributes to that impression. After Oroonoko's whipping she says that had she not fled with the women, she could have prevented his mistreatment. In view of the final scene, this comment seems to be pure bravado, the last of the emphases on her personal importance inserted throughout the novel. At the end she says that even though her mother and sister were present during the terrible final mutilation and wanted to help Oroonoko, they were "not suffer'd to save him; so rude and wild were the Rabble, and so inhuman were the Justices who stood by to see the Execution . . . ." Since the narrator's position in the colony is derived from the importance of the post that her father was to have held, it would seem logical that all of his relatives would command the same kind of respect. Undoubtedly the narrator would have found herself as powerless to halt the execution as her mother and sister were.

At the end of the novel, all of the good people are ineffectual. The narrator has fled. Trefy, whose function as a foil to the wicked men who persecute Oroonoko has been pointed out by Platt [*PMLA* 49 (1934)] has been lured away on false pretenses by Byam. The narrator's mother and sister can only watch ineffectually. In certain kinds of volatile situations, there is a point where the momentum of events becomes so great that any individual agents are powerless to stop the flow; a strange sense of inevitability takes over. The passions released are so violent and irrational that they seem to possess an inherent pattern, an inevitability all their own, and the culmination can only be atrocity, as it is in *Oroonoko*. It is at this point that normal standards cannot actively influence the course of events. These standards are useless because events have gone too far for normal, decent people to effectively assert their values. This sort of situation occurred on a giant scale in the French Revolution and recurs on a smaller scale in lynchings or other individual acts of mob violence. It happens whenever fanatics or evil men take control of a situation and are determined on destruction. Seen in this context, the narrator's flight emerges as realistic enough; at the end, whether or not her spirit was divided, she could not have done anything to stop the course of events.

Moreover, the narrator is no longer needed in the narrative to function as a standard of judgment for her readers. The final events are too terrible to require judgment by normal standards, just as they do not require heroic language for embellishment. Simply describing them accurately is condemnation enough, and editorial intrusions would be extraneous. The narrator's flight emphasizes that her standards cannot operate in the kind of world shown at the end of *Oroonoko*. The standards of ordinary, decent people become useless and paralyzed when madness assumes control.

Thus Behn uses her narrator in *Oroonoko* to unify and to add realism to the disparate elements of her novel. In addition, the narrator's words and actions also provide a standard of judgment for the honorable, for the wicked, and, most interestingly, for the average people she herself represents. The view of their potential for effective action in explosive situations is a bleak but starkly honest one. The ordinary man will do all that he can; after all, the people at Parham House try to aid Oroonoko, and Trefy resists with a brave ultimatum to Byam and his men. But as events assume a terrifying momentum of their own from those who intend evil, the good can only fly from the inevitable, as the narrator does, or stay to endure the pain of watching ineffectually, as her mother and sister do. The novel itself, however, indicates one further option for the ordinary people trapped in this kind of situation. They can remember, as the narrator has done in *Oroonoko,* and tell their stories again in regret, in remonstrance, and in warning. The standards of decent, average men fail in the world of *Oroonoko*. Nevertheless, the writing of this kind of novel is, indirectly, a retrospective assertion of the validity and importance of those standards, held securely within the context of an entertaining story.

Judith Kegan Gardiner (essay date 1980)

SOURCE: "Aphra Behn: Sexuality and Self-Respect," in *Women's Studies: An Interdisciplinary Journal,* Vol. 7, No. 1-2, 1980, pp. 67-78.

[In the essay below, Kegan Gardiner maintains that Behn's work is imbued with eroticism, reflecting the author's belief that "sexual passion . . . [is] the root of all social impulse."]

The ideal seventeenth-century cavalier could not love his "Deare so much," loved he "not Honour more"; in his code of war, art, and love, independent action posed as effortless and loyal service. Yet this elegant code rested on a sexual double standard. According to the notorious Restoration rake, John Wilmot, Earl of Rochester, "real honor" is "noble confidence in men; / In women, mean mistrustful shame." Even the gallant, long-locked Richard Lovelace himself abruptly dropped his tone of respectful admiration for women when they dared to write poetry; the "Pen" was "nere truely justly slit till now" that women prostituted themselves in sonnets. Adored or condemned for their sexual "honor" and reviled for aspiring to any other field, how could a seventeenth-century woman see herself as an artist and an autonomous person? She couldn't, replied Virginia Woolf in *A Room of One's Own*. Circumscribed by "the value that men set upon women's chastity," the woman poet could only feel, thought Woolf, that "death would be better" than "living the life of Aphra Behn."

But not for Aphra Behn, 1640-89, England's first professional woman writer, a witty, unabashed, sexually-active, and critically maligned woman. To enable herself to write, Behn created a poetic identity for herself as Astraea, muse of a lost golden age who could combine "Female Sweetness and a Manly Grace." More fundamentally, to avoid becoming either the disdainful lady or the disdained whore of male polarization, she identified with the male role while modifying its view of women. Following the code of cavalier honor, she could seek physical pleasure and write about it while retaining both a sense of personal integrity and of loyalty to a larger political order.

Behn's mysterious, colorful life as a colonial and a spy has always attracted more interest than her work. Because she wrote a novel about a persecuted slave in a lush New World setting, she has been touted as a precursor to Defoe, Rousseau, and Harriet Beecher Stowe. Yet *Oroonoko* is a sport in the Behn canon; her single dominant theme in plays, novels, and poetry is human sexuality—its powers and problems. Literary critics enlisted under the double standard have retreated embarrassed, but it is her portrayal of her artistic self and of her sexuality that we must examine if we are to justly value her work.

In the preface to *The Lucky Chance,* Behn challenges her audience to recognize "the Priviledge for my Masculine part the Poet in me". In her view of herself as a creative artist, as in her treatment of female sexuality, she combines a belief in each sex's innate capacity for the traditional traits of both with an apology for the socially-induced incapacities of her own. Any errors in her translation of Fontenelle's *A Discovery of New Worlds,* she says, should be excused "in a Woman, who is supposed to be well versed in the Terms of Philosophy." She chose the task because Fontanelle put a woman in the dialogue, and "I thought an English woman might adventure to translate any thing a French woman may be supposed to have spoken." Then she criticizes the author for making his woman speaker so stupid. Similarly, she says that other women should attribute any faults in *Sir Patient Fancy* "to the Authors unhappiness, who is forced to write for Bread and not ashamed to owne it." She bemoans her female lack of a proper classical education, but denies that this should hamper her as a playwright. After all, she tells the "Good, Sweet, Honey, Sugar-Candied Reader" of *The Dutch Lover* that women often have as much learning as Shakespeare did and that everyone prefers his plays to those of the pedantic three-unities crowd.

Criticized by an unjust claque only because of her sex, in the epilogue to *Sir Patient Fancy* she defends woman's role as a poet in terms that join an appeal to the conventional myth of an egalitarian golden age with a special pleading in behalf of women's special talents for intuiting and responding to human needs.

> What has poor Woman done, that she must be
> Debar'd from Sense, and sacred Poetry?
> Why in this Age has Heaven allow'd you more,
> And Women less of Wit than heretofore?
> We once were fam'd in story, and could write
> Equal to Men; cou'd govern, nay, cou'd fight. . . .
> That we have nobler Souls than you, we prove,
> By how much more we're sensible of Love;
> Quickest in finding all the subtlest ways
> To make your Joys, why not to make you Plays?
>
>   . . .
>
> We'll let you see, whate'er besides we do,
> How artfully we copy some of you:
> And if you're drawn to th' Life, pray tell me
>   then,
> Why Women should not write as well as Men.

She would rather not write at all, she says, than be restrained on the grounds of her sex. Versatile and hard working, apparently she had to keep producing to feed the wolves at her door. In eighteen years of authorship she wrote at least seventeen plays, fourteen fictions, several translations, and two volumes of original poetry. Despite a need to write for money, however, she was not content to see herself as a mere mercenary hack: "I value Fame as much as if I had been born a hero . . . ."

Behn's identification with the role of hero helps explain her fanatical devotion to the doomed Stuart kings. To the modern, mercantile, and male "way of Writing" by "Method, and Rule" she opposes a nostalgic identification with the exiled courtiers of Charles I who combined personal loyalty to a perfect political "great Sufferer" with a vigorous sexuality restrained only by their self-defined honor. Esthetically and politically, she believes "nobler Souls" of either sex prove their superiority by their emotional sensitivity, that is, by being "sensible of Love." This cavalier pose helps her define an autonomous position for herself as a bright, sexually-active woman. There were few societies in which such a person could function freely. Behn invents one in her drama, where she can imagine herself as the dashing Rover of her most famous play. The other, equally fantastic realm, is the pastoral no-person's-land of her libertine poetry. Swinburne ranked her

and Rochester as the two best Restoration song writers, but few critics share his enthusiasm for Behn's poetry. "With their feeble personification and insipid allegory, almost all" of her poems are "equally dull," lamented Edward Wagenknecht [*The Colophon,* 1934]. "And she—poor lady!—considered herself a poet first of all."

Her most praised and only widely-anthologized lyric, "Love Arm'd," from the play *Abdelazar,* demonstrates her original touch with these jaded literary conventions decried by her critics. The poem succeeds because Behn used the clichés of literary artifice to demonstrate a psychological truth: the fact that love constructed within the lovers' minds remains a powerful force despite their knowledge of its self-created character.

> Love in Fantastique Triumph satt,
> Whilst Bleeding Hearts a round him flow'd,
> For whom Fresh paines he did Create,
> And strange Tyranick power he show'd;
>
> From thy Bright Eyes he took his fire,
> Which round about, in sport he hurl'd;
> But 'twas from mine he took desire,
> Enough to undo the Amorous World.
>
> From me he took his sighs and tears,
> From thee his Pride and Crueltie;
> From me his Languishments and Feares,
> And every Killing Dart from thee;
>
> Thus thou and I, the God have arm'd
> And sett him up a Deity;
> But my poor Heart alone is harm'd,
> Whilst thine the Victor is, and free.

The first quatrain paints an emblem. Personified Love sits in a triumphal throne or chariot as in a masque or pageant. The effective trisyllabic "fantastic" implies both the exaggerated power of love and its origin in the lovers' fantasies. The word "flowed" vivifies the clichéd "bleeding hearts" so that we see love seated above the sea of miseries it caused. Although potentially a great constructive force, here Love only creates pain, and therefore its alien and uncanny "strange" power is "tyrannic," that is, both absolute and unjust. Behn's verbs at the end of each line of the first quatrain hammer out the idea of love's force.

Having established the emblem of Love in the first quatrain, Behn takes the next two to apportion Love's attributes between the lover and the beloved. Love capriciously hurls the beloved's eye-fire like Jove's thunderbolts while the lover's eyes show the devastating effects of desire "enough to undo the amorous world." Thwarted desire leads not to creative doing but to undoing, with its connotations of social ruin. Love seems to be taking qualities equally "from me" and "from thee," but it soon becomes clear that the powerful God of Love is identical with the tyrannic beloved.

The final quatrain sets up the lover's ideal of reciprocity

by intimately concluding, "thus thou and I." Together they make love not merely a conqueror but a "diety"—an apotheosis for which we are well prepared both by the convention of the god of Love and by Love's Jove-like actions. Then the last two lines of the poem break the pretended parity between the lovers to reveal the beloved's monopoly of Love's power. The self-pitying lover complains, "But my poor Heart alone is harm'd, / Whilst thine the Victor is, and free." As Behn emphasizes by the caesura late in the last line, to be "free" from reciprocal claims is to be victorious over the committed. The beloved is thus also a god, an unmoved mover, a triumphant conqueror, and much of the poem's force springs from the anguish of the lover whose resentment includes a recognition that such suffering requires compliant cooperation.

As so often in Behn's love poetry, the conventional war imagery alludes to the real pain of the battle between the sexes. The long English-Petrarchan tradition includes reams of such poems of unrequited passion. Behn's are unusual chiefly for their freshness of viewpoint. Her beloveds are not always female, nor her lovers, male. In **"Love Arm'd,"** neither sex is specified, and the dramatic context is of a woman wooing a man.

Behn wrote during a period in which repressive attitudes about female sexuality were overtaking earlier, more flexible views. Repeatedly she defends her work from the charge of being "Baudy," decrying the unfairness that criticized her material only because "from a Woman it was unnaturall". Although she claimed that her "Conversation" was "not at all addicted to the Indecencys alledged", she never bothered to refute the many slanders on her personal morality and apparently considered them irrelevant to her work. Her literary younger sister, the Countess of Winchelsea indulgently wrote after Behn's death that "amongst Women there was none on the earth / Her superior in fancy, in language, or witt, / Yet . . . a little too loosley she writt." By Alexander Pope's "Epistle to Augustus," the qualifier of Winchelsea's judgement had become the whole: "The stage how loosely does Astrea tread, / Who fairly puts all characters to bed." At least Pope was still reading Behn; he remade one of her quatrains [**"To Henry Higden"**] into his famous couplet on wit. Patricia Meyer Spacks dates the notion that proper women were not sexual beings to the beginning of the eighteenth century [*Eighteenth-Century Studies* 8.1 (Fall, 1974)]. As so often in literary history, a pioneer may stake a path that the wagon trains do not take, and Behn's poetic terrain was both too artificially terraced and too passionately stony for many others to follow.

Throughout her lyrics she treats sexuality frankly and often from the viewpoint of the sexually-active woman. Woman's parity with man in desire is the point of one of her better-known lyrics, called simply **"The Willing Mistriss."** Her pindaric **"On Desire"** asserts the terrible primacy of that urge: "Thou new-found pain," "thou haunt'st my inconvenient hours." But despite the pains of passion, the absence of passion is even worse: "For when the mind so cool is grown / As neither Love nor Hate to own, / The

Life but dully lingers on." Both men and women desire blindly in her work; both are fickle; both pine for what they cannot have; both wish to domineer; the innate psychology of both sexes is identical, yet social circumstances upset the parity. Women may be ruined for what men take as pleasure, and women thus fear being "conquered" only to be abandoned. Behn rails against the prevailing double standard:

> Be just, my lovely Swain, and do not take
> Freedoms you'll not to me allow;
> Or give Amynta so much Freedom back:
> That she may Rove as well as you.

Unlike her male colleagues, Behn means men when she refers to "the faithless sex."

Because there is no emotional distinction between the two sexes in Behn's writing, she can describe her characters in androgynous terms. Anyone may become attracted to anyone else who is sufficiently beautiful and intelligent. She addresses her lover John Hoyle as "Thou Beauty of the Envying Swaines" and describes Philander with Lycidas "who pays his Tenderness again, / Too Amorous for a Swain to a Swain." Her one overtly lesbian poem—to "the fair Clarinda"—is playfully ambivalent:

> In pity to our Sex sure thou wer't sent,
> That we might Love, and yet be Innocent:
> For sure no Crime with thee we can commit;
> Or if we shou'd—thy Form excuses it.

Her occasional poems indicate a network of friendships, some with women, most with men, of an intimate, relaxed, and egalitarian character. For example, she asks one man "if he cou'd tell . . . by the Style" which other man sent her an anonymous love note. In **"A letter to a Brother of the Pen in Tribulation"** she chastises a friend for "an Interlude of Whoring" that has confined him with venereal disease just when she wanted him to write her a prologue for a play. Yet for some purposes she accepts contemporary stereotypes about female nature. She alludes to women's deceit, women's inconstancy, and "Impertinence, my sexes shame," even though her men are equally deceitful, inconstant, and pert. In the social world portrayed in her poetry, women compete with one another for male favors, though they may cooperate in the face of male perfidy or generously acknowledge one another's claims. Thus "I found it just you should out-Rival me" she writes a competing beauty, just as she compliments the wit of a competing playwright.

Her consistent morality is that sexual submission for the sake of money, family, or status—in or out of marriage—is base prostitution. In contrast, "inclination" is natural and often irresistible. In her wooden versification of the Lord's Prayer, she glosses the text "And forgive us our trespasses" by claiming that "Love, soft bewitching Love! has been the cause" "Of all my Crimes, the breach of all thy Laws / . . . That sure will soonest be forgiven of God." A contemporary satirist aptly jibed that Behn "humbly requested her Maker to grant her a private Act of

Toleration for a little Harmless Love, otherwise called Fornication" [Tom Brown, "The Late Converts Exposed, 1690]. Clearly, she did not consider her full sexual life and art sinful. This view caused Victorian critics to shy from her lewdness, but it is a refreshingly pure attitude when compared to that of the male libertines of her time. Unlike male rakes like Rochester, Behn never makes sexuality dirty. Often the male libertine poet impresses his reader with his contempt for women, sometimes with his contempt for himself, and with his sense of the horrid degradation of human bodily process. Other male Restoration poets detach the mating game from the central self so that it becomes trivial and meaningless. Behn also portrays love as a game—but always for real stakes. Many of her novels and plays show love as a woman's only profession, and her ability to keep cool is then as serious a matter as her enslavement to a desire that may leave her pregnant and adrift. In her verse, on the other hand, she persistently uses the conventions of pastoral in order to free her explorations into the psychology of desire from entanglement with the social constraints that make the consequences of desire oppressive for women. Her lovers of both sexes may be pained or disillusioned, but they do not feel guilty for loving or despise themselves or the opposite sex.

The contrast between her libertine poetry and that of her contemporaries is most obvious in her handling of the theme of impotence that Jay Levine has called a "full-blown and widespread obsession" of the Restoration [*ELH*, 28, 4 (Dec., 1961)]. Behn's **"The Disappointment"** differs from others of these poems by its stress on the woman's point of view. Unlike Ovid's *Amores* III.7, the classical progenitor of such poems, or the French "L'Occasion perdue recouverte" that Behn's poem partly translates, or even Rochester's brutal "The Imperfect Enjoyment," her poem does not contrast an incident of the man's humiliating impotence with his earlier or later exaggerated vigor. Nor does it lead, as so many such Restoration poems do, to broad reflections on the inadequacy of the senses. Instead, it concentrates on the immediate comedy of the erotic situation. Like most of Behn's soft pornography, **"The Disappointment"** is set in a pastoral never-never-land, and it contrasts with **"Love Arm'd"** as an example of her versatility in deploying literary conventions for an unconventional exploration of the vicissitudes of love.

> One day the Amorous Lysander,
> By an impatient Passion sway'd,
> Surpriz'd fair Cloris, that lov'd Maid. . . .

As in many of her poems, Behn affirms the fantasy that women like to be gently forced to abandon their social pretenses to "honor" and modesty.

> And now without Respect or Fear,
> He seeks the Object of his Vows,
> (His Love no Modesty allows)
> By swift degrees advancing—where
> His daring Hand that Altar seiz'd,
> Where Gods of Love do sacrifice:
> That Awful Throne, that Paradice

> Where Rage is calm'd, and Anger pleas'd;
> That Fountain where Delight still flows,
> And gives the Universal World Repose.

Several similarly humid stanzas follow. However, at the crucial moment, "The too transported hapless Swain/ Found the vast Pleasure turn'd to Pain". The nymph responds:

> Cloris returning from the Trance
> Which Love and soft Desire had bred,
> Her timerous Hand she gently laid
> (Or guided by Design or Chance)
> Upon that Fabulous Priapus,
> That Potent God, as Poets feign;
> But never did young Shepherdness,
> Gath'ring of Fern upon the Plain,
> More nimbly draw her Fingers back,
> Finding beneath the verdant Leaves a Snake:

> Than Cloris her fair Hand withdrew,
> Finding that God of her Desires
> Disarm'd of all his Awful Fires,
> And Cold as Flow'rs bath'd in the Morning
>   Dew.
> Who can the Nymph's Confusion guess?
> The Blood forsook the hinder Place,
> And strew'd with Blushes all her face,
> Which both Disdain and Shame exprest:
> And from Lysander's Arms she fled,
> Leaving him fainting on the Gloomy Bed.

> Like Lightning through the Grove she hies,
> Or Daphne from the Delphick God. . . .

The diction here is both erotic and witty, with pastoral conventions playing peek-a-boo with the narrative. The primary joke is that the nymph behaves like Daphne or fair Florimell, although she is frightened not by the prospect of sexual intercourse but by its disappointment. The narrative of the two stanzas quoted here is unified by the action of Cloris' hand. First it is "gently laid," as she wishes to be, and then withdrawn. That Cloris' hand is "guided by design or chance" is our first hint that the panting passive maid may be more experienced than her pose. Then the encomium to Priapus, unlike that earlier one to her "altar" of love that felt Lysander's hand, is both exaggerated and ironically undercut. Internal rhyme makes the "fabulous Priapus" already comic, and the alliterations of "that potent god, as poets feign" link male poetry, faking, and fabling. Priapus, it seems, rarely lives up to its potent poetic image. Behn likes simple phallic imagery throughout her love poetry—fires, darts, arrows, snakes. Here the lush "verdant" leaves hide a sterile "snake"; the horrid discovery is emphasized by the line's inversion and its elongation. The nymph retreats nimbly and knowledgeably. Again, traditional pastoral imagery is wittily reversed. The "flowers bathed in the morning dew" are not fresh and lovely but clammy, weak, and "cold."

After leading us breathless through stanzas of enjambed erotic narrative, Behn then calls out from her third-person proscenium to bring us voyeurs on stage. "Who can the nymph's confusion guess?" Finally, she ends the poem by joining us in wicked sympathy with the lovers. Lysander curses "the Shepherdess's Charms, / Whose soft bewitching Influence / Had Damn'd him to the Hell of Impotence", while "The Nymph's Resentments none but I / Can well Imagine or Condole . . . ."

What created desire? Why does it attach one to the people it does? How does it die, revive, and change? Behn writes repeatedly of jealously, revenge, and the desire for domination in sexual relationships. The assymmetries of desire can lead to the psychic cruelty of **"Love Arm'd"** or the physiological incongruities of **"The Disappointment."** As Behn traces love affairs through fantasy and disillusionment, she always reveals one underlying libido, not an idealized love dualistically separated from vulgar carnality. Some of her critics chide that love in Behn's work is only sex. It is a criticism that we may interpret to her advantage. She was not a woman to be fooled by myths of eternal and perfect love. Nor, like some male libertines, does she reduce sexuality to a bestial or mechanical coupling. Instead, she consistently sees sexual passion—which involves a generous giving of oneself to others—as the root of all social impulse. Its emotional opposite is egotistical concentration on one's "interests." Between abandoned loss of self and total self-absorption, she seeks a cavalier balance in independent sexuality capable of mutual pleasure and mutual response. Those incapable of such reciprocity deserve to be cursed; as Behn, that excellent early anatomist of sexual politics, says in another context, "A Pox of Foolish Politicks in Love."

Spy, colonialist, mistress of the comedy of intrigue, early romancer, novelist, poet, and spokeswoman for the writing woman—Aphra Behn deserves our respect most for maintaining the creative woman's ability to be at once sexuality giving and intellectually active and independent.

Angeline Goreau (essay date 1980)

SOURCE: "Success and Attack," in *Reconstructing Aphra: A Social Biography of Aphra Behn,* The Dial Press, 1980, pp. 207-35.

[*Here, Goreau traces the critical and popular reaction to some of Behn's works, focusing especially on the writer's criticism of the "property-marriage system" in her plays.*]

The staging of Aphra's tragedy *Abdelazer* in July 1676 marked the end of a three-year literary silence. No play had appeared under her name since the foundering of *The Dutch Lover* in 1673. Perhaps she was still smarting from the attacks launched against her on that occasion; or perhaps she was writing plays that were only to be staged later. A third possibility is that she was very much preoccupied by the initial intensity of her love affair with John Hoyle. The play *Abdelazer* opened with a song which was to become one of her most famous

lyrics. It was called **"Love Armed"** and began thus:

> *Love in fantastique triumph sat,*
> *Whilst bleeding hearts around him flowed,*
> *For whom fresh pains he did create,*
> *And strange tyranick power he showed.*
> *From thy bright eyes he took his fire,*
> *Which round about, in sport he hurled,*
> *But 'twas from mine he took desire,*
> *Enough to undo the amorous world.*

Aphra then describes the *"languishments and fears"* she has suffered from this cavalier lover who remains cruelly remote while she undergoes the pain of attachment: *"My poor heart alone is harmed, / Whilst thine the victor is, and free."* Whether or not the poem was actually written for Hoyle and then inserted in her play cannot be definitely ascertained, but it certainly described their relationship. It may also have reflected something of Aphra's current state of mind, for the subject of *Abdelazer* is obsessional passion. The tragedy was adapted from an anonymous play called *Lust's Dominion; or, the Lacivious Queen,* which had been published in 1657. The story centers on the overwhelming desire that the (fictional) Queen of Spain has conceived for Abdelazer, a Moor like Othello, to whom she sacrifices husband, son, country, and eventually, of course, herself. He has only used her to acquire power and has her assassinated when she no longer serves his purpose.

Whatever personal fascination this theme may have had for Aphra, it is also likely that she chose it with the idea of making her return to the stage a commercial success. Nathaniel Lee had recently made his dramatic debut with two ranting, furious tragedies that had met with great popularity. Sex, horror, and madness were all the rage, and Aphra's *Abdelazer* had the right ingredients. Early in the play, Abdelazer sets the tone of what is to come: *" 'Tis now dead time of night, when rapes and murders are hid beneath an horrid veil of darkness."*

As Aphra had calculated, the play was a success. Her friend Nell Gwyn supported her by coming and bringing a substantial party from the Court with her. Ordinarily, the presence of such a celebrity was enough to fill the theater with curious onlookers who were eager to catch a glance of the royal mistress even if they cared nothing for the play itself. The play would probably have been financially remunerative even without Nell Gwyn's help, as Aphra had astutely estimated what the public wanted to see. In artistic terms, however, *Abdelazer* is unquestionably among the worst of her plays. Despite the fact that she herself was given to extremity, fustian tragedy was evidently not her gift. The play reeks of melodrama, and Aphra's normally lively dialogue is flat and artificial. She must have realized this because, except for *The Young King,* actually written much earlier in her career, she never attempted the genre again. She found the full expression of her talent in the series of comedies she immediately turned to writing next.

After the performance of *Abdelazer* in July 1676, Aphra

retired to the countryside for a brief rest. But peace and quiet were not to be had. Emily Price, a young actress with the Duke's Company who was shortly afterward to act in Mrs. Behn's *Sir Patient Fancy,* wrote from London to tell Aphra that the town was once again talking about her: this time her critics were accusing her of plagiarism. Aphra expressed small surprise at the attack but felt hurt that Thomas Otway had not dealt entirely straightforwardly with her. He had been gossiping unkindly behind her back. *"My dear,"* she wrote to Emily Price:

> *In your last* [letter] *you informed me that the world treated me as a plagiary, and I must confess, not with injustice. But that Mr. Otway should say, my sex would not prevent my being pulled to pieces by the critics, is something odd, since whatever Mr. Otway now declares, be may very well remember when I last saw him, I received more than ordinary encomiums on my* Abdelazer. *But every one knows Mr. Otway's good nature, which will not permit him to shock any one of our sex to their faces. But let that pass. As for being impeached of murdering my Moor, I am thankful, since, when I shall let the world know, whenever I take the pains next to appear in print, of the mighty theft I have been guilty of; but, however, for your own satisfaction, I have sent you the garden from whence I gathered, and I hope you will not think me vain, if I say, I have weeded and improved it. I hope to prevail on the printer to reprint* Lust's Dominion, *that my theft may be the more public. But I detain you. I believe I shan't have the happiness of seeing my dear Amilla 'till the middle of September. But be assured I shall always remain as I am,*
>
> > *yours,*
> > *A. Behn*

Aphra refused to be drawn into a quarrel with Thomas Otway, whom she had so generously supported and whose company she took great pleasure in. She probably preferred to take his remark as a response to his own difficulties with the critics rather than as a manifestation of spite or literary jealousy. In any case, it had been demonstrated to her for some time that not only would her sex fail to "prevent her being pulled to pieces by the critics," as Otway, had said, but it would more or less *ensure* that she would be. Experience had taught her this much so far, though it had not yet taught her how to deal with the pain and anger such attacks inevitably drew from her.

The accusation of plagiarism was hardly worth serious consideration. It was standard practice to rewrite earlier material for the Restoration stage, and there was hardly a playwright of Aphra Behn's generation who had not at one time in his career based his work on someone else's play. For the most part, the plays that were used for raw material in this way were very much inferior. Often the dialogue of the "rewritten" play was almost entirely original, and several scenes and characters were added. The "plagiary" consisted of little more than using an old plot, usually rather conventional in any case, as a framework for something new. Such literary borrowing was not generally considered much of a sin. Aphra was well aware that she was being singled out for punishment. For the time being, though, she chose to ignore the scandal as

best she could and enjoy the rural quiet, perhaps remembering the pastoral Kentish countryside where her childhood had been spent. She tried to explain that pleasure to Emily Price, writing: *"In your last, you admired how I could pass my time so long in the country: I am sorry your taste is so depraved, as not to relish a country life. Now I think there's no satisfaction to be found amidst an urban throng (as Mr. Bayes calls it)."* Aphra included some verses in her letter, praising the peace and green of meadows, woods, and groves and telling her friend to *"fly that hated town, / Where's not a moment thou canst call thy own."* . . .

In the second half of the 1670s [Aphra] was at the height of her powers. Plays issued from her pen at a remarkable rate: little more than a month after the production of *Abdelazer, The Town Fop* was staged (September 1676). Just six months later, in March 1677, **The Rover** went on the boards, followed by *Sir Patient Fancy* in January 1678. **The Feigned Curtezans** was produced in March 1679, and **The Young King** in September of that year. In addition, there were two plays said to have been of Mrs. Behn's authorship which came out anonymously: **The Debauchee** in February 1677, and **The Counterfeit Bridegroom** in September 1677.

In just a little over three years, Aphra Behn had produced six, and possibly eight, plays which were staged by the Duke's Company at the Dorset Garden Theater. Most of them were at least moderately successful—with the exception of the old-fashioned tragicomedy **The Young King**. **The Rover** was so popular that it had numerous repeat performances. The royal party was so taken with it that a full two years after it had first appeared at the Dorset Garden Theater, the play was performed at Court by special request. Later, when Aphra was on somewhat less certain financial ground, she attempted to reproduce her success by writing a sequel to **The Rover**. She dedicated it to the Duke of York and thanked him for *"the incouragement your Royal Highness was pleased to give The Rover at his first appearance."* Perhaps, in addition to her handsome box-office returns, he had given her some financial reward at the time.

The Town Fop: or Sir Timothy Tawdrey, coming so suddenly on the heels of the lugubrious *Abdelazer,* marked a sharp reversal in dramatic mode and effect. The ready wit, swift and easy pacing of the scenes, visual humor, rapid-fire repartee, comic intrigue, and general waggery of Aphra's new play would become the trademarks of the comedies that were her most successful works. Her handling of social satire in particular was so accurate in its language, social reference, and theatrical timing that it must have sent even the sophisticated Restoration audience howling. Mrs. Behn's parody of the way a would-be man of wit went about courting a young lady was gifted caricature; the tics and pretensions of the fashionable creature she is making fun of were common currency of the time and clearly recognizable to contemporary theatergoers. Her exaggeration of the exaggerated made very good theater:

> "*I'm the Son of a Whore, if you are not the most belle Person I ever saw,*" the young man begins, "*and if I be not damnably in love with you; but a pox take all tedious courtship, I have a free-born and generous spirit; as I hate being confined to dull cringing, whining, flattering, and the Devil and all of foppery, so when I give an heart, I'm an infidel, Madam, if I do not love to do't frankly and quickly, that thereby I may oblige the beautiful receiver of my vows, protestation, passions, and inclination . . . Upon my reputation, Madam, you're a civil well-bred person, you have all the agreemony of your sex, la belle taille, la bonne mine, & reparteee bien, and are toute oure toore, as I'm a Gentleman, fort agreeable . . . Well, if I do not hold out, Egad, I shall be the bravest young fellow in Christendom.*"

Out of the context of a carefully built up, complicated structure of events, it is difficult to grasp the full comic effect of the scene, but Mrs. Behn's use of language as social touchstone comes through. The parody is in this case a joke within a joke, because the young gallant in question, Wittmore, is deliberately trying to make himself as absurd as possible so that the young woman he is courting (Isabella) will be sure not to fall in love with him. Wittmore's wooing is actually a pretext to insinuate himself into the pious household of Sir Patient Fancy, Isabella's father, so that he may make love to her young stepmother. Lady Fancy is in fact Wittmore's former mistress, forced by financial duress to marry the old Sir Patient Fancy, a City merchant whose hypocritical obsession with godliness makes him entirely deserving of the deception constantly practiced on him. Mrs. Behn twists the plot into more and more intricate configurations, until finally Wittmore, who has been "*towsing*" [petting] Lady Fancy in her bedroom, is nearly discovered by her husband. She pushes her lover, half-dressed, under the bed and hides his clothes just a moment before Sir Patient intrudes. A letter of assignation addressed to Wittmore has been found—written, of course, by Lady Fancy—and Sir Patient is under the mistaken impression that his daughter has sacrificed her virginity to the man he believes to be her suitor. Rushing into Lady Fancy's bedroom, he commences a rant in which the authoress plays verbal and visual humor off against each other in an incredible burlesque:

SIR PATIENT: *Oh, I am half killed, my daughter, my honour—my reputation.*

LADY FANCY: *Good heavens, Sir, is she dead?*

SIR PATIENT: *I wou'd she were, her portion and her honour would then be saved. But oh, I'm sick at heart, Maundy, fetch me the bottle of Mirabilis in the closet,— she's wanton, unchaste.*

[Enter Maundy with the bottle.]
Oh, I cannot speak it; oh, the bottle—[Drinks.] *she has lost her fame, her shame, her name.—Oh,* [Drinks.] *that is not the right bottle, that with the red cork* [Drinks.] [Exit Maundy.] *and is grown a very t'other- end-of-the-town creature, a very apple of Sodom, fair without and filthy within, what shall we do with her? she's lost, undone; hah!* [Enter Maundy.] *Let me see,* [Drinks.] *this is* [Drinks.] *not as I take it—*[Drinks.]— *oh, how you vex me*—[Drinks.] *No, no here.* [Gives her the bottle.]

MAUNDY: *You said that with the red cork, Sir.* [Goes out.]

SIR PATIENT: *I meant the blue;—I know not what to say.—In fine, my Lady, let's marry her out of hand, for she is fall'n, fall'n to predition; she understands more wickedness than had she been bred in a profane nunnery, a court, or a playhouse.* [Drinks.]—*therefore lets marry her instantly, out of hand.*

Proper Sir Patient, intoxicated by the supposedly "medicinal" mirabilis with which he has so liberally punctuated his discourse, now begins to look lecherously at Lady Fancy and bolts the door against interruption. Wittmore, still hiding under the bed, is now prevented from making any silent escape and furthermore forced to listen to the ridiculous baby talk Sir Patient is playing Lady Fancy with. He chases her around the room, repeating "*catch her, catch her, catch her,*" "*my little ape's face,*" "*you little mungrel,*" and "*my little harlot*" with idiotic persistence until finally, falling in a drunken stupor on the bed, he sleeps. Seizing the opportunity, Wittmore creeps out from under the bed, but he knocks over a chair in the process. Sir Patient awakens and the lover runs to his hiding place again. Lady Fancy forcibly holds her husband down, explaining that it was she who had tripped over the chair. Calmed, he sleeps again. Wittmore then crawls toward the door and nearly escapes when the alarm on his watch goes off and Sir Patient is once again aroused. Lady Fancy throws herself weeping onto him and reveals that the alarm comes from a death-watch that has been in her family for more than a hundred years, which mysteriously rings just before the death of anyone close to her. After one more failed escape, Wittmore next gets as far as the dressing table, overturning it while trying to stand up. Lady Fancy sits down on his back as though he were a stool, pretending to faint. Claiming to be at the door of death, she sends Sir Patient for help, and finally her lover is able to slip out undiscovered. On stage, the scene was hugely successful. Such farce was becoming increasingly dominant in Restoration theater, no doubt partly because it was broad enough to capture the attention of the rowdy, self-absorbed audience.

Aphra owed at least some of her popularity to her consummate skill in this aspect of the theater, but she was equally famous for her repartee. She even ventured to make literary jokes on occasion. When the fatuous Sir Timothy Tawdrey, in *The Town Fop,* defends himself from attack by an insubordinate nurse by informing her that he is a "Gentleman, and a Knight," she replies:

NURSE: *Yes, Sir, Knight of the ill-favor'd countenance is it?*

SIR TIMOTHY: *You are beholding to Don Quixote for that, and 'tis so many ages since thou couldst see to read, I wonder thou hast not forgot all that ever belonged to books.*

NURSE: *My eyesight is good enough to see thee in all thy colours, thou Knight of the burning pestle thou.*

SIR TIMOTHY: *Agen, that was out of a play—Hark ye, Witch of Endor, hold your prating tongue, or I shall more well-favourdly cudgel ye.*

NURSE: *As your friend the hostess has it in a play too, I take it, ends which you pick up behind the scenes, when you go to be laught at even by the player-women.*

Defeated by a woman's wit, Sir Timothy sourly remarks: "*The Devils in her tongue, and so 'tis in most women's of her age; for when it has quitted the tail, it repairs to the upper tire.*"

. . . . .

Aphra's plays **The Town Fop, The Rover,** and **Sir Patient Fancy** all took up in various forms a critique of the social practice of marriage in her time and its destructive effects on both men and women—particularly the second sex. Mrs. Behn had initiated the attack on matrimony in her very first work to be staged, **The Forced Marriage** (1671), and developed the theme through nearly every one of her plays, even those whose principal thrust was political.

The property-marriage system had been a firmly entrenched custom for many generations before Aphra was born, and most children were educated to an unquestioning acceptance of the tradition as a fact of life. Primary matrimonial considerations under this system were the financial and political advantages of the union and the social status of the family that was to be married into. For the most part, little attention was paid to the desires or inclinations of the parties concerned. When Henry Oxinden's twelve-year-old daughter steadfastly refused to marry the man he had chosen for her, Oxinden wrote to his wife in a fury: "Let her know from me she has undone herself; and more assuredly she has. Let her know I shall never again desire to see her face: let her like Cain wander as a vagabond and a runagate; it shall move no heart of mine; let her know I shall never count her among the number of my children, and am resolved when I come home to send her out of my sight." It certainly would have been difficult for a twelve-year-old girl to stand up to such pressure. And of course her father could actually force her to do as he wished if he so chose.

It was standard procedure for parents to agree first on a match and then inform their offspring of a *fait accompli*. Often negotiations were in an advanced state or the contract already signed when the bride or groom were told of their impending wedding; sometimes they were even the last to learn. The manner in which Samuel Pepys—as an intermediary party—negotiated an "alliance" between the son and daughter of two high-ranking officials of the Navy, the Earl of Sandwich and Sir George Carteret, in 1665 seems to have been fairly commonplace. Pepys, as he recorded in his diary, was asked by Lady Sandwich to make the necessary approaches to another intermediary, Dr. Clerk, who would discreetly propose the match and terms to the Carteret family. After some bartering, it was agreed that Jemima, the Earl of Sandwich's daughter, was to bring to the merger a portion of five thousand pounds, to be paid over to the groom's family in exchange for a jointure of eight hundred pounds a year. Once the monies had been agreed upon, the King and the Duke of York, High Admiral of the Navy, were asked for their permission and the marriage contract signed. In all the five months of dickering, the bride-to-be was totally unaware that her fate was being decided for her. Only after the legalities had been concluded was she brought up to London to meet her future husband, whom she had never laid eyes on until that moment.

Aphra Behn's assault on the property-marriage system takes the form of satire in **The Town Fop**. As the play opens, the pompous and undesirable Sir Timothy Tawdrey has just arrived in London from his country estate to claim a bride he has never met. He by chance encounters her brother, Friendlove, who is horrified to learn that his sister, Celinda, is to be married off to such a fool. Sir Timothy smugly informs Friendlove how he came into possession of the prize: "*Your father (according to the method in such cases, being certain of my estate) came to me thus—Sir Timothy Tawdrey,—you are a young gentleman, and a Knight, I knew your father well, and my right worshipful neighbour, our estates lie together; therefore, Sir, I have a desire to have a near relation with you, etc.*" When Friendlove objects to this sacrifice of his sister, Sir Timothy dully reminds him: "*The old people have adjusted the matter, and they are the most proper for a negotiation of that kind, which saves us the trouble of a tedious courtship.*"

To find Sir Timothy a half-wit is bad enough, but worse still, it now comes out that he has foppish ambitions. Tawdrey unthinkingly mouths all the current clichés about the way marriage was lived among the fashionable; collectively, they add up to a devastating portrait of the cynicism that Aphra Behn saw inevitably grow out of this sort of arbitrarily arranged marriage. The would-be "man-of-mode" explains to his two "witty" companions, Sham and Sharp, his reason for marrying Celinda.

TAWDREY: *The wench I never saw yet, but they say she's handsome—But no matter for that, there's money, my boys . . . money in abundance, or she were not for me . . . my whole design is to be master of myself, and with part of her portion to set up my Miss [Mistress], Betty Flauntit; which, by the way, is the main end of my marrying . . . ready money, ye rogues! What charms it has! makes the waiters fly, boys, and the master the cap in hand—excuse what's amiss, gentlemen—Your*

Worship shall command the best—and the rest—How briskly the box and dice dance, and the gay wench consults with every beauty to make her agreeable to the man with ready money! In fine, dear rogues, all things are sacrificed to its power; and no mortal conceives the joy of argent content. 'Tis this powerful God that makes me submit to the Devil, matrimony; and then thou art assured of me, my stout lads of brisk debauch.

SHAM: *And is it possible you can be tied up to a wife? Whilst here in London, and free, you have the whole world to range in, and like a wanton heifer, eat of every pasture.*

SIR TIMOTHY: *Why, dost think I'll be confined to my own dull enclosure? No, I had rather feed coarsely upon the boundless common; perhaps two or three days I may be in love, and remain constant, but that's the most.*

Tawdrey has not even met Celinda and already he is spending her portion, in his mind, on his mistress. Not that he truly loves Betty Flauntit either, but simply sees her as a necessary concession to fashion. The acceptance of a corrupted form, as Aphra presents it, has so divorced him from any feeling that his one remaining instinct is exploitation. Aphra draws Tawdrey as an absurd figure through his ridiculous use of language, but beneath the buffoonery, there is a strong current of revulsion in her dramatic treatment of him.

The construction of **The Town Fop**'s byzantine plot is designated to further demonstrate the deleterious effects of marriage as it was then institutionalized. Celinda, awarded without her knowledge to Tawdrey, has secretly contracted herself to Bellmour, a friend of Friend-love's, who is in turn in love with Diana, Bellmour's cousin. The two cousins are both wards of their uncle, Lord Plotwell, who decides to marry them—to each other. Having already pledged himself to Celinda, Bellmour rejects his uncle's proposition. The latter, as it turns out, has the power to alienate Bellmour's fortune as the price of disobedience in the matter of marriage, according to his father's will. It seems that Plotwell's brother has specified that his son (Bellmour) must marry for *family interest* and not *"imprudently"* according to his own inclination—i.e., for love. The unhappy Bellmour asks his uncle, *"Sir, can you think a blessing can e'er fall upon that pair, whom interest joins, not love?"* But Plotwell is not to be persuaded and summarily has his ward arrested for payment of ten years' maintenance. Legally, he was well within his rights. *The Lawes Resolution . . .* (1632) stated that "If any heir . . . shall marry himself without greeing [agreeing] with his Lord . . . where the Lord offered him a convenient marriage, and without disparagement, there it shall be lawful to hold the inheritance until and after the full age of twenty-one years, by so long time as shall suffice to reap and receive the double value of the marriage."

When he realizes that without the requisite finances he will never be allowed to marry Celinda, Bellmour hope-lessly gives in and goes through the forced marriage to his cousin Diana. The shame of having broken his vow to Celinda drives him mad, and he rushes off into a fanatic debauch in which half of the fortune gained is spent, leaving Diana, his benefactress, undeflowered on her wedding night. Celinda attempts suicide; her brother tries to kill Bellmour; Diana swears vengeance on the husband who has scorned her. Finally, Lord Plotwell realizes that his misdirected government has led to the destruction of all. He relents and agrees to do his best to obtain a divorce for the unmatched wards.

The ending is not as improbable as it might seem, since Mrs. Behn was playing on a technicality of English Common Law. A pledge to marry, pronounced by both parties in the presence of witnesses—which was Bellmour and Celinda's case—was considered a *spousal de praesenti* by ecclesiastical courts and constituted a valid marriage contract. The court could compel such a contract to be solemnized in church. A subsequent marriage, even if preceded only by contract without ceremony, could be annulled on the grounds that it was bigamous. Aphra Behn used this device in several other plays as well—perhaps she meant it to be read as prescriptive for young lovers seeking a way out of forced marriage.

It was much more rare for a young man to find himself in Bellmour's position than for young women. Because of the high mortality rate in the seventeenth century, a man might be in possession of his fortune at quite an early age, and usually in that case there were few restrictions to tie him down. Also a young man who was still under parental control and had taken a fancy to a lady of sufficient fortune and position might be able to take some initiative in the matter and succeed in his purpose, unless his parents had some overwhelming aversion to the match.

It was much more difficult for a young woman to do the same: if modesty did not prevent her, the societal insistence on female obedience would probably do so. The Marquis of Halifax, in his *Advice to a Daughter* (1700), remarked that the duty to conform to parents' wishes in the matter of matches particularly applied to women: "It is one of the disadvantages of your sex," he wrote, "that young women are seldom permitted to make their own choice." The author of the *Defense of the Female Sex* (1696) refers to the same double standard of custom, complaining, "thus we women are debarred the liberty of choosing for ourselves."

The heroine of Aphra's first play, **The Forced Marriage,** passively accepted this condition, though her despair was so intense that she contemplated suicide. Subsequent heroines were already beginning to manifest signs of rebellion by the time her third play, **The Dutch Lover,** came out two years later. The assertiveness of the feminist "Epistle to the Reader" which prefaces the play is matched by the force of the heroine's declaration in the first act: *"I am contracted to a man I never saw, nor I am sure shall not like when I do see, he having more vice and folly than his fortune will excuse, tho' a great one; and I had rather die than marry him."* She boldly goes out and finds a lover of her own choice. Aphra makes a slight retreat from her point at the end of the play, when her heroine's chosen lover turns out to be the very one her father had designed for her, effectively evading the problem.

The young women who speak the first lines of *Sir Patient Fancy,* Lucretia and Isabella, are still more "forward" than the heroine of *The Dutch Lover.* They choose to enjoy each other's company rather than that of the unwelcome suitors who "*are the precious things our grave parents still chose out to make us happy with, and all for a filthy jointure, the undeniable argument for our slavery to fools.*"

> ISABELLA: *Custom is unkind to our sex, not to allow us free choice; but we above all creatures must be forced to endure the formal recommendations of a parent, and the more insupportable addresses of an odious fop; whilst the obedient daughter stands—thus—with her hands pinned before her, a set look, few words, and a mein* [look] *that cries—Come marry me; out upon't.*

> LUCRETIA: *I perceive then, whatever your father designs, you are resolved to love your own way.*

> ISABELLA: *Thou mayst lay thy maidenhead upon't, and be sure of the misfortune to win.*

It was a bold act for a girl educated in the seventeenth-century manner to affirm that she intended to *decide for herself,* but trafficking her way through the battle of the sexes and dealing with the consequences her decision was likely to bring upon her presented considerable difficulties. In *The Rover,* Aphra Behn set forth what was perhaps her most thorough articulation of the dilemma young women like these faced in seeking their freedom. As in *Sir Patient Fancy,* the first scene opens on a private conversation between two girls—Hellena and Florinda, sisters—mutinously discussing how to outwit the intentions of their father, who has decided the fate of each with the customary disregard for their wishes or feelings. Florinda has been promised in marriage to an elderly but wealthy nobleman whom she despises; Hellena, "*designed for a nun,*" proposes that they slip out into the carnival crowd disguised as gypsies, by which means she intends to find "*some mad companion or other that will spoil my devotion . . . though I ask first.*" Florinda, though sympathetic, is somewhat taken aback by this open declaration of sexual design: "*Art thou mad to talk so?*" she asks Hellena. "*Who will like thee well enough to have thee, that hears what a mad wench thou art?*"

"*Like me!*" Hellena answers. "*I don't intend every he that likes me shall have me, but he that I like.*"

The he she tangles with is of course Willmore, the Rover—so called because he was one of the banished Cavaliers forced into exile with Charles II when the Parliamentarians were in power, and like his King, he has wandered disinherited all over Europe in search of adven-

ture or fortune. Willmore is also a rover in a second sense—his sexual fancy passes from woman to woman as randomly as he chances to meet another, and he is faithful to none. Aphra's Rover is the very pattern of a libertine hero; he is witty, extravagant, irresistibly attractive to women, and promiscuous. Rochester was the most evident model, but another, less publicly visible, likeness was of course John Hoyle.

Willmore's behavior is to the letter that of a Restoration rake: there can be no question of what he means when he tells his companion, Belvile: "*Thou know'st there's but one way for a woman to oblige me.*" He has a wit's horror of marriage and subscribes to the "liberated" dismissal of feminine "virtue": "*What the devil should I do with a virtuous woman?—a sort of ill-natured creatures, that take a pride to torment a lover. Virtue is but an infirmity in women, a disease that renders even the handsome ungrateful* [distasteful]."

The "mad" heroine realizes from the very first moment what "freedom" she has tangled with and how it will limit her own; but it is precisely this in the Rover's nature that attracts her to begin with. "*How this unconstant humor makes me love him,*" she mutters to herself when she sees he has already betrayed her only an hour after swearing the contrary. The young woman is split between her own desire for sexual freedom and her instinct that it will make her his victim. So she tricks him, frustrates him, and outwits him until finally they negotiate a settlement:

> WILLMORE: *Since we are so well agreed, let's retire to my chamber . . .*

> HELLENA: *'Tis but getting my consent, and the business is soon done; let but old gaffer hymen and his priest say Amen to't, and I dare lay my mother's daughter by as proper a fellow as your father's son, without fear or blushing.*

> WILLMORE: *No, no, we'll have no vows but love, child, nor witness but the lover; . . . Hymen and priest wait still upon portion, and jointure; love and beauty have their own ceremonies. Marriage is as certain a bane to love, as lending money is to friendship . . .*

> HELLENA: *And . . . what shall I get? A cradle full of noise and mischief, with a pack of repentance at my back? Can you teach me to weave incle to pass my time with?*

In the end, he agrees to marry her, but only because she threatens to leave him altogether. Hellena does not believe in marriage any more than her Rover, nor does she care a fig for feminine virtue, but she has understood that withholding her favors is the only way she can survive in the battle of the sexes. Hellena clearly recognizes the crucial difference between the *givens* of her sexuality and her lover's: she is the one who will be left with "*a cradle full of noise and mischief,*" a ruined reputation, and most likely poverty as well. She may be in ideological agreement with Willmore about the oppressiveness of marriage, but her attitude must be practical because she pays a very different price for the "joys" of free love.

Of course Hellena's chosen means of survival was not the only solution for a woman of her time. Mrs. Behn wrote another female character into the play who represents a second avenue of possibility. She is Angelica Bianca, the whore. Willmore, only a very short time after he first meets Hellena, comes across Angelica Bianca's portrait hanging on a balcony and learns that she is to be auctioned for a vast sum of money. As a penniless Cavalier in exile he cannot bid for her, so instead he rails at her mercenary attitude toward love. Angelica replies with infallible logic: since men cannot be depended upon in love, *"I'm resolved that nothing but gold shall charm my heart."* She further reminds him that men are guilty of the same marketplace attitude, for they always choose a wife not for her qualities or beauty but for her fortune.

Despite the resolve to protect herself, Angelica yields to the Rover, who promptly leaves her after he has satisfied his urges. She finds to her horror the virtuous Hellena preferred and finally realizes what Willmore does not know himself—that despite his disdain for honor in a woman, it is still the only element that can command his love and respect. Her clear view of the social realities governing sexual affairs has not prevented her from falling into the trap of the "ruined" woman: *"In vain I have consulted all my charms,"* she laments, *"in vain this beauty prized, in vain believed my eyes could kindle any lasting fires. I had forgot my name, my infamy, and the reproach honor lays on those that dare pretend a sober passion here. Nice reputation, tho it leave behind more virtues than inhabit where that dwells, yet that once gone, those virtues shine no more."*

. . . . .

The hypocrisy of arranged marriage was a standard theme in Restoration drama, but the violence of Aphra's systematic and persistent attack on the institution was special. Generally, Mrs. Behn's fellow dramatists adopted a more cynical attitude than hers—though exceptions may be argued, and Aphra herself was quite capable of writing against what she had declared elsewhere to be her position.

In life, most of the wits who protested matrimony so vigorously nevertheless married—and clearly wed for "interest." The Earl of Rochester, having been left with a sadly reduced estate by his improvident father, sought to repair his fortune by choosing to pursue one of the richest heiresses in England—at the King's suggestion. After the marriage, it seems he eventually did conceive a certain affection for her, but his original motives were calculatingly financial. Once in possession of the fortune, he left her to the isolation of the country while entertaining mistresses in London. Rochester's booncompanion, the Duke of Buckingham, had, in the last years of the Commonwealth, married the daughter of a Parliamentary General in order to regain his sequestered estates. After the Restoration, he more or less treated her as though she had

ceased to exist and lived openly with the Countess of Shrewsbury. The dramatist Etherege married a rich old widow, and Wycherely tried to secure his financial situation in the same way by marrying the widowed Countess of Drogheda, whose ferocity turned out to be as great as her wealth. The witty Buckhurst, Earl of Dorset, married in succession two wealthy ladies of noble birth, both said to be beautiful but evidently also chosen for their dowry and social position.

Neither Rochester nor Buckingham nor Etherege nor Wycherley nor Buckhurst was forced by parents to marry as he did; they were all at their own disposal. Their objections to marriage might be seen, then, in the most unfavorable light, as reluctance to be tied to any woman who could not be as easily discarded as a whore or a mistress and who might even believe that he had some responsibility to her.

Aphra Behn's attack on marriage and the property-marriage system, on the other hand, was part of a much more comprehensive philosophical stance. She was, in principle, opposed to the intrusion of "interest" into intimacy of whatever sort between men and women—whether it be marriage or love; whether that interest be property, title, money, ambition, or other. This was her definition of "free-love." In a poem she wrote to the Earl of Dorset on the occasion of his second marriage, she made the following statement: *"Too often and too fatally we find / portion and jointure charm the mind, / The very soul's by interest swayed, / And nobler passion now by fortune is betrayed;/ By sad experience this I know, / And sigh, Alas! in vain because 'tis true."* It was a strange remark to have made to a patron from whom she was probably expecting a much-needed reward. But she was apparently unable to refrain from it; perhaps she felt herself a voice against the tide. Her poem **"On Desire"** seems to indicate that even in the face of opportunity she had never been able to force herself to make love to a man for his position or his money, though everywhere *"interest did all the loving business do."* Speaking to her perversely retreating "desire,"

> *When interest called, then thou wert shy,*
> *Nor to my aid one kind propension brought,*
> *Nor woud'st inspire one tender thought,*
> *When princes at my feet did lie.*
> *When thou could'st mix ambition with thy joy,*
> *Then peevish phantom thou wer't nice and coy.*

She half regrets; her life might have been easier. Still, her overriding feeling is pride in independence and, through all the confusion of her conflicting impulses, a steadfast rejection of the values she sees as false:

> *Take back your gold, and give me current love,*
> *The treasure of your heart, not of your purse . . .*
> *According to the strictest rules of honour,*
> *Beauty should be the reward of love,*
> *Not the vile merchandise of fortune,*
> *Or the cheap drug of a church-ceremony.*
> *She's only infamous, who to her bed*

*For interest takes some nauseous clown she
   hates;
And though a jointure or a vow in public
   Be her price, that makes her but the dearer
   whore.
All the desires of mutual love are virtuous.*

There were other voices who had begun to speak out against marriage-for-money in Aphra's time, but few took the logical conclusions of such a stance as far as she did, nor elaborated it as part of a larger, politics of sexuality. Aphra was, though of course she did not know it, at the beginning of a "sentimental revolution" that would eventually revise England's idea of marriage. Though it was clear Aphra's generation was witnessing a disintegration of the old form, the counsel Francis Osborne gave in his *Advice to a Son* (1656) was still uppermost in men's minds: "He that takes a wife wanting money is a slave to his affections, doing the basest of drudgeries without wages." Charles II confirmed this reality when, in 1664, he wrote to his sister that "a handsome face without money has but few gallants, upon the score of marriage."

It would not be until the next century that history would catch up to Aphra's vision.

. . . . .

Aphra Behn's astounding rate of dramatic production in the later part of the 1670s, her repeated successes, and increasing fame were continual irritants to her literary competitors and the aspiring lesser wits who fiercely resented that a woman had achieved what they had failed to. In addition, her emancipated attitude and spirited defense of self-determination excited their animosity still further. One of her poems is a reply to a playhouse "friend" who has informed her that she does not know her place: *"Since you'll have it so,"* she says, *"I grant I am impertinent. / And till this moment did not know / Through all my life what 'twas I meant; / Your kind opinion was the unflattering glass, / In which my mind found how deformed it was. / Impertinence, my sex's shame, / (which has so long my life persued,) / You with such modesty reclaim / . . . To so divine a power what must I owe, / That renders me so like the perfect—you?"*

Though she often put up a front of saucy reply to her detractors, Aphra was in truth far from indifferent to the siege of criticism and insult. She had complained privately to Emily Price about the charges of plagiarism over *Abdelazer* and in that letter dismissed their importance, but finally the accusation was persistent enough to cause her professional damage. In a postscript to *The Rover,* Aphra publicly protested that this kind of malicious gossip had caused her publishers to delay printing the play. Her statement clearly identified literary jealousy as one of the principal motivations behind the reports: *"Had* [the play] *succeeded ill, I should have had no need of imploring justice from the critics, who are naturally so kind to any that pretend to usurp their dominion."*

The imputation of plagiarism, though, was a minor theme in the diatribe directed against Aphra. The principal charge was that she had failed in feminine modesty—or as it was more commonly put, that she was a whore. A poem by William Wycherley, addressed "To the Sappho of the Age, Supposed to Lye-In of a Love-Distemper, or a Play," was evidently written when Aphra was at the height of her theatrical success. Wycherley nastily comments on her growing "public" fame—punning on the double sense of the word as it was applied to feminine sexuality at that time. "Once, to your shame, your parts to all were shown," he claims—demonstrating his own "parts" with the clever double entendre on the word, which then meant *wit,* but also slyly implied *private* parts. "But now," Wycherley goes on, "(tho' a more public woman grown,) / You gain more reputation in the town; / Grow public, to your honor, not your shame, / As more men now you please, gain much more fame; / . . . Barren wits, envy your head's offsprings more, / Than barren women, did your tail's before." The logic Wycherley's joke rested on was well known to everyone: it was the old adage that in gaining "fame," a woman lost it. What was so funny was that there were some "barren wits" gullible enough to see Aphra's reputation shining instead of stinking as it ought.

In a sense, Aphra herself had set up the structure for Wycherley's satire: her very first prologue, it will be remembered, had declared that women, who had formerly pleased by beauty, were now attempting wit as a superior means of conquering the other sex. She had been half-serious and half-playful, but Wycherely used the pretext to drag her through the mud: "Thus, as your beauty did, your wit does now, / The women's envy, men's diversion grow; / Who, to be clap'd, or clap you, round you sit, / And, tho' they sweat for it, will crowd your pit; / Since lately you lay-in, (but as they say,) / Because, you had been clap'd another way; / But, if 'tis true, that you have a need to sweat, / Get, (if you can) at your new play, a seat."

The slander is couched in a wily series of double meanings: "clap" in the sense of applause, but also as slang for venereal disease; "sweating" from overcrowding the theater, but also as the cure for the "clap" (a reference to the sweating-tubs); and the "pit" of the theater, but also a woman's sexual parts. The last line of the poem seems to suggest a certain envy; though Wycherley was himself undeniably a success, his literary output was small compared to the rush of plays from Aphra's energetic pen—in the end, he wrote only four to her seventeen. In view of the experience of other, far less provoking, women writers, it seems inevitable that the slurs on Aphra's sexuality would come whether there was any basis for them in her life or not. It seems possible that at one time Aphra might indeed have had a succession of lovers, but to be castigated for it by a libertine like Wycherley, however, was ridiculous.

Another contemporary satire written in 1676—anonymously—included Aphra among the leading playwrights of her day competing for the title of Poet Laureate, but in these terms:

*. . . The poetess Aphra next showed her sweet
   face
And swore by her poetry and her black ace
The laurel by a double right was her own
For the plays she had writ and the conquests
   she's won.
Apollo acknowledged 'twas hard to deny her,
But to deal frankly and ingeniously by her,
He told her, were conquests and charms her
   pretence,
She ought to have pleaded a dozen years hence.*

Aphra was then about thirty-six years old. The verses, passed around in manuscript in all the coffeehouses and taverns the wits frequented and then in the Court itself, must have caused her some pain.

Aphra chose to ignore the traducement of her personal life, but was not about to let the remarks pass unanswered when they were directed at her professional capacity. In another "Preface to the Reader," printed at the beginning of her play **Sir Patient Fancy,** she defends herself: "I printed this play with all the impatient haste one ought to do, who would be vindicated from the most unjust and silly aspersion, woman could invent to cast on woman; and which only my being a woman had procured me; *That it was Bawdy,* the least and most excusable fault in the men writers, to whose plays they all crowd, as if they came to no other end than to hear what they condemn in this: *but from a woman it was unnatural* . . . (Aphra's emphases)." It was bad enough to have to take squibs and lampoons and open hostility from men, Aphra contended, but to find herself under attack from the sex whose rights she had been trying to uphold was severely disappointing. "The play had no other misfortune but that of coming out for a woman's," her manifesto went on, "had it been owned by a man, though the most dull unthinking rascally scribler in town, it had been a most admirable play. Nor does its loss of fame with the ladies do it much hurt, though they ought to have had good nature and justice enough to have attributed all its faults to the authors unhappiness, who is forced to write for bread and not ashamed to own it, and consequently ought to write to please (if she can) an age which has given several proofs it was by this way of writing to be obliged, though it is a way too cheap for men of wit to pursue who write for glory, and a way which even I despise as much below me."

Did Aphra feel that her gift had been deformed by the necessity of making a living by her writing? She was, she says, forced by necessity to write to the fashion of the age—i.e., to write as the other (male) playwrights did; to write "like a man." Is she saying that she might have written differently had she been free from this demand? The answer must be speculative—but perhaps this might in part explain the double voice in Aphra's work.

Mrs. Behn's argument that what she wrote was no more salacious than her male colleagues' plays was quite correct. That she was the victim of a literary double standard is confirmed by a letter of John Dryden's to Elizabeth Thomas, a young woman who had confided her literary

ambitions to him. "You, who write only for your diversion," he wrote, congratulating her intention not to *publish* anything she wrote, but to keep it private, "may pass your hours with pleasure in it, and without prejudice, always avoiding (as I know you will) the licenses which Mrs. Behn allowed herself, of writing loosely, and giving (if I may have leave to say so) some scandal to the modesty of her sex. I confess, I am the last man who ought, in justice to arraign her, who have been myself too much a libertine." At least Dryden had the grace to admit the hypocrisy of attacks on Mrs. Behn. But the letter was written only after she was dead. The age had reversed its social stance on the issue, and Dryden himself, having recently converted to Catholicism, was primarily apologizing for his own libertine past rather than excusing Mrs. Behn for having scandalized the modesty of her sex.

However she might have been hurt by the aspersions cast on her character and her plays, Aphra's epilogue to **Sir Patient Fancy** in no uncertain terms told her critics she did not intend to be daunted:

*I here and there o'erheard a coxcomb cry,
Ah, Rot it—'tis a woman's comedy,
One, who because she lately chanc'd to
   please us,
With her damn'd stuff, will never cease to
   tease us.
What had poor woman done, that she must be
Debarred from sense, and sacred poetry? . . .
As for you half-wits, you unthinking tribe,
We'll let you see, what e'er besides we do,
How artfully we copy some of you:
And if you're drawn to th' life, pray tell me
   then,
Why women should not write as well as men.*

The epilogue was spoken by "Mrs. Gwin." Recent scholars have said that the actress cannot have been the famous Nell Gwyn, as she had retired from the stage several years before, when she became the King's mistress. There is, however, a contemporary engraving depicting her speaking the lines, which seems to argue otherwise. It does seem possible that the jolly Nell might have thought it amusing to return to her former profession once or twice—particularly as she was known for her generosity and it would certainly have given a boost to Aphra's career. The fact that Aphra's very next play, **The Feigned Curtezans,** performed about two months later, is dedicated to Nell Gwyn seems to support the possibility. It was Aphra's first dedication to any of her plays, and she might well have thought it a good opportunity to thank the actress for the support she had given. Mrs. Behn praises Mrs. Gwyn for her beauty, charm, and sweetness, but most of all for her wit—commenting that her example *"ought to make your sex vain enough to despise the malicious world that will allow a woman no wit . . . [and] shame those boasting talkers who are judges of nothing but faults."*

Nancy Cotton (essay date 1980)

SOURCE: "Aphra Behn," in *Women Playwrights in England c. 1363-1750*, Bucknell University Press, 1980, pp. 55-80.

[*Below, Cotton studies the development of Behn's career and the course of critical reaction to her work.*]

Aphra Behn (c. 1640-89) was a hard-driving professional playwright, independent, bawdy, witty, and tough. She differed from all her feminine predecessors because she was "forced to write for Bread and not ashamed to owne it" (To the Reader, *Sir Patient Fancy*). Nothing is known of her background or education but myths and guesses. She was born in Wye; she was born in Canterbury. Her maiden name was Amis; or Johnson. She was the daughter of a barber; or of the lieutenant-general of Surinam. She was married to a London merchant named Behn, of Dutch extraction; or Mr. Behn was a fiction. She had lovers innumerable; she suffered faithfully a long unhappy passion for a bisexual lawyer named John Hoyle. But what is known of her life shows her one of the remarkable personalities of her age.

Her first biography, "Memoirs on the Life of Mrs. Behn," appeared in 1696 with the earliest collected edition of her novels and purported to be "Written by a Gentlewoman of her Acquaintance." "One of the Fair Sex" reports Behn's early precosity "ev'n in the first Bud of Infancy," for "besides the Vivacity and Wit of her Conversation, at the first Use almost of Reason in Discourse, she wou'd write the prettiest, soft-engaging Verses in the World". There is no record of her education, but her works show that she knew French, and there is presumptive evidence that she knew Spanish and Italian also.

About 1663-64 Behn traveled to Surinam, then an English colony. She describes her journey in her famous and influential *Oroonoko* (1688), sometimes called the first abolitionist novel. The facts may be embroidered—*Oroonoko* after all is a novel rather than an autobiography—but they show her adventurousness. She tells us that her stay was short in the colony "because my Father dy'd at Sea, and never arriv'd to possess the Honour design'd him (which was Lieutenant-General of six and thirty Islands, besides the Continent of Surinam) nor the Advantages he hop'd to reap by them: So that though we were oblig'd to continue on our Voyage, we did not intend to stay upon the place". She visited the Indians, who were understandably amazed at her European dress: "They were all naked; and we were dress'd, so as is most commode for the hot Countries, very glittering and rich; so that we appear'd extremely fine; my own Hair was cut short, and I had a Taffety Cap, with black Feathers on my Head; my Brother was in a Stuff-Suit, with Silver Loops and Buttons, and abundance of green Ribbon." Behn remembered with gusto her voyage across "Three thousand Leagues of spacious Ocean" (Dedication, *The Young King*), recounting in *Oroonoko* her adventures searching for "tiger" cubs and eating an armadillo.

Upon her return to England, according to her biographer, she "gave King Charles the Second, so pleasant and rational an Account of his Affairs there, and particularly of the Misfortunes of Oroonoko, that he desir'd her to deliver them publickly to the World; and [was] satisfy'd on her Abilities in the Management of Business, and the Fidelity of our Heroine to his Int'rest" ("Memoirs"). This anecdote is as difficult to prove or disprove as any told about her life at this period, but she herself tells of presenting to "his Majesty's Antiquary's . . . some rare Flies, of amazing Forms and Colours" from Surinam. The story goes that she married Mr. Behn about this time. He disappeared rapidly from the scene, perhaps of the plague in 1665 or 1666, and was never heard of again. Behn never mentions him in any of her writings.

Everything about the character she gives of herself in *Oroonoko,* even perhaps the tale of her acquaintance with the king, is consonant with the first indisputable external evidence about her life. In 1666 she went to Antwerp as a secret agent for the English government. Her employment as a spy is documented in a series of letters preserved among official state papers. Her mission was to send information about disaffected Cromwellians, now taking their turn in exile, and to relay Dutch military plans. As a secret agent she used the code name Astrea. Later, as her literary name, Astrea became as synonymous with Aphra Behn as Orinda was with Katherine Philips.

Astrea ran into debt in the Netherlands and sent urgent appeals for money to Thomas Killigrew, who had recommended her for the job, and even to Lord Arlington, Secretary of State. Finally she had to borrow money from a London merchant in order to pay her debts abroad. She arrived home in 1667, penniless and substantially in debt. Despite further appeals to those who had employed her, she ended up in debtor's prison. She wrote Killigrew the day before her imprisonment:

> I will send my mother to the King with a petition, for I see everybody are words, and I will not perish in prison from whence he [her creditor] swears I shall not stir till the utmost farthing be paid; and oh God, who considers my misery and charge too, this is my reward for all my great promises and my endeavours. Sir, if I have not the money to-night, you must send me something to keep me in prison, for I will not starve.

No one knows how or when she was released from prison, but it may indeed have been someone at court who paid her debt, perhaps the king himself, for to the end of her life she was an ardent Tory, devoted to Charles II and his brother James.

"The Rest of her Life was entirely dedicated to Pleasure and Poetry; the success in which, gain'd her the Acquaintance and Friendship of the most sensible Men of the Age" ("Memoirs"). As to the "Pleasure," if the word means sexual pleasure as it often did in the Restoration, there is little external evidence. Her works show her sexual sophistication and won her a reputation in her own lifetime as an adept of love, who practiced what she preached: "The Passions, that of Love especially, she was Mistress of; and gave us such nice and tender Touches of them, that without her Name we might discover the Author." As to the "Poetry," the incomplete edition of her collected works runs to six volumes. The determination expressed in her letter to Killigrew—"I will not starve"—is evident in all her work. She turned out plays, poems, novels, and translations to suit the marketplace. Her wide circle of friendships is documented in innumerable compliments from distinguished contemporaries. Among her literary friends were Dryden, Otway, Edward Howard, Waller, Charles Cotton, Nahum Tate, Edward Ravenscroft, Nathaniel Lee, Thomas Creech, and probably the Earl of Rochester. She must have known all her contemporaries in the theater, both playwrights and actors. Sir Peter Lely and Mary Beale painted portraits of her. People of other professions also sought her out, and students just down from the universities haunted her rooms. She apparently was "able to write in the midst of Company, and yet have her Share of the Conversation." She was noted among her friends for her witty conversation, beauty, and generosity.

No one knows how she gained an entree to the theater. In *Oroonoko,* after describing the "glorious Wreaths" of feathers made by the natives, she says, "I had a Set of these presented to me, and I gave 'em to the King's Theatre; it was the Dress of the *Indian Queen,* infinitely admir'd by Persons of Quality; and was inimitable". The patentee of the King's Company at this time was Thomas Killigrew, whom Behn had worked for during her career as a spy. In spite of these connections with the King's Company, her plays were produced by the rival Duke's Company. Perhaps, as has been suggested, she took her plays to the rival house because Killigrew had treated her shabbily about her expenses in the Netherlands. It has also been suggested that the Duke's Company might have been more receptive to a woman playwright because it was the more innovative of the two companies. This hypothesis, however, ignores the fact that the King's Company had already produced plays by Frances Boothby and Katherine Philips in 1669. A more likely hypothesis is that the Duke's Company was competing with the King's Company by producing a woman playwright in the following year.

Whatever the circumstances, Behn entered the theater in 1670, producing, before her death nineteen years later, seventeen extant plays. Two more plays have been lost— *Like Father Like Son; or, The Mistaken Brothers* (1682) and *The Wavering Nymph; or, Mad Amyntas* (1684). Four anonymous plays have been attributed to her—*The Woman Turned Bully* (1675), *The Debauchee; or, The Credulous Cuckold* (1677), *The Counterfeit Bridegroom; or, The Defeated Widow* (1677), and *The Revenge; or, A Match in Newgate* (1680).

She began her apprenticeship with *The Forced Marriage; or, The Jealous Bridegroom* (1670), a romantic tragi-comedy of intrigue of the popular Beaumont and Fletcher school. In February 1671 Behn followed up with a romantic comedy, *The Amorous Prince; or, The Curious Husband,* more vivacious in language and more complex in plot. With *The Dutch Lover* (1673) Behn found her forte, the comedy of intrigue, and her style, brisk colloquial prose. Her apprentice work was finished—she had found her stage formulas. Behn typically manipulates several sources into a complexly plotted play of expert stage craftsmanship. A number of couples—eluding the unwanted marriages arranged for them—meet, bed and/or wed after innumerable intrigues, mistaken identities, duels, disguises, and practical jokes. Her plays abound in bedroom farce. Her scenes of comic lowlife are delightful, full of landladies, bawds, buffoons, and prostitutes. She provides spectacle in masquing, costuming, and dance, and uses stage machinery and other technical resources to create special effects. Behn had a fine lyric gift, and her plays are full of witty and romantic songs. These plays, although fun to read, are for the stage rather than the page. Behn was the first woman to write theatrically.

Her wit is more often in the plot than in the dialogue. Because of this, her plays are often compared unfavorably with the comedies of manners written by her contemporaries. But Behn was writing in another genre, the Spanish-type comedy of intrigue, one of the most commercially successful genres of the day. Behn wrote for money and she chose the mode that suited her talents. Behn's assessment of her own plays in the preface to *The Lucky Chance* . . . is accurate. She wrote as well as any of her contemporaries except Etherege, Wycherley, and Dryden. And considering her prolific output, she indeed "made as many good Comedies, as any one Man" in her own age.

Behn wrote a series of fine intrigue comedies. The best of these, *The Rover; or, The Banished Cavaliers* (1677), is set at carnival time in Naples, where impoverished English cavaliers-in-exile become entangled with Spanish ladies and win their persons and fortunes. Behn's rover, Willmore, is her distinctive version of a favorite Restoration character, the wild gallant. The rover is eager for an amour anytime, anyplace, with any woman at hand. *The Rover* stayed in the repertory until the middle of the eighteenth century, the role of the witty heroine being taken by such famous actresses as Elizabeth Barry, Anne Bracegirdle, Anne Oldfiled, and Peg Woffington. Behn exploited her success by continuing Willmore's adventures in *The Rover Part II* (1681). The play was dedicated to the Duke of York because of "the incouragement" he gave "the Rover at his first appearance, and the concern" he was "pleas'd to have for his second" (The Epistle Dedicatory). Another variant on *The Rover* was *The Feigned Courtesans; or, A Night's Intrigue* (1679). Again a group of English travelers, this time in Rome, meet, intrigue with, and marry a group of foreign ladies. Also among Behn's best is *Sir Patient Fancy* (1678), an amusing tangle of the amours of two neighboring London families, a first-rate stage play with fine scenes of bedroom farce. Behn's *Emperor of the Moon* was an instant success in 1687. A gay and extravagant combination of *commedia dell' arte,* operatic spectacle, sumptuous costuming, dance, song, satire, intrigue, and a bit of manners comedy, *The Emperor of the Moon* was performed for nearly a hundred years.

Two of Behn's plays deal centrally with her most distinctive theme, her attack on forced marriage. Announcing that theme in the title of her first play, she went on to write *The Town Fop; or, Sir Timothy Tawdrey* (1676) and *The Lucky Chance; or, An Alderman's Bargain* (1686)—a sentimental, then a harder treatment of the same subject. In *The Town Fop,* the young lovers are brought near to ruin before a fifth-act reversal dissolves a forced marriage. We see not their witty stratagems but their bitter sufferings when parental authority is abused. The effect, then, is sentimental rather than comic. Ten years later *The Lucky Chance* made a comic attack on loveless marriage, with three pairs of lovers using their wits to escape that dreadful fate. All three heroines complain explicitly about forced marriage. Lady Fulbank:

> Oh, how fatal are forc'd Marriages!
> How many Ruins one such Match pulls on!
> Had I but kept my Sacred Vows to Gayman,
> How happy had I been—how prosperous he!
> Whilst now I languish in a loath'd embrace,
> Pine out my Life with Age—Consumptions,
>   Coughs.

Leticia, preparing to elope with Bellmour, addresses the absent Sir Feeble:

> Old Man forgive me—thou the Aggressor art,
> Who rudely forc'd the Hand without the Heart.

Diana speaks similarly as she prepares to elope with Bredwel:

> Father, farewell—if you dislike my course,
> Blame the old rigid Customs of your Force.

The serious tone of these complaints, made in what is essentially a farcical comedy, shows the earnestness of Behn's feeling that love should be the basis for marriage. New Comedy in general depicts the witty stratagems of young lovers who outwit their elders and thus escape unwanted arranged marriages. Behn goes beyond this to attack the arranged marriage as an institution.

She also used the stage to voice her strong opinions about the political upheavals in the latter years of Charles II's reign, when feeling ran high between Whig and Tory over the possibility of a Catholic succession through the Duke of York. In *The Roundheads; or, The Good Old Cause* (1681) Behn satirized the Parliamentarians in the turbulent days immediately preceding the Restoration. *The Roundheads* is a poor play; the satire is too gross to be telling. A few months later, in the spring of 1682, Behn produced a much better political satire in *The City Heiress; or, Sir Timothy Treat-all.* Treat-all, "an old seditious Knight, that keeps open House for Commonwealthsmen and true blue Protestants" (dramatis personae), was clearly a satire of the prominent Whig Shaftesbury. The satire is effective and is integrated into a fast-paced intrigue comedy. That summer Behn went too far in her political

outspokenness and offended the king when, for the anonymous play *Romulus and Hersilia,* she wrote an epilogue attacking the Duke of Monmouth, Charles II's natural son and potential Protestant usurper. Both Behn and the actress who spoke the epilogue were arrested. Apparently nothing much came of the arrest, but Behn had made enemies among a number of powerful Whigs and among Whig playwrights such as Shadwell.

Some of Behn's plays are not easy to categorize. She wrote one tragedy, *Abdelazer; or, The Moor's Revenge* (1676), a murderous melodrama distinguished only by its energy and the often quoted song "Love in fantastick Triumph sat." She was apparently always pressed for money, particularly during the 1680s when times were hard for playwrights, and consequently often wrote hurriedly. In 1679 she refurbished for production *The Young King; or, The Mistake,* like her earliest plays a romantic tragicomedy in the Beaumont and Fletcher mold. The dedication calls the play the "first Essay of my Infant-Poetry" and implies that an early version was written in Surinam. The text shows signs of hasty and incomplete revision. Haste and need may also have produced *The False Count; or, A New Way to Play an Old Game* (1681), described in the epilogue as "a slight Farce, five Days brought forth with ease." Possibly the play was indeed written with such speed, for, although amusing, it is less complexly plotted than her other plays. Two Behn plays were produced posthumously. *The Widow Ranter; or, The History of Bacon in Virginia* (1689), set in America, unmercifully dramatizes the colonial officials as cowardly and drunken transported felons. Charles Gildon rewrote a few scenes of *The Younger Brother; or, The Amorous Jilt,* a busy intrigue comedy, and brought it out in 1696, seven years after Behn's death.

In several plays, Behn explores in distinctive ways two stock characters, the courtesan and the amazon. Critics have suggested that she gives prominence to the courtesan simply as a means of titillation. Rather, she uses this character as a weapon in her thematic attack on mercenary marriage. An early example is Angelica Bianca in *The Rover.* She is so famous and beautiful a courtesan that she can sell her favors for a thousand crowns a month. In spite of her mercenary nature, she falls in love with the poor but dashing rover, Captain Willmore. He argues her into bed by upbraiding her for selling love for money. Although she is persuaded, at one point she turns the argument against him:

> Pray, tell me, Sir, are not you guilty of the same mercenary Crime? When a Lady is proposed to you for a Wife, you never ask, how fair, discreet, or virtuous she is; but what's her Fortune—which if but small, you cry—She will not do my business—and basely leave her, tho she languish for you.—Say, is not this as poor?

Ultimately the humorless courtesan loses Willmore to the witty maiden Hellena. Angelica Bianca mistakenly thinks that this is due to her "lost honor," but what wins the rover is not Hellena's "honor" but her wit. Although she loses the love game in *The Rover,* Angelica Bianca is developed as a three-dimensional passionate woman, a character with real thoughts and feelings.

Two years later in *The Feigned Courtesans* the rover of the play, Frank Galliard, woos the young Roman courtesan La Silvianetta, while his more romantic friend Sir Harry Fillamour is attracted by her companion Euphemia. The courtesans are really Cornelia and Marcella, young ladies of fortune and family who have run away from home in disguise, Marcella to avoid a forced marriage, Cornelia to avoid a convent. It is their disguise as courtesans—a role they enjoy playing—that enables them to attract and then win their men. Another young lady, Laura Lucretia, also disguises as La Silvianetta in order to attract Galliard. Inferior in wit to Cornelia, she loses the rover and must be content with her fiancé.

The *Rover Part II,* in another two years, varies again the pattern of Part I. Willmore, now a widower, is once more pursued by a witty, virtuous maid—Ariadne—and a beautiful, passionate courtesan—La Nuche. Because of the earlier play, a strong expectation is set up that Ariadne will capture Willmore in marriage, taking him away from the mercenary courtesan. But Ariadne's wit fails at a crucial point. Striking up a flirtation with Willmore, she talks of love in terms of monetary value. When he praises her charms, she says they are to be enjoyed by "one that can esteem 'em to their worth, can set a Value and a Rate upon 'em". Wishing to impress the inconstant rover, she derides constancy because "it loses Time and Profit," because "new Lovers have new Vows and new Presents." Willmore, who in Part I upbraided the courtesan for being mercenary, now turns the same attack on Ariadne, on honorable ladies and their marriage settlements:

> You Women have all a certain Jargon, or Gibberish, peculiar to your selves; of Value, Rate, Present, Interest, Settlement, Advantage, Price, Maintenance, and the Devil and all of Fopperies, which in plain Terms signify ready Money, by way of Fine before Entrance; so that an honest well-meaning Merchant of Love finds no Credit amongst ye, without his Bill of Lading.

La Nuche and Willmore are attracted to each other when the play opens, and he turns the same arguments on her. Throughout five acts she wavers between love and interest while Willmore tries to win her to the rover view of love free and unconfined. Their battle of wits takes serious and comic turns, culminating in an allegorical scene in which La Nuche in center stage hears Willmore on one side argue for her on the grounds of pure love, while Beaumond, on the other side of the stage, offers wealth for her favors. La Nuche nearly loses Willmore at this point by succumbing to Beaumond's offers, and Willmore makes her conscious of her error:

> Death, hadst thou lov'd my Friend for his own Value, I had esteem'd thee; but when his Youth and Beauty cou'd not plead, to be the mercenary Conquest of his Presents, was poor, below thy Wit: I cou'd have conquer'd so, but I scorn thee at that rate—my Purse

shall never be my Pimp.

La Nuche now realizes that she loves her rover more than her profit and uses her wits to win him back. Knowing that Willmore has a midnight assignation with Ariadne, she substitutes herself for her rival. This time the courtesan disguises as the maid. In a fifth-act surprise, Ariadne must return to her fiancé Beaumond, while Willmore and La Nuche pair off "without the formal Foppery of Marriage."

The denouement of *Rover II,* although surprising in terms of stage convention, is carefully prepared for. La Nuche's character is much more highly developed than that of her prototype. La Nuche has the wit and sense of humor that Angelica Bianca lacked. She is on stage far more often than her rival, Ariadne, and she tends to dominate the action. Because of her full characterization, La Nuche elicits audience sympathy, so that her success with Willmore is psychologically satisfying. The casting may have added to the satisfaction of the Restoration audience. While William Smith played Willmore in both parts of *The Rover,* Elizabeth Barry, the most celebrated actress of the day, played first the witty maid Hellena and then the courtesan La Nuche. The denouement works out a progression: in *Rover I* the witty maid wins out over the courtesan; in *The Feigned Courtesans* the witty maid wins out disguised as a courtesan; in *Rover II* the witty courtesan wins out over the maid. In each case, the more generous woman gets the man. Behn uses the series of *Rover* plays to make in a stronger form the point she makes in her plays against forced marriage. In those plays, heroines forced into, or about to be forced into, loveless but profitable marriages feel themselves prostituted. In the *Rover* series Behn goes a step further to say that the only difference between prostitution and marriage for money is that prostitution is the more candid, less hypocritical way for a woman to earn a living.

Another female character used to translate theme into stage action is Behn's woman warrior. This character provides a visual metaphor for the battle of the sexes and appears in both romantic and comic versions. The romantic woman warrior appears in *The Young King* as Cleomena, Princess of Dacia, who has been "bred up in War" (dramatis personae); because of an oracle, she is to inherit the throne instead of her brother. She makes her first entrance "drest like an Amazon, with a Bow in her Hand, and a Quiver of Arrows at her Back." Her hereditary enemy, Thersander, Prince of Scythia, for his own reasons is disguised as Clemanthis, an unknown warrior of incredible valor fighting in the Dacian army. Cleomena and Clemanthis inevitably fall in love with each other. Believing that the Scythian prince has treacherously murdered Clemanthis, the princess herself disguises as Clemanthis and fights in single combat with Thersander. Her plans for revenge are foiled when she is wounded, recognized, and carried off the field. Still bent on revenge, Cleomena next disguises as a shepherd and stabs Therander in the breast. He recovers from his near-fatal wound, the mistakes are unraveled, and the marriage of Cleomena and Thersander makes peace between the warring kingdoms. It is curious that both Cleomena and Thersander masquerade as the same person, as Clemanthis. This may support the other suggestions in the play of Cleomena's androgynous temperament. More probably, the identity of disguise suggests the identity of souls in love. The name *Clemanthis* combines the letters and sounds of the names *Cleomena* and *Thersander*.

A jolly woman warrior is the title character of *The Widow Ranter*. Because the play is set in colonial America, the Widow Ranter has full scope for her unconventionality. Formerly the mistress, later the wife of old Colonel Ranter, she has been left with "fifty thousand Pounds Sterling, besides Plate and Jewels: She's a great Gallant . . . her Extravagancy is very pleasant, she retains something of her primitive Quality still, but is good-natur'd and generous." Ranter is notorious for beginning the morning with a pipe and punch.

Ranter loves dashing Lieutenant-General Daring and intends to have him in spite of his affection for the maiden Chrisante. When Indian wars break out, Ranter disguises as a man and appears on the battlefield, with her maid Jenny dressed as a footman:

> Ranter. Why should I sigh and whine, and make my self an Ass, and him conceited? no, instead of snivelling I am resolved—
>
> Jenny. What, Madam?
>
> Ranter. Gad, to beat the Rascal. . . .
>
> Jenny. Beat him, Madam! what, a Woman beat a Lieutenant-General?
>
> Ranter. Hang 'em, they get a name in War from Command, not Courage; but how know I but I may fight? Gad, I have known a Fellow kick'd from one end of the Town to t'other, believing himself a Coward; at last forced to fight, found he could; got a Reputation, and bullied all he met with; and got a Name, and a great Commission.
>
> Jenny. But if he should kill you, Madam.
>
> Ranter. I'll take care to make it as comical a Duel as the best of 'em; as much in love as I am, I do not intend to die its Martyr.

Daring recognizes Ranter through her disguise, and realizing that she loves him, teases her by gossiping about the widow: "Gad, I'd sooner marry a she-Bear, unless for a Penance for some horrid Sin; we should be eternally challenging one another to the Field, and ten to one she beats me there; or if I should escape there, she wou'd kill me with drinking. . . . she'll rail and smoke till she choke again; then six Gallons of Punch hardly recovers her, and never but then is she good-natur'd."

Ranter is so enraged that she draws her sword on him, and Daring, laughing, proposes to her:

> Daring. Give me thy Hand, Widow, I am thine—and

so entirely, I will never—be drunk out of thy Company:—Dunce [the parson] is in my Tent,—prithee let's in and bind the Bargain.

> Ranter. Nay, faith, let's see the Wars at an end first.
>
> Daring. Nay, prithee take me in the humour, while thy Breeches are on—for I never lik'd thee half so well in Petticoats.
>
> Ranter. Lead on, General, you give me good incouragement to wear them.

The compatibility of a marriage between these two equals in wit and war is emphasized a few minutes later. Battle breaks out in earnest, and Daring enters duelling, "Ranter fighting like a Fury by his side."

Behn uses the Widow Ranter to give visual, dramatic representation to the battle of the sexes. Sword combat is added to the usual wit combat of the gay couple of Restoration comedy. While the amazon was an old stage character, Behn uses her in a distinctive way. Possibly Cleomena and the Widow Ranter grew out of Behn's Surinam experience; both plays have colonial connections. *The Widow Ranter* is set in Virginia, and the first draft at least of *The Young King* was written in Surinam. Behn's woman warrior may be a colonial conception; she may also have been a feminist conception.

Certainly her creator was a feminist. During her career, in response to the attacks of her enemies, Behn became a staunch defender of women. She took this position gradually. She began her career confident that the novelty of being a woman playwright would help rather than hinder her success. A glamorous woman, widely complimented on her beauty and wit, she intended to exploit her glamor in the theater. She opened her first play with a flirtatious prologue that traded on her sex as an advertisement. An actor begins the prologue of *The Forced Marriage,* warning the gallants that the women are planning "new Stratagems . . . They'll join the force of Wit to Beauty." He warns that all the ladies in the audience are spies set by the "Poetess"

> To hold you in a wanton Compliment;
> That so you may not censure what she 'as writ,
> Which done, they face you down 'twas full of
>   Wit.

At this point an actress enters, points to the ladies, and scoffs:

> How hast thou labour'd to subvert in vain,
> What one poor Smile of ours calls home again?
> Can any see that glorious Sight and say
> A Woman shall not Victor prove to day?
> Who is't that to their Beauty would submit,
> And yet refuse the Fetters of their Wit?

The prologue had probably been preceded by some advance publicity, for the play opened to a full house and ran for six nights.

But as soon as it became clear to the theatrical world that a woman was going to be a serious contender for money and prestige, resistance set in, and a cabal formed against Behn because of her sex. *The Dutch Lover* failed for a number of suspiciously coincidental reasons—poor acting (particularly in the part of the Dutch lover, played by the comedian Edward Angel), poor costuming (which made the mistaken identities unintelligible), and a missing epilogue (which had been promised by a friend). Behn responded with spirit in an epistle to the "Good, Sweet, Honey, Sugar-Candied Reader" in which she denounced the acting and costuming. She also turned her guns on the hostile members of the audience:

> Indeed that day 'twas Acted first, there comes me into the Pit, a long, lither, phlegmatick, white ill-favour'd, wretched Fop, an Officer in Masquerade newly transported with a Scarf & Feather out of France, a sorry Animal that has nought else to shield it from the uttermost contempt of all mankind, but that respect which we afford to Rats and Toads, which though we do not well allow to live, yet when considered as a part of God's Creation, we make honourable mention of them. A thing, Reader—but no more of such a Smelt: This thing, I tell ye, opening that which serves it for a mouth, out issued such a noise as this to those that sate about it, that they were to expect a woful Play, God damn him, for it was a woman's. Now how this came about I am not sure, but I suppose he brought it piping hot from some who had with him the reputation of a villanous Wit: for Creatures of his size of sense talk without all imagination, such scraps as they pick up from other folks. I would not for a world be taken arguing with such a properties as this; but if I thought there were a man of any tolerable parts, who could upon mature deliberation distinguish well his right hand from his left, and justly state the difference between the number of sixteen and two, yet had this prejudice upon him; I would take a little pains to make him know how much he errs.

She did not write a play, at least not under her own name, for three years. When she returned to the stage with *Abdelazer* (1676), it looks as though she made one more attempt to conciliate her enemies with flirtation. The epilogue "Written by a Friend" was spoken by "little Mrs. Ariell" who told the gentlemen she would "intercede" for "our Poetess":

>   my Sex's Cause
> Whose Beauty does, like Monarchs, give you
>   Laws,
> Should now command, being join'd with Wit,
>   Applause.
> Yet since our Beauty's Power's not absolute,
> She'll not the Privilege of your Sex dispute,
> But does by me submit.

Apparently the intercession did not work, for Behn was extremely careful the following year, 1677, when she brought out two plays, possibly three, anonymously. Among them was *The Rover*, the prologue of which specifically refers to the author as a man.

After the success of *The Rover*, Behn wrote again under her own name. The next year she was forced into a defense of her fine comedy *Sir Patient Fancy*. The epilogue begins:

> I here and there o'erheard a Coxcomb cry,
> Ah, Rot it—'tis a Woman's Comedy,
> One, who because she lately chanc'd to please
>   us,
> With her damn'd Stuff, will never cease to teeze
>   us.
> What has poor Woman done, that she must be
> Debar'd from Sense, and sacred Poetry?
> Why in this Age has Heaven allow'd you more,
> And Women less of Wit than heretofore?
> We once were fam'd in story, and could write
> Equal to Men; cou'd govern, nay, cou'd fight.

Behn was even blunter in the epistle to the reader: "The play had no other Misfortune but that of coming out for a Womans: had it been owned by a Man, though the most Dull Unthinking Rascally Scribler in Town, it had been a most admirable Play".

Her enemies criticized with virulence. Shadwell, for example, complained:

> Such stupid humours now the Gallants seize
> Women and Boys may write and yet may please.
> Poetess Afra though she's damned to day
> Tomorrow will put up another Play. . . .

Shadwell at least acknowledged that Behn wrote her own plays. Others charged her with plagiarism, an amusing charge considering that in the Restoration everyone borrowed from everyone else, and everyone pillaged French and Spanish sources. When Behn adapted Killigrew's unwieldy closet drama *Thomaso* into *The Rover*, she was forced to defend herself in the Post-Script to the published play. Her acknowledgement of indebtedness to Killigrew is deliberately incomplete: "I . . . hang out the Sign of Angelica (the only Stol'n Object) to give Notice where a great part of the Wit dwelt." She then comments accurately that "the Plot and Bus'ness (not to boast on't) is my own" and throws out a clever challenge: "As for the Words and Characters, I leave the Reader to judge and compare 'em with Thomaso." Here Behn had her tongue in cheek, knowing that anyone with the fortitude to read Killigrew's play would see that she had transformed his "Words and Characters" infinitely for the better. She concludes by parrying the unspoken reason for accusations against her: "Had this succeeded ill, I shou'd have had no need of imploring that Justice from the Critics, who . . . wou'd doubtless have given me the whole Honour on't." She understood quite well that the charge of plagiarism was not an attack on her use of source material but an attack on her success.

The accusation of plagiarism turned smutty. Since it was unthinkable that a woman should write good plays, then of course a man must have written them for her; and why else would a man write her plays unless he was receiving her favors? The nastiest version of this line of thinking appears in an imaginary letter to Behn by Tom Brown:

> It is no great wonder to me you should prove so witty, since so many sons of Parnassus, instead of climbing the Heliconian hill, should stoop so low, as to make your mount of Venus the barren object of their poetick fancies: I have heard some physicians say, the sweet sin of fornication draws mightily from the brain . . . if so, how could the spirit of poesy be otherwise than infus'd into you, since you always gain'd by what the fraternity of the muses lost in your embraces? . . . well might you be esteem'd a female wit, since the least return your versifying admirers could make you for your favours, was, first to lend you their assistance, and then oblige you with their applause: besides, how could you do otherwise than produce some wit to the world, since you were so often plough'd and sow'd by the kind husbandmen of Apollo?

Although this was originally published some years after Behn's death, it reflects what others said of her during her lifetime. It was rumored, for example, that John Hoyle wrote Behn's plays:

> The censuring Age has thought it fit,
> To damn a Woman, 'cause 'tis said
> The Plays she vends she never made.
> But that a Grays Inn lawyer does 'em
> Who unto Her was Friend in Bosom. . . .

Edward Ravenscroft was also suggested as the author of Behn's plays.

Another disguise for attack on Behn as a woman was the charge that her plays were obscene. This is even more amusing than the charge of plagiarism: Restoration comedy notoriously exploits sex. Behn, because she was less verbally dexterous than her famous contemporaries, was less adept at the double entendre. She was much better at erotic description of sexual delights, and she was noted for this. Dryden approved that she "so well cou'd love's kind Passion paint." Others disapproved: "She'd put luscious Bawdry off for Wit." Her plays offended those who are offended by bedroom farce:

> Again, for Instance, that clean piece of wit,
> The City Heiress, by chast Sappho writ,
> Where the lewd Widow comes, with brazen face,
> Just reeking from a Stallion's rank embrace,
> T'acquaint the Audience with her slimy case.

The probable pun here on "case" (=vagina) shows the critic none too ingenuous.

Behn was often disingenuous herself in her defenses against the charge of obscenity, often denying double entendres or bedroom jokes where they obviously existed. But there was no reason for her to be more honest than her critics. She understood their real motives better than they themselves did. With her usual intelligent directness, she put her finger exactly on the point of the attack:

> The little Obligation I have to some of the witty Sparks and Poets of the Town, has put me on a Vindication of this Comedy from those Censures that Malice, and ill Nature have thrown upon it, tho in vain: The Poets I heartily excuse, since there is a sort of Self-Interest in their Malice, which I shou'd rather call a witty Way they have in this Age, of Railing at every thing they find with pain successful. . . . And nothing makes them so thorough-stitch an Enemy as a full Third Day, that's Crime enough to load it with all manner of Infamy; and when they can no other way prevail with the Town, they charge it with the old never failing Scandal—That 'tis not fit for the Ladys.
>
> (Preface, *The Lucky Chance*)

Behn saw that it was the success of her play rather than its content that offended her critics.

Attacks on Behn as a pornographer are attacks on her for writing as uninhibitedly as a man. She understood this clearly, pointing out that the jests in celebrated plays

> are never taken Notice of, because a Man writ them, and they may hear that from them they blush at from a Woman. . . . Had I a Day or two's time . . . I would sum up all your Beloved Plays, and all the Things in them that are past with such Silence by; because written by Men: such Masculine Strokes in me, must not be allow'd.
>
> (Preface, *The Lucky Chance*)

In another place she wrote:

> I Printed this Play with all the impatient haste one ought to do, who would be vindicated from the most unjust and silly aspersion . . . which only my being a Woman has procured me; *That it was Baudy,* the least and most Excusable fault in Men writers, to whose Plays they all crowd, as if they came to no other end than to hear what they condemn in this: *but from a Woman it was unnaturall.*
>
> (To the Reader, *Sir Patient Fancy*)

That goes straight to the heart of the three-hundred-year controversy about Behn's alleged pornography. Those who defend Behn from this "unjust and silly aspersion" say that she wrote exactly as her masculine contemporaries did. But this defense is precisely the reason for the attack. It is time to lay this old argument to rest, simply noting that Behn's works praise sexual pleasure and that she therefore does not display the kind of sexual nastiness found in the works of misogynists like, say, Wycherley.

During the late 1680s attacks on Behn became more viciously personal. She suffered from some painful crippling disease, she was chronically strapped for money, and her beauty had faded. Her enemies spared her on none of these misfortunes, suggesting that they were due to syphilis:

> Doth that lewd Harlot, that Poetick Quean,
> Fam'd through White Fryars, you know who I
>   mean,
> Mend for reproof, others set up in spight
> To flux, take glisters, vomits, purge and write.
> Long with a Sciatica she's beside lame,
> Her limbs distortur'd, Nerves shrunk up with
>   pain,
> And therefore I'll all sharp reflections shun,
> Poverty, Poetry, Pox, are plagues enough for
>   one.

Her troubles were increased by the crushing of her political loyalties, for she lived to see James II deposed in the Glorious Revolution.

Aphra Behn died 16 April 1689, reputedly at the hands of "an unskilful Physician" ("Memoirs"), and was buried under two verses probably by Hoyle:

> Here lies a Proof that Wit can never be
> Defence enough against Mortality.

She died in poverty and out of favor politically, but she was the first woman whose pen won her burial in Westminster Abbey. Although all her life she had written to earn a living, once when defending herself against charges of plagiarism, she had complained, "I make Verses, and others have the Fame" (Post-Script, *The Rover*). Later she wrote, "I am not content to write for a Third day only. I value Fame as much as if I had been born a *Hero;* and if you rob me of that, I can retire from the ungrateful World, and scorn its fickle Favours" (Preface, *The Lucky Chance*). At the end of her life she inserted into a translation some verses of her own, an apostrophe to Daphne:

> I, by a double right, thy bounties claim,
> Both from my sex, and in Apollo's name.
> Let me with Sappho and Orinda be,
> Oh ever sacred nymph, adorned by thee.
> And give my verses immortality.

She won the literary immortality she coveted. Although she died neglected, the posthumous appearance of a number of plays and novels, revivals of her plays, and dramatic adaptations of her novels established her reputation firmly. In 1691 Gerard Langbaine's *Account of the English Dramatick Poets* described "Mrs. Astraea Behn" as "A Person lately deceased, but whose Memory will be long fresh amongst the Lovers of Dramatick Poetry". In 1694 Thomas Southerne adapted Behn's novel *History of the Nun* into the highly successful play *The Fatal Marriage.* The next year Southerne made a hit play out of *Oroonoko,* this time making a handsome admission of his source: "I stand engaged to Mrs. Behn for the Occasion of a most Passionate Distress in my Last Play; and in a Conscience that I had not made her a sufficient Acknowledgment, I have run further into her Debt for *Oroonoko,* with a Design to oblige me to be honest; and that every one may find me out for Ingratitude, when I

don't say all that's fit for me upon that Subject. She had a great Command of the Stage" (Epistle Dedicatory, *Oroonoko*). The first collection of her novels was published in 1696, and further novels were published in 1698 and 1700. In the eighteenth century the collected novels were printed repeatedly, *Oroonoko* was translated into French and German, and the collected plays went into a third edition.

Behn's success inspired a new generation of women playwrights, although at first it did not seem that this would happen. In 1689 a "Young Lady of Quality" wrote a broadside "Elegy Upon the Death of Mrs. A. Behn; The Incomparable Astrea." The elegist lamented:

> Of her own Sex, not one is found
> Who dares her Laurel wear,
> Witheld by Impotence or Fear. . . .

Duffy on the neglect of Behn:

Literary survival is largely a matter of fashion and chance. No greater gods preside over it and we deceive ourselves if we think they do, that we have a just appraisal of what is excellent and worth preserving from the millions of words ever written. The work of a single writer, of a school or of a whole era can be dismissed to the dustheap where broken reputations lie about like discarded toys. If anyone disputes this I should remind him of just one instance: the resurrection job T.S. Eliot and others had to do on the metaphysicals, and in particular on one of the greatest of English writers, John Donne, earlier this century.

It's therefore no surprise that the woman on the Clapham bus should be unable to answer when asked the name of the first woman in England to earn her living as a professional writer and even when prompted 'Aphra Behn', should be completely unresponsive. For Aphra Behn has suffered not only a personal eclipse which is almost unparalleled in literary history but the eclipse of her whole idiom, English baroque, in the company of as acknowledged a genius as Dryden, to whom we pay an examination paper lipservice without any real appreciation or much understanding. Where we have acknowledged her existence it has usually been to mock or abuse her apparently without even the justification of having read her work.

> *Maureen Duffy, in* The Passionate Shepherdess:
>   Aphra Behn, 1640-89, *Jonathan Cape, 1977.*

Jane Spencer (essay date 1986)

SOURCE: "Three Self-Portraits: Aphra Behn, Delariviere Manley, Jane Barker," in *The Rise of the Woman Novelist from Aphra Behn to Jane Austen,* Basil Blackwell, 1986, pp. 41-74.

[*In the following excerpt, Spencer discusses Behn's view of herself as a female writer as seen in the author's use of narrative voice in her works.*]

Aphra Behn's comments on herself as a writer are sprinkled liberally in the prefaces to her plays. She had to struggle for recognition of her right to a professional role—hence her tart remarks that women were equally entitled to write bawdy, and that people would have admired her plays more if they had thought a man had written them. To someone so determined to be accepted on equal terms with men, a good deal of the praise she was given must have been more galling than gratifying. Her admirers were busy building her a reputation as a writer of love, praising her poems for being erotic, even suggesting that reading Behn was tantamount to being seduced by her. Thomas Creech's poem to her announced:

> . . . thy Pen disarms us so,
> We yield our selves to the first beauteous Foe;
> The easie softness of thy thoughts surprise,
> And this new way Love steals into our Eyes; . . .
> In the same trance with the young pair we lie,
> And in their amorous Ecstasies we die . . .

Using another common assumption about femininity, one eulogist saw her work as evidence of her delicate understanding of the mysteries of nature, women and love.

> What Passions does your Poetry impart?
> It shows th'unfathom'd thing a Woman's Heart,
> Tells what Love is, his Nature and his Art,
> Displays the several Scenes of Hopes and Fears,
> Love's Smiles, his Sighs, his Laughing and his
>   Tears.

A posthumous edition of her poems was introduced with similar claims: 'The Passions, that of Love especially, she was Mistress of, and gave us such nice and tender Touches of them, that without her Name we might discover the Author. Behn was certainly not above exploiting this image of herself when it came to selling her poems and her translation of Balthazar de Bonnecourse's *La Monstre, The Lover's Watch: or, the Art of making love*. Love was her subject here, and the encomium poems printed at the beginning of these volumes served as advertisements of the fact. Moreover, it is certainly fair that she should be remembered as a poet of love, when we consider such deservedly celebrated lyrics as **'Love in Fantastic Triumph sate'** and **'A Thousand Martyrs I have made'**. To Behn, though, love was not an especially feminine subject, it was simply an important poetic theme; and it was as a poet, simply, that she wanted to be remembered. 'Poetry (my Talent)', she wrote in proud parentheses, deceptively casual. In the preface to one of her comedies, *The Lucky Chance* (1687), she asked for a very different kind of recognition from the kind she got:

> All I ask, is the Priviledge for my Masculine Part the Poet in me, (if any such you will allow me) to tread in those successful Paths my Predecessors have so long thriv'd in, to take those Measures that both the Ancient and Modern Writers have set me, and by which they have pleas'd the World so well: If I must not, because

of my Sex, have this Freedom, but that you will usurp all to your selves; I lay down my Quill . . . for I am not content to write for a Third day only [i.e. just for money: playwrights took the proceeds of the third performance]. I value Fame as much as if I had been born a *Hero* . . .

Instead of placing herself in the tradition of Sappho and Orinda, Behn is appealing here to the precedent of all the 'Ancient and Modern Writers', mostly men, and defining her poetic talent as masculine. The freedom she is demanding here is the freedom to write without any special restraints because of her sex.

Behn tended to compromise her claim for the freedom to write as men wrote by simultaneously denying that she wrote bawdy plays as they did: 'they charge [*The Lucky Chance*] with the old never failing Scandal—That 'tis not fit for the Ladys: As if (if it as they falsly give it out) the Ladys were oblig'd to hear Indecencys only from their Pens and Plays.' However, the fact that her comedies were successful on the stage in the 1670s and 1680s indicates that she escaped the requirements of 'decency' soon to bear especially hard on women. Her success in Restoration comedy has been held against her by some recent critics who find her work *too* 'masculine': reproducing the attitudes of male libertines, so that the hero of her comedy *The Rover* (1677) is rewarded for his philandering by marriage to the chaste heroine, who (as it transpires in the sequel to the play) soon dies, leaving him free to rove once more. Behn is not without general concern for her sex and for women's freedom, as her plays' treatment of arranged marriages and her heroines' criticisms of various masculine tyrannies demonstrate. Still, it is outside the plays themselves that she supports women most thoroughly, through her claims for women's abilities as writers.

Her novels are particularly interesting from this point of view, because in them she tackles the problem of the woman writer's authority by creating an explicitly female narrator. Fiction formed a large part of Behn's output in her later years. First to be published was *Love Letters Between a Nobleman and his Sister*, in three volumes from 1784 to 1787. Based on the contemporary scandal of Lord Grey of Werke's elopement with his sister-in-law Lady Henrietta Berkeley, and containing much anti-Monmouth sentiment at the time of Monmouth's rebellion, it contained enough sexual and political intrigue to be very popular. Behn published several other works of fiction during her lifetime, the most important being *The Fair Jilt* (1688) and *Oroonoko* (1688), and there are several stories written probably about 1685 but not published until after her death.

Her experiments with narrative technique are notable. The first part of *Love Letters* is as the title suggests, epistolary, and the heroine's passionate letters have led to comparisons with the Portuguese nun, though here the man replies and the lovers are united. But emphasis on epistolary passion obscures the political and satirical slant of the work. Some of Silvia's letters to Philander are attempts to dissuade him from joining Monmouth in the Rye House Plot against Charles II. Philander's response shows that his adoration of Silvia is a cloak for political ambition. 'I design no more by this great enterprize, than to make thee some glorious thing', he tells her, but soon adds, 'in going on, Oh *Silvia!* When three Kingdoms shall lie unpossest, and be exposed, as it were, amongst the raffling Crowd, who knows but the chance may be mine, as well as any others . . . ?'

In the second and third parts, Behn turned to third-person narration, which allowed her to develop more clearly her own ironic comments on Silvia and Philander. Her narrator undercuts any claim Silvia has to be a passionate heroine in the tradition of the Portuguese nun: Silvia has 'no other design on [Octavio, another admirer], bating the little Vanity of her Sex, which is an Ingredient so inter-mixt with the greatest Vertues of Womenkind, that those who endeavour to cure 'em of that disease, rob them of a very considerable pleasure . . . whatever other Knowl-edge they want, they have still enough to set a price on Beauty.' Generalizing from Silvia, the narrator comments on all female behaviour: Eve's 'love of Novelty and Knowledge has been intaile'd upon her Daughters ever since, and I have known more Women rendred unhappy and miserable from this torment of Curiosity, which they bring upon themselves, than have ever been undone by less villainous Men.' Such narrative comments seem to reiterate standard views of false womankind from a male perspective. The reason for this may be that Behn was modelling her narrative voice on that of Paul Scarron, whose *Comic Novels* were popular at this time in England as well as in his native France. Scarron's intrusive, sar-donic and obviously masculine narrators place his work in a comic tradition later developed further by Le Sage and Fielding. Aphra Behn's story ***The Court of the King of Bantam,*** published posthumously in 1698, was said to have been written as 'a Trial of Skill, upon a Wager, to shew that she was able to write in the Style of the cele-brated *Scarron,* in Imitation of whom 'tis writ', and its facetious wit suggests that she must have won her bet. Already, though, Behn was moving away from the im-plicitly male viewpoint imitation of Scarron encouraged in her. The narrator of ***The Court of the King of Bantam,*** identified as a friend of the heroine, Philibella, rather than the more central male characters, might best be envisaged as a woman. In most of the other stories the narrator is clearly female.

In ***The Unfortunate Happy Lady,*** the narrator, describing the talk of a procuress and her girls, comments, 'our Sex seldom wants matter of Tattle'. The narrator of ***The History of the Nun: or, the Fair Vow-Breaker*** (1689), con-fides to the reader that she was once encouraged to be-come a nun (*Works,* V). Describing a duel between the heroine's rival lovers in ***The Nun: or, The Perjur'd Beauty*** (1698), the narrator exclaims, 'Ah! how wretched are our Sex, in being the unhappy Occasion of so many fatal Mischiefs, even between the dearest Friends!' (V). In ***The Unfortunate Bride: or, The Blind Lady a Beauty,*** she tells us, ''tis the Humour of our Sex, to deny most eager-ly those Grants to Lovers, for which most tenderly we

sigh, so contradictory are we to our selves' (V). In these stories the narrator identifies herself as a woman with the authority to make general statements about female na-ture—which are essentially the same as the stereotyped views she offered from a man's perspective in ***Love Let-ters.***

There are times when Behn develops her narrative com-ments in the direction of that specifically feminine au-thority to comment on women's experience and on love, which her admirers were ready to grant her, but which in the prefaces to her plays she ignored so as to claim the same authority as men. In ***The History of the Nun: or, the Fair Vow Breaker,*** the narrator professes to offer new insights into love that are not available to most people:

> Love, like Reputation, once fled, never returns more. 'Tis impossible to love, and cease to love, (and love another) and yet return again to the first Passion, tho' the Person have all the Charms, or a thousand times more than it had, when it first conquer'd. This Mistery in Love, it may be, is not generally known, but nothing is more certain. (V)

She also offers her experience as authority for advice on how to treat young women, explaining:

> I once was design'd an humble Votary in the House of Devotion, but fancying my self not endu'd with an obstinacy of Mind, great enough to secure me from the Efforts and Vanities of the World, I rather chose to deny my self that Content I could not certainly promise my self, than to languish (as I have seen some do) in a certain Affliction.

She adds that she now thinks it a mistake to prefer the 'false ungrateful World' to the peaceful cloister, but:

> nevertheless. I could wish, for the prevention of abundance of Mischiefs and Miseries, that Nunneries and Marriages were not to be enter'd into, 'till the Maid, so destin'd, were of a mature Age to make her own Choice; and that Parents would not make use of their justly assum'd Authority to compel their Children, neither to the one or the other. (V)

Claiming a woman's right to advise and slanting her ad-vice in the direction of young women's freedom to choose their destiny, Behn here is very close to many of the woman novelists of the eighteenth century.

Often Behn makes her narrator not simply a woman but specifically the self-portrait of a well-known author, re-ferring in passing to her own works. In ***The Dumb Virgin*** she is so pleased with the hero's assumed name of Dan-gerfield that 'being since satisfied it was a Counterfeit, I us'd it in a Comedy of mine' (V). In ***Oroonoko*** she mentions meeting Colonel *Martin,* a man of great Gal-lantry, Wit, and Goodness, and whom I have celebrated in a Character of my new Comedy, by his own Name, in Memory of so brave a Man' (V). The events of ***The Fair Jilt*** are said to have taken place in Antwerp, 'about the

Time of my being sent thither by King *Charles'* (V, 98), referring to a spying mission she undertook in 1666 to obtain information from a former friend William Scot, son of one of the regicides. Clearly one purpose of references like this was to impress upon her readers the literal truth of her narratives, whose events she claimed to have witnessed; and recent research shows that *Oroonoko* and *The Fair Jilt,* at least, have their basis in truth. Another reason for putting her self-portrait into her novels is to include in them her vindication of the woman writer's ability and authority.

This is most evident in *Oroonoko,* where the autobiographical element means that Behn's interest in the narrator's position develops into an examination of her own role as woman and as writer. This fascinating novel marks an important stage in the history of women's quest for literary authority. Writing before the full establishment of the convention that love is the woman writer's subject and a moral aim her excuse, Behn has a freedom denied to most of her eighteenth-century descendants. She ranges widely over different societies, to investigate the meaning of civilized values in a story beyond the scope of many more polished later novelists. *Oroonoko* is the story of an African prince tricked into boarding a slave vessel and taken to Surinam while it is under English occupation. Because of his royal bearing Oroonoko (or Caesar, as the English appropriately rename him) is treated with respect by the Cornish gentleman, Trefry, who becomes his master. In Surinam he meets his long-lost love, Imoinda, also a slave, and they marry and conceive a child. Unwilling to have his child born into slavery, Oroonoko foments and leads a slave rebellion, which is suppressed. He is cruelly beaten. Vowing revenge, he takes his wife into the forest and kills her to prevent her falling into his enemies' hands; but after her death he loses his resolution and remains by her body. When he is recaptured he inflicts horrible injuries on himself, and then on the orders of General Byam, Deputy Governor of Surinam, he is executed. The tale affords a picture of an exotic colony (lost to the Dutch by the time of *Oroonok*'s publication), and shows the English in their relations with its native people and with the African slave-trade. Three very different cultures—the European, the native Surinam, and that of Coramantien, Oroonoko's African home—are compared to one another. Thus it is a novel of ideas as well as action, and the narrator's comments are crucial to the rendering of these.

She is a narrator of a type especially common in the early novel—herself a character within the tale, relating it with the authority of an eye-witness. Neither omniscient and outside the action, nor central to it, she provides her commentary on the events she narrates. Having travelled out to Surinam, as we know Aphra Behn herself did, she meets the enslaved Oroonoko, hears the story of his past life and adventures, and either sees or hears of the rest of his story up to his dreadful end. Trefry, she tells us, once intended to write the hero's life, but died before he could do it, and so the task fell to her, which, she says modestly, is a pity for Oroonoko. 'His Misfortune was, to fall in an obscure World, that afforded only a Female Pen to celebrate his Fame' (V). Yet as events unfold we realize that her gender is an important part of her authority: what she knows, and the comments she is able to make, depend on it. The female pen is vindicated.

The scene is set for Oroonoko's story by the narrator's description of Surinam. The Surinam natives represent 'an absolute *Idea* of the first State of Innocence, before Man knew how to sin: And 'tis most evident and plain, that simple Nature is the most harmless, inoffensive and virtuous Mistress (V). Civilization could only bring repression, and 'Religion would here but destroy that Tranquillity they possess by Ignorance; and Laws would but teach 'em to know Offences, of which now they have no Notion' (V). Their simplicity contrasts markedly with the duplicity shown by the white community throughout the story.

The story of Oroonoko's Coramantien life provides another contrast to Europe. Here it is not so much a case of the noble savage against civilization, as that of the truly civilized man against a decadent society. The young prince Oroonoko embodies the Restoration's heroic ideal: proud, honourable, superhuman in his prowess in battle, and 'as capable of love, as 'twas possible for a brave and gallant Man to be; and in saying that, I have named the highest Degree of Love: for sure great Souls are most capable of that Passion' (V). His wit, his judgement, and his character all in all are as great 'as if his Education had been in some *European* court' (V). His experiences show those Europeans whose highest values he has adopted in a very poor light. From the captain who tricks him aboard the slave-ship, to Byam, Deputy-Governor of Surinam, who tricks him into surrender after the slave rebellion, they fail to live up to their own code of honour.

The contrast between the African prince and the English people is used to expose what Behn saw as the recent betrayal of civilized values by the English. Oroonoko, royal himself, echoes his creator's royalist sentiments when he expresses horror at the execution of Charles I, 'with all the Sense and Abhorrence of the Injustice imaginable' (V). He and his countrymen 'pay a most absolute Resignation to the Monarch, especially when he is a Parent also' (V), most unlike the English, with Monmouth's plot against his father Charles II in their recent history by the time Behn was writing Oroonoko's story. The Coramantiens' attitudes to sexual relationships compare well with the Europeans', too. Oroonoko's early passion for Imoinda 'aimed at nothing but Honour, if such a Distinction may be made in Love; and especially in that Country, where Men take to themselves as many as they can maintain; and where the only Crime and Sin against a Woman, is, to turn her off, to abandon her to Want, Shame and Misery: such ill Morals are only practis'd in *Christian* countries' (V).

As narrator, Behn has two assets which enable her to make Oroonoko's story serve this critique of her own society: her intimate acquaintance with and sympathy for the hero himself and her own identity as one of the Europeans, but not so completely at one with them that she cannot take a detached view of them.

Both these narrative assets are enhanced because of her social position and her sex. She has travelled out to Surinam with her father, who was to be Lieutenant-Governor of the colony, but died on the voyage. She lives in the best house on the plantation and has, she claims, 'none above me in that Country'. She thus has status but no occupation, and no permanent stake in the colony; so she is well-placed to observe and comment freely. As a woman she can comment with authority on Oroonoko's gallantry and attractiveness. When she first saw him, she explains, he 'addressed himself to me, and some other Women, with the best Grace in the World' (V). She gets to know him well because 'he liked the Company of us Women much above the Men' (V). In fact 'we [women] had all the Liberty of Speech with him, especially my self, whom he call'd his *Great Mistress;* and indeed my World would go a great Way with him' (V). Thus she hears his story from his own lips and is able to report his noble sentiments.

The narrator also enters the action, exploiting Oroonoko's gallantry and his attachment to her in order to keep him under the control of the white settlers. Oroonoko is suspicious of their promises to set him free when the Lord Governor arrives, an attitude justified by his former experience of the Christian word of honour and by the narrator's comment that they 'fed him from Day to Day with Promises' (V). The settlers, fearing a slave mutiny, ask the narrator to use her influence to persuade Oroonoko to wait till the Lord Governor makes his appearance. This she does, and it is hard to tell whether she does so in good faith or not. Her admiration for his heroic scorn of slavery sits oddly with her actions: 'I neither thought it convenient to trust him much out of our View, nor did the Country, who fear'd him', she reports (V), relating how she and the other settlers surround Oroonoko with 'attendants' who are really spies. She encourages the royal slave to take several pleasant 'Diversions'—hunting tigers, fishing, visiting the Surinam Indians—the real purpose of which is to divert his thoughts from rebellion. She seems to be acting entirely, and with typical duplicity, as a European; but once the rebellion breaks out the narrator's ability to detach herself from her society's crimes becomes evident.

The whites, it now transpires, are split. Byam, 'a Fellow, whose Character is not fit to be mentioned with the worst of the Slaves' (V), is for taking strong measures against the rebels, but 'they of the better sort', including the narrator, believe that Oroonoko has been badly treated and should not be harshly dealt with now (V). Trefry joins in the pursuit of the rebels, meaning to act as mediator; but, duped by Byam's promises of leniency, he persuades Oroonoko to surrender, and unwittingly leads him into a trap. The narrator now separates herself from the Europeans responsible for Oroonoko's downfall. She neither sides with Byam's cruelty nor shows Trefry's gullibility. If the reader wonders why someone of her high social position did nothing to protect Oroonoko from the vicious treatment he gets, the answer lies in her sex. As a woman, she has had to flee from the scene of action:

> You must know, that when the News was brought on *Monday* Morning, that *Caesar* had betaken himself to the Woods, and carry'd with him all the *Negroes,* we were possess'd with extreme Fear, which no Persuasions could dissipate, that he would secure himself till Night, and then would come down and cut all our Throats. This Apprehension made all the Females of us fly down the River, to be secured; and while we were away, they acted this Cruelty; for I suppose I had Authority and Interest enough there, had I suspected any such Thing, to have prevented it.
>   (V)

The trust between the royal slave and his 'Great Mistress' has been shattered by their racial differences, and yet her ignominious flight reveals similarities in the positions of the European woman and the enslaved African man. Like Oroonoko, who is given the outward respect due to a prince but kept from real power, the narrator is under the illusion that she has high status in the colony; but when it comes to a crisis the men are the real rulers, and being the daughter of a man who would have governed Surinam if he had lived does not help her. Ironically, she still seems to believe in her 'Authority and Interest' as she tells a story which reveals how illusory these were.

The narrator's gender is now her alibi. It saves her from sharing the guilt of her countrymen's treatment of the noble black prince, and, by implication, from sharing in the general corruption of the European society she criticizes. She is absent at other key moments too. She has to leave the hero when she sees his self-inflicted wounds, being 'but sickly, and very apt to fall into Fits of dangerous Illness upon any extraordinary Melancholy' (V). She is still away when he is executed. Her mother and sister (scarcely mentioned in the story up to this point) witness the event in her stead, but they are 'not suffer'd to save him' (V). Their position here is like the narrator's throughout: a spectator, but because of her femininity, a helpless one.

This feminine position, though, is an appropriate one for a narrator. On the fringes of her world, she is unable to act in the decisive scenes, but she observes, records, and eventually hands the story down to posterity. In ***Oroonoko*** the narrator's femininity is especially important because the similarities between the slave's and the woman's positions allow her her sympathetic insight into the hero's feelings at the same time as she creates a full sense of the difference of his race and culture. The limitations on women which Behn acknowledges, even exploits, within her narrative, do not apply to expression. As a character the narrator seems caught uneasily between admiration for her hero and allegiance to European civilization, but this means that she can present a picture of both sides. She ends with a flourish that implicitly asserts women's equal right to be recorders of events and interpreters of the world:

> Thus died this great Man, worthy of a better Fate, and a more sublime Wit than mine to write his Praise: Yet, I hope, the Reputation of my Pen is considerable enough to make his glorious Name to survive to all

Ages, with that of the brave, the beautiful and the constant *Imoinda*. (V)

The reputation of Aphra Behn's pen certainly was great at the time that *Oroonoko* was written, and she uses that reputation to present the female narrator as authoritative, disinterested and sympathetic, with as much authority as a male writer and also with special insights gained from her woman's position.

The marginality of the narrator's position is very important to Behn for another reason. It enables her to create her self-image as a writer, free from some of the restrictions on behaviour and feeling which operate on women as represented in the narrative. The contrast between the heroine, Imoinda, and the woman who writes her story is instructive. Imoinda is all that convention could desire of a noble hero's mate: beautiful, sensitive, ready to sacrifice all to preserve her chastity, capable of brave deeds in defence of her husband, and above all, devoted to him. Her qualities are best seen in her eagerness to die at his hands: when Oroonoko explains that he must kill her to preserve her honour, 'He found the heroick Wife faster pleading for Death, than he was to propose it' (V). The narrator explains this attitude as part of exotic Coramantien custom: 'For Wives have a Respect for their Husbands equal to what any other People pay a Deity; and when a Man finds any Occasion to quit his Wife, if he love her, she dies by his Hand; if not, he sells her, or suffers some other to kill her' (V). The killing of Imoinda shocks Oroonoko's European friends, but is presented as 'a Deed, (that however horrid it first appear'd to us all) when we had heard his Reasons, we thought it brave and just' (V). Here an uneasy note creeps into the narrator's assessment of Coramantien, the place where natural honour and nobility are supposed to thrive. It has crept in before whenever women's position was considered. African polygamy is useful for the purposes of a satirical attack on European sexual hypocrisy, but Behn holds back from endorsing it as a real alternative by making Oroonoko vow to be true all his life to Imoinda alone; and the whole Coramantien episode shows that heroic society torn apart by the quarrel between Oroonoko and his grandfather the king over possession of the heroine. Writing *Oroonoko,* Behn was confronted with the problem of a woman's relation to the heroic ideal which she, along with other Restoration writers, endorsed. In some ways Behn identifies with her hero, but in the story of Oroonoko and his wife her position, as a woman, might be expected to be more analogous with Imoinda's, and that is an identification she does not want to make.

The female narrator Behn creates is important for *not* being the heroine. It is a pity that the autobiographical element of *Oroonoko* has caused so much criticism to centre on the truth or otherwise of the self-portrait within it, for Behn was deliberately not focusing on her own experience, and at a time when heroine and woman writer were coming to seem almost synonymous, she insisted on making a sharp distinction between them. If Imoinda, ideally lovely and noble, is Oroonoko's true mate, the narrator is his 'Great Mistress', sympathising with him, surviving him, recording his story, and assessing his sig-nificance. From the narrative stance Behn creates in this novel it is evident that for her being a writer was a way of escaping some of the limitations imposed on women.

Her prefaces claim a man's rights in writing, and her narratives claim something of a special authority as a woman, but without acknowledging any of the limitations on feminine expression that were later to come into force. Her double claim is well expressed in some lines she inserted into her translation of the sixth book of Cowley's Latin work, *Of Plants.* Here, unusually for her, she calls on the examples of Sappho and Orinda. The poet has been invoking Daphne, source of the poet's laurels, and then 'the Translatress in her own Person' addresses her:

> I, by a double Right, thy Bounties claim,
> Both from my Sex, and in *Apollo's* Name:
> Let me with *Sappho* and *Orinda* be,
> Oh ever sacred Nymph, adorn'd by thee;
> And give my verses Immortality.

Behn's confidence in her own authority as a woman writer is not matched in the century following her death.

Catherine Gallagher (essay date 1988)

SOURCE: "Who Was that Masked Woman? The Prostitute and the Playwright in the Comedies of Aphra Behn," in *Women's Studies: An Interdisciplinary Journal,* Vol 15, No. 1-3, 1988, pp. 23-42.

[*Here, Gallagher focuses on* The Lucky Chance, *exploring how Behn "created a persona that skillfully intertwined the age's available discourses concerning women, property, selfhood and authorship."*]

Everyone knows that Aphra Behn, England's first professional female author, was a colosal and enduring embarrassment to the generations of women who followed her into the literary marketplace. An ancestress whose name had to be lived down rather than lived up to, Aphra Behn seemed, in Virginia Woolf's metaphor, to obstruct the very passageway to the profession of letters she had herself opened. Woolf explains in *A Room of One's Own,* "Now that Aphra Behn had done it, girls could go to their parents and say, You need not give me an allowance; I can make money by my pen. Of course the answer for many years to come was, Yes, by living the life of Aphra Behn! Death would be better! and the door was slammed faster than ever."

It is impossible in this brief essay to examine all the facets of the scandal of Aphra Behn; her life and works were alike characterized by certain irregular sexual arrangements. But it is not these that I want to discuss, for they seem merely incidental, the sorts of things women writers would easily dissociate themselves from if they led pure lives and wrote high-minded books. The scandal I would like to discuss is, however, with varying degree of appropriateness, applicable to all female authors, regardless of the conduct of their lives or the content of their works. It is a scandal that Aphra Behn seems quite purposely to have constructed out of the overlapping discourses of commercial, sexual, and linguistic exchange. Conscious of her historical role, she introduced to the world of English letters the professional woman writer as a new-fangled whore.

This persona has many functions in Behn's works: it titillates, scandalizes, arouses pity, and indicates the vicissitudes of authorship and identity in general. The author-whore persona also makes of female authorship per se a dark comedy that explores the bond between the liberty the stage offered women and their confinement behind both literal and metaphorical vizard masks. This is the comedy played out, for example, in the prologue to her first play, **The Forced Marriage,** where she announces her epoch-making appearance in the ranks of the play-wrights. She presents her attainment, however, not as a daring achievement of self-expression, but as a new proof of the necessary obscurity of the "public" woman.

The prologue presents Aphra Behn's playwrighting as an extension of her erotic play. In it, a male actor pretends to have escaped temporarily the control of the intriguing female play-wright; he comes on stage to warn the gallants in the audience of their danger. This was a variation on the Restoration convention of betraying the playwright in the Prologue with an added sexual dimension: the comic antagonism between playwright and audience becomes a battle in the war between the sexes. Playwrighting, warns the actor, is a new weapon in woman's amorous arsenal. She will no longer wound only through the eyes, through her beauty, but will also use wit to gain a more permanent ascendency. Here, woman's playwriting is wholly assimilated to the poetic conventions of amorous battle that normally informed lyric poetry. If the male poet had long depicted the conquering woman as necessarily chaste, debarring (and consequently debarred from) the act of sex itself, then his own poetry of lyric complaint and pleas for kindness could only be understood as attempts to overthrow the conqueror. Poetry in this lyric tradition is a weapon in a struggle that takes as its most fundamental ground-rule a woman's inability to have a truly *sexual* conquest: for the doing of the deed would be the undoing of her power.

Aphra Behn's first Prologue, stretches this lyric tradition to incorporate theatre. However, the woman's poetry cannot have the same *end* as the man's. Indeed, according to the Prologue, ends, in the sense of terminations, are precisely what a woman's wit is directed against:

> Women those charming victors, in whose eyes
> Lie all their arts, and their artilleries,
> Not being contented with the wounds they made,
> Would by new stratagems our lives invade.
> Beauty alone goes now at too cheap rates
> And therefore they, like wise and politic states,
> Court a new power that may the old supply,
> To *Keep* as well as gain the victory:
> They'll join the force of wit to beauty now,
> And so *maintain* the right they have in you.

Writing is certainly on a continuum here with sex, but instead of leading to the act in which the woman's conquest is overturned, playwriting is supposed to extend the woman's erotic power beyond the moment of sexual encounter. The prologue, then, situates the drama inside the conventions of male lyric love poetry but then reverses the chronological relationship between sex and writing; the male poet writes before the sexual encounter, the woman between encounters. She thereby actually creates the possibility of a woman's version of sexual conquest. She will not be immediately conquered and discarded because she will maintain her right through her writing. The woman's play of wit is the opposite of foreplay; it is a kind of afterplay specifically designed to prolong pleasure, rescucitate desire and keep a woman who has given herself sexually from being traded in for another woman. If the woman is successful in her poetic exchange, the actor warns the gallants, then they will no longer have the freedom of briskly exchanging mistresses: "You'll never know the bliss of change; this art Retrieves (when beauty fades) the wandring heart."

Aphra Behn, then, inaugurated her career by taking up and feminizing the role of the seductive lyric poet. The drama the audience is about to see is framed by the larger comedy of erotic exchange between a woman writer and a male audience. That is, this prologue does what so many Restoration prologues do, makes of the play a drama within a drama, one series of conventional interactions inside another. But the very elaborateness of this staging of conventions makes the love battle itself (the thing supposedly revealed) seem a strategic pose in a somewhat different drama. After all, what kind of woman would stage her sexual desire as her primary motivation? The answer is a woman who might be suspected not to have any: a woman for whom professions of amorousness and theatrical in authenticity are the same thing: a prostitute. Finally, just in case anyone in the audience might have missed this analogy, a dramatic interruption occurs, and the prologue stages a debate about the motivation behind all this talk of strategy. The actor calls attention to the prostitutes in the audience, who were generally identified by their masks, and characterizes them as agents of the playwright, jokingly using their masks to expose them as spies in the amorous war:

> The poetess too, they say, has spies abroad,
> Which have dispers'd themselves in every road,
> I' th' upper box, pit, galleries; every face
> You find disguis'd in a black velvet case.
> My life on't; is her spy on purpose sent,
> To hold you in a wanton compliment;
> That so you may not censure what she's writ,
> Which done they face you down 'twas full of
>   wit.

At this point, an actress comes on stage to refute the suggestion that the poetess's spies and supporters are prostitutes. She returns, then, to the conceits linking money and warfare and thus explicitly enacts the denial of prostitution that was all along implicit in the trope of amorous combat. Unlike the troop of prostitutes, she claims,

> Ours scorns the petty spoils, and do prefer
> The glory not the interest of war.
> But yet our forces shall obliging prove,
> Imposing naught but constancy in love:
> That's all our aim, and when we have it too,
> We'll sacrifice it all to pleasure you.

What the last two lines make abundantly clear, in ironically justifying female promiscuity by the pleasure it gives to men, is that the prologue has given us the spectacle of a prostitute comically denying mercenary motivations. The poetess like the prostitute is she who "stands out," as the etymology of the word "prostitute" implies, but it is also she who is masked. Indeed, as the prologue emphasizes, the prostitute is she who stands out by virtue of her mask. The dramatic masking of the prostitute and the stagey masking of the playwright's interest in money are exactly parallel cases of theatrical unmasking in which what is revealed is the parallel itself: the playwright is a whore.

This conclusion, however, is more complex than it might at first seem, for the very playfulness of the representation implies a hidden "real" woman who must remain unavailable. The prologue gives two explanations for female authorship, and they are the usual excuses for prostitution: it alludes to and disclaims the motive of money; it claims the motive of love, but in a way that makes the claim seem merely strategic. The author-whore, then, is one who comically stages her lack of self-expression and consequently implies that her true identity is the sold self's seller. She thus indicates an unseeable selfhood through the flamboyant alienation of her language.

Hence Aphra Behn managed to create the effect of an inaccessible authenticity out of the very image of prostitution. In doing so, she capitalized on a commonplace slur that probably kept many less ingenious women out of the literary marketplace. "Whore's the like reproachful name, as poetess—the luckless twins of shame," wrote Robert Gould in 1691. The equation of poetess and "punk" (in the slang of the day) was inescapable in the Restoration. A woman writer could either deny it in the content and form of her publications, as did Catherine Trotter, or she could embrace it, as did Aphra Behn. But she could not entirely avoid it. For the belief that "Punk and Poesie agree so pat, / You cannot well be *this,* and not be *that*" was held independently of particular cases. It rested on the evidence neither of how a woman lived nor of what she wrote. It was, rather, an a priori judgement applied to all cases of female publication. As one of Aphra Behn's biographers, Angeline Goreau, has astutely pointed out [in *Reconstructing Aphra,* 1980], the seventeenth-century ear heard the word "public" in "publication" very distinctly, and hence a woman's publication automatically implied a public woman. The woman who shared the contents of her mind instead of reserving them for one man was literally, not metaphorically, trading in her *sexual* property. If she were married, she was selling what did not belong to her, because in *mind and body* she should have given herself to her husband. In the seventeenth century, "publication," Goreau tells us, also meant

sale due to bankruptcy, and the publication of the contents of a woman's mind was tantamount to the publication of her husband's property. In 1613, Lady Carey published (anonymously, of course) these lines on marital property rights, publication and female integrity:

> Then she usurps upon another's right,
> That seeks to be by public language graced;
> And tho' her thoughts reflect with purest light
> Her mind, if not peculiar, is not chaste.
> For in a wife it is no worse to find
> A common body, than a common mind.

Publication, adultery, and trading in one's husband's property were all thought of as the same thing as long as female identity, selfhold, remained an indivisible unity. As Lady Carey explained, the idea of a public mind in a private body threatened to fragment female identity, to destroy its integrated wholeness:

> When to their husbands they themselves do bind,
> Do they not wholly give themselves away?
> Or give they but their body, not their mind,
> Reserving that, tho' best, for other's prey?
> No, sure, their thought no more can be their own
> And therefore to none but one be known.

The unique, unreserved giving of the woman's self to her husband is the act that keeps her whole. Only in this singular and total alienation does the woman maintain her complete self-identity.

We have already seen that it is precisely this ideal of a totalized woman, preserved because *wholly* given away, that Aphra Behn sacrifices to create a different idea of identity, one complexly dependent on the necessity of multiple exchanges. She who is able to repeat the action of self-alienation an unlimited number of times is she who is constantly there to regenerate, possess, and sell a series of provisional, constructed identities. Self-possession, then, and self-alienation are just two sides of the same coin; the alienation verifies the possession. In contrast, the wife who gives herself once and completely disposes simultaneously of self possession and self alienation. She has no more property in which to trade and is thus rendered whole by her action. She *is* her whole, unviolated womanhood because she has given up possessing herself; she can be herself because she has given up *having* herself. Further, as Lady Carey's lines make clear, if a woman's writing is an authentic extension of herself, then she cannot have alienable property in that without violating her wholeness.

Far from denying these assumptions, Aphra Behn's comedy is based on them. Like her contemporaries, she presented her writing as part of her sexual property, not just because it was bawdy, but because it was hers. As a woman, all of her properties were at least the potential property of another; she could either reserve them and give herself whole in marriage, or she could barter them piecemeal, accepting self-division to achieve self-ownership and forfeiting the possibility of marriage. In this sense,

Aphra Behn's implied identity fits into the most advanced seventeenth-century theories about selfhood: it closely resembles the possessive individualism of Locke and Hobbes, in which property in one's self both entails and is entailed by the parcelling out and serial alienation of one's self. For property by definition, in this theory, is that which is alienable. Aphra Behn's, however, is a gender specific version of possessive individualism, one constructed in opposition to the very real alternative of staying whole by renouncing self possession, an alternative that had no legal reality for men in the seventeenth century. Because the husband's right of property was in the whole of the wife, the prior alienation of any part of her had to be seen as a violation of either actual or potential marital propriety. That is, a woman who, like Aphra Behn, embraced possessive individualism, even if she were single and never bartered her sexual favors, could only do so with a consciousness that she thus contradicted the notion of female identity on which legitimate sexual property relations rested.

Publication, then, quite apart from the contents of what was published, ipso facto implied the divided, doubled, and ultimately unavailable person whose female prototype was the prostitute. By flaunting her self-sale, Aphra Behn embraced the title of whore; by writing bawdy comedies, which she then partly disclaimed, she capitalized on her supposed handicap. Finally, she even uses this persona to make herself seem the prototypical writer, and in this effort she certainly seems to have had the cooperation of her male colleagues and competitors. Thus, in the following poem, William Wycherley wittily acknowledges that the sexual innuendos about Aphra Behn rebound back on the wits who make them. The occasion of the poem was a rumor that the poetess had gonorrhea. Wycherley emphasizes how much more public is the "Sappho of the Age" than any normal prostitute, how much her fame grows as she looses her fame, and how much cheaper is the rate of the author-whore than her sister punk. But he also stresses how much more power the poetess has, since in the world of wit as opposed to the world of sexual exchange, use increases desire, and the author-whore accumulates men instead of being exchanged among them:

> More Fame you now (since talk'd of more)
>   acquire,
> And as more Public, are more Mens Desire;
> Nay, you the more, that you are Clap'd to, now,
> Have more to like you, less to censure you:
> Now Men enjoy your Parts for Half a Crown,
> Which, for a Hundred Pound, they scarce had
>   done,
> Before your Parts were, to the Public known.

Appropriately, Wycherley ends by imagining the whole London theatrical world as a sweating-house for venereal disease:
> Thus, as your Beauty did, your Wit does now,
> The Women's envy, Men's Diversion grow;
> Who, to be clap'd, or Clap you, round you sit,

> And, tho' they Sweat for it, will crowd your Pit;
> Since lately you Lay-in, (but as they say,)
> Because, you had been Clap'd another Way;
> But, if'tis true, that you have need to Sweat,
> Get, (if you can) at your New Play, a Seat.

If Aphra Behn's sexual and poetic parts are the same, then the wits are contaminated by her sexual distemper. Aphra Behn and her fellow wits infect one another: the theatre is her body, their wits are their penises, the play is a case of gonorrhea, and the cure is the same as the disease.

Given the general Restoration delight in the equation of mental, sexual, and theatrical "parts," and its frequent likening of writing to prostitution and playwrights to bawds, one might argue that if Aphra Behn had not existed, the male playwrights would have had to invent her in order to increase the witty pointedness of their cynical self-representations. For example, in Dryden's prologue to Behn's *The Widow Ranter,* the great playwright chides the self-proclaimed wits for contesting the originality of one another's productions and squabbling over literary property. Drawing on the metaphor of literary paternity, he concludes:

> But when you see these Pictures, let none dare
> To own beyond a Limb or single share;
> For where the Punk is common, he's a Sot,
> Who needs will father what the Parish got.

These lines gain half their mordancy from their reference to Aphra Behn, the poetess-punk, whose off-spring cannot seem fully her own, but whose right to them cannot be challenged with any propriety. By literalizing and embracing the playwright-prostitute metaphor, therefore, Aphra Behn was distinguished from other authors, but only as their prototypical representative. She becomes a symbolic figure of authorship for the Restoration, the writer and the strumpet muse combined. Even those who wished to keep the relationship between women and authorship strictly metaphorical were fond of the image: "What a pox have the women to do with the muses?" asks a character in a play attributed to Charles Gildon. "I grant you the poets call the nine muses by the names of women, but why so? . . . because in that sex they're much fitter for prostitution." It is not hard to see how much authorial notoriety could be gained by audaciously literalizing such a metaphor.

Aphra Behn, therefore, created a persona that skillfully intertwined the age's available discourses concerning women, property, selfhood and authorship. She found advantageous openings where other women found repulsive insults; she turned self-division into identity.

The authorial effect I'm trying to describe here should not be confused with the plays' disapproving attitudes toward turning women into items of exchange. *The Lucky Chance,* which I am now going to discuss, all too readily yields a facile, right-minded thematic analysis centering on women and property exchange. It has three plots that can easily be seen as variations on this theme: Diana is being forced into a loveless marriage with a fop because of her father's family ambition. Her preference for the young Bredwell is ignored in the exchange. Diana's father, Sir Feeble Fainwood, is also purchasing himself a young bride, Leticia, whom he has tricked into believing that her betrothed lover, who had been banished for fighting a duel, is dead. Julia, having already sold herself to another rich old merchant, Sir Cautious Fulbank, is being wooed to adultery by her former lover, Gayman. That all three women are both property and occasions for the exchange of property is quite clear. Diana is part of a financial arrangement between the families of the two old men, and the intended bridegroom, Bearjest, sees her merely as the embodiment of a great fortune; Leticia is also bought by "a great jointure," and though we know, interestingly, nothing of Julia's motives, we are told that she had played such a "prank" as Leticia. It is very easy, then, to make the point that the treatment of women as property is the problem that the play's comic action will set out solve. Whether she marries for property, as in the cases of Leticia and Julia or she is married *as property* (that is, given, like Diana, as the condition of a dowery), the woman's identity as a form of property and item of exchange seems obviously to be the play's point of departure, and the urge to break that identification seems, on a casual reading, to license the play's impropriety. One could even redeem the fact that, in the end, the women are all *given* by the old men to their lovers by pointing out that this is, after all, a comedy and hence a form that requires female desire to flow through established channels.

Such a superficial thematic analysis of *The Lucky Chance* fits in well with that image of Aphra Behn some of her most recent biographers promote: an advocate of "free love" in every sense of the phrase and a heroic defender of the right of women to speak their own desires. However, such an interpretation does not bear the weight of the play's structure or remain steady in the face of its ellipses, nor can it sustain the pressure of the play's images. For the moments of crisis in the play are not those in which a woman becomes property but those in which a woman is burdened with a selfhood that can be neither represented (a self without properties) nor exchanged. They are the moments when the veiled woman confronts the impossibility of being represented and hence of being desired and hence of being, finally, perhaps, gratified.

Before turning to those moments, I'd like to discuss some larger organizational features of the play that complicate its treatment of the theme of women and exchange. First, then to the emphatic way in which the plots are disconnected in their most fundamental logic. The plots of Diana and Leticia rely on the idea that there is an irreversible moment of matrimonial exchange after which the woman is "given" and cannot be given again. Thus the action is directed toward thwarting and replacing the planned marriage ceremony, in the case of Diana, and avoiding the consummation of the marriage bed in the case of Leticia. Julia, however, has crossed both these threshholds and is still somehow free to dispose of herself. The logic on which her plot is based seems to deny that there are critical or irremediable events in female destiny. Hence in the scene directly following Leticia's intact deliverance from Sir Feeble Fainwood's bed and Diana's elopement with Bredwell, we find Julia resignedly urging her aged husband to get the sex over with and to stop meddling with the affairs of her heart: "But let us leave this fond discourse, and, if you must, let us to bed". Julia proves her self-possession precisely by her indifference to the crises structuring Diana's and Leticia's experiences.

On the one hand, Julia's plot could be seen to undercut the achievement of resolution in the other plots by implying that there was never anything to resolve: the obstacles were not real, the crises were not crises, the definitive moment never did and never could arrive. Julia's would be the pervasive atmosphere of comedy that keeps the anxieties of the more "serious" love plot from truly being registered. But on the other hand, we could argue that the crisis plots drain the adultery plot not only of moral credibility but also of dramatic interest, for there would seem to be simply nothing at stake in Julia's plot. Indeed, Julia's plot in itself seems bent on making this point, turning as it so often does on attempts to achieve things that have already been achieved or gambling for stakes that have already been won. These two responses, however, tend to cancel one another, and we cannot conclude that either plot logic renders the other nugatory. *The Lucky Chance* achieves its effects, rather by alternately presenting the problem and its seeming nonexistence. The imminent danger of becoming an unwilling piece of someone else's property is at once asserted and denied.

The alternating assertion/denial emphasizes the discontinuity between the two "resolutions" of the woman's sexual identity that I discussed earlier: one in which the giving of the self intact is tantamount to survival; the other in which an identity is maintained in a series of exchanges. This very discontinuity, then, as I've already pointed out, is part of an overarching discursive pattern. The proof of self ownership is self sale; hence, Julia has no exculpating story of deceit or coercion to explain her marriage to Fulbank. But the complete import of what she does, both of what she sacrifices and what she gains, can only be understood against the background of a one-time exchange that involves and maintains the whole self.

The disjunction between the plot exigencies Leticia is subjected to and those that hold and create Julia, (our inability to perceive these plots within a single comic perspective) reveals the oppositional relationship between the two seventeenth-century versions of the female as property. Built into this very disjunction, therefore, is a complicated presentation of the seeming inescapability for women of the condition of property. In the play, the exchange of women as property appears inevitable, and the action revolves around the terms of exchange. The crisis plots, of which Leticia's is the most important, posit wholeness as the pre-condition of exchange and as the result of its successful completion. The unitary principle dominates the logic of this plot and also, as we are about to see, the language of its actors and its representational rules. Julia's plot, on the other hand, assumes not only the fracturing and multiplication of the self as a condition and result of exchange, but also the creation of a second order of reality: a reality of representations through which the characters simultaneously alienate and protect their identities.

This split in representational procedures can be detected in the first scene, where it is associated with the characters of the leading men. In the play's opening speech, Bellmour enters complaining that the law has stolen his identity, has made him a creature of disguise and the night. His various complaints in the scene cluster around a central fear of de-differentiation, of the failure properly to distinguish essential differences. Thus it is the "rigid laws, which put no difference / 'Twixt fairly killing in my own defence, / And murders bred by drunken arguments, / Whores, or the mean revenges of a coward" that have forced his disguise, his alienation from his own identity. That is, the denial of the true, identity insuring, difference (that between duelers and murderers) necessitates false differences, disguises and theatrical representations that get more elaborate as the plot progresses. The comedy is this series of disguises and spectacles, but its end is to render them unnecessary by the reunion of Bellmour with his proper identity and his proper wife.

The very terms of Bellmour's self-alienation, moreover, are identitarian in their assumption that like must be represented by like. Bellmour has taken a life in a duel, and for that he is deprived of the life he thought he would lead. He has destroyed a body with his sword, and for that a body that belongs to him, Leticia's, will be taken from him also through puncturing. Even the comic details of Bellmour's reported death are consonant with this mode of representation:

> RALPH: Hanged, Sir, hanged, at The Hague in Holland.
>
> BELLMOUR: For what, said they, was he hanged?
>
> RALPH: Why, e'en for high treason, Sir, he killed one of their kings.
>
> GAYMAN: Holland's a commonwealth, and is not ruled by kings.
>
> RALPH: Not by one, Sir, but by many. This was a cheesemonger, they fell out over a bottle of brandy, went to snicker snee, Mr. Bellmour cut his throat, and was hanged for't, that's all, Sir.

The reductio ad absurdum of like representing like is the commonwealth in which everyone is a king. It is within this comically literalist system of representation that Bellmour is imagined to have had his neck broken for slitting the throat of a cheesemonger. It is no wonder that the climax of Bellmour's performance is a simulation of the exchange of like for like. As Sir Feeble Fainwood approaches the bed on which he intends to deflower Leticia,

asking her, "What, was it ashamed to show its little white foots, and its little round bubbies?," Belmour comes out from between the curtains, naked to the waist. And, all the better to ward off that which he represents, he has Leticia's projected wound painted on his own chest and a dagger ready to make another such wound on Sir Feeble. The whole representational economy of this plot, therefore, has an underlying unitary basis in the notion that things must be paid for in kind. Even Leticia's self sale seems not to be for money but for the jewelry to which she is often likened.

Like Bellmour, Gayman also enters the first scene in hiding, "wrapped in his cloak," but the functional differences between the two kinds of self-concealment are soon manifested. The end of Gayman's disguises is not the retrieval of his property, but the appropriation of what he thinks is the property of others: "Are you not to be married, Sir," asks Bellmour. "No Sir," returns Gayman, "not as long as any man in London is so, that has but a handsome wife, Sir". His attempts are not to reestablish essential differences, but rather to accelerate the process of de-differentiation. "The bridegroom!" exclaims Bellmour on first seeing Sir Feeble. "Like Gorgon's head he's turned me into stone." "Gorgon's head," retorts Gayman, "a cuckold's head, 'twas made to graft upon". The dizzying swiftness with which Gayman extends Bellmour's metaphor speaks the former's desire to destroy the paired stability of exchanges. Looking at the bridegroom's head, Bellmour sees an image of destructive female sexuality, the Gorgon. Thus, the bridegroom represents the all-too-available sexuality of Leticia. Gayman's way of disarming this insight is to deck it with horns, to introduce the third term, taking advantage of Leticia's availability to cuckold Sir Feeble. But for Bellmour this is no solution at all, since it only further collapses the distinction between lover and husband, merging him with Sir Feeble at the moment he alienates his sexual property: "What, and let him marry her! She that's mine by sacred vow already! by heaven it would be flat adultery in her!" "She'll learn the trick," replies Gayman, "and practise it the better with thee." The destruction of the "true" distinctions between husband and lover, cuckold and adulterer, proprietor and thief is the state for which Gayman longs.

Bellmour's comedy, then, moves toward the re-establishment of true difference through the creation of false differences; Gayman's comedy moves toward the erasure of true differences through the creation of false and abstract samenesses. Gayman is in disguise because he cannot bear to let Julia know that he is different from his former self. He wishes to appear before her always the same, to hide the new fact of his poverty. He tries to get money from his landlady so that he can get his clothes out of hock and therefore disguise himself as himself in order to go on wooing Julia. On the same principle of the effacement of difference, Gayman later tries to pass himself off as Julia's husband when he, unbeknownst to her, takes the old man's place in bed.

Moreover, just as the false differences of Bellmour's comedy conformed to a unitary like-for-like economy of representation, the false samenesses of Gayman's plotting are governed by an economy of representation through difference. The most obvious example of this is the use of money. Money in this plot often represents bodies or their sexual use, and what is generally emphasized in these exchanges are the differences between the body and money. For example, in the scenes of Gayman's two prostitutions (the first with his landlady and the second with his unknown admirer), the difference between the women's bodies and the precious metals they can be made to yield is the point of the comedy. The landlady is herself metamorphosed into iron for the sake of this contrast: she is an iron lady who emerges from her husband's blacksmith's shop. She is then stroked into metals of increasing values as she yields 'postle spoons and caudle cups that then exchange for gold. However, Gayman's expletives never allow us to forget that this sexual alchemy is being practiced on an unsublimatable body that constantly sickens the feigning lover with its stink. Even more telling is the continuation of this scene in which Gayman receives a bag of gold as advance payment for an assignation with an anonymous woman. Here the desirability of the gold (associated with its very anonymity) immediately implies the undesirability of the woman who sends it: "Some female devil, old and damned to ugliness, / And past all hopes of courtship and address, / Full of another devil called desire, / Has seen this face, this shape, this youth, / And thinks it's worth her hire. It must be so". Of course, as this passage emphasizes, in both cases the women's money stands for Gayman's sexual worthiness, but as such it again marks a difference, the difference in the desirability of the bodies to be exchanged. Hence the unlike substance, gold, marks the inequality of the like biological substances.

The freedom and the perils, especially the perils for women, that this comedy of representation through difference introduces into erotic life are explored in the conflict between Julia and Gayman. And this conflict returns us to the issue of authorial representation. Julia, like many of Aphra Behn's heroines, confronts a familiar predicament: she wishes to have the pleasure of sexual intercourse with her lover without the pain of the loss of honor. Honor seems to mean something wholly external in the play; it is not a matter of conscience since secret actions are outside its realm. Rather, to lose honor is to give away control over one's public representations. Hence, in the adultery plot, as opposed to the crisis plot, women's bodies are not the true stakes; representations of bodies, especially in money and language, are the focal points of conflict.

Gayman's complaint against Julia, for example, is that she prefers the public admiration of the crowd, which she gains through witty language ("talking all and loud") to the private "adoration" of a lover, which is apparently speechless. Julia's retort, however, indicates that it is Gayman who will betray the private to public representation for the sake of his own reputation. It is Gayman who will "describe her charms," "Or make most filthy verses of me / Under the name of Cloris, you Philander, / Who, in lewd rhymes, confess the dear appointment, / What hour, and where, how silent was the night, / How full of

love your eyes, and wishing mine." (We have just, by the way, heard Gayman sing a verse about Cloris's wishing eyes to his landlady.)

To escape being turned into someone else's language, losing the ability to control her own public presentation, Julia subjects herself to a much more radical severance of implied true self from self-representation than Gayman could have imagined. At once to gratify her sexual desire and preserve her honor, she arranges to have Gayman's own money (in some ways a sign of his desire for her) misrepresented to him as payment for sexual intercourse with an unknown woman. That is, Julia makes the anonymous advance earlier discussed.

Julia, then, is hiding behind the anonymity of the gold, relying on its nature as a universal equivalent for desire, universal and anonymous precisely because it doesn't resemble what it stands for and can thus stand for anything. But in this episode, she becomes a prisoner of the very anonymity of the representation. For, as we've already seen, Gayman takes it as a sign of the difference between the woman's desirability and his own. Apparently, moreover, this representation of her undesirability overwhelms the private experience itself, so that when the couple finally couples, Gayman does not actually experience Julia, but rather feels another version of his landlady. As he later reluctantly describes the sightless, wordless encounter to Julia (whom he does not suspect of having been the woman), "She was laid in a pavilion all formed of gilded clouds which hung by geometry, whither I was conveyed after much ceremony, and laid in a bed with her, where, with much ado and trembling with my fears, I forced my arms about her." "And sure," interjects Julia aside to the audience, "that undeceived him." "But," continues Gayman, "such a carcass 'twas, deliver me, so shrivelled, lean and rough, a canvas bag of wooden ladles were a better bedfellow." "Now, though, I know that nothing is more distant than I from such a monster, yet this angers me," confides Julia to the audience. "'Slife, after all to seem deformed, old, ugly." The interview ends with Gayman's final misunderstanding, "I knew you would be angry when you heard it."

The extraordinary thing about this interchange is that it does not matter whether or not Gayman is telling the truth about his sexual experience. The gold may have so overwhelmed his senses as to make Julia feel like its opposite: a bag of wooden ladles rather than precious coins; and, indeed, the continuity of images between this description and Gayman's earlier reactions to women who give him money tends to confirm his sincerity. The bag of ladles reminds us of the landlady, who was also a bag, but one containing somewhat more valuable table utensils: 'postle spoons and caudle cups. However, Gayman may be misrepresenting his experience to prevent Julia's jealousy. Either way, Julia was missing from that experience. Whether he did not desire her at all or desired her as someone else is immaterial; what Julia experiences as she sees herself through this doubled representation of money and language is the impossibility of keeping herself to herself and truly being gratified as at once a subject and object of desire.

By participating in this economy of difference, in which her representations are not recognizably hers, then, Julia's problem becomes her state of unexchangeability. The drive for self-possession removes her "true" self from the realms of desire and gratification. Because she has not given herself away, she finds that her lover has not been able to take her. Surprisingly, however, the play goes on to overcome this difficulty not by taking refuge in like-for-like exchanges, but by remaining in the economy of difference until Julia seems able to adjust the claims of self-possession and gratification.

The adjustment becomes possible only after Julia has been explicitly converted into a commodity worth three hundred pounds. The process leading up to this conversion merits our scrutiny. Gayman and Sir Cautious are gambling: Gayman has won 300 pounds and is willing to stake it against something of Sir Cautious's.

> Sir Cautious: I wish I had anything but ready money to stake: three hundred pound, a fine sum!
>
> Gayman: You have moveables Sir, goods, commodities.
>
> Sir Cautious: That's all one, Sir. That's money's worth, Sir, but if I had anything that were worth nothing.
>
> Gayman: You would venture it. I thank you, Sir. I would your lady were worth nothing.
>
> Sir Cautious: Why so, Sir?
>
> Gayman: Then I would set all 'gainst that nothing.

Sir Cautious begins this dialogue with a comical identification of everything with its universal equivalent, money. Everything he owns is convertable into money; hence, he believes that money is the real essence of everything that isn't money. Hence, everything is *really* the same thing—money. For Sir Cautious the economy of difference collapses everything into sameness. The only thing that is truly different, then, must be "nothing," a common slang word for the female genitals. One's wife is this nothing because in the normal course of things she is not a commodity. As Sir Cautious remarks, "Why, what a lavish whoremaker's this? We take money to marry our wives but very seldom part with 'em, and by the bargain get money". Her normal nonexchangeability for money is what makes a wife different from a prostitute; it is also what makes her the perfect nothing to set against three hundred pounds. We could say, then, that Julia is here made into a commodity only because she isn't one: she becomes the principle of universal difference and as such, paradoxically, becomes exchangeable for the universal equivalent.

The scene provides a structural parallel for the scene of Gayman's prostitution, in which, as we have seen, money also marks difference. But the sequels of the two scenes are strikingly dissimilar. Gayman is once again back in Julia's bed, but his rather than her identity is supposedly masked. Whereas in the first encounter, Gayman went to bed with what he thought was an old woman, in the second, Julia goes to bed with what she thinks is her old husband. But the difference between these two scenes in the dark as they are later recounted stems from the relative inalienability of male sexual identity. Even in the dark, we are led to believe, the difference of men is sensible: Gayman says, "It was the feeble husband you enjoyed / In cold imagination, and no more. / Shyly you turned away, faintly resigned. . . . Till excess of love betrayed the cheat." Gayman's body, even unseen, is not interchangeable with Sir Cautious's. Unlike Julia's, Gayman's body will undo the misrepresentation; no mere idea can eradicate this palpable difference and sign of identity, the tumescent penis itself. Hence, when Gayman takes Sir Cautious's place in bed, he does not really risk what Julia suffered earlier: "after all to seem deformed, old, ugly." Gayman's self will always obtrude into the sphere of representation, another version of the ladle, but one that projects from the body instead of being barely discernible within it.

This inalienable masculine identity, although it seems at first Gayman's advantage, is quickly appropriated by Julia, who uses it to secure at once her own good reputation and complete liberty of action. Once again we are given a scene in which the speaker's sincerity is questionable. When Gayman's erection reveals his identity, Julia appears to be outraged at the attempted deception: "What, make me a base prostitute, a foul adult'ress? Oh, be gone, dear robber of my quiet". We can only see this tirade as more deceit on Julia's part, since we know she tricked the same man into bed the night before. But since her deceit was not discovered and his was, she is able to feign outrage and demand a separation from her husband. The implication is, although, once again, this cannot be represented, that Julia has found a way to secure her liberty and her "honor" by maintaining her misrepresentations.

It is, then, precisely through her nullity, her nothingness, that Julia achieves a new level of self-possession along with the promise of continual sexual exchange. But this, of course, is an inference we make from what we suspect Julia of hiding: her pleasure in Gayman's body, her delight that she now has an excuse for separating from her husband, her intention to go on seeking covert pleasure. All of this is on the other side of what we see and hear.

It is this shady effect, I want to conclude, that Aphra Behn is in the business of selling. And it is by virtue of this commodity that she becomes such a problematic figure for later women writers. For they had to overcome not only her life, her bawdiness and the author-whore metaphor she celebrated, but also her playful challenges to the very possibility of female self-representation.

Ellen Pollak (essay date 1993)

SOURCE: "Beyond Incest: Gender and the Politics of Transgression in Aphra Behn's *Love-Letters between a Nobleman and His Sister*," in *Rereading Aphra Behn: History, Theory, and Criticism,* edited by Heidi Hutner, University Press of Virginia, 1993, pp. 151-86.

[*Below, Pollak presents a detailed study of Behn's* Love-Letters, *contending that "Behn's narrative effectively displaces the conceptual grounds of a heterosexual matrix of assumptions that encodes incestuous desire as a form of freedom from patriarchal law."*]

Expressly incestuous and deeply embedded in the politics of regicide and political rebellion, Aphra Behn's *Love-Letters between a Nobleman and His Sister* is also a text insistently preoccupied with questions of gender, identity, and representation. Published in three parts between 1684 and 1687, Behn's novel is based loosely on an affair between Ford, Lord Grey of Werke, and his wife's sister, Lady Henrietta Berkeley, a scandal that broke in London in 1682, when Lady Berkeley's father published an advertisement in the *London Gazette* announcing the disappearance of his daughter. Lady Berkeley had in fact run off with Grey, the well-known antimonarchist figure whom Dryden alluded to as "cold Caleb" in *Absalom and Achitophel* (1681) and who serves Behn here as a model for her character Philander. Prosecuted by Lord Berkeley for abducting and seducing his daughter, Grey was eventually found guilty of "debauchery" but never sentenced. Shortly thereafter, he was also implicated in the Rye House Plot to murder Charles II and was later active in Monmouth's rebellion against Charles's brother, James. In Behn's fiction Grey figures as a political follower and friend of Cesario, the French prince of Condé, whose failed attempt to overthrow his king is modeled on the parallel exploits of Charles's bastard son. Lady Berkeley is Sylvia, the dutiful royalist daughter whom Philander seduces and corrupts. Like the crown for Cesario, she is for Philander a sign of male prerogative and desire, her body the theater across which several dramas of masculine rivalry are played out.

It is not surprising that a text situated so expressly within the political context of the Duke of Monmouth's rebellion against the royal authority of both his father and his uncle should structure itself around the repetition of a series of analogously configured masculine rivalries. Through her elaborate foregrounding of the figure of a woman, however, Behn adds a dimension to this drama of political and familial succession that is manifestly absent from such comparable royalist efforts as *Absalom and Achitophel.* To what extent Behn's choice to develop the love interest here was motivated by her recognition of the greater acceptability for a woman of the role of romance historian over that of political poet, we cannot know for sure; but when Lady Berkeley's father published his advertisement announcing her disappearance and offering £200 for her return, Behn clearly perceived an opportunity to explore the narrative possibilities (as well as discursive instabilities) inherent in comparing stolen daughters with stolen crowns.

Behn incorporates the scandalous historical fact of the Berkeley-Grey affair into the political, thematic, and figural dimensions of her fiction by situating Philander's justifications for his adulterous and incestuous desire for Sylvia squarely within the context of Restoration debates over the relationship and relative authority of nature and conventional morality. As Susan Staves has amply demonstrated, an increasing dissociation of natural law theory from theology during the second half of the seventeenth century effectively established the conditions both for changes in the institutional treatment of moral crimes and for the emergence of a new brand of heroism in the imaginative literature of the age. Herculean and libertine stage heroes captured the popular imagination through their bold allegiance to a nature defined not in accordance with, but in opposition to, religion, law, custom, and conventional morality. Such heroes appealed to nature to justify a range of behaviors traditionally regarded as crimes against nature as well as God. Along with adultery, sodomy, and parricide, the deployment of incest as a figure for rebellion against traditional forms of authority became a favorite device on the Restoration stage for articulating cultural anxieties and for giving dramatic play to the multiple tensions inherent in contemporary efforts to rethink the connections between the laws of nature, religion, and social morality.

Behn's libertine hero, Philander, fits the profile of this new literary type in his elaboration of natural justifications for his socially criminal desire for Sylvia. From as early as his very first letter, he invokes the liberatory ethos of a return to original pleasures. The legal institutions of kinship and of marriage, he insists, are mere practical creations inspired by material interests, while his own incestuous and adulterous passion has a primacy that transcends the prudent imperatives of tradition. Philander uses the fact that his relation to Sylvia is affinal (a legal relation created through his marriage to her sister) as opposed to consanguineal (a blood relation) to further question the natural basis for the rules that prohibit his having sex with her: "What kin, my charming *Sylvia,* are you to me? No ties of blood forbid my passion; and what's a ceremony imposed on man by custom! . . . What alliance can that create? Why should a trick devised by the wary old, only to make provision for posterity, tie me to an eternal slavery?" In point of legal fact, as Sybil Wolfram's work [*In-Laws and Outlaws,* 1987] has shown, because the English concept of marriage in the seventeenth century was based on the legal and religious doctrine of the unity of husband and wife, "intercourse between affinal relations was . . . on a footing with and as much incest as intercourse between close blood relations." But Philander represents an emergent strain of thought that radically questioned the received assumption that incest controverted natural law.

Scripture itself had become a site of theoretical controversy among seventeenth-century moral philosophers, especially at those points where God appeared arbitrarily to command behavior else-where prohibited by His law.

Staves cites the story of Abraham's divinely ordered murder of Isaac as one scriptural conundrum that seemed to focus the crisis of authority experienced by moralists, but there were also numerous instances of apparent biblical inconsistency regarding the legitimacy of incestuous practices. One of the most pervasively cited involved a perceived discrepancy between the injunctions of Leviticus, which forbade incest, and those of Genesis, which bade Adam and Eve (whom most commentators regarded as siblings) to increase and multiply.

Thus, in 1625 Hugo Grotius asserted that although marriages between brothers and sisters are illegal, they are forbidden by divine command and not (as appeared to be the case with parent-child marriages) by "the pure law of nature." Here Grotius accepts the Jewish teaching that the prohibition against sibling marriage was given to Adam "at the same time with the laws to worship God, to administer justice, not to shed blood, [etc.] . . . ; but with the condition that the laws regulating marriage should not have effect until after the human race had multiplied sufficiently." Jeremy Taylor echoed Grotius thirty-five years later when he asserted that, by contrast to parent-child incest, sibling marriages are only "next to an unnatural mixture"; for "if they had been unnatural, they could not have been necessary" as "it is not imaginable that God . . . would have built up mankind by that which is contrary to Humane Nature." And in 1672, Richard Cumberland took a similarly relative position on the question of sibling incest, arguing that marriages between brothers and sisters "in the first Age of the World" were "*necessary* to propagate that Race of Men, and to raise those Families, which Reason now endeavours to *Preserve,* by *prohibiting.*"

Behn's Philander does not emerge ex nihilo, therefore, when he invokes Genesis to justify his incestuous desires. In a manner typically modern and predictably Whig, he disdains the beaten track of conventional morality to assert the prerogatives of an originary state: "Let us . . . scorn the dull *beaten road,* but let us love like the first race of men, nearest allied to God, promiscuously they loved, and possessed, father and daughter, brother and sister met, and reaped the joys of love without control, and counted it religious coupling, and 'twas encouraged too by heaven itself." As Ruth Perry has observed [in *Women, Letters, and the Novel,* 1980], Philander speaks for the authenticity of nature over the artifice of social codes. Posing as the ultimate pastoral lover, he emulates the freedom of creatures in the natural world. There is "no troublesome honour, amongst the pretty inhabitants of the woods and streams, fondly to give laws to nature," he insists, "but uncontrolled they play, and sing, and love; no parents checking their dear delights, no slavish matrimonial ties to restrain their nobler flame." Only "man . . . is bound up to rules, fetter'd by the nice decencies of honour."

Given Behn's royalist politics, Philander's defense of incest may seem at first blush a simple alignment of Whiggism with transgression, the act of regicide—as René Girard has noted in another context [in *Violence and the Sacred,*

1977]—constituting an equivalent in the political realm of parricide or incest within the family. Those who violate loyalties to their king, Behn seems to want to say, are also apt to violate the other bonds on which the social order and its civilizing systems of difference depend. Behn's creation of a heroine of royalist birth who draws the better part of her appeal from her success in outdoing Philander at the game of transgressiveness, however, destabilizes this easy, politicized opposition between authority and rebellion and suggests a more complex and heterogeneous notion of transgression than a simply negative political coding would allow. As more than one critic has noted, Behn's treatment of gender often seems to complicate and refract, if not indeed to contradict, her party politics, creating in her work the sense of multiple and incommensurate ideological agenda. *Love-Letters* exemplifies this tendency through its own rhetorical excess, inviting itself to be read with a certain burlesquing tongue-in-cheekiness, as if it wants to make us ask—and it does make us ask—why (if this is first and foremost a political scandal novel) Behn would choose to defend the royal cause through so protracted a portrait of untamed female insubordination.

Is it true, as Janet Todd and Maureen Duffy both suggest [in *The Sign of Angellica,* 1989, and introduction to *Love-Letters,* respectively], that Behn wants to promote the values of sincerity and authenticity as they are embodied in the figure of Philander's friend and rival, Octavio, by showing us that Philander's appeal to nature is nothing more than base hypocrisy? Perhaps, at the most manifest level; but why then does her narrative read so much like a celebration of the pleasures and powers of role-playing and artifice whereby the indomitable Sylvia sacrifices Octavio to her revenge against Philander? If, as Perry suggests, Behn's characters are designed to show us "where disrespect for law and order can lead," why does Behn's relation to her heroine's depravity seem so very fraught with irony? The narrator tells us that Sylvia is imperious, proud, vain, opinionated, obstinate, censorious, amorously inclined, and indiscreet, and yet Behn seems to revel in the emotional resilience the heroine's duplicity affords. Jane Austen rarely assumes a more heteroglot relation to her heroines than Behn does when, reflecting on the ease with which Sylvia is able to transfer her affection from one lover to the next, she writes: "Nature is not inclined to hurt itself; and there are but few who find it necessary to die of the disease of love. Of this sort was our *Sylvia,* though to give her her due, never any person who did not indeed die, ever languished under the torments of love, as did that charming and afflicted maid." The nature appealed to here is elusively construed, gesturing ironically toward an unstable opposition between female nature and artifice in a world where a natural female impulse toward self-preservation requires the performance, nearly unto death, of the artifice of languishing femininity.

Feminist critics have taken differing positions regarding the significance of the incest in Behn's text. To Janet Todd, it is merely a sensationalist device meant to keep Behn's book in print but not an important theme developed at any length. For Judith Kegan Gardiner, on the other hand, Sylvia's willing participation in an incestuous adultery with her brother-in-law is the paradigmatic instance of her transgressiveness as a heroine and the conceptual point of departure for a complex reconfiguration of literary history [*Tulsa Studies in Women's Literature* 8 (Fall 1989)]. Reading *Love-Letters* as a story of brother-sister incest that does not follow a familiar and traditionally valorized oedipal logic but instead avoids "both father-son and mother-daughter paradigms for a transgressive sexuality in which the woman is not exclusively a victim but a willing and desiring agent," Gardiner makes the case that a revaluation of the importance of Behn's text in the history of the novel genre opens the way to imagining an alternative paradigm of literary history, one that displaces an oedipal by what she calls "an incestuous model of the novel's origins."

But is Behn's heroine stably figured as a willing agent of incestuous desire? Does the text of *Love-Letters* in fact support Gardiner's assessment that incest functions for Sylvia, as it does for Philander, as the expression of a liberatory eros? Behn may indeed refuse an oedipal model of female desire, but does she therefore necessarily embrace an incestuous ideal of feminine transgression? I shall argue that, on the contrary, far from replacing an oedipal with an incestuous ideal, Behn's narrative effectively displaces the conceptual grounds of a heterosexual matrix of assumptions that encodes incestuous desire as a form of freedom from patriarchal law.

There is a great deal more at stake here than a subtle difference of reading. Where we locate the transgressiveness of Behn's heroine has critical implications not just for the place Behn will occupy in contemporary conceptions of aesthetics and of literary history but also for a feminist analysis of narrative representations of incestuous desire, especially for recent efforts to theorize the role of incest in modern discursive inscriptions of female desire. In making the case for Sylvia's incestuous agency without taking into account how she is located specifically as a female subject in relation both to incest and to the law that produces it as an object of repression—without regard, that is, to the patriarchal power structure within which incest derives its meaning and transgressive force to begin with—Gardiner allows a dangerous slippage to occur in her argument. Assuming that incest always inevitably constitutes transgression (indeed reading incest as the ultimate transgression), she relies on a characteristically modern discursive coding of incestuous desire as natural—an emergent cultural inscription in seventeenth-century England, as we have seen, but one that I would argue Behn's narrative actively refuses to underwrite.

In fact, I would suggest, far from elaborating a simple equivalence or correspondence between incest and transgression, Behn uses both categories to register the shifting positionality of gendered subjectivities, producing a variable model of the transgressiveness of incest and the incestuousness of transgression for her male and female characters. Rather than inscribing incest as a stable and univocal marker of transgression, she destabilizes incest as a trope of liberation by exposing the ways it is differently constituted for her hero and heroine. In the process, she radically problematizes the question of desire's origins, representing what Gardiner reads as original desire in Sylvia not as an intrinsic essence but as an effect of power. Sylvia's transgressiveness as a heroine is situated not in her incestuous agency but elsewhere; it emerges rather in a conceptual and performative space made available to her only by the eventual recognition that Philander's exaltation of incest as a liberation from prohibitive patriarchal law actually functions as an instrument of power. Incest operates in Behn's text, in other words, not as a simple figure for transgression but as a complex discursive site where the oppositional ideologies of patriarchy and individualism intersect, at once confronting each other and, in the process, exposing their joint complicity in (and their shared dependence on) the appropriation and cooptation of female desire.

This is hardly to revert to Todd's assessment of the essential insignificance of the incest in Behn's text. On the contrary, it is to read Sylvia's incest as a necessary part of Behn's complex critique of Whig libertarian politics. At the level of plot, after all, the incest does take Sylvia outside her father's house; it thus establishes the conditions within which Behn is able to show that that outside is always already inside—always on the verge of reinscribing the very law it would subvert. To be successfully transgressive on Behn's terms, Sylvia will have to move beyond the illusory liberation of naturalized incestuous desire—*outside* the outside of an oedipal dyad in which women are mere theaters for the playing out of male desire. The serial nature of *Love-Letters* allows Behn to effect these consecutive displacements compellingly, by creating an opportunity for her to write her heroine out of and beyond the limits of the typical romantic plot.

I. PHILANDER'S "PHALLIC HANDSHAKE" AND THE LIMITS OF THE LIBERTINE CRITIQUE OF PATRIARCHY

I approach my subject through a reading of several key episodes that help to establish the context within which the incest in Behn's narrative acquires meaning. My aim is to illuminate the extent to which the incestuous relation between Philander and Sylvia is conditioned by the dynamics of a system of homosocial exchange in which the daughter's desire functions not as a locus of agency but as a site of confrontation between paternal and fraternal interests. Because familial conflict is coded politically in Behn's novel, this reading also necessarily involves discussion of the way Sylvia's body functions in a double symbolic register as a political as well as familial battleground.

This is not to say that Sylvia entirely lacks transgressive agency. It is rather to suggest that we must first understand the structuring homosocial frame within which her incest is enacted ultimately to appreciate the process whereby she manages to move beyond the possibilities for transgression it delimits into a space subversively generated by a parodic repetition of its terms. For, however paradoxically, it is only after Sylvia comes to recognize her status as a sign within a drama of masculine rivalry, to understand that as a woman she is always already a representation within a homosocial matrix of desire, that she opens herself to the possibility of taking performative control of her enactment of desire and gendered subjectivity.

I take as my point of entry Philander's account of an episode that occurs relatively early in part one, immediately after his first nocturnal tryst with Sylvia. As a dutiful royalist daughter, Sylvia early expresses considerable anguish over Philander's attempts to prevail upon her "honour"; she finally concedes, nevertheless, to a private interview, which she justifies as a trial of her virtue and resolution. And as Philander's letter recounting the details of their first night alone together reveals, Sylvia does remain "a maid" despite the opportunity for physical conquest on his part.

The cause of Philander's forbearance, as he explains, is neither his regard for Sylvia's honor (on the contrary, he says, her resistance inflames him all the more) nor her physical attractions (these, he insists, are overwhelming) but a fit of sexual impotence brought on by a state of overstimulation. Having "overcome all difficulties, all the fatigues and toils of love's long seiges, vanquish'd the mighty phantom of the fair, the giant honour, and routed all the numerous host of women's little reasonings, passed all the bounds of peevish modesty; nay, even all the loose and silken counterscarps that fenced the sacred fort," instead of receiving "the yielding treasure," Philander had fallen "fainting before the surrendering gates," a circumstance he goes on to associate with the weakness of old age. In a rhetorical maneuver that underscores his physical prowess even as it acknowledges a lapse in his "(till then) never failing power," he attributes his attack of impotence to the envy of the gods; one "malicious at [his] glory," he suggests, has left him full of "mad desires," but "all inactive, as age or death itself, as cold and feeble, as unfit for joy, as if [his] youthful fire had long been past, or *Sylvia* had never been blest with charms." Indeed, the excess of passion has so paralyzed Philander that he curses his youth and implores the gods to give him "old age, for that has some excuse, but youth has none."

The dialectic of youthful vigor and old age within which Philander here encodes what amounts to an averted incestuous consummation is, as we have to some extent already seen, precisely the dialectic within which he has attempted to justify his incestuous and adulterous desire from the start. From as early as his very first letter to Sylvia, he has idealized his affection for her by casting the older generation as guardians of a threatened domain of power, invested only in the jealous retention of control over the future. The institutions of kinship and of marriage are mere "trick[s] devised by the wary old" who, like the gods, arbitrarily wield the reins of political power even as they fear and envy Philander's authentic passion and youthful virility.
Philander reproduces this dialectic at a more literal level in his reference later in the same letter to a parallel sexual plot involving another male predator and another "reluc-

tant maid." For even as Philander—"the young, the brisk and gay"—is engineering an interview with Sylvia, Sylvia's father—that "brisk old gentleman"—has been counting on a garden assignation with Melinda, her refreshingly worldly serving maid. Few readers will forget the hilarious "accident" by which plot and comic subplot here intersect, enabling Behn to play irreverently with the ironies, multiple meanings, and shifting power relations produced when the "maid" Sylvia, "mistress" of Melinda, plays "mistress" to Philander while her "maid," Melinda, plays "mistress" to Sylvia's father. Much as Defoe would later point to the ironies inherent in the homonymous relation contained within the honorific *Madam,* Behn here uses the shifting and multiplying of subject positions to baldly expose the illusory forms of power invested in all varieties of mistresses and maids.

According to Philander, no consummation takes place between master and "mistress" here any more than between Philander and Sylvia. Alarmed by a noise that makes the young lovers fear discovery, Philander steals into the garden disguised in Melinda's nightgown and headress, only to be mistaken for Melinda by the eager old gentleman. Here is his account of events as they unfold: "*Monsieur* the Count, . . . taking me for Melinda, . . . caught hold of my gown as I would have passed him, and cried, 'Now *Melinda,* I see you are a maid of honour,—come, retire with me into the grove, where I have a present of a heart and something else to make you.'" It is now Philander's turn to play the role of reluctant maid: "With that I pulled back and whispered—'Heavens! Would you make a mistress of me?'—Says he—'A mistress, what woulds't thou be, a cherubin?' Then I replied as before—'I am no whore, sir,'—'No,' cries he, 'but I can quickly make thee one, I have my tools about me, sweet-heart; therefore let us lose no time, but fall to work.' . . . With that he clapped fifty guineas in a purse into one hand, and something else that shall be nameless into the other, presents that had been both worth *Melinda*'s acceptance".

Combining many of the key motifs and topoi of *Love-Letters* (among them masquerade, gender reversal, class and generational encounter, and homosocial exchange of a most literal variety)—all within an epistolary frame—Philander's garden adventure offers a veritable object lesson in the problematics of reading Behn. It is possible to take Philander's narrative at face value, to accept the hero at his word, as Gardiner does when she reads Philander's disguise as providing a sort of comic externalization of his demeaning impotence. Philander, as she sees him here, is a whining buffoon—"a ludicrously declassed and feminized figure"—whose exposure through Behn's publication of his private correspondence realizes his own worst fear, as he expresses it in his letter, of being publicly ridiculed ("Where shall I hide my head when this lewd story's told?"). In Philander's account of his comic adventure with Beralti, Gardiner suggests, Behn not only casts doubt on the virility of the notoriously promiscuous Lord Grey but "undercuts the admiration accorded to Don Juans" generally. His withdrawal from the garden, which leaves his father-in-law in a state of sexual frustration is, Gardiner argues, a burlesque of "his own frustrated romantic seduction of Sylvia."

But Gardiner's reading does little justice to the hermeneutic instabilities generated by the epistolary nature of Behn's text, instabilities that produce the immanent possibility—if not the eminent probability—that Philander is only feigning impotence. The only grounds we have for validating what really happened on that disappointing night are, after all, Philander's words—his own dubious representation of events. And in light of the strategies of seduction he has deployed up to this point, it makes perfect sense to read his attack of impotence not as a fact but as a performance (or what might more appropriately be termed a magnificent antiperformance in this case). Far from constituting a form of humiliation, this episode actually helps Philander to consolidate his power over Sylvia.

Philander's "retreat" from consummation at this moment of peak excitement and opportunity is thoroughly in keeping with the strategies of deferral by which he has gained entry into Sylvia's bedchamber in the first place. From the outset, he has moved with a certain deft belatedness. As early as her third letter, Sylvia pines for word from Philander: "Not yet?—not yet?" she laments, "oh ye dull tedious hours, when will you glide away? and bring that happy moment on, in which I shall at least hear from my *Philander;* . . . Perhaps *Philander*'s making a trial of virtue by this silence." In her next, still waiting ("Another night, oh heavens, and yet no letter come!"), she even entertains the thought that Philander may in fact be toying with her: "Is it a trick, a cold fit, only assum'd to try how much I love you?" Predictably, Philander has an excuse, although in presenting it he also betrays a certain disingenuity: "When I had sealed the enclosed, *Brilliard* told me you were this morning come from *Bellfont,* and with infinite impatience have expected seeing you here; which deferred my sending this to the old place; and I am so vain (oh adorable *Sylvia!*) as to believe my fancied silence has given you disquiets; but sure, my *Sylvia* could not charge me with neglect."

It may be revenge for Sylvia's ambivalence about surrendering herself to him, indeed for the tenacity with which she clings to the imperatives of honor, that drives Philander to these delays. For although Sylvia often longs for him, she is just as often grateful for his neglect: "Let me alone, let me be ruin'd with honour, if I must be ruin'd.—For oh! 'twere much happier I were no more, than that I should be more than *Philander*'s sister; or he than *Sylvia*'s brother: oh let me ever call you by that cold name." Philander, however, will be satisfied with gaining nothing less than absolute control over the representation of Sylvia's desire. Early on she describes herself as the very embodiment of disorder and indeterminacy: "Could you but imagine how I am tormentingly divided, how unresolved between violent love and cruel honour, you would say 'twere impossible to fix me any where; or be the same thing for a moment together." Onto this doubt and indecision, Philander fixes his own desire, reading Sylvia as he wishes—like Adam, dreaming her doubt into desire for his advances and then naming it as love. "I know you love," writes Philander to Sylvia. "He soon taught her to

understand it was love," asserts the narrator in the novel's "Argument"; "thou art the first that ever did inform me that there was such a sort of wish about me," writes Sylvia to Philander. Such phrases echo as a refrain throughout part one. And Sylvia does at last defer to the authority of Philander's reading of her, both in finally accepting his diagnosis of her alienation from desire and in conceding to his accusations of her fickleness and inconstancy along the way.

In the context of this series of deferrals, Philander's impotence simply constitutes a culminating moment in the production of desire in Sylvia. Although in prior letters she had vacillated wildly between attraction to her brother-in-law and a perfectly catechismal defense of patriarchal honor, in the two letters that she writes in quick succession immediately following Philander's "lapse" in potency, she describes herself as experiencing a degree of desire she has previously not known. "I have wishes, new, unwonted wishes," she writes, "at every thought of thee I find a strange disorder in my blood, that pants and burns in every vein, and makes me blush and sigh, and grow impatient, ashamed and angry." She now further concedes that her previous "coldness" must have been dissembled, as she was "not mistress of" it. (This concession by Sylvia is of interest for our reading of Philander, as it admits the possibility that coldness may be feigned.) Sylvia continues, "there lies a woman's art, there all her boasted virtue, it is but well dissembling, and no more—but mine, alas, is gone, for ever fled." In the process of increasingly surrendering to Philander's "cause," Sylvia now begins in several instances to echo his very words and arguments, mirroring his early references to "fond custom" and "phantom honour" as well as the opportunistic and somewhat desperate arguments he had used to justify his commitment to the political interests of the treacherous Cesario. Just as he had there described himself as being "in past a retreat" and declared that "though the glorious falling weight should crush me, it is great to attempt," so Sylvia now casts herself in the role of heroic martyr to her love: "I am plunged in, past hope of a retreat; and since my fate has pointed me out for ruin, I cannot fall more gloriously. Take then, *Philander,* to your dear arms, a maid that can no longer resist, who is disarmed of all defensive power: she yields, she yields, and does confess it too." Sylvia's response to Philander's impotence, in short, is to renounce every doctrine she has hitherto been taught by the "grave and wise." He induces her to give up a "coldness she is not mistress of" by, in effect, being master of his own. One more instance of deferral (occasioned this time by Cesario's calling him away) will secure his romantic victory; to prove his passion, Philander will offer to disregard the summons, but Sylvia—now thoroughly identified with his interests—insists that he respond, promising that Philander's obedience to the commands of Cesario (whom earlier she had regarded as a rival) will be rewarded in her arms.

If, as Sylvia is here driven to presuppose, affecting coldness is "a woman's art"—a prerogative or sign of femininity—then feigning impotence is for Philander, in more than one sense, "putting on" the maid. It is a way both of putting Sylvia on (i.e., controlling her through deception) and of doing so by performing a woman's part (affecting coldness), a strategy made literal in Philander's garden performance as Melinda. Appropriating to himself a dissembled coldness that he identifies as a female strategy, Philander does not invite Sylvia to become a better mistress of her own standoffishness, but instead maneuvers her into accepting the coercive fiction of her own natural desire for him. Her longing for him is thus understood not as the effect of a performance on his part but as an essence intrinsic to her, a "natural propensity" poorly masked in her case by a shabby cloak of artificial virtue. As she does at several other points throughout her text, Behn here problematizes the question of desire's origins in depicting Sylvia's grasping after a causal narrative: "I am the aggressor," she declares eventually, "the fault is in me, and thou art innocent." Thus does Philander take control rhetorically of their courtship by inducing Sylvia to own an "unaccountable" passion over which she has neither prior knowledge nor control.

It remains, however, to determine the role of Philander's garden performance as a reluctant maid in his project of displacing all traces of reluctance in Sylvia. I have argued that what to Gardiner is whining and buffoonery on Philander's part can also, if we refuse to assume the hero's authenticity, be understood as a form of strategic self-dramatization whereby Philander acquires power by performing impotence. Philander's account of his "pleasant adventure" in the garden similarly serves his ends with Sylvia by enlisting her collusion as a reader in a comic undermining of paternal authority. By reducing the count to a rather embarrassing travesty of the predatory excesses of youth, it offers a repetition and amplification of Philander's successful manipulation of the signs of impotence and femininity to establish the conditions for sexual victory. It is not just that Philander has prior knowledge from Melinda of Beralti's sexual indiscretions while Beralti himself remains ignorant of Philander's dalliance with his daughter. There is also the fact that the old man is prepared to pay for Melinda's services, a detail that, while it bespeaks Beralti's economic prowess, also makes him compare unfavorably with Philander. The fifty guineas intended for Melinda may stand as a mark of Bellfont's class as well as gender supremacy, but they are also a sign of his maid's affective indifference to him—an indifference that, as we have seen, stands in stark contrast to the passion Philander arouses in Sylvia (despite, if not indeed because of, his temporary lapse in potency). In fact, the comic circumstance of Melinda's physical absence at the moment when the fifty guineas is bestowed makes an utter mockery of the count's physical power over her. The scene in which the father both literally and figuratively attempts to impose the phallus is also the scene in which the paternal phallus is inadvertently exposed, not simply to the laughter of the son-in-law but, through him, to the daughter's laughter too.

But Beralti's garden vigil for the daughter's maid takes place at the very moment when Philander is preparing the stage for the theft of the daughter's maidenhead. The identity of role between Philander and the count as predatory males is thus complicated by their status as rivals. They are not simply mirrors of one another—males in quest of separate objects of desire—but competitors for control of Sylvia. (Could not Beralti's dalliance with the maid in fact be read as a phastasmatic rendering of the eroticized relation between father and daughter that underpins the entire sexual drama of part one?) To the extent that they situate Sylvia's alienation from her father within the context of a drama of masculine rivalry in which she figures not as an agent but a sign, the familial dynamics here are critical. Philander's inclination to flout paternal authority and to infringe upon the father's right of rule is an aspect of his political character as a follower of the regicidal Cesario. But the link does not end there. Like Cesario, Philander functions in the capacity of a son, a role that he has acquired by his marriage to Sylvia's sister, Myrtilla, and one that involves not just the acquisition of certain privileges but also the institution of specific prohibitions. The rules of kinship that give Philander freedom of access to Beralti's daughters also presuppose the assumption of countervailing filial responsibilities. Sylvia alludes to both these prerogatives and their limits when she contemplates the consequences of her father's discovery of their affair: "my father being rash, and extremely jealous, and the more so of me, by how much more he is fond of me, and nothing would enrage him like the discovery of an interview like this; though you have the liberty to range the house of *Bellfont* as a son, and are indeed at home there; but . . . when he shall find his son and virgin daughter, the brother and the sister so retired, so entertained,—What but death can ensue? Or what is worse, eternal . . . confusion on my honour?" In seducing Sylvia (by, in effect, usurping the father's prerogative to dispose of her virginity), Philander violates the authority invested in him as a brother—an "authority" that, as the following passage testifies, Sylvia recognizes as "lawful." Describing herself as impaled by a sense of familial obligation in the face of his advances, as "a maid that cannot fly," she entertains a moment of regret: "Why did you take advantage of those freedoms I gave you as a brother? . . . but for my sister's sake, I play'd with you, suffer'd your hands and lips to wander where I dare not now; all which I thought a sister might allow a brother, and knew not all the while the treachery of love: oh none, but under that intimate title of a brother, could have had the opportunity to have ruin'd me . . . by degrees so subtle, and an authority so lawful, you won me out of all."

Within the discursive economy of Behn's text, in short, Sylvia's honor—represented both by her virgin body and her desire to fulfill her f(am)ilial obligations—becomes Philander's political battle-ground. As "daughter to the great *Beralti* and sister to *Myrtilla,* a yet unspotted maid, fit to produce a race of glorious heroes," Sylvia recognizes that all her actions reflect on the honor of "the noble house of the *Beralti*" and that Philander seeks "to build the trophies of [his] conquests on the ruin of both *Myrtilla*'s fame and [her own]." From a political perspective, it is not sufficient that he ruin Myrtilla only, as Sylvia yet remains to "redeem the bleeding [royalist] honour of [her] family". As Myrtilla puts it in her one admonitory missive to her sister, Sylvia is "the darling child, the joy of all, the last hope left, the refuge" of "the most unhappy [family] of all the race of old nobility." Philander's corruption of Beralti's dutiful younger daughter through the illicit appropriation of sexual rights over her in this sense constitutes a Whig usurpation of the royalist right of rule.

One sees here, better perhaps than at any other point in her text, the logic of Behn's interweaving of sexual and political narratives; for what Behn's complex structuring of her tale makes evident is the profound interimplication—indeed the mutually constitutive nature—of sexuality and politics. The relationship between plots here is more than merely analogical, more than the simple matter of a metaphor in which sexual conquest serves as a figure at the level of private life for a more public, political form of victory. It is rather a relationship of discursive interdependence in which the categories of the private and the public, materiality and meaning, desire and the law reveal their inherently contingent and unstable identities. Gardiner accepts the efficacy of a stable distinction between private and public life when she rests her reading on the difference between Philander's positive political power and his lack of familial authority over Sylvia. But this is precisely the distinction Behn destabilizes when she exposes the intensely political nature of individual desire. Philander's binary opposition between private and public life is, she suggests, an illusion created to sustain the liberatory fiction that legitimates the operations of masculine privilege.

Philander represents his incestuous love for Sylvia as an expression of unconstrained desire that marks a liberation from a materialist economy of sexual exchange. Against the institution of marriage—"a trick devised by the wary old only to make provision for posterity"—he urges the authenticity of "pleasures vast and unconfin'd." And eventually, in the invective against marriage to which she devotes her penultimate letter in part one, Sylvia too comes to embrace such a libertine philosophy, asserting that only adulterous love can occasion genuine heterosexual reciprocity ("That's a heavenly match," she writes, "when two souls touched with equal passion meet, . . . when no base interest makes the hasty bargain, . . . and . . . both understand to take and pay.") Ultimately, however, by showing how the very act of erotic transgression that Philander proffers as an individualist solution to the problem of hierarchical repression ultimately reinscribes Sylvia's specular status in reciprocal relations between men, Behn exposes the limits of the libertine critique of patriarchy.

The assymmetrical and nonreciprocal character of Sylvia and Philander's relationship will become increasingly clear, both to Sylvia and to the reader, as the events of parts two and three of the narrative—especially those involving the relationship between Philander and Octavio—unfold. But even within the limits of the love plot of part one, that inadvertent "phallic handshake" between father and son-in-law in the garden—a savage burlesque of the gentleman's agreement by which the gift of the daughter is legitimately exchanged—reveals (even as it figures the

bypassing of legitimate succession) the homosocial ground of both patriarchal law and its transgression. Fifty guineas and that "nameless" entity, the father's penis, may be "presents . . . both worth *Melinda*'s acceptance," but only Sylvia—phallic representative of the Father's Name and Law—is worth Philander's. Just as Sylvia's ensuing marriage to Philander's "property," Brilliard, will expose the underlying ironies of the libertine's dependence on the legal artifice of marriage to secure control over the body of his lover, so Behn here shows that an incestuous challenge to the law of patriarchal prerogative does not necessarily constitute a challenge to the law of masculine privilege.

II. ROLE-PLAYING, CUCKOLDRY, AND CROSS-DRESSING: SYLVIA'S SEMIOTIC EDUCATION

It is crucial to recognize the extent to which Philander's performative strategy of playing the maid in part one of Behn's narrative is embedded in the male homosocial dynamics that organize her plot more generally. Abounding in the representation of erotic triangles, *Love-Letters* may be read as a veritable proving ground for analysis of what Eve Kosofsky Sedgwick not long ago identified [in *Between Men: English Literature and Male Homosocial Desire*, 1985] as the homosocial bases and gender assymmetries of triangular heterosexual desire. Of special relevance here is Sedgwick's analysis of the dynamics of cuckoldry and their relationship to the "masculinizing potential of subordination to a man" as it is elaborated in psychoanalytic accounts of male psychosexual development. Sedgwick quotes Richard Klein's gloss on Freud's account of "the little boy's progress towards heterosexuality" to call attention to the way in which modern constructions of heterosexual masculinity presuppose the existence (and repression) of a prior homosexual stage of feminized subordination to another male. The male child, writes Klein, "must pass . . . through the stage of the 'positive' Oedipus, a homoerotic identification with his father, a position of feminized subordination to the father, as a condition of finding a model for his own heterosexual role."

A dynamic of homoerotic identification similar to the one Freud posits and Klein describes is central to the male relationships represented in Behn's text. It is evident not just in Philander's struggles with his father-in-law, where playing the maid becomes simultaneously the means by which the hero usurps paternal authority and the occasion (however burlesque) for a homoerotic encounter with the father, but also in the prolific instances of cuckoldry recounted elsewhere in the narrative. For Sylvia is not just the space across which Philander aspires to homosocial sameness with "the father"; she is, interestingly, also the conduit whereby he asserts masculine identity with Cesario.

A brief review of the prehistory of the incestuous lovers' affair clearly reveals the extent to which Sylvia functions for Philander simultaneously as a locus of deflected homoerotic love and as a means of resolving his own desire to be like Cesario. The founding circumstance of Sylvia and Philander's love is a prior sexual rivalry between Philander and Cesario over the heart and body of Sylvia's older sister, Myrtilla. After promising to marry the prince, Myrtilla had been drawn instead into a marriage with Philander, only to return at last to an adulterous affair with Cesario. Here again, as in the matter of the affair between Philander and Sylvia, Behn makes the origins of desire problematic, introducing ambiguity in her "Argument" as to whether the impulse toward conjugal infidelity originates in Philander or Myrtilla. Philander nevertheless produces his own causal narrative in an early letter to Sylvia, where he makes the case that Myrtilla was the first to violate her vows. Especially striking here is his response to that alleged betrayal:

> *Myrtilla,* I say, first broke her marriage-vows to me; I blame her not, nor is it reasonable I should; she saw the young *Cesario,* and loved him. *Cesario,* whom the envying world in spite of prejudice must own, has irresistible charms, that godlike form, that sweetness in his face, that softness in his eyes and delicate mouth; and every beauty besides, that women dote on, and men envy: that lovely composition of man and angel! with the addition of his eternal youth and illustrious birth, was formed by heaven and nature for universal conquest! And who can love the charming hero at a cheaper rate than being undone? And she that would not venture fame, honour, and a marriage-vow for the glory of the young *Cesario*'s heart, merits not the noble victim.

Instead of faulting Myrtilla for her disloyalty, Philander identifies with her desire for Cesario. Granted, his letter is part of an elaborate textual strategy of seduction—one that requires that he provide Sylvia with irrefutable justifications for his own adulterous love. But the hyperbolic portrait he paints of Cesario, surpassed in erotic extravagance only by the protracted and probably parodic inventory of Myrtilla's physical attributes in the novel's "Argument," exceeds the demands of Philander's rhetorical project and prepares us for his ensuing account of the "joyful submission" and "shameful freedom" he experiences when Cesario cuckolds him:

> But when I knew her false, when I was once confirmed,—when by my own soul I found the

> dissembled passion of hers, when she could no longer hide the blushes, or the paleness that seized at the approaches of my disordered rival, when I saw love dancing in her eyes, and her false heart beat with nimble motions, and soft trembling seized every limb, at the approach or touch of the royal lover, then I thought myself no longer obliged to conceal my flame for *Sylvia;* nay, ere I broke silence, ere I discovered the hidden treasure of my heart, I made her falsehood plainer yet: even the time and place of the dear assignations I discovered; certainty, happy certainty! broke the dull heavy chain, and I with joy submitted to my shameful freedom, and caressed my generous rival; nay, and by heaven I loved him for it, pleased at the resemblance of our souls; for we were secret lovers both, but more pleased that he loved *Myrtilla;* for that made way to my passion for the adorable

Sylvia!

At the climax of this passage, it is difficult to disentangle Philander's pleasure from Myrtilla's. But Philander's text ultimately takes a turn whereby its writer comes to occupy more than a single position in the complex network of triangular desire. At one and the same time, he manages to identify with Myrtilla's pleasurable submission to Cesario and, through the mediating figure of Sylvia, with Cesario's position of conquest over him. For Philander, that is, Sylvia is not just a double for Myrtilla (not just another version of prohibited woman-hood) but a locus of deflected homosocial love—a substitute, in effect, for Cesario. As in Philander's night of impotence or his garden encounter with Beralti, where playing the maid serves as a strategy for appropriating paternal prerogatives, so here identification with the position of Myrtilla becomes a conduit for his assertion of masculine privilege. By providing the possibility for Philander to occupy multiple subject positions simultaneously, Sylvia creates the conditions whereby he is able to convert his sense of admiration and envy for his rival into a version of identification with him.

"'To cuckold,'" writes Sedgwick, "is by definition a sexual act, performed on a man, by another man. . . . The bond of cuckoldry . . . [is] *necessarily* hierarchical in structure, with an 'active' participant who is clearly in the ascendancy over the 'passive' one." In the homosocial scheme that underwrites this bond, moreover, "men's bonds with women are meant to be in a subordinate, complementary, and instrumental relation to bonds with other men." The world of *Love-Letters* both exemplifies this ethos and, through the heroine's ability to identify it, provides a critique of its structuring principles.

As Philander notes early on, being cuckolded is hardly an abuse over which it is worth risking one's life, let alone one's friendship with a male rival. "Let the dull, hot-brained, jealous fool upbraid me with cold patience," he writes in defense of his response to Cesario's cuckoldry, "let the fond coxcomb, whose honour depends on the frail marriage-vow, reproach me, or tell me that my reputation depends on the feeble constancy of a wife, persuade me it is honour to fight for an irretrievable and unvalued prize, and that because my rival has taken leave to cuckold me, I shall give him leave to kill me too."

Sylvia displays a similar cynicism when she demands in a moment of resistance to Philander, "What husband is not a cuckold? Nay, and a friend to him that made him so?" Philander, of course, claims transcendent passion for Sylvia as grounds for his casual dismissal of Myrtilla, insisting that "only she that has my soul can engage my sword." But his actions in the ensuing narrative will belie these early protestations and expose the deep contradictions inherent in Philander's libertine debunking of the interested codes of patriarchal honor. Sylvia will perceive these contradictions with clarity by the middle of part two, when pregnant and betrayed by Philander after having joined him in his flight to Holland to escape political prosecution (as in real life Henrietta Berkeley had in a similar circumstance followed Grey), she angrily begins a course of increasing cunning and self-sufficiency. Entertaining the advances of another suitor while allowing Philander to continue to believe in her fidelity to him and in her ignorance of his infidelity to her, she will ultimately outstrip Philander at the game of inconstancy. The Dutch nobleman Octavio, illegitimate son of the House of Orange as well as Philander's confidante and friend, fittingly becomes her instrument of revenge.

The ensuing rivalry between Philander and Octavio reproduces the competing demands of love and honor that dominate Philander's seduction of Sylvia, only to recast them in an ironic light. To all appearances, Octavio is the very embodiment of honor and authenticity; but Behn makes a mockery of his honorable punctilios in her portrait of his bumbling efforts to "protect" Sylvia from the secret of Philander's infidelity. Unable to restrain his love for the abandoned Sylvia, Octavio dutifully confesses all in letters to Philander, only to discover that the latter has taken up with Octavio's own virtuous, married sister, Calista, and is altogether willing to surrender Sylvia's body to the encroaching erotic advances of a friend. While Octavio nourishes resentment over the honor of Calista (of whose familial identity Philander yet remains ignorant), he nevertheless resolves that his friendship for Philander will surpass all other ties, including both his duty to his sister and his passion for Sylvia. Finding solace in being able to act honorably toward (i.e., with permission from) his rival in satisfying his desire for his new object, Octavio thus agrees to what amounts to a double transaction with Philander: namely, the prostitution of his sister to gain a lover ("rifle *Calista* of every virtue heaven and nature gave her," he declares, "so I may but revenge it on the *Sylvia!*" and the exchange, in effect, of his sister for Philander's. Behn underscores the similarity in difference between incest and exchange here by building a clearly incestuous charge into Octavio's voyeuristic consumption of letters in which Philander elaborately details his erotic encounters with Calista. Through her repeated doubling of the categories of sister and lover, she lodges a deft critique of aristocratic codes of masculine honor that deploy sisters as well as lovers as enabling grounds for the enactment of male prerogative.

Cognizant of the extent to which Octavio and Philander's gentleman's agreement reduces her to a mere object of circulation among men, Sylvia at length confronts Octavio with the double moral standard underlying his devotion to male honor:

> "Oh, you are very nice, *Octavio* . . . in your punctilio to *Philander;* but I perceive you are not so tender in those you ought to have for *Sylvia:* I find honour in you men, is only what you please to make it; for at the same time you think it ungenerous to betray *Philander,* you believe it no breach of honour to betray the eternal repose of *Sylvia.* You have promised *Philander* your friendship; you have avowed yourself my lover, my slave, my friend, my every thing; and yet not one of these has any tie to oblige you to my interest. . . . And here you think it no dishonour to break your word or promise; by which I find your false notions of

> virtue and honour, with which you serve yourselves, when interest, design, or self-love makes you think it necessary."

Finally, it is neither Sylvia's inconstancy with Octavio nor the latter's erotic rivalry that inspires Philander to raise his sword against his friend; it is rather the perception that, in betraying the "secrets of friendship" to Sylvia, Octavio has allowed a heterosexual tie to supercede their homosocial bond. This transgression alone is able to move Philander, as it were, out of the boudoir and onto the battlefield.

On the day before he is to take Holy Orders in part three of the narrative, Octavio—now broken by Sylvia's treachery—is visited by Philander, who comes to beg Octavio's pardon for offenses he has committed against him and to persuade him to abandon his determination to retire from the world. Not only has Philander debauched Octavio's sister, who has by now retired pregnant to a convent, but he has ravished from him Sylvia, the very mistress he had not long before abandoned to his friend. As a pledge of his friendship at this critical moment in the text, Philander now assures Octavio that he would never have violated his sister, Calista, had he known of her relationship to him. He would, moreover, as he wryly notes, gladly "quit [Sylvia] to him, were she ten times dearer to him than she was," if doing so would deter Octavio from his desperate intent. Although these protestations of friendship from Philander fail to dissuade Octavio from his resolve, they nevertheless elicit this reciprocal profession of his love:

> "Sir, I must confess you have found out the only way to disarm me of my resentment against you, if I were not obliged, by those vows I am going to take, to pardon and be at peace with all the world. However, these vows cannot hinder me from conserving entirely that friendship in my heart, which your good qualities and beauties at first sight engaged there, and from esteeming you more than perhaps I ought to do; the man whom I must yet own my rival, and the undoer of my sister's honour. But oh—no more of that; a friend is above a sister, or a mistress.' At this he hung down his eyes and sighed."

Uttered on the eve of the hero's initiation into the fraternal order of St. Bernard, this simple maxim—"A friend is above a sister or a mistress"—is perhaps the baldest statement we have of the sexual hierarchies that underpin Behn's plot. Granting the pardon Philander begs, Octavio seals it by taking "a ring of great value from his finger," which he presents to Philander as a pledge of his love, in much the same spirit that Philander had earlier pledged Sylvia. Like the ring, Sylvia is the gift that cements and the token that signifies relations between men.

Sylvia's specular status in relations between men is neatly literalized by her frequent appearances in male attire. It is, in fact, during the first of these episodes of cross-dressing that Octavio initially falls in love with her. Drag enhances Sylvia's attractions as an object of male desire (she "never appeared so charming and desirable" as when dressed as a man if for no other reason than that it enables her male admirers both to identify with the sexual conquests of the young cavalier whom she impersonates and to experience a certain rivalry with him. These at least are the peculiar pleasures of Octavio's experience: "*Octavio* saw every day with abundance of pleasure the little revenges of love, on those women's hearts who had made before little conquests over him, and strove by all the gay presents he made a young *Fillmond* (for so they called *Sylvia,*) to make him appear unresistible to the ladies; and while *Sylvia* gave them new wounds, *Octavio* failed not to receive them too among the crowd, till at last he became a confirmed slave, to the lovely unknown; and that which was yet more strange, she captivated the men no less than the women."

In the long run, however, cross-dressing has another—a productive as opposed to a merely specular—potential that Sylvia in time learns to exploit with increasing skill and that goes beyond according her that freedom of physical movement and those other "little privileges . . . denied to women." Over the course of her career, Behn's Ovidian letter-writer undergoes a dazzling metamorphosis from corrupted innocence to triumphant depravity—a transformation that culminates in part three of the narrative in an exhilarating escapade in which she elevates the game of sexual conquest from a means of revenge into an art. Having become a consummate fiction-maker and role player (as well as a wealthy courtesan who capitalizes on the weaknesses of unsuspecting men), she here undertakes as a "frolic to divert herself" conquest of the heart of Don Alonzo, a young Spanish-born gentleman distinguished most significantly for being the only man ever to have succeeded in outdoing Philander at the game of inconstancy. When Alonzo boasts of having "reduced . . . to . . . a lover" an unconquerable Dutch countess whose heart even Philander could not command, Sylvia resolves to go him one better by determining to fix his own wandering heart on her. She succeeds in her determination by enacting a masquerade in which she plays both male and female parts: a handsome cavalier named Bellumere and his lovely sister, Mme de— .

By means of a ring that Alonzo gives to Bellumere as a pledge of male friendship and that Mme de— later vaunts upon her tour, Sylvia deftly turns Bellumere into a suspected rival of Don Alonzo for her favors. She thus plays an interesting variation on the homosocial code whereby mistresses typically stand in as obligatory heterosexual displacements of prohibited objects of homoerotic male desire. By creating a male version of herself through which to lure her victims into a homoerotic attachment, she paradoxically ensures her own status as a primary object of desire instead of merely an intermediate term in a phallocentric sexual and symbolic economy. In this instance, she also cleverly turns Alonzo's imagined rival into a brother, to whose authority over the disposal of her favors she presents herself as determined to defer. Sylvia imposes her own authority, that is, by means of the pretense of deferring to Bellumere's, thus creating a drama in which she at once reproduces and subverts the hierarchy of authority that informed her early relation with Philander. Both producing and controlling Alonzo's desire for her, she now manages her own circulation as a

sign of femininity.

This episode makes stunningly clear the extent to which Sylvia has appropriated Philander's performative strategies of symbolic deferral by the novel's end. As we have seen, the relation between sign and referent in Philander's garden escapade with Beralti following his alleged attack of impotence in part one is neither as stable nor transparent as Gardiner suggests when she reads it as a simple externalization of the hero's demeaning impotence. Nor does it involve a simple masking of the "truth" of Philander's inherent dominance. It is, rather, a productive relation in which Philander consolidates his power by using theater to produce material effects. This, we might say, is his type of sorcery, the basis of that power to charm by which he creates effects in some instances as tangible as those wrought by philtres upon the body of Brilliard or by alchemy on the heart and eyes of Cesario. For Behn, his performances are occasions for displacing the natural ground of the opposition between inner and outer experience, psyches and surfaces, artifice and authenticity. Philander treads an extraordinarily fluid line between roleplaying and reality, dissembling so well at times that, as Behn's narrator notes late in the text, "he scarce knew himself that he did so."

By the time Sylvia encounters Don Alonzo, she has learned how to exploit the productive nature of performance so as to move beyond her status as a specular representation of male desire, a mere player in a drama controlled by men, both to create and variously represent herself. She has not, however, always recognized the productive potential of her own radical deracination as a sign (a performer) of femininity. Although she has from the start intuited the insufficiency of the written word to express her soul completely, she is fairly confident initially of its ability to simulate, if not entirely to substitute, for presence. "While I write," she declares in an early letter to Philander, "methinks I am talking to thee; I tell thee thus my soul, while thou, methinks, art all the while smiling and listening by; this is much easier than silent thought, and my soul is never weary of this converse; and thus I would speak a thousand things, but that still, methinks, words do not enough express my soul." Still a fairly naive reader, Sylvia believes this insufficiency can be made up for by the supplement of presence, by merely adding voice to text: "to understand that right, there requires looks; there is a rhetoric in looks; in sighs and silent touches that surpasses all; there is an accent in the sound of words too, that gives a sense and soft meaning to little things, which of themselves are of trivial value, and insignificant; and by the cadence of the utterance may express a tenderness which their own meaning does not bear; by this I wou'd insinuate, that the story of the heart cannot be so well told by this way, as by presence and conversation." A more savvy reader of Philander might by now have recognized the dangers of ventriloquism, which he betrays in his third letter when he describes the emptiness of his public performances: "I move about this unregarded world, appear every day in the great senate-house, at clubs, cabals, and private consultations; . . . I say I appear indeed, and give my voice in public business; but oh my heart more kindly is employed." But Sylvia, though she sometimes doubts his word, still finds Philander's letters more reassuring than ominous. Clinging to an idealized notion of presence, she buys into the rhetorical opposition between private and public life on which Philander erects the fiction of his own sincerity.

While the Sylvia of part one may still believe naively in the possibility of her own and others' authenticity ("I have no arts, heaven knows, no guile or double meaning in my soul, 'tis all plain native simplicity," her maid and "too fatal counsellor," Melinda, nevertheless detects her mistress's performative potential early on. In the letter she writes to Philander just before his fateful night of impotence, Melinda alludes to the late occurrence of "many ominous things." Among these she cites an incident that has aroused suspicions in Sylvia's mother regarding her daughter's romantic activities. Melinda presumably wants to alert Philander on the eve of his assignation with Sylvia to the perils of heightened parental vigilance, but her letter also provides him with a warning glimpse of Sylvia's budding semiotic education. It shows the heroine's incipient ability to exploit not just the dangerous excesses of script but the dangerous supplementarity of presence and voice itself. Although Sylvia had early lamented the intransigence of her "guilty pen," bemoaning the insidious tendency of writing to betray her best intentions, she here shows an almost instinctive urge to master the treachery of the letter and to exploit its openness as a form of self-defense. Discovered by her mother in the act of writing to Philander, physical evidence in hand, Sylvia brilliantly avoids being implicated in her own guilt through an ingenious act of textual deferral. In the exigency of the moment, she concocts the fiction that she is writing as a surrogate for Melinda to the latter's lover, using pseudonyms to protect that guilty "maid," and she adds demonstrative proof of her claim by, in effect, performing her text aloud with an altered—an essentially ironic—emphasis. As Melinda reports, she "turned it . . . prettily into burlesque love by her *manner of reading it*" (italics added).

This cunning transformation of material fact into plausible fiction by creating a multiplicity of referents through the act of reading forms a stark contrast with the later example of Clarissa, who is characteristically victimized by the uncontrollable openness of her own letter texts. When Clarissa finally does learn to exploit the ambiguities of script, moreover, she can do so only by closing them around the referent of the father. Writing to Lovelace that she is "setting out with all diligence for [her] Father's House," in her famous trick of lying truthfully, Clarissa points to a superabundance of father figures not to an open field of interpretive possibility. And indeed one can not help feeling that the imperatives of honesty and sincerity that control Clarissa's writing play a rather sinister role in determining the range of choices she is able to imagine for taking retributive action against Lovelace's treachery. It is not until the topos of the daughter's guilty pen recurs in Frances Burney's *Evelina* or Jane Austen's *Lady Susan* that we again encounter an exploitation of the formal openness of the letter as subtle and

subversive as the one Behn offers in this single episode from her text.

This scene, in which Sylvia reads her own love letter as if she were only playacting the lover, resonates in several crucial ways throughout Behn's text. In one sense, it serves as a paradigm in small of Behn's novel as a whole—a figure, as it were, for the distancing effect of parody Behn herself achieves at the level of narration through her characteristic cultivation of rhetorical excess. As the first instance in the narrative when Sylvia instinctively plays the role of "maid," moreover, it foreshadows the freedom she will ultimately realize by abandoning the presupposition that she possesses a natural bedrock of desire and a core of stable self-identity. By introducing the possibility that Sylvia's letter may be itself only a script—that the very text she generates as the sincere expression of her soul may be symptomatic of a role she plays but over which she does not have performative control—it exposes the radically contingent nature of her desire and the performative as opposed to natural basis of her subjectivity.

If Sylvia's original letter text is merely an imitation of originality and if presence and voice are not reliable markers of substance but dangerous forms of supplementarity, then the very possibility of an origin—of an authentic ground from which one's actions and one's utterances proceed—becomes problematic. In the space opened by these unsettling possibilities, Sylvia is freed from the promise of an incestuous fulfillment of original desire into an open field of signifying possibility. Behn gestures toward this openness in the penultimate paragraph of her text, where she sends her heroine daily in search of new conquests "wherever she shews the charmer." The physical body—that most corporeal of figures—finally emerges as the most unstable of all sites of meaning. The ultimate charmer, it obliterates the very ground of truth and falsehood required for the enactment of personal authenticity. In Behn's world of apparently infinite displacements, there is finally no essence or original that is not constituted in the dialogics of performance or the contestations of power politics. Even so allegedly authenticating a gesture as incest is finally exposed as substituting for the law it would subvert.

III. CODA

Libertine rhetoric exalts the female as an iconic substitute for the father-king, promoting the flattering fiction that woman is the source of both desire and prohibition. "Glorious woman was born for command and dominion," declares Philander, "though custom has usurped us the name of rule over all." In fact, he insists, Sylvia's sovereignty is the motivating force for all his political ambitions. He seeks political empire only to be able to trade it for romantic slavery:

> Let me toil to gain, but let *Sylvia* triumph and reign;
> I ask no more than the led slave at her chariot wheels,
> to gaze on my charming conqueress, and wear with
> joy her fetters! Oh how proud I should be to see the
> dear victor of my soul so elevated, so adorn'd with

crowns and sceptres at her feet, which I had won; to see her smiling on the adoring crowd, distributing her glories to young waiting princes. . . . Heavens! methinks I see the lovely virgin in this state, her chariot slowly driving through the multitude that press to gaze upon her, she dress'd like *Venus,* richly gay and loose, her hair and robe blown by the flying winds.

By novel's close, Philander's vision of Sylvia's triumph as spectacle (however disingenuously it has been offered) is realized, as the heroine, "dressed in perfect glory," is pursued by gazing crowds through the streets of Brussels, a rival of even Cesario's elegant mistress, Hermione. But unlike Hermione, who invests all her own ambition in Cesario's success only to meet her demise in his defeat, Sylvia does not depend for her glory on Philander's toil and enterprise; she achieves it on her own. She makes the punctilious Octavio an instrument of her revenge against Philander and to that passion she eventually sacrifices him. By the end of the narrative, moreover, she has resourcefully managed to turn even Philander's servant, Brilliard, (originally deployed to maintain Philander's authority over her) to the promotion of her material interests. Now using Brilliard as a prop in her own self-serving schemes, she manipulates him (by once again exploiting a homosocial bond) into extorting an inheritance from the retired Octavio on the spurious promise of her own penitence and retirement. Then, "impatient to be seen on the *Tour,* and in all public places," she promptly furnishes herself with "new coach and equipage, and . . . lavish . . . clothes and jewels."

The irony of Behn's political defense of royalism is that it ends with the triumph not only of the king but also of the woman who most quintessentially embodies unregenerate female defiance of male supremacy. Cesario's rebellion fails and Philander opportunistically embraces monarchy, while in a savagely ironic twist on this double defeat of the Whig cause, Sylvia makes good the libertine promise of female sovereignty. At one level Behn seems to want to point to divinely appointed kingship as the ultimate locus of truth and authority—the original object of worship of which all other objects of desire are failed imitations and empty substitutes. But the figure at center stage in *Love-Letters between a Nobleman and His Sister,* the one that absorbs the reader's gaze, is not the king at all but the spectacularly protean body of Sylvia. That this body is also figured without much comment for the better part of Behn's narrative not as the virgin body Philander invokes but as an eroticized maternal presence, a curiously denaturalized point of physical origin in the shape of a pregnant eros, is perhaps not so very insignificant a detail after all, so thoroughly disruptive as it is of any binary relation between displacement and origin. Much as Sylvia signifies the physical power to generate nameless and presumably endless substitutions, so Behn proliferates meanings beyond the binary frame that constitutes incest as a counter to patriarchal law or legitimate kingship as an ultimate site of meaning and of power.

FURTHER READING

Biography

Cameron, W. J. *New Light on Aphra Behn.* Auckland, New Zealand: University of Auckland, 1961, 106 p.

> Cameron summarizes this study as "an investigation into the facts and fictions surrounding [Behn's] journey to Surinam in 1663 and her activities as a spy in Flanders in 1666."

Duffy, Maureen. *The Passionate Shepherdess: Aphra Behn, 1640-89.* London: Jonathan Cape, 1977, 324 p.

> Account of Behn's life based on her works and the scant extant documents relating to or by her. Duffy examines Behn's works for insight into her life.

Goreau, Angeline. *Reconstructing Aphra: A Social Biography of Aphra Behn.* New York: The Dial Press, 1980, 339 p.

> Portrays Behn as a woman driven by contradictory personality traits: independence and emotional neediness.

Criticism

Duffy, Maureen. Introduction to *Love-Letters Between a Nobleman and His Sister,* by Aphra Behn, pp. v-xvii. New York: Penguin Books, Virago Press, 1987.

> Comprehensive introduction to Behn's *Love-Letters,* where, as Duffy asserts, "We hear the first authorial female voice in English prose."

Gardiner, Judith Kegan. "The First English Novel: Aphra Behn's *Love Letters,* the Canon, and Women's Tastes." *Tulsa Studies in Women's Literature* 8, No. 2 (Fall, 1989): 201-22.

> Assesses the role of Behn's *Love-Letters* in the history of the novel, focusing on "psychological paradigms" both in the work and in its historical context.

Gewirtz, Arthur. "The Comic Adaptations of Aphra Behn: Libertine Naturalism in Restoration Comedy." In his *Restoration Adaptations of Early 17th Century Comedies,* pp. 83-110. Washington, D.C.: University Press of America, 1982.

> Summarizes most of Behn's notable plays, with a particular emphasis on the "libertine naturalism" of the typical rake (or male sexual predator) in Restoration comedy.

Greer, Germaine. "Montague Summers and *The Works of Aphra Behn.*" In *The Uncollected Verse of Aphra Behn,* edited by Germaine Greer, pp. 1-11. Stump Cross, England: Stump Cross Books, 1989.

> Chastises Summers for poor scholarship in his six-volume edition of *The Works of Aphra Behn,* particularly pointing out errors related to Summers' treatment of Behn's poetry. Greer states: "It is typical of Behn's chequered literary fortunes that she should have found an editor

shadier than herself, who divided his intellectual attention unevenly between satanism, theatricals, and literature, in descending order of importance, and that we should be indebted to his eccentricity for the only edition of her works that we have."

Guffey, George. "Aphra Behn's *Oroonoko*: Occasion and Accomplishment." In *Two English Novelists: Aphra Behn and Anthony Trollope,* Papers Read at a Clark Library Seminar, May 11, 1974, pp. 3-37. Los Angeles: William Andrews Clark Memorial Library, 1975.

Presents a realistic reading of the novel and asserts that in *Oroonoko* Behn "makes a strong argument for the absolute power of legitimate kings . . . [and] attempts to

gain the sympathy of her reader for James, who, at the time of the publication of the book, was in great danger of immanent deposition or wars."

Link, Frederick M. Introduction to *The Rover,* by Aphra Behn, pp. ix-xvi. Lincoln: University of Nebraska Press, 1967.

Describes how Behn, in *The Rover,* created a skillful and witty comedy of intrigue out of the weighty and slow-moving play *Thomaso* by Thomas Killigrew. Link's introduction also includes a capsule summary of Behn's dramatic oeuvre while discussing at length the characters in *The Rover.*

————. *Aphra Behn.* Boston: Twayne Publishers, 1968, 183 p.

General Overview of Behn's life and career

Morgan, Fidelis. "Aphra Behn-Astraea." In *The Female Wits: Women Playwrights on the London Stage 1660-1720,* pp. 12-23. London: Virago Press, 1981.

Surveys Behn's life and theatrical works.

O'Donnell, Mary Ann. *Aphra Behn: An Annotated Bibliography of Primary and Secondary Sources.* New York: Garland Publishing, 1986, 557 p.

Catalogue of Behn's works and critical commentary on her writing; includes an introduction that summarizes her career.

Schofield, Mary Anne, and Macheski, Cecilia, eds. *Curtain Calls: British and American Women and the Theater 1660-1820.* Athens: Ohio University Press, 1991, 403 p.

Includes essays by Deborah C. Payne, Frances M. Kavenik, Jessica Munns, Nancy Cotton, and Rose Zimbardo that explore various aspects of Behn's career as a playwright.

Stiebel, Arlene. "Not Since Sappho: The Erotic in Poems of Katherine Philips and Aphra Behn." In *Homosexuality in Renaissance and Enlightenment England: Literary Representations in Historical Context,* edited by Claude J. Summers, pp. 153-64. New York: The Haworth Press, 1992.

Interprets "The Disappointment" as an account of rape and argues that Behn's verse manipulated literary conventions to allow her to discuss taboo subjects such as lesbianism without alerting the audience to any breach of decorum.

Todd, Janet. "'An Honour and Glory to our Sex': Aphra Behn," in her *The Sign of Angellica: Women, Writing, and Fiction 1660-1800,* pp. 69-83. London: Virago, 1989.

Surveys Behn's life and works and designates *Love-Letters* as her masterpiece. Todd also suggests that, "in a way all the works of Behn together teach a kind of acceptance of the absurdity of life."

Additional coverage of Behn is contained in the following sources published by Gale Research: *DISCovering Authors, Dictionary of Literary Biography, Vol. 39: British Novelists, 1660-1800; Dictionary of Literary Biography,* Vol. 80: *Restoration and Eighteenth-Century Dramatists; Dictionary of Literary Biography, Vol. 131: Seventeenth-Century British Nondramatic Poets; Drama Criticism, Vol. 4;* and *World Literature Criticism, 1500 to the Present.*

Anne Bradstreet

1612(?)-1672

(Full name Anne Dudley Bradstreet) English-born American poet and prose writer.

For further information on Bradstreet's career and works, see *Literature Criticism from 1400 to 1800,* Vol. 4.

INTRODUCTION

Bradstreet was America's first published poet and the first woman to produce a lasting volume of poetry in the English language. Her work is considered particularly significant for its expression of passion, anger, and uncertainty within the rigid social and religious atmosphere of Puritan New England, and for the insight it provides into the lives of women from that period.

Biographical Information

Bradstreet was born in England to a Puritan family. Her father, Thomas Dudley, was steward to the Earl of Lincoln, a leading nonconformist in the religious strife of England. Because of her father's high position and the availability of the Earl's extensive library, Bradstreet's education was unusually comprehensive for a woman of her time. In 1630 she moved with her husband and her parents to the Massachusetts Bay Colony, where her husband and her father served as governors of the settlement. As a New England colonist, Bradstreet encountered a life of hardship to which she was unaccustomed. In 1647 her brother-in-law returned to England, taking with him the manuscript of Bradstreet's poems. He published them without her knowledge, entitling the collection *The Tenth Muse* (1650). The volume met with immediate success in London. Surprised by the work's reception, but unhappy with its unpolished state, Bradstreet undertook to revise the poems, some of which were lost in the fire that destroyed the Bradstreet home in 1666. Six years after her death the revisions and some new poems were published under the title *Several Poems.* Bradstreet's prose meditations and later poems did not appear in print until 1867.

Major Works

Most of Bradstreet's works may be placed into one of two distinct periods. The "public" poems that appeared in *The Tenth Muse* are structurally and thematically formal, written in the style of Renaissance poetry. The *Quaternions,* which consist of four poems, each of which are divided into four parts, treat the humours, elements, sea-

ANNE BRADSTREET

sons, and ages of man, and are imitative of Guillaume Du Bartas's *Divine Weeks and Works.* "The Four Monarchies" is a long unfinished poem, patterned after Sir Walter Raleigh's *The History of the World,* describing what were considered the four great monarchies of civilization. The elegies contained in *The Tenth Muse* are dedications to public figures such as Queen Elizabeth I and Sir Philip Sidney. Bradstreet's later poems—described by most scholars as her "private" poems—are less stylized and more personal. In these works, Bradstreet expressed anxiety about her health and the safety of her family, as well as passionate love for her husband, and uncertainty concerning her religious devotion. The elegies "In Memory of My Dear Grandchild Elizabeth Bradstreet" and "To the Memory of My Dear Daughter in Law, Mrs. Mercy Bradstreet" are poignant meditations on death in which Bradstreet questions her faith. In "Some Verses Upon the Burning of Our House, July 10th, 1666," she mourns the loss of her possessions, eschewing the Puritan ideal of the primacy of spiritual rewards over worldly pleasures, but concludes the poem with a sense of resignation and faith. As

Wendy Martin has noted: "Much of [Bradstreet's] work indicates that she had a difficult time resolving the conflict she experienced between the pleasures of sensory and familial experience and the promises of heaven. As a Puritan she struggled to subdue her attachment to the world, but as a woman she sometimes felt more strongly connected to her husband, children, and community than to God." Bradstreet's poems to her husband Simon contain erotic symbolism noted by many critics, and her most critically acclaimed poem, "Contemplations," evidences an appreciation of nature and solitude similar to that found in the work of the later Romantic poets.

Critical Reception

Bradstreet received praise for the formal poetry of *The Tenth Muse,* which adhered to courtly standards and thus marked her as highly talented. Afterwards, however, she was largely ignored by critics until the late nineteenth century, when a volume of her later poems was published for the first time. Commentators then offered little praise, viewing her poetry as only a slight exception to what nineteenth-century readers perceived as the austere, repressive nature of Puritanism. In the mid-twentieth century, feminist critics became interested in Bradstreet's work, recognizing her exploration of the paradoxes between religious doctrine and individual belief, and the often blatant sexual imagery of poems addressing her husband or her God. While Bradstreet's public poetry is considered by many contemporary critics to be stilted and imitative, her private poetry is acclaimed for its deft use of ballad and lyric forms, and for its insightful exploration of complex personal issues.

PRINCIPAL WORKS

The Tenth Muse, Lately sprung up in America (poetry) 1650

Several Poems Compiled with great variety of Wit and Learning, full of Delight (poetry) 1678

The Works of Anne Bradstreet in Prose and Verse (poetry and meditations) 1867

The Works of Anne Bradstreet (poetry and meditations) 1967

The *Complete Works of Anne Bradstreet* (poetry and meditations) 1981

CRITICISM

Alvin H. Rosenfeld (essay date 1970)

SOURCE: "Anne Bradstreet's 'Contemplations': Patterns of Form and Meaning," in *The New England Quarterly,* Vol. XLIII, No. 1, March 1970, pp. 79-96.

[*In the following excerpt, Rosenfeld discusses Bradsteet's*

"*Contemplations*" *in terms of its similarities with the works of later Romantic poets.*]

On first reading, the thirty-three stanzas of **"Contemplations"** seem to be held together very loosely, if at all, but a closer reading begins to reveal certain patterns of imagery and ideas within the poem. The seasonal metaphor is one of these and contributes significantly to both form and meaning. A second pattern, the daily cycle of morning and night, with its attendant periods of light and dark, obviously ties in closely with the yearly cycle of the seasons. The progression of natural images—directing the poet's vision from tree to sun to river to bird to stone—is a third and needs to be examined carefully. A fourth element of structural and thematic importance involves the elaborate switches in narrative and dramatic time. A fifth concerns the noticeable contrasts between Classical and Biblical allusions. A sixth has to do with tone and mood and the varied uses of the lyrical and elegiac modes together with the larger form of the narrative. All of these factors help to make the poem the rich and complex work that it is. They also lend the poem unity, although it is a unity that is not easily apparent and only becomes so when one isolates some of the patterns of form and meaning and examines them, at first, somewhat apart.

Anne Bradstreet's use of the seasonal metaphor—which moves the poem from autumn through winter to a temporarily realized season of eternal spring and summer—is an anticipation of the English Romantic poets and inevitably provokes parallels with Wordsworth and Coleridge, Shelley and Keats. As with those poets, her seasons are both physical and spiritual and participate in the same cycle of the waning and revival of life. As more than one critic has already pointed out, several of her lines on the seasons resemble some of the most memorable lines in the poems of Shelley and Keats, a factor that may permit us to read her poetry in the light of what we have learned from theirs.

Particularly appropriate—and helpful—in this connection is the place of the poet as the central figure in the drama of seasonal change. For it is the threat to the poet in his vocation *as* poet and not just as mortal man that is always crucial in the Romantic's evocation of the seasons. That is true for the Wordsworth of the "Ode: Intimations of Immortality," for the Coleridge of "Dejection: An Ode," for the Shelley of "Ode to the West Wind," for the Keats of the great odes—and for the Anne Bradstreet of **"Contemplations."** A significant part of her poem's theme (and one finds it also in the poems just cited) has to do with the challenge to the imagination of the poet's heavy and constant sense of time, flux, and a final oblivion. A major portion of this theme in **"Contemplations"** is carried by the seasonal metaphor.

The poem actually begins with it—"Some time now past in the autumnal tide" (1)—and from this point on it is pervasive, appearing explicitly in at least a third of the stanzas and implicitly in many of the others. The poet invokes it immediately when, walking alone in the woods of an autumn day, she quietly gives herself up to the splendid scene and is moved to remark: "More heaven than earth was here, no winter and no night" (2). She is moved by the majesty of the trees and particularly by one "stately oak" which, with its height and strength, seems to defy and transcend a "hundred winters . . . or [a] thousand." But the lines that most fully express the poet's attachment to the metaphor of the seasons appear later, in stanzas 18 and 28:

> When I behold the heavens as in their prime,
> And then the earth (though old) still clad in
>   green,
> The stones and trees, insensible of time,
> Nor age nor wrinkle on their front are seen;
> If winter come and greenness then do fade,
> A spring returns, and they more youthful made;
> But man grows old, lies down, remains where
>   once he's laid.
>
> (18)

> The dawning morn with songs thou dost prevent,
> Sets hundred notes unto thy feathered crew,
> So each one tunes his pretty instrument,
> And warbling out the old, begin anew,
> And thus they pass their youth in summer
>   season,
> Then follow thee into a better region,
> Where winter's never felt by that sweet airy
>   legion.
>
> (28)

The Shelleyan note is inescapable in the first of these stanzas, the Keatsian in the second. Anne Bradstreet seems to share with these poets a consciousness of the rejuvenescence of life, of the chance to recover from the old to make always new beginnings, which comes with the cycle of the "Quaternal seasons," as she refers to them in an earlier stanza (6). Stanza 18 ends, however, on a pessimistic note about man's ability to participate in the seasonal cycle, and at this point we have a departure from the later Romantic poet's affirmation of seasonal death and rebirth. Anne Bradstreet was of another age, after all, and she is nowhere closer to that age than here, where she qualifies a strong personal impulse towards Romantic beliefs with the traditional Christian assertion of man's mortality:

> By birth more noble than those creatures all,
> Yet seems by nature and by custom cursed,
> No sooner born, but grief and care makes fall
> That state obliterate he had at first;
> Nor youth, nor strength, nor wisdom spring
>   again,
> Nor habitations long their names retain,
> But in oblivion to the final day remain.
>
> (19)

Theseus' famous speech in *A Midsummer-Night's Dream* about the imagination giving to airy nothing "a local habitation and a name" is echoed here, and its implications are that the poet has suffered not only a reversal of her commitment to the seasonal metaphor but of the very

quality of her imagination. For although the poem goes on to affirm that "man was made for endless immortality" (20), the kind of immortality referred to and pursued is that of orthodox Christianity and not Romantic renewal on earth. Christianity's idea of resurrection after death is based, in part, upon the symbolism of the seasonal cycle, but its final goal is transcendence of all natural forms to eternal life beyond. A prose passage in Anne Bradstreet's **"Meditations Divine and Moral"** helps to make this point emphatic:

> The spring is a lively emblem of the resurrection: after a long winter we see the leafless trees and dry stocks (at the approach of the sun) to resume their former vigor and beauty in a more ample manner than what they lost in the autumn; so shall it be at that great day after a long vacation, when the Sun of righteousness shall appear; those dry bones shall arise in far more glory than that which they lost at their creation, and in this transcends the spring that their leaf shall never fail nor their sap decline.

This is a graceful description of familiar Christian doctrine and represents, one imagines, what Anne Bradstreet would have claimed to be her final religious position on the questions of life, death, and immortality.

Does it also represent her deepest responses as a poet, one wonders? The question must be asked, and not just for **"Contemplations"** but for other of her poems as well. For if one closely reads **"The Flesh and the Spirit,"** **"Verses upon the Burning of Our House,"** the elegies on Sidney, Du Bartas, and Elizabeth, the poems to her husband, and **"Contemplations,"** it soon becomes clear that the currents within the poetry itself seem too often to run counter to a position of religious orthodoxy. And if it is finally unfair to throw Anne Bradstreet fully into the camp of the Romantics, so too is it unfair to cast her completely as a traditionally believing "Puritan" poet.

Several critics have called attention to "the clash of feeling and dogma" in her poetry, to the struggle between "how she really feels instead of how she *should* feel," and that is precisely what we are faced with here. This struggle adds character and strength to her poetry, and one should not attempt to dismiss it, as is sometimes done, by seeing it as merely an incidental flaw in an otherwise clearly defined position of either staunch Puritanism or rebellious Romanticism. The poetry itself does not fully resolve these tensions in either direction, after all, but instead gains much of its vitality and interest from the existence of what Blake called the warring contraries.

In **"Contemplations"** one finds the war of the contraries everywhere: in the early assertion but later retreat from the seasonal metaphor; in the dualities of morning and night; light and dark; the present earth and a future heaven; rapt speech and an imposed silence. Phoebus and the God of the Puritan's Bible are opposed here, as are their related values, which may be designated, in the poem's own terms, as "this world of pleasure" (32) as against the promised joys "of an eternal morrow" (30). In the end, the will towards "divine translation" (30) appears to triumph, but one suspects a large share of its victory is doctrinaire, imposed from without, rather than earned naturally from within, the poem.

So much of **"Contemplations"** seems, in fact, to issue from what Anne Bradstreet calls "the feeling knowledge" (6) of the world that one begins to doubt the legitimacy for her poetry of some of the less inspired religious assertions that appear within it. One cannot ignore their presence, of course, but too often the merely traditionally rendered religious passages pale before some of the more deeply felt lyrical passages in praise of Phoebus and the things of the earth. It is hard to be moved, for instance, by a triplet such as this:

But sad affliction comes and makes him see
Here's neither honour, wealth, nor safety;
Only above is found all with security.

(32)

whereas one *is* moved by this:

Thy presence makes it day, thy absence night,
Quaternal seasons caused by thy might:
Hail creature, full of sweetness, beauty, and
    delight.

(6)

Anne Bradstreet's apostrophe to the sun is worthy of Shelley and expresses some of the same elegance of line and imaginative strength that one finds in Shelley at his best. In contrast, her verses on man's earthly afflictions and promise of security beyond are flat and awkward. The second triplet is graceful, the feeling, inspired; in the first, the language is clumsy, the sentiment, unconvincing and seemingly untrue.

If one weighs the merit of these two sets of verses by Anne Bradstreet's affection for "the feeling knowledge," it is obvious that, no matter what her position as a prominent member of the Puritan faith community, as a poet she was more a worshipper of Phoebus than of Christ. Her loveliest lines in **"Contemplations"** are written in praise of the sun god, whom she addresses as "a strong man" and "a bridegroom," and who moved her to a position of near adoration:

Then higher on the glistering Sun I gazed,
Whose beams was shaded by the leavie tree;
The more I looked, the more I grew amazed,
And softly said, "What glory's like to thee?"
Soul of this world, this universe's eye,
No wonder some made thee a deity;
Had I not better known, alas, the same had I.

(4)

This is poetry written from a high level of inspired awe and strong feeling, but the concluding line tends to deflate these qualities of spirit considerably and represents a retreat from them. This initial surge and subsequent reversal of voice and vision is typical not only of this

passage but of the poem as a whole, and in observing it one becomes aware of a fundamental pattern in **"Contemplations"** that largely defines both the poem's form and meaning.

The poet's imagination belonged to the earth and the sun who reigned over it, reviving "from death and dullness" (5) not only the earth's heart but hers as well. The demands of a Puritan religious consciousness, however, apparently did not permit so free and exuberant an indulgence of the imagination and dictated instead its own terms of worship. The poet is consequently turned away from her initial sources of inspiration in the natural world to thoughts of what instead she *should* be praising. The results for the poetry are, as expected, not good:

My great Creator I would magnify,
That nature had thus decked liberally;
But Ah, and Ah, again, my imbecility!

(8)

Stuttering—and—ultimately—silence come instead of praise. The displacement of elevated feeling by an overpowering sense of religious duty issues in a collapse of the imagination. The same poet whose senses are earlier described as "rapt" by the "delectable view" of an autumn day and who sees and can sing the sun "so full of glory" (7) is brought to silence when forced to praise her Maker: "I, as mute, can warble forth no higher lays" (9).

In a letter to her children accompanying her book of poems, Anne Bradstreet wrote that the aim of her poetry was "to declare the truth, not to set forth myself, but the glory of God." There is no reason to doubt that that was her conscious intention, but she could no more apply it consistently and programmatically in her poetry than could Milton. Her song *is* a song of praise, but she could only sing well what her imagination, and not her moral consciousness, responded to faithfully. When the latter intruded from without, the poetry collapsed from within. When this happens in **"Contemplations"** her resources as a lyric poet are stunned, and, rendered "mute," she literally has no voice left to sing her hymn of glory.

Brought to the point of silence, then, the poem can either end here in a defeat of the imagination or try to find new direction. It attempts the latter, and with stanza 10 a major turn occurs that complicates the poem exceedingly in terms of both form and meaning.

In its first nine stanzas the poem is essentially a dramatic lyric, but stanzas 10 through 17 are purely narrative. There is also a significant time change, from present to past. The seasonal metaphor is dropped altogether, and the times of day which earlier prevailed, morning and afternoon, now become "perpetual night" (17). Phoebus and all other references to a radiant earth disappear and are replaced by the Biblical stories of Adam and Eve (11-12), Cain and Abel (13-15), and somber reflections of "the virgin earth . . . cloyed" with the draught of too much blood (14). Man's fallen state and the general vanity of all human endeavor are described in a mood that has shifted radically from one of a reflective and rapt lyricism to that of a heavy brooding that approaches the dirge. The former themes of vitality, immediacy, buoyancy, and pleasure have gone out of the poem, and instead one has references to sin, death, vanity, and despair.

The poem has obviously undergone an extreme change in all respects, a change that one can account for and understand only in terms of what happens in the poem to the imagination. The poet alert and fully alive when her imagination is indulged is brought first to a stammering silence and then carried in a drift towards death when her imagination is forced to turn away from the natural sources of its inspiration. The outward pressures of dogma separate her from her chosen bridegroom Phoebus and the delights of the earth and instead bring her to recall guiltily the fates of Adam and Eve, Cain and Abel. Like Eve, she "sighs to think of Paradise. And how she lost her bliss" (12). Like Cain, she is "branded with guilt and crushed with treble woes" (15). She defines Cain's struggle as one between "deep despair" and a "wish of life" (15), and that is exactly her own situation at this point in the poem; and, within the frame of the long narrative section, it is the death wish and not the "wish of life" that prevails. . . .

"Contemplations" does not collapse entirely with the collapse of its initial Romanticism, though, and Anne Bradstreet was resourceful enough to seek out new figures to continue the poem. The tree was her first important image, valued for its majesty, strength, and longevity. It was conceived chiefly as a symbol of stasis and an intimation of eternity (3). But the tree functions only as a secondary symbol in the poem, for in gazing upward at it (4), the poet first glimpsed above the leaves the splendid sun which, apotheosized as Phoebus, in turn became the poem's dominant figure. The several lyrical stanzas then devoted to Phoebus are a celebration of life's potency, beauty, glory, and light, but these are not the values that the poet's imagination is allowed to indulge. Phoebus is defeated, and with his removal from the poem, the poet returns to the tree momentarily, only to discover that, "I once that loved the shady woods so well, Now thought the rivers did the trees excell" (21). The river, different in symbolic value altogether from either the tree or the sun, is adopted as the poem's new figure, and with its steady flow and flux represents the poem's redirection: the race towards death. It is, accordingly, highly prized by the poet:

> Thou emblem true of what I count the best,
> O could I lead my rivulets to rest,
> So may we press to that vast mansion, ever
>   blest.
>
> (23)

A peaceful yet determined death is the new goal, and the river, which is able to press on, despite hindrances, to that "beloved place," is an appropriate symbol. It also contains that oldest of traditional Christian symbols of immortality, the fish, and two rather mediocre stanzas (24-25) are devoted to describing different fishes, all of whom

know instinctively how to glide to "unknown coasts." The passages on the fish are not a high point of lyrical description, but they do serve to bring the poet back to her fondness for Classical allusions, this time to Thetis, Neptune, and, most importantly, Philomel (26). . . .

The central image in the final stanza—the engraved white stone—is, as has often been pointed out, based on a verse from Revelation, and appears to end the poem with a lesson on holy dying. No doubt that is how Anne Bradstreet intended it, and the Scriptural reference implies such a reading. At the same time this final stanza is replete with echoes of Shakespeare, and consequently additional interpretations also suggest themselves:

> O Time the fatal wrack of mortal things,
> That draws oblivion's curtains over kings;
> Their sumptuous monuments, men know them
>   not,
> Their names without a record are forgot,
> Their parts, their ports, their pomp's all laid in
>   th' dust
> Nor wit nor gold, nor buildings scape times rust;
> But he whose name is graved in the white stone
> Shall last and shine when all of these are gone.
>
> (33)

Two centuries later Shelley was to write lines similar to these in his famous sonnet on Ozymandias. The Romantic poet and the Puritan poet shared a common sense of mortal decay and the futility of monuments against the tyranny of time.

The greatest poet to give voice to these themes, though, saw poetry itself as an imperishable monument against time, and his own magnificent achievement has proved him correct. Shakespeare, who was one of Anne Bradstreet's favorite authors, frequently exerted a noticeable influence on her work, and that is surely the case here in the final stanza of **"Contemplations."** It is so not only in reference to her lines on time and oblivion, which recall several of Shakespeare's sonnets, but also in reference to the form and meaning of her concluding couplet.

An exceptional formal consideration must be noted first, and that is that *only* here in the thirty-three stanzas of **"Contemplations"** does Anne Bradstreet end with a couplet and not a triplet. This is a highly suggestive factor and tends to reinforce our suspicions that she was ending her poem with Shakespeare as well as the Bible very much in mind. If indeed that is the case, then Anne Bradstreet's imagination is engaged once again in this poem in a battle of contraries, this time between two notions of immortality. The Christian hope for a "divine translation" to "an eternal morrow" (30) is unquestionably strong, but so too is the Shakespearian will towards fame. In a sense Anne Bradstreet is composing her epitaph in these final lines, and she is doing so both as a devoted Christian and a dedicated poet. The two come more closely together here than elsewhere in the poem, and one cannot easily assign them priorities. Nor is it necessary to do so, but only to hold them both in mind.

For while Anne Bradstreet found her image of the white stone in Revelation, she engraved it after the manner of Shakespeare. It ends her poem on both a religious *and* an aesthetic note, each of which is able to transcend "time the fatal wrack of mortal things" in a sublime way. If we still remember Anne Bradstreet and recall her wish to have her dry bones arise in glory, it is because she was finally poet enough to live in her verse and secure the fame that good poetry provides.

Jane Donahue Eberwein (essay date 1981)

SOURCE: "'No Rhet'ric We Expect': Argumentation in Bradstreet's 'The Prologue'," in *Early American Literature,* Vol. XVI, No. 1, Spring 1981, pp. 19-26.

[*Here, Eberwein reevaluates Bradstreet's "Prologue," concluding that, rather than a confession of humility, it is a subtle assertion of the poet's skill and power.*]

For an acknowledgment of a poet's simple capacities and modest literary goals, Anne Bradstreet's **"The Prologue"** elicits strangely varied responses—especially in regard to voice and tone. Is the poet humbly submissive or bitterly angry? Is she self-deprecating and self-denigrating, as some readers find, or a prefeminist champion of her sex? Both extremes find textual justification, depending on the weight one accords her admittedly blemished muse or her anticipated parsley wreath. Perhaps, as Elizabeth Wade White [in *Anne Bradstreet: "The Tenth Muse,"* 1971] and Robert Arner [in "The Structure of Anne Bradstreet's *Tenth Muse,*" in *Discoveries and Considerations,* 1976] have suggested, the poem divides structurally and tonally at stanza five, with the first half lamenting the poet's inferiority to male writers and the second half asserting, nonetheless, her right as a woman to express herself in verse. The tension between Bradstreet's modest disclaimers and her spirited self-defense runs through the poem, however; it may be found implicitly in the first stanza and explicitly in the last, and it permeates the language and logic of all **"The Prologue."** Only by reading the poem as consistently ironic can we hope to appreciate Bradstreet's conscious artfulness in deploying both sides of the argument: inviting both male and female champions (and the vast majority of more tolerant readers) to approach her writing with respect.

As the name indicates, this is a prologue designed to introduce the author to her readers while whetting their interest in the more substantive poems to follow. She proceeds by negation, telling what she cannot hope to do: "To sing of wars, of captains, and of kings, / Of cities founded, commonwealths begun, / For my mean pen are too superior things." But, if we expect her to anticipate Barlow in turning from lofty historical themes to choose "a virgin theme, unconscious of the Muse," we will be unprepared for the succeeding poems. **"The Prologue"** was never meant to introduce Bradstreet's love poems or meditations; it was written directly for **"The Four Monarchies"** and was then prefixed to the four quaternions as well as the historical surveys in the opening section of

The Tenth Muse. Despite her disclaimer, then, Bradstreet proceeded directly to write on the subjects she so pointedly reserved for poets and historians. The opening lines introduce an ironic counterpointing of claimed incapacity and demonstrated command which would enliven the whole poem.

The key to Bradstreet's strategy in preceding her lengthy, laborious, learned scholarly poems with this engaging prologue comes in the opening of stanza three: "From schoolboy's tongue no rhet'ric we expect." Like so many parts of the poem, this line has dual implications. We do not, in fact, count on hearing eloquent orations from schoolchildren, but we must recall that Bradstreet's contemporaries expected, in the sense of looked forward to, such skill as a probable outcome of the boy's education. From grammar, the student would proceed in course through the rest of the trivium: logic and rhetoric. In likening herself to the schoolboy, the poet suggests her own capacity to advance in the verbal arts—especially the art of persuasion. When we do not expect rhetoric, we may not even notice it; but we can be influenced by it, despite ourselves. As Henry Peacham wrote in the 1593 *Garden of Eloquence,* "By the benefit of this excellent gift, (I meane of apt speech given by nature, and guided by Art) wisedome appeareth in her beautie, sheweth her maiestie, and exerciseth her power, working in the minde of the hearer, partly by a pleasant proportion . . . and partly by the secret and mightie power of perswasion after a most wonderfull manner." Bradstreet praised apt speech given by nature and guided by Art in **"The Prologue"** and demonstrated it as well, keeping a pleasant proportion between instruction and delight to achieve a secret but significant power of persuasion. By recognizing her dexterity in manipulating logic and rhetoric, by remembering Rosamund Rosenmeier's caution [in "Divine Translation: A Contribution to the study of Anne Bradstreet's Method in the Marriage Poems," *Early American Literature* 12 (1977)] that we must read Bradstreet as "someone accustomed to thinking figurally," and by responding to her varied cultural allusions, we can appreciate the complexity and sophistication of her apparently simple argument.

Like most of Bradstreet's successful poems, **"The Prologue"** is an argument: an attempt to articulate and reconcile opposition by emphasizing discrepancies while hinting at unity. As Ann Stanford has noted [in *Anne Bradstreet: The Worldly Puritan,* 1974], the histories which **"The Prologue"** introduces fail as literature partly because they lack the tension the poet knew how to achieve when she engaged an I-narrator in vigorous argumentation. Unlike the quaternions, in each of which the four speakers demonstrate a different argumentative method, **"The Four Monarchies"** proceeds by discursive, impersonal narration. Bradstreet may have needed the chance to spar off against assumed sexist opponents in order to release the energy and excitement her familiar readers would anticipate in a new grouping of her poems.

With whom is Bradstreet actually arguing here? Certainly not with Thomas Dudley and the circle of admiring friends among whom she circulated her manuscripts. Textual analysis shows no direct personal address until stanza seven, when she says, "Preeminence in all and each is yours" to an inclusive audience of the whole male sex; but the apostrophe in stanza eight addresses a different you, limited to the great poets: " . . . ye high flown quills that soar the skies." Her debate, however, seems to be with other antagonists—each "carping tongue" who belittles "female wits." Who those carping tongues might be remains a question. Although Jeannine Hensley, Elizabeth Wade White, and Ann Stanford all assume the reality of such criticism, they offer no specific examples. Those who sympathize with the poet's presumed cultural isolation as a frontier woman artist speak of the pain she "must have" felt and the insults she "must have" endured—linking her with Anne Hutchinson and Anne Hopkins, two well-documented examples of Puritan women who suffered for their intellectual aspirations. Yet Hensley admits [in her introduction to *The Works of Anne Bradstreet*, 1967] that "we have no contemporary reference to her or her poetry which is not somewhere between admiration and adulation." There is simply no evidence of the attacks to which she retorts in **"The Prologue."**

The carping tongues, probably imagined, offered a useful opportunity for forceful, witty expression in this ironic battle of the sexes. Straw men, they were set up only to be knocked down. None of the deference Bradstreet shows in passages of the poem was meant for them. Her expressions of humility, presumably sincere acknowledgments of inferiority, were directed to recognized literary greats: Du Bartas, her poetic model; Demosthenes; perhaps Virgil; and all " . . . ye high flown quills that soar the skies, / And ever with your prey still catch your praise." Long before Franklin, Bradstreet discovered that one could achieve the appearance of humility (and its rhetorical effect in placating a suspicious audience) by emulating the loftiest models and confessing failure.

Unlike Bradstreet's formal debate poems in which the contenders successively advance their individual cases, **"The Prologue"** maintains argumentative tension by its deft ordering of assertions and its ambiguous juxtapositions of ideas. Bradstreet develops both cases together, often seeming to capitulate to her opposition. But any male supremacist who read happily along, imagining no threat to his smugness, would eventually find his case pressed to the point of absurdity, while a more alert or ironic reader would be delighted throughout by the poet's cleverness in charming while outwitting her antagonist. If **"The Prologue"** was intended to win readers for the histories while building affection and respect for the poet, it served its purpose.

Beginning boldly with her echo of Virgil, Bradstreet immediately disclaims her obvious purpose. She had, indeed, written of wars, captains, kings, cities, and commonwealths, though not in the epic strains a reader might expect from one who thought of poesy as "Calliope's own child." Reference to her "obscure lines" could hardly disguise her purpose, at least for any reader with enough foresight to glance ahead into the book. Like Chaucer's "I can namore," this statement deflects attention only

slightly from the author's plan to develop the supposedly forsaken topic at great length.

Further developing the sense of authorial humility, Bradstreet moved into a sincere tribute to Du Bartas, still her poetic master. The admiration, however, was that which an aspiring writer of either sex might feel for an established poet. Such expressions of poetic inadequacy to a great theme and inferiority to a major writer were common among authors known to Bradstreet, and there is no reason to interpret her praise as specifically female submissiveness. In his dedicatory verse to *The Tenth Muse*, we should recall, John Woodbridge indited a parallel passage to acknowledge his inability to emulate Bradstreet herself.

> What I (poor silly I) prefix therefore,
> Can but do this, make yours admired the more;
> And if but only this I do attain,
> Content, that my disgrace may be your gain.

Praising Du Bartas's choice of subject matter, his "sugared lines," and even his "overfluent store" of verse, Bradstreet—"simple I"—called attention to qualities which she could reasonably hope to imitate according to her skill. And skill is a revealing word, placing emphasis on craftsmanship, which could be developed, rather than natural gifts, which might have been denied. **"The Prologue"** is itself a display of poetic skill, technically more artful than the histories or quaternions with their monotonous couplets. The stanzaic pattern, the sound effects, and the rhetorical devices of **"The Prologue"** consistently qualify its author's pretensions to simplicity.

The next stanza sounds more sincerely self-deprecating with its imagery of "broken strings" in a musical instrument and "a main defect" in an aesthetic structure. Bradstreet speaks of her "foolish, broken, blemished Muse" and acknowledges irreparable limitations. People have no right to expect music, she asserts, in cases where nature has denied some essential power.

Yet her next example, Demosthenes, reverses the conclusion drawn in stanza three. Surely a congenital speech impediment seems a natural defect precluding oratorical success. But art, in this case purposeful, concentrated, sustained self-discipline, led first to clarity and then to fluency and sweetness. With any natural endowment at all, then, Bradstreet shows that an ambitious artist can achieve excellence. Art corrects nature, except for the "weak or wounded brain" which "admits no cure." Readers who divide the poem structurally at this halfway point see the first four stanzas as submissive and self-abasing— especially the final line. Perhaps the statements are self-critical but only in the sense that she submits to the artistic claims of recognized literary masters and recognizes faults in herself which can be corrected through the stylistic apprenticeship on which she has already embarked, as anyone could discover by reading the poems introduced by **"The Prologue."** Only if she claims the weak and wounded brain as self-description need we interpret this part of the poem as an expression of defeat.

Note, however, that mention of weak and wounded brains leads Bradstreet directly to reflection on carping tongues, which may well articulate idiocy. At this point, she joins battle with her supposed critics and stops comparing herself with writers who deserve her respect. These scolds who would restrict a woman to domestic activities turn out to be contemptuous of thought and imagination in any form—not just when offered by a female wit. They refuse to look at evidence ("If what I do prove well . . . "), and they mistake skill for chance. Confronted with the analogy the Greeks drew between femininity and artistic inspiration as embodied in the Muses, they cut a Gordian knot with their brute disregard for cultural intricacies. Those who say that "The Greeks did nought, but play the fools and lie" demonstrate contempt for fiction and deadness to poetry. They can hardly be the readers she hoped to draw further into her manuscript, but in travestying their claims she might hope to entertain or even impress her proper audience.

In stanza seven Bradstreet spins out the clumsy assertions of her fancied enemies to the extreme limits of logical fallacy. "Let Greeks be Greeks, and women what they are," she begins as if to capitulate gracefully. But Greeks and women need not to be regarded as mutually exclusive categories. Attentive readers, like John Woodbridge, could think of Sappho. The carpers, of course, could drift rapidly along, caught in a tidal wave of ironic concessions. Although it would be "but vain" for women "unjustly to wage war," it might at times be appropriate to rally female energies in justified aggression. The poet who seems to be calming tensions here and promising peace is the same author who later in *The Tenth Muse* let gracious young New England challenge her despondent mother with a decidedly militant call to arms:

> These are the days the Church's foes to crush,
> To root out Popelings head, tail, branch, and
>   rush;
> Let's bring Baal's vestments forth to make a
>   fire,
> Their miters, surplices, and all their tire,
> Copes, rochets, crosiers, and such empty trash,
> And let their names consume, but let the flash
> Light Christendom, and all the world to see
> We hate Rome's whore with all her trumpery.

Bradstreet completes the logical undoing of her opponents by wheeling in a veritable Trojan Horse to confirm the tentative peace. "Men can do best, and women know it well," she proclaims—right in the prologue to a series of history poems which will parade before her readers an astounding chronicle of disasters, defeats, and depravities involving both men and women rulers but featuring the generally more powerful males. Although Bradstreet gave greater attention to women rulers in her poems than she found in Raleigh's history, she never attempted to show one sex as morally or even politically superior in the use of power; certainly **"The Four Monarchies"** rebuts her generalization in **"The Prologue,"** however, and indicates its irony. The crowning joke comes next, when she admits "Preeminence in all and each is yours." By extending claims of male supremacy to all areas of human experience, she seems to dismiss hopes for female excellence in government, oratory, and poetry while acknowledging male dominion in everything: presumably even needlework and childbearing.

This apparent capitulation to the irrational claims of her imagined critics violates common sense, of course, and conflicts as well with the argumentative pattern of the quaternions in which each element, humor, age, and season admits weaknesses as well as strengths. The resolution of these conflicts comes from a recognition of complementary functions, from awareness of multiple contributions to a final desired unity. The same reasoning characterizes Bradstreet's marriage poems, where husband and wife appear as mutually dependent and supportive partners. To restrict women from literature, then, or even from historical narration would be folly. The battle of the sexes, like the debates of the elements and humors, should never be won.

After this deft lobotomy of weak or wounded brains, Bradstreet concludes **"The Prologue"** with a modest but confident declaration of her literary hopes. In the final stanza she invokes the world's great writers in lines which themselves fly and flash with the eloquence of her praise. The masters soaring in the heavens may see her lines as "lowly," but she gives no indication that earthbound readers need concur. In comparison to a poet like Du Bartas or a rhetorician like Demosthenes, she is limited but hardly worthless. Her "mean and unrefined ore" highlights their "glist'ring gold" and may, with time, be enhanced by careful polishing.

The most striking image in this paean, however, is surely that of the "thyme or parsley wreath" Bradstreet requests in recognition of her poetry, discounting the traditional bay laurel. It seems a humble request: substitution of a kitchen herb for richer foliage. Bay leaves are also herbs, however, and there are cooks who plunge all three in the same aromatic pot. As far as honor goes, there may be less distinction here than the phrasing suggests. Elizabeth Wade White points out that thyme symbolized vitality and courage for the Greeks and that they sometimes honored athletes or dead heroes with the "fadeless foilage" of parsley wreaths. Even more familiar was the mythical background of the laurel as a symbol of poetry. In his verses "Upon Mrs. Anne Bradstreet Her Poems, Etc." prefaced to *The Tenth Muse*, John Rogers commended the Puritan poet for her avoidance of the wantonly lascivious topics provided by classical literature, specifically mentioning "How sage Apollo, Daphne hot pursues." C.B., in his introductory quatrain, wrote: "I cannot wonder at Apollo now, / That he with female laurel crowned his brow." The laurel crown commemorated Daphne, who was protectively transformed in her flight from lusty Apollo; so the bay leaves provided a female crown for male poets. The modesty that kept Anne Bradstreet from claiming such an honor, then, may have been more nearly allied to chastity than to humility. She may have felt sensitive to the mythic presentation of woman as simultaneously the object and victim of the god of poetry and the sign of glory for his disciples. It is clear, at any rate, that the concluding stanza expresses personal self-assurance as a poet, and the reader who has followed the stylistic, rhetorical, and logical devices by which she guides **"The Prologue"** from acknowledgment of her defects to assertion of her triumph is likely to accept the claim. Like Emily Dickinson, who contrasted "Carbon in the Coal" with "Carbon in the Gem" as queenly ornaments, Anne Bradstreet contrived to sound meek and vulnerable, even in the act of choosing among crowns.

Helen Saltman (essay date 1983)

SOURCE: "'Contemplations': Anne Bradstreet's Spiritual Authobiography," in *Critical Essays on Anne Bradstreet,* edited by Pattie Cowell and Ann Stanford, G. K. Hall & Co., 1983, pp. 226-37.

[*In the following essay, Saltman examines Bradstreet's "Contemplations" in the context of Puritan theology and Biblical inspiration.*]

Anne Bradstreet's poem **"Contemplations,"** is no ordinary Puritan spiritual autobiography in which the convert emphasizes his human weakness, particularly pride, in his struggle for faith. Rather, it is an account in which the poet dwells on the theological concepts (masked in metaphor and Biblical allusion) that support the Puritan doctrine of rebirth and salvation. By dwelling on these concepts, the poet approaches the ideal conversion William Perkins outlines in *A Golden Chain, or the Description of Theology.* In this work Perkins explicates the "four degrees of God's love" (the steps toward salvation): "Effectual Calling, Justification, Sanctification, and Glorification." In similar stages, Mistress Bradstreet's **"Contemplations"** dramatizes her spiritual awakening and conversion.

As in other conversion experiences, **"Contemplations"** opens with the poet recalling a time when her sensual appreciation of nature brought her to an awareness of God's glory. Step by step she recounts how she became aware of God's attributes: "goodness, wisdom, glory, light" which grow out of the apparent "excellence" of this world. By beginning her poem, her meditation, just before nightfall, Bradstreet emulates the Psalmist, who not only "prevented the dawning of the morning" to "hope in the word," but who also sings "mine eyes prevent the night watches that I might meditate in thy word" (Psalm 119:147, 148). In Puritan theology, Psalm 119 "moves the faithful to a deeper consideration of God's glory" by setting "before their eyes the most exquisite workmanship of the heavens," the purpose of which is to lead God's "chosen people" to the "law, where in God hath reveiled himself more familiarly" and to "reproach man his ingratitude seeing the heavens, which are dumme creatures, set forth God's glorie" (Geneva Psalm 119).

Anne Bradstreet expresses poetically in **"Contemplations"** her belief that nature reveals God to mankind, a belief restated in her prose autobiography:

> That there is a God my reason would soon tell me by the wondrous works that I see, the vast frame of the heaven and the earth, the order of all things, night and day, summer and winter, spring and autumn . . .

The affirmation of reason as capable of discerning God through his works is finely detailed in **"Contemplations"** through the poet's rich description of nature and by her subsequent response of amazement. As she contemplates nature, her vision is brought higher; the "stately oak" causes her to think of "eternity." Her contemplation of the "sun" suggests a "deity." Amazed at the wonder of the sun, "this bright light luster" (l. 49), she desires to "sing some song" in admiration of her "great Creator" (l. 54). The opening celebration of nature is merely a feeble awakening to God's glory: "All mortals here the feeling knowledge hath" (l. 40). All individuals, even the depraved, are capable of perceiving the most obvious of God's attributes from his creation. "Of God's glory and blessedness," Perkins remarks, "the more obscure manifestation is the vision of God's majesty in this life by the eyes of the mind through the help of things perceived by the outward senses." Thus, "feeling knowledge" (knowledge perceived through the senses) is not the same as "saving knowledge"—the knowledge of the Fall, sin and death, and redemption from God's Grace as mediated by Christ. Bradstreet's desire to "magnify" her Creator is merely evidence of a false awakening. She is unaware of her errors; only her sinful, her sensous being apprehends the glory of God from the "bright light luster" of a fallen world.

While it is possible for a Puritan to know God in nature through the faculty of his reason, that reason has been corrupted by the Fall. "Men's minds received from Adam: ignorance, namely a want, or rather a deprivation of knowledge in the things of God," [Perkins writes]. Since original sin has corrupted human "faculties," there is nothing of a saving nature in becoming aware of God's glory through the senses. Only by attendence on the word of God is one able to have "revealed" knowledge of Him. And only by "Saving Grace" does one attain true faith. Anne Bradstreet clearly distinguishes in her prose spiritual autobiography between knowledge of God through reason and revealed knowledge from scripture:

> I have argued thus with myself. That there is a God, I see. If ever this God hath revealed himself, it must be in His word, and this must be it or none.

Bradstreet affirms the Puritan doctrine that knowledge of God through nature—in Perkins' words, the "more obscure manifestation"—cannot lead to salvation; salvation depends on revealed understanding of the deity. Bradstreet's sensual appreciation of nature in stanzas 1-8 has brought her to an awareness of God and the desire to glorify Him. But the poet is not yet aware of her "fallen" condition, or of her "sins."

The convert should feel "infinite despair" at his sins as he becomes increasingly aware of God's attributes. Since understanding of God and the "law" comes from the gospel, the convert must prepare himself to hear the "saving" word of God. First, he needs to sever himself from this world; and second, he needs to have "a sensible feeling of [his] own beggary"—he needs to be "truly humbled," [according to] Perkins. As part of her "Effectual Calling," the poet metaphorically sets herself apart from mankind: "silent alone, where none or saw, or heard, / In pathless paths I lead my wand'ring feet" (ll. 51-52). And the poet's subsequent lament, in addition to expressing her inability to praise God, dramatizes her "abject," humbled condition:

> I heard the merry grasshopper then sing.
> The black-clad cricket bear a second part;
> They kept one tune and played on the same
>   string,
> Seeming to glory in their little art.
> Shall creatures abject thus their voices raise
> And in their kind resound their Maker's praise,
> Whilst I, as mute, can warble forth no higher
>   lays?
>
>   (ll. 58-64)

Without grace, the poet is like the "abject creatures" with whom she compares herself—unregenerate. She too is doomed by time and mortality. The unregenerate speaker is not yet aware of her sins, or indeed, that the world is fallen. In the first nine stanzas of **"Contemplations,"** the poet has no knowledge of God's word, of the "law," or of redemption. She has no understanding of the covenant of grace; and without grace, she cannot, like the Psalmist, sing and "make a joyful noise unto the Lord, make a loud noise, and rejoice, and sing praise" (Psalm 98:4). Without faith that results from saving grace, the poet cannot praise God as she desires.

The poet, humbled yet unaware of the possibility of redemption, describes her further growth in "Effectual Calling." By recounting the story of the Fall and Expulsion, she is brought to an awareness of the sins which in Puritan theology she shares with Adam and all mankind: "All Adam's posterity is equally partaker of this corruption," Perkins [writes]. The poet affirms the theological position that each individual partakes of the Fall by imaginatively reconstructing the scene. As Robert D. Richardson, Jr. pointed out [in "The Puritan Poetry of Anne Bradstreet," *Texas Studies in Language and Literature* 9 (1967)], "the poet lives in the present and the Biblical stories exist also in the present, alive in her imagination." While affirming mankind's fallen state, she emphasizes its fallen faculties, its predilection for error. Ironically, individuals conquer time by an act of imagination—"it makes a man more aged in conceit . . . / While of their persons and their acts his mind doth treat" (ll. 69-71). That is, the act of fancy and thought, and even meditation itself, has been a crucial factor in the history of mankind's downfall because of this reliance on "fallen" faculties. Perkins reminds us that "sin is . . . a corruption of man's faculties." The poet reconstructs the Biblical scene to meditate on human apostasy and to affirm that reason and fancy are fallen faculties. In each stanza, the participants of the Fall are engaged in the human "conceit" of

thinking: "sometimes in Eden fair he seems to be, . . . *Fancies* the apple, dangle on the tree" (ll. 72-74). Holding "bloody Cain," Eve "sighs to *think* of Paradise, / And how she lost her bliss to be more wise" (ll. 83-84). Cain "Hath *Thousand thoughts* to end his brother's days" (l. 91); while Abel "keeps his sheep, no ill he *thinks*" (l. 93). Later, with a "dreadful mind," Cain "*thinks* each he sees will serve him in his kind" (l. 98). The poet relives the Fall: she *"Fancies"* Cain "*now* at the bar" (l. 100). [My italics.] She brings to the reader a sense of immediacy in the Biblical account of human apostasy along with an understanding that men and women have been betrayed by their own thoughts. The poet's understanding of this apostasy through her attendance on the word and her identification with the acts of thinking which lead to the Fall, her imaginative participation in the Fall, give her the knowledge of sin as "vain delight" and death as "perpetual night" (ll. 118-19).

The poet then considers the implications of Adam's Fall. In stanzas 17 and 18, she meditates on death and time—the consequences of the Fall, and on the paradox arising from the knowledge gained by the Fall: knowledge has brought mankind old age and death; the earth, "though old," is continually reborn, "still clad in green"; the sensual stones and trees are insensible of time (ll. 122-23). Each paradox comments on the uselessness of the "knowledge" gained by the Fall—mankind is sensible of time in a world of the senses, a fallen world. Finally, the poet expresses the ultimate despair, "man grows old, lies down, remains where once he's laid" (l. 127). The speaker's new knowledge of sin and death in conjunction with her awareness of God's glory and majesty correspond to a necessary development in her "Effectual Calling." But as long as the poet depends on the knowledge gained through nature and custom, her faith in salvation and in man's nobility remains limited: "By birth more noble than those creatures all, / Yet seems by nature and by custom cursed" (ll. 128-29). Thus, "Effectual Calling" is incomplete without faith which comes from grace.

The Puritan distinction concerning the knowledge gained from custom and nature without grace is crucial. Perry Miller explains [in *The New England Mind,* 1939]

> Knowledge of the passing away of one generation after another shows us our mortality and misery, but gives us no relief; the heavens and earth are divine creations, but tell us nothing of divinity unless the spirit of God bears witness in them.

Mankind is unable to find salvation through his own understanding of nature or of the scriptures. Stanzas 1-19 of **"Contemplations"** articulate the limits of nature and custom. The poet has demonstrated her ability to seek God in nature—but nature can tell her, in Perry Miller's words, "nothing of divinity." The poet has experienced merely the preparatory stages in her "Effectual Calling": "a man not destined for salvation could go this far and never get any further," [according to Edmund S. Morgan in *Visible Saints*]. Predestination and the Puritan doctrine that human efforts are entirely ineffectual in attaining salvation in spite of knowledge and sincere effort are thus affirmed by stanza nineteen:

> No sooner born, but grief and care makes fall
> That state obliterate he had at first;
> Nor youth, nor strength, nor wisdom spring
>   again,
> Nor habitations long their names retain,
> But in oblivion to the final day remain
>
> (ll. 130-34).

The poet affirms that mankind, viewed through the perspective of nature and custom, is doomed to "oblivion" and that through Adam's Fall mutability is the only law to which the unredeemed are subject. Even more significantly, the poet realizes that unregenerate thoughts (reason without grace) drive individuals to this position of despair. And yet, paradoxically, despair and the realization of hopelessness are themselves necessary steps within "Effectual Calling." Thus, the poet prepares the reader for the recognition of the change wrought by grace.

In contrast to the poet's announcement in stanzas 18 and 19 of mankind's hopeless fate resulting from the Fall, in stanza 20 Bradstreet reverses herself by announcing that "man was made for endless immortality." This positive statement of faith has no logical precedent in the poem. The poet's sudden affirmation of salvation corresponds to her receiving grace, resulting in "true faith," "which is a miraculous supernatural faculty of the heart," that is, "a serious desire to believe" [according to] Perkins.

The rebirth of the poet and her new faith is the subject of stanza 20. In the 19th stanza, mankind is "born" to "oblivion." In the 20th stanza, the poet answers her rhetorical question, "Shall I wish there, or never to had birth," with a rousing "Nay." This is her spiritual rebirth, her conversion, a different "birth" than that mentioned in stanza 19. Of course, "birth" is a common metaphor for spiritual regeneration. Daniel Shea [in *Spiritual Autobiography in Early America,* 1968] has called attention to the importance of the symbol of childbirth in the poet's prose spiritual autobiography: "scriptural as well as personal . . . , birth sums up much of what Anne Bradstreet wished to say." Beginning then, with stanza 20 of **"Contemplations,"** the poet exhibits the new theologically correct vision which grace has given her: the heavens, the trees, and the earth are no longer seen in their "strength and beauty." Now they, not mankind, "shall darken, perish, fade and die, / And when unmade so ever shall they lie" (ll. 139-40). Anne Bradstreet even puns on the false, the "lying" beauty and youth of the earth.

From stanza 21 to the end of **"Contemplations,"** Anne Bradstreet's vision of nature demonstrates the theological principles governing sanctification wherein "holiness is enlarged" and "those that are quickened . . . rise up to the newness of life" (Perkins). Bradstreet's desire for holiness is reflected in stanzas 21-23. Each of these three stanzas restates the regenerate soul's desire for union with God: "Thou emblem true of what I count the best, / O could I lead my rivulets to rest, / So may we press to that

vast mansion, ever blest" (ll. 160-63). Further expressing her desire for redemption, the poet places herself in the scene, "under the cooling shadow of a stately elm . . . by a goodly river's side" (ll. 142-43). This symbolic scene alludes to the First Psalm of David, to "a tree planted by the rivers of water," wherein a person meditates with "delight" on God's "laws." The tree by a "goodly river's side" also suggests the river and tree of life of revelation:

> And he showed me a pure river of the water of
>   life.
> In the midst of the street of it, and on either
>   side
> of the river, was there the tree of life. . . .
> And there shall be no night there
>
> (Revelation 22:1,2,5).

Echoing this symbolic desire for redemption, the poet expresses a preference for the river of life and for a place of perpetual light:

> I once that loved the shady woods so well,
> Now thought the rivers did the trees excel,
> And if the sun would ever shine, there would I
>   dwell
>
> (ll. 146-48).

Grace endows "spiritual wisdom," by which the desire for holiness becomes part of the convert's vision. Through "an illumination of the mind," the convert acknowledges the "truth" of God's word and applies the truth to the "good ordering of . . . both things and actions" (Perkins). Through this "illumination of mind," nature loses its sensual quality in order to present theological truth.

In addition to the convert being "renewed in holiness," as part of his sanctification, he is expected to engage in spiritual battle ("Christian Warfare"). In stanzas 24 and 25, the poet's vision of nature presents a drama of the "spiritual battle." The combatants are personified as two kinds of "fish." The first, in stanza 24, are "nature taught." That is, like the poet in the first eight stanzas of **"Contemplations,"** they have no knowledge of redemption; they "know not" of their "felicity." They lead an instinctual existence in which their actions are governed by the seasons. And so they leave their "numerous fry" landlocked in "lakes and ponds"; they are unable to reach the ocean. In contrast to this depiction of the unregenerate "fish" who are cut off from God (the Ocean), the "fish" in stanza 25, the "great ones," are the elect. The activity of "combat" in which they are engaged is "Christian Warfare"; they "take the trembling prey before it yield" (l. 175). They are engaged in a spiritual battle. These combatant "fish," "whose armour is their scales, their spreading fins their shield" (l. 176), have the "whole armour of God" and "the shield of faith" (Ephesians 6:13,16). Anne Bradstreet is theologically correct in alluding to Ephesians to dramatize an important part of sanctification. The marginal notes in the Geneva Bible specify this chapter as "an exhortation to the spiritual battel and what weapons the Christian should fight with all." In his discussion of Sanctification, Perkins renders the "complete armour of God" as six specific virtues with which the "Christian soldier" fights "the tempter" ("Satan, the flesh, and the world"). The poet, then, presents her spiritually renewed vision of nature in complete accordance with puritan doctrine.

When the poet's view of nature in the first nine stanzas of **"Contemplations"** is contrasted with that of stanza 21 and following, the change that takes place is clearly revealed. The poet's early view of nature is sensual ("rapt were my senses at this delectable view") (l. 7) while the latter view is spiritual ("thou emblem true of what I count the best") (l. 160). The former implies the speaker as being in a state of nature, the latter as being in a state of grace.

"Contemplations" thus reveals the poet's conversion experience in her changing vision of nature. It also suggests her sanctification by its success in affirming Puritan doctrine. In other words, the poet implies the sanctification of her poetic vocation. As in other accounts of conversion, a tension exists between the convert's view of the world before and after receiving grace. That is, Anne Bradstreet is describing an experience which has, by necessity, been changed by the experience itself. It is evident then that the first nine stanzas in which she states her feeble awakening to God's glory in nature, and her errors due to her fallen condition, are seen in retrospect from her new redeemed vision. Thus, her description of the sun in these early stanzas can also be seen as emblematic of the "son," signifying the glory of Christ and anticipating the redemption. Stanza 5, which personifies the sun as a "bridegroom" is the key to this reading:

> Thou as a bridegroom from thy chamber rushes,
> And as a strong man, joys to run a race;
> The morn doth usher thee with smiles and
>   blushes;
> The Earth reflects her glances in thy face
>   (ll. 30-33).

Although this personification seems pagan, as critics have pointed out, Anne Bradstreet was keenly aware of the religious implications of the word, "bridegroom." In her last dated poem, "As Weary Pilgrim" (August 31, 1669), the poet expresses her redeemed soul's desire for the promise in revelation to the elect:

> Lord make me ready for that day,
> Then come, dear Bridegroom, come away.

To be sure, Mrs. Bradstreet's personification of the sun as a "bridegroom" would not have appeared as a pagan influence to her contemporaries. They probably would have thought instead that the "morn" in this passage symbolized the "New Jerusalem." The pious Puritan would have recognized Psalm 19 not only as the authority for finding God's attributes in nature ("the heavens declare the glory of God; and the firmament sheweth his handywork"); but he also would have recognized this Psalm as the source of the "bridegroom" in the fifth stanza:

> In them hath he set a tabernacle for the sun,
> Which is as a bridegroom coming out of his
>   chamber,
> and rejoiceth as a strong man to run a race
>   (Psalm 19:4,5).

Anne Bradstreet's lines personifying the sun as a bridegroom in fact paraphrase this Biblical passage: "thou as a bridegroom from thy chamber rushes, / And as a strong man, joys to run a race." In addition to providing the metaphor of the sun as a bridegroom, Psalm 19 affirms God's attributes and laws in converting the soul. In the Geneva Bible, the marginal notes reveal that the "intent" of the Psalm is to "move the faithfull to a deeper consideration of God's glory." Thus, Bradstreet makes clear that it is the Psalm that has awakened her spiritually rather than the sensual beauty of nature. And in Psalm 19, David affirms God as his personal redeemer. David ends the Psalm with the prayer: "Let the words of my mouth, and the meditation of my heart, be acceptable in thy sight, O Lord" (Psalm 19:14).

Psalm 19 is Anne Bradstreet's primary inspiration for **"Contemplations."** The Psalmist's desire for redemption is her desire; his prayer for his "meditation" and his "words" to be acceptable in God's eyes is her unspoken prayer. David is the type of Christ; throughout **"Contemplations"** the movement of the poem is to the Redemption. Though Christ and the passion are not explicitly considered, Christ's covenant of redemption is continually implied. Time and mortality enter human life through the Fall. Individuals overcome time and mortality through the covenant of grace made possible by Christ. And time and mortality are central issues in **"Contemplations."** Though David the Psalmist is Bradstreet's immediate inspiration (poetically as well as spiritually), he is also typologically important, prefiguring Christ and the redemption she seeks. Thus the last two lines of the poem directly paraphrase revelation, and the promise of salvation (glorification) made possible by Christ's covenant with God:

> But he whose name is graved in the white stone
> Shall last and shine when all of these are gone
>   (ll. 232-33).

Every line in **"Contemplations"** anticipates this evidence of redemption.

Anne Bradstreet's choice of the Psalmist for her inspiration is symbolically and emblematically explained in the poem. The poet is interrupted in her meditation on "Christian Warfare" by the chant of the "sweet-tongued Philomel." This Philomel represents David the Psalmist. The poet addresses the bird: "the dawning morn with songs thou dost prevent" (l. 198), paraphrasing David's prayer to God in Psalm 119:147: "I prevented the dawning of the morning, and cried: I hoped in thy word." The spiritual significance of the Philomel appears as we consider closely the poet's description of her attributes. This bird is "merry" and "fears no snares" (l. 184), while the nightingale, that *secular* bird of poetic inspiration is melancholy. This

Philomel is unconcerned with worldly things, "reminds not what is past, nor what's to come dost fear" (l. 190). It is a spiritual bird whose "meat" is "everywhere" (l. 188). The "meat" refers to the promise of grace and salvation in Revelation 2:17 with which **"Contemplations"** ends. We may also recall that in Bradstreet's poem **"The Flesh and the Spirit,"** the spirit affirms her meditative habit, arguing against the flesh by exclaiming: "the hidden manna I do eat, / The word of life it is my meat." And that "hidden manna" is Bradstreet's metaphor for Grace in her prose spiritual autobiography, **"To My Dear Children."** The Psalmist, then, who eagerly meditates on the word of God, is characterized by the poet as a Philomel. To God he cries out for inspiration and life: "quicken me" (Psalm 119:149).

The melodious songs of David are thus Anne Bradstreet's inspiration. She, too, desires to be quickened, to have "wings" to "take flight" (l. 183) with the Philomel, to be inspired spiritually as well as poetically in order to sing God's praises. "The principal end of [man's] election is to praise and glorifie the grace of God," the Puritan theologians remind us (Geneva Ephesians 1:5). But the "merry" Philomel, whose song is God's "inspired word," is the means to the poet's salvation as well as her inspiration. Bradstreet's song of praise will be the poem **"Contemplations."** No wonder, then, her inability to sing her "great creator's" praises (ll. 55-57) at the time of her first "obscure" awakening, when she compared her "mute" attempt to the "merry" grasshopper and the cricket.

The last five stanzas of **"Contemplations"** testify further to the poet's sanctification, affirming her belief in Puritan theology and her ability to sing of its perfect wisdom. Dramatizing the necessity for affliction as part of God's plan for mankind, the poet describes the individual as either unregenerate, "a weatherbeaten vessel wracked with pain," with no hope of salvation (l. 207), or as one of the Elect who "sings merrily" until a "storm" makes "him long for a more quiet port" (l. 217). Affliction tests the soul, providing a life of misery to the unregenerate, but the impetus for the elect to turn from worldly things to spiritual matters in search of redemption. In her prose spiritual autobiography, Bradstreet makes a similar distinction concerning the uses of affliction:

> If at any time you are chastened of God, take it as thankfully and joyfully as in greatest mercies; for if ye be His, ye shall reap the greatest benefit by it.

As a significant part of sanctification, affliction ("the patient bearing of the Cross") is God's instrument to spur the convert to holiness and virtue (Perkins). Affliction also enables the convert, the elect, to make the soul-saving distinction between this world and the next, a distinction the poet was unable to make at the outset of **"Contemplations":**

> Fond fool, he takes this earth ev'n for heav'n's bower.
> But sad affliction comes and makes him see
> Here's neither honour, wealth, nor safety;

> Only above is found all with security
>
> (ll. 222-25).

The poet, then, in stanza 32 renounces her youthful error in mistaking the earth for "heav'n's bower." And, finally, in the last stanza of the poem, the worth and beauty of the natural world, "a bright light luster" is fully rejected as meretricious. Only the promise of redemption in Revelation 2:17, the "name . . . graved in the white stone / Shall last and shine when all of these are gone" (ll. 232-33).

Anne Bradstreet's affirmation of her Puritan faith in **"Contemplations"** is virtually identical in its important aspects with the simple and brief expression of her faith intended only for her family. In her prose spiritual autobiography addressed **"To My Dear Children,"** she desires to help her children be reborn—"I now travail in birth again of you till Christ be formed in you." She affirms the ability of mankind's fallen reason to discern God in nature: "That there is a God my reason would soon tell me by the wondrous works that I see." In addition, she affirms her belief in the "word" of God which promises free grace; it is her "meat"—"I have sometimes tasted of that hidden manna that the world knows not"— just as it is the "meat" of the Philomel in **"Contemplations"** and the "meat" of the Spirit in **"The Flesh and the Spirit."** But most significantly, Anne Bradstreet's inspiration in her prose spiritual autobiography is the same as in her poetic account. It is David the Psalmist, the type of Christ. It is to David that she turns in the midst of affliction:

> Sometimes He hath smote a child with a sickness, sometimes chastened by losses in estate, and these times (through His great mercy) have been the times of my greatest getting and advantage; yea, I have found them the times when the Lord hath manifested the most love to me. Then have I gone searching and have said with David, "Lord, search me and try me, see what ways of wickedness are in me, and lead me in the way everlasting."

Profoundly inspired by the Psalms of David, Anne Bradstreet identifies with him. David's spiritual searching is her searching. His poetic mode of expression in praise of God is hers. And as a type of Christ, he symbolizes the salvation of her spirit. Confident in her faith, Anne Bradstreet chose to express her conversion poetically, using her greatest skill to praise God. If she revealed that her talent as well as her inspiration was God given, it was not through any sinful display of pride. Yet her singular expression of religious conversion in **"Contemplations"** testifies to her craft as a poet as well as to her spiritual state. Bradstreet's quest for faith to sing God's praises is inexorably tied to her desire for poetic inspiration. Thus, rather than presenting any conflict between her vocation as a poet and her spiritual state, **"Contemplations"** reconciles the two.

Walter Hesford (essay date 1987)

SOURCE: "The Creative Fall of Bradstreet and Dickinson," in *Essays in Literature,* Vol. XIV, No. 1, Spring 1987, pp. 81-91.

[*Here, Hesford argues that Bradstreet finds her deepest inspiration in the autumn season and in intimations of mortality.*]

Applying a Calvinistic misreading of a biblical lesson, Bradstreet explains why stability must elude us in this life:

> All the comforts of this life may be compared to the gourd of Jonah, that notwithstanding we take great delight for a season in them and find their shadow very comfortable, yet there is some worm or other, of discontent, of fear, or grief that lies at the root, which in great part withers the pleasure which else we should take in them, and well it is that we perceive a decay in their greenness, for were earthly comforts permanent, who would look for heavenly? ("Meditations Divine and Moral," #69)

In the Book of Jonah, the episode of the gourd (4:6-11) teaches its audience (if not the recalcitrant prophet) to value creation; Bradstreet uses it to teach her audience—her children—to devalue this green but decaying earth, to look toward eternity. Yet she undermines her pious instruction through her concluding rhetorical question, which makes apparent her emotional allegiance to seasonal comforts. Being drawn in opposite directions destabilizes and energizes Bradstreet's creative work, especially when its subject allows her to experience the opposing pulls most keenly.

The season of autumn, a type of Revelation to the book of nature, provides her with just such a subject, since it inspires her to luxuriate in comforts of apocalyptic intensity, as precariously glorious as Jonah's gourd; not surprisingly, Bradstreet's reading of autumn results in her most successfully sustained poem, **"Contemplations,"** written about twenty years after her first celebration of the season in the Quaternion poems. As critics have noted, Bradstreet now fleshes out her scholarly interest in nature's patterns and types with a convincing voice, rich in personal knowledge and desire. The creative fall is not only the subject of **"Contemplations,"** but also the experience it bears witness to and affords.

As in **"The Four Seasons of the Year,"** autumn here is the season of creation and the fall; implanted in its paradisal perfection is the seed of its demise:

> Some time now past in the autumnal tide,
> When Phoebus wanted but one hour to bed,
> The trees all richly clad, yet void of pride,
> Where gilded o'er by his rich golden head.
> Their leaves and fruits seemed painted, but was true,
> Of green, of red, of yellow, mixed hue;
> Rapt were my sense at this delectable view.

The first three words of **"Contemplations"** inform us that the paradise it presents at the outset has already been lost through the passing of time. The choice of "tide" further sets the scene in flux, suggesting its inadequacy as a permanent contest, and by the end of the second line, indeed, the reader knows that the world created here has but an hour's duration. Thus from the start, Bradstreet acknowledges the transience of earthly beauties, and her meditative ramble during the New England Indian summer moves on the edge of night and winter.

Yet also evident is the poet's attraction to the colorful, delectable world artfully served up by Phoebus Apollo, the sun. (Like other Colonial writers, Bradstreet found in classical mythology sanction for sensuous involvement in her New England surroundings.) Apparent author of the text she delights in, the sun seems Bradstreet's muse, encouraging her own fall creativity. As the poem proceeds, the sun draws her praise, almost her worship. She repeatedly raises her eyes from his text the better to see God, creation's true author and rightful recipient of her affection; repeatedly her eyes return to the sun-lit world, unable to wean themselves from the passing scene. Only after a prolonged excursion into history and subsequent ruminations by the banks of a "stealing stream" (l. 149) on the effects of time does she resign herself to the orthodox position that the text that matters is not nature's Revelation (or the record of man's questionable accomplishments), but the one mentioned in Revelation 2:17: ". . . he whose name is grav'd in the white stone / Shall last and shine . . ." (ll. 232-33). The poet's ultimate desire is not to create, but to be recreated, not to write, but to be written on the apocalyptic stone so her name will outshine the sun. The stone replaces both world and poem as text, thus capping her creative fall.

The poem's historic excursion mentioned above is prompted by the poet's inability to join a choir of nature's "abject" creatures praising their creator (stanzas eight and nine); . . . she is not in close enough communion with the rest of nature to participate in its mass, sing in its language; thus she must speak instead of that which makes communion impossible: man's fall into historical consciousness and sin becomes the burden of her song, a purely human source of creativity. Bradstreet first focuses on the primal family (stanzas 10-15), then reflects on the human condition (stanzas 16-20) in the tone of radical biblical wisdom literature, Ecclesiastes and the Book of Job. Like Solomon (the traditional author of Ecclesiastes), she is made melancholic by the vanity of our existence; like Job, she is bitter that this existence has not even the cyclical longevity of the green earth (see Job 14:7-10), though immortality is our recompense. Biblical wisdom, with its interest in natural patterns and human affairs, provides a language, a voice through which, here and elsewhere in her work, Bradstreet can assess and articulate the fall of her experience.

Bradstreet perhaps most identifies with the original human source of wisdom, "our grandame" Eve, whom she imagines in stanza 12 contemplating the course of history in a "retired place," much like the poet herself:

Here sits our grandame in retired place,
And in her lap her bloody Cain new-born;
The weeping imp oft looks her in the face,
Bewails his unknown hap and fate forlorn;
His mother sighs to think of Paradise,
And how she lost her bliss to be more wise,
Believing him that was, and is, father of lies.

Bradstreet's Eve shows no guilt for her sin, only grief for her loss. Holding bloody Cain in her lap, she thinks of Paradise; she is indeed the archetype of the poet, with longing that comes from being sensuously and consciously alive, and with that blood-stained wisdom that comes from being an experienced mother.

Bradstreet and "the kinship between spirit and flesh."

[While] she hoped for salvation from the sufferings of flesh, Bradstreet was no annihilist. Indeed, her depictions of God and heaven often reveal her belief in their kinship to human and earthly life. Her poem, "In my Solitary houres in my dear husband his Absence," depicts God as an eternally present version of Simon: "Tho: husband dear bee from me gone / Whom I doe loue so well / I have a more beloued one / whose comforts far excell." And in her poem on the burning of her house, she reminds herself, "Thou hast an house on high erect / Fram'd by that mighty Architect, / Wth glory richly furnished / Stands permanent tho: this bee fled." As these verses suggest, Bradstreet carefully crafted her ideas about God and heaven from images of husband and home.

Bradstreet's sense of the kinship between Spirit and Flesh complemented her belief in both the immortality of the soul and the resurrection of the body and allowed her to imagine her salvation at death as a pleasure that was simultaneously spiritual and physical. For example, in a poem written near the end of her life, she imagined her dying body as a bed and represented Christ as a splendid bridegroom arriving to lay in her. Reversing the Renaissance conceit of sex as death, Bradstreet invested her anticipated death with sensual pleasure by concretizing the Puritan belief in spiritual marriage to Christ. Thus she looked forward to the moment of her death as a kind of sexual rapture: "What tho my flesh shall there consume / It is the bed Christ did perfume. . . . Lord make me ready for that day / then Come deare bridgrome Come away". . . .

Amanda Porterfield, in Female Piety in Puritan New England, *Oxford University Press, 1992.*

It is as such that Bradstreet speaks in much of her mature work, encouraging and admonishing her offspring, bewailing their absence or loss, chastizing herself for her strong attachment to them (as well as to other extensions of her body and her body itself), finding her ordinary and extraordinary concerns as a woman enmeshed in fleshly relationships meet subjects for her poetry. Her religion carries her toward silent resignation and the stony silence of eternity, but her emotional ties to others and the world involve her in words, through which she can work out or at least articulate her fears and sorrows, and verbally commune with the very human sources of her keenest joys. Thus her fall into her married, motherly, and grandmotherly roles, while consuming most of her time, stimulates her creativity; when she can write, she can write with the wisdom and authority of one who has not so much listened to that old serpent, the father of lies, but to herself as she falls, and so can speak the truth about what she has suffered and loved.

Bradstreet's love poetry makes such bold use of literary conventions that they carry conviction. When she closes her **"Letter to Her Husband Absent upon Public Employment"** with "Flesh of thy flesh, bone of thy bone, / I here, thou there, yet both but one...," the language itself achieves the emotional union she longs for. When, in **"To My Dear and Loving Husband,"** she concludes "Then while we live, in love let's so persevere / That when we live no more, we may live ever...," her unorthodox plot to storm heaven through intense fleshly love intensifies her verse. That she felt embodied in her verse is indicated in her poignant plea to her husband in **"Before the Birth of One of Her Children"** to "kiss this paper for thy dear love's sake" should she die in childbirth. And her moving elegies for all those who, like her **"Dear Grandchild Elizabeth Bradstreet,"** were her "heart's too much content," suggest she was far more adept in making present her personal losses than in realizing her spiritual hope. In her mature work, Bradstreet writes as an Eve bearing the fruits of her mortality.

Timothy Sweet (essay date 1988)

SOURCE: "Gender, Genre, and Subjectivity in Anne Bradstreet's Early Elegies," in *Early American Literature,* Vol. 23, No. 2, 1988, pp. 152-74.

[*In the following excerpt, Sweet considers the ways in which Bradstreet created a feminine poetic persona for herself in the context of the male poetic tradition.*]

Facing a genre that writes the feminine only as object, Bradstreet exercises certain discursive strategies that may be called "strategies of reformation": local modifications of a discourse that permit the formation of the experience of subjectivity in a previously unproductive discourse and that expose, momentarily, the power relations inherent in that discourse. These strategies are necessary because a woman, bound by the gender system, will experience de-subjectification within discourse that clearly identifies "the subject" with masculinity. Bradstreet wants to write, but not from within the gender system that proscribes feminine subjectivity. In this sense she is trying to displace the category of writing subject, in moves that look much like those of classic deconstruction. These moves expose the political consequences of a discursive construct, in this case the parallel hierarchical oppositions of masculine/feminine and subject/object.

The problematic of subjectivity and gender is initially displayed in the elegy on Sidney, the earliest of the three public elegies. As Anne Stanford points out, the model for this poem was Joshua Sylvester's elegy on Sidney ("Anne Bradstreet's Portrait of Sidney" [in *Critical Essays on Anne Bradstreet*, 1983]). But Bradstreet's elegy is most interesting for the ways in which it deviates from the conventional structure of invocation, classical tribute, Christian meditation, and consolation, which Sylvester had so closely followed. Bradstreet seems to refuse the prescribed gesture of invocation by elevating Sidney above the muses, for example:

> Thy Logick from *Euterpe* won the Crown,
> More worth was thine, then *Clio* could set
>   down.

But the muses in turn refuse such treatment and assert their authority near the end of the poem. At this point the poem reflects on the production of poetic discourse by feigning an interruption in its own production. The "I" of the poem "muses" on the possibility of being fully constituted as a subject of this discourse—first with reference to the object created by the discourse (Sidney the poet):

> Fain would I show, how thou fame's path didst
>   tread,
> But now into such Lab'rinths am I led
> With endless turnes, the way I find not out,
> For to persist, my muse is more in doubt:
> Calls me ambitious fool that durst aspire,
> Enough for me to look, and so admire.

The object of the poem is metonymically the very genre in which subjectivity is being produced: Sidney is the author of poems that represent the discursive formation. Following Sidney along fame's path—that is, tracing his appearance as political and poetic subject ("Armes, and Arts")—the poet loses her place in the maze of discourse. There is no clear position for the subject to occupy. At such a juncture, a masculine poet would receive the aid of a muse, which would restore him to a productive position, enabling him to finish the poem. Bradstreet's muse, however, dictates silence. As a site of the refication of the feminine in discourse, the muse prescribes the position of the feminine (non)subject: do not produce discourse, for to do so would be to produce your own subjectivity. This much could perhaps be written off as a conventional gesture of humility which, in the elegy, is just one more means by which the poet is constituted—a mere diversion (which would raise the question of what kind of subjectivity is produced by a gesture of self-deprecation). But the interruption continues and becomes the focus of the poem; thus, while discourse is still being produced, gestures of hyperbolic praise required by the genre disappear. The poem is approaching the boundaries of the discourse.

The discourse of Sidney seems at this point foreign to the poet, whose pen—the instrument of literary production—writes unguided in an image of production *without* subjectivity:

> Goodwill, did make my head-long pen to run,
> Like unwise *Phaeton* his ill guided sonne, . . .
>
> So proudly foolish I, with *Phaeton* strive,
> Fame's flaming chariot for to drive.

When Sidney had confronted the issue of fame in *Astrophel and Stella,* he had simply placed himself in a strong alignment with classical discourse by objectifying Stella in the body of a muse. But in Bradstreet's poem classical allusions, which evoke the world of the muses, demonstrate the way subjectivity conventionally is constituted only as masculine. A representation of the muses cannot coexist with a subject identified as feminine. The muses themselves are puzzled (for even if they are favorably disposed toward female poets, a reader will recall that they had seen very few since Sappho, and thus are probably uncertain about their relations with Bradstreet). They deny the poet's subjectivity by taking away the instrument used in the production of discourse:

> That this contempt it did the more perplex,
> In being done by one of their own Sex;
> They took from me the scribbling pen I had,
> I to be eas'd of such a task was glad.
> For to revenge his wrong, themselves ingage
> And drave me from *Parnassus* in a rage.

The muses—the reification of the feminine in this discursive formation—will not permit a feminine subject to play the role of poet (with all the privileges that entails, such as access to the inspiring waters of Hippocrene).

But the muses' prohibition becomes a demonstration of the reification of gender, once it is clear that a poetic subject *has* been produced, in spite of the discursive prohibitions voiced by the muses. It is simply not a subject to which the attributes of a gender clearly apply. Or, more precisely, it is a subject caught up in a confusion over sex and gender. A muse literally "has" a gender (at least in the way that I am using the term)—in fact it has nothing else, being only a representation of objectified femininity in discourse. But a muse cannot have a sex, because it is not a biological being (so Milton mused about the angels). Here is the root of the problem: because sex and gender are represented on the same level in the figure of the muse, the two are conflated. The converse is true as well: sex and gender are conflated also when a masculine poet produces himself as a subject in relation to a muse. When Bradstreet produces herself (it is difficult to escape the pronoun system) as a subject of such a discourse, the resulting poem tropes the conflation of sex and gender that the masculine poetics refuses to voice.

The discourse is re-formed, but only through a self-reflexive strategy that takes the poem away from its object and into an exploration of the discourse itself and its prescription of subjectivity. Some critics have found this excursion to be artistically unfortunate; thus it is with a sigh of relief that they report Bradstreet's revisions for the posthumous 1678 edition, which removed (among other things) the lines about Phaeton and the chariot. The force of the poem remains nevertheless. In the concluding lines, the muses still determine the production of subjectivity by controlling the production of discourse:

> *Errata* through their leave threw me my pen,
> For to conclude my poem two lines they daigne
> Which writ, she bad return't to them again.

"Femininity" is represented in the poem as being the worst enemy of a woman poet; the convention of the muses is demonstrated to be the means by which the discourse controls access to itself. "Errata" occupies an interesting position here, for the name is clearly a corruption of "Erato," the muse of erotic poetry, who inspired (among others) *Astrophel and Stella*. Thus the name simultaneously identifies a discourse and distances the present production from that discourse, while invalidating the convention (what authority can the muse of error have?). "Errata" also signifies the fly-leaf on which printer's mistakes are corrected, thus indicating that Bradstreet, even when she revised the poem, realized that the possibility of truly error-free production lies somewhere outside the literary object as it is normally constructed. If "Errata" is Bradstreet's muse, the resulting literary production is on the margins of the dominant discourse—but is also a correction of it. The revised poem is not as extravagant as the original, yet it maintains the original strategy of representing an interruption in the production of discourse. A new couplet appears, summarizing the position of the subject with respect to the discourse:

> Then wonder not if I no better sped,
> Since I the muses thus have injured.

To injure the muse, in this context, is to deconstruct the reification of the feminine as it is represented discursively in the figure of the muse.

The elegy on Du Bartas examines the effects of two potential distortions of the conventional dyad of (masculine) poet and (feminine) muse. The subject first tries out the position of muse herself and then creates her own muse, a male child. This poem does not display the formal "incoherence" of the elegy on Sidney, because in some sense there is less at stake. Unlike Sidney, the figure of Du Bartas does not represent the discursive formation in which subjectivity is being produced. Bradstreet knew Du Bartas as the author of a Christian epic rather than as a writer of elegies. His *Devine Weekes and Workes* in fact places God in the position of muse. Bradstreet does not confront the implications of such a strategy, but instead excludes herself from the discourse of Du Bartas with the lines

> Thy Sacred works are not for imitation,
> But monuments for future admiration;

thus maintaining the generic *structure* of her elegy more or less intact. But of course this does not eliminate from elegiac discourse the problem of the muse. Nor does it eliminate the general question of the deployment of gender-based power in discourse. As a reading subject, the poet finds herself subjugated by Du Bartas' epic, which has the power to "Lead [] millions chained by eyes, by ears, by tongues." The effects of power operated by discourse are represented early in the poem—in another image of physical domination:

> My ravisht eyes, and heart, with faltering tongue,
> In humble wise have vow'd their service long.

Du Bartas' poetry is clearly aligned with male power, a power that seemingly cannot be deployed by a feminine subject.

Given these power relations, Bradstreet first explores the prescribed site of the appearance of the feminine (the muse), by displaying her subjugation as reading subject and consequently representing herself as muse-object:

> My dazled sight of late, review'd thy lines,
> Where Art, and more then Art in Nature shines;
> Reflection from their beaming altitude,
> Did thaw my frozen hearts ingratitude;
> Which Rayes, darting upon some richer ground,
> Had caused flowers and fruits, soone to abound;
> But barren I, my Daysey here doe bring,
> A homely flower in this my latter spring.

The transformation from reading subject to writing subject cannot be effected without going through the detour of the muse—a strategy that might function as an affirmation of male discursive power, but for the refusal of the subject to be objectified. The potential intercourse between Du Bartas and this muse is shown to be unproductive; no "flowers and fruits" of poetry will come from such a relation. A subject cannot occupy the position of the object-muse, so a gesture of humility, and a representation of the sterility of the conventionally fertile relation between poet and muse, become strategies by means of which subjectivity is produced in the site of *poet* (where gender is normally specified, but by conventions that—as we have seen in the elegy on Sidney—are open to local modification).

But such a constitution of the subject would simply return the poet to the problematic conventional relation between poet and muse, if not for the striking re-formation that appears next:

> My Muse unto a Childe, I fitly may compare,
> Who sees the riches of some famous Fayre;
> He feeds his eyes, but understanding lacks,
> To comprehend the worth of all those knacks.

Bradstreet deconstructs the convention by reducing her muse to the level that the muses had previously prescribed for her in the elegy on Sidney. The child is permitted to look, but not to speak; thus inhibits the production of discourse:

> [He] findes too soone his want of Eloquence,

The silly Pratler speaks no word of sence;
And seeing utterance fayle his great desires,
Sits down in silence, deeply he admires.

Several strategies are being deployed in this substitution of muses. First, by changing the gender of the muse but at the same time identifying him as a prattling child, Bradstreet has preserved and yet reversed the conventional opposition of genders in the poet/muse dyad while demonstrating the absurdity of the convention. Readers could hardly admit that *this* muse dwells on Parnassus. Second, where normally the poet gains a voice through a represented relation with the muse-object, here voicelessness—the inability to produce subjectivity through discourse—is located specifically in the muse, thus freeing the site of "poet" for unconstrained, unaided production (the elegy continues for fifty lines plus an epitaph). Finally, that the muse is a child adds some tension to the assumption that the fertility of the intercourse between poet and muse depends on the possibility of a sexual relationship between poet and muse. Bradstreet had played on the assumption earlier in the poem, but it becomes even clearer here that both the gender and the sexuality of the muse are always only represented, never "natural." The reification of gender is neither affirmed nor denied in this citation of the convention; instead, it is exposed and deconstructed through a reversal that gives voice to the voiceless gender.

The elegy on Queen Elizabeth involves a different sort of reversal: conventions of Sidney and Spenser are written with a feminine inflection. In the opening invocation of *The Faerie Queene,* Spenser had placed Elizabeth in the position of muse. Before that, Sidney had pursued a logical consequence of the objectification of the feminine by conflating the object of the poem with the muse. If there is a muse in Bradstreet's poem, it can only be Elizabeth because the poet immediately dissociates herself from the conventional muses:

Her personall perfections, who would tell,
Must dip his pen i'th' Heliconian Well;
Which I may not, my pride both but aspire
To read what others write, and then admire.

The dissociation is given added force by the opposition of the "I" of the poem to the masculine pronoun "his" (the unmarked gender in this discourse). Femininity appears to be inscribed in all three possible positions: poet, muse, and object.

But if the muses always hover about elegiac discourse, in this poem Elizabeth is never overtly identified as a muse. Although she could be said to inspire the poem as object, she seems not to be an example of objectified femininity. Rather, she is represented as a speaking subject who brings into the poem new, reconstructed discursive relations. The couplet "But can you Doctors now this point dispute, / She's argument enough to make you mute," metaphorically explores a discourse in which a feminine subjectivity has not only been successfully constituted but is in fact fully present. By virtue of her unusual position of

power, Elizabeth can be represented *as discourse in the act of being produced,* in the form of a self-sufficient argument.

Such a discourse remains elusive, however, and there is a sense in which, since Elizabeth's death, the possibilities have become more restricted:

Let such, as say our sex is void of reason
Know 'tis a slander now, but once was treason.

When occupied by a feminine subject, the position of the monarch as a locus of power had temporarily altered the relations between juridical and quotidian discourses. Thus any argument that women are "void of reason" was placed not only in the discourse of gossip ("slander"), but also in a more powerful juridical discourse. But, as, [Cheryl] Walker points out [in "Anne Bradstreet: A Woman Poet," in *Critical Essays on Anne Bradstreet,* 1983]:

the reign of Elizabeth, which opened up opportunities for women in both education and publishing, was a mere moment in history. . . . [A]fter the Queen's death, there was an ominous murmur around and about, and the distinct sound of doors closing once again in the faces of hopeful women.

With the death of Elizabeth, the locus of power transferred to James I, a masculine subject, and what was once inappropriate to juridical discourse became inappropriate *only* to the discourse of gossip, where power is more widely dispersed. In "social" discourse generally, proscriptions against this sort of slander compete with the gender system which constructs a "woman" who is, popularly, "void of reason"—an argument to which Elizabeth can no longer provide a living counter-example.

This sense of nostalgia for the authorizing power of a female monarch pervades the poem, culminating in a final strategy in which Bradstreet enlists millennialist theology in a re-formation of Arthurian romance:

No more shall rise or set such glorious Sun
Untill the heavens great revolution:
If then new things, their old form must retain,
Eliza shall rule *Albian* once again.

Elizabeth, and all the power she makes possible, replaces Arthur as the once and future monarch of England. But nostalgia is usually for a time that never was, so we need to ask what difference Elizabeth finally made. As the embodiment of the law, she served as a demonstration that the feminine gender was not "naturally" excluded from positions of power. But she did not abolish the reification of gender, and thus she always spoke—in her own poetry, for example—partly from within the place left open to her by the gender system. The source of her power was, after all, the patriarchal theocratic system. Bradstreet may have found the example of Elizabeth empowering—a figure waiting to be read as a living deconstruction of the gender system—but she could not after all occupy Elizabeth's privileged position. A text prescribing the education of women shows that in 1620, things remained much as they had always been: " . . . instead of reading Sir Philip Sidney's *Arcadia* let them read the grounds of huswifery. I like not a female poetesse at any hand" (Thomas Powell, *Art of Thriving*).

When the figure of the poet is aligned by gender with the power of Elizabeth, the production of subjectivity in poetic discourse is not problematic for Bradstreet. There are no difficulties with the reified femininity represented by the muses. It might be said that Bradstreet does temporarily identify a female precursor in Elizabeth, who authorizes a rebellion against patriarchal authority. . . .

Bradstreet's early elegies show that in seventeenth-century elegiac poetry, a feminine subjectivity cannot be said to appear, or if it does it "appears" only as an "absence." The feminine is only objectified, in the figure of the object-muse. This does not necessarily imply that a woman can be only a non-subject (witness the exceptional case of Elizabeth), but it does raise an important question. . . . Specifically how can a "feminine" subjectivity appear in a discourse that makes no provision for it? One answer, for Bradstreet, is that poetic discourse speaks only of the writing subject, the author-poet—and yet there are also reading subjects, whose genders are culturally defined not only by elegiac poetry, but by other (religious and quotidian) discourses where the "feminine subject" has a place (e.g., Puritans of either sex with sufficient education wrote devotional poems and prose meditations). But more important for Bradstreet the poet is the realization that if femininity is reified in poetic (or any other) discourse, so is masculinity. In this sense, "the poet" is also an object, constructed by the discourse that "he" produces. It is not that Bradstreet attempts to produce a specifically feminine subjectivity in poetic discourse. Rather, she shows how subjectivity can be detached from gender, and how even the male poet is always objectified even as "he" produces "his" own subjectivity. She deconstructs the gender system by exposing how it is constructed and how the discourse has perpetuated itself by maintaining a system in which masculine gender is ordinarily a constitutive component of subjectivity. The three elegies, then, can be read as immanent critiques of the gender system as it (dis)appears in poetry. They acknowledge the power of, and seem to participate in, the gender system—and yet they play feminine off of masculine in the sites of poet and muse, demonstrating that while gender is often restrictive for subjects categorized as "feminine," it is only a contingent feature of subjectivity.

Bradstreet's contemporary readers did not recognize the extent of her demystificatory enterprise (perhaps she was not quite aware of her own accomplishments in this vein), or were not, in any case, willing to acknowledge it. One of the more telling signs of the position of "the feminine" in the public poetry of the time is the very title of *The Tenth Muse*. The great honor done Bradstreet by John Woodbridge (who presumably chose the title when he arranged for publication) can be seen from our perspective as a simple adherence to the rules of a discourse that had not yet permitted a feminine subject to occupy the

position of poet. If, on the basis of the reading proposed here, the title seems ironic, it probably did not appear so at the time, when women could be represented only as muses and as objects—products of discourse who yet could not produce discourse. Thus the ability of women to produce their own subjectivity in public poetry was officially denied, and Bradstreet was assigned to the category of puzzling, but ultimately harmless anomaly, in accordance with Woodbridge's preface:

> I doubt not but the Reader will quickly find more then
> I can say, and that the worst effect of his reading will
> be his unbelief, which will make him question, whether
> it be a womans Work, and aske, Is it possible?

Some of the commendatory verses that preface the volume share this rhetoric of puzzlement, while one sarcastically dismissive poem places female poets completely outside the domain of useful production: "But stay a while, they seldom rise till ten a clock." Most of these poems proclaim the worth of the volume while simultaneously pointing out how odd it is that a woman could have produced it. And most also cite the convention of the muses, for example:

> And if the Nine vouchsafe the tenth a place,
> I think they rightly may yeeld you that grace.

Even though such references may well have been inspired by the title of the volume, they identify the existing discursive practice that collapses sex into the gender: there is no place on earth for a poet who is a woman, so the figure of the (female) poet must be placed in the mythical realm. If these poems can be taken as evidence of the early reception of the volume, it is clear that most of Bradstreet's readers did not recognize the nature of her critique.

Of all the poetry Bradstreet wrote after the appearance of *The Tenth Muse,* only **"The Author to Her Book"** seems to be concerned explicitly with the gender of the poetic subject—*not* because the discourses of public poetry no longer required re-formation in order to permit the female poet the ability to produce her own subjectivity, but rather (as I will argue below) because after *The Tenth Muse,* Bradstreet wrote primarily in other, less problematic discourses. In this light **"The Author to Her Book"** can be read as a summation of the project of re-formation in the early poetry, and also, perhaps, as a comment on the difficulty of the project. The position of this poem in public discourse is clear because it is so closely aligned with Spenser's "To His Booke." Spenser represents his poet as the metaphorical father of his poetry:

> Goe little booke: thy selfe present
> As child whose parent is unkent. . . .

> But if that any aske thy name,
> Say thou wert base begot with blame.

Bradstreet's **"The Author to Her Book"** also represents the poet as parent and reiterates Spenser's concern with genealogy, but most of her poem is devoted to images of *deformation.* Such images, absent from Spenser's poem, remind the reader of how the elegies in *The Tenth Muse* modified the discourse they inherited:

> Thou ill-form'd offspring of my feeble brain. . . .
>
> 　in raggs, halting to th' press to trudge,
> Where errors were not lessened (all may judg).

But at the same time this poem suggests that no amount of revision could re-form *The Tenth Muse;* and while the poet places the blame on herself, we have seen that it is the discourse itself that would prohibit a *fully successful* re-formation:

> 　　. . . affection would
> Thy blemishes amend, *if so I could:*
> I wash'd thy face, but more defects I saw,
> And rubbing off a spot, still made a flaw.
> I stretcht thy joynts to make thee even feet,
> Yet still thou run'st more hobling than is meet.
> 　(emphasis added)

Of all Bradstreet's poems, **"The Author to Her Book"** is the most self-reflexively concerned with deformation and re-formation; and like other apparently "deformed" poems, it displays the gender-specific relations of subject to discourse such that we can "read" those relations not only in the poem itself, but also in the discourse that determines it. While Spenser's poem produces a masculine subject—a "shepheards swain"—who has engendered a book of poetry (upon the muse, according to the present but unthematized convention), Bradstreet's poem represents the poet as a mother who gives birth. Thus the conventional sexual relationship between poet and muse is re-formed in a way that seems to continue the deconstructive project of the public elegies: "If for thy Father askt, say, thou hadst none." Spenser's poem is the product of a father poet ("unkent," but very much an active presence) and a mother muse (not represented, but implied by the discourse). Since the discourse makes no provision for a reversal of that relationship, Bradstreet's mother-poet must be represented explicitly as sole progenitor. There can be no denying that the poet is represented as having a sex. As such, she cannot escape the requirements of the gender assigned to the mother: she has sole care of her child-poem, fashions for it a suit of homespun cloth, and is generally represented as fulfilling her domestic role. This poem displays the problem but despairs of a solution and indicates the future direction of Bradstreet's poetry.

Most of her later poems are written from within a discourse of domesticity and display an acceptance of the "woman's place." They have been valued highly (certainly more highly than the early elegies) by feminist and traditional critics alike. According to Adrienne Rich's assessment in 1966, only certain poems written after the publication of *The Tenth Muse* "rescue Anne Bradstreet from the Women's Archives and place her conclusively in literature . . . [:] poems in response to the simple events in a woman's life" ("The Tensions of Anne Bradstreet").

But Rich later recanted, saying that her earlier reading had privileged a "masculine view of history and literature" (preface to "Tensions"). And it is true that the marriage poems and others such as the verses on the burning of her house have been widely anthologized and discussed—generally from a patriarchal perspective on the canon. While these poems are good of their kind, they are comfortable and unproblematic in terms of their acceptance of the gender system. . . .

Perhaps a discovery of the power of discourse to resist change (to resist the exercise of certain kinds of power) was Bradstreet's reason for abandoning the genre of the public elegy. In any case, with the exception of **"The Author to Her Book,"** all of Bradstreet's later poems are written within discourses in which the constitution of a feminine subjectivity is unproblematic. The necessity of a woman to produce herself as the subject of everyday social discourse was perhaps an overwhelming constraint for Bradstreet as her domestic duties gained stronger influence over her literary ambition; an accurate description of the situation might be [Elizabeth Wade] White's chapter title, "Family Life and Literary Development" (*Anne Bradstreet*). Where the early elegies demonstrate that subjectivity could in some cases be detached from the gender assigned to the poet, the domestic poems merely reproduce the ideology of social discourse, which reifies gender.

In the later elegies and epitaphs, written on members of her family rather than on public figures, the writing subject is produced within a social discourse that determines the relations between subject and object: daughter and father, grandmother and grandchild, etc. Most of these elegies were not intended for publication, and here in particular the position of the writing subject is never an issue, since the title of each poem identifies the figure of the poet as a relative in mourning. The classically inspired discourse of public poetry is erased in favor of a purely Christian system that has no place for such creatures as muses.

In all the later *domestic* poems (a genre readily separable from the private elegies, although determined ultimately by similar discursive practices), the constitution of a feminine subject is legitimated by social norms. While these domestic poems occasionally incorporate devices from a discourse we would now identity as "metaphysical poetry" (e.g., the extended pun on "hart" and "deere" in one of the **"Letter[s] to her Husband"**), in general these poems remain within the bounds of a discourse of domesticity (and outside classical discourse). Here the position of the feminine subject is unproblematic because wholly specified. The represented figure of the poet is absent from these poems, because the writing subject is constructed by the roles of wife, mother, and home-maker, rather than by the role of poet. The position of "poet" in the public sense is not available in this discourse (a fact of which Bradstreet was probably aware, since she never intended any of the domestic poems to be published as Poetry). The positions of wife and mother, on the other hand, existed ready-made.

Different discourses specify different ways of reading and different positions for the critic as reading subject. To read the early public poems in the same terms as the later private ones is to see failure (e.g., lack of "genuine expression") where there was real achievement. The production of subjectivity could be accomplished in the early poetry only by means of strategies that appear ungainly when judged by the inapplicable standard of the domestic poetry. When the constitution of a feminine subject is unproblematic, as in Bradstreet's domestic poetry, no strain is put on the dominant discursive conventions. Thus the domestic poetry does not expose the gender-based power relations of the discourse that determines it; rather, it merely reproduces the existing ideology (the gender system), without questioning the "order of things" created and supported by discourse. Since these later poems display no traces of any problematic attempts to re-form a discursive practice, it has been too easy to apply to Bradstreet's career a romantic fiction of a struggle for and progress toward a "personal voice." The story I have proposed may make it look as if instead she surrendered or retreated into less hostile terrain.

Paula Kopacz (essay date 1988)

SOURCE: "'To Finish What's Begun': Anne Bradstreet's Last Words," in *Early American Literature,* Vol. 23, No. 2, 1988, pp. 175-87.

[*In the following essay, Kopacz discusses the endings of Bradstreet's poems.*]

On a number of occasions Anne Bradstreet indicated concern about finishing her poems. In marking the hiatus after writing the first three sections of the long poem **"The Four Monarchies,"** for example, she writes, "After some days of rest, my restless heart / To finish what's begun, new thoughts impart" (lines 1-2). Three-fourths of the way finished, she found herself "restless" to get on with the job. Forced to cut short her description of the fourth monarchy, under a formal **"Apology"** she writes, "To finish what's begun, was my intent" (line 3553), and she explains the circumstances that made finishing impossible. To be sure, many critics have voiced relief that this particular poem was *not* finished. But finishing, in the sense of completing something begun, was important for Anne Bradstreet. "Perseverance, inherited and cultivated, was a strong trait in her character," wrote [Elizabeth Wade] White [in *Anne Bradstreet: "The Tenth Muse,"* 1971]. It was just as important to finish a poem as it was to finish her "errand into the wilderness." So she withstood the rising of her heart at first sight of New England, became "convinced it was the way of God" (**"To My Dear Children"**), submitted to His will and her husband's will, gave birth to eight children, and lived to the ripe age of sixty—daughter, wife, and mother of leading magistrates of the Massachusetts Bay Colony. While other women refused to come (such as the wife of the Reverend John Wilson, who had to return to England himself to persuade her) or took one look at the glorious New World and threw themselves overboard (the wife of William

Bradford), Anne Bradstreet accomplished her errand to New England. And she finished her poem on **"The Four Monarchies."**

Yet completing a poem was only part of the concern. The poem had to be concluded in an appropriate way. The critics have had much to say here. Indeed, critical evaluation of Anne Bradstreet has in some quarters depended almost exclusively on those sixteenth-century conventions of apology and seventeenth-century reaffirmations of doctrine that end so many of Bradstreet's poems. Because of these conventions and doctrinal assertions, Bradstreet's poetry was for many years regarded primarily for its historical value. *The Tenth Muse* was, after all, the first volume of poetry published by a New World author. Moses Coit Tyler and Samuel Eliot Morison, pioneers of early American literary awareness, perceived Bradstreet as a quaint historical anomaly; they seem amused that a *woman* would write the first volume of American poetry. Perhaps Bradstreet handicapped herself by frequently writing in the self-effacing, humble tone that Waller tells us was conventional among seventeenth-century women writers. For whatever reason, the solid erudition of the poems in *The Tenth Muse* was overlooked in favor of their frankly imitative manner, and most readers have preferred the later poetry, wherein Bradstreet is said to have come into her own both as a woman and as a poet. These poems published later—poems about the deaths of family members, fear of childbirth, love poems to her husband and domestic crises such as the burning of her house—interested the cultural historians because of what they tell us about life in New England in the mid-seventeenth century. In both the early and the later poetry the literary conventions and doctrinal assertions in the poems bound Bradstreet to her culture—her English literary heritage and her New World theology.

As critical interest in Bradstreet grew, scholars clarified the literary influences and explored the religious dimension of her work. Du Bartas had been recognized as an important source for Bradstreet as early as Nathaniel Ward's commendatory verse published in *The Tenth Muse* in 1650. In addition to careful analysis of Du Bartas' influence, critics have examined the influence of Raleigh, Spenser, Sidney, and Shakespeare, as well as lesser known literary figures. At the same time, a resurgence of interest in Puritan studies made it possible to explore the play of religious themes in Bradstreet's poetry—the conflict between the visible and invisible worlds, for example, or the tension between this world and the next.

Feminist criticism brought another wave of fresh scrutiny. Some studies sought to place Bradstreet in a tradition of female writers and to acknowledge the difficulties of writing as a woman. Walker points out [in "In the Margin: The Image of Women in Early Puritan Poetry," in *Puritan Poets and Poetics,* ed. Peter White, 1985] that Bradstreet and other Puritan women were depicted even in the literature of their time as being distinctly marginal in the life of the community, historical fact to the contrary. Yet just as it was predictable that early critics, mostly men, would find Bradstreet slavishly but imperfectly trying to emulate the male writers who influenced her, it was predictable that early feminist critics would find Bradstreet rebelling both openly and covertly against her male-dominated culture. In this reading conventions cannot be praised as the ties that bind, but become thorns in the side. They must be explained—explained away, if possible. . . .

The issue of orthodoxy is inextricably related to Bradstreet's endings, for they seem to focus the tension that some critics see between emotion and doctrine. Whether literary or doctrinal, the endings demonstrate Bradstreet's imbedding herself within literary and religious contexts that can help her understand the world and the great questions of life that all thinking persons confront. The endings of the poems are important also because Bradstreet herself regarded them as particularly revealing. Whether exercising a religious convention or a literary one, Bradstreet was compelled by her thorough grounding in eschatalogical thinking to feel that any kind of concluding was tantamount to some final evaluation or summing up, some ultimate, transcendent meaning.

As a devout Puritan, Bradstreet believed that everything one does receives divine notice and is, given John Cotton's explanation of a "calling," a form of prayer. Therefore, writing was not an activity distinct from making meals, changing diapers, or conducting affairs of state. Even though John Woodbridge, Bradstreet's brother-in-law, assures the "Kind Reader" that her "poems are the fruit but of some few hours, curtailed from her sleep and other refreshment," writing was not an activity for one's leisure time, in a recreational sense. In separating the poetry into two distinct camps, public and private, modern historians and literary critics contend that the private poetry is more "authentic" or "genuine" than the public, but it is a distinction that Bradstreet herself would not make—all writing being equally devoted to the service of God. Bradstreet's early "public" poetry on the four elements, the humours, the ages of man, the seasons of the year, and the four monarchies is the same fabric as the "private" poetry, the work of her later years. All are forms of prayer, whether explicit or not. In defending Bradstreet's work against the charge of "pious moralizing," Piercy distinguishes between a writer's *imposing* didacticism or religion upon a reader and being thoroughly enmeshed in a religious outlook; Bradstreet is clearly the latter. Whether writing about the apparent injustice of a grandchild's death or about the history of the world, Bradstreet was mindful of her God and her mission on earth.

Given the Puritan propensity to see all activity as a form of prayer and to take spiritual stock of oneself, it should be no surprise that Bradstreet's endings show a desire to evaluate, to crystallize the meaning of an experience or thought or feeling. The endings move toward eschatological considerations sometimes explicitly, but more often, to their merit, implicitly, with a power that surpasses the cognitive implications of the words on the page. Indeed, rather than being mere conventions, literary or religious, slapped onto the end of a poem simply to mark the finish in an artistically typical or doctrinally conventional way,

Bradstreet's endings often show consummate aesthetic skill in giving not only an answer to the intellectual and emotional questions raised, but also a feeling of ultimate conclusion and accomplishment. In short, Bradstreet's endings *finish* her poems and *conclude* them as well. In saying this, we need to distinguish between Bradstreet's finding peace of mind, which may or may not be achieved by an ending, and bringing a satisfactory sense of conclusion to a reader.

"The Four Monarchies" is a concluded yet unfinished work. Bradstreet never gets beyond Tarquinius Superbus in the succession of chiefs during the Roman Monarchy, the last of the four monarchies she planned to describe. And even the kings whom she does catalogue receive surprisingly short shrift compared to descriptions in the earlier monarchies. Yet despite its fragmentary nature, Bradstreet manages to convey to a reader of **"The Fourth Monarchy"** a sense of completion by using the conventional addendum of **"Apology."** Here the person changes from third to first, and Bradstreet explains why she could not finish the historical account: after a number of unsuccessful attempts, her papers were burned in the fire that destroyed her house. There is no attempt to blend the personal material of the **"Apology"** with the rest of the history, as she does in the elegy on Sidney. Yet merely explaining the reasons for not completing the work brings to the reader the satisfaction of an answered question, a sense of conclusion.

Furthermore, the final couplet deftly returns us to the history of the fourth monarchy, without the abrupt rupture that marked the move from history to personal statement earlier. In returning to the old familiar subject matter, Bradstreet gives a sense of completion even though the historical narrative is not completed in the chronological manner of the first three monarchies. Personifying her monarchies as lacking legs, Bradstreet reassures the reader that it doesn't matter, for the fourth monarchy has for "many ages been upon his knees" (line 3572). In the time of a couplet Bradstreet "completes" the history up to the present time ("the world *now* sees" [line 3571], emphasis added). The slow march of time established through the succession of kings in earlier monarchies becomes irrelevant from a different perspective, one that views the distant spanning of the centuries from a divine position. During these "many ages," durative verbs prevail (the world "sees"; the monarchy has "been" on its knees; her monarchies "lack" legs). In using these verbs of duration rather than verbs that mark percussive action, Bradstreet reinforces our sense of being so temporally distant from the monarchy that we can look back with a certain amount of cool unconcern. In fact, she tells us this is no matter ("Nor matter is't this last" [line 3571]), and the medial caesura emphasizes the fact. The meter conveys a tone of flat, imperial judgment. The reader senses something worthy of note, a "divine" perspective that conveys stability and permanence. In short, Bradstreet has achieved successful closure paradoxically by explaining why she could not finish and by dismissing the history she did not give us, thus making the absent present.

While it is certainly an accomplishment for Bradstreet to bring a historical narrative to successful closure without following through on the deliberate march of time set up in the poem, ending an elegy is even more difficult because the elegy dwells on a theme that itself frequently brings closure—death. Because the subject of an elegy is death, the concept of death raised at the end would not sufficiently differ from the body of the poem to bring a sense of closure, as it does with tragedy, for example. Another conventional from of closure was also denied Bradstreet in those elegies that have become most problematical—final emotional acceptance of death. Thus, elegies for both public figures and family members tested Bradstreet's skill.

The **"Elegy Upon . . . Sir Philip Sidney"** has been criticized for its ending. Stanford, for example, says the ending is merely a long digression, so that the "faults of this poem—its lack of unity and the overworking of the lengthy digressions—overshadow its virtues" [in *Anne Brastreet: The Worldly Puritan,* 1974]. But what better way to end a poem on the death of a famous man than with a whimsical, humorous, life-giving anecdote—itself something of the spirit of the man? The poet turns to herself in bringing the poem on Sidney to conclusion. She is unable, she says, to report on Sidney's fame, and the Muses refuse to help her "Since Sidney had exhausted all their store" (line 79). Furious, they take her "scribbling pen" (line 80), drive her from Mount Parnassus, but allow Errata to return her pen so she can write two concluding lines. The anecdote has the effect of bringing immediacy and genuine personality to the eulogy, as well as foreshadowing a conclusion. Readers are told what to expect—exactly two more lines, so they are psychologically prepared to read those lines as an ending. And when their expectations are fulfilled, they feel the experience has been brought to a satisfactory end.

But the lines would function well in any event. The subject of Sidney's fame has been important throughout the poem; in the penultimate line Bradstreet abandons her attempt to describe this fame ("So Sidney's fame I leave to England's rolls" [line 90]). "So" effectively introduces the couplet by suggesting a logical connection between everything that has preceded these lines and implying an epigrammatic finish that will follow. But even if Sidney's fame lives on, "His bones do lie interred in stately Paul's" (line 91). There is no escaping the finality of mortality. The effect on the reader is that of closure, both because we have been prepared to expect it formally and because we are forced to confront the fact of physical decay. The whimsical account of the poet's being driven from Parnassus, far from being a digression, brings together various themes of the poem—the difficulty of writing poetry (and to appreciate this fact enables one to better appreciate Sidney), Bradstreet's personal interest in Sidney, and the power of art to prolong "life" through fame. We laugh at Bradstreet's caricature of herself, and we accept death as the natural conclusion of life. The near rhyme of the final couplet, differing as it does from the exact rhymes that precede it, reinforces a sense of finality by duplicating that uneasy feeling we experience in contemplating

death. Sidney's "bones" are a cognitive reminder of our mortality, and the slant rhyme is a sensuous reminder. Thematically and formally the poem achieves successful resolution in its ending.

The poem in honor of Du Bartas follows some of the same patterns in the ending as that for Sidney, namely the theme of fame's outliving the artist, the poet's returning to her own inability to praise adequately, and her poetic leave-taking. But this time the ending also effects a kind of frame, most noticeably because of the poet's first-person voice. In *Poetic Closure* [Barbara Herrnstein] Smith, comparing closure in poetry and painting, refers to "a point at which, without residual expectations, [the reader] can experience the structure of the work as, at once, both dynamic and whole." The frame around a painting and the framing narrative of this poem function similarly: both provide a perspective from which the audience perceives the whole. The reader thus feels the stability that is a major source of successful closure when Bradstreet returns to the first person.

Yet the ingenuity of the frame extends beyond person to subject matter: both the beginning of the poem and the ending are about finishing. Ironically, the poem begins with Bradstreet's expressing her inability to finish; indeed, the task of adequately praising Du Bartas seemed "so great" that Bradstreet "Gave o'er the work before begun withal" (lines 6, 7). And thus, despite the disclaimer, she launches into a relatively lengthy poem of praise, much of which directly addresses Du Bartas. After a section on her muse, who is so amazed at Du Bartas' literary riches that he is humbled to silence, and a comparison to France's great heroes, who won fame for France only by their "heaps of wounded slain" (line 62), Bradstreet returns to wonder "at the hand of heaven, / In giving one [the gifts that] would have served seven" (lines 68-69). The substitution of the third-person "one" for the expected second person of direct address subtly prepares the reader for the careful, third-person distancing from Du Bartas six lines from the end. Here, reflection on the enduring quality of Du Bartas' fame emotionally signals a leave-taking that is reinforced by the closed couplet form. Consequently, Bradstreet's return to the theme of her own inadequacy and leave-taking in the final four lines, her finishing the poem, frames the experience so a reader accepts the dynamic of continuing fame amid the finality of mortality and the conclusion of elegy. Like the circle of a frame, Bradstreet ends where she began, ending.

The word play of the final line enhances the sense of conclusion. Sounds are repeated in key words presented antithetically—"Good will, not skill" (line 85). Smith notes that antithetical summaries are a conventional closure for many sixteenth-century poems (31). The epitaph that follows the poem exploits the convention. It flirts with polarities—birth and death, heaven and humanity, Art and Nature, dying and reviving. In the final couplet ("so Bartas died; / But . . . he is revived" [lines 93-94]) the passive present-tense verb counters the opposing past tense, and the reader by now almost triumphantly accepts Du Bartas' death and the conclusion of an aesthetic experience. Thus in both the frame and final antitheses Bradstreet shows herself aware of literary fashion and adept at using conventions to resolve a poem.

The third elegy on a public figure, the one for Queen Elizabeth, has achieved much critical attention because Bradstreet uses the occasion to defend women. Yet the poem also reveals the poet's skill in concluding. Repetition of the word "happy" ("happy England," "happy, happy . . . days," "happiness" [lines 106-08]) builds expectation, and repetition of "she set" (line 111) emphasizes the loss. In the final four lines of the poem Bradstreet plays with antithetical summaries again ("No more shall rise or set so glorious sun" [line 112] and "*new* things their *old* forms shall retain" [line 114], emphasis added) as she looks forward to the joy of the millennium. Her readers would have recognized the familiar device of closure and would have rejoiced in their anticipation of the millennium. Like the sun, Elizabeth has "set," but she will "rise" once more to "rule Albion once again" (line 115). The conclusion works because, as in the poem on the four monarchies, Bradstreet offers at the end a totally different temporal point of view, one that makes human time, and consequently human mortality, of little consequence. In Elizabeth's ruling "once again," we have come full circle, always a positive image of closure. Not only are we reassured through the thematic, religious consolation of the millennium, but also through the reconciliation of words of opposite meaning.

While attention has been drawn to the public elegies because Bradstreet's suggestion that fame can overcome death has been seen by some critics as unusual, the private elegies have evoked the strongest disagreement. Controversy frequently centers on doctrinal assertions that appear in the final lines of the poems. The elegies written on the deaths of her grandchildren—Elizabeth, at a year and a half of age; Anne, just over three and a half; and Simon, a month and a day—show Bradstreet at her most emotional and putting her faith to its greatest test.

In the poem in memory of Elizabeth, emotional tension builds as Bradstreet reiterates "Farewell" and then questions her own discontent over this farewell: "why should I once bewail thy fate, / . . . Sith thou art settled in an everlasting state"? (lines 10, 12). The second stanza is especially disconcerting; in an apparent answer to her question, Bradstreet reminds us that natural order affords decay and death only after timely growth. The next two lines focus the problem because they point out the injustice of this death: "But plants new set to be eradicate, / And buds new blown to have so short a date" (lines 17-18). The conjunction "but" clearly indicates that this death goes against natural order. The final line of the poem is the one that has caused so much debate: "Is by His hand alone that guides nature and fate," clearly attributing this untimely death to God. Murdock's reading [discussed in Stanford's *Anne Bradstreet*] is shared by many. He believes that Bradstreet found herself "perilously close to writing rebelliously against God's decrees. She pulls herself up in the last line." He then asserts, "It falls flat, even

metrically, because it is dictated not by real feeling but by deference to orthodox doctrine" (64).

But instead of its failing thematically and metrically, the line closes the poem in thematically and structurally effective ways. Bradstreet deliberately vents her emotions in this poem; she was not ashamed of them, and she did not deny them. The task of the Puritan was not to repress the emotions, but to direct them. Emotions were not considered autonomous, but subject to the control of the will. Believing in faculty psychology, Bradstreet thought it her duty to restrain her emotions, to bring them in line with productive behavior. Writing a poem was just such a form of productive behavior because it was a form of prayer, and consequently an active attempt to prepare the heart. While modern sensibility sees "tension" between emotion and doctrine, the Puritan viewed them as integrally related. Consequently, the final line is not an ironic laying down of doctrine, but a fact that must be brought into line with the emotional feeling of the poem; not contradictory to emotion, but coinciding with it. Bradstreet may still feel upset about the death, but it is not accompanied by anger with God.

The poem demonstrates a number of strategies that ensure this composure. First of all, it is organized in two stanzas, the second answering the question raised by the first. A question-and-answer format structurally affords a sense of closure. The rhyme scheme of the poem is: a b a b c c c d e d e c c C. The return of familiar sound (c) in the triplet of the second stanza contributes to a sense of closure. And finally, the last line conveys the effect of closure by an additional foot. The change from iambic pentameter to hexameter adds solidity and finish. The final alexandrine comes in an assertive statement, and the last word of the poem is "fate." No devout Puritan would argue with fate. Anne Bradstreet may still regret the death of the infant; the poem cannot wipe away those feelings. But the work comes to an end that is aesthetically satisfying because it is both structurally and thematically sound. The aesthetic closure is a deliberate working toward the integration of emotional and theological stability. To oversimplify, the poem is a process, not a product. And the process is prayer.

The poem on the death of the infant Simon is the second most controversial of the private elegies. [In "'Farewell Dear Babe'; Bradstreet's Elegy for Elizabeth," in *Early American Literature,* 15 (1980)], Mawer finds a tone of "outrage," while Stanford finds the poem "intensely ironic" and "close to blasphemy" until the "quiet settling down" of the last four lines. Both critics suggest an orthodox ending that doesn't quite work. Yet in this poem perhaps even more than the others, the ending is an integral part of a complex web and cannot be considered distinct from what precedes it.

The entire poem juxtaposes the timely and the timeless. Consider the verbs of the opening line: "No sooner came, but gone, and fall'n asleep." The child "came" at a specific point in time; the activity could be dated. Yet he is "gone"; this verb marks a different sense of time because it reveals duration, as does the final verb of the line, "fall'n asleep." If Bradstreet were not from the very beginning contrasting different views of time, the verbs in the line would have been parallel in form—"come" paired with "gone," or "came" paired with "left" or "went," both durative or both percussive. Yet they are not to be seen as mutually exclusive; indeed, they are quite compatible, for the devout Puritan lived constantly aware of the two levels of time—humanity's mortal time on earth and God's eternal presence.

Although the babies have been "Cropt" by God, with all the sudden abruptness the consonants imply, it is neither mere orthodox assertion nor ironic rebellion for Bradstreet to say "yet is He good" (line 8). The eternal, enduring presence of His goodness is an undeniable fact, reinforced by the response of "awe" reported in the next line. Line 10, "Such was His will, but why, let's not dispute," again juxtaposes human time and God's time; "His will" is timeless, firm, while men and women are engaged in timely disputation. Although it was difficult to hold to the timely and the timeless simultaneously, the Puritan was accustomed to thinking on both temporal levels.

"Let's say He's merciful as well as just" is the most potentially explosive line of the poem, but it is only the modern reader who can read it so. "Let's say" is the imperative mood, parallel to prior exhortations in the poem—"let's be mute" (line 9) and "let's not dispute" (line 10), or the familiar command, "Let us pray." This hortatory accepts completely what it commands; it cannot be read as ironic or sarcastic, as Stanford suggests. Indeed, the line immediately preceding the one in question describes the Puritan posture—"With humble hearts and mouths put in the dust" (line 11), hardly an attitude from which to lash out in ironic rebellion against God. In fact, it serves to remind us of divine power in creating a human being out of the dust of the earth, to which we will all return.

The final four lines effect successful closure in a number of ways. First, Bradstreet reworks the theme of coming and going with which the poem begins, but this time with millennial suggestions. God "will return" to "make up . . . our losses" (line 13). Instead of the mortal coming and going of her grandchild, Bradstreet concerns herself now with the return of divinity on earth. And because she is confident of His return, she can direct the infant, "Go pretty babe, go . . . " (line 15), in marked contrast to her sense of powerlessness over the infant's departure in the first line ("No sooner came, but gone . . . "). The movement from "gone" to "go" measures the progress she has made in understanding this death over the course of the poem. The command to "go" is repeated—"go rest with sisters twain"; the author directs the child to join that timeless realm, emphasized by the durative verb "rest." We remember that in the opening line the child was "asleep"; "rest" at this point successfully close the poem by repeating a concept, but this time with deepened meaning. That the child will successfully cross over to the world of the timeless becomes clear in the last line, for he will "Among the blest in endless joys remain" (line 16).

"Remain" is a durative verb, and the line preponderates with the sense of the timeless (the joys are "endless"; the child will be "Among the blest"). Even the sounds of the line are continuing sounds—the *m* and *n* surrounding the dipthong in "remain" and the repetition of the *s/z* sound in "blest," "endless," and "joys." Thus, the ending works in this poem; it makes the poem a whole and leaves the reader in a position of stability and permanence because it so deliberately echoes the earlier, more painful view, when human time and God's time struggled against each other. The reader has come full circle with Bradstreet and is now wiser and reconciled to timeless existence.

What these "public" and "private" poems show is that Bradstreet was at all times a Puritan poet, in the fullest sense of the term. She was Puritan in her respect for the great cultural tradition she emerged from; the conventions of apology and statements of humility at the end of many poems show her attachment to this tradition and her belief that poetry was a consecrated art. She was a poet in her adept manipulation of conventions to achieve successful closure. She was a Puritan in seeing her conclusions as extremely important, in having them carry the burdens of eschatological implications. She was a poet in conveying these implications through ingenious concluding strategies of thematic resolution; question and answer; repetition of sounds, words, and images; in playful antitheses that strike the mind as paradoxical; and in framing narratives. She was Puritan in granting doctrine the final say. She was a poet in striving to make doctrinal statements fit the poem as a whole, in working through the process of creativity. And finally, she was a Puritan poet in seeing each poem as not so much an artifact as a prayer. After the last line was written, the success or failure of the poem would be determined by a divine judge, who would note the poem as a work in progress toward the ideal end—eternal life with God on high. The last word remains to be written.

Patricia Caldwell (essay date 1988)

SOURCE: "Why Our First Poet Was a Woman: Bradstreet and the Birth of an American Poetic Voice," in *Prospects: An Annual of American Cultural Studies,* Vol. 13, 1988, pp. 1-35.

[*In the following excerpt, Caldwell discusses Bradstreet's struggle with traditional male images symbolizing poetic creation, and concludes that Bradstreet became the founder of American poetry precisely because of her marginal position.*]

It takes a worried man—or woman—to sing a worried song, and it is not surprising that Bradstreet's earliest poetry is more worried, in a more obviously "feminine" way, than anything she wrote later. Self-consciously erudite, duly apologetic, and above all, written "to please [her] wintry father," these "public" poems are marked by frequent, nervous recurrences to two conventions that Bradstreet certainly would have encountered in her wide reading. One is the well-known modesty topos, a long-established posture of authorial self-effacement and disparagement. Critics have differed about the degree of genuine self-doubt in Bradstreet's apparently formulaic apologies, but since all but one of them appear in poems she wrote before the age of thirty-five (and significantly, before her father's death), it seems reasonable to suppose that the novice poet found some real and necessary comfort in a convention that provided an acceptable outlet for her fears. Far more interesting, however, are her early imaginative encounters with a second convention, namely, the often-used image of the *pen* (an image that virtually disappears from Bradstreet's work after 1650), for this is a masculine symbol whose employment by a woman poet can never quite be taken for granted.

Among Bradstreet's favorite reading, we know, was the work of Sir Philip Sidney, perhaps her distant kinsman. Sidney's use of the pen in the first sonnet of *Astrophel and Stella* (1598) is probably the best-known occurrence of that image in English literature: a pen that, truant or idle though it appears, eventually delivers the poet from his allegedly pregnant state in a sort of hermaphroditic triumph. Today we are acutely aware, especially from the work of Gilbert and Gubar, that for women writers, the pen can represent a fearsome problem—this phallic instrument that the male writer wields in literally "begetting" his "thoughts on paper," this symbol of the male author's sexual authority that is also "the essence of literary power." Little wonder, then, that when the twenty-six-year-old Bradstreet took up *her* pen, early in her writing life, to record a tribute to her hero, Sidney, she could not get this time-worn convention of her literary culture to work for her. . . .

> *Apollo* laught to patch up what's begun,
> He bad me drive, and he would hold the Sun;
> Better my hap, then was his darlings fate,
> For dear regard he had of *Sydney*'s state,
> Who in his Deity, had so deep share,
> That those that name his fame, he needs must spare,
> He promis'd much, but th' muses had no will,
> To give to their detractor any quill.
> With high disdain, they said they gave no more,
> Since *Sydney* had exhausted all their store,
> That this contempt it did the more perplex,
> In being done by one of their own sex;
> They took from me, the scribling pen I had,
> I to be eas'd of such a task was glad.
> For to revenge his wrong, themselves ingage,
> And drave me from *Parnassus* in a rage,
> Not because, sweet *Sydney*'s fame was not dear,
> But I had blemish'd theirs, to make't appear;
> I pensive for my fault, sat down, and then,
> *Errata,* through their leave threw me my pen.
> For to conclude my poem two lines they daigne,
> Which writ, she bad return't to them again.
> So *Sydney*'s fame, I leave to *England*'s Rolls,
> His bones do lie interr'd in stately *Pauls*.

[In *"Anne Bradstreet's Public Poetry and The Tradition of Humility,"* Early American Literature 17 (1982)], Ei-

leen Margerum makes the interesting argument that this passage is a "diversion" and "not a statement of poetic self-doubt," that Bradstreet's aim here is to deflect attention from her "unorthodox views" in praising Sidney's amorous poetry at all, since he was then "out of favor with the Puritans." But, regardless of her conscious motives, Bradstreet's treatment of the pen figure has nothing in common with the confident, even breezy literary sexuality of the male poets. Instead, there is shame before her own sex for having a pen at all; it must be confiscated by those Fury-like muses, only to be returned for brief service—hurled at her like a weapon by "Errata." Clearly, it is an insulting mistake for Mistress Bradstreet to wield a pen, and the problem is not handled, as it might have been, with irony and wit. The episode takes shape through a barrage of classical images strewn nervously and even bewilderedly about. One detects real, not mock, distress in this passage, confusion as to what the poet's stance should really be, and a sense that the whole weight of inherited literary convention is pressing the poet into an uneasy, abrupt silence.

This is not an isolated case, merely attributable to the fact that the Sidney elegy was probably only the second poem Bradstreet ever wrote. In **"To her most Honoured Father,"** Bradstreet dedicates her earliest efforts to Thomas Dudley, even though her "lowly pen" is unequal to the "Eagles quill." Dudley presumably used in writing his own (now lost) poem on the four parts of the world. **"In honour of *Du Bartas*, 1641"** finds Bradstreet wishing for "an Angels voice, or *Barta*'s pen," although her tongue is hopelessly "mute." At the end of the Grecian section of **"The Foure Monarchies,"** "My tyred braine, leaves to a better pen, / This taske befits not women, like to men." Even the elegy to a woman, Queen Elizabeth, questions the efficacy of the poet's pen, though in a milder way: "No *Phoenix,* Pen, nor *Spencers* Poetry" can sufficiently praise "Eliza." He who would do so "Must dip his Pen i'th' Heleconian Well; Which I may not . . . " A few years after the Sidney elegy, however, Bradstreet's **"Prologue"** to the so-called Quaternions—her four long poems on the elements, humours, ages, and seasons—finally uses the pen image with complexity and skill.

> 1. To sing of Wars, of Captaines, and of Kings,
> Of Cities founded, Common-wealths begun,
> For my mean Pen, are too superiour things,
> And how they all, or each, their dates have run:
> Let Poets and Historians set these forth,
> My obscure Verse, shal not so dim their worth.
>
> 2. But when my wondring eyes, and envious heart,
> Great *Bartas* sugar'd lines doe but read o're;
> Foole, I doe grudge, the Muses did not part
> 'Twixt him and me, that over-fluent store;
> A *Bartas* can, doe what a *Bartas* wil,
> But simple I, according to my skill.
> 3. From School-boyes tongue, no Rhethorick we expect,
> Nor yet a sweet Consort, from broken strings,
> Nor perfect beauty, where's a maine defect,

My foolish, broken, blemish'd Muse so sings;
And this to mend, alas, no Art is able,
'Cause Nature made it so irreparable.

4. Nor can I, like that fluent sweet tongu'd
Greek
Who lisp'd at first, speake afterwards more
plaine
By Art, he gladly found what he did seeke,
A full requitall of his striving paine:
Art can doe much, but this maxime's most sure,
A weake or wounded braine admits no cure.

5. I am obnoxious to each carping tongue,
Who sayes my hand a needle better fits,
A Poets Pen, all scorne, I should thus wrong;
For such despight they cast on female wits:
If what I do prove well, it wo'nt advance,
They'l say it's stolne, or else, it was by chance.

6. But sure the antick *Greeks* were far more
milde,
Else of our Sex, why feigned they those nine,
And poesy made, *Calliope*'s owne childe,
So 'mongst the rest, they plac'd the Arts divine:
But this weake knot they will full soone untye,
The Greeks did nought, but play the foole and
lye.

7. Let *Greeks* be *Greeks*, and Women what they
are,
Men have precedency, and still excell,
It is but vaine, unjustly to wage war,
Men can doe best, and Women know it well;
Preheminence in each, and all is yours,
Yet grant some small acknowledgement of ours.

8. And oh, ye high flown quils, that soare the
skies,
And ever with your prey, still catch your praise,
If e're you daigne these lowly lines, your eyes
Give wholsome Parsley wreath, I aske no Bayes:
This meane and unrefined stuffe of mine
Will make your glistering gold but more to
shine.

This poem has been much discussed, and its fifth stanza is probably the most quoted of all of Bradstreet's lines. The poem's witty send-up of male "superiority" hinges cleverly on the juxtaposition of male pen and female needle—witty, but awesomely serious in its revelation of a woman writer's tangled feelings about her vocation. Here, the pen figure is mingled with two other emotionally laden image-clusters: needle, tongue, musical instrument—all of which have sexual overtones, and two of which can be dangerous; and images of threat and hurt: wars, wounds, brokenness, the preying of hawks. Moreover, the famous fifth stanza is notable not only for the needle/pen opposition, but also for the key word "obnoxious." Since its primary 17th-Century meaning was "exposed to (actual or possible) harm; subject to injury or evil," we must read the line, "I am vulnerable to criti-

cism," not "repellent to my critics," as we would mean now. It is the effect on herself of those cutting tongues, and not her effect on them, that worries the speaker. For this poet, the tongue—in some poems directly associated with the masculine pen—is a fearsome object; in others, as here, the speaker also has a good deal of pain and trouble with her own tongue. The reader's eye is also drawn to stanza three, poignantly and familiarly rendering the woman poet-singer as defective or deformed, a musical instrument that has been played too roughly, its strings broken, no longer virginal (and the pun is intended, for this might be a virginal, that small tabletop harpsichord popular in the 16th and 17th Centuries), foolish, broken, and blemished. The poem, with its freight of cutting, wounding, and maimed objects, seems to say, "Don't hurt me, men." Yet all the while, the speaker shoots out barbs or needles of her own, by fearlessly launching her poem in the masculine, old-world epic mode of the *Aeneid,* by tossing off puns, by playing on the art-versus-nature convention, by skillful rhetorical shifts—in all these ways, she seems to laugh at the male literati. In the guise of subservience, couched in the conventions of poetic self-effacement, she needles her supposed critics. In fact, the needle in stanza five may be less important as a symbol of women's domesticity than as a symbol of women's weaponry. If in the masculine world of wars, captains, and kings, the pen is mightier than the sword, the woman poet can hope to make the needle, and the act of needling, mightier than the pen.

But it is not a successful standoff. There is still the anxiety and the pain in this poem about the making of poems. Susan Gubar tells us [in "'The Blank Page' and the Issues of Female Creativity," in *The New Feminist Giticism,* ed. Elaine Showalter, 1985] that for a woman the making of art can feel like the destruction of the woman's own body.

> Because of the forms of self-expression available to women, artistic creation often feels like a violation, a belated reaction to male penetration rather than a possessing and controlling. . . . Women's paint and ink are produced through a painful wounding, a literal influence of male authority. If artistic creativity is likened to biological creativity, the terror of inspiration for women is experienced quite literally as the terror of being entered, deflowered, possessed, taken, had, broken, ravished—all words which illustrate the pain of the passive self whose boundaries are being violated. . . . [Women artists] often describe the emergence of their talent as an infusion from a male master rather than inspiration from or sexual commerce with a female muse.

Such may well be the case with the early Bradstreet, even though we must respect the long distance and differentness between the centuries. True, in **"The Prologue,"** Bradstreet's broken, out-of-tune muse is female, is herself; in her very early elegy to the epic poet Guillaume Du Bartas, she "compares" her muse to "a Chide" (but interestingly, a boy child) whose speech falters and who is also "weake brain'd I." But Bradstreet's muse in a truer sense was the man who was "the strongest influence in her life"—her father, Thomas Dudley. To him, she consecrated all of her early work, which she clearly felt he had inspired; from him flowed any "worth" she might contain; to him, all duty owed. It may be, as Wendy Martin argues, [in *An American Triptych,* 1984] that the contrasts between Bradstreet's elegy for her mother (a remarkably pallid poem) and the elegy for her father "dramatize the differences in roles that Puritan women and men were expected to play in their society." They also dramatize the differences in Bradstreet's feelings towards each of her parents. "Father, Guide, Instructor too," he was the one who gave his second child and eldest daughter her extraordinary education, and he was the one, apparently, to encourage her writing (or whose encouragement mattered). He was also at least one of her poetic "precursors" or "mythic progenitors," for he had written poetry, almost all of it now lost. For this reason, he may also have been what Joanne Feit Diehl calls "the composite father . . . the main adversary" [in "Come Slowly—Eden," *Signs* 3 (1978)].

Diehl, in her study of women poets and the muse, points out that male poets are naturally able to "separate their poetic fathers—mythic progenitors—from the [traditionally female] muse" and by engaging in an oedipal struggle to court the muse away from the poetic father or precursor, "invoke the aura of inspiration" they desire. But such a synthesis is denied the woman poet, who "cannot 'beget' art upon the (female) body of the muse" and who therefore must get her "literal influence," in Gubar's phrase, from a "male master"; so she conflates precursor and muse into a "doubly potent" masculine figure, "fears his priapic power and wards him off with intense anxiety as she simultaneously seeks to woo him." These insights into the woman poet's dilemma seem especially ominous for Bradstreet: to have had a muse who was both her "poetic father" and *actual* father must have been burdensome indeed. There is a telling glimpse of this problem in a pair of passages. In the final stanza of **"The Prologue,"** the speaker both "wards off" and "woos" the manly "high flown quils, that soare the skies" catching "prey"; we find the same image in **"To her most Honoured Father,"** written about the same time (1642) and paying ambivalent homage to Thomas Dudley's own poem on the four parts of the world.

> Their paralells to finde I scarcely know,
> To climbe their Climes, I have nor strength, nor skill,
> To mount so high, requires an Eagles quill:
> Yet view thereof, did cause my thoughts to soare,
> My lowly pen, might wait upon those four.

Thus, the poet teases and resents, worships and fears the patriarchal "Eagles quill"—the only means available to her for writing poetry. Given the confusion of the paternal presence in her creative imagination and given the "conventional romantic relationship of poet and muse," we can understand why Bradstreet fled, Daphne-like, from the Apollonian laurel that her poems might have earned: The violent sexual origins of the "Bayes" may have seemed much too close for comfort.

But we should not forget that even as he was her muse and progenitor, Governor Thomas Dudley exerted something other than mythic force. He was also, to his daughter's imagination and in actual fact, a figure in history: "One of thy Founders, him *New-England* know, / Who staid thy feeble sides when thou wast low," and a formidable founder at that, who according to his own account, "Dy'd no Libertine" and whose daughter defended him as

> True Patriot of this little Commonweal,
> Who is't can tax thee ought, but for thy zeal?
> Truths friend thou wert, to errors still a foe,
> Which caus'd Apostates to maligne so.
> Thy love to true Religion e're shall shine,
> My Father's God, be God of me and mine.

But it was not Dudley's allegedly stern and "arrogant" character alone that made him central to his daughter's poetic quest. She, of course, claimed in her elegy to him that he was "Well known and lov'd, where ere he liv'd" (prudently adding, "by most"); but something more interesting is revealed in the succeeding line, bland as it may at first appear: "Both in his native, and in foreign coast." Dudley's native coast was, of course, on the British side of the Atlantic, whereas New England, in Bradstreet's vocabulary, was still "foreign" after more than twenty years. Whether it seemed foreign to her own sensibility or whether the poet was assuming Dudley's own outlook, one thing seems clear: This was Dudley's "historical" significance for her; he was, in all his power and presence, a figure of the Old World; he "was" the Old World. Hence, it was only after he died in 1653, a few years after the publication of *The Tenth Muse,* that Bradstreet's poetry began to steer its well-known course away from patriarchal European literary models and toward the personal and empirical, never to return. . . . Fifty-six years ago, Samuel Eliot Morison attributed the shift in Bradstreet's poetic life to the trauma of seeing *The Tenth Muse* in print, which "completely cured her of the Du Bartas disease, and of writing imitative poetry." A recent interpretation by Wendy Martin is that the liberating shift occurred on the death of the father. Martin is right, but we may add that with Dudley's passing came the "death" of old England to Bradstreet's poetic imagination. When Bradstreet lamented in her elegy that "His Generation serv'd his labours cease." did she not feel the double impact of these words? Yes, Dudley the governor and magistrate had served and labored for his contemporaries, and his entire generation of Winthrops and Cottons, now dead, had served and labored for the country; but Dudley's "Generation" of a poet-daughter, his "labours" as her mythic progenitor—these, too, had served and passed. That these complementary readings are so tightly joined in one or two words indicates the inseparability in Bradstreet's psyche of Dudley the muse from Dudley the type of his "native" England. Now Bradstreet had to go her own way in the "pathless paths" of the New World experience. Now her book "had no father."

"The Author to her Book" marks this point of no return. Though precise dating of her writings is sometimes impossible, there is no reason to doubt that Bradstreet wrote this poem shortly after the surprise appearance of *The Tenth Muse* in 1650 and therefore near the time of her father's death. Addressed to the work that had been "snatcht" by her brother-in-law and "expos'd to publick view" by being published in England without Bradstreet's permission, the poem at first appears to give conventional treatment to a familiar metaphor: the book as the author's brainchild.

> Thou ill-form'd offspring of my feeble brain,
> Who after birth did'st by my side remain,
> Till snatcht from thence by friends, less wise
>   then true
> Who thee abroad, expos'd to publick view,
> Made thee in raggs, halting to th' press to
>   trudge,
> Where errors were not lessened (all may judg).
> At thy return my blushing was not small,
> My rambling brat (in print) should mother call,
> I cast thee by as one unfit for light,
> Thy visage was so irksome in my sight;
> Yet being mine own, at length affection would
> Thy blemishes amend, if so I could:
> I wash'd thy face, but more defects I saw,
> And rubbing off a spot still made a flaw.
> I stretcht thy joynts to make thee even feet,
> Yet still thou run'st more hobbling then is meet;
> In better dress to trim thee was my mind,
> But nought save home-spun Cloth, i'th' house I
>   find.
> In this array 'mongst vulgars mayst thou roam,
> In Criticks hands, beware thou dost not come;
> And take thy way where yet though art not
>   known,
> If for thy father askt, say thou hadst none:
> And for thy Mother, she alas is poor,
> Which caus'd her thus to send thee out of door.

Although it is not strictly an envoi, **"The Author to her Book"** may be tellingly compared with numerous self-disparaging "sendings on the way" of "newborn" books by Bradstreet's admired predecessors. [In *Shakespeare's Images of Pregnancy,* 1980], Elizabeth Sacks has shown that at a time when "the English language itself was undergoing rebirth," scores of Renaissance works, "born from the poet's laborious throes," were "viewed as . . . vulnerable, helpless infant[s] struggling for existence in an unfriendly world." Spenser, Sidney, Chapman, Turberville, Lyly, Dekker, Shakespeare, and others dressed the idea with "florid obstetrical metaphors," imagining their creations with "bleeding" and "gaping wounds" inflicted in "delivery" by careless printers, or literary offspring maimed, crippled, lame, deformed, and monstrous, vulnerable to harsh treatment by the larger world. Sacks points out that "rediscovery of the generation metaphor"—which can be traced back at least as far as Plato—"seemed appropriate" in a period of prosperity, expansion, and "great literary productivity," but her findings suggest that in the hands of authors afflicted with "male womb-envy," the metaphor often took on a dark and even bitter aspect. Coinciding with the "novelty of popular printing" and the burgeoning of published literary texts, it gave shape to

the poets' fears about winning sympathetic support from patrons and public, and it could even be twisted into a "savage" weapon of "displeasure and contempt," as in the Harvey—Nash debate of the 1590s. It may even have reflected Tudor and Elizabethan obsessiveness about barrenness and the production of heirs.

Bradstreet, then, had at her disposal a rich and well-worked, if somewhat equivocal, metaphor. She must have known Spenser's dedication to Sir Philip Sidney of *The Shepheardes Calender* (1579), wherein the poet, in the modest guise of "Immerito," sends his "little booke" to the patron for protection: It goes, "As child whose parent is vnkent"; if "Enuie barke at thee," it is to hide under the patron's wing; if asked who made it, it will reply that a "shepheards swaine" sang it while feeding his flock; if asked its name, "Say thou wert base begot with blame / For Thy thereof thou takest shame"; in the end, "when thou art past ieopardee, / Come tell me, what was sayd of mee / And I will send more after thee." She must also have known Sidney's own dedication to *The Countess of Pembroke's Arcadia* (1590), which likened "this idle work of mine" to an unwanted child.

> As the cruel fathers among the Greeks were wont to do to the babes they would not foster, I could well find in my heart to cast out in some desert of forgetfulness this child which I am loth to father. But you desired me to do it. . . . I hope, for the father's sake, it will be pardoned, perchance made much of, though in itself it have deformities. . . . [My head] having many, many fancies begotten in it, if it had not been in some way delivered would have grown a monster. . . . But his chief safety shall be the not walking abroad; and his chief protection the bearing the livery of your name.

The exploitation of this metaphor went to even greater lengths when the poet felt no need to portray himself as a serious, courteous gentleman. Such was Bradstreet's Southern contemporary, George Alsop, four years an indentured servant in Maryland, whose own "The Author to his Book" introduced a satirical pamphlet (1666) describing that colony. Alsop's ribald, violent couplets begin with a lifelike account of the poet's seduction, rape, and abondonment by Apollo. The resulting boy-child is a "Brat as black as Ink," and the poet, fearing he will be accused of fornication with an African slave, throws his "Bastard" out into "a monstrous World," imaginning all sorts of degradations for him and his final death by hanging, although "In Resurrection he will surely live." Half the poem is taken up with acid portrayals of English critics as sour, stuffy, and posturing murderers, ignorant "Asses and captious Fools" incapable of understanding "The Heathen dresses of another Land" and who are not "real men." The poet, presumably, is a real man, and he indicates it in part by toying bawdily with the childbirth metaphor as a slap against the fastidious critics of himself and of the New World.

Yet the reader gets very different impressions from the men's protestations, on the one hand, and Bradstreet's, on the other. All these poets achieve ironic effects based on the notion of parental love, all employ a grotesque imagery that is unacceptable on a logical plane, and all betray a genuine affection for the "base-born" literary child. But Spenser, Sidney, and other courtly male poets are concerned primarily with paying an elaborate if convoluted compliment to actual patrons and often to their literary precursors, as Chaucer had done in his envoi to *Troilus and Criseyde*. Their transparent pose of humility is grounded in a real situation, i.e., their precarious, discomforting dependence on the patronage of powerful royals and nobles. Hence, the men who write these poems, including Alsop, reassert their autonomy by teasing and mauling the parent-child figure until it yields up an aggrandized, even defiant picture of the poet himself, whether he is a tough guy, a charming, singing swain, or a manly, Zeus-like brain enticingly swollen with fancies.

Bradstreet's treatment of the metaphor is something apart from all these. We must remember that she probably felt compelled to write her poem in response to the prefatory one by her brother-in-law John Woodbridge, whose ***Tenth Muse*** dedication, "To my deare Sister, the Author of these Poems," called the book "so faire an infant," defended his own efforts "To force a womans birth" and "Expose her Labours," and regretted that without Bradstreet's "owne sweet hand; 'Tis not so richly deckt, so trimly tir'd." In reply, Bradstreet's lowly imagery of a fatherless child roughly handled may look conventional and may seem to be-speak some half-playful mixture of self-deprecation and secret pride; but the homely, realistic details—the washing and rewashing of the "child's" face, the store of homespun cloth "i' th' house"—and the relative gentleness with which the speaker tries to mend the (once again) blemished, broken child are not in the reckless spirit of the male poets. It is as if the poet is not really comfortable with this particular tradition, and, although she purports to use it in the mannered, clever, and masculine way, some real distress seeps out in what seems a muted reprimand to her brother-in-law, to male literati in general, and perhaps particularly to those in the Old World "abroad." The reluctant use of imagery that would be unnatural to a loving mother and caretaker of many children is more a sign of withdrawal from the bastions of literary patriarchy (implied in the poem's very first line) than it is either a genuine confession of artistic inadequacy or even a plea for critical acceptance. When this poet remarks that her poems have no father, she does not do so in an ironic pretense of rejecting the "child," like Spenser or Sidney. It is the truth. Her poems have no courtly patron and no familial *pater*. The patron/*pater* is dead, and with him, as we have seen, something of the Old World itself. Hence, the poem is built on a foundation that must be discarded. If there are traces of some breach between old England and New England in the emotional thrust of the poem's contents, such a breach is also implied in the skewed employment of a convention, deeply embedded in European literary culture, that will not serve in the new place. . . .

Still, we might expect Bradstreet to use the figure more than she does, at least in the early period of her writing, when she was closer to European conventions and when, as a bride, she was also very much preoccupied with her own (biological) fertility. The convention, however, is scarcely there, and both of the two Bradstreet poems that do clearly use the maternity/creativity metaphor—one is **"The Author to her Book,"** as we have already seen—come late in her writing life and are unusually fearful and melancholy. We need only recall the historical alliance of childbirth and death—death of the mother and of the baby—to realize why this should be so. But the curse of Eve, "the great daunger" and "the great paine and peryl of child birthe," was not only an axiom of life in an age when twelve to fifteen percent of English women died in childbirth and many more from ensuing "complications" and "debilitations"; it was also inescapably linked with male domination: "Vnto the woman he said, I wil greatly increase thy sorrows, & thy conceptions. In sorowe shalt thou bring forthe children, and thy desire shal be subject to thine housband, and he shal rule ouer thee" (Genesis 3:16). Well might these associations have dampened the creative urges of any woman who dared on her own to write poems. But perhaps just as significant were contemporary assumptions about the exact role of the woman in the process of reproduction. Marina Warner points out [in *Alone of All Her Sex,* 1983] that before 19th-Century microscopes discovered the ovum, a mother was regarded as "merely a nutritive force in the genesis of a human life," the passive storehouse of substance and food; whereas the "vital procreative" part that gave "form and movement" to the child was believed to be only by the active "operation" of the father. Moreover, Warner vividly recalls the traditional Christian association of mother Eve with "nature, a form of low matter," and with "all that is vile, lowly, corruptible" and physically repellent: "Woman was womb and womb was evil." It was all very well for men to play with these notions in their ironic melodramas of giving birth to poems, but quite another for women poets, who lived inside women's bodies, and most of whom had, of course, experienced actual, physical childbirth, to want to associate these negativities and condemnations with their literary labors. And if, as in Bradstreet's case, the muse was envisioned as her very own father, the "paine and peryl" of artistic childbirth would be grievous indeed, if not unthinkable. . . .

If a poet's voice is "something he inherits, but which environment modifies and on which experience tells," then Bradstreet's destiny as a poet had to be tied intimately to the new place, with all its problems and perplexities. Yet Bradstreet did warble out the old and did begin anew by turning a problem, this very problem of speech and of language, into an opportunity to write a different sort of poetry than she had been trained to write.

This development is perhaps most clearly seen in those poems, written a few years after she composed **"Contemplations,"** in which Bradstreet lamented the deaths, within a period of four years, of three small grandchildren, all the offspring of her first-born son, Samuel. The three poems have been subjected to some Puritan-like wrangling among scholars over the alleged heresy and unorthodoxy of grandmother Bradstreet's struggle between grief and belief. Yet surely as human beings we can assume that the loss of a child or grandchild is deeply and searingly felt even within a religious life, and that it is worthwhile to look at the poems *as* poems, as constructs of language that reveal something about the expression of feeling in poetry and even in American poetry. The question is not only one of dogma and Puritan orthodoxy, but, given the human anguish at the deaths of these children, a question of how the experience gets translated into poetic language and form.

When we explore this question, we find that the three elegies form a related group and should be read as such, for there are noticeable progressions in feeling and form from Elizabeth's to Anne's to Simon's memorial. Even the titles record this change: The two granddaughters are "deceased," but the grandson, third to go, has "dyed"; the first two died "being a year and half old" and "being three years and seven Moneths old," the third died "being *but* a moneth, and one day old", (emphasis added). The first elegy, to Elizabeth, is set within a framework of natural phenomena, plants, fruits, and flowers; the second, to Anne, is set in a more ephemeral realm of bubble, glass, and turning shadow; the third stands nakedly before God. The first is in two neat seven-line stanzas with a carefully woven rhyme scheme of couplets and triplets, the second is in nine consecutive couplets, and the last is in just six couplets, as if to echo the brevity of the tiny infant's life. The first two start with conscious statement directed outward: "Farewel dear babe," "With troubled heart & trembling hand I write"; the third opens with a musing not so much heard as overheard: "No sooner come, but gone, and fal'n asleep." The first two speak in the first person singular: "Blest babe why should I once bewail thy fate," "How oft with disappointment have I met," "I knew she was but as a withering flour"; the last elegy entirely eschews the "I" in favor of a general "we." The first takes on the question of the natural order of things with a certain stately, declarative didacticism; the second quivers with a series of rhetorical shifts that act out the "troubled heart" of the speaker as she moves through a swift succession of moods; but the third gives us what can only be called the sound of silence.

> No sooner come, but gone, and fal'n asleep,
> Acquaintance short, yet parting caus'd us weep,
> Three flours, two scarcely blown, the last i'th'
>   bud,
> Cropt by th' Almighties hand; yet is he good,
> With dreadful awe before him let's be mute,
> Such was his will, but why, let's not dispute,
> With humble hearts and mouths put in the dust,
> Let's say he's merciful, as well as just,
> He will return, and make up all our losses,
> And smile again, after our bitter crosses.
> Go pretty babe, go rest with Sisters twain
> Among the blest in endless joyes remain.

Brevity and compression are the expressive strategy here, and the flickering, halting rhythm, the absence of an "I," and the silent spaces in the poem all suggest a speaker withdrawn or withdrawing, not unlike Emily Dickinson's

speaker in "After great pain, a formal feeling comes." This is a tight-lipped poem, hinging on silence. A full third of the poem enjoins quiet and constraint. The tone throughout is one of chary resistance to speech, of breath held back. The hand of God "Crops" in silence, as in a desert or a vacuum and not amidst the rustically abundant nature of the Elizabeth poem. The Savior, of course, does not speak, but only smiles enigmatically and eerily. The one direct speech in the poem utterly undercuts the notion of communication: "Go pretty babe, go rest with Sisters" is a timeworn domestic formula and seemingly all the speaker can manage, like a weary mother sending the noisy children out to play so she can be quiet and alone. In all these ways, the poem enfolds itself in a taut, laconic moodliness. Yet line seven, "With humble hearts and mouths put in the dust," draws us in; it is the exact center of the poem and the only line rooted in the Bible. The source is the Lamentations of Jeremiah (3:26-29):

> It is good bothe to trust, and to waite for the
>   saluation of the Lord.
> It is good for a man that he beare the yoke in
>   his youth.
> He sitteth alone, and kepeth silence, because
>   he hath borne it vpon him.
> He putteth his mouth in the dust, if there maie
>   be hope.

The Geneva exegesis for these last two lines reads, "He murmureth not against God, but is pacient. He humbleth him selfe as thei that falle downe with their face to the grounde, & so with pacience waiteth for succour." So again, speech is enjoined, but with an important anticipation of change. We are reminded of Job, whose story also stands behind the grandchild elegies ("Man that is born of woman, is of short continuance, and ful of trouble. He shooteth forthe as a flowre, and is cut downe: he vanisheth also as a shadow, & continueth not" [14:1-2]), and who does eventually encounter a God who speaks to him. Much has been said about these poems' stony resistance to the divine dispensation; but, at least, by grounding her elegies in certain portions of scripture, Bradstreet can remind herself of the promise of succour that eventually will come from God in speech, in dialogue with man, even if it is only in the next world: "Thou drewest nere in the daye that *I called* vpon thee: *thou saidest,* Feare not" (Lamentations 3:57, emphasis added); or perhaps more to the point, she can remove herself in some sense from the little world of men and recall the great lesson that "Job's *answer* was found, not in the friends' *talk* about a God who puts everything to right in the world's affairs, nor even in what God *says* and does, but in God himself." [Hugh Anderson, "The Book of Job," in *The Interpreter's One-Volume Commentary on the Bible,* 1971].

In the meantime, in this realm, the poem stands, honest and uncompromising, held together by the tensile strength of its speechless speech. . . . What she can do is speak in a voice of stark honesty, unwilling to fall into archness, reticent to the point of silence, yet all the more eloquent for what she withholds, the buried feeling in the line. Albert Gelpi has characterized "the American strain as it splits away from the British" in terms of Edward Taylor's qualities: "honesty which lacks tact and finish, self-involvement which can snarl itself in knots and crotchets, fresh energy which can move into clumsiness, a complex personal idiom ready to sacrifice conventional clarity." I would suggest that Bradstreet's quieter honesty and her forced, oblique inwardness are also characteristic, emerging in a plainer surface by far than Taylor's and one that looks simple, but which does not sound so to the attentive ear. Bradstreet's muted voice, her sound of silence, is an eloquent construct of the unsaid but not the unarticulated. It is a voice suited to the experience of a New World not yet fully accessible to the consciousness of its inhabitants.

Some of the subtlety and intensity of Bradstreet's achievement can be foreseen in an early poem, **"Before the Birth of one of her Children,"** written some time before 1647 and therefore possibly the first of her warblings "anew." This is Bradstreet's other "childbirth" poem, but it is a birth poem in a far more authentic way than is "The Author to her Book" or similar works by contemporary male poets. We have seen that for the woman writer, birth is too weighty a matter to be used as a mere device: When Bradstreet does give it serious attention as a metaphor, it is completely integral to the meaning of the poem.

> All things within this fading world hath end,
> Adversity doth still our joyes attend;
> No tyes so strong, no friends so dear and sweet,
> But with deaths parting blow is sure to meet.
> The sentence past is most irrevocable,
> A common thing, yet oh inevitable;
> How soon, my Dear, death may my steps attend,
> How soon't may be thy Lot to lose thy friend,
> We both are ignorant, yet love bids me
> These farewell lines to recommend to thee,
> That when that knot's unty'd that made us one,
> I may seem thine, who in effect am none.
> And if I see not half my dayes that's due,
> What nature would, God grant to yours and you;
> The many faults that well you know I have,
> Let be interr'd in my oblivious grave;
> If any worth or virtue were in me,
> Let that live freshly in thy memory
> And when thou feel'st no grief, as I no harms,
> Yet love thy dead, who long lay in thine arms:
> And when thy loss shall be repaid with gains
> Look to my little babes my dear remains.
> And if thou love thy self, or loved'st me
> These O protect from step Dames injury.
> And if chance to thine eyes shall bring this
>   verse,
> With some sad sighs honour my absent Herse;
> And kiss this paper for thy loves dear sake,
> Who with salt tears this last Farewel did take.

This poem is about itself, quite literally. Its goal is both physical union and immortality through the poem as an object, as a palpable thing. The poem begins with what appear to be the usual aphorisms about the mutability of

all things, but these conventional statements have a sharp point, for as Bradstreet unfolds her poem, its own existence and its own mutability will be brought into question. From the outset, the poem turns the reader's attention increasingly toward itself and toward the immediate situation, i.e., the situation that impels the poet to write "these [particular] farewell lines," until it ends in its own concrete objectification: a paper to be kissed, imbued with salt tears that can be tasted by the mouth. The taste of salt has many associations and surely suggests here the poet's bitter grief at the possibility of losing her husband (she loses *him* if she dies): We hear echoes of the story of Lot's wife and of the Passover symbolism. But probably, just as surely, this 17th-Century housewife would think of salt as a preservative against deterioration. The speaker juxtaposes images of nothingness, emptiness, absence, numbness, and oblivion with images of decay: "Yet love thy dead, who long lay in thine arms" is oddly necrophiliac; the children as "remains" grotesquely bring to mind the poet's own rotting corpse. Yet the paradox is that something pure will actually be preserved from mere nothingness and from decay: the poem, written on its salt-soaked paper. This general notion may not seem very startling—it has been encountered before, notably in Shakespeare's sonnets—but the immediacy and physicalness of the poem's language are unusual. These are first apparent in the double meaning of line five: "The sentence past is most irrevocable" calls attention to the preceding line as a physical thing; it is there and it is irrevocable, as is the heavy blow of the death sentence, to which it is a witness. Similarly, "these farewell lines" are *these* lines and no others. Moreover, the lines are woven with exhortations, initially in the form of gentle subjunctives but soon transformed into relentless imperatives: Love thy dead, look to my babes, protect the children, honor my hearse, kiss this paper. There is, especially, a constant implied demand to *look at* the poem and to remember its injunctions as one remembers its author. Indeed, "Look to my little babes my dear remains" has the same kind of double force as line five, for those babes, those remains, can be construed as the poems as well as the children that have been created. In a sense, poem and author, poems and children, are all one, and they can be kept alive only through the perceptions of Simon Bradstreet. Although it is beyond the poet's power to ensure her husband's reading of this poem, with its ensuing effects, her concern about reaching his eyes is one indication of that command she is trying to exercise over his person: his mind (memory), his affections (love), his senses (seeing, kissing, tasting), all through the immediacy and activism of the language of the poem as it is being read and presumably reread.

Hence, by the end of the poem, it is clear that the poem itself has taken an active part in the process it relates: the process of preserving the feeling that fueled it, not "consumed with that which it was nourished by" so much as preserving that which nourished it, in the living act of being read. And this physical participation in the process of its own creation, or at least in the process of its emergence into someone else's consciousness, is something like what babies do to be born into the world. There is even a laborious "panting" quality in the sequence of breathless pleas beginning with "and" in the last ten lines: "And when thou feel'st," "And when thy loss," "And if thou love," "And if chance," "And kiss this paper." One might say the poem "is" a baby, and the baby is the poet's self or the part of herself that loves her family, idealized into art. [In *The Nightingale's Burden,* 1982], Cheryl Walker in fact points to "the association between self-representation in children ('my dear remains') and self-perpetuation in art" as the key to the poem. Yet the children are less important in the poem than the literal birth of the poem itself. Unlike the male poet who uses childbirth as a fancy or a conceit, Bradstreet implants the metaphor so deeply within the poem that we feel something, some identity, some meaning, is really struggling to be born here, struggling to be engendered. From the feminist point of view, that something may well be a "wounded" self, or worse, an eternally absent self, represented only by the paper, which will be read by the man, thus returning the woman to her customary entombment as man's "text and artifact." Yet the interwoven issues of self-birth, self-preservation, and self-expression to which this poem attests are not necessarily confined to women or even to individuals. We have here a whole society trying to give birth to itself, to preserve itself, to *utter* itself; yet the members situated in a relationship with old England that consists in being what Leslie Fiedler has called "The Other's Other," a people whose self-definition must be determined "not directly, but reflexively," against its own mythologized version of the Old World. So here, the poet's "translated" self is to be reconstructed by the imagined Other, the husband, as he literally reads her in the form of the poem that she herself has made. It is not a simple, domestic, "woman's" poem, and although it is certainly not a resolution of problems (not that poems should be), it takes us a long way from needles and pens. The old, clever conventions are gone; in their place are the makings of a more powerful and ingrown symbolism, rooted in concrete and inescapable experience. **"Before the Birth"** may not be a second "Nativity Ode," but it is a step toward honest dealing with American concerns, a step that could not have been taken in the same way by a mannered minor English poet like Katherine Philips. Yet it is a poem that only a woman could have written. This is not to suggest that New England's men did not experience the problem of identity or of finding an authentic voice; just the contrary. But no man of the first generation recorded these struggles in a significant way in poetry: It fell to a woman to do it, forced by her gender into a confrontation with urgent problems of poetic expression.

Indeed, an argument can be made that all the first-generation colonists were in the position of women—a variation on the feminist critics' theme that all women have been "colonized." Consider that the American Puritans were accused of cowardly, womanish flight from the troubles in England; that they had to grapple with problems of authority in Massachusetts while paying homage to a patriarchal home government that either patronized, chastised, or ignored them; that they had to face unprecedented experiences for which traditional language and forms were inadequate; that in New England there were subtle

strictures on free expression by *any*body. Psychologically and symbolically, the colonists were, in these respects, "women." For such a community, a woman poet was a natural representative, her nerve endings alert to the peculiar struggle for identity and for authentic expression that feminist critics have exposed as the urgent concerns of women writers, so many of whom have found themselves writing in a "New World." It is not, then, so surprising that Anne Bradstreet was bringing forth a newborn, New World poetry while men on both sides of the ocean were still engaged in the witty pleasures of literary couvade. . . .

Beth M. Doriani (essay date 1989)

SOURCE: "'Then Have I . . . Said with David': Anne Bradstreet's Andover Manuscript Poems and the Influence of the Psalm Tradition," in *Early American Literature,* Vol. 24, No. 1, 1989, pp. 52-69.

[*In the following essay, Doriani discusses Bradstreet's use of the poetic conventions of the Biblical Psalms.*]

"What we need to realize now," said Robert Daly in 1978 [in *God's Altar: The World and the Flesh in Puritan Poetry*], "is that . . . Puritan orthodoxy was conductive to the production of poetry, and that Bradstreet's poetry is illuminated by an understanding of the theology which structured the experiences her poetry expressed." Daly argued that Bradstreet remained faithful to her tradition in that she celebrated the sensible world while consistently ascending to a celebration of its Creator through her contemplations of the world. But Bradstreet's orthodoxy, as it emerges in her devotional poetry, goes even beyond her attitude toward the world and poetic uses of it. What she does in her Andover Manuscript poems is not only to draw on the themes and emphases of Puritan theology but to adopt the rhetorical techniques and voice of the Psalms as the Puritans understood them. Her imitation of the Psalms—in technique, stance, and thematic patterns—indicates her ability to work comfortably within her tradition, searching for a poetic language that God would accept.

That Anne Bradstreet's poetry reflects the influence of the Psalms—the Book of Psalms as well as the *Bay Psalm Book*—has been generally acknowledged. Her indebtedness to the psalm tradition is, however, far greater than an imitation of the metrics of the *Bay Psalm Book* translations or the diction and imagery found in the Book of Psalms. The Andover Manuscript poems, written as reflections on intensely personal events in her life, show a more comprehensive reliance on the Psalm tradition than has hitherto been acknowledged. For Bradstreet, the psalter and the Puritan tradition surrounding it prove conducive to the production of poetry and provide her with a voice to imitate, the Davidic voice, as she strives to praise God even in her suffering.

The importance of the Hebrew Psalms for the New England Puritans derives from the Protestant Reformation.

With Calvin and Luther's sanctioning of psalm-singing for corporate as well as private worship came the quick adoption of the psalms as the hymnody of many churches in western Christendom. Translators drew on popular secular tunes for the music of their new metrical psalms; the balled or common meter of their renditions contrasted favorably with the unmeasured music of the Roman Catholic plain-chant. The rendering of the Psalms into vernacular poetry was a favorite pastime of poets and pastors from the Reformation through the eighteenth century. It is significant that only ten years after arriving in the New World the Massachusetts Bay Puritans produced their own psalter—the *Bay Psalm Book*—that would supersede the Pilgrims' *Ainsworth Psalter* in ease of singing and the Sternhold and Hopkins psalter in faithfulness of translation.

For the Puritans, the singing of psalms satisfied at least two priorities: their enjoyment of music and their high estimation of the language of Scripture. In the Psalms the Puritans found a catalogue of praises in a language acceptable to God. Tradition held that David, God's faithful servant, provided a model of the language of praise that God had sanctioned. Although he was admittedly human in his sinfulness, David was also regarded as a type of Christ. His composition of psalms, in their reflection of the range of human spiritual experience, opened up the channel between God and man. Thus the Psalms were important not only for joyful, corporate singing but also for serious study and meditation. The numerous metrical translations of the Psalms in the seventeenth century attest to their central place.

That David the type prefigures Christ the antitype is central to understanding the seventeenth-century view of the Psalms. In his role of suffering servant, David was seen as exemplifying Christly behavior in the struggle to overcome sin and gain redemption. In one respect, then, the Psalms were regarded as illuminations of the connection between the psalmist's situation and the struggles of the contemporary Christian. The Psalms not only gave Christians of all ages encouragement and comfort in their suffering, but also provided experiential patterns to imitate in the Christian journey towards obedient living. David was the foremost model for all pious exercise, from repentance to supplication to joyful praise. In his total dependence on God, David provided a sanctioned way of communicating with God. As a type of Christ, he provided the words suitable for imitation in the Christian struggle. Because he was human, Christians could identify with him; because he was a type of Christ, they could look to him as a guide in their own service of God.

David was a seminal figure for imitation not only in his spiritual struggles but also in his poetics. As the chief work of poetry in the Bible, the Book of Psalms itself became a model for devotional writers and poets. Luther had stressed the usefulness of the language of the Psalms in the composition of original verse. Since the age of assured inspiration had ended with the canonization of the New Testament, any devotional poet aspiring to write in a sanctioned manner had to be satisfied with imitating holy Scripture. The Psalms, then, were the essential model for sacred songs and poetry. The authors of the *Bay Psalm Book*, in justifying their metrical translations of the Psalms for worship, declared in their preface that "certainly the singing of Davids psalmes was an acceptable worship of God, not only in his owne, but in succeeding times." Further, because God Himself had sanctioned poetry by using it in the Psalms, poetry was seen as an acceptable vehicle for devotion—especially if it imitated the Psalms. Thus poetic activity had biblical justification. It is not surprising that the genres of the prayer-poem, the religious lyrical poem, and the hymn were popular in the seventeenth century: all were patterned on the models that David had presented in the Psalms. David was viewed, then, not only as a saint but also as a sanctified artist. The psalter thus became an aesthetic guide "through its stances, its voices, and its use of the Word of artistry God accepted." It provided the best of the language of humanity in its most noble service: communication with God.

In a personal journal begun in 1656, Bradstreet's first entry is a spiritual autobiography addressed to her children; she indicates her turning to the Psalms for solace in the midst of personal affliction. In the letter **"To My Dear Children,"** she says that, in her times of greatest affliction, "I [have] gone to searching and have said with David, 'Lord, search me and try me, see what ways of wickedness are in me, and lead me in the way everlasting.'" As the model of the faithful pilgrim, David provides the words for her as she struggles with emotional crises and physical suffering. He also provides her with a sanctified poetics. As she indicates in the letter, her intention in writing is not "to show my skill, but to declare the truth, not to set forth myself, but the glory of God." At the same time, she indicates that her immediate purpose is that her children might have the "spiritual advantage" of her experience. She follows the letter with entries about her succeeding struggles with illness and doubt, recording the entries in both poetry and prose. Reliance on the Psalms for the poetry of this notebook provides her with the means to serve the spiritual advantage of her children in the larger context of glorifying God. In providing a poetic language acceptable to God, the Psalms also provide a mode which will give her poems a lasting pedagogical importance. As the psalmist's verses teach the children of God of all times, so does her imitation of the Psalms allow her to attain a sanctified immortality for these poems intended for her children. As she writes in her letter, she has bequeathed these poems to her children so that she "may be daily in [their] remembrance" and thus teach them even after she has died, encouraging their faithfulness to and hope in God. "Make use of what I leave in love," she writes in the poem that opens her letter, "And, God shall bless you from above." She shows her indebtedness to the Psalms in David's role both as faithful servant and as sanctified poet.

Certainly Bradstreet had written earlier about her personal suffering, even as early as 1632, as in **"Upon a Fit of Sickness, Anno 1632, *Aetatis Suae*, 19."** This poem, unlike the poems on "public" topics, follows the common meter of the *Bay Psalm Book,* a meter that she would adopt again in the poetry of her notebook. But the similarity of this early poem to the Psalms—or to her later psalmlike poetry—stops there. Even the metaphor with which she opens and closes the poem, the "race" of the faithful follower of Christ, is not psalmic but Pauline (as in 2 Tim. 4:7). It is not until later in her life that she experiments with a full range of psalmic techniques in her personal poetry.

As [Adrienne] Rich points out [in her introduction to Jeannine Hensley, *The Works of Anne Bradstreet,* 1967], Bradstreet's active sensibility was decidedly changing after 1650, the year of the first edition of her ***The Tenth Muse, Lately Sprung Up In America***. The titles themselves of the thirteen poems added posthumously to the second edition (1678) indicate the change. These poems show a turn to more personal subjects: her responses to illness, the anticipation of the birth of a child, her loneliness for her husband in his absence, her responses to the deaths of grandchildren. No longer would she take on such subjects as the ancient monarchies, the four humors, or Queen Elizabeth. Instead, the poems become responses to the events of a woman's life, just as the poems in her notebook are. Five of the thirteen poems bear dates congruent with those of her notebook: **"In Reference to Her Children, 23 June, 1659"** and the poems on the deaths of grandchildren Elizabeth (1665), Anne (1669), and Simon (1669), and daughter-in-law Mercy (1669). It is noteworthy that three of these poems refer to deaths that occur in the autumn of 1669; one of the poems in the Andover Manuscript is also dated August 31, 1669. Yet none of the poems not in the notebook show any significant adoption of the psalm tradition. The poems of the notebook take on a special importance as she reserves the psalmic model for them. Through these poems we get a glimpse of a deeply personal side of Bradstreet, a side in which she shows us a deep commitment to her Puritan heritage as she struggles to assume the Davidic voice.

Since childhood Bradstreet had listened to the singing of the Psalms; she had heard the Psalms in the Sternhold and Hopkins version as a young child and then in the *Bay Psalm Book* in the fifteen years preceding her first journal entry. The authors of the *Bay Psalm Book*—university-trained ministers Thomas Weld, John Eliot, and Richard Mather—wanted to replace the Sternhold and Hopkins version with renditions more faithful to the original Hebrew, even if this meant a sacrifice of poetic effect. They declare in the psalter preface that their goal was to provide the psalms in their "native purity," not to give a paraphrase or in any way vary the sense of the sacred verse. For Bradstreet, the *Bay Psalm Book* translations provided a quite close rendering of the Hebrew Psalms at the same time that they provided verse models. These, and the Geneva Bible prose versions she read and meditated upon as a faithful Puritan, give her access to the biblical poetry and the psalm tradition.

The most insistent and persistent characteristics of the *Bay Psalm Book* selections—and Bradstreet's Andover Manuscript poems—are, of course, the metrical regularity and simple rhyme schemes. All but two of Bradstreet's poems of 1656-62 are in the two most common meters of the Bay Psalm Book: common meter and long meter. Bradstreet uses both the open (abcb) and closed (abab) rhyme schemes of the *Bay Psalm Book*. Although she does not imitate any particular psalm, the similarity in sound to the *Bay Psalm Book* selections is striking, as Psalm 23 demonstrates:

> The Lord to mee a shepheard is,
>   want therefore shall not I.
> Hee in the folds of tender-grasse,
>   doth cause mee downe to lie:
> To waters calme me gently leads
>   Restore my soule doth hee:
> he doth in paths of righteousnes:
>   for his names sake leade mee. . . .

[Rivkah] Zim points out [in *English Metrical Psalms,* 1987] that, with respect to metrical psalms, metrical regularity can constrain a poet by the need either to fit his or her words to preexisting tunes, or to make the verses suitable for musical improvisation. Nevertheless, he recognizes, such metrical regularity would also have assisted a singer to read these holy songs and to sing them to brief melodies stanza by stanza. The metrical regularity and their ability to be sung would also make the verses easier to remember. Writing for an audience whom she very much wanted to edify, Bradstreet perhaps saw in the metrical psalms a form by which, in its ease of memorization, she and her lessons might be remembered.

Yet her larger purpose, as she indicates in her letter, is to glorify God. The diction and imagery found in the Psalms provide her with a sanctified poetic vocabulary. That she adopts the psalmic diction and imagery in the poems of her notebook is obvious, as in her use of the psalmic expressions of "paying vows" and "rendering praises" to God (appearing in eleven out of the fourteen Andover Manuscript poems); the biblical images of God as "light," "strength," "shelter," "shadow," and even a protective bird in His role of divine caretaker; the metaphor of God's "face" to suggest His favor; the metonomy of His rod and staff to reflect His fatherly, chastising care; and other psalmic figures. She uses such imagery to take the stance of the Davidic suffering servant. Like David, she suffers because of her own sin—and God's consequent chastisement—or because of the trials which are necessarily a part of her life, such as the loneliness she must endure in her husband's absence. In this stance as servant she voices her dependence on God by calling to Him in her afflictions or by praising Him as her help and strength. David provides a fitting model for her to emulate in her struggles with suffering and doubt. Even more strikingly, she imitates not only the psalmic diction and imagery but psalmic structural techniques as she imitates David's voice.

In her Andover Manuscript poems, Bradstreet uses interrogation, the shifting of audience, and amplification, which Fithian describes as, along with antithesis, the major rhetorical techniques used in the Psalms to express the poetic voice. As does the psalmist, Bradstreet sometimes uses the technique of interrogation to communicate her familiarity with God. This technique of direct questioning appears, for example, in Ps. 6: "My soule is also sore troubled: but Lord, how long wilt thou delay?" (v. 3). The psalmist often uses interrogation to call God to action. Since he enjoys a close relationship with God, he is in a position to urge God to take action, and he does so by interrogation. Likewise, Bradstreet uses interrogation in her poem **"My Soul"** when she writes, "Come Jesus quickly, Blessed Lord. / Thy face when shall I see?" (ll. 25-26). More often, however, she uses the technique in the way that the psalmist uses it in Pss. 8, 27, and 89—as a sort of rhetorical device to communicate inadequacy and dependence on God. Here the direct questioning has the character of praise. Ps. 27:1 provides a good example: "The Lord is my light and my salvation, whome shall I feare? the Lord is the strength of my life, of whom shall I bee afraid?" Bradstreet uses the technique similarly in **"In Thankful Remembrance for my Dear Husband's Safe Arrival"**:

> What shall I render to Thy name
> Or how Thy praises speak?
> My thanks how shall I testify?
> O Lord, Thou know'st I'm weak.
>
> (ll. 1-4)
>
> What did I ask for but Thou gav'st?
> What could I more desire?
>
> (ll. 16-17)

As in Ps. 8:4, she does not intend her questions to be answered; she uses interrogation to communicate her own inadequacy before a gracious and loving God. The technique also appears, used in a similar way, in the opening lines of her **"July 8, 1656"** poem: "What God is like to Him I serve? / What Saviour like to mine?" (ll. 1-2). The implicit answer, of course, is "none"—thus she goes on to praise her God. Like David, she communicates her worship of God, acknowledging the magnitude of His love and care. Such worship springs from her sense of gratitude to God: He has done so much for her in removing her affliction, yet He receives so little from her, as she asserts in an early prose passage from her journal. And again, like David, she realizes that the only offering she can make is praise. Interrogation provides her a vehicle to express her gratitude and praise in an intimate way.

Imitating David's shifting of audience within the context of a single psalm allows Bradstreet to give voice to her praise of God in a full way as well as to deal with her doubts in her times of suffering. In the Psalms, David often turns from addressing God to address his own soul or a general audience. It is common to see several shifts of audience in a single psalm; David will often address God, then turn to ask his soul a question, then turn back again to God in a report of the condition of his soul, as in Ps. 42:

> As the hart brayeth for the rivers of water, so
> panteth my soule after thee, O God. . . .
> Why art thou cast downe, my soule, and unquiet
> within me? waite on God: for I will yet give

thanks for the help of his presence.
My God, my soule is cast downe within me. . . .

    (vv. I, 5, 6)

In the first verse, the psalmist is obviously directing his words to God. Then he turns to his soul, rebuking it for its doubt and distress; subsequently he turns his attention back to God. At times, David shifts his attention to address a general audience, as in the ninth verse of Ps. 42: "I will say unto God, which is my rocke, Why hast thou forgotten mee?"

In Bradstreet's poetry, the shifting takes on special importance in that it provides her with the opportunities both to encourage her own children—her analogue to David's audience—and to praise God directly herself. As in **"On My Son's Return,"** she urges her children on the path to obedience as she calls, in the first four lines, for "all praise to Him" (l. 1). Then she turns to address God herself, reviewing His faithfulness towards her in His care of her son. The shift implicitly allows her to praise God as His faithful servant as well as to remind her children—and herself—of the trustworthiness of God. In "For Deliverance from a Fever," she directs most of the poem to God Himself, recounting to Him her experience with a fever and, in doing so, offering her praise to Him. The shift to a general audience occurs near the end, after line 25:

> Thou show'st to me Thy tender love,
> My heart no more might quail.
> O, praises to my mighty God,
> Praise to my Lord, I say,
> Who hath redeemed my soul from pit,
> Praises to Him for aye.
>
>   (ll. 24-29)

Having experienced serious illness and recovery, Bradstreet desires to remind her readers that it is God who heals, as she states in her July 8, 1656, prose entry. Thus she turns in the last quatrain to call on a general audience to give praises to God. Reminding her children of the grounds for praise—the rescue of a suffering woman from her affliction—she urges them to join in her adoration, as if teaching them how to bless God. Moreover, the technique allows her to express the fullness of her gratitude: it is as if she feels so overwhelmed with gratitude that her own individual praise is insufficient as a response to God for His goodness to her.

Bradstreet's choosing to shift between a variety of audiences instead of writing only prayers addressed to God also allows her to challenger her readers to see life's trials from a broad perspective and thereby learn the "very lesson she must force upon herself." As Jeffrey A. Hammond has pointed out [in "'Make use of What I Leave in Love': Anne Bradstreet's Didactic Self," *Religion and Literature* 17 (1985)], the intentionally didactic nature of Bradstreet's verse is often a reflection of her efforts to identify and communicate what she saw as the real truth behind her periods of suffering and recovery—that is, that God is dealing in a fatherly way with His child. Certainly she indicates such a purpose in her letter **"To My Dear Children."**

That her devotional poetry is "virtually a seamless blend of the confessional and the didactic" is in keeping with her shifts of audience. When she turns to address a general audience (as in **"From Another Sore Fit"**: "What shall I render to my God / For all His bounty showed to me?" [ll. 14-15]), she no doubt has in mind her own children, desiring to challenge them to see past their own moments of affliction, as she does, to the One who provides sustenance, strength, and loving-kindness. At the same time, the technique affords her the opportunity to give full voice to her feelings as she moves easily between audiences, prodding her soul, addressing God, or calling Jesus to return—all of which she does in **"My Soul,"** shifting four times in only twenty-eight lines (253). Thus her readers see her confession of her suffering, which she often perceives as chastisement from God, as in **"Deliverance from a Fit of Fainting"**: she declares that her "life as spider's webb's cut off" (l. 6). Yet her readers also see how thanksgiving springs from such suffering: "My feeble spirit Thou didst revive / . . . Why should I live but to Thy praise?" (ll. 10, 14). That the Christian expresses such thanksgiving is important to godly living, Bradstreet affirms in her July 8 prose entry. She herself "dares not pass by without remembrance" of the love God showed to her in her suffering. Such thanksgiving reflects David's model throughout the Psalms.

The psalmic technique of amplification—an addition to or expansion of a statement—also allows Bradstreet to voice her feelings about God in a way sanctioned by David. Of the three forms [Rosemary] Fithian describes [in "'Words of my Mouth, Meditations of My Heart,'"*Early American Literature* 20 (1985)]—hyperbole, *accumulatio,* and *exclamatio*—Bradstreet uses two in her Andover Manuscript poems, hyperbole and *accumulatio*. Hyperbole in the Psalms often communicates the psalmist's utter dependence on God by a graphic description of his physical condition. For example, in Ps. 31:10 the psalmist writes, "For my life is wasted with heaviness, and my yeeres with mourning: my strength faileth for my paine, and my bones are consumed." Similarly in Ps. 22 he describes his bones as being "out of joynt" and his heart as "like wax . . . molten in the middes of my bowels" (v. 14) as he seeks God's deliverance.

In her poems written about her periods of illness, Bradstreet also intensifies her own condition. In **"From Another Sore Fit"** she describes herself as having "wasted flesh" (l. 10) and as "melting" in her own sweat (l. 8), before God in His grace reaches out to help her. In **"Deliverance from a Fit of Fainting"** she describes her life as a "spider's webb's cut off" (l. 6) to communicate her physical weakness during her sickness, and she writes that she was "though as dead" before God "mad'st [her] alive" (l. 12). Her self-belittling conveys the Puritan belief that deliverance is to be sought in God and not in self: she is utterly dependent on God. Moreover, that such a heartbroken speaker could call upon God for help would certainly bring consolation for her readers, as Hammond

points out. Hyperbole also communicates the capacity of God to deliver His children, as in Ps. 93 where God is "more mightie" than "the noyse of many waters" and "the waves of the sea" (v. 4). Bradstreet similarly exalts the Lord by making hyperbolic statements: "Thy mercies, Lord, have been so great / In number numberless, / Impossible for to recount / Or any way express" (**"In Thankful Remembrance,"** ll. 20-23). Even in the midst of her trials, she knows that God will ultimately not forsake her and that in Him alone lies triumpth over affliction.

Accumulatio, the amassing of detail, is Bradstreet's most frequent poetic technique, specifically in the form of Hebrew synonymous parallelism. In this technique the lines of poetry are paired, with the second of the lines repeating the basic meaning of the first while adding detail, as in Ps. 145:18-19:

> The Lord is neere unto all that call upon him:
> yea, to all that call upon him in trueth.

> He will fulfill the desire of them that feare him:
> he also will heare their crie, and will save them.

In each instance, the first thought is not only repeated but supplemented. Like the other psalmic techniques, the parallelism is seen in both the Geneva Bible and the *Bay Psalm Book* selections, preserved in the metrical psalms by virtue of the accuracy of the translations. In the *Bay Psalm Book,* verses eighteen and nineteen of Psalm 145 are rendered thus:

> Hee's neere to all that call on him:
> in truth that on him call.

> Hee satisfy will the desire
> of those that doe him feare:
> Hee will be safety unto them,
> and when they cry he'le heare.

As in the second verse of this case, the authors of the *Bay Psalm Book* often accommodate long lines of the psalms by arranging the parallelism between two pairs of lines. Bradstreet uses both forms of the parallelism. In the very first poetic entry of her notebook (**"By Night When Others Soundly Slept"**) she employs the technique, arranging the parallelism between single lines:

> By night when others soundly slept,
> And had at once both ease and rest . . .
> I sought Him whom my soul did love,
> With tears I sought Him earnestly. . . .
>
> (ll. 3-4, 7-8)

She too expands the content of the first line by adding detail in the second. "From Another Sore Fit" provides additional examples (ll. 6-7, 10-11), as well as "In My Solitary Hours," in which the pairings occur frequently (stanzas 1-3, 8, 10, 13). The parallelism can be found throughout Bradstreet's poetry; it appears in virtually all of the poems of her notebook. When she arranges the parallelism between two pairs of lines instead of between two single lines, she treats a two-line phrase as if it were actually a single line, as we have seen in the *Bay Psalm Book*:

> Whence fears and sorrows me beset
> Then didst Thou rid me out;
>
> When heart did faint and spirits quail,
> Thou comforts me about.
>
> (**"For the Restoration of My Dear Husband,"**
>   ll. 1-4)

A two-line phrase often echoes the preceding two lines in her poetry, usually in the same stanza. Thus a line is actually paralleling the second line after it, still preserving the structure of psalmic *accumulatio*.

Bradstreet fits such paired lines into the thematic patterns found in the Psalms—the most striking similarity between Bradstreet's Andover Manuscript poems and the Psalms. In the tradition of the Psalms, the articulations of the devout person's struggle toward obedience reflect categories with distinct themes, as Fithian has noted: lament, supplication, and thanksgiving. Although elements of two categories are often combined within a single psalm (such as thanksgiving and supplication), the three kinds are arranged within quite specific structural patterns in the Psalms. The great majority of Bradstreet's Andover poems clearly expresses thanksgiving and praise, as in the Psalms. This type of psalm typically begins with an exclamation of the intention to praise, often either in an epithet or in an imperative call to worship. Next, the psalmist gives the specific grounds for praise—for example, a catalogue of dangers that God has helped the psalmist to overcome, or a list of God's activities. Often an index of God's qualities constitutes the grounds for praise. Finally, a proclamation of praise appears.

Psalm 146 exemplifies a psalm of thanksgiving. The exclamation of the intention to praise appears in the first two verses. In this Psalm both a call to worship and declaration are given in the opening: "Praise ye the Lord. Praise thou the Lord, O my soule. I will praise the Lord during my life. . . . " Next, as his grounds for praise, the psalmist describes God in terms of what He has done; this catalogue provides the major portion of the content of the Psalm. The psalmist describes God as He "Which made heaven and earth, the sea, and all that therein is" and "Which executeth justice for the oppressed" (vv. 6-7). The psalmist also describes what God does in the present, such as giving sight to the blind (v. 8) and "releeving the fatherless" (v. 9). The statement of praise appears as the last verse of the Psalm: "The Lord shall reigne for ever. . . . Praise ye the Lord" (v. 10).

Among Bradstreet's poems, **"From Another Sore Fit"** and **"Deliverance from a Fit of Fainting"** clearly exemplify the thanksgiving theme. In each she declares her intention to praise in the first stanza by affirming God's

worthiness for praise ("Worthy art Thou, O Lord, of praise," she writes in the first line of **"Deliverance from a Fit of Fainting"**). She continues in both poems with a list of the grounds for her praise by describing God's merciful acts toward her. She writes, "My plaints and groans were heard of Thee, / . . . My wasted flesh Thou didst restore," (**"From Another Sore Fit,"** ll. 7, 10); similarly in lines 10-12 of **"Fit of Fainting"** she lists the reasons for her praise. Bradstreet concludes each by declaring her desire to praise: in **"Fit of Fainting"** the declaration appears in the last stanza ("Why should I live but to Thy praise?" [l. 14]), while in **"Sore Fit"** it occupies the last four stanzas ("Thy name and praise to celebrate, / O Lord, for aye is my request. . . . " [ll. 26-27]). This declaration allows her to rehearse the events of her suffering and put them into cosmic perspective, thereby affirming to herself and to her readers that, although her suffering is real, it is not ultimate. Whether she emphasizes these events or the statements of praise which follow, it is clear that such praise emerges from a strong sense of pain and suffering. The thanksgiving pattern as modeled in the Psalms gives her ample means both to recapitulate her pain and to express her gratitude to God for delivering her. Most often her thanksgiving is gratitude for removing the affliction—the "sore fit" or the "fit of fainting." Yet, as she points out in many of her prose entries, it is also gratitude for God's fatherly care, for chastising her by means of affliction to make her a "vessel fit for His use." Asserting that God "hath no benefit" by her adversity, she states that He afflicts her for her spiritual "advantage," that she may be a "gainer" by it. Moreover, she can live no more "without correction than without food." Thus she is grateful for the "mercies in His rod" (**"Sore Fit,"** l. 16) and for His chiding her in her doubt (**"Fit of Fainting,"** l. 11).

Among her Andover Manuscript poems Bradstreet also includes several poems of supplication, a form that allows her to affirm God's trustworthiness as she petitions Him for help. A psalm of supplication is distinguished from a lament by its mood of certainty. Although the psalmist is asking for God's help, as in the lament, he is doing so in full expectation that God will heed his call. This type of psalm typically opens with an invocation followed by a list of reasons why the psalmist expects God to respond to his cry for help. This list could be a description of what God has revealed to the psalmist about Himself in the past—either God's qualities or His saving actions—or it could be a description of the psalmist himself, of his attempts to be obedient to God as he tries to persuade God or call Him to account to be the caring father He has promised to be. In this last instance the psalmist often presents himself as the figure of a righteous man, as in Ps. 17:3: "Thou hast proved and visited mine heart in the night: thou hast tryed me, and foundeth nothing. . . . " A request follows, in addition to an indication that the psalmist realizes the possibility of God's help. Sometimes the psalmist includes a promise to praise. In Psalm 71 the supplicating nature of the psalm is readily identifiable. First, the tone is that of certainty, of assurance that God will respond: "For thou art mine hope, O Lord God, even my trust from my youth," the psalmist writes (v. 5). The psalm adheres to the basic structure of a psalm of supplication. The invocation occupies verses one to four ("encline thine ear unto me," [v. 2]), followed by a description of the Lord's graciousness, as in verses seven and nineteen, in which the psalmist points out God's trustworthiness and the "great things" He has done. The psalmist's petition is that God would deliver him, as he repeats in verses two and four and rephrases throughout the psalm (for example, "Goe not farre from mee" [v. 12]). He tells God of his intention to praise ("Therefore will I praise thee for thy faithfulnesse, O God, upon instrument and viole" [v. 22]) and ends the psalm as if he had already been delivered ("they are confounded and brought unto shame, that seeke mine hurt" [v. 24]).

Since most of the Andover Manuscript poems are thankful responses to God's graciousness, the supplication poems are few. Yet the two that do reveal such a theme—the poems about the departures of Bradstreet's son and her husband—adhere closely to the psalmic pattern of supplication. Each poem begins with an invocation, a call for God's attention:

> Thou mighty God of sea and land,
> I here resign into Thy hand. . . .
> **("Upon My Son Samuel,"** ll. 1-2)

> O thou Most High who rulest all
> And hear'st the prayers of thine,
> O hearken, Lord, unto my suit
> And my petition sign.
> **("Upon My Dear and Loving Husband,"** ll. 1-4)

Each continues with a description of the poet's obedience. In the poem on her son, Bradstreet concentrates on her obedience in the nurture of her son: she mentions the prayers, vows, and tears involved in raising him (l. 5) and her faithfulness to him as a mother (l. 6). In **"Upon My Dear and Loving Husband"** she describes not only her own obedience in stanza 5—similar to the way that the "righteous man" of the Psalms does—but also her husband's (stanza 3), as if in an effort to persuade God to take care of him: "At Thy command, O Lord, he went. . . . Then let Thy promise joy his heart" (ll. 12, 14). She intensifies her persuasion when she calls her husband God's "servant" (l. 10)—as a reminder to God about His responsibility to him—and her own "dear friend" (l. 11)—suggesting that God should take care of him because of His responsibility to Anne herself.

In both poems, as in the psalms of supplication, the speaker's request for God's help is confident. In the poem on her husband, she declares that she is commending Simon into God's "arms": she has made the initial move and trusts that God will receive her husband (ll. 8-9). She calls on God to "keep and preserve" her husband (l. 10) as well as herself in his absence (ll. 16, 19), declaring that God is her "strength and stay" and that His "goodness never fails" (l. 17, l. 31). In **"Upon My Son Samuel"** her request also seems confident. Again she asks God to "preserve" and "protect" her son (ll. 13, 14); she asserts her confidence in God when she declares that she has "no

friend . . . like Thee to trust" (l. 11). Moreover, she is confident of God's favorable stance towards her son: "For sure Thy grace on him is shown" (l. 10).

Both poems conclude by concentrating on praise, with an indication that the poet realizes that God will help in some way. In **"Upon My Dear and Loving Husband"** Bradstreet emphasizes her intent to praise: she tells God that her and Simon's response to His safekeeping will be that they together will sing His praises (ll. 46-51). In **"Upon My Son Samuel"** she asserts that she will celebrate God's praise if Samuel returns safety, seeming to assume that he will (ll. 15-18). Almost as an afterthought she adds that she hopes that she will see him "forever happified" with God if she should die before his return. Whatever happens, it will be God's will; He will do what is best (l. 20). In both poems she has an attitude of peace and confidence in God, characteristic of the psalms of supplication. She has seen God work before in her life, answering her prayers for deliverance and healing her illness and doubt. She has no reason to believe that God will not exercise His fatherly care in some way for her loved ones.

Only one "lament" poem seems to occur among Bradstreet's devotional poems; the absence of her husband is the only occasion on which she reflects in these poems a state close to depression. In this poem we see the influence of the psalmic lament as she pleads with God to comfort her in her loneliness and to return her husband to her. A psalmic lament typically involves five basic parts, as in Psalm 3. The invocation or cry for help opens the psalm ("Lord, how are mine adversaries increased? how many rise against me?" [v. 1]); it is followed by the complaint ("Many say to my soule, There is no helpe for him in God" [v. 2]). Then the psalmist voices his trust in God, reviewing God's care for him in the past ("I did call unto the Lord with my voice, and he heard mee . . . " [v. 4]). He follows this by petitioning God, laying his request before Him ("O Lord, arise: helpe me, my God" [v. 7]). These three elements following the invocation can occur in any order in a lament; sometimes they are repeated (as in Psalm 3, in which the psalmist repeats his trust in God). The lament typically concludes with a vow to praise God or with the statement of praise itself. In Psalm 3 the praise occurs in the last verse: "Salvation belongeth unto the Lord, and thy blessing is upon thy people" (v. 8). **"In My Solitary Hours"** is Bradstreet's single patterned psalmic lament in the Andover poems.

The invocation and complaint are combined in the first stanza. Calling on God to hear her, she tells Him to observe her "tears," "troubles," "longings," and "fears." In stanza two she asserts her trust in God: "Thou hitherto hast been my God; / . . . Through Thee I've kept my ground" (ll. 7-10). She continues to express her trust in stanzas three and four, reflecting on her past close relationship with God. She even declares that God is more "beloved" to her than is her husband. Thus the foundation is laid for her petition, which occurs in stanzas five, eight, and nine: she asks God to "uphold" her, to grant her His favor, and finally to bring back her husband. She reiterates her trust in God in stanzas six and eight and concludes the poem with a vow to praise—individually (ll. 39-40, 49-50, 53-54) and with Simon (ll. 43-46). Again she demonstrates that praise does emerge from her suffering, but this time she is in the midst of suffering and can only promise to praise. Yet though she suffers, she is still able to trust. Certainly she is a "gainer" by her adversity: like the psalmist, she has seen that, although God may hide His face, He does not desert His children. She knows that it is God to whom she must go for care, and so she lays her petitions before Him. The psalmic lament provides a fitting structure for her to voice her distress as well as her intent to praise.

By imitating David in the language, voice, stance, and thematic patterns in the poems of her notebook, Bradstreet takes on the voice of David, demonstrating her powerful identification with David: "then have I . . . said with David," she writes in her letter. In her quest for faith as well as for a poetic, David provides a model for her as both an approved servant and a sanctioned poet. As she struggles with her relationship to God, questioning His care for her in her periods of illness or His presence in her family's absence, she turns to David and writes psalm-like poetry. And we cannot help but hear a godly mother's desire for her children to hold fast to the faith, even after she herself has died, when she asks God

> O help Thy saints that sought Thy face
>   T' return unto Thee praise
> And walk before Thee as they ought,
>   In strict and upright ways
>   ("**In Thankful Remembrance**," ll. 24-27)

In her opening letter she remarks, "I have often been perplexed that I have not found that constant joy in my pilgrimage and refreshing which I supposed most of the servants of God have." It is in David that she finds a servant of God who knows affliction, a suffering believer with whom she can identify. Yet she has also "tasted of that hidden manna" and has had "abundance of sweetness and refershment after affliction." This is the lesson she would have her children learn. Praise and thanksgiving can indeed emerge from pain and suffering, if one is confident in Him who returns "comfortable answers" to prayer. David's words provide sanctified poetry; his experience provides a point of identification for the suffering yet trusting Christian. And his poetic forms—both those of the Bible and the metrical translations of the *Bay Psalm Book*—provide an effective pedagogical model. Inspired and sustained by the psalms, Bradstreet is better able to voice her praise of God in a period of affliction and thereby urge her children on to greater faith.

Rob Wilson (essay date 1991)

SOURCE: "'Enrapted Senses': Anne Bradstreet's 'Contemplations,' " in *American Sublime: The Genealogy of a Poetic Genre,* University of Wisconsin Press, 1991, pp. 67-93.

[*Here, Wilson argues that the sublime first emerges in American poetry in Bradstreet's verse.*]

> That there is a God my Reason would soon tell me
> by the wondrous workes that I see, the vast frame
> of the Heaven and the Earth, the order of all things,
> night and day, summer and winter, spring and autumne
> . . .
> The consideration of these things would with amazement
> certainly resolve me that there is an Eternal Being.
>   [**"To My Dear Children"**]

Anne Bradstreet (c. 1612-1672) was surely *there first,* but we still don't know how, poetically, to situate or claim her. The strange country of the Indian wilderness which her courtly/Christian poetry helped to domesticate and to legitimate conveys traces of a tone and tradition which later signaled, no less explicitly, *the transport of the sublime.* Bradstreet "said something" of her new country: she invented and indulged in "rapt senses" of place that, later, turned into a kind of commonsense and commonplace of the American will to remake the material landscape into a locus of spiritualized awe and self-empowerment. I take "**Contemplations**" to reveal such a pious landscape of American "election"—of self-election into the "rapted wit sublime." Bradstreet's poetry remains exemplary, it seems to me, of an awe-stricken sublimity struggling to be born in an inhospitable climate of "desert wilderness" and a cultural landscape of hegemonic plainness, as her woman's voice becomes marked with anxious transgression exactly as it is lifting into rapture.

As an early and even oxymoronic incarnation of such a *Christianized* sublime, Bradstreet is both blasted to mute admiration by the grandeur of the past yet enabled by the sublimity of this radical tradition—the "other tradition" of her beloved Du Bartas and, later, of John Milton—to achieve some version of an original voice. Worshipping the poetic sublime, Bradstreet says something from *New England* by which to supplement and make new the Nine Muses of tradition. American poetry is often caught (as in Bradstreet, from the start) in this fruitful tension between an indebtedness to prior languages silencing the self before the burden of the European past, and hyperboles of inventiveness, or vacancy—the will to modernity marking a displaced self struggling to innovate poetry in a future-haunted landscape of emptiness and bulk, as a way to voice what John Cage would later proclaim is "knowing nowness."

As a Puritan woman given to the very *male* art of English poetry which had come down to her, as she realized, "shod by Chaucer's boots and Homer's furs"; as a would-be poet of high feeling before the creatural world, whom Nathaniel Ward rightly praised in the "Introductory Verses" as an "Auth'ress [who] was a right Du Bartas girl," sporting her own brand of stylistic "spurs"; and as a woman of "unweaned" maternal attachments to her own flesh and blood touchingly portrayed as "eight birds hatched in one nest," Bradstreet wrote from the curious position of a marginalized subject permitted to aggrandize and *to feel.* That is, she could as such a poet succumb to sudden, transgressive flights of rapture (yet thereby produce out of these moods her own convictions of faith and grace) before the creatural world. Indeed, this storehouse of natural images was fast becoming (after Du Bartas and the awakened European interest in Longinus) the basic substance of the sublime mode, as *humilitas* gave way to a divinely sanctioned *sublimitas,* anywhere on earth.

Just registering such poetic moments of "feeling knowledge" (sublime transport) in poetic "contemplations" or prosaic "meditations," Bradstreet was (by gender) already outside the law of *plain-style* subordination; her voice of sensuous rapture was secretly operating, as we might now say, "from the peculiar *sub rosa* position of the doubly-displaced subject" who is never fully present to the (male) interpretive community as plain sign nor as self. The sublime seemingly ratified such illicit moods and motives outside, or beyond, the law. Such power, at least, came with the occupational territory.

Postfeminist revisionings of American poetics now underway might allow us to rescue Bradstreet's verse from the hegemony of Perry Miller's New England Way as anti-fleshly and characteristically "plain," as monological and metaphysical in its poetic mode. For, if the dissemination of the vaunted "Plain Style" worked to restrain male egos into stylistic plainness, or shackled and bloated the energy of Edward Taylor into nervous excess, say, the female poet as *Tenth Muse* could spring up in the Massachusetts wilds from inhabiting, by contrast, the secret space of her own recurring rapture. Bradstreet early suggests the locus of an American countertradition, the making not only of what Wendy Martin and Cheryl Walker have tracked and differentiated as "a female counter-poetic" to the reign of phallo-logic, but also, from a more genealogical point of view, of the generic possibility of an American sublime not wholly displaced by anxiety towards the past, a mood of which, as a scribbling woman and wilderness poet, she had an impressive dose.

Empowering herself as poet, Bradstreet installs and instantiates the genre of the American sublime. Yet Martin oddly disqualifies Anne Bradstreet—if not American woman poets more generally—from innovating such a sublime mode, stipulating, almost, like Edmund Burke, that these privatized poets tend to write at the level of the domestic, the ordinary, and the beautiful. "Because these women writers [Bradstreet/Dickinson/Rich] reject the male hierarchies that accord more importance to public than to private life," Martin claims [in *An American Triptych,* 1984], "their poetry is not a narrative of sublime moments but a chronicle of the quotidian."

Writing palpably within a Protestant tradition of exalted feeling and high truths modeled after the *Devine Weekes* of the Calvinist poet, Du Bartas, Bradstreet nevertheless *could* and indeed did, I will claim, write a sublime poetry of "feeling knowledge" towards that very quotidian which, in an instant of transport, linked the "rapt contemplation" of nature, as item and framework, to the contemplation of God. Surrounded by privations and dread, the American sublime is emergent, seemingly stranded, yet *there* in the poetry of Anne Bradstreet. The ingredients and conse-

quences of this event have gone largely unrecognized, at least as instantiating the makings of a poetic genre.

Like latter-day American and equally Christian poets, such as William Livingston, William Cullen Bryant, Walt Whitman, Emily Dickinson, or Frederick Goddard Tuckerman, Bradstreet registers "the sublime" as a moment of pious awe before the landscape in which the poet is dislocated, undone, yet perilously uplifted into regions of spirit. The poetic result is, quite often, an elevated tone of praise and a sense, more materially speaking, of symbolic self-empowerment where the ego fits in a scene of its own self-constituted unity. The sublime, as Bradstreet early glimpsed, might have cash-value consequences if sustained through faithful labor. This scenario of *conversion,* heights and risks of ecstasy in an indigenous setting, is memorably depicted in **"Contemplations,"** a poem which suggests the emerging genre of an American sublime in its tone of "rapted wit" and master narrative of conversion.

Displaced from community power into the no-place of poetry, this hyperbolic ***Tenth Muse Lately Sprung Up In America*** (1650) was presented to her largely male readers by amazed male critics ("To force a woman's birth" in such a labor of "pleasant witty poetry," the book was printed in London not by herself but by her brother-in-law, John Woodbridge) as a "right Du Bartas girl." That is, Bradstreet emerges as an amazing (and threatening) offspring of the Protestant sublime which was increasingly legitimating such private "rapture" to supplement the textual mediations of the Bible and the Church. The mood seemed necessary to the settlement of New World havens.

The Puritan sublime of this "right Du Bartas girl," as depicted in **"Contemplations,"** could be conjured to serve the rapture of conversion: representing the moment as an interiorized opening of "rapt senses" to natural creatures of the Massachusetts wilds such as birds, brooks, and trees, of which woman herself was a salient embodiment after the figural fall of Eve. Her "rapt," if not sun-raped, senses were made into signs of exalted feeling, of course, and (more latently) into signs transgressing the very plain-style *limits* (in the *sub/lime*) which the poem went on to moralize. That is, however evocative of New World powers, the mood of the sublime had to be converted into a credible metaphor of divine law and of man's fall into sensuous subjectivity, a legitimate *figura* for the collective (male) project to subdue a beast- and Satan-filled wilderness.

Relegated by gender to the *humilitas* of lowly domestic productions (the textual slogan of this "Feminist Bradstreet" emerging in the 1980s, as in Martin, becomes "In better dress to trim thee was my mind, / But nought save home-spun Cloth, in the house I find") and, as a Calvinist, hyper-cognizant of her own reprobation, Bradstreet subjected herself to moods of recurring stylistic anxiety towards representing any such elevated subjects or attitudes beyond reclamation. This anxiety yet reveals her deepest aspiration to evoke the *sublime* style in a cultural code of Puritanism which largely constrained her voice to use the "home-spun Cloth" of lesser modes of lyric / domestic production. Needless to say, these quotidian lyrics are deft and local, such as those love poems to her Christ-like absent husband or ones keeping track of her chattering flock.

In the larger frame of **"Contemplations,"** however, she blames this lingering sense of stylistic inadequacy and any smallness of voice (*humilitas*) on her own female "imbecility." But this self-definition is surely overdetermined by the Puritan consciousness of womanhood as inferior, as well as of sinfulness as a perpetual threat (as is exposed in stanzas 10 through 17, where figural men pursue base instincts and vain pleasures, and "The Virgin Earth, of blood, her first draught drinks"). This drive to settle upon a humbled voice of textual austerity is also urged upon her by the sermon-induced hegemony of "the Puritan Plain Style," which would downplay the raptures of selfhood and the richness of nature. The "inner feminist world" of Bradstreet was fully mediated by such Puritan strictures and a discourse of piety which subjected this brilliant poet to the laments of a *failed sublime*. Unsponsored by props of tradition or genre, this can make for a voice of perpetual anxiety and seemingly idiotic awe before prior and surrounding shapes of textual grandeur.

If the sublime of Bradstreet emerges blasted and torn, and her drive to write poetry is hemmed in by anxiety and threatened by a self-humiliating sense of modesty and scorn, this is because the sublime comes down to Bradstreet as already gendered in voices of mastery and empowerment that are fully Eurocentric and not her own. Courting female power, this "right Du Bartas girl" Bradstreet must enter into if not invent a genre of permitted trespass in which women such as herself can seize or inhabit roles formerly alotted to the strength of men

As Patricia Yaeger theorizes in "Toward a Female Sublime," without in any way considering the untimely figure of Bradstreet, the forces that would conspire against a woman inhabiting any sovereign sublime have made for what Yaeger calls a "failed sublime." "In texts where it occurs," she theorizes, "we witness a woman's dazzling, unexpected empowerment followed by a moment in which this power is snatched away—often by a masculine counter-sublime that has explicitly phallic components." Though women poets like Bradstreet are surely capable of miming and joining the great, we must go on to recognize, as Yaeger argues, "that something in the social order (either something external, or a set of beliefs internalized by the actant herself) intervenes, and the heroine finds herself not only stripped of transcendent powers, but bereft, in a lower social stratum than before" [in *Gender & Theory: Dialogues on Feminist Criticism,* 1989]. The context and ideological hegemony of Puritanism would mitigate against claims of self-glory or threats of female empowerment; hence they must be smuggled in and questioned, if not explained away, by Bradstreet herself as "poetic rapture" or as merely the inflated claims of the bewildered, brazen, and dispossessed.

To evoke one telling example, Bradstreet's "bleating" strain and "rudeness" of style as she contemplates the "royal hearse" of Queen Elizabeth would yet register, rather outrageously and with all the anxious power-dynamics towards self-anointed queenhood of Emily Dickinson, her own *rapture* before that British "rex" who had already, in quite worldly terms, invalidated the (very sexist) claim that "our sex is void of reason" and incapable of such precedent-making grandeur:

> Although, great Queen, thou now in silence lie
> Yet though loud herald Fame doth to the sky
> Thy wondrous worth proclaim in every clime,
> And so hath vowed where there is world or time.
> So great's thy glory and thine excellence,
> The sound thereof rapts every human sense,
> That men account it no impiety,
> To say thou wert a fleshy deity.

This wonder-struck elegy **"In Honour of that High and Mighty Princess Queen Elizabeth of Happy Memory"** is coded with *rapture* if not divinization before female *power/grandeur*, that exalted consciousness of the specular model's superiority. No less so emerges Bradstreet's humility, which this poet was forever feeling, even before a fellow woman who might model her own empowerment and will to elevation. Bradstreet is transported to incarnate a mode of elevated praise, however, by a woman herself elevated into a "fleshy diety," a highly un-Puritanical creature of political grandeur subjecting England to a reign of happiness who had sent "Her seamen [subversive pun on textual *semen*] through all straits the world did round."

As a poetic stance, nonetheless, Bradstreet aspires to mime the fleshly grandeur of her subject—here the praise of a female sublimity—which paradoxically inspires her to a rapture that humbles if not annihilates the emergence of her own voice: "Her personal perfections, who would tell / Must dip his pen in the Helaconian well, / Which I may not, my pride doth but aspire / To read what others write and so admire." So blasted, the voice falls off into that of a *readers' sublime*: that is, Bradstreet becomes dwarfed by the prior sublimity of England and France, which only male "pride" could aspire to emulate (as does her emulous cock son). But her effusive praise for this "glorious sun" as son/rex of England is motivated by a sense that woman can and will instance this power, this "excellence" and majesty, which the Queen like a *fleshly* deity had once embodied. Through Elizabeth, Bradstreet models yet disables the emergence of her own American sublime.

Not surprisingly, the affect-rich and over-allusive textuality of **Tenth Muse** had inspired in Nathaniel Ward his own quite misogynistic warning, distanced in the timeless voice of Apollo. "Let men look to't, lest women wear the spurs." Or as John Woodbridge warns readers concerning woman poets too ambitious of such grandeur, unlike his "modest," "solid" and "comely" Mistress Bradstreet, "Some books of women I have heard of late, / Perused some, so witless, intricate, / So void of sense, and truth, as if to err / Were only wished (acting above their sphere) / And all to get, what (silly souls) they lack, / Esteem to be the wisest of the pack." Such "silly souls" (Puritan females) would aspire to lord it above their subordinate workaday sphere ("in better dress") writing intricate sense and even voicing "truth," that is, the logocentric perogative of the governing male. If these souls aspire to the esteem and envy of the phallic pack and somehow style themselves sublime, they will prove incapable of those "pleasant witty strains" Woodbridge attributes to his scribbling sister-in-law, whom he yet forcibly publishes (and advertises, as in colonial travelogues) as a New World wonder, a goddess lately (somehow) sprung up in crabbed *New* England.

Bradstreet depicts these very sublime moods of "amazement," against all odds, as a self-made labyrinth of enraptured feeling in which sensuousness exceeds moralization, or public recuperation, yet is interpreted as a sign of God: "The consideration of these things would with amazement certainly resolve me that there is an Eternal Being." "These things" of which Anne Bradstreet speaks to her children are the "wondrous workes" of nature, which present to the senses the vast and orderly evidence for God's existence. Such works, moralized, provide the basis for an *immense* metaphor of correspondence between earth and heaven. The New World is not necessarily, thereby, a place of hermeneutic deprivation. Contemplating nature in such rapt moods of election, faith is possible, indeed inevitable—a "feeling knowledge" fitfully obtained. Nature awes Bradstreet into faith in God as the source of vastness and as author of her own potential greatness on earth. Not alone "the verity of the scriptures," not extraordinary events like miracles or tempests, not analytical meditation on the state of the self, but nature affectionately *beheld* fills the mind with the self-subjugating idea of God. Vacancy could be converted and moralized into poetic immensity. However shorn of creature comforts, surely colonial America had that. . . .

FURTHER READING

Bibliography

Skeick, William J., and JoElla Doggett. "Anne Bradstreet." In their *Seventeenth-Century American Poetry: A Reference Guide,* pp. 34-54. Boston: G. K. Hall & Co., 1977.
   Covers Bradstreet criticism from 1844 to 1975.

Biography

White, Elizabeth Wade. *Anne Bradstreet: The Tenth Muse.* New York: Oxford University Press, 1971, 410 p.
   Standard biography of Bradstreet.

Criticism

Aldridge, A. Owen. "Anne Bradstreet: Some Thoughts on the *Tenth Muse.*" In his *Early American Literature: A Comparatist Approach,* pp. 25-52. Princeton, N.J.: Princeton University Press, 1982.
   Considers the possible infleunce of Bradstreet on the Spanish poet Sor Juana Inés de la Cruz.

Cowell, Pattie, and Ann Stanford, eds. *Critical Essays on Anne Bradstreet.* Boston: G. K. Hall & Co., 1983, 286 p.
   Includes Colonial, nineteenth-century, and twentieth-century responses to Bradstreet's work.

Eberwein, Jane Donahue. "The 'Unrefined Ore' of Anne Bradstreet's *Quaternions.*" *Early American Literature* IX, No. 1 (Spring 1974): 19-26.
   Argues that Bradford's early poetry displays many of the techniques she uses to different effect in the more highly regarded later poetry.

———. "Civil War and Bradstreet's 'Monarchies'." *Early American Literature* XXVI, No. 2 (Fall 1991), 119-44.
   Argues that the "Four Monarchies" were so important to Bradstreet because of their relevance to the English Civil War.

Maragou, Helena. "The Portrait of Alexander the Great in Anne Bradstreet's 'The Third Monarchy'." *Early American Literature* XXIII, No. 1 (Spring 1988): 70-81.
   Explores the contradictions between Bradstreet's portrait of Alexander the Great and tenets of Puritan theology.

Margerum, Eileen. "Anne Bradstreet's Public Poetry and the Tradition of Humility." *Early American Literature* XVII, No. 2 (Fall 1982): 152-60.
   Discusses Bradstreet's subversive use of the modesty topos.

Martin, Wendy. "Anne Bradstreet: 'As Weary Pilgrim'." In her *An American Triptych: Anne Bradstreet, Emily Dickinson, Adrienne Rich,* pp 15-76. Chapel Hill: University of North Carolina Press, 1984.
   Presents a comprehensive portrait of Bradstreet and her work, with an emphasis on the historical context.

Piercy, Josephine K. *Anne Bradstreet.* New York: Twayne Publishers, 1965, 144 p.
   Focuses on Bradstreet's life and summarizes critical perspectives on her work.

Porterfield, Amanda. "Anne Hutchinson, Anne Bradstreet, and the Importance of Women in Puritan Culture." In her *Female Piety in Puritan New England: The Emergence of Religious Humanism,* pp. 80-115. New York: Oxford University Press, 1992.
   Argues that Bradstreet played an important role in the development of Puritan culture.

Rosenmeier, Rosamond R. "The Wounds upon Bathsheba: Anne Bradstreet's Prophetic Art." In *Seventeenth-Century American Poetry in Theory and Practice,* edited by Peter White, pp. 129-46. University Park and London: Pennsylvania State University Press, 1985.
   Explores the influence of biblical prophecy on Bradstreet's style and technique.

Schweitzer, Ivy. "Anne Bradstreet Wrestles with the Renaissance." *Early American Literature* XXIII, No. 3 (1988): 291-312.

    Argues that in the course of her career Bradstreet grew beyond the Renaissance models used in her early work.

Stanford, Anne. *Anne Bradstreet: The Worldly Puritan—An Introduction to Her Poetry.* New York: Burt Franklin & Co., 1974, 170 p.

    Analyzes Bradstreet's poetry, arguing that her "entire canon represents the struggle between the visible and invisible worlds." Also includes a chronology of Bradstreet's works, a list of books with which she was familiar, and a selected critical bibliography.

Waller, Jennifer R. " 'My Hand a Needle Better Fits': Anne Bradstreet and Women Poets in the Renaissance." *Dalhousie Review* 54, No. 3 (Autumn 1974): 436-50.

    Compares Bradstreet to female poets of the English Renaissance.

White, Elizabeth Wade. "*The Tenth Muse*—A Tercentenary Appraisal of Anne Bradstreet." *William and Mary Quarterly* VIII, No. 3 (July 1951): 355-77.

    Suggests that Bradstreet was the first Englishwoman to write poetry professionally.

Additional information on Bradstreet's life and works is contained in the following sources published by Gale Research: *Dictionary of Literary Biography*, Vol. 24; *DISCovering Authors*; *Literature Criticism*, Vol. 4; and *Poetry Criticism*, Vol. 10.

Elizabeth Tanfield Cary, Viscountess Falkland

1585/6-1639

English dramatist, translator, and biographer.

INTRODUCTION

Elizabeth Tanfield Cary was the first woman to publish a full-length original play in English, *The Tragedie of Mariam, Faire Queene of Jewry* (1613). Considered her most important work, the play was widely circulated during her lifetime, and may have influenced such works as *Othello* and *The Second Maiden's Tragedy*. Although few of the works Cary is purported to have written still exist, modern critics have found in Cary a unique response to Renaissance England informed by her lifelong struggle against religious, political, and domestic tyranny.

Biographical Information

According to *The Lady Falkland, Her Life* (1861), a biography of Cary commonly attributed to one of her daughters, Elizabeth Tanfield was born in 1585 or 1586 to Elizabeth Symondes and her husband Lawrence Tanfield, a successful Oxford lawyer and later Lord Chief Baron of the Exchequer. At a young age, the precocious child taught herself French, Spanish, Italian, Latin, Hebrew, and Transylvanian, and translated Seneca's *Epistles* and Ortelius' *Le Miroir du Monde*. Her rebellious view of Protestantism began during her youth; at the age of twelve she allegedly found internal contradictions in Calvin's *Institutes of the Christian Religion*.

When she was sixteen, Elizabeth Tanfield married Sir Henry Cary, a knight's son and member of the Privy Council. Cary was ten years her senior, and some critics contend that their marriage was socially motivated: Cary's title raised the Tanfields from the upper middle class to the gentry and the Tanfield fortune raised Cary from the gentry to the peerage. Immediately following the marriage, Henry Cary served in military expeditions abroad while Elizabeth lived with her mother-in-law. Forcefully deprived of books by her mother-in-law, Elizabeth began writing recreationally; she completed several works during this period, including two plays, a life of Tamburlaine, and *The Tragedie of Mariam*.

In approximately 1607, Henry Cary returned from his military service abroad. He and his wife began living together for the first time and Elizabeth eventually gave birth to eleven surviving children. In 1620, Henry Cary was named viscount of Falkland and shortly afterward was appointed Lord Chief Deputy of Ireland. In order to finance the move to Dublin so that her husband could

Elizabeth Tanfield wife of S.ᵗ Henry Carey, Lord Falkland. From an Original picture at Burford Priory.

assume his post, Elizabeth Cary mortgaged her jointure, which caused her father to disinherit her in favor of her son Lucius. Cary's marriage began to disintegrate shortly thereafter. While her husband tried to force Anglican rule on a large population of Irish Catholics, Elizabeth Cary's Catholic sympathies became more pronounced and she flaunted Protestant authority. When her conversion to Catholicism, which had taken place secretly in 1604, became public in 1626, Henry feared she would damage his career as a courtier and he abandoned her, taking custody of their children and stripping her of their wealth. Cary lived in semi-starvation and eventually appealed for an allowance before the Privy Council in 1627. Although the Council instructed Henry to give her 500 pounds per annum, seven months later he still had not complied with the order.

Still, Cary continued writing, including verse lives of Mary Magdalene, Agnes Martyr, and St. Elizabeth of Portugal; hymns to the Virgin Mary; *The History of the Life, Reign, and Death of Edward II* (1680); and translations of Cardinal du Perron. Published in France in 1630, Cary's translation of *The Reply of the Most Illustrious Cardinall of*

Perron, to the Answeare of the Most Excellent King of Great Britaine was smuggled into England but was suppressed by Archbishop Abbot and ordered to be publicly burned. Cary was jailed by Charles I in hopes that she would recant, but after her imprisonment she kidnapped her two youngest sons, Patrick and Henry, and, defying the Star Chamber, smuggled them to the continent. By the time of her death, six of her children had converted to Catholicism and were living in France. Toward the end of her life, Cary began translating the writings of Blosius, some of which may be extant in manuscript. She died of lung disease in 1639 and was buried in the chapel of Queen Henrietta Maria.

Major Works

Cary is primarily recognized for her drama *The Tragedie of Mariam, Faire Queene of Jewry*. A Senecan tragedy that draws on Josephus' *Antiquities*, *The Tragedie of Mariam* depicts the relationship between King Herod and his wife Mariam. In the play, Mariam reacts to a rumor that her husband has been executed: while she regrets his death, she rejoices in her newfound freedom from tyranny. Later in the play, however, Herod returns and is convinced by his sister Salome that Mariam had been unfaithful. In a fit of anger, Herod has her executed, only to regret his action and lament Mariam's death. *The Tragedie of Mariam* circulated in manuscript form for years and, although the play was never performed onstage, many leading literary figures of the time were aware of its publication. Despite the popularity of *The Tragedie of Mariam*, only two of Cary's other writings survive: a translation of Jacques Davy du Perron's *The Reply of the Most Illustrious Cardinall of Perron, to the Answeare of the Most Excellent King of Great Britaine*, a defense of Catholicism and criticism of Anglicanism; and the drama/biography of Edward II and his wife Queen Isabel, *The History of the Life, Reign, and Death of Edward II.*

Critical Reception

Cary's contemporaries held her in high regard and dedicated several works to her: *England's Helicon*, John Marston's *Works*, Michael Drayton's *England's Heroicall Epistles*, and the sixth book of Richard Belling's continuation of Sidney's *Arcadia*. In addition, Cary is the subject of verses by William Basse and John Davies of Hereford. Although Cary scholarship waned somewhat following her death, recent manuscript discoveries and feminist critical perspectives have revived an interest in Elizabeth Cary, and she is now considered an important figure in the history of women's literature.

PRINCIPAL WORKS

The Tradegie of Mariam, Faire Queene of Jewry (drama) 1613
The Reply of the Most Illustrious Cardinall of Perron, to

the Answeare of the Most Excellent King of Great Britaine* [translator] (letter) 1630
*The History of the Life, Reign, and Death of Edward II (drama/biography) 1680

*Written in 1627; survives in two versions, both published in 1680 and originally attributed to Lord Falkland.

CRITICISM

Sandra K. Fischer (essay date 1985)

SOURCE: "Elizabeth Cary and Tyranny, Domestic and Religious," in *Silent But for the Word: Tudor Women as Patrons, Translators, and Writers of Religious Works*, edited by Margaret Patterson Hannay, The Kent State University Press, 1985, pp. 225-37.

[*In the following excerpt, Fischer argues that Cary's writings, in particular* The Tragedie of Mariam, *confront the political and domestic hardships that she suffered as a repercussion of her conversion to Catholicism.*]

Lady Elizabeth Tanfield Cary, Viscountess Falkland (1585-1639), was the chiefly self-educated daughter and heiress of a genteel Renaissance family. She has been remembered primarily for her Catholic polemics, manifested most boldly in a translation, published in Douay in 1630, of Cardinal Perron's answer to criticism of his works by James I; for her temerity and conviction Lady Cary found her book confiscated and publicly burned. This was not, moreover, her first receipt of closed-minded and tyrannical oppression: if the Renaissance changed women, it may have been . . . to a dual dependence on favor from husband *and* ruler. Indeed, Lady Cary's life speaks as a series of conflicts between the ideal and the real: personally, religiously, politically, and artistically. Her biographers have not been blind to this conflict and the way Lady Cary met it. Lady Georgiana Fullerton [in *Life of Elizabeth, Lady Falkland, 1585-1639*, 1883] finds her plight both typical of women and exemplary, prefacing her biography with the heartening comparison of our own "hardships resembling those she underwent" and the encomium, "as a generous, courageous, noble-hearted woman, who fought a good fight, kept the faith, and continued it to the end, she may well be honoured and admired, and her example offered to the imitation of all who suffer for justice' sake."

So voracious a reader in her youth that she bribed the servants for more candles to use surreptitiously in her bedroom for night study, Elizabeth Tanfield was most attracted to the writings of the church fathers and the lives of saints. Consequently, at the age of nineteen, she privately and intellectually converted to Catholicism: a happy change for her conscience and temperament, but an unfortunate choice for domestic expediency. She had already, at fifteen, been contracted in marriage to a knight's son of a strong anti-Catholic predisposition. Because the marriage was arranged primarily to consolidate Tanfield money with Cary prestige, Sir Henry Cary left his young wife first in the care of her family and then of his mother. Thus it was rather easy for Elizabeth to conceal her new religion, a deception she continued for twenty years. Her parents innocently assisted in the ruse by having letters to her husband written by another in Elizabeth's name; when he finally saw a letter of his wife's own composition, he was flabbergasted by her erudition and style and insisted that it was a forgery.

Lady Cary attempted to be a dutiful wife inasmuch as it was compatible with her beliefs: she gave birth to eleven children, followed her husband to Ireland, and dedicated an early play she wrote to him. Moreover, the concept of conjugal duty was consistent with her religious ideals of humility and self-effacement. She advised her eldest daughter, Anne, "Whenever conscience and reason will permit it, always prefer the will of another to your own," and she attempted to conform to this credo herself. The entire marriage could have been a battle of wills on many fronts, but Lady Cary consistently bowed to her husband's wishes, which often necessitated altering her character and disposition. Although she preferred study to nursery, she handled all the domestic tasks, including rearing of the children; she loathed horses but learned to ride because it pleased her husband; she cared little for clothing and appearance yet dressed up according to her husband's preferences. As Fullerton reports, "Her women were fain to walk round the room after her, pinning on her things . . . whilst she was thinking seriously on some other business, and it was always her custom to write or to read whilst they curled her hair."

Despite the efforts of Lady Cary to be a proper wife in all external natters, when Sir Henry discovered her religious conversion, in 1626, he sent his wife into isolation and near-destitution. His intent, according to Fullerton, was to "starve his wife into submission." Her father followed suit by disinheriting his daughter, and the king had her imprisoned in her rooms for six weeks, hoping to force her to recant. Sir Henry wrote letters to the king disclaiming his wife, and all her friends abandoned her in the face of scandal. After nearly starving to death for her religious beliefs, Lady Cary boldly brought her case before the Privy Council, which in 1627 ruled that Sir Henry must support her with an allowance of £500 per annum. He was remiss in doing so even after the order, revealing his qualities of pride and bigotry, but Lady Cary, reluctant to displease her husband further, did not complain to the council a second time. In politics Lord Falkland was similarly tyrannical, demanding that all priests be banished from Ireland in direct opposition to crown orders and good sense. Eventually Queen Henrietta Maria, because of her own Catholic background, interceded to promote nuptial reconciliation between the Carys. In 1633 the whole family was reunited in a single household, but a few weeks later Sir Henry broke his leg in a fall from his horse: it gangrened, was amputated, and he bled to death. Before he died he allegedly asked to see a priest.

Even in the face of such domestic and economic disaster,

Lady Cary persevered in her love of letters. In addition to her Perron translation, she undertook lives of three saints in verse, hymns to the Virgin Mary, a history of Edward II (erroneously attributed to her husband, who would certainly not have been capable of the praise of the pope that it contains), and two plays, one now lost and the other remarkable for being the first extant original English tragedy by a woman, *The Tragedie of Mariam, the Faire Queene of Jewry* (1613). This play is even more remarkable in the plight of its heroine, who, like Lady Cary, must come to terms with domestic and political tyranny in the form of her husband Herod, tyrant par excellence.

Although the minimal criticism focused on this play has judged Elizabeth Cary's sentiments as in part rebellious, it is more accurate to say that she is interested, here and elsewhere, in how a woman handles tyranny and maintains her own integrity. Mariam's actions are for the most part sympathetic, although her end is tragic; her problems are lack of agency and situations offering only Hobson's choices. In *The History of . . . King Edward the Second,* Cary swings the focus to his queen, whose actions, in a predicament similar to Mariam's, she disdains: "Certainly this man was infinitely tyrannical and vicious, deserving more than could be laid upon him; yet it had been much more to the Queen's reputation and honour, if she had given him a fair and legal trial. . . ." She seems to have consciously chosen for artistic expression historical women who also faced tyranny with a clear conscience, yet who found their choices for solution similarly ambiguous.

> Such marginal genres as religious writings, translations, and closet drama in a sense afford vicarious action: the writing itself, whether or not disseminated and read, becomes a philosophically justified enactment of the author's life.
>
> —*Sandra K. Fischer*

Lady Cary's tendency to choose well-known stories from prominent sources indicates one of the circumlocutious devices of the genres of marginality: in a simple retelling of the facts, the author is not obliged to accept responsibility for what may be considered rebellious notions. She may, in her verse or prose reinterpretation of history, test the responses of characters in plights similar to her own; she may discernibly call for restitution against domestic and religious tyranny; but the composition remains distanced from reality. . . . Such marginal genres as religious writings, translations, and closet drama in a sense afford vicarious action: the writing itself, whether or not disseminated and read, becomes a philosophically justified enactment of the author's life. She may speak with liberty and impunity of an ancient queen of Judea and the archetypal dramatic tyrant, or of the wife of a medieval

English king—but the subject is ever herself. A woman writer may establish her own realistic precedent in art; she may create her own role models. . . . Cary's writings primitively and innocently work toward "revision"—that is, examining the stereotypes, redefining feminine identity, and locating an authentic voice outside the male tradition. The voice of silence thus speaks through historical reinterpretation.

Lady Cary, as a writer and a recusant, of necessity found herself confronted with other paradoxes, which involved establishing a maverick self-image and retaining an apparently perverse personal integrity against the conflicting voices of authority. Even with the accomplished, wily, and intelligent Elizabeth on the throne, and a few other women prominent in Tudor society as literati, there must have been an inherent tension then, as now, in being a "smart woman." As a child Cary was both encouraged and dissuaded from learning; she could privately stretch her accomplishments to the limits of her potential but then must publicly conceal the extent of her "unladylike" abilities. One is reminded of the wide-ranging humanistic education of the daughters of Thomas More, and the paradox of these talents being put to use only as dinner entertainment for household guests. Moreover, as a Catholic, Cary revered all authority and believed in self-effacement, always, for instance, kneeling when in the presence of her mother.

Yet this same woman stressed internal consistency: she must be true to her talents and beliefs. Thus, as a writer, she found in the world of letters an acceptable arena of action. According to Edward Hyde, Earl of Clarendon, she had a "most masculine understanding" and, although she probably did not expect a wide readership for any of her works, could not allow the constrictions to silence her. The life of the mind could be chronicled creatively: she, like other Renaissance women writers, "apparently believed that [her] writings would be useful records of experience available nowhere else." In religious terms the same paradox expressed itself in her life, for to be true to her religion and its authority, she must flout civil authority. Although recusants in late Tudor England were increasingly being persecuted for their practice, Lady Cary consistently risked such punishment by attending private masses.

Although isolated intellectually, spiritually, and physically from her husband and alienated from her king, Lady Cary continued private and social inquiry into her favorite subjects. We may have this artistic perseverance to account for the publication of **Mariam.** The poet John Davies, Elizabeth Cary's childhood writing master, was also well-acquainted with Philip Sidney's sister, Mary Herbert, Countess of Pembroke, herself a published dramatic translator who encouraged her coterie to write philosophical closet drama like **The Tragedie of Mariam.** Although Cary's daughter asserts the standard noble excuse for publication of the play, that it was stolen away and entered illegally in the register, it appeared in print shortly after Davies had published complimentary verses to his literary women acquaintances, lauding the dramatic

ability of Lady Falkland. He dedicates "The Muse's Sacrifice, Or Divine Meditations" of 1612 to the "most noble, and no lesse deservedly-renowned Ladyes, as well Darlings, as Patronesses, of the *Muses;* LUCY, *Countess of Bedford;* MARY, Countesse-Dowager of Pembroke; and ELIZABETH, *Lady Cary,* (Wife of Sr. *Henry Cary:*) Glories of Women." . . .

One may wonder at the inclusion of Lady Falkland's name alongside the more famous Countesses of Bedford and Pembroke, particularly because Elizabeth Cary typically had little money or favor to bestow upon struggling poets. She was, however, quite renowned as a hostess and leader of intellectual coteries, no matter how mean her surroundings and scarce her funds. By age four she had mastered five languages; she adored the theater and was well pleased when Sir Henry himself appeared in a masque at court in 1612. After his death she pursued intellectual stimulation with great vigor, being particularly fond of Oxford men and "freedom of conversation." Dr. [William] Laud found her Catholic arguments so convincing and influential that he recommended her banishment from London and the court. . . .

One mark of Elizabeth Cary's contemporary position as a learned and influential lady is the number of works dedicated to her or mentioning her. These include John Marston's *Works:* "To the Right Honourable, the Lady Elizabeth Carey, Viscountess Falkland . . . because your Honour is well acquainted with the Muses"; the 1614 edition of *England's Helicon,* published by Richard More: "TO THE TRULY VERTUOUS AND Honourable Lady, the Lady ELIZABETH CARIE"; lines by a Mr. Clayton, on her prolific output, in *In Laudem nobilissimae Heroinae . . . ;* and by a Father Leander, praising her learning and quality of mind. To express her religious philosophy she chose primarily to translate Catholic treatises from the Continent; but for private concerns her subject was tyranny, protected under the cloak of true historical source.

One final biographical instance completes the pattern of Lady Cary's battle against religious and political tyranny. After the death of Sir Henry, their son Lucius became Lord Falkland; he was alone among the Cary children in remaining Protestant rather than converting to Catholicism. Fearing that her younger sons, Patrick and Placid, would be subverted by Lucius and a morally dubious acquaintance of his, a Mr. Chillingworth, Lady Cary first removed her sons to Catholic boarding houses "in obscure parts of London" with the intent of eventually sending them to seminaries in France. Lucius assiduously set out to find his brothers; when he failed, he had his mother called before the Privy Council for interrogation. She would not reveal their whereabouts, answering truthfully about her intentions, and thus was briefly imprisoned in the Tower for defiance. When the Chief Justice released Lady Cary, she continued undaunted with her plan, managing to sneak her sons out of the country: Placid became a monk in Paris, and Patrick went to Rome with the intention of becoming a priest, although he later decided that his primary duty was to produce a proper—that is, Catholic—heir.

An effigy of Elizabeth Tanfield Cary on the Tanfield tomb at Burford, Oxfordshire.

As [Kenneth] Murdock [in *The Sun at Noon,* 1939] summarizes the pattern of Lady Cary's life, "She was caught in one of the central dilemmas of her time, between intellectual conviction and expediency, between loyalty to an ideal and loyalty to her husband, between the pursuit of Heaven and the race for favor with the King." This also perfectly describes the position of Mariam at the opening of Cary's play. Although Cary is predictably faithful (according to our theory of marginal intent) to her source in the *Antiquities* of Josephus, she makes several artistic alterations in focus and emphasis that help to reveal her main concerns. First, she chooses Mariam, the wronged wife, over king, husband, and tyrant Herod as her tragic focal point. Additionally, she augments the depiction of other women in the history and shows them as defined solely in relation to men: as wives, widows, sisters, former wives, mothers-in-law, maidens, whores. As Simone de Beauvoir suggests, women's social value and extent of power as well as their identities derive from these relationships. The men, in turn, become foils, alternatives for the judging of women and the treatment of wives, with Constabarus and Herod at opposite ends of the spectrum.

Mariam's primary foil is Salome, who may have some feminist principles but no moral sense. Finally, Lady Cary hints, by the end of the play, at a continuum linking the martyrdom of Mariam and the sacrifice of Christ, adumbrating a comparable release from tyranny and the old law in these symbolic deaths.

While Mariam exhibits defiance on two primary levels—political and domestic—Cary adds a persistent undertone of moral difference as well. From the beginning of the play Mariam is nearly alone in possessing scruples in her society—and indeed this must be as Lady Cary herself felt in her religious conversion and subsequent alienation. It is noteworthy in this regard that Herod can be nothing less, in stage tradition and in symbol, than tyranny personified: certainly Lady Cary was familiar with Hamlet's admonition to the players to avoid passionate rantings in the Herodian vein, and she found she could easily use the religious implications of the literary Herod as "the tyrant ogre . . . , the usurper from whom the world is now to be saved," and "the extreme symbol of the misgoverning, tenacious ego" who "has brought mankind to the nadir of spiritual abasement." The spiritual, moral, or religious level is of greatest interest to the playwright: Mariam would have no tragedy were she not in inner conflict over duties of the conscience and duties of the world.

The play opens with a striking soliloquy illustrative of this conflict. Mariam is above all (and despite minor flaws of overconfidence and pride) a woman of scrupulous conscience and rigorous self-examination. Upon hearing rumors of Herod's demise, the heroine wants to exult at the death of personal and social tyranny, but while she hated her husband's hypocrisy, she finds herself guilty of the same crime:

> When *Herod* liv'd, that now is done to death,
> Oft have I wisht that I from him were free:
> Oft have I wisht that he might lose his breath,
> Oft have I wisht his Carkas dead to see. . . .
> Hate hid his true affection from my sight,
> And kept my heart from paying him his debt. . . .
> For hee by barring me from libertie,
> To shunne my ranging, taught me first to range.
> But yet too chast a Scholler was my hart,
> To learne to love another then my Lord.
> (ll. 17-20, 22-23, 27-30)

What crime has this woman committed? Cumulative anaphora reveals her justified attitude toward husband and tyrant, but now she chastises herself for mental disobedience. Although his treatment of her—murdering her brother and grandfather, usurping the throne, leaving a command for her execution if he fails to return from battle, exhibiting extreme jealousy, and doting on her image of beauty rather than her spiritual or intellectual excellence—legitimizes her response, she has not been unfaithful; yet still she feels guilty. Such meticulous moral logic sets the tone for the entire play.

Indeed, all the characters project guilt upon Mariam as the plot unfolds, and in self-examination she must concur by realizing that reputation is as important as actual innocence. Her error was to alienate husband and king; thus, while her conscience is clear, Mariam is guilty of political and marital inexpediency. Her dilemma lies in how to reconcile promptings of the heart with public forms and duties. Mariam knows morally what constitutes right action, yet she does not understand the misinterpretation of her pure motives through the spectacles of will, jealousy, and ambition.

The play advances primarily through Senecan confrontational dialogue: Mariam is first joined by her mother, Alexandra, who understands political expediency to the extent that it eclipses morality. She would betray her own daughter to save herself. Salome, sister of Herod, next enters, suspicious of political plotting between the queen and her mother. She will actually plan and enact a poisoning ruse to indict Mariam of the very crimes of which she herself is guilty. Just as survival motivates Alexandra, so Salome is driven by an individualistic will that overtops morality. These powerful exchanges between the foremost women in the society of the play are remarkable in that they fail to offer [what de Beauvoir calls] a "counter-universe" to the male-oriented and dominated order. Their invectives do not afford the progression discernible in Shakespearean plays. . . .

Instead, each woman postures against the representation of tyranny in her own way and alone.

At the midpoint of the play, reports of the death of tyranny have filtered through the whole society, causing a realignment of personal possibilities: Pheroras may marry the servant Graphina, Doris must plot to institute her son as heir by killing Mariam's children, Constabarus may release the sons of Babus from hiding, and Salome must jockey for power to fulfill her concupiscent will. However, as we have begun to suspect, the announcement comes that Herod still lives, and a new realignment begins. Mariam fatally decides to quit a life of hypocrisy: she will abstain from the bed of Herod, forcing congruency between thought and action. She realizes how easy it would be to dissemble and ensure her political position, but instead she trusts her innocence and good character to speak for themselves:

> I know I could inchaine him with a smile:
> And lead him captive with a gentle word,
> I scorne my looke should ever man beguile,
> Or other speech, then meaning to afford. . . .
> Oh what a shelter is mine innocence, . . .
> Gainst all mishaps it is my faire defence, . . .
> Mine innocence is hope enough for mee.
> (ll. 1166-69, 1174, 1176, 1183)

Sohemus, keeper of Mariam and counselor to Herod, has been charged to murder the queen if Herod dies away from Palestine. He, however, has been moved by Mariam's modesty, chastity, purity of heart, and mistreatment at the tyrant's hands. He knows that he is in danger because he failed to complete his commission, but he would gladly die to save the good queen. This decision writes

both their death warrants, for Herod believes that Mariam must have engaged in "criminal conversation" for Sohemus to be so swayed. Simultaneously the Butler brings in the poisoned cup sent by Salome, which is supposed to be a love potion concocted by Mariam for Herod. Both the Butler and Sohemus are thus effective agents in the doom of Mariam, yet both betrayers are repentent immediately before their deaths, reformed by recognition of Mariam's goodness.

Only a willful misreading of instances such as this could allow the critical observation that Cary [thinks negatively of women]. Comments upon which this judgment may be based are directed against Salome in order to enhance the portrayal of Mariam and to underscore the perverse irony of her execution. The sons of Babus, for example, meet their deaths with equanimity, claiming that they are happy to die because it will free them from women. But their comments stem from the experience of their only true friend, Constabarus, who, even while he inductively curses all women because of Salome's actions, reiterates that Mariam is the sole redemption of her sex:

> But no farewell to any female wight.
> You wavering crue: my curse to you I leave,
> You had but one to give you any grace:
> And you your selves will Mariams life bereave,
> Your common-wealth doth innocencie chase.
> (ll. 1578-82)

Imagistically, Salome is, based on Matthew 23:27,

> a painted sepulcher,
> That is both faire, and vilely foule at once:
> Though on her out-side graces garnish her,
> Her mind is fild with worse then rotten bones.
> And ever readie lifted is her hand,
> To aime destruction at a husbands throat: . . .
> Her mouth though serpent-like it never hisses,
> Yet like a Serpent, poysons where it kisses.
> (ll. 880-89)

Mariam, however, is exempt from this portrayal. Part of her tragedy is her lack of whitewash: the beauty of Mariam is an indication of spiritual purity and innocence.

From the point of Herod's return the play turns symbolically religious, casting over the sacrifice of Mariam a Christ-like aura. She becomes a combined symbol of scapegoat and sacrificial lamb whose death will cleanse the kingdom of tyrannical misjudgment as it also releases the heroine from her insoluble dilemma. Herod vacillates in Pilate-like fashion through an entire scene in giving the command for her execution. Should he behead her? No weapon would consent to pierce her lovely skin. Should he drown her? Rivers would change course to save her. Should he burn her? Fire would be unable to harm the very origin of passion. Even though Herod typically employs hyperbole regarding Mariam—indeed, his only redeeming quality is his love for her, and it is excessive, possessive, and uxorious—his uncertainty indicates the religious symbolism of the final portion of the play. "[A]nd

Hebrew why," he asks himself, "Seaze you with Lyons pawes the fairest lam / Of all the flocke?"

As the Nuntio brings report of Mariam's death, the religious effect of her sacrifice makes itself known. Her last message to Herod is that in three days he will pray for her resurrection. Herod recognizes his tyrannical error and repents for the slaughter of innocence not in three days, but in three minutes. Mariam's individual sacrifice has a profound social effect: it prepares the way for the death of all tyranny. Herod laments through all of Act V for his misguided actions, comparing Mariam's death to the archetypal murder:

> Retire thy selfe vile monster, worse then hee
> That staind the virgin earth with brothers blood,
> Still in some vault or denne inclosed bee,
> Where with thy teares thou maist beget a flood,
> Which flood in time may drowne thee: happie day.

(ll. 2191-95)

This flood of tears will baptise the kingdom to open the way for a new order. The redemption of humanity by Christ's sacrifice becomes equivalent to the redemption of womanhood by Mariam's sacrifice.

Although Lady Cary inserts this hint of hope at the end of the tragedy with the seeds of conversion of the tyrant, the play is remarkable in its avoidance of feminist propositions, especially considering the proliferation of broadsides of the Swetnam and Munda variety at this time, both attacking and defending the female sex. Mariam experiences tragic anagnorisis because she cannot facilely dismiss duties to husband and state: all personal decisions have public ramifications. The antifeminist viewpoint, even to the extent of misogyny, is given free and vituperative voice in the complaints of Constabarus against Salome; but Mariam stands in example to explode the stereotype. Cary speaks for a quiet feminism that recognizes the many contradictory roles of the intelligent, educated, noble Renaissance wife and mother. Choric commentary in *The Tragedie of Mariam* is conventionally traditional, almost reactionary in its observations, and certainly not to be heard as the voice of the playwright. The Chorus is effective, however, in symbolically pinpointing the dilemma of a woman of independent thought who also believes unerringly in the Catholic ideals. While Mariam tentatively chooses to trust in her virtues and defy the convention, the Chorus speaks to her as conservative conscience: a woman must be willing to dedicate her mind as well as her body to her husband. It is Mariam's decision not to submit with mind *or* body that instigates her peripety.

Like Cary, Mariam is unsuccessful in escaping the tragedy of personal and political tyranny; however, her death asserts the integrity of her conscience and apotheosizes her as a victim whose suffering and sacrifice affect the tyrant and open the way for change. This was perhaps more than Lady Falkland could hope for personally, and she used the marginal genre as a forum for the philosophical investigation of the subject closest to her heart. Mar-

iam's dilemma is no less ambiguous and her end indeed tragic, but she exhibits the same strength of character and dedication to ideals in the face of conflicting duties that Elizabeth Cary herself attempted in her recusant position. She and her husband were apparently reconciled at his deathbed, and among his private papers was found a copy of her Perron translation. Her domestic vigilance, similarly, brought her a final victory, for of her eight surviving children, six found vocations in the Catholic church, including all four of her daughters.

Tina Krontiris (essay date 1990)

SOURCE: "Style and Gender in Elizabeth Cary's *Edward II*," in *The Renaissance Englishwoman in Print: Counterbalancing the Canon,* edited by Anne M. Haselkorn and Betty S. Travitsky, Amherst: The University of Massachusetts Press, 1990, pp. 137-53.

[*In the following essay, Krontiris considers possible autobiographical elements in* The History of the Life, Reign, and Death of Edward II *and compares the work with* The Tragedie of Mariam, *outlining Cary's maturation as a writer. She also examines "the possible influence of religion in [Cary's] development."*]

Elizabeth Cary, Lady Falkland, has been known primarily as the author of *Mariam,* a closet drama she wrote at the age of sixteen or seventeen. But it is now apparent that this is not her only surviving dramatic work. Some twenty-three years after her first published play, *Mariam,* and during a solitary confinement that followed her secret conversion to Catholicism, Cary wrote *History of . . . King Edward II,* which appears to be an unfinished play or a biography influenced by drama. The work, which attests to Lady Falkland's development as a woman writer and dramatist, survives in two versions, both printed in 1680 by different printers. The longer of the two, published in a folio volume, seems to be closer to the form of a play. It contains several speeches and is written predominantly in blank verse; it is also clearer, more coherent, and less sentimental in tone. The shorter version, which came out in a small Octavo book, seems to be a condensed account of the longer piece.

Edward II was found among Lord Falkland's papers and for this reason it was attributed to him by the 1680 printers and subsequently by the editors of an eighteenth-century miscellany that reprinted the short version. This attribution went unchallenged until relatively recently when Donald Stauffer [in "A Deep and Sad Passion," 1935] proved it to be Lady Falkland's composition. As there is still some uneasiness among critics about its authorship, I shall initially produce additional evidence, mainly internal, to strengthen Stauffer's argument. Stauffer has already called attention to the parts in the work that do not point to Lord Falkland as its likely author. I will concentrate here on the parts that point to Lady Falkland.

First, the work is sympathetic toward the adulterous Queen Isabel, an attitude unlikely to have been held by the ultraconservative Lord Falkland. But more important, there is an emphasis on certain aspects of the queen's life that are in agreement with Lady Falkland's personal experiences as her biographers have conveyed them to us. There is, for instance, a noticeable emphasis on the queen's suffering and abandonment in times of affliction. This is evident from the amount of space devoted to Isabel's search for loyal friends as well as from the language used to describe her condition. She is referred to as a woman "dejected out of wedlock," a representative of the "unworthily oppressed" in her kingdom. In her affliction she is abandoned by all, even by her own brother, king of France, who places political expediency above his duty to a "forsaken queen" and sister. Alleged friends recognize "the justice of her cause" but are unwilling to risk their position in order to support her. Her first loyal friend "finds her in her melancholy chamber, confused in her restless thoughts, with many sad distractions." "Domestic spies" seek to make her condition worse, while her husband writes to the pope and asks him to summon her back to England.

The queen's condition as described in this part parallels that of Lady Falkland shortly after her conversion to Catholicism in 1626. From this year to about 1629 (*Edward II* was written in 1627), Lady Falkland was isolated and reduced to poverty, her husband having cut off all financial support. She lived in an empty house without furniture and, except for the loyal Bessie Poulter, without servants—all having been removed by Lord Falkland's order. Meanwhile her angered husband tried to force her to recant. He wrote several letters to the king, the privy council, and the archbishop of Canterbury asking them to put pressure on the "apostate," as he called her. Without money and rejected by her husband, Lady Falkland was in desperate need of material and moral support. Some of her friends remained loyal to her during this time but others deserted her, lest their reputations should suffer. Her own mother turned her out of doors. I suggest that Lady Falkland's preoccupation with loyal friends and Queen Isabel's similar preoccupation in *Edward II* have a common head.

There are even more direct parallels. Isabel's joy at receiving her first true friend, Robert of Artois, is very similar to that of Lady Falkland at receiving Mr. Clayton, the first friend to visit her in her isolation. Also, like Isabel, Lady Falkland thought of herself as suffering unjustly. In her letter to Conway she says that by helping her he "shall please God in helping the oppressed." An even more striking parallel is the mention of "domestic spies" both in the history and in Lady Falkland's letters to Charles I and to Secretary Coke. She urges the latter not to believe "those pestilent servants of my lord's, who seek to make advantage of my misery . . . to work their own ends," while she tells the king that she can find no fault with her husband, "except with regard to his believing too much information of his servants against me, who, for their own interest seek to estrange his affections from me." The history states that "Many of her Domestic Spies were here attending, as she well knew and saw, to work her ruine" (113) and "to make her once more forsaken."

Apart from these parallels there is also a sympathetic attitude toward the Catholic figures mentioned briefly in the history. The pope, albeit misled by Edward's information, is "wisely foreseeing" and the black monks at the abbey of St. Hammonds "had the honour to give their long-lost Mistriss the first Welcome." It is very unlikely that Lord Falkland, who hated all "Popelings," as he called them and who at the time of the history's composition was at war with his estranged wife over her conversion to Catholicism, would have included even the slightest favorable reference to Catholics. Additionally, there is external evidence which leaves little doubt that the piece was written by Elizabeth Falkland. "The Author's Preface to the Reader" is signed E.F., but Henry Falkland's initials were H.F. Be it noted that during the period of the history's composition the letters of Lord Falkland to the king and the members of the privy council were signed H. Falkland; those of his wife, E. Falkland. That the history was found among Lord Falkland's papers cannot be taken as evidence for its being written by him, for apparently in the last years of his life, when he was reconciled to his wife, he read her literary works and kept copies of them. The translation of Du Perron's *Reply*, which is indisputably Lady Falkland's and which was done in the same chronological period, was also found among his personal papers. Last, I would like to suggest that the author's sympathy for the neglected queen in the history could very well be a tribute to Queen Henrietta-Maria, who in the first years of her marriage (married 1625) was ignored and even avoided by her husband, and who was Lady Falkland's friend. We know that the translation of *The Reply* (1630) was dedicated to the Catholic Henrietta-Maria.

As in the case of *Mariam*, the author's choice of subject matter for this literary work is suggestive of her concerns. *Edward II* deals as much with the relationship between the king and the queen as with that between the king and his subjects. Lady Falkland, then, is once more attracted to a story that focuses on the relationship between the two genders and that treats a situation she understood. In her version of Edward II's life she shows familiarity with a long line of writers who treated the same subject before her. Highly eclectic in her use of available material, she seems to have relied primarily on Grafton and to a lesser extent on Marlowe, although her sources cannot be easily identified. From Marlowe she has apparently borrowed the incident of the king being shaved in cold puddle water, Gaveston's Italian identity, and Edward's neglect of and callous behavior toward Queen Isabel. But she has not lifted or borrowed material on a large scale from any particular author. This suggests that Lady Falkland felt the need to write an original story, not merely to retell one already told. Apparently she was not satisfied with the way the subject had been dealt with. Indeed she lets us know as much in her "Preface to the Reader" when she refers to the "dull character of our Historians," who write by inference and try to please "Time" rather than "Truth." Although, as I show later, her own statement about Truth needs to be taken with caution, she evidently felt that the story had not been told quite right. Her dissatisfaction seems to have been greater with the treatment the queen had received, for it is in this respect that her account differs most from the versions of her predecessors. Her portrait of Edward is not very different from Marlowe's. Nor does she have anything particularly new to say about absolute monarchy as a governing system; her criticism seems specifically aimed at Edward for using his power arbitrarily and setting a bad example for his subjects. But the case is very different with respect to Queen Isabel. Unlike Marlowe and others who offer a perfunctory sketch of the queen and maintain an ambivalent attitude toward her, Lady Falkland treats Isabel with a great deal of sympathy, provides justification for her adultery, and labors to develop her into a consistent character. In the remaining portion of this discussion I intend to show how Lady Falkland advances her defense of Edward's wife in contradistinction to previous writers and how she attempts to express herself without openly violating cultural norms or personal convictions regarding proper conduct in general and feminine conduct in particular. I shall also draw a brief comparison between *The History of . . . Edward II* and *Mariam* in order to show Lady Falkland's development as a woman writer. Finally, I shall refer to the possible influence of religion in her development.

The defense of Queen Isabel is attempted chiefly through a process of victimization. Almost throughout the work Isabel is shown to be a woman and a wife trapped in a situation to whose making she has not contributed and out of which she tries to escape. Her marriage to Edward has been a stop-gap solution to the king's homosexual passion: "the interest of a wife was thought the most hopeful inducement to reclaim these loose affections" that had gone to Gaveston. As a wife—"in name a Wife, in truth a Hand-maid"—she is forced to play the standby role accorded her by her husband and his minions. Even her trip to France is originally engineered by Spencer, who wishes "to pare her nails before she scratch'd him," with the consent of her husband who "could be contented well to spare her whose eyes did look too far into his pleasures." This kind of presentation has the effect of legitimating many of Isabel's actions. Her flight to France becomes not a traitorous act but an attempt to escape oppression at home.

The process of victimization is also deployed in what perhaps constitutes the most daring aspect of the author's task—her justification of Isabel's adultery. This is apparent from the queen's first full appearance, one-third into the work:

> Love and Jealousie, that equally possest the Queen, being intermixed with a stronger desire of Revenge, spurs her on to hasten on this Journey [to France]. She saw the King a stranger to her bed, and revelling in the wanton embraces of his stoln pleasures, without a glance on her deserving Beauty. This contempt had begot a like change in her, though in a more modest nature, her youthful Affections wanting a fit subject to work on, and being debarr'd of that warmth that should have still preserv'd their temper, she cast her wandering eye upon the gallant Mortimer, a piece of masculine Bravery without exception.

With psychological insight, the author here renders Edward responsible for his wife's infidelity. Unlike previous writers, she recognizes the affective and sexual needs of Isabel as a young woman ("her youthful Affections wanting a fit subject to work on") and treats Edward's homosexuality as a form of adultery. Through his behavior, Edward is shown to be the first to invalidate the marriage agreement. Hence the author justifies Isabel's lack of marital chastity and implicitly also opposes the role of the patient Griselda prescribed by her culture in similar situations.

But adultery was a serious offense when committed by a woman and Lady Falkland was no doubt aware of her culture's judgment on this matter. If she wanted to engage the reader's sympathy for the queen, she had to be very careful. Besides casting her heroine as a victim, Lady Falkland uses a number of other tactics that seem to work in favor of the queen's character. Elements of time and space seem deployed to control the reader's response to Isabel's adulterous actions. Accordingly, the queen's appearance in the history is strategically delayed until Edward's abuse has been sufficiently—and emphatically—exposed. Her affair with Mortimer is described only briefly, while he is made to appear more like a companion to her griefs than a sexual partner. Conveniently, he is set aside and only occasionally referred to until the last few scenes, despite the fact that he accompanies the queen to France. Traditional notions of feminine sexual conduct are likewise appropriated to render the queen more acceptable and sympathetic. Thus Isabel's sexual behavior is of "a more modest nature" than her husband's and her speech to her brother is characterized by "a sweetly-becoming modestie." The "showre of Chrystal tears" she sheds are pitiable and proper for a woman's supposed soft nature.

Furthermore, the author strengthens the queen's position in the history by endowing her with a caring nature and a motherly instinct. Her character, unlike her husband's, is fortified with a care for the oppressed: "'tis not I alone unjustly suffer," she pleads, "my tears speak those of a distressed Kingdom, which, long time glorious, now is almost ruin'd." Although the presence of the eldest son is structurally necessary so that he can claim the throne when his mother's party returns from France, the specific reference to her son, especially in the short version, suggests more than is necessary for the structure of the plot: "Her eldest Son, her dearest comfort, and the chief spring that must set all these wheels a going, she leaves not behind, but makes him the Companion of her Travels." Additionally, the queen is credited with the good opinion and support of respectable people. Robert of Artois, a "steady States-man, not led by Complement, or feign'd professions," speaks of the queen's "deeds of Goodness"; and the earl of Heinault, a man of "an honest Heart and grave Experience," decides to join his brother, Sir John, in defending "a Queen that justly merits Love and Pity." Even Edward's own feelings regarding his wife's infidelity appear to be deployed somewhat in her favor: "he thinks the breach of Wedlock a foul trespass; but to contemn her he so much had wronged, deserv'd as much as they could lay upon him." Through these strategies, then, the author manages to preempt criticism of the queen as adulteress and disloyal subject.

In previous treatments of Edward's life, the queen's character had been denigrated by attributing to her both cruelty, which I shall discuss shortly, and hypocrisy. But in Lady Falkland's portrayal of Isabel hypocrisy is relatively absent. There are two obvious allusions to the queen's hypocritical behavior. One is shortly before her flight to France when "She courts her Adversary [Spencer] with all the shews of perfect reconcilement," pretending to be "well pleased, and glad to stay at home." The other occurs when she is about to escape from France: having been deceived by the French Council, she quits the French court "in shew contented" and "praiseth Spencer, as if 'twere he alone had wrought her Welfare." As may be discerned, however, this type of hypocrisy is presented as a valuable skill, one that Isabel learns of necessity and that finally saves her life. It is not a blemish but an admirable quality allied to cunning and envied even by the cleverest politician. Rather than hold it against the queen, Lady Falkland uses it to poke fun at Spencer who, for all his ingenuity, is outwitted by a woman more than once: "[his] Craft and Care . . . here fell apparent short of all Discretion, to be thus over-reach'd by one weak Woman"; "Thus Womens Wit sometimes can cozen Statesmen." In this way, Lady Falkland cleverly turns a characteristic other writers had presented as a vice into a skill.

The defense of the queen lapses at one point and discloses Lady Falkland's difficulty in handling her heroine. As we have seen, Isabel is not criticized for assuming political power. Although in the end she is shown to be susceptible to the corruptive influence of power, for the most part she is portrayed as an intelligent and skillful politician whose maneuvers in the battle with the Spencers win her a victory. (With one summons she manages to bring Arundel, Spencer, and the city of Bristol into her possession.) But she is severely criticized for the cruel treatment of her fallen adversaries, particularly and especially of Spencer:

> While She thus passeth on with a kinde of insulting Tyranny, far short of the belief of her former Vertue and Goodness, she makes this poor unhappy man attend her Progress, not as the antient Romans did their vanquish'd Prisoners, for ostentation, to increase their Triumph; but merely for Revenge, Despite, and private Rancour. . . . Certainly this man was infinitely vicious, and deserv'd as much as could be laid upon him, for those many great and insolent Oppressions, acted with Injustice, Cruel[t]y, and Blood; yet it had been much more to the Queens Honour, if she had given him a quicker Death, and a more honourable Tryal, free from these opprobrious and barbarous Disgraces, which savour'd more of a savage, tyrannical disposition, than a judgment fit to command, or sway the Sword of Justice.

This is a severe condemnation and not the only of its kind. But it does not mark a change in the author's overall attitude toward her heroine. As the phrasing in the passage just quoted might suggest ("far short of the belief of her former Vertue and Goodness"), Lady Falkland strives to make Isabel as consistent a character as possible. This pause in the queen's defense seems rather a manifestation of the author's difficulty in reconciling the material she inherited from her sources, on the one hand, with her personal convictions and cultural values on the other. In order to better understand Lady Falkland's attitude toward cruelty, it would be useful to pay attention to other instances of it in the work. Early in the history, the beheading of Lancaster and twenty-two other nobles in "a bloody Massacre" is the act of the "cruel Tyrant" Edward. Bishop Stapleton's death is "inhumane and barbarous" at the hands of the "enraged multitude; who neither respecting the Gravity of his Years, or the Dignity of his Profession, strike off his Head, without either Arraignment, Tryal, or Condemnation." Old Spencer is likewise treated "not with pity, which befits a Prisoner, but with insulting joy, and base derision."

The above passages indicate, among other things, that the author holds strong views on the subject of cruelty and by extension suggest the difficulties she may have encountered in dealing with this aspect of her heroine's character. The historical sources had more or less established the major events of the story. Even Marlowe, who probably gives Isabel the most favorable treatment accorded by any male writer, shows her at the end to be a hypocritical and cruel woman. Lady Falkland could appropriate hypocrisy and turn it into an advantage, as we have seen. But cruelty was too strong a blemish. Silence on the matter was therefore neither possible nor desirable, since it would have left the queen exposed at a most critical point. A justification of cruelty, on the other hand, would have contradicted the author's own principles about proper Christian behavior. Indeed, implied in the author's criticism of cruelty is a notion of justice that combines Christian ethics with a sense of fairness in the exercise of power. According to this notion, revenge in the form of cruelty toward a powerless subject (in this case a fallen adversary) is both unfair and unchristian: "It is assuredly . . . an argument of a Villanous Disposition, and a Devilish Nature, to tyrannize and abuse those wretched ruines which are under the Mercy of the Law, whose Severity is bitter enough without aggravation. . . . In Christian Piety, which is the Day-star that should direct and guide all humane Actions, the heart should be as free from all that's cruel, as being too remiss in point of Justice."

In her own life too Lady Falkland abided by these principles. Her biographers tell us that an obligation to treat the offender with kindness was one of her life-long convictions. The spectacle of cruelty itself was a violation of her ideas about comeliness and fitness. Furthermore, in the author's culture cruelty was a characteristically unfeminine vice. The connection between cruelty and femininity is apparent even in the language that the author uses: "The queen's act is far unworthy of the Nobility of her Sex and Virtue." Noticeably, there is no apology for Mortimer's cruelty. The author thus chose what seems like a twist: she maintained the defense of the queen but condemned her cruelty.

Departing once more from her predecessors, Lady Falkland confines Isabel's cruelty mainly to the case of Spencer. With the exception just discussed, she continues to defend the relative innocence of her heroine until the crucial last part—Edward's death. Significantly, the queen is shown to disapprove of the plans to murder the king: "The Queen, whose heart was yet believed innocent of such foul Murther, is, or at least seems, highly discontented." This is made especially poignant and dramatic in the final speeches she exchanges with Mortimer in which she is made to declare: "ne're can my heart consent to kill my Husband." The killing of Edward is presented as being almost entirely Mortimer's doing. When Mortimer suggests the idea, she tries to dissuade him. She finally succumbs to his pressure but on condition that she will be spared the spectacle and "be not made partaker, or privy to the time, the means, the manner."

It is difficult to say how the dramatic situation would have ended had it been put in the final form of a play, but as it is the history lingers on after Edward's death, which is followed by long moralizing on how much he deserved his punishment. Both Edward and Richard II are mentioned as examples of oppressive kings who abused their right to kingship and who died providentially: "But his [Edward's] Doom was registred by that inscrutable Providence of Heaven who, with the self-same Sentence, punish'd both him, and Richard the Second, his great Grandchild, who were guilty of the same Offences." In the folio volume there is a more severe criticism of the subjects who betray the king and of their decision to depose and murder him. But even here the final responsibility for Edward's misfortune is made to fall on him: "had he not indeed been a Traytor to himself, they could not all have wronged him." Clearly, then, the author makes Edward's end a providential piece of work, and while she implicates Mortimer she exonerates the queen. The deaths of Mortimer and Isabel do not fall within the same chronological range, but significantly, only Mortimer is reported to have paid for his actions by death. The queen, "who was guilty but in circumstance," experienced only the pangs of conscience.

When we compare *The History of Edward II* (1627) with *Mariam* (written c. 1604, published 1613), we notice that the later work evinces an assertiveness that seems to be lacking in the earlier one. "The Author's Preface to the Reader," dated and prefixed to the folio volume of *Edward II*, provides the most direct evidence of Lady Falkland's ability to assert herself as a writer. The latter part of this preface is worth quoting:

> I have not herein followed the dull Character of our Historians, nor amplified more than they infer, by Circumstance. I strive to please the Truth, not Time; nor fear I Censure, since at the worst, 'twas one Month mis-spended; which cannot promise ought in right Perfection.

> If so you hap to view it, tax not my Errours; I my self confess them.

What is interesting in this preface is that there is no apology for the author's sex or, more important, for the subject taken up. On the contrary, there is a boldness, not unlike that we find in her address to the reader in the translation of *The Reply of the . . . Cardinall of Perron*, published three years later. For the purpose of comparison I shall quote parts of this address:

> Reader Thou shalt heere receive a Translation wel intended. . . . I desire to have noe more guest at of me, but that I am a Catholique, and a Woman: the first serves for mine honor, and the second, for my excuse, since if the worke be but meanely done, it is noe wonder, for my Sexe can raise noe great expectation of anie thing that shall come from me: yet were it a great follie in me, if I would expose to the view of the world, a worke of this kinde, except I judged it, to want nothing fitt, for a Translation. Therefore I will confesse, I thinke it well done, and so had I confest sufficientlie in printing it.

A boldness and a self-confidence characterize both addresses to the reader. In the address of *The Reply* there is of course the conventional apology for the author's sex. But such an apology is shown to be worn out, for in the next sentence the author turns around and repudiates the excuse. She confidently asserts that she finds the work very well done and that, woman or not, she would not have published it unless she thought it met her standards of publishable quality. In both addresses the reader's attention is diverted from the controversial subject itself—Catholicism in the one and criticism of absolute rule coupled with justification of adultery in the other—to the quality of the work. The focus is shifted to perfectability, the execution of the ideas. Most important, in both addresses the author presents her task as telling the "Truth" or "informing [the reader] aright." This is an appropriation of the notion of absolute truth, the one Truth that everyone has the right, indeed the obligation, to tell. This notion, which is found in much religious writing of the period and which Cary probably acquired from her long experience with religious materials, becomes in fact a very effective strategy, which allows the author to tell the story from her perspective. In *Mariam* she had expressed several traditional notions of womanhood. Her heroine, idealized according to the standards of sixteenth-century culture, had to suffer patiently under a tyrannical husband and remain free from moral blemish: Mariam was not allowed to find recourse in adultery. In *Edward II* Lady Falkland still voices traditional notions of female conduct, but here these notions are deployed as writing strategies. As I have argued, this becomes especially apparent when it is viewed in conjunction with the author's appropriation of structural elements, such as space and time. If indeed the author had an audience in mind, she could not have afforded to alienate her readers. Expressing the ideas was as important as gaining acceptance of them.

The tone of voice in *Edward II* also marks a change from that in *Mariam*. This is particularly apparent in the narrative portions of the history, where Lady Falkland sounds what we today would call argumentative and moralizing. Here is an example:

But what could be expected, when to satisfie his own unjust Passions, he had consented to the Oppressions of his Subjects, tyranniz'd over the Nobility, abus'd his Wedlock, and lost all fatherly care of the Kingdom, and that Issue that was to succeed him. Certainly it is no less honourable than proper, for the Majesty and Greatness of a King, to have that same free and full use of his Affection and Favour, that each particular Man hath in his oeconomic government; yet as his Calling is the greatest, such should be his care, to square them always out by those Sacred Rules of Equity and Justice.

Passages of this sort are not rare. In *Mariam* Lady Falkland had used didactic lines for the chorus, which served to express conventional wisdom on wifely conduct. But in *Edward II* this didacticism develops into a sophisticated argumentative technique. In the later work the appropriation of ideas and events seems to be a rhetorical strategy to gain her audience's acceptance rather than an attempt to refrain from offending the male reader. Furthermore, the moralizing is frequently expressed in religous terms. This I have already partly shown in my discussion of Lady Falkland's attitude toward cruelty. I shall here provide one more instance, which concerns the author's interpretation of Spencer's failure to prevent the escape of the queen and her party: "But when the glorious power of Heaven is pleased to punish Man for his transgression, he takes away the sense and proper power by which he should foresee and stop his danger."

Given the events that intervened between the composition of her two dramas, it would be fair to say that this change in tone is at least partly the result of Lady Falkland's long and active experience as a recusant. This experience, which included the writing of saints' lives and the translating of Du Perron's *Reply*, apparently helped her to become more assertive. The translation of *The Reply* in particular was an exercise not only in theological argument but also in the style of polemics, as that work is a long and vigorous defense of Catholicism against Protestant charges. Thus religious dissidence seems to have been a liberating catalyst for Viscountess Falkland as it was for many other Renaissance women. Anne Askew, Elizabeth Cary, Mary Ward, and the women who joined the sects differed in their religious allegiances but shared at least one characteristic: an independent, critical spirit. Criticism of the officially sanctioned dogma, whatever that might be, could and often did encourage independent thinking and insubordination.

Margaret W. Ferguson (essay date 1991)

SOURCE: "Running On with Almost Public Voice: The Case of 'E.C.'," in *Traditions and the Talents of Women*, edited by Florence Howe, University of Illinois Press, 1991, pp. 37-67.

[*An American educator and critic, Ferguson has written and co-written a number of studies of Renaissance literature, including* Trials of Desire: Renaissance Defenses of Poetry *(1983) and* Rewriting the Renaissance: The Discourses of Sexual Difference in Early Modern Europe *(1986). In the following essay, Ferguson assesses "the feminist political significance" of* The Tragedie of Mariam *and explores the work's "extremely ambivalent ideological statement about women as male 'property.'"*]

She was the only daughter of a rich lawyer; she was precociously bright but not beautiful; she was married at fifteen to an aristocrat who wanted an heiress's dowry. He was Protestant, as were her parents; she converted secretly to Catholicism in the early years of what proved a stormy marriage. Most of what we know about this female contemporary of Shakespeare (she was born around 1585 and died in 1639) comes from a biography written (anonymously) by one of her daughters who became a Catholic nun in France. This daughter does not, however, mention the single fact about her mother that might be of greatest interest to modern feminist critics and historians—namely, that this woman was evidently the first of her sex in England to write an original, published play. Her name was Elizabeth Cary and her play was entitled *The Tragedie of Mariam, Faire Queene of Jewry*. It was printed in London in 1613. Mary Sidney, countess of Pembroke, had translated Robert Garnier's *Marc Antoine* in 1592, and Cary's play is clearly indebted to that aristocratic experiment in Senecan closet drama. But Cary's interest in the drama and in women's relation to it goes far beyond that of any female English writer we know before Aphra Behn. According to her daughter [who wrote *The Lady Falkland: Her Life,* 1861] Cary "loved plays extremely" and for a time at least managed to go occasionally to the London theater. Her authorship of *Mariam*, along with an early play now lost and a later one on the history of Edward II, makes her the first woman in England to attempt substantial original work in a genre socially coded as off-bounds to women, authors and actresses alike.

An excerpt from Cary's introduction to her translation of *The Reply* (1630)

Reader Thou shalt heere receive a Translation wel intended. . . . I desire to have noe more guest at of me, but that I am a Catholique, and a Woman: the first serves for mine honor, and the second, for my excuse, since if the worke be but meanely done, it is noe wonder, for my Sexe can raise noe great expectation of anie thing that shall come from me: yet were it a great follie in me, if I would expose to the view of the world, a worke of this kinde, except I judged it, to want nothing fitt, for a Translation. Therefore I will confesse, I thinke it well done, and so had I confest sufficientlie in printing it.

Elizabeth Cary, in The Reply of the Most Illustrious Cardinall of Perron, to the Answeare of the Most Excellent King of Great Britaine, *Martin Bogart, 1630.*

Cary's play was never performed on stage. Whether or not it was published with her permission, much less at her active request, is a question I wish I, or anyone, could answer. Having that information would make it considerably easier to accomplish one of my chief aims in this essay: to assess the feminist political significance of this play, both in its own time and in ours. More empirical information about the circumstances of the play's publication would be useful because the question of a woman's right to assume a "public" voice is both central to the drama and unanswered within it. That unanswered question, central not only to this play but also to Renaissance debates about the nature and proper behavior of womankind, underlies the lack of consensus among the play's (few) readers about its ideological statement. *Mariam* seems at times to mount a radical attack on the Renaissance concept of the wife as the property of her husband; but the play also seems—or has seemed to some of its readers, both feminist and nonfeminist—to justify, even to advocate, a highly conservative doctrine of female obedience to male authority. I don't intend to make a case for or against either of these interpretations; I hope, rather, to show how, and to begin to show why, the play's ideological statement is so mixed, so contradictory.

The Tragedie of Mariam tells the story of the marriage between King Herod and his second wife, the royal-blooded Jewish maiden Mariam. Like many other Renaissance dramas about this ill-fated match, *Mariam* is based on a narrative in Josephus's *Jewish Antiquities* (ca. 93 A.D.), which was published in an English translation by Thomas Lodge in 1602. Evidently following Lodge's Josephus quite closely, the author nonetheless revises her source significantly. She compresses, amplifies, and transposes material in order to observe the dramatic unities; and she alters the characterization of the heroine and other female figures, as well as the portrait of the troubled marriage between Mariam and Herod, in ways that are both more extensive and more ideologically charged than critics have noted.

The prefatory Argument [of *Mariam*] describes the events which occur prior to the play's action: "Herod the sonne of Antipater (an Idumean), having crept by the favor of the Romanes, into the Jewish Monarchie, married Mariam the [grand]daughter of Hircanus, the rightfull King and Priest and for her (besides her high blood, being of singular beautie) hee reputiated Doris, his former Wife, by whome hee had Children." The play opens at the moment in Josephus's narrative when Herod has been summoned to Rome by Caesar to answer for his earlier political association with Mark Antony, who had helped him acquire Judea. Having overthrown Antony, Caesar is likely to punish Herod, and indeed a rumor of his execution reaches Jerusalem, bringing joy to many who had suffered under his tyranny and bringing relief mixed with sorrow to his wife. Her ambivalent reactions to the news of Herod's death become even more complex when she learns from Sohemus, the man charged by Herod to guard her during his absence, that orders had been given that she should be killed in the event of Herod's death. Outraged by Sohemus's revelation of her husband's jealous

possessiveness and grieving still for the brother and grandfather Herod had murdered in order to secure his claim to the Judean throne (as Mariam's mother, Alexandra, continually reminds her), Mariam is unable to rejoice when Herod does unexpectedly return from Rome at the beginning of Act 4. She not only fails to show the proper wifely pleasure at seeing him but she also refuses to sleep with him. His sister Salome, who hates being placed in a subordinate position both by Mariam and by the Jewish marriage laws which prevent women from suing for divorce, schemes to get rid of her husband, Constabarus, and Mariam too. Fanning Herod's anger at his unresponsive wife by "proving" that Mariam is engaging in adultery with Sohemus and is at the same time plotting to poison Herod, Salome convinces the still-infatuated king to order Mariam's death by beheading. After the execution, which is described by a messenger, Herod spends most of the final act regretting, as Othello does, the loss of his "jewel." Unlike Othello, however, this jealous husband created by a female playwright laments not only his innocent wife's death but, specifically, the loss of her too lately valued powers of speech.

According to its first printer, *The Tragedie of Mariam* was written by a "learned, vertuous, and truly noble Ladie, E. C." The scholarly detective work done by A. C. Dunstan for the 1914 Malone Society reprint of the play (there was only one edition) persuasively identified E. C. as that Elizabeth Cary whose father was a wealthy lawyer named Lawrence Tanfield and whose husband, Sir Henry Cary, became Viscount Falkland in 1620. According to the biography of Cary by her daughter, Sir Henry married his wife (in 1602), "only for [her] being an heir, for he had no acquaintance with her (she scarce having spoken to him), and she was nothing handsome." The same text traces Elizabeth's gradual conversion to Catholicism and its drastic consequences on her status as a social and economic subject. The biography is a crucial but problematic document in my case; a rhetorically complex instance of didactic religious discourse (the "exemplary Catholic life"), the biography, like Cary's play, raises questions by its very mode of material existence about the effects of gender as well as class on the social construction Michel Foucault has called "the author function." The text of the *Life,* according to its nineteenth-century Catholic editor, was "corrected" by the unnamed female author's brother; his name is given to us (Patrick Cary) and he is said to have "erased" from his sister's biography of his mother "several passages which he considered too feminine."

This enigmatic mark of censorship is one of many reasons why we need to approach both Cary's play and the *Life* as parts of a larger social text that can be only very partially reconstructed—and interpreted—by the modern reader. The traces of the social text which impinge most insistently on Cary's writing, and her daughter's, pertain to the set of prescriptive discourses and legal, economic, and behavioral practices surrounding the concept of female chastity and epitomized in the famous Renaissance formula that wives should be "chaste, silent, and obedient." This triple prescription, the core of a set of theories richly elaborated, and also variously challenged, in texts ranging from domestic conduct books and educational treatises to sermons and works of (so-called) imaginative literature, might be called an ideological topos. The topos that Cary's play at once summons into formal being and reacts against manifests itself in Renaissance texts both as abstract opinions about women's proper behavior and as "protonarrative" material fashioned into ballads ("The Cucking of a Scold," for instance), prose fictions like Deloney's *The Pleasant and Sweet History of Patient Grissell,* and numerous plays ranging from Shakespeare's *The Taming of the Shrew* and *Othello* to the anonymous *Lingua; or, The Combat of the Tongue and the Five Senses for Superiority* (1607), in which Lingua, dressed as a woman, sows deceit until she is imprisoned in the house of Gustus (Taste), where "thirty tall watchmen prevent her from wagging abroad."

The "chaste, silent, and obedient" topos also informs the English common law doctrine of the *feme couvert* as elaborated, for instance, in a handbook entitled *The Womans Lawyer* [1632]: "Women have no voyse in Parliament, they make no lawes, they consent to none, they abrogate none. All of them are understood either married or to be married." The normative woman thus constructed in legal discourse was also the object of Juan Luis Vives's influential educational program for young women. In his *De Institutione Feminae Christianae,* written in 1523 for Mary Tudor and printed eight times in English translation before 1600 as *The Instruction of a Christian Woman,* Vives invokes the authority of Saint Paul to support the view that "it neither becometh a woman to rule a school, nor to live amongst men or speak abroad, and shake off her demureness and honesty, either all together, or else a great part; which if she be good, it were better to be at home within and unknown to other folks, and in company to hold her tongue demurely, and let few see her, and none at all hear her. The Apostle Paul . . . saith: Let your women hold their tongues in congregations. For they be not allowed to speak but to be subject as the law bideth." As this passage suggests, Vives is more concerned with a woman's conduct than with her education; "the notion that a woman's chastity is constantly endangered," as Gloria Kaufman observes [in "Juan Luis Vives on the Education of Women," 1978], "occupies most of Vives's attention and delimits his view of the formal education girls should receive."

It seems both important and difficult to analyze this ideological topos of gender, which constitutes "woman," with particular reference to the property of chastity, as a class or group opposed to "man," in relation to the marxist conception of opposing social classes. The difficulty derives partly from the fact that this topos serves the interests of different classes and groups in the early modern period—particularly the aristocracy, the gentry, and the urban middle classes—in rather different ways and by means of a differential social positioning of men and women within each class. Moreover, the ideological topos works in still different ways when cross-class marriages are at issue. The economic and ideological value of female chastity varies accordingly, with the result that

certain logical fissures open in the very concept of chastity. These fissures may have been particularly visible to those who, like Cary, experienced a change in their social status.

The Tragedie of Mariam subjects the concept of female chastity to severe scrutiny and goes a long way toward unraveling the logic which binds "chastity" to "silence" and "obedience." That unraveling owes much to the ambiguity of Cary's class position, an ambiguity intensified in her case, as in many women's, by the institution of marriage. The only daughter of a lawyer who rose in social status to become Chief Baron of the Exchequer and his wife, Elizabeth Symondes, evidently a member of the lower gentry, Cary was married to a nobleman who, like many of his kind, needed funds to pay his debts and maintain his family's estate. Marriage in the Elizabethan and Stuart periods was generally a prime avenue for the interpenetration (if not the harmonious blending) of what we may loosely call "aristocratic" and "bourgeois" economic interests and values. Cary's marriage was a paradigmatic instance of such interpenetration, illustrating it, indeed, in complex double measure because Cary's mother had apparently come down the social ladder by marrying Tanfield. Elizabeth herself, following the more common social pattern for women, rose through her marriage to Sir Henry. The son of the Master of the Royal Jewel House, Sir Henry was, according to Kenneth Murdock [in *The Sun at Noon,* 1939], "a 'compleat courtier' of the new type soon to flourish under James I and Charles I. Such men observed the external forms of the old chivalric supporters of the throne, but their motives smacked of the increasingly capitalistic atmosphere of the time, and service at court was for them as much a profit-making enterprise as a duty imposed by family or tradition."

The marriage between Elizabeth and Henry brought increased social prestige to her father and a valuable dowry—as well as the prospect of a large future inheritance—to her husband. Rightly anticipating, however, that his son-in-law would lack bourgeois virtues of self-restraint (Sir Henry was constantly in financial straits, and part of his wife's dowry may have been spent on ransoming him home from the Netherlands, where he had been taken prisoner early in the marriage), Lawrence Tanfield supplemented the dowry payment by settling a jointure on his daughter as an independent provision for her and her children. Such jointures, usually settled on a bride by the groom's father to provide income in the event of the husband's death, occasionally worked to give not only widows but wives some control of property, even though the common-law doctrine of coverture forbade it. When, however, Elizabeth Cary sought to exercise control over her jointure later in her marriage—ironically, by mortgaging it to help her husband, who needed funds to take up the post of Lord Deputy of Ireland in 1622—her father was evidently outraged: he disinherited her. His decision, which dramatizes the extent to which daughters were tokens in what Eve Kosofsky Sedgwick has called "homosocial" exchanges between men, may have been reinforced by the fact that he learned of Elizabeth's secret conversion to Catholicism at about this time. She had evidently been brooding about that conversion since the early years of her marriage; her daughter writes that "when she was about twenty, through reading, she grew into much doubt of her religion." At about the same time, according to the *Life,* she "writ many things for her private recreation, on several subjects and occasions, all in verse." A "Life of Tamberlaine" (now lost) is mentioned as the best of these literary endeavors; *Mariam,* however, is not mentioned at all.

When Cary wrote *Mariam* (sometime between 1603 and 1612, during the early years of her marriage), she chose a plot in which the husband is of a different religion and a somewhat lower birth than the wife. Cary, however, stresses much more than Josephus does the discrepancy between the husband's bloodline and the wife's. Mariam's mother indignantly insists, for instance, that Herod "did not raise" her sons' status by marrying Mariam because "they were not low, / But borne to wear the Crowne in his despight" (1.2.154-55). And Mariam taunts Salome with her "baser" birth, prompting her to protest, "Still twit you me with nothing but my birth" (1.3.241, 48). Cary's choice of plot, especially when seen in conjunction with these and other changes she makes in Josephus's narrative to emphasize Mariam's queenly status and also her possible political ambitions (Cary's Herod, unlike his prototype, fears that his wife may aspire to usurp his place on the throne [4.4.1494]), suggests that the play represents a gender-marked version of a common Renaissance fantasy, itself a species of what Freud called the "family romance": the dream of being more nobly born than one actually is. The class relation between Mariam and Herod is in fact an inversion of that which really obtained between Cary and her husband, and the inversion provides a historically specific fictional frame for the play's central conflict, which arises from the heroine's refusal to become wholly the "property" of her lord. The frame is historically specific not only because it is arguably shaped by the author's dissatisfaction with her subordinate position in her own marriage but also because Mariam's exceptionally noble birth, which is pointedly described in Cary's prefatory Argument as bringing Herod *"in his wives right* the best title" to the Judean throne (my emphasis), obliquely allies Mariam with those royal women of recent English history—Elizabeth and Mary Tudor and Mary, queen of Scots—who were political figures in their own right and who were legally exempted from the rule of female "coverture" even if they married.

Cary's play therefore might be said to "rewrite" the class story of her own marriage without, however, directly challenging the fundamental concept of class hierarchy; indeed, she explicitly ratifies that concept by equating Salome's baseness of birth with baseness of character. The rewriting, which also stresses the problem of an interfaith union, allows Cary to explore the dilemmas of an allegorical version of herself, a woman who desires at once to obey and to defy that code of wifely duty which subtended the property and class system of seventeenth-century English society. Although Mariam challenges that system much more ambivalently than Herod's sister

Salome does when she forcefully protests the sexual double standard with regard to divorce, it is worth noting that Salome's insistance on women's right to pursue their desires is not simply condemned by the play but is instead recast, with its "lustful" motives expunged, by Mariam's ultimate insistance on dying rather than breaking an oath she has made not to sleep with her husband.

Before turning to look closely at the play itself, I should comment briefly on the fact that its very existence in the world—its existence as an ambiguously "public" object, printed but not perhaps by the author's will, and written in the oxymoronic and elitist subgenre of Senecan closet drama—points to Cary's problematic relation to dominant ideologies of both class and gender. Noblemen of Cary's era did not, by custom, write for the public, or for money. The custom existed, however, in some tension with one of the prime tenets of humanist ideology—namely, the "nobility" of the classical ideal of literary fame. For noble-women, the custom discouraging publication was even more binding than it was on men; but a classical education, however altered to suit the alleged needs and capacities of the weaker sex, instilled in some women, as it did in some men too, a desire for fame that conflicted with the rules of social decorum. Cary, who according to her daughter learned early to read Latin and Hebrew as well as numerous modern European languages, was clearly vulnerable to the contradictions which pertained to the act of publication throughout this period. An insight into this arena of contradiction is afforded by Sir John Davies, who evidently served as Cary's childhood handwriting instructor and who in 1612 urged her and two other ladies to publish their work. In a poem dedicating his *Muses Sacrifice; or, Divine Meditations* to "The Most Noble, and no lesse deservedly-renowned Ladyes, as well Darlings, as Patronesses, of the Muses; Lucy, Countesse of Bedford; Mary, Countesse-Dowager of Pembroke; and Elizabeth, Lady Cary, (Wife of Sr. Henry Cary)," Davies praises the last named as the creator of a drama set in Palestine and encourages her—or so it initially appears—to show her work to the public and to posterity:

> Cary (of whom Minerva stands in feare,
>   lest she, from her, should get Arts Regencie)
> Of Art so moves the great-all-moving Spheare,
>   that ev'ry Orbe of Science moves thereby.
> Thou mak'st Melpomen proud, and my Heart
>   great
>   of such a Pupill, who, in Buskin fine,
> With Feete of State, dost make thy Muse to mete
>   the Scenes of Syracuse and Palestine.
> Art, Language; yea; abstruse and holy Tongues,
>   thy Wit and Grace acquir'd thy Fame to raise;
> And still to fill thine owne, and others Songs:
>   thine, with thy Parts, and others, with thy
>   praise.
> Such nervy Limbes of Art, and Straines of Wit
>   Times past ne'er knew the weaker Sexe to
>   have;
> And Times to come, will hardly credit it,
>   if thus thou give thy Workes both Birth and
>   Grave.

The problem inherent in the logic of Davies's encomiastic rhetoric is that by praising a member of a class at the expense of that class (the "weaker Sexe") he implicitly places the exceptional woman in the double-bind situation so often discussed by modern feminists: achievement is bought at the price of dissociation from what the culture considers to be one's nature. Moreover, by erasing the fact of prior female achievement even as he urges Cary to publish so that history will not forget *her*, Davies testifies to a problem wryly noted by the seventeenth-century American poet Anne Bradstreet [in "The Prologue"]. Evidence of female achievement, she suggests, may well be simply ignored in an ideological climate that presupposes female inferiority:

> For such despite they cast on Female wits:
> If what I do prove well, it won't advance,
> They'll say it's stoln, or else it was by chance.

Davies further complicates his exhortation to female publication by suggesting that it may involve a derogation of noble status in general and, in particular, a danger to female chastity. "You presse the Presse with little you have made," he chides his "Three Graces," but the phrasing surrounds publication with an aura of unseemly sexual importunity which thickens when Davies goes on, in the next stanza, to personify the Press both as a noble damsel in distress, in need of rescue from the low-born versifiers who have "wrong'd" her, and as a woman already so sullied that she is by implication worthy only of scorn from "great hearts":

> [Y]ou well know the Presse so much is wrong'd,
> by abject Rimers that great Hearts doe scorne
> To have their Measures with such Nombers
> throng'd,
> as are so basely got, conceiv'd, and borne.

The syntax creates a momentary ambiguity about whether "great Hearts" are the object or subject of "scorn" when they approach the press, and the stanza also conjures visions of sexual danger or blood-line contamination. The lines can therefore hardly be read as unequivocally encouraging a noblewoman to "presse the press" with her writing, since in so doing she is implicitly linked either with a fallen woman or with one who has deserted her sex altogether to assume the aggressively masculine sexual role suggested by the verb *press*. The advice to publish is tied to a covert argument for remaining aloof from a scene of illicit sexual traffic: she who submits her creative offspring to the press is likely to be taken for an adulterous mother of bastards. Better to let the poetic children go to the grave unknown to the world than to allow one's noble (and by implication restrained, controlled) "Measures" be "throng'd" by "basely got" Numbers.

Davies's message to his noble female readers is not utterly distant in spirit from that which Sir Edward Denny, Baron of Waltham, sent to Lady Pembroke's niece, Mary Wroth. Outraged because he suspected an unflattering allusion to himself in Wroth's prose romance *Urania*, published in 1621 when the widowed author was in great need of money, Denny wrote her an insulting poem. Unpublished but widely circulated among his friends, it portrayed the female author as a monstrous creature:

> Hermaphradite in show, in deed a monster
>   As by thy works and words all men may
>   conster
> Thy wrathful spite conceived an Idell book
>   Brought forth a foole which like the damme
>   doth look.
>   . . . leave idle books alone
> For wise and worthyer women have written none.

Denny's harsh advice to Lady Mary that she should cease writing for public consumption evidently had an effect: she soon promised to withdraw her book from circulation.

We have no way of knowing whether Davies's ambiguously encouraging verses contributed in any way to the publication of Cary's play in 1613. Indeed, we can't even discover whether it was Cary herself or one of her friends or relatives who made the decision to publish. There is a cryptic remark in the *Life* about some verse by Cary "stolen" from her sister-in-law's bedroom, printed, and afterward by the author's "own procurement called in." Elaine Beilin has speculated [in "Elizabeth Cary and *The Tragedy of Mariam*, 1980] that the "stolen" item may be the prefatory sonnet found in only two known copies of *Mariam*, the sonnet addressed to Cary's "worthy Sister, Mistris Elizabeth Carye" and hence an item which could identify the play's author to the public. If Beilin's hypothesis is right, it is interesting that Cary would have recalled the sonnet but not the play; perhaps she wanted it published but was unwilling to go so far in defying custom—and her husband's strong views on women's proper behavior as "private" beings—as she would have had she publicized her authorship.

The absence of any mention of *Mariam* at all in the *Life* of Cary and her daughter's obvious unwillingness to be known herself as a named author testify to the force of cultural strictures against women's publishing. And ideologies of gender were evidently often reinforced by those of class and religion to maintain the taboo against a privileged woman's "pressing the Press" with her writing. In rare cases such as Cary's, something might be published despite the taboo. But it probably affected the literary work's mode of material existence more often, and more substantially, than modern critics have tended to acknowledge. Recall that Cary's son Patrick "erased" certain passages from his sister's biography of his mother because they were "too feminine." What might Cary herself have "erased" from her play, following her conscious or unconscious judgment or that of other readers during the years when the play was evidently circulating in manuscript? The question can't, of course, be answered, but it's not altogether idle: the problem to which it points is that of censorship—a major theme in Cary's play.

The heroine of Cary's play is torn between the demands of wifely duty, which coincide at least intermittently with her feelings of love for the tyrannical but infatuated Herod, and the demands of her conscience, which are initially defined in terms of family loyalty and voiced through the figure of Mariam's mother, Alexandra. She hates her son-in-law because, to secure his claim to the throne of Judea, Herod had not only married the royal-blooded Mariam but murdered her brother and grandfather. The nature of Mariam's dilemma shifts, however, as the play progresses, partly because her long soliloquies, like Hamlet's, work to dissolve binary oppositions. Also like *Hamlet,* Cary's play gives us characters who mirror certain aspects, and unrealizable potentials, of the central figure. At first glance, Cary's two major foil characters seem to come from a medieval morality play: on the one hand, there is Salome, Herod's wicked sister who works, Vice-like, to plot Mariam's death; on the other, there is Graphina, a slave girl loved by Herod's younger brother, Pheroras. Virtuous, humble, obedient, she seems to embody the ideal of womanhood prescribed in Renaissance conduct books.

The ethical opposition symbolized by these two characters—an opposition that emerges, specifically, as one of different modes of speech—is, however, also shot through with complexities. Salome's structural resemblance to the morality Vice figure is partly occluded when she is made to speak crudely but eloquently against the injustice of Jewish law, which gives (rich) men but not women the right to divorce (1.4); and Graphina—the only character whose name is not found in Josephus's text or in Lodge's translation of it—becomes more opaque the more one studies her brief appearance in Cary's text (2.1). She is strongly associated with the feminine virtue of modest silence, but the dramatic presentation prevents us from conceiving of that virtue as a simple alternative to the "vice" of female speech, either Salome's or Mariam's. Pheroras tells Graphina that he prefers her to the bride Herod had designated for him because that "baby" has an "Infant tongue" which can scarcely distinguish her name "to anothers care" (2.1.562-63). The "silent" Graphina evidently has won her lover's admiration for her powers of speech: "move thy tongue," he says, "For Silence is a signe of discontent" (2.1.588). She obeys. The strange little scene queries the logic of the "chaste, silent, and obedient" topos by suggesting first that womanly "silence" may function just as erotically as speech in a nonmarital relation (the conduct books never consider this possibility) and second that a certain kind of speech signifies the same thing that "silence" does in the discourse of wifely duty—that is, compliance with the man's wishes: Graphina tells her lover only what he wants to hear, when he wants to hear it. She may therefore be said to figure a mode of "safe" speech, *private* speech that neither aims at nor produces offense. Cary's invented name for this character might, on this line of interpretive speculation, be significant: the name evidently plays on the Greek word for writing, *graphesis.*

If the figure of Graphina represents for Cary the possibility of both a nontransgressive mode of discourse (like private writing?) and a mutually satisfying love relation, neither of those possibilities is available to the play's heroine. The first words Mariam speaks, which are also the play's first words, epitomize the problem:

> How oft have I with publike voice run on?
> To censure Rome's last Hero for deceit:
> Because he wept when Pompeis life was gone,
> Yet when he liv'd, hee thought his Name too
>   great.

These lines, which are spoken in soliloquy and initiate a complex parallel between Mariam's situation and that of Julius Caesar, link the theme of female public voice immediately with the idea of transgression ("run on") and the idea of "censure." The question mark after the first line seems at first merely an oddity of seventeenth-century "rhetorical" punctuation. But the question itself, voiced at the play's threshold moment by a female character whose "unbridled speech" eventually plays a major role in her husband's decision to censor her voice definitively, is not by any means simply rhetorical. It is, we might say, complexly rhetorical—for several reasons. To make it the kind of question that obviously requires the affirmative answer "very often," the reader must "run on" over the line's end and its punctuation. The structure of the verse creates for the reader a slight but significant tension between pausing—to respect the seemingly self-contained formal and semantic unit of the first line—and proceeding, according to the dictates of the syntactic logic which retrospectively reveals the first line to be part of a larger unit. The verse thereby works to fashion a counterpoint between formal and semantic strains. We pause on the theme of "running on," we run on to encounter the theme of censure (as "censorship" and "critical judgment" both). The lines work not only to anticipate the drama to come (deploying the strategy of the "pregnant" opening most famously used in *Hamlet*) but also to mark the play, for Cary herself and perhaps for her first "private" readers, with something we might call the woman author's *signature.*

That signature consists not of a name but of a Chinese box set of questions about the logic of the Pauline injunction against female public speech and the cultural rule of chastity that injunction ostensibly supported. Like a lawyer presenting ambiguous fact situations to a judge, in the opening speech Cary invites us to consider whether the play text itself is "covered" by the law: Is *writing* a form of "public voice"? Is a *drama* not necessarily intended for performance on the public stage a legitimate form of female verbal production? Is a *soliloquy*—by theatrical convention, a "private" speech overheard (overread?) by an audience—legitimate? In short, the play opens in a way that seems designed to test, but not overtly to disobey, the rule proscribing "public voice" for women. Here we have a written representation of a female character soliloquizing, as if in private, about a prior event of (ambiguously) culpable public speech—ambiguously culpable because the comparison with Caesar's speech "degenders" Mariam's prior speech act, although the issue of gender, and a potential male audience's response to the speaker's gender, is clearly on the heroine's (and the author's) mind. Mariam goes on to transform the figure of Caesar from an (imperfect) model for a speaker to an authoritative model for an audience or judge. She suddenly apostrophizes the "Roman lord" with an aggressively defensive apology for exhibiting a fault (rash judgment) commonly ascribed to the daughters of Eve but also characteristic of many male rulers, including Julius Caesar:

> But now I doe recant, and Roman Lord
> Excuse too rash a judgment in a woman:
> My sexe pleads pardon, pardon then afford,
> Mistaking is with us, but too too common.
>
> (1.1.5-8)

Mariam's opening lines arguably address a problem that has to do not only with female speech in general but with the play's own mode of material existence—indeed, its *right* to exist in the world. The act of writing, for oneself or for an audience of family and friends, would seem—like the dramatic form of the soliloquy—to occupy a shady territory between private and public verbal production. Because of the ambiguous status of writing, Cary could in one sense have applied Mariam's opening question to herself and answered it with a decorum the fictional character lacks. "How oft have I with publike voice run on?" "Never." But that answer would not have satisfied the culturally constructed censoring power that the play text ascribes chiefly to the figure of the tyrant-husband but also to the chorus and, at certain moments, to the heroine herself, speaking, evidently, for an aspect of the author's own conscience or superego.

According to her daughter, Cary "did always much disapprove the practice of satisfying oneself with their conscience being free from fault, not forbearing all that might have the least show or suspicion of uncomeliness or unfitness; what she thought to be required in this she expressed in this motto (which she caused to be inscribed in her daughter's wedding ring): *Be and seem*." This passage, which attributes to Cary a rule of spiritual and social conduct as fraught with problems as the rules Hamlet formulates for himself, might be paraphrased as follows: never be satisfied that you really are as virtuous as you may seem to yourself—but always be what you seem. The difficulty of putting such a principle into practice is dramatized, in Cary's play, by the fact that the chorus formulates one version of this rule in order to condemn Mariam for following (and articulating) another version of it.

The chorus's speech occurs at a pivotal moment in the plot: at the end of Act 3, just before Herod's first appearance on stage and just after Mariam learns, through her guardian, Sohemus, that Herod is alive. The rumor of his death in Rome had prompted Mariam's opening soliloquy detailing her mixed emotions about him and had also prompted the various intrigues—by Salome, by Mariam's mother, Alexandra, and others—which are described and partly enacted in the first half of the play. Through talking with Sohemus, Mariam has just learned of Herod's secret orders that she should be killed if he dies. Sohemus has both disobeyed those orders and broken his oath to keep silent about them—a double transgression that Salome will subsequently exploit to fulfill her desires to rid herself of her husband, Constabarus, and to bring about Mariam's downfall. In this same scene, Mariam has announced to Sohemus her "solemne vowes" to abandon Herod's bed (3.3.1136). Despite Sohemus's prudential advice to the contrary, she refuses to be reconciled sexually with her husband. Mariam's oath arises from her commitment to an ethic of uniting her "being" with her "seeming": she has told Sohemus that she will not use sexual wiles to disguise her true feelings about Herod, nor will she speak in a way that hides her thoughts: "I scorne my looke should ever man beguile, / Or other speech, then meaning to afford" (3.3.1168-69). It is such words of principle—and the principle that generates such words—that Sohemus laments thus after Mariam has left the stage:

> Poor guiltles Queene! Oh that my wish might
>   place
> A little temper now about thy heart:
> Unbridled speech is Mariam's worst disgrace,
> And will indanger her without desart.
>
> (3.3.1184-87)

His lines anticipate, albeit with more sympathy for Mariam, the chorus's criticism of her in the subsequent speech, which I shall quote in full:

> Tis not enough for one that is a wife
> To keep her spotles from an act of ill:
> But from suspition she should free her life,
> And bare her selfe of power as well as will.
> Tis not so glorious for her to be free,
> As by her proper selfe restrain'd to bee.
> When she hath spatious ground to walke upon,
> Why on the ridge should she desire to goe?
> It is no glory to forbeare alone,
> Those things that may her honour overthrowe.
> But tis thanke-worthy, if she will not take
> All lawfull liberties for honours sake.
>
> That wife her hand against her fame doth reare,
> That more then to her Lord alone will give
> A private word to any second eare,
> And though she may with reputation live.
> Yet though most chast, she doth her glory blot,
> And wounds her honour, though she killes it not.
>
> When to their Husbands they themselves doe
>   bind,
> Doe they not wholy give themselves away?
> Or give they but their body not their mind,
> Reserving that though best, for others pray?
> No sure, their thoughts no more can be their
>   owne,
> And therefore should to none but one be
>   knowne.
>
> Then she usurpes upon anothers right,
> That seekes to be by publike language grac't:
> And though her thoughts reflect with purest
>   light,

Her mind if not peculiar [i.e., "private"] is not
   chast.
For in a wife it is no worse to finde,
   A common body, then a common minde.

And every mind though free from thought of ill,
   That out of glory seekes a worth to show:
When any's eares but one therewith they fill,
   Doth in a sort her purenes overthrow.
Now Mariam had, (but that to this she bent)
Beene free from feare, as well as innocent.

                    (3.3.1219-54)

[As she notes in "Two English Women in the Seventeenth Century: Notes for an Anatomy of Feminine Desire," 1985,] Angeline Goreau finds in this speech testimony to the "social hegemony" of the idea of female modesty in seventeenth-century England. Assuming that the chorus speaks unequivocally for the author's own opinions, Goreau concludes that Cary here ratifies a definition of chastity not only as abstinence from illegitimate sexual activity but also as a virtue that involves divesting oneself of "power as well as will." By thus reinterpreting chastity as passivity, [Goreau, in *The Whole Duty of a Woman: Female Writers in Seventeenth-Century England*, 1985, claims that] Cary "sets up an infinitely expanding architecture of self-restraint, often more far-reaching and effective than any form of external censorship might be."

Goreau is right to stress this feature of the chorus's speech, but she fails to consider the ways in which both the rhetoric of the speech and its larger dramatic context render this extreme prescription of wifely self-censorship problematic. The chorus, indeed, offers contradictory statements about the precise nature of the error Mariam has committed. According to the second stanza, the error involves indulging in, rather than refraining from, something that is characterized as "lawfull" liberty. When the chorus goes on to specify the error as a fault of *speech*, however, its "lawfull" status seems to disappear. By stanza five, the error is the distinctly illegitimate and usually masculine political one of "usurping upon anothers right." There is a corresponding contradiction in the chorus's views of the "virtue" it is advocating. In the third stanza, which stresses the duty of relinquishing desires for speech and fame, the virtue being advocated is quite distinct from the possession of physical chastity; the woman may be "most chast" even if she does grant a "private word" to someone other than her husband. By stanza five, however, the "redefinition" of chastity that Goreau remarks has occurred: "her mind if not peculiar [private] is not chast." Which formulation about chastity are we to take as authoritative?

Interpreting the chorus's speech becomes even more difficult when we try to read it—as Goreau does not—in its dramatic context, as an ethical prescription for this particular heroine. The final lines seem to suggest that Mariam's tragic fate could have been averted had she refrained from speaking her mind to anyone other than her husband. But the play's subsequent development makes this notion absurd: it is precisely because Mariam speaks her mind—not only to others but also, and above all, to her husband—that she loses her life. She articulates in Herod's presence a version of the same principle we have heard her assert to Sohemus: "I cannot frame disguise, nor never taught / My face a looke dissenting from my thought," she says, refusing to smile when Herod bids her to (4.3.1407-8). It is, however, not wholly accurate to say she brings on her death by transgressively speaking her mind. The problem is that she *both* speaks too freely *and* refuses to give her body to Herod—its rightful owner, according to the chorus. She censors the wrong thing: his phallus rather than her tongue.

The problem of her sexual withholding is addressed by the chorus only obliquely, in the form of the (apparently) rhetorical question "When to their Husbands they themselves doe bind, / Doe they not wholy give themselves away?" By the end of its speech, the chorus has evidently suppressed altogether the crucial issue of Mariam's denial of Herod's sexual rights. The strange logic of the speech anticipates that of Herod's later accusation of Mariam: "shee's unchaste, / Her mouth will ope to ev'ry strangers eare" (4.7.1704-5). The equation of physical unchastity with verbal license, expressed through the provocative image of the woman's mouth opening to a man's ear, alludes, perhaps, to anti-Catholic propaganda against Jesuit priests as Satanic corrupters of women and of the institution of confession, where male "strangers" received women's secrets. The image of a female mouth promiscuously opening to a male ear rewrites Mariam's fault as one of double excess or "openness," whereas what the play actually shows is that Mariam's verbal openness is a sign of sexual closure. Her behavior entails a "property" crime in certain ways more threatening than adultery is to the ideological conception of marriage because it takes to a logical extreme, and deploys against the husband, the concept of female chastity.

Neither the chorus nor any other character in the drama can clearly articulate this central problem in Mariam's behavior. The chorus concludes by asserting that Mariam would have been "free from feare, as well as innocent," if only she had been willing to forbear filling "any's ears but one" with her words. The pronoun *one* evidently refers here, as it does in the earlier phrase "none but one," to the husband. If, however, we grant that the play as a whole makes it extremely hard to read the chorus's question about whether women should give themselves "wholly" away in marriage as requiring a simple affirmative answer, then it becomes necessary to ask . . . whether the term *one* might alternatively refer to the wife herself. Since Mariam is in danger because she speaks to her husband—and against his sexual will and his property rights—perhaps Cary's point, if not the chorus's, is that if a wife has such thoughts she "would be wiser to keep them to herself, precisely because in marriage they are no longer her own" [Catherine Belsey, *The Subject of Tragedy: Identity and Difference in Renaissance Drama*, 1985]. But in Mariam's case, such silence or self-censoring would not have any practical efficacy unless it were accompanied by sexual surrender and its psychic corollary: the split between being and seeming which Mariam terms "hypocrisy." The chorus's ethical precepts begin to look at best incoherent, at worst cynical, a dark twisting of the "be and seem" motto into a prescription for wives to seem as others think they should be. Belsey suggests, indeed, that with this speech "the transparency of the text falters as it confronts its own theorization of its challenge to marital absolutism. Although I'm less sure than she is that the text is ever "transparent," I agree that there is a peculiar opacity in the chorus's speech against a wife's right to use "publike language."

That opacity, I think, has something to do with the fact that the chorus's speech is the moment in the drama where Cary most directly interrogates her play's own right to exist. However we construe the injunction that wives should reveal their thoughts to "none but one," it is clear that the chorus draws around the wife a circle of privacy so small that she would err by *circulating* a manuscript, much less publishing it. Had Cary obeyed the rule of privacy set forth by her chorus, she might possibly have written a play, but we would not be reading it. Even the act of writing, which generally requires some will and ambition, comes under implicit attack in the chorus's portrait of the ideal wife who "bare[s] herself of power as well as will" and who is urged to relinquish in particular all desire for "glory." The chorus's speech exposes the logical implications of the legal doctrine of coverture, which held that "the very being . . . of the woman is suspended during the marriage."

The *Life* of Cary by her daughter provides three interesting and ideologically complex glosses on the chorus's speech. "He was very absolute," the *Life* says of Sir Henry, "and though she [Elizabeth Cary] had a strong will, she had learned to make it obey his. The desire to please him had power to make her do that, that others could have scarce believed possible for her; as taking care of the house in all things (to which she could have no inclination but what his will gave her)." The *Life* also tells us that Cary often resorted to sleep to cure depression; she could sleep "when she would," which seems a near analogue for the paradoxical ideal of willed willessness projected by the chorus's speech. And finally the *Life* recounts that Cary gave to her eldest daughter a principle of behavior that contains a significant exception to the absolutist doctrine of wifely obedience: "Wheresoever reason and conscience would permit her, she should prefer the will of another before her own."

Cary's exception has analogues in numerous Protestant works that challenged the doctrine of absolutist royal sovereignty by positing for the individual (male) subject a limited right of passive disobedience to the prince or magistrate on grounds of Christian conscience. Moreover, Cary's statement (as reported by her Catholic daughter) corresponds with certain statements by both radical Protestant and Catholic theorists on the wife's right to disobey her husband—the sovereign's domestic representative and analogue in the little body politic of the family— if his commands should conflict with God's. In ["Recusant Women," 1985], Marie Bowlands mentions the case of Margaret Clitherow, who "asked her confessor whether she might receive priests and serve God without her husband's consent. She was told that the less he knew the better, and that nothing could override her duty to serve God." Bowlands also cites a passage from the Catholic *Treatise on Christian Renunciation* which advised women that "your husbands over your soul have no authority and over your bodies but limited power."

During this turbulent era of British history, such formulations appear with enough frequency to justify us in saying they comprise an ideological topos of "minority dissent." Articulated by Catholic and Protestant writers, male and female, such statements clearly drive a wedge into the apparently hegemonic social rule linking female chastity with silence and obedience. The dissenting female voice, historical or fictional, invokes religious principles to redefine chastity in a way that dissociates it from obedience to (certain) figures of male authority. Consider, for instance, the speech of Milton's "Lady" to her would-be king and seducer, Comus: "Thou canst not touch the freedom of my mind / With all thy charms, although this corporal rind / Thou hast immanacl'd, while Heav'n sees good" (*A Maske* [1637], ll. 663-65); or consider the speech of a beleaguered heroine in an anonymous play of 1620: "Tho my body be confin'd his prisoner, / Yet my mind is free" (*Swetnam the Woman Hater Arraigned by Woman*, 2.1.97-98).

The language Mariam uses to justify her course of action—resistance to the sexual demands and other wishes of a husband who is also her king—clearly belongs to this religious tradition of minority dissent: "They can but my life destroy, / My soule is free from adversaries power" (4.8.1843-44), she says after Herod has falsely accused her of adultery and, spurred on by Salome, proclaimed his intention to execute her. Although the chorus continues to argue that Mariam should have submitted to Herod's authority—thereby paying her marital "debt" and winning "long famous life" (4.8.1939)—Elaine Beilin is surely right to argue that the play's final act reconceives (and simplifies) the conflict between the chorus's perspective on wifely duty and Mariam's by presenting the heroine's death as an allegorical version of Christ's crucifixion. Josephus had shown Mariam meeting her death with noble fortitude, but Cary adds to her source numerous details that give Mariam a specifically Christological heroism. The messenger who describes her death to Herod in Act 5 apostrophizes her as "your heavenly self" and goes on to compare her to a phoenix, a traditional symbol of Christ. A parallel between Mariam and Christ is also implied by the suicide of the butler who had been suborned by Salome to accuse Mariam of seeking to poison Herod. Cary's butler, like Judas, hangs himself from a tree in remorse for his betrayal; in Josephus, there is no mention of the butler's death.

Cary further revises her source by specifying the mode of Mariam's death. Josephus simply says that Herod ordered her executed, whereas Cary places considerable emphasis on the "fact" that she is beheaded. This detail, unremarked by Cary's critics so far as I know, seems an overdetermined allusion—to Christ's harbinger, John the Baptist, beheaded by Salome; to a recent queen of Scotland, Mary, whose son ruled England when Cary wrote her play and who was in the eyes of many English Catholics a victim of Protestant tyranny; and also, perhaps, to Anne Boleyn, killed by a royal husband who had broken with the Catholic church to divorce his first wife and who was explicitly likened to the tyrant Herod by some of his disapproving subjects. Infused with rich but warily coded theological meanings, Cary's play surrounds Mariam's death with an aura of mysterious sanctification altogether absent from Josephus's narrative.

There is, however, a price for such sanctification, with its implicit justification of the ethical path Cary herself would eventually follow: the path that led her to defy her husband's authority on the grounds of conscience. In the play's final act, Mariam is not only absent from the stage but also represented, through the messenger's account of her last moments, as a woman who has somehow learned to bridle her tongue. On the way to her execution, she is cruelly taunted by her mother, who, after having urged Mariam throughout the play to despise Herod, now suddenly—evidently to save her own skin—condemns Mariam for "wronging" Herod's princely authority (5.1.1986). Enraged at the report of Alexandra's behavior, Herod asks, "What answere did her princely daughter make?" The messenger replies, "She made no answere" (5.1.1992); and he goes on to stress Mariam's new virtue of silence by remarking that she died "as if . . . she were content" after "she some silent prayer had sed" (2026-27). The wickedness associated with the female tongue and with women in general, according to Constabarus's misogynist tirade against the sex to which Salome belongs (4.6.1578-1619), is here symbolically transferred from Mariam to her mother, who takes Mariam's place as the object of Herod's censoring wrath: "Why stopt you not her mouth? where had she words / to darke that, that Heaven made so brighte?" (5.1.1979-80), Herod asks the messenger; and the reader remembers that Herod has just exercised his power to stop Mariam's mouth. Once he has done so, in what seems to me the play's most complex and ambivalent irony, he suddenly starts to value Mariam's words with passionate desire: "But what sweet tune did this faire dying Swan / Afford thine eare: tell all, omit no letter" (5.1.2008-9), he says; and again, in an exchange that seems designed to effect a kind of wish-fulfilling revenge on the tyrannical censorious husband, he exclaims: "Oh say, what said she more? each word she sed / Shall be the food whereon my heart is fed" (2013-14). To which the messenger replies, reporting Mariam's words, "Tell thou my Lord thou saw'st me loose my breath." "Oh that I could that sentence now controule," Herod responds, ostensibly referring to his own "sentence" of death. His remark might also, however, refer to Mariam's utterance: by killing her, he has after all lost the power to control her speech. His "word," as he says later, made her "bleed," but it cannot bring her back to life.

It seems significant that Cary only imagines Herod coming to value Mariam's voice at the moment when the disputed property of her body is absent both from the stage and from the narrative "present": "Her body is di-

vided from her head," the Nuntio asserts, and the graphic image of the dead and sundered woman (which occurs nowhere in Josephus's text) highlights the price Mariam has paid for her freedom of conscience. Through its characterization of Mariam, the play offers two different models, neither very satisfactory from a modern feminist perspective, for a woman's ability to exercise her will: according to both models, which might be called the domestic and the religious respectively, the will is exercised with the ultimate aim of losing it or, rather, of adopting, as an object of desire, the effacement of personal desire. Cary's heroine, unable to choose the first model by subordinating her will to her husband's, opts instead for an extreme version of the second, a martyr-like death: "Now earth farewell, though I be yet but young, / Yet I, me thinks, have knowne thee too too long" (4.8.1902-3). In so choosing, Mariam, like Richard Wilbur's nuns "keeping their difficult balance," finds an uneasy compromise solution to the conflicting behavioral models provided by Salome on the one hand and Graphina on the other: by the former's example of aggressive rebellion against patriarchal rules and the latter's example of passive subservience to a man (rewarded by his romantic adoration).

How are we to assess Mariam's compromise solution from a modern feminist perspective informed by an awareness of the social and imaginative options open to a woman like Elizabeth Cary? Although Cary's representation of Mariam, like Cary's daughter's representation of her mother, shows us women *behaving* in ways that anticipate the "principled disobedience" characteristic of some radical Protestant women during the English civil wars, neither of the Cary texts shows a heroine explicitly justifying independent female behavior. The radicalism of these texts, in so far as we may call it that, occurs chiefly in small details of plot and, in the case of the play, through oblique intertextual allusions, moments of rhetorical tension, and the words of female characters such as Salome, Alexandra, and Herod's first wife, Doris; in other words, what is radical must be inferred or teased out by a reader who assumes that an emphatic "no" may mean a "yes"— a reader, in short, sympathetic with psychoanalytic modes of interpretation and also aware that the censorship so often constitutive of the female author's text may derive not only from what we call the "unconscious" but also from direct social pressures or from that combination of the two known as internalization.

Sympathetic though we may be with the covertly radical dimension of Cary's play and her life story, we nonetheless need to remark that other seventeenth-century women, both historical and fictional, were considerably less oblique than Cary and her daughter in arguing for and/or in demonstrating some form of female independence. One has only to think of the lively and complex heroine of Middleton's and Dekker's *The Roaring Girl* (1611) or the Protestant radical Katherine Chidley; the latter, in her *Justification of the Independent Churches of Christ* (1641), writes: "I pray you tell me what authority the unbeleeving husband hath over the conscience of his beleeving wife. It is true he hath authority over her in bodily and civill respects but not to be a Lord over her conscience." On the spectrum suggested (very incompletely) by such examples, Cary's play appears quite conservative in its statement about women's social being. That conservatism derives from many sources—above all, I think, from the fact that the ideologies of gender, religion, and (privileged) class worked together, in the case of Cary's play, to limit its potential either to reach a broad audience or to make a clear critique of women's status as a male property category.

Consider again the play's contradictory mode of existence as a published Senecan closet drama. Intriguing as it is that this female-authored play was published at all—and evidently with Cary's acquiescence, if not with her active approval—the fact remains that it had a limited and mainly elite readership. Like the Judith Shakespeare imagined by Virginia Woolf, Cary was barred from significant participation in the world of the London stage. Had she been able to write for the public theater, instead of being simply an occasional member of an audience in the city and a closet dramatist at home, her play itself might have been differently constructed; it would surely have reached a wider audience in her own day and later. As the case of Shakespeare amply testifies, access to the commercial stage bears no necessary relation to the articulation of progressive political positions. Such access, however, which opens a play to scrutiny from members of different classes, did frequently serve in Renaissance England as an enabling condition for the development of certain politically radical interpretations of drama. And such interpretations may or may not have been intended by an individual author.

Cary's gender alone would have served to keep her away from the London stage, but her gender and class aspirations and religious beliefs all worked together to create *Mariam's* extremely ambivalent ideological statement about women as male "property." That statement concludes with, though it's not fully constituted by, Mariam choosing (under great duress) to turn her critical rebellious energies inward to self-reproach and upward toward a transcendental religious ideal of chaste female martyrdom. Cary thus rejects the option of turning Mariam's energies outward to some form of collective action by allying her heroine's rebellion against Herod with the "base-born" Salome's critique of the sexual double standard in divorce laws. The vilifying of Salome is of course dictated—but only in part—by generic conventions and by the historical plot Cary inherited; I would argue, however, that Cary's own class position and biases contribute substantially to what she does with Salome. Even more than Herod, Salome is implicated in Cary's use of her drama to rewrite the social story of her marriage. For Salome stands in relation to Mariam as Cary stood in relation to her own husband and mother-in-law; the latter's dislike of Elizabeth, vividly recorded in the *Life*, may well have entailed open or veiled insults about base birth like those which Mariam directs at her sister-in-law. If, as I am suggesting, a desire to ennoble herself and take revenge on the family into which she had been married against her will underlies Cary's identification with the "pureblooded" Mariam, that desire contributes to the play's occlusion of the similarities between Mariam's and Salome's situations as rebel-

lious wives. And the separation between Mariam and Salome, drawn in terms of their social status, contributes in turn to the sharp distinction the play draws between the (religiously valuable) idea of female freedom of conscience and Salome's advocacy of female freedom to pursue one's sexual desires. By vilifying Salome's character and opinions as "base," Cary ultimately ratifies the ideological "truth" proclaimed by the authoritative voices of the Counter-Reformation church (and most Protestant sects as well), by the voices of men in the English middle and upper classes, and by the voices of almost everyone who participated in the Renaissance debates on the nature of womankind. That "truth" is that, whatever one may think about the qualities of a woman's mind or soul, her body is base and in need of governance.

The limits of Cary's choices—and her heroine's—are complex products of a specific set of historical circumstances *and* of an individual psyche capable, to some degree, of interrogating, and even defying, the "customs" rooted in the material and ideological aspects of gender, religion, and class. The complexes of social facts to which those three abstract terms refer have changed enormously since the seventeenth century. Nonetheless, the heuristic interest of Cary's case for late-twentieth-century feminists may well lie in the challenge it offers for thinking about how modern ideologies of gender, radical or conservative, continue to be formed—and deformed—by forces of class and religion that are partly, but not wholly, within our powers to understand and to alter.

FURTHER READING

Biography

Fullerton, Georgianna Charlotte. *Life of Elizabeth, Lady Falkland 1585-1639*. London: Burns and Oates, 1883.
 Extensive biography of Cary that reprints several of her letters and other pertinent documents.

Murdock, Kenneth. *The Sun at Noon: Three Biographical Sketches*. New York: Macmillan, 1939, 327 p.
 The most complete and widely read twentieth-century portrayal of Elizabeth Cary. The book also contains biographies of Lucius Cary and John Wilmot.

Simpson, Richard, ed. *The Lady Falkland, Her Life from a ms. in the Imperial Archives at Lisle*. London: Catholic Publishing and Bookselling Co., 1861.
 The first full-length study of Elizabeth Cary's life, probably written from 1643 to 1649 by one of her daughters.

Criticism

Beilin, Elaine V. "The Making of a Female Hero: Joanna Lumley and Elizabeth Cary." In *Redeeming Eve: Women Writers in the English Renaissance*, pp. 151-176. Princeton: Princeton University Press, 1987.

Focuses on autobiographical elements of Cary's *The Tragedie of Mariam*, drawing extensively on the biography *The Lady Falkland, Her Life*.

Brashear, Lucy. "A Case for the Influence of Lady Cary's *Tragedy of Mariam* on Shakespeare's *Othello*." 26 (1976): 31.

Short argument contending that Cary influenced Shakespeare's *Othello*.

Cary, Elizabeth. *The Tragedy of Mariam, the Fair Queen of Jewry*. Edited by Barry Weller and Margaret W. Ferguson. Berkeley: University of California Press, 1994, 328 p.

Standard modern edition of Cary's *Tragedy*, including a thorough critical introduction, the full text of the play, a reprint of *The Lady Falkland, Her Life*, and an extensive bibliography.

Ferguson, Margaret W. "A Room Not Their Own." In *The Comparative Perspective on Literature: Approaches to Theory and Practice*, pp. 93-116. Edited by Clayton Koelb and Susan Noakes. Ithaca: Cornell University Press, 1988.

Uses Christine de Pizan's *Livre de la cité des dames* and Elizabeth Cary's *The Tragedie of Mariam* to illustrate that Renaissance literature written by women generally tries to justify women's self-expression without problematizing prevailing views of female chastity.

Gutierrez, Nancy A. "Valuing *Mariam*: Genre Study and Feminist Analysis." *Tulsa Studies in Women's Literature* 10, No. 2 (Fall 1991): 233-51.

Explores the role of feminist literary criticism in the evaluation and interpretation of *Mariam*, concluding that the play is "a highly sophisticated literary exercise demonstrating Cary's participation in contemporary literary dialogue as well as her interest in issues of sexual politics."

Raber, Karen L. "Gender and the Political Subject in *The Tragedy of Mariam*." *Studies in English Literature, 1500-1900* 35, No. 2 (Spring 1995): 321-343.

Insists that, in *Mariam*, Cary criticizes political and domestic patriarchy, which thwarts women's participation in public discourse.

Travitsky, Betty S. "The *Femme Covert* in Elizabeth Cary's *Mariam*." In *Ambiguous Realities: Women in the Middle Ages and Renaissance*, pp. 184-96. Edited by Carole Levin and Jeanie Watson. Detroit: Wayne State University Press, 1987.

Argues that Cary's *Mariam* comments on the subordination of women in Renaissance-era marriages.

Margaret Cavendish

1623-1673

English poet, playwright, biographer, and essayist.

INTRODUCTION

One of the pioneering women writers in the seventeenth-century, Margaret Cavendish occupies an important position in the female literary tradition. Chiefly known for her contribution to the genre of biographical writing in *A True Relation of the Birth, Breeding, and Life of Margaret Cavendish, Duchess of Newcastle* (1656) and *The Life of the Thrice Noble, High and Puissant Prince William Cavendishe, Duke, Marquess, and Earl of Newcastle* (1667), Cavendish was also a prolific writer of philosophical essays and an active participant in the scientific speculations of her time. During her lifetime Cavendish published books in a variety of genres ranging from poetry and fiction to philosophical treatises and orations, leaving an impressive oeuvre which continues to attract scholarly attention.

Biographical Information

The youngest child of Thomas Lucas and Elizabeth Leighton, Cavendish was born at St. John's Abbey, Colchester, Essex in 1623. Raised by her widowed mother, she received a traditional education that provided her with the rudimentary accomplishments prescribed for women in the seventeenth-century. In 1643, Cavendish joined the court of Queen Henrietta Maria as a maid of honor and accompanied her into exile in Paris in 1644. In Paris she met William Cavendish, Marquis of Newcastle, whom she married in 1645. The Marquis encouraged Cavendish to further her intellectual development and prompted her interest in the philosophical and scientific debates of the day. Her first two works, *Poems and Fancies* and *Philosophicall Fancies (both 1653)*, are marked by an imaginative response to contemporary speculative sciences. Both works were completed and published in England, where Cavendish was attempting to raise some funds to relieve the financial constraints imposed by a life of exile. Undaunted by their dismissal as insignificant curiosities by her contemporaries, Cavendish returned to France and proceeded to publish three more works. In 1660, Cavendish and her husband returned to England, and finding no favor at the court, retired to their country seat at Welbeck Abbey in Nottinghamshire. She expanded her interest in social issues, especially those related to gender, and addressed them directly in her *Orations of Divers Sorts* (1662) and *CCXI Sociable Letters* (1664). At the same time, Cavendish's continued interest in scientific speculation resulted in three more philosophical treatises, and in 1667 she was honored by the Royal Academy for her

scientific achievements. Cavendish spent the last years of her life revising her previous works and publishing final versions of her philosophical and literary texts before her death in 1673.

Major Works

Prior to the writings of Cavendish, the literary output of female writers in Britain was primarily restricted to occasional devotional or religio-political tracts. Cavendish's works, with their wide variety of genres, thus occupy an important place in the history of English literature. Her chief subjects of interest were philosophical speculations and social issues specifically, particularly those concerning women's position in society. Beginning with *Philosophicall Fancies,* Cavendish wrote six volumes of philosophical and scientific treatises. Her later works, such as *Philosophical Letters* (1664) and *Observations upon Experimental Philosophy* (1666), actively participate in contemporary debates concerning the relative merits of speculative philosophy and experimental science. The terms of Cavendish's scientific theories are imaginatively illustrated in *The Description of a New World, Called the Blazing World* (1666), a utopian fantasy that brings together Cavendish's philosophical speculations, political beliefs, and social concerns. Cavendish was also constantly challenging the conflicts between her own literary aspirations and the traditional ideal of the "silent woman," and in *The Blazing World* she explores her fantasy of female power through the creation of a brilliant heroine who is taken to a world where she is made Empress, and participates in philosophical discussions with learned men. In her narrative poems and plays, however, Cavendish is more ambiguous in her representations, placing strong intelligent women next to quiet retiring heroines, and undermining her proto-feminist critique of the institution of marriage by employing the trope of marriage at the end of a number of her plays. Her two biographical works—*The Life of the Thrice Noble, High and Puissant Prince William Cavendishe, Duke, Marquess, and Earl of Newcastle* and *A True Relation of the Birth, Breeding, and Life of Margaret Cavendish, Duchess of Newcastle*—also illustrate the conflict faced by Cavendish, who was both a wife and a writer. While the former is a glorified and loving portrayal of William Cavendish by his devoted wife, the latter embodies Cavendish's desire for independent recognition as a writer. This tension, found in all of Cavendish's major works, makes her writings interesting documents of social history as well as significant landmarks in feminist literary history.

Critical Reception

Cavendish's early critical reception was marked by a tendency to trivialize her literary productions as the curious result of an uncontrolled, overactive imagination. Samuel Pepys's judgment of Cavendish as a "mad, conceited, ridiculous woman" whose husband was "an asse to suffer her to write what she writes to him and of him" is characteristic of the criticism of her contemporaries. However, three years after her death, her husband published a collection of poems and letters eulogizing the Duchess's work, which indicates the presence, even during her lifetime, of some recognition of her merit as a writer. During the eighteenth and nineteenth centuries Cavendish's reputation consistently improved, as writers such as Charles Lamb and Isaac Disraeli praised her untutored genius and traced her influence on the works of poets such as Milton. This reputation has been superseded in recent criticism by a sociological interest in Cavendish that views her works as important representations of seventeenth-century social, political, and philosophical ideologies. As a result, there has been a renewed interest in the content of Cavendish's philosophical works and an attempt to place her within the historical context of philosophical ideas. The major part of Cavendish scholarship in the latter half of the twentieth century, however, focuses on her works precisely as the literary productions of a female writer. As one of the pioneering women writers who actively sought publication in order to achieve lasting recognition, Cavendish occupies a very significant position in any feminist history of English literature.

PRINCIPAL WORKS

Philosophicall Fancies (essays) 1653
Poems and Fancies (poetry) 1653
The Philosophical and Physical Opinions (essays) 1655
The World's Olio (essays) 1655
Natures Pictures drawn by Fancies Pencil to the Life, to which is added *A True Relation of the Birth, Breeding, and Life of Margaret Cavendish, Duchess of Newcastle* (short stories and autobiography) 1656
Orations of Divers Sorts, Accomodated to Divers Places (orations) 1662
Playes (drama) 1662
CCXI Sociable Letters (letters) 1664
Philosophical Letters: or, Modest Reflections upon some Opinions in Natural Philosophy (essays) 1664
Observations upon Experimental Philosophy, to which is added *The Description of a New Blazing World* (essays and fiction) 1666
The Description of a New World, Called the Blazing World (fiction) 1666
The Life of the Thrice Noble, High and Puissant Prince William Cavendishe, Duke, Marquess, and Earl of Newcastle (biography) 1667
Grounds of Natural Philosophy (essays) 1668
Playes, Never Before Printed (drama) 1668

CRITICISM

Virginia Woolf (essay date 1925)

SOURCE: "The Duchess of Newcastle," in *Collected Essays, Vol. III*, Harcourt, Brace & Company, 1925, pp. 51-8.

[*A British novelist, essayist, and short story writer, Woolf is considered one of the most prominent literary figures of twentieth-century English literature. Concerned primarily with depicting the life of the mind, she revolted against traditional narrative techniques and developed her own highly individualized style. In the following essay, Woolf paints a sympathetic portrait of Margaret Cavendish as an intelligent though untutored woman attempting to leave a mark in a world that mocked any display of intellectual activity by women.*]

' . . . All I desire is fame', wrote Margaret Cavendish, Duchess of Newcastle. And while she lived her wish was granted. Garish in her dress, eccentric in her habits, chaste in her conduct, coarse in her speech, she succeeded during her lifetime in drawing upon herself the ridicule of the great and the applause of the learned. But the last echoes of that clamour have now all died away; she lives only in the few splendid phrases that Lamb scattered upon her tomb; her poems, her plays, her philosophies, her orations, her discourses—all those folios and quartos in which, she protested, her real life was shrined—moulder in the gloom of public libraries, or are decanted into tiny thimbles which hold six drops of their profusion. Even the curious student, inspired by the words of Lamb, quails before the mass of her mausoleum, peers in, looks about him, and hurries out again, shutting the door.

But that hasty glance has shown him the outlines of a memorable figure. Born (it is conjectured) in 1624, Mar-

Engraving by J. Harrewijn (1692) of the house in which the Duke and Duchess of Newcastle lived during their years of exile.

garet was the youngest child of a Thomas Lucas, who died when she was an infant, and her upbringing was due to her mother, a lady of remarkable character, of majestic grandeur and beauty 'beyond the ruin of time'. 'She was very skilful in leases, and setting of lands and court keeping, ordering of stewards, and the like affairs.' The wealth which thus accrued she spent, not on marriage portions, but on generous and delightful pleasures, 'out of an opinion that if she bred us with needy necessity it might chance to create in us sharking qualities'. Her eight sons and daughters were never beaten, but reasoned with, finely and gaily dressed, and allowed no conversation with servants, not because they are servants but because servants 'are for the most part ill-bred as well as meanly born'. The daughters were taught the usual accomplishments 'rather for formality than for benefit', it being their mother's opinion that character, happiness, and honesty were of greater value to a woman than fiddling and singing, or 'the prating of several languages'.

Already Margaret was eager to take advantage of such indulgence to gratify certain tastes. Already she liked reading better than needlework, dressing and 'inventing fashions' better than reading, and writing best of all. Sixteen paper books of no title, written in straggling letters, for the impetuosity of her thought always outdid the pace of her fingers, testify to the use she made of her mother's liberality. The happiness of their home life had other results as well. They were a devoted family. Long after they were married, Margaret noted, these handsome brothers and sisters, with their well-proportioned bodies, their clear complexions, brown hair, sound teeth, 'tunable voic-

es', and plain way of speaking, kept themselves 'in a flock together'. The presence of strangers silenced them. But when they were alone, whether they walked in Spring Gardens or Hyde Park, or had music, or supped in barges upon the water, their tongues were loosed and they made 'very merry amongst themselves, . . . judging, condemning, approving, commending, as they thought good'.

The happy family life had its effect upon Margaret's character. As a child, she would walk for hours alone, musing and contemplating and reasoning with herself of 'everything her senses did present'. She took no pleasure in activity of any kind. Toys did not amuse her, and she could neither learn foreign languages nor dress as other people did. Her great pleasure was to invent dresses for herself, which nobody else was to copy, 'for', she remarks, 'I always took delight in a singularity, even in accoutrements of habits'.

Such a training, at once so cloistered and so free, should have bred a lettered old maid, glad of her seclusion, and the writer perhaps of some volume of letters or translations from the classics, which we should still quote as proof of the cultivation of our ancestresses. But there was a wild streak in Margaret, a love of finery and extravagance and fame, which was for ever upsetting the orderly arrangements of nature. When she heard that the Queen, since the outbreak of the Civil War, had fewer maids-of-honour than usual, she had 'a great desire' to become one of them. Her mother let her go against the judgement of the rest of the family, who, knowing that she had never left home and had scarcely been beyond their sight, justly thought that she might behave at Court to her disadvantage. 'Which indeed I did', Margaret confessed; 'for I was so bashful when I was out of my mother's, brothers', and sisters' sight that . . . I durst neither look up with my eyes, nor speak, nor be any way sociable, insomuch as I was thought a natural fool.' The courtiers laughed at her; and she retaliated in the obvious way. People were censorious; men were jealous of brains in a woman; women suspected intellect in their own sex; and what other lady, she might justly ask, pondered as she walked on the nature of matter and whether snails have teeth? But the laughter galled her, and she begged her mother to let her come home. This being refused, wisely as the event turned out, she stayed on for two years (1643-45), finally going with the Queen to Paris, and there, among the exiles who came to pay their respects to the Court, was the Marquis of Newcastle. To the general amazement, the princely nobleman, who had led the King's forces to disaster with indomitable courage but little skill, fell in love with the shy, silent, strangely dressed maid-of-honour. It was not 'amorous love, but honest, honourable love', according to Margaret. She was no brilliant match; she had gained a reputation for prudery and eccentricity. What, then, could have made so great a nobleman fall at her feet? The onlookers were full of derision, disparagement, and slander. 'I fear', Margaret wrote to the Marquis, 'others foresee we shall be unfortunate, though we see it not ourselves, or else there would not be such pains to untie the knot of our affections.' Again, 'Saint Germains is a place of much slander, and thinks I send too often to you'. 'Pray consider', she warned him, 'that I have enemies.' But the match was evidently perfect. The Duke, with his love of poetry and music and play-writing, his interest in philosophy, his belief 'that nobody knew or could know the cause of anything', his romantic and generous temperament, was naturally drawn to a woman who wrote poetry herself, was also a philosopher of the same way of thinking, and lavished upon him not only the admiration of a fellow-artist, but the gratitude of a sensitive creature who had been shielded and succoured by his extraordinary magnanimity. 'He did approve', she wrote, 'of those bashful fears which many condemned, . . . and though I did dread marriage and shunned men's company as much as I could, yet I . . . had not the power to refuse him.' She kept him company during the long years of exile; she entered with sympathy, if not with understanding, into the conduct and acquirements of those horses which he trained to such perfection that the Spaniards crossed themselves and cried 'Miraculo!' as they witnessed their corvets, voltoes, and pirouettes; she believed that the horses even made a 'trampling action' for joy when he came into the stables; she pleaded his cause in England during the Protectorate; and, when the Restoration made it possible for them to return to England, they lived together in the depths of the country in the greatest seclusion and perfect contentment, scribbling plays, poems, philosophies, greeting each other's works with raptures of delight, and confabulating, doubtless, upon such marvels of the natural world as chance threw their way. They were laughed at by their contemporaries; Horace Walpole sneered at them. But there can be

no doubt that they were perfectly happy.

For now Margaret could apply herself uninterruptedly to her writing. She could devise fashions for herself and her servants. She could scribble more and more furiously with fingers that became less and less able to form legible letters. She could even achieve the miracle of getting her plays acted in London and her philosophies humbly perused by men of learning. There they stand, in the British Museum, volume after volume, swarming with a diffused, uneasy, contorted vitality. Order, continuity, the logical development of her argument are all unknown to her. No fears impede her. She has the irresponsibility of a child and the arrogance of a Duchess. The wildest fancies come to her, and she canters away on their backs. We seem to hear her, as the thoughts boil and bubble, calling to John, who sat with a pen in his hand next-door, to come quick, 'John, John, I conceive!' And down it goes—whatever it may be; sense or nonsense; some thought on women's education—'Women live like Bats or Owls, labour like Beasts, and die like Worms, . . . the best bred women are those whose minds are civilest'; some speculation that had struck her, perhaps, walking that afternoon alone—why 'hogs have the measles', why 'dogs that rejoice swing their tails', or what the stars are made of, or what this chrysalis is that her maid has brought her, and she keeps warm in a corner of her room. On and on, from subject to subject she flies, never stopping to correct, 'for there is more pleasure in making than in mending', talking aloud to herself of all those matters that filled her brain to her perpetual diversion—of wars, and boarding-schools, and cutting down trees, of grammar and morals, of monsters and the British, whether opium in small quantities is good for lunatics, why it is that musicians are mad. Looking upwards, she speculates still more ambitiously upon the nature of the moon, and if the stars are blazing jellies; looking downwards she wonders if the fishes know that the sea is salt; opines that our heads are full of fairies, 'dear to God as we are'; muses whether there are not other worlds than ours, and reflects that the next ship may bring us word of a new one. In short, 'we are in utter darkness'. Meanwhile, what a rapture is thought!

As the vast books appeared from the stately retreat at Welbeck the usual censors made the usual objections, and had to be answered, despised, or argued with, as her mood varied, in the preface to every work. They said, among other things, that her books were not her own, because she used learned terms, and 'wrote of many matters outside her ken'. She flew to her husband for help, and he answered, characteristically, that the Duchess 'had never conversed with any professed scholar in learning except her brother and myself'. The Duke's scholarship, moreover, was of a peculiar nature. 'I have lived in the great world a great while, and have thought of what has been brought to me by the senses, more than was put into me by learned discourse; for I do not love to be led by the nose, by authority, and old authors; *ipse dixit* will not serve my turn.' And then she takes up the pen and proceeds, with the importunity and indiscretion of a child, to assure the world that her ignorance is of the finest quality imaginable. She has only seen Des Cartes and Hobbes, not questioned them; she did indeed ask Mr. Hobbes to dinner, but he could not come; she often does not listen to a word that is said to her; she does not know any French, though she lived abroad for five years; she has only read the old philosophers in Mr. Stanley's account of them; of Des Cartes she has read but half of his work on Passion; and of Hobbes only 'the little book called *De Cive'*, all of which is infinitely to the credit of her native wit, so abundant that outside succour pained it, so honest that it would not accept help from others. It was from the plain of complete ignorance, the untilled field of her own consciousness, that she proposed to erect a philosophic system that was to oust all others. The results were not altogether happy. Under the pressure of such vast structures, her natural gift, the fresh and delicate fancy which had led her in her first volume to write charmingly of Queen Mab and fairyland, was crushed out of existence.

> The palace of the Queen wherein she dwells,
> Its fabric's built all of hodmandod shells;
> The hangings of a Rainbow made that's thin,
> Shew wondrous fine, when one first enters in;
> The chambers made of Amber that is clear,
> Do give a fine sweet smell, if fire be near;
> Her bed a cherry stone, is carved throughout,
> And with a butterfly's wing hung about;
> Her sheets are of the skin of Dove's eyes made
> Where on a violet bud her pillow's laid.

So she could write when she was young. But her fairies, if they survived at all, grew up into hippopotami. Too generously her prayer was granted:

> Give me the free and noble style,
> Which seems uncurb'd, though it be wild.

She became capable of involutions, and contortions and conceits of which the following is among the shortest, but not the most terrific:

> The human head may be likened to a town:
> The mouth when full, begun
> Is market day, when empty, market's done;
> The city conduct, where the water flows,
> Is with two spouts, the nostrils and the nose.

She similized, energetically, incongruously, eternally; the sea became a meadow, the sailors shepherds, the mast a maypole. The fly was the bird of summer, trees were senators, houses ships, and even the fairies, whom she loved better than any earthly thing, except the Duke, are changed into blunt atoms and sharp atoms, and take part in some of those horrible manœuvres in which she delighted to marshal the universe. Truly, 'my Lady Sanspareille hath a strange spreading wit'. Worse still, without an atom of dramatic power, she turned to play-writing. It was a simple process. The unwieldy thoughts which turned and tumbled within her were christened Sir Golden Riches, Moll Meanbred, Sir Puppy Dogman, and the rest, and sent revolving in tedious debate upon the parts of the soul, or whether virtue is better than riches, round a wise and learned lady who answered their questions and cor-

rected their fallacies at considerable length in tones which we seem to have heard before.

Sometimes, however, the Duchess walked abroad. She would issue out in her own proper person, dressed in a thousand gems and furbelows, to visit the houses of the neighbouring gentry. Her pen made instant report of these excursions. She recorded how Lady C. R. 'did beat her husband in a public assembly'; Sir F. O. 'I am sorry to hear hath undervalued himself so much below his birth and wealth as to marry his kitchen-maid'; 'Miss P. I. has become a sanctified soul, a spiritual sister, she has left curling her hair, black patches are become abominable to her, laced shoes and Galoshoes are steps to pride—she asked me what posture I thought was the best to be used in prayer'. Her answer was probably unacceptable. 'I shall not rashly go there again', she says of one such 'gossip-making'. She was not, we may hazard, a welcome guest or an altogether hospitable hostess. She had a way of 'bragging of myself' which frightened visitors so that they left, nor was she sorry to see them go. Indeed, Welbeck was the best place for her, and her own company the most congenial, with the amiable Duke wandering in and out, with his plays and his speculations, always ready to answer a question or refute a slander. Perhaps it was this solitude that led her, chaste as she was in conduct, to use language which in time to come much perturbed Sir Egerton Brydges. She used, he complained, 'expressions and images of extraordinary coarseness as flowing from a female of high rank brought up in courts'. He forgot that this particular female had long ceased to frequent the Court; she consorted chiefly with fairies; and her friends were among the dead. Naturally, then, her language was coarse. Nevertheless, though her philosophies are futile, and her plays intolerable, and her verses mainly dull, the vast bulk of the Duchess is leavened by a vein of authentic fire. One cannot help following the lure of her erratic and lovable personality as it meanders and twinkles through page after page. There is something noble and Quixotic and high-spirited, as well as crack-brained and bird-witted, about her. Her simplicity is so open; her intelligence so active; her sympathy with fairies and animals so true and tender. She has the freakishness of an elf, the irresponsibility of some non-human creature, its heartlessness, and its charm. And although 'they', those terrible critics who had sneered and jeered at her ever since, as a shy girl, she had not dared look her tormentors in the face at Court, continued to mock, few of her critics, after all, had the wit to trouble about the nature of the universe, or cared a straw for the sufferings of the hunted hare, or longed, as she did, to talk to some one 'of Shakespeare's fools'. Now, at any rate, the laugh is not all on their side.

But laugh they did. When the rumour spread that the crazy Duchess was coming up from Welbeck to pay her respects at Court, people crowded the streets to look at her, and the curiosity of Mr. Pepys twice brought him to wait in the Park to see her pass. But the pressure of the crowd about her coach was too great. He could only catch a glimpse of her in her silver coach with her footmen all in velvet, a velvet cap on her head, and her hair about her ears. He could only see for a moment between the white curtains the face of 'a very comely woman', and on she drove through the crowd of staring Cockneys, all pressing to catch a glimpse of that romantic lady, who stands, in the picture at Welbeck, with large melancholy eyes, and something fastidious and fantastic in her bearing, touching a table with the tips of long pointed fingers, in the calm assurance of immortal fame.

B. G. MacCarthy (essay date 1944)

SOURCE: "Biography," in *Women Writers: Their Contribution to the English Novel, 1621-1744,* Third Impression, Cork University Press, 1946, pp. 70-121.

[*In the following excerpt from an essay first published in 1944, MacCarthy traces the conflicting opinions about Cavendish's literary abilities and contends that her genius, evident in her biographical works, was unappreciated by her contemporaries.*]

Of the many women whose intellectual powers were rendered ineffectual by a want of education, the Duchess of Newcastle is an outstanding example. Like other well-bred women, she had had her tutors, who were paid to give a semblance of schooling, but who were not even supposed to exact the discipline of study. A young lady could read, write and cipher, she could chatter a foreign language, dance, and play the virginals, embroider and make bead bags. In the name of common sense what more could any one expect? Let her carry her "education" as she would a handkerchief—in case she should need it. It were unnecessary, and indeed rather ill-bred to make great play with either or flourish them about. But Margaret Newcastle was haunted by a dual hunger—for knowledge and for fame. She wanted to know "whether it be possible to make men and other Animal creatures that naturally have no wings, flie as birds do?" "Whether the Optick Perception is made in the Eye or Brain, or in both?" "Whether there could be self-knowledge without Perception?" "Whether snails have a row of small teeth orderly placed in the gums"? Such knowledge was not forthcoming, and the undisciplined and voracious mind raced on to other fields of enquiry. There was not time enough in eternity to know all she wished to know, or to write all she felt impelled to write. She writes so fast that she cannot stay to form the letters properly. She never revises. She fills twelve folio volumes, and the more she writes the more her readers tap their foreheads significantly, and rock with laughter. She knows, but she does not care. If writing is a disease, then countless great men have been at death's door. "All I desire is fame," she says; and again: "I have an Opinion, which troubles me like a conscience, that 'tis a part of Honour to aspire to Fame."

As for Learning, that I am not versed in it, no body, I hope, will blame me for it, since it is sufficiently known, that our Sex is not bred up to it, as being not suffer'd to be instructed in Schools and Universities; I will not say, but many of our Sex may have as much Wit, and be capable of Learning as well as Men; but since they want Instructions, it is not possible they should attain to it; for Learning is Artificial, but Wit is Natural.

Writing over two centuries later, Sir Egerton Brydges says [in his preface to *A True Relation of the Birth, Breeding and Life of Margaret Newcastle, Duchess of Newcastle,* 1872]:

That the Duchess was deficient in a cultivated judgment; that her knowledge was more multifarious than exact; and that her powers of fancy and sentiment were more active than her powers of reasoning, I will admit; but that her productions mingled as they are with great absurdities, are wanting either in talent, or in virtue, or even in genius, I cannot concede.

[In his *Curiosities of Literature,* 1849, Isaac] Disraeli supports the same view:

Her labours have been ridiculed by some wits, but had her studies been regulated she would have displayed no ordinary genius . . . Her verses have been imitated even by Milton.

And finally in the following criticism [from *The Cavalier and his Lady,* 1872] we find the same judgment more fully expressed:

There are [in the writings of the Duchess] the indisputable evidences of a genius as highborn in the realms of intellect as its possessor was in the ranks of society: a genius strong-winged and swift, fertile and comprehensive, but ruined by deficient culture, by literary dissipation and the absence of two powers without which thoughts are only stray morsels of strength, I mean Concatenation and the Sense of Proportion. She thought without system, and set down everything she thought. Her fancy turning round like a kaleidoscope changed its patterns and lines with the most whimsical variety and rapidity. Nevertheless, I believe, had the mind of this woman been disciplined and exercised by early culture and study, it would have stood out remarkable among the feminine intellects of our history.

Happily, however, two of the Duchess of Newcastle's works are free from those fixed ideas and exaggerated fancies which distort her other writings. These are the two biographical works which we are about to consider. In them, the turgid current of her thought flows clearly and surely to the end she had in view.

In 1656, appeared ***Natures Pictures drawn by Fancie's Pencil*** . . . which contained, as the eleventh and last book ***The True Relation of My Birth, Breeding and Life***. It preserves, as all autobiographies should, the quintessence of the writer's individuality.

Anne Clifford had presented a chain of events with few comments [in her autobiography]. Margaret Newcastle presents thoughts in which events are caught like flies in amber. She does not lose her way in the tangled happenings of her career, because external events never constituted her life. Life to her was thought. Well might she say: "I have made a world of my own." Out of the press and hurry of the years she gathered something timeless—a conception of values which took its nature from her own personality. She might have been embittered by her misfortunes, intoxicated by her powers of endurance, made querulous by her poverty, or disillusioned by that spiritual weariness which always follows the triumph of a political cause. But she had an inner existence against which the tide of external events beat in vain. She does not particularise her backgrounds, and yet she gives sufficient to convey a feeling of vivid intimacy. The depth of her judgments, the unpretentious sincerity of her story and the steady undercurrent of emotion which carries it onward give this biography an unforgettable pathos and beauty.

In 1667, the Duchess published *The Life of the Thrice noble, high and puissant Prince, William Cavendish, Duke . . . of Newcastle,* a book "both good and rare" for which, says [Charles Lamb in *Last Essays of Elia*], "no binding is too good: no casket is rich enough, no casing sufficiently durable, to honour and keep safe such a jewel." . . .

There have been diverse opinions as to these biographical works of the Duchess. [Samuel] Pepys was very forthright in his condemnation. On March 18th, 1667, he writes [in his diary]: "Staid at home reading the ridiculous History of my Lord Newcastle, wrote by his wife; which shows her to be a mad, conceited, ridiculous woman, and he an asse to suffer her to write what she writes to him and of him. So to bed my eyes being very bad."

His myopia, however, was nothing to that of Horace Walpole [*A Catalogue of the Royal and Noble Authors of England*, 1759], who fulminates against the Newcastles "with less taste and justice than are commonly to be found in his censures, and with more than his usual spleen," [according to Edmund Lodge in his *Portraits of Illustrious Personages of Great Britain*, 1835]. Disraeli dismisses as mere levity Walpole's criticism which in brief is as follows:

> Of all the riders of [Pegasus] perhaps there have not been a more fantastic couple than his Grace and his faithful Duchess, who was never off her pillion. One of the noble Historian's finest portraits is of the Duke: The Duchess has left another; more diffuse indeed but not less entertaining. It is equally amusing to hear her sometimes compare her Lord to Julius Caesar, and often to acquaint you with such anecdotes as in what sort of coach he went to Amsterdam.

Having jeered at the Duchess's claims to genius and at her peculiarities, he ends thus:

> What a picture of foolish nobility was this stately poetic couple, retired to their own little domain, and intoxicating one another with circumstantial flattery

on what was of consequence to no mortal but themselves.

And what a picture of finicking celibacy was Walpole himself, retired into his little pseudo-Gothic stronghold at Strawberry Hill, surrounded by an arid collection of artistic curiosities, and drawing his life-breath from the sterile eulogies of his select coterie! Whereas the Newcastles left a memory of faithful love, this doyen left a miasma of malicious preciosity. Before he sneered at Margaret Newcastle's literary absurdities, he should have wiped the bloody drop from Alfonso's nose. Before he stigmatised a childless woman as a "fertile pedant," he should have considered for a moment his own barren existence.

Happily, however, there have been few such critics. The general consensus of opinion has always emphasised the profound value of *The True Relation* and the *Life of William Cavendish*. To the worth of the latter biography, Firth has finely testified [in the preface to the *Life of William Cavendish*, 1886]:

> The special interest of the book lies in the picture of the exiled Royalist, cheerfully sacrificing everything for the King's cause, struggling with his debts, talking over his creditors, never losing confidence in the ultimate triumph of the right, and on his return, setting to work uncomplainingly to restore his ruined estate. It lies . . . in the portrait drawn of a great English nobleman of the seventeenth century; his manners and his habits, his domestic policy, and his alliances with neighbouring potentates, all are recorded and set down with the loving fidelity of a Boswell.

Douglas Grant (essay date 1957)

SOURCE: "The Voyage of Fancy," in *Margaret the First: A Biography of Margaret Cavendish, Duchess of Newcastle, 1623-1673,* Rupert Hart-Davis, 1957, pp. 151-70.

[*Below, Grant focuses on Cavendish's early works written during the years of her exile, emphasizing the broad range of Cavendish's literary output and tracing the source of her highly imaginative literary creations to her own life experiences and aspirations.*]

> *I desire all my readers and acquaintance to believe, though my words run stumbling out of my mouth, and my pen draws roughly on my paper, yet my thoughts move regular in my brain.*

One of the illustrations made by Abraham van Diepenbeke for the book on horsemanship was a group portrait of Newcastle and his family. Newcastle and Margaret are shown seated under the middle arch of a portico of five arches. Newcastle's three daughters and their husbands, the Earl of Bridgewater, the Earl of Bolingbroke and Charles Cheyne, are arranged in wedded pairs, each pair to an arch. His two sons, Charles and Henry, exhibit their horsemanship in front of the portico, and their wives are placed together under the fifth arch. A dog scampers excitedly about the horses; a vain attempt on the artist's part to enliven the stiff formality of the scene.

Diepenbeke had earlier drawn a conversation piece of Newcastle and his family, which had appeared as the frontispiece to Margaret's large collection of tales published in 1656. The title-page to the collection deserves to be transcribed in full, so typical is it of the author's style: *Natures Pictures drawn by Fancies Pencil to the Life. Written by the thrice Noble, Illustrious, and Excellent Princess, The Lady Marchioness of Newcastle. In this Volume there are several feigned Stories of Natural Descriptions, as Comical, Tragical, and Tragi-Comical, Poetical, Romancical, Philosophical, and Historical, both in Prose and Verse, some all Verse, some all Prose, some mixt, partly Prose, and partly Verse. Also, there are some Morals, and some Dialogues, but they are as the Advantage Loaves of Bread to a Bakers dozen; and a true Story at the latter end, wherein there is no Feignings*. A more specific and inclusive title could hardly have been devised.

Diepenbeke's conversation piece shows the family seated round a table in a room warmed by a winter fire; the blaze is so hot that one of the servants is seen in the act of opening a window to let in air. Newcastle and Margaret, their heads crowned with laurel, are seated at the head of the table, and as Newcastle addresses his children, stressing his words with a gesture of the hand, they lean forward or loll back comfortably in their chairs. The principal difference between the artist's preliminary study for the engraving and the engraving itself is in the narrator. In the study it is Margaret herself who holds up her hand for attention, and her relinquishment of the rôle of narrator to her husband in the engraving was probably made to avoid further offending those who would have thought that she was entrenching again on 'the male prerogative'. Margaret withdrew the concession, however, in her verses describing the frontispiece:

> My lord and I here in two chairs are set,
> And all his children, wives and husbands, met,
> To hear me tell them tales as I think fit,
> And hope they're full of fancy and of wit.
> Ladies, I ask your pardons, mercies, I,
> Since I talk all, and many ladies by.

Newcastle did contribute one or two tales in verse to the collection to justify his prominence in the frontispiece, but his chief contributions were two commendatory poems, one on the tales themselves and the other on all Margaret's published works, which is largely his earlier preface to *The Philosophical and Physical Opinions* set in rhyme. His verses in praise of the tales are in the style of a pedlar's crying of his wares:

> Gallants and ladies, what do ye lack? pray buy.
> Tales *à la mode*, new fashioned here do lie,
> So do romancies, your grave studies too;
> Academies of Love, teaching to woo
> And to be wooed, corrupts more virgins than
> Hot satires turned to amorous courtly men:
> But these are innocent; then be not nice;

> Will you not buy because they teach not vice?
> Nature will teach you that; then do not look
> To do 't by art and learning by the book:
> A vestal nun may read this and avow it,
> And a Carthusian confessor allow it.

The tales in verse which open the collection are supposed to be told in turn by a group of men and women as they sit round a winter's fire. The greater number are hardly more than anecdotes phrased in poor rhyme: a young widow is found weeping at her husband's grave and, rejecting consolation, dies; or, a man swears to his dying wife to be constant to her memory and when he marries again, he marries a shrew and quickly dies. A few of the tales are more ambitious. In **"A Description of Constancy"** a young girl is sent by her widowed father to the Queen's court as a maid of honour. She falls in love with a handsome and martial prince, who is unfortunately intended as a match for the Queen's niece. She writes to him protesting her love and, luckily for her modesty, he writes to her simultaneously in the same strain. They conceal their affection out of policy but once they are discovered, the prince is despatched to the army and the girl is abducted and given out for dead. When the prince learns of her supposed death, he adopts the life of a hermit, and the girl, persuaded in turn of his death, spends her days weeping and mourning. But disasters overtake the army and the prince, under threat of execution, is ordered by the Queen to resume his command; this he refuses to do and is told to prepare for death. The girl, too, is warned of her execution. But when the lovers are reunited on the scaffold, the Queen has a change of heart and forgives them, and the tale ends with their marriage.

As we read through one story after another of this kind, we may remember that the list of contents given on the title-page concludes with a promise of 'a true story at the latter end wherein there is no feignings.' The true story is *A true Relation of my Birth, Breeding, and Life,* one of the most charming autobiographical sketches of the century, in which Margaret simply and hastily sets out the main facts of her life. Believing later that it lessened her dignity, she omitted it in 1671 from the second edition of the book. What relation does it bear to all the preceding stories? It serves in effect, though not in intention, to show that all her tales were essentially autobiographical. They were the daydreams prompted by her own experience and are variations, more or less fantastic, upon it. Each story has its heroine and each heroine is Margaret in disguise; in the disguise of the learned lady or of the lovely innocent. The two are occasionally kept apart but generally they alternate in a single character. And as the scenes of a daydream succeed each other imperceptibly and have neither a beginning nor an end, so her tales are the contiguous scenes of a single story, loosely and uncertainly narrative. They move idly forward, repeating one another, stagnating for whole pages; and were only concluded, one imagines, when some outside interruption forced her to break off hastily her endless unravellings.

One of the longer stories, **"Assaulted and Pursued Chastity"**, can serve as an example of all the rest. The ostensible moral is 'to show young women the danger of travelling without their parents, husbands or particular friends to guard them.' A well-bred orphan, the Lady Affectionata—Margaret's heroines are always short of at least one parent—returning to her native country at the end of a civil war, is shipwrecked upon the coast of the Kingdom of Sensuality and falls into the hands of a bawd. This infamous creature tries to procure her for a young Prince, 'a grand monopolizer of young virgins', who is already married to a woman much older than himself. On the plea that a wizard once advised her to fire off a shot on her birthday to ensure good luck, Affectionata persuades a maid in the establishment to lend her a pistol, and promptly shoots the Prince with it when he refuses to desist from his advances. The wound only strengthens the Prince's love and he manages to have Affectionata removed from the bawd's to his aunt's house, and by his assiduous attentions and presents he makes Affectionata fall in love with him. One day when he is heated with wine he assaults her, but she frustrates him by quickly breaking a convenient phial of poison in her mouth and falling into a coma. Revived by the aunt, she determines to escape, and cutting off her hair, donning a page's suit and adopting the name of Travelia, she makes her way to the coast in the hope of boarding a ship bound for her own country. By mistake she boards a vessel bound 'for new discoveries towards the south.'

In spite of its obvious absurdities, the tale so far retains touch with reality and moves at a much quicker pace than Margaret usually shows; but Affectionata-Travelia's escape towards the south is the opportunity for fantasy to board as pilot. The cruise ends in shipwreck and the captain of the vessel and Affectionata-Travelia, whom the captain has adopted as his 'son', make for the shore in the ship's boat only to be astonished by the natives lined up to greet them as they step ashore: 'they in the boat never saw such complexioned men, for they were not black like negroes, nor tawny, nor olive, nor ash-coloured, as many are, but of a deep purple; their hair as white as milk, and like wool; their lips thin, their ears long, their noses flat, yet sharp, their teeth and nails as black as jet and as shining; their stature tall and their proportion big; their bodies were all naked.' These strange creatures mount them on beasts yet stranger—half calf and half fish, with a horn like a unicorn's—and carry them to the governor of the kingdom. The wonders of the country unfold as they ride along: houses made of fish-bones and tiled with fish-scales, trees without either branches or leaves, having their flowers inlaid in the smooth wood, and all manner of fabulous beasts—especially one: 'There was one kind of beast in the shape of a camel, and the neck as white as a swan, and all the head and face white, only a lock of hair on the top of his crown of all manner of colours; the hair of his body was of a perfect gold yellow, his tail like his fore-top, but it would often turn up like a peacock's tail, and spread it as broad, and the hairs being of several colours made a glorious show; the legs and feet of the colour of the body, but the hoofs as black as jet.'

The metropolis to which they are carried is crammed with wonders, the most remarkable being the persons of royal blood: they 'were of a perfect orange colour, their hair coal-black, their teeth and nails as white as milk, of a very great height, yet well shaped.' The dew might fall in flakes like snow on this kingdom and taste of double-refined sugar but the inhabitants are anthropophagi; and after a year in captivity, Affectionata-Travelia and the captain understand that they are to be sacrificed. The heroine copes with the danger in an original manner. Having learnt the country's language and made the captain devise two pistols, she shoots the high priest dead as she is about to be sacrificed publicly to the sun, and pretending to be a messenger from the gods, she harangues the people on the nature of the soul and of God to such effect that she breaks them of cannibalism, civilizes them and becomes their beloved legislator.

We are now returned to the libidinous Prince. He sets out in search of Affectionata-Travelia and after being taken by pirates, adopts their profession. Among his first prizes are Affectionata-Travelia and the captain, who are on their way home. The pirate ship sinks, but all the crew and their goods are safely landed on a fertile uninhabited island. The Prince recognizing Affectionata-Travelia through her male disguise, proposes that they should pass their lives together on the island as man and wife. This proposal is sufficient to inspire Affectionata-Travelia's escape to the Kingdom of Amity; and still in disguise, she becomes confidante to the Queen of that country. The Prince, after several adventures, lands in the neighbouring Kingdom of Amour, and on the orders of its King leads an army against Amity. He succeeds in defeating the Queen but after Affectionata-Travelia has assumed command, he loses the day to her superior military genius and is taken prisoner. A plausible ending is at last within sight. The King and Queen marry and live in Amour, and Affectionata-Travelia and the Prince, whose elderly wife has died in his absence, follow suit and reign in Amity as joint-viceroys. And they all live happily ever after.

After reading this tale, and the many others in a similar style, it is with some surprise that we come upon Margaret's protestations that she did not, could not read romances, the leisured class's favourite literary diversion. She had tried to read them but having once sampled them, whenever she picked one up later by mistake she promptly threw it aside as 'an unprofitable study.' Romances, she affirmed, contained little 'which ought to be practised, but rather shunned as foolish amorosities and desperate follies.' Her own tales, on the contrary, excited to virtue and quenched 'amorous passions.' Her moral objections to the form were sincere—had they not been she would never have risked alienating her readers' attention with the unbearable tedium of pages of moral discourse—but in improbabilities and wonders she far outdid any romancer. How could the heroic and languorous worlds of even the most polished French romancers compete with her kingdom of purple savages and plumed camels? The truth is that there was a marked affinity between her imagination and theirs, and she was as instinctively conforming to the spirit of the age in the composition of her tales as she was in her natural philosophy.

Her weaknesses as a writer of fiction—though they are so apparent that it seems redundant to set them down—lie in narrative and characterization. 'Assaulted and Pursued Chastity' has a livelier opening than most of her tales but becomes intolerably confused and disjointed by the end, a failing which may not be obvious in the résumé; and many of the others hardly progress at all, settling immediately into a pool of stagnant speculation. The heroines are always interesting to the extent of revealing Margaret's own personality, but the other characters are insubstantial and have even less connection with life than the abstractions which people the usual contemporary romances. The only reward her tales generally offer is an occasional passage of poetic fantasy, like the journey made to the centre of the earth by the hero of **"The Travelling Spirit"**: 'So when he came to the centre of the earth, he saw a light like moonshine: but when he came near, he saw the circle about the centre was glow-worms' tails, which gave that light; and in the centre was an old man, who neither stood nor sat, for there was nothing to stand or sit on; but he hung, as it were, in the air, nor never stirred out of his place, and had been there ever since the world was made; for he having never had a woman to tempt him to sin, never died.'

But Margaret's genius is disconcerting. There is one tale in the collection which shames the others with its brilliance. **"The Contract"** is the story of the orphaned Lady Delitia, who is brought up by an uncle. The Duke of the province persuades the uncle to betroth his niece while yet a child to his second son. The Duke and his elder son die and the younger son inherits. He promptly forgets his obligation to Delitia and makes love to the young wife of an aged grandee. The uncle is naturally distressed by this conduct but determines to educate Delitia as well as he can; he instructs her in moral philosophy, 'to lay a ground and foundation of virtue', in history, 'to learn her experience by the second hand', and in the poets, 'to delight in their fancies and recreate in their wit'. When the Duke has married the pretty widow of the grandee, the uncle brings Delitia, now aged thirteen, to the capital, to live incognita and to continue her education, in music, dancing, natural philosophy, chemistry, etc.

Delitia's beauty grows in proportion to her knowledge and at length her uncle decides to present her to the world, choosing as the occasion a masque-night at court. She arrives attired in black. Both the Duke and his Viceroy fall in love with her at sight, but she slips secretly away like Cinderella without revealing her identity. Determined to see her again, the Viceroy commands a ball and she attends, dressed this time in white satin, embroidered in silver. Her beauty was such that 'she produced the same effects as a burning-glass; for the beams of all eyes were drawn together, as to one point placed in her face, and by reflection she sent a burning heat, and fired every heart.'

The Duke is overcome with grief and shame when he learns her identity but the Viceroy, unimpeded by a wife, proposes to her; a proposal which she is reluctantly persuaded by her uncle to accept. The Duke in despair writes to her protesting his love and she replies admitting her affection. At an interview, he persuades her to go to law over him with his wife, pleading her prior claim; and at the trial she argues her case so well that his marriage is declared null and he is free to marry her. The Viceroy, who really behaves rather badly, is rewarded with the Duke's cast-off wife.

A résumé of **"Assaulted and Pursued Chastity"** sets the tale off to advantage by abridging its devious and tiresome length, but as certainly **"The Contract"** is spoilt in a résumé by the stress which inevitably falls on the apparently implausible ending. In fact the narrative moves forward so swiftly and directly, the characterization is so consistent and the dialogue so crisp and natural that the ending is satisfactorily integrated into the whole. The material is the same as that of the other stories—once again Margaret is dramatizing herself and her ambitions—but this time she has succeeded in expressing it perfectly. Were all the tales in the collection of this quality, she would have enjoyed a considerable reputation as a writer of fiction.

Why do her other tales fall so far short of **"The Contract"**? She was quite incapable of deliberation or revision: 'the brain being quicker in creating,' she wrote, 'than the hand in writing, or the memory in retaining, many fancies are lost, by reason they oftimes out-run the pen.' She was always running a race with her fancy, and, carried far ahead by her speed, she could not face the boredom of turning back to methodize what she had already written. Good, bad or indifferent, everything was sent to the press exactly as it was written, and having cleared her desk of papers she sat down again to take up the next subject, careless of what had gone before.

The second of Newcastle's commendatory verses prefixed to *Natures Pictures* was in praise of all Margaret's works which had appeared so far, 'except her tragedies and comedies, which will shortly come out.' Unfortunately the publication of her plays was delayed. The manuscript was lost when the ship carrying it to England to be printed foundered. Margaret was prudent enough to keep copies of her 'poor labours' until after they had appeared in print, when she burnt the copies, but the loss postponed publication of her plays until after her return to England. The volume appeared in 1662 and a shorter collection of dramatic fragments in 1668.

Since Margaret owed so much to Newcastle for intellectual stimulus, it was inevitable that she should turn her attention sooner or later to the stage. He was more ambitious to appear as a dramatist than in any other literary rôle, and in 1649 he had had printed two of his comedies, *The Country Captaine* and *The Varietie*. The first was largely the work of James Shirley, to which Newcastle gave his name, and was written and acted in 1639 or 1640. The second is almost certainly of Newcastle's own composition. On the evidence of *The Varietie* Newcastle's conception of a play was to associate arbitrarily a few characters, each of them a 'humour' after the style of Ben Jonson, to entangle them in matrimony and to keep them justifiably on the stage by a slight pretence to plot.

The tediousness and coarseness of *The Varietie* are hardly redeemed by the few passages of brisk dialogue. He had one gift which was not well displayed in this comedy—a pleasant sense of humour, which he showed particularly in his depiction of 'low' characters, grooms, servants and country folk; a class which he understood with the instinctive sympathy of the true aristocrat.

Newcastle's dramatic practice, however, cannot give a fair idea of his conception of the worth and dignity of the stage. In one of the many epistles to the reader prefixed to her plays, Margaret argues that a public theatre greatly benefits youths of quality: 'it learns them graceful behaviours and demeanours, it puts spirit and life into them, it teaches them wit, and makes their speech both voluble and tuneable; besides, it gives them confidence, all which ought every man to have, that is of quality . . . to conclude, a poet is the best tutor, and a theatre is the best school that is for youth to be educated by or in.' The argument is unquestionably Newcastle's, and as Margaret heard him expound such themes and listened to him read his own plays, which in her fond opinion were the equal of Shakespeare's in wit, she decided that she, too, must write for the stage.

The disadvantage of writing plays during the interregnum was the impossibility of their being produced. The London theatres were closed and the actors were either dead or dispersed. But the disadvantage was only theoretical in Margaret's case. As she herself readily admitted, her plays could never have been performed. They were far too long to be staged and 'might tire the spectators,' as she wrote so innocently, 'who are forced or bound by the rules of civility to sit out a play, if they be not sick.' A unique epidemic would have unhoused the theatre long before one of Margaret's plays reached half-way. But length is the least of their failings. They are nothing more than a collection of disconnected scenes. 'I would have my plays to be like the natural course of all things in the world,' she wrote, distinguishing this weakness, ' . . . some of my scenes have no acquaintance or relation to the rest of the scenes, although in one and the same play, which is the reason many of my plays will not end as other plays do.' They neither end nor proceed in the usual fashion; but even if they had conformed to the rules, they are so utterly undramatic that it is impossible to imagine them upon the boards—the only appropriate stage was, as she herself suggested, her own brain. But she was not at all sorry that they could never have been produced, for she could not have borne to hear them hissed: 'it would have made me a little melancholy to have my harmless and innocent plays go weeping from the stage, and whipped by malicious and hard-hearted censurers.' And the impossibility of their performance could not detract from their high purpose, which was 'to extol virtue, and to honour merit, and to praise the graces.'

Her plays are of the same substance as her tales, and their matter and manner can be most conveniently illustrated by a brief outline of one of the longest and the most coherent, *Love's Adventures*. The play has a double plot—and several underplots, which must be disregarded—and

each has its own heroine, Lady Bashful and Lady Orphan, who are both Margaret in disguise. To begin with the less important, Lady Bashful suffers extremely in company from shyness, which hides her sharp intelligence and good sense. She has several suitors, the most extraordinary being Sir Serious Dumb, a silent man. His silence, however, is only assumed and once he has won Lady Bashful's affection and defeated his rivals, he becomes as eloquent as any, revealing himself as a man eminently suitable in character to becoming Lady Bashful's husband.

The adventures of Lady Orphan are more complicated and are reminiscent of Affectionata-Travelia's in **"Assaulted and Pursued Chastity."** Lady Orphan falls in love with Lord Singularity, whom she was intended from childhood to marry, and comes to the bold decision of joining him in Italy, where he is serving as General to the Venetians and winning a golden name. Travelling south in the company of her foster-father, Father Trusty, she presents herself to Lord Singularity in the disguise of a page and is taken into his service, quickly winning his confidence. After several adventures—for example, falling under suspicion of being a spy—she accompanies her master to the wars and acquits herself so gloriously that the Venetians make her Lieutenant-General to their army. She travels home in the company of Lord Singularity and at the Pope's urgent request breaks her journey in Rome, where she defeats the whole College of Cardinals in argument. The Pope is so impressed that he offers to make her a saint or a cardinal as she chooses, but as either of these honours would have interfered with her relation to Lord Singularity, she declines them and continues on her way. She doffs her disguise of a boy only when her foster-parents are accused of murdering her, and Lord Singularity's affection for her immediately becomes love. The play ends with their marriage.

An outline cannot reflect the confusion of the play, which is so long that it had to be broken into two parts, like so many of the others. The three unities, of time, place and action, are completely disregarded; time is indefinite in extent and operation, place is an appendage of character, and action creeps through a delta of tedium. As for the characters, they unaccountably emerge and disappear like figures in a dream and are to be recognized only by their names, indicative of their humours—Lady Wagtail, Sir Roger Exception, Nurse Fondly, Sir Peaceable Studious, Mrs. Reformer, *et al*.

All her other plays fall under the same condemnation; none lives up to the promise of its title: *Youths Glory and Deaths Banquet, The Publick Wooing, The Comical Hash, Bell in Campo,* etc. There is not an exception to contradict the impression that Margaret's genius was quite unsuited for the stage. The greatest rewards her plays offer are a deeper insight into her own character, an occasional passage of smart dialogue, commenting satirically on the follies, fashions and conventions of the day, and many eloquent speeches expressive of her poetic sensibility.

A few of her scenes have sometimes been complained

against as exceptionally coarse for a woman, even allow-ing for the greater licence of the age; but the charge is not well grounded. She could not help but catch the tone of Newcastle's loose conversation, but when she imitated it she was revealing her longing to speak with the freedom of men rather than an innate coarseness of character. If society tolerated adultery and seduction on the stage when they were drawn by a man, why should she as a woman not except the same licence? Was the discussion of vice also to be a male prerogative? Her frankness may not be prepossessing but it is introduced rarely, and then so for-mally that her intention is patent.

In a general prologue to all her plays Margaret explained that their faults were due to the rapidity of their compo-sition; they were, she continues,

> So quickly writ that I did almost cry
> For want of work, my time for to employ:
> Sometime for want of work, I'm forced to play,
> And idly to cast my time away.

And in another place she confessed that as she found pleasure only in writing, she was constantly anxious lest her brain should grow barren, 'or that the root of my fancies should become insipid, withering into a dull stu-pidity for want of maturing subjects to write on.' During her last years in Antwerp she was running out of subjects; poetry, natural philosophy, fiction and the drama, she had attempted them all, and having exhausted her stock of ideas on them, she was at a loss for new subjects, or, more correctly, for further opportunities to relieve her fancy.

Luckily one of her correspondents suggested that she should write a volume of orations. At first she demurred, and not only on account of her ignorance of the rules of rhetoric; even supposing that she possessed the necessary 'wit, eloquence and learning', how could she speak on matters of war and peace, or on affairs of state, the usual themes of orators, without knowledge of them, which, being a woman, she had been denied? However, she agreed to make a trial of one or two orations and to send them to her correspondent for her approval, and if they were approved, she would attempt others, sufficient to make a book.

The suggestion was fruitful because she admired orators above all others; not formal orators but natural orators, 'that can speak on a sudden upon any subject, whose words are as sweet and melting as manna from Heaven, and their wit as spreading and refreshing as the serene air, whose understanding is as clear as the sun, giving light of truth to all their hearers, who in case of persuasion speak sweetly, in case of reproof, seasonably, and in all cases, effectually.' The greater number of the heroines of both her stories and plays are called upon to speak in public, and a few actually make oratory their profession, reveal-ing Margaret's own longing to have the freedom and opportunities of men to address assemblies. Lady Sanspa-reille, the demi-heroine of *Youths Glory and Deaths Banquet,* persuades her doting father to let her preach her

opinions. She first addresses an audience of philosophers on nature, and they are so struck with admiration that one of them suggests—needless to say, the remark is an inter-jection by Newcastle—that they should all shave off their reverend beards 'and stuff boys' footballs with them.' Other gatherings which she enlightens in the course of her brief career are composed of moral philosophers, orators, poets, young students and soldiers; and as she dies prematurely, she is comforted by the thought of the several monuments to be erected to her memory.

Denied Lady Sanspareille's opportunity, Margaret had to address 'reading auditors', and her collection of orations, *Orations of Divers Sorts, Accomodated to Divers Places,* which appeared in 1662, after her return to England, was the closest she came to shining in public as an orator.

Margaret's *Orations* is one of the most systematic of her works and yet one of the most disappointing. Alarmed by criticisms that her plays were without plot, design or catastrophe, which hurt though she had herself anticipat-ed them in the preliminaries to the collection, she at-tempted a methodical arrangement of her orations and explained it in a well-ordered address to the reader. Her orations were, in the first place, general orations, adapted to any kingdom or government. She wished her readers to imagine themselves in the market-place of a metropolitan city listening to a debate on peace and war. War is the people's choice, and a number of orations on the field of battle follow, succeeded in turn by further orations deliv-ered in the city, ruined by the war and now rebuilding. The series is so far a reflection of Margaret's own time. Orations in the king's council and in the judicature are the necessary sequel and prepare for orations suitable to domestic occasions. Orations on civic affairs, on the merits of a country life, on trade and commerce and on scholar-ship wind up the cycle, which has touched upon all the activities, deserving of eloquence, of any community.

The scheme is admirable, but unfortunately Margaret's self-consciousness under criticism, and her lack of knowl-edge of many of the subjects treated, inhibited her fancy, and the delightful irrelevancies, satiric, shrewd, or poetic, which are the reward of the most tedious pages of her other works, are missing. The style is clear and smooth but flat and monotonous; and the self-imposed restraint, the deliberate avoidance of eccentricities, injects an insi-pidity into her thought and sentiment which is quite un-characteristic. On very few occasions does she reveal her true qualities. A peasant's address to prove the happiness of rural life offers her an opportunity to express yet again her deep love of the countryside, a theme which whenev-er it occurs, as it frequently does, in her stories and plays is as refreshing as a gust of chill evening air through a hot room. 'Can there be more odoriferous perfumes than the sweet vegetables on the earth?' the peasant exclaims, in accents unlike those of any peasant: 'or finer prospects than stately hills, humble valleys, shady groves, clear brooks, green hedges, cornfields, feeding cattle, and fly-ing birds? Can there be more harmonious music than warbling nightingales and singing birds? Can there be more delightful sounds than purling brooks, whispering winds, humming bees and small-voiced grasshoppers? Can there be a more delicious sweet than honey? More wholesome food than warm milk, fresh butter, pressed curds, new-laid eggs, seasoned bacon, savoury bread, cooling salads, and moist fruits? Or more refreshing drink than whey, whig, and butter-milk? Or more strenghtening drink than ale, mead, perry and cider? And are we not our own vintage?'

The speeches of the quarter-drunk and half-drunk gentlemen are disappointingly flat, but in 'a sleepy speech to students' and in 'a waking oration', its reply, Margaret enters for the first time in the collection into her own realm of fantasy. The first orator contends that the drowsy world of dreams, provided the dreams be pleasurable, offers more than the contemplative or poetic worlds, for not only the mind but the senses, too, are engaged: 'The truth is, the poetical world, and contemplative life, is rather a world for thoughts, and a life for the mind, than the senses: yet, if the senses were as sensible in contemplation as in dreams, it would be the best life of all; because it might make the life what it would, and the pleasures of that life to continue as long and to vary as oft as it thought good; and for the poetical world, or rather worlds, they would be a delight to view as well as to live in.' This strange opinion is rejected by the second speaker, who condemns the drowsy world as only suitable for 'dull, lazy, unprofitable creatures', a mad chaotic world. 'And as for dancing balls and French fiddles,' which the first speaker had professed to enjoy to perfection only in dreams, 'when the gallants, in dreams, are dancing in smooth measures and with fair ladies, and the music keeping tune to the dancing-time, on a sudden the courtly dancers, or dancing courtiers, turn topsy-turvy, dancing with their heads downwards and heels upwards; a very unbecoming posture for fair-faced ladies! And as for the music, that is quite out of tune, and the fiddle-strings broken, and the musicians as mad as March hares.' This surprising vision, which occurs at the very end of the collection, is Margaret's typical way of protesting against the unnatural restraint which she had imposed upon herself throughout its course, and is identical with the protests which she lodged at the conclusion of several of her writings on natural philosophy.

The letters in which Margaret discussed the composition of the *Orations,* along with many other letters, were collected by her and published in 1664 under the title of *CCXI Sociable Letters. Sociable Letters* is her most delightful work in prose and deserves to be far better known than it is. Who her correspondent was it is impossible to say, perhaps her friend and former maid, Mrs. Topp; but the informality of the letters strongly suggests that though written with the idea of publication in mind, they were actually addressed to someone and were not simply self-communings. The form suited her excellently. Unable to give her attention to any one subject for long without digressing restlessly into fantasy, the flexible length of the letter allowed her to concentrate upon a single topic and to dismiss it once she had made her relevant observations. And as there were no rules to govern their composition, she was not continually set on edge by the sus-

picion that she was unwittingly transgressing them. A further advantage was that intimate correspondence with a trusted friend released her from bashfulness. Bashfulness, she once wrote, is a tyrant, whipping the body with 'pains of restraint' and imprisoning thoughts, words and wit; and many of her defects as a writer were caused by her bashfulness at appearing before the public. At ease with her correspondent, she was spared these agonies and could avoid their effect.

The naturalness of the *Sociable Letters* allowed her to give a clearer and fairer impression of her own character than in any of her other works. Neither her comedies nor her comical tales would lead the reader to suppose that she had a genuine sense of humour; the humour there is largely unintentional, as when she adds to a scene of duelling the stage direction, 'Meantime the women squeeks'. But her letters show that she could laugh at a ridiculous situation—at the behaviour of her neighbour's jealous wife—and gently at herself, at her attempts to employ her maids. They also reveal an uncommon shrewdness in observing society; and her opinions were expressed so sharply that had she thought of it, she could have written social satire to effect.

Her comments on the manners of society are many and various, ranging from opinions to descriptions of incidents. The behaviour of Lady D. D. and Lady C. C., for example, is compared in a sketch of what happened at the dinner parties they gave. Though hurt by an unkind remark of her husband's, Lady D. D. suppressed her tears and continued to entertain her guests, excusing her husband to them afterwards by saying that even the dearest and lovingest of friends would on occasion give cause for exception: 'thus her discretion did not suffer her passion to disturb her guests, and her good nature did excuse her husband's folly, and her love did forgive his disrespect to her.' Lady C. C. behaved to the contrary. Being a 'mode' lady she would have a 'mode' dinner, and was highly disgusted when the cook sent up a chine of beef, knowing his master loved it. The serving of beef was 'not only an old but a country fashion' to her refined taste, and she commanded its removal. Her husband objected, she repeated the order, and very quickly the pair fell from words to blows, and she retreated weeping to her chamber, to her guests' discomfiture: 'the truth is, she showed herself a fool and behaved herself as mad.' Or there is the anecdote of Sir S. P., who was foolish enough to lose £500 at tennis and £2,000 at cards and dice, which led Margaret to consider the evils of tennis and gambling, whoring and drunkenness. She condemned tennis because it wasted a man's vital spirits 'through much sweating,' and whoring because it destroyed his health and property and brought his family to misery; and 'so with the pot and the rot, the ball, the card and the dice, men busy the whole time of their life, or rather waste the whole time of their life, together with their life; and not in any one of these actions is honour, nor, as I can perceive, pleasure.' Her social comments are constantly entertaining and surprising.

The variety of the *Sociable Letters* includes speculations

in natural philosophy, literary criticism, and anecdotes taken from her own experience; but as many of these letters have been quoted already, or will be used later, it only remains to refer to those in which she generalizes on life with an ease and eloquence superior to many moralists of reputation. Good sense always governed her private life and is equally revealed in her letters. 'Indeed time runs so fast upon youth,' she wrote in reply to her correspondent's desire to anticipate the passage of time, 'as it doth oppress youth, which makes youth desire to cast it by; and though the motion of time is swift, yet the desire of youth is swifter, and the motions of thoughts are as far beyond the motions of time, as the motion of time is beyond the motion of nature's architecture; so as youth through its sharp, greedy hungry appetite devours time, like as a cormorant doth fish, for he never stays to chew but swallows down whole fishes, so youth swallows, as it were, whole days, weeks, months, years, until they surfeit with practice, or are fully satisfied with experience.'

Margaret's writing had swallowed down the years of exile. *CCXI Sociable Letters* was the last of her works composed in Antwerp. When she had travelled to England in company with Sir Charles Cavendish in 1651, she had been entirely unknown beyond the narrow circle of her family. Between her departure from England in 1653 and her return at the Restoration, she had published four books and was famous, or notorious, as the leading literary woman of the age.

Patricia A. Sullivan (essay date 1980)

SOURCE: "Female Writing Beside the Rhetorical Tradition: Seventeenth Century British Biography and a Female Tradition in Rhetoric," in *International Journal of Women's Studies*, Vol. 3, No. 2, March/April, 1980, pp. 143-60.

[*In this essay, Sullivan compares Cavendish's* Life of William Cavendish *with Thomas Sprat's "Life of Cowley," highlighting the influence of gender on the form and style of biographical writing. She asserts that Cavendish's use of extensive detail, heightened emotional pitch, and temporally sequenced narrative creates a human "life story" that contrasts with Sprat's objective analysis of his subject's contribution to society.*]

The historical difference between the improvised education afforded girls and the highly structured training in rhetoric given to boys reveals at least some of the roots of the female tradition in rhetoric. Seventeenth century Britain can be used to document some of the connection between training and the development of a female mode of writing, for it was a time of strict segregation of schooling (sex-wise) and it also was the time when "respectable" ladies began to publish letters, poetry, biographies and autobiographies—giving us published material for women as well as for men. The education girls received was an extremely practical and personal training, usually from their mothers, who stressed home management, reading for cultural improvement, writing letters and diaries,

pious living, and the arts. The boys received a highly agonistic training that stressed public speaking, analytic reasoning, and ceremonial combat. Interestingly enough, biographies published by women and men trained in these modes show styles that reflect the schooling they received. The women, educated practically, tend to heighten the emotional involvement with the subject, use massive detail for realistic effect, and create a temporal and episodic sequence through narrative. The men, educated academically, tend to distance the question/subject, construct adversaries, and handle arguments through analytic division. The two styles rarely overlap. Thus, as biographies by women and others untrained in the rhetorical tradition are published, a considerable conflict in structure, style, and purposes is presented for the reading public (previously published accounts fit the academic mold). How does the influx of non-rhetorically trained writers into the public market affect form in biography? (in the novel?). In what ways can this clash inform us about the roots of the now famous female tradition in writing?

Let us pursue these questions through a contrast of two representative biographies—Margaret Cavendish, Duchess of Newcastle's *The Life of William Cavendish* (1667) and Thomas Sprat's "Life of Cowley" (1669). If the practical (female) education and the abstract, ceremonial (male) education result in contrasting approaches to structure, attitude and content in the later published writing, Margaret Cavendish's writing should be taken up with more day to day living, masses of detail, expression of feeling, involvement with the story, and additive rather than antithetical style, while Thomas Sprat's biography should produce a more formal, oratorical account that features the accomplishments of Cowley (mental, physical and religious), his leading or key thoughts, his adversaries and their criticisms, and some generalized account of Cowley's life, all presented in antithetical, argumentative fashion. Sprat, the rhetorically trained biographer, should replace the almost unrestrained personal involvement with a more analytical admiration, very carefully grounded in the virtues of the subject-at-hand. And, in his account, identifiably rhetorical structures (like distancing the question, analytic division, and adversary procedure) should take precedence over story-telling. In short, the Duchess' work should strive for a realistic, humanly informed "life story," while Sprat's work should seek to evaluate and judge the quality of Cowley's contribution to society.

The Life of William Cavendish and the Rhetorical Tradition:

Structurally, *Life* divides itself loosely into four books, some authorial notes and a recounting of the author's life. The first two books tell the story of William's war exploits and misfortunes in exile: William is portrayed as knight in shining armor. His involvement in the Civil War (Book I), as told by his secretary to Margaret, who sets down Rolleston's account with total credulity, gives William an unblemished record. The question of whether William was justified in fleeing the country when he did is never posed, much less discussed in any fashion. No attempts are made to explain William's actions, for it is assumed that no justification is necessary. In the second book, the Duchess includes a more detailed account of events, for she has entered this phase of William's life. Still, throughout his misfortunes and maneuvers to avoid creditors she talks only of his sad lot as a loyal subject and never of his spendthrift nature or the egotistical qualities necessarily present for him to leave her in Antwerp as pawn for his debts while he returned to England with the king. William emerges as the suffering servant of the king, and one who, in the end, is rewarded not a hundred-fold but with only a fraction of his losses restored. This makes the concluding scene touching; William has outlived his usefulness and therefore is replaced by younger, wittier courtiers. His story, as the Duchess has created it, is one of the lively, loyal and ultimately human knight.

The third and fourth books drift away from the story and are tied to the narrative in subject matter and purpose only. The third book has sixteen sections, five which discuss the personal qualities brought out in the first two books, four which give new data concerning his past life and pedigree, and seven which present capsules of his habits and humors. By far the most intricate section is the discussion of the pedigree that, after stating William's ancestry goes back to William the Conqueror, proceeds to chart extensively five generations of the Duke's family. The fourth book, entitled "Essays and Discourses," has sixty-three somewhat formal statements by the Duke and twenty-two conversational statements. From the first group, fifty-six are comments on government and seven on universal aspects of human nature. The second group has more of a conversation set up between "I" and "my Lord" in which the Duchess recalls the conditions under which each of the statements were made. The conversation gives a good estimation of the Duke's repartee, which, at best, was variable (e.g., LXXIV is trite, while LXXXIII is witty). "Notes of the Authoress" has seventeen sections—the first seven exalt William and the final ten wander off into vague generalizations that have nothing to do with the theme. The final section of the work concerns the Duchess' life—this she writes so that should she die and the Duke marry again people would know that she, and not another of the Duke's wives, was the author of this work.

This structure—two books of narration, two books of additional information to enhance the subject's character and include anecdotes inappropriate to the flow of the narrative but important or interesting to the author, and an autobiography of the author—contrasts substantially with the structure of biographies written in the traditional format. The rhetorical tradition would hardly present a story as a simple narration, though it would include a narration of sorts (*narratio* in oratory) as part of the pattern. Since tradition in biography was explicitly or implicitly evaluative, undertaking to convince the reader that, given all the possible situations and criticisms, the person under scrutiny remains a humble, moderate, and virtuous man or—as in the case of St. Thomas More's *Life of Richard III*—is, on the contrary, villainous. Instead of limiting the viewpoints so that only one impression can be extracted (i.e., William is the courageous and loyal servant of the king, a man who had suffered much phys-

ically and monetarily), the rhetorical approach seeks to allow multiple viewpoints so that areas of doubt concerning the character and actions of the person can be uncovered and countered, making a few concessions for humanity's sake. As a case in point, notice the rhetorical structure of Thomas Sprat's "Life of Cowley." In sixteen pages (folio) Sprat handles a discussion of Cowley's early life, a defense of his loyalty to the king, a discussion of Cowley's writing (with its various phases), a favorable evaluation of his character, a flaw, the reactions to his death, and the answer to why such lives as his are profitable to preserve as models for the ordinary people. Following an oratorically inspired pattern, the work manages to keep itself tightly woven—connecting each strand of the argument with its preceding and following segments. The areas of doubt (e.g., the question of Cowley's loyalty to the king) are expressed directly in the account and answered in proper argumentative fashion. The complexity of the person, while not being emphasized, is not denied. And there exist no after-sections to house other material which contribute to the major point of the essay. The entire text makes one unit—an argument for the value of Cowley's life.

Distancing the Question:

The traditional biography does not encourage an intimate author/subject familiarity, though tempered admiration usually evidences itself in the tone of the work. Instead, "distance" governs the author/subject relationship, subduing intense emotions. In Sprat's biography of Cowley it is obvious that Sprat respects and admires Cowley as a writer and as a man, but that in no way impinges on Sprat's ability to criticize the actions of Cowley:

> If anything ought to have been chang'd in his Temper, and Disposition: It was his earnest Affection for Obscurity and Retirement . . . I acknowledge he chose that state of Life, not out of any Poetical Rapture, but upon a steady and sober experience of Humane things. But however I cannot applaud it in him. It is certainly a great disparagement to Virtue & Learning it self, that those very things which only make Men useful in the World, should encline them to leave it.

Sprat is a trusted friend of Cowley's (in his will Cowley confided his manuscripts to Sprat for editing and publishing), but has no blood relationship to him, and Cowley is dead when the biography is written. These factors help establish a physical distance from the subject that the Duchess does not enjoy and enable Sprat more latitude in his judgment of Cowley. Still, readers can sense that Sprat would have kept a distance regardless, and, conversely, that the Duchess would have made even a distant person familiar.

More than physical distance is at play here, however. Sprat approaches his subject while the Duchess tells the story of and chats about her husband. The centuries of oratorical tradition, all but unknown to Margaret Cavendish, are the foundation of Sprat's stance toward knowing. Agonistically framed, rhetoric (at root oratory, organized with the help of writing) identifies problems, lists arguments, and selects appropriate attacks. Sprat feels his writing is primarily a contest in which the best competitor wins. And, in this rhetorical tradition, to assure the orator that he could argue even his brother down, the question has to be distanced for better management. The quotation above illustrates the distancing. Sprat assures the hearer that Cowley has chosen to retire for rational considerations rather than out of an emotional response to some stimuli and then enters his objection, "I cannot applaud it in him." The key phrase is "it in him," for Sprat does not rashly insinuate that Cowley is a doomed man because of one action; he separates the wrong from the man and distains the action rather than the person. He further distances the debate by moving away from Cowley and the concrete situation to a platitude on "Virtue and Learning" that he means to be universally applicable. This emphasizes even more strongly that he is primarily interested in right conduct and has used an action performed by Cowley to illustrate his beliefs of right and wrong. The move is both psychologically and operationally a sound one. He is able to divide the "sinner" and his "sin"—often a primary objective in good oratory. For to face the question objectively (at a distance from personal involvement), the speaker has to maintain his own self without regard to the oration.

The Duchess' *Life* displays a much more intense personal involvement of the author and the subject than is common among traditional treatments. Springing from her status as a relative and the fact that her husband was living when the account was written, her stance toward William in the biography is a close, totally sympathetic and humble one that envisions no criticism. Though the Duchess at times attempts the type of formal distance maintained in the traditional biography, she can never quite abandon her primary motive for writing, praising her husband for his faithfulness to king and country and recounting his misfortunes. Her partisanship makes it hard to separate the knower from the known. Take, for example, the opening of each of the four books:

> Since my chief intent in this present work is to describe the life and actions of my noble Lord and husband, William, Duke of Newcastle, I shall do it with as much brevity, perspicuity, and truth, as is required of an impartial historian . . .

> Having hitherto faithfully related the life of my noble Lord and husband, and the chief actions which he performed during the time of his being employed in his majesty's service for the good and interest of his King and country, until the time of his going out of England, I shall now give you a just account of all that passed during the time of his banishment till the return into his native country . . .

> Thus having given you a faithful account of all my Lord's actions both before, in, and after the Civil Wars, and of his losses, I shall now conclude with some of the particular heads concerning the description of his own person, his natural humour, disposition, qualities,

virtues; his pedigree, habit/diet, exercises, etc., together with some remarks which I thought requisite to be inserted, both to illustrate the former books, and to render the history of his life more perfect and complete . . .

> Containing several essays and discourses gathered from the mouth of my noble Lord and Husband. With some few notes of mine own. I have heard my Lord say . . .

The openings to the first three books attempt a distance. The distance, however, is slight and somewhat unreal because it is so personal and alien to the rest of the account. In these openings the Duchess uses first and second person—the most familiar persons—couching the introduction in terms of what "I" want to say about "my noble Lord" instead of what is important to be said about William, Duke of Newcastle. The fact that she uses "my noble Lord and Husband" in all four openings emphasizes both the emotional ties between author and subject and her desire to emphasize the relationship. Such maneuvers, even in the guise of formal discourse, hardly breed the distance necessary to make the Duchess the "impartial historian" she claims to be. She does not even remotely approximate the type of distance Sprat obtains in the opening of his biography:

> Mr. Abraham Cowley was born in the City of London, in the Year one thousand six hundred and eighteen. His parents were Citizens of a virtuous life and sufficient Estate and so the condition of his Fortune was equal to the temper of his mind, which always was content with moderate things.

Sprat immediately assumes a reporter's distance in the account, placing references in the third person and the verbs in past passive voice. He gives his opinion of Cowley—that his fortune and temper of mind were both content with moderate things—instead of stating a very generalized purpose for the writing as the Duchess does—to describe the life and actions of my Lord. Though more direct, Sprat's beginning achieves more distance.

Analytic Division:

In addition to the distancing of the subject, rhetorically styled biography very painstakingly divides and analyzes the material at hand. Calling on grammar school practice in exercises for theme writing and oratory, the academically trained biographers tend to construct analytic lists of reasons or traits important enough to be considered. This hearkens back to the countless classical writing and rhetorically styled Christian sermons they had copied and summarized; the books on rhetoric they had copied, translated, retranslated, and analyzed; the commonplace books they had made for each form of writing and for rhetorical purposes; and the speeches and defenses they had prepared by listing all the arguments they could imagine and choosing the most vital ones. It is little wonder that their writing features appropriated rhetorical procedures: arguments, lists, and objections that are handled analytically.

Sprat's discussion of Cowley's writing offers an example

of such divisions. Sprat handles Cowley's writing in two spurts. At the outset of the discussion he declares: "Of his works that arc Publish'd, it is hard to give one general Character, because of the difference of their subjects; and the various forms and distant of their writing." Thus, initially he takes pains to tell the reader *why* a simple classification cannot be rendered. This disposes the reader to hear his reasoning further and likewise prepares the reader for the forthcoming divisions, which are handled quite deftly. He then sets up the two attacks; the first is directed at the general qualities of Cowley's works while the second deals with particular works, countering any objections those works received. He gives first the generally positive aspects of Cowley's writing; then he settles into fielding criticism he has heard from others. Take, for example, the opening argument:

> If any should think that he was not wonderfully curious, in the choice and elegance of all his words: I will affirm with more truth on the other side, that he had no manner of affectation in them: he took them as he found them made to his hands; he neither went before nor came after the Age. He forsook the conversation, but never the Language of the City and Court . . . If his Verses in some places seem not as soft and flowing as some would have them, it was his choice not his fault. He knew that in diverting mens minds, there should be the same variety observ'd as in the prospects of their Eyes: where a Rock, a Precipice or a rising Wave, is often more delightful than a smooth, even ground, or a calm Sea. Where matters required it, he was as gentle as any man. But where higher Virtues were chiefly to be regarded, an exact numerosity was not his main care. This may serve to answer those who upbraid some of his pieces with roughness, and with more contractions than they are willing to allow . . . that as the peculiar excellence of the Feminine Kind, is smoothness and beauty: so strength is the chief praise of the Masculine.

In this passage Sprat takes Cowley's words and discusses their excellence in terms of affectation, conformity to usage of the age, choice of jerky rhythm for aesthetic purposes, effectiveness in communicating the proper mood and virtue, and strength of verse. Using examples, he argues that roughness (visual aesthetics) can often become more interesting than smoothness and that roughness is characteristically more masculine (as smoothness is feminine). Through these examples, Sprat implies that Cowley is the strong, male artist and those who wince at his strengths are, perhaps, a bit effeminate (as well as not aesthetically quite so astute).

That argument is followed by three other discussions of the general strengths of Cowley's prose and verse. Sprat discusses Cowley's perfect mastery of Latin and his ability to write equally well in both Latin and English. Then he moves to Cowley's poetic "Fancy" which he says: "flowede with great speed, and therefore it was very fortunate to him, that his Judgment was equal to manage it." Cowley always, in Sprat's opinion, had "invention powerful and large as can be desired. But it seems all to arise out of the nature of the subject, and to be fitted for the thing of which he speaks." Finally, he discusses generally

the variety of arguments present about Cowley's work, pointing out their contradictory nature.

In his discussion of the particular works, Sprat begins with the love verses, then the Pindaric imitations, Cowley's *Davideis,* his moral and divine works, the Latin poems, his nature books, his letters, and the first discourses. Each of these has at least a paragraph devoted to some of the positive comments and counters to negative criticisms. Generally this portion of his discussion is more defensive than the section that treats the general characteristics of Cowley's writing, probably because there are usually more specific criticisms given than general ones. (Sprat also throws in a defense of his exclusion of Cowley's letters from his edition of Cowley's *Works*.) Yet, each of the criticisms leads the discussion to a point where Sprat can move on to a more positive presentation, and in each criticism the mythical objector is discredited.

This method of handling the products of someone's life (in lieu of giving the events of the person's life) by careful division is almost totally foreign to the Duchess' work. She is, in her account, quite noticeably prone to enumeration: the losses of William; the misfortunes encountered by William; the sufferings of William; William's blessings; his honors and dignities; his pedigree. The crucial difference between the lists the Duchess makes and those compiled by rhetoricians is the latter's use of analysis. The Duchess' lists enumerate those qualities which are present in her husband. They do not attempt, with the possible exception of her totalling of financial losses, to divide the material in such a way as to interrelate its parts for more effective argumentation; they simply give a tally. On the other hand, the listing practiced by orators is a divisive measure aimed at reducing the size of the question into packets more easily argued (*partitio*). The Duchess does not need this process because she is making no overt arguments in *Life*. To her, William is a hero beyond the reach of argument: there is no reason to invent arguments against so perfect a knight.

Adversary Procedure:

A third characteristic tactic found in rhetorically styled writing is the identification or, often, creation of adversaries. Such adversary procedure handles possible objections and arguments counter to the authors' arguments by mentioning first that "some have objected to this because . . ." Then the authors answer "these people" with portions of the reasons that discredit or mollify somewhat their objection. Thus, the authors can create an agonistic model and test their arguments on paper with opponents of their making. This tactic is particularly useful in persuasive or judical situations where the authors try to convince the readers that they can answer all objections—and what better means than by thwarting some mythical opponent?

Sprat invokes this adversary procedure frequently in his discussion of Cowley's Civil War involvement and of his published works. He answers all possible objections, and those unfavorable arguments which he has definitely heard voiced merit "some people have said." He also frames Cowley's disagreements with others in terms of adversary proceedings. When the objection is vague or not fully formed, Sprat uses "if any shall think," "if any are displeased," or "if there needed any excuse to be made." Those points where Sprat has definitely heard criticism rate "some" people in the arguments—"as some would have it," "this may serve to answer those who upbraid," "some people object," "enough to that sort of men." Sprat even reconstructs Cowley's reasoning behind his controversial preface in an agonist fashion:

> The objection I must not pass by in silence . . . This is the true reason that is to be given of his delivery of that opinion [anti-crown statement in the preface to poetry volume]. Upon his coming over he found the state of the Royal Party very desperate. He perceived the strength of their enemies so united, that till it should begin to break within it self, all endeavors against it were likely to prove unsuccessful. On the other side he beheld their zeal for his Majesties Cause, to be still active, that it often hurried them to inevitable ruine. He saw this with much grief. And though he approved their constancy, as much as any man living, yet he found their unseasonable shewing it, did only disable themselves, and give their Adversaries great advantages of riches and strengths by their defeats. He therefore believed that it would be meritorious service to the King, if any man who was known to have followed his interest, could insinuate into the Usurper's minds, and could perswade the poor opressed Royalists to conceal their affections, for better occasions.

Sprat faces the objection directly, declaring he cannot pass it by; rather he must answer the challenge. Sprat then sets the nature of his attack; he will give "reason" behind Cowley's "opinion." This assures the readers that the argument will be staged on rational grounds. Sprat continues, relating the history in terms of Cowley's "perceiving" and "seeing" a grave situation in which well-intentioned people acted in a fashion that weakened the Royal Party. He "sees" this with much "grief"; thus Sprat reduces the emotion of Cowley's reaction. Cowley's adversity to the Royalists is framed in agonistic terms, for "though" he approves of their "constancy," "yet" he sees the advantage it gives to their "adversaries." As a consequence of this reasoned analysis, Cowley "therefore" decides how those people who recognize the situation and are faithful to the king must act. That decision presses Cowley to write the controversial preface—an act born of loyalty rather than disloyalty. Thus, Sprat shows the analytic and agonistic method Cowley invoked as defense for his words.

Sprat uses the adversary procedure noticeably more in the sections where he defends Cowley's loyalty to the crown and where he discusses Cowley's writings than in sections where he talks of Cowley's personal qualities. This is understandable since traditionally the adversaries are more important in a judicial situation than they are in a laudatory one. Thus, the places where defenses are required are the places where adversaries spring up.

On the other hand, in the Duchess' *Life,* though there are situations present in William's life that are ripe for defense, there is no over attempt to defend by argumentation any of his actions. The Duchess refuses to recognize that William may not have lived the blemish-free existence that she paints for him. The points most worthy of comment are his involvement in the Civil War and his acceptance of diminished influence in the restored reign of Charles II. Regarding William's abrupt departure from England, occasioned by the loss of the battle of Marston Moor, the Duchess raises no question that there might have been another way for William to deal with the situation, nor does she defend his decision:

> . . . well knowing that those which were left could not hold out long, and being also loath to have aspersions cast on him, that he did sell them to enemy, in case he could not keep them, he took a resolution, and that justly and honourably, to forsake the kingdom . . . the gentry of the country, who also came to take their leaves of my Lord, being much troubled at his departure, and speaking very honourably of him, and surely they had no reason to the contrary.

Instead of presenting the alternatives open to William, simulating some rational process by which he reached the path of action he took, and answering the objections adversarily as Sprat does, the Duchess presents as the inevitable course of action a decision which all others involved questioned. She also does not face and answer criticism of others (though "surely they had no reason to the contrary" shows she knew) for actions of that sort will always receive criticism from some quarter.

Later, when William finds little satisfaction from Charles II after the Restoration, the Duchess does not openly admit to conflict between them. Instead of playing up the loyal service versus the terrible treatment received from "some people" as the rhetorical writer would, the Duchess subtly draws the conflict by mentioning her own disgruntlement at the housing provided William and by relating her urgings for his retirement to the country.

And, when he decides to follow her advice and try to recoup some of his vast losses, she only mentions what William says to Charles: "but whatsoever your Majesty is pleased to command me, were it to sacrifice my life, I shall most obediantly perform it; for I have no other will, but your Majesty's pleasure." After such a loyal and eloquent statement, the fact that there is no reply noted for Charles stands as testimony that Charles thought William expendable. But, the Duchess does not dwell on this snub, showing how unjustified it was; rather she leaves Charles' reaction without personality or clarity and glosses over the area of dispute. In no way can she be accused of stirring the ashes of the dispute; in fact, she smothers any flames.

The Life of William Cavendish and the Female Tradition:

It is clear that the Duchess' *Life* does not conform to the characteristic patterns for biography written in the rhetorical (academic) tradition; not only does she keep a familiar voice, fail to divide the argument into parts, and refuse to create adversaries who she then answers, the Duchess veers from the tradition in a more substantial manner: she refuses to argue in an overt fashion. While we can sense that she recognizes some of the criticisms leveled at her husband—particularly with regard to his leaving the court of Charles II—she never openly admits that anyone criticized any of William's decisions or actions. Traditional biography would state and answer all criticisms of William's decisions and actions; Margaret does not do either. Thus, while the Duchess shows some familiarity with conventions of traditional biography—she calls herself "an impartial historian" in the opening even if the distance is familiar, she lists traits though the lists are not for the purpose of topical division, and she denies that anyone would criticize her husband which negates the possibility of adversaries—she does not openly and rationally argue the validity of her evaluation, a procedure at the heart of rhetorical thinking and writing. The reason why she and other female biographers of the day "fail" to follow the formats prescribed in academic training can be traced, at least in part, to the variance in education given to women: they were not intimately acquainted with the rhetorical devices ingrained into men educated in the school systems. "Why," however, is not so interesting a question as "To what effects?"

Did the special features of the Duchess' *Life* (features shared with other contemporary female biographers and autobiographers) contribute to the growth of a particular style we often times label the female tradition? The reluctance to engage in any overt argument certainly is a central feature in that tradition, as it is in *Life*. This is not to say that such works have no argument; instead, they proceed indirectly. As Thomas Farrell observes in his discussion of modern female rhetoric ["The Female and Male Modes of Rhetoric," *College English*, Vol. 40, No. 8, 1979], this argumentation through indirection is quite sophisticated: the writer attempts to engage readers in the process that led to the conclusion rendered so that readers will understand how the conclusion was reached. In *Life* we see the rudiments of such argumentation. It is not the entity possessed by modern examples, for after two books the work turns into a collection of relevant data. But, in its refusal to argue directly, a refusal that was tolerated because the Duchess was a woman and "did not know any better," even though the Duchess hints at her awareness of criticism, and in its attempt in the first two books to tell the story of William's involvement in the Civil War and his life afterward using the "brevity, perspicuity, and truth, as is required of an impartial historian," the Duchess invites readers to listen to the life of William in its proper perspective. She intends for readers to understand the trials and sufferings of her lord. And that fits with the attitudes governing argumentation through indirection.

As with rhetorical biography, *Life* depends on a number of devices to achieve its purposes: increased involvement between author and subject (heightening of emotional pitch); an intimate, complex knowledge of the subject (massive detail about the subject); and telling the true story rather than constructing an abstract, rational, and evaluative argument (narrative construction). All of these characteristics help the readers achieve the goal of these female biographer—understanding the life and actions of the subject under consideration. Let us observe these traits in action.

Heightening of Emotional Pitch:

The Duchess is intensely involved with the life of her husband and displays that partisanship in several ways, including a heightening of emotional pitch over that used in rhetorical works. Instead of establishing a distant, formal tone of a judge, she varies the pitch of the work to establish a lively tone throughout the first two books. Though not as informal as some modern styles, the *Life* sounds an enthusiastic, informal tone that finds some similarities with much of the romantic fiction of the day (this fits with our notion that the familiar form impinges on the writing style adopted). This enthusiasm reaches full swing in the narrative and winds down considerably in the more contemplative books. In the narrative the Duchess methodically records examples of William's loyalty and greatness. A series of visits by Charles II serve as an illustration:

> Nor was this the only honour my Lord received from his Majesty . . . being met one time in Antwerp, were pleased to honour my Lord with their presence, and accept of a small entertainment at his house, such as his present condition was able to afford them. And some other time his Majesty passing through the city was pleased to accept a private dinner at my Lord's house; after which I receiving that gracious favor from his Majesty that he was pleased to see me, he did merrily, and in jest, tell me that my Lord's credit could procure better meat than his own. Again, some other time, upon a merry challenge playing a game at butts with my Lord (when my Lord had played the better of him), What . . . have you invited me to play rock?

This jovial little account is followed by a passage that declares these events are mentioned to show "my Lord's happiness in his miseries," and proceeds to expound on William's loyalty and on royal and foreign dignitaries' recognition of his goodness. But all this serves as introduction to the Duchess' comments about the extent of William's miseries and sufferings:

> He was put to great plunges and difficulties, insomuch that his dear brother Sir Charles Cavendish would often say, that though he could not truly complain of want, yet his meat never did him good by reason my Lord, his brother, was always so near wanting, that he was never sure after one meal to have another: and though I was not afraid of starving or begging, yet my chief fear was that my Lord for his debts would suffer imprisonment, where sadness of mind, and want of exercise and air, would have wrought his destruction, which yet by the mercy of God he happily avoided.

The rise in pitch is quite effectively wrought. Moving from innocuous entertainments of the king (which are esteemed because they involve the king directly), to assertions of William's loyalty (which is evident if the king has chatty and private visits with him), and finally to fears of starving or going to prison for debts (which would be tantamount to death), the pitch builds gradually to intensify and reinforce the wife's fears. And, it becomes more evident that this build-up has been placed when the next paragraph moves the time forward to set a new event. The Duchess intuits that the context of loyalty, greatness, and misfortune in which she enshrouds William's life cannot be half so tonally effective without variations— peaks and troughs of emotion that point to a private rather than a public knowledge of the subject and that add a realism (which in modern times is closely linked with truth).

Massive Detail about the Subject:

Achieving a portrait steeped in intimate, complex knowledge of the subject depends, quite heavily, on the amount of private detail used in the account. Such detail supplies a realism and a sense of privileged knowledge lacking in rhetorically structured biographies and encourages readers to believe the author has intimate and complete knowledge of the events. In *Life* the Duchess uses masses of details to tell the story of William to some interesting effects. Take William's involvement in the Civil War. The Duchess uses realistic detail structured dramatically to reenact the battles, creating a fairly realistic war scene. Even though that section of the biography is the one that receives criticism, for when compared to other histories and documents it seems one-sided, the Duchess' rendering of the battle scene far outstretches Clarendon's version in color and drama. The Duchess relates:

> "Gentlemen," he said, "you have done me the honour to choose me your captain, and now is the fittest time that I may do you service; wherefore if you will follow me, I shall lead you on the best I can, and show you the way to your own honour." They being glad of my Lord's proffer as my Lord was of their readiness, went on with the greatest courage . . . in which encounter my Lord himself killed three with his pages half-leaden sword, for he had no other left to him . . . At last, after they had passed this regiment on foot, a pikeman made a stand to the whole troup; and though my Lord charged him twice or thrice, yet he could not enter him; but the troup despatched him soon.

Clarendon's account of William's final battle runs like this:

> This may be said of it, that the like was never done or heard or read of before; that two generals whereof one had still a good army left, his horse, by their not having performed their duty, remaining upon the matter, entire, and much the greater part of his foot having retired into town, the great execution falling on the north foot, and the other, having absolute commission over the northern countries, and very many considerable places in them still remaining in his obedience, should both agree in nothing else but leaving that good city and the whole country as prey to the enemy . . .

The Duchess' account is far more engaging, and probably more convincing to readers with no knowledge of the events, even though the question Clarendon raises is one she never attempts to answer. Small details make the difference. Speech, action, and the props accompanying action are geared to reenactment much more closely than to situation analysis. Thus, the Duchess recreates the excitement of the battle while Clarendon judges military strategies and their subsequent effects.

The Duchess' use of detail is most convincing in Book II of the biography where she recounts the events she remembers (the substance of the first book was told to her by William's secretary). Almost without regard for patterning, she weaves these details into the narrative as "proof" of her main point. The amount of detail she uses slows the story to an almost realistic pace at times. Take one of her passages on life in Antwerp as example:

> After my Lord had been in Antwerp some time, where he lived as retiredly as it was possible for him to do, he gained much love and respect of all that knew or had any business with him. At the beginning of our coming thither, we found but few English (except those who were merchants) but afterwards their number increased much, especially of those of quality; and whereas at first there were no more but four coaches that went the Tour, viz. the Governor's of the Castle, my Lord's, and about two more, they amounted to the number of above a hundred, before we went from thence; for all those who had sufficient means, and could go the price, kept coaches, and went the Tour for their own pleasure. And certainly I cannot in duty and conscience but give this public testimony to that place. That whereas I have observed, that most commonly such towns or cities where the prince of that country does not reside himself, or where there is not great resort of the chief nobility and gentry, are but little civilized; certainly the inhabitants of the said city of Antwerp are the civilest and best-behaved people that I ever saw. So that my Lord lived there with as much content as a man of his condition could do, and his chief pastime and divertisement consisted of the manage of two aforementioned horses; which he had not long enjoyed, but the Barbary horse, for which he paid 200 pistoles in Paris, died, and soon after the horse which he had from Lord Crofts; and though he wanted present means to repair these his losses, yet he endeavoured and obtained so much credit at last that he was able to buy two others, and by degrees so many as amounted to the number of eight. In which he took so much delight and pleasure, that though he was then in distress for money, yet he would have sooner tried all other ways, than parting with any of them; for I have heard him say that good horses are so rare as not to be valued for money and that he who would buy him out of his pleasure (meaning his horses), must pay dear for it. For instance I shall mention some passages which happened when my Lord was in Antwerp.

This passage maintains the Duchess' extremely consistent purpose, but the interest is fostered by her use of detail. How does she convey to the readers the influx of people of quality? By the radical increase in the number of carriages that "went the tour." And how does she show that

Antwerp was civilized? By the fact that my Lord is able to turn his attention to the care and feeding of his horses. The people allow him to be taken up with the care and feeding of his horses rather than throwing him into debtors' prison or subjecting him to some other similar fate. And, she can make those connections without blinking an eye.

Narrative Construction:

The narrative construction used in the first two books of **Life** is the most popular means of patterning biographies among women biographers of the day. The straightforward, temporal sequence of narrative allows them to naturally spin the stories of the subject's life. It fits much more easily with the purposes of the female biography than the structure preferred by the rhetorical tradition (subordinating sequential narrative to argumentative consideration of issues, principles, and explanations of worth). The narrative also is the form with which they have had most practice, since most women wrote diaries, letters, and copies of sermons, and read the Bible, romances, diaries, letters, and pious works. Hence, they feel as comfortable with narrative sequencing as rhetorically trained men feel with oratorically based writing.

In the biographies written by women, time plays a more important role in the accounts than it would in traditional biography: it becomes more important to know when an event happened and what came next. This results in careful selecting of events, setting of atmosphere, and establishing of characters in order to have meaning shine through this time-linked rendition of the subject's life. It also results in the use of time devices rather than rhetorical devices for transition and coherence in the writing. The Duchess shows this use of time; as she moves from event to event, time-oriented transitions are her mainstays. The first two books are filled with transitions such as: immediately upon receipt, not long after, as soon as, about the same time, about this time, some short time after, in December, during the time, in the meantime, next was, and that day. She employs temporal progression for coherence and transition rather than linking together the parts of the biography with argumentative connectors.

The narrative, and the influence of narrative romances, encourages a move toward fiction. For example, the Duchess' narrative features a high charge of hero worship. "My Lord" fights with a flourish and lives in style even when the debtors' prison threatens. He epitomizes the gallant knight of the age—loyal, brave, chivalrous, generous, faithful, and a lover of horses. In fact, he is so perfect in the role of the gallant knight that he could have been found in some fictive account. Fate causes his misfortunes; he does not have character defects. Never a foul word does he utter; to his enemies he is generous and forgiving. The Duchess paints no flaws into her husband's countenance, and, consequently, he seems a bit too good to be human. Such semi-deification figures in many of the biographies written by women of the day (prime examples are Mrs. Hutchinson's *Memoirs of the Life of Colonel Hutchinson* and Lady Fanshawe's *The Memoirs*

of Ann, Lady Fanshawe), for it seems that when these women write, especially about close relatives, they exaggerate the strengths and either minimize or, as in the case of the Duchess, disregard entirely their weaknesses. This quickly leads to an account one-sided enough to push the biography toward fiction—a folk hero in the vein of the older folk narratives and romances. Such is the case with the Duchess; she creates a hero-story to serve as the life of her dear husband, William.

Sylvia Bowerbank (essay date 1984)

SOURCE: "The Spider's Delight: Margaret Cavendish and the 'Female' Imagination," in *English Literary Renaissance*, Vol. 14, No. 3, Autumn, 1984, pp. 392-408.

[*In the following essay, Bowerbank views the controversial "eccentricities" of Cavendish's literary productions as reflections of what the author considered to be her "true wit," her femininity, and her philosophy of nature.*]

> The world arose from an infinite spider
> who spun this whole complicated mass from
> his bowels.
>
> (Brahmin Teaching)

Recently Margaret Cavendish, Duchess of Newcastle (1623-1673), was remembered in the popular [*The Incomplete*] *Book of Failures* [by Stephen Pile, 1981] as "the world's most ridiculous poet." And for the past three hundred years—although Charles Lamb may have enjoyed the eccentricity of her person and prose—readers of her works have agreed that she failed as a philosopher and as a writer. In *A Room of One's Own*, Virginia Woolf goes searching for a seventeenth-century "Judith Shakespeare" and finds in Cavendish's writings "a vision of loneliness and riot . . . as if some giant cucumber had spread itself over all the roses and carnations in the garden and choked them to death." In her study of seventeenth-century travel fantasies, *Voyages to the Moon*, Marjorie Nicolson refuses to describe Cavendish's **New Blazing World** because she cannot bear to reread that "ponderous tone" in order "to bring order out of . . . chaos." But Cavendish herself confesses her shortcomings. In a typically disarming epistle to the reader she warns, "I shall not need to tell you, I had neither Learning nor Art to set forth these Conceptions, for that you will find yourself." Her naivete of method can be and has been blamed on her lack of education and lack of access to learned and critical communities. Yet anyone who has ventured to read ten pages of Cavendish's work knows that her method, or rather her defiance of method, is deliberate.

I. Cavendish's Conception of Herself as a True Wit:

In most of her writings Cavendish celebrates, in theory and in practice, what she calls her "natural style." Her first book, **Poems and Fancies** (1653), announces the approach she exemplifies:

> Give Mee the Free, and Noble Stile,

Which seems uncurb'd, thought it be wild . . .
Give me a Stile that Nature frames, not Art:
For Art doth seem to take the Pedants part.

She associates the writings of the learned with sterile artificiality and labored imitation. Cavendish's "true wit" is natural wit unrestrained. Occasionally in her writings she depicts playful confrontations between fancy and reason; for example, in *Philosophical Fancies* (1653), Reason cautions Thoughts to "walke in a Beaten Path" lest the world "think you mad." But Thoughts rebel: "we do goe those waies that please us best. / Nature doth give us liberty to run / Without check." For Cavendish, "Learning is Artificial, but Wit is Natural" (**"To the Reader"**).

While Restoration comedy might be seen to share this perspective in spirit, if not in method, the prevailing literary opinion and practice of her age denied such a polarization between natural wit and learned judgment. As early as 1595, Philip Sidney's *Defence of Poesie* claimed that natural wit "reined with learned discretion" becomes true wit. In *Timber,* Ben Jonson uses the same image (ultimately taken from Plato) of the rider-poet reining in his horse (spontaneous wit) with a bit (judgment). Like the bee—now known to scholars as "the neo-classic bee"—the true writer imitates; he is able "to draw forth out of the best, and choicest flowers . . . and turn all into honey." In *Epicoene,* Jonson creates the archetypal Truewit who has many descendants in Restoration comedy. In all his speeches Truewit seems to speak spontaneously; actually Jonson constructed his "instinctive" eloquence by means of a careful rejuvenation of classical sources. For Jonson, study and imitation, rather than making wit artificial, purify it and make it more right and more natural. In later neoclassical writers, like Dryden, the trend to understand true wit in terms of judgment dominating fancy increased to the point of eliminating fancy altogether.

It will be clear how estranged Cavendish was from the prevailing literary attitudes if we look at a passage from a writer of the next generation who excelled at anatomizing perversions of wit. Readers of *A Tale of a Tub* are familiar with Swift's masterly creation of the narrator who can be identified as "a mad modern." In a remarkable passage at the end of "A Digression concerning . . . Madness," Swift reveals the narrator's mentality by playfully applying the traditional horse/rider image: madness is the overthrow of reason by fancy; it is a "revolution" against the natural hierarchical order of the two faculties: "I myself, the author of these momentous truths, am a person, whose Imaginations are hard-mouthed, and exceedingly disposed to run away with his reason, which I have observed from long experience to be a very light rider, and easily shook off; upon which account my friends never trust me alone."

What is mad for Swift is feminine for Cavendish. Reason may predominate in men, but fancy predominates in women. In *Poems and Fancies,* Cavendish reminds ladies of poetry as "belonging most properly to themselves." Female brains, she claims, "work usually in a Fantasticall motion" and therefore "go not so much by Rules and Methods as by choice" (**"To all Noble and Worthy Ladies"**). Elsewhere she emphasizes that reason is enslaved by necessity while fancy is voluntary (**"To the Reader"**). In **"Poetesses hasty Resolution"** prefacing *Poems and Fancies,* she describes how her self-love in its ambition for fame overcame her judgment when she published her poems without revision. Reason is depicted as an authoritarian bully who would have told her how ill her poems were if she had not rushed them into print. In a later work she defends herself against a rude comment by a reader who said, "my wit seemed as if it would overpower my brain" by asserting that "my reason is as strong as the effeminate sex requires."

She is claiming, for women at least, a freedom from "rules and method" denied writers by the seventeenth-century literary climate, dominated as it was by the opinions of Horace, whose satiric target in *Ars Poetica* is the Democritus who believes "that native talent is a greater boon than wretched art and shuts out from Helicon poets in their sober senses." Cavendish was convinced that her originality was enough "ground" for "lasting fame." Over and over again, she tells her readers that she has no time for studying other people's work because "our sex takes so much delight in dressing and adorning themselves." Besides, her ambition is not to be a lowly scholar but a great philosopher: "A Scholar is to be learned in other mens opinions, inventions and actions, and a philosopher is to teach other men his opinions of nature" (**"To the Reader"**). This ambition led her to send her *Philosophical and Physical Opinions* (1655) to Oxford and Cambridge. Hoping this action is "not unnatural, thought it is unusual for a woman," she asks the universities to house her book "for the good encouragement of our sex; lest in time we should grow irrational as idiots, by the dejectedness of our spirits, through the careless neglects and despisements of the masculine sex to the effeminate" (**"To the two Universities"**). Besides, she does not see why her opinions should not be studied with other "probabilities" (such as Aristotle's teachings); after all, only the custom of teaching ancient authors prevents readers from a "right understanding" of "my newborn opinions."

As we have seen, Cavendish associates fancy unregulated by judgment with vanity, especially in women. Yet she expects readers to share her good-natured tolerance of this charming foible, "it being according to the Nature of our Sex." At the same time, she presents literary labor as pedantry not becoming to noble persons like herself. Although this attitude was not uncommon among her contemporaries (at least professedly), it led Cavendish to reject revision of her work as a task beneath her dignity and also unnatural to her as a woman. In her supposedly revised *Philosophical and Physical Opinions* (1663), she thinks it is enough that she is "very Studious in my own Thoughts and Contemplations" and that she records them in their natural and noble disorder: she had "neither Room nor Time for such *inferior Considerations* so that both Words and Chapters take their Places according as I writ them, *without any Mending or Correcting*" (**"Epistle to Reader,"** my italics). She goes on to hope that "Understanding Readers" will not reject the "Inward worth" of her philosophy "through a Dislike to the Outward Form." The truth is there somewhere, she claims, because she makes no attempt to censure "Nature," which gives her thoughts "which run wildly about, and if by chance they light on Truth, they do not know it for a Truth" (**"Epistle to Mistris Toppe"**).

Her justification for her lack of method is that she recreates pure nature. Although she cannot create a well-wrought urn, so to speak, she gives fresh thoughts: she asks, "Should we not believe those to be Fools, that had rather have foul Water out of a Golden Vessel, than pure wine out of Eathern or Wooden Pots?" (**"To the Reader of My Works"**). The natural trait she imitates is fecundity. Nature brings forth monsters, as well as well-proportioned offspring, and lets them die of their own deformity; in like manner, Cavendish claims, she "scribbles" down whatever comes to her and lets the reader sort it out. Fecundity and originality are the gifts of the true wit. Cavendish is best understood, then, as a defender not of her sex, but of self and self-expression.

Hers is the mentality which is the target of Swift's *Battle of the Books* (1704). In the famous confrontation between the bee and the spider, the ancient and the modern respectively, Swift uses the bee to symbolize the principles and practices of neoclassicism. "By an universal Range, with long Search, much Study, true Judgment, and Distinction of Things," the bee-writer "brings home Honey and Wax." The spider, on the other hand, is akin to Jonson's Little-wit, in *Bartholomew Fair,* who "like a silkworm" spins creations "out of myself." Swelling up, Swift's spider boasts, "I am a domestick Animal, furnisht with a Native Stock within my self. This large Castle . . . is all built with my own Hands, and the Materials extracted altogether out of my own Person." His characteristics—his stress on originality; his fondness for a domestic rather than a "universall" perspective; his aimless creativity which, although it creates a space for himself, gives nothing of use (honey and wax) to others—are so extreme that he is fittingly called a subjectivist. The neoclassical bee warns that the spider's perspective ("a lazy contemplation of four Inches round") and his method ("feeding and engendering on it self") turns "all into Excrement and Venom; producing nothing at last, but Fly-bane and a Cobweb."

Yet with what exuberance did Cavendish embrace this subjectivist perspective and method as her own. With a curious aptness she favors imagery of silkworm, spider, and spinning for depicting literary creativity, particularly hers. In *Poems and Fancies,* she writes that "all brains work naturally and incessantly" and goes on to call the writing of poetry "spinning with the brain." She intends to win fame as a writer "by spinning" a "Garment of Memory": "I cannot say the *Web* is strong, fine or evenly Spun, for it is a Course piece; yet I had rather my Name should go meanly clad, then dye with cold" (**"The Epistle Dedicatory"**). I have italicized "web" to emphasize how naturally Cavendish could fuse the images of the spinner and the spider. Cavendish resorts to spinning imagery when excusing herself for encroaching on male prerogative: women have so much "waste time" that "our

thoughts run wildly about," producing not only "unprofitable, but indiscreet Actions, winding up the thread of our lives in snarles on unsound bottoms" (**"An Epistle to Mistris Toppe"**). To describe "great masters of speech," she writes that they can speak "untangled"; they "can winde their words off their tongue" without a snarl or knot; they can work the "thread of sense into a flourishing discourse." Yet Cavendish is aware of the commonplace implications of the imagery of silkworm and spider. In *Natures Pictures Drawn by Fancies Pencil* (1656), a collection of conflicting tales about life by various speakers usually identified by sex alone, she has "a Man" denigrate the creativity of spider and silkworm:

> The Silkworm and the Spider Houses make,
> All their Materials from their Bowels take . . .
> Yet they are Curious, built with Art and Care,
> Like Lovers, who build Castles in the Air,
> Which ev'ry puff of Wind is apt to break,
> As imaginations, when Reason's weak.

In her autobiography Cavendish presents a poignant picture of her life as an isolated duchess who would be a famous writer. Her one delight was her solitary creativity which she describes using her favorite imagery: "I had rather sit at home and write . . . I must say this on behalf of my thoughts, that I never found them idle; for if the senses bring no work in, they will work of themselves, like silkworms that spins [sic] out of their own bowels."

II. No Room in Salomon's House·

In his *New Atlantis,* Francis Bacon imagines Salomon's House, a patriarchal institution dedicated to enlarging "the bounds of Human Empire" over nature. When the Royal Society was founded in 1662, it was based on the Baconian principle that the search for knowledge must be communal and experimental. Because the advancement of knowledge requires a mind "steadily fixed upon the facts of nature," Bacon was suspicious of the speculative mind which works "upon itself, as the spider worketh his web," and brings forth only "cobwebs of learning." For Baconians, there could be no room in Salomon's House for natural philosophers who give out their "own imaginations for a pattern of the world."

Margaret Cavendish's writings, as we shall see, attempted to provide an alternative perspective to the prevailing Baconian paradigm. Her lifelong ambition was to win public acceptance as Nature's true champion. In 1653, as R. H. Kargon points out [in *Atomism in England from Hariot to Newton,* 1966], Cavendish "expounded an Epicurean atomism at once so extreme and so fanciful that she shocked the enemies of atomism and embarrassed its friends." Everything could be explained by the motion of atoms, such as: what causes dropsy, how the brain works, and why the earth has attraction. And "the Cause why things do live and dye, / Is, as the mixed Atomes lye." At times her descriptions of atoms are no less plausible than the descriptions of how the world works given in the learned texts of her more restrained contemporaries who were also fumbling around in search of a credible mechanics—for example, Robert Boyle with his corpuscular universe. At other times she is fancy-free and plays with her atoms, as when she imagines "A World in an Eare Ring": "Wherein a Sun goeth round, and we not see. / And Planets seven about that Sun may move." And her ultimate defense of her opinions is that, although they may or may not be true, they are natural. After all, "I do not applaud my self so much as to think that my works can be without errors, for Nature is not a Deity" (**"To the Reader"**).

Her intuitive, if erratic, exposition and defense of Nature's ways continued after 1660, although, probably in response to the more restrictive intellectual climate of the Restoration, she abandoned atomism: if each atom were "absolute," there could never be "good government" in the universe (**"Another Epistle to the Reader"**). This use of a political analogy suggests that her social perspective—that of a royalist duchess restored to her place in a regulated kingdom—had some influence on these later speculations about the natural order. In another work she repudiates atomism because in that philosophy every atom is "a kind of Deity" undermining the harmonious whole of Nature. In this typically entertaining passage she depicts rebellious democratic atoms: "Nature would be like a Beggars coat full of lice; Neither would she be able to rule those wandering and stragling atomes, because they are not parts of her body, but each is a single body by itself, having no dependance upon each other."

Yet she continued to present Nature as self-moving and perceptive. *Philosophical Letters* (1664) should be read as a vindication of the wisdom of nature and the "intelligence" of matter from what Cavendish considers the belittling attacks of Henry More, Hobbes and Descartes. She ridicules More for assuming the passivity of nature (**"Letter VIII"**). She denies Hobbes' claim for human supremacy by means of language over the rest of creation. As everyone knows, she quips, "a talking man is not so wise as a contemplating one." Other creatures, she says, have their own reason: "For what man knows, whether Fish do not know more of the nature of water, and ebbing and flowing, and the Saltness of the Sea?" She attacks Descartes' separation of mind from body and his reductionist attitude toward the body: "the Eye, Ear, Nose, Tongue, and all the Body, have knowledge as well as the Mind."

The only difference is that the mind, rational matter, is not "encumbered with the grosser parts of matter to work upon" but the senses, sensitive matter, "works or moves only in its own substance." Reason, as she tells us in another work, is "nothing but corporeal self-motion, or a particle of the purest, most subtil and active part of matter." This being the case, she asks why the human should "be the onely Creature that partakes of this soul of Nature," and why the rest of Creation "should be soulless or (which is all one) irrational." The natural soul of reason permeates nature: "I do not deny that a Stone has Reason." Clearly these insights into nature's vital connectiveness resemble the ideas of Anne Conway and others.

Her philosophy of nature is empathetic, subjective, and fragmentary. Sometimes she happens to create a startlingly beautiful analogy; for example, she likens animate matter to a spinner and inanimate matter to yarn: "Natural air seems to be made by such kinds of motions as spiders make cobwebs, for the animate matter's motions spin from a rare degree of inanimate matter." But mostly her natural philosophy consists of passages excusing and flaunting her ignorance; for example, she writes about the anatomy of the body by confessing that she never read a book on the subject nor studied the body because "the modesty of my Sex would [not] permit me." In *Observations upon Experimental Philosophy* (1666), she presents a curious argument to show that speculation is a higher means toward knowledge than experiment is. Playing on the overlapping social and intellectual connotations of the word "mechanick," she writes that "experimental or mechanick Philosophy" should be subservient to speculative philosophy just as "the Artist or Mechanick is but a servant to the student." Her main target in *Observations* is the microscope, that "artificial informer" that "more deludes than informs." The year before, Robert Hooke published his influential *Micrographia* describing his experiments with the microscope. Cavendish thinks it "unnatural" to change the size of creatures so they "cannot be judged according to their natural figure." For illustration, she ridicules one of the experiments describing the 14,000 eyes on a fly. The microscope must be misleading us here or else, she asks, why doesn't a fly see a spider? She adds that these "eyes" might be "blisters or watery pimples."

This is the kind of speculation Joseph Glanvill, an apologist for the Royal Society, compliments in a letter to "your Grace" when he admires "the quickness and vigor of your conceptions." But he adds that hers is a pattern that men should not imitate. Glanvill denies that ratiocination is higher than "perfection of sense" by reasserting the Baconian paradigm. A natural philosopher must be willing "to tie down the mind in Physical things, to consider Nature as it is, to lay a Foundation in sensible collections, and from thence to proceed to general Propositions, and Discourses." Walter Charleton, another member of the Royal Society, also treats her with the tact required in writing to a duchess: he professes not to know "which of the two, Aristotle or your Grace, hath given us the best definition of the humane Soul." But he also warns her that all opinions, even hers, must be subjected to "skeptical Judgement."

In another letter, Charleton tells her the use to which he puts her philosophy: "Whenever my own Reason is at a loss, how to investigate the Causes of some Natural Secret or other, I shall relieve the Company with some one pleasant and unheard of Conjecture of yours so that by reading your Philosophy, I have acquired thus much advantage: that where I cannot Satisfy, I shall be sure to Delight." With her peculiar sense of humor and self-importance, Cavendish would have been pleased with this unusual tribute. There is no doubt that in small selected doses Cavendish delights us, as she intends to, with her fanciful conjectures and self-mockery. Charleton also teased her about her eccentric style: "You plant Fruit-trees in your Hedge-rows, and set Strawberries and Rasp-berries among your Roses and Lilies." Yet even for this "art" he flatters her: she has a fancy "too generous to be restrained" by "the laborious rule of Method."

It was probably not any of her ideas—radical and eccentric as they may seem—that alienated her from the community of natural philosophers. After all, Charleton, a popularizer of Epicurean atomism of the type made respectable by Gassendi, was forgiven after he trimmed his work to the hostile winds of Restoration science. As we have seen, Cavendish willingly discarded her politically dangerous atomism. And other writers, if more cautiously, were sympathetic to finding the life principle immanent in nature. There were two main factors, then, contributing to her exclusion from the intellectual community: her sex and her untamed method. Lady Ranelagh is the only other contemporary Englishwoman who has a claim to being called "a scientific lady," and she was content to work through her brother, Robert Boyle. To a limited extent Cavendish was able to overcome social restrictions because of her status as a duchess and as the wife of a patron of virtuosi: she corresponded with leading thinkers; she published her works; she got invited, albeit as a spectator, to the Royal Society in 1667. But mostly she was isolated. With good reason, then, she defends contemplation as the means, indeed her only means, to seek natural truths. The Royal Society, based as it was on the inductive method and the fraternal accumulation of knowledge, could provide no home for her person or her perspective.

Cavendish's response to her failure as a natural philosopher was to retreat into fantasy. In 1666 she created her own *New Blazing World*. As she tells us in **"To all Noble and Worthy Ladies"** of the 1668 edition, the opinions advanced in *New Blazing World* have "sympathy" and "coherence" with those expressed in *Observations,* to which it was originally appended in 1666. But in *New Blazing World,* she could be "Margaret the First" in a more congenial world; no one should begrudge her this pleasure "since it is in every ones power to do the like" (**"To the Reader"**).

The tedious chaos of the "plot" is an obvious feature of this work which has been attacked elsewhere. The central character is an Empress of a newly found polar kingdom whose main interest is in ruling over the virtuosi: "the Bearmen were to be her Experimental Philosophers, the Bird-men her astronomers, the Flyworm- and Fish-men her Natural Philosophers, the Ape-men her Chymists, the Satyrs her Galenick Physicians," for example. The Empress becomes angry at her virtuosi when the Bearmen observe celestial phenomena through a telescope and begin to quarrel. The Empress condemns telescopes as "false informers" which "delude" their senses. Obviously this is the same opinion Cavendish advances in *Observations,* but in *New Blazing World* the Empress has power to command them to smash their instruments. She lets them keep their toys only when her experimental philosophers admit that "we take more delight in Artificial delusions, than in Natural truths."

In *New Blazing World,* Cavendish deliberately lets fancy take the reins and creates a world which indulges her fondest wishes—even allowing her some harmless retaliations against the Royal Society. Cavendish imagined a situation, improbable even in the twentieth century, in which a female leader dominates the scientific community. Her experimental philosophers are hack workers on detail, servants who bring in their observations so that the Empress can triumphantly speculate and create a synthetic truth. But the independent, intelligent Empress gets lost in the oblivion of Cavendish's prose.

What we remember instead is the eccentric duchess created in Pepys' *Diary,* who made an infamous visit in 1667 to the Royal Society during which leading scientists such as Robert Boyle and Robert Hooke did experiments to provide what Marjorie Nicolson derisively calls [in *Pepys' Diary and the New Science,* 1965] "the afternoon's entertainment." According to Pepys' enduring version, Cavendish did not "say anything that was worth hearing, but . . . was full of admiration, all admiration." What we remember, then, of the seventeenth-century "scientific lady" of England is the image of woman as audience and, at best, as patron of men's accomplishments.

To reinforce how fanciful, how "mad," how revolutionary, and ultimately, how irrelevant Cavendish's vision of a female scientific genius was to her contemporaries, we need only compare the relationship of the Empress to her virtuosi with the more famous depiction of the relationship between an intelligent woman and a modern philosopher in Bernard Fontenelle's *Plurality of Worlds, Entretiens sur la pluralite des mondes* (1686) was one of Fontenelle's most ingenious tactics in his life-long attempt to popularize the ideas of the new philosophy. There were 28 editions of *Entretiens* in Fontenelle's long lifetime (1657-1757). The passages quoted in this essay are from the 1638 translation by Aphra Behn. The immense popularity of *Plurality of Worlds* can be explained, to a great extent, by Fontenelle's choice of format. As Behn's subtitle tells us, he uses "five nights conversation with Madam the Marchioness of****" in a garden in order to defend the mechanical philosophy and the theory that there are other inhabited worlds. We are to enjoy a pleasant and flirtatious dialogue between "Fontenelle" and Madam even as we learn the truths of the Cartesian universe: "we are always in the Humour of mixing some little Gallantries with our most serious Discourses."

But what interests us here is the relationship between the two conversationalists: "Fontenelle" is the authority; he will teach the Copernican system. There are, for him, "no more unnecessary Difficulties" because he can reduce nature to a few easy laws. Because nature works like the contrivance of machines behind the scenes of an opera, he can "draw the Curtains and shew you the World." What room is there for dialogue when one party has all the answers? Well, this expert is a chivalrous servant to a noble and charming lady. Madam is an eager, intelligent, and pliable student. But she has her little rebellions—"just like a woman." When "Fontenelle" offers to demonstrate a point by drawing a zodiac in the sand, she stops him: "It would give a certain Mathematical Air to my Park, which I do not like." Although she admires the simplicity of the Copernican system, she objects to the insecurity of the earth in it. She teasingly claims to favor the Indian system in which the earth is supported by four elephants. If danger threatens these solid foundations, the Indians "would quickly double the number of their elephants." "Fontenelle" laughs "at her fancy"; this is reminiscent of Charleton's pleasure at Cavendish's wit. Late on the first night, Madam at last agrees to be reasonable and to be Copernican. Later when she holds back in attractive timidity from the implications of such a vast universe, he urges her on to intellectual courage.

Thus although modernists like Fontenelle might eagerly debunk the traditional cosmic hierarchies of Aristotle and Aquinas, "Fontenelle" and Madam embark into the new universe with their respective sexual roles intact. He leads intellectually and she follows. Even though Behn might object to the inconsistency of Madam's superficial yet profound character, Fontenelle's book did teach women (and men) what was actually being debated in the science of the seventeenth century, and Behn approved of bringing women into intellectual circles. But Cavendish's *New Blazing World* offered no instruction and no access to or compromise with the outside world.

In her own world Cavendish can refuse to moderate her desires to accessible goals and can create her women free from the restrictions which hampered Cavendish in both the social and intellectual realms. Only in paradise, only in a state with people of many complexions—literally azure, purple and green—and only in a state ruled by an Emperor "extraordinary" like her husband in his easygoing, nonauthoritarian character, only in fantasy, could Cavendish find a haven for the intellectually ambitious woman. But beyond making this crucial point, *New Blazing World* offers little reading satisfaction or intelligibility. A passage from Robert Boyle reiterating the contempt the new science felt for subjective truth illustrates why Cavendish failed as a natural philosopher in the age of reason. There was no room in Salomon's House for the spider who "taking notice only of those objects, that obtrude themselves upon her senses, lives ignorant of all the other rooms in the house, save that wherein she lurks."

III. Margaret Cavendish and the Crabbed Reader:

Cavendish was used to such complaints as mine. In *Orations of Divers Sorts* (1668), she ridicules her censorious critics: "those Faults or Imperfections I accuse my self of, in my Prefatory Epistles, they fling back with a double strength against my poor harmless Works; which shews their Malice and my Truth." She asks such "ill-natured" readers why they bother to accuse her plays of having no plots when she already acknowledges that. Such critics "prefer Plots before Wit." Then she states her most characteristic stance as a writer: "I write to please myself, rather than to please such Crabbed Readers." Still there is a proliferation of prefaces before her works in which she addresses readers, shares her problems as a writer and as a thinker, and tells us how to read her work. Yet for three

hundred years, her readers have remained crabbed—except for her husband, Charleton perhaps, and Charles Lamb. Perhaps we have yet to understand the nature of the legacy she left to posterity.

Maybe her sense of humor eludes us. Maybe we are like her sour contemporary, Mary Evelyn, who on overhearing the friendly banter between Charleton and the Duchess to the effect that universities should be abolished if they didn't abandon Aristotle and teach Cavendish's newfound ideas, became so provoked by Cavendish's manner that she dismissed the Duchess as mad. Maybe Cavendish intends us to laugh at the incongruous juxtaposition of her self-deprecation and self-dramatization. She not only ridicules herself and the foibles of her sex but also—and this is important—casts doubt upon serious claims to knowledge of nature's secrets. William Cavendish seems to have shared her skeptical and playful attitude in this passage inserted at the end of her *Philosophical and Physical Opinions* (1663): "Since now it is A-la-mode to Write of Natural Philosophy, and I know, no body Knows what is the Cause of any thing, and since they are all but Guessers, not Knowing, it gives every Man room to Think what he lists, and so I mean to Set up for my self, and play at this Philosophical Game as follows, without Patching or Stealing from any Body." Perhaps Margaret Cavendish developed her science of the fancy to restore the balance in an age of reason. Her work represents, in a whimsical way, a groping toward an alternative vision to Salomon's House with its pretence to finding certain and objective knowledge. And she does attempt a relationship with nature that runs counter to the exploitive mastery proposed by Bacon; her approach is sensitive and reverent as well as subjective.

By her own admission, she was vain, inconsistent and silly; yet she took herself and her philosophy seriously. She was incapable of sustained study and thinking, so she said; yet she wanted to be a famous philosopher and to join the scientific establishment. In the same work she expounds a vitalistic and a mechanistic universe. Her writing is muddled and indecisive; yet she expected posterity to admire it. The effect of letting contradictions stand is to undermine continually any authoritative stance she might be achieving. And yet at times this method gets at the complexity of psychological and social reality: for example, in *Orations of Divers Sorts,* she lets several female speakers describe the lot of women from conflicting perspectives. They claim everything from "we live like Batts, or Owls, labour like Beasts, and dye like Worms" to "what can we desire more, than to be Men's Tyrants, Destinies, and Goddesses?" Since Cavendish makes no judgmental distinctions among her female orators, it would be a mistake to guess her viewpoint; perhaps she shared all their attitudes to some extent. Contradiction is typical of her style. It is hard to say whether this is an intentional strategy or the unfortunate result of her refusal to revise and to edit her writing.

Cavendish's work is a defense of free fancy or subjective expression in principle and in practice. Some modern writers like Anaïs Nin [*The Novel of the Future,* 1976] advocate a revolution in style toward one that would reflect psychological reality: the new literary form would be "endlessly varied and fecundating as each crystal varies from the next." Cavendish can be seen as a pioneer of such an approach. Even those of us who are attracted to her personality and ideas cannot help but wish she had been a more disciplined writer. It is also useful, then, to see Cavendish's place in literary history as a cautionary tale for those of us who would suggest that craftsmanship and order are masculine, and artlessness and chaos are feminine. Do we really want to create a literary ghetto called the "female imagination" and claim as its characteristic style of expression, anarchic formlessness? Style has no sex. After all, the real spider's web, although spun out of herself, is architectonically sound, even elegant.

The theme of Cavendish's *CCXI Sociable Letters*:

Perhaps the commonest theme in these epistles is women, their characteristics and their abilities. As usual, the Duchess has no very high opinion of her sex's wisdom, but she still is ambitious enough to envy men's greater capacities. Women are too much occupied with gossip and dancing, romances and courtships, too completely overruled by the vagaries of tyrannic fashion, for their minds to be more than "shops of smallwares, wherein some have pretty toyes, but nothing of any great value." Feminine influence must come indirectly, for "not only Wives and Mistresses have prevalent power with Men, but Mothers, Daughters, Sisters, Aunts, Cousins, nay Maid-Servants have many times a persuasive power with their Masters, and a Landlady with her Lodger, or a she-Hostess with her he-Guest; yet men will not believe this, and 't is the better for us, for by that we govern as it were by an insensible power, so as men perceive not how they are Led, Guided and Rul'd by the Feminine Sex." Some instances of this fact are given in other letters, but most marriages discussed by the Duchess do not turn out so well. In one case divorce is narrowly averted, there are several matches of convenience, while censorious wives, fickle husbands, and general incompatibility disturb many marital relationships.

Henry Ten Eyck Perry, in The First Duchess of Newcastle and Her Husband as Figures in Literary History, *Ginn and Co., 1918.*

Lisa T. Sarasohn (essay date 1984)

SOURCE: "A Science Turned Upside Down: Feminism and the Natural Philosophy of Margaret Cavendish," in *The Huntington Library Quarterly,* Vol. 47, No. 4, Autumn, 1984, pp. 289-307.

[*In this essay, Sarasohn discusses Cavendish's writings on atomistic cosmology and natural philosophy, and her development of an original speculative philosophy, which Sarasohn associates with Cavendish's feminism.*]

In Margaret Cavendish's play *Love's Adventures,* the heroine dons male clothes, saves her intended and the Republic of Venice from the Turks, and lectures the College of Cardinals on theology to universal acclaim. This literary echo of the famous "world turned upside down" topos of early modern European culture reverberates often in the work of the wife of the "arch-conservative" duke of Newcastle. It is a potent symbol. As Natalie Davis has shown [in *Society and Culture in Early Modern France,* 1965], the reversal of male-female roles in early modern culture, during those strange times in either fiction or fact when women were on top, not only represented a safety valve for releasing the tensions and preserving the order of hierarchical society, but also provided a tool for criticizing, challenging, and sometimes even changing the dominant values and powers of society. Margaret Cavendish believed that the social order could expand to accommodate the intellectual equality of women, without its structure fragmenting from this innovation. Thus, it comes as no surprise to see her embrace the ambiguity of a world turned upside down.

In the seventeenth century, the traditional intellectual values of society also were being challenged by the revolutionary findings of the new science. When Copernicus reversed the places of the sun and the earth, and Galileo and Descartes substituted motion for rest as the basic fact of physics, the universe itself was turned upside down. Margaret Cavendish's work unites the dual assaults on traditional authority implicit in both feminism and the new science.

Joan Kelly has argued [in "Early Feminist Theory and the Querrelle des Femmes, 1400-1789," *Signs: Journal of Women in Culture and Society,* 8, 1982] that "every learned tradition was subject to feminist critique, since all were dominated by men and justified male subjection of women." In this paper it will become clear that Cavendish used the skeptical methodology of the new science not only to attack traditional natural philosophy, but also as a weapon in her battle for the recognition of female intellectual equality. We shall see, however, that this skepticism became a two-edged sword, both damning and justifying female subservience.

Cavendish fused revolutionary scientific ideas and an underlying feminist ideology in her conception of a living universe, infused with motion, and ordered by a female spirit, which could best be understood from the empathetic viewpoint of a female scientist. Thus, both the substance of her philosophy and its exposition justified a revolution in the interpretation of the traditional female role. Cavendish's work shows how the radical implications of one area of thought can reinforce and strengthen the subversive tendencies of another, quite different attack on authority.

Cavendish urged "learned professors to free their minds from the prejudice that nothing coming from the pen of a woman could be worth serious attention." She realized that women were kept in "a hell of subjection" because of the suppression of their natural faculties and intelligence by men. Thus, for Cavendish, the exposition of natural philosophy became a conduit for a reappraisal of the position of women, in which her actions spoke as loudly as her words. Her husband, who was her staunchest ally, wrote in the preface to one of her books of philosophical opinions, "but here's the crime, a lady wrote them, and to entrench so much on the male prerogative is not to be forgiven."

The duchess met the philosophic and scientific geniuses of the age—René Descartes, Thomas Hobbes, and Pierre Gassendi—while in exile in France in the mid-1640s. Her husband had been Hobbes's patron for many years, and both Descartes and Gassendi dined with the Newcastles. It is likely that the duke's enthusiasm for the Scientific Revolution and its proponents originally awakened Cavendish's interest in natural philosophy. The duchess incorporated several themes of the new science into her own enormous corpus of literary works: poems, plays, essays, orations, and disquisitions on natural philosophy.

The duchess's writings are a curious combination of scientific speculation and fantasy, largely uncritical and hopelessly repetitive. Nevertheless, her natural philosophy is no more fantastic than that of some of her male contemporaries, like Kenelm Digby and Johannes Van Helmont, who were considered scientific prodigies in their own time and are now accorded a position of respect as pioneers of science.

Cavendish first elaborated her scientific theories in a book of poetry, *Poems and Fancies,* published in 1653. It is dedicated to her brother-in-law, Charles Cavendish, who with her husband was her main source of information on natural philosophy. Sir Charles was the duchess's companion on a journey to England in 1651. Undoubtedly they discussed the various systems of philosophy at some length, and this is one of the reasons she determined to attempt to develop a system of her own.

In *Poems and Fancies* the duchess advocated an atomistic cosmology which Robert Kargon [*Atomism in England from Hariot to Newton,* 1966], the historian of English atomism, characterizes as "so extreme and so fanciful that she shocked the enemies of atomism, and embarrassed its friends." Her atomism was indeed very extreme and reflects her rejection of all kinds of intellectual authority. According to Cavendish, the world is composed of four differently shaped kinds of atoms: square atoms which constitute earth, round atoms which make up water, long atoms which compose air, and sharp atoms which compose fire. The various concatenations and motions of these different atoms, and the void, make up all the variety of forms and change we find in nature; their motion in the brain constitutes our understanding and emotions as well; their harmony produces health, their disharmony, sickness.

To this extent, the duchess's system, although it may sound strange to modern ears, is not very different from the corpuscular philosophies advocated by Descartes, Hobbes, and Gassendi. The shocking element of Cavendish's atomism was the almost complete lack of theological qualifiers necessary to dissociate mechanism from the charge of atheistic materialism, a complaint often made against Hobbes himself. The duchess's atoms are eternal and infinite, two attributes which the proponents of corpuscular philosophy were careful to separate from their doctrines of matter, because in a Christian cosmology only God can be eternal and infinite. Furthermore the atoms, as the duchess described them, seem to act out of their own volition; whether they are ordered by God is left a very open question:

> Small atoms of themselves a World may make
> As being subtle, and of every shape:
> And as they dance about, fit places find,
> Such forms as best agree, make every kinde. . . .
> And thus, by chance, may a new world create;
> Or else predestined to worke my Fate.

This casual attitude toward divine providence is complemented by similar neglect of the concept of the immortal soul: the soul the duchess describes is material, although she suggests it can somehow continue after death. Since ancient atomism was already considered atheistic because it denied divine providence and the immortality of the soul, Cavendish was treading on very dangerous ground here. This heterodoxy was emphasized when she suggested that there are an infinity of worlds, probably populated, not only outside our world but inside it as well, for instance within a lady's earring: "And if thus small, then ladies well might weare / A world of worlds, as pendents in each eare." It is difficult to understand how Christ's revelation might be preached within an earring.

The underlying methodological premise of Cavendish's natural philosophy is a form of extreme skepticism about the possibility of absolute knowledge of nature, which she shared with her husband and brother-in-law, who in turn were influenced by the natural philosophers they associated with in France. Cavendish felt that our senses cannot penetrate nature's mysteries, and, since every age believes something different, "all opinions are by fancy fed/ And Truth under opinion lieth dead." While skepticism led other natural philosophers to develop new methodologies based on experimentation and the careful use of reason, the duchess used skepticism to justify wild flights of imagination: "Who knowes, but in the braine may dwell / Little small fairies who can tell?"

Cavendish's skepticism was, in part, the consequence of her sex and upbringing. Like most women in the Stuart period, she was relatively uneducated. Although she had tutors in "reading, writing, working, and the like," she was not "kept strictly thereto, they were rather for formality than benefit," since her mother preferred that her daughters be virtuous rather than cultivated. The duchess never learned any foreign language, and her command of English grammar and spelling was at best rudimentary, even given seventeenth-century conditions. Because of these factors, Cavendish was unable to develop a systematic understanding of the work of others. She was very aware of these shortcomings, and on several occasions complained that university education was denied to women, and their minds consequently were underdeveloped: "I will not say, but many of our sex may have as much wit, and be capable of learning as well as men; but since they want instructions, it is not possible they should attain to it. . . ."

Just as the old learning had denied educational opportunities to women, likewise the new learning was largely a male prerogative. Although the duchess was the only woman in the period ever to be invited to a session of the Royal Society, she was invited only to observe a few experiments; it was inconceivable that she could ever become a member. Pepys was afraid that even this small courtesy would cause scandal for the Society. Not surprisingly, Cavendish treated the empirical methodology of the Royal Society with great scorn, claiming that the microscopes and telescopes of experimental science could never discover the interior secrets of nature. In *Observations on Experimental Philosophy* she wrote:

> But seeing that in this age, sense is more in fashion than reason, it is no wonder there are so many irregular opinions and judgments amongst men. However, although it be the mode, yet I for my part shall not follow it, but leaving to our moderns their experimental or mode-philosophy built upon deluding art, I shall addict myself to the study of contemplative philosophy, and reason shall be my guide.

Thus, Cavendish had no choice but to advocate a full-scale skepticism; the path to conventional knowledge was closed to her. She argued that if no one can know anything absolutely, then there was no reason why her speculations might not be as correct or more correct than anyone else's. In this case, skepticism became a warrant for extravagant imagination and uncritical thought, but the very fact that Cavendish could adopt a radical skeptical epistemology and use it to justify her own work demonstrates her abilities and substantiates the claim that the new science had radical implications for areas far beyond the purview of science.

Carolyn Lougee has argued, in her recent book on women in seventeenth-century France, that feminists, both male and female, were attracted to skepticism because it denied customs prevalent in a society at any one time; thus, the subjection of women was not natural and inevitable, but rather circumstantial and malleable. In rejecting custom, tradition, and religious authority, feminism and modernism became one.

Skepticism, however, was a two-edged sword. As Richard Popkin has shown [in *The History of Scepticism,* 1964], skepticism could coexist with conservatism: since there are no absolutes in politics, religion, or custom, the customs of the past have as much validity as those of the present, with the added advantage of proven stability and safety. The inherent ambivalence of skepticism toward tradition, seeing it as both destroyer and conservative apologist, was reflected in Cavendish's ambivalent attitude toward traditional institutions. She fervently defended the superiority of monarchy and hierarchy, reflecting class rather than gender solidarity, but realized all forms of political association were a tyranny of men over women.

Another factor underlying the duchess's radical natural philosophy is a fideism so pervasive that it approaches eighteenth-century deism, and is the theological counterpart of her skepticism. Whenever God is mentioned in any of her works, she insists that he cannot be known in any way whatsoever by his creatures. Her theology is completely negative; we can only know that God is not at all like us. In her *Orations,* she wrote, "whatsoever is Infinite and Eternal, is God; which is something that cannot be described or conceived; nor prescribed or bound: for it hath neither beginning nor ending." Consequently, she believed that faith and reason should be entirely separate, explaining the almost complete lack of theological motifs in her work. While other natural philosophers also advocated the autonomy of faith and reason, Cavendish adhered to this policy much more consistently than they did. It is interesting in this regard to compare her with Walter Charleton, the major English atomist of her time, whose natural philosophy is one long paean of praise to God's providential ordering of the universe.

While the duchess may have borrowed many of her ideas and preconceptions from the general intellectual climate of her day, she believed that her system was entirely unique. The desire for originality was the driving force of her creativity and the impetus for the development of her own unique natural philosophy. In the introduction to her work *Philosophical and Physical Opinions*, she proclaimed, "as for the ground of this philosophical work, as matter, motion, and figure, 'tis as old as eternity it self, but my opinions of this ground are as new as my first conception," and she begs the reader to acknowledge her originality. This plea is echoed in all her writings, where she disparages any kind of imitation.

In *Observations on Experimental Philosophy,* the duchess arued defensively that her philosophy was different than anything taught before, and indeed,

> were it allowable for our sex, I might set up a sect or school for my self. . . . But I, being a woman, do fear they would soon cast me out of their schools, for though the Muses, Graces, and Sciences are all of the female gender, yet they were most esteemed in former ages, then they are now; nay could it be done handsomely, they would now turn them all from females into males; so great is grown the self-conceit of the masculine, and the disregard of the female sex.

The only option left to the duchess, since she could not be admitted into the male preserves of learning, was to develop her own speculative philosophy, rejecting not only the teachings of the ancients, but the system of the moderns as well, at least in theory. If the Scientific Revolution can be considered an attack on the authority of Aristotle and the medieval worldview, the natural philosophy of Margaret Cavendish was a further attack on the authority of a male-dominated science, and, by implication, an attack on all male authoritarianism. In adopting the role of the female scientist, Cavendish implicity turned the world upside down.

Thus Cavendish abandoned atomism by 1661, instead developing a scientific theory where a hierarchy of matter, integrated into an organic whole, composed the entire natural world. According to her theory the universe is composed of matter and motion, which are inseparable. There are three kinds of matter, differing in figure and type of motion, but inextricably integrated in composed forms of matter: rational matter, the most excellent, which is self-moving, the seat of conception, and the director of the rest of matter; sensible matter, which carries out the commands of rational matter, and is the vehicle for sensual perception; and inanimate matter, which is the least excellent because it lacks perception, although it is self-conscious and the material substratum of all being. All of matter is to some degree animate, but this does not cause divisive or natural anarchy because all types of matter are essentially one; diversity is resolved in unity. Self-moving matter is the principle of the world. This materialism is no less extreme than the duchess's atomism, because in it matter remains eternal and infinite, and the soul is considered material.

Did Cavendish's gender affect the content of her science itself? We have seen that the roles which women filled in the seventeenth century circumscribed the duchess's education and influenced the development of her epistemology and methodology. In addition, Cavendish's gender may have acted as an heuristic device, causing her to be sympathetic toward those ideas which substantiated and supported a fuller role for women in the social and natural cosmos. Thus, whenever there is a choice, Cavendish chose the more organic and nurturing view of nature, not necessarily because these ideas are inherently attractive to women, but perhaps because the psychological presuppositions of the early seventeenth century associated the roles of women and nature. Many of Cavendish's male contemporaries were equally attracted to the notion of an organic universe, which had been a dominant world-view for centuries, but most of the proponents of the new science had rejected organicism for the mechanistic model of the universe. The duchess was unusual in her attempt to integrate some of the basic axioms of the new science, for example the pervasiveness of matter in motion, within an organic and vitalistic universe.

Thus matter is animistic, eternal, and a unity in the most far-reaching sense: "Nature is a body of a continued infiniteness, without holes or vacuities." The conservation of matter, the empathy of its parts for one another, and the transformation of constantly changing forms, results in an ordered, harmonious universe: "And since Nature is but one body, it is entirely wise and knowing, ordering her self-moving parts with all facility and ease, without any disturbance, living in pleasure and delight, with infinite varieties and curiosities, such as no single part or creature can ever attain to."

While Cavendish sometimes treats nature as the totality of matter, which is immanently self-ordering, in other parts of her work nature is considered as an ordering principle, somehow transcendent as well as immanent in matter. She considered this principle to be female. Since the duchess had abstracted God so thoroughly from her metaphysics, nature was left with an extraordinarily large sphere of action:

> Tis true, God is the first Author of motion, as well as he is of Nature; but I cannot believe, that God should be the prime actual movent of all natural creatures, and put all things into local motion, like as one wheel turns all the rest; for God's power is sufficient enough to rule and govern all things by absolute will and command, or by a Let it be done, and to impart self-motion to Nature to move according to his order and degree, although in a natural way.

Once God has infused nature with the power of regulating motion, nature operates in an almost entirely autonomous manner, "Nature is neither absolutely necessitated, nor has absolute free-will . . . and yet hath so much liberty, that in her particulars she works as she pleaseth. . . ." This autonomous and almost independent nature is functionally equivalent to a seventeenth-century housewife:

> Nature, being a wise and provident lady, governs her parts very wisely, methodically and orderly; also she is very industrious, and hates to be idle, which makes her employ her time as a good huswife doth, in brewing, baking, churning, spinning, sewing, etc. . . . for she has numerous employments, and being infinitely self-moving, never wants work but her artificial works are her works of delight.

This remarkably pragmatic and industrious nature is as far as an entity could be from the ethereal plastic spirit that some of Cavendish's male contemporaries envisioned. By the end of this disquisition, the duchess tied her robust concept of nature directly to her own feminism: women may be particularly apt as experimental philosophers because they are experienced in the creation of artificial constructs, like "sweetmeats, possets, . . . pyes, and puddings." Moreover, if women became experimental philosophers, they could release men from the burden of "useless experiments," thus enabling them to devote their time to fundamental studies. In this case, Cavendish revealed an ambivalent attitude toward women; they are intellectually equal to men, but nevertheless should be socially subservient to men. Paradoxically, they are good only for those tasks Cavendish most despises. She concluded, "woman was given to man not onely to delight, but to help and assist him."

In fact, woman's relationship with man seems analogous to nature's relationship with God. Just as a good wife orders her household and produces children, nature regulates the world and produces an infinite variety of creatures: "in all figures, sizes and actions is apparent the curious variety of Nature, and the omnipotency of the Creator, who has given Nature a self-moving power to produce all these varieties in her self." Cavendish adopted the principle of the great chain of being, which she infused with vitalistic meaning: God's plenitude, expressed through Nature's fecundity, fills every place in the universe with living matter. The duchess revealed her belief in the matrix of living creation in a strong appreciation of natural beauty and a profound sympathy for animals, most apparent in one of her best poems, *The Hunting of the hare,* which ends with a denunciation of hunting and human carnivores:

> As if that God made Creatures for Mans meat,
> To give them Life, and Sense, for Man to eat;
> Or else for Sport, or Recreations sake,
> Destroy those Lifes that God saw good to make:
> Making their Stomachs, Graves, which full they fill
> With Murther'd Bodies, that in sport they kill.

The organic and vitalistic quality of Margaret Cavendish's natural philosophy distinguished it from the mechanistic systems of Hobbes and Descartes. While the duchess shared their fascination with matter and motion, she denied that insensible matter, without self-movement, could produce an ordered universe. Likewise, she rejected the argument of the Cambridge Platonists who claimed that the universe was animated and moved by an immaterial spirit. It was impossible in her view that an immaterial spirit could affect and cause alteration in material being. Cavendish's natural philosophy is more closely related to the organic theories of the Renaissance natural magicians and the vitalistic thought of the chemists of the sixteenth and seventeenth century, and to some aspects of the thought of Pierre Gassendi, with whose works she was probably familiar through the intermediacy of Charles Cavendish and Walter Charleton.

As a scientific philosophy, Margaret Cavendish's materialism is an interesting, but unimportant by-product of the Scientific Revolution. Many of her ideas, like vitalistic matter, the great chain of being, or a female and fecund nature, were part of the intellectual currency of her day, even if they were not usually associated with the new science. Thus, her philosophy had no influence in her own time, and most scholars who study Cavendish's work, such as Virginia Woolf [*The Common Reader,* 1925], deplore the stultifying effect natural philosophy had on her poetic genius: "Under the pressure of such vast structures, her natural gift, the fresh and delicate fancy, which had led her in her first volume to write so charmingly of Queen Mab and fairyland, were crushed out of existence." While this may be the case from a literary point of view, her natural philosophy is significant in what it reveals about the female, or at least one female, attitude toward nature and cosmology. Repeatedly in her work, in the least metaphorical way possible, Cavendish claims that her philosophy is her child. Not surprisingly, she envisions a universe that lives.

One of the reasons which may have led Cavendish to abandon her original atomism in favor of organic materialism was the political implications of corpuscular natural philosophy. In *Philosophical and Physical Opinions,* she explained that it was impossible that all effects could arise from atoms, unless they possessed a kind of consciousness. However, if each separate part of matter was endowed with consciousness, "they would hardly agree in one government, which is as unlikely as several kings would agree in one kingdom, or rather as men, if every one should have an equal power, would make a good government. . . ."

The implicit unity of her own system circumvented the anarchy of pure atomism: hierarchy therefore replaces egalitarianism as the best ordering device in both nature and society. Nevertheless, Cavendish realized that the principle of hierarchy which she so eagerly embraced in her natural and political philosophies, had dire implications for the status of women. Thus, in *The World's Olio,* the duchess proclaimed,

> True it is, our sex makes great complaints, that men from the first creation usurped a supremacy to themselves, although we were made equal by nature: which tyrannical government they have kept ever since; so that we could never come to be free, but rather more and more enslaved. . . . Which slavery hath so dejected our spirits, that we are become so stupid, that beasts being but a degree below us, men use us but a degree above beasts. Whereas in nature we have as clear an understanding as men, if we are bred in schools to mature our brains. . . .

This strong statement of radical feminism arose from Cavendish's despair at her own position and that of her sex. In fact, this despair paradoxically often resulted in long diatribes against women interspersed in her work, perhaps reflecting her own insecurity. Although the duchess realized the condition of her sex was due to historical circumstances, she sometimes lost sight of this perception and blamed women for their own innate inferiority.

Thus, all through her work, Cavendish vacillates between the defense and condemnation of women. There is a debate in her book of *Orations* between different women on the subject of whether women should "unite in prudent counsels, to make our selves as free, happy, and famous, as men," where some of the speakers argue that women are equal to men, and others that men are far wiser than women. The orator, who perhaps best represents Cavendish's own opinion, declares that there is not sufficient evidence to decide the issue one way or the other. If women are without wit and strength, it is because they "neglect one and make no use of the other." The only option is for women to strive to improve themselves, through speech and exercise "all which will make our strength and wit known, both to men, and to our selves: for, we are ignorant of our selves, as men are of us. And how should we know our selves, when we never make a trial of our selves?"

Cavendish believed that the current unenlightened state of most of her female contemporaries made them incapable of intelligent political action or even rational thought: "neither doth our sex delight or understand philosophy, for as for natural philosophy, they study no more of

Nature's works than their own faces . . . and for moral philosophy, they think that too tedious to learn, and too rigid to practice." On some level, Cavendish realized that this female incapacity was the result of the traditional roles women filled in marriage. Although her opinion sometimes wavered, Cavendish often denounced marriage as a vehicle for male immortality, in which women lost all identity and independence. She even went so far as to attack motherhood, which she believed benefited only the husband and his family, while only endangering the health and life of the wife. While Cavendish did not explicitly recommend the destruction of traditional social norms as the vehicle for female emancipation, as did her peers in the French salons, she realized that equality could only be found when women rejected marriage as the totality of life, and sought to develop their intellectual capabilities. For most women of her age, however, Cavendish seemed to realize this was an impossible ideal. Thus, Cavendish's radicalism sometimes splinters into social conservatism: the unenlightened woman can only improve herself by virtuous behavior within the traditional framework of home and family.

The duchess was not unique in her ambivalent attitude toward herself or her sex. Margaret L. King has argued [in *Beyond Their Sex,* 1980, edited by Patricia H. Labalme] that "the ambitions of the learned women of the Renaissance were thwarted in part because, being women, they were vanquished from within: by their own self-doubt, punctuated by moments of pride; and by their low evaluation of their sex. . . ." Although King is describing the intellectual women of the early Italian Renaissance, she could have been speaking of Margaret Cavendish. King shows that many of the women responded to their sense of social incompatibility with the rest of their sex, and to "fragile self-confidence," by retreating to the isolation of abbeys or "book-lined cells." The duchess treasured nothing more than the solitude of her own study, which she sometimes did not leave for weeks on end. Apparently she had some good reasons for her retreat, since she was not received sympathetically by her own sex when she met them. The wife of John Evelyn commented icily, "I was surprised to find so much extravagance and vanity in any person not confined within four walls." Cavendish seems to have taken some pride in exaggerating her alienation from her sex through her unusual attire and offensive language. She also took her revenge by an almost obsessive denunciation of the mores of the Restoration court and the lewdness of most women in general. When she adopts this mode of exposition, no Puritan divine could have been more fervent in defence of traditional morality and social values.

As we have seen above, Cavendish's skeptical epistemology was also congenial to social conservatism. Skepticism could be quite negative about the human condition as a whole. Cavendish's attack on feminine rationality sounds like a minor chord in Montaigne's symphony on human perversity and self-delusion. The concluding chord for both sometimes was a paean in praise of tradition and stability. In this case, the sophistication of Cavendish's critique undermined her innate radicalism, and contribut-

Frontispiece of The World's Olio, *1671 edition, engraved by Abraham Diepenbeke.*

ed to the ambiguity of her attitudes toward gender and social structure.

Cavendish's ultimate answer to the ambivalent position she found herself in was recourse to fantasy to express her ideas, to assert her equality with men, and to receive the adulation and fame she believed she deserved. Attached to *Observations on Experimental Philosophy,* her most mature and sophisticated scientific work, is a strange romantic fantasy, *The Description of a New Blazing World*. Douglas Grant [*Margaret the First,* 1957], the duchess's most recent biographer, accounts for its presence because Cavendish "had become restive under the discipline increasingly imposed on her by natural philosophy." *The Blazing World* is not the result of restlessness. Rather, it is a prime example of a world turned upside down, where Cavendish could fulfill her wishes on the grand scale.

According to the story, a beautiful young maiden is kidnapped by a lascivious merchant, but after he and his crew have died in the polar wastes, she escapes by transversing the poles between her world and the "Blazing

World," so-called because of the brightness of its stars. There she meets its strange inhabitants, all sorts of anthropomorphic beasts and many-colored humans, and eventually marries the emperor of the Blazing World. He gives her an absolute dominion over his realm and his subjects worship her as if she were a divinity. This is a classical reversal of male-female roles, and an expression of Cavendish's desire for dominance within a traditional hierarchy.

However, the story does not end there. The first thing the empress does is to call a meeting of all the natural philosophers in the land: fish-men, worm-men, ape-men, bird-men, fox-men, etc. Then ensues a wonderful satire of seventeenth-century science with all the various beings arguing abstruse points of both ancient and modern science. The worm-men largely reiterate Cavendish's own natural philosophy, which the empress emends and approves. The discussion ends by "the Empress having thus declared her mind . . . and given them better instructions than perhaps they expected, not knowing that her Majesty had such great and able judgment in natural philosophy." In the Blazing World, at least, the duchess's science has triumphed as she triumphs over all other natural philosophers.

Moreover, Cavendish was not content in her Blazing World merely to overawe mythical scientists. Later in the story, the empress decides to write a "caball," and wants to use either the soul of Galileo, Descartes, Gassendi, Helmont, or Hobbes as her scribe. The immaterial spirits, who are her advisors in this enterprise, inform her "that they were fine ingenious writers, but yet so self-conceited, that they would scorn to be scribes to a woman." Instead, they suggest she use the soul of the duchess of Newcastle, who, "although she is not one of the most learned, eloquent, witty, and ingenious, yet she is a plain and rational writer; for the principle of her writings is sense and reason. . . ." Thus, by the curious device of introducing herself as a character in her own fiction, Cavendish not only castigates the prejudice male philosophers feel for women, but repudiates them in taking refuge with herself. Nothing could speak more eloquently of the duchess's sense of isolation and forced reliance on herself.

Margaret Cavendish's feminism consisted of a flanking attack on traditional authority. Rather than calling for the destruction of social hierarchy and institutions, which she supported for class and personal reasons, she advocated everything that was intellectually subversive within traditional society. She developed a natural philosophy that could not be restrained by either method or authority, repudiating both the old and new system of thought. In her own life, she scandalized social mores with her outlandish dress and eccentric behavior, proclaiming the independence of intellectual women, not from fundamental societal norms, but from cultural conformity. In the Blazing World, the soul of the duchess of Newcastle explains to her alter ego, the empress, "I endeavor, said she, to be as singular as I can; for it argues but a mean nature to imitate others . . . for my nature is such, that I had rather appear worse in singularity, than better in the mode."

Margaret Cavendish achieved her aim.

Sidonie Smith (essay date 1987)

SOURCE: "The Ragged Rout of Self: Margaret Cavendish's *True Relation* and the Heroics of Self-Disclosure," in *A Poetics of Women's Autobiography: Marginality and the Fictions of Self-Representation,* Indiana University Press, 1987, pp. 84-101.

[*In the following essay, Smith traces Cavendish's conflicting depictions of herself in her autobiography to the tension between the traditional ideal of feminine silence and Cavendish's desire to give voice to her own life-story.*]

> When the rumour spread that the crazy Duchess was coming up from Welbeck to pay her respects at Court, people crowded the streets to look at her, and the curiosity of Mr. Pepys twice brought him to wait in the Park to see her pass. But the pressure of the crowd about her coach was too great. He could only catch a glimpse of her in her silver coach with her footmen all in velvet, a velvet cap on her head, and her hair about her ears. He could only see for a moment between the white curtains the face of "a very comely woman," and on she drove through the crowd of staring Cockneys, all pressing to catch a glimpse of that romantic lady, who stands, in the picture at Welbeck, with large melancholy eyes, and something fastidious and fantastic in her bearing, touching a table with the tips of long pointed fingers, in the calm assurance of immortal fame.
>
> —Virginia Woolf, *The Common Reader*

Margery Kempe tested for her culture the boundaries between madness and divinest sense, to paraphrase an Emily Dickinson poem. A mother of fourteen children who wore white to symbolize her chastity, an illiterate middle-class woman who conversed with holy men, about Scripture, a worldly adventurer who spread herself on the floor of her neighborhood church to weep and wail at the suffering of Christ made her presence felt and her voice resonate throughout the medieval world, if not throughout the centuries to follow. Domesticating Christ, Kempe facilitated her own empowerment in the larger arena of public debate. Two hundred years later Margaret Cavendish also tested the boundaries of madness for her culture. Mad Madge, as her contemporaries sometimes called her, was no extroverted woman like Kempe. Painfully shy and retiring, she nonetheless acknowledged the same desire for public significance as Kempe did. She, too, sought empowerment within the public arena of heroism; and like Kempe she achieved both public praise and notoriety. With more self-consciousness and less volubility, Cavendish was another "eccentric" woman who went about shaping her life and her life story for posterity.

Critics of seventeenth-century autobiography, when they have discussed Cavendish's autobiography, *A True Relation of My Birth, Breeding, and Life,* have remarked on the surprising and unprecedented self-scrutiny evident in her work. Paul Delany states [in *British Autobiography in the Seventeenth Century,* 1969] that "it would be giving the Duchess more than her due to describe her as a penetrating self-analyst, but in her ingenuous way she does reveal much more about her personality than most autobiographers of her time"; and he goes so far as to trace her autobiographical lineage to Rousseau: "The line of development is unbroken from her work to a modern, subjective autobiography like Rousseau's—his kind of preoccupation with his own singularity is already implicit in the Duchess's ***Relation***." Suggesting that the duchess's narrative "adumbrates, if it does not achieve, a scientific emphasis," Wayne Shumaker [*English Autobiography: Its Emergence, Materials, and Form,* 1954] concludes that it is "full of psychological significance—more so, perhaps, for the modern than for the seventeenth-century reader—and, whatever the motivating purpose, can properly be regarded as a study of character in a broadly sketched environmental setting." Recently, Cynthia S. Pomerleau contends [in *Women's Autobiography: Essays in Criticism,* 1980, edited by Estelle C. Jelinek] that autobiographies by women in the century, Cavendish's included, "seem more modern, more subjective, more given to self-scrutiny, more like what we have come to know as autobiography" than those works by men that have been conflated with the autobiographical tradition of the seventeenth century. All three, motivated by different critical scenarios, identify in Cavendish's narrative, even if they do not stop to explore it, a protomodern preoccupation with the self qua self that promotes a thickness of self-representation distinguishing her autobiography from others of the period.

"That romantic lady," as Virginia Woolf describes her [in her *The Common Reader,* 1925], would have reveled in such recognition of her "true" distinction, though not perhaps at its failure until recently to command serious attention. She was born Margaret Lucas about 1624 at St. John's in Essex, the youngest of eight children. Her father, a landed gentleman, died when she was two, after which she was raised in an apparently sheltered, even idyllic environment by her mother and older siblings. With the advent of the Civil War, the circumstances of the young woman's life altered dramatically. Two of her brothers died as a result of the fighting. Family property was confiscated. Then she left home to serve, from 1643 to 1645, as maid of honor to Queen Henrietta-Maria. In 1645, she accompanied the queen into exile in Paris, where she met and married William Cavendish, then marquis, but later duke, of Newcastle. They spent seventeen years in exile in Paris, Rotterdam, and Antwerp, during which time Cavendish turned to writing as a "profession." During the fifteen years between 1653 and 1668, she wrote and published fourteen works: five scientific treatises, five collections of poetry and fantasies, two collections of essays and letters, and two collections of plays, as well as a biography of her husband and an autobiography. With the Restoration she and her husband returned to England and retired from court to live on their country estate at Welbeck, where she died in 1674. Before her death Cavendish became a controversial figure, as the passage from Woolf so sympathetically suggests. She wrote. She wore

theatrical costumes. She promoted the importance of a chaste life. She thereby gained a reputation for madness. And yet she received the adulation of some prominent writers and scholars of the period.

Cavendish wrote her autobiography at the relatively young age of thirty-two; she thus looked back, not on a long life, but on a short span covering childhood, young adulthood, early marriage, and the beginning of a "career." She had, in fact, only just begun to write and had not yet achieved public recognition of her talents. But she had married well; and the duke was himself a celebrity. Earlier she had written a biography of her husband, an occasion to idealize him and to defend him against detractors. Her decision to write her own story suggests that Cavendish also wanted to immortalize herself and to defend herself against her own detractors.

Men and women writing autobiographies in the seventeenth century—Cavendish particularly—would have grappled with complex problems of self-representation in a fragmented tradition. They would have struggled with the contours of individual experience, personal intentions, the formal options, and the expectations of their readers, influenced by a cultural ambiance that encouraged exploration of all kinds, including self-exploration, but offered few clearly defined models, in part because many of the autobiographies written during the period remained unpublished for several hundred years. There were, however, two generalized conventions that provided provisional topographical opportunities: the narrative of religious conversion tracing its roots to Augustine's *Confessions* and the secular *res gestae* tracing its roots back to the classical period. Yet in both nascent conventions the figures of selfhood would have complicated the autobiographical project for a woman. Religious autobiographers tended to be members of formal church hierarchies who perceived the significance of their lives to derive from their status as members of the "militant elite" or "spiritual aristocracy." While the Protestant sects that emerged from the Reformation validated woman's authority to read her life for the signs of God's grace, except for the Quakers, they continued to deny her access to public roles and responsibilities. Excluded from the ministry because of patriarchal notions about her "natural" subordination to the authority of her husband and her suspect relationship to language, a woman could not claim membership in the church hierarchy and could not, therefore, claim her life's significance to derive from that kind of activity. Nor did the conventions of secular autobiography offer unequivocal guidance, for they depended in the seventeenth century on the premise that the sum of public acts constituted an individual's "life." In other words, formal "autobiography" remained clearly androcentric.

When Cavendish initiated her autobiographical project, neither sacred nor secular figures promised to conform comfortably to the experience of her life. Whatever her relations to and ideas about the other world, they remained outside the purview of her narrative, which she grounds exclusively in the world of people, education, individual characteristics, not in the exploration of divine providence and personal salvation. Moreover, since her only relationship to public events came from her ascribed status as the daughter of Master Lucas and the wife of the duke of Newcastle, she could not write in the tradition of *res gestae* unless she wrote about the men who had given her her names. (She did so, of course, when she wrote the biography of her husbnd, to which her own autobiography was appended soon after its first publication. But she originally separated her autobiography from his biography, in 1656 publishing her "life" in a folio entitled ***Natures Pictures drawn by Fancies Pencil to the Life.***)

As did other educated and predominantly aristocratic women who wrote secular autobiography during the century, Cavendish turned to her private experience for the matter of her narrative. Pomerleau argues that "for women, and not for men, the domestic choices were, partly by default, a medium for self-expression; and as men began gropingly to write about their public lives, so, amazingly, did a few women write about their private lives." She goes on to contend that "the idea that oneself, one's feelings, one's spouse and domestic relations were properly and innately worth writing about was essentially a female idea, however tentatively conceived at the time." For that reason, Donald A. Stauffer [*English Biography before 1700*, 1930] finds women's autobiographies of the period "more personal, informal, and life-like" since the women are "engrossed in the more enthralling problems of their own lives." Moreover, educated women writing their lives approached autobiography with a different orientation toward rhetoric and writing than educated men did. Denied the classical training offered to young men, a training built on imitation and repetition of classical models, elaborated through the structure of argumentation and agonistic combat, articulated in the voice of "objectivity," women often wrote in a style and with a rhetorical voice more fluid and familiar.

Evidence suggests, however, that other women did not presume, as Cavendish did, to garner for themselves significance beyond that attached to conventional figures of women's selfhood, so that they shunned formal autobiography, never writing expressly about themselves for the public. Some, such as Lucy Hutchinson, based their claim to significance on their domestic roles as mothers and as companions to men of public stature, whose biographies they wrote. For instance, Hutchinson abandoned her autobiographical project after describing her parentage and early years, and turned instead to the biography of her husband in a release of great and skillful verbosity as if her own life story ended after adolescence when marriage subsumed her identity in her husband's. Ann Lady Fanshawe wrote specifically for her son's edification and assumed an appropriately self-abnegating stance as she focused on her husband's career. In both purpose and design these texts served to enhance the image of man. Others may have written of their own, rather than their husbands', exploits in the larger social and political arena, but they limited the audience for their work to family members as Anne Lady Halkett did. Consequently, such works by women fell well within cultural expectations governing women's relationship to self-writing and re-

affirmed an ideology of autobiography as a male preserve.

Cavendish, having dutifully written the biography of her husband and having had no children whom she could edify, journeyed well beyond those other autobiographers by publicizing her life. She usurped the authority to write her own story for the world, authoring her autobiography as she authored scientific treatises and works of poetry, philosophy, utopian fantasy, drama, biography. She recognized, however, that her readers would read her as "woman," inflecting their response to her narrative with patriarchal expectations of woman's identity, condemning her "unfeminine" desire to use her intelligence and ambition in pursuit of public acclaim. For, as Hilda Smith suggests [in her *Reason's Disciples: Seventeenth-Century English Feminists,* 1982], Cavendish "understood, better than any of her sisters, the multifaceted nature of women's oppression. She noted their poor education, exclusion from public institutions, political subordination within the home, physiological dictates of childbirth, and society's pervasive vision of women as incompetent, irresponsible, unintelligent, and irrational." A self-consciousness about her identity and status as a woman therefore dominated her works and prompted her critique of the ideology of gender. Yet, as Smith also notes, her critique, while extensive and even radical, was not without its contradictions: "She often suggested that society's perception was correct; women had made few contributions to past civilization, not because they were ill educated but because they had less ability than men." Such contradictions worry the autobiography itself. Influenced by the discourse on man and its empowering narratives, Cavendish wanted to become not merely an ascriptive footnote in the course of history but a person of acknowledged achievements and historical distinction whose eminently "readable" life would gain her "fame in after ages." Yet as she pursued this vision she threatened herself with still another kind of exile, not from the court, not from England, but from that larger domain of "womanhood" with its privileged stories of selfhood. Moreover, she was herself a product of that discourse and so, as she grew accustomed to seeing herself reflected in "the looking-glass of the male-authored text," internalized the narrative of feminine goodness, a silent plot of modesty, naïvité, virtue, dependency, innocence, and self-concealment. The anxiety occasioned by such doubling of narrative purpose manifests itself in the fundamental ambiguity at the heart of Cavendish's self-representation. Indeed, there are in ***A True Relation*** two competing self-representations: that of the woman who fulfills the patriarchal imperatives of female selfhood and who defends the integrity of her innocence; and that of the woman who demands from the world recognition of her own independent achievements. The tension that drives Cavendish's narrative and that leads to the unprecedented self-scrutiny noted by critics of her work, is the tension generated as Cavendish struggles to reconcile, if in the end she only fails to do so, her desire to maintain the silence of the ideal woman and her desire to give voice to her own unconventional and heroic narrative.

Cavendish begins her story with a brief biography of her father, revealing the degree to which she located her identity in his status and character: "My father was a gentleman," she writes, "which Title is grounded and given by Merit, not by princes." Probably because he was dead before Cavendish turned three, she invests the slim biography with such mythic resonances. He represents the ideal hero who "did not esteem Titles, unless they were gained by Heroick Actions." But he represents also the hero robbed of heroic possibilities. The critical moment around which the lost possibility coalesces is the scene of the duel her father fought when a young man. A sign of masculine bravery and integrity, the duel reveals her father's allegiance to the "Laws of Honour." And yet the times are not conducive to that particular expression of heroism: Because of political complications, her father is exiled from England by Queen Elizabeth. When he finally returns after Elizabeth's death, "there was no Employments for heroick Spirits" since the times of "wise" King James remain peaceful. In the end, her father never gains a "title" and never, as a result, gains a historically prominent lineage or a heroic story such a title would command. The story she tells of her father is one of exile and frustrated desire.

In its themes of heroism and of exile, this paternal biography resonates with the daughter's desire for story and her own sense of confusion and frustration about self-representation. In many ways Cavendish is her father's daughter. Like her father before her, she would leave behind the legitimate trace of her "Heroick Actions," those "manly" accomplishments that would ensure her "fame in after ages." Like him, she suffers from frustrated desire, as political, social, and cultural circumstances deny her access to the realm of public activity and significance that lie outside the womb. Like him, she suffers "exile" for her attentiveness to that androcentric code of honor. And just as her father's life is lived out in a heroic eventlessness that silences his claims to titles, so too Cavendish's life of inactivity threatens to silence her claim to a cultural story of her own. Thus, as she begins her narrative, Cavendish confronts the cultural silence of the very life she would represent.

In this context it is interesting to consider the relationship of Cavendish's autobiography to the biography she wrote of her husband. Since her husband had been a central (and controversial) leader of the Royalist forces and a companion to the king, his life provided the material and the occasion for Cavendish to engage in heroic storytelling. (Unlike her father, her husband gained esteem and public titles from his heroic feats during fiercely troubled times.) Cavendish organized her story in four parts. The first two parts tell of her husband's participation in the Civil War; but more than that, they offer a partisan's defense of the hero's actions as a way of answering his critics and enhancing his reputation. Thus she presents him as the hero-warrior devoted to his sovereign, abused by the mediocre people around him; and her story appropriates conventional features of the classical *res gestae*. In the third part she turns to a description of his character, humor, disposition, birth, breeding, and education, in an apparent attempt to flesh out the details of the inner, the personal, life of the hero. The fourth part introduces the voice of the hero himself as she assembles a collection of his own writings and commentaries. Ultimately, Cavendish creates in the story of her husband an ideal figure who enacts "the heroic ethic of the masculine world."

While Cavendish desires to place heroic action in the plot of her own life, she can in fact replicate only the third part of the biography's structure in her story, the personal rather than the public story. Thus she amasses rather disjointed descriptions of her birth, education, family, disposition, and humor, and winds them around a slim chronological narrative of her personal development from childhood to young adulthood. Yet Cavendish does introduce brief narratives of male heroism into her story as she digresses with adulatory descriptions of the characters and adventures of father, brothers, brother-in-law, and husband. Of her brothers she affirms that "they loved Virtue, endeavoured Merit, practic'd Justice, and spoke Truth; they were constantly loyal, and truly Valiant." Of her brother-in-law: "He was nobly generous, wisely valiant, naturally civill, honestly kind, truly loving, Virtuously temperate." Of her husband: "my Lord is a person whose Humour is neither extravagantly merry, nor unnecessarily sad, his Mind is above his Fortune, as his Generosity is above his purse, his Courage above danger, his Justice above bribes, his Friendship above self-interest, his Truth too firm for falsehood," and on and on. Such passages clearly evince not only Cavendish's desire to defend her family but also her obvious admiration of quintessentially male-identified values and qualities of character. They also provide a parallel story of masculine activity alongside her own story of public silence.

Such "male" stories seem to add value, authority, and legitimacy to Cavendish's "life" by a process of association. She enhances her own figure and status as a result of the ideal figures of such male relatives. Yet ironically, such privileging of male biography and ideals of personality in the story effectively subverts a central quality of character she would claim for herself: Like her father, who refuses to buy the status of nobility and who would only earn it through significant heroic action, Cavendish seeks to earn her recognition and fame through significant public action and merit of her own, not to purchase it ascriptively through the heroic feats of men. By incorporating those "masculine" stories so fully into her own, she partially undermines her effort to follow in her father's footsteps. Moreover, she turns her woman's autobiography into a biography of men.

The attentiveness to males—to father, brothers, husband—testifies simultaneously to a very "feminine" orientation to storytelling and to the world in that it pays homage to the superior value and virtue of male-identified activities. Such an orientation becomes particularly critical for Cavendish since, as certain passages in the text reveal, she is acutely aware of the reputation she is gaining as an "unwomanly," even a somewhat "mad," woman. She alludes to rumors and "false reports," projecting throughout her text a public and a reader critical of her desire for public display of her person (in the ostentatious clothes she wears), of her word (in the court appeals she makes, in the books she writes), and of her ambition. Responding to the pressure of those cultural voices, Cavendish struggles to defend her identity as an ideal woman, thereby assuring her reader that she has followed, not in her father's, but in her mother's footsteps. And so, interweaving throughout the digressive narratives of male relatives (and the idealization of the masculine ethic) is the story of her "maternal" inheritance with its idealization of true womanhood—the story, as Mary C. Mason suggests [in *Autobiography: Essays Theoretical and Critical,* 1980, edited by James Olney], "of an emerging young woman."

If her father as exemplar of masculine integrity sits at the threshold of her autobiography, her mother, the exemplar of the true feminine, inhabits the center of her story— literally and figuratively. The daughter represents her mother as the embodiment of perfect beauty: "She was of a grave Behaviour, and had such a Magestic Grandeur, as it were continually hung about her, that it would strike a kind of awe to the beholders, and command respect from the rudest." She is also the "affectionate Mother, breeding her children with a most industrous care, and tender love, and having eight children, three sons and five daughters, there was not anyone crooked or any ways deformed, neither were they dwarfish, or of a Giant-like stature, but every ways proportionable." And finally, she is the model wife and widow, who

> never forgot my Father so as to marry again; indeed, he remain'd so lively in her memory, and her grief was so lasting, as she never mention'd his name, though she spoke often of him, but love and grief caused tears to flow, and tender sighs to rise, mourning in sad complaints; she made her house her Cloyster, inclosing her self, as it were therein, for she seldom went abroad, unless to Church.

Read in tandem these descriptive passages pay empassioned tribute to a remarkable woman, an ideal of timeless beauty and devotion, an image of female perfection that is cloistered, quiescent, eternal.

Throughout *A True Relation,* Cavendish tenaciously insists that she has imitated the maternal model of the ideal feminine and she has achieved the sanctity and aristocratic gentility of inner life on which the imitation depends. She does so by characterizing herself as "the sheltered innocent" who lives "the cloistered life," drawing repeatedly on the language and imagery of both figures to sustain that narrative identity. For instance, as Cavendish nostalgically represents it, her childhood was lived out in an idyllic, protected, totally innocent world. Here mother and older siblings created for her a conventual environment closed off from the public realm where males acted heroically; and in that enclosed space the child and young woman was bred "according to . . . the Nature of my Sex . . . Virtuously, Modestly, Civilly, Honourably, and on honest principles." Her education included "singing, dancing, playing on musick, reading, writing, working, and the life." Yet intellectual accomplishment and independence of mind were discouraged to such an extent that she can write of her sisters that they "did seldom make Visits, nor never went abroad with Strangers in their Company, but onely themselves in a Flock together agreeing so well, that there seemed but one Minde amongst them."

Describing her entrance as a young woman into the world of the court, Cavendish identifies herself as the sheltered innocent leaving the virtuous life of the cloister to confront a "fallen" world where cunning, sophistication, intrigue, debauchery proclaim the reign of evil. Deprived of the guidance of her siblings, she was "like one that had no Foundation to stand, or Guide to direct me, which made me afraid, lest I should wander with Ignorance out of the waies of Honour, so that I knew not how to behave myself." As a result, she "durst neither look up with my eyes, nor speak, nor be any way sociable, insomuch as I was thought a Natural Fool." Thus, although she might have gained an education, she clings to innocence, maintaining that "being dull, fearfull, and bashfull, I neither heeded what was said or practic'd, but just what belonged to my loyal duty, and my own honest reputation; and, indeed, I was so afraid to dishonour my Friends and Family by my indiscreet actions, that I rather chose to be accounted a Fool, then to be thought rude or wanton." When she describes her later attempt to petition the English courts for access to her husband's lands (which had been confiscated during his exile), she again characterizes herself as "unpracticed," "unlearned," "ignorant," "not knowing." And when she analyzes her bashfulness and her way of living, she emphasizes again and again her isolation from the fallen multitude and her "aversion to such kinds of people." For Cavendish, the representation of herself as foolish, uncomfortable, ignorant, fearful, bashful, and speechless in public testifies to her superior virtue, the basis on which her true merit as model woman rests.

Cavendish also establishes that her virtue derives from her chaste relationship to men and to sexual passion. During her childhood, she tells her reader, her mother "never suffered the vulgar Servingmen to be in the Nursery among the Nurse Maids, lest their rude love-making might do unseemly actions, or speak unhandsome words in the presence of her children, knowing that youth is apt to take infection by ill examples, having not the reason of distinguishing good from bad." She describes herself as a young woman who "did dread Marriage, and shunn'd mens companies as much as [she] could." And she maintains that she "never was infected [with amorous love], it is a Disease, or a Passion, or both, I only know by relation, not by experience." These passages taken together reveal her vision of sexuality as a form of "infection" and of men's company as conducive to another kind of dis-ease. Adding chastity to the catalog of goodness, Cavendish reveals, by the way, the degree to which the life story of the ideal woman demands the repression of sexual desire. In fact, in her relationship to the duke, she represents herself as totally without desire, as a kind of clean slate waiting to be written on: "My Lord the Marquis of Newcastle did approve of those bashful fears which many condemn'd, and would choose such a Wife as he might bring to his own humours, and not such an one as was wedded to self-conceit, or one that had been temper'd to the humours of another, for which he wooed me for his Wife." Here she joins the imagery of sexual purity, religious devotion, and self-effacement when describing her vision of marriage, recapitulating the metaphor of the cloistered life (associated with her mother) with obvious rhetorical flamboyance: "though I desire to appear to the best advantage, whilest I live in the view of the public World, yet I could most willingly exclude myself, so as Never to see the face of any creature, but my Lord, as long as I live, inclosing myself like an Anchoret, wearing a Frize gown, tied with a cord about my waste."

The powerful appeal of feminine "silence" for Cavendish may have derived in part from her profound experience of displacement during exile from England and her desire to reclaim her rightful place in the order of English society. Thus a preoccupation with traditional patterns of social arrangements, and with the sexual arrangements at the center of them, characterizes her autobiography as it does much of secular autobiography of the late Renaissance. As Delany notes, "secular autobiographers were often unusually concerned with their social status, either because it had changed significantly for better or worse, or because they had perceived a shift in the relative standing of the class to which they gave allegiance." The very identity of Cavendish's family had altered dramatically, irrevocably: Two of her brothers had perished as a result of the Civil Wars; her mother had been stripped of her lands and assets; her husband had been exiled. In such a context Cavendish seems to cling to the old, the established, the fundamental patterns of sexual relationships that root her personal identity. Pomerleau, writing of women's autobiographies in the century, suggests that "the old patterns may actually have provided an element of serenity and stability in a world where the sanctity of these patterns could no longer be taken for granted." A proud supporter of the authority of the monarch and a critic of the democratic impulses of the opposition (and of democracy generally, evidenced by her aristocratic scorn of the fallen multitude), Cavendish maintained, despite her acute recognition of the oppression of women, despite her often strong condemnations of the institution of marriage, a commitment to the authority of the familial patriarch as well as to that of the royal one.

Cavendish's insistence before the reader on identifying discomfort with virtue, bashfulness with merit, childlike fear with ideal feminine purity and ignorance testifies to the intensity of her desire to imitate the self-abnegating model of ideal womanhood represented by her mother and thereby to secure the love and acceptance of the world. Yet her rhetoric in key passages betrays another vision of that model of womanhood. If we return to the central passages describing her mother and read them once again, we see that the language evokes, however subtly, images of feminine enclosure and physical and psychological entombment. Of her mother, Cavendish writes that

> her beauty was beyond the ruin of time, for she had a
> well favoured loveliness in her face, a pleasing

sweetness in her countenance, and a well-temper'd complexion, as neither too red nor too pale, even to her dying hour, although in years, and by her dying, one might think death was enamoured with her, for he imbraced her in a sleep, and so gently, as if he were afraid to hurt her.

Cavendish obviously wants to testify to her mother's perfection and mystical power. Yet in doing so she testifies to much more. Forever devoted to a dead husband, willingly cloistered in her womb-like convent, marvelously preserved from the physical ravages of time, and caressed easily by death, this mother is also the figure of frozen stillness, a necromantic presence whose real power derives from the hold her memory has on the daughter. Paradoxically, the daughter subverts the grasp of this mother, whose image commands obedient imitation, by betraying in the very language of entombment a fundamental dissatisfaction with the ideal. For to be cloistered in such an ideal, however well preserved and comfortable it may be, is to be dead to independent expression, knowledge, and heroic possibilities. Ultimately, that ideal of self-representation is unmasked as a "fiction," compellingly prescriptive yet untruthful and invalid. While Cavendish would duplicate her mother's story, her language reveals the desire for a duplicitous transgression of its lines.

The language of the text subverts the representation of her mother as ideal woman in yet another way. Cavendish acknowledges that, however much her mother might have emphasized "being" and deemphasized "doing" in her educational scheme, she embraced a socially acceptable practical role foisted upon her by widowhood: "though she would often complain that her family was too great for her weak Management, and often prest my Brother to take it upon him, yet I observe she took a pleasure, and some little pride, in the governing thereof: she was very skilful in Leases, and setting of lands, and Court-keeping, ordering of Stewards, and the like affairs." In this telling description, Cavendish notes the deference and self-abnegation of her mother's public mask and the private sense of satisfaction and power concealed by that mask. In other words, she identifies the fictional nature of her mother's public persona: Before her, her mother, too, masked her pleasure in power. In this characterization, therefore, Cavendish captures her own dilemma—how to maintain the virtuous woman's silence and simultaneously pursue public power. Moreover, she reveals her strategy for negotiating the dilemma—the fabrication of a self-effacing mask. But in doing so she calls into question the very truthfulness of her representation of herself as the virtuous, silent woman.

Of course, the first evidence of a self-asserting protagonist is the autobiography itself. The title announces the very desire for public acknowledgement Cavendish tries unsuccessfully to mute; for once she commits herself to the autobiographical project, she dissociates herself from the figure of the self-abnegating woman. By writing she authorizes her own story: She speaks publicly. Then the opening of the narrative, discussed earlier, reveals her strong identification with the father and the heroic values of the world of men. Male heroics are denied her, however; thus she takes up the pen, a choice that seems natural to her as the preface to one of her other works suggests: "That my ambition of extraordinary Fame, is restless, and not ordinary, I cannot deny: and since all Heroick Actions, Publick Employments, as well Civill as Military, and Eloquent Pleadings, are deni'd my Sex in this Age, I may be excused for writing so much." While she does not turn her autobiography into a conscious exploration of her development as an artist, she does provide, if only unconsciously, a thin strand of a story tracing her emerging authorship.

The figure of an empowered and ambitious self becomes visible in such passages as the one in which she describes her early fascination with dress: "I never took delight in closets, or cabinets of toys, but in the variety of fine clothes, and such toys as onely were to adorn my person." She thus grounds in early childhood her preoccupation with fashioning herself in her own representations, albeit in a conventional script of women's lives:

> My serious study could not be much, by reason I took great delight in attiring, fine dressing, and fashions, especially such fashions as I did invent myself, not taking that pleasure in such fashions as was invented by others: also I did dislike any should follow my Fashions, for I always took delight in a singularity, even in accoutrements of habit.

Unique, "loud" clothes break the silence and the anonymity at the core of feminine goodness, publicly distinguishing her from all other girls by giving original lines to her body. Through such fashioning, the young woman gives form to her fantasies of creative selfhood, and the autobiographer, recalling such moments, unmasks her desire for "making up" in both senses of the phrase: making up stories about herself and making herself up for public exposure.

Suzanne Juhasz, in an essay on contemporary autobiographies by women ["Towards a Theory of Form in Feminist Autobiography: Kate Millet's *Flying* and *Sita;* Maxine Hong Kingston's *The Woman Warrior*," in *Women's Autobiography: Essays in criticism,* 1980], alludes to the dynamic relationship of literary women to the realm of fantasy, suggesting that "because there is usually a profound discrepancy between the options that society offers to women and the potential that they find within themselves, women frequently have complex inner lives, worlds of fantasy." Cavendish's autobiography reveals that fantasy became a means she early developed to mediate between the cultural imperative of self-annihilating silence and more heroic possibilities of selfhood. Shy, contemplative, yet ambitious—as she tells her reader a number of times—in fantasy and later in writing Cavendish can become the empowering author of her own story and fashion herself as a protagonist of heroic proportions, thereby wresting greatness and distinction from insignificance. Unable to grasp the sword or to ride a horse into battle as her husband (and male relatives) can, she can

grasp the pen and ride words across pages. And she can create in her writing women of heroism who take on all the roles of men, including fighting, ruling, discovering, as they do in such works as **Bell in Campo** and **The Description of a New World**. Thus writing, with its promise of regenerative, capacious, galvanizing selfhood, not the "Lord" of her text, represents life itself to Cavendish, since it enables her to exercise her reason and imagination, and to body forth her originality by shaping interpretations. (In fact, the marquis, at least as he is represented in the autobiography, performs a function much like the woman "in some corner" of Freud's male daydreams. He becomes a kind of male muse who acknowledges, who seems even to inspire, her writing.) What Stephen Jay Greenblatt claims [in his *Renaissance Self-Fashioning: From More to Shakespeare,* 1980] for the prominent literary men of the Renaissance applies as well to Cavendish: "the Renaissance figures we have considered understand that in our culture to abandon self-fashioning is to abandon the craving for freedom, and to let go of one's stubborn hold upon selfhood, even selfhood conceived as a fiction, is to die."

Cavendish's language and imagery suggest the degree to which she imagined writing as a female equivalent to male warfare, a heroic arena in which women might gain access to distinction through merit. In describing her method of writing and her handwriting, she appropriates a trope from the dominant discourse, noting that

> when some of those thoughts are sent out in words, they give the rest more liberty to place themselves in a more methodicall order, marching more regularly with my pen, on the ground of white paper, but my letters seem rather as a ragged rout, than a well armed body, for the brain being quicker in creating than the hand in writing, or the memory in retaining, many fancies are lost, by reason they ofttimes outrun the pen; where I, to keep speed in the Race, write so fast as I stay not so long as to write my letters plain.

Yet this language also reveals the degree to which she felt ambiguous about the presumption inherent in such an analogy. Having established the analogy, Cavendish associates herself with the routed and defeated rather than with the heroic and victorious. Hers is a battle lost, at least in terms of the orderliness of her ideas and her handwriting, which by the end of this passage is what her "writing" has been reduced to. Or more precisely, she is really an interloper on the field of battle as the distinction she draws between her husband's writing and her own attests. While the marquis "recreates himself with his pen, writing what his Wit dictates to him," she "pass[es] [her] time rather with scribbling than writing, with words than wit." This disclaimer recapitulates the earlier rhetoric of ignorance and reaffirms—at the moment she would reveal her desire for significant action and accomplishment—her continued allegiance to the conventions of ideal female gentility, in particular the modesty that forbids the assertion of female authority and authorship. Elsewhere Cavendish takes pains to distinguish herself from other, less virtuous women who speak publicly in their own behalf as "Pleaders, Attorneys, Petitioners, and the like, running about with their several Causes." Such women

> doth nothing but justle for the Preheminence of words, I mean not for speaking well, but speaking much, as they do for the preheminence of place, words rushing against words, thwarting and crossing each other, and pulling with reproaches, striving to throw each other down with disgrace, thinking to advance themselves thereby.

Again Cavendish appropriates the combat trope, but with an intriguing difference. Here she would accuse other women of unfeminine activity and self-asserting public display, and so doing reaffirm her own modesty in public. But ironically, while she means to mark the difference between herself and other women who use language publicly, the imagery in the passage identifies her with them. Like them, she would through writing enter the world of male combat and seek distinction on the field of battle. Like them, she seeks preeminence. That confusion in her recourse to the combat trope betrays the confusion at the heart of her project and betrays the "fictionality" of both self-asserting and self-effacing representations.

The problematic nature of Cavendish's public exposure is represented both literally and figuratively in her relationship to her carriage. Twice in the narrative she alludes to the pleasure she feels in riding about and reveals her motives for such public exposure: "because I would not bury myself quite from the sight of the world, I go sometimes abroad, seldome to visit, but only in my Coach about the Town." Reality beyond the cloister must be engaged in order for her to enlarge the experiential bases of her fantasies and to feed her vanities: "I am so vain, if it be a vanity, as to endeavor to be worship't, rather than not to be regarded." Like the hero who rides through the streets in his triumphal chariot, Cavendish would be worshipped by the populace. Yet the "fallen" public, that awesome, often truculent, intractable, vulgar reality, threatens to shatter the fantasy of purity and distinction. Thus, for an "ideal" woman cloistered within the protective walls of bashfulness but desiring an audience larger than her Lord to validate her true originality, the carriage becomes the vehicle that promises both assertive self-display and the requisite self-concealment emblematic of an inner goodness so critical to the chaste, virtuous woman. If the public is allowed to see but not to touch, Cavendish is allowed to be seen but not to be touched by the fallen multitude.

The autobiography is itself a metaphorical carriage, a vehicle that parades the body of Cavendish's life before the public, allowing her to escape the confinement of silence. But that secular gesture of self-display threatens to take her on a transgressive ride beyond the conventional path of woman's selfhood. The final passage of Cavendish's autobiography captures the central dilemma in its poignant self-reflexiveness. In the first clause she acknowledges a prominent motif embedded in the ideology of gender: Women manifest a natural tendency to vanity,

and vanity in woman is evil. Thus the public display of the woman who would write autobiography marks her as a true daughter of Eve. The scene of autobiography is no place for woman. Just as she earlier acknowledges public censorship of her sartorial fashioning, Cavendish here recognizes the inevitability of public censorship of her literary self-fashioning, of the very autobiography she has just written. In response, she assumes a defensive posture, strategically citing authoritative precedents: "but I hope my readers will not think me vain for writing my life, since there have been many that have done the like, as Cesar, Ovid, and many more, both men and women, and I know no reason I may not do it as well as they." In a gesture of petulance, she would bring the authority of Caesar and Ovid to bear on her enterprise. Perhaps she identifies with the betrayal of the former and the exile of the latter, since as a Royalist she is living through just such betrayal and exile. Certainly, she identifies her autobiographical authority with the literary authority of the man of public action and the poet. But, as Patricia Meyer Spacks notes [in her *The Female Imagination,* 1975], the models to whom she refers are male—her reference to female precedents notwithstanding—and their deeds a matter of public significance. She can cite no female models of significance, no tradition of women's autobiography. Moreover, the text betrays Cavendish's own ambivalence about such comparisons. The very next clause speaks to the lack of public significance in women's lives and by implication in their narratives: "but I verily believe some censuring Readers will scornfully say, why hath this Lady write her own Life? since none cares to know whose daughter she was, or whose wife she is, or how she was bred, or what fortunes she had, or how she lived, or what humour or disposition she was of?" The catalog of content, a summation of her own autobiographical material, betrays the absence of heroic action and public deeds, the conventional subject matter of formal autobiography.

Her defensive posture intensifies: "I anser that it is true, that 'tis to no purpose to the Reader, but it is to the Authoress, because I write it for my own sake, not theirs." While she declares that the reader's expectations are insignificant to her, the pose remains more rhetorical than convincing. For the next and final passage reveals powerfully the fundamental motivation of the effort:

> Neither did I intend this piece for to delight, but to divulge; not to please the fancy, but to tell the truth, lest after-ages should mistake, in not knowing I was daughter to one Master Lucas of St. Johns, near Colchester, in Essex, second wife to the Lord Marquis of Newcastle; for my Lord having had two Wives, I might easily have been mistaken, especially if I should dye and my Lord Marry again.

These closing words of her text testify eloquently to her desperate need to be "read" accurately by those readers who will, if they so choose, distinguish her for posterity from her husband's other wives. Ultimately, then, the issue is one of identity versus anonymity. Cavendish is writing for her very life. Ironically, however, only her identity as daughter and wife will differentiate her from her husband's other wives. So for all her effort to follow her father's example and to maintain the value of merit as the source of "fame in after ages," Cavendish can rely only on her ascriptive status as wife and daughter to place her historically. In that light it is interesting to note again that originally the autobiography appeared by itself in her collection of her writings, *Natures Pictures drawn by Fancies Pencil to the Life:* only later was it appended to the second edition of the biography of her husband, a kind of historical footnote. Thus her story becomes a satellite revolving around the body of man's story. Paradoxically, while she authors his life, his life, in fact, authors and authorizes hers.

Cavendish could not tell her autobiographical story the way her culture had come to expect it to be told. She could not discover in her life the plot for *res gestae* or for spiritual quest. Somehow, she had to make the private story suffice instead of the public one. Decked out in those "odd" autobiographical clothes, she insisted on being regarded, if only by a public bent on laughing at her. However flawed, however entangled as it inevitably was in the very patriarchal plots that mocked her attempts at self-fashioning, her autobiographical carriage ride is in its own way as frustratedly heroic as her father's youthful duel. Like her father, she was doomed to "die" in the realm of feminine silence and the repetitive anonymity that characterized women's narrative possibilities in the seventeenth century or to become an exile from the autobiographical conventions of her culture. Engaged as she is in that effort, she cannot help but be more self-revealing than contemporary autobiographers who inscribed their self-representations in the more "impersonal" conventions of *res gestae* or spiritual awakening or in the narratives of domestic drama that provided the autobiographer more comfortable, because more clearly delimiting, narrative personae. Cavendish can give neither us nor herself those comfortable masks. She gives us, instead, a woman struggling uncomfortably with an androcentric genre.

In its narrative chaos the prose surface of Cavendish's *True Relation* reveals the desperate pleasure the very act of writing must have offered her. Suppressed energy and vitality permeate the text and its constant transformations. Sentences start in one direction, shift, scatter, reconvene, then go off suddenly elsewhere. That may be, as some critics remark, the sign of her undisciplined mind, the mind of a woman denied the intellectual training reserved exclusively for men. As such it reveals the price she paid for being a woman. But it also reveals the fierce desire for power at the heart of Cavendish's personal struggle for "fame in after ages." And so, out of all the mutability and the mobility, the interpenetration of story lines, the proliferation of digressive details, Cavendish constitutes both her "character" and her "life," representing herself as a woman of desire and of potentially unbounded imagination. For all her confusions and ambivalences, for all her protestations of cloistered selfhood, she evinces that unenclosed originality she so admired.

Sophia B. Blaydes (essay date 1988)

SOURCE: "Nature is a Woman: The Duchess of Newcastle and Seventeenth-Century Philosophy," in *Man, God, and Nature in the Enlightenment,* Donald C. Mell, Jr., Theodore E. D. Braun, and Lucia M. Palmer, eds., Colleagues Press, 1988, pp. 51-64.

[*Here, Blaydes reacts against the dismissal of Cavendish's philosophical works as eccentric and fanciful, emphasizing their importance to the history of philosophy, and placing her in the tradition of rational materialism proclaimed by such eminent philosophers as Descartes and Locke.*]

Margaret Lucas Cavendish, the Duchess of Newcastle (1623?-73), often reminded her readers that women were part of God's creation. On one occasion, she offered a lovely prayer that is ostensibly from Nature to God:

> Eternal God, Infinite Deity,
> Thy Servant, NATURE humbly prays to Thee,
> That thou wilt please to favour Her, and give
> Her parts, which are Her Creatures, leave to live. . . .

Assuring God of her adoration, Nature prays for all of "Her" creatures:

> That in their shapes and forms, what e're they be,
> And all their actions they may worship thee . . .

Depicted as the all-encompassing and nurturing female, Nature seems to be reminding God that women are part of His creation and that they are among those creatures who adore Him and for whom Nature prays:

> For 'tis not onely Man that doth implore,
> But all Her parts, Great God, do thee adore. . . .

Printed on the last page of the Duchess's *Philosophical Letters,* the prayer comes sometimes from Nature and sometimes from the Duchess herself, who is both the narrator of the poem and one of Nature's parts. Affirming in just a few lines the conventional view of a feminine nature—Mother Nature or Mother Earth—and masculine power—God the Father or the Creator—the Duchess also voices her fears that God will not favor her or give her "leave to live," although she is one of Nature's parts, and that He will not accept her "actions" as worship of Him. She feared that, because she was a woman, she would enjoy neither a long and healthy life nor lasting fame and honor after her death.

Unable to have children, the Duchess sought to fulfill her nature and to avoid oblivion in ways that were available to her. From 1653 through 1671 she wrote fourteen books that she published in twenty-four separate editions. Exercising her gift from God, the Duchess applied her natural talents, writing poetry, fiction, and philosophy in order to instruct and entertain others in those ideas that she knew were virtuous and honorable. Yet, the honor and fame that she expected did not come, as her poem suggests, because she was a woman. Instead of being honored for her books, she was judged mad. If her fiction and poetry were disparaged—and they were—what chance did her volumes of philosophy have?

They had little, apparently, for she was accused on the one hand of plagiarism for using words that no woman could possibly know and on the other for being too original. In response, the Duchess wrote letters, poems, and dedications defending her books and her reasons for writing them. Such behavior from a noblewoman during the Restoration period was inappropriate. As Caroline Merchant noted recently [in her *The Death of Nature: Women, Ecology, and the Scientific Revolution,* 1980], "Disorderly woman, like chaotic nature, needed to be controlled." The ideal wife, Merchant continues, "combined goodness, virtue, intelligence, and common sense, but not too much 'learning and pregnant wit,' for 'Books are a man's prerogative.'" The Duchess may have seen herself as the ideal wife, if we are to believe her many comments on the subject, but to Samuel Pepys, the Restoration diarist [*The Diary of Samuel Pepys,* 1976, edited by Robert Latham and William Matthews], she was a "mad, conceited, ridiculous woman" whose husband was "an asse to suffer her to write." Dorothy Osborne, after reading the Duchess's *Poems and Fancies,* wrote to her future husband [*The Letters of Dorothy Osborne to William Temple,* 1928], Sir William Temple, that the Duchess "is a little distracted, she could never be so ridiculous else to venture at writing books." The Duchess's errors, to write and to publish, are blamed first on her husband, and then on her apparent madness.

Over the centuries, the judgement of her age has prevailed. Only recently have most of the Duchess's books been read and studied, partly because they illuminate woman's condition during the Restoration. Some readers have even found that some of her writing is as notable as her celebrated biography of the Duke. No one, however, has examined each of her seven philosophic books individually for ideas or style. A brief discussion of a few of her ideas and her method of presenting them over fifteen years might help readers judge both the Duchess's sanity and her achievement.

A reading of the seven works in the order in which they were published reveals that the Duchess changed and developed as a writer and philosopher from 1653 through 1668. Her first three volumes—*Philosophical Fancies* (1653), *The Philosophical and Physical Opinions* (1655), and *Philosophical and Physical Opinions,* another edition (1663)—were written during the Newcastles' exile forced by the Civil War and then during their isolation from the Royalist mainstream after the Restoration in 1660. The fourth—*Philosophical Letters* (1664)—was written after the Duchess had read other philosophers' works and had thus ended her intellectual isolation. Her last three philosophical works—*Observations Upon Experimental Philosophy, 2nd edition* (1668)—are careful responses to others' ideas and their methods as well as clarifications of

her own. In the first three she was proud of her abilities, what she and her age considered natural reason. She was especially proud because she was untutored and thus independent of others' ideas. She remained proud in the next four volumes, even after she had read others and compared her ideas with their philosophies. It is through the comparisons that she affirmed herself and established her identity as a thinker.

The first woman to write for publication, the Duchess was the most radical of "Reason's Disciples," Hilda L. Smith's label for seventeenth-century English feminists [in *Reason's Disciples: Seventeenth-Century Feminists,* 1982]. In 1653, when the Duchess published her first philosophic work, she was the wife of the exiled commander-in-chief of the Royalist forces who was declared by Parliament the greatest enemy to Cromwell. Under those circumstances, one might question her haste to publish her thoughts on atoms, matter, and motion. She explains in *Philosophical Fancies* that the book occupied her idle time for three weeks while she was in England trying to salvage some of her husband's fortune. In a prefatory poem she writes:

> THOUGHTS, run not in such strange phantastick waies,
> Nor take such paines to get a *Vulgar Praise.*
> The *World* will scorne, and say, you are all *Fooles,*
> Because you are not taught in common *Schooles.*
> The World will think you mad, because you run
> Not the same *Track,* that former times have done.
> Turn foolish *Thoughts,* walke in a *Beaten Path,*
> Or else the *World* ridiculously will laugh.

Her rejection of scholarship echoes, among others, sentiments expressed by Sir William Davenant and Thomas Hobbes, both friends of her husband. They, too, disdained books for the development of either poetic wisdom or practical leadership. In his "Preface" to *Gondibert* (1651), Davenant emphasizes the need for original, not imitative poetry. Hobbes's introduction to *Leviathan* (1651) repeatedly states that wisdom comes not from books but from self-study and that is what leads to knowledge of "Mankind." Like them, the Duchess upheld the natural and free exercise of one's faculties. Thus, she was in the mainstream of the tradition of writers in the seventeenth century that honored reason and sought to solve problems through it.

An octavo of 112 pages, *Philosophical Fancies* is her smallest and shortest book. Only seventy-one of those pages contain her philosophic discussions. The others have prefatory poems, epistles, and dedications. The volume ends with a five-page list of questions she could have posed and answered if she had had time. Irritating as the mix of materials is today, such prolegomena and epilogues, as we know, were common in the seventeenth century. Davenant outdoes his heroic poem *Gondibert* with a prefatory letter to Hobbes that is not only long but also of greater interest than the poem. He appends Hobbes's answer and an epilogue as well.

The Duchess opens her philosophic discussion with a prose passage:

> There is no *first Matter*, nor *first Motion;* for *matter* and *motion* are *infinite*, and being *infinite*, must consequently be *Eternall;* and though but *one matter,* yet there is no such thing, as the *whole matter,* that is as one should say, *All.* And though there is but one *kinde* of *matter,* yet there are *infinite degrees* of *matter,* as *thinner* and *thicker, softer* and *harder, weightier* and *lighter;* and as there is but one *matter,* so there is but one *motion,* yet there are *infinite degrees of motion,* as *swifter* and *slower;* and *infinite changes of motion. . . .*

The next passage ends simply: "the *Minde*" is "*Matter moving,* or *Matter moved.*" Like other philosophers of her day, Gassendi and Descartes among them, she declares herself a materialist. Her language, if not her concerns, might have amused or annoyed her readers. Even today, we find her redundant and foolish. We forget that the young Duchess was not alone in her concerns or their mode of expression. She is writing in a way that would have been acceptable if she had not been a woman. Her error is that she insists upon an original vocabulary. For example, in her paragraph "Naturall *or* Sensitive War," she writes:

> ALL *Naturall War* is caused either by a *Sympatheticall Motion* or an *Antipathetical Motion.* For *Naturall Warre,* and *Peace* proceed from Selfe-preservation, which belongs to the *Figure;* for *nothing* is annihilated in *Nature,* but the particular *Prints,* or *severall shapes* that *Motion* makes of *Matter;* which *Motion* in every *Figure* strives to maintain what they have created: for when some *Figures* destroy others, it is for the maintenance or security of themselves: and when the Destruction is, for Food, it is *Sympatheticall Motion,* which makes a particular *Appetite,* or nourishment from some *Creatures* to others; but an *Antipatheticall Motion,* that makes the *Destruction.*

Behind the passage lurks the familiar Hobbesian theory of the state, which begins in the *Leviathan* with the observation that man, who is by nature self-seeking and hostile toward others, seeks to establish a contract with a sovereign for protection. The Duchess's idea is not so radical; it is her language that is an impediment. Such notions demand certain terms that the Duchess did not use.

The small volume includes her early atomist theory and introduces her interest in remedies and recipes. Again, part of a familiar concern, medicine and cookery were included in many more-honored books. Sir Kenelm Digby [*The Closet of the Eminently Learned Six Kenelme Digby, Kt.,* 1669] included recipes and cures as part of his "chemical secrets" in his philosophic treatises. In one case, he informs his readers through a kind of rebus or pictorial code "How to fix silver into gold by mercury and mercury precipitate." Today, we may be amused by his charming errors. Despite the similarities in some methods and ideas, Hobbes, Digby, and the Duchess evoked different responses from their readers. They still do. Hobbes informs; Digby amuses; and the Duchess annoys. One might question whether the judgment of the Duchess arises— and arose—from criteria that are repressive. In a recent study, Marcie Kaplan notes that most psychologists and psychiatrists assess a woman's mental health and social stability so that [quoting Wray Herbert, "Curing Femininity," *Science News,* September, 1983]:

> the typical psychologically healthy woman is more submissive, less independent, less aggressive, more emotional and emotionally expressive, more excitable and more concerned about appearance. If a woman rejects this stereotype, she is an unhealthy woman. . . .

Is it possible that the Duchess's contemporaries judged her by her unconventional behavior and that today we judge her according to her nonsensical philosophy that conformed to the notions of her time?

In 1655 the Duchess published her second volume, ***The Philosophical and Physical Opinions.*** The work includes the Duchess's "physical" or medical comments that she had omitted from the first book. More ambitious, the book is still another that the Duchess completed in isolation. Testifying to that isolation are a number of defenses of her original genius and her honesty, evidently prompted by the response to her first philosophic book. In the first of many such testimonials, the Duke writes, "If you have read any such things before, i'le be bold to burn the Book." Defending her against the contradictory charges of plagiarism and originality, the Duke argues that "in natural Philosophy, one opinion may be as true as another, since no body knows the first cause in nature of any thing." After defending her gifts and her books, the Duke moves to the real cause of the attacks on his wife: "here's her crime, a Lady writes them, and to intrench so much upon the male prerogative, is not be forgiven. . . ."

The Duchess defends herself on the altar of nature. In language that is clear, rational, and authoritative, yet laden with homely imagery, she describes her condition and her proximity to philosophic ideas. Comparing her situation to those of other women, she writes:

> as many others, especially wives go from church to church, from ball to ball, from collation to collation, gossiping from house to house, so when my Lord admits me to his company, I listen with attention to his edifying discourse, and I govern my self by his Doctrine; I dance a measure with the muses, feast with the Sciences, or sit and discourse with the arts.

In easy, colloquial terms, the Duchess emphasizes the nobility and predictability of her situation; she is, after all, following the example of her husband, her lord, whose will she accepts. He is her model and her law. Her case is more poignantly stated when she explains:

> Since nature is so generous to distribute to those that fortune hath cast out, and education hath neglected, why should my readers mistrust nature should be

sparing to me, who have been honourably born, carefully bred and nobly married to a wise man. . . .

Insisting upon her own sense of decorum and fulfillment of her natural role, she writes, "I am my Lords Scholer." Although a woman, the Duchess claims that she has received wisdom as God's bounty, which she exercises according to ideals learned first from her family and then from her husband. Expecting censure yet seeking praise, the Duchess suggests that her book may be worth reading. Emphasizing the credos of her age and class, she insists that "my head is so full of my own natural phancies, as it had not roome for strangers to boord therein, and certainly natural reason is a better tutor than education."

Particularly noteworthy in her second book of philosophy is a passage that relates to John Locke's theories. To the Duchess, "remembrance is but a pattern taken from the Memory, and the memory but a pattern taken from the objects." It is an important point because she feared that only memory provided immortality, and that memory, like everything else, was matter that would turn to dust.

The third volume of her philosophy was published in 1663 and continues to be a product of her isolation. When the Newcastles returned to England from exile in 1660, they were neglected by their restored monarch. Isolated and with more time than she had expected to have, the Duchess reviewed and restated her theories in a folio of five hundred pages. She abandoned some, like the atomist ideas. Even so, she claims in this volume that "the best Natural Philosophers are those that have the Clearest Natural Observation, and the Least Artificial Learning," which, of course, places her among the best. Introducing each of her ideas with the qualifier, it "seemeth to human sense and reason," she explains that "Natural Philosophers go and study not beyond Sense and Reason; and according to the proportion of that Sense and Reason that I have, I shall declare my Philosophical Opinions." Just as she had in the other volumes of philosophy that she published within a ten-year span, the Duchess emphasizes her originality and her virtue as an uneducated, natural philosopher. She sees herself as one of nature's creatures, endowed with reason and writing talent. In each she relies upon her reason for her conclusions, which she expresses in direct, simple language. Isolated first as an exiled Royalist in Europe and then by the court and king in England, she produced books that served to isolate her even more.

By 1664, when the Duchess published her fourth book of philosophy, *Philosophical Letters,* she had read four philosophers of her day, Descartes, Hobbes, Henry More, and Van Helmont. Although she had disclaimed knowledge of others' philosophies in her previous works, now she reveals that she will present her arguments that have arisen from her study of them. A lengthy commentary on the four *Philosophical Letters* demonstrates that the Duchess abandoned her proud isolation, educated herself, acquired a more conventional philosopher's vocabulary, and discovered a frame of reference for her own ideas. Using

the genre that she found most congenial, the informal friendly letter, the Duchess presents her arguments with the philosophers in a series of clear statements. Through an order imposed by the form, the Duchess carefully explains her ideas so that her fictitious correspondent can readily understand each point. She intends to dispute with the philosophers, she writes, "according to the ability of my Reason. . . ." Explaining that each philosopher seems to espouse his own truth, she states with justifiable self-righteousness, "All what I speak, is under the Liberty of Natural Philosophy, and by the Light of Reason onely, not of Revelation; and my Reason being not infallible, I will not declare my Opinions for an infallible Truth. . . ." She will not declare her opinion as truth, as the philosophers have; she will instead suggest that her views have as much validity as another's, even a man's.

Reflecting the form of others' speculative philosophies, *Philosophical Letters* has four sections. In the first, twenty-nine letters discuss Hobbes's *Leviathan*. Too detailed to summarize, the Duchess's appraisal includes Hobbes's views of perception, motion, and imagination. In her arguments with Hobbes, the Duchess is surprisingly effective and sensible. For example, she states that Hobbes in his chapter on reason defines reason to be "nothing else but *Reckoning*: I answer, That in my opinion Reckoning is not Reason itself, but onely an effect or action of Reason. . . ." By the thirtieth letter the Duchess writes that she has begun to read Descartes. Intending "to pick out onely those discourses which I like best," she soon argues with the philosopher over his views of mind and matter— she insists that they are inseparable—and over his notion that only man has reason. By the forty-second letter, the Duchess summarizes the philosophies of Hobbes and Descartes and then restates her own beliefs:

> First I am for self-moving matter, which I call the sensitive and rational matter, and the perceptive and architectonical part of nature, which is the life and knowledge of nature. Next I am of an opinion, that all Perception is made by corporeal, figuring self-motions, and that the perception of foreign objects is made by patterning them out. . . .

The second portion of the book opens with an attack on Henry More and his book *Antidote*. If, as More states, everyone believes in a god, why does More write a book that is designed to prove the existence of God? "[U]nless," she writes, "it be to shew Learning and wit: In my opinion, to prove that, which all men believe . . . is the way to bring it into question." She argues with More's view that man is a superior being. Like Mother Nature in her poem, the Duchess notes the excellence of "the rest of natural Creatures. . . ." Emphasizing her materialism as she reviews More's philosophy, the Duchess denies his view of "Incorporeal substance" and in doing so corrects one of her early errors:

> When I did write my first conceptions in Natural Philosophy, I was not so experienced, nor had I those observations which I had had since; Neither did I give those first Conceptions time to digest, and come to a

maturity or perfect growth, but forced them forth as soon as conceived, and this made the first publishing of them so full of Imperfections, which I am much sorry for; but since that time, I have not onely reviewed, but corrected and altered them in several places. . . .

After reviewing others' philosophies, the Duchess reconsidered her own. She does not hesitate to inform her readers of her changes and the reasons for them.

Her education, however, did not prepare her for the chemistry of Van Helmont, whose work she reviews in the third section of the book. Unable to understand much of it, the Duchess accuses the scientist of making "such a mixture of Divinity, and natural Philosophy, that all his Philosophy is nothing but a meer Hotch-potch, spoiling one with the other." Relying upon her own natural reason, the Duchess is able to point out convincingly that Van Helmont's views are not so enlightened as they appear. At one point, she notes, Van Helmont attributes the trembling of the earth to the judgment of God for man's sins. He also writes of a gold-making stone. The Duchess cannot resist chiding him: "I wish with all my heart, the poor Royalists had had some quantity of that powder; and I assure you, that if it were so, I myself would turn a Chymist to gain so much as to repair my Noble Husbands losses. . . ."

The last section of the book restates some of the Duchess's ideas and confirms her change from an original, isolated writer who claimed a unique and uninformed approach to the world of ideas into a philosopher who correlates her work with that of others. She discarded some notions and reaffirmed others. Still a materialist, she finds no distinction between the world of matter and reason. She emphasizes that natural philosophy is above those dissensions caused by theology and law. *Philosophical Letters,* the product of her self-education, also reveals the Duchess's antipathy toward the new sciences, for she insists that one discovers truth through reason, not through experiments.

In 1666 the Duchess published *Observations upon Experimental Philosophy,* considered by some to be her most important scientific treatise. In another five hundred folio pages, the Duchess offers a critique of experimental science that she calls "this brittle Art." She accuses the experimental scientists "in these latter times" of busying "themselves more with other Worlds, then with this they live in." As a natural philosopher, she writes:

> I confess, I have but little faith in such Arts, and as little in Telescopical, Microscopical, and the like inspections, and prefer rational and judicious Observations before deluding Glasses and Experiments. . . .

She even recommends her "Pastime" to others; "if all Women that have no imployment in worldly affairs, should but spend their time as harmlessly as I do, they would not commit such faults as many are accused of."

She encourages her readers to avoid those writers who

> confound both Divinity and Natural Philosophy, Sense and Reason, Nature and Art, so much as in time we shall have rather a Chaos, than a well-order'd Universe by their doctrine: Besides, many of their writings are but parcels taken from the ancients; but such Writers are like those unconscionable men in Civil Wars, which endeavour to pull down the hereditary Mansions of Noble-men and Gentlemen, to build a Cottage of their own; for so do they pull down the learning of Ancient Authors, to render themselves famous in composing books of their own.

This, her fifth philosophic work, she explains, addresses "our Modern Experimental and Dioptrical Writers" just as she had presented "some famous and eminent Writers in Speculative Philosophy" in her fourth. Dismissing her first three works in favor of her *Philosophical Letters* and this volume, the Duchess informs her readers:

> as for Learning, that I am not versed in it, no body, I hope, will blame me for it, since it is sufficiently known, that our Sex is not bred up to it, as being not suffer'd to be instructed in Schools and Universities; I will not say, but many of our Sex may have as much wit, and be capable of Learning as well as men; but since they want Instructions, it is not possible they should attain to it; for Learning is Artificial, but Wit is Natural.

Expending time and effort to learn what others had written, the Duchess still prefers the untutored, natural wit to the learned, artificial instruction that men enjoyed. In an effort to reach all readers, the Duchess applauds simplicity in language, just as she honors naturalness in philosophy. She suggests to her readers, "If you do write Philosophy in English, and use all the hardest words and expression which none but Scholars are able to understand, you had better write it in Latine. . . ." She advocates her own approach, which is to shun artificial, difficult language so that one's writing "may be the better understood by all, learned as well as unlearned. . . ."

The text of *Observations* contains a clear, often amusing, view of experimental philosophy. The Duchess derides the "toys" of men—microscopes, telescopes—and experiments, equating such activities with women's work. She also writes of the ancients, whose wisdom she praises. Yet, "I, being a woman," she writes, "do fear they would soon cast me out of their Schools. . . ." After reviewing Thales, Plato, and Aristotle, among others, in the second part of the book, she ruefully observes that they will have lasting fame even though their reasoning is often faulty, "For Fame doth all, and whose name she is pleased to record, that man shall live, when others, though of no less worth and merit, will be obscured, and buried in oblivion."

In 1668, *Observations* was brought out in a second edition, but unlike her other works, this seems to be a reprint rather than a reworking. One might theorize that her books had been burned in 1666 in the Great Fire of London that destroyed the publishing industry for a brief time. In 1668 not only was the volume reprinted but altogether six of the Duchess's books came out in new editions. The only change in the second edition of *Observations* was that she omitted some of her lengthy explanations.

That same year, 1668, the Duchess published her last philosophic work, *Grounds of Natural Philosophy,* which she dedicated to "all the Universities in Europe." Less discursive and thus more controlled now, even without the added control of the epistolary form, *Grounds* presents most of the same ideas that the Duchess had expressed in her other, earlier works. Her approach to matter remains the same. She writes:

> Matter is what we name *Body;* which Matter cannot be less, or more, than Body; Yet some Learned Persons are of opinion, That there are substances that are not Material Bodies. But how they can prove any sort of Substance to be no Body, I cannot tell. . . .

The Duchess continues in the work to refer to other philosophers and their ideas, but she dismisses any of their ideas that contradict her observations or defy her natural reason.

From her discussion of matter, the Duchess moves through 232 pages that she divides into thirteen sections. First, she explains her philosophy and her basic vocabulary so that her ideas will be clearly understood by her readers. Then she addresses topics that range from men to dropsies and appearances to vegetables. More provocative is the lengthy passage that the Duchess has appended to the thirteen sections. The appendix, about one hundred pages long, is divided into five parts that cover topics that obsessed her. She refers to her own oppressive illnesses. Under some stress, the Duchess considers God, sin, society, birth, dreams, Hell, and other worlds. Finally, using a philosophic format, she presents a discussion between various parts of her mind. She discusses her restoration to health after illness and to life after death. Seeking, it appears, reassurance of her immortality, the Duchess considers her own return from death, her husband's after his death, and the return to life of her dead family. Although a work of philosophy, *Grounds* becomes in its last pages an expression of the Duchess's greatest fears. As she had in her poems, plays, and fantasies before, the Duchess here lets her imagination momentarily satisfy her. The last section of the work becomes an expression of her desire for survival, restoration, and immortality.

It is that final hope for immortality that drove the Duchess throughout her life to write and to publish what she wrote. To the Puritans, the king, and his court, she was mad, a rebel against society. Yet, it is possible that she believed she was fulfilling the role that was hers by birth, breeding, and marriage. Born to an aristocratic family, the Duchess enjoyed an idyllic, pastoral childhood despite her father's death while she was an infant. Her desire to write and to instruct was bred in her by her family, especially her mother who applied sweet reason in her role as head of the family. Later, with a husband who was

as supportive and reasonable as he was attractive, the Duchess could pursue in an intellectual and social vacuum activities she had enjoyed as a child. Consistent with her breeding and her experience, the Duchess did not defy convention through her published philosophy. Instead, she fulfilled her nature; and her books, especially her philosophic books, explain what her nature was.

The Duchess's philosophical works offer evidence that their writer had a mind capable of instruction, albeit self-instruction. Her readings of other philosophers and her discussions with her husband reveal the plight of the intelligent seventeenth-century woman. She could not attend their schools, but she could nonetheless learn from the philosophies of men. After 1664, most of her foolish redundancies lessened, her vocabulary became more conventional, and her faith in her basic natural philosophy was affirmed. She did abandon her earlier atomist theories and her notions of the uncorporeal world, but she found that her disdain for experimental philosophy intensified so that she continued to attack what she now perceived even more clearly to be the foolishness of vain pursuits.

Is that all one can say of her philosophical works, that they permitted her to develop and change? Clearly there is more merit to them than that. At the very least, some of her seven volumes should be important in the history of philosophy. Placing her books beside those of such figures as Sir Kenelm Digby reveals that her prolixity and her topics are typical of other philosophers who were not derided. What was it after all that she proclaimed but a faith in reason, proclaimed also by Descartes and Locke, among others, a fundamental materialism, considered also by Hobbes, and a skepticism toward the experimental sciences, echoed by Henry More. That the history of science proves her wrong on some of her notions is beside the point. That was not why she was ridiculed and rejected.

There is no mystery to her rejection. She was a woman who dared to trespass into the world of learning, traditionally the man's preserve. There is, however, a mystery to her motives. One explanation is that she did not defy the laws that dictated the behavior of seventeenth-century noblewomen. Rather than defiance, each of her books conveys the impression of a wife who is obedient to her husband's wishes and a woman who expects to be judged by a code of honor and truth that she remembers from her past and sees again in her husband. A thoughtful, ambitious woman, the Duchess found that her self-imposed isolation, of which she had been so proud, had become her prison. In an effort to attract fame and honor during her lifetime and immortality after death, the Duchess sent copies of her books to universities in England and Europe. Her wishes were in part fulfilled, but not as she had expected. Safely stored for centuries, the volumes survived so that we can now read some of them and wonder.

Of the seven volumes, the last three might interest today's reader the most because they provide more of a seventeenth-century context for the Duchess's ideas. Of the three, however, the last volume would intrigue those readers who are fascinated by the revelation of a person through literary forms, philosophical treatises, and bio graphical statements. To read the Duchess is to learn about woman's condition in the late seventeenth century and, in particular, the condition of one intelligent noblewoman. Not always easy to read, the Duchess is a natural philosopher who is able to express basic ideas in clear, homely language and to argue with some of the more prominent figures of her day. As such, she is refreshing. She is also a woman who seems to be out of tune with her times. It seems from her poem on Nature that the Duchess learned a bitter lesson during her lifetime. Like Nature, she was endowed with talents. However, like Nature, she was not free to exercise them because she was a woman.

Linda R. Payne (essay date 1991)

SOURCE: "Dramatic Dreamscape: Women's Dreams and Utopian Vision in the Works of Margaret Cavendish, Duchess of Newcastle," in *Curtain Calls: British and American Women and the Theater, 1660-1820,* edited by Mary Anne Schofield and Cecilia Macheski, Ohio University Press, 1991, pp. 18-33.

[*In this essay, Payne argues that Cavendish's flouting of the rules of dramatic composition in her plays is a deliberate rejection of masculine structures rather than a failure of her artistic talent. She also contends that Cavendish's portrayal of modest and dutiful women illustrates the conflict she faced between social expectations and her own aspirations.*]

Margaret Lucas Cavendish, Duchess of Newcastle, was jeered by her Restoration contemporaries both high and low, male and female. Often known as "Mad Madge," she was described by Pepys [in *Everybody's Pepys: The Diary of Samuel Pepys 1660-1669,* 1926] as "a mad, conceited, ridiculous woman" whose husband was "an ass to suffer her to write what she writes to him and of him." Dorothy Osborne declared [in *The Weaker Vessel,* 1984, by Antonia Fraser] that "there are many soberer people in Bedlam" and that her friends were "much to blame to let her go abroad." Other charges, also leveled against almost every woman who dared to write, included sexual immorality and plagiarism from male authors.

Even today, more attention is focused on her outlandish dress and unpredictable behavior than on her work. [In *The Madwoman in the Attic,* 1979, Sandra M.] Gilbert and [Susan] Gubar, using her as a type for their "madwoman" figure, agree that she probably *was* mad, while Angeline Goreau [in *Feminist Theorists,* 1983] implies as much in suggesting that the progressive worsening of her "eccentricities" might have been caused either by "natural evolution" or "the effects of the conflict of her ambitions and her sex."

Yet this "fantasticall" figure was the first English woman to publish extensively, and she tried her hand at every available genre: poetry, fiction, biography, scientific and philosophical treatises, but most prolifically in drama. Cavendish has gained recognition in recent years as one of the first important biographers, and her scientific and philosophical works are regarded with some amused interest for their marked originality and oddness in a speculative era. Her drama and fiction, however, are generally regarded as failures and given very little attention. Although she published nineteen dramatic works in two collections, ***Plays*** (1662) and ***Plays Never Before Printed*** (1668), none of them was produced, and their publication was undoubtedly due to the fortune and influence of her husband, William. Her fiction is almost never read.

The wits, Cavendish complained, condemned her plays because they were not made up according to the "Rules of Art." Critics through the years have been less kind. Virginia Woolf [in *A Room of One's Own,* 1929] called them "intolerable" and found Cavendish's writings "a vision of loneliness and riot . . . as if some giant cucumber had spread itself over all the roses and carnations in the garden and choked them to death." Marjorie Nicolson declared [in her *Voyages to the Moon,* 1948] that criticizing Cavendish was beyond her scope, that just to read her one needed to bring order out of chaos. Even sympathetic biographer Douglas Grant describes the plays [in his *Margaret the First,* 1957] as "confused," a "delta of tedium," "utterly undramatic," and "a collection of disconnected scenes."

Cavendish herself saw the problems in her plays, calling them "tedious" and "somewhat long," "like dull dead statues," "dull and flat by reason they have not the high seasoning of Poeticall Salt," and, generally, "not so well done but that there will be many faults found."

In fact, in the first collection, through nine prefaces **"To the Readers,"** an epistle dedicatory to **"My Lord,"** and **"A General Prologue to all my Playes,"** she alternately apologized for their flaws and justified them as deliberate breaks from convention. It is while comparing her plays to those of her husband that she described them as "dull dead statues," for which reason, she said,

> I send them forth to be printed, rather than keep them concealed in hopes to have them first Acted; and this advantage I have, that is, I am out of fear of having them hissed off from the Stage, for they are not like to come thereon; but were they such as might deserve applause, yet if Envy did make a faction against them, they would have had a public Condemnation; and though I am not such a Coward, as to be afraid of the hissing Serpents, or stinged Tongues of Envy, yet it would have made me a little Melancholy to have my harmless and innocent Playes go weeping from the Stage, and whipt by malicious hard-hearted jurors.

She excused the seeming tedium her plays would present on the stage as a product of their length, since "having much variety in them, I could not possibly make them shorter, and being long, it might tire the Spectators, who are forced, or bound by the rules of civility to sit out a Play, if they be not sick."

However, the length is probably not really so much the problem as their apparent lack of form or structure. Cavendish's apologies for such flaws typically reveal both insecurity and a defiant carelessness: "for besides that I want also the skill of scholarship and true writing, I did many times not peruse the copies that were transcribed, lest they should disturb my following conceptions; by which neglect . . . many errors are slipped into my works."

She explains the lack of coherence by declaring herself a poet rather than a tailor:

> I have heard that such Poets that write Playes, seldom or never join or sew the several scenes together; they are two several Professions, at least unusual for rare Poets to take that pains . . . but I like as a poor Taylor was forced to do all my self, as to cut out, shape, join, and sew each several scene together, without any help or direction . . . but howsoever, I did my best indeavour, and took great pains in the ordering and joining thereof, for which I hope my Learned Readers will pardon the errors therein and excuse me the worker thereof.

Her unconventional structures extend even to the technical side of her writing: grammar, syntax, and, alas, spelling. However, as she saw it,

> I do perceive no strong reason to contradict but that everyone may be his own grammarian if by his natural grammar he can make his hearers understand his sense. . . . But language should be like garments, for though every particular garment hath a general cut, yet their trimmings may be different, and not go out of the fashion.

In fact, she seemed to consider the kind of ordered logic and "rules" which much of her audience expected from literature to be a masculine trait. She even went so far as to declare it "against nature for a woman to spell right." Women are strong on fancy, while reason is a man's domain. Women's brains "work usually in a Fantasticall motion . . . not so much by Rules and Methods as by choice." In her first collection of poetry, **Poems and Fancies** (1653), she declared her disdain for the rules of art:

> Give me the free and noble style,
> Which seems uncurbed, though it be wild
> . . . Give me a style that Nature frames, not art,
> For art doth seem to take the pedant's part;
> And that seems noble, which is easy, free,
> Not to be bound with o'er-nice pedantry.

Cavendish wrote "Fancy," as she called her creative writing, "to recreate the Mind, and withdraw it from its more serious Contemplations," her more serious inquiries into "truth" or "reason." Her gender bias not only evidences itself in her artistic method, or at least in justification of it, but also in her portrayal of female characters. Mastery over language itself is often shown as inaccessible to women, primarily because of its corruption by men. Women achieve various degrees of success in traditional-

ly masculine endeavors according to their access to traditional masculine tools. Paradoxically, other equally heroic women deliberately choose the domestic sphere in rejection of society's decadent—and primarily masculine—structures.

Perhaps it is also within the scheme of Cavendish's canon as "fancy" or a woman's dream world that we can appreciate her "disconnected scenes." Such dreamscapes seem appropriate to works so obviously filled with the dreams of both heroines and playwright. In **The Presence** (1668), the princess and her ladies spend their days dreaming, finding in dream lovers fulfillment not to be found at court. In a fantasy never explained by rational process, the princess awakens one day to find her dream made flesh—and, no less, a prince in disguise.

The Duchess, not finding her dreams flesh, could at least give them substance on paper, explaining that she created the fantasy domain of **The Description of a New World, Called the Blazing-World** (1668) because,

> though I cannot be Henry V or Charles I, yet I will endeavour to be Margaret the First, and though I have neither Power, Time, nor Occasion to be a giant Conqueror like Alexander or Caesar, yet rather than not be Mistress of a world, since Fortune and the Fates would give me none, I have made one of my own.

Admitting that she wrote for recognition and identity outside the domestic sphere, in the preface to **Nature's Pictures Drawn by Fancies Pencil** (1651) she declared, "That my ambition of extraordinary Fame, is restless, and not ordinary, I cannot deny: and since all Heroic Actions, Publick Employments, as well Civil as Military, and Eloquent Pleadings, are deni'd my Sex in this Age, I may be excused for writing so much."

So her works present one vision after another of women achieving such goals. Queens, counselors, belles, scholars—all are projections of Cavendish's visions of power. There are also intriguing glimpses of strong, platonic relationships between women, and perhaps a bit of flirtation with lesbianism. These amazon heroines may be actual warriors, like Lady Victoria in **Bell in Campo** (1662), who recruits and leads a victorious female army of "Heroickesses," convinced that with equal education women will prove "as good Souldiers and Privy Counsellors, Rulers and Commanders, Navigators and Architectors . . . as men are." In addition to her noble actions, her eloquent speeches gain approval for a sort of Bill of Rights for Women, and represent Cavendish's finest dramatic writing.

Or the heroines might be scholars, like Lady Sanspareille of **Youths Glory, and Deaths Banquet** (1662), who gains fame and regard as a philosopher and orator both from the great men of her time and a very compelling queen. Or take the case of Lady Orphant of **Loves Adventures** (1662)—she's something of both. In order to be near the man she loves she takes on male identity and disguise. As the page "Affectionata," she astounds the army with both her genius for strategy and her valor in battle, quickly moving up to a command post. Her reputation nets her a summons to Rome, and during her visit to the Vatican she debates with the College of Cardinals and is offered a cardinal's hat by the pope himself. She also "gets her man," of course, although he first adopts her as his son!

One aspect of the unusual vision of author and heroines is rejection of the traditional marriages of the time. *The Matrimonial Trouble* (1662) chronicles nine bad marriages, while the masque performed by the women of the *Convent of Pleasure* (1662) is also designed as antimarriage propaganda. Ten scenes depict women beaten by drunken husbands, dying in childbirth, or suffering as their own children die. In the words of the epilogue, "Marriage is a curse we find, / Especially to Women kind, / From the Cobler's wife we see, / to Ladies, they unhappy be." The heroine, Lady Happy, asserts that marriage to the "best of men, if any best there be . . . [brings] more crosses and sorrows than pleasure, freedom, or happiness" and has thus separated herself from men, "who made the female sex their slaves."

The negative matrimonial examples in the plays include both the common commercial alliances of the time and also relationships based on passion. Although Lady Wagtail, one of the fashionable gossips of *Love's Adventures,* insists that "there's none of the effeminate Sex but takes it for a disgrace to lie an old maid, and rather than dye one, they will marry any man that will have them," a number of Cavendish heroines prove her wrong. Doltche, for instance, in *The Comedy Named the Several Wits,* rejects the notion of arranged marriage: "If my Father desires me to dye, I shall satisfie his desire, for it is in my power to take away my own life, when I will; but it is not in my power to love those my Father would have me; for love is not to be commanded, nor directed, nor governed, nor prescribed, for love is free, and not to be controuled."

Some of the heroines speak convincingly against marriage as a trap for women but eventually accept exceptional men with potential for truly equal relationships. This seems to have been the case with the duchess herself, who obviously loved her husband deeply and dramatically proved her devotion to him through many years of poverty, yet was proud to say that she had never known what it was to be "in love." Lady Bashful of *Loves Adventures* reluctantly agrees to marry the man she has come to love truly, but insists on a private ceremony rather than making a pageant that would hypocritically dramatize triumph in taking on an institution of enslavement. Lady Happy will marry the prince who has infiltrated her *Convent of Pleasure* only after he has gradually won her esteem and love while masquerading as a woman.

Other heroines maintain their resolve and their celibacy. Grand Esprit and Ease of *The Wits Cabal* (1662), Single in *The Matrimonial Trouble,* and, most notably, Sanspareille in *Youths Glory* insist on their right to remain single. Sanspareille perhaps makes her case most convincingly, in a multi-page oration which she delivers while dressed in white Satin "like as a Bride," to her father and

an entire audience "which are all Lovers." She cunningly begins by treating the responsibility and drudgery of marriage for men, but then moves on to her strongest point:

> but to treat or discourse of married women, is to discourse of a most unhappy life, for all the time of their lives is insnared with troubles . . . I do as faithfully believe it, as if I were experienced therein: On which faith, I made a vow never to marry, since I hear men are so hard to please and apt to change; wherefore if I were marryed, instead of discoursing of several arguments, I should be groaning and sighing, and weeping, with several pain and vexations. . . .

Not only can Cavendish's heroines envision life without marriage, but they can also envision life without men. Two of her plays include utopian schemes, communities of women. Each of the works takes its name from its utopian society.

In *The Female Academy,* the academy is established for the "well-born (or antient descent)" and rich. Men are excluded, except for observing from a grate, as are less elite women, who have yet a separate grate. The word goes out, "If you would have your Daughter virtuously and wisely educated, you must put her into the Female Academy." Viewing Cavendish's ideals for education, we see the ladies learning by making orations (just as the author seemed to prefer her own speculations to any kind of research or systematic observation). Each morning and afternoon the members of the academy assemble to listen to one after another of the young women discoursing on such issues as "whether or not women may equal men in wit or wisdom" (yes to wit, no to wisdom), "the behavior of our sex," friendship, honesty, "vanity, vice, and wickedness," "boldness and bashfulnesse," "virtuous courtships and wooing Suiters," poetry, and theater. One favorite topic is to discourse on discourses. The men of the neighborhood, lustful, jealous, and threatened, determine to break the strength of the Academy by marching in protest and blowing trumpets around the compound.

Revealing quite a different vision, the convent in *The Convent of Pleasure* is a retreat not for asceticism but rather for sensual delights. The Lady Happy has established it because she believes that

> men are the only troublers of Women; for they only cross and oppose their sweet delights, and peaceable life; they cause their pains, but not their pleasure . . . those Women where Fortune, Nature, and the gods are joined to make them happy, were mad to live with Men, who make the Female sex their Slaves. . . .

She vows,

> But I will not be so inslaved, but will live retired from their Company. Wherefore, in order thereto, I will take so many Noble Persons of my own Sex . . . whose Births are greater than their Fortunes, and are resolv'd to live a single life, and vow Virginity; with these I

mean to live incloister'd with all the delights and pleasures that are allowable and lawful; My Cloister shall not be a Cloister of restraint, but a place for freedom, not to vex the Senses but to please them.

The cloister, it is reported, has "conveniencey for much Provision, and hath Women for every Office and Employment: for though she hath not above twenty Ladies with her, yet she hath a numerous Company of female servants, so as there is no occasion for Men." The staff includes "Women-Physicians, Surgeons and Apothecaries." Cavendish describes at great length the lavish decor and "conveniencies" of the convent, the dress provided the ladies, the choicest meats of each season, as well as the lush grounds and gardens. In a song, Lady Happy promises,

> We'll please our Sight with Pictures rare.
> Our Nostrils with perfumed Air.
> Our Ears with sweet melodious Sound,
> Whose Substance can be no where found
> . . . Variety each Sense shall feed.
> And Change in them new Appetites breed.

The recreations of the cloistered ladies not only delight their senses and aesthetics, but also provide for fulfilling their dreams. Through their pageants and skits the dramatic medium itself becomes central in multiple layers of plays within plays. A sequence in which fantasies come to life gives the work a dreamlike—and eerily modern—quality. A pastoral scene appears and a princess (dressed as a shepherd) woos Lady Happy (dressed as a shepherdess), discussing "innocent love" and the platonic desire to "mingle souls together" in a kiss. The pasture vanishes and the scene (without changing) opens into a rocky shore with the princess as Neptune and Lady Happy as a sea goddess. They make verses about their beautiful lives in the sea, until the scene again vanishes.

Cavendish exposed her view of dreams and creativity in her self-reflexive fiction, *Description of the Blazing World* (1668). Immaterial spirits instruct the Empress's friend, the Duchess of Newcastle, that

> every human Creature can create an Immaterial World fully inhabited by Immaterial Creatures, and populous of Immaterial subjects, such as we are, and all this within the compass of the head or scull . . . also he may alter that World as often as he pleases, or change it from a Natural World, to an Artificial . . . a World of Ideas, a World of Atoms, a World of Lights, or whatsoever his Fancy leads him to . . . and enjoy as much pleasure and delight as a World can afford you.

The world created by the fictional Duchess of Newcastle is, of course, the Blazing World created by the historical Duchess of Newcastle.

Although many of Cavendish's plot lines and characters seem to represent an author creating new structures to undermine the patriarchal order, others paradoxically undercut this purpose. While Cavendish has envisioned

and portrayed a fascinating and encouraging complexity of women's roles in a man's world, she also reveals a striking ambivalence about a woman's choice of those roles. Both the utopian communities of *The Female Academy* and *The Convent of Pleasure* promise rich and unusual fulfillment for women, frightening those outside by their potential for upheaving the social order, yet ultimately each turns out to be fruitless.

Much is made of education for the Female Academy, holding up lofty, though abstract, goals and ideals for women. However, after a number of gestures in a feminist direction, the status quo is restored. In the final scene, the matron reveals to the insecure men that the ladies have committed themselves to the academy in order to become better wives, and "have learn'd so much Duty and Obedience, as to obey to what they shall think fit."

In the other ostensibly feminist stronghold, the Convent of Pleasure, Lady Happy finds herself more and more attached and attracted to a beautiful princess who has joined her ranks, and questions, "Why may I not love a woman with the same affection I could a Man?" Alas, we never learn the answer to that question because the princess turns out to be a prince in disguise. The ambivalence is particularly interesting in this most unusual instance of sexual cross-identity: the audience is not in on the masquerade, and the "princess" in turn further cross-dresses (as a man dressed as a woman-dressed-as-a-man), assuming masculine dress and roles for the playacting with which the women frequently amuse and instruct themselves. As Lady Happy assumes her new position as princess, the Convent is, of course, forgotten.

Cavendish undermines much of the potential feminine power of the other works to comparable effect. In addition to the amazon or heroic heroines, there is also another major character type generally found either as a foil to the main heroine or as a focus of an important subplot. This woman is generally more conventional: quiet, seeking to please, devoted to her traditional duties and the man she loves. In most cases Cavendish emphasizes that the character is shy to the point of painfulness—just as the author described herself in her single days as a lady of Queen Henrietta's court.

Jacqueline Pearson, in "Women may discourse . . . as well as men," classifies the two types of heroines as speaking women and silent women. Both have exemplary qualities, but play two different types of roles in the world, distinguished by their access to language—which is itself molded and manipulated by men—the golden key to success, or even survival, in a man's world. In at least six of Cavendish's plays the "heroic" heroines make public orations, pointedly demonstrating their mastery over language. The silent women, however, recognizing that they lack meaningful language, deliberately reject the corrupt language typically available to women and which characterizes other females as gossips, liars, and cheats.

Two plays feature sub-heroines, both known as Lady Bashful, who suffer great malice and gossip from the court and fashionable society because they lack the expected social graces. In *The Presence,* the Ladies Wagtail and Self-Conceit and Quick-Wit mock the Lady Bashful for her unsociable behavior and try to embroil her in scandal when she omits conventional social forms. When asked if she came to court to be thought a fool, she responds,

> No, I came to learn Wisdom, and to improve my Understanding, and if I can meet no Vertue, Worth, nor Honour to take Exampels from, yet I may observe the Follies, so as to shun them where or whensoever I meet them; and though ignorance is thought a defect, either in Nature, or Breeding, yet it is not accounted a crime, nor a deadly sin; and as long as they cannot think by my Carriage I am base, wanton, or wicked, I do not care how they think of my Wit or Bashfulness.

Lord Loyalty sees Lady Bashful's sterling qualities through her quiet demeanor and weds her, much as the dashing Duke of Newcastle had wed the blushing maid of honor who held such similar sentiments.

The Lady Bashful of *Love's Adventures* similarly asserts that her bashfulness is based on fear of dishonoring herself and not on any shame in her person or actions. When visited by the Ladies Wagtail and Amorous and the Sirs Bolde and Exception of fashionable society she trembles and shakes, either stammering, or being struck entirely mute with terror. Yet she, too, attracts wooers, although desiring none. She finds least troublesome the attentions of Sir Serious Dumb, who courts her by notes, thereby disturbing her privacy the least. When he is attacked by another suitor, Bashful realizes her love for him, disarms the challenger, and threatens him with his own sword. "Fear gave me confidence . . . love gave me courage," she tells Dumb. He, it turns out, is not really mute, but has foresworn language to merit her esteem through action rather than corrupt words. Through him Cavendish most pointedly dramatizes the issue that serves as such a strong undercurrent in her work.

Lady Innocent of *Youths Glory, and Deaths Banquet* is a victimized heroine more akin to those of the era's romances. Yet it is corrupt language that persecutes her—in this case the lies of her rival Lady Incontinent. Finding herself accused of immorality and lies, Innocent trusts in the virtue and judgment of her guardian and fiancé Lord de l'Amour to be able to discern the truth: "To what purpose should I speak? . . . silence, and patience, shall be my two companions." But when framed for stealing from Incontinent, despairing of finding language to answer the charges, she decides that only her death can demonstrate her innocence to her fiancé. So suicide becomes a triumphant action, prompting her stricken lover also to take his own life in her tomb.

These heroines show that within the domestic realm (the real world, perhaps), women must trust to modest and virtuous lives to speak for them and achieve a respect above their normal station—respect that they cannot gain by competing on the same basis with the men who manipulate that world and its language. They can claim a

kind of power over their own lives and sometimes those around them, but it is a power in stark and somewhat perplexing contrast to that wielded by the heroines of the main plots.

Perhaps *Youths Glory* provides the most disturbing manifestation of Cavendish's ambivalence. Silent Lady Innocent, who must commit suicide in order to communicate her innocence, is set opposite that most articulate of scholars and individualists, Lady Sanspareille. Sanspareille succeeds in earning the world's respect, but then inexplicably sickens and dies. Was it just too inconceivable that this remarkable woman could continue to bloom in a public role, particularly when further estranged from her sex by her vow of celibacy?

Cavendish's ambivalence toward her heroines seems to mirror the insecurity that shines through all the apologies and prefaces about her own efforts to master the written word: she alternately portrays her vocation as a heroic assay into the male competitive sphere and a harmless diversion for days insufficiently filled with domestic duties in a wealthy and childless household. She apologizes for one of her first ventures into publication. *The Philosophical and Physical Opinions,* confessing to His Excellence the Lord Marquis of Newcastle, "I have somewhat erred from good housewifery, to write Nature's Philosophy, where, had I been prudent, I should have translated natural philosophy into good housewifery."

Like her statements concerning her own vocation, within the plays Cavendish's contrasting visions of female power are juxtaposed jarringly against each other. Perhaps her complex and contorted structures may also be part of her struggle to project the full complexities of her ambivalences. Part of what makes her plays seem disconnected is the rapid alternation of short scenes from each plot or subplot with those of the others, or sometimes simply with a few lines by anonymous passersby commenting chorus-like on the action or filling in a strand of exposition. Certainly one aim of this technique must be to maintain a high level of suspense—after all, this is the typical structure of pot-boilers and the modern soap opera—but the ponderous number of scenes that results (as many as thirty to fifty in one part of a two-part play) and the choppiness of the transitions are not comfortable even for reading, and would certainly be unstageable. (I would suggest, however, that although the works are at heart plays of ideas rather than of dramatic action, with extensive editing and rearranging of scenes, three—*Love's Adventures, Bell in Campo,* and *The Convent of Pleasure*—may contain the dramatic elements and liveliness necessary to succeed on stage.)

Furthermore, while most of Cavendish's plays were untheatrical, written during the interregnum while the theaters were closed and without any sense of the visual dimensions of that medium, they may have a greater appeal to the modern imagination than they did for her own time. Surrealistic scenes—sometimes little more than a fleeting series of tableaux or images—and fantasy sequences seem now as if they could have been written for film. Perhaps the most striking example of this is *The Convent of Pleasure,* in which the medium itself becomes central in multiple layers of plays within plays. In addition to the masque on the hardships of women are the scenes in which the ladies of the Convent, particularly Lady Happy and the princess prince, appear in shifting scenes representing their fantasies.

But beyond the problems of structural coherence, the lack of a unified vision or direction would have prevented Cavendish from gaining a popular audience. The tensions inherent in her ambivalence could not be exploited because they are never resolved, probably not even for the playwright. The rigid expectations of her society concerning the way in which theater as a public ritual builds and climaxes are not conducive to portraying uncertainty. On the other hand, the presence of unresolved conflicts can be a powerful force on the page rather than the stage. There is a private dimension to reading which allows the suggestion of multiple meanings for both writer and reader. Our finest literature is usually rich in the unresolved conflicts and ambivalences of real life.

Regardless of what degree of self-awareness she possessed or expressed, Cavendish's heroines play out the dramas of identity and self-determination that women faced then—and now. Just as the two heroine types suggest Margaret as she was and Margaret as she dreamed herself, so the major heroic plots about powerful, influential women project her seemingly unrealizable dreams against the subplots featuring appropriately dutiful and modest women sorting through the domestic trials of the real world. That Cavendish could not live within the bounds of her own world is evident in her unconventional behavior—and the ridicule it drew, including the world's refusal to take her writing seriously. She may have deprecated her abilities and her writing, but she never stopped writing. Wielding her pen was her own form of heroic action by which she could stay within the proscribed confines of domesticity and yet break out to test ideas and dreams women had never dared claim before.

Her dream world is populated by women who seek to live their lives without restraint and others who warn them that to do so means failure or death. The inventive alternatives Cavendish devised reveal not only exceptional creativity but also courage. Her ultimate ambivalence—a woman equal to any earthly man who finally runs up against some insidious inexplicable force that will not let her live (whether it be a patriarchal god or her own "unnaturalness")—is more a collapse of faith than a failure of fancy.

Rachel Trubowitz (essay date 1992)

SOURCE: "The Reenchantment of Utopia and the Female Monarchical Self: Margaret Cavendish's *Blazing World,*" in *Tulsa Studies in Women's Literature,* Vol. 11, No. 2, Fall, 1992, pp. 229-45.

[*In the following essay, Trubowitz views Cavendish's*

Blazing World as an attempt to redefine the conventions of the utopian genre from a female perspective.]

Margaret Cavendish, the first Duchess of Newcastle, stands out in English literary history as the first woman author not only to write but to publish profusely. In the tumultuous fifteen years between 1653 and 1668 Cavendish published (in folio) thirteen strikingly eclectic volumes of fiction, poetry, plays, essays, scientific treatises, and other nonfictional prose. One of the most compelling of these volumes is a utopian work, *The Description of a New World, Called the Blazing World* (1666). Yet while an important contribution to the utopian genre, *Blazing World,* like many of the Duchess's other texts, has been bypassed in favor of works by her male counterparts. Dismissed by her contemporaries as the incomprehensible scribblings of "a mad, conceited, ridiculous woman," to quote Samuel Pepys [in *The Diary of Samuel Pepys,* 1976], in our own century Cavendish's writings have often been unsympathetically treated as unintelligible, dull, and naive. The fluid, fantastical, and fairy-tale qualities of *Blazing World* have perhaps made the text especially susceptible to scholarly scorn. Even its special distinction as the first utopia written by a woman in England has not encouraged historians of utopian thought to give *Blazing World* sustained, serious scrutiny. Frank E. and Fritzie P. Manuel devoted only one sentence of their nine-hundred-page study of *Utopian Thought in the Western World* [1979] to the Duchess's *Blazing World;* it is for them a utopia "so private that [it] border[s] on schizophrenia." Studies devoted more exclusively to the seventeenth century share the same inattentiveness to Cavendish's utopia. J. C. Davis, for instance, focuses on utopian writing in England between 1516 and 1700 [in *Utopia and the Ideal Society: A Study of English Utopian Writing 1516-1700,* 1981], but he too devotes almost no space to *Blazing World:* he lists *Blazing World* in his bibliography, but offers no commentary on it elsewhere in his book.

This essay means to redress such omissions by arguing several interlocking points in relation to Cavendish's text: first, that *Blazing World* is neither a self-indulgent "retreat into fantasy" nor a "ponderous tome," but rather a canny revision of the utopian social paradigm, driven by the competing demands of the Duchess's radical feminism and social conservatism; and secondly, that Cavendish's complex engagement with the utopian paradigm in *Blazing World* results in a revision of the utopian genre that is at once culturally subversive and politically nostalgic and, as such, uniquely accommodates her construction of female subjectivity in imperial terms. The female self that emerges in *Blazing World* not only supports a new (if finally problematical) paradigm of female independence, but also significantly informs the idealized treatment of women's friendship in Cavendish's fantastical utopian kingdom.

In part, the omission of *Blazing World* from standard studies of the utopia can be attributed to the generic transgressiveness of Cavendish's text. As Davis and the Manuels acknowledge, *Blazing World* is a utopia; it is, however, a utopia that in many ways fails to conform to prevailing assumptions about the form. For most students of the genre, the utopia celebrates the attempt to rationalize human culture. Davis describes the utopia as "distinguished by its pursuit of legal, institutional, bureaucratic and educational means of producing a harmonious society"; for James Holstun [*A Rational Millennium: Puritan Utopias of Seventeenth-Century England and America*], the utopia is "the experimental site for the formation of a new cultural order . . . a human organization of space that will follow from human reason." The rationalized space of utopia is for Holstun also a disciplinary formation. Following Foucault's treatment of the prison and the asylum, Holstun defines the utopia in both its literary and nonliterary, or "applied," configurations as *a factory for the disciplinary production of subjectivities.* Davis's and Holstun's definitions of the utopia generally enrich our understanding of the genre; they do not, however, greatly help to elucidate *Blazing World.* Unlike other utopias, including or especially those contemporaneous with it, Cavendish's ideal world does not domesticate human and physical nature into a rationalized cultural grid that can be easily managed and patrolled.

Cavendish's paradigm of felicitous community "reenchants" the demystified locus of utopia by giving its rationalized physical and psychic topography magical, mythological, and transcendent qualities. In so doing, it dissociates the utopia from the repressive force of discipline and newly associates it with a suspension of rationally conceived laws and institutionally imposed order. In this unrestrained site, Cavendish constructs a new utopian world, "framed in [her] own Mind, according as [s]he pleases," in which she takes "more delight and glory, then ever *Alexander* or *Caesar* did in conquering this terrestrial world."

We shall see that Cavendish's reenchantment of the utopia shapes her *Blazing World* in two key ways. It feminizes the utopia by giving her license—once the typically utopian effort to "normalize" human experience through rational, legal, and institutional means is abandoned—to address her complaint "that men from the first Creation usurped a Supremacy to themselves, although we were made equal by Nature: which Tyrannical Government they have kept ever since." In *Blazing World,* the "Tyrannical Government" of men is replaced by a magical and mythological mode of female rule. Cavendish's utopia is governed by an all-powerful and magnificently accoutered Empress who, not unlike Apollo, traverses her kingdom in a "very Glorious" chariot, fashioned from green, blue, and white diamonds and "drawn by Twelve Unicorns, whose Trappings are all Chains of Pearl." At the same time, Cavendish's reenchantment of utopia aligns the form with her aristocratic nostalgia for what could be called a "magical" past, for an idealized pre-Civil War England unrooted from actual history, in which the mystical sovereignty of monarchy prevailed over an undivided national and when custom, tradition, and other rationally irreducible supports for social hierarchy were embraced by all classes. Along with its radical feminism, *Blazing World* ratifies the kind of patriarchalism that is articulated in Robert Filmer's defense of kingship, *Patriarcha, or the Natural Power of Kings,* which celebrates the divinely

appointed power of monarchy and equates obedience to God with submission to the king: the subjects of the Blazing World believe that

> a Monarchy is a divine form of Government, and agrees most with our Religion; for as there is but one God, whom we all unanimously worship and adore with one Faith; so we are resolved to have but one Emperor, to whom we all submit with one obedience.

The same equivocal conjunction between royalism and feminism that shapes Cavendish's treatment of the utopian genre also underpins the imperial model of female subjectivity that the Duchess celebrates in *Blazing World.* It is a model that, as Catherine Gallagher aptly points out [in "Embracing the Absolute: The Politics of the Female Subject in Seventeenth-Century England," *Genders,* Spring, 1988], emerges from the overlap between the ideology of absolute monarchism and that of the absolute self: "the paradoxical connection between the *roi absolu* and the *moi absolu.*" The figure of the absolute sovereign is internalized by the Duchess as a monarchical ideal of the independent woman who has complete dominion over herself.

In Cavendish's writings, however, Gallagher argues, this imperial paradigm of the self-governing female subject leads less to an affirmation of female independence than to the division and cancellation of personal identity: it initiates "a regressive self-pursuit" that ends in "a classic *mise en abyme.*" While valid, Gallagher's focus on the solipsistic implications of Cavendish's absolutist model of female selfhood directs important attention away from one of the central concerns of *Blazing World* and many of the Duchess's other writings: the possibility of female friendship and community, a subject that Cavendish addresses with characteristic ambivalence. I shall show that, more than simply trap her in "the vortex of solipsistic regression," Cavendish's imperial model of female self inspires her depiction in *Blazing World* of perfect friendship as the "molecular" coupling of two independent female subjectivities, even while elsewhere in her utopia and other writings it drives the Duchess's efforts to distance herself from other women and to denounce her own sex. But like her reenchantment of the utopian genre, Cavendish's ideal of female self and community is finally destabilized by the competing interests of the royalist and feminist ideologies that jointly structure her world view.

While most utopias represent the attempt to confine nature and culture to rationally organized and institutionally controlled political spaces, Cavendish's *Blazing World* reenvisions utopia as the locus of marvelous and inexplicable natural and cultural transformations. From the moment we follow Cavendish's central character, identified simply as "a young Lady," into the Duchess's ideal kingdom, we enter a world outside of logocentric time and history, a fluid, uncanny, and uncharted territory in which the boundaries between logically and ideologically incompatible ideas and experiences dissolve and new rationally unthinkable and culturally transgressive alliances emerge.

The distance between the utopia and Cavendish's reinvention of it can be perhaps most clearly gauged by the depiction of nature in ***Blazing World***. Nature in the utopian works that proliferated in England during the seventeenth century is usually systematically reshaped to serve experimentation in maximizing agricultural and human productivity. In Robert Burton's utopia [*The Anatomy of Melancholy*, I, 1932], for instance, every bit of land is forced "by art" to yield all of its resources: "I will not have a barren acre in all my territories, not so much the tops of the mountains." New scientific approaches to the art of husbandry also resulted in a myriad of utopian schemes for applying technological and technocratic methods to the cultivation of the natural world. Thus in *Macaria* [*A Description of the Famous Kingdom of Macaria*, 1641], Gabriel Plattes systematizes the exploitation of the mineral and agricultural resources in his utopian commonwealth by placing the management and control (although, unlike Sir Thomas More, not the ownership) of land under a central council. In Cavendish's utopia, however, nature conforms to no system or rationalized framework; it is obedient only to its own anarchic properties. "The Blazing World" is home to "strange Creatures," fantastic anthropomorphic animals of many brightly colored complexions, purple, green, and azure, among others, which demonstrate the rationally irreducible laws of nature in Cavendish's ideal world:

> some were Bear-men, some Worm-men, some Fish- or Mear-men, otherwise called Syrenes; some Bird-men, some Fly-men, some Ant-men, some Geese-men, some Spider-men, some Lice-men, some Fox-men, some Ape-men, some Jack-daw-men, some Magpie-men, some Parrot-men, some Satyrs, some Gyants, and many more, which I cannot all remember.

This kind of logically disruptive reorganization of nature provides a framework for Cavendish's counter-utopian treatment of culture and reconstruction of psychic and social space. The utopian genre generally reconciles the tensions between the internal and external dimensions of cultural experience by subsuming the psychological sphere into the social one. Stephen Greenblatt's observation [in his *Renaissance Self-Fashionings: From More to Shakespeare*, 1980] that More "has greatly restricted any sense of *personal* inwardness" is true not only of *Utopia* but also of its descendants. Cavendish's foray into the fantastic, however, allows her to expand the utopian landscape of experience into the personal as well as the public domain.

This expanded utopian terrain can be charted most clearly in the Duchess's heroine. With her entry into the Blazing World, the distinctions between "inside" and "outside," under which she suffers in the old world that she leaves behind, no longer have currency. In her own world, the young Lady's inner excellence is not matched by her outward circumstances: she is abducted by a merchant who desires her visible wealth and beauty, but who refuses to honor the virtue of her personal being. By contrast, in the Blazing World, the inner excellence of the young Lady finds immediate veneration in the outside world,

over which she is bequeathed absolute dominion. The Lady's harmonizing of private virtue, public honor, and political power pushes Cavendish's utopia in the direction of romance. Romance, as Michael McKeon points out [in his *The Origins of the English Novel, 1600-1740*, 1988], "justifies the attainment of place by the ascription of internal merit. It designates a true nobility and an aristocracy of worth." It is precisely this romance ethos of "true nobility" that Cavendish's heroine personifies. The social value of her private virtue is celebrated publicly by all the inhabitants of the Blazing World, rulers and subjects alike; it transcends and unifies class differences. The Bear-men, the first creatures she encounters in the new world, "flockt together to see this Lady, holding up their paws in admiration"; they instantaneously "entertained her with all kindness and respect." When she is taken to "Paradise," the imperial realm of the Blazing World, to meet the Emperor, he not only immediately recognizes her superior personal qualities, but also makes her both his wife and his ruler, giving "her an absolute power to rule and govern all that World as she pleased."

Cavendish replicates her integration of personal inwardness and social outwardness in terms of gender through the confluence she creates between public "male" and private "female" spheres of her utopia. As recent critics have noted, the seemingly discontinuous demands of the new capitalist economy, reformed and Puritan views of marriage and family, and the new scientific efforts to control "Dame Nature" converged during the mid-1600s to compel a spiritualization of women into companionate helpmeets and to force an absolute bifurcation between the public and commercial world of men and the private and domestic world of women. In her utopia, Cavendish cancels these new gendered demarcations between public and private by casting her heroine in a variety of "male" roles, most notably that of warrior or general. Crossdressed in her imperial grab, she is as Empress an emblem not of domestic harmony but of military prowess, a figure reminiscent of Ariosto's Bradamante, Spenser's Britomart, and other literary Amazons and androgynes. She also recalls Elizabeth I, England's androgynous "Amazonian Queene." In detailing the Lady's military costume, Cavendish not only links her heroine to the female kingship of Elizabeth, who donned battle gear to review the English troops at Tilbury in 1588, but she also symbolically evokes the androgynous "body politic" of Elizabethan England and a cultural moment, unlike her own, in which the lines demarcating gender boundaries were at least partially effaced:

> In her left hand she held a Buckler, to signifie the Defence of her Dominions . . . In her right hand she carried a Spear made of a white Diamond, cut like the tail of a Blazing-star, which signified that she was ready to assault those that proved her Enemies.

In the second part of the text, Cavendish's Empress leads her navy to war when she comes to the aid of her native country, vowing to "destroy all [its] Enemies before this following Night," a vow she fulfills by winning a tremendous sea battle. The Empress's show of "manly" strength does not, however, simply replicate "male" acts of military aggression. Cavendish's female warrior is a savior not conqueror. Indeed, Cavendish goes so far as to depict her as a kind of female Christ: carried above the ocean on the heads and backs of her Fish-men, "she seemed to walk upon the face of the Water."

In addition to commanding the battlefield, Cavendish's heroine takes charge of the intellectual terrain of her new kingdom. The Empress establishes and heads her own scientific college, into which she recruits her male subjects, assigning to each anthropomorphic animal species a specialized discipline: the Bear-men are her experimental philosophers, the Bird-men her astronomers, the Spider- and Lice-men her mathematicians, and so on. This scientific college resembles and critiques both the Royal Society (to which the Duchess was extended an invitation, the only woman of the period to be awarded this honor) and its utopian inspiration, Salomon's House in Bacon's *New Atlantis,* an academy of male Elders dedicated to enlarging "the bounds of Human Empire over nature." In a challenge to the patriarchal order that underpins both institutions, real and fictive, Cavendish's scientific college subjects the male scientific community to absolute female dominion, a situation, as Sylvia Bowerbank notes [in "The Spider's Delight: Margaret Cavendish and the 'Female' Imagination," *English Literary Renaissance,* Vol. 14, No. 3, 1984], that is "improbable even in the twentieth century." The Empress solicits information from her scientific workers, who do only the investigative labor of science; she then assesses their observations and experiments and draws inferences from them. Yet just as her military prowess does not simply replicate "male" aggression, so the Empress's keen intelligence and expertise in science manifest themselves in "female" terms. While Bacon declares that he means to enlist science to enter nature "like a general who means to take possession," Cavendish confines her heroine's scientific interests to noninvasive speculation and reflection or to precisely the kind of learning that Bacon repudiates as "contentious": it does not "work upon matter, [but] . . . upon itself, as the spider worketh his web, then it is endless and brings forth indeed cobwebs of lerning . . . of no substance or profit."

Cavendish's heroine also takes charge of the church. Under her guardianship, the spiritual privatizing of women in her new kingdom is abolished, and her female subjects are given more public and visible modes of religious engagement. After repudiating the men of the Blazing World for forcing the women to "stay at home, and say their Prayers by themselves in their Closets," the Empress establishes a new uncloistered religious order for women, of which she makes herself head. Unlike her male scientists, her female novices prove themselves to have "quick wits, subtle conceptions, clear understandings, and solid judgments." These women become "in a short time, very devout and zealous Sisters." Cavendish's Empress is, however, not only a Mother Superior; through her "excellent gift of Preaching" the Empress also assumes the male role of a priest.

Cavendish's foray into the fantastic in *Blazing World* thus allows her to envision a future world in which the rational grid that the utopia places on human culture is cast aside in favor of a magical decompartmentalizing of logically incompatible categories of experience, figured forth most notably in the Duchess's feminist blending of "male" and "female" roles. The same fantastical rewriting of utopia, however, enables Cavendish to articulate her aristocratic nostalgia for a magical past, for some purely imagined moment in pre-Civil War England when custom, tradition, bloodline, and other nonrational justifications of monarchy and social hierarchy prevailed without contest.

To put it another way, while the magical and marvelous qualities of *Blazing World* help Cavendish to feminize utopia, they also assist her efforts to de-Puritanize it. Puritanism, especially in its most radical modes, took as its central target of reform the sacramental and traditional constructs of religious and political authority. In an effort to demythologize the powers of church and state, Puritan reformers sought to devote themselves and the world to a rational ideal of human experience through which the mystified, unregulated repertoire of customary and ritualized cultural assumptions and practices might be replaced by a methodical, precise, and disciplined system. In the 1640s and '50s the utopia, despite its Roman Catholic antecedents in More's text, proliferated among the various radical sects, and it provided an idealized depiction of exactly this kind of rationalized cultural system. As Holstun argues, Puritan utopia "presents itself as the genre of universal (but Eurocentric) rationalization." In reenchanting the utopia, Cavendish reclaimed the genre for the royalist side as an instrument by which the magic of monarchy, custom, and tradition, which the Puritans had tried to eradicate through utopian visions of rationalized politics, culture, and religion, could be reinstated.

That magic is most demonstrable in Cavendish's presentation of the absolutist authority of imperial sovereignty, which, like other Restoration monarchists, she associated with God-like power to wrest order from chaos. Within her heroine, Cavendish reproduces the divine or, more specifically, Christological pretenses of the restored Stuart monarchy, as exemplified in *Astraea Redux* where Dryden welcomes Charles II as Christ:

> That star that at your birth shone so bright
> It stain'd the duller Suns Meridian light,
> Did once again its potent Fires renew,
> Guiding our eyes to find and worship you.

The return of Charles as Christ to the throne was also heralded by his apologists in Christological terms as the beginning of a divinely inspired dispensation. Joseph Swetnam, a preacher from Derby, associated the triumph of Charles's monarchy over the Cromwellian republic with the silencing of the oracles at Christ's birth and the triumph of the infant Christ over the gods of paganism [in *David's Devotions upon his Deliverances,* 1660]: "heresie and blasphemy like *Apolloes* oracles at Christ his birth being silenced." The accession of Charles II in 1660 marked, for Swetnam, the end of sectarianism and dissent and a new divinely inspired era of union, both religious and political.

Like Swetnam's Charles, Cavendish's Empress has divine attributes: the Emperor and the citizens of the Blazing World "conceived her to be some Goddess, and offered to worship her." She also manifests the divinely inspired nature of her absolute sovereignty through Christ-like abilities to quell heresy and dissent and to establish both unity and univocality. In the passage noted above, in which the Empress appears as the Saviour of her native nation ("she seemed to walk upon the face of the Water"), she silences the paralyzing confusion of her former countrymen, "so many cross and different Opinions," by means of her God-like presence alone:

> Which sight, when her Country-men perceived at a distance, their hearts began to tremble; but coming something nearer, she left her Torches, and appeared onely in her Garments of Light, like an Angel, or some Deity, and all kneeled down before her, and worshipped her with all submission and reverence.

She achieves similar unanimity in the intellectual sphere by closing the scientific academy she founds when the dissonance created by the differences of opinion among her scientific workers threatens to overwhelm the unity and order of her state: she follows the counsel that "'tis better to be without their intelligences, then to have an unquiet and disorderly Government." The transcendent authority of Cavendish's Empress is, in short, shrouded in the same imperial mysteriousness as the Duchess's own king. While Cavendish's utopian kingdom recasts the public world of men in female terms, at the same time her paradigm of female dominion closely adheres to the prevailing ethos of male sovereignty.

Cavendish's reenchantment of utopia thus creates a new generic space capable of accommodating her desire for, in Lisa Sarasohn's words ["A Science Turned Upside Down: Feminism and the Natural Philosophy of Margaret Cavendish," *Huntington Library Quarterly,* Vol. 47, No. 4, 1984], female "dominance within a traditional social hierarchy," a desire embodied by the vexed figure of the female prince. This imperial figure also informs the representation of female subjectivity in the text. For Cavendish, every woman is capable of being an absolute sovereign, at least over her inward state, where she can literally subject herself and both rule and author the domain of her own person. In Cavendish's prefatory remarks to *Blazing World,* she describes

her desire to script her own subjectivity in monarchical terms:

> I am not Covetous, but as Ambitious as ever any of my Sex was, is, or can be; which makes, that though I cannot be Henry the Fifth, or Charles the Second, yet I will endeavour to be Margaret the First; and although I have neither power, time nor occasion to conquer the world as Alexander and Caesar did; yet rather then not to be a Mistress of one, since Fortune

and the Fates would give me none, I have made a World of my own.

Frustrated by the strictures on her sex, Cavendish translates her ambitions for worldly power into subjective terms, seizing upon the figure of queen—and more specifically, as we have seen, on the figure of Elizabeth I—one of the few "life scripts," as Sidonie Smith has called it [in her *A Poetics of Women's Autobiography: Marginality and the Fictions of Self-Representation,* 1987], available to women in the Renaissance and Restoration as a way to articulate that subjectification. With this self-investiture as "Margaret the First" and the inward-directed force of absolute sovereignty gained through accession to her own private seat of power, Cavendish spells her rebirth as an autonomous and self-governing woman despite the cultural constraints thwarting her worldly ambitions.

This same conception of the private self as an arena in which women can simultaneously achieve both absolute sovereignty and personal freedom also underpins Cavendish's fictive reinscription of her person near the end of *Blazing World* when the Duchess herself enters her utopia as secretary to the Empress, to whom she announces her desire for empire. The two ladies consult the Immaterial Spirits for a way to fulfill this ambition, and they are told that while the Duchess can neither inherit nor conquer an empire, she could become an empress by creating her own subjective kingdom, in which her sovereignty would in fact be more perfect than in a worldly empire:

> Why should you desire to be Empress of a material world, and be troubled with the cares that attend Government? when as by creating a World within your self, you may enjoy all both in whole and in parts, without controle or opposition; and may make what world you please, alter it when you please, and enjoy as much pleasure and delight as a world can afford you?

At the same time that she mimes the discourse of imperial absolutism, Cavendish converts that discourse into a celebration of the unfettered female subject.

The integrity and autonomy celebrated in the construction of subjectivity in this passage is further underscored by the originality that the "fictionalized" Duchess claims for her immaterial world. As a female realm, the microcosmic kingdom of her self can have no male antecedents: "no patterns would do her any good in the framing of her World." One by one, she casts aside the cosmological theories of Thales, Pythagoras, Plato, Epicurus, Aristotle, Hobbes, and Descartes as inadequate blueprints for her own subjectively crafted kingdom. Her mind is a realm complete unto itself, self-directed, self-governing, and self-begot.

This fictive image of imperial selfhood converts the "true," modest, and retiring self-image that Cavendish constructed in her autobiography, *A True Relation of my Birth, Breeding, and Life* (1656), into a powerful, yet also problematical, paradigm of female independence. In *A True*

Relation, as Smith has argued, Cavendish's self-inscription adheres closely to the more traditional feminine ideal in its emphasis on perfect quiescence and reclusivity. Repeatedly emphasizing the sheltered and cloistered aspects of her personal experience, the Duchess figures her life primarily in the imagery of conventual retreat. Her childhood is staged in the enclosed space of an entirely female world, her father having died when she was an infant. Of her sisters she writes that they "did seldom make Visits, nor never went abroad with Strangers in their Company." Their self-reliance and interdependence create a spiritual sanctuary of peace and harmony: "themselves in a Flock together agreeing so well, that there seemed but one Minde amongst them."

This domestic sanctuary is shattered with Cavendish's entrance into the public sphere when she accepts an appointment as maid of honor to Queen Henrietta Maria at the exiled Stuart court in France. Cavendish describes herself outside the cloister of her family as painfully shy and unworldly: she "had no Foundation to stand, or Guide to direct me, which made me afraid, lest I should wander with Ignorance out of the waies of Honour, so that I knew not how to behave myself. . . . I was thought a Natural Fool, indeed I had not much Wit." She recreates the conventual environment of her childhood in her "not Amorous . . . [but] honest and honourable" marriage to William Cavendish. Cavendish charts the fourteen and one-half years that she and her husband spent in exile on the Continent, though mostly in Antwerp, which she characterizes as "the most pleasantest and quietest place [for the duke] to retire himself and ruined fortunes in." After the Restoration, the couple retired to the northern estate of Welbeck Abbey, far from the court in London, and into another secluded, enclosed, and silent domestic space, in which she "could most willingly exclude myself, so as Never to see the face of any creature, but my Lord, as long as I live."

In *Blazing World* the silent and carefully circumscribed subjective space mapped out in her autobiography is reshaped into a boundless, discursive arena in which the female subject can demonstrate its unqualified singularity and verbal power as mistress over itself. Within this new utopian site Cavendish also radically reconfigures the intimate, conventual bond between her sisters as the perfect friendship between her Empress and her own fictionalized persona. If for Cavendish the female subject is absolute monarch over its inward kingdom, female friendship is the intimate pairing of two such singular, self-governing, incorporeal subjectivities. When the Duchess presents her immaterial world to the Empress, "Her Majesty was so ravished with the perception of it, that her soul desired to live in the Duchess's World," but the Duchess urges her instead to make her own spiritual kingdom. the two ladies achieve an ideal "Platonick Friendship" as two perfectly matched and perfectly autonomous, self-created souls:

the Emperess['s soul] imbraced and saluted her [the

Duchess's soul] with a spiritual kiss . . . and truly their meeting did produce such an intimate friendship between them that they became Platonick Lovers, although they were both Females.

True community is represented by Cavendish as the intimate bond between self-sufficient female atoms.

Ironically, the same paradigm of the imperial female subject that enables this atomic theory of female friendship and community also inspires Cavendish's fierce attacks against her own sex. Sarasohn attributes the Duchess's antifemale diatribes to "Cavendish's despair at her own position and that of her sex." While such despair represents an important psychological source of Cavendish's conflicting attitudes toward women, these conflicts also result from the ideological double bind into which she is driven by her imperial model of the female subject. This model allows her to celebrate the self-sufficiency of women both as individuals and in friendship, but its close adherence to an absolutist paradigm of royal power also requires her to distance herself from other women. If the absolute sovereignty of Cavendish's Empress gives her the autonomy to rule herself and to enjoy the "molecular" friendship I have been describing with the Duchess, who is equally autonomous, it also demands that she protect her imperial singularity by allowing no other woman "employment in Church or State." As a female author, Cavendish achieves in the act of writing the same imperial singularity as her Empress by replicating the paternal discourse that objectifies women as "Other," thus distancing her from other women. In the preface to *The Worlds Olio* (1655), she refutes the claim for women's natural equality to men, which, as we have seen, she elsewhere champions:

> There is great difference betwixt the Masculine Brain and the Feminine. . . . and as great a difference there is between them as there is between the longest and strongest Willow, compared to the strongest and largest Oak.

While allowing her to depict true community as the bonding of independent female atoms, Cavendish's imperial model of female autonomy paradoxically also inspires her antifemale arguments for male authority and control.

Cavendish's conflicting representations of women do not, of course, all issue from the same generic and political pressure points. In her *Orations* (1668), a staged debate among different female speakers on the issue of women's equality with men, antifemale argument serves entirely different formal and ideological functions than in *Blazing World* and in other works of Cavendish. A text that participates in what Linda Woodbridge has described [in *Women and The English Renaissance: Literature and The Nature of Womankind, 1540-1620,* 1984] as the "formal controversy" on female nature, the *Orations* presents arguments on both sides of the question of women's equality. Some of the speakers maintain that women should "Unite in Prudent Counsels, to make our Selves as Free, Happy, and Famous, as Men"; some argue that men are "more Ingenious, Witty, and Wise than Women, more strong, Industrious, and Laborious than Women, for Women are Wittless, and Strengthless, and Unprofitable Creatures." Like many writers of such debates, Cavendish presents herself as detached from the arguments she rehearses in the *Orations*. She demonstrates her ability to refute and support women's equality with men with equal conviction, even as she suggests, as Moira Ferguson notes [in *Women Writers of the Seventeenth Century,* 1989], that "she sympathizes with more than criticizes women and the tribulations they face."

In *Blazing World,* however, these same conflicting positions on women's nature produce greater tension in Cavendish's imperial paradigm of female subjectivity, as manifested in the text in both empress and authoress. An inviolable and unitary locus of knowledge and power, Cavendish's female subject is completely autonomous, yet capable of equitable female friendship and community; as such, it challenges the gendered relations between independence and dependence, power and weakness, public and private, which had been recently—and strictly—drawn in the Duchess's own historical moment. Informed by a patriarchal model of male sovereignty, however, the same paradigm underpins Cavendish's antifemale objectifications of "woman" and negates the ideal of female friendship and community she celebrate in *Blazing World*.

Cavendish's construction of female subjectivity and the utopian world she creates to accommodate it thus splinter under pressure of competing ideological assumptions. While her royalism and feminism converge to produce the ideal of female monarchy that she offers in *Blazing World* as a model for both social and personal experience, the Duchess's feminist desire for self-government and female community is finally undermined by her aristocratic investment in monarchy or, more precisely, by her adoption of the patriarchal ethos of absolutism that monarchy, both male and female, mystifies and enshrines.

FURTHER READING

Biography

Haynes, Alan. " 'The First Great Lady': Margaret, Duchess of Newcastle." *History Today* XXVI, No. 11 (November 1976): 724-33.

Biographical discussion of Cavendish focusing on her life and literary career.

Jones, Kathleen. *A Glorious Fame: The Life of Margaret Cavendish, Duchess of Newcastle, 1623-1673.* London: Bloomsbury, 1988, 192 p.

Extensive literary biography that praises Cavendish as a pioneer of the female literary tradition in the seventeenth century.

Criticism

Fitzmaurice, James. "Fancy and the Family: Self-characterizations of Margaret Cavendish." *The Huntington Library Quarterly* 53, No. 3 (Summer 1990): 199-209.

Examines Cavendish's conflicting self-portrayals, and attributes them to the necessity for a publishing woman writer in the seventeenth century to justify herself within traditionally acceptable frameworks.

Gagen, Jean. "Honor and Fame in the Works of the Duchess of Newcastle." *Studies in Philology* LVI, No. 3 (July 1959): 519-38.

Explains Cavendish's desire for fame in terms of Renaissance ideal of honor.

Meyer, Gerald Dennis. "The Fantastic Duchess of Newcastle." In *The Scientific Lady in England 1650-1760: An Account of Her Rise, with Emphasis on the Major Roles of the Telescope and Microscope,* pp. 1-15. Berkeley: University of California Press, 1955.

Highlights Cavendish's efforts to make science accessible to women in her time, stating that she was "the first Englishwoman to write extensively about science."

Rogers, Katharine M. "Erotic Scandals, Feminist Romances, and Revolutionary Fragments." *Belles Lettres* 8, No. 3 (Spring 1993): 16-18, 20.

Offers a brief review of *Blazing World* and asserts that the portrayal of Cavendish's aspirations in this novel is more significant than the actual achievement of her dreams.

"The Incomparable Margaret." *The Times Literary Supplement* No. 2864 (January 18, 1957): 29-30.

Highlights the conflict between Cavendish's desire for literary recognition and her lack of education.

Additional coverage of Cavendish's life and career is contained in the following source published by Gale Research: *Dictionary of Literary Biography,* Vol. 131.

Aemilia Lanyer

1569-1645

(Born Aemilia Bassano. Also Emilia; also Lanier) English poet.

The following entry presents a selection of criticism on Lanyer from 1960 to the present. For additional information on Lanyer's life and works see *Literature Criticism from 1400-1800*, Volume 10.

INTRODUCTION

A minor seventeenth-century English poet, Lanyer contributed to the limited canon of literature by female writers of the Shakespearean age with *Salve deus rex judaeorum*, a small volume of poetry considered unique for its feminist recasting of Christ's Passion. Attempting to revise misogynistic interpretations of Christian belief, Lanyer revealed a keen intellect in her argument for women's essential role in perpetuating Christianity. Only recently rediscovered, Lanyer's work provides valuable historical and sociological insight into Elizabethan England.

Biographical Information

Lanyer's life is briefly sketched both in *Salve deus* and in the notebooks of Simon Forman, an astrologer who cast her horoscope. Born at Bishopsgate in 1569, she was the illegitimate daughter of an Italian court musician, whose mismanagement of family funds and death in 1576 necessitated her employment at a young age. While working as a maid in the household of Susan Wingfield, countess of Kent, Lanyer appears to have gained the initial academic background that would eventually include a strong working knowledge of the Bible, Classical literature, and the poetry of such contemporaries as Mary Sidney, countess of Pembroke—an impressive scholarly display for any Elizabethan woman, much less one of such modest means and social standing. Sometime during her teenage years, presumably while in attendance upon the countess of Kent, Lanyer met and became the paramour of Lord Henry Carey Hunsdon, first cousin to Queen Elizabeth. Well-kept by Hunsdon, Lanyer, through his connections, became acquainted with the aristocratic ladies to whom she would later appeal for patronage. Upon becoming pregnant in 1592, she was discarded by Hunsdon and married off to a court musician and gentleman soldier, Alphonso Lanyer. Their union was unhappy and they were separated periodically due partly to Alphonso's extended military excursions, but also, apparently, by design. During one such separation, Lanyer resided for a short period with Margaret Clifford, countess of Cumberland, at the Berkshire estate of Cookham. Clifford's influence proved crucial to Lanyer's development as a poet, for while at Cookham Lanyer received additional academic tutelage and experienced a religious conversion, becoming devoutly Protestant. Lanyer attributed her literary endeavors and the religious nature of her subject matter to the behest of the countess, whose patronage may have made it possible for *Salve deus* to be published in 1611. Not surprisingly, Clifford is the central female character of *Salve deus*: the dedication, "To the Ladie Margaret," relates her preparation to assume the role of a bride of Christ, almost one-quarter of the title poem addresses the countess's numerous Christian virtues, and "The Description of Cooke-ham" recounts the poet's remembrance of her idyllic life at the Berkshire estate. In 1613, some time after Lanyer had left Cookham, her husband died, leaving her to engage in multiple lawsuits concerning potential revenue from his estate. Aside from a brief record noting Lanyer's unsuccessful attempt to establish a school for young women in 1617 and a court petition indicating her involvement in financial litigation in 1635, little else is known of her life between the publication of *Salve deus* and her death in 1645 at age seventy-six.

Major Works

Salve deus rex judaeorum, Lanyer's only known work, is a poetic reinterpretation of Christ's Passion that emphasizes the role Christian women have played in upholding social morality throughout history. Composed of eleven dedications, the title poem, and a short country-house poem, *Salve deus* is intended solely for women: Lanyer made no attempt to address a male audience, concentrating instead upon enlightening women of all classes to the essential nature of their Christian mission. The dedications, addressed to potential patronesses and typical of Tudor literature, emphasize the exemplary characteristics of each noble woman. The title poem reinterprets biblical history beginning with Adam and Eve, meditating on the Passion, death, and resurrection of Christ, and concluding with commentary on the state of Christianity in contemporary England. Asserting that Christ chose women to continue his work on earth, Lanyer contrasted the failures of Adam, the apostles, and the male sex in general, with the virtues of the redeemed Eve, the Virgin Mary, and the daughters of Jerusalem. Central to Lanyer's fusion of biblical history with an ideal contemporary society is her admonition of Clifford and other contemporary noble women to prepare to assume honored positions as brides of Christ. *Salve deus* concludes with the elegiac poem "The Description of Cooke-ham," in which Lanyer painfully acknowledges the discrepancy between her dream vision of an ideal Christian world of women (based upon her experience at Cookham) and the reality of the imperfect world of men to which she must return.

Critical Reception

Virtually no criticism on Lanyer's work exists prior to the 1970s. Upon its publication in 1611, *Salve deus* appears to have attracted little or no attention, and Lanyer was all but forgotten for over three centuries until her work was rediscovered in 1973 by A. L. Rowse. Claiming that Lanyer was the Dark Lady alluded to in Shakespeare's sonnets, Rowse theorized that *Salve deus* was written as an angry rebuttal to Shakespeare's portrait. This hypothesis, which was quickly refuted by other Shakespeare scholars, brought Lanyer's life and work to light, but also shifted initial attention away from the work itself. Hence the small body of criticism that now exists on *Salve deus* which has examined the poet's interpretation and presentation of Christian mythology, her technical competence, and the potential sociological value of her work. In general, critics deem Lanyer's feminist portrayal striking and, as Barbara K. Lewalski concludes, "[of] considerable intrinsic interest as a defense and celebration of good women." Lanyer's poetic talents, however, have been variously assessed. While critics praise her work as occasionally brilliant in imagery and acknowledge her basic command of rhyming and iambic pentameter, she is considered but a modestly skilled poet. Most commentators concur with Lewalski's opinion that "'The Description of Cooke-ham' is the gem of the volume," and also with Rowse's assessment that "she was too facile and fluent: she wrote too much, she padded out what she had to say—it [the volume] would have been more effective if shorter." Scholars have begun not only judging the artistic merits of *Salve deus,* but assessing the work's value as a potential source of historical insight as well.

PRINCIPAL WORK

Salve deus rex judaeorum (poetry) 1611

CRITICISM

Mary R. Mahl and Helene Koon (essay date 1977)

SOURCE: "Aemelia Lanier: 1570(?)—1640(?)," in *The Female Spectator: English Women Writers Before 1800,* The Feminist Press, 1977, pp. 73-87.

[*Below, Mahl and Koon place Lanyer in relation to her husband's occupation as a court musician and the cultural developments that took place in England during her lifetime.*]

When George Ballard wrote in 1752 that he had been forced to omit certain women "of distinguished parts and learning" from his *Memoirs of Several Ladies of Great Britain* because he had "been unable to collect very little else relating to them," his list included Elizabeth Grymeston, Bathsua Makin, and Æmelia Lanier. And today little more is known of Makin and Lanier.

Æmelia's maiden name is in doubt. She may have been the daughter of a member of the King's Music, Baptist Bassano, and Margaret Johnson, but we cannot be sure. We do know that she married Alphonso Lanier, a musician who played the recorder in the King's Music from 1594 until his death in 1613. Apparently Æmelia was well educated and had been trained in Latin and French. Her use of imagery from the field of music demonstrates her close familiarity with that art, either from personal training or from her association with the royal band at court. She was also well versed in classical mythology. Direct reference to the metrical version of the Psalms by the Countess of Pembroke reveals that she moved in that social group which circulated poetry in manuscript. The simple quatrains of her dedicatory poem are followed by the more sophisticated stanzas, ottava rima, of the ***Salve Deus Rex Judæorum*** itself.

Court records of the King's Music date back to the coronation of Edward IV in 1460. Queen Elizabeth's band seems to have been the first to include violins, in addition to the usual brasses, woodwinds, and timpani. Many of the musicians came from French and Italian families who arrived in England in the sixteenth century. Nicholas Lanier, father-in-law of Æmelia, was a member of the French Royal Music in the court of Henry II as late as 1561. Lanier appears to have moved that year to England, where he lived in London with Guillaume de Vache, another French musician. And that same year he joined the Queen's band. As was customary, his six sons eventually followed him in the Royal Music, as did many of their sons after them. Of his five daughters we know nothing.

The fifth child was Alphonso who, trained in flute and recorder, joined the band in 1594. He continued in his position at court until his death in 1613. He apparently held an army commission as well, and was known as Captain Lanier. In 1604 he was awarded a "grant of the office of weighing of hay and straw brought to London and Westminster, for 20 years," according to the *Grove Supplement.* This patent devolved upon Æmelia at his death but she made it over to his brother Innocent, who proposed to apply for a supplementary grant and to give her one-half of the joint proceeds. He failed to acquire the added grant, however, and never made any payments to her. At Innocent's death in 1625, another brother, Clement, held the patent, which had evidently been renewed. He also exploited Æmelia and withheld payment to her when she appealed to the courts for redress in 1635. No settlement was ever recorded.

Henry Lanier, the only son of Æmelia and Alphonso, pursued a career in the King's Music as a flutist, as his father had before him. He had one son, Andrea, whom he placed under the tutelage of an uncle so that the boy might be trained in flute and cornet. Henry died in 1633.

By 1635 Æmelia was left alone, her husband and her son having died, and her grandson having been placed with Alphonso's brother as ward and pupil. Her life had been spent in court circles during the reigns of Elizabeth, James I, and Charles I, all of whom had encouraged the development of music and drama. By 1635 court musicians were engaged in preparing music not only for plays but also for elaborate masques, and a new form of music drama, called "opera," was in its infancy. The term "orchestra" was now being used to describe the band that was located between the singers and the audience—a departure from the usual position behind or beside the stage. Within Æmelia's lifetime England had witnessed the development of the madrigal, the opera, and masques that required fantastic musical settings. Her brother-in-law, Nicholas, became Master of the King's Music, traveled on the Continent as agent for Charles I and the Duke of Buckingham to purchase paintings, and wrote what might be considered the first true English opera, entitled *Lovers Made Men* in 1617. His portrait was painted by Van Dyck. He was a friend of the famous Henry Lawes, and of John Milton, Sr., the poet's father.

We do not know when Æmelia Lanier died, but her name has not been found in official records after 1639. Her little book published in 1611 would seem to be too polished for a first attempt at writing poetry; it is highly possible that other works exist in manuscript, unidentified.

S. Schoenbaum (essay date 1980)

SOURCE: "Shakespeare's Dark Lady, A Question of Identity," in *Shakespeare and Others,* Associated University Presses, 1985, pp. 63-79.
[*In the following excerpt, first published in 1980, Schoenbaum challenges A. L. Rowse's theory that Lanyer was the "Dark Lady" of Shakespeare's sonnets.*]

On January 29, 1973, *The Times* carried a feature article, headed "Revealed at Last, Shakespeare's Dark Lady," by A. L. Rowse. Once published, *The Times* article was summarized in newspapers and magazines the world over. For weeks afterwards the correspondence columns of the paper reverberated with responses—heated, facetious, or merely informative. Even Dame Agatha Christie entered the lists. Dr. Rowse had made a stir.

In his controversial biography of Shakespeare, Dr. Rowse claimed to have solved all the problems of the Sonnets but one; everything "except for the identity of Shakespeare's mistress, which we are never likely to know." That was in 1963. At the Bodleian Library, Dr. Rowse was then working his way through the case-books of Simon Forman. A contemporary of Shakespeare—Forman was born in 1552 and died in 1611—this remarkable individual was a physician, astrologer, and lecher, at all three of which vocations he enjoyed considerable success. He has long been known to Shakespeare scholars by reason of his manuscript *Book of Plays,* in which he gives eye witness accounts of performances at the Globe of *Macbeth, The Winter's Tale,* and *Cymbeline.* But apparently nobody before Rowse had undertaken to

examine the mass of other papers. Here, in one of the case-books, among the mingle-mangle of English and Latin and diagrammed astrological forecasts, Dr. Rowse discovered his Dark Lady.

Lanyer as the "Dark Lady" of Shakespeare's Sonnets:

[Lanyer's] prose address is a piece of rampant feminism, like nothing else in the age—though a strong assertion of feminism runs all through the poems too, culminating in a passionate defence of Eve and putting the blame for eating the fatal apple on Adam! It is obvious that something personal had aroused her anger. Shakespeare's Sonnets had been published, though not by him, in 1609, with their unforgettable portrait of the woman who had driven him 'frantic-mad', dark and musical, tyrannical and temperamental, promiscuous and false, a powerful and overbearing personality, quite well known, of bad reputation. (Perhaps those Sonnets were intended as a warning to the young patron for whom they were written: he certainly did not fall under her spell as his susceptible poet had done—though she told Forman that she had been 'favoured . . . of many noblemen' and received great gifts. This was exaggeration typical of her, and of her poems). The portrait was defamatory enough. The very next year, 1610, her book was announced, and in 1611 published.

> A. L. Rowse, in The Poems of Shakespeare's Dark Lady: Salve Deus Rex Judaeorum, *JonathanCape, 1978.*

She was Emilia Lanier, *née* Bassano, the daughter of Baptist Bassano and Margaret Johnson, who, although unmarried, lived together as man and wife. The Bassanos were a family of court musicians who had come to England from Venice to serve Henry VIII. Their descendants stayed on at court in the same capacity; Baptist's will describes him as "the Queen's musician." Emilia was only six when her father died, and by the time she was seventeen, in 1587, she was an orphan with a dowry of £100—not a negligible sum in those days when a skilled artisan earned sixpence for a day's work—but she was hardly an heiress. She mended her fortune, however, by becoming the mistress of Henry Carey, 1st Lord Hunsdon, then well advanced in years. As Lord Chamberlain he supported the players in their sporadic skirmishes with the municipal authorities, and he was himself the patron of an acting troupe; for a while, just before his death, in 1596, he sponsored Shakespeare's company, the Chamberlain's men. Finding herself pregnant by the noble lord, Emilia (according to Rowse) covered up by taking as a husband a court minstrel, William Lanier, several years her junior. Not surprisingly, the marriage didn't go too well. Emilia told Forman, whom she visited in 1593 to have her horoscope cast, that

> she hath been favoured much of her Majesty and of many noblemen, hath had great gifts and been made much of—a nobleman that is dead hath loved her well and kept her. But her husband hath dealt hardly with her, hath spent and consumed her goods. She is now

very needy, in debt and it seems for lucre's sake will be a good fellow, for necessity doth compel.

She will be a good fellow; so she was promiscuous. She was also, Dr. Rowse reported, dark: Forman describing her as "very brown in youth," with "a wart or mole in the pit of the throat or near it." Would she, Emilia asked the wizard, ever be a Lady? Forman, for his part, tried to have *halek* with her, and recorded progress in his case-book. At first she drew away—she was a coquette—but later dispatched her maid to fetch him to her. "I went with them," he records in his diary, "and stayed all night." She told him tales about the invocation of spirits. In January 1600 Emilia Lanier sent for Forman, and he wondered "whether she intendeth any more villainy." By then he was finished with her.

This, in sum, is the story of Emilia Lanier, as it emerges from the pages of the case-books of the astrologer Simon Forman. His case established, Dr. Rowse re-wrote his 1963 biography of Shakespeare, mainly (one guesses) to give Emilia a showcase, and published it in 1973 as *Shakespeare the Man.* In the preface to the emended second printing he claims that the resurfacing of Emilia "has triumphantly vindicated the answers I have put forward all along, and the method by which they were found . . . The discovery of the Dark Lady completely corroborates, and puts the coping-stone on, my previous findings"—i.e. the chronology of the Sonnets and the identity of Fair Youth, Rival Poet, and Mr. W. H. And a page later, with breathtaking confidence:

> Perhaps I should add now merely that it will be found quite impossible to impugn any of them, for they are the definitive answers. It should be encouraging for research to think that Elizabethan problems, which have awaited their answer for centuries, can still be resolved at this late date.

In the same year Rowse brought out a revised version of his edition of the Sonnets, titled *Shakespeare's Sonnets: The Problems Solved,* complete with paraphrases for those who prefer to read their poems as prose, and with sufficient reference to Emilia in the annotations.

But is she the Dark Lady? She was promiscuous, and her dates do accord with Dr. Rowse's dating of the Sonnets. Coming as she did from a musical family, she may well have been accomplished at the virginals. Dr. Rowse observes that the husband's christian name, William, makes an admirable basis for puns, lending another dimension to the word-play of the Will sonnets:

> Whoever hath her wish, thou hast thy Will,
> And Will to boot, and Will in over-plus.

Over-plus indeed! But Rowse is wrong about the name of the lady's husband: she married Alfonso, not William, Lanier. Alfonso is not such a good name for puns. And was Emilia dark? An odd phrase, "very brown in youth," as though brownness of coloration diminished with the passage of the years. Stanley Wells was the first to look

more closely at the words in Forman's diary, which Rowse conveniently reproduced in his *Shakespeare the Man.* The word, Dr. Wells noted, is not *brown* at all, but *brave:* she was very brave in youth. It is not even a very difficult reading. *Brave* here means "splendid," "fine," "showy"; no help. We cannot, then, even say on the basis of the evidence that Emilia Bassano, or Lanier, was dark. So we are left with a promiscuous lady. There must have been others in Elizabethan London—else why such an outcry about venereal disease? Even had Dr. Rowse got all of his facts straight, his argument would have been no more than a tissue of conjecture, very interesting conjecture, to be sure, but conjecture none the less. No wonder that *The Times,* which had announced in a front-page headline "A. L. Rowse discovers Shakespeare's Dark Lady," quickly beat a prudent retreat, and for the correspondence which followed used the noncommittal heading, "Another Dark Lady."

This episode has a curious aftermath. The facts about Emilia and her husband were not long in coming to light after Dr. Rowse published his *Shakespeare the Man.* The next year, in 1974, he had a chance to retrace his steps in his biography of Simon Forman. Again he tells Emilia's story. She is now brave, not brown, and her husband's name is correctly given, in passing, as Alfonso. Nowhere does Dr. Rowse allude to past errors, and about his thesis he remains impenitent. "I am all the more convinced," he asserts, " . . . that here in this Italianate woman we have the Dark Lady." As one item of evidence he cites "her brief affair with the player-poet of the Company." Thus what one sets out to prove becomes, almost magically, the proof itself. In Dr. Rowse's latest life, *Shakespeare the Elizabethan* [1977], speculation is accorded the status of fact, and the dustwrapper duly hails "his unanswerable identification of Shakespeare's Dark Lady."

Ann Baynes Coiro (essay date 1993)

SOURCE: "Writing in Service: Sexual Politics and Class Position in the Poetry of Aemilia Lanier and Ben Jonson," in *Criticism,* Vol. XXXV, No. 3, Summer, 1993, pp. 357-76.

[*Below, Coiro discusses the significance gender and class in relation to a writer's decision to print his or her works during thte Renaissance. She then compares the Social Commentary in Lanier's* Salve Deus Rex Judaeorum *with that in Ben Jonson's* The Forrest.]

The growing and increasingly central interest in writings by sixteenth- and seventeenth-century women is beginning to have some material effects on the literary profession. In the fifth edition of the *Norton Anthology* (published in 1986), for example, a literature teacher could find a couple of poems by Lady Mary Wroth, one psalm by the Countess of Pembroke, and two poems by Queen Elizabeth. In the just-published sixth edition (1993), the number of texts by women has significantly increased, both in number and variety. One notable change is the inclusion of Aemilia Lanier as a major author, a figure until very recently entirely absent from literary history, much less the canon.

The *Norton Anthology* is at once a commercially sensitive gauge of what will sell to changing populations of teachers and students and also a powerful shaping tool of the literary canon. Nevertheless, it will take at least a generation for the profession of literary studies to internalize these newly visible texts into our sense of literary history, for the only way they can be internalized is through a series of subtle and radical shifts in our assumptions about Renaissance and seventeenth-century literature and culture. An overriding assumption which must be questioned, for example, is our still-lingering sense of Renaissance writing as somehow aristocratic. One thing the archaeology of early modern women's writing can show us is the pattern of our professional attention. Twenty years ago, even ten years ago, the only Renaissance woman writer an English professor was likely to know anything at all about was Mary Sidney, Countess of Pembroke and then only because of her editorial shepherding into print of her brother's *Arcadia.* First Elizabeth and then Lady Mary Sidney Wroth joined the Countess of Pembroke in our readings, forming a sort of vestibule to our construction of the now-assembling texts of women's writing, a vestibule which resembles in its names and its purpose the prestigious dedicatory collection at the front of a newly-published Renaissance text.

In these initial stages of discovery we have also tended to group women writers together simply as women, and we have then attended to their shared difficulties of speaking in a male-dominated discourse. Without exception, current studies devoted to early modern women writers have emphasized an idealized sisterhood among them, even though these studies discuss highly varied configurations of women across several generations and even across continents. It would ultimately be a disservice to women writers and distortion of their real power, however, to segregate them permanently as a subset of Renaissance literature and to romanticize their shared gender into a politically and intellectually univocal force. The mantra "race-class-gender" is not a unified chant, but a braided and abrading puzzle.

In an attempt to acknowledge contingencies of gender and class and, to some extent, even of race, I will focus on the politics of publication engaged in by two members of the service entourage surrounding powerful, wealthy women—a man, Ben Jonson, and a woman, Aemilia Lanyer, writing at the same time and to many of the same people. My concern is also, at least implicitly, with the politics of current literary criticism in Renaissance studies and feminist criticism in particular, politics which have left largely unchallenged the orthodoxies of traditional literary history so that women writers remain the lacy, decorative frill on the edge of a fabric that has not changed.

One of the central questions feminist criticism has asked of early modern women's writing is how a woman enters the psychomachia of writing performance. In order to begin to understand that question, however, it is important to acknowledge that it is virtually impossible to separate out gender as a category unrelated to class position. The criss-crossing of gender and class is particularly intricate and codependent in the Renaissance when writing venues themselves carry class and gender stigmas. Manuscript was seen as a more private, class-bound form of publication, for example, and writers like Philip Sidney or John Donne were extremely leery of appearing in print for fear of seeming common and thereby losing the insider positions they were vying for by seeming carelessly clever. The public, commodified circulation of print, on the other hand, was seen by those with court ambitions as a cheapening, chancy, even dangerous business. Spenser tried it in *The Faerie Queene* with a notable lack of success. Increasingly during this period, writing venues began to acquire gendered associations as well. As the dominance of print culture expanded decade after decade from Elizabeth's reign up through the civil war, manuscript became, in practice, a feminine mode of writing, suspect but carefully surveilled, containable and decorous; print, on the other hand, was figured as a more daring, aggressive, *masculine* mode. Women like the Countess of Pembroke wrote freely and at the highest level of accomplishment for class controlled manuscript circulation, but would appear in print only as the ministering handmaiden for the body of a dead brother's works. By the middle of the seventeenth century, the axes of manuscript/aristocratic/feminine, on the one hand, and print/Parliament/masculine, on the other, are strikingly visible in the print battles of the civil war; John Milton's late and agonized decision to begin to print his writing, for example, is also a decision to become somehow a *man* at last.

In the single voices of two individual writers of the late Renaissance, Aemilia Lanyer and Ben Jonson, we may hear the complicated, self-conscious and subconscious constructing dialectic of gender and class, a dialectic which can illuminate the field of writing at the moment when women began to advance inexorably upon it. In many significant ways, Lanyer and Jonson have more in common with each other than does Lanyer with other important women writers of her generation. Mary Sidney, Countess of Pembroke and Lady Mary Sidney Wroth, for example, defined themselves not only as women, but also and very centrally as members of a powerful aristocratic family. They were so defined by their culture, and their decisions about what to circulate among their group in manuscript and when to release Sidney manuscripts into the print market were defined as much by their social status as by their gender.

Wroth, for example, was a visible figure, invested with complex significance. We need only read Jonson's epigram "To Mary Lady Wroth" where he acknowledges that we "know [her] to be a *Sydney,* though un-named" (*Epigrammes,* CIII); we need only remember her living presence in the landscape of "Penshurst," one of the "great lord" 's "own" children, to realize that a feminist analysis of Wroth and of poetry addressed to Wroth must take into account not only concepts now shaping our sense of early-modern women such as "dismemberment" or "voyeurism" or "silencing" *but also* the real power of this and other individual women as part of a social network. In Jonson's representation of Wroth, she rises above the name of wife, her birth heritage so luminous in her writing that she reclaims her Sidney name. The public appearance of Wroth's *Urania* (a massive pastoral romance modeled to some extent on her uncle's *Arcadia* and incredibly detailed in its allusions to court scandals, many of them her own) was indeed a breach of social and sexual decorum. By printing her own words, Wroth disturbed the system where someone like Ben Jonson had been assigned the job of writing about someone like her in carefully muffled metaphoric terms. Nevertheless, it was a system set up to have Lady Mary Sidney Wroth within it.

For any woman writer, clearly, the risks of leaving the private world of manuscript circulation and entering the print market were high. For women who were not aristocratic, however, women who did not carry the fragile carapace of privilege and tradition, the entry into a print forum required a different series of negotiations. With whom could and did women who were *not* Sidney's align themselves in devising a print appearance? To what extent would a woman be *breaking* company with other women by publishing?

Two closely contemporary print appearances—Ben Jonson's *The Forrest,* published as one part of his 1616 *Workes,* and Aemilia Lanyer's **Salve Deus Rex Judaeorum,** published in 1611, present a near perfect test case for enriching our sense of writing performance in a system where, we must now in these latter days again acknowledge, women, as well as men, were authors. When we place Lanyer next to Jonson we learn a great deal about each of them as individual writers. We also learn more about concepts of authorship in the late Renaissance, more about the strains (both sexual and social) which, within three decades, would change English society, and more about the relationship of genre to social crisis. In other words, when Lanyer is fully in the canon, the canon will change at a number of perhaps unexpected pressure points.

Before we can think with some objectivity we must, however, look our own critical bogeys in the face. Our sense of Renaissance women, particularly of non-aristocratic Renaissance women, has been as deeply and romantically shaped by Virginia Woolf as our sense of Jacobite Scotland has been shaped by Sir Walter Scott. Virginia Woolf's powerful parable in *A Room of One's Own* of Shakespeare's sister Judith has affected generations of readers, stirring the fundamental beginnings of feminist scholarship and women's studies. In Woolf's telling, Shakespeare was lucky enough to have a modest but sufficient education and to be able, after a charmingly rakish youth, to set off to London "where he got work in the theatre, became a successful actor, and lived at the hub of the universe, meeting everybody, knowing everybody, practicing his art on the boards, exercising his wits in the streets and even getting access to the palace of the queen."

But Woolf imagines that Shakespeare had a gifted sister who remained at home, uneducated, while her parents tried to force her into a life of conventional wifehood. Woolf imagines her rebelling and fleeing to London, fleeing to the same stage door where her brother had first found his way, but there "men laughed in her face" at her wish to become an actress and the manager "hinted—you can imagine what. . . . At last, for she was very young" and because she reminded him of Shakespeare, she was taken as a mistress by the manager and became pregnant. "Who shall measure the heat and violence of the poet's heart when caught and tangled in a woman's body?"— she killed herself and was buried like a witch at the crossroads.

Woolf is a powerful and imaginative story-teller and her influence on feminist readings of the Renaissance has been profound, both on our sense of the wounded desperation of early modern women writers and on our sense of the damaging domination and misogyny of canonical male writers like Milton. Yet there is something worrisome about Woolf's pathetically charming and seemingly sympathetic little story, for it romanticizes, and thereby eradicates, the possibility of Shakespeare's sister's writing voice. After her story of fragile genius driven mad and destroyed by rigid sexual mores, Woolf concludes "That, more or less, is how the story would run, I think, if a woman in Shakespeare's day had had Shakespeare's genius. . . . But it is unthinkable that any woman in Shakespeare's day should have had Shakespeare's genius. For genius like Shakespeare's is not born among labouring, uneducated, servile people. It was not born in England among the Saxons and the Britons. It is not born today among the working classes. How, then, could it have been born among women?"

There is now another story to be told, however, a story strikingly like Woolf's in some details but powerfully different in its conclusions. Aemilia Lanyer is one of the few early modern women writers whose work was available on the library shelf as early as the 1970s. Even as I write this in the spring of 1993 it is still not possible to find Lanyer published free-standing under her own name, however. Until a modern edition of Lanyer appears later this year, Lanyer will be found shadowed under the name of Shakespeare. In 1978 A. L. Rowse, a famously crotchety Shakespeare scholar, published a theory he had been developing for a decade, asserting that Lanyer is the Dark Lady of the sonnets. Rowse reprinted Lanyer's 1611 book, **Salve Deus Rex Judaeorum,** which he regarded as a nearly negligible piece of writing, as another bit of evidence in the endlessly fascinating hunt for Shakespeare's biography. No one has since fully accepted Rowse's theory about Lanyer's relationship with Shakespeare, but neither is it implausible. Certainly, given the connections Rowse traces, Shakespeare would have known her. What follows, framed by a pronounced dose of irony in giving Shakespeare once again the possessive place, is the counter-story of Shakespeare's maybe-mistress, Aemilia.

Lanyer was the daughter of an Italian musician, Baptista Bassani, who had come to England in the mid-sixteenth century to serve as paid amusement and polish in the rather rough-around-the-edges Tudor court and had married an Englishwoman named Margaret Johnson. It is at this point in the early modern period still fairly anachronistic to speak of a middle or working class, but clearly the Bassani family inhabited the same social sphere as Shakespeare or Ben Jonson—talented, educated people using their wits to carve out a successful life in a changing society. Aemilia Lanyer's one surviving work, *Salve Deus Rex Judaeorum,* is stridently Christian in its argument, constructing the Old Testament as a time when women might indeed bear some of the guilt for human frailty, but celebrating Christ's coming as the moment when women completely redeemed themselves from the Fall, by nurturing Christ and defending him, while men persecuted and killed one of their own in cowardly jealousy and hatred. In considering Lanyer's class position, gender position, and her startlingly feminist poem, it is also critically important to note that Aemilia Lanyer is a second-generation Jew, one of the very few people of Jewish heritage in England at this time. (In this, too, Lanyer's real story interlaces with Woolf's fantasy in elaborate and fascinating counterpoint.)

Lanyer became the mistress of the powerful Lord Hunsdon, Elizabeth's Lord Chamberlain and patron of Shakespeare's acting company. When she became pregnant by Hunsdon, however, she was married off to another musician, Alfonso Lanyer, who was a Catholic. It is really impossible to emphasize strongly enough how marginal, how unusual her position was in Renaissance England—as a Jew, converted or not, as an Italian, as the wife of a Catholic, as a woman artist making a living as a fringe member of the court. Lanyer herself makes clear that Elizabeth read her poetry and was generous in her patronage, but Alfonso Lanyer lost all her money in a series of foolish investments. By the time Aemilia Lanyer wrote *Salve Deus Rex Judaeorum* Elizabeth had been dead for almost a decade, there was a new sovereign who was much less generous to poets, and Aemilia Lanyer was forty and probably no longer in the position to sell her beauty for favors (as contemporary gossip claims she had done earlier).

Lanyer serves as a strikingly de-romanticizing counter-narrative to Woolf's sad story of Shakespeare's sister. She met everyone, knew everyone, practiced her art, exercised her wit, and even got access to the palace of the queen. She got pregnant, lost everything, but she didn't kill herself, she self-consciously identified herself with the laboring classes, and she wrote. And she is far from the only example of what we can tentatively call middle-class women writing at this time. *A Room of One's Own* has been a critical text in opening a still widening wedge for women in the academy, both as writers and readers. Lanyer's complex counter-story is now visible to us in part because of Woolf's elegant challenge. But *A Room of One's Own* embodies, too, the conservative class prejudices embedded in our profession. Even as it asks that we turn the house of writing open, it presumes still a serving class ministering and silent somewhere in that house. We need to question continually the story literary history has been telling us. The call to question was, after all, Woolf's

manifesto. And Aemilia Lanyer's writing will call into question many old assumptions.

Lanyer's book, *Salve Deus Rex Judaeorum,* is one interwoven text constructed of, first, up to ten prefatory pieces to different aristocratic women. She had some eliminated and others rearranged in at least four separate printings in order to tailor them for presentation to different patrons; the chief focus of her hopes, however, seems to have been Margaret Clifford and her daughter Anne who had retreated to the country as the result of a dispute with the Clifford men about Anne's right to inherit property. The next section of the book is an aggressively feminist preface, **"To the Vertuous Reader";** and then the body of the poem retells the story of the fall and of Christ's passion in a way that makes women the redemptive figures in the New Testament dispensation and men the betrayers of Christ. *Salve Deus Rex Judaeroum* ends with the first country-house poem published in England, **"The Description of Cooke-ham."** Lanyer's poem centers on the grounds of Cooke-ham where three women—Margaret Clifford, Countess of Cumberland, Anne Clifford, Countess of Dorset and later to be Countess of Pembroke and Montgomery, and Aemilia Lanyer—wander in Christian contemplation. It is a gorgeous Eden, walled and safe from a fallen world. One of the striking things about this country-house poem is that Cooke-ham was not the ancient family seat of the Clifford family, but a temporary refuge loaned or rented to these women by the king while they persisted in their stubborn fight to be allowed, as women, to inherit land, an outrageous claim. For reasons that are not made clear in the poem, the Clifford women have left Cooke-ham; there are other estates for them. But for Lanyer the exclusion from paradise seems final. They have left her behind and asked her to write a poem in memory of their time there.

The two framing thirds of *Salve Deus,* the long section of poems addressed to women of rank and virtue and the concluding country-house poem, may be closely and fruitfully paired with Ben Johnson's *The Forrest,* for Jonson's book is similarly a collection of deftly panegyric poems to powerful aristocrats within which is positioned his extremely famous country-house poem, "To Penshurst." The fifteen odds and ends of lyric and epideictic poetry in *The Forrest* are gathered around the motivating factor of praise for the Sidney family. Several of these poems are addressed to women; indeed, one long poem, "To the World A Farewell for a Gentlewoman, Virtuous and Noble," is spoken in the voice of a noblewoman who renounces courtly pleasures and retreats, like the Clifford women, to the country. Jonson's country-house poem, "To Penshurst," which describes the ancestral home of the Sidney family in Kent, is the book's masterpiece.

The country-house poem is a genre which has attracted a great deal of critical attention, especially in recent years, and "To Penshurst" is the set-piece of this very impressive critical dialogue among marxist, formalist, and new historicist critics. "To Penshurst" is also a bedrock of the English canon. Any conventionally trained college English major is at least glancingly familiar with the subtle and superb craftsmanship of Jonson's artful compliment that begins:

> Thou art not, *Penshurst,* built to envious show,
> Of touch, or marble; nor canst boast a row
> Of polish'd pillars, or a roofe of gold:
> Thou hast no lantherne, whereof tales are told;
> Or stayre, or courts; but stand'st an ancient pile,
> And these grudg'd at, art reverenc'd the while.

It is the classic example of a poem enshrined in and defining of literary history, the founding instance of an important genre in English. But in fact, it is *not* the first country-house poem; Lanyer's, published five years earlier, is.

The two collections, then, invite comparison: both heavy with praise of patrons, some the same people, both grounded by the two earliest country-house poems in English, both structured around the role of the poet speaking. One striking difference between the two is Lanyer's long central section on the fall of Eve and on Christ's passion and the redemption of women. The central narrative is particularly fascinating because of its pre-Miltonic subversion of the story of Christian history, and also in light of Lanyer's heritage as a Jew. *Salve Deus Rex Judaeorum* should become a text crucial in our reconfiguration of literary history not only in its conflicted narrative of gender and class but also and connectedly in its narrative of gender and race. In Lanyer's poem, it is not Jews who kill Christ, but men; at the same time, any real possibility of freedom and dignity for women begins with Christ's coming. For the purposes of comparing Lanyer and Jonson, I will emphasize the social and poetic negotiations of the panegyric poems of *Salve Deus Rex Judaeorum* and *The Forrest,* but Lanyer's bold, passionate Biblical narrative lies at the vibrant center of her text, complicating her praises and sharply highlighting the containments of Jonson's poetry and his unease with religious themes. When we read Jonson's *Forrest,* we read one of the most handsome, tactful and, at the same time, melancholy works of social poetry in the Renaissance. When we read Lanyer's triptych of praise, passion, and country-house poem we read one of the most audacious, deliberate, and intensely personal social critiques to be published in the early seventeenth century.

Salve Deus Rex Judaeorum is a radical poem—a poem in which Christ comes for the poor, the ignorant, those at the bottom of the English social structure, not just for the rich and well-born. It is, as Barbara Lewalski and other critics have argued, an affirmation of good women, but it is very explicitly not an affirmation of *all* women. A crucial part of her social radicalism is that Lanyer is writing as a *woman* writer to aristocratic women; her writing is as edgy, self-fashioning, and socially self-conscious as Jonson's ever is. We cannot read her right until we read her sophisticated irony about her position in a world where she is dependent on a matriarchy she often resents.

In the prefatory poems and in the closing country-house poem, Lanyer alludes to a life of cultured servitude, amusing companion in the households of Countesses. Something of a Renaissance Lily Bart. To place her in the same position with the Countess of Pembroke, or Lady Mary Wroth, or Lucy, Countess of Bedford simply because she is a woman is a flattening distortion of her marginal, precarious position. Both Lanyer and Jonson lived dependent on these women and, to a large extent, their writing personalities were generated by the resentments and needs that these service relationships created. It is now a critical commonplace to discuss Ben Jonson's misogyny, his need to lash out at writing women as threats to his masculinity. Placing Jonson's anger next to Lanyer's, however, should destabilize any simple sense of gender wars.

The best known passage in *Salve Deus Rex Judaeorum* is its feminist attack on men in Lanyer's address **"To the Vertuous Reader"**: "evil disposed men, who forgetting they were borne of women, nourished of women, and that if it were not by the meanes of women, they would be quite extinguised out of the world, and a finall ende of them all, doe like Vipers deface the wombes wherein they were bred, onely to give way and utterance to their want of discretion and goodnesse." But we should not excise the passage on men out from the long passage of which it is only a small part. It seems relatively easy for Lanyer to dismiss men, viperous Pilates that they are, but the real danger to Lanyer's project is women. She is praising women in her "little booke" because she says women have been defamed as defamers of women: "And this have I done, to make knowne to the world, that all women deserve not to be blamed though some forgetting they are women themselves, and in danger to be condemned by the wordes of their own mouthes, fall into so great an errour, as to speak unadvisedly against the rest of their sexe." Lanyer herself, of course, has been the object of ill-speaking, a woman who would, according to surviving gossip, trade a good time for a living. It may seem that she here utterly refutes my argument about her ironic, sometimes bitter tone toward women of the class above her, the class she served. Yet she is acknowledging exactly the situation to which I point. There is tense anger and danger in women's voices and women's textual interpretations, clearly. The whole point of her project in the opening of *Salve Deus Rex Judaeorum* is to shore up for herself some kind of protection from attack by women. She begs her readers to "increase the least sparke of virtue where they will finde it, by their favorable and best interpretations, [rather] than quench it by wrong construction."

Yet, in a move familiar to us from Jonson and other Renaissance writers when introducing particularly dangerous texts, Lanyer invites the very interpretations and the very danger she openly disclaims. Given our warning about seeking virtue, what kind of construction can we put on the prefatory poems? If we begin with the lead poem, **"To the Queen's most excellent Majestie,"** it is hard to see how *not* to find a wrong construction. Queen Anne is called on to "grace" this volume. She can do this not because she is necessarily virtuous, but because she has "rifled nature of her store," "dispossest" all the goddesses of their "richest gifts,"

The Muses doe attend upon your Throne,
With all the Artists at your becke and call.

Anne is invited to look into this mirror and see not herself, as Elizabeth was asked to see herself in the mirror of
The Faerie Queene, but another Majestie:

He that all Nations of the world controld,
Yet tooke our flesh in base and meanest berth:
Whose daies were spent in poverty and sorrow,
And yet all Kings their wealth of him do
    borrow.
For he is Crowne and Crowner of all Kings,
The hopeful haven of the meaner sort.

The Lanyer persona, in sharp contrast, has nothing in
Anne's world—her "wealth within his Region stands. . . .
Yea in his Kingdome onely rests my lands/ Of honour."

Anne is invited to a feast given by a great Lady, richly
dressed by Lanyer with Honour, Eve herself. There is
clearly a price to be paid for this feast, however. The
queen is being subjected throughout the poem to a sustained critique for failing to provide the patronage to
Lanyer that Elizabeth had done. Lanyer asks explicitly
and repeatedly for money in this opening poem. And she
plays the humility topos in gendered terms—I'm just a
woman, just ignorant, please elevate my mind. The juxtaposition of the request "in a Woman all defects excuse,"
however, and the addressee, "peerlesse Princesse," absolutely levels either Lanyer's claim to find women defective or the queen's right to claim superiority. Lanyer's
request for help from her "superiors" is as two-edged as
Milton's Eve's was to be; indeed, and significantly it is
couched in the same terms as Eve's censored request for
knowledge from Adam about the heavens in Book 8 of
Paradise Lost:

For even as they that doe behold the Starres,
Not with the eie of Learning, but of Sight,
To find their motions, want of knowledge barres
Although they see them in their brightest light:
So, though I see the glory of her State,
Its she that must instruct and elevate.

In Lanyer's complicated text, there are two kinds of elevation—spiritual and worldly. The women in the prefatory company of women shift in and out of the two spheres,
accompanied by dizzying switches of tone. What she insists virtuous ladies see throughout ***Salve Deus Rex Judaeorum*** is a leveling Christ. "Glory can end what Grace in
you begun," she warns; only of "heavenly riches make
your greatest horde."

We should not forget, however, that Lanyer has a specific
suggestion about where these rich ladies might get rid of
some of their excess money. For the irony of the prefatory poems is at least triple: criticism of the aristocratic
ladies studded with inestimable wealth, promotion of a
leveling Christian radicalism, and, at the same time, a
wonderful degree of self-promotion. To Lady Margaret
Clifford, her chief patron in times past, she begins "Right

*Anne Clifford, Countess of Dorset, to whom Lanyer dedicated one
of her poems.*

Honourable and Excellent Lady, I may say with St. Peter,
'Silver nor gold have I none, but such as I have, that give
I you.'" To Lady Susan Bertie, in whose household she
served as a young woman, she ends with a stinging claim
for the freedom of her poem:

And since no former gaine hath made me write,
Nor my desertlesse service could have wonne,
Onely your noble Virtues do incite
My Pen, they are the ground I write upon;
Nor any future profit is expected,
Then how can these poor lines go unrespected?

The final poem in the front matter lays aside the mockery
and intermittent resentment that has rippled throughout.
Addressing Lady Anne Clifford, Countess of Dorset,
Lanyer is startlingly explicit:

Greatnesse is no sure frame to build upon,
No worldly treasure can assure that place;
God makes both even, the Cottage with the
    Throne,
All worldly honours there are counted base;
        . . . . .
What difference was there when the world
    began,
Was it not Virtue that distinguisht all?
All sprang but from one woman and one man,

Then how doth Gentry come to rise and fall?
Or who is he that very rightly can
Distinguish of his birth, or tell at all
In what meane state his Ancestors have bin . . . ?

One need which propels Lanyer into print is service to
women she hopes to win as patrons, but there is under
that need a complicated and subverting anger against
gender roles *and* class roles. Lanyer has addressed not
only Queen Anne and the Clifford women but also, among
others, the Princess Elizabeth, Lady Arabella Stuart, Mary
Sidney, Countess of Pembroke and Lucy, Countess of
Bedford. It would be a mistake to claim that all these
women's lives were somehow secure because of their
wealth and position. Lanyer pulled the poem to Arabella
Stuart because of her dangerous disgrace; the Clifford
women spent years fighting their own husband and father
for Anne Clifford's rightful inheritance of lands. Yet their
marginalization is crucially different from Lanyer's. Above
all, Aemilia Lanyer is a *writer,* who writes in service to
those above her while acutely conscious of those below.
The strains of that service on her writing criss-cross and
undergird the poem's collage.

Ben Jonson's *The Forrest* is, by contrast, an oddly retreating book: it is, after all, Jonson's last collection of
poetry crafted for and allowed a public appearance (its
companion book, *Epigrammes,* being the first). It begins
with "Why I Write Not of Love," that linking of tight
poetic form with his own age and impotence. The collection could indeed be read as a linked meditation on fertility and impotence. "To Penshurst" hymns the generative successes of the Sidney family, but "To the World"
hymns the Virtuous Gentlewoman's choice to retreat into
her own bosom. The "Celia" songs from *Volpone* are
wonderful with calculated lust, but *The Forrest* ends with
Jonson's rarely discussed but very moving prayer of hopelessness and despondency at the thought of ongoing life.
While Lanyer is vividly excited and determined about
seizing the print forum, Jonson is divided, half-hearted
about *The Forrest*'s project of public praise. A book that
begins with a poem like "Why I Write Not of Love"
where the poet displays tightly packed irony and despair
at his own failure at heat and life and ends with the loath-
ing of the world so movingly spoken in "To Heaven" is
a book structured by a weird ambivalence about public
life and private life, about a poet's paying job and a poet's
desire, about the poet's own physical, sexual life and his
role as a crafter of public sentiments. Jonson was proudly
uneasy about the service of praise he offered to those
who could reward him. Yet, deeply desirous of being
allowed to be enclosed within a country-house garden,
Jonson publishes an edgy support of the aristocratic status
quo. Lanyer stands startlingly close to Jonson in class
position and formal convention, and yet her text is startlingly different. Left alone within a rented and then ab-
sented country-house garden, she publishes a radical
manifesto.

Perhaps the most striking effect of comparing Lanyer and
Jonson is the inescapable and disturbing pairing of **"To
Cooke-ham"** and "To Penshurst." For one thing, such a
pairing highlights the absence of Lanyer's writing from
the outstanding body of critical work on the country-house
poem. Because this is a genre so finely packed and so
oddly short-lived, the country-house poem lends itself
richly to formal, generic and sociopolitical readings. The
genre has become a paradigm for central debates in seventeenth-century studies: to what extent is the genre "new"
and to what extent an amalgam of classical forms? to
what extent is it a "happy ethic of consuming," in Raymond Williams's words [in *The Country and The City,*
1973], where the existence of labor is simply extracted so
as to leave the pleasures unadulterated? to what extent is
it a reflection of growing ostentation and the Crown's
attempt to control its aristocracy? Each side would agree,
however, that the genre uses vast country seats as vehicles to praise or analyze the power of the feudal structure
of family property inherited through primogeniture. Labor, capital, and social change are thus the terrifying
undertext that the form exists to repress.

"To Cooke-ham" must complicate the debate: a poem *by*
a forty-year-old woman with fading prospects of court
preferment; a poem *to* women who are claiming their
right to property inheritance in the face of the entire patriarchy, including the King; a poem *on* an estate which
is not the family seat, but a temporary, rented or borrowed refuge.

As revealing as the different extrinsic circumstances of
property and inherited power are the intrinsic position-
ings of the poet figure within the garden in each poem.
Jonson's Penshurst exists always in the now, a place where
Jonson can go and be treated like an equal, can eat all he
wants of the best food,

Where the same beere, and bread, and selfe-same
    wine,
That is his Lordships, shall be also mine. . . .
Here no man tells my cups; nor, standing by,
A waiter, doth my gluttony envy:
But gives me what I call, and lets me eate,
He knowes, below, he shall finde plentie of
    meate.

The Jonson figure in the poem attributes parsimony at
other houses' tables not to the lord but to the servant class
who, in places less liberal than Penshurst, stint on serving
less important guests like Jonson so that there will be
food to go around below stairs later. Jonson structures
into the poem the powerfully embracing feeling that while
a guest at Penshurst:

. . . all is there;
As if thou were mine, or I raign'd here;
There's nothing I can wish, for which I stay.

Penshurst becomes a fantasy redress of Jonson's own social
unease, caught between his patrons and the servants he
mocks and who mock him. Lanyer's Cooke-ham, on the
other hand, is a desolate place; this country-house poem
is a poem of loss, the poet figure left behind in a ruptured
Eden to memorialize paradise lost. The persona of the

woman poet begins by describing her role as the kept writer of aristocratic women exiled in country retreat:

> . . . where the Muses gave their full consent,
> I should have powre the virtuous to content:
> Where princely Palace will'd me to indite.

One of the things for which we feel uneasy admiration in Jonson's poem is the astonishing tact with which he makes Penshurst a metaphoric vehicle for the great chain of being *and* a repressive class system; it takes a skilled eye to open up the ideology of his almost seamless poem. Lanyer's poem uses a strategy sharply different, making the artifice of the pathetic fallacy part of the subject of her poem. The place becomes a living tribute to Lady Clifford's power, she "From whose desires did spring this worke of Grace." "The Walkes put on their summer Liveries, / And all things else did hold like similies." And so throughout the body of the poem the garden becomes a garden of similes, the central oak, a man defending her from Phoebus's advances, for example, or the vista she saw from under the tree—hills, vales and woods—are men "as if on bended knee" pleading before her.

Raymond Williams has described the ways in which similes function in the country-house poem genre to mystify the social order into the natural order. The heavy use of simile in Lanyer's poem, however, is openly subversive. After an extended list of elaborate similes comparing nature in the Cooke-ham garden with adoring subjects, the poet's voice breaks out in an address to Fortune which is clearly an address to the fortunate as well:

> Unconstant Fortune, thou art most too blame,
> Who casts us downe into so lowe a frame:
> Where our dear friends we cannot dayly see,
> So great a difference is there in degree.
> Many are placed in those Orbes of state,
> Parters in honour, so ordain'd by Fate;
> Neerer in show, yet farther off in love,
> In which, the lowest alwayes are above.
> But whither am I carried in conceit?

The abrupt question addresses the essential danger and power of this poem. She begins by hymning the fated order of a society where some are privileged and some are low; she veers into a Christian critique of wordly power, and then she addresses the dangerous power of poetry itself. The passage is a microcosm of the poem. It goes on:

> My Wit too weake to conster of the great.
> Why not? although we are but borne of earth,
> We may behold the Heavens, despising death;
> And loving heaven that is so farre above,
> May in the end vouchsafe us entire love.
> Therefore sweet Memorie doe thou retaine
> Those pleasures past, which will not turne
>   againe.

Lanyer's final memory, however, is at once gaspingly funny and demeaning. Lady Clifford takes her farewell of Cooke-ham and, in a highly stylized, highly self-conscious gesture of pathetic fallacy, the poet has all the flowers and trees fade into autumn as a way of mourning the lady's grand exit. The patron lady and the poet pause under the great oak, however:

> To this faire tree, taking me by the hand,
> You did repeat the pleasures which had past,
> Seeming to grieve they could no longer last.
> And with a chaste, yet loving kisse took leave.

We are moved by the act of sisterhood. By the next line, however, **"To Cooke-ham"**'s whole over-wrought, high art structure of ingratiating simile falls into a ludicrous joke: we realize that Lady Clifford has kissed the tree.

The poem ends with quietly scathing anger. Lanyer has indeed written the poem she has been asked to write by her patroness, but she publishes it. By the act of publication, she breaches the walls of the garden.

> This last farewell to *Cooke-ham* here I give,
> When I am dead thy name in this may live,
> Wherein I have perform'd her noble hest,
> Whose virtues lodge in my unworthy breast,
> And ever shall, so long as life remaines,
> Tying my heart to her by those rich chaines.

In the Renaissance, women were bound by rich chains of marriage, of service. Aemilia Lanyer shows us the chains of obligation, need, love, and sometimes humiliation which bind her to the women above her. We should be moved by the sisterhood, but we should not be blind to the rich chains.

Lanyer and Jonson bear witness together to the shaping difficulties of gender, writing and service. Lanyer's anger at and fear of the power of women is in many ways greater than Jonson's. Her act of print publication is a rejection of her private role as a woman of service within a matriarchy. It must take, however, all the backing of Jesus Christ to propel her into that place. Jonson seems in many ways to be yearning for exactly the social gender expectations which Lanyer rejects. The poet in "To Penshurst" fantasizes retreat into a comforting estate where there will be clean sheets and lots of food, where he will be able to write marvelous poetry and escape the taint of the service class he feels nipping at his parvenu heels. Jonson is the poet literary history regards as the *man* who first took control of print culture, who laid out his writing in the physical space of the 1616 *Workes*. But Jonson is torn. In "To Penshurst" he scorns the builders of "proud, ambitious heaps" and praises an aristocratic family with a chaste wife and an immanent Lord existing somewhere out of and above the poem as a shaping force. The male narrator's voice is rather pathetically willing to be allowed to sit at table and be protected temporarily from the service class. He joins within Penshurst the women and children and ripe daughters. "To Penshurst" is a beautifully elaborated dance of social and sexual acquiescence.

In his "Penshurst," Jonson inscribes the Sidney oak within whose "writhed bark" angry or desolate men have cut the names of women they have failed to possess; in her **"Cooke-ham"** Lanyer inscribes the oak kissed by Lady Clifford. The sexual interplay with the oaks is, clearly, wholly different. But furthermore, in transcribing this act within her poem, Lanyer goes far beyond the delimitations of Jonson's exquisite panegyric. She wrests the (rented) oak away from the Cliffords by kissing it herself; she steals from the similes of praise the power those similes bestow upon the praised. It is Lanyer's choice to display openly the "rich chaines" even if she cannot fully throw them off. In displaying, in *printing,* she takes control—no longer a simile herself, one of the emblematic daughters of service or the wife who makes Penshurst such a lovely frieze of male power. For Lanyer, the act of printing is an act of defiance in several registers. When we have thought about country-house poems we have summoned a genre of conservative pieties, poems shoring up the walls against the powerful realities of labor and capital. We can no longer think about the genre without Lanyer as one of its two originary instances. The walls of the estate had already been breached.

Finally, Milton can help us think in this instance about the costs and legacies of gender and writing. Milton's early poetry, written from the mid-1620s until the 1645 *Poems,* is heavily influenced by Jonson. In form, in classical learning, and even in its politics, Milton's early writing marks him as a son of Ben. Milton had tremendous difficulty letting go of this early writing. We see much of that anxiety dramatized in *Areopagitica.* It was the work of the feminine place, the Lady's closet, the aristocratic manuscript realm which Milton found so appealing. After the searing experience of the war, interregnum, and restoration, however, Milton's poetry changes utterly. Instead, we have a radical Christian vision of a garden within us all. That garden has been read as famously unfeminist, famously explicit in its underscoring of the patriarchy. Virginia Woolf, for one, condemns John Milton with aristocratic distaste as a woman writer's bogey. In the questioning voice of Milton's Eve, however, the woman who asks for knowledge, who accepts the responsibility of bringing Christ into the world, the woman who leads us out of the garden and into the world in the most powerful act of *printed* poetry yet written, we hear the voice of women writing for print—we hear the voice of Aemilia Lanyer.

Barbara Kiefer Lewalski (essay date 1993)

SOURCE: "Imagining Female Community: Aemilia Lanyer's Poems," in *Writing Women in Jacobean England,* Harvard University Press, 1993, pp. 213-41.

[*In the following excerpt, Lewalski analyzes the three parts of Lanyer's* Salve Deus Rex Judaeorum: *the dedications, the title poem, and her country-house poem, "The Description of Cooke-ham."*]

Aemilia Lanyer (1569-1645) was the first Englishwoman to publish a substantial volume of original poems, and to make an overt bid for patronage as a male poet of the era might, though in distinctively female terms. Her volume of (ostensibly) religious poems, published in 1611, was entitled *Salve Deus Rex Judaeorum.* The author identifies herself on the title page as a married gentlewoman whose status is defined through her husband's position as an officer and court musician: "Mistris *Aemilia Lanyer,* Wife to Captaine Alfonso Lanyer Servant to the Kings Majestie." Besides containing some good poems and passages, the volume is of particular interest for its feminist conceptual frame: it is a defense and celebration of the enduring community of good women that reaches from Eve to contemporary Jacobean patronesses. Lanyer imagines that community as distinctively separate from male society and its evils, and proclaims herself its poet.

We know very little about Aemilia Lanyer, but enough to recognize her as a marginal figure at Elizabeth's, and still more at James's, court. Her family connections were with the circle of court musicians dependent upon patronage, and she had virtually no prospects beyond what she could win for herself. A. L. Rowse's edition of the *Salve Deus* [*The Poems of Shakespeare's Dark Lady: Salve Deus Rex Judaeorum by Emilia Lanier,* 1978] marshals some of the known facts about her life, chiefly drawn from the casebooks and diary of Simon Forman, the astrologer, in the service of his highly tenuous argument that she was the "Dark Lady" of Shakespeare's sonnets. But the links to Shakespeare suggested by the few records we have are much too weak to support Rowse's confident claim, even if we grant his very questionable assumption that Shakespeare's sonnets are to be read as straightforward autobiography. A more complete and reliable account of the biographical facts and the documents supporting them is supplied in Susanne Woods's edition of Lanyer's poems [*Salve Deus Rex Judaeorum,* 1993]. . . .

The title of Lanyer's volume of poems promises, somewhat misleadingly, a collection of religious poetry—a genre thought especially appropriate for women writers: ***Salve Deus Rex Judaeorum. Containing, 1. The Passion of Christ. 2. Eves Apologie in defence of Women. 3. The Teares of the Daughters of Jerusalem. 4. The Salutation and Sorrow of the Virgine Marie. With divers other things not unfit to be read.*** In a postscript to the volume addressed **"To the doubtfull Reader,"** she claims that the Latin title was delivered to her in a dream long before she conceived of the work, but that she later read that dream as a God-given sign appointing her to it:

> Gentle Reader, if thou desire to be resolved, why I give this Title, *Salve Deus Rex Judaeorum,* know for certaine, that it was delivered unto me in sleepe many yeares before I had any intent to write in this maner, and was quite out of my memory, untill I had written the passion of Christ, when immediately it came into my remembrance, what I had dreamed long before; and thinking it a significant token, that I was appointed to perform this Worke, I gave the very same words I received in sleepe as the fittest Title I could devise for this Booke.

Lanyer's statement at once claims a divine sanction for her work, and at the same time asserts complete responsibility for it since she remembered the dream only after she finished the book. But despite the title and the dream, the volume in fact contains several kinds of poems on subjects not exclusively religious, in various poetic genres and verse forms. As a whole, the work is devised as a comprehensive Book of Good Women, fusing religious devotion and feminism so as to assert the essential harmony of those two impulses. Lanyer does not imitate (though she might conceivably have read) Boccaccio or Christine de Pisan or Chaucer; her volume offers in a quite unexpected form a feminist defense and celebration of women and of Lanyer as woman poet.

An excerpt from *Salve Deus Rex Judaeorum*

Most blessed daughters of Jerusalem,
Who found such favour in your Saviors sight,
To turne his face when you did pitie him;
Your tearefull eyes, beheld his eies more bright;
Your Faith and Love unto such grace did clime,
To have reflection from this Heav'nly Light:
Your Eagles eyes did gaze against this Sunne,
Your hearts did thinke, he dead, the world were
    done.

When spightfull men with torments did oppresse
Th' afflicted body of this innocent Dove,
Poore women seeing how much they did
    transgresse,
By teares, by sighes, by cries intreat, nay prove,
What may be done among the thickest presse,
They labour still these tyrants hearts to move;
In pitie and compassion to forbeare
Their whipping, spurning, tearing of his haire.

> *Aemilia Lanyer, in her* Salve Deus Rex
> Judaeorum, *1611.*

The volume was entered in the Stationers' Register on October 2, 1610, by the bookseller Richard Bonian, and the poems were probably written within a year or two of that date. It was issued twice in 1611, with a minor change in the printer's imprint, and is now very rare; possibly only a few copies were printed, chiefly for presentation purposes, though the epistle **"To the Vertuous Reader"** implies a larger intended audience. In at least two copies (and perhaps more) certain dedications were omitted to tailor the volume for the recipient. Lanyer's husband seems to have taken some pride in her work, as he presented a copy to Thomas Jones, Lord Chancellor of Ireland and Archbishop of Dublin, whom he knew from his Irish service.

The book is in three parts. The first section contains nine dedicatory poems in a variety of genres addressed to royal and noble ladies, a prose dedication to the Countess of Cumberland, and a prose epistle **"To the Vertuous Reader,"** which is a vigorous apologia for women's equality or superiority to men in spiritual and moral matters. The title poem is a long meditation on the Passion and death of Christ (1,056 lines) which in fact incorporates the three other items listed as separate poems on the title page. But while that table of contents is misleading, it properly registers the title poem's emphasis on the good women associated with the Passion story. The Passion narrative is itself contained within a frame of 776 lines (more than a third of the whole), comprising elaborate tributes to Margaret Clifford as virtuous follower of the suffering Christ. The volume concludes with a country-house poem, **"The Description of Cooke-ham,"** celebrating an estate that was occupied on occasion by Margaret Clifford, as a lost female paradise. This poem may or may not have been written before Jonson's "To Penshurst" (commonly thought to have inaugurated the genre in English literature), but it can certainly claim priority in publication.

Given Lanyer's dubious past, her evident concern to find patronage, and her focus on women, contemporary and biblical, we might be tempted to discount the Passion subject as a thin veneer for a subversive feminist statement. But Lanyer was a woman of her age, and her imagination was governed by its terms. At the time of this writing, she appears to have been sincerely, if not very profoundly, religious, and she presents Christ's Passion as the focus for all the forms of female goodness (and masculine evil) her poems treat. Her good women meditate upon and imitate this model, and as poet she interprets her experience of life in religious categories. Her feminist perceptions can be rendered only in terms of the discourse of Scripture, but they force a radical imaginative rewriting of its patriarchal norms to place women at the center.

Salve Deus: **The Dedications:**

The nine dedications make a bold bid for patronage on a very wide front: they are obviously intended to call Lanyer to the attention of past patrons or acquaintances from her better Elizabethan days, and to attract new ones. She has chosen her targets very carefully, reaching out to all the obvious female power brokers of the court. In the opening dedication to Queen Anne, Lanyer laments that she does not now enjoy the associations and favors of that earlier time, when "great *Elizaes* favour blest my youth" (sig. a 4v), intimating that the present Queen might like to renew that happy condition. She next addresses Princess Elizabeth, whom she does not claim to know personally, as heir to all the virtues of her great namesake. Then she reaches out **"to all vertuous Ladies in generall"** who attend on "Queen" Virtue and with the Muses wait on Pallas (Queen Anne's chosen personification in masques and addresses); these allusions direct this long poem to all of Queen Anne's female entourage, suggesting that those about to be singled out are particularly worthy examples of that large community of female virtue. Next, Lanyer addresses the ladies she does know from happier Elizabethan days. First, as rank dictates, Arbella Stuart: "Great learned Ladie, whom I long have knowne, / And yet not knowne so much as I desired"; then her former mistress and patron, the Dowager Countess of Kent, Susan (Bertie) Wingfield, "the Mistris of my youth." Then, though she cannot claim acquaintance with either of them, she appeals to the greatest literary patronesses (respectively) of the Elizabethan era and of the Jacobean court: Mary (Sidney) Herbert, Dowager Countess of Pembroke, and Lucy (Harrington) Russell, Countess of Bedford. A prose dedication follows, identifying Margaret (Russell) Clifford, Dowager Countess of Cumberland, as the major dedicatee of the volume; she is honored throughout as Lanyer's past patron and best present hope. The poem that follows, to the Countess of Suffolk, Katherine (Knevet) Howard, is an effort to reach out to the powerful Howard faction, though Lanyer admits that she is a "stranger" to that lady. She concludes with the address to Anne Clifford, now Countess of Dorset, whom she claims as a close former acquaintance, inviting her to take up her mother's legacy of virtue and generosity as Lanyer's patron.

These dedications reveal something about Lanyer's actual associations; though hyperbolical like most of their kind, they would fail of their purpose if they were to falsify too outrageously the terms of a relationship. Offering multiple dedications was tricky though not uncommon; it was perhaps easiest to bring off when (as in Spenser's *Faerie Queene*) the monarch was the principal dedicatee, and the others (seventeen in Spenser's case) were ancillary. Lanyer devises a comparable strategy, making the several ladies an ideal version of Queen Anne's own court and entourage. More than that, however, she comprehends all the dedications within the thematic unity of her volume, addressing these ladies as a contemporary community of good women who are spiritual heirs to the biblical and historical good women her title poem celebrates.

Whatever actual patronage Lanyer may have enjoyed, her dedications rewrite the institution of patronage in female terms, transforming the relationships assumed in the male patronage system into an ideal community. Here the patrons' virtue descends through the female line, from mothers to daughters—Queen Anne and Princess Elizabeth, Margaret and Anne Clifford, Catherine and Susan Bertie, Katherine Howard and her daughters—and it redounds upon their female poet-client and celebrant, Lanyer. Many though not all of the dedicatees were linked through kinship or marriage with the Sidney-Leicester faction, which promoted resistance to Spain, active support of Protestantism on the Continent, continued reform in the English Church, and patronage of the arts, especially Christian poetry. The author describes her book as the glass which shows their several virtues, and she invites them to receive and meditate upon Christ their Bridegroom, here depicted.

The qualities Lanyer associates with her gallery of good women—heroic virtue, extraordinary learning, devotion to the Muses, and high poetic achievement—implicitly challenge patriarchal ideology and help to justify her own undertaking. Although Lanyer often excuses her poems as faulty and unlearned by reason of her sex, her several

apologias seem closer to the *humilitas* topos than to genuine angst. She appeals to her subject matter itself as justification for attempting what is "seldome seene, / A Womans writing of divinest things." Since religious poetry is often considered the highest genre, this claim gives an honorific, rather than a restrictive, value to the widespread assumption that women, if they write at all, should treat religious subjects. Lanyer continually proclaims her poems worthy of attention for their divine, and their female, subject, implying that a woman poet may write worthily since all these women are seen to be so worthy.

The dedication to Queen Anne, in six-line pentameter stanzas rhymed *a b a b c c,* establishes the contemporary community of good women. Its Queen is another Juno, Venus, Pallas, and Cynthia, attracting Muses and artists to her throne. With some sense, it seems, of the Queen's oppositional politics and subversive masques, Lanyer calls her particular attention to "*Eves* Apologie, / Which I have writ in honour of your sexe" (sig. a 4). As self-appointed female poet of this community of women, Lanyer claims to derive her poetics not from classical learning but from "Mother" Nature, source of all the arts:

> Not that I Learning to my selfe assume,
> Or that I would compare with any man:
> But as they are Scholers, and by Art do write,
> So Nature yeelds my Soule a sad delight.
> And since all Arts at first from Nature came,
> That goodly Creature, Mother of perfection,
> Whom *Joves* almighty hand at first did frame,
> Taking both her and hers in his protection:
> Why should not She now grace my barren Muse,
> And in a Woman all defects excuse.
>
> (sig. a 4v)

The other dedications elaborate the ladies' qualities and Lanyer's poetics. The sonnet-like poems to Princess Elizabeth and Arbella Stuart emphasize their learning: Lanyer offers her own "first fruits of a womans wit" to Elizabeth, whose "faire eyes farre better Bookes have seene," and she apostrophizes Arbella as "Great learned Ladie . . . / so well accompan'ed / With *Pallas,* and the Muses." The third poem (in seven-line pentameter stanzas rhymed *a b a b c c*), **"To all vertuous Ladies in generall,"** praises all who are ladies-in-waiting to Queen Virtue, companions of the Muses in attending on Pallas, and Virgins waiting for the Bridegroom. The fifth dedication (in the same verse form as that to the Queen) praises the Countess of Kent as a glass displaying all virtues to the young Aemilia, and as a heroic follower of Christ even in infancy, when her staunchly Protestant mother, Catherine Bertie, Countess of Suffolk, fled England with her family during Queen Mary's reign:

> Whose Faith did undertake in Infancie,
> All dang'rous travells by devouring Seas
> To flie to Christ from vaine Idolatry,
> Not seeking there this worthlesse world to
>   please,
> By your most famous Mother so directed,
> That noble Dutchesse, who liv'd unsubjected.

From *Romes* ridiculous prier and tyranny,
That mighty Monarchs kept in awfull feare;
Leaving here her lands, her state, dignitie;
Nay more, vouchsaft disguised weedes to weare:
When with Christ Jesus she did meane to goe,
From sweet delights to taste part of his woe.

(sigs. c 2-c 2v)

The next dedication is given special importance by its central position, its length (224 lines), its verse form unique in this volume (four-line pentameter stanzas rhymed *a b a b*), and its genre: it is a dream-vision narrative entitled **"The Authors Dreame to the Ladie Marie, the Countesse Dowager of Pembroke."** The poem is well made and graceful, with the dream-vision journey serving admirably to mark the Countess's unique status as a paradigm of female worth, as well as her absence from the present court—both because she remained for the most part on her country estates and because she belonged in spirit to the Elizabethan era. The poem recounts Lanyer's dream journey under the conduct of Morpheus to the Idalian groves, where she finds the Countess of Pembroke enthroned in Honor's chair, crowned by eternal Fame and receiving tribute from various classical representatives of Art, Beauty, and Wisdom: the Graces, Bellona, Dictina, Aurora, and Flora. Under the Countess's aegis the strife between Art and Nature is resolved, and all the company join to sing the Countess's Psalm versions:

Those holy Sonnets they did all agree,
With this most lovely Lady here to sing;
That by her noble breasts sweet harmony,
Their musicke might in eares of Angels ring.

While saints like Swans about this silver brook
Should *Hallalu-iah* sing continually,
Writing her praises in th'eternall booke
Of endlesse honour, true fames memorie.

(sig. d v)

Morpheus then reveals the lady's name, indicates that she spends all her time "in virtuous studies of Divinitie," and (continuing Lanyer's argument for the equality or superiority of women in moral and spiritual matters) ranks the Countess "far before" her brother Sir Philip Sidney "for virtue, wisedome, learning, dignity" (sig. d 2).

Upon awakening from her vision, Lanyer resolves to present her own "unlearned lines" to that lady, expecting that she will value these "flowres that spring from virtues ground" even though she herself reads and writes worthier and more profound books:

Thogh many Books she writes that are more
    rare,
Yet there is hony in the meanest flowres:

Which is both wholesome, and delights the taste:
Though sugar be more finer, higher priz'd,
Yet is the painefull Bee no whit disgrac'd,
Nor her faire wax, or hony more despiz'd.

(sig. d 3)

The Countess of Pembroke, as learned lady and poet, is hereby asked to recognize Lanyer as her successor in a female poetic line. And Lanyer points to the Countess as her model by the length, art, and extended personal reference of the dream-vision poem.

The later dedications are again epistolary in form. That to the Countess of Bedford (in seven-line pentameter stanzas rhymed *a b a b c c*) identifies Knowledge, wielded by Virtue, as the key to her heart, and emphasizes (as does Jonson's epigram) her "cleare Judgement" (sig. d 3). The unique prose dedication to the Countess of Cumberland marks her as Lanyer's primary patron and audience; it offers the Passion poem as a worthy text for the Countess's meditations, at once a mirror of her "most worthy minde" and a subject certain to grace "the meanest & most unworthy hand that will undertake to write thereof." Lanyer here claims for herself and her patron-subject the conventional eternizing power of poetry, asserting that these poems "may remaine in the world many yeares longer than your Honour, or my selfe can live, to be a light unto those that come after" (sig. c-c v). The dedication to the Countess of Suffolk (in six-line pentameter stanzas rhymed *a b a b c c*) takes note of the power and honor her Howard husband wields, but (true to the female focus) identifies the Countess as the "fountaine" of his chief delights and honors, and urges her to guide her "noble daughters" in meditations based on Lanyer's Passion poem (sig. e 2v). At this point Lanyer claims forthrightly that her poetic vocation and poetic achievement are God-given: she was led by her birth star "to frame this worke of grace," and enabled to do so by God, whose "powre hath given me powre to write, / A subject fit for you to looke upon" (sig. e 2).

The final long dedication to Anne, Countess of Dorset (116 lines in eight-line pentameter stanzas rhymed *a b a b c c*), presents her as the worthy heir and successor to her mother's excellences, virtues, and stewardship of the poor. Here, uniquely, Lanyer presumes to teach proper moral attitudes and conduct to her subject, as if privileged to do so by former familiarity. For one thing, in praising Anne's inheritance of Margaret's "Crowne / Of goodnesse, bountie, grace, love, pietie," she urges Anne to practice these virtues, including "stewardship" toward Lanyer herself:

To you, as to Gods Steward I doe write,
In whom the seeds of virtue have bin sowne,
By your most worthy mother, in whose right,
All her faire parts you challenge as your owne;

. . . . .

You are the Heire apparent of this Crowne
Of goodnesse, bountie, grace, love, pietie,
By birth its yours, then keepe it as your owne,
Defend it from all base indignitie;
The right your Mother hath to it, is knowne
Best unto you, who reapt such fruit thereby:
This Monument of her faire worth retaine
In your pure mind, and keepe it from al staine.

(sig. e 4v)

More boldly, she makes their former association and the present gulf between them, owing to rank and class, the basis for a trenchant critique of hierarchy founded upon patriarchal values. Alluding both to Anne's loss of her lands and to her own loss of contact with Anne, now Countess of Dorset, Lanyer contrasts male succession through aristocratic titles with a female succession grounded on virtue and holiness, drawing radical egalitarian conclusions:

> What difference was there when the world
>   began,
> Was it not Virtue that distinguisht all?
> All sprang but from one woman and one man,
> Then how doth Gentry come to rise and fall?
> Or who is he that very rightly can
> Distinguish of his birth, or tell at all,
> In what meane state his Ancestors have bin,
> Before some one of worth did honour win.
>
> (sig. e 4v)

This first part of Lanyer's volume concludes with a prose epistle **"To the Vertuous Reader"** which extends the idealized community of learned and virtuous women to a broader readership, offering the book "for the generall use of all virtuous Ladies and Gentlewomen of this kingdome" (sig. f 3). The imagined presence of male readers as well prompts a switch to polemics: the epistle makes a brief but forceful contribution to the *querelle des femmes,* that centuries-old controversy over women's inherent worthiness or faultiness which Rachel Speght was soon to address in her polemic against Swetnam. Lanyer first lectures those women who "forgetting they are women themselves . . . speake unadvisedly against the rest of their sexe," urging them to leave such "folly" to "evill disposed men" (sig. f 3). With considerable passion she then denounces those men "who forgetting they were borne of women, nourished of women, and that if it were not by the means of women, they would be quite extinguished out of the world, and a finall ende of them all, doe like Vipers deface the wombes wherein they were bred"— associating such men with those who "dishonoured Christ his Apostles and Prophets, putting them to shamefull deaths" (sig. f 3). Marshaling biblical examples with rhetorical force and flair, she argues that God himself has affirmed women's moral and spiritual equality with or superiority to men, and more than that, their call to exercise military and political power:

> God . . . gave power to wise and virtuous women, to bring down their pride and arrogancie. As was cruell *Cesarus* by the discreet counsell of noble *Deborah,* Judge and Prophetesse of Israel: and resolution of *Jael* wife of *Heber* the Kenite: wicked *Haman,* by the divine prayers and prudent proceedings of beautifull *Hester:* blasphemous *Holofernes,* by the invincible courage, rare wisdome, and confident carriage of *Judeth:* & the unjust Judges, by the innocency of chast *Susanna:* with infinite others, which for brevitie sake I will omit. (sig. f 3v)

In clipped, forceful phrases, she also details the singular honors accorded to women by Christ, and their fidelity to him:

> It pleased our Lord and Saviour Jesus Christ, without the assistance of man . . . to be begotten of a woman, borne of a woman, nourished of a woman, obedient to a woman; and that he healed woman, pardoned women, comforted women: yea, even when he was in his greatest agonie and bloodie sweat, going to be crucified, and also in the last hour of his death, tooke care to dispose of a woman: after his resurrection, appeared first to a woman, sent a woman to declare his most glorious resurrection to the rest of his Disciples. Many other examples I could alleadge of divers faithfull and virtuous women, who have in all ages, not onely beene Confessors, but also indured most cruel martyrdome for their faith in Jesus Christ. (sig. f 3v)

In Lanyer's imaginative vision, as in Anne Clifford's and Rachel Speght's, God testifies for women and takes their part. This prose address delivers a hard-hitting defense of women, and of Lanyer herself as author. By defining the attitudes toward women which well-disposed men ought to hold, she undertakes to reclaim some segment of the male sex from the evil mass, and so ends by offering her book to good Christians of both sexes.

The Title Poem:

Lanyer's Passion poem, the **Salve Deus** (in eight-line pentameter stanzas, rhymed *a b a b a b c c*) proposes Christ as the standard that validates the various kinds of female goodness her poems treat, and condemns the multiple forms of masculine evil. The poem also undermines some fundamental assumptions of patriarchy, in that it presents Christ's Passion from the vantage point of good women, past and present. Lanyer as woman poet recounts and interprets the story. The Countess of Cumberland is the subject of the extended frame, as chief reader and meditator on the Passion, as well as exemplary image and imitator of her suffering Savior. And the Passion narrative itself emphasizes the good women who played a major role in that event, setting them in striking contrast to the weak and evil men: the cowardly apostles, the traitor Judas, the wicked Hebrew and Roman judges, the tormenting soldiers, the jeering crowds.

As poet-narrator, Lanyer treats her material variously, sometimes relating events, sometimes elaborating them in the style of biblical commentary, sometimes meditating upon images or scenes, often apostrophizing participants as if she herself were present with them at these events. She uses rhetorical schemes—especially figures of sound, parallelism, and repetition—with considerable skill; her apostrophes often convey strength of feeling, she describes and sometimes dramatizes a scene effectively. And the inset rhetorical speeches such as **"Eves Apologie"** are forceful and effective. There are few striking images or metaphors, but Lanyer's allusions are usually appropriate and her language straightforward, taking on at times colloquial directness. Her greatest fault is a tendency to pad lines and stanzas to fill out the metrical pattern.

The poem has some generic precedents, whose elements are here well mixed. One strain is the religious complaint poem—the tears of the Magdalen, of Christ himself, of penitent sinners—usually focused on the Passion and Crucifixion. This was often, though not exclusively, a Counter-Reformation genre: the best-known English example was probably Robert Southwell's *Saint Peters Complaynt* [1595], in which Peter laments Christ's Passion and his own denial of Christ, bitterly berating himself and the woman who questioned him. Lanyer incorporates elements of this genre in the stanzas on the tears of the Daughters of Jerusalem and on the grief of the Virgin, though she apostrophizes those personages rather than having them voice their own complaints, as was more usual. The segment called **"Eves Apologie"** mixes complaint and rhetorical argument; it might well be a direct response to the frequent outbursts of misogyny in Southwell's poem, as Peter lays his and all men's sins at woman's door:

> O Women, woe to men: traps for their falls,
> Still actors in all tragicall mischances:
> Earths Necessarie evils, captivating thralls,
> Now murdring with your toungs, now with your
>   glances.

The other important genre is the meditation on the Passion, mixed with lamentation; often, as here, it incorporated erotic elements from the Song of Songs. In this kind perhaps the closest analogue for Lanyer is the almost contemporary "Christ's Triumph over Death" (1610) by Giles Fletcher [in his *Christ's victorie and triumph in heaven and earth, over and after death*]. Other suggestive Protestant analogues for Lanyer are a series of poems Nicolas Breton addressed to his patron, the Countess of Pembroke, in which he associates Mary Sidney with his meditative subjects by devising various kinds of frames. In *The Ravisht Soule,* an ecstatic meditation on Christ's works and glory, he invites the Countess to be the ravished soul that so meditates; in *The Blessed Weeper* he takes on the persona of the Magdalen meditating on the Passion and urges the Countess to become such a weeper; in *The Pilgrimage to Paradise* he invites her to identify with the travails of the Christian pilgrim he describes. Closest of all, perhaps, is the *Countess of Pembrookes Love,* in which Breton directly associates the Countess with the poem's speaker, who is undertaking a meditation on Christ in a *contemptus mundi* vein. His prefatory epistle explicitly describes the work as hers: "The heavenly Meditations, of an honourable Lady, the weake discourse whereof, far short of her worthiness . . . I have here [set forth]." Another of Mary Sidney's clients, Abraham Fraunce, also associated his patron directly with his subject in poetic meditations on Christ which he entitled *The Countesse of Pembrokes Emanuell* [1591]. Lanyer's demonstrated interest in the Countess of Pembroke as both patron and poet makes it likely she knew these works and that they provided some basis for the extended frame in which she positions the Countess of Cumberland as part of her subject: Margaret Clifford both reprises her savior's sufferings and is the chief meditator on them. Visual analogues for this device are those Renaissance religious paintings with the patron prominently portrayed within the scene as a worshipper.

The long preface (stanzas 1-33) addresses Margaret Clifford and sets up the frame. The first nine stanzas propose to immortalize her in verse and recall the solace she has found for her many sorrows in the beauties of Cookham and the love of God. Stanzas 10-18 comprise an embedded psalmic passage praising God as the strong support of the just and the mighty destroyer of all their enemies, with obvious (and later overt) application to the much-wronged Margaret Clifford. The passage echoes or paraphrases a melange of Psalm texts—chiefly Psalms 18, 84, 89, and 104—in what seems to be a gesture of discipleship to the Countess of Pembroke:

> With Majestie and Honour is He clad,
> And deck'd with light, as with a garment faire;
>
>   . . . . .
>
> He of the watry Cloudes his Chariot frames,
> And makes his blessed Angels powrefull Spirits,
> His Ministers are fearefull fiery flames,
> Rewarding all according to their merits;
> The Righteous for an heritage he claimes,
> And registers the wrongs of humble spirits:
> Hills melt like wax, in presence of the Lord,
> So do all sinners, in his sight abhorr'd.
>   (sigs. A 2-A 2v)

Stanzas 19-33 identify Margaret Clifford as one of those just who are specially beloved and protected by God, and praise her for abandoning the delights of the court to serve her heavenly King in rural retirement. This section includes a dispraise of the most notable beauties of history—Helen, Cleopatra, Rosamund, Lucretia, Matilda—all women whose beauty led them or their lovers to sin or ruin. By contrast, the Countess's inner beauty of grace and virtue made Christ the husband of her soul, and his death "made her Dowager of all" (sig. B).

This statement leads into the Passion narrative proper (stanzas 34-165). First, however, Lanyer invokes and admonishes her "lowely Muse" for risking the fate of Icarus or Phaeton by flying so far above her "appointed straine":

> Thinke when the eye of Wisdom shall discover
> Thy weakling Muse to flie, that scarce could
>   creepe,
> And in the Ayre above the Clowdes to hover,
> When better 'twere mued up, and fast asleepe;
> They'l thinke with *Phaeton,* thou canst ne'r
>   recover,
> But helplesse with that poore yong Lad to
>   weepe:
> The little World of thy weake Wit on fire,
> Where thou wilt perish in thine owne desire.
>   (sigs. B-Bv)

But she takes courage from the story of the Widow's Mite, and the conviction that God's glory will shine the more "the Weaker thou doest seeme to be / In Sexe, or Sence" (sig. Bv). Proposing, like many Protestant poets of her era, to render sacred matter "in plainest Words" so as not to distort it, she prays God to "guide my Hand and Quill" (sig. B 2).

Her account of the Passion is part commentary or meditation on the biblical story and part apostrophe, a figure she uses to intensify emotion and create an effect of immediacy. The first section (stanzas 42-79) begins with Christ's prayers and subsequent capture in the Garden of Gethsemane. Using apostrophe to poignant effect, Lanyer conveys Christ's profound isolation even from his beloved apostles:

> Sweet Lord, how couldst thou thus to flesh and
>   blood
> Communicate thy griefe? tell of thy woes?
> Thou knew'st they had no powre to doe thee
>   good,
> But were the cause thou must endure these
>   blowes.
>
>   (sig. B 3)

In this section the primary emphasis is on the sins and failures of Christ's own (male) apostles. Peter delcared that his faith would never fail, but Christ knew Peter would deny him three times. Christ implored the apostles to wait and watch with him, but they slept. The apostle Judas proved to be "a trothlesse traytor, and a mortall foe" (sig. B 4v). Peter offended Christ and the law by drawing his sword against Christ's enemies. Then, with a fine flourish of parallelism and antithesis Lanyer castigates the "accursed crew" of scribes and Pharisees who apprehended Christ:

> How blinde were they could not discerne the
>   Light!
> How dull! if not to understand the truth,
> How weake! if meekenesse overcame their
>   might;
> How stony hearted, if not mov'd to ruth:
> How void of Pitie, and how full of Spight,
> Gainst him that was the Lord of Light and
>   Truth:
> Here insolent Boldnesse checkt by Love and
>   Grace,
> Retires, and falls before our Makers face.
>
>   . . . . .
>
> Here Falshood beares the shew of formall Right,
> Base Treacherie hath gote a guard of men;
> Tyranny attends, with all his strength and might,
> To leade this siely Lamb to Lyons denne.
>
>   (sigs. C, C 2)

This section ends by reverting to the disciples' failures: "Though they protest they never will forsake him, / They do like men, when dangers overtake them" (sig. C 2v). That formulation prepares for Lanyer's sharply drawn contrast between the weak and evil men in the Passion story and the good women.

The second section (stanzas 80-118) treats the torment Christ suffered from yet more wicked men, the several judges: wicked Caiphas, proud Pontius Pilate, scoffing Herod. It begins by describing Christ through a series of epithets—Herbert's technique in "Prayer I":

> The beauty of the World, Heavens chiefest
>   Glory;
> The mirrour of Martyrs, Crowne of holy Saints;
> Love of th'Almighty, blessed Angels story;
> Water of Life, which none that drinks it, faints;
> Guide of the Just, where all our Light we
>   borrow;
> Mercy of Mercies; Hearer of Complaints;
> Triumpher over Death; Ransomer of Sinne;
> Falsely accused; now his paines begin.
>
>   (sig. C 3)

Caiphas is summed up in a nice metaphor, "Thy Owly eies are blind, and cannot see," and Pilate in another, "A golden Sepulcher with rotten bones" (sigs. C 4, D 3v).

Then Lanyer addresses a lengthy apostrophe to Pilate (stanzas 94-105), contrasting good women with all these evil men. Associating herself with Pilate's wife, Lanyer pleads with Pilate to spare Christ, relating that plea to a remarkable apologia pronouncing Eve innocent of any evil intention in the Fall. This part—**"Eves Apologie"**—takes Eve and Pilate's wife as representatives of women, while Adam and Pilate represent men:

> O noble Governour, make thou yet a pause,
> Doe not in innocent blood imbrue thy hands;
> But heare the words of thy most worthy wife,
> Who sends to thee, to beg her Saviours life.
>
>   . . . . .
>
> Let not us Women glory in Mens fall,
> Who had power given to over-rule us all.
>
> Till now your indiscretion sets us free,
> And makes our former fault much less appeare;
> Our Mother *Eve,* who tasted of the Tree,
> Giving to *Adam* what shee held most deare,
> Was simply good, and had no powre to see,
> The after-comming harme did not appeare:
> The subtile Serpent that our Sex betraide,
> Before our fall so sure a plot had laide.
>
>   (sigs. C 4v-D)

She presses that argument hard, using the Fall and Passion stories to weigh the characteristic sin of women (excessive love) against that of men (violence). Her argument is that Eve's "harmeless Heart" intended no evil at all, that her fault was only "too much love, / Which made her give this present to her Deare, / That what shee tasted, he likewise might prove, / Whereby his knowledge might become more cleare" (sig. Dv). By taking the name of the Tree of Knowledge literally, Lanyer makes knowledge the gift of Eve or woman: "Yet Men will boast of Knowledge, which he tooke / From *Eves* faire hand, as from a learned Booke." In Lanyer's argument, all the guilt of the Fall belongs to Adam, who was strong, wise, and undeceived. Moreover, any faults which women might have inherited from Eve are far outweighed by the guilt, malice, and violence of men, epitomized in Pilate:

> Her weakenesse did the Serpents words obay,
> But you in malice Gods deare Sonne betray.
>
> Whom, if unjustly you condemne to die,
> Her sinne was small, to what you doe commit.
> (sig. Dv)

Lanyer's biblical exegesis would have been outrageous (by contemporary standards), and she may have intended the shock to underscore the susceptibility of the biblical narratives to very different interpretations, depending on the interests involved. They had been hitherto constrained to patriarchal power, so she by a neat reversal wrenches them to women's interests. She concludes with a forthright declaration of gender equality, denouncing hierarchy and men's unjust claim to rule:

> Then let us have our Libertie againe,
> And challendge to your selves no Sov'raigntie;
> You came not in the world without our paine,
> Make that a barre against your crueltie;
> Your fault being greater, why should you
>   disdaine
> Our beeing your equals, free from tyranny?
> If one weake woman simply did offend,
> This sinne of yours, hath no excuse, nor end.
>
> To which (poore soules) we never gave consent,
> Witnesse thy wife (O *Pilate*) speakes for all.
> (sig. D 2)

The third section (stanzas 119-165) presents the procession to Calvary, the Crucifixion, and the Resurrection, again contrasting the responses of good women and evil men to these events. The journey scene is described with considerable dramatic effectiveness:

> First went the Crier with open mouth
>   proclayming
> The heavy sentence of Iniquitie,
> The Hangman next, by his base office clayming
> His right in Hell, where sinners never die,
> Carrying the nayles, the people still blaspheming
> Their maker, using all impiety;
> The Thieves attending him on either side,
> The Serjeants watching, while the women cri'd.
> (sig. D 4)

A lengthy apostrophe to the Daughters of Jerusalem follows (stanzas 122-126), offering them as examples of women's pity and mercy, as opposed to men's fierce cruelty:

> When spightfull men with torments did oppresse
> Th'afflicted body of this innocent Dove,
> Poore women seeing how much they did
>   transgresse,
> By teares, by sighes, by cries intreat, nay prove,
> What may be done among the thickest presse,

> They labour still these tyrants hearts to move;
> In pitie and compassion to forbeare
> Their whipping, spurning, tearing of his haire.
>
> But all in vaine, their malice hath no end,
> Their hearts more hard than flint, or marble
>   stone.
> (sig. D 4v)

Then, in another long apostrophe, Lanyer locates herself with the mother of Jesus as observer and grief-stricken mourner at the Crucifixion, meditating as well on Mary's wondrous role in the Redemption and her exaltation as "Queene of Woman-kind" (stanzas 127-142):

> How canst thou choose (faire Virgin) then but
>   mourne,
> When this sweet of-spring of thy body dies,
> When thy faire eies beholds his bodie torne,
> The peoples fury, heares the womens cries.
> (sig. E 2v)

Lanyer's baroque description of the Crucifixion itself (somewhat reminiscent of Giles Fletcher) is not without poetic force and religious feeling:

> His joynts dis-joynted, and his legges hang
>   downe,
> His alablaster breast, his bloody side,
> His members torne, and on his head a Crowne
> Of sharpest Thorns, to satisfie for pride:
> Anguish and Paine doe all his Sences drowne,
> While they his holy garments do divide:
> His bowells drie, his heart full fraught with
>   griefe,
> Crying to him that yeelds him no reliefe.
> (sig. E 3)

But the emphasis on good women continues. This icon of the Crucifixion is presented as an object of meditation to the Countess of Cumberland, who is apostrophized as "Deere Spouse of Christ" (sig. E 3) and urged to judge "if ever Lover were so true" (sig. E 4v). Finally, the precious balms brought by still other good women to annoint the dead Christ are interpreted as a figure of the precious ointments "of Mercie, Charitie, and Faith" brought to the risen Christ (the Bridegroom of Canticles) "by his faithfull Wife / The holy Church" (sig. F).

A long coda (166-230) completes the frame begun with the long prologue; it recounts the many forms in which Christ appears to Margaret Clifford as she practices the works of mercy, and portrays her in Canticles imagery as Christ's spouse. It also proclaims her superiority to the various worthy women of history, reworking here that familiar topos of the *querelle* defenses of women, the review of female worthies from classical antiquity and the Bible. She is more noble and more beloved by her spouse than Cleopatra was, since she does not flee from him in his troubles, and she dies not one death for love but a thousand, every day (sig. F 3v). The Countess also surpasses the famous female warriors—the Scythian women who put Darius to flight; Deborah, who judged Israel; valiant Judith, who defeated Holofernes—in that she wages "farre greater warre . . . / Against that many headed monster Sinne" (sig. F 4). Esther, who fasted and prayed three days to free her people from Haman, gives way to Margaret Clifford, who for "dayes, weekes, months, and yeares" (sig. F 4v) has worn the sackcloth of worldly troubles. She overmatches the chaste Susanna's single trial of chastity since she subdues all base affections in her own breast. And the journey of the noble Queen of Sheba to find the greatest earthly king, Solomon, is but a figure of the Countess's love and service to an almighty and everlasting King.

This section concludes with a sensuous baroque passage expatiating upon the sweetness of Christ's grace and love:

> Sweet holy rivers, pure celestiall springs,
> Proceeding from the fountaine of our life;
> Swift sugred currents that salvation brings,
> Cleare christall streames, purging all sinne and
>   strife.
> Faire floods, where souls do bathe their snow-
>   white wings,
> Before they flie to true eternall life:
> Sweet Nectar and Ambrosia, food of Saints,
> Which, whoso tasteth, never after faints.
>   (sig. G 4)

This sweetness "sweet'ned all the sowre of death" (sig. G 4) to the first martyrs—Saint Stephen, Saint Lawrence, the apostles Andrew and Peter, and John the Baptist. The praise of these male saints (stanzas 219-228) provides some small counterweight to the massive wickedness Lanyer lays to men's charge throughout the poem. She concludes the poem by declaring that the Countess of Cumberland treads in the footsteps of these martyrs and folds up "all their Beauties" in her breast (sig. Hv).

The Country-House Poem: "Cooke-ham":

"The Description of Cooke-ham," in 210 lines of pentameter couplets, presumably executes the Countess of Cumberland's charge, referred to in *Salve Deus* as not yet fulfilled, to write "praisefull lines of that delightfull place," the *"Paradice"* of Cookham (sig. A). Although the house and estate do not survive, the area is still a beauty spot. Located in Berkshire a few miles from Maidenhead, it has extensive frontages on the Thames, rich woodlands, lush meadows, picturesque scattered hamlets, and high hills in the west. The poem sustains a gentle elegiac tone throughout, since this is a valediction by author and residents to an Edenic pastoral life and place.

"Cooke-ham" may have been written before Jonson's "To Penshurst," published in 1616 but from the reference to Prince Henry (l. 77) obviously written before his death in November 1612. Jonson's poem, usually identified as the first English country-house poem, establishes the terms of a genre that celebrates patriarchy: Robert Sidney's Penshurst is a quasi-Edenic place whose beauty and harmony are centered on and preserved by its Lord, who

"dwells" permanently within it. In sharpest contrast, Lanyer's country-house poem describes a paradise inhabited solely by women: Margaret Clifford, who is the center and sustainer of its beauties and delights; her young virgin daughter, Anne; and Aemilia Lanyer. **"Cooke-ham"** portrays the destruction of this Edenic place when its lady departs—presumably to her widow's dower residences.

Lanyer's poem looks back to several classical and Renaissance poems which contributed to the development of the country-house genre. One is the *beatus ille* tradition praising a happy rural retirement from city business or courtly corruption, with its origins in Horace's Epode II, and Martial's Epigram III.58 on the Baian villa. In Lanyer's version the male speaker and the virtuous happy man are replaced by women. Another strand contains landscape or topographical descriptive poetry, such as Michael Drayton's *Polyolbion,* and, more generally, classical and Renaissance pastoral and Golden Age poetry. Closest of all are poems built upon the controlling topos of the valediction to a place, the best-known example of which was Virgil's First Eclogue. Read against that model, Lanyer's poem makes the pastoral departure a matter of social and domestic rather than state politics.

Whichever poem came first, it is instructive to compare Lanyer's poem with Jonson's, as they draw upon the same generic resources and are so nearly of a date; they offer, as it were, a male and a female conception of an idealized social order, which respond to contemporary ideology and which are epitomized in the life of a specific country house. Jonson's poem is cast in the form of an ode celebrating the estate of Sir Robert Sidney as a *locus amoenus* which perfectly harmonizes pastoral and providential abundance with georgic cultivation, associating the course of life at Penshurst with the permanence and stability of nature. It begins by contrasting the house itself with more recent and much more ostentatious "prodigy" houses (such as Knole and Longleat) built chiefly for show. Jonson then describes the estate and its life: the woods inhabited by nature gods; the fish, fowl, and beasts eagerly offering themselves for the lord's table; the tenants tendering their produce out of love rather than need; the generous and egalitarian hospitality of the hall (which the poet describes from his own experience); the "high huswifery," virtue, fruitfulness, and maternal devotion of Barbara Sidney; the presence of Robert Sidney as the moral center who gives order and stability to the entire estate and social community. . . .

Lanyer's poem, by contrast, displays the real superimposed upon the ideal, affording a very different representation of the lady's situation. In this country-house poem the house itself is barely mentioned: it belonged, after all, to the crown, not to the Countess. But the estate is described in evocative pastoral imagery as a *locus amoenus;* it enacts the pathetic fallacy continually as it responds to Margaret Clifford's presence according to the seasonal round. No lord dwells here, but three ladies prepare to leave, forever. Moreover, there is no larger society here: no extended family, no servants, no villagers, no visitors, no men at all. This poem gives mythic dimension to

Lanyer's dominant concerns throughout the volume: this lost Eden was a female paradise and as such an ageless, classless society in which three women lived together in happy intimacy.

The elegiac tone is established in the opening lines, as Lanyer bids farewell to the place she associates with her religious conversion and the confirmation of her vocation as poet:

> Farewell (sweet *Cooke-ham*) where I first
>   obtain'd
> Grace from that Grace where perfit Grace
>   remain'd;
> And where the Muses gave their full consent,
> I should have powre the virtuous to content:
>
>   . . . . .
>
> Never shall my sad eies againe behold
> Those pleasures which my thoughts did then
>   unfold.
>
>   (sig. H 2)

She represents Margaret Clifford as sharing these elegiac sentiments, and advises her to regard those "pleasures past" as "dimme shadowes of celestiall pleasures."

Then begins the description of the estate as it responds to the arrival and departure of its mistress. It becomes a *locus amoenus* as each part decks itself out in all its spring and summer loveliness for her arrival:

> The Walkes put on their summer Liveries,
> And all things else did hold like similies:
> The Trees with leaves, with fruits, with flowers
>   clad,
> Embrac'd each other, seeming to be glad,
> Turning themselves to beauteous Canopies,
> To shade the bright Sunne from your brighter
>   eies:
> The cristall Streames with silver spangles graced,
> While by the glorious Sunne they were
>   embraced:
> The little Birds in chirping notes did sing,
> To entertain both You and that sweet Spring.
>
>   (sig. H 2-H 2v)

Other aspects of nature contribute to the welcome with an obsequiousness like that of the Penshurst fish and game offering themselves to capture, but Lanyer's tone carries no hint of Jonson's amused exaggeration. The hills descend humbly that the Countess may tread on them. The gentle winds enhance her pleasure in the woods by their "sad murmure." "The swelling Bankes deliver'd all their pride" (their fish) upon seeing this "Phoenix." The birds and animals sport before her— only slightly more timorous than they would have been with Eve:

> The pretty Birds would oft come to attend thee,
> Yet flie away for feare they should offend thee:

> The little creatures in the Burrough by
> Would come abroad to sport them in your eye;
> Yet fearefull of the Bowe in your faire Hand,
> Would runne away when you did make a stand.
>
>   (sig. H 2v)

Although at Cookham most aspects of nature are ungendered, the female personifications Philomela and Echo are prominent exceptions: in the Edenic phase their voices bring praise and delight, but at the ladies' departure they sound again their familiar tones of grief and woe— associating their sad stories with this new example of women's wrongs and sorrows. As in that other Eden, the focus of interest in this place is a "stately Tree" (sig. H 2v), which is somehow an entire forest, incorporating the qualities of many trees. This tree is almost the only element of nature gendered male: it is an oak which surpasses all its fellows in height; it is straight and tall "much like a comely Cedar"; and it has outspread arms and broad leaves "like a Palme tree" (sigs. H 2v-3). The tree serves the Countess as a kind of ideal lover, more dependable than her own husband as it shelters and protects her against the too fierce onslaughts of the (also male) sun, Phoebus; and she implants on it her last farewell kiss before departing. Seated by this tree the Countess enjoys regal honors and delights. "Hills, vales, and woods, as if on bended knee" salute her, and she has a view of "thirteene shires" (not actually possible but here a substitute for Adam and Eve's view of all the world from their paradise): "A Prospect fit to please the eyes of Kings" (sig. H 3). This tree offers no temptation, sexual or otherwise, only contentment and incitement to meditate upon the creatures as they reflect their Creator's beauty, wisdom, love, and majesty. Elsewhere in the woods the Countess meditates on the Scriptures "with Christ and his Apostles there to talke; / Placing his holy Writ in some faire tree"; and she daily follows in the spiritual footsteps of the greatest Old Testament saints:

> With *Moyses* you did mount his holy Hill,
> To know his pleasure, and performe his Will.
> With lovely *David* you did often sing,
> His holy Hymnes to Heavens Eternall King.
>
>   . . . . .
>
> With blessed *Joseph* you did often feed
> Your pined brethren when they stood in need.
>
>   (sig. H 3)

As a counterpart to the oak in the realm of nature, these biblical figures supply spiritual male companionship in Cookham's Edenic world.

The next passage is a complaint that Lanyer can no longer associate with Anne Clifford, now Countess of Dorset, because "Unconstant Fortune" (sig. H 3v) has placed too great a social divide between them. While the passage gives vent to Lanyer's discontent with her station and makes a transparent bid for further attention from Anne, it is thematically appropriate. In Edenic Cookham, Lanyer (who is twenty years older than Anne Clifford) can describe herself nostalgically but improbably as a constant participant in the young Anne's "sports." But now the social constraints which accompany Anne's aristocratic rank by birth and marriage are set off against those natural associations dictated solely by virtue and pleasure, "Whereof depriv'd, I evermore must grieve" (sig. H 3v).

Then, Cookham's grief at the ladies' preparations for departure is described in a notably effective passage in which pathetic fallacy fuses with the seasonal change from autumn to winter:

> Me thought each thing did unto sorrow frame:
> The trees that were so glorious in our view,
> Forsooke both floures and fruit, when once they
>   knew
> Of your depart, their very leaves did wither,
> Changing their colours as they grewe together.
> But when they saw this had no powre to stay
>   you,
> They often wept, though speechlesse, could not
>   pray you;
> Letting their teares in your faire bosoms fall:
>
>   . . . . .
>
> Their frozen tops, like Ages hoarie haires,
> Showes their disasters, languishing in feares:
> A swarthy riveld ryne all over spread,
> Their dying bodies halfe alive, halfe dead.
>   (sig. H 4)

The Countess's gracious leave-taking of all the beloved creatures and places on the estate culminates in her charge to Lanyer to preserve them in poetry. Then the scene turns sentimental as Lanyer portrays herself stealing the farewell kiss the Countess bestows on the noble oak.

The final passage echoes the imagery of the opening passage, as all the elements of the *locus amoenus* transform themselves from beauty to desolation:

> And those sweet Brookes that ranne so faire and
>   cleare,
> With griefe and trouble wrinckled did appeare.
> Those pretty Birds that wonted were to sing,
> Now neither sing, nor chirp, nor use their wing;
> But with their tender feet on some bare spray,
> Warble forth sorrow, and their owne dismay.
> Faire *Philomela* leaves her mournfull Ditty,
> Drownd in dead sleepe, yet can procure no
>   pittie:
> Each arbour, banke, each seate, each stately tree,
> Lookes bare and desolate now for want of thee;
> Turning greene tresses into frostie gray,
> While in cold griefe they wither all away.
> The Sunne grew weake, his beames no comfort
>   gave,
> While all greene things did make the earth their
>   grave:
> Each brier, each bramble, when you went away,
> Caught fast your cloths, thinking to make you
>   stay:

> Delightful Eccho wonted to reply
> To our last words, did now for sorrow die;
> The house cast off each garment that might
>   grace it,
> Putting on Dust and Cobwebs to deface it.
> All desolation then there did appeare,
> When you were going whom they held so deare.
>   (sigs. H 4-I I)

In sharpest contrast to Jonson's "Penshurst," whose lord "dwells" permanently within it and thereby preserves its quasi-Edenic beauty and harmony, Layner's **"Cooke-ham"** portrays the destruction of an idyllic place when its lady departs. Cookham takes on the appearance of a ravaged Eden after the first human couple is expelled. But here it is a female pair—or rather trio—who depart: the Countess called away by the "occasions" attendant upon her widowhood; the virgin daughter to her conflict-ridden marriage; Lanyer to social decline. Offering her poem as "this last farewell to *Cooke-ham*" (sig. I I), Lanyer suggests that none of them will return to this happy garden state in which women lived without mates but found contentment and delight in nature, God, and female companionship.

Randall Martin on Lanyer's depiction of Christ in *Salve Deus Rex Judaeorum*:

In Lanyer's reading the passion seems less representative of Christ's atonement for universal human sinfulness than a revelatory indictment of ubiquitous male cruelty and patriarchal oppression, which in some sense remain unredeemed because they continue to tyrannise women. Jesus on the other hand displays the love, nurturing functions, and healing actions traditionally associated with women, and he shares their experiences of marginalisation and injustice. . . . Christ therefore affirms women's authentic subjectivity, so that in meditating upon his ordeal Lanyer's women readers are in effect gazing at themselves. This reciprocal relationship is signalled by Lanyer's recurring image of herself as a servant holding up a mirror before her readers wherein they may see both Jesus and their true natures, undistorted by traditional constructions of male scholars who depreciate the role played by biblical women as active agents of God's will, portraying them as passive bystanders or handmaidens. Lanyer thus offers women a new way of dignifying themselves using Christ as their model of personhood, newly reclaimed as both 'female' and divine.

> *Renaissance Women Writers in England, edited by
> Randall Martin, Longman's, 1995.*

As yet we can only speculate about the factors—education, female patronage, ambiguous social status, somewhat unusual sexual freedom, life experience—that led Lanyer to write and especially to publish poetry. Nor can we explain the remarkable feminist conceptual frame that unifies her **Salve Deus,** with its egalitarian challenge to sexual and class hierarchy and its insistent contrast of good women and evil men, past and present. Whatever Lanyer's actual experience in the households of Margaret Clifford and Susan, Countess of Kent, her book projects an imaginative vision of an enduring female community. The patronage poems present a female lineage of virtue from mother to daughter, a community of good women extending from Catherine Bertie, Protestant fugitive in Mary Tudor's reign, to the young Anne Clifford. They also rewrite patronage in female terms, imagining for the poet Lanyer a family of maternal and sisterly patronesses who will honor and reward her celebrations of them and of the female sex. The Passion poem extends this community back to biblical times and even to Eve, portraying women as Christ's truest apostles and followers. In **"Cooke-ham"** a female Eden suffers a new Fall when the structures of a male social order force its women inhabitants to abandon it. Lanyer's poems boldly reimagine and rewrite the fundamental Christian myths—Eden, the Passion, the Community of Saints—with women at their center.

Janel Mueller (essay date 1994)

SOURCE: "The Feminist Poetics of Aemilia Lanyer's *Salve Deus Rex Judaeorum*," in *Feminist Measures: Soundings in Poetry and Theory*, edited by Lynn Keller and Cristanne Miller, University of Michigan Press, 1994, pp. 208-36.

[*Here, Mueller analyzes Lanyer's feminist theology, stating that "in her handling, universalism and essentialism empower a feminism that proves rich, outrageous, and originary by any present-day standard."*]

The year 1611 saw the publication, in London, of the first volume of poetry in English written by a woman: *Salve Deus Rex Judaeorum*. Its title page identified the poet as "Mistris Aemilia Lanyer, Wife to Captaine Alfonso Lanyer, Servant to the Kings Majestie." In the expatiating fashion of the time, the title page also highlighted the following portions of the volume's title poem: **"1 The Passion of Christ. 2 Eves Apologie in defence of Women. 3 The Teares of the Daughters of Jerusalem. 4 The Salutation and Sorrow of the Virgine Marie,"** while lumping together its shorter poems as "divers other things not unfit to be read." Who was Aemilia Lanyer, and what was she doing in her **"Salve Deus Rex Judaeorum,"** thus characterized? Questions like these are no merely naive voicings of curiosity. They have proven useful as starting points for interpretation all along the discontinuous time line that charts the history of women's authorship in the West. In historical criticism sensitive to the category of gender, it is now regularly accepted that the exercise of authorship—by women no less than by men—requires some empowering sense of authorization, of authority, to write and publish. As applied to Lanyer and her volume, such questions engage the interplay of her social identity with the poetic identity of her work, on the assumption that the two are mutually self-constituting in ways that can be traced—to at least some degree—from recoverable features of text and context.

Who was Aemilia Lanyer? She was born in London in 1569 as Aemilia Bassano, the second of two daughters of a common-law marriage between an otherwise unknown Margaret Johnson and Baptist Bassano, one of Queen Elizabeth's musicians. The Bassanos were a Venetian Jewish family of musicians who had Christianized and relocated at the court of England, as members of the King's Musick, on the invitation of Henry VIII. Although Aemilia was only seven when her father died, income from some London properties provided her mother, her sister, and herself with a livable maintenance. As indicated in her later verse epistles, the growing girl Aemilia also retained her court connections—which she redraws poetically as an illustrious society comprised solely of females. The first dedicatory epistle to the *Salve Deus* volume wistfully reflects on that vanished time when "great *Elizaes* favour blest my youth." Another salutes Susan Bertie, countess of Kent, as "the Mistris of my youth, / The noble guide of my ungovern'd dayes," thus signaling her adolescent formation under the then widespread practice of being sent from one's family to be trained up in service in an aristocratic household. Lanyer significantly credits the countess's own capacity for moral governance to her mother's influence: "By your most famous Mother so directed, / That noble Dutchesse, who liv'd unsubjected." Susan's mother was Catherine Bertie, duchess of Suffolk, an outspoken Protestant who went into voluntary exile under Mary Tudor, taking her children with her. The duchess had married her former steward, Richard Bertie, in an earlier notable act of self-assertion (and one often proposed as a source-idea for the tragic heroine of John Webster's *Duchess of Malfi*, staged ca. 1614, published in 1624).

In 1587, when Aemilia was eighteen, her mother died. Close to this time the orphaned girl became the mistress of a high-ranking court official, the lord chamberlain, who was also Queen Elizabeth's first cousin. Henry Carey, Lord Hunsdon, was forty-five years older than Aemilia. When she showed signs of pregnancy in 1592, Hunsdon arranged for her to marry Alphonso Lanyer or Lanier, a court musician like her father, and a descendant of an expatriate French Huguenot family from Rouen. There are baptismal records for two children in early 1593—a son, Henry, presumably named after Hunsdon, and in late 1598 a daughter, Odillya, who died in infancy. Notes kept by the astrologer Simon Forman, whom Aemilia consulted on several occasions, additionally record the Lanyers' anxieties over their declining fortunes between 1597 and 1599. Alphonso received some income from a patent granted him by King James in 1604, and Aemilia, again on the testimony of her poetry, spent some time before 1609 at Cookeham, a royal estate, in cherished intimacy with Margaret Clifford, countess of Cumberland, and her daughter, Anne, soon to become countess of Dorset by marriage.

Nothing else is known of the intervening year before Aemilia published *Salve Deus Rex Judaeorum* in 1611. Particularly unfortunate is the lack of any clue in the scanty biographical record for dating the intensity of religious feeling to which the long title poem of this collection bears witness. However, inferential connections have been drawn between its other contents and the Lanyers' financial situation. Judging from various arrangements of its dedicatory verse epistles to highborn ladies and from presentational inscriptions in nine extant copies, wife and husband both used *Salve Deus* as an instrument to solicit patronage. Alphonso, however, would die shortly, in 1613. Aemilia's widowed years remain shrouded in anonymity and authorial silence, although records of intermittent lawsuits bespeak her self-reliance in, briefly, founding a school "to teach and educate the children of divers persons of worth and understanding" and otherwise maneuvering to secure her financial rights. Her struggles eased somewhat when her son Henry reached his majority, married, and started a family. When she died at seventy-six in 1645, Lanyer left an inheritance to two teenage grandchildren, Mary and Henry, whom she apparently helped to raise.

So much, then, for a basic answer to the question, Who was Aemilia Lanyer? But a no less basic answer is called for when this question is denied the privilege of historicist interest on which I build in the bulk of my discussion here. The present-day context for asking Who was Aemilia Lanyer? is the happy phenomenon of numbers of women writing poetry that is rich, outrageous, and originary because it is increasingly unfettered and self-assured. Given a contemporary twist by a late twentieth-century and presumably postmodernist reader, the question might run as follows: Who was Aemilia Lanyer, that we should care about her poetry after almost four hundred years? As Lanyer's advocate I would concede at once the datedness of key aspects of her outlook. She believes that the feminine and the masculine are essential, innate features of two sexes. She also makes universalist assumptions about God's purposes, both in creating persons whose common humanity is marked by sexual difference and in holding them accountable by a single moral standard for their actions in what simply is the course of history. Our current tactics as feminists no less than our theories disparage notions that human nature has significantly differentiated traits outside of culture and thus emphasize gender rather than sex as the reciprocal social production and acquisition of a given sexed subject. Relativistic and deterministic implications afford us little basis for moral judgments, which we reach nonetheless on other terms: our ideological commitments, our best attempts at reasoning, our emotional responses. Emphasizing cultural embeddedness, we formulate our political, critical, and poetic projects accordingly. But, I would urge, Lanyer does exactly the same, even though her notion of culture is Christian world history and her understanding of embeddedness finds two sexes locked in a domination-subordination relationship that shows everywhere as a given of social organization. Lanyer proves every bit our contemporary, moreover, in her resolve to find and articulate transformative possibilities in gender relations that will carry their own secure imperative for actualization. For this purpose, which is to say oddly from a contemporary point of view, she looks to the figure of Christ in history—to divinity humanized or humanity divinized—as she reads the record of Scrip-

ture with wholly unconventional eyes. The mystery that explodes into a demonstrated truth in her poem **"Salve Deus Rex Judaeorum"** is Lanyer's understanding of Christ's incarnation: she views it in light of the Crucifixion as a public, historical action taken by men alone; this vindicates, once and for all, female nature and feminine values, and it authorizes gender equality ever after. In her handling, universalism and essentialism empower a feminism that proves rich, outrageous, and originary by any present-day standard. Beyond the inherent interest that I hope to verify for Lanyer's poem, an object lesson emerges for contemporary readers: our best wisdom, our most sophisticated and influential theories, are no sine qua non for a feminist poetics. Hers is a striking case in point. . . .

Lanyer locates her . . . project of defending her female sex squarely in the domain of religious poetry and, beyond that, in a specifically scriptural subject—here, the last events of Christ's life. There are several recoverable reasons for such a choice in a London vernacular publication of 1611. First, in the interval between flare-ups in 1588-97 and 1615-37, the English controversy about women saw a relatively quiescent phase with regard, at least, to the circulation of antifeminist themes in satirical tracts or polemical diatribes. Lanyer had no immediately pressing motive to engage in prose controversy from a feminist position. **"To the Vertuous Reader"** shows her much more concerned with the bad effects of *both* sexes' speaking ill of women, which undermines not merely women's reputations for virtue but their very capacity and incentive to be virtuous.

While lauding the exemplary virtues of Margaret Clifford, countess of Cumberland, in a framing section near the opening of **"Salve Deus,"** Lanyer addresses what she represents as a pressing contemporary problem—how female moral agency is represented in recent English secular poetry and drama. She decries portrayals of Lucrece, Cleopatra, Rosamund, and Matilda, alluding perhaps to Shakespeare's *Rape of Lucrece* (1594) and to *Antony and Cleopatra* (1606-7), or to Samuel Daniel's *Cleopatra* (1593) and *Complaint of Rosamond* (1592), as well as to Michael Drayton's *Matilda* (1594). The framing section that concludes **"Salve Deus"** with another celebration of the countess of Cumberland's active virtue returns to the figure of Cleopatra, detailing the fickleness, adultery, cowardice, and treachery of this "blacke Egyptian" as an egregious instance of a woman's loss of moral direction. Lanyer's preoccupation with Cleopatra testifies to a conspicuous development in London stage plays that drama historians regularly note. This is the quite sudden emergence, from a virtual void, of women with the full stature of evil-doing tragic protagonists like Alice Arden in *Arden of Faversham* (1591), Anne Frankford in Thomas Heywood's *A Woman Killed with Kindness* (1603), and Shakespeare's Lady Macbeth (1606). As Lanyer acutely saw, the moment was ripe for intervening in the discursive construction of women by male authors as (im)moral subjects: it was time to counterclaim for them as gender-specific exemplars of virtue.

At just this time, moreover, calls were sounding for a redirection of poetic energies from secular love to sacred subjects. Probably the best known of these are George Herbert's two sonnets, "My God, where is that ancient heat towards thee" and "Sure Lord, there is enough in thee," sent to his mother as a New Year's gift in 1610. Scriptural subjects, specifically, received fresh validation in the year that Lanyer published *Salve Deus*. The team of scholars who had been working since 1606 under royal mandate to verify the accuracy of the text of the entire English Bible against its sources in the original languages published their Authorized (or King James) Version in 1611, with an epistle dedicatory offering it "to your MAIESTIE, not only as to our King and Soveraigne, but as to the principall moover and Author of the Worke: . . . it being brought unto such a conclusion, as that we have great hope that the Church of England shall reape good fruit thereby." Court culture, humanist scholarship, and vernacular biblicism all intersect in this milestone event. To lodge a timely challenge to invidious constructions of her sex, onstage and off, by male poets and by her society more broadly, Lanyer considered it necessary not just to contradict standing portrayals or to celebrate living women but to develop a new poetic ontology for figuring femininity as worthy, true, and good. This ontology would ground itself in a portrayal of a maligned, about-to-be-murdered Jesus of Nazareth that quite closely follows scriptural sources. It would proceed, however, on Lanyer's own authority to figure women and women alone as capable of rightly recognizing and receiving the incarnate divine Word. . . .

A marginal *incipit* opposite stanza 42 of "Salve Deus" signals the onset of the poem's central narration: "Here begins the Passion of Christ." Lanyer employs the in medias res opening that had become standard in Renaissance poetic narratives on lofty subjects, secular or sacred. With this she conjoins a skillful use of temporal and spatial setting for emotive heightening, a convention shared with such Ovidian poetic narratives as Shakespeare's *Lucrece,* Daniel's *Rosamond,* and Drayton's *Matilda.* It is deep night in the garden of Gethsemane on the Mount of Olives. Jesus is alone with his fears and forebodings. Behind him is his Last Supper; ahead lies his betrayal by Judas and his forcible seizure by the soldiers of the high priest Caiaphas. The garden's atmospheric darkness is liminal—a space no longer of private life, like the upper room where he has just shared a meal with his twelve disciples, but not quite yet a public space of arrest, interrogation, and judicial sentencing. In this liminal setting, Lanyer's narration follows the gospel story closely while furthering her systematic portrayal of a Christ who is not understood through any species of private or public relationships with other men. Peter, James, and John, his favorite disciples, whom he entreats to keep him company while he prays, fall into a sleep that Lanyer feelingly equates with spiritual blindness. They

> could not watch one houre for love of thee,
> Even those three Friends, which on thy Grace
> depends,

Yet shut those Eies that should their Maker see;
What colour, what excuse, or what amends?

Immediately thereafter, Judas leads Christ's enemies to him and betrays him in a far graver perversion of intimacy:

> A trothlesse traytor, and a mortall foe,
> With fained kindnesse seekes thee to imbrace;
> And gives a kisse, whereby he may deceive thee,
> That in the hands of Sinners he might leave
>   thee.

But, as brought out through Lanyer's continuous emotional coloration of her narrative, the public action of arresting Christ also proceeds in total incomprehension and misprision of its subject:

> Now muster forth with Swords, with Staves,
>   with Bils,
> High Priests and Scribes, and Elders of the
>   Land,
> Seeking by force to have their wicked Wils,
>
>   . . . . .
>
> And who they seeke, thou gently doest demand;
> This didst thou Lord, t'amaze these Fooles the
>   more,
> T'inquire of that, thou knew'st so well before.
>
>   . . . . .
>
> His name they sought, and found, yet could not
>   know
> *Jesus* of Nazareth.

Incomprehension darkens into willful misconstrual and perjury as Christ is brought before Caiaphas to be formally examined. Lanyer's narration tracks the gradation from abuses of language to abuses of justice that repeatedly leaves her Christ with the option, only, of keeping silent. "They tell his Words, though farre from his intent, / And what his Speeches were, not what he meant." In responding to repeated encounters with men who both coerce and misjudge him—a pattern intensified in his dealings with Caiaphas, Pilate, and Herod as the legal process runs its course—Lanyer's Christ exhibits perfect quiescence in both demeanor and language. . . . On those rare occasions when Lanyer's Christ has anything at all to say, the speech that befits his behavior is correspondingly sparing, yet always transparent—and true in the strongest sense of truth, self-identity. Every sentence that Lanyer's scripturally styled Christ utters under interrogation packs a characteristic semantic and spiritual force, registering profound self-disclosure in tautology or near-tautology: "I am he," "Thou hast said it." . . .

Where, moreover, Lanyer's Christ proves incomprehensible to the men about him, to her as commentator he remains so continuously readable that she is able to specify the virtues that ground his speech and behavior at each point: "Here faire Obedience shined in his breast, / And did suppresse all feare of future paine"; "His paths are Peace, with none he holdes Debate, / His Patience stands upon so sure a ground." One rhetorical and poetic high point takes the form of a bold stanzaic enjambment in which Lanyer asserts herself authorially by interrupting the lying enemies of Christ in Caiaphas's hall. These men call Christ a blasphemer, but she can name him truly. And so she does, inserting her catalog of ascriptions into a sentence that had begun as a description of the men's perjury:

> High Priests and Elders, People great and small,
> With all reprochfull words about him throng:
> False Witnesses are now call'd in apace,
> Whose trotheless tongues must make pale death
>   imbrace
>
> The beauty of the World, Heavens chiefest
>   Glory;
> The mirrour of Martyrs, Crowne of holy Saints;
> Love of th'Almighty, blessed Angels story;
> Water of Life, which none that drinks it, faints;
> Guide of the Just, where all our Light we
>   borrow;
> Mercy of Mercies; Hearer of Complaints;
> Triumpher over Death; Ransomer of Sinne;
> Falsely accused: now his paines begin.

As the foregoing quotation clearly indicates, there is nothing explicitly feminist about this poetically striking juncture in Lanyer's narration of the passion of Christ. Yet here and elsewhere for considerable stretches Lanyer skillfully predisposes her story, description, and commentary to feminist implications. These implications become remarkably and fully explicit when Pilate's wife breaks in upon her husband to remonstrate with him in **"Eves Apologie,"** the second of the subdivisions highlighted on the poem's title page. I want to work toward a concluding discussion of **"Eves Apologie"** by tracing the diverse, local feminist predispositions that lead into and away from its unique outspokenness in other parts of Lanyer's **"Salve Deus."**

Perhaps the most obvious of these predispositions—certainly the first to become conspicuous in the poem—is the pattern of fundamental misprision exhibited by all of the males in the story, friends and foes alike, while the female poet unfailingly understands what and who Jesus is. Although the conventional epic guise of an omniscient narrator serves as her vehicle for expressing this understanding, deeper ideological implications remain untouched by this identification of poetic means. As now amply documented in a range of studies focused on the social construction of femininity in sixteenth- and earlier seventeenth-century England, it appears scarcely less obvious that Lanyer understands her Christ because he is thoroughly feminized in demeanor and language according to the period norms set out in conduct books and doctrinal tracts, especially those of the late Elizabethan and Jacobean Puritan divines—John Dod and Robert Cleaver, William Perkins, William Whateley—who were actively

publishing as Lanyer wrote. Her Christ, like the ideal woman of the Puritan manuals, is silent except when induced to speak, and modest and taciturn when he does; he is gentle, mild, peaceable, and submissive to higher male authorities.

Not only does Lanyer herself appear to understand the traits of her Christ's character from familiarity with them as the virtues that women were to acquire and manifest as defining their femininity. She also conducts two psychological studies—of the women of Jerusalem, of Christ's mother Mary—in which she writes the same process of understanding into her narration of the ostensibly historical events of **"Salve Deus."** These women empathize with Christ through their shared affinities in demeanor, language, and feeling. Because his social identity resonates with their own, they, like Lanyer, can comprehend him inwardly. And again, on the evidence of the numbered subsections of her title page, Lanyer highlighted these instances of reciprocal recognition as **"The Teares of the Daughters of Jerusalem"** and **"The Salutation and Sorrow of the Virgine Marie."** They are highlighted accordingly in the body of the poem, where schematic gender opposition first links the women with Christ in action and utterance and then sets them as a group over against the other males. In a transitional stanza between these two highlighted sections, Lanyer's pointed phrases exemplify what I am terming the feminist predisposition of her commentary:

> When spightfull men with torments did oppresse
> Th'afflicated body of this innocent Dove,
> Poore women seeing how much they did
>   transgresse,
> By teares, by sighes, by cries interest, nay prove,
> What may be done among the thickest presse,
> They labour still these tyrants hearts to move;
> In pitie and compassion to forbeare
> Their whipping, spurning, tearing of his haire.

Thus as Christ sets out toward Calvary, bearing his cross on his scourged and bleeding shoulders, the executioners and their hangers-on "thinke he answer'd for some great transgression, / Beeing in such odious sort condemn'd to die," while the women bystanders see that "his own profession / Was virtue, patience, grace, love, piety." They weep aloud for Christ as he passes; he in turn pauses and speaks to them consolingly. Lanyer's reiterated identical nouns—grace, love—affirm the spiritual and ethical oneness of the suffering women with the suffering Christ:

> Thrice happy women that obtain such grace
> From him whose worth the world could not
>   containe;
> Immediately to turne about his face,
> As not remembering his great griefe and paine,
> To comfort you, whose teares powr'd forth apace
>   . . . . .
> Your cries inforced mercie, grace, and love
> From him, whom greatest Princes could not
>   moove.

Although the women of Jerusalem are powerless to alter the outcome of the procession to Calvary, Lanyer nevertheless grants them a clear moral victory by poetic means, as the sound and significance of the men's cries are supplanted by those of the women's cries by stanza's end:

> First went the Crier with open mouth
>   proclayming
> The heavy sentence of Iniquitie,
> The Hangman next, by his base office clayming
> His right in Hell, where sinners never die;
> Carrying the nayles, the people still blaspheming
> Their maker, using all impiety;
> The Thieves attending him on either side,
> The Serjeants watching, while the women cri'd.

Lanyer's section on the salutation and sorrow of the Virgin Mary works a comparable but far more complex and subtle transmutations of tones and themes. The narrative point of departure is a scriptural given, a grief near despair.

> How canst thou choose (faire Virgin) then but
>   mourne,
> When this sweet of-spring of thy body dies,
> When thy faire eies beholds his bodie torne,
>   . . . . .
> Bleeding and fainting in such wondrous sort,
> As scarce his feeble limbes can him support.

Lanyer's local poetic objective is to convert this extremity of evil to an assurance of blessedness that the suffering mother will register as immediately and experientially as she does her present grief. To begin this process Lanyer reminds Mary of the greeting pronounced by the angel of the Annunciation and elaborates its significance:

> He thus beganne, Haile *Mary* full of grace,
> Thou freely art beloved of the Lord,
> He is with thee, behold thy happy case;
> That thou a blessed Virgin shouldst remaine,
> Yea that the Holy Ghost should come on thee
> A maiden Mother, subject to no paine,
> For highest powre should overshadow thee:
> Could thy faire eyes from teares of joy refraine,
> When God look'd downe upon thy poore
>   degree?
> Marking thee Servant, Mother, Wife, and Nurse
> To Heavens bright King, that freed us from the
>   curse.

Key to this passage and to Lanyer's broader authority as a religious poet in **"Salve Deus"** is the salutation as a locution. A rarely employed poetic resource in her contemporary English but a salient feature of spoken dialogue in half a dozen important gospel episodes, the salutation begins with a special, reverential word of greeting, then adds the addressee's name and significant attributes. Its structure here is "Haile *Mary* full of grace, . . . Servant, Mother, Wife, and Nurse / To Heavens bright King, that freed us from the curse." In Lanyer's poetic, not only does knowing aright bespeak naming aright, but

naming and knowing cast in the form of a salutation bespeak a direct, intimate encounter with another person that authorizes the salutation itself. The salutation thus comes to figure as the linguistic hallmark of Lanyer's poetics of femininity—a speech act uniquely expressive of the capacity to apprehend truth that distinguishes women and the feminized Christ. Lanyer's treatment of Mary in this final highlighted subsection of the poem insists on her uniqueness in assuming just those womanly roles of "Servant, Mother, Wife, and Nurse" that enabled Christ to incarnate his corresponding ones as "Her Sonne, her Husband, Father, Saviour, King, / Whose death killd Death, and tooke away his sting." If Mary can sustain her sense of the blessedness of her agency in relation to Christ as specified in the roles foretold by this angel of the Annunciation, even her present sorrow can be turned into acceptance of Christ's death as a necessary means to the "good" of human redemption. Two remarkable stanzas narrate Mary's achievement of this delicate spiritual and emotional modulation as she reflects on Christ's gender roles while performing her own:

> His woefull Mother wayting on her Sonne,
> All comfortlesse in depth of sorow drowned;
> Her griefes extreame, although but new begun,
> To see his bleeding body oft she swouned;
> How could she choose but thinke her selfe
>   undone,
> He dying, with whose glory shee was crowned?
> None ever lost so great a losse as shee,
> Beeing Sonne, and Father of Eternitie.
>
> Her tears did wash away his pretious blood,
> That sinners might not tread it under feet
> To worship him, and that [,] it did her good
> Upon her knees, although in open street,
> Knowing he was the Jesse floure and bud,
> That must be gath'red when it smell'd most
>   sweet:
> Her Sonne, her Husband, Father, Saviour, King,
> Whose death killd Death, and tooke away his
>   sting.

Lanyer's prose postscript to her volume partially elucidates the vital connotations she attached to the biblical salutation as she lays out her first and only explanation of her title:

> Gentle Reader, if thou desire to be resolved, why I give this Title, ***Salve Deus Rex Judaeorum,*** know for certaine: that it was delivered unto me in sleepe many yeares before I had any intent to write in this maner, and was quite out of my memory, untill I had written the Passion of Christ, when immediately it came into my remembrance, . . . and thinking it a significant token, that I was appointed to perform this Worke, I gave the very same words I received in sleepe as the fittest Title I could devise for this Booke.

Further elucidation comes at the recurrent junctures where Lanyer as omniscient narrator and commentator reproves Christ's enemies for hailing him by name yet knowing him not at all. Thus she writes of the high priests and scribes who arrest him:

His name they sought, and found, yet could not
  know
Jesus of Nazareth . . .
When Heavenly Wisdome did descend so lowe
To speake to them: . . .
Nay, though he said unto them, I am he,
They could not know him, whom their eyes did
  see.

And thus she writes, more scathingly, of Christ's inter-rogation by Caiaphas, who charges him once "in his glorious name" to tell "Whose pleasure 'twas he should endure this shame" and again "by his powrefull name, / To tell if Christ the Sonne of God he be, / Who for our sinnes must die, to set us free." Lanyer's Christ returns to Caiaphs the truth of Caiaphas's own linguistic formu-lation:

Then with so mild a Majestie he spake,
As they might easly know from whence he
  came,

. . . . .

To thee O *Caiphas* doth he answere give,
That thou hast said, what thou desir'st to know.

But these words of truth are rejected as blasphemy, and the Word of Truth as a blasphemer. Caiaphas pronounces a sentence of death for blasphemy against this same "Christ the Sonne of God . . . Who for our sinnes must die, to set us free" and sends him to Pilate for its ratification. The soldiers who crucify Christ mock him with a crown of thorns, a reed for a scepter, and the salutation, "Haile king of the Jewes"—in the Latin of the Vulgate, *"Salve Rex Judaeorum."* Above his head his cross eventually bears a caption—"This is Jesus the king of the Jewes" (Matthew 27:37) or simply "The king of the Jewes" (Mark 15:26, John 19:19)—which the high priests futilely try to have altered to read: "He said, I am King of the Jewes" (John 19:21). These multiplied misprisions that yet vindi-cate salutation as an acknowledgment of incarnate divin-ity inscribe the core of Lanyer's poetic and supply the narrative crux of her poem. *Salve Deus Rex Judaeorum.* Hail, God, the king of the Jews. Lanyer's title both op-poses and embraces the truth of the gospel narrative that had been uttered uncomprehendingly, as a verbal gesture of mockery, by the soldiers who crucified Christ. By her addition of just one word in apposition, *Deus,* she makes fully explicit her expression of personal faith in the divin-ity of one whom the Jews (the people of her own descent on her father's family's side) did not recognize as their king. She does so recognize him, and she salutes him as such.

However, the intricacies that register in **"The Saluta-tion and Sorrows of the Virgine Marie"** and in the mystique—if I may so call it—of salutation in Lany-er's religious poetics may seem far removed from the feminist predispositions and feminist poetics that I claim for her text. Briefly, it may look in this historical nar-rative of political and social world as if Christ and the

women are the losers, and that the grieving Mary, no less than the women of Jerusalem, must content them-selves with either an inward or an otherwordly assur-ance that this feminized Christ will be victorious over masculinist evil and violence. Despite a sensitive and often perceptive discussion of **"Salve Deus,"** Elaine Beilin comes to adopt this line [in her *Redeeming Eve: Women Writers of the English Renaissance,* 1987]. As she puts it, "I would not agree . . . that Lanyer was a feminist, because her advocacy for women begins with spiritual power and ends with poetry; and in fact, she assumes that men control society, art, and the worldly destiny of women, including herself." But I in turn cannot agree with Beilin. I read Lanyer's portrayal of the spiritual power of femininity—of Christ and the women—in **"Salve Deus"** as having extreme revision-ary implications for men's control of society, art, and the worldly destiny of women. My reading, apart from the overt declarations of **"Eves Apologie"** that still await discussion, goes like this.

Lanyer vindicates femininity to male critics and the misogynists of both sexes, whom she deplores in her preface, **"To the Vertuous Reader,"** not merely by portraying the closeness of Christ and actual good women. She historicizes her retracing of the gospel account of the passion. This poetic narrative devolves in a space that is social and political, through and through. Its implications and those of the authorial commentary are social and political as well. More spe-cifically, Lanyer uses her portrayals of Christ and ac-tual good women to trace the impact of feminine or feminized virtue on the masculine side of a range of standing dichotomies that mark conceptions of social and political relations: public/private, mind/body, cul-ture/nature, reason/passion. As narrated, the superiori-ty of feminine virtue is constantly confirmed as it makes its impact in the masculine domain. Christ leaves the privateness of the upper room and the garden to en-gage the public proceedings of the soldiers, Caiaphas, Pilate, Herod, which the women likewise engage on his behalf. The connection between Christ and the women proves the more effective in that these figures together demonstrate, through what they are made to suffer, the problematic reciprocal relation between political sub-mission and sexual subordination, and they do so more tellingly than almost any other rare sixteenth- and sev-enteenth-century text that in any way critiques this relation as a problem. The net impact of Christ and the women in the narrative is to leave Jerusalem's public life and its intersecting political and priestly jurisdic-tions exposed as a sham of justice, as corruption, ma-lignity, and violence.

Similarly, as my account of highlighted sections in **"Salve Deus"** has already suggested, Lanyer represents the bod-ies of Christ and the women as more legible expressions of understanding and morality—the qualities that suppos-edly make for the mind's superiority—than are the minds of the male figures of authority. "Here insolent Boldnesse checkt by Love and Grace, / Retires, and falls before our Makers face." . . . In one of several characteristically gendered contrasts, Lanyer authorially reprehends Pilate as he confirms Caiaphas's sentence on Christ. "Art thou a Judge?" she begins.

> The death of Christ wilt thou consent unto,
> Finding no cause, no reason, nor no ground?
> Shall he be scourg'd, and crucified too?
> And must his miseries by thy meanes abound?

Lanyer's Pilate also becomes a prominent locus in the poem for the working out of culture/nature and reason/passion dichotomies that redound to the discredit of male domination. In a stanza that includes both pairs of binaries in its imagery, she demands of him:

> Canst thou be innocent, that gainst all right,
> Wilt yeeld to what thy conscience doth
>   withstand?
> Beeing a man of knowledge, powre, and might,
> To let the wicked carrie such a hand,
> Before thy face to blindfold Heav'ns bright light,
> And thou to yeeld to what they did demand?
> Washing thy hands, thy conscience cannot cleare,
> But to all worlds this staine must needs appeare.

Although unanswered, these questions put to Pilate are far from merely rhetorical or, in Beilin's terms, a manifestation—in poetry only—of a woman's spiritual power. The sun attests to the innocence of the Son, as a later passage on "The terror of all creatures at that instant when Christ died" will confirm in its evocation of earthquake and other cataclysms—"The Sunne grew darke, and scorn'd to give them light, / Who durst ecclipse a glory farre more bright." Pilate's handwashing is a sorry irrelevance to the stain of bloodguilt incurred through his complicity in putting to death not merely an innocent victim but divinity incarnate. In the aftermath of Christ's Crucifixion read as history, culture must look to a morally cognizant (and to that extent a feminized) nature for moral refounding.

Which is to say that men must look to women for the refounding of existing political and social relations. Exactly thus runs the argument advanced by Pilate's wife in **"Eves Apologie"** (meaning defence—the sense is clearly that of apologia). Lanyer draws the warrant for a spirited portrayal of this figure from the passing notice accorded her in single biblical verse, Matthew 27:19: "When he [Pilate] was set downe on the Judgement seate, his wife sent unto him, saying, Have thou nothing to doe with that just man [Jesus]: for I have suffered many things this day in a dreame, because of him." In keeping with Lanyer's generic representation of femininity as spiritually superior, Pilate's wife's first utterance discloses her true understanding and faith: "Heare the words of thy most worthy wife, / Who sends to thee, to beg her Saviours life./ . . . / Open thine eies, that thou the truth mai'st see, / . . . / Condemne not him that must thy Saviour be." But she just as directly adds the most ominous pragmatic warning she can give Pilate, one based on the status quo of gender politics:

"Let not us Women glory in Mens fall,/ Who had power given to over-rule us all." Lanyer's figure begins from a bond to scriptural authority as absolute as Lanyer's own to the Gospels: she acknowledges that men got power over women from the Fall of Adam and Eve. But she goes on to argue that the Gospel as history shatters that power. If men commit the far worse sin of killing Christ, their doing so sets women free from men's rule.

Here Pilate's wife exposes her own author's historicity. With a return to origins that demonstrates typical period procedure for tracing the cause or rationale of current practices, she reflects analytically—which for her and Lanyer means comparatively—on the Fall as narrated in Genesis. She details several considerations and lines of reasoning that work in Eve's favor. First, the serpent lied to Eve only; hence she was deceived into sinning, but Adam was not.

> she (poore soule) by cunning was deceav'd,
> No hurt therein her harmlesse Heart intended:
> For she alleadg'd Gods word . . . that they
>   should die. . . .
>
> But surely *Adam* can not be excusde,
>
>   . . . . .
>
> Being Lord of all, the greater was his shame:
> Although the Serpents craft had her abusde,
> Gods holy word ought all his actions frame.

The allusion to "Gods holy word" refers to the prohibition against eating the fruit of the tree of knowledge of good and evil that God gave to Adam before Eve was created (Genesis 3:16-18). There is no explicit indication in scripture that the prohibition was ever transmitted to Eve. This is Pilate's wife's second consideration on Eve's behalf.

> The perfect'st man that ever breath'd on earth
>   . . . From Gods mouth receiv'd that strait
>   command,
> The breach whereof he knew was present death:
> Not *Eve*. . . .
> He never sought her weakenesse to reprove,
> With those sharpe words, which he of God did
>   heare.

In the third place, Pilate's wife finds Eve's psychology in sinning far more admirable than Adam's.

> We know right well he did discretion lacke,
> Beeing not perswaded thereunto at all;
> If *Eve* did erre, it was for knowledge sake,
>
>   . . . . .
>
> Yet Men will boast of Knowledge, which he
>   tooke
> From *Eves* faire hande, as from a learned Booke.

Finally, Pilate's wife reasons from Adam's priority in creation to his probable role as source of evil: "If any Evil did in her remaine, / Beeing made of him, he was the ground of all." Her logic infers that an original creature is an originary one also in the case of woman's nature—if not, what is the primacy that is taken to ground male superiority? It will be clear here without further comment how Lanyer lines up the fundamental binaries of culture/nature and reason/passion in this fourfold apologia so that Pilate's wife personifies femininity triumphant in masculine terms.

Lanyer's possible antecedents for this passage make a fascinating if necessarily inconclusive subject. So little is known about her education and contacts—for example, whether she might somehow have had knowledge of the disputation conducted in 1451-53 in an exchange of Latin letters between Ludovico Foscarini, a Venetian doctor of canon law, civil law, and medicine, and the learned Veronese noblewoman Isotta Nogarola on the subject "Of the Equal or Unequal Sin of Adam and Eve." Nogarola argues that Eve's sin was unequal in being less than Adam's, on three counts. First, Eve sinned through ignorance and inconstancy while Adam sinned through a prideful desire for God-like moral knowledge. Second, in delivering the prohibition, God made Adam responsible for himself and Eve, but Adam did not restrain Eve, hence his guilt was greater. Third, God gave Eve a lesser punishment than Adam: she would bear children in pain, but he was condemned to labor and to death.

Nogarola also rebuts Foscarini's argument that Eve's sin was unequal in being greater than Adam's, again on three counts, in which she undertakes to reconfirm that Adam's sin was greater. To Foscarini's charge that Eve sinned more than Adam by setting him an evil precedent and being, in Aristotle's formulation in the *Posterior Analytics,* "That on account of which any thing exists is that thing and more greatly so," Nogarola responds that Adam's inherent superiority—as God's original creation, as the one to whom dominion over the earth was given—enabled him to resist Eve, and he is responsible for not doing so. To Foscarini's second charge, that Eve's sin was greater than Adam's because she, as an inferior creature, aspired to divinity equally with the superior creature Adam, Nogarola answers shortly with the principle that guilt is never increased by inferiority or weakness but rather the opposite: "In many people it is seen that he who knows less sins less, like a boy who sins less than an old man or a peasant less than a noble." Adam is, therefore, more guilty.

To Foscarini's third charge, that Eve's sin was the greater because her punishment was cumulative—she incurred Adam's punishments of death and labor as well as her own of pain in childbirth—Nogarola retorts that, as opposed to inference, the actual wording of God's pronouncements in Scripture makes Adam's sin look clearly worse. God does not mention Eve's sin at all, only Adam's, in listening to his wife and eating of the tree that he was commanded not to touch (Genesis 3:17). Likewise, God phrases Adam's punishment more harshly than Eve's, for he says to Adam but not to her that he is dust and will return to dust (Genesis 3:19). Nogarola stands fast in her determination that Adam is more guilty than Eve. Hereupon Foscarini moves to close their disputation by admonishing her regarding the fallibility and deceitfulness of the female sex and her possible overconfidence in her own powers of argumentation. Most interestingly for future readers of Lanyer's **"Salve Deus,"** he refers to Pilate's superior moral awareness at the time of Christ's passion as a matter on which he and Nogarola could agree and thus resolve their differences:

> Though I have spoken, you may not hear. You may spurn and disdain my words. . . . Let us read the history of the passion and the dreams of the wife, the words of Pilate, the washing of hands, the avoidance of judgment, and we shall confess that he understood . . . that the sentence was unjust. These things make it quite clear that the force of my arguments has not been weakened.

Whatever may or may not have been known to Lanyer from Nogarola's Veronese-Venetian antecedent, Lanyer unquestionably figures as a feminist innovator within an English vernacular context. Her Pilate's wife prefigures by several years other women authors' analyses of the Fall of Adam and Eve that began to circulate as the English controversy about women entered its earlier seventeenth-century phase with Joseph Swetnam's *Araignment of Lewde, Idle, Forward, and Unconstant Women* [1615]. Largely a racy series of anecdotes and denunciations, Swetnam's tract drew its fiercest counterfire from his attempts to reason, especially this one:

> Who can but say that women sprung from the Devil? Whose heads, hands, and hearts, minds and souls are evil. . . . For women have a thousand ways to entice thee and ten thousand ways to deceive thee. . . . They are ungrateful, perjured, full of fraud, flouting and deceit, unconstant, waspish, toyish, light, sullen, proud, discourteous, and cruel. And yet they were by God created and by nature formed, and therefore by policy and wisdom to be avoided. For good things abused are to be refused.

Responding in *A Muzzle for Melastomus* [1617], Rachel Speght exclaims against Swetnam's illogic, "An impious conclusion to infer: that because God created, therefore to be avoided. O intolerable absurdity!" and elsewhere argues to exonerate Eve in terms closely resembling Lanyer's:

> We shall find the offence of Adam and Eve almost to parallel: . . . Woman sinned, it is true, by her infidelity in not believing the word of God but giving credit to Satan's fair promises that "she should not die" (Genesis iii.4); but so did the man too. And if Adam had not approved of that deed which Eve had done, and been willing to tread the steps which she had gone, he—

being her head—would have reproved her. . . . And he, being better able than the woman to have resisted temptation, because the stronger vessel, was first called to account: to show that to whom much is given, of them much is required.

Later in 1617 Speght is followed by another, tartly self-styled opponent of Swetnam, Esther Sowernam, who in *Esther Hath Hang'd Haman* commends and sharpens Speght's detection of multiple fallacies in Swetnam's gloss on the Genesis account of the fall. But Sowernam reserves her chief triumph for her exposure of Swetnam's mistaking of an echo of Euripides for a verse of Scripture, "If God had not made them only to be a plague to a man, he would never have called necessary evils." "Out of what scripture, out of what record, can he prove these impious and impudent speeches? . . . If he had cited Euripides for his author, he had some colour. . . . Thus a pagan writeth profanely, but for a Christian to say that God calleth women 'necessary evils' is most intolerable and shameful to be written and published."

Not only does Pilate's wife in Lanyer's **"Salve Deus"** reason her way to a defense of Eve without explicitly presupposing what Nogarola, Speght, and Sowernam all do, that Eve by nature is inferior to Adam; she also takes the controversy about women two steps further—both, as far as I know, completely unprecedented and original. Granting for the purposes of argument that Eve deserved to be subjugated to Adam for having been the first to fall, Pilate's wife challenges Pilate on the relative blameworthiness of the Fall and the Crucifixion, in which, she charges, "you in malice Gods deare Sonne betray":

Whom, if unjustly you comdemne to die,
Her sinne was small, to what you doe commit;
All mortal sinnes that doe for vengeance crie,
Are not to be compared unto it:
If many worlds would altogether trie,
By all their sinnes the wrath of God to get;
This sinne of yours, surmounts them all as farre
As doth the Sunne, another little starre.

Sardonically invoking the superiority of the sun's light to image the greater male culpability for the Crucifixion in her female eyes, Pilate's wife inverts the culture/nature and reason/passion dichotomies to explicit female advantage once again in Lanyer's poem. The Crucifixion is worse than the Fall because malice is worse than ignorance as the state of mind in which evil is done. Moreover, by the implicit standards of the long-traditional conception of sin as self-murder, killing oneself is far less culpable than killing the son of God. Finally, no woman wants the Crucifixion; only men do. Pilate's wife now spells out to Pilate the implications of the Crucifixion and the Fall for gender relations:

Then let us have our Libertie againe,
And challendge to your selves no Sov'raigntie;

. . . . .

Your fault being greater, why should you disdaine
Our beeing your equals, free from tyranny?

. . . . .

This sinne of yours, hath no excuse, nor end.

To which (poore soules) we never gave consent,
Witness thy wife (O *Pilate*) speakes for all.

Foscarini's complacent hunch to the contrary, an intelligent woman of the Renaissance, reflecting on Pilate, Pilate's wife, and Christ's Crucifixion, would not easily find for the superiority of Pilate's moral understanding and thus confirm the subjection of females to males ordained by God after the Fall. These two personages are styled to enforce exactly the opposite finding in Lanyer's feminist poetics, while a fully reasoned claim—no mere call—issues for sexual equality in the aftermath of the Crucifixion. Interestingly, the lack of punctuation marks to enclose reported speech in early seventeenth-century texts makes it impossible to determine whether the last two lines of the foregoing quotation are spoken by Pilate's wife or by Lanyer as omniscient narrator. No less interestingly, an exact determination does not affect the interpretation or the prescient feminism of **"Salve Deus Rex Judaeorum"** because a brief for an end to male domination, thus historicized, holds for any date subsequent to the Crucifixion and for any nominally Christian place. In this poem Aemilia Lanyer takes more seriously—that is to say, more historically—the radical social and political implications of the new order broached in the gospel narrative of primitive Christianity than would any other English thinker or writer of either sex until a quarter century later, in the midcentury ferment of revolution and interregnum. Even in that later company, she and her Pilate's wife sound voices of the utmost present-time urgency and cogency as they lay claim to what has long since remained for women the receding future of gender equality.

FURTHER READING

Beilin, Elaine V. "The Feminization of Praise." In her *Redeeming Eve: Women Writers of the English Renaissance*, pp. 177-207. Princeton: Princeton University Press, 1987.

> Examines Lanyer's glorification of women's virtue and spiritual prominence in her *Salve Deus Rex Judaeorum*.

Lewalski, Barbara K. "Re-writing Patriarchy and Patronage: Margaret Clifford, Anne Clifford, and Aemilia Lanyer." *The Yearbook of English Studies: Politics, Patronage and Literature in England 1558-1658* 21 (1991): 87-106.

> Discusses the literary works of Lanyer, Margaret Clifford, and Anne Clifford.

Woods, Susanne, ed. Introduction to *The Poems of Aemilia Lanyer: Salve Deus Rex Judaeorum,* pp. xv-xlii. New York: Oxford University Press, 1993.
    Biography.

Additional information about Lanyer's life and career is contained in the following sources published by Gale Research: *Dictionary of Literary Biography,* Vol. 121, and *Literature Criticism from 1400 to 1800,* Vol. 10.

Katherine Philips

1632-1664

(Born Katherine Fowler; also wrote under pseudonym Orinda) English poet and translator.

INTRODUCTION

Although Philips was hailed by her contemporaries as a "model" woman poet and was acclaimed for her translations of French poetry and drama, her work fell into obscurity by the end of the seventeenth century and subsequently attracted little critical attention until recent years. She is best known for her ardent poetry on the theme of friendship between women, her translations of plays by Corneille, and her letters, published posthumously, to her friend Sir Charles Cotterell.

Biographical Information

Born in London in 1632, Philips was the daughter of John Fowler, a successful cloth merchant, and his wife, Katherine Oxenbridge. A maternal uncle, John Oxenbridge, was a Parliamentarian who counted among his friends the poets John Milton and Andrew Marvell. Philips attended Mrs. Salmon's Presbyterian boarding school in Hackney, but at fifteen, following her mother's marriage to Sir Richard Philips, she moved to her stepfather's family home in Pembrokeshire, Wales. In 1648, when she was sixteen, she married John Philips, a relative of her stepfather and a Parliamentarian then aged fifty-four. Despite their age difference and conflicting political views—Katherine was a staunch Royalist—their relationship appears to have been amicable. They had two children: a son, Hector, who died within six weeks of birth, and a daughter, also named Katherine, who survived and later bore fifteen children. Extremely important to Philips was her network of acquaintances, female and male, whom she designated her "Society of Friendship" and to whom she assigned fanciful pseudonyms, taking the name "Orinda" for herself. Much of her poetry was written for circulation among this select group, which included, in addition to her many female friends, such prominent men of letters as the theologian Jeremy Taylor (designated "Palaemon") and Sir Charles Cotterell ("Poliarchus"), master of ceremonies at the court of Charles II. Following the Restoration in 1660, which put an end to her Parliamentarian husband's political career, Philips began to take a more active role in the management of his estate. She also began to enter a more public realm of literary expression. With the encouragement of Roger Boyle, the Earl of Orrery, whom she met during a stay in Ireland, she wrote a translation of Corneille's *La Mort de Pompée* that was performed in Dublin in 1663. She also addressed to members of the royal family a number of poems expressing her longstanding loyalty to the Royal-

ist cause. She was at work on a translation of Corneille's *Horace* when she succumbed to smallpox in London in 1664.

Major Works

While she first came to the public notice with the performance of *Pompey* in 1663, Philips had been writing poetry for private circulation for many years. Her works include marriage poems (addressing the bride rather than, as was customary, the groom), poems of parting, elegies and epitaphs marking private family occasions, and poems of praise and thanksgiving directed to the royal family, as well as numerous translations of French verse. Particularly noted are her many poems celebrating her friendships with women, in which she adopts many of the conventions of seventeenth-century love poetry. Philips maintained that her poetry was not intended for publication, and when a pirated edition of her poems appeared early in 1664, she reacted with dismay, claiming that she "never was more vexed." Some critics suggest, however, that this public reticence may have been a ploy to avoid censure for seeking public attention. Her translation of Corneille's *Horace*, left unfinished at her death later that year, was completed by John Denham and was performed at the Theatre Royal from 1667 to 1669. The sometimes gossipy *Letters from Orinda to Poliarchus* (1705), published three years after Sir Charles Cotterell's death, chronicle the progress of her translation of Corneille, reveal Philips's support for the Restoration, and echo her poetry's preoccupation with female friendship.

Critical Reception

On the title page of the 1664 edition of her poems Philips is called "the Incomparable," and on that of 1667 "the Matchless Orinda." Such florid praise is characteristic of early responses to her work; the 1667 edition includes a series of poems by other poets in praise of the recently deceased Orinda, including verses by Thomas Flatman, James Tyrell, and Abraham Cowley. However, in his "Bibliotheca: a poem occasioned by the sight of a modern library" (1712), Thomas Newcomb complained that Philips's poems "Instead of Rapture, give us Sleep." This attack on her work, Paula Loscocco suggests in a 1993 essay, is symptomatic of a general decline in Philips's fortunes at the hands of eighteenth-century Neoclassical aesthetics. Despite sporadic critical attention in intervening years, most notably an essay published by Edmund Gosse in 1881 and a 1931 biography by Philip Webster Souers, her work attracted little critical attention until the late 1970s. Much recent criticism examines Philips's negotiations with the nearly exclusively male literary milieu of her time and the development of her literary persona and poetic style. Lucy Brashear (1979) suggests that the strategies Philips adopted in order to gain acceptance as a female poet ironically made it more difficult for subsequent women poets to win literary recognition. Elaine Hobby (1988) and Celia A. Easton (1990) view Philips's poetic persona as a creation intended to circumvent contemporary strictures against female literary production. Study of Philips's adaptation of the conventions of courtly love poetry has led some critics, such as Hobby and Harriette Andreadis (1989), to perceive a homoerotic element in her poems on female friendship, but Claudia Limbert (1991) finds this interpretation at odds with the reactions of Philips's contemporaries, and argues that the question of her sexuality should be secondary to an understanding of her efforts to preserve her reputation while breaching social norms through her professional writing activities. In an essay published in 1991, Maureen E. Mulvihill examines Philips's use of her friendships with contemporary men of letters to gain acceptance of her work and to advance her literary career.

PRINCIPAL WORKS

Pompey: A Tragedy [translator] (drama) 1663
Poems. By the Incomparable Mrs. K.P. (poetry) 1664
Poems. By the Most Deservedly Admired Mrs. Katherine Philips, the Matchless Orinda. To Which is Added, Monsieur Corneille's Pompey and Horace, Tragedies. With Several Other Translations out of French (poetry) 1667

Horace [translator; completed by John Denham] (drama) 1668*
Letters from Orinda to Poliarchus (letters) 1705
The Collected Works of Katherine Philips: The Matchless Orinda 3 vols. (poetry, letters, and drama) 1990-93

*Philips's incomplete translation was included in the 1667 edition of her poetry.

CRITICISM

Edmund Gosse (essay date 1881)

SOURCE: "The Matchless Orinda," in *Seventeenth Century Studies: A Contribution to the History of English Poetry,* William Heinemann, 1897, pp. 229-58.

[*A distinguished English literary historian, critic, and biographer, Gosse wrote extensively on seventeenth- and eighteenth-century English literature. In the following excerpt, originally published in* Cornhill Magazine *in 1881, he seeks to revive interest in Philips's work and provides an overview of her career.*]

It was not until the second half of the seventeenth century that women began to be considered competent to undertake literature as a profession.

In the crowded galaxy of Elizabethan and Jacobean poets there is no female star even of the seventh magnitude. But with the Restoration, the wives and daughters, who had learned during the years of exile to act in political and diplomatic intrigue with independence and skill, took upon themselves to write independently too, and the last forty years of the century are crowded with the names of "celebrated scribbling women." Among all these the Matchless Orinda takes the foremost place—not exactly by merit, for Aphra Behn surpassed her in genius, Margaret, Duchess of Newcastle, in versatility, and Catherine Trotter in professional zeal; but by the moral eminence which she attained through her elevated public career, and which she sealed by her tragical death. When the seventeenth century thought of a poetess, it naturally thought of Orinda; her figure overtopped those of her literary sisters; she was more dignified, more regal in her attitude to the public, than they were; and, in fine, she presents us with the best type we possess of the woman of letters in the seventeenth century.

Yet modern criticism has entirely neglected her. I cannot find that any writer of authority has mentioned her name with interest since Keats, in 1817, when he was writing *Endymion,* came across her poems at Oxford, and in writing to Reynolds remarked that he found "a most delicate fancy of the Fletcher kind" in her poems, and quoted one piece of ten stanzas to prove it. In Mr. Ward's *English Poets,* where so many names owe their introduction to one or two happy compositions which have survived the body of their works, I find no page dedicated to

Orinda; and I suppose she may fairly be considered as dead to the British public. If I venture to revive her here, it is not that I greatly admire her verses, or consider her in the true sense to have been a poet, for even the praise just quoted from Keats seems to me exaggerated; but it is because of the personal charm of her character, the interest of her career, and its importance as a chapter in the literary history of the Restoration. Nor was she, like so many of her contemporaries, an absurd, or preposterous, or unclean writer: her muse was uniformly pure and reasonable; her influence, which was very great, was exercised wholly in favour of what was beautiful and good; and if she failed, it is rather by the same accident by which so many poets of less intelligence have unexpectedly succeeded.

Katherine Fowler was born on New-Year's Day, 1631, in a respectable cockney family of Bucklersbury. Of her father, who was a Presbyterian, nothing else is known save that he was a prosperous merchant. She was baptized at the font of St. Mary Woolchurch on January 11, 1631. John Aubrey, the antiquary, who was her exact contemporary and one of her numerous friends, has preserved various traditions of her childhood. Like Cowley, another cockney child of the period, she was very eager and precocious in the pursuit of letters. The imaginative bias of her mind first took a religious form. She had read the Bible right through before she was five years old; she would pray aloud—rather ostentatiously, one fears—by the hour together, and had a potent memory for the actual text of the florid sermons that she heard on Sundays. At school she was a prodigy of application; she would commonly say, by heart, many chapters and passages of Scripture, and began at a very early age to write verses. As she grew old enough to form convictions of her own, she threw off the Presbyterian and Parliamentary traditions of her home, and announced herself an admirer of the Church and the King just as those stars were setting on the political horizon. Through the darkest period of the Commonwealth she remained stanchly Royalist; and we may fancy that she was well content to leave a home no longer sympathetic to her, when, in her seventeenth year, she married a Royalist gentleman of Wales, Mr. James Philips, of Cardigan Priory.

The early part of her life as Mrs. Philips is dark to us. None of her letters, and but few of her poems, from this period have been preserved. The earliest of her verses form an address to her neighbour Henry Vaughan, the Silurist, on the publication of his *Olor Iscanus* in 1651. These lines are interesting to the student of versification as showing that Katherine Philips, from the very first, had made up her mind to look forwards and not backwards. There is no particular merit in these verses, but they belong to the school of Waller and Denham, and prove that the authoress had learned very exactly the meaning of the new prosody. To the end of her career she never swerved from this path, to which her constant study of French poetry further encouraged her.

She seems to have adopted the melodious pseudonym by which she had become known to posterity in 1651. It would appear that among her friends and associates in and near Cardigan she instituted a Society of Friendship, to which male and female members were admitted, and in which poetry, religion, and the human heart were to form the subjects of discussion. This society, chiefly, no doubt, owing to the activity of Mrs. Philips, became widely known, and was an object of interest to contemporaries. Jeremy Taylor recognised it from afar, and Cowley paid it elaborate compliments. In the eyes of Orinda it took an exaggerated importance:—

> Nations will own us now to be
> A temple of divinity;
> And pilgrims shall ten ages hence
> Approach our tombs with reverence,

a prophecy which still waits to be fulfilled. On December 28, 1651, Miss Anne Owen, a young lady of Landshipping, entered the Society under the name of Lucasia, it being absolutely necessary that each member should be known by a fancy name. The husband of the poetess, for instance, is never mentioned in her poems or her correspondence except as Antenor. Lucasia was the chief ornament of the Society, and the affection of Orinda was laid at her feet for nearly thirteen years, in a style of the most unbounded and vivacious eulogy. It is very delightful to contemplate the little fat, ruddy, cockney lady, full of business and animation, now bustling the whole parish by the ears, now rousing her rather sluggish husband to ambition, now languishing in platonic sentiment at the feet of the young Welsh beauty who accepted all her raptures so calmly and smilingly. In Miss Owen, Mrs. Philips saw all that can be seen in the rarest altitudes of human character.

> Nor can morality itself reclaim
> The apostate world like my Lucasia's name:
> . . . Lucasia, whose harmonious state
> The Spheres and Muses only imitate.
> . . . So to acknowledge such vast eminence,
> Imperfect wonder is our eloquence,
> No pen Lucasia's glories can relate.

Nor is Lucasia the only member of her little provincial quorum of whom she predicates such brave things. There is Ardelia, whose real name neglectful posterity has forgotten to preserve; there is Miss Mary Aubrey, who becomes Mrs. Montague as time goes on, and whose poetical name is Rosania; there is Regina, "that Queen of Inconstancy," Mrs. John Collier; later on, Lady Anne Boyle begins to figure as "adored Valeria," and Lady Mary Cavendish as "dazzling Polycrite." The gentlemen have very appropriate names also, though propriety prevents Orinda, in their cases, from celebrating friendship in terms of so florid an eloquence. The "excellent Palæmon" was Francis Finch originally, but the name was transferred, as the "noble Palæmon," to Jeremy Taylor; the "noble Silvander," Sir Edward Dering, was more fortunate in preserving his name of honour; and last, but not least, the elegant Sir Charles Cotterel achieved a sort of immortality as Orinda's greatest friend, under the name of Poliarchus.

There are few collections of seventeenth century verse so personal as the poems of Orinda. Her aspirations and sentimentalities, her perplexities and quarrels, her little journeys and her business troubles, all are reflected in her verse as a mirror. She goes from Tenby to Bristol by sea in September 1652, and she gives Lucasia an account of the uneventful voyage in verse:—

> But what most pleased my mind upon the way,
> Was the ships' posture that in harbour lay;
> Which to a rocky grove so close were fixed
> That the trees' branches with the tackling
>   mixed,—
> One would have thought it was, as then it stood,
> A growing navy or a floating wood.

These are verses for which we have lost all taste, but they were quite as good as those by which Waller was then making himself famous, and in the same modern manner. These and others were handed about from one friend to another till they reached London, and gained the enthusiastic poetess literary and artistic friends. Among these latter were Henry Lewes, the great musician, and Samuel Cooper, the finest miniature painter of the day, to both of whom she has inscribed flowing copies of verses, informed by her familiar stately wit.

But the subject that chiefly inspired her was the excellence of her female friends, and in treating this theme she really invented a new species of literature. She is the first sentimental writer in the English language, and she possesses to the full those qualities which came into fashion a century and a half later in the person of such authors as Letitia Landon. Orinda communes with the stars and the mountains, and is deeply exercised about her own soul. She is all smiles, tears, and sensibility. She asks herself if her affection has been slighted, she swears eternal troth, she yearns for confidences, she fancies that she is "dying for a little love." With Antenor, her husband, she keeps up all the time a prosaic, humdrum happiness, looking after his affairs, anxious about his health, rather patronisingly affectionate and wifely; but her poetical heart is elsewhere, and her leisure moments are given up to romantic vows with Rosania and Lucasia, and correspondence about the human heart with the noble Silvander. The whole society, one cannot help feeling, was entirely created and kept alive by the sensibility of Orinda, and nothing but her unremitting efforts could have sustained its component parts at the proper heights of sympathy. Mrs. Philips, in fact, had come to the conclusion that, as she put it, "Men exclude women from friendship's vast capacity," and she was determined, in spite of the difficulties in her path, to produce some shining specimens of female friendship. The seventeenth century was quite astonished, and looked on with respectful admiration, while the good Orinda laboured away, undeterred by the irritating circumstances that her *sociétaires* would get married at the very moment when they seemed approaching perfection, and that after marriage they were much more difficult for her to manage than before.

Her first great disappointment was the "apostasy" of

Rosania, on which occasion she lifted up her voice to the "great soul of Friendship," and was rewarded by unusual response from Lucasia, on whom it is possible that the absence of Rosania had acted in an exhilarating manner. But it is time to quote some of those addresses to her friends by which she distinguishes herself so clearly from all the writers of her generation, and by which she must be known in future, if she be known at all. After receiving one of those compliments from the great men of her age, which began to flow in upon her retirement at Cardigan, Orinda thus expressed her satisfaction to Lucasia, and stirred her up to fresh efforts of sentiment:—

> Come, my Lucasia, since we see
>   That miracles man's faith do move,
> By wonder and by prodigy
>   To the dull angry world let's prove
>   There's a religion in our love.
>
> We court our own captivity,—
>   Than thrones more great and innocent;
> 'Twere banishment to be set free,
>   Since we wear fetters whose intent
>   Not bondage is, but ornament.
> Divided joys are tedious found,
>   And griefs united easier flow;
> We are ourselves but by rebound,
>   And all our titles shuffled so,—
>   Both princes, and both subjects too.
>
> Our hearts are mutual victims laid,
>   While they,—such power in friendship lies,—
> Are altars, priests and offerings made,
>   And each heart which thus kindly dies,
>   Grows deathless by the sacrifice.

It cannot be denied that these are vigorous lines, full of ingenious fancy, nor were there many men then living in England who could surpass them. We are dealing with a school whose talent has evaporated, and we must not forget to judge such verse by the standards of its time. Of Milton nobody was thinking; Dryden was still silent; Herrick and Wither had ceased to write; and it may safely be said that there was nothing in the lines just quoted which Cowley, or Waller, or Denham would have disdained to sign. Lucasia was also the theme of some verses which close, at all events, in a very delicate harmony:—

> I did not live until this time
>   Crowned my felicity,
> When I could say, without a crime,
>   I am not Thine, but Thee.
>
> For as a watch by art is wound
>   To motion, such was mine;
> But never had Orinda found
>   A soul till she found thine.
> Then let our flame still light and shine,
>   And no false fear control,
> As innocent as our design,
>   Immortal as our soul.

The piece which Keats admired so much that he took the trouble of copying it in full, was inspired by Miss Mary Aubrey, and may be given here as a final example of the manner of Orinda:—

I have examined and do find
    Of all that favour me,
There's none I grieve to leave behind,
    But only, only thee:
To part with thee I needs must die,
Could parting separate thee and I.

But neither chance nor compliment
    Did element our love;
'Twas sacred sympathy was lent
    Us from the Quire above.
That friendship Fortune did create
Still fears a wound from Time or Fate.

Our changed and mingled souls are grown
    To such acquaintance now,
That, if each would resume her own,
    Alas! we know not how;
We have each other so engrost,!
    That each is in the union lost.

And thus we can no absence know,
    Nor shall we be confined;
Our active souls will daily go
    To learn each other's mind.
Nay, should we never meet to sense
Our souls would hold intelligence.

Inspirèd with a flame divine,
    I scorn to court a stay;
For from that noble soul of thine
    I ne'er can be away.
But I shall weep when thou dost grieve,
Nor can I die whilst thou dost live.

By my own temper I shall guess
    At thy felicity,
And only like thy happiness,
    Because it pleaseth thee.
Or hearts at any time will tell
If thou or I be sick or well.

All honour sure I must pretend,
    All that is good or great;
She that would be Rosania's friend
    Must be at least complete;
If I have any bravery,
'Tis cause I have so much of thee.

Thy leiger soul in me shall lie,
    And all thy thoughts reveal,
Then back again with mine shall fly,
    And thence to me shall steal;
Thus still to one another tend:
Such is the sacred name of Friend.

Thus our twin souls in one shall grow,

And teach the world new love,
Redeem the age and sex, and show
    A flame Fate dares not move:
And, courting Death to be our friend,
Our lives too shall together end.

A dew shall dwell upon our tomb
    Of such a quality,
That fighting armies thither come
    Shall reconcilèd be.
We'll ask no epitaph, but say,
ORINDA *and* ROSANIA.

For ten years Katherine Philips continued to live at Cardigan in the midst of this enthusiastic circle of friends, and in a social quiet that was broken only by her own agitations of spirit. In 1654, in the seventh year of her marriage, she bore her first child, a son who was named Hector, and who lived only forty days. She bewails his loss in many verses, which are not the less affecting because they are stiff in form. She was ultimately consoled for her boy's death by the birth of a girl, who survived her, and eventually married a Mr. Wogan, of Pembrokeshire. It is unfortunate that we cannot trace the course of Orinda's intimacy with Jeremy Taylor, although it is most probable that he visited her Society at Cardigan during the years that he lived near to her in Carmarthenshire. At all events, when, in 1659, he dedicated his *Discourse on the Nature, Offices, and Measures of Friendship* to "the most ingenious and excellent Mrs. Katherine Philips," he paid her the most delicate and affectionate compliments, and showed himself well acquainted with the tenor of her mind. His treatise was, indeed, a public testimony, from a man of the highest authority, to the success with which she had proved women to be capable of the serene and exalted virtue of friendship.

This tribute from the famous Bishop of Down and Connor inaugurated that brief period during which Orinda ceased to be a provincial notoriety, and became for the small remainder of her life a prominent figure in contemporary society. At the Restoration she sang out loud and clear, in strains that were proved to be sincere by her long and unflinching resistance to the Commonwealth. As Arion she goes forth to meet his Majesty upon a dolphin:—

Whom does this stately navy bring?
O, 'tis Great Britain's glorious King!
Convey him then, ye Winds and Seas,
Swift as desire and calm as peace.
Charles and his mighty hopes you bear;
A greater now than Cæsar's here,
Whose veins a richer purple boast
Than ever hero's yet engrossed,
Sprung from a father so august
He triumphs in his very dust.

She hails the fine weather for the coronation as a "bright parenthesis" placed by Heaven itself between two storms of rain, and she indites separate copies of verses to all the ladies of the royal family. Soon the Duchess of York becomes aware of this ardent poetess in the West, and commands her to send some specimens of her poems; and in a little time we find Orinda, unable to stay at Cardigan when the world of London had suddenly become so distractingly interesting, on a visit to town. We find her the guest of Cowley at Barn Elms, and invited to inscribe her name on one of his ancient trees. And at the close of this visit to London in 1661 she suddenly becomes vividly present to us for the rest of her life.

We have already mentioned her friendship for Sir Charles Cotterel, whom she named Poliarchus. He was a Royalist courtier of great elegance and erudition, who had long been steward to the Queen of Bohemia, and was now master of the ceremonies at the Court of Charles II. He dabbled gracefully in literature, was a very accomplished linguist, and long after the death of Orinda achieved an ephemeral reputation as the translator of the novels of La Calprenède. He survived Katherine Philips nearly a quarter of a century, dying in 1687, and what then became of his collection of her letters does not appear. In 1705, however, forty years after her death, Bernard Lintott published, without any bibliographical information, forty-eight *Letters from Orinda to Poliarchus,* which are not only extremely well written and vivacious, but full of autobiographical matter, and amply furnished with dates. By means of these letters we can follow Orinda closely through the last and most interesting months of her life.

The first letter is dated from Acton, Dec. 1, 1661. She has come up to London to prosecute some business for her husband, and is staying with his brother, to the members of whose family she had at various occasions indited poems. Sir Charles Cotterel has paid her a visit, in the course of which he has confided to her his hopeless passion for a lady named Calanthe, and she is full of concern for his peace of mind. Mr. Matthew Arnold has pointed out how suddenly the prose of the Restoration threw off its traditional involutions and false ornament, and became in a great measure the prose that we wish to use to-day. The *Letters* of Orinda form a singular instance of the truth of this criticism, and compare very favourably with such letters as those of Howd in point of simplicity of style. Thus, for instance, she refers to Sir Charles Cotterel's agitation of mind:—

> The great disturbance you were in when you went hence, and the high and just concern I have for you, have made me take the resolution to trouble you with my most humble and earnest request to resist the attempts your present passion is like to make on your quiet, before it grows too imperious to be checked by the powers of either reason or friendship. There is nothing more easy than to captivate one's self to love or grief, and no more evident mark of a great soul than to avoid those bondages. I hope, therefore, you will not think it altogether unbecoming the friendship you have given me leave to profess for you, to entreat you to overcome those passions, and not give way to melancholy, which will unhinge your excellent temper, and bring so great a cloud on the happiness of your friends. Consider for how many important interests you are responsible, and exert all the powers of reason with which your excellent judgment abounds, to shake

off your sorrows, and live cheerfully and long the delight of all who have the honour of your acquaintance.

Calanthe had been in correspondence with Orinda, and that faithless confidante had shown her letters to Poliarchus, hence many entreaties that her weakness may not be divulged to the injured fair. It is plain that Orinda greatly enjoyed her position as go-between in this interesting love affair, which, however, very shortly languished, and left upon the ensuing correspondence only this trace, that Sir Charles Cotterel having written such passages in his letters to Orinda as were not to be read by Calanthe in Italian, Orinda was obliged to learn that language, to which, indeed, she forthwith gave herself very assiduously. Her visit to London came to an end in March 1662, and she wrote to Poliarchus a sprightly letter from Gloucester on her return journey. A very interesting letter, dated Cardigan Priory, March 18th, announced her return. She found Wales exceedingly dull at first, after the pleasures of courtly and literary society in London. She complained that she could not find any satisfaction in "my beloved rocks and rivers, formerly my best entertainment," and she longed to be able once more to enjoy Sir Charles Cotterel's conversation, which was to her "above all the flights of panegyrick." Her one consolation was that the faithful Lucasia was still at Cardigan, though threatening every day to be gone to her own home. Descending to mundane things, poor Orinda confessed that she had been much disappointed in the condition of her husband. He is dull, apathetic, and depressed, was roused to no interest by her account of the conduct of his affairs in London, and terrifies her by his absolute indifference to business. From the sluggishness of Antenor she turns again to the pleasures of literature, and by an amusing affection characteristic of the school she belonged to, she tells Poliarchus that she is reading English books with patience and French ones with pleasure.

She spent the month of April with her beloved friend at Landshipping, but, alas! the hour of the apostasy of Lucasia was approaching. While Orinda was amusing herself with the idea that Poliarchus was showing her poems at Court, and while she was signing herself to him "more than all the world besides your faithful Valentine," Miss Anne Owen was herself accepting a valentine in a less platonic sense. It seems to have all happened at Landshipping under the very nose of Orinda, without attracting the attention of that active creature. When at last she found it out, she was beside herself with chagrin and indignation. The bridegroom was a son of Sir Thomas Hanmer, and the match was one thoroughly approved of by both families. Orinda, as she says herself, "alone of all the company was out of humour; nay, I was vexed to that degree that I could not disguise my concern, which many of them were surprised to see, and spoke to me of it; but my grief was too deeply rooted to be cured with words." Her position, indeed, was a very trying one; nor ought we to smile at the disappointment of this worthy little lady, who had worshipped a divinity so long only to find her suddenly composed of common clay.

The event was certainly hurried, for before the middle of May Lucasia was married, Orinda mean-while indulging herself in transports of jealousy, and in long correspondence on the subject with Rosania and Poliarchus. When the young people were actually married, Orinda remained with them at Landshipping, and when they prepared to go over to Ireland, where the bride's new home was, she announced her intention of accompanying them. The vigilance of friendship, however, was not the only or the main cause of this determination. There were several suits to be tried in Dublin, involving heavy gains or losses to her husband, and as he could by no means be roused to an interest in these, Mrs. Philips resolved to undertake them herself. On July 19th, 1662, she writes from Rosstrevor, in County Down, where she had been enjoying the society of Jeremy Taylor, who had been settled something less than two years in his diocese. This august companionship did not prevent Orinda from exercising a sharp supervision over the newly married pair. She informs Poliarchus, in a strain of the finest unconscious humour, that she believes the bridegroom to be of a most stubborn and surly humour, although, "to speak sincerely, she has not been able hitherto to detect in him the marks of any ill nature," and what exasperates her most of all, in her character of the social banshee, is that Lucasia herself "pretends to be the most satisfied creature in the world."

In July 1662, Mrs. Philips began what was evidently the happiest year of her life by taking up her abode in Dublin. At the Restoration the great difficulty of settling the claims of those Irish gentlemen who demanded the King's favour, and the endless litigations respecting the forfeited lands in Ireland, brought over to Dublin a large company of distinguished lawyers with their families, and gave the city a temporary show and glitter. It was many years before affairs were in any degree arranged, and the English colony in Dublin settled down to enjoy themselves as best they might. Orinda found herself thrown at once into the distinguished company which gathered round the Lord-Lieutenant, the great first Duke of Ormonde, and she received an exceptionally warm welcome in the family of the Countess of Cork. Of all the Boyles, however, at that moment, the most influential was Roger, Earl of Orrery, whose enthusiastic admiration for Orinda displayed itself at once in every species of compliment and hospitality. He was eminent alike as a soldier, a statesman, and a poet, was one of the most influential men in the three kingdoms, and at that moment was engaged in Ireland upon a most arduous and painful office. He had just been appointed Lord Chief-Justice of Ireland under the Duke of Ormonde, and his friendship was not merely flattering and agreeable to Orinda, but extremely advantageous. He placed her among the ladies of his family, obtained for her the protection and personal friendship of Lady Cork, and in fact did all that was possible to make her stay in Dublin pleasant.

Another distinguished person with whom she swore eternal friendship in Dublin was the young Earl of Roscommon, not yet famous as the author of the *Essay on Trans-lated Verse,* and indeed only twenty-eight years of age, but already looked upon as a patron of poetry, and as a very agreeable and eligible bachelor, "distempered," unfortunately, "with a fatal affection for play." Another Dublin acquaintance was James Tyrell, the politician and historian; yet another was John Ogilby, a man belonging to a generation earlier than all these, who had successfully outwitted Sir William Davenant, and had contrived to persuade Charles II. to send him out to Dublin as Master of the Revels. Ogilby is still sometimes remembered as the translator of the *Odyssey* and of the *Æneid*. That Orinda impressed all these persons with a great sense of her intellectual power and moral excellence, is evident from the nature of the eulogies they poured upon her while she lived and long after she died. When a man in the position of Lord Orrery says in print of a little plain Welsh lady of the middle class—

> Madam, when I but knew you by report,
> I feared the praises of the admiring Court
> Were but their compliments, but now I must
> Confess, what I thought civil is scarce just

we may be sure that he is trying to express with sincerity a very genuine admiration. Nor is the Earl of Roscommon, who addresses her as "Dear Friend," less sincere, though more ridiculous, when he states it to be his experience that when he meets hungry wolves in the Scythian snows,

> The magic of Orinda's name
> Not only can their fierceness tame,
> But, if that mighty word I once rehearse,
> They seem *submissively to roar in verse.*

On one of the earliest occasions upon which Mrs. Philips met Lord Orrery, in August 1662, she ventured to show him her latest effusion, a scene she had translated from the third act of Corneille's tragedy of *Pompée*. Orrery admired it excessively, and laid his entreaties, almost his commands, upon her to complete it in the same style—that is, in rhymed heroic verse. She set to work and completed the task, a very considerable one, by the middle of October. She found that it relieved her, in combination with select passages from Seneca and Epictetus, from absolutely breaking her heart over Lucasia, whose husband at last insisted on taking her back to their house at Rosstrevor. Orinda, ensconced in her snug nest of quality at Dublin, full of literary ambition, and scribbling day and night at *Pompey,* seems to have missed her friend as little as could be expected. She was treated as a very great celebrity; and when she had occasion to hand round some manuscript verses which Cowley had just sent her for approval, she must have felt that her cup of literary importance was full.

Thus caressed by Lady Cork and complimented by all the lettered earls, she passed the months of August and September 1662 in a sort of golden dream, scarcely finding time, amid all her avocations, to write a hasty letter to the devoted Poliarchus, to whom, however, *Pompey* was sent in quick instalments. She gives him an interesting account, in October, of the theatre which the new master of the revels, Ogilby, was building at Dublin—a theatre that cost £2000 to put up. She holds it to be much finer than Davenant's in London; and she is present when the season opens with a performance of Beaumont and Fletcher's comedy of *Wit without Money.* As soon as the rough draft of *Pompey* was finished, she busied herself with her husband's affairs—"putting in Antenor's claim as an adventurer in my father's right here in Ireland"—and this, with two other minor lawsuits, occupies her spare time until the summer of the ensuing year. Her most serious attention, however, settles upon *Pompey.* Sir Charles Cotterel takes so much interest in it that she says, "I look on you as more a friend to me than David was to Jonathan;" but she shows a little temper when he offers some verbal criticism. For instance, and this is interesting historically, he objects to the word *effort* as not English, and she replies that it has been naturalised here these twelve years. She might have added that Cotgrave had included it in his dictionary, in 1660.

Orinda spent the winter of 1662 at Dublin, touching up the text of *Pompey,* writing songs for it, and having them put to music—not without regret that her friend, the great Henry Lawes, who died just as the first manuscript of the play reached London, could not adorn them with immortal strains. Lord Orrery, who looked upon himself as the "onlie begetter" of this tragedy, moved heaven and earth to bring it out upon the stage; and, when Ogilby had made arrangements for its representation, Orrery spent £100 out of his own pocket to buy handsome Egyptian and Roman dresses and bring out the tragedy in style. It was dedicated to his mother, Lady Cork. Lord Roscommon wrote the prologue, and Sir Edward Dering the epilogue; each of them so ordered their verses that they should be delivered by the actor while turning to the Duke of Ormonde's box. New dances and a masque were introduced here and there by Ogilby, and on the second week of February 1663 it was finally presented to the public. It enjoyed an unbounded success; but, unfortunately, the letter in which Mrs. Philips gave Sir Charles Cotterel an account of the performance has not been preserved. Her friends, however, pressed her to print the play, and from the success which attended this experiment we may judge of the reception of the piece on the boards. An edition of five hundred was printed, a single packet only being sent to London, and in a fortnight the whole of the impression was sold. In London the demand was so great, that hardly had the few copies sent arrived at the capital, than Mr. Herringman, the poets' publisher in those early days of the Restoration, wrote to ask Orinda's leave to bring out a London edition.

Meanwhile, Orinda had certain literary experiences. She made the acquaintance of Samuel Tuke, whose very successful play, the *Adventures of Five Hours,* was awakening delusive hopes of a great new dramatist; and she welcomed in *Hudibras* the advent of one much greater than Tuke. Her first impulse of criticism was that which the world has endorsed: "In my life I never read anything so naturally and so knowingly burlesque." In May, her troubles as an authoress began. A miscellany of poems by

living writers appeared, in which some of her lyrics were pirated and widely advertised; and her serenity was shaken, a week or two later, by the fact that two London publishers were quarrelling for *Pompey,* and did, in fact, bring out, in the month of June, two simultaneous editions of that lucky play. And now it came to her knowledge that, while she had been thus busily employed, she had cut the ground from under the feet of some of the most celebrated wits of the day; for Waller had set his heart on translating *Pompée,* and had finished one act before Orinda's version was heard of. The other four acts had been supplied by Sir Edward Fillmore, Sir Charles Sedley, and the young men who were afterwards known as the Earls of Dorset and Middlesex. As early as January 1663 it was announced that this translation was complete and immediately to appear. The success, however, of the Irish version checked the London one; and Orinda, hearing nothing of her illustrious rivals, became frightened, and wrote to Waller a letter deprecating his anger. His reply, which reached her early in June, reassured her; the courtly poet was characteristically smooth, courteous, and obliging, and, if he felt annoyance, contrived most wittily to avoid the show of it. At last, on July 16, 1663, having gained the two most important of her three suits, Mrs. Philips set sail from Dublin to Milford, and went home to her husband at Cardigan after an absence of exactly twelve months.

She found the excellent Antenor much improved in health, and she settled down to spend the autumn and winter at home. Her new importance as a woman of letters, and her large London correspondence, however, exposed her to a fresh annoyance. The postmaster at Carmarthen scandalously neglected his duty, and letters were constantly delayed and lost. The gentry of the neighbourhood, however, stirred up by the ever-energetic Orinda, sent in a memorial to O'Neil, the Postmaster-General, and the indolence at Carmarthen received a sharp reprimand. She found the winter tedious after her happy life at Dublin; she does not complain, but her letters to Sir Charles Cotterel are dejected in tone, and her appeals to her friends to find something in London for her husband to do are constant and pathetic. And now another annoyance occurred. A piratical London publisher managed to obtain copies of all her miscellaneous poems, which she had refused to print, and brought them out surreptitiously in November 1663, the title-page dated 1664. Her friends wrote to her to condole, but did not send her the book, and her anxiety and vexation, combined with the rumour that the verses were very incorrectly printed, threw her into a sharp attack of illness. The volume, however, is not particularly incorrect, and it was prefaced by an ode of Cowley's which should have been balm to the breast of the wounded poetess. In it that eminent rhetorician, speaking in the consciousness of his enormous prestige, addressed her in terms of the highest and most affectionate eulogy, and contrived to throw into one stanza, at least, of his encomiastic ode, some of the most delicately felicitous compliments that a poet ever addressed to a sister in Apollo:—

> Thou dost my wonder, would'st my
> envy raise,

If to be praised I loved more than to
    praise;
I must admire to see thy well-knit
    sense,
Thy numbers gentle, and thy fancies
    high,
These as thy forehead smooth, these sparkling
    as thine eye.
    'Tis solid and 'tis manly all,
    Or rather, 'tis angelical!
    For, as in angels, we
    Do in thy verses see
Both improved sexes eminently meet,—
They are than Man more strong, and more
    than Woman sweet.

In January 1664 she took in hand another play of Corneille's, and that the one most popular in England through his lifetime—*Horace*. It had been translated before, by Sir William Lower, in 1656, and was attempted later on by Charles Cotton, in 1671. Orinda worked slowly at this, and brought four acts of it, all she was destined to complete, with her when she came to London in March. She was absolutely unable to stay any longer in suspense, and she thought that her energy and influence might secure some post for her husband if she came right up to town. The last three months of her life were brilliantly spent; she was warmly welcomed at court and in the best society. Her last verses, signed June 10, 1664, were addressed in terms of affectionate respect to the Archbishop of Canterbury. They breathe the old ardour, the old moral elevation, the old eager note of the enthusiastic Orinda. Twelve days later she was dead, a victim to smallpox, that frightful disease to which the science of the day saw no hope of resistance. She had but half completed her thirty-fourth year. She was buried under a great slab in the church of St. Bennet Sherehog, among the remains of her ancestors.

Thus, in the middle of a brilliant social and literary success, the abhorred shears slipped in and cut the thread. The memory of the matchless Orinda was celebrated in numberless odes. All the Royalist poets combined to do her honour. Cowley mourned her in a massive lyric. Denham demanded the privilege of concluding her *Horace*. Her name was mentioned with those of Sappho and Corinna, and language was used without reproach which might have seemed a little fulsome if addressed to the Muse herself.

For half a century Orinda was an unquestioned light in English song; then she sank into utter darkness. But her memory is worthy of some judicious revival. She presents us with a clearly defined and curious type of the literary woman, and there are few such in our early literature. She secured the affectionate esteem of the principal people of her time, and we know enough of her character to see that she could not but secure it; and if she sinned against poetry, as we understand it, much may be forgiven her, for she loved it much.

Elizabeth H. Hageman (essay date 1987)

SOURCE: "Katherine Philips: The Matchless Orinda," in *Women Writers of the Renaissance and Reformation,* edited by Katharina M. Wilson, The University of Georgia Press, 1987, pp. 566-608.

[*In the following excerpt, Hageman provides an overview of Philips's career and works.*]

Because her poem **"On the First of January 1657"** includes the statement that God has "By moments number'd out the precious sands, / Till [the poet's life] is swell'd to six and twenty years," students of Katherine Philips have assumed that her actual birth date was January 1, 1631/ 1632. The accuracy of that precise date remains unvalidated, but church records do reveal that the future poet was baptized at Saint Mary Woolchurch in London on January 11 of that year. Her mother was Katherine Fowler, née Katherine Oxenbridge, daughter of Daniel Oxenbridge, a doctor of physic and fellow of the Royal College of Physicians in London; her father was James Fowler, a prosperous London cloth merchant. In his *Brief Lives,* Philips's contemporary John Aubrey indicates that after receiving early training at home—she learned to read from "her cozen Blackett, who had lived with her from her swadling clothes to eight"—young Katherine Fowler was enrolled in the Presbyterian Mrs. Salmon's school for girls in nearby Hackney. Aubrey reports that Katherine Fowler was a pious, intelligent child. "She was," he writes, "very religiously devoted when she was young; prayed by herself an hower together, and tooke sermons *verbatim* when she was but 10 yeares old." She "Loved poetrey at schoole, and made verses there." Mrs. Blackett, in particular, had favorable memories of her former charge, whom she remembered as "Very good-natured; not at all high-minded"—even if she was "pretty fatt; not tall; reddish faced."

In December 1642, John Fowler died, leaving his wife, his daughter, and his son Joshua a combined legacy of some 3,300 pounds. A few years later, probably in 1646, Fowler's widow married Sir Richard Phillips of Picton Castle in Pembrokeshire, the southernmost county of Wales, and in August of 1648, young Katherine Fowler married James Philips, a relative by birth and by marriage to Sir Richard. She was then sixteen years old; her new husband was fifty-four.

From 1648 until 1664, the year of her death, Katherine Philips's home was the Priory in Cardigan, on the banks of the River Teify, not far from the sea. Among her best-known works are the poems to Lucasia. . . . Orinda is Philips's name for herself in her poems and letters; Lucasia is Anne Owen, who lived some twenty-five miles away and who was a close friend of Philips from at least as early as 1651 until Philips's death. **"To My Dear Sister Mrs. C.P. on Her Marriage"** celebrates the marriage in 1653 of Philips's sister-in-law Cicily Philips to John Lloyd in Saint Mary's Church, next door to Cardigan Priory; the **"Epitaph on Mr. John Lloyd"** was written three years later to be carved on Lloyd's funeral monument in the church in Cilgerran, a few miles from Cardigan. Even some of Philips's poems on political subjects can be related to her life in Wales. **"Upon the Double Murther of King Charles I,"** for example, responds to verses written by the Welsh republican Vavasor Powell when he was visiting the priory; and **"On the Third of September 1651"** moralizes on an event that certainly pleased Philips's Parliamentarian husband: Cromwell's defeat of Charles II at the Battle of Worcester—a defeat which effectively ended the second and final tide of the English Civil War.

The genres Philips chose for the bases of her poems include many that were popular among her contemporaries: the pastoral dialogue, the wooing poem, the poem of parting, the epithalamion, the epitaph, and the elegy. Time and again her approach to those genres is that of an intelligent poet writing to an audience she expects to appreciate her exploitation of traditional poetic conventions and her deft manipulation of language. For example, in a number of the poems she wrote during the 1650s, Philips expresses a longing for a quiet life of ordered peace: in **"A Retir'd Friendship. To Ardelia,"** she explicitly contrasts a secluded life of "kindly mingling Souls" with the world of "Bloud and Plots"; in the Lucasia poems she reiterates the idea that personal friendship offers joy superior to that of "Crown-conquerors" (**"To My Excellent Lucasia, on Our Friendship"**); and in **"To Mr. Henry Lawes,"** she imagines the musician's holy power to "repair a State." Highly traditional in their echoing pastoral motifs established by classical poets like Virgil and Horace and developed throughout the English sixteenth century, Philips's poems of retirement are most timely in their nostalgic longing for a lost golden age and then in their celebrating the return of the monarchy as a revival of a pastoral paradise. Both royalist and Parliamentarian poets of the seventeenth century, it should be noted, wrote pastoral verse: Katherine Philips's age was the age of Milton's "Lycidas," of Herrick's *Hesperides,* of Vaughan's *Olor Iscanus,* and of Marvell's *"The Garden."* The latter two works, in fact, include tributes to Philips: in *Olor Iscanus* (1651), Vaughan presents a poem in praise of Katherine Philips, for whom "No *Lawrel* growes, but for [her] *Brow,*" and "The Garden" incorporates perhaps the greatest compliment of all—two, possibly three, echo allusions to lines from Philips's work.

In her two most moving poems on death—the epitaph for the tomb of her infant son and "Orinda upon Little Hector Philips"—Philips uses the conventional *topos* of the metaphoric relationship between the "numbers" of time and the "numbers" of poetry to convey the pain of a bereaved parent. In the latter poem, the number forty, which is associated in Christian numerology with periods of privation and trial, reinforces her theme of the untimeliness of the boy's death: the long-awaited child—born after "Twice forty months" of marriage—died "in forty days." Unsustained by any muse but her "Tears" and unaided by any "Art" but her grief, this mother offers only "gasping numbers" for her child's elegy. Those "gasping numbers" are appropriate to the occasion, for the poem is "Too just a tribute for [the child's] early Herse." In the **"Epitaph"** Philips writes of having been "Seven years childless" and

puns on the words *morning* and *mourning* as she predicts that "if" the Sun (significant here because the sun heralds new days and new beginnings) should be "Half so glorious as [the child's] eyes," it will, like the child, be shrouded in a "morning Cloud." If the mark of a successful poem about death is, as many think, the poet's ability to find consolation, then Philips has failed. But if the poet's task is to find a verbal formulation of a state of mind, then few poems are more successful than these two.

In her epithalamion for Cicily Philips and the verses written in her behalf three years later when her husband died, Philips again uses the theme of time in interestingly appropriate ways. She begins **"To My Dear Sister Mrs. C.P. on Her Marriage"** by defining the kind of verses she will not write: she announces that she is not so naïve as to think that celebrating a marriage in traditionally festive ways (with the cups, garlands, and altars invoked by poets like Edmund Spenser in his "Epithalamion") is anything but indulgence in "wild toyes [which] / Be but a troublesome and empty noise." Orinda, a more serious poet, will offer instead "great Solemnities"—her "wishes for *Cassandra*'s bliss." The phrase "those men" to name the poets whose mode Orinda rejects is of course apt in a poem whose persona is the female Orinda in an age when most poets were men and most marriage poems celebrated the groom's joy. Orinda takes for granted her society's notion of the new wife's duties to her husband and to the marriage and prays "May her Content and Duty be the same." Content will come, Orinda continues, if the marriage is the kind of companionate marriage that Protestant writers of sixteenth- and seventeenth-century England recommended—if it is the kind of loving marriage that Philips's poems to her own husband (Antenor in the verses) suggest she enjoyed. In the second line of her poem, Orinda rejects the idea that those who "crown the cup" really do "crown the day" in favor of a different kind of wish expressed at the end of her poem: she hopes this couple "may count the hours as they pass, / By *their own* Joys and not by Sun or Glass" (italics mine). Far less ornate than the kind of epithalamion this poet refuses to emulate, Philips's poem is remarkable for her careful adoption of a plain style as a vehicle for a poem that advocates a marriage characterized by "Friendship, Gratitude, and strictest Love."

Written, as its subtitle says, "in the person of his wife," the **"Epitaph on Mr. John Lloyd"** is poignant in its sympathetic expression of the wife's sorrow for a husband who "so untimely dy'd / And living pledges was deny'd." Knowing that even her "Grief at length must dy" and fully aware that future generations will look at the monument with "unconcerned Eys," the widow begs the funeral monument to use its persuasive powers to teach them not only to admire John Lloyd for his virtue, but to pity her for her grief. The effect of the epitaph is multifaceted: literally "inscribed on his Monument / in Kilgarron" (subtitle), it images a widow's successful search for relief. The stone *can* "Preserve," at least for some time, her grief, and its words *do* articulate the message she intends. In providing the widow with words with which to bid the "abiding faithful stone" to instruct those who will read it "then," Philips has given her a way to assert that her husband has a "name [that] can live" after all. Radically different in tone, but similarly successful in their wit, are three poems about wooing . . . : the companion poems **"To Regina Collier, on Her Cruelty to Philaster," "To Philaster, on His Melancholy for Regina,"** and . . . **"An Answer to Another Perswading a Lady to Marriage."** In the latter, the poet addresses a callow youth who wastes his time wooing a lady whom he sees as the goddess of love herself. Philips treats both lady and lover with comic scorn: if he really believed her to be a goddess, he would not presume to confine her in a domestic love—to make her a "petty Houshold God"; if she really were as lovely as he thinks, she would not be so publicly and indiscriminately flirtatious. In the companion poems, the poet chides each lover in turn: first the "Triumphant Queen of scorn," and then her disconsolate suitor. Regina, she asserts, has become a "Round-head"—a Parliamentarian (here a term of dispraise for a person who "insult[s] upon" a subject she has conquered with her own seductive beauty). But unlike those poets who content themselves with poems urging ladies to submit to their men, Orinda then turns to the unsuccessful wooer and calls him a "vain / And double Murtherer"—a murder in that his self-indulgent grief is suicidal and in that his pain "wounds" Regina too. As she urges him to give up Regina, this poet expresses disdain for the "Queen" who does not deserve Philaster's loyalty and also for the lover whose "dulness"—stupidity—allows him to mourn an undeserving mistress.

The same temperament that led to those witty poems is evident in a manuscript in Philips's hand now in the National Library of Wales. Inscribed before her marriage to James Philips, the manuscript is a single sheet on which are written two poems and a snippet of prose—all on the subject of love and marriage. On one side of the sheet is a playful dispraise of marriage, which "affords but little Ease / The best of husbands are so hard to please," and "A recipt to cure a Love sick Person who can obtain the Party desired":

> Take two oz: of the spirits of reason three oz: of the Powder of experience five drams of the Juce of Discretion three oz: of the Powder of good advise & a spoonfull of the Cooling watter of Consideration make these all up into Pills & besure to drink a little content affter ym & then the head will be clear of maggotts & whimsies & you restored to yr right sences but the persons that wont be ruld must become a sacrifise to cupid & dye for love for all the Doctors in the world cant cure ym.

> If this wont do apply the plaister & if that wont do itts out of my power to find out what will.

On the other side of the sheet are sixteen lines in the couplets that Philips would use in many of her later verses—in panegyrics to members of the royal family and to her fellow poets, in verse letters to her husband, in moral poems with titles like **"Happiness," "The Soul,"** and **"The World."** The speaker of this poem claims that "If himans

rites shall call me hence / It shall be with some man of sence." Her requirements that her husband be "Nott with the great butt with the good estate" and that he stand "Ready to serve his friend his country & his king" indicate how thoroughly the young poet had assimilated the values of seventeenth-century neoclassical poetry. For in this poem young Katherine Fowler has transformed the formulaic description of the loyal, sensible, and moderate friend advocated by poets like Ben Jonson into a description of the ideal husband.

The fact is that while Philips's poems and letters suggest that she did enjoy a companionate marriage with James Philips and that she found congenial friends among her neighbors and relatives in Wales, many of her closest connections were with Londoners—and, in spite of the fact that many of the members of her family were Parliamentarians, with royalists. As a Members of Parliament, James Philips made extended trips to London; in all likelihood Katherine Philips accompanied him in his sojourns there. She must have been in London in the spring of 1655, for their only son Hector was buried then in the church of Saint Benet-Sherehog in Syth's Lane in London. Among her many London friends were two, Mary Aubrey and Mary Harvey, who had been Philips's classmates at Mrs. Salmon's school. Mary Aubrey (later Mrs. Montague) appears as Rosania in Philips's verses. Whether any of Philips's poems refer to Mary Harvey, we do not know, but one—**"To Sir Edward Dering (the Noble Silvander) on His Dream and Navy, Personating Orinda's Preferring Rosania Before Solomon's Traffic to Ophir"**—is addressed to the man Mary Harvey married in 1648, and two of Philips's poems are printed in Henry Lawes's *Second Book of Ayres and Dialogues* (1655), which is dedicated to Lady Dering.

Sir Edward's name appears several times in letters Philips wrote to Sir Charles Cotterell in the early 1660s. Moreover, six of the letters that survive in Dering's letterbook, now owned by the University of Cincinnati, are addressed to Philips; others are written to their mutual friends the Countess of Roscommon, Mary Montague, Lady Gifford, and Lady Dungannon (Anne Owen, who in 1662 was remarried to Marcus Trevor, Lord Dungannon). In those letters, also written in the early 1660s, Dering uses the same classical names that Philips used to refer to their mutual friends, and his admiration for Philips is a constant theme. In a letter written to Philips on January 3, 1662, for instance, he writes of "Orinda's pen, whose every line gives more lasting honour than Egyptian Pyramids, though they alone of all the wonders of the world, seem to despise the injuries of time." In July of 1664, Dering writes to Lady Roscommon that "Since Orindas death, I am growne so cold & stupid, and my complexion not very active and spirituall at the best, is now so dull & frozen, that I hardly know what I do or say, I entertaine nothing with delight, even the satisfactions of sincere & vertuous friendship, which among humane joyes I did esteeme the most, have not the sweetnesse which they had. . . . Sure, another wound like this, would make me alltogether insensible, and leave me (allmost) as unconcerned for the world, as if I had never been." The following February, when he writes to Lucasia of his slow recovery from that sorrow, he includes a statement of the significance of their friend's life:

> But not to dwell too long upon so melancholy reflexions, your Ladyship could not but observe that Orinda had conceived the most generous designe, that in my opinion ever entred into any breast, which was to unite all those of her acquaintance which she found worthy or desired to make so, (among which later number she was pleased to give me a place) into one societie, and by the bands of friendship to make an alliance more firme than what nature, our country or equall education can produce: and this would in time have spread very farr, and have been improved with great and yet unimagind advantage to the world: for it would have been of great use sure, to show the world that there were satisfactions in vertuous friendship farr transcending all those delights, which the most specious follyes can tempt us with; and doubtlesse many would have quitted the extravagancies of their inclinations for feare of being banishd so happy a conversation, that would have resisted more pressing arguments, and all the instruments of a more rugged discipline.

Dering's words here might seem to support those who have read in Philips's friendship poems evidence that she organized and headed a Society of Friendship that met to discuss literary and/or philosophical questions. Surely, however, if Philips had founded such a society, Dering would not be using words that would suggest that Lady Dungannon might not have noticed its existence. In the absence of better evidence that Philips had organized a society with a membership list or a definite program, it seems more reasonable to believe that the word "society" in her poems and in this letter refers to her social set— what we might now call her network of friends. What Dering's statement *does* show is the reality and significance of the close ties between members of the social circle to which they both belonged.

Dering's words also suggest that Philips's contemporaries agreed with the judgment of twentieth-century anthologists that the poems on friendship are her best—or, if not her best, then certainly her most characteristic—works. In those poems, Philips appropriates the language love poets of the mid-seventeenth century had inherited from the Elizabethans and Jacobeans and applies it to a new subject: female friendship. Her friendship poems abound with echo allusions to poems like John Donne's "Canonization," "The Sun Rising," "The Ecstasy," and "A Valediction: Forbidding Mourning." In, for example, **"Friendship in Embleme, or the Seal. To My Dearest Lucasia,"** . . . Philips transforms the conceit of the compass from Donne's "A Valediction: Forbidding Mourning" into an insignia of her friendship. Donne worked with his compass image for the last three of the nine stanzas in his poem; Philips rings changes on it for ten of her sixteen stanzas, all written, as are Donne's, in tetrameter lines rhyming *a b a b*. In "A Valediction: Forbidding Mourning," Donne says his "love [is] so much refin'd / That our selves know not what it is." Orinda goes further, maintaining that "Friendship hearts so much refines, / It noth-

ing but itself designs." And while Donne contrasts his love with that of "Dull sublunary lovers," Orinda asserts that the only reason for explicating her emblematic image is "that we may the mind reveal / To the dull eye."

In **"Friendship's Mystery. To My Dearest Lucasia,"** Orinda echoes Donne's "The Canonization," in which the poet demonstrated that he and his lady "prove / Mysterious by this love," when she bids Lucasia,

> Come, my *Lucasia,* since we see
> That Miracles Mens faith do move,
> By wonder and by prodigy
> To the dull angry world let's prove
> There's a Religion in our Love.

In his "Sun Rising," Donne asserts of himself and his lady: "She is all States, all Princes, I, / Nothing else is." Orinda declares an even more complete equality between herself and her friend when she says that "all our Titles [are] shuffled so, / Both Princes, and both Subjects too." The "shuffling" of those friends' "Titles" is nowhere more clear than in **"A Dialogue of Absence 'twixt Lucasia and Orinda,"** where, rather than teach Lucasia what to think, Philips allows her to teach Orinda. Orinda's sorrow is lightened at least a little by Lucasia's assurance that

> Our Souls, without the help of Sense,
> By wayes more noble and more free
> Can meet, and hold intelligence.

In the end, Orinda admits that parting is—if not joyful—then "sadly sweet," and the friends join to sing the chorus, which looks forward to a final union when "we shall come where no rude hand shall sever, / And there wee'l meet and part no more for ever."

The theme of Platonic friendship, of course, may be found throughout Renaissance literature. In 1560, for example, the English writer George Turberville had written that true friends as "two in bodies twaine / Possessing but one heart." Seventeenth-century poets like William Cartwright had also conflated the theme of friendship with the vocabulary of Platonic love. But most Renaissance writers followed the classical assumption that when they wrote of friends they were celebrating relationships between men. Turberville, for instance, cited Tullie and Atticus, Theseus and Pirithous, Damon and Pythias, Pylades and Orestes, Titus and Gysippus, Laellius and Scipio, Achilles and Patroclus, and Nysus and Aeurialus as illustrations of true friendship. When women appeared in literary works about friendship, they were, as a rule, the seductresses who wooed men like John Lyly's Euphues away from his true friend Philautus. It remained for Katherine Philips to assert a philosophy of friendship that took for granted the notion that women could be friends with each other and with men.

We can see both how well-known Philips was for her poems on friendship and how atypical her idea of female friendship was when we read Jeremy Taylor's *A Discourse of the Nature and Offices of Friendship. In a Letter to the*

Most Ingenious and Excellent M.K.P. (1657; republished in the same year and again in 1662 as *The Measures and Offices of Friendship*). His essay is organized as a series of answers to questions from Orinda herself. Taylor credits her with being "so eminent in friendships [that she] could also have given the best answer to [her] own enquires"; he even suggests she "could have trusted [her] own reason, because it is not only greatly instructed by the direct notices of things, but also by great experience in the matter of which [she] now enquire[s]." The poet who had hoped that Cassandra and her husband would enjoy a life so intertwined that "we may not know / Who most Affection or most Peace engrost" would probably have been glad to read Taylor's assertion that "marriage is the queen of friendships," and surely Orinda would approve of the judgments that "some wives have been the best friends in the world" and that a woman "can die for her friend as well as the bravest Roman knight." But Taylor's belief in women's value in times of true need is not complete. "I cannot say," he writes, "that women are capable of those excellencies by which men can oblige the world; and therefore a female friend in some cases is not so good a councellor as a wise man, and cannot so well defend my honour, nor dispose of reliefs and assistances if she be under the power of another." Taylor writes, here, in a practical vein; knowing full well women's limited power in seventeenth-century society, he continues, "A man is the best friend in trouble, but a woman may be equal to him in the days of joy." And then Taylor's tone becomes wittily patronizing as he concludes that section of his essay and moves on to its next topic. "I hope you will pardon me," he writes, "that I am a little gone from my undertaking: I went aside to wait upon the women and to do countenance to their tender virtues; I am now returned, and if I were to do the office of a guide to uninstructed friends, would add the particulars following." Nothing has been said in this essay about the possibility of women's being friends with one another. And the comments on women's ability to be friends to men, it turns out, was only a digression that briefly impeded the progress of Taylor's real task.

Having read Taylor's *Discourse* and not knowing of any other piece on friendship addressed to Orinda, some writers have believed that Taylor must be the Palaemon whom Orinda addresses in . . . **"To the Noble Palaemon, on His Incomparable Discourse of Friendship"**—even though the title of another of her poems identifies Sir Francis Finch as Palaemon. In 1939, however, W. G. Hiscock published his discovery, in the library of Christ Church College, Oxford, of an essay on friendship by Finch dated October 1653 and published the following March. In fact, there are at least two extant copies of Finch's essay—the second owned by Yale University. The existence of Finch's essay clarifies the question of the title of Philips's poem and provides another interesting example of her creativity. For the verse letter occasioned by Palaemon's "incomparable Discourse of friendship" responds quite directly to an essay that Orinda obviously (and rightly) sees as a genial compliment to her.

Finch's piece is prefaced by a letter to "the truly honour-

able Mrs. A.O." and signed "Your most devoted, faithfull *Palaemon*." That "Mrs. A.O." is Philips's friend Anne Owen is made clear by Palaemon's saying he wrote the piece at the command of "the onely Names I *reverence* to such a height as it takes off all colour and thoughts of dispute, *Lucasia* and *Orinda*." The title of Orinda's poem is a genial response to Palaemon's humility: "How to begin," he says, "I know not; and if I find it difficult to end, I may possibly swell this into a *bulk incongruous* for a *letter,* and I am sure aforehand it will neither have *Method* nor *Solidity* enough to deserve the appellation of a *Treatise,* or *Discourse*." Finch's essay does have *Method:* he systematically discusses "The *Nature* of [friendship], the *Causes* of it, and the *Benefit* and *Use* of it." That its *Solidity* makes it worthy of the title "discourse" Orinda affirms by calling it a one—and by claiming it is "incomparable." Indulging as surely as had Palaemon in friendly overstatement, Orinda credits him with discovering and then rescuing friendship from oblivion and wishes "for a voice which loud as thunder were" to declare Palaemon's "conquering truths." Her assertion that his written words create a "glorious Monument more permanent than a temple, statue, or a tomb" wittily aligns Finch's essay with works as significant as Shakespeare's sonnet "Not marble, nor the gilded monuments / Of princes" and asserts that Finch can be compared to poets like Shakespeare to whom Ben Jonson had written in 1623, "Thou art a Moniment, without a tombe, / And art alive still, while thy Booke doth live" ("To the Memory of My Beloved, the Author Mr. William Shakespeare: And What He Hath Left Us").

Philips's name can be associated with Finch's as early as 1651, for in that year they both contributed commendatory poems for the posthumous edition of the poems and plays of William Cartwright. John Berkenhead, too, contributed a poem to the 1651 volume, as did Philips' countryman Henry Vaughan, the musician Henry Lawes, and their mutual acquaintance Sir Edward Dering. All but Vaughan also contributed pieces for the 1655 edition of Lawes's *Second Book of Ayres and Dialogues*. Two songtexts by Edmund Waller, who was to become Philips's rival in the 1660s, and one by William Cartwright appear in the 1655 volume. In his poem to Cartwright, Berkenhead asks, "Where are such Flames, such Puissance and Sway, / As thy Cratander, or Lucasia?" Cratander and Lucasia are both characters in dramas by Cartwright. Lucasia, of course, is also Philips's name for Anne Owen; and Cratander is the name she calls Berkenhead in "To Mr. J.B. the Noble Cratander, upon a Composition of His Which He Was Not Willing to Own Publickly." Indeed, one of the five songs by Berkenhead in the 1655 volume is addressed to a Lucasia. As the author of a recent book on Berkenhead points out, study of English writers of the 1650s makes it increasingly clear that "the Cavaliers were a comparatively small group of people, united by political and cultural, and, very often, by family ties, who naturally sought out each others' company during the Interregnum." "Little wonder, with such friends," that same author says two pages earlier, "that Orinda was a staunch Episcopalian by the Restoration." It may be going too far to call Philips a "staunch Episcopalian" in 1660, but it is true that by the time the monarchy was restored to England she had left her Presbyterian childhood far enough behind that she could celebrate the coronation of Charles II with enthusiastic phrases and that her last poem, dated July 10, 1664, should be addressed to the archbishop of Canterbury. A number of Philips's poems, some written during the Interregnum, some after the Restoration, show her royalist sympathies. Thanks to the collection of her letters published in 1705 and reissued (with the addition of one letter) in 1729, we know that some of her poems were written under the direct encouragement of her friend "Poliarchus," Sir Charles Cotterell, Master of Ceremonies in the court of Charles II. On May 3, 1662, Philips sent Cotterell verses which she proposes he edit and return so she may "send the Duchess [of Gloucester] another Copy, in obedience to the Command she was pleas'd to lay upon me, that I should let her see all my Trifles of this nature." And then Orinda adds with obvious pleasure, "I have been told, that when her Highness saw my Elegy on the queen of Bohemia, she graciously said, it surpriz'd her." On June 4, 1662, Philips thanks Cotterell for his account of the queen's arrival in Portsmouth—an account that she would turn into her **"To the Queen's Majesty on Her Arrival at Portsmouth, May 14, 1662."** And in November of 1663, she sends **"To the Queen's Majesty, on Her Late Sickness and Recovery"** in response to his account of the queen's recovery from an illness that had seemed to be fatal.

A month later, on December 24, Philips responds to a letter in which Cotterell has told her of his showing that poem to the royal family: "now give me leave," she says, "to quarrel with you heartily, for presenting the Copy of Verses to the Queen, and that too without making any Alteration in them, contrary to the Request I made you, when at the same time you knew very well that Mr. Waller had employ'd his Muse on the same subject." Ironically, she imagines that "Mr. Waller has, it may be, contributed not a little to encourage me in this Vanity, by writing on the same Subject the worst Verses that ever fell from his Pen. . . . But sure he, who is so civil to the Ladies [Waller was well known for not being civil] had heard that I design'd such an Address, and contenting himself with having got so much the Advantage of me in *Pompey,* was willing to yield me this Mate at Chess, and to write ill on purpose to keep me in Countenance." Nonetheless, Philips admits, she is "not . . . so mortify'd to this World as to be insensible of the infinite Honour their Majesty's have done me in receiving so very graciously that worthless Tribute from the humblest of their Subjects."

The story to which Philips refers when she writes of Waller's "having got so much the Advantage of me in *Pompey*" is also told in the letters. In 1662, having accompanied the newly remarried Lucasia to Dublin, Philips became acquainted with the earl of Orrery who, she reports to Cotterell in a letter of August 20, encouraged her to complete a translation of Corneille's *Pompey.* In October she wrote to Cotterell of having sent him a copy of her work "which I fear will not be deem'd worthy to breathe in a place where so many of the greatest Wits

have so long clubb'd for another of the same Play," and in December she expresses concern that "the other Translation, done by so many eminent Hands, will . . . appear first, and throw this [her *Pompey*] into everlasting Obscurity." In January 1661/1662 Philips hopes "to hear what becomes of the other Translation of *Pompey,* and what Opinion the Town and Court have of it: I have laid out several ways to get a Copy, but cannot yet procure one, except only of the first Act that was done by Mr. Waller. Sir Edward Filmore did one, Sir Charles Sedley another, and my Lord Buckhurst another; but who the fifth I cannot learn, pray inform your self as soon as you can, and let me know it." Later in the month, she writes that Lord Orrery has decided to produce her translation in Dublin and that Lord Roscommon has written a prologue and Sir Edward Dering an epilogue for it. No account of the performance survives, but we do know that it was a great success and that soon thereafter Philips's translation was printed in Dublin by John Crooke and performed in London. In a letter of April 15, 1663, we learn that Henry Herringman had written to Philips "to give him leave to reprint it at London" and that she commissioned her brother-in-law Hector Philips "to treat with him about it." But before the end of the year Crooke had reprinted Philips's play in London, and in 1664 Herringman printed the other translation, announcing on its title page that it had been "Translated out of French by Certain Persons of Honour." Pleased by her success with *Pompey,* Philips began a translation of Corneille's *Horace.* She reached act 4, scene 6, before her sudden death in 1664. Completed by John Denham, the play was performed at court in 1668 and at the Theatre Royal the following year.

Given her obvious interest in the production and subsequent publication of *Pompey,* one might expect Philips to have been eager to see her poems in print. That, however, seems not to have been the case, for after a quarto volume of seventy-five of her poems was printed by Richard Marriott in January 1663/1664, letters from Philips to Cotterell and to Lady Dorothy Temple express her dismay. In fact, on January 29, Orinda addressed two letters to Cotterell: one in which she agreed with his proposal that the best response to the publication might be "to hasten to London and vindicate my self by publishing a true Copy." "Mean while," she wrote, "I have sent you inclos'd my true Thoughts on that Occasion in Prose, and have mix'd nothing else with it, to the end that you may; if you please, shew it to any body that suspects my Ignorance and Innocence of that false Edition of my Verses; and I believe it will make a greater Impression on them, that if it were written in Rhyme: Besides, I am yet in too great a Passion to solicite the Muses, and think I have at this time more reason to rail at them than court them; only that they are very innocent of all I write, and I can blame nothing but my own Folly and Idleness for having expos'd me to this Unhappiness; but of this no more till I hear from you again." Philips did indeed go to London in 1664, but she contracted smallpox and died in June of that year—without issuing an authorized edition of her work.

In 1667, however, a folio edition of 116 poems, 5 verse

translations, and Philips's **Pompey** and her **Horace** was published by Henry Herringman. The preface to the volume is unsigned, but students of Philips have assumed it to have been written by Cotterell, because it includes a transcription of the letter Philips had written for him to let others read. In that public document Philips maintains that she now finds herself "that unfortunate person that cannot so much as think in private, that must have my imaginatinos rifled and exposed to play the Mountebanks, and dance upon the Ropes to entertain all the rabble; to undergo all the raillery of the Wits, and all the severity of the Wise, and to be the sport of some that can, and some that cannot read a Verse." Her principal concern seems to derive from a sense of having lost control of her work. "The truth is," she writes, "I have an incorrigible inclination to that folly of riming, and intending the effects of that humour, only for my own amusement in a retir'd life; I did not so much resist it as a wiser woman would have done; but some of my dearest friends having found my Ballads, (for they deserve no better name) they made me so much believe they did not dislike them, that I was betray'd to permit some Copies for their divertisement; but this, with so little concern for them, that I have lost most of the originals, and that I suppose to be the cause of my present misfortune." In addition to the understandably disturbing fact of having poems she had written for a limited audience circulating for the amusement and criticism of all England, Philips is (again understandably) concerned that the 1664 volume contains errors—the poems, she has heard, are "abominably transcrib'd," and that it includes poems "that are not mine." The poet is also conscious of having inadvertently invaded the privacy of some of her friends and relatives. As she says, there are "worthy persons that had the ill luck of my converse, and so their Names expos'd in this impression without their leave [and] few things in the power of Fortune could have given me so great a torment as this most afflictive accident." There are those who have taken Philips's statements as the pretty complaints of a lady falling victim to the error of one who protests too much. It is more likely, I should think, that Philips means what she says: she did not choose to publish a collection of her verse. Moreover, had she anticipated a volume of her work, she would have wanted control over which poems would appear—and in what form.

It is of course true that a seventeenth-century woman writer would have particular reason to dread making herself public in such a way; indeed, in the letter published in 1667, Philips says that a "wiser woman" would have refrained from making herself a possible object of scandalous talk. According to the ethic of Philips's age, *any* talk about a woman is by definition scandalous, and we might wonder that Philips would have agreed to enter the public arena by permitting the production and publication of **Pompey**—and of course, to a lesser extent, by allowing the publication of the poems in the volume of Cartwright's works and in Lawes's *Second Book of Ayres and Dialogues*. During the Interregnum, one J. Jones, perhaps the republican Jenkin Jones, had threatened to publish **"Upon the Double Murther of King Charles I,"** in which she expresses sympathy for the executed king and disdain for

Engraving by William Faithhorne from the Vander Gucht portrait bust of Katherine Philips.

the Welsh republican Vavasor Powell's "Libellous Copy of Rimes" against Charles I. Exactly how severe the repercussions against James Philips would have been is difficult to say; but we do know that in a verse letter written to her husband after Jones's threat Philips argued that it would be no more fair to blame him for her work than it is to blame Eve for Adam's fall. Philips of course well knew that in the seventeenth century it was common wisdom that the fall of humanity *was* caused by Eve's seduction of Adam—and that husbands *are* responsible for their wives' actions. Surely her words here are heavily and consciously ironic.

In the mid sixties, Philips's concern is somewhat different from what it would have been in the 1650s when Jones made his threat. For Philips's poems are bold in a number of ways—in their confident claim that Orinda's friendships are as wondrous and wonderful as the romantic love Donne had celebrated earlier in the century; in her focusing on Cicily Lloyd, rather than on her new husband, both in her epithalamion and then in his epitaph; in her most "cavalier" verses, the poems in which she chides Regina Collier for her cruelty to her suitor and then chides the suitor for allowing himself to be victimized by her;

and in the clever lines in which she mocks not only a lovesick youth but his lady who thinks she is the sun itself. In conception and execution, much of Katherine Philips's work is quite remarkable. Had it been less remarkable, less irreverent about seventeenth-century mores and less personal in its being written to and for individuals whom she cared about, Philips might have been more willing to present it to all of England. As it was, Philips' choice had been to circulate her poems within a restricted circle of friends. Having written for Lucasia and Palaemon, for Rosania and Silvander, and for the king and his family, Philips could only have been startled to think of herself being read by the likes of Samuel Pepys.

Elaine Hobby (essay date 1988)

SOURCE: "Romantic Love—Poetry," in *Virtue of Necessity: English Women's Writing, 1649-88*, 1988. Reprint by The University of Michigan Press, 1989, pp. 128-42.

[*In the following excerpt, Hobby analyzes Philips's public persona as a function of the constraints placed upon women writers in the seventeenth century and examines Philips's reworking of the conventions of courtly love poetry in her poems celebrating female friendship.*]

Katherine Philips, 'the Matchless Orinda', the author of a book of poetry, two play translations and some published correspondence, has long been perceived as a model lady poetess, dabbling in versification in a rural Welsh backwater, confining her attention solely to the proper feminine concerns of love and friendship. It is generally agreed that she was modestly alarmed at the prospect of any public attention for her work. By briefly examining her *Letters from Orinda to Poliarchus* (her correspondence with the Master of Ceremonies at Charles II's court, Charles Cotterell) and the images of constraint and retirement found in her poetry, I will suggest that the 'Orinda' persona who appears in modern critical accounts is a creation made necessary by the particular circumstances confronting this seventeenth-century woman poet. Through 'Orinda', Philips gained acceptance in her own period, and has a reputation that has survived into our own. I will then go on to examine more closely Philips's best-known work, her poetry celebrating women's friendship, and how it engages with the conventions of the courtly love tradition to produce an image of female solidarity (and, perhaps, of lesbian love) that could be sustained within the tight constraints of marriage.

Since her death in 1664, Katherine Philips's writings have never dropped entirely from the public eye. There is a certain significant irony in this, since she is remembered as the archetypal blushing poetess, who shied away from any public recognition of her works. She never desired publication, and was horrified when a surreptitious edition of her poetry appeared in 1664, the story goes. The figure who appears in her poetry and her *Letters to Poliarchus* is 'the matchless Orinda', the self-effacing lady poet who thoroughly understands that she

is inferior to the male sex. As such, she has been allowed a tiny and peripheral place in the literary canon. In part, the image of Orinda that has come down to us is dependent on the belief that her writing was really a secret and private affair, her poems passed around only in manuscript form to a few trusted friends. This is an anachronistic distortion of the method of 'publication' that she used: circulation of manuscripts was the normal way to make writing public before the widespread use of printed books, and was a method that continued to be popular in court circles throughout the reign of Charles II, at least. Such a description also fails to consider the fact that, as a royalist poet married to a leading parliamentarian, she had positive reasons for avoiding too much public attention during the 1650s, which was when she did most of her writing. Bearing these factors in mind, we find that the evidence suggests that she was actually a well-known writer.

As early as 1651, when she was nineteen years old, Philips's writing was sufficiently well thought of for a poem of hers to be prefaced to the posthumous edition of William Cartwright's plays, and a poem written in praise of Philips by Henry Vaughan was included by him in his collected works in that same year. She must already have been circulating some of her writings. In 1655, a song of hers was printed by Henry Lawes in his *Second Book of Ayres*. Although Katherine Philips's identity was not revealed in Cartwright's text, both Vaughan and Lawes printed her full name. It is clear that her achievements were well known, at least among prestigious royalists. She addressed poems to Francis Finch, John Birkenhead and Sir Edward Dering, and the fact that they were also involved with the publication of Cartwright's plays and the *Second Book of Ayres* could indicate that her acquaintance with them dated from 1651 or even earlier. It is not surprising to find that by 1657, when Jeremy Taylor answered in print Katherine Philips's enquiries about the nature of friendship, his complimentary address to her should have heralded her as someone known to be 'so eminent in friendships'. And after the Restoration, she sought out recognition from aristocracy and royalty, sending poems to the Duchess of York, the Archbishop of Canterbury, and to King Charles himself, and dedicating her translation *Pompey* to the Countess of Cork. Her skill as a translator had a sufficiently high public profile for John Davies to praise her by name when dedicating his 1659 translation of *Cléopatre* to her in 1662, and for Lord Roscommon to claim to have undertaken a translation from French purely in compliment to her. Any assessment of Philips's writing that suggests that she was of a shy and retiring spirit, forced into the public eye in 1664 against her strongest inclinations, is choosing to ignore her involvement with this then more traditional form of public recognition. The 'public' she was interested in reaching was the coterie of court and leading poets, not the wider world.

The assertion that Philips did not wish her works published is based on the letters she wrote to Sir Charles Cotterell between 1661 and 1664, published in 1705 after his death as *Letters from Orinda to Poliarchus*. The correspondence deals in part with her preparing a translation of Corneille's *Pompée*, and seeing it onto the stage and through the press in 1663, and her attempts to suppress an unofficial edition of her poems in 1664. The established judgement of these letters' significance is that they demonstrate Katherine Philips's blushing horror at the thought of her works and name becoming public property. They are used to reconfirm the image of her that has come down to us from posterity. The fact that **Pompey** was published without identifying the translator is seen as proof that Philips held a suitably modest assessment of her own abilities. What is not noticed is that the prologue to the play, written by the Earl of Roscommon, and its epilogue by Sir Edward Dering, both identify the author as female. Given Philips's reputation as a translator, and the fact that she was living in Dublin during the play's much-acclaimed performance there, it is likely that her identity was common knowledge, at least among those whose opinion of her she valued. In the copy that she sent to the Countess of Roscommon she certainly made no attempt to hide her name, and the stationer Henry Herringman knew whom to contact when he wanted to bring out a London edition of **Pompey**.

The **Letters to Poliarchus** have been read as if they give straight-forward access to 'the real Katherine Philips', her personal doubts and fears, and that they can therefore tell us the 'truth' about her identity as an author. Such a reading discounts the fact that all writing is governed by specific conventions, and that in the case of a mid seventeenth-century woman these conventions included the requirement that she apologise for daring to take up the pen, and find ways to excuse her boldness. We would therefore expect to find, as we do, that the **Letters,** written to her important political ally and sponsor Charles Cotterell, are preoccupied largely with finding ways to justify writing as a 'female' activity. The **Letters to Poliarchus** indeed provide material for a fascinating study of the process through which 'Orinda' is constructed and refined throughout the correspondence, making it possible for Philips to write and gain wide public acclaim while disavowing any desire to do either. Orinda can also humbly request advice and guidance from Cotterell with her translation of *Pompée,* whilst blithely continuing to follow her own judgement when he disagrees with her.

There are many examples of this in the **Letters**. The most extended is found in a long-drawn-out discussion of one word in her translation: the word 'effort', at that time seen as a French term not an English one. Cotterell counselled her to omit the word, and the subsequent correspondence continued for some months. There was every reason for Philips to take Cotterell's advice and change her text. He was, after all, a recognised linguist and translator. However, although she finally asks Cotterell to change the text himself, the word appears unaltered in the published version. Part of the justification for her consistency, which might have been seen as unfeminine stubbornness, is that she is leaving the word alone at the insistence of another eminent man and writer, Roger Boyle. She tells Cotterell,

I would fain have made use of your correction, and

thrown away 'effort', but my Lord Orrery would absolutely have it continued; and so it is, to please his humour, though against my will and judgement too.

There is no need to assert her own opinion against Cotterell's. She can cite another male authority instead.

Translation, as defined by Philips in the **Letters,** was a suitably modest undertaking for a woman, the task being to produce a text that kept well within the specific and narrow bounds of the original. This restrictive format could then be used, however, to vindicate her own expertise, and to criticise judiciously the work of others. This is demonstrated strikingly in Philips's detailed analysis of 'what chiefly disgusts me' in a rival translation of *Pompée* undertaken by a group of men. Her comments become so scathing as to strain the limits of self-effacement, and her letter criticising the men's translation ends with the necessary retraction: 'I really think the worst of their lines equal to the best in my translation.'

One of the 'wits' involved with the male *Pompey* translation was William Waller, and he and Philips became rivals again shortly after the publication of her play when both sent poems to the king celebrating the queen's recovery from a serious illness. Charles, apparently, far preferred Philips's poem, a victory not without its costs, since as Philips knew, Waller could be a dangerous enemy to a woman poet. In her letter to Cotterell delighting in the king's praise of her poem, she recalls Waller's public insult to her contemporary, Margaret Cavendish the Duchess of Newcastle.

> Mr Waller has, it may be, contributed not a little to encourage me in this vanity, by writing on the same subject the worst verses that ever fell from his pen. I could be an outrageous critic upon them, if I were not restrained, by other considerations . . . I remember I have been told that he once said, he would have given all his own poems to have been the author of that which my Lady Newcastle writ of a stag: and that being taxed for this insincerity by one of his friends, he answered, that he could do no less in gallantry than be willing to save the reputation of a lady, and keep her from the disgrace of having written anything so ill. Some such repartee I expect he would make on this occasion.

The best-known of Philips's **Letters to Poliarchus** is the one most centrally concerned in producing the image of the poetess that has come down to us. It appears as part of the preface to the posthumous, 1667 edition of the poems, having been written after Richard Marriot had brought out a surreptitious edition from an imperfect manuscript early in 1664. Cotterell hurried to suppress the edition, and Philips's letter refers to this with gratitude. The letter has been read, as the editor of the posthumous edition no doubt designed, as clear proof of the poet's diffidence. In the 1667 edition of **Poems** the letter lies framed by his assertion of her bashfulness and self-effacement, directing the reader how to interpret it. Much is made of her description of herself as someone 'who never writ any line in my life with an intention to have it printed'. Printing Philips might have been nervous about: it could in no way be construed as a feminine act. She was not, however, averse to having her writings published in a more traditional way. This letter, which finally was printed, was not the 'private' communication it is presented as, but was designed for a public audience. In a covering note, which is not included in the 1667 preface, Philips urges Cotterell to 'show it to anybody that suspects my ignorance and innocence of that false edition of my verses.' The greatest danger, indeed, was that she might be suspected of the same kind of scheming that many male authors practised: of having arranged the appearance of this incomplete edition as a way of testing how it would be received, before fully committing herself to it in public. Those with long memories would know, after all, that some of her works had already appeared in print, in 1651 and 1657. If her identity as the acclaimed translator of **Pompey** was also known or suspected despite its anonymous publication, such a consequence was likely, and would do irreparable damage to her carefully sculpted public image.

It is worth noting that Katherine Philips had other objections to the surreptitious printing of her poems, which she also mentions in the published letter. Since she died before the 1667 **Poems** appeared, it is impossible to know how she would have re-edited the text, but it is clear that there are many variants between the editions. The most obvious change is that the 1667 edition contains some fifty-five poems, and the two play translations, not found in the earlier text. Many of the omitted poems were written in Ireland, which suggests that the manuscript used by Marriot was an early one, perhaps an early draft, since some verses also scan badly. In addition, the absence of some lines and inclusion of nonsense verses suggests that it was illegible in places. The reader of the surreptitious edition would get an impression of the poet's skill far inferior to that provided by the amended text.

So what kind of poetry was written under the name of Orinda? Katherine Philips was a royalist and High Church Anglican whose immediate family included many important parliamentarians and Independents. Having been born and educated in London, the daughter of a wealthy merchant, John Fowler, she had moved to Wales to join her mother by the time she was fifteen. Her father had died, and her mother was remarried to a prominent parliamentarian, Richard Phillipps. In August 1648, at the age of sixteen, Katherine was wadded to a fifty-four-year-old relative of Sir Richard's, James Philips of Tregibby and The Priory, Cardigan. James was called to the Barebones Parliament in 1653, and served locally as a commissioner for sequestration.

During the 1650s, the political differences between husband and wife seem to have become known, and Colonel John Jones apparently attempted to discredit James Philips by publishing some writing of Katherine's. Her poem addressed to her husband on this occasion is fascinating. While expressing remorse and admitting she had undermined her spouse's reputation, she in no way promises to alter her opinions. Indeed, the poem is in fact a statement

of her separateness from him, and a call for her to be assessed as an independent being, not as a part of her husband. At one level, there is nothing indecorous in these lines, as she is asking that her husband be considered free from her guilt. At another, she asserts that from the first, from the time of Adam and Eve, women and men should be regarded as autonomous, each responsible for their own actions. Even her enemy's wife, she maintains, need not be treated as though she agreed with Colonel Jones's opinions (Jones's wife indeed differed from him politically). Under a legal system where the husband and wife were assumed to be one person, the husband, this is a quietly radical statement.

> *To Antenor, on a Paper of mine which J.J.*
> *threatens to publish to prejudice him.*
> Must then my crimes become thy scandal too?
> Why, sure the devil hath not much to do.
> The weakness of the other charge is clear,
> When such a trifle must bring up the rear.
> But this is mad design, for who before
> Lost his repute upon another's score?
> My love and life I must confess are thine,
> But not my errors, they are only mine.
> And if my faults must be for thine allowed,
> It will be hard to dissipate the cloud:
> For Eve's rebellion did not Adam blast,
> Until himself forbidden fruit did taste.
> 'Tis possible this magazine of hell
> (Whose name would turn a verse into a spell,
> Whose mischief is congenial to his life)
> May yet enjoy an honourable wife.
> Nor let his ill be reckoned as her blame,
> Nor yet my follies blast Antenor's name.

This poem to Antenor was not the only one Philips wrote on this occasion. She also addressed one to her close friend, Anne Owen, 'the truly competent judge of honour, Lucasia', asking her to believe in her untainted honesty. This appeal to Lucasia's support is unsurprising. Philips's solution to finding herself surrounded by those whose political and religious beliefs contrasted sharply with her own had been to establish her Society of Friendship. The friends admitted to this select band were all royalists, and their correspondence and companionship must have done much to offset her isolation. Naming herself 'Orinda', she gave similar pastoral-sounding names to her friends, and addressed poetry to them which uses the language and imagery of courtly love conventions. Some of the Society's members have not been identified, but their number seems to have included Anne Owen (Lucasia), Mary Aubrey (Rosania), Francis Finch (Palaemon) the brother of the philosopher Anne Conway, John Birkenhead (Cratander), Sir Edward Dering (Silvander), Lady Mary Cavendish (Policrite), James Philips (Antenor) and Sir Charles Cotterell (Poliarchus). (Those added after the Restoration, when the Society of Friendship presumably changed somewhat, included Anne Boyle—Valeria—and Elizabeth Boyle—Celimena—relatives of the diarist and autobiographer Mary Rich.)

In general, the extant poems that she addresses to these

friends make few overt comments on state politics. (Almost all her explicitly royalist poems were written after the Restoration.) During the 1650s, addressing issues of state politics was far more common among women sectaries than their more conservative sisters. Affairs of government were supposed to be beyond the realm of proper female concern, and in her lines deploring the execution of Charles I Philips found it necessary to assert that, in general, women should leave public issues well alone. Only with the whole world order upset by the 'murder' of the monarch, she asserts in **'Upon the Double Murther'**, could the unfeminine act of commenting on affairs of state be excused.

Philips's poems on solitude, retreat and the country life, however, also reveal her royalism. Maren-Sofie Røstvig has shown [in *The Happy Man*, 1962] how the defeated royalists in their rural exiles took up classical images of contentment and virtue in the countryside. The controlled and balanced happy man, contemptuous of the fervent battles of the political world, was their answer to the Puritan image of the committed Christian warrior. Henry Vaughan and Abraham Cowley both wrote in this vein, and both men were known by Philips. The writings of Saint-Amant were also incorporated into this tradition in England, and Philips was familiar with his work, translating his 'La Solitude'.

Her poetry shows many signs of commitment to this philosophy of retirement, wherein submission and acceptance of limitations are heralded as positive and necessary virtues. Many of the poems which in other respects are widely different from one another are characterised by advocacy of contentment or confinement or restriction, and the assertion that true freedom and choice can be found through this. (These include, for instance, **'A Sea-Voyage from Tenby to Bristol'**, **'To my dear Sister Mrs C.P. on her Marriage'**, **'Happiness'** and **'Upon the Graving of her Name Upon a Tree in Barnelmes Walk'**.) These sentiments would have been deeply familiar to Philips's royalist contemporaries.

There is, however, a radical difference between Katherine Philips's situation and that of her fellow-poets. They were men, and their retirement from affairs of state was a recent change in circumstances, and in some cases self-imposed. Philips was a woman. Her residence in the countryside was due to the fact that she had to be with her husband. She had no choice in the matter, and no hope that this apparently natural state of affairs had ever been different, or could ever be changed. This is most poignantly apparent in the many poems written on parting from one of her close women friends. Orinda recommends a stoical acceptance of separation, claiming that only through such a resignation of will can true self-determination be found. The way in which the parting is experienced, she argues, is something that friends do have control over, and this is where their freedom lies. This gives a very special inflexion to the traditional courtly love motif of separation from a beloved. Only by giving this particular extension to notions of self-control and contentment under compulsion could Katherine Philips find a

way to maintain some autonomy, living as she was surrounded by her political enemies, people who had legal control over her existence. In **'Parting with Lucasia: A Song'** this theme is especially interesting because Philips suggests that through resignation women can become 'conquerors at home'. The double meaning in this phrase—it can be read both as 'conquerors of ourselves' and 'conquerors in the house'—shows how, for this woman poet, a measure of self-determination could be achieved. If women can control their grief at being separated from one another, she argues, any task is slight by comparison, and can be performed. The poem ends

> Nay then to meet we may conclude,
> And all obstructions overthrow,
> Since we our passion have subdued,
> Which is the strongest thing I know.

About half of Philips's poems are concerned with love and friendship. The great majority of these address the theme of intimacy between women, exploring its delights and problems. This anatomisation and celebration of female closeness is made in direct defiance of the accepted view of women. Although from its earliest days the language and themes of courtly love poetry had been used to glorify friendships between men, women's relationships with one another had never been treated to such serious consideration in print. Orinda's response to this nonsense is unequivocal.

> If souls no sexes have, for men t'exclude
> Women from friendship's vast capacity,
> Is a design injurious or rude,
> Only maintained by partial tyranny.
> Love is allowed to us and innocence,
> And noblest friendships do proceed from thence.

It is entirely characteristic that she should argue that qualities normally attributed to women are the very features that most fit them to move outside the conventional requirements.

The courtly love conventions are an important and frequent feature of Orinda's poetry. In some poems, she adopts wholesale the stance and language of the frustrated lover, wooing a merciless mistress. An integral part of this tradition was the poem renouncing love, and Philips's works include a wholly conventional example of this kind, **'Against Love'**. Addressed to Cupid, the poem includes stock references to lovers burning and raving and the 'killing frown' of the mistress who provides only diseased joys. What is unusual is for such a renunciation of love to be made by a woman. By writing from the position usually reserved for the male lover, the woman poet gains access for herself to the power and freedom that were usually enjoyed only by men in love relationships. Traditionally, this poetry, while lamenting the control wielded by the mistress over her lover through her 'killing frown', nonetheless gives voice only to the lover, who explores and revels in his (usual) 'subjugation' to the mistress's gentle charms. The price that Philips pays for this access to male speech in at least some of her poems is that she is limited thereby to the kinds of relationship allowed by this essentially male tradition. Some of the poems addressed to Mary Aubrey include a great deal of this conventional language, and are restricted to situations taken directly from the courtly love tradition. Since one of the fundamental assumptions of this poetry is that the beloved object is an exception to the general run of womankind and infinitely superior to other females, this can have the result of deprecating other women. Such is the case in **'Rosania shadowed whilst Mrs Mary Aubrey'**.

> Unlike those gallants which take far less care
> To have their souls, than make their bodies fair;
> Who (sick with too much leisure) time do pass
> With these two books, pride and a looking-glass:
> Plot to surprise men's hearts, their power to try,
> And call that love, which is mere vanity.
> But she, although the greatest murtherer,
> (For every glance commits a massacre)
> Yet glories not that slaves her power confess,
> But wishes that her monarchy were less.

Many of Orinda's poems, however, rigorously rework these conventions, giving them new meanings that express a particularly female perspective. In **'A Dialogue betwixt Lucasia, and Rosania, Imitating that of Gentle Thyrsis'**, Lucasia is a shepherdess and Rosania the wooer who tries to persuade her to leave the flocks and go away with her. Lucasia explains that she would much rather leave with Rosania, given the choice, but must stay where her duty lies. The poem presents loving friendship between women as the part of their lives that is characterised by choice and freedom, but prevented from blossoming by the duties of female existence: 'Lucasia: Such are thy charms, I'd dwell within thine arms / Could I my station choose.' The poem, like many in the tradition from which it springs, looks forward to a final union after death.

> Rosania: Then whilst we live, this joy let's take
>   and give,
> Since death us soon will sever.
> Lucasia: But I trust, when crumbled into dust,
> We shall meet and love for ever.

These lines echo another dialogue, **'A Dialogue of Absence 'Twixt Lucasia and Orinda, set by Mr Henry Lawes'**, which ends in a chorus anticipating a future where women will no longer be forced to part by other concerns: 'But we shall come where no rude hand shall sever, / And there we'll meet and part no more for ever'.

Some of the most interesting of Katherine Philips's poems take particular images from the received patterns and rework them. In doing so, Philips both shows that relationships between women are different from those between men and women, and implicitly criticises her male poetic sources. A notable instance of this is her reworking of John Donne's famous 'compasses' image in his 'A Valediction: forbidding Mourning'.

> If they be two, they are two so

> As stiff twin compasses are two,
> Thy soul the fixed foot, makes no show
> To move, but doth, if th'other do.

> And though it in the centre sit,
> Yet when the other far doth roam,
> It leans, and hearkens after it,
>   And grows erect, as that comes home.

> Such wilt thou be to me, who must
>   Like th'other foot, obliquely run;
> Thy firmness makes my circle just,
>   And makes me end, where I begun.

This has been praised as the expression of all-transcendent love. A quick and simple feminist reading, however, would point out how the compasses actually celebrate woman's immobility and fixity in 'the centre', and man's freedom to move and still be loved. It is the male 'foot' that roams: the female can only lean in sympathy with it. Katherine Philips's response to these lines seems to involve the same analysis. **'To my dearest Lucasia'** celebrates love between women. It describes an emblem that could be used to represent the relationship, and uses an image of compasses to describe equal freedom and equal control.

> The compasses that stand above
> Express this great immortal love:
> For friends, like them, can prove this true,
> They are, and yet they are not, two.

> And in their posture is expressed
> Friendship's exalted interest:
> Each follows where the other leans,
> And what each does, this other means.

> And as when one foot does stand fast,
> And t'other circles seeks to cast,
> The steady part does regulate
> And make the wanderer's motion straight:

> So friends are only two in this,
> T'reclaim each other when they miss:
> For whosoe'er will grossly fall,
> Can never be a friend at all.

Katherine Philips's poetry provides a developing definition of female friendship. One of its most fundamental characteristics—and one which by implication must exclude men from this greatest intimacy with women—is that women friends are so alike that they mirror one another. This idea appears explicitly, for instance, in **'A Friend'**.

> Thick waters show no images of things;
> Friends are each other's mirrors, and should be
> Clearer than crystal or the mountain springs,
> And free from clouds, design or flattery,
> For vulgar souls no part of friendship share:
> Poets and friends are born to what they are.

A comparison with a poem addressed to her husband, **'To**

my dearest Antenor, on his Parting', illustrates how very different this essentially equal relationship is from marriage. Philips-as-wife is her husband's image, passively reflecting him. There is no equal mirroring here.

> And besides this thou shalt in me survey
> Thyself reflected while thou art away . . .
> So in my breast thy picture drawn shall be.
> My guide, life, object, friend, and destiny:
> And none shall know, though they employ their
>   wit,
> Which is the right Antenor, thou, or it.

Even though she calls Antenor her friend, the relationship defined here is quite different from the one she celebrates with women who are close to her.

Orinda's most extended exposition of the argument that women's friendship has a special and superior quality is the poem **'To my Excellent Lucasia, on our Friendship.'** This moves from the opening 'I' of the first stanzas to the exultant, united 'we' of the final one. The friendship, through mirroring and recognition of similarity, gives joy and peace that is found in no other relationship—certainly not in the 'bridegroom's mirth'.

> I did not live until this time
> Crowned my felicity,
> When I could say without a crime,
> I am not thine, but thee.
>
> This carcase breathed, and walked, and slept,
> So that the world believed
> There was a soul the motions kept:
> But they were all deceived.
>
> For as a watch by art is wound
> To motion, such was mine:
> But never had Orinda found
> A soul till she found thine;
>
> Which now inspires, cures and supplies,
> And guides my darkened breast:
> For thou art all that I can prize,
> My joy, my life, my rest.
>
> No bridegroom's nor crown-conqueror's mirth
> To mine compared can be:
> They have but pieces of this earth,
> I've all the world in thee.
>
> Then let our flames still light and shine,
> And no false fear control,
> As innocent as our design,
> Immortal as our soul.

Marriage contains elements of duty and compulsion. Struggling to resolve the conflict between wifely submission and passionate friendship, and accept that she cannot change her situation, Katherine Philips asks her dearest friend to be patient with her imperfections. She reflects on the divine essence of friendship, claiming that in its origins the relationship is superhuman. True friendship should consist of harmony and freedom, and she laments that, in her human imperfection, she is seeking to control and possess her friend. In a world where so many imperative demands were made of them, women seek, she says, to allow perfect liberty to one another in this most perfect of relationships. Having described the state she aspires to, she sighs,

> But what's all this to me, who live to be
> Disprover of my own morality?
> And he that knew my unimproved soul,
> Would say I meant all friendship to control
> But bodies move in time, and so must minds;
> And though th'attempt no easy progress finds,
> Yet quit me not, lest I should desperate grow,
> And to such friendship add some patience now.

The range and themes of Katherine Philips's poetry show the ways in which a woman whose religious and political allegiances placed her outside the sisterhood of the radical sects could negotiate a space of autonomy for herself and her female friends. She was a tremendously important reference point for contemporary High Church women. Her translation *Pompey* was greeted with overwhelming joy by an Irishwoman who signs herself simply 'Philo-Philippa'. The terms of this praise illustrate the fact that Orinda's spirited defence of women's friendship was not lost on the women of her times.

> Let the male poets their male Phoebus choose,
> Thee I invoke, Orinda, for my muse;
> He could but force a branch, Daphne her tree
> Most freely offers to her sex and thee,
> And says to verse, so unconstrained as yours,
> Her laurel freely comes, your fame secures:
> And men no longer shall with ravished bays
> Crown their forced poems by as forced a praise.
>   Thou glory of our sex, envy of men,
> Who are both pleased and vexed with thy bright
>   pen:
> Its lustre doth entice their eyes to gaze,
> But men's sore eyes cannot endure its rays;
> It dazzles and surprises so with light,
> To find a noon where they expected night:
> A woman translate *Pompey!* which the famed
> Corneille with such art and labour framed!
> To whose close version the wits club their sense,
> And a new lay poetic SMEC springs thence!
> Yes, that bold work a woman dares translate,
> Not to provoke, nor yet to fear men's hate.
> Nature doth find that she hath erred too long,
> And now resolves to recompense that wrong.
> Phoebus to Cynthia must his beams resign,
> The rule of day and wit's now feminine.
>   That sex, which heretofore was not allowed
> To understand more than a beast, or crowd;
> Of which problems were made, whether or no
> Women had souls; but to be damned, if so;
> Whose highest contemplation could not pass,
> In men's esteem, no higher than the glass;

And all the painful labours of their brain,
Was only how to dress and entertain:
Or, if they ventured to speak sense, the wise
Made that, and speaking ox, like prodigies.
From these thy more than masculine pen hath
    reared
Our sex; first to be praised, next to be feared.
And by the same pen forced, men now confess,
To keep their greatness, was to make us less . . .
Ask me not then, why jealous men debar
Our sex from books in peace, from arms in war;
It is because our parts will soon demand
Tribunals for our persons, and command.
      Shall it be our reproach, that we are weak,
And cannot fight, nor as the schoolmen speak?
Even men themselves are neither strong not
    wise,
If limbs and parts they do not exercise.
      Trained up to arms, we Amazons have been,
And Spartan virgins strong as Spartan men:
Breed women but as men, and they are these;
Whilst Sybarite men are women by their ease . . .
      That noble friendship brought thee to our
    coast,
We thank Lucasia, and thy courage boast.
Death in each wave could not Orinda fright,
Fearless she acts that friendship she did write:
Which manly virtue to their sex confined,
Thou rescuest to confirm our softer mind;
For there's required (to do that virtue right)
Courage, as much in friendship as in fight.
The dangers we despise, doth this truth prove,
Though boldly we not fight, we boldly love . . .
Thus, as the sun, you in your course shine on,
Unmoved with all our admiration:
      Flying above the praise you shun, we see
      Wit is still higher by humility.

Philips's poetry was also an essential reference point for women poets who followed her. Many of those writing later in the seventeenth century, including Aphra Behn, Anne Killigrew, Ephelia and Jane Barker, refer to her as their guide. In the post-Restoration world, where acceptable female behaviour was again being narrowly defined, she was an important example that it was possible for a woman to be praised for her writing, as long as she was sufficiently modest in her claims. While helping to open a pathway into print for women, therefore, she also staked it out as a strait and narrow way. Through the critics' appraisals, 'the matchless Orinda' became the scourge of such followers as the 'incomparable Astrea', Aphra Behn.

Harriette Andreadis (essay date 1989)

SOURCE: "The Sapphic-Platonics of Katherine Philips, 1632-1664," in *Signs: A Journal of Women in Culture and Society,* Vol. 15, No. 1, Autumn, 1989, pp. 34-60.

[*In the following essay, Andreadis argues that the poems that constitute "Philips's real contribution to English letters" reveal expressions of homoerotic love "and have*

a place beside the long classical tradition of the literature of male love." Extensive footnotes have been deleted in this reprinting, and can be found in the original essay cited above.]

Katherine Philips, known as "The Matchless Orinda," was the first English female poet to achieve a considerable reputation in her own time. She was extravagantly praised, indeed lionized, by her male contemporaries: Abraham Cowley, the earl of Roscommon (Wentworth Dillon), Jeremy Taylor, John Dryden, and much later, even John Keats referred to her as the female standard of excellence toward which all other women ought to aspire. Andrew Marvell may have been influenced by some of her poetic language and Henry Lawes set a number of her poems to music. Laudatory references continue into the eighteenth century, particularly by women writers who, responding to male commentary on the proper female poetic persona, saw in Philips a model of success to be emulated. In her own time, despite her bourgeois background, her great charm and cultivated feminine modesty gained her admittance, after the Restoration, to the best literary and court circles. The nobility, some of whom were literati, welcomed her presence and felt graced by her genius.

The acclaim of her contemporaries has by now, however, worn very thin: she is seen as having "wielded persistently her all too fluent pen," as having had friendships with women "florid in their intensity," or as having "wanted to take on, by cajolery rather than by assault, an artistic role generally reserved for men." In works of literary history, she is listed generally as a minor Caroline poet who kept alive the traditions of the cavalier poets through the years of the Interregnum. For the most part, she has been studied as a member of male literary circles, for the sake of her distinguished literary connections or for her literary influence. In works dealing with women writers, she is most often described as a minor example of *préciosité* or, conversely, as an example of "the growing influence of neoclassicism," and, thus, she is given a perfunctory place in anthologies. At best, she is regarded as the poetic model for a later, female "school of Orinda" or as an influence on certain male poets. At worst, she is accused of versifying gossip. Even such a recent, and sympathetic, critic as Lillian Faderman does little to alter the view of Philips's 1931 biographer, Philip Webster Souers, that "her greatest claim to attention is that she was among the few who kept alive in the teeth of Puritan scorn and persecution the old court tradition, and handed it over ready for use to the returning wits of the Restoration."

Her production was small since her life was short. It includes a single volume of poems written for her friends, published in an unauthorized edition in the year of her death, and then reedited, expanded, and reprinted posthumously by her friend and literary executor, Sir Charles Cotterell; a translation of Pierre Corneille's *Pompey* and a partial translation of *Horace* completed by Robert Denham; a volume of her letters to Sir Charles, dubbed Poliarchus in *précieuse* fashion, edited and published posthumously by him in 1705; and four letters to "Berenice," an anonymous noblewoman, published with the *Familiar*

Letters of John Wilmot, earl of Rochester, in 1697. In all, five editions of her work appeared after the unauthorized 1664 folio edition of her *Poems,* the final one being the 1710 octavo of her *Works*. Her reputation during the seventeenth century was based on a privately circulated group of poems addressed to her intimate women friends and chronicling in some detail her emotional relations with them. Her other poems were mostly occasional or moral-philosophical exercises in what we now consider the traditional, and rather undistinguished, mode of the seventeenth century; elegies, encomia, political poems, verse essays on friendship, poems of personal retirement and contemplation, and a journey poem are characteristic. Philips's real contribution to English letters, however, though acknowledged by her contemporaries and by the women writers who succeeded her, has been either over-looked or trivialized by students of English literature since the late eighteenth century. It is remarkable that, as a woman, she could have achieved the considerable reputation she enjoyed among her contemporaries. That her contribution was acknowledged by them is without question. We must then ask what that contribution really was and why it was so highly esteemed.

An examination of the materials of Philips's life and work reveals a woman whose emotional focus was primarily on other women and whose passionate involvement with them guided much of her life and inspired her most esteemed poems. Philips's original and unusual use of literary conventions accounts for the acclaim she was accorded by her contemporaries, and her unique manipulation of the conventions of male poetic discourse, of the argumentative texture of John Donne, of the language of the cavaliers, and of the tradition of platonic love became the means by which she expressed in an acceptable form her homoerotic impulses. Philips's contribution was to appropriate the cavalier conventions of platonic heterosexual love, with their originally platonic and male homoerotic feeling, and to use those conventions and that discourse to describe her relations with women. While homoerotic male poetic discourse in the form of male friendship poetry was by no means unusual during the Renaissance and early seventeenth century, Philips's is the earliest printed example of a woman's poetic expression in English of intense same-sex love between women.

The poems that brought her acclaim, and that still are considered her best work, established a "society of friendship" that used, superficially, the rhetorical conventions of the cavalier poets and of French *préciosité*. In her attempt to create an ideal "society" of friends, in her use of pastoral nicknames for her friends, in her reading of Italian and French romances, and in her attraction to the idea of platonic love, Philips embraced current literary and courtly fashions. To see her work merely as an example of *préciosité* does not, however, do justice to the breadth of interests and influences her work reveals. Moreover, though she uses its superficial trappings, her poetic language does not fit the *précieux* prescription for periphrasis, tortured hyperbole, or excessive imagery. Instead, a disinterested reading of Philips's works suggests a more judicious view than has been offered by literary critics:

like others among her contemporaries, most notably Abraham Cowley, one of her admirers, she moved in the course of her literary career—as did a number of male poets—from the private, contemplative, metaphysical mode of her poetry during the Interregnum to a more public neo-classical style during the Restoration. Her earlier work is composed for the most part of the platonic love lyrics to her female friends that initially won her praise; but later, during and after the Restoration, she turned to longer poems on public themes and to the translations of Corneille. Certainly Philips was ambitious and certainly her work was embedded in the traditions, culture, and fashions of her time. Yet it would be more accurate to say that the forms she used coincided with and appropriated literary fashion rather than that she wrote as she did only because she courted poetic success. The evidence of her life indicates that the forms she used also fulfilled important personal needs.

Philips used the conventions of her time to express in her own poetry a desexualized—though passionate and eroticized—version of platonic love in the love of same-sex friendship. In Philips's poetry friendship between women is infused with the passionate intensity and rhetoric of heterosexual love as it was understood by seventeenth-century male poets. The major influence on her friendship poems may not be the cavaliers or *préciosité* but John Donne and the metaphysical conceit, for the intensity of her friendship feelings is expressed through echoes of Donne's early seduction poems.

An attentive reading of her poems addressed to Rosania, her pseudo-classical name for her school friend Mary Aubrey, and to Lucasia, Anne Owen, who replaced Rosania in Philips's affections after Rosania's marriage, reveals the intensity of Philips's emotions and her unique use of convention as a vehicle to express her intimate feelings. **"To my Lucasia, in defence of declared friendship,"** one of Philips's best-known and most admired poems, is typical of her work: she appropriates both the sentiments of metaphysical platonism and the form of male poetic discourse to shape her passion. Stanzas 8 through 12 are especially clear in illustrating her rhetorical strategies:

> Although we know we love, yet while our soule
>   Is thus imprison'd by the flesh we wear,
> There's no way left that bondage to controule,
>   But to convey transactions through the Eare.
>
> Nay, though we read our passions in the Ey,
>   It will obleige and please to tell them too:
> Such joys as these by motion multiply,
>   Were't but to find that our souls told us true.
>
> Beleive not then, that being now secure
>   Of either's heart, we have no more to doe:
> The Sphaeres themselves by motion do endure,
>   And they move on by Circulation too.
>
> And as a River, when it once has pay'd
>   The tribute which it to the Ocean ow's,

Stops not, but turns, and having curl'd and
   play'd
   On its own waves, the shore it overflows:

So the Soul's motion does not end in bliss,
   But on her self she scatters and dilates,
And on the Object doubles, till by this
   She finds new Joys, which that reflux creates.

Evident here is the manner in which Philips channels a passionate emotional intensity into acceptable metaphysical images and argument. The platonic union of souls, the eyes as vehicles of the spirit, and the analogy between the movement of human hearts and the circulation of the spheres were stocks in trade of the male discourse of metaphysical passion for women. Here, a female poetic voice uses these conventional images to address her intensely beloved female friend. In her invocation to her beloved to speak their love, she adds to these images the particularly female and subliminally erotic analogy of a river's flow, which captures the rhythms of female sexual passion.

Philips's use of Donne, rather than the lesser cavalier poets, for her model is apparent not only in the echoes of his particular images but more precisely in the force of her argumentative stance, in the relentless development of thought through the manipulation of conceit. **"To My excellent Lucasia, on our Friendship,"** again echoes Donne:

I did not live untill this time
   Crown'd my felicity,
When I could say without a crime,
   I am not Thine, but Thee.
This Carkasse breath'd, and walk'd, and slept,
   So that the world believ'd
There was a soule the motions kept;
   But they were all deceiv'd.
For as a watch by art is wound
   To motion, such was mine:
But never had Orinda found
   A Soule till she found thine;
Which now inspires, cures and supply's,
   And guides my darken'd brest:
For thou art all that I can prize,
   My Joy, my Life, my rest.
Nor Bridegroomes nor crown'd conqu'rour's
   mirth
   To mine compar'd can be:
They have but pieces of this Earth,
   I've all the world in thee.
Then let our flame still light and shine,
   (And no bold feare controule)
As innocent as our design,
   Immortall as our Soule.

Except that these poems are addressed to a woman, they could have been written by a man to his (female) lover. Clearly, the discourse used by Philips is both male and heterosexual. And, in this poem, it reaches beyond the merely conventional image of "two friends 'mingling

souls'" in the extravagant intensity of the conceit of the watch.

"To My excellent Lucasia" adumbrates Donne's imagery as well as the intellectual form of his metaphysical poetic. The union of lover and beloved, the soullessness of the "Carkasse" before discovery of the beloved, the negative comparison of the condition of the beloved to more worldly joys ("Nor Bridegroomes nor crown'd conqu'rour's mirth") to enforce the sacredness of the relation, and the insistence on the "innocent . . . design" of their love, are also integral to Donne's love poetry.

"Friendship in Emblem, or the Seale, to my dearest Lucasia" perhaps most obviously draws on Donne in its use of the compass image from *A Valediction: Forbidding Mourning*. Here again, the crucial element that distinguishes her source as Donne rather than the cavaliers is the sustained force of her intellectual argument in developing the conceit. Stanzas 6 through 13 illustrate this clearly:

The compasses that stand above
Express this great immortall Love;
For friends, like them, can prove this true,
They are, and yet they are not, two.

And in their posture is express'd
Friendship's exalted interest:
Each follows where the other Leanes,
And what each does, the other meanes.

And as when one foot does stand fast,
And t'other circles seeks to cast,
The steddy part does regulate
And make the wanderer's motion streight:

So friends are onely Two in this,
T'reclaime each other when they misse:
For whosoe're will grossely fall,
Can never be a friend at all.

And as that usefull instrument
For even lines was ever meant;
So friendship from good = angells springs,
To teach the world heroique things.

As these are found out in design
To rule and measure every line;
So friendship governs actions best,
Prescribing Law to all the rest.

And as in nature nothing's set
So Just as lines and numbers mett;
So compasses for these being made,
Doe friendship's harmony perswade.

And like to them, so friends may own
Extension, not division:
Their points, like bodys, separate;
But head, like soules, knows no such fate.

The conceit of the compass, an emblem of constancy, as used by Donne to explore the meaning of his approaching absence from his wife is here present as subtext in Philips's poem. Her use of the same conceit—and it is her most obvious echo of Donne—to describe her passionate friendship for Lucasia is played against the silent text of Donne's poem, which reverberates through it and underlines its platonism as well as its eroticism.

These are only a few examples of Philips's appropriation of Donne and the metaphysical mode of argument. A reading of all of her poems to her female intimates yields others. It is the intense, passionate quality of her feeling, the emotional tension inherent in the argument of the conceit, that distinguishes these poems from her other poetic efforts. She appropriated a male heterosexual poetic discourse, with its platonism, its implicit eroticism, and its impassioned argument via conceits, rather than the less intense, more distant tone of the male friendship poetry of her contemporaries because this discourse suited the deeply intimate nature of the emotions she sought to chart and for which she sought a vehicle.

Though Philips's expression may bear some resemblance to the platonism of some earlier male friendship literature, such as Michel de Montaigne's essay, "On Friendship," she probably was not acquainted with earlier renaissance models. Most of her reading was limited to her near contemporaries, whose friendship poetry employs, instead of a renaissance platonic ideal, the Horatian ideal of civilized life and the Aristotelian notion of friendship as the bond of the state to defend against the "cavalier winter." These contemporaries are more concerned to place friendship in the context of retirement to nature as an escape from the turmoil of the times than to explore the ecstasies and trials of intimacy through the language of platonism. Theirs is a generalized approach to the subject that is in contrast to Philips's impassioned use of direct address and metaphysical conceit.

That these poems were not merely clever exercises in courtly convention by a woman seeking reputation and patronage (as were, perhaps, some of her Restoration poems addressed to royalty) is confirmed by the circumstances of Philips's life and letters. Born Katherine Fowler, the daughter of a prosperous London cloth merchant, in 1648 she married James Philips, whom she was to call Antenor in keeping with her penchant for devising pseudo-classical names for her intimates. She was sixteen; he was fifty-four. Clearly, in this marriage, probably arranged by her mother, she loved and respected her husband as she was socially and morally bound to do. Yet, clearly also, there was much distance between them in addition to their respective ages. He lived on the remote west coast of Wales at Cardigan Priory, while she was attached to the intellectual and social amenities of London and took, or created, every opportunity to return to literary and court circles. Her politics were also different from his: she remained a royalist like her friends and courtly admirers, while he and her family were parliamentarians. This publicly recognized political difference at least once threatened his political career.

Antenor's absence never evoked the same metaphysical anguish in Philips as did that of Rosania or Lucasia; she wrote of him most often in terms of her "duty." A telling contrast is that between the frequently unrestrained emotion in her many poems lamenting the absence of a female friend and the relative coolness of her single poem to Antenor upon his absence and of her descriptions of her "duty" to Sir Charles. On her imminent departure from Ireland and Lucasia, she wrote: "I have now no longer any pretence of Business to detain me, and a Storm must not keep me from ANTENOR and my Duty, lest I raise a greater within. But oh! that there were no Tempests but those of the Sea for me to suffer in parting with my dear LUCASIA!" This passage succinctly points to a contrast that is apparent throughout Philips's writing; it juxtaposes, on the one hand, her feelings of obligation to her husband and, on the other, her passion for Lucasia. As to the rest of her immediate family, her son is mentioned only twice in her writings, both times in poems, one of them a particularly dull one about his death at the age of forty-one days; her daughter, who survived her, is never mentioned at all, either in her poems or in her letters.

Having endured, in 1652, Mary Aubrey's (Rosania's) defection from their friendship into marriage, Philips wrote at least one poem on her "apostasy," and quickly replaced her with Anne Owen (Lucasia). In 1662, Anne Owen, too, married, and Orinda despised Owen's new husband, Marcus Trevor, which added to her grief. Nevertheless, she accompanied the newlyweds to Dublin and stayed on for a year, ostensibly to conduct her husband's business (he was now in some financial and political distress owing to his parliamentarianism) and to finish *Pompey* and see it played at the Theatre Royal, Smock Alley, Dublin. She had also begun to develop aristocratic connections: the earl of Orrery offered her encouragement, she frequented the duke of Ormonde's salon, and she was becoming friendly with the countess of Cork.

She described her feelings to Sir Charles, whose suit to Anne Owen she had unsuccessfully encouraged, presumably in an attempt to keep Anne within her immediate social circle and in close geographical proximity: "I am much surpriz'd that she, who is so well-bred, and her Conversation every way so agreeable, can be so happy with him as she seems to be: for indeed she is nothing but Joy, and never so well pleas'd as in his Company; which makes me conclude, that she is either extremely chang'd, or has more of the dissembling Cunning of our Sex than I thought she had." She wrote repeatedly to Sir Charles of her grief and disappointment, not unmixed with bitterness, at the loss of her bond with Anne Owen. Her grief in these letters is as acute as the passion in the earlier poems is intense. From Dublin on July 30, 1662, she wrote:

> I now see by Experience that one may love too much, and offend more by a too fond Sincerity, than by a careless Indifferency, provided it be but handsomly varnish'd over with civil Respect. I find too there are few Friendships in the World Marriage-proof. . . . We may generally conclude the Marriage of a Friend to be the Funeral of a Friendship. . . . Sometimes I think it is because we are in truth more ill-natur'd than we really take our selves to be; and more forgetful of past Offices of Friendship, when they are superseded by

others of a fresher Date, which carrying with them the Plausibility of more Duty and Religion in the Knot that ties them, we persuade our selves will excuse us if the Heat and Zeal of our former Friendships decline and wear off into Lukewarmness and Indifferency: whereas there is indeed a certain secret Meanness in our Souls, which mercenarily inclines our Affections to those with whom we must necessarily be oblig'd for the most part to converse, and from whom we expect the chiefest outward Conveniencies. And thus we are apt to flatter our selves that we are constant and unchang'd in our Friendship, tho' we insensibly fall into Coldness and Estrangement.

Her letters to Sir Charles during this period are full of disappointed idealism, of highmindedness scorned. The scale of values Philips holds dear in these letters, and in her poetry, places the noble feelings of disinterested friendship far above the frequently compromised and banal motives of marriage and duty. Nevertheless, her notion of disinterested friendship is driven by intensely passionate commitment to the individual woman in question, so that when, in the usual course of things, her friend marries, she responds as a lover scorned. The feelings she expressed in her letters to Sir Charles concerning the defection of Anne Owen reverberate from the poems she had written ten years earlier on the apostasy of Mary Aubrey:

> Lovely apostate! what was my offence?
> Or am I punish'd for obedience?
>
> . . . . .
>
> For our twin-spirits did so long agree,
> You must undoe your self to ruine me.
>
> . . . . .
>
> . . . Glorious Friendship, whence your honour
>   springs,
> Ly's gasping in the croud of common things;
>
> . . . . .
>
> For from my passion your last rigours grew,
> And you kill me, because I worshipp'd you.

Thus Philips reveals a covert, innate rebelliousness; she protests with chagrin Mary Aubrey's and Anne Owen's replacement of such romantic sentiments with ones more suitable to the exigencies of social and economic life.

Her last known passionate attachment seems to have been to "Berenice," whom she knew at least since 1658, when she wrote begging her to come to Cardigan and console her for Lucasia's absence. Philips evidently continued her correspondence with "Berenice" after returning from Ireland to her home at Cardigan Priory in Wales because the last letter is dated from there a month before her death in London. The tone of the four letters to "Berenice" is a combination of nearly fawning supplication to a social superior and breathless passion, the two inextricably fused:

All that I can tell you of my Desires to see your Ladiship will be repetition, for I had with as much earnestness as I was capable of, Begg'd it then, and yet have so much of the Beggar in me, that I must redouble that importunity now, and tell you, That I Gasp for you with an impatience that is not to be imagin'd by any Soul wound up to a less concern in Friendship then yours is, and therefore I cannot hope to make others sensible of my vast desires to enjoy you, but I can safely appeal to your own Illustrious Heart, where I am sure of a Court of Equity to relieve me in all the Complaints and Suplications my Friendship can put up.

It is impossible to disentangle the elements of Orinda's passion for "Berenice," complicated as their relationship was by social inequality and as our understanding of it is by an absence of any information external to the four letters. However, Philips's tone in these letters seems desperate beyond any conventional courtliness; she yearns to fill the void left by Lucasia's absence and, later, rejection.

After her success with *Pompey* on the Dublin stage, Philips found it difficult to remain immured at the Priory and finally was able to solicit an invitation from her friends, and her husband's permission, to return to London, where she died of smallpox at the age of thirty-one. A major change had taken place in Philips's life when the loss of her friendship with Lucasia was coincidentally accompanied by the foundering fortunes of her husband, which she attempted to remedy through her well-placed friends. That she had not succeeded in doing so when she died suggests that the double blow she had suffered left her depressed (as the anxiety in her last letters to Sir Charles shows), weakened, and vulnerable to disease.

After the defection of Lucasia, she wrote no more of the poetry that had won her such high praise; instead, she poured her energies into using her court connections to gain patronage for herself and, probably unsuccessfully, preferment for Antenor. She wrote numerous poems to royalty, self-consciously addressing public themes, and increasingly fewer intimate poems to particular friends. Also, she vied with the male wits for recognition of her theatrical translations, which are still considered the best English versions of Corneille. Philips's immersion in Corneille and the adoption of a more neoclassical style may have been politically expedient in the early 1660s, but at this time in Philips's life, Corneille's subordination of personal passion to duty and patriotism in the long speeches that she translated also must have appealed to her own need to control her disordered emotions.

Her royalist sympathies throughout the Interregnum no doubt now enabled her to advance the interests of her parliamentarian husband as well as her own literary ambitions. Souers comments on the notable change in her poems and in her stance toward literary circles: "The Cult of Friendship may be said to have died with the marriage of its inspirer. All that remained was the empty shell, which, in this case, means the names, so that when, later, poems addressed to new friends appear, it must be kept in mind that the old fire is gone." Souers's judgment is borne out by the poems Philips addressed to the Boyle sisters, daughters of the countess of Cork, a patron during Philips's stay in Ireland. Though she attempts to continue, or perhaps to revivify, the traditions of her cult of friendship by bestowing pastoral nicknames, Philips reveals in her later poems the conflict and ambivalence with which more intimate approaches to her social superiors are fraught. She confronts this problem of friendship with aristocratic women directly in **"To Celimena"** (1662-64), addressed to Lady Elizabeth Boyle; the eight-line poem concludes: "Wouldst thou depose thy Saint into thy Friend? / Equality in friendship is requir'd, / Which here were criminal to be desir'd". Her earlier passionate avowals of friendship have become reverential.

The poems that made Orinda famous depended for their creation on Philips's personal affections. When the person to whom those affections were directed removed herself permanently from the sphere of Philips's life, the well of her unique creativity dried up, though she continued to refine her craft. Orinda may have sought other muses, such as "Berenice," but if indeed she did, the quest seems to have been fruitless, or even half-hearted, given the severity of her loss and the need to turn her attention to the matter of her husband's (and her own) livelihood and economic well-being. That Philips was aware of the change in her interests and, indeed, undertook it deliberately, is poignantly obvious in her comments to Sir Charles from Dublin on May 2, 1663: "I have us'd all the Arts that Diversion could afford me, to divide and cure a Passion that has met with so ill a Return, and am not a little oblig'd to my Lady CORK'S Family for assisting me in that Intention: But oh! I begin already to dread what will become of me, when I return home, and am restor'd to the sight of those Places, where I have been so often blest with the Enjoyment of a Conversation in which I took so much Delight, and is now for ever ravish'd from me." She needed, however, to keep up appearances and, as Souers notes, did so in a perfunctory manner—conscious that impassioned friendship was incompatible with social advancement—by continuing to write poems to women that retained the form, if not the passion, of her earlier work.

An examination of Philips's life in conjunction with the poems that initially won her praise thus reveals that her friendship poems to Rosania and Lucasia were an unvarnished expression of her love channeled into the already acceptable, even fashionable, mode of male heterosexual poetic discourse. Once we understand that the feelings in these poems are "real" and that they are confirmed by her letters to Sir Charles and "Berenice," it becomes clear that they are also homoerotic and have a place beside the long classical tradition of the literature of male love.

Male friendship literature written in English before the 1580s, according to Stephen Latt, relies heavily on classical precedent and "tends to be unoriginal or, at best, a rehearsal of old commonplaces—without originality, without personal application." In the 1580s, however, male

friendship literature exhibited a movement "towards a more emotional expression of friendship," which appropriated the civilities of Horatian and Aristotelian ideals and which continued into the seventeenth century with the poems of Thomas Carew, James Howell, Richard Lovelace, and Henry Vaughan (who was also part of Orinda's circle of male literary friends). In describing the friendship literature of the years 1620-64, Latt notes a "gradual movement away from the public level of experience. With the pressures of the times, writers turned increasingly inward. The turmoil of dissension, the chaos of rebellion, and the catastrophe of regicide freed loyal monarchists to desert the public scene." Philip's poetry paralleled rather than emulated this male tradition, and it is distinguished from the poetry of her contemporaries in its personal intensity and in the metaphysical platonism she used to address female friendship.

Philips's awareness of the connection between her own feelings and the male tradition of friendship is manifest to some extent in her attempts to assure herself of the acceptability of her attachments by writing to Jeremy Taylor concerning the religious nature and limits of friendship. His answer to her, in "A Discourse of the Nature, Offices, and Measures, of Friendship, with Rules of Conducting It, in a Letter to the Most Ingenious and Excellent Mrs. Katharine Philips" (1657), cannot have been very satisfactory; his view is, as one might expect, rigorously androcentric in its treatment of women as friends only in relation to men: "A man is the best friend in trouble, but a woman may be equal to him in the days of joy: a woman can as well increase our comforts, but cannot so well lessen our sorrows." Reaffirming traditional views, Taylor denied women's capacity for true friendship with men and ignored friendship between women. Perhaps more satisfying to Philips was the opening of Francis Finch's treatise *Friendship* (1653-54), dedicated to Anne Owen, "D. Noble *Lucasia-Orinda*," in which Finch publicly acknowledged and graciously complimented the relationship so important to Philips.

She turned her fluent control of contemporary seventeenth-century male poetic idiom to her own particular uses, thus placing herself uniquely in a tradition whose only previous female exponent was the classical poet Sappho. That this daring manipulation of convention caused admiration for her work is quite apparent in the commendatory poems that introduce her poetry and in other contemporary comments that repeatedly praise her likeness to Sappho. Philips seems to have been the first English poet to have evoked that classical comparison. Until it later became a more conventional literary compliment, toward the end of the century, this comparison seems to have been somewhat problematic because of Sappho's presumed sexual transgressions. Sappho's work was recognized as the highest literary achievement in lyric poetry by a woman; although her subject matter was regarded as questionable by contemporary writers, it was echoed by Orinda. Sir Charles wrote in the preface to the 1667 edition of Philips's poems which he edited: "We might well have call'd her the English *Sappho*, she of all the female Poets of former Ages, being for her Verses and her Vertues both, the most highly to be valued. . . . And for her Vertues, they as much surpass'd those of *Sappho* as the Theological do the Moral, (wherein yet *Orinda* was not her inferior)." One Philo-Philippa, the anonymous author of one of the commendatory poems for this volume, writes:

> Ingage us unto Books, *Sappho* comes forth,
> Though not of *Hesiod's* age, of *Hesiod's* worth,
> If Souls no Sexes have, as 'tis confest,
> 'Tis not the he or she makes Poems best:
> Nor can men call these Verses Feminine,
> Be the sense vigorous and Masculine.

Abraham Cowley, the author of *Davideis,* which contains at least one homoerotic passage, describes Philips's poetic art:

> 'Tis solid, and 'tis manly all,
> Or rather, 'tis Angelical:
>   For, as in Angels, we
>   Do in thy verses see
> Both improv'd Sexes eminently meet;
> They are than Man more strong, and
>   more than Woman sweet.

Moreover, in the following he is at pains to describe Philips as a more virtuous Sappho, to distinguish her exemplary modesty and purity from the manners of her model:

> They talk of *Sappho,* but, alas! the shame
> Ill Manners soil the lustre of her fame.
> Orinda's inward Vertue is so bright,
> That, like a Lantern's fair enclosed light,
> It through the Paper shines where she doth write.
> Honour and Friendship, and the gen'rous scorn
>   Of things for which we were not born,
> (Things that can only by a fond disease,
> Like that of Girles our vicious stomacks please)
> Are the instructive subjects of her Pen.

Praise of Philips as the standard of female excellence and poetic skill continued through the seventeenth century and into the mid-eighteenth century. Her name is linked with those of Aphra Behn ("Astrea") and Sappho in many of the commendatory poems and epistles written by women that preface plays written by women for the London stage of Queen Anne; she became a model to be emulated and replaced. In 1696, Mary Pix addressed Delariviere Manley on "her Tragedy call'd *The Royal Mischief* ": "Like *Sappho* Charming, like *Afra* Eloquent, / Like Chast *Orinda* sweetly Innocent."

Nancy Cotton and Jane Spencer point out that Orinda and Astrea became the two ideals in a female tradition to which later women writers aspired. Yet Sappho continued to provide the second figure in a separate dyad and continued to be linked with Orinda when the issue was female poetic genius, so that the comparison of Orinda to Sappho became increasingly conventional. The persistence of this association is apparent in these lines from John Duncombe's 1754 *The Feminiad: A Poem,* which echo very clearly the sentiments expressed by Cowley almost

a century earlier:

> Nor need we now from our own Britain rove
> In search of genius, to the Lesbian grove,
> Tho' Sappho there her tuneful lyre has strung,
> And amorous griefs in sweetest accents sung,
> Since her, in Charles's days, amidst a train
> Of shameless bards, licentious and profane,
> The chaste ORINDA rose; with purer light,
> Like modest Cynthia, beaming thro' the night:
> Fair Friendship's lustre, undisguis'd by art,
> Glows in her lines, and animates her heart;
> Friendship, that jewel, which, tho' all confess
> Its peerless value, yet how few possess!

Though, after this, Orinda's reputation seems to have declined, its particular characteristics were reclaimed intact when, in 1905, George Saintsbury wittily introduced her poetry as "her Sapphic-Platonics."

These comparisons with Sappho are important because they refer to the great classical female model of lyric poetry, but they are also important because they explicitly indicate a similarity of subject matter. Even though Cowley and Duncombe acknowledged this similarity of subject matter, they were also, paradoxically, eager to dispel the erotic content implicit in the comparison by emphasizing Orinda's purity. What we would now call the bisexuality of Sappho, to which Cowley and Duncombe allude, was also part of Sappho's legend for Orinda's contemporaries. Sappho's reputation for erotic involvement with women, as well as with men, was conveyed to the seventeenth century primarily by certain passages in Ovid's *Heroides* ("No more the *Lesbian* Dames my passion move, / Once the dear Objects of my guilty Love"), by Horace's references to *mascula Sappho* and to Sappho's complaints about the young women of Lesbos, and by the ode preserved by Longinus from Sappho to a female lover. Donne himself wrote the explicitly sexual poem *Sapho to Philaenis:*

> And betweene us all sweetnesse may be had;
>   All, all that *Nature* yields, or *Art* can adde.
> My two lips, eyes, thighs, differ from they two,
>   But so, as thine from one another doe;
> And, oh, no more; the likenesse being such,
>   Why should they not alike in all parts touch?
> Hand to strange hand, lippe to lippe none denies;
>   Why should they brest to brest, or thighs to
>   thighs?

Bayle's *Dictionary* (1710), though somewhat later, also is unequivocal in its view of Sappho's erotic activities ("her Amorous Passion extended even to the Persons of her own Sex" and "*Sappho* always passed for a Famous *Tribas,*" or tribade), citing evidence that had been available since the Renaissance. We can infer, then, that the writers of contemporary encomia to Orinda understood the nature of allusions to Sappho but were eager to dispel any suggestions of unnatural sexuality. They wished to pay her the high compliment of comparing her to the great classical lyricist not only for her poetical voice, but also for the uniqueness of her subject matter, at the same time that they wished to reconfirm her platonic purity. The encomium was appropriate and perhaps inevitable, if somewhat uncomfortable. Eventually, as it became more conventional, the comparison to Sappho was often used to suggest only literary accomplishment until Saintsbury recalled its original significance. Since Saintsbury, readers of Philips's work have simply neglected or trivialized her contribution to the history of poetic ideas: the recovery of the homoeroticism of platonic ideals in their classical lesbian context.

It was Philips's use of the conventions of male poetic discourse, particularly of the metaphysicals and the cavaliers, and her echoing of the literary tradition of male friendship, that sanctioned her unconventional subject and, in fact, made it a novelty in her time. Because her discourse was familiar her subject was acceptable. Without those conventions, and without Philips's modest and feminine demeanor in court circles, and her exemplary personal virtuousness, it seems unlikely that her poetry would have been praised as it was. Her literary example initiated a tradition of published female friendship poetry whose parameters have yet to be defined. The men who were her contemporaries accepted her ideals of passionate friendship between women and were persuaded to regard them as ennobling because they could recognize in their rhetorical strategies a parallel or analogue to their own ideals of heterosexual platonism and male friendship. That her poetic model was Donne, with his unquestioned heterosexual eroticism, only emphasizes the erotic nature of her passions.

The aspect of homosexuality that is pertinent to this study of Philips is a curious one. The poetic use of classical pastoral and friendship conventions in renaissance and seventeenth-century literature tells us next to nothing about the actual circumstances of people's lives. But in the case of Katherine Philips, external sources in the form of her letters and her highly unusual use of convention indicate that the feelings expressed in her poems were more than conventional or courtly gestures. This fact calls for an inquiry into the history of homosexuality in England.

We still know very little about the private erotic relations between women in seventeenth-century England. Lesbianism was not named as a reason for prosecuting women and few private documents have come to light that describe lesbian activities during this period. The appearance, not too long after Philips's death, of literary documents by English women that portray explicitly lesbian activity—such as the duchess of Newcastle's play, *The Convent of Pleasure* (1668), Anne Killigrew's poem of erotic flagellation, *Upon a Little Lady Under the Discipline of an Excellent Person* (1686), Aphra Behn's poem *To the Fair Clarinda, Who Made Love to Me, Imagined More than Woman* (1688), and Delariviere Manley's "new Cabal" in her roman à clef *The New Atlantis* (1709)—surely is suggestive. However, these documents stand in an at best ambiguous relation to actual intimate behaviors, although they do indicate clearly that lesbian activities, as the twentieth century understands them, had been

publicly articulated by women by the late 1660s and were regarded as scandalous infractions of the laws of nature. In English cultural mythology, tribades were classed with pederasts, and probably papists, but we do not today have more reliable documentation of their activities, as we do about those of male homosexuals.

Alan Bray has described the change that took place in male homosexual life in England from 1650 to 1700. According to his research into court records and other documents, it was at this time that "molly" houses came into being as a symptom of the increasing isolation of practicing homosexuals from traditional institutions. This was the beginning of what we now call a homosexual subculture that evidently did not include women, though the appearance of explicitly lesbian literary subject matter might suggest the existence of an analogous female subculture. Of course, as Bray suggests, at the point of emergence of a subculture, the dominant culture officially recognizes that such individuals do indeed exist. Bray hypothesizes, on substantial grounds, that before 1650, and before the official acknowledgment of the existence of homosexual behavior, "the conflict between individual desire and the values of society as a whole" was resolved by a "cleavage . . . between an individual's behaviour and his awareness of its significance." Before 1650, that is, there was a happy collusion between the individual and his culture to deny the meaning of his behavior, since pederasts were considered monstrous. Thus, male homosexuality was an unacknowledged, but hardly unusual, activity in such respectable institutions as the public schools and the apprentice/master system.

What is known as lesbianism to the twentieth century, though frequently unacknowledged or trivialized by patriarchal culture, always has existed as a sexual behavior. On the one hand, social construction theory suggests that expressions of lesbian behavior, as well as definitions of and discourse about that behavior, vary from one era and culture to another since sexuality is a cultural construct rather than—as has been traditionally claimed in patriarchal culture—determined by nature. On the other hand, current debates about an appropriate definition of lesbianism do not offer a satisfactory method for describing the erotic experience or self-understanding of women before the mid-eighteenth century, when acknowledgment of female sexuality was severely inhibited in English-speaking and other Western cultures. Bonnie Zimmerman summarizes the attempts by Adrienne Rich, Catharine Stimpson, and Lillian Faderman to establish a useful working definition of lesbianism for historical scholarship; she cautions us to avoid the "simplistic universalism" that results when we use the overly inclusive "lesbian continuum" described by Rich as well as the exclusive genital sexuality of Stimpson's definition, which may have political utility in the twentieth century but inhibits attempts to reconstruct female eroticism in earlier historical periods. Faderman's work mediates between the definitions proposed by Rich and Stimpson by using the convention of "romantic friendship" to describe the erotic relations between women from the mid-eighteenth century to the historical moment in the twentieth century in which lesbians became self-identified. Yet Faderman's use of this convention, like Carroll Smith-Rosenberg's reading of the language of nineteenth-century American women, leaves much to be desired: it evades the nature of the erotic content of much of the earlier literature she discusses and defuses its implications.

To describe the historical consistency of erotic experience in women's friendship as it is expressed in literature and to identify a particular stance toward other women that partakes of the erotic, whether or not it is known actually to have culminated in behavior now described as sexual, we must revise Faderman's definition so that it includes the earlier periods and initiates a revaluation of earlier texts that does not diminish their possible erotic dimensions. We can begin this redefinition of lesbianism by reassessing earlier texts and reconsidering erotic relations between women as a possible dimension of their meaning. Because "the historical relationship between genital sexuality and lesbianism remains unclear," we must first accept certain earlier *texts* as lesbian insofar as they convey an experience of passion or eroticism that expresses "libidinous energy," whether or not it includes verifiable experience of genital activity. Second, we must be willing to acknowledge that the *writers* of these texts may have been lesbians insofar as they apparently understood and were able to convey "libidinous energy" between women, even though it may never be possible to know the precise nature of their sexual activities. In this way, we do justice to the nature of their contents and perhaps also avoid a Procrustean distortion of the writer's experiences.

Although the validity of social construction theory is difficult to dispute, it is also true that earlier women writers lived and wrote in a patriarchal culture that obscured the nature of female sexuality and the contexts of women's writing. That being so, it is necessary to put aside heterosexist bias and homophobia in order to recognize the ways in which lesbian eroticism does indeed manifest itself.

Given this perspective, there is no question that Katherine Philips produced lesbian texts, that is, texts that are amenable to lesbian reading in the twentieth century. It is also possible that contemporary female readers of Philips's texts found in them those qualities that we call lesbian echoed in their own feelings and that this contributed to their popularity and influential status among later women writers, as well as to their neglect and/or disparagement by some twentieth-century female critics. Whether, and to what extent, Philips might have expressed her homoerotic feelings genitally is impossible to assess without the availability of further biographical evidence and must remain for now a moot—and perhaps irrelevant—question. However, the evidence surveyed here confirms that Philips's was indeed a lesbian experience. The passion Philips expressed in her poetry and in her letters, and the absence of its expression in other areas of her life (i.e., toward husband or children), indicates a fervor in her feelings for women that would not have been acceptable either to herself or to others *except* as given shape in conventional form. To name this experience "romantic friendship," in

conformity with the euphemizing language of the eighteenth century, would dilute the power of her poetry and deny her the full dimensions of her experience by perpetuating the trivialization of lesbianism. Therefore, we must acknowledge that her manipulations of the conventions of male poetic discourse constitute a form of lesbian writing.

We might argue, then, by analogy, that erotic behavior among respectable women was, until the last third of the nineteenth century, carried on in the same way as was male homoeroticism before 1650—that there was a "cleavage" between consciousness and behavior that allowed the individual and her society to evade naming the behavior—and that such erotic behavior was, in fact, later institutionalized and made acceptable by the convention of "female romantic friendship." The work and life of Katherine Philips furnished an example that made possible the later acceptance of eroticized friendships between women as a respectable alternative to the specter of unnatural vice. Her example may also suggest that it is appropriate to reassess, from this perspective, the language and conventions through which "romantic friendship" has been expressed and to examine the extent to which we may have misread its erotic content.

Celia A. Easton (essay date 1990)

SOURCE: "Excusing the Breach of Nature's Laws: The Discourse of Denial and Disguise in Katherine Philips' Friendship Poetry," in *Restoration: Studies in English Literary Culture, 1660-1700*, Vol. 14, No. 1, Spring, 1990, pp. 1-14.

[*In the following essay, Easton associates Philips's strategies of political disguise and sexual repression with her exploration of poetic language.*]

In his preface to the first authorized edition of Katherine Philips' *Poems,* her editor and confidant, Charles Cotterell, praises the poems that follow by attempting to situate them beyond gender, beyond history, beyond language, beyond geography, and beyond mortal existence:

> Some of them would be no disgrace to the name of any man that amongst us is most esteemed for his excellency in this kind, and there are none that may not pass with favour, when it is remembered that they fell hastily from the pen but of a Woman. We might well have call'd her the English *Sappho,* she of all the female Poets of former Ages, being for her Verses and her Vertues both, the most highly to be valued; but she has called her self ORINDA, a name that deserves to be added to the number of the Muses, and to live with honour as long as they. Were our language as generally known to the world as the Greek and Latine were anciently, or as the French is now, her Verses could not be confin'd within the narrow limits of our islands, but would spread themselves as far as the Continent has Inhabitants, or as the Seas have any shore. And for her Vertues, they as much surpass'd those of *Sappho* as the Theological do the Moral,

(wherein yet *Orinda* was not her inferiour) or as the fading immortality of an earthly Lawrel, which the justice of men cannot deny to her excellent Poetry, is transcended by that incorruptible and eternal Crown of Glory where with the Mercy of God hath undoubtedly rewarded her more eminent Piety.

This urging for transcendence typifies the neo-platonism espoused by Philips and her circle of friends; the movement toward the "eternal Crown of Glory" fittingly acknowledges Philips' recent, untimely death. The condescending "pen but of a Woman" is echoed by women and men alike in the seventeenth century. But Cotterell's introduction to the poems of "The Matchless Orinda" reveals more than sexist commonplaces and conventions of praise. The areas of transcendence Cotterell outlines are precisely those that trigger what I shall call a "discourse of denial and disguise" in Katherine Philips' poetry. Orinda's poems, in fact, insist upon their ties to gender, history, and language, although they often seem to follow the path to a superior realm Cotterell maps out both for the collection and its author. At times, Philips draws her reader beyond history while she herself is covering up her royalist politics prior to the Restoration; at other times, she appeals to a transcendent, non-physical notion of friendship while creating exclusive, affectionate bonds with other women.

I do not focus on the categories of politics and affection arbitrarily. One of the interests of this essay is the way in which the poems from one category draw upon the other for their metaphors. Philips is best known for her poems on friendship, though the first poem in the 1667 collection defends the memory of Charles I against the satirical pen of a man who would "murder" the king again, in print. The poet protests in the opening line of this poem, "I think not on the State," then proceeds to chastise Vavasor Powell for libelling the dead king. The lines in which Orinda explains why she must speak out—though it is irregular for her to do so as a woman and an apolitical person—tellingly parallel her protests against—and partial reconciliation with—the physical world in her friendship poems:

> 　　　　　　　　. . . this is a cause
> That will excuse the breach of Nature's laws.
> Silence were now a sin, nay Passion now
> Wise men themselves for Merit would allow.

"Nature's laws," a phrase that echoes the popularity of the new science of the seventeenth century, here refers to rules of decorum and propriety rather than principles of physics. A woman's "natural" condition is silence; passion most grievously violates that nature. But a "cause" can invert the natural order, transforming "whatever is" into "whatever's not."

The poetry of Mrs. Katherine Philips, the Matchless Orinda, whether political or affectionate, struggles with "nature" and its contradiction. To sort out the conflicting voices in the poetry, we might think of "Philips" as the voice of the woman whose proper place is guarded, "Orinda" as the voice of the poet for whom silence is a sin. For Orinda, the medium for violating the natural order is the language of poetry. It is Philips who needs transcendence, who dares not acknowledge a political, public, or physically affectionate life; it is Orinda who circumvents the censor, whose metaphors return the subjects of her poetry to the physical world.

These voices may overlap, and yet are separate from the biographical Katherine Philips. Katherine Fowler, age 16, married James Philips, age 54, in 1648. During the Commonwealth, while James Philips served the Cromwell government by quelling Royalist uprisings, she lived both in her husband's home in Wales and in their London lodgings. Her acquaintances in London, mostly Royalist sympathizers, included childhood friends, the poets Henry Vaughan and Abraham Cowley, and the theologian Jeremy Taylor. Philips' "Society of Friends," described in her poetry as a group of close friends, each assigned classical names and addressed with the hyperbolic conventions of friendship literature (Charles Cotterell, for example, was "Worthy Poliarchus"), may or may not have met regularly. [Philip] Souers casts doubt on the theory that Philips headed a salon for intellectuals, pointing to the infrequency of her visits to London. More likely, he asserts, the Society's "members" kept in touch through correspondence and the circulation of poems in manuscript.

In the eighteenth century, the English equivalent of the *salon* was the "Bluestocking party," a gathering run by one of several intellectual women for the purpose of drawing together men and women for "serious" (i.e., regarding art and literature) conversation. Souers argues that Philips would not have been sponsoring such parties in the seventeenth century, since the focus on friendship in her poetry (and there is very little other evidence for the "Society") is almost exclusively female. "Orinda's Society was not a salon," he asserts, "it was the official order of Friendship in the kingdom of feminine sensibility." It is possible that Professor Souers, whose 1931 biography of Philips is the only book-length study of her life and work, might startle at Lillian Faderman's observation [in *Surpassing the Love of Men,* 1981] that had Orinda "written in the twentieth century, her poetry would undoubtedly have been identified as 'lesbian'," but there is no critical dispute that Orinda desires to define her friendships in exclusively female terms. The poems make clear that whatever respect the biographical Philips received from her husband and male acquaintances, the poet, Orinda, felt compelled to defend women's friendships as, alternatively, equal to and superior to men's.

Katherine Philips consulted Jeremy Taylor in the 1650's on the nature of friendship. Taylor dedicated to her his 1657 "Discourse of the Nature, Offices and Measures of Friendship," "Written in answer to a Letter from the most ingenious and vertuous M.K.P.," i.e., Mrs. Katherine Philips. Taylor's acknowledgment of his friendship with his correspondent certifies both that Philips' friendship society was well known and that Taylor believed friendship could extend across gender—as far as the limits of gender allowed. Much of Taylor's book depends upon Cicero's *De Amicitia,* with two major exceptions in the argument. In Cicero's dialogue, Laelius insists that one never think of one's friend as "useful," and he is explicit in declaring that friendship is possible only between two good (virtuous) men. Taylor explains that he does not mean to sound "mercenary," but that he believes a sign of a worthy man is his ability to do the most good; a man who loves him will do him "all the good he can."

Taylor's other break with the classical conception of friendship, which speaks most directly to Philips' concerns, is his slight admission of women to friendship's realm. First of all, they may enter through marriage: "Marriage is the Queen of friendships, in which there is a communication of all that can be communicated by friendship: . . . being made sacred by vows and love, by bodies and souls, by interest and custome, by religion and by laws. . . ." Taylor concludes that marriage is the archetype of friendship, friendships being marriages of the soul. Even when he considers women outside marriage, he continues to view them in relation to or in comparison with men. Since Taylor's conception of friendship begins with Christian charity, he is willing to admit that women are capable of generous acts. He addresses the subject explicitly in an aside (for which he later apologizes, seeming to have lost sight of his argument):

> But by the way (Madam) you may see how much I differ from the morosity of those Cynics who would not admit your sex in to the communities of a noble friendship. I believe some Wives have been the best friends in the world. . . .

But Taylor's sense of women is that they are imperfect men:

> I cannot say that Women are capable of all those excellencies by which men can oblige the world; and therefore a femal[e] friend in some cases is not so good a counsellor as a wise man, and cannot so well defend my honour; nor dispose of reliefs and assistances if she be under the power of another. . . .

These defects, he admits, are no reason to exclude women from friendship. Women may never be wise men, but, then again, neither will many men.

Orinda's poetry consciously swerves from several points of Taylor's wisdom. Although she does write a handful of epithalamiums, most of the poems celebrate the friendship of women. When Taylor contends that a woman cannot "defend my honour," his examples are explicitly military, of men sacrificing themselves for others in battle. Philips, the voice of restraint, acknowledges that woman's place is not in warfare, but Orinda will often adopt military metaphors when addressing another woman, simultaneously imitating and defying the poetic practices of men.
Orinda expresses affection in military language most explicitly in her poem, **"To the truly Noble Mrs. Anne Owne, on my first Approaches."** The language is a convention of male speech, as Taylor's document reveals. But Orinda does not merely adopt military metaphors for her own seductive purposes. The poem's simultaneous distance from and embrace of the language of conquerors makes it clear that the speaker is a woman self-consciously appropriating a language that is not hers, not merely imitating male conventions:

> *Madam,*
> As in a Triumph Conquerors admit
> Their meanest Captives to attend on it,
> Who, though unworthy, have the power confest,
> And justifi'd the yielding of the rest:
> So when the busie World (in hope t'excuse
> Their own surprize) your Conquests do peruse,
> And find my name, they will be apt to say,
> Your charms were blinded, or else thrown away.
> There is no honour got in gaining me,
> Who am a prize not worth your Victory.
> But this will clear you, that 'tis general,
> The worst applaud what is admir'd by all.
> But I have plots in't: for the way to be
> Secure of fame to all posterity,
> Is to obtain the honour I pursue,
> To tell the World I was subdu'd by you.
> And since in you all wonders common are,
> Your Votaries may in your Vertues share,
> While you by noble Magick worth impart:
> She that can Conquer, can reclaim a heart.
> Of this Creation I shall not despair,
> Since for your own sake it concerns your care.
> For 'tis More honour that the World should
>   know,
> You made a noble Soul, than found it so.

The conceit of the poem is a simple one: Anne Owen is a "Conqueror," and Orinda is her "Captive." Orinda effects a self-deprecating voice, praising her friend by disparaging herself. According to the poem, Anne Owen wins no glory in conquering Orinda, since Orinda is not worth Anne's attentions; but she is honored, in the world's eyes, by ennobling Orinda's soul, by imparting the conqueror's virtues to the conquered.

The metaphor is familiar in the romance tradition, echoed in the Cavalier poems of Orinda's male contemporaries. But Orinda, intimately addressing Anne Owen from the beginning of the poem, explicitly subverts conventional sex roles. Can one argue that this poem, by the "English Sappho," is meant to be read, as many of Sappho's lyrics were through the nineteenth century, as a fictional, male persona addressing a woman? I believe there is no mistaking that this is a poem about the conquering of one woman's heart by another. The traditionally feminine tokens "honour" and "prize" are associated with the speaker. Anne is compared to a triumphant military leader, yet she retains certain conventionally female attributes: her "charms" and her "Vertues." Orinda is no passive captive, however; she plots and pursues and creates. Not only has Orinda challenged the conventional male/female structure of a conquest poem, she has also created a woman's voice that can be simultaneously submissive and aggressive. In this way, Orinda does not merely imitate a tradition of heterosexual conquest. Rejecting the static positions of conqueror and conquered through a fluidity of roles, she dismantles the power relations of erotic expression.

If this is a "breach of Nature's laws," it is not without a "cause." Ostensibly, Orinda can push beyond the boundaries of gender's commonplaces because, as she has presented the problem in the poem, she must preserve Anne Owen's reputation, lest "the world" believe it has been sullied by an unworthy conquest. Blame me, says Orinda: let the world understand the pursuit as mine, satisfying my desire to be "subdu'd by you." If Orinda merely proposed this plot and let go of it, Anne would be relieved of her connections with male metaphors, since Orinda has asserted herself as the true aggressor. But the fiction is too pleasurable to renounce. She is not ashamed of the lie she has produced: "Of *this Creation* I shall not despair." She will pretend, for the world's sake, that Anne is not responsible for her conquest, but in the end Orinda wants both women to be seen as both "Conquerors" and "Captives."

The strange part of this poem is that even though it turns upon the imagined opinion of "the World," it ends transcendently. Orinda becomes Anne's "Votary"; Anne ennobles Orinda's Soul. This is the tension between what I have called, for shorthand purposes, the voices of Philips and Orinda. Orinda's language is, after all, not merely military but also sexual: the title refers to her "first Approaches"; line 9 refers to Anne "gaining me"; and in line 16 Orinda admits she desires to be "subdu'd." In steering the subject away from the physical and into a transcendent realm, Philips echoes Jeremy Taylor's definition of friendship as a marriage of souls. But that definition does not have the ultimate voice in this poem. The last lines, "For 'tis more honour that the World should know, / You made a noble Soul, than found it so," remind the reader that even though it is desirable to have a "noble soul," Orinda, living in a fleshly world, does not gain hers without external intercession.

In a strategy of denial, Philips appeals to a neo-platonic, spiritual notion of friendship. Orinda circumvents this denial by imposing the physical world, through metaphor, upon the transcendent. This suggests to me two separate concerns in the poetry. The first is simply repression: politics, public life, homoeroticism and physicality make Philips nervous, so she admits them only as vehicles to a "higher" truth. The inevitable return of the repressed, however, is staged through Orinda's metaphors. They insist, no matter how much *Philips* cries, "I think not on the State," *Orinda* does.

The second concern of the poetry, as I read it, relates to this tension of repression. It is the implicit exploration in Orinda's work of the nature and power of poetic language. In the Anne Owen poem I have been describing above, Orinda defends her "Creation," which is to say, her fiction or her lie, which she enacts in the course of the

poem. Composed of language, this creation opposes the ideal realm of friendship, where souls ought to be able to merge without mediation. But if Philips—the voice that favors *soul* over *body*—wishes to celebrate her friendships, she is dependent upon Orinda's mediating language. Another poem to Anne Owen, **"To my Lucasia, in defence of declared Friendship,"** seems to suggest that, though friendship is discovered in the ideal realm, it is maintained by its verbal celebration. The following lines are selected from the twenty-stanza poem:

1

O My Lucasia, let us speak our Love,
  And think not that impertinent can be,
Which to us both doth such assurance prove,
  And whence we find how justly we agree.

7

Think not 'tis needless to repeat desires;
  The fervent Turtles always court and bill,
And yet their spotless passion never tires,
  But does encrease by repetition still.

8

Although we know we love, yet while our Soul
  Is thus imprison'd by the Flesh we wear,
There's no way left that bondage to controul,
  But to convey transactions through the Ear.

9

Nay, though we read our passions in the Eye,
  It will oblige and please to tell them too.
Such joys as these by motion multiply,
  Were't but to find that our Souls told us true.

16

If I distrust, 'tis my own worth for thee,
  'Tis my own fitness for a love like thine;
And therefore still new evidence would see,
  T' assure my wonder that thou canst be mine.

17

But as the Morning-Sun to drooping Flowers,
  As weary Travellers a Shade to find,
As to the parched Violet Evening-showers;
  Such is from thee to me a Look that's kind.

18

But when that Look is drest in Words, 'tis like
  The mystic pow'r of Musick's unison;
Which when the finger doth one Viol strike,
  The other's string heaves to reflection.

Insecurity commonly motivates demands for written expressions of devotion: some lovers declare their affection in poetry, others in newspaper advertisements, still others in death-defying graffiti, spray-painting "I love you Carol always" across highway overpasses. Many a love affair is over, however, before an author has time to develop the metaphysical justification for announced love that Philips produces in this poem.

Her justification is logically flawed, though sentimentally attractive. Philips first attempts to tiptoe around the physical world in stanza 7: how does one explain "desires" and "passion" in the context of transcendent friendship? The turtle doves seem to provide a safe metaphor. Although they are "fervent," their passion is "spotless." Yet we are left with an image of Orinda and Lucasia contentedly cooing and cooing and cooing. Orinda will not be satisfied with a single declaration. As she echoes the "repeat" of the first line of this stanza in the "repetition" of the fourth, one senses that this is another occasion on which "silence were now a sin."

Her logic breaks down more explicitly in stanza 8. Here we are invited by Philips' Christian neo-platonism to consider "the Flesh" a prison house for "the Soul." As prisoners, we desire to control this "bondage," and we might expect to do so through an appeal to an outside force, i.e., the warden, God, Grace, or some other unfleshly power. There seems to be a bit of corruption in the prison house, however, since our resource is an insider: "the Ear." Or perhaps this sense organ is a privileged prisoner. Promoted, though not freed, for good behavior, the Ear sympathizes with the soul's desire for freedom. The Ear loosens the soul's bonds. The Ear enables one soul to pass a message of affection to another.

Before discussing how the Ear might have gained its favored status, I want to contrast it with the other privileged portion of the flesh that appears in stanza 9: "the Eye." The Eye has traditionally held a superior office as the conveyor of the soul's intentions. Through the Eye, Orinda says, friends can read each other's passions. Lucasia's look, she admits in stanza 17, is like sunshine, an oasis, a resuscitating shower. But "that Look" is improved as a token of affection, she contends in stanza 18, if it is "drest in Words." In this cause, Orinda will not settle for silence. The Ear has greater control over the flesh than the Eye does.

Katherine Philips died several years before Milton's Satan stigmatized the Ear by tempting rather than liberating Eve's soul with a few well placed whispers in her innocent aural cavity. We have no reason to be suspicious of this sense organ in this poem to Lucasia. On the contrary, the Ear assumes the special role of being the part of the flesh that can affect our control over the bondage of the flesh because it is the organ that receives language—at least spoken language. Orinda commands in the first line of the poem, "let us speak our Love." Her poem, while commanding, is also her speech-act, for here Orinda does "speak her love." Creating by speaking is action with precedents no one need be ashamed of, the most famous of which is recounted in the first two chapters of Genesis. So Philips treads on safe ground poetically, and in an extended sense, theologically (the creation of the world producing a harmonious music of the spheres), when she suggests in the 18th stanza that composed ("drest in") words are like harmonious music, "reflecting" one note with another through sympathetic vibration. This is to say, language is creative, language, like music, creates special relationships, and language improves understand-ing that depends merely upon visual impressions.

But something is wrong with the Eyes and Ears of this work; Philips ignores language's written, rather than spoken, capacities, an odd position to take in a composed poem. Is she practicing denial? writing sloppily? composing cleverly? The synaesthesia of stanza 18 curiously directs us to this problem. I read the musical simile two ways. The first is that there are two musicians; one responds to the performance of the other as each contributes separate lines of a duet. The second interpretation is that the sounding of one string on one instrument effects the sounding of a second string on that instrument through sympathetic vibration, though that string is not played by the musician. I will not dispute there may be other readings of these lines. My quibble is over the word "reflection," a word borrowed from the sense world of the Eye rather than the Ear. Even allowing for changes in English pronunciation since the 17th century, "reflection" is not a particularly strong rhyme for "unison." I believe it is purposefully chosen. Orinda seems to have invented *aural* reflection to describe her relationship with Lucasia.

The relationship is as contradictory as the mixing of Ear and Eye because it resists seventeenth-century expectations of women's behavior. Orinda must convince Lucasia that declared love is not "impertinent." She gives permission for a woman to "oblige and please" (stanza 9) not a man, but another woman. She intimates a physical dimension to their friendship when she claims the Viol string (stanza 18) does not merely echo or respond but "*heaves* to reflection." Here, as in the earlier poem to Anne Owen, Orinda calls for performance within the corporeal world rather than transcendence of it.

The third contradiction of this poem is its denial of its graphic dimension. This contradiction actually consolidates the poem's contradiction of senses (Eye/Ear) and contradiction of behaviors (expected/resisted). I have been trying to suggest in the discussions of these two poems to Anne Owen that "Philips" desires contradict "Orinda's." Orinda situates her friendships in a public, political, physical world. Philips retreats from this world through an appeal to an ideal of friendship between souls rather than bodies. Orinda resists Philips' denial by disguising her physical desires as metaphors, rather than subjects, in her poetry. Philips seems to reply that if poetry is the vehicle by which she will "speak her Love," she will make it as transcendent as possible by denying its relation to the *visible* world.

Although Katherine Philips' poems circulated in manuscript throughout the interregnum, she refused to have them published until her friends convinced her that she must do so in order to refute the faulty, pirated edition of her work, which appeared in 1664. Unpublished poems might seem more likely to appeal to the aural rather than visible world. But even they leave their graphic trace on handwritten pages. The written poem is an "aural reflection." It is the means by which Orinda and Lucasia can coo and coo and coo together, even though they are separated in Wales and London. It is a fiction, of course.

Orinda is not "speaking" but *writing* her love. But it is an acceptable "Creation," as Orinda says in the earlier poem, one which pretends merely to give forth invisible sounds.

Philips repeats the idea that real poetry, verse that will be eternal, is voiced rather than inscribed in her poem, **"To my Lady Elizabeth Boyle, Singing now affairs, &c."** Here again are political and military metaphors; here again are sounds of sexual submission. And here again is an explicit denial of the power of the pen:

> Subduing fair! what will you win
>   To use a needless Dart:
> Why then so many to take in
>   One undefended heart?
> I came expos'd to all your Charms,
>   'Gainst which the first half hour
> I had no will to take up Armes,
>   And in the next no Power.
> How can you chuse but win the Day,
>   Who can resist your Siege,
> Who in one action know the way
>   To Vanquish and Oblige?
> Your Voice which can in melting strains
>   Teach Beauty to be blind,
> Confines me yet in stronger Chains,
>   By being soft and kind.
> Whilst you my trivial fancy sing,
>   You it to wit refine,
> As Leather once stamp'd by a King
>   Became a Current Coin.
> By this my Verse is sure to gain
>   Eternity with men,
> Which by your voice it will obtain,
>   Though never by my Pen.
> I'd rather in your favour live
>   Then in a lasting name,
> And much a greater rate would give
>   For Happiness then Fame.

This poem of praise and gratitude to a woman who, with others of Katherine Philips' acquaintance, learned and privately performed songs from Philips' *Pompey* (a translation of Corneille), is another poem from a vanquished lover to her conqueror. It too depends on contrasts: the oxymoronic "Subduing fair" suggests an androgynous Elizabeth Boyle; chains are made stronger "By being soft and kind." Will contrasts with power, voice with pen, and happiness with fame. Yet even these contrasts are of two sorts: paradoxes and choices. The paradox of the aggressive woman or the soft chain is acceptably unreconciled, but choices must be decided. Orinda's duel of will and power dissolves in a double defeat, but voice wins out over pen and happiness over fame. Philips consistently selects the least physical and least visible quality or object, but Orinda equally consistently undermines that choice. Philips may be thinking of transcendent friendship, but Orinda's poem is still panting from Elizabeth Boyle's obliging siege.

The siege's success, according to the poem, depends neither on the pen nor on another superfluous, long, pointed object, the "needless dart." The third line of the poem clarifies the complaint: Boyle's quantity of erotic arrows is excessive; Orinda's heart puts up no defense. There really is no question of Boyle shooting too many phallic weapons against Orinda; there is no need for any dart at all. Orinda claims that she cannot resist the woman "Who in one action know(s) the way / To Vanquish and Oblige." I find nothing unusual in Orinda's use of military metaphor: she draws equally from poetic convention and her own adult life in England during the Civil Wars. But she emasculates the convention. The "Dart" is needless.

And so, for the same reasons perhaps, the pen is also needless. Charles Cotterell's introduction to the *Poems* makes it clear that most verses are the products of the pens of men. He also tellingly notes that Orinda's poems "fell hastily" from her pen, as if she wanted to rid herself of that tool as quickly as possible. To have a poem and not a pen is paradoxical, but paradoxes do not upset this poet. Although Orinda knows the power of poetic language and Philips knows the harmony of souls fed by linguistic communication, there are serious objections from both perspectives to the symbolism of the pen. Its mark is too physical for Philips. Its connections are too masculine for Orinda.

Orinda's rejection of masculine symbolism contributes to her "Sapphic," if not "feminist" identity. Hilda Smith [in *Reason's Disciples*, 1982] cites Katherine Philips as an early feminist role model because of her "retreat" poems, which promote pastoral escape with other women from a male world of politics, war, and sexuality. Since Katherine Philips' concerns about gender difference led her to no political action, nor even to question the sexist commonplaces spoken by her husband and male friends, "feminist" sounds as anachronistic as Faderman's label, "lesbian." Her poetic vision is one of separatism and a rejection of phallocentrism. Her poetic passions are lesbian, whether or not they accurately describe physical consummation. The seventeenth century provides no descriptive erotic vocabulary for such female discourse, unless we expand the customarily asexual label, "The English Sappho," that Katherine Philips shared with Anne Killigrew and others. By validating women's friendship as a theme that combines Katherine Philips' contradictory voices, the poems represent a Sapphic discourse produced by a rejected pen.

Despite Jeremy Taylor's concession that wives make good friends, the words flowing from the pens of most men Orinda knew of, since Aristotle and Cicero, claimed that women did not have the capacity to be friends—whether with men or (had it been thought of) with other women. Theological opinion admitted, by the seventeenth century, that women did indeed have souls, but having less power of reason, women's souls were more vulnerable than men's to corruption and wickedness. Orinda disputes both classical wisdom and theological prejudice. She argues in a didactic, fifteen stanza poem, **"A Friend,"** that such biases are based on faulty premises. Gender distinctions are part of the material world; souls are only temporarily imprisoned in that world. It is the "Philips" voice that appeals to transcendence as an argument for equality in the fourth stanza:

If Souls no Sexes have, for Men t'exclude
  Women from Friendship's vast capacity,
Is a design injurious or rude,
  Onely maintain'd by partial tyranny.
Love is allow'd to us and Innocence,
  And noblest Friendships do proceed from
    thence.

This is another safe argument: Philips takes the tyrant's own words and throws them back at him. Having granted (Christian) women the capacity to love—as daughters, wives, and mothers—and having acknowledged women's "innocence" by their ready protection of it, Philips' male contemporaries have already granted women the vital ingredients of friendship. Moreover, if they truly believe in the separation of the body and the soul, they must dismiss their idea that women's souls are as encumbered as their bodies by their gender. Friendship, being the merging of souls, is gender neutral. **"A Friend"** asserts that when women are defined in terms of their relations with men, as daughters, mothers, or wives, they love on a less pure level than they do as friends. Friendship is, the third stanza claims,

Nobler th[a]n Kindred or th[a]n Marriage-band,
  Because more free; Wedlock-felicity
It self doth only by this Union stand,
  And turns to Friendship or to Misery.
Force or Design Matches to pass may bring,
But Friendship doth from Love and Honour
    spring.

Relationships, this poem explains, can be created by family, formality, or force, but these are not inherently felicitous joinings. The stanza concludes with Philips' appeal to the abstract ideals of Love and Honour, which produce friendship. If earthly relationships are to produce any happiness at all, they must include friendship. But why is friendship "more free" than "Kindred" or "Marriage-band"? From a seventeenth-century woman's perspective, it is the only relationship over which she has control, having no choice over the family into which she is born and little choice in the man she must marry. But women's friendships are also freer from obligations and consequences than family or marriage. As a daughter, a mother, or a wife, a woman must serve someone else; in friendships between women, love is mutually exchanged.

Another poem, **"Friendship,"** argues that friendship is not merely more free but also more pure than heterosexual union:

All Love is Sacred, and the Marriage-tie
Hath much of Honour and Divinity.
But Lust, Design, or some unworthy ends
May mingle there, which are despis'd by
    Friends.

Not only does Katherine Philips fret over the corruptibility of marriage, she also clings to an ideal notion of friendship unblemished by desire, manipulation, or expectation. Yet these are certainly attributes—positive attributes—of the friendships Orinda reveals in her poems to other women. Perhaps coming exposed to Elizabeth Boyle's charms is not "lust"; perhaps creating a fiction of desiring to be subdued by Anne Owen is not "design"; perhaps demanding a declaration of love is a "worthy end" unto itself. But this is a philosophical poem, not specific in its address. It holds back the very physical tokens Orinda offers her intimates.

Curiously, Philips' rejection of the physical also rejects a belief in equality of the sexes. She measures men and women by different standards, degrading men and idealizing women. The poems suggest that men degrade themselves by seeking material conquests. For Philips, women's friendships prove that their values are superior to men's. Many feminists would reject this view of women's nature. It fails to query whether or not women, in general, would object more than men to war, violence, ambition, and politics if greater opportunity for participation in so called "men's activities" had been available to them. Philips accepts the seventeenth-century commonplaces: with fewer ties to the world, women can more easily transcend it. By idealizing women as superior peacemakers. Orinda validates the lesbian discourse of her poems addressed to women: appeals to women's "nature" provide a socially acceptable excuse for preferring women to men.

In her philosophical, defining poems, like **"A Friend"** and **"Friendship,"** Orinda proves that the pen can nearly murder a subject by cramming it into lengthy, laborious stanzas. But when she addresses her friends, when her poem becomes not merely a description but also an act of friendship, it delights with lyrical freshness, the aural reflection of unaffected affection. In **"To my Excellent Lucasia, on our Friendship,"** Orinda combines commonplaces with the gushing of an enamored individual. Here, again, body contrasts with soul, men's happiness contrasts with women's. Here, again, Philips situates friendship in an ideal realm. But here again, as well, Orinda's worldly, poetic language steals back the subject: friendship does not entirely abandon the earth.

I did not live until this time
  Crown'd my felicity,
When I could say without a crime,
  I am not thine, but Thee.

This Carcass breath'd, and walkt, and slept,
  So that the World believ'd
There was a Soul the Motions kept;
  But they were all deceiv'd.

For as a Watch by art is wound
  To motion, such was mine:
But never had *Orinda* found
  A Soul till she found thine;

Which now inspires, cures, and supplies,
  And guides my darkned Breast:
For thou art all that I can prize,
  My Joy, my Life, my Rest.

> No Bridegrooms nor Crown-conquerors mirth
>   To mine compar'd can be:
> They have but pieces of this Earth,
>   I've all the World in thee.
>
> Then let our Flames still light and shine,
>   And no false fear controul,
> As innocent as our Design,
>   Immortal as our Soul.

Without Lucasia, Orinda was a soulless automaton, a cadaver imitating human life. Since they have become friends, Orinda's previously empty shell has found joy, life, and rest. This is no mere marriage of souls, however; Orinda seems to have consumed Lucasia, to have become Lucasia, to have absorbed Lucasia's soul. The last stanza explains that their souls are like flames: Orinda's appropriation of Lucasia's soul intensifies rather than consumes it.

Nevertheless, **"To my Excellent Lucasia, on our Friendship"** does not abandon its reader, disembodied, in friendship's transcendent realm. Men's happiness, as "Bridegrooms" or "Crown-conquerors," is admittedly a material happiness scorned by Philips. But it is also inferior to the speaker's because it is produced by mere "pieces of this Earth," in contrast with having "all the World in thee." Philips is slipping here: her preference is not for the spiritual over the temporal, but for the whole over a part. Admittedly, "this Earth" is a subset of "the World," the latter including both the tangible and the intangible. An automaton plus a soul equal a self. Correspondingly, the Earth plus the transcendent realm equal the World. Totality is not merely in the transcendent realm of friendship. Orinda has *all the world* "in thee," in the person of Lucasia.

In her poem, **"A Friend,"** the word "design" was part of a tyrannical toolkit, wielded by rude men who wanted to exclude women from the delights of friendship. In the last stanza of this poem to Lucasia, however, both the women's "Flames" and their "Design" are "innocent." Design, in Orinda's woman-identified world, is prelapsarian, creative, uncorrupt.

Yet her design is physical. She rejects the "crown-conquerors," conveniently displacing her political allegiances to both the crown-conquering Puritans and the crown-conquered Royalists. But the eliminated subject returns as metaphor. The first two lines of the poem confess, "I did not live until this time / Crown'd my felicity." Philips pretends to be apolitical, but Orinda adorns her messages of affection with political imagery. She also situates that affection in the temporal world: "this time" crowns her felicity. The ideal realm is eternal, beyond time; Orinda's friendships are here and now.

In the third stanza, she compares her former self to a watch, underscoring this concern with time. The simile is unfavorable: a watch is mechanically driven, and so was Orinda before she received Lucasia's soul. The difference between the mechanical and the inspired life Orinda de-

sires is the difference between an individual and a community. The watch is a creation, designed to perform a task. It is functional and observable, but not—in the terms of 1980's tech toys—interactive. Lucasia's soul, in contrast, inspires, cures, supplies and guides. Once again, it is the interchange of friendship that most attracts Orinda. But the watch has been enhanced, not replaced. The interchange of friendship occurs in mortal time.

I want to return now to Charles Cotterell's list of praise, with which I began this essay. He says Orinda's poems would not disgrace "the name of any man." He claims her poems are timeless, for her name should "live with honour as long as" the Muses. He laments the isolation of the English language, for he believes Orinda's verses speak beyond the concerns of national boundaries. And finally, her poetry, which he claims reflects her "Vertues," surpassing Sappho, he compares to heavenly glories. Cotterell's goal is not consistent literary criticism. He confuses the poet and her poetry as he shifts his praise of the virtues of each, but his interests are appropriate for discussing a poet whose poems extol transcendence.

The physical side of Orinda's poetry does not reach Charles Cotterell; she excludes it through denial and disguise. According to seventeenth-century social conventions, the poet, Katherine Philips, respects "Nature's Laws": she marries, she mothers, she muses. Her Sapphic persona, Orinda, who forms bonds outside marriage, who renames her friends, and who writes—with a pen—unconventional verses, breaks the Laws. The tension of voices in the poems includes the kind of writer Cotterell describes: a virtuous, timeless, universal, woman poet. But Orinda's voice also insists on poetry not merely in thought but in deed, as she physically reinscribes herself in morality, history, and place.

Claudia A. Limbert (essay date 1991)

SOURCE: "Katherine Philips: Controlling a Life and Reputation," in *South Atlantic Review*, Vol. 56, No. 2, May, 1991, pp. 27-42.

[*In the following essay, Limbert discusses Philips's efforts to assert control over aspects of her personal and public life. Limbert questions the validity and relevance of critical preoccupation with Philips's sexual identity and instead examines the socially acceptable methods by which she protected her literary reputation.*]

Katherine Philips (1632-64) was, in effect, two women. The first woman was the very conventional product of London's seventeenth-century merchant class, which was firmly Puritan-Presbyterian in religion and staunchly Parliamentarian in politics. Consistent with her family background as well as with her society's expectations for women, Philips received—at most—six years of a boarding school education, probably stressing accomplishments rather than academics. Her dowry mostly on paper and her looks unremarkable, she was nevertheless considered fortunate in her marriage, at the age of sixteen, to James

Philips, a fifty-four-year-old Welsh widower with a small child and chronic money problems, a man active in Parliamentarian politics. Living in Wales, Mrs. Philips cared for her stepdaughter, gave birth to two children, ran her household, and, to all intents and purposes, lived the unexceptional life of a wife and mother before succumbing to smallpox at thirty-two. This is one Katherine Philips.

The second woman was as wildly unconventional as Mrs. Philips was conventional. Influenced by her maternal grandmother, who had been a friend of Quarles, this woman had been writing poetry since childhood. A Royalist with a wide circle of influential Royalist friends, she enjoyed thinking for herself, was well educated, read widely not only in English but in French and Italian, and enjoyed art and the theater. Known as the "Matchless Orinda," she was the only female contributor to an edition of Cartwright's work titled *Comedies, Tragi-Comedies with Other Poems,* and her first poem in print was among the prefatory poems in this volume. In 1655, two of her poems were included in Lawes's *Second Book of Ayres.* Orinda also wrote some poems presented to the royal family, the Duchess of York saying that their quality "had surpriz'd her." By 15 May 1663, several of Orinda's poems had been pirated for an Irish miscellany. Just previous to that, her translation of Corneille's ***Pompey***—the first verse translation from French to appear on the British stage—had been enthusiastically received and printed in Dublin. The great popularity of ***Pompey*** seems to have caused some of her poems again to be pirated and brought out in a London edition shortly thereafter. Following her death, edited volumes of her poems and letters were published.

Additionally, Orinda's work, virtue, and subject matter became the focus of laudatory treatises and poems by Francis Finch, Jeremy Taylor, Abraham Cowley, and Henry Vaughan. For example, Finch in 1654 and Taylor in 1657 both acknowledged Philips as the high priestess of friendship by publishing treatises inspired by friendship as defined and practiced by Philips. Cowley wrote two poems to Philips's memory in the prefatory section of the posthumous edition of her work, and Vaughan generously acknowledged her both in his *Olor Iscanus* and *Thalia Rediviva.*

Katherine Philips—Orinda—managed to accomplish all this in her brief thirty-two years and did it by attempting to control the things that most threatened to constrain her: the restrictions imposed on her by seventeenth-century society on a personal level as a woman and on a professional level as a writer handicapped by her sex.

On a personal level, Philips could do nothing about her family's middle-class merchant status nor about its Puritan-Parliamentarian allegiance. Probably living over or near her father's business in Coleman Street, a hotbed of radicalism, she could not change the fact that her mother's family had strong connections with the Puritan-Parliamentarian faction. Yet, Katherine Philips had become an avowed Royalist by the time of her earliest extant poems, written when she was about fourteen years old and beginning to think about the attributes of a future husband. However, she managed to remain on good terms with her family, being close to her much-married mother, who, after the death of John Fowler, went on to marry a "Danyell Henly" before marrying Sir Richard Phillips (sic)—a man who was probably a Parliamentary sympathizer, followed by Cromwell's well-known supporter Major-General Philip Skippon, who remembered Katherine Philips, her husband, and daughter in his will.

Just as Philips could not control her familial situation, neither did she have much control over whom she would marry. Although her juvenilia shows that she preferred a Royalist husband who was "Ready to serve . . . his King," James Philips was not this man, serving as he did in Cromwell's government as a member of the High Court of Justice, army commander, and local justice of the peace and sheriff. Yet, luck had been with Katherine as James was politically a moderate who allowed her a large measure of freedom in her politics as well as in her choice of friends. Certainly he remained on good terms with her Royalist friends throughout her lifetime as well as after her death.

It would seem, however, that on at least one occasion, Katherine's political allegiance had caused James embarrassment, if not serious trouble. Although her original poem no longer exists, a second poem titled **"To Antenor on a paper of mine which J. Jones threatenes to publish to his preiudice"** reveals that Philips had written a poem against Jones, a Parliamentary sympathizer, that had fallen into Jones's hands. Jones had threatened to publish it and make trouble for James. In a subsequent conciliatory poem to her husband, Katherine Philips refers to the original poem as just a "trifel,"; even though it seems to have been quite a bit more than that because she also labels Jones as "This magazine of hell / Whose name would turne a verse into a spell." Still, she professes herself to be confused as to why James should be blamed for what she has written since "My love and life I must confesse are thine, / But not my errours, they are only mine." Yet, while she uses the words "errours," "faults," and "follies" in reference to what she had previously written about Jones, the tone of the conciliatory poem and its choice of words strong-mindedly maintain what must have been her original blistering estimation of Jones as a "dark lanthorne" who is "below a poets curse." Thus, this poem is really just a reiteration of Philips's uncompromising position on Jones and shows that, while she respects her husband and wants his good opinion, she will not back down on her beliefs in order to secure such an opinion.

Although Katherine Philips had no control over her birth and little over her marriage, she could and did make changes in two other areas of her life that restricted her on a personal level. One such restriction concerned her isolation in Cardigan, a small town tucked claustrophobically into a narrow Welsh valley. Philips's letters to her friend and mentor Sir Charles Cotterell, the Master of Ceremonies at the court of Charles II, record her constant struggle to get back to London. On the surface, Philips claims that she only wants to go to London to help her husband find a position that will enable him to put his "shatter'd Affairs" and "entangled Concerns" into better order. However, obviously linked to that more altruistic purpose is her desire to have the "Opportunity to converse with some few worthy Friends." To accomplish these two goals, particularly the latter, Philips characteristically asked her friends for help, requesting that Sir Charles, Elizabeth Clifford Boyle, and her old schoolmate Mary Aubrey Montagu "lay their Heads together to contrive some way to see Orinda." Too, in order to get herself to London, Philips did not hesitate to turn her hand to a little mild deception of her husband. Not only did she ask her friends to write to James and to express their willingness to help him, but she asked Sir Charles Cotterell to "use your Endeavors to facilitate my coming to London. . . . You must contrive some plausible Pretence to make him [James Philips] believe, that by being there I might be very useful to his Affairs by the means of your Friendship, and by the Assistance of my other Friends." Philips adds that she would like Sir Charles to reply to her letter in Italian, presumably because her husband did not understand that language. In this way, Philips managed to manipulate her husband, avoiding conflict with him while getting what she wanted.

Perhaps it was in the area of her education that Philips was able to make the greatest change, and she did so at a time when women were the most illiterate group in society, with the majority not even able to sign their own names. Philips obviously was not content to stop with what little education she had received. Her letters demonstrate that she was educating herself, reading an amazing number of books. They record her acquaintance with Beaumont and Fletcher's *The Scornful Lady*, Henry Hammond's sermons, Suckling's *Brennoralt*, Orrery's "verses", Sir Charles Cotterell's translation of *The Temple of Death*, and Butler's *Hudibras*. She also mentions reading Jonson's *The Silent Woman*, Cowley's *Cutter of Coleman Street*, and some poetry by Lord Falkland. Philips requests and obtains Samuel Tuke's *Adventure of Five Hours* before passing it on to Orilby for his Dublin theater.

Philips also sent reading material to Sir Charles. One letter mentions her sending L'Estrange's "Apology for Women" because she felt that, like L'Estrange, Sir Charles valued women. In addition, she sends him "some Translations from Virgil by Mr. Cowley" as well as an Irish miscellany containing some of her poems.

Although, in Philips's last years, she was increasingly interested in learning Italian, she continued to read French works, priding herself on her understanding of this language. In one letter, Philips lightly castigates Sir Charles for having sent her an English translation as well as the French original by an unnamed male author, saying that she had not minded the English translation as much as she had minded Sir Charles "interlining the French Paper, which I take as the far greater Affront."

Sir Charles also guided Philips's efforts in learning Italian, with the result that Philips felt confident about her

ability to understand Italian prose but was impatient with her progress with its poetry. She laments: "I am not yet perfect enough in the Italian to discover all the Beauties of Cotesti's Poems, which I can scarcely forgive my self for, having had the Advantage of so good a Master as your self."

Thus, it can be seen that Philips was able to overcome some of society's restrictions against women on a personal level; however, it was much more difficult to overcome what the handicap of her sex meant to Philips as a writer. In general, one might characterize seventeenth-century society as a society in which it was acceptable for a woman to write for her own amusement; however, the woman who took her writing into the public sphere, perhaps even allowing her name to be affixed to it, ran the risk of crossing that shadowy but very real border between "lady" and "woman." The question here is, how did Philips— someone with no beauty, no social position, and no money,—manage to have her work received so favorably without leaving her reputation in tatters?

One might begin to answer by first acknowledging that Philips realized how easy it would be to lose her good name. After all, a woman of middle-class birth and marriage had little social protection; therefore, Philips had no choice but to conform or to suffer the consequences. On one occasion, having just returned to Cardigan after a long stay in Dublin but still feeling drawn to her friends in London, Philips resigned herself to staying at home because James's affairs could not be straightened out quickly, "nor indeed would it appear well to the world, if we should part so soon, after having been so long asunder." On another occasion, after her poems had been pirated in London, she wrote to Sir Charles: "Let me know what they say of me at Court and every where else, upon this last Accident, and whether the exposing [of] all my follies in this dreadful Shape has not frighted the whole World out of all their Esteem for me."

As a female writer, a person who had already overstepped the bounds of acceptable conduct, Philips was particularly open to criticism regarding her sexual conduct, and she seems to have combatted this in several ways, with an almost twentieth-century appreciation of public relations.

First, besides the fact that no scandal was ever attached to her marriage, Philips was careful in her choice of subject matter—friendship. In working with this topic, Philips took a poetic genre that had been used by male writers who were writing either to women (Donne) or to other men (Shakespeare). Previously, such poems had usually concerned the male poet's passion for the subject of his poems. Producing an exciting frisson of the senses, these poems often involved an elaborate catalog of the subject's bodily parts and had a clearly physical base that might or might not be overlaid by the declaration of a non-physical intent, much as a layer of cold air presses against a layer of warm air. But Philips—mindful of her literary and personal reputation—was careful not to address her attentions to men. Instead, she gave the old genre a new and intriguing twist by writing of the friendship of one woman for another, keeping everything on a platonic level. In her pastoral poems, Philips's women friends become elevated to the rank of goddesses surrounded by a full panoply of goddess imagery: twinned spirits, celestial waters, and heavenly fires. Philips's poems also differ from their earlier models in that the reader is never given a physical catalog of the woman in question. Was she blonde? Tall? Brown-eyed? Well-rounded? Philips's reader never gets an answer to such questions because, in actuality, the topic is not one particular woman. Rather, Philips's topic is virtue—and how it is found perfected in each of her friends. For example, in **"To the excellent Mrs A.O.,"** Philips writes to her dearest friend Lucasia (Anne Owen), the woman who perhaps inspired the best of Philips's poetry:

> But as though through a burning glass
> The sun more vigorous doth passe,
> It still with generall freedom shine's
> For that contract's but not confine's
> So though by this, her beams are fixed here
> Yet she diffuse's glorys every where.

> Her mind is so entirely bright
> The splendour would but wound o'sight
> And must to some disguise submit,
> Or we could never worship it
> And we by this relation, are allow'd
> Lustre enough to be Lucasia's cloud.

> Nations will own us now to be
> A Temple of divinity.
> And Pilgrims shall Ten ages hence
> Approach our Tombs with reverence
> May then that time, which did such blisse convey,
> Be kept with us perpetuall Holy day!

However, what is one to make of **"To My Excellent Lucasia,"** also to Anne Owen?

> I did not live untill this time
> Crown'd my felicity
> When I could say without a crime
> I am not Thine, But Thee.
> This Carkasse breath'd & walk'd & slept
> So that the world believ'd
> There was a soule the motions kept
> But they were all deceiv'd
> For as a watch by art is wound
> To motion, such was mine
> But never had Orinda found
> A Soule till she found thine.
> Which now inspire's cure's and supply's
> And guides my darken'd brest
> For thou art all that I can prize
> My Joy, my Life, my rest.
> Nor Bridegroomes nor crown'd conqu'urours mirth
> To mine compar'd can be
> They have but pieces of this Earth
> I've all the world in thee.

> Then let our flame still light, & shine,
> (And no bold feare cont'roule)
> As inocent as our design
> Imortall as our Soule.

Here, although the reader still has no sense of Anne's physical appearance, the tone—the emotional level—has been turned up to an almost excruciating pitch. After all, there are those lines: "I am not thine, but thee," "But never had Orinda found / A Soule till she found thine," and "My Joy, my Life, my rest." How should one read this poem? The answer is that we can look at it and the remainder of Philips's friendship poems in three different ways: with the eyes of some twentieth-century scholars, the eyes of Philips's peers, and the eyes of Philips herself.

A relatively new twentieth-century movement among those studying Philips's poetry attempts to categorize Philips's poems as lesbian poems that deal either overtly or covertly with lesbian love. Roger Thompson, one of the first to do this, did so by using a false biographical hypothesis [in *Women in Stuart England and America: A Comparative Study,* 1974]. Although Thompson does not openly state that Philips had lesbian relationships, he does believe that Philips was "sexually odd" and had "lesbian leanings." The basis for Thompson's assertion seems to have been a statement made by John Broadbent who, in turn, had based his belief that Philips was a lesbian poet on the rather curious grounds that Philips's two children were born ten years apart. (For an absorbing discussion of this issue regarding Philips as well as lesbianism in women's poetry, see Libertin [in *Women's Studies,* 1982]. Of course, a thesis equating a ten-year separation between births with lesbianism is ridiculous on two grounds. First, no one can seriously regard any span of time between the births of children—whether one year or twenty years—as having anything to do with any woman's sexual identity. Second, in the case of Philips, Broadbent (and, hence, Thompson) has his facts wrong. Philips's son Hector was born 23 April 1655 and died the following 2 May. Her daughter Katherine was born 13 April 1656. Therefore, Philips was pregnant with her second child about three months after the birth of her first.

But what about other twentieth-century scholars who, drawing their conclusions from the poems themselves, try to explain Philips's poetry by saying that Philips was a lesbian poet writing lesbian poetry? Currently, most seem to be only tentatively putting literary toes into literary waters by suggesting rather than insisting upon such an identification for Philips. Although Ellen Moody, for example, never openly states that Philips was lesbian, her recent article [in *Philological Quarterly,* 1987] implies this, saying that Regina Collyer, "Rosania, and Lucasia all eventually rejected the exclusive devotion and overt courtship Orinda lavished on them: with an understandable desire for independence and autonomy, they shut her out with husbands, new friends, other interests." Here, Moody—like Broadbent and Thompson—has her facts wrong. Philips herself seems to have initiated the break with Collyer because of Collyer's new allegiance to the Parliamentary cause as is demonstrated by Philips's poem

"To the Queen of inconstancie / Regina in Antwerp."
(See Limbert's "Regina Collyer" [in *Restoration,* 1989]
for a further explanation of this break.) There is also
concrete evidence that Rosania and Philips remained close
throughout Philips's lifetime. Indeed, when Philips died
of smallpox, she died cradled in the arms of her old boarding school friend, Rosania. Lucasia (Anne Owen) did stub-
bornly resist Philips, not because of the sexual intensity
of Philips's friendship, but because Philips was aggressively and single-mindedly putting forward Cotterell as
Anne's second husband while Anne, pressured by male
family members, leaned toward and eventually married
Marcus Trevor. In this case also, the two women overcame their differences and remained friends until Philips's death.

Yet, whether Philips was a lesbian poet is not the real
question that should be asked here—interesting and intriguing as such a question may be. Instead, when one is
discussing how Philips protected her literary reputation,
the real question is how Philips's peers viewed her sexuality. It would seem that they viewed Philips as a virtuous woman—read: a heterosexual wife and mother—who
also wrote poetry. Indeed, Philips appears to have been
taken up by the conservative elements of her society,
including such clergymen as Jeremy Taylor and the Archbishop of Canterbury, men who would have been the first
to withdraw their support had there been any hint that
Philips was a lesbian or was writing lesbian poetry. After
all, some things could be forgiven in a man. Such things,
however, were not forgivable in a woman. Additionally,
the men surrounding and supporting Philips's literary
career must have approved not only of her poetry but of
the sentiment behind it, obviously finding neither her
subject matter nor her intensity out of the ordinary. Again,
if they had, chances are that they also would have withdrawn their support. Furthermore, Philips's husband must
have read her poems, and there is no record that he disapproved of what she wrote in any way.

Finally, one must look at Philips's own definition of friendship. Does she see friendship as needing some form of
sexual expression? On the contrary, Philips's definition
of friendship—the best attempt that humans can make to
emulate God's divine love and an experience of immortality unobtainable in marriage or sexual relationship—
can be seen in her poem **"Friendship"**:

Let the dull brutish world yt know not love
Continue haeretiques & disapprove
That noble flame, but the refined know
'Tis all ye heaven, we have here below.

. . . . .

All Love is sacred, & the marriage ty
Hath much of Honour, & divinity,
But Lust, design, or some unworthy ends
May mingle there, which are despis'd by friends.

. . . . .

For Love like earthy fires (which will decay

If ye materiall fuell be away)
Is with offensive smoake accompanyd
And by resistance onely is supply'd
But friendship like ye fiery element
With it's own heat, & nourishment content
(Where neither hurt, nor smoke, nor noise is
    made)
Scorn's ye assistance of a foreign ayd.
Friendship (like Heraldry) is hereby known
Richest when plainest; bravest when alone
Calme as a Virgin, & more inocent
Then sleeping Doves are. . . .

Considering the question of Philips's sexual identity, unless
convincing biographical or historical evidence can be
found to the contrary, one must conclude that Philips—in
the eyes of her peers and in her own eyes—enjoyed what
might be termed a spotless sexual reputation, no doubt
contributing to her other label, the "virtuous Orinda," a
label that became an automatic addition to her name.

Thus, Philips protected her reputation as a female writer,
first, by choosing her subject carefully and, second, by
handling it in a manner acceptable to her society. Philips
always adopted a respectful approach to the women of
her poems (whether of her own social class or a higher
one), an approach that could never be seen as inappropriate since Philips used pastoral pseudonyms to address the
women in question, which enabled her to lower social
barriers. As she says in **"To Rosania & Lucasia"**: "Formal addresses then disclaime; / And never must ye Madam name." This meant that Philips could speak her
thoughts freely as an equal without giving offense for at
least the length of a poem if not longer.

Third, Philips protected her literary reputation by often
having male friends act on her behalf. Although it is never
quite clear just how much latitude she actually would
have allowed Sir Charles Cotterell as her editor, Philips
did give him permission to make changes in her poetry if
he felt such changes were necessary, and she did ask him
to give **Pompey** the "last finishing Strokes from your
Excellent Pen." In addition, Philips had other male supporters, including the Duke of Ormonde, who supplied
£100 for the elaborate costuming of **Pompey;** Lord Orrery (Roger Boyle), who encouraged her to complete her
translation of this same play; the unidentified "Artaban,"
who was her copyist; Sir William Temple, who wrote the
epilogue for her play; and Sir Edward Dering, who carefully copied out many of her poems and his own letters
to her so that they would be preserved. Philips also sometimes had men in appropriate positions present her work
to those even more elevated. For example, Marcus Trevor
presented a poem to the Duke of Ormonde for her, and
Sir Charles was asked to pass her work along to members
of the royal family. Even more remarkable for the time,
none of these men ever seems to have regarded the writ-
erly Philips as a freak. Her status as a lady was never
compromised; her status as a writer, always respected.

Fourth, Philips was well able to protect herself in a literary way because she understood and used to her own

advantage the patronage system employed by her male contemporaries. She counted among her patrons Sir Charles Cotterell, the Countess of Cork, Lord Orrery, and the Duke of Ormonde. Eventually, after much delicate negotiation carried out according to her own plan by Sir Charles, Philips received the protection of the King's sister-in-law, the Duchess of York, for her play that was produced in February 1663. In order to secure this patronage, Philips had begun to prepare the groundwork as far back as the previous May by sending a poem to the Duchess through Sir Charles. By 3 December, Philips was openly speaking of dedicating the play to the Duchess, and eventually, a copy of the play was indeed presented to Anne Hyde with a letter from Philips slipped inside. Philips, aware of her own image, had decided to address the Duchess in a letter rather than in verse "neither out of laziness or Disrespect, but merely because I thought it would have look'd more pedantick and affected to have address'd my self to her in Verse" because "Prose would favour less of Ostentation. . . ."

Finally, and perhaps a little sadly to our modern eyes, Philips did not hesitate to minimize herself and her work in order to control a possibly volatile situation, as she did when the pirated 1664 edition appeared on the London market. In a letter sent to Sir Charles and intended to be shown around Court in her defense, she claims to have "never writ a Line in my Life with Intention to have it printed." She appeals to the readers of this letter by claiming to have had "a sharp Fit of Sickness" just from hearing about her poems' publication. In a statement clearly designed to disarm her detractors, she assumes the posture of a humble female who had dared to write poems even though such action was "so much above my Reach, and a Diversion so unfit for the Sex to which I belong." Claiming that she would have thrown all her work into the fire before she would have let this happen, she excuses herself for writing, saying it was a personal weakness that precipitated her setting pen to paper. She writes:

> The truth is, I have always had an incorrigible Inclination to the Vanity of Rhyming, but intended the Effects of that Humour only for my Amusement in a retir'd Life, and therefore did not so much resist it as a wiser Woman would have done: But some of my dearest and best Friends having found my Ballads (for they deserve no better a Name) they made me so much believe they did not dislike them, that I was betray'd to permit some Copies to be taken for other's Diversion, but this with so little Concern for them, that I have lost most of the Originals, which I suppose to be the result of my present Misfortune. . . .

Of course, Philips is carefully painting a picture of herself as a stupid, foolish woman whose friends' flattery caused her to allow her poems to be circulated and whose poems mattered so little to her that she had lost "most" of the originals. Here, Philips twists the truth of the matter in order to gain some measure of protection. Philips was far from being stupid or foolish. One doubts whether she ever underestimated herself or her work. She systematically had written out clean copies of poems designed not only for her humbler friends but for those in higher social circles. She deprecated her poems by calling them mere ballads when she knew they were more than that. After all, she had closely studied other poets' work in English, French, and Italian. Nor does it seem plausible that she had lost most of her originals, for it was her habit to keep a copybook, and she still possessed the one holding much of her work up until 1658. One feels that since Philips carefully imposed controls over every aspect of her life, she would also have kept copies of her later work in a safe place. If Philips herself did not have every single one of her poems—highly doubtful—then her friends could have supplied true copies. Philips made these statements because they were expected of her by her society and because they were a way of protecting herself.

Writing in 1929, Virginia Woolf expressed the hope that society would eventually allow women writers rooms of their own. As one reads Philips's poems and letters, one gets a real sense that she was actively engaged in constructing her own room. In Philips's case, this room was a safe place within her society where she could write in peace as a woman and be free from censure. At the time of Philips's death, she had been successful in building herself just such a space. It was small and tight and it was not totally proof against attack but, for that moment, it did serve its purpose. One wonders, however, if Philips had not died at thirty-two but had continued to write and to publish, how much longer its walls might have held.

Maureen E. Mulvihill (essay date 1991)

SOURCE: "A Feminist Link in the Old Boys' Network: The Cosseting of Katherine Philips," in *Curtain Calls: British and American Women and the Theater, 1660-1820,* edited by Mary Anne Schofield and Cecelia Macheski, Ohio University Press, 1991, pp. 71-104.

[*In the following excerpt, Mulvihill traces the development of Philips's career in the context of the "Orinda" myth and the "old boys' network" that contributed to her popular success.*]

The Restoration is significant in the history of English feminism because it witnessed the advance of women playwrights in the professional theater. The first decade of the Restoration was graced by four newcomers: Katherine Philips (*Pompey,* 1663; *Horace,* 1668), Frances Boothby (*Marcelia,* 1670), Aphra Behn (*The Forc'd Marriage,* 1670), and Elizabeth Polwhele (*The Faithful Virgins,* [1670/71]). Behn was the most prolific and commercially successful in this first wave of dramatic ingénues. Boothby and Polwhele the most obscure. Katherine Philip's place in this cluster of female dramatists is preeminent, as it was Philips who first broke ground for women in the English and Irish theater. For a brief moment in theater history, Philips was a *cause célèbre,* and her dazzling career provided the important precedential model for aspiring literary women. Philips was the first "Sappho" of the English-speaking world, and the first woman to have her work produced on the Dublin and London stage. Her success, in fact, may well have pointed the way for Behn; for when Behn made her début with *The Forc'd Marriage,* mounted by the Duke's Company in the summer of 1670, she was succeeding Philips, whose dramatic translations from Pierre Corneille had been enthusiastically received several years before.

Katherine Philips's contemporary fame rested on two translations from the French classical tragedy of Corneille: his *La Mort de Pompée* (1642), translated by Philips in 1663 and brilliantly staged the same season in Dublin's new Theatre Royal in Smock Alley; and Corneille's *Horace* (1640), partially translated by Philips shortly before her sudden death in 1664, and produced in 1668 at Dublin's Theatre Royal and also before the court of Charles II. Philips's **Pompey** and **Horace** were published soon after their premières, and each saw sell-out editions in Dublin and London. (The first issue of the Dublin **Pompey**, 500 copies, was sold within weeks.) Philips's reputation as "the Matchless Orinda," rapturous poet of "female Friendship," came slightly later and now is seeing a revival. But Philips initially made her mark in the Anglo-Irish theatre, not the poetic coteries of the Restoration court.

Notices on Philips after her death do not scant her dramatic talent. Estimates in David Erskine Baker's *Biographica Dramatica* (1764), for example, celebrate her success in playwrighting. And contradicting Sir Edmund Gosse's assessment that Katherine Philips "sank into utter darkness" in the early eighteenth century is William Roberts's work, which traces something of Philips's popularity up through the late 1800s. Philips's rapid ascent to celebrity was astonishing, given harsh male prejudice against women writers at that time. Her chaste, comely verse and unimpeachable reputation set the standard for female excellence. In fact, so dominant was the cult of "Orinda" during the later-Stuart period that women writers, especially poets, found themselves hard-pressed to compete with Philips, and so began working alternative literary markets—drama, essay-periodical, and particularly the novel. But no matter how overdrawn the portrait, Katherine Philips showed that a public career in literature was possible for a woman in the seventeenth century, even if she were a commoner. While Philips's *oeuvre* is lean—a single published folio of 116 original poems and five verse-translations from the French, two dramatic translations from Corneille, and an incomplete collection of letters— "Orinda" was the undisputed darling of her era and the most celebrated woman in seventeenth-century Anglo-Irish letters.

Reassessing a legend is dangerous business. But in the case of Katherine Philips, whose achievement has been overstated since the late seventeenth century (to the detriment of more skilled women writers), some *contextualizing* of Philips's life, work, and career is long overdue. The obvious weakness in almost all Philips studies to date is an inability to appreciate the "Orinda" myth for what it really was: a remarkable literary campaign conceived and promoted by Philips herself, her relatives, and some of the literary bosses of the Restoration old boys' network.

Philips's grand if brief career was a collaborative product created by Philips and several powerful male allies. Her principal literary productions—the Corneille translations— were orchestrated by influential men of the late seventeenth-century literary world. Philips found effective comrades in Stuart London, Dublin, and southwest Wales, the triple base, as we shall see, of her elaborate operations. Without in any way wishing to discredit Katherine Philips (indeed her support by preeminent men of letters further attests to her talent), I am eager to explore this underplayed aspect of her career as a case-study in supportive relations between men and women of letters at this time. Moreover, based on Philips's published correspondence, it appears that her camaraderie with male confidants and literary advisors resulted in a progressive unfolding of a surprisingly assertive authorial ego.

With the single exception of Lucy Brashear's essay on Philips in *The Anglo-Welsh Review* in 1979, this dimension of Philips's artistic temperament and career has been overlooked in Philips studies thus far. Brashear suggests that Philips always was on the climb, dating from her early days in Wales in the 1650s, when she strategically began creating the "Orinda" persona by broadly circulating her poems, and, moreover, by addressing them to notables of only slight acquaintance, such as Henry Vaughan, one of Philips's many new Welsh relatives after her marriage in 1648. Brashear even (ingeniously) suggests that Philips may well have "engineered" the pirated edition of her own poems in 1664.

My reconstruction of Philips, slightly more tempered and comprehensive, takes into account the full play of "Orinda" 's support-base and its strong influence throughout the three phases of her career, a career distinguished by its astute management, networking, and heretofore unacknowledged artistic individualism. But before I can begin to properly make my case, the stage must first be set for Philips's entrance with some introductory remarks on the sensitive literary climate of the Restoration and its representation in today's feminist criticism.

Prologue: Feminist Angst vs. the Politics of Female Authorship

My genealogical researches into the powerful Phillipps clan, seated at Picton Castle, Pembrokeshire, Wales, the line into which Katherine Philips *née* Fowler married in 1648, have led me to a fresh perspective on the phenomenon of the professional English woman writer who first emerged during the later-Stuart period. As we know, many women writers began to go public during the Restoration. Some asserted their new literary identity by publishing their initials on the title pages of their work. Others, such as Sarah Egerton, Jane Barker, Anne Lady Winchilsea, and Mary Lady Chudleigh, boldly published their surnames. Observing the broad literary and political connections of the Phillipps group in Wales and its key role in launching Katherine Philips, I have begun to examine the professional beginnings and sponsorship of other women writers of their period (particularly the poet-playwright "Ephelia," apparently of the interrelated Proud-Phillips-Milton line) with an eye to the largely unacknowledged role of their male allies and the networks they sometimes made available to the young female entrants.

This new line of inquiry is frankly deconstructive of the new feminist reconstructive criticism. So we begin by looking at things squarely. The new recovery work on women writers of the Restoration and eighteenth century has produced both admirable results and questionable tendencies. On the positive side, it has performed superlatively: by resurrecting a new canon of obscured writings; by identifying female coteries and patronesses; by producing at a brisk rate a body of new reference tools, biographies, and criticism; and by reprinting many essential feminist texts heretofore out of print for generations. This flurry of aggressive feminist activity in the American, British, and Canadian academies bodes well for a deep reconstruction of the canon, with women writers more equitably represented.

Yet, despite its appreciated gains, a fair amount of the recent criticism promotes a point of view (by now almost a premise) which is disturbing and historically unsupportable. I refer to the perception that insists on an adversarial relationship between men and women of letters. Promoters of such a vantage point romanticize female professionals, especially the writers, as a disenfranchised, beleaguered minority whose work was carried out in some sort of vague literary and psychological isolation. The more strident adherents speak of male "victimization" of women. Exclusivity, otherness, and, above all, *feminist angst* are assigned these "pioneers" as inevitable conditions of their gender and "unique" historical position. One commentator on Restoration literature [Angeline Goreau] writes [in Reconstructing Aphra, 1980]: "[Aphra Behn] was a writer who not only insisted on being heard, but [who] successfully forced the men who dominated the jealous literary world of Restoration England to receive her as an equal. . . . I began a life of Aphra and saw in her a heroine . . . a feminist heroine." A historian [Hilda Smith, in *Reason's Disciples*, 1982] characterizes early English women writers as a distinct social and intellectual subgroup, hellbent on feminist reform: "They were mavericks, operating in a largely hostile environment, who employed bits and pieces of the social and intellectual criticism they found about themselves to understand and to change women's lives." A third example comes to hand from a feminist literary critic [Mary Poovey] who claims [in *The Proper Lady and the Woman Write*, 1984] that women writers suffered ordeals of identity, as cultural definitions of female propriety condemned individualism and certainly the pursuit of a career: "The struggle each of these women waged to create a professional identity was in large measure defined by the social and psychological forces of this ideal of proper—or innate—femininity." Feminist anthologists are now joining the fray with descriptions of women writers as *"guerrilleras"* storming the bastions of the patriarchal establishment. Broad historical judgments and psychologizing of this nature have begun to appear with increasing frequency in feminist studies. These tendencies, I suggest, are misleading because they do not stand up against available historical evidence on how women of the pre-Modern era broke

into literary professions and began shaping careers. Now, unarguably, the young women writers of the early-modern era were mercilessly ridiculed by *some* male writers. Robert Gould, an undervalued Restoration poet-playwright, attacks Behn and "Ephelia" in his blistering antifeminist *Satyrical Epistle* as "hackney Writers" whose verse was "as vicious as their Tails" (1691). Anne Countess of Winchilsea was roundly jeered by Pope's circle in *Three Hours After Marriage,* a successful farce of 1717. Artemisia, the female speaker in Rochester's most polished social satire, *A Letter from Artemisia . . . to Chloe* (1679), begins her verse-epistle with a thirty-one-line summary of contemporary male bias against women writers. "Whore is scarce a more reproachful Name / Than Poetess," she writes her friend. Moreover, women were systematically barred from such early old boys' networks as the universities at Oxford and Cambridge, the Royal Society, and that prototype of the English club, the ubiquitous coffee house. Yet, the record also shows that women's writings *did get into print*. This hard fact of history suggests that overt patriarchal oppression of women did not carry over into the literary establishment; if it had, then work would not have been published and sponsored at all. The flourishing London book trade (the commercial arm of the literary old boys' network) appreciated the market potential of the new books by women. And, as the women went on to show, theirs was not ephemeta but work of lasting value. Publishers cultivated this new breed of writer through complimentary prefaces which, in turn, stimulated interest in the buying public. Benjamin Crayle promoted Jane Barker in his edition of her *Poetic Recreations* (1688). Richard Bassett remarked on the uniqueness of a book he published in 1700. *The Nine Muses,* a collection of elegies on the death of Dryden written exclusively by women. Bernard Lintot, publisher of Pope's *Homer,* ensured a receptive audience for Katherine Philips's *Letters,* which he published in 1705, by soliciting commendatory verses for the book. Other London bookmen, such as James Courtney. John Taylor, and James Nott, publishers respectively of *Female Roems . . . By Ephelia* (1679), Sarah Egerton's *Female Advocate* (1687), and Egerton's *Poems* (1703), gave visibility to their new authors and, moreover, heightened their commercial profile, by seeing their work through subsequent editions.

Then, as now, an integral dynamic in the politics of authorship was finding a place on the circuit. This meant establishing bonds and useful contacts with contemporaries who had already "arrived." Comandeering the authorship circuit, of course, was that well-oiled machine of the literary brotherhood, the old boys' network, a privately-held club of literary brokers who materially determined the success or failure of many careers. We know, for example, that senior male writers sometimes made themselves available to sponsor and advise their talented male juniors. Dryden gave a healthy boost to the early career of William Walsh by gracing Walsh's *Dialogue Concerning Woman* (1691) with a substantial preface. Or consider the early career of John Gay. In a letter dated 23 August 1714, Pope advised the young Gay on his *Fan,* a courtship-and-marriage allegory. Sir Richard Steele also assisted Gay when he recommended *The Fan* in *The English-*

man (10 December 1717), one of Steele's several successful essay-periodicals. Consider, too, the team of classical translators who assisted Dryden in his *Juvenal* of 1692. And Pope proceeded similarly, with a battery of "Auxiliaries," in launching his Homer during the period 1712 to 1726. There was also the Scriblerus Club, that literary fraternity of Pope, Swift, Gay, Parnell, Harley, and Arbuthnot, which produced satire on bad writers and "false Taste." Examples of such professional camaraderie, fraternal links, and career-boosting are legion in the careers of professional men of letters. To a large extent, this is the very stuff of literary history.

But not a few of the literary "good ole boys" also gave a generous hand-up to so-called petticoat-authors, especially at the outset of their careers. Rochester and Dryden, though members of rival coteries, found a mutual friend in Aphra Behn, and they collaborated with her to a far greater extent than Behn scholars have yet to acknowledge. Dryden is especially interesting on this score. As his foremost bibliographer observed, Dryden was "something of a favorite with the [literary] ladies." This is an important dimension of the laureate's literary life which James Winn broaches in his impressive *John Dryden and His World* (1987) and which he presently is examining in a study of gender in Dryden's aesthetics. Dryden counselled the young poet Elizabeth Thomas (his "Corinna"); he expressed to Walsh and Jacob Tonson respectful interest in the verse of Mary Lady Chudleigh; and he was so well regarded by his female contemporaries that upon his death in 1700 he was honored by the collection of their elegies, mentioned above. Further evidence exists in supportive relationships between John Dunton and Elizabeth Singer Rowe, Swift and Delariviére Manley, Joseph Johnson and Mary Wollstonecraft, and George Hickes and Elizabeth Elstob.

Female authorship was a sensitive literary and social issue throughout the Restoration and most of the eighteenth century. No one close to the material denies that. But the facts also show that the victimization school of feminist studies lacks historical grounding. As the literary register tells us, the old boys' network was not without some female rewards.

Katherine Philips: A Life and A Career
(in Three Acts)

The brief but successful dramatic career of Katherine Philips is a fine case-study in supportive partnership between literary men and women. Indeed, Philips's entire literary life, from her ***Pompey*** (1663) to her ***Poems*** (1667), and ***Letters*** (1705), was carefully managed by influential male confidants, relatives, and literary associates. Moreover, as her correspondence reveals, Philips's guided initiation in the politics of authorship was evidently so gratifying an experience that she began to develop a confident sense of herself as an important, independent presence of her day. Because her personal background is essential to my case, let me illustrate the privileged career development and marketing of Katherine Philips within the main lines of her biography.

1. London. The first phase of Philips's life centered in London, site of her early beginnings. Katherine Phillips *née* Fowler was born in London in 1631 into an upper-middle-class English family. Her father, John Fowler, was a prosperous tradesman, a "clothmaker." Her mother, Katherine Oxenbridge, had married down in her match with Fowler, as she descended from a prestigious English pedigree of the fourteenth century, one which included Dr. Daniel Oxenbridge of the Royal College of Physicians and Lady Elizabeth Tyrwhitt *née* Oxenbridge, a lady-in-waiting to Queen Katherine Parr and governess to Princess Elizabeth Tudor. Lady Tyrwhitt, one of two writing women in Katherine Philips's maternal line, produced *Morning and Evening Prayer,* dedicated to Elizabeth and preserved in the British Library. A second literary model for young Katherine Philips would have been her maternal grandmother Katherine Oxenbridge *née* Harby, an amateur poet and an acquaintance of the poet Francis Quarles. To date, Philips scholars have failed to suggest that Katherine Philips was quite plausibly inspired by these two precedential models of female authorship in her own family. This often is the case among early women writers, I have found, whose models are traceable through their matrilineal line.

Literate around the age of four, according to contemporary accounts, young Katherine received training in the rudiments at home, from her cousin the governess Mrs. Blackett. At the age of eight, she began formal training at Mrs. Salmon's fashionable boarding-school for girls at Hackney, where the precocious Philips displayed signs of literary aptitude. It was here that she made her first principal career contact in the person of Mary Aubrey, of the distinguished Welsh royalist Aubreys, who became the dear "Rosania" of Philips's poems. Mary Aubrey helped to ensure Philips's fame by relating essential facts of her life and career to her cousin John Aubrey, whose biographical sketch of Philips continues to be the foundation of all Philips studies, from Philip Souers's monograph (1931) down to the Rev. Patrick Thomas's useful Ph.D. dissertation (1982, University of Wales). This schoolgirl relationship between Philips and Mary Aubrey blossomed into enduring friendship. Most important of all, it was the first of several profitable connections between Katherine Philips and the Welsh peerage.

2. Wales. The second phase of Katherine Philips's life and nascent literary development centered in Wales, that lesser London to the west which gave us such literary personalities as John Aubrey, the Vaughans, Nell Gwyn, and the blind poet Anna Williams of Samuel Johnson's circle. The 1640s were turbulent years for young Katherine and her mother. John Fowler, Katherine's father, died in 1642, after which Katherine's mother married one George Henley of London at St. Andrew's Church on 4 May 1643. But this second marriage was also short-lived, and again we find Katherine Philips's mother a widow. But again she remarried, so that by 1646 Katherine's mother was the second wife of a prominent landowner in the Welsh peerage. At the age of fifteen, young Katherine left London with her mother to relocate to Pembrokeshire in southwest Wales. This would soon become the scene of her literary apprenticeship.

Katherine's second stepfather was Sir Richard Phillipps, second Baronet, of the Picton Castle Phillipps line, a prestigious family in the Welsh peerage and wealthy landowners with broad social and political ties throughout Wales, England, and Ireland. This Welsh clan was also a strong literary and philanthropic power in southwest Wales, as active benefactors of unfortunate writers. A widower when he married Katherine's mother, Sir Richard was related by law to the Dryden line, as his first wife was Elizabeth Dryden, an aunt of John Dryden's. The poet-laureate of the Restoration, then, was a cousin of Katherine Philips's. Dryden acknowledged their kinship and acquaintance in a letter to the young poet Elizabeth Thomas, published by Charles Ward. It was Philips's relative Dryden who promoted her as "Matchless," a seldommentioned but significant fact in Philips studies; and, as Cowley would do in an elegiac ode to "Orinda" prefixed to the first authorized edition of her work in 1667, Dryden praised Philips as the female laureate of the Restoration in his elegiac ode to the poet-painter Anne Killigrew (1685).

When Katherine Philips's second stepfather died in 1648, Dame Phillipps soon took a fourth husband, Major Philip Skippon, also a Welsh notable. Skippon died in 1660. Four times widowed, Katherine Philips's mother had become one of the wealthiest women in Wales. By the time of her death in 1678, she would live to see her daughter a wife, mother, poet, dramatic translator, and literary toast of the English-speaking world.

Marriage, motherhood, and the poetic celebration of platonic friendship between women were the principal concerns of Katherine Philips's late teens and early womanhood. Her mother and their new Welsh relations had selected a husband for young Katherine, one James Philips of Cardigan. A widower and Oxford men, Philips was a Parliamentarian and a political power in southwest Wales and in London. He also was related by blood and marriage to the Picton Castle Phillipps line. At the time of their marriage in August 1648, Katherine was seventeen years old, James Philips fifty-four. For an arranged marriage, theirs was a reportedly happy union, which produced two children, a son Hector, who died in infancy (see "**On Little Hector Philips,**" Katherine's most affecting lyric), and a daughter Katherine, who married into the prominent Wogan family of Boulston, Pembrokeshire, also a cadet branch of the ancient Phillipps line.

Before her public life in literature, Katherine Philips composed intimate lyrics for a small circle of Welsh friends and relatives. Fame never was a goal early on, or so she adamantly claimed in her letters. Philips confined herself to Cardigan during the late 1640s and throughout the 1650s, attending to new domestic duties, but also producing a substantial body of verse devoted largely to her signature theme, female friendship. The center of Philips's emotional life, one gathers, was not hearth and home, but rather the affectionate relationships she

cultivated with the two principal adepts of her "sacred society of Friendship," Mary Aubrey (her "Rosania") and especially Mrs. Anne Owen *née* Lewis of Orielton, another family relation, and the beloved "Lucasia" of Katherine Philips's most expressive lyrics. Mrs. Owen lived in Llandshipping, southeast of Picton Castle and only twenty-five miles from Katherine's new home, The Priory in Cardigan. While Philips's verse is ostensibly innocent of explicit sapphic sentiment, a subtle psychosexual subtext sometimes appears to operate in her wooing and courtship poems to women, and probably merits some attention from Philips scholars.

Philips's juvenilia, if not her entire canon, display a broad, eclectic reading in English and especially French literature, as *préciosité* had been brought into vogue by Henrietta Maria, the French queen-consort of Charles I. Essentially derivative in imagery and technique, Philips's early verse also displays the influence of William Cartwright, a Cavalier poet, playwright, and divine, who enjoyed a high reputation in his day. Philips paid homage to her English master (whom she soon would replace with a French one) in a poem beginning, "Stay, Prince of Phansie," prefixed to Cartwright's *Poems* (1651). This minor publication was Philips's first literary credit, and it gave her immediate local visibility. As in Cartwright's verse, Philips's poems are heavily freighted with the poetic effects of three traditions: (1) Classical and Renaissance traditions of platonic love and platonic friendship; (2) *préciosité,* abundantly represented in the French *élégie* and the mannered salon verse of Voiture and other devotées of the Hôtel de Ramboüillet; and (3) English "wit," as displayed in the poetic ingenuities of Donne and others of the "metaphysical" school. But Philips wisely distinguished her adaptations of these traditions by introducing into her verse a decidedly feminine feature: ardent friendship between women. By in effect "feminizing" the existing traditions in love-poetry formulated by male poets, Philips founded the first English school of an explicitly feminine poetic, a worthy facet of her work that should be explored.

It was in 1662, during an extended visit to Dublin with the newly-married "Lucasia," that Katherine Philips's life and literary aspirations took the sudden turn that catapulted her from the enclosure of Cardigan to the public light of celebrity: Enter Roger Boyle, first Baron Broghill and first Earl of Orrery.

3. Dublin. It was Dublin, not London or Cardigan, that was the site of Philips's career. In Dublin, Philips was "discovered" and her career launched. There, she met several influential Irish and transplanted English nobles and literary bosses who fostered her talent and materially made her career possible.

Two, perhaps three, matters prompted Philips to leave Cardigan for Dublin in 1662. First, she refused to part with her beloved "Lucasia." Mrs. Owen, newly widowed, had recently married the royalist Welsh colonel Marcus Trevor, first Viscount Dungannon and Baron Trevor of Rostrevor. Philips insisted she accompany the new Lady

Dungannon in her journey from Llandshipping, Wales to Dublin to see "Lucasia" happily installed in Manor Rostrevor. Second, Philips had serious family business in Ireland. At the Restoration, her husband, a staunch supporter of Cromwell, had suffered significant financial losses. She hoped to salvage their resources by prosecuting a claim of her husband's to certain properties in Ireland. These legal and civil negotiations extended her visit to well over a year (to her delight). Yet, a third reason for the Dublin visit was quite possibly Philips's developing professional yearnings. Her literary apprenticeship was in Wales, in the 1640s and '50s; by the time of the Restoration in 1660, she was understandably eager to test her potential in a literary climate less competitive than London's and more hospitable certainly to untitled newcomers.

During Philips's stay in Dublin, it was Roger Boyle (familiarly "Orrery") who came forward as her patron. Orrery, an influential power in the Irish peerage and ten years Philips's senior, was the son of Richard Boyle, first Earl of Cork, and a notable figure in Irish affairs, second only to Dublin's Lord Mayor, James Butler Duke Ormande. Like so many pivotal figures in Philips's career, Orrery had close ties to many of Philips's new Welsh relatives. As she wrote in August 1663: "My good friend ["Lucasia"] has favor'd me with the Acquaintance of my Lord Orrery: He is indeed a Man of Parts." And so he was. Hardly the frivolous man Bishop Burnet thought him to be, Orrery was a man of broad talent and achievement, as soldier, statesman, poet, French translator, and dramatist. William Smith Clark, the principal editor of Orrery's work and a leading scholar of the early Irish theater, identified Orrery as Restoration Dublin's most important literary figure and a generous patron of several minor writers, including Philips.

Orrery's literary credits show that he and Philips enjoyed intersecting interests. Like Philips, Orrery was an enthusiast in French literature, platonic friendship, and rhymed heroic drama, particularly tragedy, in which he preceded Dryden and Dryden's brother-in-law Sir Robert Howard. Clark suggests that "the always vain Orrery" promoted Katherine Philips's work in heroic tragedy to aggrandize his own success in the genre. Regardless, by the time Orrery had "discovered" Philips, he had established himself as a literary lion, principally through an early work, *Parthenissa,* a six-volume French romance he produced during the Interregnum. When he met Philips, Orrery was at work on his most successful play, *The General,* a heroic tragedy which premièred at John Ogilby's new Theatre Royal in Smock Alley, Dublin, in February 1663 and later in London at Lincoln's Inn Fields in September 1664. The vogue ushered in by Orrery's *General* may have steered Philips in the direction of heroic tragedy. When she writes in her letters that a fragment of her first Corneille translation just happened to find its way into Orrery's hands, we have to smile.

Orrery's interest in the untitled housewife from Wales was not fortuitous. As a former peer of Cromwell's, Orrery certainly knew Welsh Parliamentarians, a group that included Katherine Philips's husband and others of the larger Phillipps clan (though many Welsh Phillippses were royalists and members of The Society of Sea-Serjeants, a secret Stuart conclave flourishing in southwest Wales after the disgrace of 1649. In her poem "**To the Countess of Roscommon, with a Copy of** *Pompey,*" Philips coyly states that it was not personal ambition but Orrery's prodding that led her to translate Corneille:

> But when you wonder at my bold design,
> Remember who did that high Task enjoin;
> Th' Illustrious *Orrery,* whose least Command,
> You would more wonder if I could withstand.

But Orrery in Dublin had a companion Philips-booster in London, Sir Charles Cotterell. This man, whom Philips affectionately called her "Poliarchus," figured just as prominently in her career as did Orrery. Cotterell was more than Philips's correspondent and confidant: he was her literary editor and royal agent. A Master of Ceremonies at the courts of both Charles I and Charles II, Cotterell was a loyal Stuart, expert diplomat, and seasoned specialist in royal protocol. When the time was most propitious, it was Cotterell who brought Katherine Philips's success in Dublin to the attention of the English court and its prestigious literary circles. Moreover, as a cousin of Sir Thomas Phillipps's sister, Cotterell was related by marriage to Katherine Philips's Welsh relatives. Philips probably consolidated her familial links to Cotterell in London at the Restoration, which she attended and celebrated in several panegyrics to the Stuarts.

Katherine Philips's ambitious decision to render a strict couplet-by-couplet translation of Corneille's heroic tragedy *Pompée,* and later his *Horace,* was correct, both for Philips and for the historical moment. No fledgling in French translation, Philips was more than up to the task. In addition to her work in Corneille, she had translated his paraphrase of Thomas à Kempis's *Imitations,* Madeleine de Scudéry's pastoral *Almahide,* and St. Amant's *La Solitude.* Philips's facility in French literature was publicly acknowledged by John Davies of Kidwelly, a Welsh contemporary, who dedicated to Philips a section of his translation of La Calprende's romance *Cleopatra* (1659-68). Philips also was familiar with the mannered verse of the *précieuses* and with the *élégies* of Henrietta Coligny de la Suze. The Rambouillet circle, it should be noted, included Pierre Corneille, who figured so largely in Philips's dramatic career.

But Philips's attraction to Corneille was more than literary good sense, it was commercially savvy. As a native Londoner with strong literary leanings and influential relatives, foremostly Dryden and Cotterell, Philips naturally kept abreast of literary markets. In her Cardigan-Dublin-London letters, she frequently presses correspondents for information on theatrical vogues. In 1660, when Charles II opened the theaters, which had been legally closed by Parliament since 1642, the climate was indeed overripe for a high-spirited, full-blooded drama. Such was the temper of the times. Philips correctly anticipated that the heroic plays of Corneille, with their oversize tragic heroes, melodramatic plots, lofty ethical arguments, and exotic effects, had exactly what Restoration playgoers wanted. In fact, it is likely that Philips's success in Corneille pointed the way for a run in rhymed heroic drama, especially tragedy, which was rapidly being produced by her contemporaries Orrery, Howard, Dryden, Lee and Otway. Philips's success in Dublin and within months in London brought much attention to French heroic drama by ushering in a Corneille fad throughout the 1660s. This vogue surely gave the lie to Dryden's claim in 1668 that French drama did not have an audience in the English-speaking world. With the necessary hindsight, it was left for Pope in the 1730s to mark the value of French heroic drama in the English plays of the preceding age:

> Late, very late, correctness grew our care,
> When the tir'd nation breath'd from civil war.
> Exact Racine, and Corneille's noble fire
> Show'd us that France had something to admire.

Fortunately for literary historians and Philips scholars, a running account of Philips's *Pompey* is available in her 1662-63 letters from Dublin to Sir Charles Cotterell in London. With precision of detail, Philips discusses with "Poliarchus" her progress on the translation, its revisions, subsequent production, and its publication by John Crooke, the King's Printer in Ireland. But Philips's *Pompey* letters are equally important for what they reveal about the politics of female authorship and about Philips herself. We notice, for example, the significant literary and material support she received from male allies in the actual translation and mounting of the play; and we also observe in her letters the emergence of a strong authorial ego in this most "modest" of English women writers.

First, let us acknowledge Philips's wide network of male allies in the *Pompey* project. As she informs Cotterell, her plans for a Corneille translation began only casually, with a translation of a single scene in act 2. The translation was done in Dublin, and circulated (most strategically, one expects) among Philips's new Irish friends—the Butlers, Dungannons, Ogilbys, Roscommons, Temples, and Tyrells. Amusingly, Philips admits to Cotterell:

> By some Accident or another, my Scene of *Pompey* fell into his [Orrery's] hands and he was pleas'd to like it so well, that he sent me the *French* Original; and the next time I saw him, [he] so earnestly importion'd me to pursue that translation that to avoid the Shame of seeing him who had so lately commanded a Kingdom, become a Petitioner to me for such a Trifle, I obey'd him so far as to finish the Act in which that Scene is; so that the whole Third Act is now *English*.

So impressed was Orrery with Philips's ability to translate Corneille's French alexandrines into neat English heroic couplets that he encouraged her to complete the remaining four acts. He judiciously postponed any premature mention of a stage production and subsequent publication. Again Philips wrote to Cotterell: "[Orrery] enjoin'd me to go on; and not only so, but brib'd me to be contented with the Pains, by sending me an excellent

copy of Verses." Orrery's eighty-two-line encomium to Philips, published in her posthumous *Poems* (1667), was the final gesture that spurred Philips to complete the translation. Thus Orrery's compliment to Philips:

> You English *Corneil's Pompey* with such flame,
> That you both raise our wonder and his fame;
> If he could read it, he like us would call
> The copy greater than th' Original;
>   You cannot mend what is already done,
> Unless you'll finish what you have begun:
> Who your Translation see, cannot but say,
> That 'tis Orinda's Work, and but his Play.

Within just two months, Orrery had what he wanted of Philips: an entirely producible, faithfully-translated heroic tragedy, written by an attractive young English talent with prestigious social and literary connections. His extravagant tribute to Philips was necessary due to her ostensible reticence at the outset of her career. (Brashear would say "feigned" reticence, and she may be correct.) But time was of the essence. Both Orrery and Philips knew that a rival translation of Corneille's play was in progress in London by a competing network, headed up by Sir Edmund Waller with collaborators Sir Charles Sedley, Sir Edward Filmore, Sir Charles Sackville, and Sir Sidney Godolphin. This new urgency attending Philips's translation—from Orrery's first encouragements down to the revisions and last-minute staging details—is dramatically laid out in her correspondence.

A flurry of letters passes between Philips in Dublin and Cotterell in London during the fall and winter of 1662-63. Philips, eager to precede the "Persons of Honour" translation, presses Cotterell to respond to her revisions and to add corrections of his own. They quibble over fine points of grammar and phrasing, the play's interact songs, and the appropriateness of the play's prose dedication to Anne Duchess of York. Philips's letters also document her reliance on Sir Edward Dering (the "Silvander" of her poems), a loyal English friend and the husband of Mary Harvey, one of Philips's former classmates at Hackney. Like Cotterell and Orrery, Dering was more than an influential politician: he was a consummate man of letters, member of the Duke of Ormande's Dublin circle, and, as his diaries show, an avid playgoer. After Orrery persuaded Philips to a Dublin production of her play in Ogilby's new Theatre Royal in Smock Alley (a real playhouse, finer than D'Avenant's theater in London, which, after all, was only a remodelled tennis court), Dering contributed to the project by writing the play's epilogue. The prologue was written by another literary lion, Wentworth Dillon, Earl of Roscommon, an established authority on dramatic translation (*Essay on Translated Verse*, 1684). Roscommon's participation in the *Pompey* project was important, as it gave a literary cachet to Philips's translation.

Orrery's role in the project was formidable. Not only did he initially encourage the project, he also financed it. Acting in effect as Philips's producer, Orrery put up £100 to cover the production's elaborate Roman and Egyptian costumes; he probably paid for the scenery, as well. Operatic in presentation, Philips's *Pompey* was performed and staged in the latest heroic mode, with a good deal of special effects. Orrery, drawing upon impressive resources, did everything to ensure a resplendent production. He even engaged the services of his own French composer to score the play's music. Also assisting with the music were Sir Peter Pett, John Ogilby, the unidentified "Philaster" (Colonel Jeffries of Abercynrig?), and Le Grand (the Duchess of Ormande's personal French composer).

And, so, on Tuesday evening, 10 February 1663, with Joseph Ashbury, a professional actor and theater-manager in the title role, Katherine Philips's *Pompey* premièred in Dublin's newest playhouse. Sumptuously mounted, it was a historic production and it pulled in a celebrity audience. Moreover, attendance at matinee performances proved that Philips's translation was also good family entertainment, a rare thing in the Restoration theatre. Not only did her *Pompey* beat Waller's team to the boards by almost an entire year, it also succeeded as a popular favorite for some fifteen years after its début. Its latest recorded London production was at the Duke of York's theater in 1678. Efforts by jealous contemporaries to undermine Philips's success, such as D'Avenant's burlesque of the play in act 5 of his *Play-house To Be Lett* (1663), were obviously fruitless. Philips's *Pompey* was widely praised, especially by female playgoers and writers, such as Anne Finch, Lady Winchilsea, also a distant relation of the larger Phillipps group, who acknowledged Philips's achievement in two blankverse plays of her own.

As fame often has it, Philips became a celebrity in a single evening. It must have been the grandest night of her life. But even with her facility in French translation and her instinctive flair for stage-production, Philips's extravaganza could never have been mounted without the backing of the old boys' network. The stunning success of the English *Pompey* was attributable to many factors well beyond Katherine Philips's talent. The play was not a first-rate dramatic translation because Philips herself was not a first-rate poet; but the play succeeded quite nicely nonetheless because it was a lavish stage production in the contemporary heroic mode and because it effectively conveyed the high spirit of its original. It also was the first English-language rhymed heroic tragedy produced in the history of the Anglo-Irish theater. And if all of this wasn't novel enough, it was the product of a female pen.

Throughout the several weeks of intensive editorial revision and negotiation preceding *Pompey*'s première, a less obvious aspect of the project begins to emerge with increasing force: *the rising authorial ego of Katherine Philips*. Biographical notices on Philips have traditionally identified her along the lines of the literary persona she and her coterie carefully constructed. In such English literary surveys as Aubrey's *Lives* (1898), Edward Phillips's *Theatrum Poetarum* (1675) (the first such survey to include a dedicated section on women poets), George Ballard's *Memoirs* (1752), Louisa Stuart Costello's *Eminent Englishwomen* (1844), Sir Edmund Gosse's *Seventeenth-century Studies* (1883), and George Saintsbury's *Minor*

Poets of the Caroline Period (1905), Katherine Philips is consistently presented as "the Matchless Orinda," a modest writer of chaste lines. Only Gosse perceived that she was "full of literary ambition." Philips's interest in fame and her strong desire to closely monitor the printing of her work are almost never mentioned by literary chroniclers. In fact, it would appear to be an amusing blunder of literary history that Philips's "sharp Fit of Sickness" over a so-called pirated edition of her poems printed in Fleet Street by Richard Marriot on 25 November 1663, long construed by "Orinda" devotées as hard evidence of her modesty and authorial reticence, was more likely an acute anxiety attack, resulting from Philips's frustration at not being able to *control* the printing of the first public appearance of her work. Quite understandably we find Philips in her letter of 29 January 1664 in a state of high pique. As she writes to Cotterell from Cardigan, Philips attempted to suppress Marriot's "false Edition." In fact, her dilemma was the talk of the town (*Intelligencer*, 18 January 1664). She complains that Marriot's unauthorized "false Book" is based on "false Copies" of her poems and "bad Verses." His is a "villainous Impression," flawed by production errors ("abominably printed"). Marriot's greatest sin was the inclusion of verses which were not hers. As Paul Elmen points out, some of Henry More's poems were included in this surreptitious edition. Philips had good reason to become ill, but not for the reason usually given.

Philips's public self-presentation is that of her persona "Orinda," the shy, self-effacing literary personality behind such lines as "[I] never writ any line in my life with an intention to have it printed. . . . I am so little concerned for the reputation of writing [and] I am so far from expecting applause for anything I scribble." This is the same voice which routinely evaluates her own work as mere "rags of Paper." The pose of modest amateur was supported by Philips's male backers. The anonymous author of the preface to the first authorized edition of Philips's collected work in 1667, probably Cotterell, mentions "how little she desired the fame of being in Print . . . how much she was troubled to be exposed." But as Philips's *Letters* reveal, the woman behind the "Orinda" mask was a wholly different individual. We sometimes see the mask slip in the *Pompey* letters to Cotterell when Philips discloses a sincere interest in fame and when she even boldly positions herself superior to her celebrated contemporaries. Philips's recorded thoughts during the *Pompey* project give us a wholly different reading on her as compared to the traditional Philips hagiography. The *Letters* reveal an aggressive new talent who is very much on the climb. Philips is strident, imposing, sometimes an out-and-out scold. She *must* surpass Waller's rival translation, Philips insists to Cotterell. She *must* present a corrected, bound manuscript copy of *Pompey* to the Duchess of York before Waller's *Pompeius* is printed. Cotterell *must* act as her agent at the English court. "The other translation," she fairly wails to Cotterell on 23 December 1662, "done by so many eminent Hands, will otherwise appear first, *and throw this* [her *Pompey*] *into everlasting Obscurity*" emphasis added). This statement, above all others, along with similar sentiments in subsequent letters to Cotterell of 27 December 1662 and later, are striking revelations because they bring into focus the authentic artistic personality of "the Matchless Orinda." Under the tensions and accelerated pace of the *Pompey* race against Waller's team, Philips's pride of authorship and explicit desire for fame had finally been articulated.

Evidence of Philip's developing egotism throughout the project also exists in her need to make literary decisions independent of Cotterell and Orrery. In the matter of the play's Dedication to Anne Duchess of York, Philips chooses prose over verse. With an unconcealed eye to her (anticipated) readership, she confidently justifies her decision to Cotterell: "Believe me, Poliarchus, I write the Letter [of Dedication] to the Duchess in Prose, neither out of Laziness or Disrespect, but merely because I thought it would have looked more pedantik and affected to have address'd myself to her in Verse. . . . I thought Prose would savour less of Ostentation." Then there is the matter of the songs in *Pompey*. Philips wrote the lyrics for five new inter-act songs; she also contributed to the play's incidental tunes, dances, and the grand masque in act 5. Her musical additions to Corneille's text illustrate both original participation in the project and musical talent. The first song, "Since Affairs of the State," was a popular hit about town, and later included in *Choice Ayres* (1675), a successful collection of contemporary songs compiled by John Playford, a leading London music publisher. Philips cleverly brings attention to her song in a poetic tribute to Elizabeth Boyle of the distinguished Cork family and later wife of Nicholas Tufton, Earl of Thanet, in a poem entitled **"To my Lady Elizabeth Boyle, Singing now affairs &c."** and in these lines to Cotterell of 10 January 1663: "I was so puff'd up with the Honour of [the dutchess of York's] Protection, that I have ventur'd to lengthen the Play by adding Songs in the Intervals of each Act, which they flatter me here are not amiss. . . . Philaster has already set one of them agreeably, and [an] abundance of People are learning it." As one critic persuasively demonstrates, Philips's five inter-act songs were quite unlike the purely transitional tunes in most English drama up to that time. Hers were integrally linked to the action in *Pompey,* and they also commented on the play's political intricacies, thereby assisting playgoers' interpretation of the play.

Philips's rising ego is never more apparent than when she takes on the competition. The *Pompeius* of Waller and his team—many senior literary men who surely would have regarded the ruddy-faced housewife from Wales an amusing interloper—was thought to be unfaithful to Corneille, according to Philips. Her criticism of the rival translation is severe, even condescending. In a letter to Cotterell of 17 September 1663, she is harsh: "There is room in several places for an ordinary Critick to shew his Skill. But I cannot but be surprised at the great Liberty they have taken in adding, omitting, and altering the Original as they please themselves: This I take to be a Liberty not pardonable in Translators, and unbecoming the Modesty of the Attempt." She also complains that the Waller team has "garbl'd" Corneille's text. In assuming "so great a License," the Waller translation is a weak imitation of the

original, she judges; and it is marred, moreover, by "bad" rhymes. "But what chiefly disgusts me," Philips goes on, "is that the Sence most commonly languishes. . . . I really think the best of their lines equal to the worst in my translation."

When Katherine Philips left Dublin in mid-June 1663 to return to the isolation of Cardigan, Wales, little did she know that her career was essentially over. Never again would she hear the applause of her contemporaries or work with Orrery and Cotterell on a new play. Philips's aspirations for a second success equal to if not surpassing her *Pompey* were dashed by circumstance. Her timing, as always, was perfect; she simply was unlucky.

The last year of Philips's life was sheer anticlimax compared to the gay round of her Dublin visit. Not that Philips's enthusiasm had waned any. If anything, she returned to Cardigan heady with celebrity. Now back on Welsh soil she wasted little time parlaying her maiden success into a second theatrical vehicle. With the success of *Pompey*. Philips became discernibly different from the imposing personality of the Cotterell letters. Evidently validated by the acclaim of 1663, her post-*Pompey* correspondence gives us a relaxed, voide. At this stage in her career, Philips had become a self-conscious, professional writer with a product to sell, a commercial market to cultivate, and a reputation to maintain and aggrandize. Unlike her Tudor female predecessors, who circulated their writings in private, Katherine Philips was now a published author and a celebrity. By 1663, she had a public to please, and she was eager to delight again.

Philips peaked very early in her career, and she was keen to build on her notoriety. Moving rapidly, she wisely solidified her position by (safety) continuing with material she could manage. Again, she turned to her French master Corneille and selected his *Horace,* a heroic tragedy of early Rome, Like his *Pompée,* Corneille's *Horace* carried strong nationalistic applications for Restoration playgoers. The existence of an earlier English translation by Sir William Lower (*Horatius,* 1656), did not temper her zeal any more than Waller's competing translation of Corneille's *Pompée* daunted her progress in 1662-63. Philips writes Cotterell on 8 January 1664 that she has begun a second Corneillean translation. This time, she requires no direction from Dublin and London allies. Like her *Pompey,* Philips's *Horace* was intended to be a lavish spectacle; and what is more Philips evidently was planning a London première of *Horace* under her own personal direction. A seasoned tactician by this time, Philips enlisted Cotterell in London and "Lucasia" and Elizabeth Boyle in Dublin to help her arrange a trip to London, where she would stay with her brother-in-law Hector Philips. Ostensibly, Philips had to make the trip to help negotiate a civil post in London for her husband. But what a fine opportunity, she must have thought, to be back on native English soil, in the city of my birth, and *there* put forward my new play!

But only three months into the visit, Philips contracted the fatal smallpox, then at near-epidemic levels. The most celebrated English woman writer of the seventeenth century died quietly and unremarkably in a house in Fleet Street on 22 June 1664, attended in her final hours by her dear "Rosania" (Mary Aubrey). Philips was not quite thirty-three years old. She was buried in the churchyard of St. Benet-Sherehog, at the end of Syth's Lane in London, alongside the graves of her infant son Hector, her father John Fowler, and two grandparents. Ironically, several months before her own death, Philips had composed an elegy on the death of Lord Rich, heir of the Earl of Warwick, who had died of smallpox that same year. In lines presaging her own untimely death, the poem begins, "Have not so many lives of late / suffic'd to quench the greedy thirst of Fate?"

Philips's *Horace* was produced posthumously at London's Theatre Royal during the 1668-69 Season, based on the four acts Philips completed before her death (her work on the play ended with act 4, scene 6) and the remaining translation done by Sir John Denham (scene 7 of act 4 and all of act 5). The Duke of Monmouth, whose manuscript notebook, taken from him after Sedgemoor, included lines from Philips's verses, delivered the play's prologue. It included high praise for its deceased author:

> So soft, that to our Shame we understand
> They could not fall but from a Ladies hand.
> Thus while a Woman HORACE did translate,
> HORACE did rise above the Roman fate.

Philips's *Horace* was a favorite at the court of Charles II. It saw an amateur court production on 4 February 1668 with Barbara Villiers, Charles's most rapacious mistress, in a leading role (she borrowed the Crown jewels from the Tower of London just for the occasion). The four acts of Philips's *Horace* were first published in London in 1667 by Henry Herringman. The complete translation, with Denham's contribution, appeared in a subsequent publication by Herringman in 1669, under the title *Horace. A Tragedy. Translated from Monsieur Corneille. The Fifth Act translated by Sir John Denham*. Interestingly, Jacob Tonson selected Charles Cotton's translation of act 5 (1671) over Denham's in his (Tonson's) edition of Philips's work in 1710.

It is regrettable that Philips did not live to complete *Horace,* as she never would have authorized the production it received in London. Like her *Pompey, Horace* was operatic; but its exotic effects and overall intent were severely compromised. Samuel Pepys, an informed theater enthusiast, attended a production of the play on 19 January 1669, and judged it a low "silly Tragedy." The play's entertainments (its songs, masques, incidental tunes) were not any of Philips's doing, but ill-advised additions by John Lacy, a professional English actor-playwright whose forte was not tragedy but comedy. The levity Lacy introduced into the play seriously muddled and unbalanced the play's tragic ethos. "Lacy hath made a farce of several dances." Pepys observed. "[I am] not much pleas'd with the play." Properly produced. Philips's *Horace* might have surpassed her first effort, had she lived to see the play through production. It certainly outdistanced *Pompey*

as a translation. By 1664, Philips had become a confident translator, and Corneille an old friend. Her *Horace* was far less literal and strenuous a translation than *Pompey* since Philips's original procedure (strict line-for-line translation) is not as apparent in the second play. But instead of being the culmination of her work during the 1660s, Philip's *Horace* was merely an entertainment for the court and, moreover, a surprising embarrassment to serious playgoers.

Philips's sudden death at the height of her celebrity was a devastating blow to the literary community. But before long, the "Orinda" machine was in full swing. First came Herringman's edition of Philips's work in 1667, a tall handsome folio graced with an engraved frontispiece portrait by William Faithorne of the Vander Gucht portrait-bust of Philips. This first authorized edition of her collected work, reissued by Herringman in 1669 and in 1678, and by Tonson in 1710, was initiated by Sir Charles Cotterell, Philips's literary executor. It consisted of an anonymous preface (probably by Cotterell); commendatory verses by Abraham Cowley, Thomas Flatman, Cotterell, a pseudonymous Irishwoman poet "Philo-Phillipa" (Elizabeth Boyle?), Roscommon, and James Tyrell; 116 original poems and five verse-translations; and the two Corneille translations. Then, Philips's letters to Cotterell were gathered, selected, and certainly edited. Forty-eight were published in 1710 by Bernard Lintot (who may have obtained them through his son) under the title *Letters from Orinda to Poliarchus*. Philips's correspondence was reissued by Lintot, with one additional letter, in 1729. As the chronological gaps in the letters suggest, some of Philips's correspondence to Cotterell have either been lost or surpressed.

Curiously, Philips scholars have yet to raise a most obvious question: had Philips lived to full creative maturity, what direction might her work have taken? Two contemporaries close to the "Orinda" myth, namely Cotterell and "Philo-Phillipa," provide clues that allow us to envision Philips in her later years as an author of serious cultural engagement. First, Cotterell (if, in fact, the author of the preface to Philips's collected work) discloses important information about a body of "lost" work by Philips, being many "excellent discourses . . . on several subjects." He has seen these essays, and he reports that they would comprise a volume much larger than Philips's published folio of 1667, 124 pages. Perhaps today's recovery work in feminist studies will locate some of Philips's "lost" essays. Certainly they would be valuable to the history of English feminism, as Philips's essays preceded the published essays of such important turn-of-the-century feminist writers as Bathsua Makin (*Essay to Revive the Antient Education of Gentlewomen,* 1673), Mary Astell (*A Serious Proposal to the Ladies,* 1694), and Mary Lady Chudleigh (*Essays upon Several Subjects,* 1710). Furthermore, given Philips's life and times, her prose writings may offer fresh perspectives on French literature, dramatic translation, and the turbulent political setting of the day. As one who lived through three administrations,

Philips may have recorded in these "lost" pieces some important topical information.

The elusive "Philo-Phillipa," clearly a female Irish intimate of Philips's (possibly, a Boyle), gives us further insight into Philips's projected literary maturity. In her rousing tribute to Philips, "Philo" expresses the hope that one day Philips will discover her own voice, and then produce original not translated material:

> But if your fetter'd Muse thus praised be,
> What great Things do you write when it is free?
> When it is free to chuse both sence and words,
> Or any subject the vast World affords?

Had her *Horace* received the success it deserved, Katherine Philips would have had two major theatrical successes to her credit. Surely she would have gone on to produce original drama of her own in the mid-1660s. And it is entirely likely that she would have become involved in feminist issues, especially in light of the rise of feminist drama by Behn and her lesser contemporaries "Ephelia," Polwhele, Boothby, and "Ariadne." While it is true that Philips never displayed overt feminist leanings, the woman was ambitious. Understandably, she would have moved her career forward along commercially attractive lines.

At full maturity, an impressive Katherine Philips steps forward. Even as a young, underdeveloped writer of slight life experience and cloying sentimentality, Philips succeeded in becoming the most celebrated English woman writer of the seventeenth century. Had she lived through the 1670s and '80s, Philips might have been as versatile as Behn. Writing Katherine Philips into her future is to observe a career of remarkable development: the adolescent bagatelle of Cardigan and the early friendship lyrics; the dramatic translations from Corneille; the prose-essays Cotterell mentions; and, then, perhaps a historical chronicle, some original drama, even some feminist writings. Philips at full maturity emerges as a significant, eclectic talent in an exuberant age of English literature. Had she grown to a plane of relative artistic independence (Behn's achievement), Katherine Philips could have put aside the "Orinda" myth and the old boys' network that welded and promoted it as mere theatrical props of her past.

Paula Loscocco (essay date 1993)

SOURCE: "Manly Sweetness: Katherine Philips among the Neoclassicals," in *The Huntington Library Quarterly*, Vol. 56, No. 3, Summer, 1993, pp. 259-79.

[*In the following excerpt, Loscocco discusses "the decline in Philips's reputation in the eighteenth century," which she explains by "charting the interplay between changes in the reception of her poetry and changes . . . in neoclassical literary aesthetics of the seventeenth and eighteenth centuries."*]

When Katherine Philips's posthumous *Poems* appeared in 1667, the volume included prefatory verses by Abraham

Cowley celebrating her as England's esteemed "Woman Laureat." Few at the time dissented from Cowley's assessment, and many—some of them prominent writers—agreed. By now, however, as critic Harriette Andreadis remarked in 1989, the "acclaim of [Philips's] contemporaries has . . . worn very thin": at best she has a poem or two in anthologies, representing a minor link between metaphysical and neoclassical poetry; at worst, critics disparage her work as "florid," "cajoling," or overly "fluent."

No one has yet adequately accounted for the decline in Philips's literary fortunes. When did this decline occur? What was the nature of her original reception? What were subsequent views of her work like? How did different senses of her poetry evolve? My essay attempts to answer these kinds of questions. I locate the decline in Philips's reputation in the eighteenth century, and I account for it by charting the interplay between changes in the reception of her poetry and changes—especially as these involve questions of gender—in neoclassical literary aesthetics of the seventeenth and eighteenth centuries.

In the course of my discussion, I identify three major phases in Philips's reception. The first spanned the 1650s and 1660s. The many writers who applauded Philips's works during these years did so in the gendered terms provided by contemporary neoclassical literary aesthetics, paying particular attention to what they described as the "masculine" strength and "feminine" sweetness of her verses. The second phase occurred in the late seventeenth and early eighteenth centuries.

Though enthusiasm for Philips's poetry continued to be expressed during these years, a reworking of the central concepts of neoclassical poetics dramatically altered the gender-configurations of the terms used to describe her poems. As a consequence, readers who praised her writings at this time did so by focusing exclusively on what they perceived to be the masculine qualities of her writing. The third phase began while the second was still in progress. At the height of the laudatory and "masculine" period in Philips's reputation, a certain Thomas Newcomb used the prevailing preference for literary masculinity against her and condemned her poetry as being irredeemably feminine. Arising from and speaking to an aesthetics hostile to what a contemporary characterized as "Feminine Expression" of any kind, Newcomb's critique appears to have tipped the balance of opinion against Philips: after his attack of 1712, no edition of her works was printed for the rest of the century, and when individual poems were reprinted, they invariably appeared in specialized collections devoted to the works of "lady poetesses." With scattered exceptions, it is only in recent years that scholars have argued for broader recognition of Philips's literary skills and merits.

We can most readily gauge the nature of Philips's mid-seventeenth-century reception if we examine the commendatory verses prefacing her 1667 *Poems*. All of these verses follow the same general progression. A poem begins by addressing the fact of Philips's sex and its presence in her poetry; it goes on to discuss her poems in traditionally neoclassical terms. In this way, I would suggest, the commendatory poems portray Philips not only as a woman writer, but also—perhaps even primarily— as a neoclassical poet.

In her study of the conventions of seventeenth-century commendatory poems on women writers [in *Eighteenth Century Life,* 1988], Joanna Lipking comes to just the opposite conclusion. She agrees that men praise these women for their ability to excel (like men) as poets, but she also finds that this praise tends to revert to the fact that these poets are women. A "characteristic feature of men's commendations" of a woman writer, she notes, is "their ineluctable drift toward the feminine side of her identity." Lipking focuses exclusively on the gender-content of poems about women writers. At least in the case of Philips, however, mid-seventeenth-century readers did not limit themselves to issues connected with her gender. Rather, they repeatedly and pointedly broadened their discussions to include other aspects of her poetry. If we likewise expand our discussion, we can discover the ways in which Philips's contemporaries paid serious attention to her not only as a woman, or a woman poet, but also as a poet writing successfully within the neoclassical idiom of her day.

The central statement of the literary tastes of the era, John Dryden's 1668 *An Essay of Dramatick Poesie,* serves as a yardstick against which to measure the neoclassical content of the encomia on Philips. Dryden begins by setting the ancients against the moderns. Eugenius, spokesman for the moderns, takes the upper hand immediately: "'I cannot think so contemptibly of the Age in which I live, or so dishonourably of my own Countrey, as not to judge we equal the Ancients in most kinds of Poesie, and in some surpass them.'" Roger Boyle, in "The Earl of Orrery to Mrs. Philips," takes a similar if somewhat hyperbolic stand when he sets her achievements against those of the Greeks and Romans:

> Past ages could not think those things you do,
> For their Hill was their basis and height too:
> So that 'tis truth, not compliment, to tell,
> Your lowest height their highest did excel.

We have, of course, no way of determining Orrery's sincerity in these lines. But comparison of his words with those of Dryden suggests that Orrery's terms of praise are consistent with those of Restoration literary discussion generally, and are not specific to encomia on women poets.

Dryden also contrasts French and English dramatic poetry, arguing in favor of the latter. "'[O]ur errours are so few, and little,'" states Neander, the proponent of English poetry, "'and those things wherein we excel them [the French] so considerable, that we ought of right to be prefer'd before them.'" Philips's translations of Corneille's plays made her work a natural focus for this kind of critical discussion. Orrery's praise of her translations remains pointedly within the terms of nationalist debate and does not refer to her gender:

> You English Corneil[le]'s Pompey with such
>   flame,
> That you both raise our wonder and his fame;
> If he could read it, he like us would call
> The copy greater than th'original. . . .
> The French to learn our language now will seek,
> To hear their greatest Wit more nobly speak.

Philo-Philippa, in "To the excellent Orinda," similarly claims in traditionally neoclassical fashion that Philips's translations "Refin'd and stamp'd" the French original, transforming its "ore" into English gold.

Most centrally, Dryden's *Essay* and the encomia to Philips share a definition of literature as "sweet" yet "correct," "easy" yet "significant," a definition highly prized by neoclassical poetics. The writers of the "'last Age,'" Dryden, in the person of Eugenius, notes,

> "can produce nothing so courtly writ, or which expresses so much the Conversation of a Gentleman, as Sir *John Suckling;* nothing so even, sweet, and flowing as Mr. Waller; nothing so Majestique, so correct as Sir *John Denham;* nothing so elevated, so copious, and full of spirit, as Mr. *Cowley.* . . ."

> All of them were thus far of *Eugenius* his opinion, that the sweetness of *English* Verse was never understood or practis'd by our Fathers. . . . : and every one was willing to acknowledge how much our Poesie is improv'd, by the happiness of some Writers yet living; who first taught us to mould our thoughts into easie and significant words.

Dryden's pairings of terms here, "sweet" and "easie" with "Majestique" and "significant," strikingly recall the single most common feature of the commendatory poems on Philips: the attention paid to her synthesis of "masculine" and "feminine" poetic qualities. In this context, the encomia's terms of gender, though deriving from and specific to the poems' female subject, also participate in general poetic discourse in ways separate from the sex of the poet. "Feminine" does refer to Philips's gender; it also refers to the qualities of "smoothness" and "sweetness" valued by contemporary literary aesthetics. "Masculine" suggests the anomalous achievement of poetry by a woman; it also suggests the qualities of "wit" and "strength" that were understood to ground and steady the mellifluousness of neoclassical verse.

Stanza 3 of Cowley's "Upon Mrs. Philips her Poems" provides a clear example of the dual allegiances that terms like "strength" and "sweetness" have in the commendatory poems:

> Where'er I see an excellence,
> I must admire to see thy well-knit sense,
> Thy numbers gentle, and thy fancies high,
> Those as thy forehead smooth, these sparkling as
>   thine eye.
>   'Tis solid, and 'tis manly all,
>   Or rather, 'tis angelical:

> For, as in Angles, we
> Do in thy verses see
> Both improv'd sexes eminently meet;
> They are than Man more strong, and more than
> Woman sweet.

Lipking focuses on Cowley's reference to Philips's forehead and eyes as evidence of a male poet's inability to see beyond gender. It is perhaps more to the point, however, to note that Cowley's mixed-sex "angelical" is an almost perfect analogue to Dryden's ideal of poetry that is both "strong" and "sweet." All that Cowley has done to the terms here is to make explicit, as suits his occasion, the gender-markings of the two adjectives.

Philo-Philippa is even more revealing. Her poem describes Philips's translation of *Pompey* as that play's ultimate point of development, mixing as it does Philips's feminine "fancy" and Corneille's masculine "sense." She then offers one of the encomia's most neoclassical critiques of Philips's poetry:

> A gliding sea of crystal doth best show
> How smooth, clear, full, and rich your verse
>   doth flow:
> Your words are chosen, cull'd, not by chance
>   writ,
> To make the sense, as anagrams do hit.
> Your rich becoming words on the sense wait,
> As Maids of Honour on a Queen of State.
> 'Tis not white satin makes a verse more white,
> Or soft; Iron is both, write you on it.

Smooth sense, soft iron: Philo-Philippa's terms dovetail with Dryden's, exemplifying the ways in which the commendatory verses prefacing Philips's 1667 *Poems* portray her as a successful poet according to the literary standards of her day.

As the poems by Philo-Philippa and especially Cowley suggest, the reputation of Philips's poetry was bolstered by the fact that neoclassical literary discourse in mid-seventeenth-century England was itself gendered: commentators regularly used terms of gender to describe and praise poetic achievement. Lipking notes that the encomia on women poets compliment women for combining masculine strength and wit with feminine beauty and softness, but she downplays the crucial fact that these qualities were held up as ideals for writers of both sexes. Men as well as women found their writings praised for being, in Cowley's words, "than Man more strong, and more than Woman sweet." Cowley, in fact, perhaps the single most applauded mid-century poet, was himself frequently described in this manner.

On the occasion of Cowley's death in 1667, John Denham wrote of his poetry:
> His fancy and his judgment such,
> Each to the other seem'd too much,
> His severe judgment (giving Law)
> His modest fancy kept in awe:

> As rigid Husbands jealous are,
> When they believe their Wives too fair.

Critical discourse had by 1667 established as conventional the proposition that (implicitly feminine) fancy required the counterpoising weight of (implicitly masculine) judgment. Denham's description of Cowley modifies this convention in several ways. First, he emphasizes the equality of fancy and judgment, noting that "Each to the other seem'd too much." He extends this perception into the following lines, where ambiguity as to whether "fancy" or "judgment" is the subject of the verb subtly undermines the traditional priority given "severe judgment." In addition, his reference to "Husbands" and "Wives" is unusually explicit in its gendering of judgment and fancy. By characterizing husbands' judgment as "severe," "rigid," "jealous," and apt as a consequence to "believe" their "modest" wives, fancy "too fair," moreover, Denham alters conventional emphasis. Instead of virtuous judgment holding licentious fancy in check, virtuous fancy is presented as the faultless equal of a judgment that tends to over-censoriousness and misperception.

If Denham locates in Cowley's writing a marriage of gendered fancy and judgment, Thomas Sprat goes considerably further, praising Cowley's poetry for its ability to embrace what he calls a "variety of Sexes in Poetry." He begins his discussion of Cowley's literary achievement neutrally enough, noting that "[i]n his life he join'd the innocence and sincerity of the Scholar with the humanity and good behaviour of the Courtier. In his Poems he united the Solidity and Art of the one with the Gentility and Gracefulness of the other." Almost immediately, however, he brings to the surface the gender-markings of scholarly "solidity" and courtly "gracefulness." Certain readers might argue that Cowley's verses were far from uniformly "graceful"; this, Sprat argues, was Cowley's "choice, not his fault":

> Where the matter required it, he was as gentle as any man. But where higher Virtues were chiefly to be regarded, an exact numerosity was not then his main care. This may serve to answer those who upbraid some of his Pieces with roughness, and with more contractions than they are willing to allow. But these Admirers of gentlenesse without sinews should know that different Arguments must have different Colours of Speech: that there is a kind of variety of Sexes in Poetry as well as in Mankind: that as the peculiar excellence of the Feminine Kind is smoothnesse and beauty, so strength is the chief praise of the Masculine.

Though Sprat here promotes "strong" or "masculine" poetry, he does so only in defiance of critics who require unrelievedly "smooth" or "Feminine" verse. The ideal is gendered "variety": he applauds Cowley for choosing a style that is, as he sees it, alternately sweetly "Feminine" or strongly "Masculine," as the content requires. Because he describes literary style through metaphors of gender, Sprat also distances his discussion (though perhaps inadvertently) from any reference to a writer's actual sex. "Masculine" and "Feminine" describe styles appropriate to the material being written, not to the sex of the person doing the writing.

Cowley's writing was portrayed by others, then, in much the same terms that he himself used to portray Philips's. Not coincidentally, in the years following the deaths of Philips (1664) and Cowley (1667), a number of writers joined the two poets together in the kind of literary union of the sexes perceived to be at the heart of their respective poetics. James Tyrrell's poem prefacing Philips's 1667 **Poems** notes that Cowley—"the great Pindar's greater Son"—has "retir'd" to Heaven, leaving the world bereft: "He, and Orinda from us gone, / What Name, like theirs, shall we now call upon?" Francis Bernard, commending his friend, Thomas Flatman, on his 1674 *Poems and Songs,* argues that anyone "who e're did hear, / Of *Cowley* or *Orinda's* fame" would appreciate Flatman's poems. In her 1688 *Poetical Recreations,* Jane Barker, warning her friends against the now debauched Muses, cites Cowley and Philips as the twin poets of chaste love:

> Though to *Orinda* they [the Muses] were ty'd,
> That nought their Friendship cou'd divide:
> And *Cowley's* Mistress had a Flame
> As pure and lasting as his *Fame:*
> Yet now they're all grown *Prostitutes.*

Perhaps the definitive pairing occurs in James Gardiner's prefatory poem to Samuel Woodford's 1667 *A Paraphrase Upon The Psalms of David.* Gardiner understands English letters to have restored drooping poesy to its original glory, and he cites Philips and Cowley as beacons of a new poetic golden age in which "pure spirit[s]" mix with "manly Theam[s]":

> One of each Sex this fruitful Age has shown,
> (And fruitful had she been, if none
> But that immortal Paire were known;)
> Though she has many more to boast,
> *Cowley,* and bright *Orinda* do adorn it most.

The frequency with which writers like Gardiner cite Philips and Cowley as their age's "immortal Paire" in poetry makes it clear that Philips was praised by her contemporaries as the peer of a writer like Cowley. The extraordinary pairing of a man and a woman poet also reinforces the idea that mid-seventeenth-century literary culture understood "variety of the Sexes," an even blend of masculine and feminine literary attributes, as a constitutive element of its poetry.

When Cowley described Philips's poems as "than Man more strong, and more than Woman sweet," then, he was speaking within what was to his contemporaries an established literary aesthetic. By explicitly gendering "strength" as masculine and "sweetness" (or "softness") as feminine, Cowley used neoclassical terms in ways common to the authors of his era. And by positing an ideal balance between these terms, Cowley joined other writers in assigning equal value to contemporary concepts of literary masculinity and femininity.

The aesthetic Cowley described, however, did not last. As early as the 1670s, there appeared what seems to have been a backlash against the notion of a literary aesthetic based on positive attributes linked to both genders. Though "sweet" and (especially) "strong" remained critical terms of choice from the mid-seventeenth century to the mid-eighteenth, articulating central neoclassical literary values, the concepts of gender associated with the two terms changed dramatically in the late seventeenth century. Mid-seventeenth-century writers, as I have shown, linked the terms "strong" and "sweet" to contemporary concepts of masculinity and femininity. By the end of the century, however, these terms had acquired an entirely different set of gender-associations: "strong" and "sweet" had come to be attached *only* to masculinity; femininity had been removed from encomiastic critical vocabulary altogether. By the end of the century, literary femininity—frequently but not always signaled by the term "softness"—had in fact become a potent tool of critical dispraise. I describe this shift in gender-associations in order to provide a context in which to understand the vicissitudes of Philips's literary reputation.

Wentworth Dillon, the earl of Roscommon, provides a trenchant example of the ways in which terms of praise previously associated with femininity could be re-gendered as masculine. In 1657, James Howell had proposed a marriage between "[m]ale" English and implicitly "feminine" romance languages like French. Twenty-seven years later, in his 1684 *An Essay on Translated Verse,* Roscommon redefined the relationship between the two languages as a competition in which the English tortoise overtakes the French hare:

> But now We [English] shew the world a nobler way,
> And in *Translated Verse* do more than *They* [French],
> Serene and clear, Harmonious *Horace* flows,
> With sweetness not to be exprest in *Prose.*

English "sweetness" here is not simply a question of verse as opposed to prose. Rather, Roscommon states,

> The *Fault* is more their *Languages* than theirs:
> 'Tis courtly, florid, and abounds in words,
> Of softer sound than ours perhaps affords;
> But who did ever in *French Authors see*
> The comprehensive *English Energy?*
> . . . I'l Recant, when *France* can shew me *Wit,*
> As strong as *Ours,* and as *succinctly Writ.*

The superior "serene and clear . . . sweetness" that Roscommon hears in English, then, is a function not only of versification but also of the language's native energy, succinctness, and strength. French, on the other hand, owes its "courtly" and "florid" nature to its inherently "softer sound." Though Roscommon distinguishes between admirable sweetness and unfortunate softness, however, he does not explicitly attach gender to either quality. He leaves this for John Dryden to do, in the commendatory poem which prefaces Roscommon's work.

In his 1668 *Essay* (written 1665), Dryden had spoken for his time when he had embraced a literary aesthetic based on "feminine" sweetness and "masculine" strength. Twenty years later, he spoke for a different time when he articulated an altered understanding of these two key neoclassical concepts. In his 1684 poem, *"To the Earl of Roscommon, on his Excellent Essay on Translated Verse,"* Dryden nimbly repatriates "sweetness" into masculine critical territory. He recounts how in medieval times "barb'rous Nations, and more barb'rous Times / Debas'd the majesty of Verse to Rhymes," but how, later, Italy and France resuscitated poetry by showing "What Rhyme improv'd in all its height can be; / At best a pleasing Sound, and fair barbarity." It was up to the English, however, to complete the restoration of poetry, by transforming "fair" and implicitly feminine "Rhyme" into explicitly masculine "Verse." *"Brittain, last,"* Dryden notes, "In Manly sweetness all the rest surpass'd." Manly sweetness: the phrase is remarkable, given the precision with which poets twenty years earlier had repeatedly characterized "sweetness" as "like a *woman*." It is possible that Dryden here has simply condensed the traditional pairing, distilling masculine strength and feminine sweetness into "manly sweetness." But his unusual way of formulating the convention suggests that the phrase instead represents a self-conscious attempt to legislate the way in which the term "sweetness" is to be understood. Used in this way, the adjective "manly" not only prevents the almost automatic association of "sweetness" with femininity, but it also replaces femininity with the opposing idea of manliness. The phrase "manly sweetness" works to redefine a central neoclassical literary term away from femininity and toward masculinity.

My reading of "manly sweetness" is supported by the remarkable fact that in the ode, *"To the Pious Memory of the Accomplisht Young Lady Mrs Anne Killigrew,"* written two years later, Dryden scrupulously avoids characterizing her virtues and achievements as sweet or feminine in any way. In his portrayal of Killigrew's literary and moral lineage, for example, Dryden never once mentions a female relation. Instead, her "Father was transfus'd into [her] Blood"; she acquired her "Morals" and "Noble Vigour" by reading "the best of Books, her Fathers Life." At her birth, her "Brother-Angels" played their harps, and "all the Blest Fraternity of Love" rejoiced. Dryden draws deliberate attention to the ways in which he separates Killigrew from her natural gender, as comparison of his poem on Killigrew with Cowley's on Philips makes clear. Philips, Cowley states, is "than Man more strong, and more than Woman sweet." Killigrew's "Wit," Dryden declares, "was more than Man, her Innocence a Child!" A child: Dryden here de-genders what had once been understood as the feminine quality of "Innocence," while at the same time he preserves the paired symmetry of Cowley's neoclassical formulation. His efforts suggest the degree of opprobrium that seems by the mid-1680s to have attached to literary terms associated in any way with women or femininity.

The recoil away from femininity in neoclassical poetics was in full force by the mid-1680s, but we can find evidence of its existence before then. As early as the 1670s, individual male writers began to lash out at poetry that could be characterized as either feminine or sweet. In 1670, for example, Samuel Woodford, in a poem prefacing Izaak Walton's *Life of Herbert,* declares that *"Sacred Poesie"*

> No longer shall a Virgin reckoned be,
>   (What ere with others 'tis) by me,
>   A Female Muse, as were the Nine:
>   But (full of Vigor Masculine)
> An Essence Male, with Angles his Companions
>   shine.

Woodford banishes femininity from the realm of sacred poetry altogether, insisting that the spirit of such poetry is essentially male. His vision of poetry (and later of Herbert) as a male angel anticipates Dryden's description of Killigrew's "Brother-Angles" and contrasts sharply with Cowley's angels, in whom "Both improv'd sexes eminently meet." In 1677, the writer "A. B." similarly defends the masculine *"Vigour"* of John Cleveland's muse against *"smooth, weak Rhymer*[s]." *"Let such to Women write,"* he sneers, spelling out the thinly veiled gender-marking behind his comments, *"you write to Men."*

The generation of women poets who came of age after the mid-seventeenth century offered eloquent testimony concerning changes in attitudes toward gender in the neoclassical literary environment. A number of these writers identified the mid-century as the Age of Orinda, and bemoaned the fact that, by the mid-1680s, that age had come and gone. They were acutely aware that an aesthetic that welcomed literary values identified with women, like sweetness or softness, had represented an encouraging environment for actual women writers. They were equally aware that an aesthetic that scorned what it conceived of as feminine literary values, or appropriated terms traditionally linked to femininity as "male," would almost certainly prove to be inhospitable to women writers.

Perhaps the clearest statement of the effect on women poets of the shift in critical values appears in Anne Killigrew's poem *"Upon the saying that my VERSES were made by another,"* published in 1686. Killigrew compares her circumstances with those of Philips, and finds not only that Philips was admired apart from the fact of her sex but also that she lived in an age that singled out for particular applause the kinds of writing that it associated with women:

> Orinda, (*Albions* and her Sexes Grace)
> Ow'd not her Glory to a Beauteous Face,
> It was her Radiant Soul that shown With-in. . . .
> Nor did her Sex at all obstruct her Fame,
> But higher 'mong the Stars it fixt her Name;
> What she did write, not only all allow'd,
> But ev'ry Laurel, to her Laurel, bow'd!

What a woman of Philips's day wrote, Killigrew remarks with revealing astonishment, was not only "allow'd"—it was actually *preferred.* In contrast, Killigrew describes her own era as an "Envious Age" in which readers unjustly accuse her of plagiarism and scorn her person. The comparison with Philips suggests that Killigrew's "Sex" has indeed "obstruct[ed] her Fame." And though she claims that the hostility she has encountered is directed "only to Me alone," her decision to compare her situation with that of a poet who had been dead for almost two decades implies a contrast more of eras than of persons.

Other writers corroborate Killigrew's sense that a female "golden age" of literature lies in the mid-century past. Among the poems prefacing Jane Barker's 1688 *Poetical Recreations* is one by "Philaster" which begins,

> Soon as some envious *Angel's* willing hand
>   Snatch'd Great *Orinda* from our happy Land . . .
> Then our Male-*Poets* modestly thought fit,
> To claim the honour'd *Primacy* in *Wit.*

A "Young Lady of Quality," writing on the occasion of Aphra Behn's death in 1689, voices similar sentiments. Tracing a poetical lineage from Philips to Behn, she now finds the line broken:

> Let all our Hopes despair and dye,
> Our Sex for ever shall neglected lye;
> Aspiring Man has now regain'd the Sway,
> To them we've lost the Dismal Day.

As the examples of Philaster and the "Young Lady of Quality" suggest, expressing fears that "Man has now regain'd the Sway" was by the 1680s a conventional means to flatter or mourn a woman poet. Nevertheless, receptiveness to writing by women and to literary qualities associated with femininity did decline dramatically in the late seventeenth century, and this lends some poignancy to conventional tributes to the Age of Orinda. As Margaret Newcastle warned with astonishing prescience in 1653, ears like her own, in which things associated with femininity were welcomed and encouraged, were fleeting:

> if it be an Age when the effeminate spirits rule, as
> most visible they doe in every Kingdome, let us take
> the advantage, and make the best . . . in witty Poetry,
> or any thing that may bring honour to our Sex.

An age in which "effeminate spirits" rule: Newcastle's phrase, suggesting as it does both actual women and "feminine" values, almost perfectly expressed the mid-century literary situation. Within thirty years, her warning about the future proved equally accurate.

The change in critical values that women writers in the 1680s describe—away from a literary aesthetic that held femininity and masculinity in equal esteem—gained considerable momentum in the early eighteenth century. Perhaps the clearest expression of this fact appears in critical discussion about an ostensibly unrelated issue: the increasing professionalization of literature. Such discussion has a bearing on an analysis of the gender-configurations of neoclassical poetics because it characterizes the differ-

ence between amateur and professional writing as a difference between a feminine (or effeminate) worse and a masculine better.

Alexander Pope, in a 1710 letter to Henry Cromwell, distinguishes between two kinds of poets. The first includes those who, writing "to establish a reputation," at times produce an "extreamly majestic" poetry; Pope clearly imagines himself to be among this group of writers. He cites Richard Crashaw as an example of the second kind of poet. Crashaw, states Pope, "writ like a Gentleman, that is, at leisure hours, and . . . to keep out of idleness." Pope refers to writers like him as *"Versifiers* and *witty Men,* rather than as *Poets,"* and associates them with *"Miscellan*[y]" or amateur writing.

In the imitation of Horace's *First Epistle of the Second Book* (1637), Pope attaches gender to the two kinds of writing he described to Cromwell. He links "Gentlemen" poets with amateur writing and locates the heyday of such poets at the Restoration:

> In Days of Ease, when now the weary Sword
> Was sheath'd, and *Luxury* with *Charles* restor'd; . . .
> The Soldier breath'd the Gallantries of France,
> And ev'ry flow'ry Courtier writ Romance. . . .
> No wonder then, when all was Love and Sport,
> The willing Muses were debauch'd at Court;
> On each enervate string they taught the Note
> To pant, or tremble thro' an Eunuch's throat.

Pope could not be clearer: the age of amateur versifying was an age in which "flow'ry" romance and "debauch'd" Muses emasculated poetry, "soften[ing]" the "Soldier" into a lisping "Eunuch." His own age, he acknowledges, continues in this tradition of effeminate amateurism: "Sons, Sires, and Grandsires, all will wear the Bays, / Our Wives read Milton, and our Daughters Plays." Pope nostalgically depicts a vague but distinctly masculine "Time was," a mythic past that contrasts with both the Restoration and his own age, when a "sober Englishman" could govern "his servants," "his Wife," and "his Son," imitating "his Fathers" and instructing "his Heir." Pope then attaches "true" poetry to this patriarchal idyll. The "Poet," he declares, is not a playful "Man of Rymes," but rather "a Poet's of some weight, / And (tho' no Soldier) useful to the State." A true poet is like a "Soldier" before the Restoration "soften'd" him: like Horace, he has *"a manly Regard to his own Character."*

The identification by 1700 of good or serious poetry with masculinity and poor or amateur versifying with femininity had significant impact on early eighteenth-century characterizations of previous poets. A critic who wished to commend a seventeenth-century poet resorted to eighteenth-century encomiastic terms and concepts that proved, in terms of gender, to be the inverse of the ones chosen by that poet's contemporary admirers. In 1697, for example, in an anthology entitled *Miscellany Poems,* the editor distinguishes between past and present poetry:

> *I was considering how much this* Art [Poetry] *was*

esteemed amongst our Forefathers, *and how Venerable, nay, almost Sacred, the* Name *of a Poet was then. . . . I think the great Difference* [between then and now] *lies here, That Poetry is now no longer the* Fountain of Wisdom, *the* School of Virtue.

In the poem that follows, he notes that the works of the "Ancients" which he so admires are "more *Masculine*" than those of modern writers, who, he complains, are mere "*Womens* Fools." When he praises "our Forefathers" and the "Ancients" as pillars of poetry, however, he does not mean to commend only classical writers like Homer or Sophocles or Virgil. Rather, the final exemplar of "ancient" masculinity is, in his view, the writer who had for decades been singled out as the "sweetest" of the early neoclassical poets, Edmund Waller:

> But if you wou'd Respect or Love express,
> And shew your Passion in a Comely Dress,
> Learn how from Courtly *Waller's* Deathless
>   Layes
> Chastly to Love, with Modesty to Praise.

The terms of commendation available to a writer in 1697 simply did not include the words traditionally applied to Waller, like "sweet" or "soft," marked as these were by their prior association with femininity. The closest a writer in that year could come to describing Waller's "Courtly" poetry was to describe his purity of style and content as "Comely"—in a "Masculine" sort of way.

As with Waller, so with Philips: by the late seventeenth and early eighteenth centuries, the critical vocabulary available to commend a woman poet like Philips was almost entirely masculine in its orientation. This situation accounts for the curious fact that several early eighteenth-century writers praise her poetry only for its manly strength—and not, as Cowley did, also for its womanly sweetness. Theophilus Cibber echoes other critics when he discusses her poetry:

> Mrs. Philips's poetry has not harmony of versification, or amorous tenderness to recommend it, but it has a force of thinking, which few poets of the other sex can exceed, and if it is without graces, it has yet a great deal of strength.

Dryden's 1699 epistolary comments to Elizabeth Thomas on Philips demonstrate that praise of Philips's "strength" means praise of literary qualities identified with masculinity. "'Tis not over gallant, I must confess," he begins,

> to say this of the fair Sex; but most certain it is, that they generally write with more Softness than Strength. On the contrary, you want neither Vigour in your Thoughts, nor force in your Expressions, nor Harmony in your Numbers, and methinks I find much of Orinda in your Manner (to whom I had the Honour to be related, and also to be Known).

Dryden's remarks are extraordinary in a number of ways. First, he links writers of "the fair Sex" with literary "Softness"—and he makes it clear that it is far from complimentary to women to do so. He also describes Thomas's "Manner" as implicitly masculine, characterized as it is by a "Strength" not "generally" seen in writings by women. Most strikingly, however, he identifies this admirably masculine style, possessing as it does both "Vigour" and "force," as the "Orinda" in Thomas's writing.

Richard Gwinnet, also writing to Elizabeth Thomas, singles out the "masculine" qualities of Philips's poems for praise as well. Philips's **"Country Life,"** Gwinnet writes,

> is so sweet a *Poem,* and sprinkled with such profound Philosophical Thoughts, expressed in easy Poetical Language, . . . that though I have read several Poems, in more Tongues than One, upon the same Subject, yet I do not know where to find a better.

Gwinnet describes Philips's poetry as "sweet," "profound," and "easy," neoclassical terms which, he goes on to suggest, are fundamentally "Masculine." "I have looked a little into Mrs. *Philips,*" Gwinnet writes, "and it is not the first Time I have been wonderfully pleased with her solid Masculine Thoughts, in no Feminine Expression." Like Dryden on Roscommon, Gwinnet commends the "sweet[ness]" of Philips's poem as one of the qualities that identifies and places her work within the masculine literary universe. By suggesting that her poems have "no Feminine Expression," Gwinnet also pays Philips one of the highest compliments available to a reader—especially a reader of women's verses—in the early eighteenth century. A far cry from Cowley's "than Man more strong, and more than Woman sweet," Gwinnet's phrase nevertheless matches Cowley's in its attempt to praise Philips's poems in terms that reflect the gender-configurations reigning in contemporary neoclassical discourse.

A markedly different response to Philips appeared in 1712. In that year, the Reverend Thomas Newcomb published a versified lampoon on "modern" writers entitled *Bibliotheca.* The poem's mock-hero is a befuddled old "Doctor" who happily fondles a series of books; Newcomb inserts his critiques of individual writers as the Doctor moves from volume to volume. Women poets come in for particular attack. "One day," writes Newcomb, the Doctor "Does to the Female World repair, / To please himself among the Fair, / (Where if no Sense was to be found, / He's sure to be oblig'd with Sound)." Newcomb is especially biting in regard to Philips. "ORINDA next demands his view / For Titles fam'd and Rhiming too; / And had been read, but that her Song, / To be admir'd, was quite too long." If the Doctor never actually reads Philips, however, Newcomb does, and he describes her poetry in damningly gendered terms:

> Their Mistress['s] want of Pride to shew,
> Her Numbers glide but wondrous low,
> Instead of Rapture, give us Sleep,
> And striving to be humble, creep. . . .
> Softness her Want of Sense supplies,

She faints in every line and dyes.

Comparison with Alexander Pope's 1711 *An Essay on Criticism* brings Newcomb's agenda out into the open:

> If *Chrystal Streams with pleasing Murmurs*
>   *creep,*
> The Reader's threaten'd (not in vain) with *Sleep:*
> Then, at the *last,* and *only* Couplet fraught
> With some *unmeaning* Thing they call a
>   *Thought,*
> A *needless Alexandrine* ends the Song,
> That like a wounded Snake, drags its slow
>   length along.

What Newcomb adds to Pope's lines is simply the association of poor verse with women and femininity. The punning phrase, "want of pride to shew," implies that a woman's attempt to express her modesty serves only to reveal her immodesty. Substituting "sense" with "Softness" suggests that her poetry is feminine in the specific sense of being weak. And Newcomb's last line adds a sly sexual innuendo that obliterates the passage's nominal focus on Philips's poetry itself.

Newcomb must substantially misrepresent both Philips and her poetry in order to depict them in the feminized way that he does. He refers to the poet, for example, as a "Virgin" and an "Unhappy Maid," and claims that she wielded her poetry (in vain) to charm some "Youth" into "Wedlock." In fact, Philips was married at age sixteen, before she wrote almost any of the extant poetry; she also never wrote courtship verses of any kind. Newcomb's claims to the contrary suggest a willful misreading of her poems in the service of blasting Philips as a failed—because female—poet.

Newcomb, seeking to censure Philips, is as careful to paint her with her sex as Cibber, Dryden, and Gwinnet, aiming at praise, are to circumvent it. In so doing, he takes what is for his time a highly idiosyncratic negative position on the seventeenth-century poet. Unfortunately for Philips, however, Newcomb's lone denunciation of her poetry, supported as it was by a neoclassical aesthetic profoundly antagonistic to "Feminine Expression," seems to have carried considerable weight: as noted earlier, the last eighteenth-century edition of Philips's **Poems** appeared in 1710, just two years before Newcomb published the *Bibliotheca.*

We can explain Newcomb's influence in part by pointing to the fact that multiple editions of the *Bibliotheca* kept Newcomb's censure of Philips before the reading public throughout the eighteenth century. Critic William Roberts notes [in *English Language Notes,* 1964] that John Nichols, manager of *Gentleman's Magazine,* included Newcomb's poem in the third volume of his *Select Collection of Poems,* and that John Bell's 1781 and 1807 reprints of the works of William King also included the *Bibliotheca.* As Roberts notes, enthusiasm for Philips's works may have been "offset to some degree by the cleverly derogatory comments of Thomas Newcomb's *Bibliotheca;*" by the mid-eighteenth century, the sustained exposure of readers to

his negative assessment of her poetry may have helped to obscure it from neoclassical view altogether.

Multiple editions of the *Bibliotheca,* however, do not in themselves adequately account for the kind of critical clout Newcomb's rather obscure poem seems to have carried. A more significant factor behind the poem's effect on Philips's literary reputation lies in Newcomb's manipulation of a critical climate in which the highest praise was to refer to a poet's work as "manly" strong and the lowest censure was to call it womanly "soft." Like Cowley's, Philips's poems would surely have gone out of fashion in the eighteenth century without Newcomb's help. But Newcomb hurried Philips's decline, and insured its persistence, by branding her poetry with her sex—something which had not previously been done to this particular poet. The means of censuring Philips as a feminine writer had existed from the 1670s; few critics before Newcomb, however, had cared to censure Philips, and thus few if any had described her in this way. Once Newcomb's damaging charges of the feminine nature of Philips's poetry were made, however, only a readership willing to take on the daunting task of defending a woman's writing from her sex could have saved Philips's reputation. In the world of eighteenth-century neoclassicism, where a woman's writing and her sex were, as in Newcomb, increasingly linked and jointly censured, this kind of readership simply did not exist. As a consequence, and according to Newcomb's wishes, Philips's poems "faint[ed] in every line, and dye[d]."

FURTHER READING

Brashear, Lucy. "Gleanings from the Orinda Holograph," *American Notes and Queries* 23, Nos. 7 & 8 (March/April 1985): 100-02.

> Discusses the identities of pseudonymous figures in the Philips holograph at the National Library of Wales.

Buckingham, Elinor. "The Matchless Orinda." *The Sewanee Review* 10, No. 3 (July 1902): 269-84.

> A biographical overview addressing the theme of friendship in Philips's life and poetry.

Limbert, Claudia [A.]. "Two Poems and a Prose Receipt: The Unpublished Juvenilia of Katherine Philips (text)." *English Literary Renaissance* 16, No. 2 (Spring 1986): 383-90.

> Discusses evidence of Philips's early writings with reference to the discovery of the "Orielton" manuscript.

——. "The Poetry of Katherine Philips: Holographs, Manuscripts, and Early Printed Texts." *Philological Quarterly* 70, No. 2 (Spring 1991): 181-98.

> Examines printed, manuscript, and holograph sources for a potential variorum edition of Philips's poetry.

——. "'The Unison of Well-Tun'd Hearts': Katherine Philips' Friendships With Male Writers." *English Language Notes* 29, No. 1 (September 1991): 25-37.

> Discusses the role of Philips's friendships with

contemporary men of letters in the development of her poetry and her career.

Limbert, Claudia A., and John H. O'Neill. "Composite Authorship: Katherine Philips and an Antimarital Satire." *The Papers of the Bibliographical Society of America* 87, No. 4 (December 1993): 487-502.

>   Compares an early Philips poem and a later, similar manuscript that the authors believe to be the work of several hands.

Lund, Roger D. "*Bibliotheca* and 'the British Dames': An Early Critique of the Female Wits of the Restoration." *Restoration: Studies in English Literary Culture, 1660-1700* 12, No. 2 (Fall 1988): 96-105.

>   Addresses William Newcomb's satirical comments on Philips and other women writers in his "Bibliotheca: A Poem Occasioned by the Sight of a Modern Library" (1712).

Mambretti, Catherine Cole. "Fugitive Papers: A New Orinda Poem and Problems in her Canon." *Papers of the Bibliographical Society of America* 71, Fourth Quarter (1977): 443-52.

>   Addresses problems of attribution involved in establishing the canon of Philips's work.

——. "Orinda on the Restoration Stage." *Comparative Literature* 37, No. 3 (Summer, 1985): 233-51.

>   Discusses the role of Philips's translations of Corneille's *La Mort de Pompée* and *Horace* in introducing elements of French tragedy into English Restoration drama.

Moody, Ellen. "Orinda, Rosania, Lucasia *et aliae*: Towards a New Edition of the Works of Katherine Philips." *Philological Quarterly* 66, No. 3 (Summer 1987): 325-54.

>   Takes issue with George Saintsbury's edition of Philips's poetry (Volume One of his *Minor Poets of the Caroline Period,* 1905) and proposes a new edition. Includes an annotated catalog of poems, grouped according to subject.

Roberts, William. "The Dating of Orinda's French Translations." *Phililogical Quarterly* 49, No. 1 (January 1970): 56-67.

>   Presents evidence that most of Philips's translations of French verse date from the early 1660s.

Souers, Philip Webster. *The Matchless Orinda.* Cambridge: Harvard University Press, 1931. 326 p.

>   The first substantial Philips biography. The last chapter, "The Poetess Orinda," offers a critical study of Philips's poetry.

Thomas, Patrick. *Katherine Philips ('Orinda')*, University of Wales Press, 1988, 73 p.

>   A concise biography which addresses Philips's philosophy of friendship and her royalist politics. Includes three "hitherto unpublished" poems from a manuscript in Cardiff Central Library, Wales.

Additional information about Philips' life and works is contained in the following source published by Gale Research: *Dictionary of Literary Biography,* Vol. 131.

Lady Mary Wroth

1587-1653(?)

(Born Mary Sidney) English fiction writer, poet, and playwright.

The following entry provides an overview of Wroth's career and works, and contains criticism published from 1946 through 1993.

INTRODUCTION

Considered the first woman writer of English original prose fiction, Lady Mary Wroth published her lengthy prose romance, *The Countesse of Mountgomeries Urania* (1621) at a time when women's writing was confined strictly to translation and pious works. For centuries dismissed as an imitation of the pastoral romance genre epitomized by Sir Philip Sidney's *The Countess of Pembroke's Arcadia* (1590), Wroth's *Urania* and the sonnet sequence at the end of the work, *Pamphilia to Amphilanthus,* have garnered increased scholarly attention since the 1970s for their successful transposition of the gender expectations that prevailed in seventeenth-century literary forms. Wroth's use of secular female viewpoints is recognized as an innovative approach to genres in which the point of view had been exclusively male. In *Urania,* Wroth reversed traditional male notions of community, creating a word of feminine friendship through which she depicted the quest for self identity and the formation of same sex friendships that support and transcend passion and marriage to the opposite sex. Wroth characterized women as the purveyors of culture and constancy, and while her works reflect the systematic subordination of women to the patriarchal mores of the times, her female characters manage to assert their identities, thereby avoiding victimization. Published after the pastoral and sonnet forms were past their popularity, Wroth's *Urania* expanded the conventions of the genres by fusing the romantic tradition with the realistic through the use of diversionary subplots and dialogue in the style of the novelle. Both for her daring examination of gender expectations and the stylistic deviations she made from traditional literary forms, Wroth is receiving increased scrutiny in modern scholarship.

Biographical Information

The eldest daughter of Sir Robert Sidney, a poet and government official, and Lady Barbara Gamage, Mary Sidney was born on 18 October 1587 into a family established in both literary pursuits and life in the courts of Elizabeth I and James I. For this reason, she had access to educational and cultural opportunities rare for

a woman of her time. Wroth's uncle was Sir Philip Sidney, author of influential Renaissance works including the sonnet sequence *Astrophil and Stella* (1590), and the pastoral romance *Arcadia,* both of which were to provide important models for Wroth's writing. Due to the literary interests of her family and her mother's active role in educating her children, Wroth spent her childhood practicing writing, language, and music. Wroth also traveled with her mother on the Continent when her father assumed a governorship in the Netherlands, spending much of her early childhood abroad. While receiving a thorough education in the arts from her mother, it was Wroth's aunt Mary Sidney, the Countess of Pembroke and sister to Sir Philip Sidney, who inspired her to literary pursuits. The Countess of Pembroke not only wrote poetry and translations from French and Italian, she also published them—a bold venture for a woman in the 1590s. According to Josephine Roberts, the Countess of Pembroke's work in various verse forms, particularly in a metrical version of the Psalms she had begun with Sir Philip Sidney, probably stimulated Wroth's interest in poetical techniques. Wroth used her aunt as the model for characters in her own work, as the Queen of Naples in the *Urania,* and as

Simena in the play *Love's Victory* (1620s?). The family's standing at court increased during Wroth's early years. When Queen Elizabeth visited Penshurst in 1600 to show her favor for Sir Robert, young Mary Sidney entertained the queen with dancing, foreshadowing later dramatic performances at the court of James I.

In 1604, Mary married Robert Wroth, who had been knighted the previous year by James I and whose hunting skills found favor with the king. The union was not a happy one; Sir Robert Wroth's dissatisfaction with his new wife was apparent to Mary Wroth's father, who commented upon their marital difficulties in a letter to his wife. However unhappy the marriage, Lady Mary Wroth's position at court was enhanced by her new husband's and her father's rising influence with James I. She performed in several court entertainments for Queen Anne, most notably *The Masque of Blackness* in 1605 and *The Masque of Beauty* in 1608 by the poet Ben Jonson, with whom Lady Wroth shared a mutual admiration for many years. Jonson wrote a poem praising Wroth's poetry, and commented to William Drummond on the unworthiness of her marriage to Robert Wroth. Due to her position at court, Lady Wroth became known as a literary patron as well as poet in her own right. She was most certainly composing verse by 1613, and her work may have circulated as early as 1605. In between her duties at court and at the Wroths' country estate, where she played hostess to the royal couple when James I came to hunt, Wroth wrote songs and sonnets, many of which would make up her sonnet sequence *Pamphilia to Amphilanthus*. Lady Wroth was well known as a poet long before the first publication of her work in 1621. However, although active and respected in literary circles, Wroth's first effort at publication may have been spurred by financial obligations incurred following the death of her husband in 1614, a month after the birth of their only child, a son. Robert Wroth left his wife a large debt. Her circumstances worsened with the death of her son, which caused Wroth to lose much of her husband's estate to his uncle due to the lack of an immediate male heir.

The difficulties for women brought on by patriarchal mores greatly influenced Wroth's later works, which extensively address the problems of marrying for financial gain, and the impoverishment that widowhood often brought to women of her class. During her early years as a widow, Wroth continued a romantic liaison with her cousin William Herbert, third Earl of Pembroke, which had begun during her marriage, eventually bearing two illegitimate children by him. Herbert is thought to be the model for the character Amphilanthus, the object of Pamphilia's affections in *Pamphilia to Amphilanthus,* while Wroth herself is thought to be reflected in Pamphilia. Despite her relationship with the wealthy Herbert, Wroth's financial position became increasingly desperate, and she may have decided to publish as a means out of her difficulties. Unfortunately, this avenue was forever closed to her with the appearance of the *Urania,* appended with the sonnet sequence *Pamphilia to Amphilanthus,* in 1621. Composed during the period 1618-1620, the *Urania* incorporates elements of the roman à clef, detailing Wroth's fall from

favor in court upon the death of her husband, attributing her circumstances to court slander, and basing several episodes in the work on actual court scandals. Publication of the *Urania* sparked a venomous flurry of criticism by courtiers who claimed to identify their own embarrassing episodes in the work. Sir Edward Denny, in particular, was incensed by Wroth's depiction of his affairs and waged a public campaign to disparage the *Urania* and Wroth. Wroth responded in kind, answering his public outcries with spirited rebuttals and attempting to rally the support of influential friends, to whom she insisted she had not meant any harm. In the end, however, she was forced to remove the work from circulation, and it remained unpublished for the rest of her life. Despite the scandal, Wroth continued to write prolifically throughout the 1620s, producing a second part to the *Urania,* and composing the drama *Love's Victory,* for which there is no record of performance. Her financial position, however, became increasingly dire, and she was forced to petition the king several times for protection from creditors. Little is known of Wroth's later years, and no literary material exists from the last three decades of her life. Wroth likely died in 1651 or 1653 without ever having regained financial stability or her former standing at court.

Major Works

Wroth's three major works all derive from established literary forms popular in her time, but their unifying and distinguishing feature is the adaptation of exclusively male forms and techniques to a female point of view. In each of her works, the protagonists are women who suffer subordination to a patriarchal society, but nevertheless shape their own destinies in fulfillment of a quest for identity and spiritual freedom. Wroth's concern is to evoke a female community of friendship in which women attain acceptance and respect outside the norms of male-dominated society, which glorified court rituals or traditional heroic exploits. Strong women characters in Elizabethan literature often were paragons of virtue or female extensions of the male concept of heroism; for example, warriors or Amazons in the tradition of Spenser. In contrast, Wroth's women range from the virtuous to the deceitful. None defines herself by male standards of female virtue or heroism, and instead looks inward to determine her identity. In the *Urania,* for example, Wroth presents resilient women characters whose notions of self are challenged by male inconstancy and their subordinate position in society. The 600 page prose romance chronicles the adventures of a huge cast of characters, with the central theme being Queen Pamphilia's vow of love and loyalty to King Amphilanthus. Pamphilia's vow is tested continually by separation from her beloved and by various intrigues that reveal his inconstancy to her. Parallel to this plot is that concerning Pamphilia's close friend Urania, an important commentator on the many adventures narrated in the work. Ostensibly a shepherdess, Urania embarks on a search for her parents and her true identity, symbolizing the feminine quest for self identity and the rejection of societal expectations. The heroic deeds of knights are compared with the spiritual heroism of women's striving for the freedom to shape their lives. Female unhappiness is portrayed as a result of betrayal by the men to whom they have pledged loyalty; a theme that is explored further in the sonnet sequence *Pamphilia to Amphilanthus,* which follows the *Urania* in the 1621 edition.

The first known edition of Wroth's sonnets consisted of 110 poems and seven miscellaneous pieces, but by the publication of the *Urania,* she had revised the sequence to the eighty-three sonnets and twenty songs. The only Renaissance sonnet sequence composed by a woman, *Pamphilia to Amphilanthus* transforms the traditional Petrarchan conceit of a male sonneteer addressing a female love object to a female sonneteer writing of her love for a man. The characters' names reflect the main concern of the poetry; Pamphilia means "all-loving", while Amphilanthus means "lover of two". The contrast between women's constancy and men's inconstancy is voiced with emotion and depth by Pamphilia, who attempts to resolve the struggle between her desire to surrender to passion and the need to retain her identity and freedom. Although the poems are addressed to Amphilanthus, the focus of the poetry is Pamphilia's examination of her own character, her thoughts on love, her inner virtue, her ambivalence towards marriage. These themes are continued in *Love's Victory,* Wroth's pastoral tragicomedy modelled after the love story in Sir Philip Sidney's sonnet sequence *Astrophil and Stella.* In the play, Wroth focusses on a woman's right to choose whether and whom to marry. As in the *Urania* and *Pamphilia to Amphilanthus,* there are strongly autobiographical motifs to the play, as Wroth decries the repercussions of marrying for financial gain rather than for love. As in her other works, women play the dominant role in the action; the deity Venus, who comments on the action and guides the characters' behavior, dominates Cupid. The drama portrays one woman's decision to marry for love and another's decision to not marry at all, while the forced marriage of two characters ends in their mock deaths, a symbol of the stifling nature of arranged unions. Female friendship again is an important element of the action, with the women characters meeting to discuss their roles in romance and to empower each others' decisions regarding marriage. Although men are portrayed as disrespectful of women, in some cases comparing women with animals, Wroth endows her female characters with self-respect and the strength to shape their lives and make decisions, thus avoiding victimization. In her works, Wroth adhered to traditional forms and took her stylistic cues from the literary establishment of her times, but her writing was far from merely derivative of these forms in its transposition of gender roles to endow a female narrator with the ability to examine her own character and her society.

Critical Reception

With the rediscovery of her works and the release of important editions of her poetry by Gary Waller in 1977 and Josephine Roberts in 1983, among others, Wroth's place in the development of literary forms received new scrutiny. Most Wroth critics have sought to examine and clarify the role of the female voice and the revolutionary

impact of the transposition of gender. The majority of scholars studying this aspect of Wroth's work have agreed that her representation of female perspectives and the creation of feminine community are both artistically successful and refreshing variations on established forms. In addition, critics have noted that the feminine viewpoint in her work serves as an important aid in a historical and sociological understanding of the role of women and the difficulties they faced during the Elizabethan and Jacobean eras. From both an historical and a literary standpoint, critics are continuing to research Wroth's contributions to English literature and to acknowledge her role in establishing the tradition of a literary feminine voice.

PRINCIPAL WORKS

The Countesse of Mountgomeries Urania (fiction) 1621
***Pamphilia to Amphilanthus* (poetry) 1621
‡*Love's Victorie* (drama) 1621(?)
†*The Poems of Lady Mary Wroth* (poetry) 1983

---

* Sonnet sequence first printed as the conclusion to *Urania;* published as separate work *Pamphilia to Amphilanthus by Lady Mary Wroth,* edited by G. F. Wallter, 1977.

†Wroth's poetry circulated in manuscript as early as 1605. This edition was edited by Josephine A. Roberts.

‡No record of performance. First published as *Lady Mary Wroth's 'Love's Victory': The Penshurst Manuscript,* edited by Michael J. Brennan, 1988.

CRITICISM

B. G. MacCarthy (essay date 1946)

SOURCE: "The Pastoral Romance," in *Women Writers: Their Contribution to The English Novel 1621-1744,* 1944. Reprint by Cork University Press, 1946, pp. 47-69.

[*In the following excerpt, MacCarthy examines Wroth's* The Countesse of Mountgomeries Urania *in the context of Elizabethan prose traditions and the influence of Sydney's* Arcadia, *and shows how Wroth blends realism and romanticism through the use of sub-plots and dialogue.*]

In 1621, in the person of Lady Mary Wroath, woman made her first contribution to English prose fiction. Having barely mentioned the name of the first English woman-novelist, we must at once retrogress after the manner of a writer who introduces his heroine only to leave her standing while he laboriously sketches in the background. But truly it would quite impossible to judge the work of Lady Mary Wroath without at first considering briefly the state of Elizabethan and Jacobean prose fiction of which her novel was an integral part.

The main point to be observed in regard to the prose fiction of the Elizabethan age is that on the whole it did not recognise itself as a separate literary medium. Narrative had undergone many changes in aim and in form, since the days of the old epics which had for their object the recital of certain events. This uncomplicated aim led to a direct form, to a treatment which Heine [in *The Prose Writers of Heinrich Heine*, 1887] rightly called a classic treatment. This treatment was classic because the form of that which was portrayed was identical with the idea of the portrayer. The wanderings of Ulysses, for example, represented merely the wanderings of a man who was the son of Laertes and the husband of Penelope. There was no wider meaning, no esoteric significance, and for this reason there was complete harmony between the idea and the form. Classic art aimed only at representing the finite, and it succeeded by direct means. But this simplicity of aim and medium did not last. Man began to be troubled by subjective views of life. He realised that direct descriptions would not express what he now wished to say, and he attempted to convey his thoughts by parabolic means. This new treatment of the subject-matter was romantic; that is to say that the form did not reveal the idea through identity, but suggested what was beyond literal expression. To attain their effects the narrators changed and adapted the material of their tales, thus departing from the classic ideal of authenticity. But the fictional nature of these tales appeared to them a sign of decadence; deliberate fiction appeared too much of a pretence, and so we find, for long ages, a persistent effort to give authenticity to feigned stories.

From the epic to the cycles of romance, from classicism to romanticism, was the natural transition. It was held by some that romanticism was merely the decadence of classic art. But this would be to arraign also the realm of poetry, and particularly of lyric poetry. Romanticism grew from taking thought, from finding in life a depth of meaning below the surface. Romanticism either endeavoured to suggest such meaning through the agency of language, or else attempted to escape this subjective reality by taking refuge in literary compositions as far as possible unlike the world around them. This was the starting-point and material witness of their mental state. The ideal of the ancients was the man of action, and they feared for the man of action who might lose his manliness and become thought-sick. It is to be observed that with the Greeks romanticism did not arise until a period of national deterioration had set in. With the humiliation of Athens, the destruction of the Macedonian monarchy and of Asiatic Greece, political liberty was lost, and the main activities of the Greek people were rendered henceforth impossible. Disillusionment led to scepticism in religious and other forms of thought. Prose fiction grew from the decadence of poetry at this time. It was far from being an introspective kind of writing. On the contrary, it was merely an objective record of imaginary events which never had been, and which never could take place in the mortal world. This unreal, this romantic fiction was of different kinds; the short story, the imaginary journey to incredible countries, the romance of adventures, and the love intrigue; the Milesian tale—a particular type of amatory short-story—and the Pastoral romance. These tales were a refuge from the life which pressed too sorely upon men: and to escape more fully from reality, writers not only depicted unreal events, but projected them against a background which had no identifiable locus. The *Golden Ass* of Apuleius, the first romance of antiquity, was to have a strange and varied posterity, but, though the symbolic presentation of truth or beauty was often obscured, the escapist characteristic always remained, frequently with dire effect.

In common with every other literary movement the Romance of Chivalry had established itself abroad before reaching England. *Amadis de Gaul,* published in 1508, was available in manuscript and in oral recitative since about the year 1300. The Pastoral Romance, a sub-development of the Romance of Chivalry, had its originator in Longus, who was to pastoral prose fiction what Theocritus had been to pastoral poetry, but the fine simplicity of *Daphnis and Chloe* did not survive, and the pastoral novel really began its sophisticated course in the *Arcadia* of Sannazzaro. This work was surpassed in interest by Montemayor's *Diana Enamorada,* which was translated into English in 1583. Sydney's *Arcadia* was a fusion of the main characteristics of the Amadis cycle of chivalric romance, and of the pastoral romance.

Sydney was not aware that in his *Arcadia* he was adhering to a moribund form. The astonishing fact is that the Pastoral Romance which had first arisen in a decadent period was received in England with great enthusiasm at a period of re-birth. There were several reasons for this anomaly. In the first place, English prose fiction was in a very undeveloped state. It was too young to know its own nature or its bent, and not only so, but it was suffering from under-nourishment. Men's attention and abilities were focussed on the drama and on poetry. These Siamese twins, considered really as one, were carefully nurtured and exhibited with pride, while fiction, that disowned foundling, pined in the cellar. The coming of the Pastoral Romance, with its pseudo-poetic style, made it possible for the poets to redeem the rickety outcast from inferior darkness, and to give it a place in the family circle. Under the protection of the poetic tradition, the Pastoral Romance, though always sickly, persisted in living for a long time. It was, for example, primarily because Sydney was a poet that he wrote the *Arcadia*. He maintained always the fallacious contention that all imaginative creation was poetry. This obsession which he shared with the established, conservative, literary forces of his period serves to show all the more clearly that the slow and painful transition from prose to poetry had not yet become an established fact in English story-telling.

In 1400, Chaucer had written an excellent story in verse. Although it owed much to Boccaccio, *Troilus and Cresseyde* showed at one stroke a remarkable power of construction and characterisation, and much subtlety in narrative device. But at least two hundred years elapsed before English fiction profited by this example, simply because it was impeded by the transition from verse to prose. Prose had an obvious advantage in story-telling. It was more economical than verse, and it could represent life more closely and more fully. Furthermore, the invention of printing gave to prose works a certainty of remembrance which until then had been possible only in verse. The trend towards prose was thus greatly hastened. But as verse had taken time to perfect itself as a medium for story-telling, so prose had now to be forged into a fit instrument for the writer of prose fiction. It had to become clear, ample, vivid, flexible and yet strong, capable of expressing the entire gamut of human experience. And while prose was thus evolving, the writers of prose fiction were endeavouring to clothe their stories in a kind of prose not yet suited to the purpose. The Elizabethan novel at its best was a living entity, with endless possibilities of thought and action, but unable yet to speak or act freely. Not only was the medium of expression lacking in resilience, but the very method of telling a story was as yet only glimpsed. The lesson of Chaucer's technique in story-telling was lost to succeeding prose writers, because they were confused by the change in medium, and seemed unable to apply to prose tales the methods which Chaucer had employed in verse-form.

This transition period gave to the prose story-teller a choice between two schools of writing, radically different in every respect. On the side of the privileged class, and springing from the poetic tradition, there was the Heroic Romance and the Pastoral Romance (the elements of which were often fused, as in the *Arcadia*); there was also, as a sub-classification, the sort of romance initiated and typified by Lyly's *Euphues* which for a long time had a great success, and which, strangled in an impossible style, contained portents of future developments in fiction. On the popular side, and chiefly of prose origin, there were the short, pithy, unpretentious stories which found their best expression in the form of the Italian *novelle,* and which were available in the collections of Painter, Whetstone, Fenton, and others; there were the moral tales, closely allied to the *novelle* and typified in the *Gesta Romanorum;* there was popular satire which Langland's verse had established long before and which was now developed vigorously by such men as Nash and Greene; there were the stories of low life, such as the gest books, the picaresque tales, the cony-catching pamphlets; there were semi-fictious and real biographies; there were Deloney's guild tales; and there was much letter-writing to imaginary people (an activity which later became a very important development in form). This popular school presented the realistic trend in fiction, which, because it had its roots in actual life, became increasingly alive, and held its ground through succeeding centuries to develop triumphantly into the modern novel.

Between the extreme right wing and the extreme left wing in fiction there was the simple prose romance of the burgher class, which later became the chap-book of the seventeenth and eighteenth centuries, as for example, *Guy of Warwick* and *Huon of Bordeaux.* These last were off-shoots of the mediaeval cycles of romance which had found new life in homely soil, and which lived, therefore, when the larger cycles had passed from the memory of the people.

The popular school had its origin in folk-tales which had always existed orally side by side with the elaborate stories of the privileged classes. Its prose tradition and its unambitious aim saved it from an involved form. In fact, in identity of form and idea it might almost be called classic. It was direct, simple and all the more vital because it did not dissipate its energies in devious symbolism or elaborate intricacies. It was spontaneous, but often crude. The romantic kind of writing had its origin in poetry, but it had also found copious expression in prose. In the use of this prose medium it was, however, hampered by the conviction that its mission was poetic, and it therefore expended its energies on a mistaken object. It contained a diffused beauty and a deliberate melodiousness which were not evident in the people's tales, but it was cumbrous, artificial and in no way a representation of life. Indeed it intentionally aimed at portrayal of a world unconnected with reality. It is clear that the modern novel could not develop from such a school of fiction, because such writing could not become real. And it is equally clear that the novel could develop from the popular school of fiction, because the realistic writing of the ordinary people *could* become aesthetic and *could* find artistic devices to suit its purposes. The reality on which the novel must feed, if it were to grow, was the main virtue of this popular fiction, and time would enable it to achieve artistic form. When Sydney wrote, the Pastoral Romance was dying. To save it there would have been needed a transfusion of common blood, rich and varied food, great draughts of wine, fresh air and sun-shine, and a complete change of scene. An inbred parent-stock, and a thin and rarefied existence had produced anaemia not more pernicious, however, than its posthumous influence. But it was not to die yet awhile. Unnatural fungus that it was, it was to draw new life from Sydney's death. When Sydney died at Zutphen, he established a tradition for romantic heroism which prolonged the life of the heroic romance, and which perpetuated its repute. It would have been well for subsequent fiction if Sydney had not been as noble in character as in lineage. To be young, gifted, and heroic, to love with passionate austerity, and coin one's heart into lyrics; to die with an immortal sentence on one's lips—this is to create a legend, and the dazzling legend of Sydney blinded even the critical to the grave defects of the *Arcadia*.

Published in 1590, the *Arcadia* had an immense success. By 1600, there had been four editions. There were fourteen editions during the seventeenth century. In 1725 a three-volume edition appeared, and was reprinted in Dublin in 1739. From that time until 1907, only abridgements were printed. In 1725 appeared Mrs. Stanley's modernised version, with which Richardson was doubtless familiar, and from which he took the name of his heroine Pamela.

The *Arcadia* attracted a great number of imitators, who wished either to continue the story or to use it as a model for similar themes. In 1606, John Day wrote *The Ile of Guls:* "A little string or rivulet drawn from the full stream of the Right Worthy gentleman, Sir Philip Sydney's well knowne *Archadea*." Shirley dramatised many episodes in his *Pastoral called the Arcadia* (1640). Shakespeare may have embodied in the scenes between Gloster and his son, in *King Lear,* the story of the dispossessed king of Paphlagonia. Mr. C. Crawford has found traces of the *Arcadia* in *The Duchess of Malfi* and other plays by Webster. Francis Quarles, author of the *Emblemes,* made the story of Argalus and Parthenia the subject of a long poem (1622). Many writers linked their works to the fame of Sir Philip Sydney by mentioning his name on their title-pages, and one writer in particular found in her near relationship to this idolised man the courage to emerge into the world of letters under the protection of his glory.

In 1621, years after the first appearance of the *Arcadia,* Lady Mary Wroath published her stout folio, the **Urania**. This attempt at Pastoral Romance has for the most part been buried in oblivion. Very occasionally some searcher among the minutiae of literature brushes aside the dust of ages, and glances inside her book. The elaborate frontispiece does certainly justify Mr. E. A. Baker's remark that Lady Mary made great play with her pedigree on the title-page. The title runs:

> *The Countesse of Montgomeries*
> *URANIA*
> *Written by the right honourable the Lady*
> *MARY WROATH*
> *Daughter to the right Noble Robert*
> *Earle of Leicester*
> *And niece to the ever famous and renowned*
> *Sr. Phillips Sydney, Knight. And to*
> *The Most exelet Lady Mary Countesse of*
> *Pembroke late deceased.*

Lady Mary Wroath grew up within a charmed circle, in an atmosphere of social and literary impeccability. Sir Philip Sydney was not only a true poet himself, but an extremely generous literary patron. The centre of all that was best in Elizabethan poetry, and with his house and purse ever open to needy writers, it was only natural that he should have been beloved, and that he and his family should have been liberally praised by the best poets of the day. Sydney himself was indeed worthy of the encomiums lavished upon him as a poet and as man, but, as we have already shown, the Countess of Pembroke merely shone in a reflected glory which her literary talents did not deserve. It is not surprising that Lady Mary Wroath should trust that the spell would hold in her case also. Yet she did not determine to write until she was driven to it as a last expedient.

The eldest daughter of Robert Sydney, first Earl of Leicester, she married Sir Robert Wroath in 1604, at the age of eighteen. She was often at court after her marriage, and King James frequently visited her husband's estate at Durrants. She was a liberal and sympathetic patroness of literature, and as such was honoured by many of the chief poets of the age. It is recorded that on Twelfth Night, 1604-5, she acted at Whitehall in Ben Johnson's *Masque of Blackness.* Johnson dedicated to her his play *The Alchemist* (1610), as well as a sonnet and two epigrams.

Chapman addressed to her a sonnet which was prefixed to his translation of Homer's *Iliad* (1614). George Wither and William Gamage offered similar tributes to "the most famous and heroike Lady Mary Wroath." But these pleasant circumstances came to an end with the death of her husband in 1614. She was left with an infant son, an income of £1,200 a year, and an estate swamped in debt. Nor had death ceased to ravage her happiness. Two years later her son died, and then her father. This last blow led to the complete wreck of her financial affairs, because, ignoring the trustees whom her father had appointed to administer her small possessions, she insisted on managing them herself. She soon proved her inability to do so, and her financial embarrassment became so serious that, in 1623, she was forced to petition the King for protection from her creditors for the space of one year. Prior to that date, however, she had determined on authorship as a solution of her difficulties.

The Countess of Montgomeries Urania was modelled on the *Arcadia*. As this literary venture was a financial speculation, it was to be expected that Lady Mary Wroath would adhere to the form which had already been received with acclamation, and which, to judge by sedulous imitators, was in the main stream of literary development. No doubt, she also hoped that a descendant of Sydney, using the pastoral medium, would strike home to the hearts of the reading public. It is quite possible, too, that she believed that she might be an inheritor of poetic gifts, and the fact that she was a woman would not deter her, in view of her aunt's reputation as a writer. Prolonged adulation is apt to destroy the critical faculty, and Lady Mary was not likely to judge aright either her aunt's talents or her own.

The **Urania** is an exceedingly complicated pastoral romance, after the Sydneian pattern. The scene is laid partly in the island of Pantaleria, governed by the Lord Pantalerius who, because of a grievance, is self-exiled from his own country. The heroine is Urania, apparently a shepherdesse, but really a princess, daughter of the King of Naples. The hero is also of noble blood, Parselius, Prince of Morea. Minor characters linked to the main plot are Amphilanthus, brother of Urania, and heir to the throne of Naples; and Leonius, the younger brother. There are various subplots very slenderly connected with the main plot. The story of the king of Albania and his children is dull and digressive. There are other inset stories which are equally digressive, but so far from dull that we must make particular mention of them, when the main plot of **Urania** has been outlined.

The beginning of **Urania** is a good example of the style in which the book is written:

> When the Spring began to appear like the welcome messenger of Summer, one Sweet (and in that more sweet) morning, after Aurora had called all careful eyes to attend the day, forth came the faire shepherdesse URANIA (faire indeed; yet that farre too meane a title for her, who for beautie deserved the highest stile could be given by best knowing Judgements). Into the Meade

she came, where usually she drave her flocks to feede, whose leaping and wantonesse showed they were proud of such a guide. But she, whose sad thoughts led her to another Manner of spending her time, made her soon leave them and follow her late begun custom: which was (while they delighted themselves) to sit under some shade, bewailing her misfortune; while they fed to feed upon her owne sorrow and teares, which at this time she began again to summon, sitting down under the shade of a well-spread Beech; the ground (then blest) and the tree with full and fined leaved branches growing proud to beare and shadow such perfection. But she, regarding nothing in comparison of her woe, thus proceeded in her grief: Alas, Urania, said she, (the true servant of misfortune) of any misery that can befal a woman, is not this the most and greatest which thou are falne into? Can there be any neare the unhappinesse of being ignorant, and that in the highest kind, not being certain of my owne estate or birth? Why was I not still continued in the beleefe I was, as I appeare, a Shepherdes, and Daughter to a Shepherd? [(.i., I.)]

Other shepherds and shepherdesses having come into the plain, the unhappy Urania endeavours to avoid them. She climbs a hill and comes to a cave, the first of these subterranean recesses mentioned in the story, but unfortunately not the last. A jaundiced reader might be forgiven for thinking of the *Urania* as a succession of caves, all full of royal personages, bemused and forewandered, who sit about endlessly narrating their misfortunes. On entering this, the first cave of the series, Urania penetrates to an inner chamber, and discovers a sonnet (newly written) lying on a stone table. A more remarkable discovery, however, is a young man, lying on a bed of boughs, raving with love and anguish of Limena. The Sydneian sentence is rather an involved medium for delirium, and we learn, only after much circumlocution, that this miserable wight is Persissus, newphew of the King of Sicilie. He recounts the story of Limena whom he believes murdered, and Urania very sensibly suggests that she may not be dead. If not, let him find her. If so, let him avenge her. Having thanked her in a speech of some thousand words, Persissus leaves the cave to follow her advice, and Urania drives home her flock.

Next day, Urania encounters a wolf, which is slain by two beautiful youths, who are seeking food for their aged father. Urania gives them for their food a lamb to which she has been confiding her troubles a few minutes before. They all repair to a sea-cave which shelters the aged father of Urania's rescuers. Having bewailed their respective fates in the loftiest language, they exchange mutual compliments, and Urania bids farewell to the old man (who is, in fact, the exiled King of Albania) and to his sons. She has not proceeded far when she meets still another beautiful youth: Parselius, Prince of Morea. He has left that country with his great friend and kinsman, Amphilanthus (heir to the Kingdom of Naples), with the object of finding the lost sister of Amphilanthus, who was stolen when an infant. It has been revealed to her father by divination that she is still living. (The reader immediately smells a rat, but alas! it takes hundreds of pages, a wilderness of misunderstandings and oceans of tears be-

fore it becomes perceptible to Urania.) Arrived in Sicily, Amphilanthus and Parselius go in different directions in their search, arranging to meet a year later at the court of the King of Naples. Parselius, while talking to Urania, sees in her a resemblance to Leonius, a younger brother of Amphilanthus, and he suspects her identity. He accompanies her to the cave where the King of Albania and his wolf-slaying sons have taken up quarters. Parselius engages to restore him to his rights, and the aged man dies of joy. Unfortunately, his sons are less susceptible to strong emotion. Parselius then goes to see Persissus (the distraught adorer of Limena) and Urania goes home, in love with Parselius.

It would serve no good purpose to continue to outline so complicated, repetitive and extravagant a plot. The scene shifts in kaleidoscopic fashion, and we find ourselves now in Pantaleria, now in Morea, now in Constantinople, Rhodes, Delos, Negropont, Pamphilia or Mytilene. But in fact the scene is always Arcadia, and the blue-blooded shepherds and shepherdesses remain ever faithful to the heroic-pastoral code. After many wanderings, exploits, and sufferings which serve merely to discover their enduring constancy, all the lovers are united, all the kings reinstated, and all the mysteries are resolved.

Since we have shown that Lady Mary devotedly copied the romantic characteristics of Sydney's novel, it is only just to show that like him she sometimes gives us beautiful little passages which are quite free from exaggeration. She has been describing a disputatious, angry man who has deafened the company with his talk, and she says:

> When he was gone, the Roome was like a calme after
> a storme or as after foule weather the Aire is silent,
> and sweete; so all being quiet, they pleased themselves
> as Birds in the Spring with their own tunes.

It has been maintained by such critics as have thought it worth while to mention Lady Mary Wroath, that the *Urania* is only a slavish imitation of the *Arcadia,* and that in her novel Lady Mary Wroath "copies and outdoes Sydney's utmost extravagances both in the story and in the mode of telling it." Certainly the *Urania* is "tedious . . . awkward and long-winded," but is it really more so than the *Arcadia?* One sometimes suspects the *Arcadia* of being so sacrosanct that it is not judged on its own merits even now. Horace Walpole had the courage to judge the *Arcadia* apart from the aura of its author. It was a critical honesty never displayed before and seldom since in this connection. Who will say that it is not wearying to plough through the *Arcadia,* or how many do so conscientiously, even in the cause of literary research? Indeed, it is so sacred that it is not often approached. The claims of the most learned commentators are not based on the intrinsic worth of the *Arcadia*—a question which they pass over almost in silence—but are entirely concentrated on its position in the development of English fiction, and on its influence on succeeding generations. Its position is said to emphasise the period of poetic invention which came between the period of traditional writing, and the development of realism. This is true, but it is perhaps more cogent to note that the *Arcadia* copied a mode of fiction which was passing, if not already past, and that, in consequence, the *Arcadia* is simply a digression in the development of the English novel. Its direct imitators were therefore splashing about in a backwater, while the main river and its tributaries flowed on surely to the open sea. As for the influence of the *Arcadia,* it is entirely to be deplored, and its occasional poetic beauties do not compensate for the fact that for long centuries English fiction was cursed with this heritage of artificial sentimentality. Certainly the French Heroic Romance was a most powerful influence in perpetuating this sort of writing in England, but it could not have had such a ready reception if Sydney had not already prepared the English mind for these extravagances, and established the Heroic Romance by force of his own personal and literary prestige.

The *Urania* sedulously copied, and possibly exaggerated, all the defects of the *Arcadia,* and if it could claim nothing individual it would simply not be worth mentioning. But this work of Lady Mary Wroath's does contain an individual feature of great interest and significance from the standpoint of fictional development; that is, the introduction of minor stories in subject and manner of the type of the *novelle.* These sub-plots are attached by very slender filaments to the main theme of the *Urania* and they are not ambitious in quality, but they give to the *Urania* the significance of uniting the realistic and the romantic genres. In a word, the *Urania* is not merely, like the *Arcadia,* representative of a decadent and retrogressive kind of fiction. It is also symptomatic of the way in which realism was developing in its own genre and was henceforth to obtrude itself in alien territory.

The best of these stories is that of Limena and Persissus. It is simple, direct, vivid. When the characters speak, they do so without circumlocutions. Limena is the daughter of a duke, who before departing for the wars in support of his king, bestows her in marriage on "a great Lord in the Country," named Philargus. This he does to ensure her safety and protection, but he does not take into account that Limena and a noble youth called Persissus are deeply in love with each other. Persissus, indeed, does not know that Limena loves him until he visits her some time after her marriage, in the home she shares with her husband and her father. They see each other frequently though innocently, but the husband is suspicious. "That night," says Persissus, "I saw her, but spake not to her, so curiously her husband watched us, yet could he not keepe our eies, but by them we did deliver our soules." The next day Philargus in his jealousy takes her away with him from their home; "And so went all worth with this odd man to have her delicacy like a Diamond in a rotten box." Persissus, however, takes the opportunity of seeing her on his way to camp, and she tells him of her husband's jealousy. Persissus had observed her paleness.

> Desirous to know the cause, I remain'd almost impatient not venturing to speak to her before her husband for hurting her; but he going out of the roome, after we had supped, either to cover the flames which

were ready to break out in huge fires of his mistrust, or to have the company fitter for him, affecting still to be chiefe: his absence, however, gave me opportunitie to demand the reason of her strangeness; she sigh'd to hear me call it so: and with tears told me the reason, concluding; and thus do you see my Lord (said she) the torments I suffer for our love; yet do you more torture me with doubting me, who have no happiness left me, but the knowledge of my faith to you, all afflictions being welcome to me, which for your sake I suffer. Between rage and paine, I remain'd amazed, till she, taking me by the hand, brought me more wofully to myselfe with these words. And yet am I brought to a greater mischiefe; with that fixing her weeping eyes upon mine . . . I must my Lord (said she) entreat you to refraine this place since none can tell what danger may proceed from mad, and unbridled jealousie; refraine your sight? Command me then to die (said I) have I deserved to be thus punished? Shall this brutishness undoe my blessings? Yet this place I will, since you will have it so, hoping you will find some means to let me know Philargus house is not in all places. That I will doe, or die (said she).

Persissus departs the next day. He gets news from Limena that her husband intends to murder her. Persissus gives the following description of the interview between husband and wife:

> After my departure from his house to the Citie, and so to the Campe, the Jealous wretch finding my Ladie retired into a Cabinet she had where she used to passe away some part of her unpleasant life; coming in, he shut the dore, drawing his sword, and looking with as much fury, as jealous spite could with rage demonstrate, his breath short, his sword he held in his hand, his eyes sparkling as thick and fast as an unperfectly kindled fire with much blowing gives to the Blower, his tongue stammering with rage bringing forth these words; thou hast wrong'd me, vild creature: I say thou hast wrong'd me; she who was compounded of virtue and her spirit, seeing his wild and distracted countenance guest the worst, wherefore mildly she gave this answere: Philargus, saide she, I know in mine owne heart I have not wrong'd you, and God knows I have not wrong'd myself.

There was no dialogue in the *Arcadia.* There is breathless dialogue here. There is dramatic urgency in the abrupt sentences, in the emphatic repetition, in the suspense which awaits violence. The simple dignity of the wife's reply makes the husband's fury seem all the more savage. This is how the scene might be described orally, by one who was actually present, and its spontaneous rightness, its realism is in complete contrast with the flowery Arcadian style. Space does not permit further quotation, so we must content ourselves with recounting briefly the remainder of the story. The husband is not depicted as a complete villain. We are shown love struggling in him before finally, through jealousy, it turns to hatred. He gives his wife two days in which to decide whether to lure Persissus to death or to die herself. She chooses to die, and Philargus takes her into a nearby wood. There he intends to murder her, but having inflicted some minor wounds, changes his mind. He takes her with him then into a distant retreat, and continues daily to torture her until she is rescued by a passing knight, who engages Philargus in combat and slays him. At that moment Persissus chances to pass that way. Philargus gives his blessing to the lovers before expiring, and they live happily ever after.

Limena's account of her sufferings is not in as realistic a style as Persissus's narrative, but although the end of the tale is rather romantic in language, it is quite just to say that this minor story is in substance and manner reminiscent of the *novelle*. Other stories worthy of mention in the same connection are that of Belizia which is good but brief, and the story of Bellamira which is also illustrative of the same trend.

It is not for a moment suggested that Lady Mary Wroath deliberately aimed at realism in those parts of the *Urania* which we have described. On the contrary, we know that she did everything in her power to imitate the style of the *Arcadia*. But apparently there were times when the strain of the Arcadian prose proved too great, and Lady Mary took a short respite to draw breath, before returning to her precarious and exhausting performance. It has been excellently said [by Baker in his *History of the English Novel*] that "Sidney in the 'Arcadia' is like the coryphée in some elaborate ballet, swimming indefatigably through the mazes of an intricate dance." Lady Mary's weaker muscles craved relief from the exquisite agony of unnatural posturing, and in the intervals she became her real self. Perhaps, also, she was more at home in some of her tales, simply because she was drawing on events within her experience.

One cannot at this late date assert that Lady Mary's realistic little stories were those founded on the amorous adventures of some of her contemporaries. It is not possible now to identify the details of age-old scandals, but we know that the book had, to some extent, a satiric intention and that it set Jacobean society by the ears. On December 15th Lady Mary wrote to Buckingham, assuring him that she had never intended her book to offend anyone, and stating that she had stopped its sale. On March 9th, 1623, Chamberlain wrote to his friend Carleton, enclosing "certain bitter verses of the Lord Denny upon the Lady Mary Wroath, for that in her book of *Urania* she doth palpably and grossly play upon him and his late daughter, the Lady Mary Hay, besides many others she makes bold with: and, they say, takes great liberty, or rather license to traduce whom she pleases, and thinks she dances in a net." Chamberlain adds [in *Court and Times of James I*] that he has seen the answer by Lady Mary to these verses of Lord Denny, but that he did not consider it worth the writing out. These proofs make it clear that Lady Mary's declaration of innocence was disingenuous, and it is a sobering thought that the first woman-novelist in English literature could not refrain from that kind of veiled slander which later developed into the histoire scandaleuse. There was a vast moral and social gap between a Lady Mary and a Mrs. Manley. Why did Sir Philip Sydney's niece stoop to besmirch a family record of nobility which so recently had been a national glory? Perhaps she had observed that, though the dead Sydney moved the hearts of men "more than with a trumpet," those same hearts were quite impervious to the misfortunes of his nearest descendant. Perhaps she realised that though the Countess of Pembroke was revered for literary feats which were either puerile or supposititious, the Lady Mary Wroath could expect no indulgence from the literary world of which she was no longer the patron. It was precisely because she anticipated cold criticism that she larded her title-page with the names of those who had died at the zenith of fame, before they could commit the social solecism of becoming poor. The satiric intention in the *Urania* was not without antique precedent, for the Eclogues of Baptista Mantuanus satirised allegorically in pastoral dialogues the social and moral vices of fifteenth century Italy. No doubt, in attacking her contemporaries, she aimed at making her book more saleable. Veiled slander, however, is not a passport to fame, however productive it may be of immediate notoriety. Even if the *Urania* were as good a book as John Barclay's *Argenis* which appeared in the same year, it would have had less permanent success, and less influence, because while political or social satire is sufficiently wide in aim to save it from an appearance of spite, personal satire always creates a revolution of feeling in its own time, and falls into oblivion when the earth lies heavily alike on the slanderer and the slandered.

It is unnecessary to comment on the fact that Lady Mary copied, in the Urania, the practice of introducing verse into the romance. This custom, to which Sydney adhered in the *Arcadia,* was of Italian origin, and was certainly no advantage to prose fiction. Most of Lady Mary's poetry is facile and superficial. In dismissing it, however, one may mention some verses which combine sincerity and grace: chiefly "Love, what art thou?" "Come, merry Spring, delight us," and "Who can blame me if I love?" She used the sonnet with little depth, but with great mastery of form. The perfect Italian form of sonnet 4 is worthy of note.

It is a paradox that Lady Mary Wroath's best claim to remembrance lies in her accidental realism. Two other women wrote Arcadian novels. In 1651, Anne Weamys published *A continuation of Sir Philip Sydney's Arcadia,* which had its second edition in 1690. When she wrote it a king had been beheaded, and England had been convulsed in political revolution and civil war; when it was republished, a King had returned, bringing with him a new era in national and literary history—a curious proof, if proof were needed, of the divorce between the Pastoral and the real, of the difficulty of killing a romantic school of writing, and of its escapist nature. Between the two editions of the *Continuation* appeared Mlle. de la Roche Guilhem's *Almanzor and Almanzaida. A Novel written by Sir Philip Sidney, And found since his Death amongst his Papers.* This work merits no particular attention, but it will not be out of place to comment on the novel of Anne Weamys.

The full title of this novel defined the particular subject-matter of the narrative:

A CONTINUATION of Sir Philip Sydney's Arcadia wherein is handled the Loves of Amphialus and Helena Queen of Corinth, Prince Plangus and Erona

With the Historie of the Loves of Old Claius and Young Strephon to Urania

Written by a young Gentlewoman

Mtis A.W.

Thomas Heath, the bookseller, woos the "ingenius Reader" in an introductory letter. He begs him not to marvel that heroic Sydney's renowned fancy should be pursued to a close by a feminine pen. Here is "Sir Philip's fantasie incarnate: both Pamela's Majestie and Philoclea's Humilitie exprest to the life in the person and style of this Virago. In brief, no other than the lively Ghost of Sidney, by a happie transmigration, speaks through the organs of this inspired Minerva."

It is to be feared that the lively ghost of Sydney would not endorse Heath's volatile words. In fact, if it were possible for lively ghosts to tear their hair, then indeed Sir Philip's locks would fall thick as autumnal leaves. Granted that a continuation always lacks cohesion with the original work, at least it should aim at artistic unity, and it should have for its object the same aesthetic principles. Sydney was guided by the principle that all imaginative invention was poetry, and to this end he evolved a prose style which was intended to be poetic, and which in its billowing, emotional prolixity was in itself a figure of the romantic complications which it expressed. But, though Anne Weamys continues the adventures of some of Sydney's characters, she does not do so in Sydneian prose. Lady Mary Wroath imitated Sir Philip Sydney's style with more or less success, and occasionally lapsed into everyday language. Anne Weamys never lapses into everyday language, and never attempts Sydneian prose. She never attempts it—not because she could not. Her writing has a consistent style of its own which shows her ability to govern language. She tells her story in a pastoral manner, but she avoids the swaying garrulity of Sydney's style, and expresses herself in a style which, though certainly romantic, is clear, straightforward and economical. Let us for a moment ignore the story which has really nothing to do with our contention, and support our argument by comparing certain characteristic manners of writing. Here is Sir Philip Sydney's description of the love of Pyrocles for Philoclea:

> Pyrocles, who had that for a law unto him, not to leave Philoclea in anything unsatisfied, although he still remained in his former purpose, and knew that time would grow short for it, yet hearing no noise, the shepherds being as then run to Basilius, with settled and humble countenance, as a man that should have spoken of a thing that did not concern himself, bearing even in his eyes sufficient shows that it was nothing but Philoclea's danger which did anything burden his heart, far stronger than fortune, having with vehement embracing of her got yet some fruit of his delayed end, he thus answered the wise innocency of Philoclea: "Lady, most worthy not only of life, but to be the very life of all things; the more notable demonstrations you make of love so far beyond my desert, with which it

pleaseth you to overcome fortune, in making me happy: the more am I, even in course of humanity, to leave that love's force which I neither can nor will leave, bound to seek requital's witness that I am not ungrateful to do which, the infiniteness of your goodness being such as I cannot reach unto it, yet doing all I can and paying my life which is all I have, though it be far, without measure, short of your desert, yet shall I not die in debt to my own duty."

(*Arcadia*, Bk. IV P. 545)

"Faire Mistress" (says Nicholas Breton [in his "Letter of Love to a Gentlewoman"] once in the service of Sir Philip Sydney, and on Sydney's death devoted to the service of the Duchess of Pembroke):

> Faire Mistresses, to court you with eloquence were as ill as to grieve you with fond tales: let it therefore please you rather to believe what I write, than to note how I speake . . . I could commend you above the skies, compare you with the Sun, or set you among the Stars, figure you with the Phoenix, imagine you a goddesse, but I will leave such weak praising fictions, and think you only yourself, whose vertuous beauty, and whose honourable discretion in the care of a little kindnesse is able to command the love of the wise, and the labours of the honest.

Anne Weamys gives the following description of the love-sick Plangus:

> In this sweet place, he sat himself down, with an intention to rest his wearied limbs under a branched tree, whilest his servants refreshed themselves and baited their horses, but no ease could be harboured in his disquieted heart, his eys being no sooner closed, but that he saw Erona burning in their unmerciful fire: at which sight he staringly opened them, and determined with himself, that since sleep would procure no comfort to him, other than Tragical scenes, he would never enjoy any contentment before he had settled Erona in her throne in safetie. [(p. 10-11)]

One observes that Anne Weamys' style is neither as flowery as Sydney's, nor as direct as Breton's. If, however, we compared her with Breton alone, her pastoral romantics would seem emphasised. She thus describes a summer morning:

> At last he entered the pleasant country of *Arcadia*, which was adorned with stately woods: no cries were heard there but the lambs, and they in sport too sounded their voices to make their playfellow lambs answer them again in imitation of the like. And the abundance of shadie trees that were there, were beautiful with the sweet melodie of birds.

But Breton exclaims, in his *Merry Dialogue:*

> Oh, to see in a faire morning, or a Sunnie evening the lambes and Rabbits at bace, the birds billing, the fishes playing, and the flowers budding. Who would not leave the drinking in an Alehouse, the warngling in a dicing house, the lying in a market, and the cheating in a

fayre; and think that the brightness of a faire day doth put down all the beauties of the world.

This world of Breton's is the real world, and he wrote in the springtime of realism, when the sap was running free in the youthful stock and showing its energy in proliferation. Anne Weamys' style was very far from this, but it was far also from the style of Sydney. She could steady herself to write with dignified incisiveness such passages as the following:

> It is Justice to bring murderers to their deserved punishments. And because you Prince Plangus testifie yourself to be such an affectionate friend to my dear children, shew yourself one in their revenge; you I will entrust to be the General of my Armie; prove as valiant now as you have ever done; let all your aim be at Plexirtus; and, if possible, convey him hither alive, that he may die a publick spectacle of shame and terror before all the People. [(p. 288)]

As for the plot of the *Continuation,* it is complicated, but well constructed. It is a noticeable fact that, in a period of literary long-windedness, and in a medium which has always connoted prolixity, Anne Weamys tells her involved story without a single digression, and without a single ambiguity. No doubt there are parts which are too synoptic, and which might have pleased more if they had been elaborated, but this is the fault of her very good quality of verbal economy. Anne Weamys subscribes to the Pastoral convention, but she keeps one eye on real life. Her heroes and heroines (and there are about ten of them) show energy and commonsense in achieving their purposes, and never evince the slightest inclination to confide their troubles to lambs. They pursue a life which contains love and adventure—too much love and too much adventure to be realistic, but also too much realism to be truly pastoral. Anne Weamys' book is at the parting of the ways. Mopsa, in the *Continuation* is presented with humour. Her fairy-tale of the King's daughter is really funny, and is told with all the deviousness and love of proverb one would expect in such a narrative.

To conclude, the works of Lady Mary Wroath and of Anne Weamys are of value, because of their position in regard to the romantic and the realistic schools. The social position of these writers made it inevitable that they should choose the aristocratic medium. Had a woman of a lower social stratum wished to write a novel, she would, no doubt, have gravitated towards the realistic fiction of her class, but in point of fact no such woman could have written a book at that period, because she would have lacked the necessary education. Women of the upper classes, in Elizabethan and Jacobean times, had such "education" as permitted them to read romances. They had no education in the real sense of the word. Naturally, the books they read were those written for their own social class, and very often dedicated actually to their sex, for in that period well-bred women assumed an important position as readers of fiction. Such works, for example, as Lyly's *Euphues* were dedicated to feminine readers. If a female were actually entreated to read such works, then a female, greatly daring, might write one—if she could. But to begin one's career in fiction with no choice but the Pastoral medium might well have daunted the stoutest feminine spirit. Lady Elizabeth Carew, for example, wrote a play [*Mariamne, or The Fair Maid of Jewry*], but the drama, with its acts, and scenes, gave, as it were, a neat form into which one might pour one's ideas, and this form was far shorter, and required less of a sustained effort. The construction of the pastoral novel, and the exigencies of the style were such feats for these first women-novelists, that one can only liken it to a child who achieves an entrechat before he has learnt to stand. Both women are best in their more realistic vein—so that however small their contribution it was in accordance with the vital trend in fiction. "Be eloquent in plainness" said Nicholas Breton, "You must not speak in the clouds to them that are acquainted with the moon."

Josephine A. Roberts (essay date 1983)

SOURCE: "The Nature of Poetry," in *The Poems of Lady Mary Wroth,* Louisiana State University Press, 1983, pp. 41–60.

[*In the following essay, Roberts discusses Wroth's treatment of the subject of love relationships and the influence of Petrarchan and pastoral literary traditions in* Pamphilia to Amphilanthus, Urania, *and* Love's Victory.]

PAMPHILIA TO AMPHILANTHUS

Lady Mary Wroth's contemporaries recognized that her verse belonged to the Petrarchan tradition and strongly identified her as Sir Philip Sidney's successor, "In whom, her *Uncle's* noble Veine renewes." Despite the early seventeenth-century fashion of "hard lines," and metaphysical wit, Lady Mary chose to reach back to a much older poetic model. Although her sonnet collection uses the voice of a female persona, the sequence contains many Elizabethan elements, especially in its structure, diction, and imagery. Yet the distinctive tone of her poems is much closer to that of Donne's lyrics, with a harsh, occasionally cynical attitude toward earthly constancy.

Lady Mary's preference for the older Petrarchan forms may be best understood in the context of a seventeenth-century critical essay on poetry, which was addressed to her: Dudley, third Baron North's "Preludium to the first Verses," which appeared as the introduction to his collection of poems [entitled *A Forest of Varieties*]. In this essay North attacks the metaphysical poets who "like ill-ranging Spaniels . . . spring figures, and ravished with their extravagant fancies, pursue them in long excursions, neglecting their true gain and pretended affection." He prefers instead poetry that is clear and easily understood; "good sense and matter elegantly delivered," he argues, should be favored over "extravagancy of fancy and conceit." North eloquently defends the plain style, in which much of Lady Mary's own poetry was written. At one point, North refers directly to her: "I wish your Ladiships authority would so abate the price that our poorer abilities might hold trade without straining." By referring to her "authority," North may be alluding either to Lady Mary's role as a patron or, more likely, as a fellow poet dedicated to the style of plain eloquence. He seems to have composed the "Preludium" before the death of Prince Henry in 1612, when he was preparing many of his own manuscript poems.

Like North's poems, Lady Mary's sonnet collection, *Pamphilia to Amphilanthus*, first circulated in manuscript among her friends. Her sequence exists in at least two distinct versions: the first, now at the Folger Library, is a fair copy in the author's hand, containing many corrections and revisions; the second text appears in a separately numbered section following the prose romance, *The Countesse of Montgomery's Urania* (1621). The two versions include many of the same sonnets, but they differ most significantly in the selection and order of the individual poems.

In identifying the central figure in her collection, Lady Mary Wroth followed Sidney's *Astrophil and Stella* by choosing a name of Greek derivation. In both versions of the sequence, the protagonist is Pamphilia, whose name means "all-loving." To emphasize that she is the speaker of the collection, Lady Mary signed the name Pamphilia in the Folger manuscript after the first group of poems (P1–55) and after the farewell sonnet (P103). Her beloved is appropriately called Amphilanthus whose name signifies "the lover of two," as explained in the prose text of the *Urania*, where he is shown to be unfaithful to Pamphilia. The prose romance supplies many additional details concerning both characters: for example, Pamphilia is described as an unusually learned woman, "being excellent in writing".

Lady Mary may also have wished to identify her protagonist with one of the most famous women writers of antiquity—Pamphila, who lived under the reign of Nero. She was described by Edward Phillips in his *Theatrum Poetarum Anglicanorum* as a poet: "Epidaurian the Daughter of Soteridas, of whose writing several works as well in Verse as Prose, are reckon'd up by Suidas, in which so great was her Repute, that her statue is said to have been erected by Cephisodorus." Regrettably, none of Pamphila's poetry has survived, but a small fragment of her voluminous history, written in Greek, remains. According to Suidas, Pamphila divided her history into thirty-three books, and it was well known to later writers, such as Aulus Gellius, who quoted from it. Although there is little biographical information concerning Pamphila, she describes herself as a married woman who wrote down the conversations of her learned guests and other material gleaned from her reading in the form of an extensive commentary. Like her distinguished namesake, Pamphilia is portrayed as a dedicated and prolific writer, and for obvious reasons Lady Mary Wroth's contemporaries regarded the fictional character as autobiographical. When Sir Edward Denny launched his attack against the prose romance *Urania*, he openly identified the author as Pamphilia in his verse poem. Once involved in the quarrel with Denny, Lady Mary denied the connection, but she still used the name as her own in the taunting verse reply to him.

It is far more difficult, however, to establish any real life figure behind the character of Amphilanthus. He is described only in very general terms, and surely some seventeenth-century readers of the sequence must have delighted in speculating over his identity. Lady Mary's husband, Sir Robert Wroth, would probably be excluded on the grounds that the relationship portrayed in the sequence is extramarital. Other possible candidates, previously mentioned in the account of the author's life, include Sir Dudley Carleton; Henry Vere, Earl of Oxford; and William Herbert, Earl of Pembroke. Although a case could be made for any of these men, Lady Mary Wroth provides a significant clue in the *Urania*, when she indicates that Pamphilia and Amphilanthus are first cousins. . . . Only William Herbert would meet this qualification, but it is important to note that Lady Mary provides few explicit indicators within the poems, in contrast to Sidney in the "Rich" sonnets of *Astrophil and Stella*.

Unfortunately, only the barest circumstantial evidence exists to support the identification of the Earl of Pembroke as Amphilanthus. Early in his life, because of the scandal with Mary Fitton, Pembroke had acquired a reputation as a rake: in fact, his biographer Clarendon believed that the central flaw of his character was that "he was immoderately given up to women" [Edward Hyde, first Earl of Clarendon, in *History of the Rebellion*]. In addition to unfaithfulness, a second characteristic attributed to Amphilanthus is his skill in composing love poetry. Although Pembroke's lyric poems were not published until thirty years after his death, his verse may be found scattered throughout a number of early seventeenth-century commonplace books. Within the second part of the *Urania* Lady Mary Wroth has the character Amphilanthus recite a poem that she claims was written by him: "Had I loved butt att that rate". The same poem appears in four different manuscripts at the British Library, where it is specifically attributed to Pembroke in three of the copies. Such an ascription may be simply a coincidence, but the evidence strongly suggests that Lady Mary Wroth was paying tribute to Pembroke's artistic gifts by including his poem in the *Urania*.

As early as 1613, Lady Mary's poems were being read in manuscript by her friends. The Folger copy of *Pamphilia to Amphilanthus* consists of 110 poems plus a group of seven miscellaneous pieces that appear after the farewell sonnet, P103. Whereas the Folger manuscript contains numerous authorial corrections, which were later incorporated in the printed text, it is clear that the sonnet sequence underwent a much more substantial revision when Lady Mary began composing the *Urania* in the period of 1618–1620. The structure of the sequence was tightened by reducing the number of poems: some pieces were eliminated entirely, and others were transferred, in revised form, to the text of the prose romance. The result was a final group of eighty-three sonnets and twenty songs, which were carefully arranged in four distinct, yet interrelated, sections.

The sequence opens with Pamphilia's dream vision, in which she witnesses the triumph of Venus and Cupid over her heart. As a helpless victim of love, she is powerless to overcome the troubling fears and hopes that beset her mind. The first section of fifty-five poems is designed to show Pamphilia's conflicting emotions as she attempts to resolve the struggle between passionate surrender and self-affirmation. Rather than offering a steady progression of attitudes, Lady Mary chooses to dramatize the mental processes through which Pamphilia seeks to discover the truth of her own feelings. The first section ends with the persona's determination to love as an individual choice, rather than as an edict imposed by the gods (P55).

Following an interlude of songs, the second section explores a darker side of passion: the lover's susceptibility to doubt, jealousy, and despair. Within the second section (P63–72) Lady Mary made the most significant revisions in the replacement of five of the original ten poems. She inserted sonnets stressing the capricious activities of Cupid, who is portrayed as a tiny, mischievous boy. This Anacreontic Cupid amuses himself by trifling with human emotions; in one sonnet he is compared to a skillful juggler, who captivates his audience "Butt if hee play, his gaine is our lost will: / Yett childlike, wee can nott his sports refuse" (P64.13–14). Pamphilia expresses her frustration in love by denigrating Cupid as the representative of infantile, self–centered feelings: "Indeed I lov'd butt wanton boy nott hee" (P72.14). As part of the internal debate, Pamphilia's mockery produces a sudden guilty reaction, for she abruptly repents of treason against the god of love and vows to reward him with a "Crowne" of praise (P76.12).

In contrast to the Anacreontic figure of the second section, Pamphilia turns to regard Cupid as a mature, esteemed king, whose behavior is just and reasonable. The treatment of Cupid as a monarch, found in the accounts of the medieval Courts of Love, is especially stressed in the third section (P77–90). Quite literally, this group of fourteen sonnets forms a circular crown, for it imitates the Italian verse form, the *corona*, in which the last line of the first sonnet serves as the first line of the next. Pamphilia begins by acknowledging the tremendous power exercised by the ruler in his Court of Love, but she soon finds it impossible to sustain her glorification of Cupid. By the end of the third series of sonnets, she admits that ambivalent feelings still disturb her: "Curst jealousie doth all her forces bend / To my undoing; thus my harmes I see" (P90.11–12). Once more, Pamphilia's skepticism returns, and she admits that in her own mind she finds no single, all–powerful monarch. An interlude of songs follows in which she continues to debate which representation of Cupid comes closest to the truth. Surprisingly, one of the few nineteenth–century critics of Lady Mary's poetry, Frederick Rowton, failed to notice the significance of this debate. After reading two of the opposing poems, he attacked [in *The Female Poets of Great Britain*, 1848] what he believed were the author's inconsistencies: "The reader will not fail to notice the remarkably contradictory sentiments which these two poems present upon that important subject. . . . which doctrine are we to believe?" Rowton failed to see that Lady Mary's purpose was not merely to present a doctrine, but rather to show the mind of a woman in the process of evaluating the varied interpretations of the essence of love.

Following her failed attempt to idealize passion, Pamphilia gradually begins in the final section of the sequence to accept pain as a necessary complement to joy in love and to recognize the unpredictability of human emotions. Many of the sonnets in the last group (P95–103) are extremely melancholy in tone, and the predominant imagery is that of the winter world of clouds, shadows, and darkness. In the last two sonnets, however, a fragile hope emerges, for Pamphilia's sufferings have taught her to prize a type of love finer than she once accepted. She vows to surmount her inner conflicts and to focus attention on heavenly love, "which shall eternall goodnes prove" (P103.6).

This final version of Lady Mary Wroth's sonnet sequence, with its careful charting of the ebb and flow of human emotions, owes much to the model of Sidney's *Astrophil and Stella*. Like Astrophil, Pamphilia engages in an internal struggle between rebellion and submission to love. Yet whereas Sidney's protagonist regards Stella as the epitome of virtue and beauty, Pamphilia shares no delusions about Amphilanthus: she recognizes his inconstancy, and many of the sonnets deal with the theme of betrayal. In fact, the bitter tone of Lady Mary's sequence more closely resembles the final section of *Astrophil*, in which the lover is estranged from his beloved. Thus in her collection Lady Mary eliminates much of the playful humor associated with the depiction of Sidney's frustrated suitor (for example, in the poems to Stella's lap dog or her bird). She does follow Sidney by including a number of sonnets that deal with the adventures of the Anacreontic Cupid, who had become a very popular figure in English poetry as a result of the overwhelming success of *Astrophil and Stella*. Although the tracing of specific sources in Lady Mary Wroth's poems is often impossible because of traditional imagery and *topoi* shared by many of the later Elizabethan sonneteers, the notes to her poems list a number of likely borrowings from her uncle's collection.

Lady Mary also adopted several of Sidney's technical innovations in her sonnets. One Distinctive mark of her style is the use of the compound epithet, which Sidney had made famous. Her compounds range from the simplest, such as "my woe–kil'd heart" (P13.4) to the most complex, as in "theyr love–burnt–harts desires" (P29.10). She also followed Sidney in the use of a great variety of stanzaic and metrical patterns in her verse. In the first section of *Pamphilia to Amphilanthus*, she alternated groups of sonnets according to the Italian and English modes: Italian, P1–6, 15–20, 29–34; English, 8–13, 22–27 (25 excepted), 36–41. Departing from Sidney's marked preference for one major sonnet form (*abbaabba cdcdee*), which his brother, Sir Robert Sidney, also adopted, Lady Mary favored a rhyme scheme using a slightly different sestet (*abba abba ccdeed*). She included a total of twenty–one variations in the rhyme scheme, far more than in *Astrophil*.

Another important source of influence for Lady Mary's poetry was her father's verse, which has been only recently discovered in a unique manuscript. It is likely that many of these poems were written while Sir Robert Sidney was stationed in Flushing, and they reflect his wartime experience: the anguish of separation from loved ones, the horrors of death, and the depths of personal despair. Despite the fact that half of Sir Robert Sidney's poems are sonnets, he uses a far different tone and imagery than is found in *Astrophil*. Many of the poems contain vivid references to excruciating physical pain: one sonnet describes a galley slave who is beaten continually, "whoe on the oare doth stretch / his lims all day, all night his wounds doth binde" (Sonnet 19, 11.7–8). Even though he wrote love poems addressed to a lady named Charys, these are marked as well by a dark, brooding hopelessness. He rarely includes the lighter poems on Cupid found in the sequences composed either by his brother or by Lady Mary Wroth.

Few of Sir Robert Sidney's intimate circle of family and friends seem to have been acquainted with his verse. It is not known exactly when Lady Mary gained access to her father's writings, but her knowledge of them can be seen in her imitations of several specific poems [see *British Library Journal I*]. The most important is her "**Crowne of Sonnets**," probably based on Sir Robert Sidney's incomplete *corona*, which consists of only four poems and a quatrain of a fifth. At the bottom of the manuscript is Sir Robert Sidney's own handwritten comment that "the rest of the 13 sonnets doth want". Perhaps this unfinished "**Crowne**" served as a challenge to his daughter's poetic talents, for she attempted an even more complex version— a chain of fourteen sonnets. Rather than writing her *corona* to Charys or any other individual, she deliberately chose to dedicate it to the most idealistic concept of love. Yet as we have seen, the persona of her "**Crowne of Sonnets**" learns that it is impossible to sustain a perfect vision and returns at the end to her awareness of the human weaknesses that undermine love. One of the greatest similarities between the verse of father and daughter may be seen in this attitude of somber introspection. Appropriately, Sir Robert Sidney pointed to the dominant tone of both collections when in the final couplet to Song 19 he wrote, "But greef and angwish are the measure / that do immortalize our loves."

Apart from the influence of the Sidneys, it is more difficult to determine the other sources of Lady Mary's poetry. Much of her mythological imagery derives from Ovid, who was one of her favorite authors. She pays tribute to him in the *Urania* when the character Antissia meets a scholar, "one who had bin mad in studying how to make a piece of poetrie to excell Ovid, and to bee more admired then hee is". She was also an avid reader of Spenser's *Faerie Queene,* as shown in her borrowings. It is possible that she had read Shakespeare's sonnets, but the evidence is not conclusive. Of the other lyrical poets available to her, Samuel Daniel, Fulke Greville, Ben Jonson, and William Herbert may have served as influences, although specific borrowings from these writers are more doubtful.

Lady Mary Wroth was thus unlikely to proclaim that she was "no pickpurse of another's wit", but she did offer a number of important innovations to the sonnet sequence. Through the creation of a female persona, she was the first English writer to reverse the sexual roles within a complete sonnet collection. Regardless of the traditional apostrophes to night, sleep, hope, absence, and despair contained in many of her poems, she introduced a significant change in the focus of the sequence. Unlike the male sonneteers who often lavished praise (or mock dispraise) upon the woman's physical attributes, Lady Mary's collection deliberately subordinates the role of the beloved. Because the rhetoric of wooing or courtship is largely absent from her collection, the poet places far greater emphasis on the persona's internal struggles, as she comes to recognize the potential dangers inherent in romantic love.

For Pamphilia, constancy is a cardinal virtue, and she is in fact renowned as the "true paterne of excellent affection and affections truth". But faced with Amphilanthus' betrayal, she must begin to re-examine her own self-deceptive misconceptions of love, both in the guise of the infantile and the idealized versions of Cupid. By the end of the sequence, the persona prepares to abandon faith in any lasting human relationship and to redirect her constancy toward divine love. The final sonnet is ultimately reminiscent of Sir Philip Sidney's famous farewell to physical passion, "Leave me ô Love, which reachest but to dust."

Ironically, Lady Mary Wroth's prose fiction demonstrates that Pamphilia is unable to sustain such ethereal constancy. Within the *Urania* the internal debate concerning love becomes even more explicit than in the revised version of the sonnet sequence, for the fiction shows how Pamphilia confronts the fundamental inequity of the double standard, in which women are expected to remain constant whereas men are not. She wittily observes the difference: "being a man, it was necessary for him to exceede a woman in all things, so much as inconstancie was found fit for him to excell her in". Although Pamphilia decides to remain a virgin monarch and dedicate her life to the service of her country, in imitation of the historical Queen Elizabeth, she eventually relinquishes her vows. She comes to recognize the impossibility of maintaining perfect constancy in a world of human frailty: "butt itt is a strange, and rare thing in reason that all men showld bee borne under that fatall rule of inconstancy, for when did any one see a man constant from his birthe to his end, therfor women must think itt a desperate destinie for them to bee constant to inconstancy, butt alas this is woemens fortunes". In the Newberry manuscript of the second part of the *Urania,* which is characterized by an atmosphere of profound disillusionment, both Pamphilia and Amphilanthus betray their pledges of constancy to marry other partners.

The URANIA

The intense, ambivalent passion of Pamphilia for Amphilanthus thus furnished the nucleus for Lady Mary's immense work of prose fiction, the *Urania*. In both the published and unpublished parts of the romance the un-happy relationship of these two characters serves as the central focus of an intricately woven plot in which Pamphilia's vow of constancy in love is tested by a series of trials, separations, and deceptions, involving an enormous cast of additional characters. In accordance with the genre of pastoral romance, the *Urania* features a variety of narrators whose tales mirror the changing moods and problems of the central heroine. Lady Mary Wroth orga-nized her cast of characters as members of an imaginary royal family, descending from the kings of Morea and Naples. . . . In the unpublished part of the *Urania* the same family relationships exist, but the author established a second generation of characters.

In constructing her romance, Lady Mary drew freely upon Sir Philip Sidney's pastoral fiction for inspiration. Her opening scene echoes the beginning of the *New Arcadia,* in which the shepherds Strephon and Klaius lament the disappearance of a mysterious shepherdess, Urania, who is described as both a simple country girl and a great goddess, the Venus Urania, dividing "her heavenly beau-tie, betweene the Earth and the Sea." Lady Mary extends the fiction by describing the quest Urania undertakes to learn her true identity; through amorous adventures, she is led to recognize her royal parentage, and in one of the climactic moments of the romance she recovers a book describing her life history. The closest friend of Pamphil-ia, Urania functions as a confidante and as a source of sound advice concerning human relationships.

Although Lady Mary used the *Arcadia* as a point of de-parture for her romance, she excluded many of the dis-tinctive elements found in Sidney's work. Most of her characters belong to the highest aristocratic class, and there are thus few base-born figures, such as Dametas or Mop-sa, who provided burlesque humor in the *Arcadia*. In addition to restricting the tone of the work, Lady Mary devoted little attention to the political issues that fascinat-ed Sidney: the nature of kingship, the administration of justice and mercy, the question of rebellion. She also severely limited the accounts of battles and heroic deeds, in order to focus major attention on the topic of love.

Throughout the text of the *Urania,* Lady Mary inserted poems to emphasize key moments of crisis and discovery. She included nineteen sonnets, many of which were ap-propriately assigned to Pamphilia, who confesses, "I sel-dome write any but sonnets". The remaining thirty-seven poems consist of a wide variety of forms—madrigals, dialogues, ballads. The longest poem (U52) is a well-paced pastoral narrative which ends in an Ovidian meta-morphosis of the grief-stricken lover. Lady Mary exper-imented with quantitative verse in at least one poem (U49), in which she imitated sapphics. As in the *Old Arcadia,* where eclogues appear at the conclusion of each book, she placed at the end of the first book of *Urania* a group of three songs (U13-15), which answer each other.

When Lady Mary introduced previously written poems into the text of the *Urania,* she often heavily revised the

verse to adapt to the speaker and the situation. An excel-lent example is U24, which was changed to fit the char-acter of Antissia, an impulsive, high-strung woman who is in love with Amphilanthus. Lady Mary revised the poem to emphasize Antissia's extreme feelings as she begins to recognize that her affection can never be required. By substituting highly explosive language, the poet reveals Antissia's childish, self-centered attitude toward love and her refusal to accept responsibility for her actions. Anti-ssia's final comparison of herself to a salamander, which according to Renaissance mythographers can take its nourishment from flames, expresses the obsessive nature of her feelings; later in the *Urania* when she plots to murder Amphilanthus, she fulfills her vow emphatically expressed in the final version of the poem: "soe shall those flames my being give" (U24.26). The early copies of U17 and U18 (in the Folger manuscript) and U9 (in the British Library manuscript) also may be compared with the later versions to show Lady Mary's process of revis-ing the poetry to suit the context of the fiction.

The speakers of the poems in the *Urania* include a wide variety of human types, ranging from saintly lovers to gigolos. Because the romance often provides significant information concerning the speakers, I have included in the notes a brief account of the background of each poem. In many cases, the prose text also directs the critical in-terpretation of a poem, as shown in U35, where the for-saken lover Dorolina delivers a catalogue of famous women deceived by men. Although the speaker herself confesses that "the Verses are long and teadious", her admission reinforces the despairing mood of the poem. A very different speaker is the Florentine knight (U53), whose poetry reflects his humorous inability to stop talk-ing: he "talked on, and regarded, or not, said Verses, spake Prose, and Rime againe, no more heeding answers."

The second part of the *Urania,* found in the Newberry manuscript, contains far less poetry. Although Lady Mary Wroth continued to use a mixture of speakers, the poems tend to be mainly songs, with only a few sonnets (N1, N3, N17). The verse shows her interest in exploring the mind under states of extreme pressure, as in N6 and N7, which are assigned to Antissia, who has now been driven insane. Yet the second volume of the Newberry text con-tains only one poem, which suggests that the prose nar-rative was occupying a greater degree of Lady Mary's attention. In the second part of the *Urania,* which was left unfinished, one of the characters alluded to the difficulty of continuing to write poetry in a hostile environment: "wee have some [poets] that dare venture in thes trouble-som times, for itt [is] dangerous, butt noe danger can make dauntless spiritts stoope". Partly because of the controversy that arose over the first part of the *Urania,* the second part did not appear in print, and it is signifi-cant that the manuscript contains several blanks for po-ems which were never included.

Despite Lady Mary's willingness to remove copies of the published *Urania* from sale, the controversy surrounding the book did not deter seventeenth-century readers. Hen-ry Peacham [in *The Compleat Gentleman*] for example, claimed in 1622 that the "late-published *Urania*" had shown the author to be the "inheritrix of the Divine Wit of her Immortle Vncle." In a catalogue of women writers [entitled *Gynai Keior or Nine Books of Various History, Concerning Women*] Thomas Heywood described her as "the ingenious Ladie, the late composer of our extant *Urania,*" and Edward Phillips mentioned her [in *Theatrum Poetarum Anglicanorum*] under the section, "Women Among the Moderns Eminent for Poetry," where he referred to the author as "an Emulatress perhaps of Philip Sidney's *Arcadia.*" In *The Ladies Dictionary,* the *Urania* was also described in comparison with Sidney's work: "a Poetical History, much of the same Nature, being a very curious piece, tho not meeting with the like general reception."

It is possible that the *Urania* furnished a contemporary dramatist, James Shirley, with plot material for his play, *The Politician* (1655). Gerard Langbaine in his *Account of the English Dramatick Poets* (1691) first observed a similarity between the play and one of the stories contained in the romance: "A story resembling this, I have read in the first book of the Countess of *Montgomery's Urania,* concerning the King of *Romania,* the Prince *Antissius,* and his Mother-in-law." Langbaine referred to the tale of the treacherous second wife of the king of Romania, who cleverly turned the king against his faithful son Antissius and attempted to seize the throne through a conspiracy with one of his servants. Shirley's basic plot is very similar, for the king of Norway was deceived by his second wife, Marpisa, who slandered the young prince and plotted to have him killed as part of her effort to usurp the throne with the assistance of the politician, Gotharus. Shirley's court, like that of *Urania,* is rife with corruption and villainy, yet despite the shift in setting to Norway, the play contains close parallels to Lady Mary's principal characters. The major difference is that the dramatist devotes greater attention to Gotharus and the double betrayal of Marpisa and her co-conspirator. In creating his plays, Shirley frequently borrowed plot material from prose romances, and a dramatic version of *Arcadia* is often attributed to him.

The *Urania* was little known to readers in succeeding generations, but the literary historian Sir Egerton Brydges printed some extracts from Lady Mary Wroth's work in 1815 [*Restituta, or Titles, Extracts, and Characters of Old Books in English Literature Required*], with the following judgment on the merits of the poetry, as compared with the prose: "It will be more to the purpose of modern literature to give copious extracts from its numerous, intermingled poetry; as specimens of Lady Mary Wrothe's talents never occur in modern revivals of forgotten genius."

LOVE'S VICTORIE

It is not surprising that Lady Mary would undertake the writing of a play as a result of her active interest and participation in dramatic entertainments. She had performed in masques and probably in amateur theatricals, and she also attended plays, as suggested by her references to the theater in the *Urania:* "yet he unmoveable, was no further wrought, then if he had seene a delicate play-boy acte a loving womans part, and knowing him a Boy, lik'd onely his action"In writing her own play, *Love's Victorie,* Lady Mary followed many of the established conventions of one of the most popular forms of early seventeenth-century drama, the pastoral tragicomedy, yet it is clear that no single play served as a dominant source. Rather, she seems to have drawn upon a broad range of literary predecessors.

Lady Mary carefully designed her play to provide two internal commentators on the action—the characters Venus and Cupid, who observe and direct the behavior of ten young people. When Venus notices that some of the humans disdain the power of Cupid, she urges her son to show that "Love can in all spiritts raine." Once her son agrees to make each of the young lovers suffer, he uses his arrows of "jealousie, malice, feare, and mistrust" to throw the mortals into confusion. Lady Mary creates dramatic irony by showing that though the young lovers cry out to the gods, they are largely unaware of their presence on stage as manipulators of the plot. The mythological characters also advise the audience of the progress of the tragicomedy and reassure us that "sweetest is that love obtained with paine."

Lady Mary's use of the mythological figures is reminiscent of a device found in the earliest model of pastoral tragicomedy, Tasso's *Aminta.* Tasso included a prologue to his play in which a belligerent Cupid announces his determination to prove his power. Venus does not appear, but Tasso's Cupid explains that she has given him instructions. Although the mythological figure occurs only at the beginning of the *Aminta,* this device was copied by a number of successive playwrights. Samuel Daniel, for example, introduced his pastoral tragicomedy, *Hymen's Triumph* (1614) with the mythological figure of Hymen, who struggles with the forces of envy, avarice, and jealousy. Indeed, the use of the mythological commentators was so popular that Jonson [in *Works of Ben Jonson,* IV] mocked the device in the induction to *Cynthia's Revels* (1600): "Take anie of our play-bookes without a CUPID, or a MERCURY in it, and burne it for a heretique in Poetrie." Of course, Jonson himself used Cupid as a commentator in this play and in a series of entertainments: *The Christmas Masque* (1616), *Love Freed from Ignorance and Folly* (1616), and *A Challenge at Tilt* (1616). He included both Venus and Cupid as participants in the Haddington Masque, or *The Hue and Cry After Cupid* (1608), a masque Lady Mary may have attended. Because of her friendship with Jonson, there is a strong possibility that she was influenced by the dramatist's use of the internal commentators, particularly since in plays like *Cynthia's Revels* they recur throughout the action, rather than appearing only in the prologue.

Just as the *Urania* offers an anatomy of amorous relationships, so Lady Mary Wroth's play presents four different couples who demonstrate that "love hath as many ways / to winn, as to destroy." She depicts Philisses and Musella as the virtuous lovers, whose union withstands a period of misunderstanding and a threat of external interference. The love of the second couple is disrupted by baser emotions: Lissius first needs to overcome his scornful pride, and his beloved Simena must learn to control her jealousy. Lady Mary shows that self-doubt and mutual mistrust nearly bring the love of this second pair "to deaths river brink." The third couple, the Forester and Silvesta, are neoplatonic idealists who have chosen both love and chastity. Their comic counterparts are Rustick and Dalina, who frantically pursue earthly, physical lust. Lady Mary's use of the four contrasting couples reinforces her theme of the variety of human response in love and resembles the complex plotting of other pastoral tragicomedies, such as John Fletcher's *The Faithful Shepherdess* (1608).

One of the theoretical questions faced by the dramatists of pastoral was whether to include comic elements in their plays. Samuel Daniel argued in the prologue to *Hymen's Triumph* that the pastoral should deal with "tender passions, motions soft, and grave." Jonson, however, took the opposite position and maintained, according to the *Conversations with Drummond,* that comedy belonged as an essential ingredient of the pastoral. On this issue Lady Mary clearly agreed with Jonson, for the gentle, playful humor found in *Love's Victorie* is one of the drama's most appealing features. The character Rustick, a country buffoon, supplies much of the comedy through his spirited, though misguided, wooing of Musella; he delivers songs of adoration comparing the redness of her cheeks to "okar spred / On a fatted sheeps back" (H4). Although the courtier-shepherds constantly outmatch him in contests of wit, Rustick is proud of his own "art to hold a plowe." Humor is also provided by such female characters as the fickle Dalina and the over-eager lover, Climeana, whose pursuit of men ends in comic disappointment: "a woman woo, / the most unfittest, shamfullst thing to doo."

Lady Mary's character Rustick bears some similarity to Lorel, the rude swineherd in Jonson's *The Sad Shepherd,* but it is unlikely that this play served as a direct source. [as C. H. J. Maxwell noted in his thesis *Love's Victorie*] Although critics disagree over the exact dating of Jonson's only surviving pastoral play, most believe that the dramatist was continuing to work on it in the years before his death in 1637. Yet, as W. W. Greg noted in [his *Ben Jonson's Sad Shepherd with Waldron's continuation,*] . . . some similarities exist between this late play and Jonson's earlier lost pastoral, *The May Lord,* which was described in the *Conversations with Drummond:* both works feature a country setting, the wise shepherd Alken, and an enchantress or witch. Because the *Conversations* provide so little specific information concerning *The May Lord,* recent scholars have debated whether the work was actually a pastoral play, a poem, or a narrative. Drummond does, however, record that Jonson assigned a part to Lady Mary Wroth and that he deliberately chose to include comic elements, which are described in terms more appropriate to dramatic action: "Contrary to all other pastoralls, he bringeth the Clownes making Mirth and foolish Sports." It is very possible that Jonson's earlier work, *The May Lord,* exerted strong influence over Lady

Mary's pastoral, particularly in the use of comedy. Although she probably never saw *The Sad Shepherd,* Jonson reiterated the importance of humor when he wrote in the prologue, "But here's an heresy of late let fall, / That mirth by no means fits a pastoral."

Like Jonson's pastoral play, *Love's Victorie* also features a series of intermingled songs which add variety to the drama. Composed in rhymed verse, the play contains some poems embedded within the actual text; for example, the Forester's speech, beginning "Did ever cruelty itt self thus showe?" forms a complete sonnet. Rather than fragmenting the text of the play, I have included in [*The Poems of Lady Mary Wroth,* 1983] those songs of more than one stanza in length, which appear at intervals in the Huntington manuscript.

By the beginning of the seventeenth century, amateur theatricals had developed into a popular form of entertainment in the great country houses. Sir Philip Sidney's *The Lady of May,* performed at the Earl of Leicester's home, Wanstead, is one of the finest early examples of an English pastoral designed for a private audience. Because Sidney's entertainment is extremely short and lacks the five-act structure of a play, it did not serve as an actual model for *Love's Victorie,* but it does contain some similar features: the contrast between shepherds and foresters, the use of comic characters, and the intermingling of songs. Unfortunately, the Huntington text of *Love's Victorie* provides little information concerning the actual performance of the play. No cast list is included, and there are few stage directions, with the exception of the departures of characters from stage (identified by *ex.*). The manuscript is divided into acts, but not scenes.

Lady Mary Wroth was by no means the first English-woman to compose a play, for she had been preceded by Elizabeth Cary, Viscountess Falkland, whose *Tragedy of Mariam* was composed several years before it was first published in 1613. Similarly, Lady Mary's aunt, the Countess of Pembroke, had shown a strong interest in classical drama through her verse translation of Robert Garnier's *Antonie* (1592). Both of these plays, however, were composed essentially as closet dramas, without concern for performance. In the later seventeenth century women dramatists increased in number, partly because Queen Henrietta Maria gave added impetus to the writing of plays by acting in a pastoral of her own composition at Somerset House in 1626. Although performances by female royalty had been fairly common in the French court, Henrietta Maria's acting was unusual for the English. She helped set a new fashion, and moreover, she and her maids performed together in *The Shepherd's Paradise* (1633), an eight-hour pastoral composed by Walter Montague. Shortly afterward, several other women dramatists began their careers, including the Duchess of Newcastle and her stepdaughters.

As in the case of Lady Mary Wroth's play, many writings by Renaissance women authors remained unpublished. John Davies of Hereford [in his *The Muse's Sacrifice, or Divine Meditations*] called attention to this phenomenon in a joint dedication to three of England's most famous literary women—Lucy, Countess of Bedford, Mary, Countess of Pembroke, and Elizabeth, Lady Cary—in which he observed, "You presse the *Presse* with little you have made." In his 1612 preface to *Polyolbion,* Michael Drayton complained more generally of the reluctance of contemporary poets to publish their works: "Verses are wholly deduc't to Chambers, and nothing esteem'd in this lunatique Age, but what is kept in Cabinets, and must only passe by Transcription." Although there were some exceptions, such as the publication of the Countess of Pembroke's translations, the same author's metrical versions of the Psalms remained in manuscript until 1823. As the textual introduction to the *Urania* will show, there is no conclusive evidence that Lady Mary actively sought to have her works published, and she even disclaimed such an intention in her letter to Buckingham. The strong social pressures against publication may be seen clearly in the reaction of Dorothy Osborne in [*The Letters of Dorothy Osborne to William Temple,* 1928], when the Duchess of Newcastle's poetry was first printed: "she could never bee soe rediculous else as to venture at writing book's and in verse too."

Lady Mary Wroth was well aware that in the early seventeenth century relatively few other women were poets: in the *Urania,* Amphilanthus observes that "poetry is an art rare in women and yett I have seene some excellent things of their writings." On the Continent, women poets had flourished much earlier, as seen in the achievements of the French writers Marguerite de Navarre, Pernette du Guillet, and Louise Labé, as well as of the Italians Veronica Gambara, Vittoria Colonna, and Gaspara Stampa. By contrast, until Lady Mary Wroth's time, the majority of English women poets had been primarily interested in religious, as opposed to secular writings. Very few of these poets had composed sonnets; in addition to Queen Elizabeth, Lady Mary's other main predecessor may have been the Countess of Oxford, who is credited with four sonnets on the death of her son. Lady Mary emerges alone among her contemporary women writers in creating a complete English sonnet sequence and in leaving behind a varied collection of lyric verse.

After the controversy surrounding the publication of some of her writing in 1621, Lady Mary Wroth's literary fame suffered partly because of the inaccessibility of her work. [As noted in the preface to Margaret Cavendish's *Sociable Letters,*] more than forty years later the Duchess of Newcastle alluded to the public hostility Lady Mary had faced when the *Urania* was first printed, but by this time the number of secular women poets had increased to include such figures as Katherine Philips, Anne Bradstreet, and the duchess herself. There were, however, very few critical evaluations of Lady Mary's poetry until the twentieth century. As part of his biographical article on Lady Mary Wroth in the *DNB,* Sir Sidney Lee claimed that her sonnets revealed a "lyric faculty and fluency." Later, R. Brimley Johnson [in *The Birth of Romance,* the first volume of the *English Literature Library,* 1928] called more specific attention to the "Crowne of Sonnets dedicated to love" in *Pamphilia to Amphilanthus,* which he believed

"ensures her position among the lyrists of her age."

In assessing literary reputation, there is admittedly a strong temptation for any editor to magnify the achievements of his subject. In the case of Lady Mary Wroth, the poems as a group vary widely in quality, from those that merely repeat the well-worn Elizabethan conceits to others that rise above the traditional imagery to present an intensely ambivalent response to love. Such sonnets as P8, P22, and P26 deserve to be included in twentieth-century anthologies of Renaissance verse because they vividly express the immediacy and urgency of the speaker's internal debate. Among some of Lady Mary's finest poems are the sonnets included in the "Crowne" (P77-90), where she skillfully conducts a labyrinthine journey through the persona's mind. Her songs, especially the pastoral eclogues U13 and U14, are fine examples of her plain style at its best: a union of delicate, unpretentious diction and careful craftsmanship.

Lady Mary may have chosen to adhere so closely to the well-defined Petrarchan mode in her poems because of a desire to perpetuate the Sidneian literary tradition in an age that was already turning to new fashions: in each of the three major genres of her work, she emulated the forms earlier used by her uncle—the sonnet sequence, pastoral romance, and pastoral drama. But in each of these forms, Lady Mary introduced original perspectives, as in her reversal of the roles of lover and beloved in the sonnets. Although she is undoubtedly a minor Renaissance poet, Lady Mary Wroth occupies a prominent position as a pioneering woman author, who was the first to write a full-length work of prose fiction, as well as a large body of secular love poetry.

Perhaps one of the best introductions to her poems is provided by Ben Jonson in his tribute to Lady Mary's verse. As the *Conversations with Drummond* suggest, Jonson believed that the sonnet form was too restrictive and inflexible: "he cursed petrarch for redacting Verses to Sonnets, which he said were like that Tirrants bed, where some who were too short were racked, others too long cut Short. Although there are only five sonnets among Jonson's collected poems, he deliberately employed the form in this case as part of his compliment to Lady Mary. Jonson clearly distinguished his own poetic practice from hers in line 2, but he indicated his willingness to "exscribe," or copy out the poems by hand. The final image of *"Venus Ceston,"* the magical girdle that conferred beauty on the wearer and aroused love in the beholder, is Jonson's graceful praise of both the woman and the artist.

A Sonnet,
to the noble Lady, the Lady
MARY WROTH

I that have beene a lover, and could shew it,
  Though not in these, in rithmes not wholly
    dumbe,
    Since I exscribe your Sonnets, am become
A better lover, and much better Poet.
Nor is my Muse, or I asham'd to owe it

To those true numerous Graces; wherof
some,
  But charme the Senses, others over-come
Both braines and hearts; and mine now best doe
know it:
For in your verse all *Cupids* Armorie,
  His flames, his shafts, his Quiver, and his
Bow,
    His very eyes are yours to overthrow.
But then his Mothers sweets you so apply,
Her joyes, her smiles, her loves, as readers take
For *Venus Ceston,* every line you make.

Carolyn Ruth Swift (essay date 1984)

SOURCE: "Feminine Identity in Lady Mary Wroth's Romance *Urania,*" in *English Literary Renaissance,* Vol. 14, No. 3, Autumn, 1984, pp. 328-46.

[*In this excerpt, Swift discusses Wroth's portrayal of the search for female identity through the characters Pamphilia and Urania, and draws parallels to Wroth's own struggle for acceptance and recognition in seventeenth-century society.*]

In 1621 Lady Mary Wroth published *The Countesse of Mountgomeries Urania,* a beautiful folio divided into four lengthy books, approximately 600 pages of prose and poetry that concludes with the sonnet sequence *Pamphilia to Amphilanthus*. An unpublished 145-page manuscript, evidently in Wroth's own hand and now at the Newberry Library, continues the story into a second generation but remains incomplete. Generally ignored today, Lady Wroth was recognized by many of her contemporaries. But while patronage may explain the attention of Jonson, Wither, and Chapman, still many of her 120 songs and sonnets, as well as much of *Urania,* can justify both her own contemporaries' praise and the study of modern scholars.

Herford and Simpson in their edition of Jonson describe briefly Lady Wroth's *Urania* as "gracefully" continuing "the Arcadian-Sidneyan tradition of her uncle". But Wroth seems to have begun her book with a deeper interest in the nature of women than is apparent in Sidney's *Arcadia*. While her title, *The Countesse of Mountgomeries Urania,* is deliberately reminiscent of *The Countesse of Pembrokes Arcadia,* Sidney's subject is the "alienation of men" from "the idyllic world to which they have retreated." Wroth's subject is the alienation of women from men.

Sidney's prose romance begins when Urania leaves Arcadia. She appears so seldom, however, that she soon becomes a symbol of lost simplicity and virtue. In what seems a deliberate reversal, Wroth's *Urania* begins with Urania's search for her parents, a symbol of the female quest for identity that shapes much of the long narrative. While Urania is only one of many women seeking to find themselves, she is also the most important commentator on the book's many courtly adventures. Queen Pamphilia's constant love for the unfaithful King Amphilanthus is the central story, from which myriad friends and relatives depart and return to narrate mirroring adventures. Wroth's double emphasis on the spiritual quests of women and the heroic adventures of knights offers us insights into the ambivalence with which a seventeenth-century woman viewed a society that subordinated even the most talented of her sex.

Within her Jacobean awareness that the world is dangerous and that human life implies betrayal, Wroth reveals the loss of identity that women experience in a society that victimizes them; both the narrator and characters sometimes devalue women as Wroth and her work were devalued in her own life. Two months after publication, for example, Wroth had to withdraw *Urania* from sale when Edward Lord Denny complained bitterly that she had satirized his family. In reply, Wroth vigorously defended her "harmless book." She transformed Denny's satiric poetic attack that she was an "hermaphrodite, in show, in deed a monster," into an attack on his drunken dyspepsia, his "hateful words" and "Dirty doubt." Wroth vigorously rejected the stigma of female writer as "female anomaly" that Margaret Cavendish would accept only fifty years later. Even so, in an age when women rarely published, her book was doomed, and Wroth published nothing else, ending what Josephine A. Roberts has called a "pioneering venture in publication."

But despite Wroth's apology in her letter to the Duke of Buckingham that she never intended her book to be published, her prolific poetry and prose as well as her forceful response to Denny indicates her pride in authorship. She also emblazoned her own name on an elegantly engraved title page, although she lived in an age when women authors were usually "Anonymous." Perhaps she tried to validate her own writing by including also the names of her uncle and aunt, Sir Philip Sidney and Lady Mary Herbert, the Countess of Pembroke. Certainly Wroth's insistence on Denny's folly reveals her pain at her book's suppression. Ironically, her book's fate proved the truth of her theme—that society limited women unreasonably and harmed them in the process.

Although critics caution each other to treat literary characters as wholly imaginary creations, the characters in *Urania* clearly reveal a talented woman author's creative reaction to the restrictions of her age. Scholars have revealed a close connection between the plot and characters of *Urania* and Wroth's own life. Roberts associates the male lover in Wroth's poetry (Amphilanthus) with Wroth's lover, the Earl of Pembroke; it follows that in *Urania* Pamphilia may represent Wroth herself. Roberts and Paul Salzman also have noted that Lord Denny was probably correct in charging that Wroth had drawn upon his family history when she condemned a father "strange" enough to threaten to kill his only daughter because he identified with his irrationally jealous son-in-law. Denny's recorded self-recognition confirms my claim that Wroth's diligent portrayal of unfaithful knights and unhappy ladies reflects the world she knew. The point is further supported by a letter from George Manners, Earl of Rutland, asking Wroth to decipher her code: "You once showed me a manuscript in your study at Barnard's Castle. Meeting here with your

Urania, I send the enclosed and beg you to interpret the names as I have begun them." Like Denny, Rutland evidently recognized his friends in Wroth's chivalric romance. In addition, Wroth's characters even embody their author's awareness of real societal injustice to women.

But reality was often intertwined with chivalric romance in the sixteenth and early seventeenth centuries. As Queen Elizabeth surrounded her life with romantic fictions, so letters reveal that courtiers gilded life with chivalry. Wroth's father, for example, wrote to his wife about their "young knight," his son. A 1613 ledger in the Rutland MSS. also reminds us that men in fact wore accoutrements of fully armed knights still seen in their paintings: "Item paid to knight that drew the armes with helmet, crest, and mantlines in 4 escocheons, upon 2 banners for 2 trumpetes." As popular romances today embellish heterosexual family life in middle-America, [according to Janice Radway in *Feminist Studies,* 9, 1983] so the seventeenth-century chivalric romance gave courtly readers in Renaissance England a model and validation.

Because *Urania,* like all fiction, can be understood on some levels through its own stated standards, its action, and its character, this essay does not unravel topical allegories that caused contemporary scandals. Section I compares Wroth's view of women's abilities in *Urania* with the view in traditional romances. Sections II and III examine Wroth's tales of women's "ruine" in romance and marriage. Section IV concludes that Wroth viewed society as destructive of woman's sense of self. To show how Wroth's views differ from the views of Renaissance men, I occasionally contrast *Urania* with the *Arcadia,* and with some of Shakespeare's plays. Where possible, I compare the action in *Urania* with seventeenth-century demographic studies and with my study of English family letters as well as the facts of Wroth's life.

Lady Mary Wroth's childhood probably encouraged her interest in romance as well as her sensitivity to unequal treatment of women. The daughter of Robert Sidney, Earl of Leicester, and Lady Barbara Gamage, Mary Sidney (born c. 1585) grew up, as did her heroine Pamphilia, with many brothers and sisters. Letters in the Sidney papers reveal that her parents fostered her interest in books but catered to her brother's education. Sir Robert Sidney's agent Rowland Whyte wrote to him, "God bless her, she is very forward in her learning, writing, and other exercises, she is put to, as dauncing and the virginals." Sir Robert secured books for her and encouraged her artistic talents, but he believed formal education important only for boys. He wrote his wife:

> For the girls I kan not mislike the care you take of them: but for the boies you must resolve to let me have my wil. For I know better what belongs to a man than you do. Indeed I wil have him ly from his maide, for it is time, and now no more to bee in the nurcery among wemen. I wil not stick to give the schoolmaster whom you speak of 20 [pounds] a yeare, if I kan heare of his sufficiency. But then wil I have the boy delivered to his charge onely, and not to have him when he is to teach him, to be troubled with the women.

In contrast, Sir Robert was evidently satisfied to hear that Mary enjoyed reading and that she danced before the Queen. This home must have ripened Wroth's awareness of the inequality of men and women even as it fostered her wide reading and her own romantic fantasies.

Urania draws heavily upon tradition although it alters traditional content and attitude. In accord with medieval romance conventions, Wroth's heroines have perfect beauty, but she uses this stereotype to reject masculine standards of female beauty and virtue. For example, Sidney creates ugly women as a source of brutal comedy: Misa is "so handsome a beldame, not onely her face and her splayfoote have made her accused for a witch". Although such merciless descriptions may parody earlier stereotypes of female perfection, he exploits such women. Thus the hero Pyrocles makes love to the infatuated Mopsa only in order to court Pamela in a brutal comedy that pains this modern reader. In contrast, heroines in *Urania* are beautiful because Wroth finds in women a wit, courage, and spirit that create beauty. She alters the medieval stereotype of female perfection, however, by recognizing that women have faults equal to men's: women are "the children of men, and like them fault-full."

As in earlier romances, women in *Urania* rely on men for aid, yet Wroth changes the romance's stereotype of female passivity since her women characters sometimes venture forth alone. Leandrus wonders that Pamphilia will reject his courtship to "adventure without guard." She responds with some humor that she does not need him: "my person, my greatness, and these walls are sufficient warrants and guardians for my safety." Her friend Antisia walks alone by the sea in humble dress in order to talk with travellers about their adventures. The more venturesome Neriana "exercises the part of an adventurous lover", travelling unaccompanied into the woods.

Unlike other romances, however, Wroth's female characters have also developed unusual skills. One group of women actually fights and a lady discourses "of martial things, being excellently learned in all the arts." In Sidney's *Arcadia* Basilius shares his hunting enthusiasm with Zelmane, the Amazon, but in *Urania* the lady takes the knight Dolorindus hawking. In *Urania* as in *Arcadia* women go fishing, a sport some seventeenth-century women in fact enjoyed, although in *Urania* they evidently always hope to catch men as well as fish. Pamphilia hunts deer with as much zest as she writes poetry, reads and pursues delicate conversations.

Wroth's respect for women's capabilities probably grew from her own close friendships with other women. *The Countesse of Mountgomeries Urania* is named for her friend and cousin Susama Herbert, the Countess of Montgomery, and her father's letters to her mother record "merry" meetings at Penshurst and in London between his "daughter Wroth" and "Lady Lucy," the Countess of Bedford, Lady Hoby, and Lady Arundel as well. In *Urania,* Wroth transforms the earlier romance pattern of heroine and confidante into genuine friendship among women. Pamphilia and Antisia deeply mourn their impending separation, "lying together, and with sad but loving discourse passing those dark hours." Urania and Pamphilia loyally remain friends through two generations.

Wroth's understanding of intense female friendship helped her to treat the possibility of romantic love between women with more respect than her uncle did in *Arcadia,* Sidney dresses his hero as an Amazon because he views him as debased—rendered partly effeminate—by love for a woman. In *Urania,* by contrast, because Veralinda once loved Leonius when he dressed as a woman, she can see his virtues more clearly. "I am (my Lord) said shee, the woman that loves you as much, or more, if possible, then I did, having so many more bonds to tye me unto it." Their love is validated because he is really a man, but Veralinda asserts her love for Leonius' feminine self to be as great as for his masculine.

Although Wroth herself was bold enough as an author to write a sympathetic tale of a woman who thinks she loves another woman, the women in her romance are discreet, and whatever sexual acts they commit are euphemized. Lovers share "stolen and sweet delights." Evelina is "a woman free" who "freely offer[s]" herself in love. "Honor" may be lost by a long courtship. One pair of lovers "enjoy" each other after three years, "nor was ought denied." The few wicked women in *Urania* share the vice of "immoderate and ungovernable passions", while most women in *Urania* are temperate and speak decorously as Renaissance tracts on manners advised.

However, Wroth's definition of decorous female speech differs from that in conventional romance. Whereas silence is one of Sidney's ideals for women, Wroth praises a woman's usual courtesy of silence only once, when she justifies Pamphilia's speaking without "respect" to an equally rude Amphilanthus. "Sweet mildness" and "loveliness" are virtues in both men and women. As Wroth praises the "womanish part" in men, she praises women whose "perfections are styled masculine." Thus in *Urania* women characters usually speak firmly and assertively. As a result, they articulate their pain at a society that values them only in courtly love affairs and in marriage.

Urania validates women but shows their limited spheres of action. With courage, Urania enters a cave in which she fearlessly examines the corpse of a knight who suddenly revives. That image of feminine courage describes the role of women in the society that Wroth creates in *Urania,* With bold hearts, they venture into the dark caves to find that society accepts them only, as the knight Steriamus later says, if they "comfort the souls of men" privately in romance and marriage.

Wroth makes clear that a seventeenth-century woman was usually dependent on men for self-respect and survival, no matter what her talents or his failings. Consequently, the vibrant female fishers and hunters in *Urania* willingly become "prisoners" in the "House of Love," "fettered" "with linkes of gold enamelled with Roses." The image of men as prisoners of love is familiar in courtly literature. Nevertheless, Wroth uniquely depicts the effects of ob-sessional love on women. In her image of gold-enamelled fetters, she recognizes that fantasy itself induces captivity to love, not the saintly but cruel mistress so often blamed in romances by men.

As a woman, Wroth knew that women can become enthralled in a love-game that may end in marriage to an overly possessive man or in an adulterous love affair that compensates for a miserable marriage. With venturesome spirits, women imagine the "sumptuous" House of Love to be "some magicall work," although they know that jealousy and grief usually ensue. Men experience love's torments too; some are "fellow prisoners in the Castle of love", but others go on to new adventures. All the women in the towers of desire remain fettered by what Wroth fittingly calls an "enemy within".

Even her virtue contributes to a woman's "ruine" in love. Pamphilia grieves that she may "have a vertue, and loose all thereby" as her constancy traps her in love for an inconstant man. Trapped by her values, she ignores the ironic warnings of a romance she reads whose subject (like *Urania*'s) was Love. "The story she then was reading, the affection of a Lady to a brave Gentileman, who equally loved, but being a man, it was necessary for him to exceede a woman in all things, so much as inconstansie was found fit for him to excell her in, hee left her for a new." Pamphilia throws the book away as disgracefully scoffing at love, but Amphilanthus her lover, whose name means "lover of two," is away loving others.

To explain the hazards of love, Wroth generalizes male infidelity. Pamphilia's friend Limena tells her of a woman who learns that "mens words are only breath, their oathes wilde, and vows water." Musalena, the Queen of Bulgaria, warns that even "the best men, will and must change, not that he does it purposely, but tis their naturall infirmitie, and can not be helped." Musalena echoes the romance that Pamphilia previously had read: tradition calls women unfaithful, but men, "who excell us in all perfections, would not for their honours sake, let us surpass them in any one thing"—not even infidelity.

This emphasis on male inconstancy is a main point of contrast between *Urania* and its predecessor, *Arcadia.* Sidney presents as a chivalric ideal the constant Argalus, who loves his wife even after she becomes scarred. In *Urania* women's bodies always defeat them. One woman finds her lover slighted her and told her she was "growne old and her beauty altered; willed her to recover that [beauty] to regain him." Bellamira too loses her lover when she loses her youthful beauty. Although even Sidney considers Argalus' Arcadian constancy unusual enough to cause Musidorus' delight, his protagonists, Pyrocles and Musidorus, also remain continually faithful to their women in startling contrast to the many fickle male lovers in *Urania.* Even if Wroth's greater stress on male infidelity is the result of Jacobean cynicism opposed to Sidney's Tudor idealism, she differs from those Jacobean writers we know best by insisting also that women are more constant than men and by stressing that their constancy to unfaithful lovers is painful and self-destructive.

Even Shakespeare, who recognized that Desdemona and Ophelia are destroyed by a husband's or lover's idealization, does not seriously recommend inconstancy. Emilia will make her husband a cuckold to win him a world, but her advice to Desdemona is comic in its dramatic effect. Urania's "excellent wit," in contrast, defines Pamphilia's constancy as a virtue "with limits." When Pamphilia boasts she would love Amphilanthus if he had never loved her or even if he had despised her, Urania does not respond, as we might expect, by praising her friend's faithfulness as a model for all women. She says, "'Tis pity . . . that ever that fruitlesse thing constancy was taught you as a vertue, . . . understand, this vertue hath limits . . . those . . . with whom it is broken are by the breech free to leave or choose again where more staidness may be found".

Such counsel to reject conventional virtue also occurs in Sidney's *Arcadia,* but when the evil Cecropia urges Pamela not to "love Virtue servillie," she is attempting a seduction. Urania, on the contrary, has offered Pamphilia a remarkable interpretation of feminine virtue as free of martyred loyalty. She explains that she herself has died to one love in order to "revive". Her imagery stresses that virtuous women must be inconstant to inconstant men in order to "revive" in self-respect.

Even in the last published book of *Urania,* Amphilanthus deserts Pamphilia again and returns to vow fidelity. In spite of Amphilanthus' clear perfidy in love, Pamphilia accepts him again from "pure love and"—as Wroth says very pointedly—"unfortunate subjection." He has used her so "vildly" that Perselina wonders why she will "endure him", and so do we when Pamphilia says, "can he smile on these wrinckles, and be loving in my decay? When hee told me I was altered for the worse and sleightly regarded me, I feared". Wroth excised Sidney's noble and faithful Argalus from her vision.

Hermione, the Queen in *The Winter's Tale,* remains faithful to her scoundrel King, and as a reward is accepted with her wrinkles at the play's conclusion. But Wroth makes clear, as Shakespeare never does, that she regrets her heroine's "unfortunate subjection" in this endless game of loving inconstant men. She also makes clear by ending her published narrative with the word "And," as if more were to follow, that Pamphilia's subjection is endless. Unlike Shakespeare's Leontes, Wroth's Amphilanthus will betray again and again. Even in the manuscript, Amphilanthus becomes faithful only after both he and Pamphilia marry others in despair. His faithfulness exists only within inconstancy.

In *Urania,* romantic love is a delusion, but marriage is a trap. Married women tell their own pain-filled stories to adventuring knights and ladies, who are only rarely able to rescue them. Wroth creates an exquisite symbol of marital misery early in her book in the story of Limena, whose cruel husband ties her to a pillar by her own hair in order to whip her and then pour salt in her wounds. Just as Limena's own hair binds her to her torture, the female virtue of constancy binds women to painful romances, and the virtue of obedience renders them complicit in their marital misery.

Wroth's own marriage was evidently difficult. Her family protected her from marriage at age 13 when the guardians of the fifteen-year-old son of Sir Thomas Manxfild indifferently sought either Mary or her sister. But in an age when, according to Peter Laslett, the average woman married at 24, privileged women married earlier, and Wroth's father arranged her marriage in 1604 when she was eighteen. Even this later marriage left much to be desired; her father's letters allude to Sir Robert Wroth's dissatisfaction a month after the wedding. Margaret Witten-Hannah conjectures that the marriage was at that time unconsummated. Wroth's comments in *Urania* on marital misery, where husbands are jealous and only enjoy hunting, suggest other sources of incompatibility. These sources are confirmed when we read Sir Robert Wroth's brief letters about hunting conditions and Ben Jonson's comment that Lady Wroth was "unworthily maried on a Jealous husband."

Whatever the cause of her own marital problems, Wroth objected in *Urania* to the "cruel and tiranical power" that parents have to force marriages upon their children. Virtuous daughters "esteem . . . obedience beyond all passions," and therefore "most dutifully though unwillingly . . . obey" even brutal fathers, who will use force if necessary, as they often did in life. Like Egeus in *A Midsummer Night's Dream* and like Lord Capulet in *Romeo and Juliet,* Orilena's father forces upon her "a loathed match," which she says will cause her "destruction". The equally articulate Lisia also describes her own fate; her "tyrannous father" married her "before discretion appearing" to a "churlish" and "dull piece of flesh". In arranging marriages, fathers rarely considered a daughter's preferences. Therefore, Bellamira must ignore her contempt for Treborius' limited abilities; as his wife, she complains that she had to "commend his ordinary talke when hee praised rude sports, or told the plaine Jests of his Hunts-man". Many women, Lisia explains, endure their marriages by "hunting and other delights abroad, to take away trouble . . . at home."

Perhaps because Wroth writes from a woman's point of view, she presents families in *Urania* as more tyrannical than they are in Shakespeare or in Sidney. Amphilanthus learns from Sydelia how her brother, Terichillus, like the Duchess of Malfi's brothers, imprisoned and tortured her, ultimately hunting down and killing the husband of her choice. Liana too tells how her father "imprisons" her in his sister's home because she will not "breed" with the man of his choice. Another daughter explains that she was "shut up in a Towre." Her father instructed his sister to beat her brutally. Wroth comments that he "kept [in her] his choisest Treasure till the day of her marriage."

Wroth's use of the words "breed" and "Treasure" reveals her recognition that families used women as sources of new wealth. Bellamira states explicitly that she married dull Treborius out of obedience to her parents who only saw "the goodness and greatness of his estate." Wroth also makes clear through her women characters that she condemns such parental brutality. In Shakespeare, when Kate's father colludes in her taming, we are expected to laugh; the beaten daughters in *Urania* recognize and describe their fathers' "cruel and tirannical power" and thus force us to acknowledge it. Yet Wroth recognized that if women married without family approval, they took enormous risks. For example, Dalinea would have been dishonored if Parselius, Pamphilia's own brother, had not acknowledged his marriage to her. Adventurous and courageous, she followed him to a distant country because "finding myselfe with child; then came the hazard of my honour in mind, the danger of my disgrace, the staine I might bring to my house: for few will believe us, poore women, in such extremity, but will rather increase our infamy."

Lawrence Stone's statistics [in his *The Crises of The Aristocracy, 1558-1641*] confirm Wroth's view that marriages arranged by families, common for "children of the rich," were often unhappy: one-third of the "older peers were estranged or actually separated from their wives . . . between 1595 and 1620." Stone conjectures that the extensive marital instability in the early seventeenth century resulted from "marriages deliberately designed to capture an heiress or to cement a political alliance, when the compulsion used may be supposed to have been particularly severe." Wroth's narrative certainly makes clear that marriages advanced a family's interests more than a daughter's since married women often later became destitute widows. Wroth had herself experienced the humiliation of widowhood when Sir Robert Wroth's death in 1614 left his young wife with a £23,000 debt which she could never erase. The death of her only son, two-year-old James, two years later meant that much of her husband's estate reverted to his uncle. Even the success of *Urania* would not have supplied her with wealth enough to discharge Sir Robert Wroth's debts since few seventeenth-century writers made more than forty pounds a year. Wroth's indebtedness meant that remarriage was unlikely, even with her jointure of £1,200. Her own needs and the needs of the two illegitimate children that she later bore to William Herbert, Third Earl of Pembroke, forced her to depend on the king's good will all her life. Every year after 1623, she obtained a royal order protecting her from creditors. Naturally, then, she had to withdraw her book from sale in spite of her jaunty defense against Lord Denny's attack and the hours she had spent writing it. Marriage to an incompatible and jealous mate may have been limiting, but widowhood crippled her.

Nowhere in Shakespeare or Sidney is the widow's humiliating dependency defined as it is in *Urania*. Limena tells Pamphilia of a lady, "the mother to many, and delicate Children," who loses her fortune "with the losse of her Husband, (as many, wofully have with that felt their undoing)". But in spite of Wroth's bleak view of marriage, she still judges it to be a woman's main source of happiness. A prophet promises Pamphilia, "You might be happy had you power to wedd." When one woman marries, Wroth says she "now must change her name, and gaine the best, and blessed estate." Wroth comments explicitly, as Shakespeare does implicitly, that there is a vast differ-

ence "betwixt servant love whose ends are love; and such, where only use and gaine attends desier." Even though the husband is "Lord" in all estates, marriage delights as partners show each other respect, "she to maintaine what she had gained, he to requite what she had given."

The contradiction between Wroth's images of marital torment and her praise of marriage as the "best and blessed estate" reflects her contradictory attitudes toward women. Like most books before the Victorian period, *Urania* makes marriage the only reward for women's merit and therefore desirable in spite of its pain. To be marriageable means to be attractive, to be successful. To be chaste, Wroth explains, is to be "dull" and to lack "affection".

In spite of its misery, the exaltation of marriage in *Urania* results in part from the impossible economic situation of unmarried women in the sixteenth and seventeenth centuries. A statute of 1563 stipulated that unmarried women between the ages of 12 and 40 could be forced to work at any job at any wage determined by municipal officials. Yet even the menial role of servant grew less available for women as households grew smaller. Family letters confirm that even in aristocratic and upper-middle class families unmarried daughters were burdens. Elizabeth Knyvett, for example, wrote to R. Townshend, on December 29, 1626, for aid to hasten her daughter's marriage. "I am suar it hath greatly afflicted me, these delayings. besides the daunger which may ensue my charge is lengthened out to the uttermost. Both in maintaining her, and also in calling in my monies." Lack of paid employment for women, combined with the economic drain of their continued support, would naturally create a climate which favored women's marriage despite the evident misery that often resulted.

In *Urania*, Wroth envisages few alternatives. Women usually embrace chastity only when widowed or disappointed in love. Melasinda retires to a monastery "to her own libertie" when her husband dies rather than remarry. Another woman serves as housekeeper in the home of a bachelor cousin, but she can do that only because her age makes her unattractive in her society.

Yet some women characters dream of liberation from marriage. In the manuscript continuation of *Urania*, Wroth tells a story of a woman significantly named "Fancy," who thinks at the age of 14 that "a husband will cherish age" as he must become old himself. She imagines "hansome discourse with a reasonable husband, children to pass away the time." However, she also worries that she might have a jealous husband who restricts what she wears, "fearing other men's children calling him dad." She then says "therfore never will I marry . . . Libertie and good company are my chosen mates." Another woman, whose brother was an esteemed prince, "many sought for wife but shee knowing her perfections and greatnesse, was nice in accepting ay, nor indeed had shee much mind to marry, loving her libertie more than marriages bondage." These free women Wroth praises as recognizing their own self-worth; like Alarina, finally freed from her self-enslavement to obsessional love that made marriage seem desirable, they might say, "I love myself; my selfe now loveth me."

Since some women value "libertie more than marriages bondage," we must wonder with Wroth why Pamphilia, a powerful queen, willingly remains painfully obsessed with the romantic possibility of marriage to Amphilanthus. Pamphilia herself wonders why, but 600 pages later her passion endures. Unlike other women, she never needed "an increase, and sufficiency of estate . . . bought . . . with her marriage, and so grow subject to an Husband". Urania and Perselina are correct that Pamphilia's unnecessary choice to wait for the inconstant Amphilanthus is weakness in a woman whose discretion they otherwise admire.

The explanation, I think, lies in Wroth's presentation of a society that tends to destroy women. She makes clear that women receive an ambiguous message when marriage is their only validation, especially when marriage occurs to benefit fathers' and husbands' estates against the women's own desires. In presenting marriage as a reward while she also narrates tales of its accompanying misery, Wroth communicates an appalling awareness that women are worthy (that is, marriageable) only when they participate in a system that may victimize them. Since a woman's happiness is often irrelevant, the message is in part that they are worthy only when willing to be unhappy. While Wroth does not explicitly describe this process of female self-destruction, she repeatedly uses narratives in which a woman protests that in marriage she gained "so much libertie . . . as she had almost typed herself." She also shows that male admiration may become the main form of female self-validation: "I was sought by many and beloved as they said by them. I was apt enough to believe them, having none the worst opinion of myself." As Wroth shows that a woman's self-worth may rest on the admiration of a man whom she may in many ways dislike, she also shows that this good opinion can therefore arise only when a woman rejects her own feelings, desires, and abilities. The resulting confusion renders true self-awareness impossible.

Wroth's use of romance conventions reveals their destructive effects on women. The knights who aid some desperate ladies abuse others, and it is often questionable whether the women are rescued or simply degraded once again. The unfaithful Amphilanthus rescues Bellamira from lonely widowhood by returning her to the father who, in effect, sold her to her husband Treborius. Limena is left tied by her hair to a pillar while Parselius and Perissus quarrel over which one had the right to rescue her and then over the proper respect owed her husband as he dies. Even though Perissus clearly puts protocol before Limena's health and safety, and even though her husband brutalized her, she obediently grants her husband's dying request that she marry Perissus.

Urania thus presents a rare, early female perspective on trapped and bewildered women. Shakespeare presents us with Hermia, who loses herself in love, but he views her plight as an amusing mortal foible; in *A Midsummer Night's Dream* he does not blame society for the destruction of a woman's self-confidence. Shakespeare also presents us with a strong woman—Portia—who knows herself and is therefore confident enough to challenge injustice. But a woman judge in seventeenth-century England is a male fantasy. In *Urania*, no women can be as strong and accomplished as Portia because the world validates women by demeaning them. As Pamphilia reads the romance she discards, for example, she is confused about her own identity. She has been taught that constancy is crucial and that marriage would make her happy. Although her experience confirms the book's teaching about male infidelity, she cannot accept it. Pamphilia sits "in a delicate thick woods" as she reads, woods not associated with the medieval woods of error which trap people in sin, but symbolize instead inner confusion.

Throughout *Urania*, venturesome women lose themselves. Philistella is "castaway," Selarina "stolen"; even the queenly Pamphilia is "lost". When Urania does not know her parentage, she grieves, "I am lost . . . not being able to know any more of myselfe: . . . now I am troubled to rule my owne thoughts." Nereana, the Queen of Stalamina, wanders in woods, "in amaze, and at last quite lost her self". But unlike Pamphilia, Nereana undermines society's restrictions as she pursues her beloved.

This minor character, whose subplot intertwines with the main plot, trusts her own feelings and rejects romantic conventions. In the end she gains both power and confidence in a story that may be unique for women in early literature. Unlike Gynecia in Sidney's *Arcadia* or Webster's Duchess of Malfi, who similarly choose to pursue their own loves, Nereana chooses total autonomy. She prefers her own misery and mistakes to secure dependency. In her adventures Nereana finds she must cope with men's fantasies at odds with her own. She is seized and worshipped by Allanus: "That he might be sure of her stay, hee tied her to a tree." In a startling image Allanus strips Nereana so that she might better conform to his vision of the woman he loves, Liana, or to his vision of a goddess of the woods. When she escapes, Nereana is then blamed for the tattered clothes that Allanus tore; Philarchos, Pamphilia's brother, from whom she seeks help, assumes her to be mad and rides off. In a comment that sounds remarkably modern, Wroth tells us that Nereana then decided to find security in "her own worth and deserts".

She sails back to her homeland "with resolution to exercise her just anger upon her people." But her people are as fickle as her lovers. Nereana is "told still she was mad, and threatened to bee used accordingly, if she raved, accused of fury, and that made the cause to satisfie the people, who had sufficient cause to believe it, seeing her passions, which though naturall to her, yet appeared to their capacities meere lunaticke actions." Finally, however, Wroth vindicates this woman accused of madness, and Nereana grows from her suffering. When a "noble man" aids her to regain her throne, "she by her poor living, and neglect being now invested in so staid an habitation of gravity, as she was fit for the honour they recalled her too." Nereana is restored to her throne because Wroth recognizes that Nereana is mad mainly in the eyes of an unreasonable world.

What a contrast to Shakespeare and Sidney! Shakespeare recognizes that Lady Macbeth's madness is more reasonable than her husband's barbarism and that Ophelia's sensitivity is more desirable than Laertes' well-adjusted opportunism. Even Sidney's *Arcadia* condemns rather than rewards the mad and jealous Gynecia, once she is overwhelmed by adulterous lust for Pyrocles as her husband is. In the *Arcadia,* as in *Macbeth* and *Hamlet,* a woman's disruption functions only to highlight the immoral masculine norm. In the story of Nereana, women are justly angry at being idolized as women and then rejected when they use the wisdom for which they are revered. For all his praise, for example, Allanus' worship tortures Nereana and drives her temporarily wild.

In spite of her recognition that women may be justifiably angry at society, Wroth seems to suffer from a confusion that equals her characters'. When we read romances, we expect to be confounded by episodic narratives and multiple characters who fight, love, and recite verses through 600 pages. But conflicts arise in *Urania* between Wroth's empathy with society and her empathy with beleaguered women. She sympathizes fully with Urania "amazed" in thick woods; she understands Nereana's madness; and she is certainly aware that Pamphilia is lost when she is enchanted in the House of Love. She praises the "excellent wit" which causes Urania to advise Pamphilia to reject her unfaithful lover Amphilanthus. At the same time that Wroth's tales explore the consequences of ill-advised constancy, however, her narrator praises Pamphilia for remaining constant, "the true patterne of excellent affection, and affections truth." She even admires the passion that will allow a woman to bind herself to a dead lover's tomb (p. 305). These contradictory values prove that as author and as woman, Wroth herself still esteemed the conventions that she presents as exploitative.

Sidney openly disparages women when he presents love as effeminizing and debasing men who love them. Shakespeare in contrast fools us into believing that society values its Portias and Beatrices. Wroth knew personally that her society rarely permitted women autonomy. Yet in *Urania* she sometimes validates social values that can destroy a woman's sense of self.

Stephen Greenblatt has shown that Renaissance "middle-class and aristocratic males . . . felt that they possessed . . . shaping power over their lives". By contrast, the contradictions in *Urania* show how limited the ability of Renaissance women was to fashion themselves as they wished. Evidently the independent Lady Mary Wroth was as much the victim of her age intellectually as she was financially. The same narrator who can women and men "equally faultful" reveals her own acceptance of male superiority when she describes Pamphilia as having "soe great a spiritt, as might be called masculine". And the independent Urania uses the word "feminine" to mean "weak" when she questions why the obsessed Pamphilia

will descend "below the poorest feminine in love?" Rather than be antagonized by a woman writer's acceptance of the word "masculine" as synonymous with "strong" and "feminine" with "weak," readers should recognize that Wroth's use of these verbal conventions reveals the power of language to alienate us from ourselves. Even in its contradictions, *Urania* reveals a feminine consciousness in conflict with societal values.

Naomi J. Miller (essay date 1989)

SOURCE: "'Not much to be marked': Narrative of the Woman's Part in Lady Mary Wroth's *Urania*," in *Studies in English Literature 1500-1900,* Vol. 29, No. 1, Winter, 1989, pp. 121-37.

[*In this excerpt, Miller studies Wroth's creation of a female community in the* Urania, *and examines her use of narrative strategies that revise the conventions of romance and affirm the resiliency of female characters.*]

Virginia Woolf's speculations in *A Room of One's Own* about the hypothetical fate of Shakespeare's unknown sister achieve unexpected relevance in the example of Lady Mary Wroth, Sir Philip Sidney's niece. Woolf muses that any woman born with a gift of poetry in the sixteenth century would never have been able to realize that gift as did a Shakespeare, or, one might say, a Sidney. Many feminist critics have used Woolf's reference to Shakespeare's sister as the starting point for their own analyses of women writers, particularly of the nineteenth century, without making any direct connection with a Renaissance woman who fits Woolf's model. In fact, Lady Mary Wroth, born in 1587, produced both a sonnet sequence, ***Pamphilia to Amphilanthus,*** and a prose romance, ***The Countesse of Mountgomeries Urania,*** which is the first published work of fiction by an Englishwoman in the Renaissance.

Woolf's prediction [in *A Room of One's Own*] that even a noble lady of a later age than Shakespeare's time who might publish something with her name to it would "risk being thought a monster," reflects in fact what happened to Wroth. The objections of some of King James's male courtiers to the book's apparently satirical references to their private lives forced her to withdraw the *Urania* from sale in 1621 only six months after its publication. Her primary attacker, Lord Denny, addresses Wroth as a "Hermophradite in show, in deed a monster," and advises her to "leave idle books alone / For wiser and worthyer women have writte none." As a result of the court furor, only sixteen copies of the published *Urania* and only one copy of her unpublished continuation of the romance survive today, while no modern edition of her romance has yet appeared. This publication history accords with Betty Travitsky's observation [in *The Paradise of Women: Writings by Englishwomen of the Renaissance*] that a major deterrent to literary publication by Renaissance Englishwomen was "the negative attitude taken by the male arbiters of the time regarding works by women on subjects outside the spheres of religion and domesticity, which were considered the province of women." Female awareness of male attitudes such as that of Lord Denny is seen as early as 1578 in Margaret Tyler's translation of *The Mirrour of Princely Deedes and Knyghthood*. In her "Epistle to the Reader," [reproduced in *The Paradise of Women*] Tyler introduces her work by expressing the hope that her "ill willers" do not attempt to force her as a woman "either not to write or to write of divinitie." Wroth in fact was attacked in part for her effrontery in presuming to write secular fiction and poetry, in contrast to her aunt's translations of religious poetry.

Recent work on women writers in the Renaissance has started to redress the previous inattention on the part of literary critics to women's voices of the sixteenth and seventeenth centuries, reviving interest in neglected texts which have suffered fates similar to that of the *Urania*. In Wroth's case, however, the work of recovery has only just begun. Before the past decade, the *Urania* received scant critical attention, save as a historical curiosity or a pale imitation of [Sidney's] *Arcadia*. Even recent scholars have for the most part undervalued the literary worth of Wroth's romance, defining her achievement primarily in terms of her uncle's generic influence. A few critics have praised Wroth's uniquely female orientation as a writer, particularly in her sonnet sequence. Nevertheless, even studies sympathetic to the achievement of the *Urania* have presented both Wroth and her characters primarily as products of the "victimization" of women in the Renaissance. The feminist orientation of such criticism often emphasizes twentieth-century assumptions about the nature of the patriarchy and the role of female writers, to the neglect of relevant considerations of generic influence and historical context in Wroth's particular case.

My analysis of the *Urania* makes reference to literary and historical conceptions of gender roles current in the period, while focusing on Wroth's female vision of community as developed both in the published *Urania* and in the manuscript continuation, rarely attended to by critics of Wroth. Historians such as Joan Kelly, Angeline Goreau, and Juliet Dusinberre have documented the impediments so often facing a woman who aspired to write in the seventeenth century. The Jacobean period saw an increase in the number of misogynistic diatribes, as well as a deepening of the sentiment that knowledge, and therefore literature, belonged to the masculine province. Recently, Gary Waller [in *Silent But For the Word*] has called attention to the rhetorical difficulties confronting Renaissance women who attempted to write within genres structured by male categories and dominated by masculine discourse. Many of the feminist pamphlets of the period take a defensive stance in seeking to refute the stereotypes presented by such misogynistic treatises. Wroth's creation of a literary work rather than a political pamphlet allows her to take the offensive in designing the structure of her own fictive community. By re-viewing and revising romance conventions according to a female perspective, Wroth undermines the strictures of female silence and passivity so much emphasized in Renaissance directives for women. While translating from social into literary terms the precariousness of the female position in Jacobean society, Wroth nevertheless affirms the resil-

ience rather than victimization of the female character.

The prime literary influences upon the *Urania* can be traced most obviously to Wroth's uncle, Sidney, as well as to Spenser and Shakespeare, while including also the continental romances of Jorge de Montmayor and Honoré d'Urfé. Wroth rewrites both her continental and native sources, drawing upon heroines from Montemayor's *Diana* and d'Urfé's *Astrée* as well as Sidney's *Arcadia*, and re-viewing characters as various as Spenser's Britomart and Shakespeare's Beatrice and Desdemona. At the heart of Wroth's narrative of the woman's part, distinguishing her focus from that of her male predecessors, lies the enabling power not of romantic love but of female friendship.

Critics have noted that Renaissance theories of friendship are concerned almost exclusively with men, at least in part because of the strong influence of classical ideals. Although the fiction and drama of the period include literary depictions of female friendship, such portrayals usually present those friendships in subordinate or at best parallel relation to male versions. In fact, many of the examples of female friendship in both continental and British romances serve to emphasize love plots by providing two women to fulfill the romantic quests of a pair of male friends, rather than to enhance portrayals of female as well as male identity.

While women play a prominent role in the works of Montemayor and d'Urfé, for example, the friendships between female characters in the *Diana* and the *Astrée* commonly serve only to underscore the primacy of love between the sexes. In the *Arcadia*, the friendship between Pamela and Philoclea parallels the initially depicted bond between Musidorus and Pyrocles, while completing a tetrad of love. The double friendship/marriage of Cambell and Triamond with Cambina and Canacee in Book IV of *The Faerie Queene* acts in a similar way to parallel friendship with love. In Shakespeare's plays, female friendships consistently yield primacy to the claims of marriage. As Louis Montrose observes [in *Representations* 1, 1983] about *A Midsummer Night's Dream*, the marriages at the end "dissolve the bonds of sisterhood at the same time that they forge the bonds of brotherhood." These male-authored representations all adumbrate Woolf's observation [in *A Room of One's Own*] that "almost without exception . . . the great women of fiction were, until Jane Austen's day, not only seen by the other sex, but seen only in relation to the other sex."

By contrast, one of Wroth's innovations in the *Urania* is her decision to develop the relationships among her characters not only before but also after marriage, so that her characters not only before but also after marriage, so that her narrative patterns are not cut off by the traditional terminus of romantic couplings so common to the works of many of her predecessors. Furthermore, because Wroth does not always match up her male and female characters in pairs, avoiding the "Noah's ark" convention which defines many romances, she is able to expand her characterizations of female friendship without necessarily subordinating them to parallel examples of male friendship.

Unlike the primarily youthful protagonists created by Sidney and Spenser, Montemayor and de'Urfé, Wroth's characters grow from youth to maturity, with three generations represented, enabling a consideration of the continuity of relationships over time. Wroth thus explores the issue of constancy and inconstancy in love, so central to the romance tradition, in a temporal framework which extends beyond the immediate formation and dissolution of bonds among the protagonists. Wroth focuses on affiliation as a governing characteristic in the development of female identity, addressing generational connection as well as generational conflict, and thus expanding her depiction of familial bonds beyond the examples of parental tyranny which dominate the romance tradition.

Whereas Sidney presents debates between uncle and nephew, aunt and niece, which can only be resolved in a social frame that supersedes familial tensions, Wroth depicts the generation of social roles through familial bonds. Thus Pamphilia assumes her role as queen because her childless uncle, the king of Pamphilia, decides to leave his kingdom to his niece, bequeathing to her the name as well as the legacy of that country. Wroth acknowledges her own generic heritage from her famous uncle by forming the name of her protagonist, Pamphilia, from a combination of syllables which echoes the names of Pamela and Philoclea, yet she moves beyond Sidney's influence in forging her own narrative discourse.

Wroth highlights the importance of interdependence in the community through her depiction of growing and persevering friendships among her female characters which underlie the fluctuations of "romantic love" between the sexes. The friendship shared by Urania, Pamphilia, and Veralinda in particular endures many changes in their respective situations, from adolescent virginity to marriage, from motherhood to widowhood, while their conversations cast light upon their maturing perspectives. When Wroth's female protagonists confront the transforming power of love, bonding in friendship relieves bondage to passion.

Furthermore, Wroth moves away from the "heroine/confidante" pattern governing the presentation of female friendship in both her native and continental antecedents, to establish more equality of voice and role in the bonds joining her protagonists. Her emphasis on mutuality rather than hierarchy in female friendship may reflect her own experiences as a Jacobean noblewoman: surviving letters and diaries written by women of the period attest to close personal friendships among women of the courtly class to which Wroth belonged. The importance of female friendship as a context for as well as a subject of Wroth's romance is signalled further in her choice of title: *The Countesse of Mountgomeries Urania* honors Susan Herbert, one of Wroth's closest friends.

Before proceeding to a closer examination of Wroth's narrative strategies in the text of the *Urania* itself, I want to situate Wroth's focus on interdependence and affilia-

tion in relation to recent feminist studies on identity formation and gender, none of which has been taken account of in previous criticism on Wroth. One suggestive study is Nancy Chodorow's influential analysis of the sociology of gender [*The Reproduction of Mothering: Psychoanalysis and The Sociology of Gender*] which proposes that while masculine identification processes stress differentiation from others, especially distinction from the opposite sex, feminine identification processes stress relationship to others, especially the continuity of identity linking one woman with another. Chodorow predicates her theory upon the presence of a female primary caretaker during a child's early years, a situation which predominated in Renaissance courtly circles through the use of wet nurses rather than through direct nurture by aristocratic mothers. From a related perspective, Carol Gilligan concludes [in her *In a Different Voice: Psychological Theory and Women's Development*] that male gender identity is threatened by intimacy while female gender identity is threatened by separation.

These theories indicate the possibility of a psychological basis, in addition to the literary and historical bases already proposed, for the bias of Wroth's perspective in contrast to that of male writers of romance such as Sidney. Sidney depicts male characters in particular who strive for autonomy, who attempt to define their identities primarily through individuation. Shakespeare's male characters also, as noted by Coppélia Kahn [in *Man's Estate: Masculine Identity in Shakespeare*] are continuously engaged in a struggle to form independent masculine identities. Wroth, on the other hand, presents female characters in the *Urania* who depend more readily upon affiliation in defining themselves, who grow through their interrelation with family, lovers, and friends. All this is not to say that Wroth's female protagonists lack individualized identities, because in fact their distinctiveness as separate characters far surpasses that of many heroines of male-authored romances. My point is that Wroth's women more consistently realize their identities through affirmations of their relatedness than through assertions of difference.

Not only Sidney and Shakespeare, but Montemayor and d'Urfé as well, construct their fictions upon extremes of romantic conflict, placing unremitting emphasis upon struggle and tension between the sexes that is resolved by the union or reunion of male and female characters in pairs, the traditional "unit," as discussed above, of the romance. Wroth focuses instead upon connections among women which predate, coexist with, and outlast the continually changing examples of conflict between the sexes. Assuming that autonomy equals strength, and that its opposite must imply weakness, critics have tended to interpret the roles of Renaissance women, and thus of Renaissance female characters as well, in terms of passivity and helplessness at best, and victimization and loss of self at worst. Wroth's narrative, however, addresses the resilience of women in a world where fluctuations in romantic fortune may be determined by male lovers, but constancy in love is redefined by female friends.

Wroth alters generic conventions in order to re-present the relation between gender, genre, and culture from a woman's perspective. Whereas the *Diana* and the *Astrée* open with the laments of faithful male lovers rejected by the title female characters, and the *New Arcadia* commences with the mourning of Strephon and Claius over the departure of their beloved Urania, Wroth's narrative opens with Urania herself mourning not for love of a man, but over the question of her identity as a woman. Unlike Sidney's Urania, Wroth's protagonist is no absent ideal, but a very present female. Having just discovered that the shepherds who raised her are not her real parents, and that her origins are unknown, Urania cries out to herself: "Of any misery that can befall woman, is not this the most and greatest which thou art falne into?". This quest for female identity rather than romantic love underlies the fictive patterns of Wroth's narrative.

Having assumed the security of her identity through "the love of those [she] tooke for parents," Urania grieves to learn "the contrary, and by that knowledge not to know my selfe." Her complaint on the one hand addresses her lack of "identity" in the sense of "essential sameness or oneness" with others—in this case her parents—while at the same time providing a starting point for her "identity" in the sense of "individuality or personality," which she must construct anew through her subsequent interaction with others separate from herself. Although recent critics, such as Carolyn Ruth Swift [in *English Literary Renaissance* 14, 1984] conclude from Urania's plight that "Wroth reveals the loss of identity that women experience in a society that victimizes them," and that "throughout the *Urania,* venturesome women lose themselves," in fact Wroth's narrative focuses upon the discovery rather than the loss of female identity. Urania's awareness of her loss becomes the starting point for her discovery of her identity through a process of social interaction rather than social victimization.

In one of Urania's first encounters, Wroth juxtaposes cultural assumptions about gender with the actualities of male and female behavior as portrayed in her narrative. Urania enters a cave where she finds a knight in mourning, yet when she attempts to give him counsel he rebuffs her the moment he becomes aware of her gender. Perissus first mistakes Urania for a spirit, and upon realizing his error exclaims: "But now I see you are woman; and therefore not much to be marked, and lesse resisted." The knight's gender-biased response to Urania introduces the importance of gender distinctions in the narrative. In fact, the folly of Perissus's male perspective is foreshadowed in his lamentations before noticing Urania's presence in the cave. He denigrates one of his adversaries by comparing him to "a Fool, who in a dark Cave, that hath but one way to get out, having a candle but not the understanding what good it doth him, puts it out," yet he fails to recognize the arrival of aid when Urania appears in his own cave. Urania herself remains unperturbed by his dismissal, persuading him finally to communicate with her so that she may give him counsel and comfort. This incident becomes a point of reference throughout the *Urania,* as an example of the title character's power to relieve the difficulties of others, both male and female. Urania is able to help Perissus not in spite of her gender, but because her own quest for her female identity has allowed her to "identify" with the losses suffered by others.

Furthermore, the incident recalls another fictive encounter in a cave in which the question of gender becomes an issue. Basilius's comment in the cave scene of the *Old Arcadia* on female "difference," after imagining his wife to be his hoped-for mistress, conveys male assumptions about the nature of woman. Wroth rewrites the significance of gender in Sidney's episode into her own narrative, beginning with the difference in motivation separating the forays of Basilius and Urania into their respective caves, and ending with the quite different results of their encounters. Whereas in the former case an imagined difference between women turns out to be nonexistent, in the latter case the imagined sameness of all women implied in Perissus's dismissal of the gender breaks down in the face of Urania's individual identity as a woman. Wroth also heightens the importance of gender beyond Spenser's treatment in a parallel episode in *The Faerie Queene,* where Britomart comes upon Scudamore bewailing his loss of Amoret, and at first encounters a reaction of indignant scorn when she attempts to comfort him. Scudamore's reaction, however, has nothing to do with Britomart's gender, because he takes her for a male knight, whereas Wroth makes gender one of the primary issues in the opening encounter between Urania and Perissus.

The question of female worth in relation to identity surfaces frequently after the encounter between Urania and Perissus. One notable example occurs in a male character's comment upon the admirable self-control of a lady following the death of her beloved: "O women how excellent are you, when you take the right way? else, I must confesse, you are the children of men, and like them faultfull". This characteristically masculine judgment depends upon a male conception of "the right way" in the first place, and assumes a masculine capability to evaluate the faults of women as fathered by men. On the other hand, when one male character inveighs against women's lightness and jealousy, having lost the favor of his own beloved, it is another male character, Steriamus, who reminds him that "your mother was a woman, and you must be favour'd by an other, to be blessed with brave posterity." Such a reminder balances the earlier perspective of women as "the children of men" with a recognition of the engendering role of women themselves. While the importance of that engendering role is emphasized by the female polemicists of the period, Wroth expands its significance from the realm of gender debate to a more encompassing consideration of human identity.

Steriamus's comment also recalls Pyrocles' exploration of his male identity in the *Arcadia*: "if I be anything, . . . I was to come to it born of a woman and nursed of a woman." Yet Pyrocles relegates that dependence to his origins while maintaining the autonomy of his present state, assuring Musidorus that in spite of his Amazon attire "there is nothing I desire more than fully to prove myself a man in this enterprise." By contrast Steriamus, who subsequently becomes Urania's husband, emphasizes the terms of male dependence upon women not only as a past connection, but as a present and future one as well: "you must be favour'd by an other, to be blessed with brave posterity." In shifting the emphasis of perception from Sidney's male character to her own, Wroth re-presents the question of identity in terms of affiliation rather than individuation, indicating the interdependence of the sexes within her fictive community.

While Wroth uses Urania's quest for her female identity and the growth of her relationship with Steriamus to explore the power of affiliation, she provides another perspective through her portrayal of Pamphilia's quest for identity in conjunction with her love for Amphilanthus. Pamphilia's idealization of her constancy as the defining quality of her character brings its own limitations. Unlike Urania, who grows through her capacity for identification with others, Pamphilia, having fallen in love with the most autonomous of the male characters, assumes the desirability of a parallel pursuit of independence for herself. Yet far more than Urania, Pamphilia finds herself in bondage to her passion, her identity constrained even as she most publicly proclaims her autonomy. Within the political and familial structures of the narrative, she can maintain this front of autonomy with the support of her father as well as her uncle, a situation in itself unusual for any female figure in the Renaissance. Nevertheless, the unsettling effect of Pamphilia's passion upon her private sense of self underlies her assertion of control over her public role.

Pamphilia only begins to move toward realization of her identity as a woman rather than as an ideal with the help of her female friends. After the first revelation of Amphilanthus's inconstancy, Pamphilia descends into such melancholy that even with Urania, who is Amphilanthus's sister, "she still put it off, and would not (unto her) confes, but dissembled." Finally Urania confronts her friend on the assumption that Pamphilia has been mourning the inconstancy of her secret beloved, "a thing familiar with men," and advises her to "hate that humour by your owne worthy constancy, . . . and let not so uncertaine a qualitie hurt you," concluding: "This I advise as my selfe would be advised if in such extremity, and this I say to you my dearest Cosin, and would say, though I knew it were my owne brother caused this mischiefe". Urania's advice reveals at the same time her capacity for identification with her friend—"this I advise as my selfe would be advised"—and her unerring perspicuity about the nature of the relationship involved—"though I knew it were my owne brother caused this mischiefe." Her characteristic frankness initiates a thoughtful exchange between the cousins on the respective merits of constancy and love, leading not to an abstract resolution of the problems involved, but rather to an opening of the lines of communication in their female friendship.

By representing bonds of female friendship which do not depend upon a "primary" context of male/female love or a "parallel" context of male friendship, Wroth rewrites the conventions of gender relation which govern the ro-

mances of her predecessors. Once Pamphilia learns from friends like Urania to recognize the regenerative potential of change over stasis, she can begin to accept the dynamic potential of her own constancy in friendship as well as romantic love. When two female characters near the end of the published *Urania* declare themselves to be "called the true loving friends, a rare matter (as men say) to bee found amongst us", that declaration acknowledges the patriarchal bias of Renaissance society, while suggesting Wroth's own determination to locate female friendship at the heart, rather than the margins, of her fictive society.

Wroth's female characters achieve voices of their own which differ greatly from the stylized discourse of conventional prose romance heroines. Although Sidney's Pamela provides one model of feminine eloquence, Wroth's protagonists often speak in dramatic terms which suggest her familiarity with female characters of the theater. The sisterly sharing of fortunes and misfortunes in love, particularly in the unpublished manuscript continuation of Wroth's narrative, takes the form of extended dramatic dialogues not commonly found in other prose romances, but strongly reminiscent of the conversations of Beatrice and Hero, Rosalind and Celia, and even of such later Shakespearean women as Desdemona and Emilia, Hermione and Paulina. Critics have pointed to conversations between Shakespeare's women as suggestive of a "female subculture" in contrast to the dominant male order. One feminist critic, [Carole McKewin in *Woman's Part*] for example, praises Shakespeare's "enduring mimetic skill in creating the sound of women's voices placing themselves in a man's world." Wroth, however, uses her narrative to explore the nature not of a female subculture but a female culture, to create the sound not of women's voices in a man's world, but of a female world of communication.

At the same time, Wroth transforms the example of a tragic heroine such as Desdemona in order to convey the power of feminine discourse in her fictive world. In the manuscript continuation of the *Urania*, for example, Wroth both echoes and reworks *Othello* in a scene where Pamphilia finds her lover Amphilanthus flung on her bed in the throes of jealousy. Grieving that his breath should be spent on sighs "for noe cause," she inquires "what is the cause" of his unease when her heart is so clearly his. "Is itt soe my onely soule," Amphilanthus responds, "fast clasping her in his armes." This exchange recalls, in both language and content, the scene in which Othello, consumed by jealousy, comes upon Desdemona in her bed, exclaiming: "It is the cause, it is the cause, my soul. / Let me not name it to you, you chaste stars. / It is the cause" (*Othello*, V.ii.1-3). Borrowing from a climactic Shakespearean scene of male jealousy, Wroth reframes her source by placing the male lover in the supine position on the bed, while revealing how the heroine's perception and common sense dissolve the barrier of jealousy on this occasion through effective communication.

Furthermore, Pamphilia experiences the regenerative effects of communication with her female friends throughout the course of her fluctuating relationship with her male lover. Unlike instances of male inconstancy in the *Diana* or the *Astrée,* such inconstancy in the *Urania* is understood, rather than simply scorned or feared, by the female characters. In their conversations among themselves, the women come to terms with gender differences while affirming their identities. Female friendship thus allows women in Wroth's romance to grow in the security of their identities through interrelation rather than individuation, freed from the dependence upon a male context which characterizes female experience in the romances of Montemayor and d'Urfé.

Wroth indicates the extent to which her female characters define their own patterns of action, instead of simply participating in a "female subculture" of a man's world, when Pamphilia comes under attack by enemy forces and receives aid not only from neighboring male princes but also from her friend and neighbor, Veralinda, the Queen of Frigia. In the description of their friendship, Wroth represents their communication as a sustaining force in a mutable world, stressing not only their political alliance as rulers, but also their emotional bond as friends: "for never was ther greater, nor Constanter love betweene woemen, then beetweene these towe most excellent Ladys, continuing to ther ends, . . . soe as while the warrs might bee cruell, and curst, yett they might in sweet conversation injoye one the other." Veralinda provides physical aid with her army, but the emphasis of Wroth's narrative rests upon the comfort she brings Pamphilia through thoughtful conversation.

Even in comfort, Veralinda preserves a sense of humor which complements her friend's emotional intensity and helps to create a more balanced perspective than Pamphilia could attain alone. Their respective views on love emerge in their discussion of Amphilanthus's relationship to Pamphilia:

> Those days are past, my deere Veralinda, cride Pamphilia, and hee is changed, and proved a man; hee was ever thought soe, sayd Veralinda . . . you were, and are the discreetest of your sex, yett you would have impossibilities; you say Amphilanthus is a man, why did you ever know any man, especially any brave man continue constant to the end? . . . all men are faulty, I would nott my self have my Lord Constant, for feare of a miracle . . . say he hath left you, lett him goe in his owne pathe, tread nott in itt, an other is more straite, follow that, and bee the Emperess of the world, comaunding the Empire of your owne minde.

On the one hand, Veralinda's practical comments recall the feminist pronouncements of Jane Anger on the nature of men. On the other hand, her humor deflects the potential for self-pity or a sense of grievance by asserting the power of the feminine perspective rather than simply denigrating the qualities of men. Another possible forebear of Veralinda could be Shakespeare's straight-talking Emilia, whose longest conversation with Desdemona is spiced with such bold questions as: "have not we affections, / Desires for sport, and frailty, as men have?" (*Othello,* IV.iii.100-101). One notable difference, however, is that while Shakespeare's Emilia defines women in rela-

tion to men's faults—"The ills we do, their ills instruct us so" (*Othello,* IV.iii 103)—Wroth's Veralinda asserts the possibility that women may choose their own paths. Furthermore, Wroth diverges from the "heroine/confidante" hierarchy governing the relationship between Desdemona and Emilia to convey a greater mutuality of friendship between her female characters. Finally, while both Emilia and Desdemona perish, for all their courage, at the hands of their husbands, Wroth's female protagonists demonstrate the potential not only to endure, but to prevail.

Male inconstancy thus ironized by Veralinda becomes less of a force to victimize women than when subject to control or release only through magic, as in the examples of Montemayor's Don Felix or d'Urfé's Hylas. Supported by constancy of love among female friends, Wroth's women are able to evaluate their male lovers with ironic humor, and even ultimately to respond with forgiveness. Their response deprives male inconstancy of its ultimate force to dominate or victimize, as the women affirm through their shared discourse their capacity to command minds of their own.

Within a literary context, Wroth's generic heritage encompasses conventional patterns of characterization which center upon the love affairs of male and female characters in pairs. Even in those romances where characterizations of women prove central to the development of the plot, from the *Diana* and the *Astrée* to the *Arcadia,* the emphasis upon love between the sexes results in perceptions of women from a consistently masculine point of view. To paraphrase that early remark from the *Urania,* women in male-authored romances are "excellent" when they take the "right way" as perceived from a male vantage-point; otherwise, they are "faultfull" according to the male judgments which have fathered them.

Within a historical context, Wroth writes during a time in which a woman was perceived primarily as a wife, again from a patriarchal vantage-point. The few women writers during this period tend to create models of negation which refute male perspectives, rather than models of affirmation. Wroth, however, represents women not just as the lovers of men, but as the loving friends of one another. She defines the role of individual women in her fictive community not primarily or even necessarily in relation to husbands, but rather in relation to a larger community of family and friends which includes parents and children, siblings and cousins. Most particularly in their friendships with one another, Wroth's female characters stand as models of affirmation who transcend the literary and historical stereotypes of the period and affirm the uniqueness of Wroth's perspective as a woman writer in the Renaissance.

Lady Mary Wroth generally receives only brief mention even in recent studies of Renaissance women. But her own experience—attacked by male courtiers for her pioneering literary venture—necessarily heightened her awareness of the discouragements as well as the challenges of writing literally out of a male tradition and consequently facing the danger of being written out of that tradition for all time. In the two parts of the *Urania,* Wroth moves beyond the characterizations of her male predecessors in the romance tradition, transforming those "children of men" through her re-presentation of the relationships not only between the sexes, but also among family and friends. The reminder by one of her male characters to another that "your mother was a woman" indicates the consistently female perspective which underlies Wroth's own characterizations in the *Urania,* of woman born.

Janet MacArthur (essay date 1989)

SOURCE: "'A *Sydney,* though un-named'; Lady Mary Wroth and her Poetical Progenitors," in *English Studies in Canada,* Vol. XV, No. 1, March, 1989, pp. 12-20.

[*In this analysis of the* Urania *and* Pamphilia to Amphilanthus, *MacArthur contends that the absence of important Petrarchan conventions in Wroth's poetry functions as an assertion of the persona's feminine voice.*]

Critics have often commented upon the tensions in Lady Mary Wroth's prose romance *The Countesse of Montgomeries Urania* (London, 1621), of which the sonnet sequence *Pamphilia to Amphilanthus* became a part. Carolyn Ruth Swift [in *English Literary Renaissance,* 14, 1984] has suggested that Lady Wroth was ambivalent, caught between her "empathy with society and her empathy with beleaguered women." Josephine A. Roberts [in *The Poems of Lady Mary Wroth*] also finds ambivalence, which she claims surfaces in the stylistic unevenness of the sequence: "the poems as a group vary widely in quality, from those that merely repeat the well-worn Elizabethan conceits to others that rise above the traditional imagery to present an intensely ambivalent response to love." In her dissertation of 1978, Margaret Witten-Hannah concludes that "the see-sawing of the different attitudes towards constancy and change [in the *Urania*] must be regarded as significant and as illustrative of the author's own uncertainty in the face of conflict between traditional moral values and ideals, and the realities of experience."

Many of the critics attribute the tensions, ambivalence, and contradiction in Lady Wroth's work to the gender of the writer and the speaker. In this study, I would like to extend the investigation of the role of gender to an examination of Lady Wroth's use of Petrarchan conventions in *Pamphilia to Amphilanthus.* Elaine Showalter claims that "women's fiction can be read as a double-voiced discourse, containing a 'dominant' and a 'muted' story, what [Sandra] Gilbert and [Susan] Gubar call a 'palimpsest'." I see the tension between the dominant and muted, showcased in the sonnet sequence, as a tension between feminine difference and Lady Wroth's desire to emulate the poetic models of her uncle and her father. Because she opts for the latter, tension is evidenced in the attempt to create an androgynous discourse in a gender-specific mode. This produces the "palimpsest" of *Pamphilia to Amphilanthus.*

That Lady Wroth chose to write at all at a time when women's writing was seen as a violation of the Pauline injunction requiring women's silence, obedience, and chastity is remarkable. Indeed, Lord Denny, one of her first critics, questioned her chastity and femininity. Outraged by what he perceived as the *Urania's* less than subtle or sympathetic allegorization of his family's private affairs, he responded with a vituperative poem. Astute as any latter-day critic, he also suggests that she had divided loyalties. In his poem, he labels her an "Hermaphrodite . . . in deed a monster" and urges her to "leave idle bookes alone / For wise and worthyer women have writte none." In another letter, he encourages her to try her hand at producing "a volume of heavenly lays and holy love" as did her "virtuous and learned aunt" (cited by Roberts), the Countess of Pembroke. His message is clear: even if you are a Sidney, producing fiction is not your prerogative.

Many critics have also found it odd that Lady Wroth wrote a sonnet sequence twenty years after the sonnet vogue had run its prolific course, at a time when there was little interest in and even outright disdain for sonnet-writing. Yet both her decision to write and publish her work and her choice of the anachronistic sonnet sequence can be explained by her identification with the Sidneys. Gary Waller [in his edition of *Pamphilia to Amphilanthus*] proposes that for many Jacobeans the Elizabethan Sidneys had become "a nostalgic reminder of older, more solid courtly and literary ideals," especially Sir Philip Sidney who had become "a long-lost reminder of disintegrated virtue and dedication" to a new generation of courtiers. That Lady Wroth retained the Sidney coat of arms after her marriage [as now by Roberts] seems to suggest that she was anxious to retain her membership in this prestigious literary family, as does the title page of the published version of the *Urania,* which proclaims her the niece of Sir Philip Sidney and the Countess of Pembroke. Furthermore, *Pamphilia to Amphilanthus,* which closely follows the models provided by *Astrophil and Stella* and by the poems of Sir Robert Sidney, offers internal evidence of her desire to be identified as the inheritor of the family literary talent and, specifically, as a sonneteering Sidney.

Most of *Pamphilia to Amphilanthus* echoes the conventional Elizabethan sonnet sequence because Lady Wroth's poetic discourse is aligned with that of her uncle and her father. Thus, it does not offer any direct challenge to the gender-specific Petrarchan mode. It is what is left out of *Pamphilia to Amphilanthus* that leaves the mark of gender upon it and calls attention to the "inside/outside position" that a female poet occupies when she tries to write within a tradition, but because of her gender necessarily writes outside and against it.

The absence of classical myths important to Petrarchism is particularly revealing in *Pamphilia to Amphilanthus.* As in many Elizabethan sonnet sequences, Cupid, a metaphor for the devastating effects of love, is depicted as a mischievous child. But in one poem, he makes an appeal to the maternal instincts of the speaker. Finding him "Cold, wett, and crying", she takes him in and nurtures him back to health, whereupon he gains easy access to her heart. In another sonnet, Pamphilia identifies with the jealous Juno, who has come down to earth to seek out her errant husband Jupiter (xcvii). However, the few myths that are used to indicate the presence and difference of a female persona appear in isolation. They do not inform the sequence in the same way that the story of Daphne and Apollo underwrites the *Canzoniere* and the tradition of Renaissance love poetry which Petrarch inspired.

Amphilanthus does not function as Daphne does for Apollo, Laura for Petrarch, or Stella for Astrophil, as a figure whose indifference and unattainability are predicated on his chastity. While it is true that his absence provides the motive for the deployment of the commonplaces of Petrarchan despair—for the poems describing the lover's long, sleepless nights, living death, false hope, and killing grief—Amphilanthus is not idealized or deified. None of the poems in the sequence address him as a divine creature, and with good reason. Throughout the *Urania,* Amphilanthus, whose name means "lover of two", is depicted as a dedicated philanderer; consequently, the Apollonian chase basic to Petrarchistic poetry would have been inappropriate in *Pamphilia to Amphilanthus*. The sequence does not present a poetics of persuasion based on the impure motives of a lover like Astrophil, for example, whose mercurial rhetoric, aimed at overcoming Stella's constancy and chastity, vacillates between praise and blame. As Josephine Roberts points out [in *the Poems of Lady Mary Wroth*], "the rhetoric of wooing or courtship is largely absent from [Lady Wroth's] collection." Moreover, Pamphilia's pursuit of Amphilanthus would make her appear unchaste as well, but an unchaste Pamphilia would have made the poem uniquely anti-Petrarchan and would have destroyed its androgynous poetics.

Instead of producing a series of calculated attempts at tropological seduction, sexual frustration is turned in upon itself, making the tone of *Pamphilia to Amphilanthus* very hopeless and static. There is more longing for death and more living death in this poem than is usual in Petrarchan sonnet sequences. In his discussion of the uniqueness of Spenser's *Amoretti,* Reed Way Dasenbrock observes that

> The love situations Petrarchan poets describe and the attitudes their poems express are characterized by instability and discontinuity. . . . Any reader of Renaissance sonnet sequences is familiar with the sense of vertigo induced by the endless shifts in tone, mood, and stance. [*PMLA* 100, 1985].

This vertiginous atmosphere is not evidenced in *Pamphilia to Amphilanthus;* in fact, Pamphilia's appeal to her own constancy and stability endures throughout. Some Petrarchan *topoi* work well to represent the lachrymose powerlessness and passivity of the lover, the imprisonment and tyranny of love, and the still misery of the lover's blighted existence. But *Pamphilia to Amphilanthus* loses the oxymoronic dynamism of Petrarchism, achieved

by the uneasy fusion of contraries, because Lady Wroth often only presents the negative side of the binaries that give Petrarchistic love poetry its vitality. The sequence lacks the lighter side produced in *Astrophil and Stella,* for instance, by the comic elements and sexual puns that reveal Astrophil's jouissance.

Nor can Pamphilia ever use Amphilanthus to transcend her static death-in-life. None of the songs and sonnets in the sequence invoke Amphilanthus as an agent of spiritual transcendence, as the kind of conduit between the lover and God that Petrarch's Laura or Dante's Beatrice were. While Astrophil does not experience a productive metamorphosis induced by his beloved either, he is at least able to enjoy the varieties of verbal ingenuity with which he attempts to gain his desired ends. Lacking the agency of a chaste beloved, Pamphilia fails at her only attempt at transcendence, represented in the crown of fourteen interrelated sonnets (lxxvii-xc) in which she tries to transform her earthly love into a love of virtue. The crown begins and ends with the speaker in the same labyrinth of despair.

Nor does the poem gain any momentum from the egotism of the lover. In many Petrarchan sequences, the absent and silent female beloved is often appropriated and objectified by an ego that seeks its confirmation in the achievement of poetic immortality or political preferment. Her image therefore reflects the poet/speaker's other ungratified desires. Hence, the myth of Narcissus is often used by Petrarchan poets. As Robert M. Durling has shown [in *Petrarch's Lyric Poems: the Rime sparse and other Lyrics*], there is "a fundamental narcissism" at the heart of Petrarchism.

Though *Pamphilia to Amphilanthus* anatomizes Pamphilia's suffering self, the transformation of the beloved into the laurel which produces a constant shift of focus in other sonnet sequences is absent. The poem never draws attention to the imaginative powers of its creator and rarely reflects back on the writing process. Most important, the speaker never uses the "eternizing" conceits that bespeak the desire for fame, the last infirmity of Astrophil and of the poetically self-aggrandizing speaker in Shakespeare's sonnets. At one point, Pamphilia even confesses that she gets no compensatory satisfaction from her own poems: "Nor can I as those pleasant wits injoy / My owne fram'd wordes" (xlv.5-6). *Pamphilia to Amphilanthus* effaces any sense of vocation, poetic or otherwise. The speaker never indicates a loss of purpose or direction in poems addressed to friends—like the wooden, curious, and dusty wits of *Astrophil and Stella*—who have become disdainful of the speaker's self-indulgent lovesickness and urge the lover not to be seduced away from his public duties.

Furthermore, the presence of the myths of Daphne and Apollo and of Narcissus in this poem would undermine Lady Wroth's poetic project, for both myths present woman as the object rather than the subject of discourse. Daphne reverts to an object in nature; Narcissus falls in love with an object which is only a reflection of himself. In the *Canzoniere*, the reworking of these myths effects an objectification of the female beloved. The *Canzoniere* is therefore emblematic of a long tradition in Western culture. Craig Owens [in *The Anti-Aesthetic Essays on Post-Modern Culture*] explains:

> Among those prohibited from Western representation, whose representations are denied all legitimacy, are women. Excluded from representation by its very structure, they return within it as a figure for—a representation of—the unrepresentable (Nature, Truth, the Sublime, etc.). This prohibition bears primarily on woman as the subject, and rarely as the object of representation, for there is certainly no shortage of images *of* women. Yet in being represented by, women have been rendered an absence within the dominant culture . . .

Lady Wroth would not want to use myths that silence the female voice in what is automatically an assertion of subjectivity by a female. As a result, one of the speaking silences in her poem is the absence of the classical myths that render the female absent in Petrarchan representation.

The absence of the myth of Diana and Actaeon also indicates her desire to efface the threat that her discourse presents to representation as a masculine prerogative. Petrarchan poetry is motivated by the loss of an object of desire. Thus, Petrarch's *rime sparse* or scattered rhymes are an attempt to re-present or remember the absent and unattainable Laura. Yet as John Freccero contends [in *Diacritics* 5, 1975], Petrarch's description also dismembers her: "Her virtues and her beauties are scattered like the objects of fetish worship: her eyes and hair are like gold and topaz on the snow, while the outline of her face is lost". The blazon participates in this process. Nancy J. Vickers suggests that the discursive dismemberment of Laura's body, a reworking of the Diana/Actaeon myth, neutralizes the threat of Diana or female difference. Scattered rhyme thereby maintains the lady's non-subjectivity—her silence, mystery, and invisibility—and, hence, the poet's productive anxiety. They also perpetuate the male observer/female object stance and the speaker's control over the signification of the "fetishized" signs into which she has been converted [according to Nancy J. Vickers in *Crit I,* 8, 1981].

However, there is very little description of the beloved in *Pamphilia to Amphilanthus* and there are no blazons. Some critics suggest that the words "well" and "will" function as allusions to her lover William Herbert, but this remains unconfirmed in a sequence that tends to avoid referentiality. Some poems describe Amphilanthus's eyes and lips, but these are generic eyes and lips, without colour and form, unlike the flashing black eyes of Astrophil's Stella, for example. Nor is Amphilanthus historicized by allusions to the place where he abides or to real events in which he may have played a part. And while there is no shortage of representations of the male in the prose romance *Urania* (bear in mind the apparent misrepresentation of Lord Denny), these represent male behaviour, not the body.

Males behave badly in the *Urania:* they are generally unfaithful and/or tyrannical lovers and husbands. Yet while "Wroth's subject is the alienation of women from men", the *Urania* and *Pamphilia to Amphilanthus* do not offer a direct challenge to society's values. On the other hand, the *Urania* praises marriage and usually depicts women's passive suffering because of their constancy, chastity, and obedience as heroic. I would like to offer a neo-Freudian explanation of this phenomenon. It can be used to explain not only the indictment of males in *Urania* but also the absence of the blazon and the rejection of the male beloved in *Pamphilia to Amphilanthus*.

Recent theories about the position traditionally granted to women in Western culture are relevant to Lady Wroth's situation as a poet. The French psychoanalytic philosopher Jacques Lacan has defined language as the Law of the Father, a structure inscribed with cultural imperatives—the Father's rules, concepts, rationality, and definitions. To enter into this system, males and females repress their maternal attachment (what Lacan calls the Desire for the Mother) and accept the notion of femininity as an absence, something defined by what it is not: not male, hence, non-subjective. Furthermore, the Western representational system has traditionally disavowed female difference. Defined as an absence rather than as an entity, female otherness and heterogeneity cannot be expressed in a signifying system that renders them non-existent. In order for a woman to participate in the symbolic system, that is, to speak or write and be given the respect accorded a unitary subject, she has had to write in what Lacan calls the Name-of-the-Father. She must submit to or identify with the Father's laws, repressing her sexual desire and negating her own difference.

Swift's contention that the emphasis on male infidelity in the *Urania* is "the result of Jacobean cynicism opposed to [Sir Philip] Sidney's Tudor idealism" draws attention to the role Lady Wroth's endorsement of a status quo associated with the Elizabethan Sidneys plays in producing the tension in her work. Lady Wroth identifies with the Tudor idealism represented by her forefathers. Nevertheless, the exploration of the experience of women in the pastoral and Petrarchan modes used by her uncle and her father introduces an element that necessarily interrogates a society that does not recognize female difference. Remaining loyal to the Father's law, she attempts to resolve the tension this creates by holding Amphilanthus rather than ideology responsible for Pamphilia's symbolic suffering. This ultimately accounts for his absence or banishment from the sequence, which is then directed away from romance and the erotic.

In rejecting the lover but accepting the Father's law, Pamphilia loses the opportunity to express herself as a desiring subject. This explains the absence of the blazon, which stands as a non-emblem of Lady Wroth's conservative project. To include a blazon in a sonnet sequence written by a woman would call attention to the erotic. It would also express a sexual desire that is other. This would interrogate the erotics of Petrarchan poetry, which depend upon male representation and female silence, on "fetishized" representations of the female's disunited body, and upon the repression of female otherness. Gordon Braden's recent contention that the Petrarchan ego often fails to confront psychic otherness can be understood in these terms. Female otherness is not acknowledged but scattered (absent) or rendered the same (repressed) in Western culture in modes of representation like classical myth and Petrarchan poetry. In a conventional sonnet sequence that endorses "the law of the same," Lady Wroth does not question the Petrarchan erotic. *Pamphilia to Amphilanthus* is therefore not the sonnet mistress's reply to the madly devoted and sexually importuante Petrarchan male. On the contrary, the absence of the blazon is a way of circumventing the kind of challenge offered to masculine conventions that exists in the work of the sixteenth-century French poet Louise Labé, for instance. Her work parodies hyperbolic Petrarchan praise and asserts female sensuality rather than chastity. Ann Rosalind Jones concludes that Labé's experiments with the blazon revealed "the absence of a standard for masculine beauty," the absence of a language of female persuasion, and the "sexual irreversibility" of this Petrarchan device.

It is not surprising, then, that there is little trace of Amphilanthus in the sequence: only ten out of the 103 songs and sonnets address him. His name, used only in the title, is not subjected to the obsessive punning that is often a feature of Petrarchan meditation on the beloved. Never invoked and rarely described, Amphilanthus becomes an absence, unlike the conventional sonnet mistress, who often becomes an absent presence. Effacing him represses any indication of a female jouissance that might impugn not only the chastity of Pamphilia but also the integrity of her female creator. As a result, constancy rather than Amphilanthus becomes the poem's fetish. Even though constancy is usually treated positively in her work, the *Urania* reveals that Lady Wroth had some misgivings about it. In a passage that contributes to the deep contradictions in *Urania,* Urania, an important and authoritative character in the narrative, tells the long-suffering Pamphilia, " 'Tis pity . . . that ever that fruitlesse thing constancy was taught you as a vertue . . . understand, this vertue hath limits . . . those . . . with whom it is broken are by the breech free to leave or choose again where more staidness may be found". Lady Wroth finds that "staidness" in the Elizabethan Sidneys, presided over by Elizabeth's faithful shepherd knight, Sir Philip Sidney, the exemplar of male constancy.

She also seeks sanction for her work through allusions to Elizabeth I. Elaine V. Beilin [*Spenser Studies* 2, 1981] suggests that Elizabeth I, whose motto was *Semper eadem* (meaning "always the same"), is "a clear presence" behind Pamphilia, an unmarried queen who remains constant to her people. By reiterating constancy through Pamphilia and the informing presence of Elizabeth I, Lady Wroth asserts her subjectivity, her unity or one-ness, and her right to produce fiction. But some critics have suggested that Elizabeth I certainly did not assert a specifically female subjectivity, but maintained her control over a patriarchal power structure by repressing her own desire and denying her own difference as a woman.

Lady Wroth re-enacts this Freudian process by writing in the Name-of-the-Father inscribed in the Petrarchan mode of representation. The emphasis on the constancy and chastity of the speaker reproduces the signification of woman in Petrarchan poetry and in Western culture, thereby declaring Lady Wroth's loyalty to a tradition of English poetry presided over by her uncle. The discourse of *Pamphilia to Amphilanthus* is therefore produced in the name of Lady Wroth's father-figures, who replace Amphilanthus. In a sense, her poem is addressed to them, as she invokes their aesthetic generative power and produces writing which reflects theirs. But as the incident with Lord Denny that led to the withdrawal of her work reveals, the virtue of a Renaissance woman who creates fiction was suspect, even if her poetical progenitors were the Sidneys. When Ben Jonson observed that his friend Lady Wroth was "a *Sydney,* though un-named" in one of his tributes to her, he inadvertently called attention to her problematic situation as a female poet, reflected in the "palimpsest" or tensions in *Pamphilia to Amphilanthus,* tensions that she tried to resolve by attempting to validate her fiction and poetry in the name of her fathers.

Carolyn Ruth Swift (essay date 1989)

SOURCE: "Feminine Self-Definition in Lady Mary Wroth's *Love's Victorie,*" in *English Literary Renaissance,* Vol. 19, No. 2, Spring, 1989, pp. 171-88.

[*In the following essay, Swift studies how Wroth's belief that women should have freedom of choice regarding marriage and the direction of their lives finds expression in her tragicomedy* Love's Victory.]

In her pastoral play *Love's Victorie,* Lady Mary Wroth created a feminine dreamworld analogous to the "masculine dreamworld" that Renato Poggioli [in his *The Oaten Flute*] finds in traditional Renaissance pastorals. As male authors retreat to Arcadia in protest against sexual conformity and responsibility, in *Love's Victorie* a female author retreats to a world in which women can enlarge their freedom by overcoming family pressure and marrying as they wish. In seventeenth-century England an aristocratic woman usually married a man her parents chose for her because of his status or wealth; in *Love's Victorie* one woman chooses to remain single and another marries the man she loves. Wroth draws her protagonists from the story her uncle Sir Philip Sidney told in *Astrophil and Stella,* a sonnet sequence which most scholars accept as based upon his own love affair with Lady Penelope Rich. At the end of *Love's Victorie* characters who represent Sir Philip Sidney and Lady Penelope die a mock death that represents the spiritual death her forced marriage caused, and then with the aid of Venus they are resurrected to live happily ever after.

Although *Love's Victorie* is an original pastoral drama, Wroth made her source clear through her characters' names and through a dialogue that occasionally refers to Sidney's work. By linking her play with the unhappy love story of Astrophil and Stella, Wroth satisfies the longing that even the most sophisticated audience may feel for happy endings to familiar tragic stories. Even though we know the difference between tragedy and comedy, some of us wish that Romeo had taken Juliet with him to Mantua, that King Lear had ended his life with Cordelia in France, or that Ophelia had survived to live happily ever after with Hamlet. In *Love's Victorie* the rewriting of the Sidney-Devereux romance enables the members of Wroth's audience to fulfill their own fantasies of a successful and empowering romance that overcomes all obstacles.

In *Love's Victorie* the characters meet in the woods to comment on each other's errors in love and to play verbal games. However, by the third game at the end of the third act, they have become more self-disclosing and more enlightened about themselves. As the characters frankly reveal truths about their lives and discuss women's roles in romance, Wroth creates a vision of women who strengthen one another and thus create love's victory.

The play's name, *Love's Victorie,* derives from prologues in which Venus challenges Cupid to force all humans to fall in love. But at the end of her play Wroth expands the conventional view of love's triumph to include recognition of women as capable of governing their own lives. *Love's Victorie* celebrates one woman's celibacy and the fantasy marriage of Sir Philip Sidney and Lady Penelope Rich. Because Wroth believed that women and men should freely choose whether to marry and whom to marry, she rewrote a story that may have dominated her own romantic imagination throughout her childhood.

Lady Mary Wroth was first identified as the author of *Love's Victorie* in 1983 when Josephine A. Roberts reported her careful analysis of the handwritings and themes in the Huntington Library's manuscript. That manuscript contains only the first four acts and includes prologues only to Acts 2 and 3. A privately owned English manuscript supplies the missing fifth act. In addition, it contains the only known copy of the initial prologue, in which the play is first named, and the final prologue, in which priests honor individuals who honor love.

The manuscripts reveal Wroth to be an author at home with the love songs and games which Renaissance playwrights often used to explore love's lost paradise. In *Love's Victorie,* as in Shakespeare's *As You Like It* and Lyly's *Gallathea,* lovers struggle to overcome misunderstandings and to experience mutual love. Puttenham's *The Arte of English Poesie* indicates that English Renaissance audiences expected pastoral to "figure matters of greater importance." Sir Philip Sidney's "Apology for Poetry" explains that pastoral contains "vnder the prettie tales . . . whole considerations of wrong dooing and patience." Sir John Harington's "Brief Apology for Poetry" also refers to the "diuers and sundry meanings" and "senses or mysteries" of poetic texts [as noted by G. G. Smith in *Elizabethan Critical Essays*]. Wroth followed that tradition when she used pastoral to explore issues of faithfulness and unfaithfulness, dependence and independence in love, themes she explored earlier in her long pastoral narrative *The Countesse of Mountgomeries Urania* (1621).

As both aristocrat and woman, Wroth could not act in the all-male professional companies of the early seventeenth century, but she derived knowledge of stagecraft from performances at court; [according to Herford and Simpson in *The Works of Ben Jonson*] her name appears among the cast of Jonson's *The Masque of Blackness* (1605). If she ever staged *Love's Victorie,* she may have used the great hall of Penshurst and its balcony; Roberts suggests that the hall at Surrenden, where Sir Edward Dering's friends pursued their theatrical interests, may also have been the site of a performance.

Wroth's work reveals her share of the Sidney family's talent. Her father Robert Sidney wrote love lyrics; her aunt Lady Mary Herbert experimented with verse form in psalm translations. *Love's Victorie* certainly justifies Herford and Simpson's description of Wroth as "gracefully" continuing the "Arcadian-Sidneian tradition" of her uncle, but like her long romance, *The Countess of Mountgomeries Urania,* Wroth's play reveals a feminine consciousness at work within seventeenth-century literary and social conventions. In spite of its pastoral scene and Arcadian references, *Love's Victorie* differs significantly from Sir Philip Sidney's *Arcadia* and even from his pastoral play *Lady of May.*

The most apparent difference is Wroth's style. While Sidney's romance and play are written primarily in prose with songs interspersed, a style Wroth used in *Urania,* the dialogue of *Love's Victorie* consists of decasyllabic couplets interspersed with songs of varied meters. In her play Wroth skillfully uses the rhetorical figures and tropes that she also used in the songs and sonnets in the printed version of *Pamphilia to Amphilanthus,* the sequence that concludes *Urania.* In an age that viewed writing as a male role, the sequential nouns of brachylogia and varieties of antistrophe show that Wroth practiced her tropes and figures with clear determination to be a writer herself:

> Meadowes, pathes, grass, flouers
> walkes, birds, brooke, truly finde
> all proue butt as vaine shouers
>
> . . .
>
> you once I loued best
> butt loue makes mee you leaue
> by loue I loue deseaue
> Joy's lost for liues unrest
>
> (f. I)

While this song reads like a poetic sampler, it well suits Elizabethan melodies I have tried, such as "Blow, Blow Thou Winter Wind." However, Wroth sometimes achieves brilliant lyricism even in the demanding test of reading aloud:

> Loues begining like the spring
> giues delight in sweetnes flowing
> euer pleasant flourishing
> pride in her braue coulers showing

Butt loue ending is att last
like the stormes of winters blast

(f. 17)

Love's Victorie differs from her uncle's play in its view of gender roles as well as in its use of poetry. Although the characters in Sidney's *Lady of May* resolutely refuse to make bond-slaves of the women they love, their benevolence arises from noblesse oblige. Sidney's play assumes that men have power over women's lives. Wroth, on the other hand, gives her female characters a high degree of autonomy. They create their own losses and their own successes as the characters in *Urania* did, and as the author tried to do in her own life.

The records of the Sidney family reveal Wroth to have lived through patterns of disappointed expectation from which might have evolved a fantasy about women who shaped their own lives. Her talents were cherished in early childhood. Sir Robert Sidney received frequent letters from his secretary Sir Rowland Whyte recounting with delight Mistress Mary's early progress in reading and the admiration her dancing inspired at court. The doting father, however, soon doted on his first son more than on Mary, his talented first-born. Although his letters warn his wife to procure the best tutors for young Robert, he is satisfied that she can handle well the training of the girls. Even if Wroth's father or her aunt the Countess of Pembroke encouraged her privately, the absence of formal effort to fulfill her early acknowledged talents must have left its residue of disappointment.

Wroth's later life also shows this pattern of frustrated anticipation. When it came time for their daughter to marry, the Sidneys refused at least one offer. Yet this parental caution did not succeed in assuring their daughter's marital happiness; family letters record her husband Sir Robert Wroth's early complaints to the family about his wife, and he was later reputed to be unreasonably jealous. Even the financial security that she and her family must have hoped she would gain from her marriage evaporated. Sir Robert died owing so much money that Wroth petitioned the king for the rest of her life for relief from debt.

Whether in spite of these disappointments or because of them, Wroth's life indicates her efforts to live and work free of many restrictions that most women accepted. Although most aristocrats circulated their writings privately and published anonymously, Wroth published *The Countesse of Mountgomeries Urania* (1621) in a handsome folio with her own name on the title page. When an influential nobleman attacked her because of her romance's portrayal of his family, she answered him with an equally vigorous attack on his mind and morals. Although she finally had to withdraw the book from circulation because of the scandal, her spirited defense of her "harmless booke" reveals a woman who respected her own work. She finally yielded to royal pressure, but little other choice was available to a woman or an author in seventeenth-century England. Always in debt, she remained unmarried after the death of her husband but may have borne two children as a result of her affair with her cousin the Earl of Pembroke. Clearly, Wroth lived her personal life as freely as possible.

Burdened with large debts, dependent on the king for relief, Wroth got whatever power she had later in life through a liaison with a powerful man. Since no record exists of her participation in later plays at court, and since she published nothing after the scandal of *Urania,* evidently she withdrew from public notice. Withdrawal would not seem unusual for most early-seventeenth-century women, but Lady Mary Wroth had enjoyed public appearances in masques. She had also proudly named herself author on the title page of her 558-page romance and had publicly battled with its critic. Retreat for such an active and courageous woman must have meant disappointed personal ambitions. I believe the plot of *Love's Victorie,* whose female characters define their desires to be free from conventional restraints and empower each other to shape their own lives, derives from the limits that society imposed on its author.

In *Love's Victorie* Wroth uses the plot design, romantic tropes, and humor that we find in other Renaissance pastoral plays, but with a difference marked by the consciousness of a talented woman whose society told her continually that she ought to be invisible and subservient. The difference calls attention to deficiencies in the portrayal of women by even the finest Renaissance male author.

The clearest example of Wroth's feminine view is her treatment of forced marriage as the basis of her plot. Although some of Shakespeare's male characters try to help women escape the cruelty of such coercion in *Romeo and Juliet* and in *Much Ado about Nothing,* Wroth places more stress upon the power of women to shape destiny as well as to endure it; her lovers escape through the agency of a clever and strong woman. Diana's votary Silvesta is far more skillful at intrigue than Romeo's Friar Lawrence, whose curious involvement with Romeo's defiance of his family is so ineffective that he creates the confusion that leads to the lovers' deaths. Perhaps Silvesta learns her lessons in helping lovers from Shakespeare's more effective Friar Francis in *Much Ado about Nothing.* Friar Francis saves Hero by hiding her, and, like the friar, Silvesta converts the blocking characters by the bride's presumed death. However, if Shakespeare inspired Wroth, she empowers women more. In *The Winter's Tale,* for example, Shakespeare created women strong enough to change a society through their creativity and faith, but in *Love's Victorie* women dominate action: the blocking character, as well as the victim and the rescuer, are all women. In addition, in Wroth's play even the presiding deity is female.

Wroth stresses her society's negation of female determination by making Musella's mother the blocking character. We cannot know whether Wroth emphasized the mother's tyranny only because of some middle-aged woman present to play the character, but Musella's mother displays fully the effect of subordination on women. While Lady Capulet is her husband's agent, she never protests her helplessness in the face of her absent husband's "will" as Musella reports her mother does (f. 21); Lady Capulet even abets Juliet's father's cruel imposition of his wishes, and praises his fatherly care (3.5.107). She never recognizes the ignominy of subordination that binds women even without visible external compulsion. Because Musella's mother at first blocks Musella's love and then enables it to be fulfilled, Wroth has suggested the possibility of female empowerment.

In addition, Wroth points out the deleterious effects on women of continual subordination. Musella acknowledges that she at first dutifully complied with and endured her father's will. Wroth knows that most young women, raised to be invariably obedient, are unlikely to resist as suddenly as Juliet does. Even so, Wroth empowers Musella and Philisses equally. The young lovers in *Love's Victorie* are partners. Because they determine to live or die together, they differ from the "star-crossed" Romeo and Juliet, who separate as Romeo escapes to Mantua and are reunited in death only because of miscommunication.

Wroth presents her women characters as respecting themselves; they are not self-deprecating. Men, however, confirm their rusticity or insensitivity by making insulting comparisons of women with animals. Rustick's materialism in fact makes him lack wit, so he must reject riddles as profitless. When Philisses suggests that the greedy Rustick speaks just like a husband (f.I9V), we may hear the author use a conventional cynical perspective on generosity of husbands. At the same time female romantic fantasy finds expression in Philisses' criticism of Rustick's venality. Since Philisses is Rustick's rival for Musella's love, his comment suggests that it is possible for a woman to marry a generous man. Wroth's pastoral responds to the fantasies of women living the failed marriages that Lawrence Stone [in his *The Crises of the Aristocracy, 1558-1641*] describes as occurring among "one-third of the older peers" in the early seventeenth century.

Throughout *Love's Victorie* a female author's voice is also heard in the distinctive use of tropes conventional in courtly love literature. As in other pastoral plays, a male lover's lament about love's cruelty initiates the action. However, directly following this conventional opening, a female protagonist, who is a chaste disciple of Diana, complains that "freedomes lost" in love's "blind foulery" (f.IV.). Where the conventional male lament stresses the cruelty of women and the follies of love, Wroth's contrasting voice asks the audience to judge whether a love that enslaves human reason actually serves women well.

In another conventional pastoral pattern Philisses values his friendship with Lissius more than his love for Musella and will not approach Musella unless he is sure that Lissius does not love her. But Wroth uses this example of the greater importance of friendship to create a parallel that shows women capable of similar loyalty. As Philisses and Lissius each refuse to rival the other in romance, Silvesta too explains that she gave up her love of Philisses because she knew Musella loved him: "betray Musella, souner will I dy" (f.IV). For Wroth friendship is a love that sustains women just as it does men; thus, Silves-

ta loves Musella so much that she later risks death to protect Musella from a miserable marriage. Through Silvesta, Wroth innovatively dramatizes women's capacity for relationships that are as deep as masculine friendship. In Shakespeare by contrast, women are devoted to other women only as servants or relatives. Emilia sacrifices her life for Desdemona's reputation, but such sacrifice is expected of loyal servants. Celia exiles herself rather than be separated from her cousin Rosalind (*AYL*), and Beatrice wants Benedict to kill Claudio to avenge her cousin Hero (*Ado*). In *The Winter's Tale* Paulina hides her Queen for years. But Wroth creates a situation that may be unique in early English drama: a female friend is willing to sacrifice her own life for another woman who is not her relative or mistress.

As Wroth centers upon the nature of male friendship and love in Act I, she introduces a new type of male character, a man who will remain chaste and sacrifice his life for a female friend. Loving Silvesta from a distance, the Forester claims a privilege "to doe as birds, and trees, and beasts may doe" (f.6). Wroth may be imitating Romeo's regrets that "every cat and dog / And little mouse" may look at Juliet while he cannot (3.3.30-33). However, the Forester's wish is not for the sexual relationship his words may suggest. He merely desires to look at Silvesta, fully accepting her independence from him. With humor, Wroth thus establishes the possibility that a man may recognize a woman as having an independent existence and goals.

Wroth turns the tables on men by emphasizing the rarity of such celibacy as the Forester's, even though the conventional charge in literature is that it is women who are frail. The Forester's chaste desire merely to see Sylvesta is so startling in the world of *Love's Victorie* that Lissius comments, "Thes tow to meete in one I ne're did finde / loue, and chastity link'd in one mans mind" (f.3). *Love's Victorie* assumes, as Wroth did in *Urania,* that women equal men; like men they are "faultfull" (*Urania* 36), but they are also capable of celibacy and constancy. Being equals, women can participate with men in the sacred friendship that men of honor have always held dear in Renaissance pastoral. And if friendship between women and men is possible, then the grounds for much sexual jealousy vanishes. Both male and female characters assume that women and men can relate non-sexually. Lissius points out to the jealous Philisses that Musella has only spoken to him of Philisses (f.9), and Musella chides the jealous Simena for misreading a "priuate freindship." Musella enables Simena to overcome her jealousy by pointing out that private contact and whispers between Climena and Lissius do not imply unfaithfulness: "though priuate must itt follow hee's vntrue, / or that they whisper'd must bee kept from you," (f.I8).

Throughout the play Wroth displays women's strengths and failings through the "new images of loue" that she promised in Act I (f.3). The Forester loves a woman enough to respect her separation from him, and women love each other enough to place their love for each other ahead of their love for a man. Granted this strength of spirit, women are capable of friendship with men. And since genuine friendship can exist only between equals, Wroth has created a world on stage that invites the audience to question the need for female subordination.

The transformations in *Love's Victorie* are manifested clearly when the shepherds and shepherdesses gather to play games at the end of each act. In Act I they consider whether to play a game of telling the truth about the past or of telling fortunes. Although they reject these games as possibly revealing "secretts of the mind" (f.3V), the songs they sing reveal truths about the singers. Climena, for example, who only later acknowledges being overly aggressive when she left her home in Arcadia to follow her lover, now sings of the sorrow that befalls a heart that ranges "from the wounted course to strang / vnknowne ways" (f.3V). Similarly Rustick sings a counterblazon that reveals him to be a fool as he compares his beloved to farm animals: her "eyes do play / like goats with hay," and her "cheecks as red / as okar spred / On a fatted sheeps back" (f.4). Thus, the songs that end Act I disclose truths that people attempt to evade.

As the play progresses, the protagonists choose to face truths they feared earlier, and as a result they become stronger. By the end of Act 3, having slowly revealed their characters and their loves in Acts I and 2, the women are now able to speak of their varied pasts, and they play the game of truth-telling rejected earlier. At these confessions of "passions past" (f.I2), the audience perceives a truth that no character states but that all recognize later when they declare their present loves: conventional romantic love games may force lovers into a dishonesty in which love itself is at risk.

As the characters learn about each other through the game of confessions, a twentieth-century audience can see that seventeenth-century standards confused women about their roles. Dalina, Fillis, and Climena approach men differently, and yet all three methods lead to suffering and loneliness. The stories of Dalina and Fillis reveal the effects upon women of being taught to hide their emotions. To avoid feeling, Dalina avoids honesty and intimacy with men. She reports loving two men at once: "when one was absent t'other had the name, / in my staid hart he present did most moue" (f.I2V). She is rejected by both. In contrast, Fillis loves with constancy. Even so, she does not win; she never shows her thoughts to any but Musella (f.I2V). Thus both the constant and the inconstant suffer, either from ambivalence or from fear, because of the reticence that is considered appropriate female behavior.

Moreover, society discourages women from pursuing action based on open honesty with men. Climena explains that she too lost her lover even though she aggressively followed him. She denies Lissius' charge that she is therefore "Vnfitt, and shamefull" (f.I4). Simena, whom Wroth clearly views as admirable, also castigates Climena for her pursuit of a lover. Both Lissius and Simena question whether Climena, who confesses this earlier love, can now love Lissius as much as does Simena, who loved only him (ff.I3-I4V).

Dalina's answer to the question of whether Climena's love can be sincere is appropriate to her own history as a woman who deceived two lovers at once. She argues that women err if they openly pursue their lovers: "lett them once see you coming; then they fly / butt strangly looke, and they'll for pitty cry." Simena recognizes this coy game to be "folly" (f.I3V). Nonetheless, the play's protagonists still maintain that appropriate feminine behavior in love involves a subtle pursuit which appears akin to the dishonest reluctance in love that Dalina advises. Appropriate behavior evidently involves a deliberately planned strategy of entrapment that will seem an accidental meeting to its male object.

Wroth shows that Renaissance women recognized a barely visible line that existed between proper and improper behavior, between self-assertion and self-sacrifice, deceit and openness. The audience can easily sympathize with the overly assertive Climena in spite of the male and female protagonists' objections to her. When Lissius rejects Climena as unfit because of her inappropriate pursuit of her first lover, we support her angry response that the only way she has shamed herself was in desiring him (f.14).

At the point Lissius and Simena both chastise the independent Climena, Wroth demonstrates that women face enormous difficulties when they try to determine their own destinies. However, Wroth's protagonists are expressing the dominant seventeenth-century view of "unruly women" as they castigate Climena. Perhaps this conflict between audience sympathies and the views of the protagonists suggests that Wroth was "at strife against herself." Such "contrary instincts" of self and society, according to Virginia Woolf, would necessarily affect the creativity of any woman "born with a gift of poetry in the sixteenth century." We can see Wroth's contrary instincts also expressed in the contradictions within the independent Silvesta, who insists on living her own life apart from men, while still restricting to passivity all women who love men: "indeed a woman to make loue is ill" (f.IIV). Silvesta advises her friend Musella to acquiesce in the conventional female role in courtly love—to display pity for the suffering lover and thus reveal that she cares. Musella will win Philisses, according to Silvesta, if she nurtures him in his woe as he "walks in this place, and heer alone doth cry / against his lyfe, and your [Musella's] great cruelty" (f.IIV).

Silvesta's advice to Musella probably disappoints most modern readers, especially since Silvesta is a woman who has rejected games of love totally. The behavior she advises may seem both dishonest and self-abusive, since she is advising that women conquer in love by ignoring their own pain. Yet Wroth's advocacy of female modesty and dedication to nurturance is at least predicated on the possibility that women may choose whom to nurture. Furthermore, as the plot develops, reluctance to confess love harms everyone; Musella asks Philisses, "why did you . . . hide your loue, / . . . now 't'is allmost to late your wish to gaine?" (f.I6).

Wroth's *Urania* contains many tales that reveal the snares of romantic love. In her play only Silvesta similarly emphasizes its failings. Yet in both works Wroth emphasizes the importance of attending to the feelings of women since she makes it clear through her mockery of Rustick as he woos Musella that romantic love by definition must be shared. By positing romantic love as a requisite for marriage, Wroth emphasizes women's right to choose their own marriages, to experience personal victory in love and life rather than to be chained to rustic clowns by family duty. Many episodes in *Urania* suggest that women should be free from parental compulsion to marry; similarly, *Love's Victorie* does not make romance a woman's only option. Silvesta suggests that chastity is important to women, not because it is moral and not because it is the only route to a good marriage, but because it leads to freedom.

When Musella charges that Silvesta is chaste only because she was rejected by Philisses, Silvesta answers that Philisses' inability to love her gave her the opportunity to learn the advantages of independence. She pities Musella whom she sees as "bound," and she now believes that a relationship with a man is less beneficial for women than is the freedom given by celibacy (f.II). In a brilliant song Philisses elevates the sovereignty of both love and reason (f.8V); but Silvesta has refused to risk loss of any rationality and rejects all "loues changings" as "blind foulery" that enslaves (f.IV). Rosalind, longing for Orlando in *As You Like It,* urges Phoebe to kneel and "thank heaven . . . for a good man's love" (3.5.57-58); Silvesta in contrast knows women can live alone and seek their own goals independent of men.

Silvesta's celibacy is one source of suspense in *Love's Victorie.* After Venus' insistence on total surrender to love in the prologues to both Act 1 and Act 2, the audience must question whether Venus will conquer both the celibate Silvesta and the Forester, who confined himself to satisfying his love for her by merely looking. We expect their surrender because the Forester speaks in terms common to courtly love poems: "Alas deere nimph, why fly you still my sight?" Other characters too place this pair in conventional roles: "what pleasure doe you take to mock att loue. . . . Sweet Nimph haue pitty or hee dies for thee" (f.6). The unfulfilled audience expectation—that all the lovers will marry at the end of the play—enables Wroth to intensify "new images" (f.3) of love. When Wroth depicts the Forester as loving Silvesta enough to respect her celibacy, she also points out that the friendship of a woman can mean as much as romantic love even to a man. In addition, in Act 5, Silvesta's willingness to risk death for Musella's release demonstrates Wroth's view that loyalty to friends may involve for women a love that is as strong as any romantic desire.

The Huntington manuscript ends with the opening section of Act 5 in which Musella determines to die rather than live her life in a forced marriage. In the conclusion another new image of love emerges in parental willingness to permit children to determine their own fates: Act 5 gives a happy ending to the love story of Sir Philip Sidney and Lady Penelope Rich.

Seventeenth-century readers had little doubt that Astrophil and Stella were Sir Philip Sidney and Lady Penelope Devereux Rich. According to William A. Ringler Jr., five of seven dedications to Lady Rich between 1594 and 1606 connect her with Astrophil. Wroth's own interest in narrating family love relationships, apparent also in *Urania* (Roberts, HLQ, 166), may have been heightened by her uncle's poems with their "narrative and psychological progression," that [William] Ringler describes [in *The Poems of Sir Philip Sidney*] as "more dramatic . . . than any other in the renaissance." Sidney's contemporaries also noted the theatricality of Sidney's sonnet sequence. As early as 1591 Thomas Nashe, in his Preface to Thomas Newman's edition, described *Astrophil and Stella* as a "Theater of pleasure . . . a paper stage streud with pearle, an artifical heav'n . . . while the tragicommody of loue is performed by starlight." Nashe uses theater metaphors to define "The argument cruell chastitie, the Prologue hope, the Epilogue dispaire." Nashe even imagines that Sidney "in the ashes of thy Loue, liuest againe like the *Phoenix.*" Wroth's play stages Nashe's vision of the resurrected lovers.

Wroth leaves no doubt about the source of her pastoral's plot. As Josephine Roberts points out, the male protagonist is called Philisses, an anagram of Philip Sidney, who called himself Philisides in the old and the new *Arcadia.* Sidney's Stella becomes Philisses' beloved Musella, whose name puns on the muse Sidney found in Penelope or Stella. In addition, Wroth refers to Musella as a "star" (ff.12, 19V) just as Sidney had alluded to Penelope Rich, and she imitates Sidney's puns on Lord Rich's name when Musella laments she is "beestowd . . . to bace . . . riches" (f.21). One of Philisses' early speeches (f.2) is even a "self-conscious imitation" of Sidney's sonnet on runaway love in *Astrophil and Stella.* Furthermore, Wroth links her play with the Sidney family, as Roberts also notes, by naming her characters in anagrams. Simena is an anagram for Mary Sidney Lady Herbert, the Countess of Pembroke, who was Sidney's sister and Wroth's aunt. Simena's lover Lissius represents the Countess of Pembroke's lover, Dr. Lister. Lady Penelope Rich was a friend of the Sidney family from her youth until her death. Her father Walter Devereux is said to have hoped Sir Philip "myght matche with my daughter," but the agreement that existed between the families was broken off. Yet even after her marriage to Lord Rich, her contacts with Sir Philip continued, as we know from Lady Penelope's appearance in *Astrophil and Stella* possessed by the "rich foole" (sonnet 24).

Lady Penelope's relationship to Lady Mary's family had many bonds that caused continued contact after Sir Philip's death in 1586. Sir Philip's uncle and Lady Mary's great-uncle married Lady Penelope's mother. His aunt and Lady Mary's great-aunt, the Countess of Huntington, was her guardian. Lady Penelope's brother, Robert Devereux, the Earl of Essex, was a friend of Sir Robert Sidney, Philip's brother and Lady Mary's father. According to a letter from Sir Robert Sidney's secretary, Lady Penelope supported Sir Robert's attempts to persuade Queen Elizabeth I to allow him to return home from Flushing in the Netherlands during the 1590s. She and Lord Mountjoy, her long-time lover and second husband, were godparents of Lady Mary's brother, Robert Sidney. The Rich and Sidney families remained politically and socially allied for several generations, and Lady Penelope clearly maintained her interest in the whole Sidney family until her death in 1607.

Wroth had good reason to see Lady Penelope as a model for the protagonist of a play whose heroine is betrothed unwillingly. Married at age eighteen, Lady Penelope protested "at the solemnity" that she was marrying against her will. Although Lord Rich was a supporter of Sir Robert Sidney's interests in the 1590s when Lady Mary was a baby, Wroth's loyalties would probably have been to Lady Rich after the Riches divorced, because Lady Rich was a friend of Wroth's mother. In addition, because Lord Robert Rich was well known to be a Puritan, even the Archbishop who scolded Lady Penelope for her sexual behavior dismissed Lord Rich to "go amongst his Puritans".

Apparently, her contemporaries accepted the illicit relationship between Lady Rich and Lord Mountjoy during her marriage to Lord Rich. But her subsequent remarriage to Mountjoy defied church law and custom; it scandalized the king enough for Mountjoy to write "A Discourse or Appologie . . . in defence of his marriage with the Lady Rich." However, by the time Wroth wrote *Love's Victorie,* Penelope Rich was long dead and William Laud, the clergyman who officiated at the second marriage, was a bishop (even becoming Archbishop of Canterbury in 1633). Thus a play that presented Lady Penelope's first marriage as inherently undesirable would probably have been acceptable to most of its aristocratic audience, including the Sidneys and their friends. Lady Penelope's son Robert Rich, Earl of Warwick, was aligned with the Sidneys in the 1620s during the struggle for control of the Virginia company; but his political power and that of his friends may have demanded that he separate himself from his aged father's Puritanism by accepting it as one more aberration of a harmless fool, even a rustic. When Lady Mary wrote her play to delight her intimates, she freely took Sir Philip Sidney's stance in *Astrophil and Stella* that Lord Rich was a "rich fool" and mocked him through the clown Rustick.

By the 1620s the legend of Astrophil and Stella had become public enough to make its reworking in *Love's Victorie* a source of pleasure to the Sidney circle in private performances. The audiences of *Love's Victorie* perhaps needed to believe as the author did that Penelope's family—like Musella's and like Lady Mary Wroth's— meant no harm when they forced marriage upon her. Yet the fact that the play was never published may suggest that Lady Wroth, already hurt by the scandal of *Urania,* wished to protect herself and her family from further public display of private injuries.

Perhaps Lady Wroth rewrote the story of Sir Philip and Lady Penelope to include their self-determined marriage because her own life had been narrowly defined by limitations gender imposed upon her status, her financial well-being, and her creative talents. Ben Jonson said to Drummond that Lady Mary was unworthily wed to Robert Wroth. [Josephine] Roberts believes that Lady Mary Wroth and William Herbert, the Earl of Pembroke, had two children. If these two conjectures are correct, Wroth would surely have had strong sympathies for Lady Penelope Rich, the old friend of her mother who also flaunted convention by having children before she married their father. If Lady Mary performed the part of Musella and the Earl of Pembroke played the part of Philisses, perhaps in *Love's Victorie* they fulfilled their own dream of a relationship accepted by society.

Wroth's *Love's Victorie* enlarges the pastoral conception of love's conquests. For Wroth, submission to the gods of love as demanded by Venus (f.20V) requires that parents love their children enough to believe them chaste and allow them to marry as they wish. In the prologue to Act 5, Cupid says that he can feel victorious only when some have experienced more pain. Among those who suffer is Musella's mother as Silvesta aids Musella to escape forced marriage through drinking a potion. When resurrected by Venus, Musella and Philisses have experienced both the death caused by forced marriage and the cathartic resurrection of real love. Their bodies on the altar, like Romeo and Juliet's in the tomb, make graphically clear the destruction that families can create when, because of mistrust, they force the young to disregard personal desires. But at the end of pastoral, fantasy can be fulfilled. Even Rustick, the most stupid of men, agrees that Musella should be free to marry the man she loves.

Through Diana's votary Silvesta and through Venus' votaries, the young lovers Musella and Philisses, Wroth uses the conventional Renaissance trope of chaste love to point out that women can recognize the advantages of virtue and loyalty; they do not need authoritarian control. Thus Wroth's vision of Arcadia in *Love's Victorie* embodies a fantasy that makes life acceptable, a fantasy that people can in fact control their own fortunes if they are determined enough to love strongly and live freely.

Anne Shaver (essay date 1991)

SOURCE: "A New Woman of Romance," in *Modern Language Studies,* Vol. XXI, No. 4, Fall, 1991, pp. 63-77.

[*In the following excerpt, Shaver examines Wroth's female protagonists, observing the ways in which they assert power within the strict behavioral confines of the feminine Renaissance ideal.*]

An examination of Pamphilia, the cynosure and central character of the Lady Mary Wroth's romance *Urania,* shows to how great an extent her author appears to have internalized the Renaissance ideal of womanhood with its insistence on chastity above all, then silence and obedience. On the other hand, Wroth's women characters also embody glimmerings of new kinds of political, poetic, and persuasive powers just becoming available to women as well as men. Pamphilia suppresses her impulses to power or disguises them as something more acceptable; she keeps her most extreme transgression, her writing, very private. Other women, like Nereana, who try to exercise undisguised power, are usually presented as eccentrics who risk public shame, punishment and even insanity. Pamphilia, however, for all her conventional perfections, finally subverts the ideal in another way: she carries the patriarchal idea of feminine virtue to fiercely independent extremes.

Lady Mary Wroth published *The Countesse of Montgomery's Urania,* a long but unfinished prose romance, in 1621. Almost immediately objections to its publication were raised by Edward Denny, Baron of Waltham, who fancied that he saw himself and his family's private affairs pilloried in the episode of Seralius and his father-in-law, and the book may have been partially suppressed. A continuation, which follows the heroines and heroes of the romance into the next generation but also is without formal ending, exists only in a single holography copy held by the Newberry Library. Josephine A. Roberts, editor of Wroth's poems, is presently at work on an edition of both parts of the romance; meanwhile the text of the published *Urania* is available from Brown University's Women Writers Project. Seminars, conference papers and publications that comment on it have begun to appear.

The earliest published reaction to the *Urania,* when critics noticed it at all, was to dismiss it as an impoverished derivative of Sidney's *Arcadia,* but recently scholars have realized that the ways in which the niece's romance is different from her uncle's are significant, and have begun to disagree in interesting ways about how Wroth's work may best be understood. Gary Waller, in the 1977 introduction to [*Pamphilia to Amphilanthus*] his edition of her sonnets, emphasizes its Jacobean anomie, the "disillusioned amorality, where betrayal, loss, and infidelity are accepted with resignation as inevitable," in contrast with the moral tone and conventional romance closure of the *Arcadia.* Josephine Roberts [in her *The Poems of Lady Mary Wroth*] agrees with Waller that the *Urania* depicts a court life "rife with corruption and villainy," but claims that the important difference from the *Arcadia* is its intense focus on love to the virtual exclusion of conventional romance heroics. Comparing the two Renaissance romances has begun a continuing interest in Wroth's text as the voice of a woman writing about woman's experiences. Lyn Swift and Elaine Beilin [in *Redeeming Eve*] both have claimed that Mary Wroth holds conservative views about women's roles, though Swift, who says "the *Urania* makes marriage the only reward for women's merit and therefore desirable inspite of its pain," questions her own premise by pointing out that the fiercely autonomous unmarried character Nereana is both the heroine's antithesis and an example of how "women may be justifiably angry at society," while Beilin prefers to emphasize that "in her main character, Pamphilia, Wroth created another variation on a familiar figure, the true Christian woman." Very recently, essays have appeared from readers who

find Wroth a more subversive critic of Jacobean misogyny than either Swift or Beilin do. Naomi Miller points out her focus on female friendship, while Jeff Masten and Maureen Quilligan are most interested in the project the author shares with her heroine, the effort to find an authentic voice as a woman writer. The *Urania,* which may well be the last English romance as it is also the first English novel, still awaits its share of genre studies. For all these reasons and more, excitement is growing about this soon not to be rare book.

One reason is the literary and historical centrality of Wroth's family connections. Niece of the Countess of Pembroke and of Sir Philip Sidney, daughter of Robert Sidney of Penshurst and Barbara Gamage, young Mary Sidney was presented at court near the end of Elizabeth's reign, and acted in masques at the court of King James. Ben Jonson, among a large number of contemporary writers, knew and admired her poetry. These connections, however, impeded appreciation of the *Urania* itself until recently, because of its being dismissed as a pale imitation of Sidney's *Arcadia.* One need only read the first page to see that this is probably not so, since the shepherdess Urania, whose absent ideality haunts the beginning of the *New Arcadia,* is present and very real in the *Urania*'s opening paragraphs. Indeed, all of Wroth's imitations are in the service of something very different: the world of romance from a seventeenth-century woman's point of view.

Generically, the *Urania* is a repository of the old and the start of something new. It inherits conventions from medieval romance, Renaissance pastoral fiction, dynastic epic, and Petrarchan love poetry, but it is also one of the earliest psychological novels, in which thinly veiled autobiography and daring passages of *roman a clef* are undisguised by allegory. Fragments of the dozens of stories embedded in the central narrative imitate Malory and his French originals, Spenser and his magic landscapes, Sidney and his stories of generational conflict of love. On the other hand, that its author is a woman, "and therefore not much to be marked," probably made possible the astonishing degree of psychological realism and just plain gossip that this seventeenth century narrative adds to the romance tradition.

Similarly, Wroth's utterly chaste, reputedly silent, and conventionally obedient heroine subverts the ideal embodied in the traditional woman of romance. Pamphilia's chastity is presented as neither religious nor dynastic, but rather as synonymous with her constancy to her love for her cousin, the matchless Amphilanthus. Her choices are virginity or marriage; as she will not marry anyone but Amphilanthus, and he remains elusive, virginity is a given. She evades her father's desire that she wed Leandrus, a dynastically suitable prince, by quoting Elizabeth Tudor's claim that she has espoused her country. Unlike Queen Elizabeth, however, Queen Pamphilia—and her creator Mary Wroth—is apparently more interested in love than in politics. Furthermore, she is arguably more interested in defining herself than in love, though love is necessary, Pamphilia says, to that definition. Other young queens marry and give control of their holdings to their husbands, but the country of Pamphilia would be an after dinner mint for Amphilanthus, Emperor by acclamation of Germany and most of Italy. Pamphilia does not want to win Amphilanthus by political means, even if such were possible; she wants him to acknowledge that she herself is matchless and to love her for her excellence, just as she does him.

As time goes by, and Amphilanthus' broad travels and demanding acts of heroism give him continued scope for his attraction to various women, a chaste and unilateral constancy becomes more and more the means by which Pamphilia defines herself. Her natural propensity to "daintinesse and feare," pointed out to her by the seeress Mellissea joins with Amphilanthus' unavailability to lock her into a longterm maidenhood. Although she professes to envy her friends, sister, and cousin, whose lovers all become their husbands, there is also evidence that she scorns their willingness to settle for less than perfection. Even when she has Amphilanthus' undivided attention, however, she avoids inviting behavior, shying away from his invitations to speak freely of her feelings, expressing—not clearly, and only to herself and the reader—her unwillingness to risk the public humiliation of his possible lack of interest and probable defection.

Thus for Pamphilia chastity and self-protective restraint become as inextricable as chastity and reputation. One of Amphilanthus' previous adventures includes a meeting with a strange household made up of a complacent husband, a chaste wife, and her passionate but chaste lover who is also her cousin. These cousin-lovers are completely fulfilled and happy with daily meetings and conversation, with looking at each other and occasionally enjoying an innocent kiss. Seeing this, Amphilanthus wishes he could have the same good fortune. It is a strange desire for a man so virile; it is, however, probably what Pamphilia would have if she could, or what Wroth would have for her heroine. Perhaps the taint of incest somewhat influences her desire for passion without sexual contact, love without marriage. But Pamela's chastity is also based upon her desire to be herself, discreet, discrete and constant to an idea of excellence not even the "matchlesse prince" can live up to.

Chastity, although it is enjoined on women by both religious and secular patriarchal society, can also be a practice that intelligent women embrace willingly, not simply out of resignation. Reputation is certainly a matter of social life or death in the enclosed society of a court; it can even stand between life and starvation. Beyond such practical considerations, however, is the tenuous hold on a separate self available to women of this time. Daughters, wives, mothers of men, the most illustrious shine primarily as the pride of their patriarchal houses. For example, in delineating the talent and intelligence of the Queen of Naples, the narrator caps her compliments by saying that such a woman is worthy to be the mother of Amphilanthus. The few women who hold countries in their own names surrender land and title gladly to the men, usually landless younger sons, who marry them. Pamphilia never says she does not want to do that, but she also never says she does, and, disappointed in love as she may be, by remaining single she is never faced with having to.

There are a number of things that Pamphilia never says. This discreetest of princesses is presented as an ideal of feminine verbal restraint, and it is true that she manages never to make public her love for Amphilanthus while all about her are advertising their passions to the world. In the first Book, her constant companion is the princess Antissia, Amphilanthus' then current lady. While it is no wonder she does not make her rival her confidante, her discretion is in high contrast with Antissia's impassioned adoration which, as Amphilanthus' affection toward her cools and shifts toward his cousin, rises to a pitch of jealous frenzy.

Like her creator, Pamphilia speaks through her poetry, containing her sorrow mostly in the discipline of sonnets and the simple measures of ballad quatrains. Although she is usually reluctant to share these poems, she has achieved a reputation for them, and a reputation for encouraging and enjoying the writings of others. This is a form of expression becoming increasingly available to women; Amphilanthus' mother, the Queen of Naples, also has earned fame as a writer and patron of poetry. Pamphilia's writing is a major part of her sense of who she is, both because she takes a craftswoman's pride in it and because its subject is herself and a subjective exploration of the way love makes her feel. She suppresses it by keeping it mostly private; nonetheless what belief she has in her own worth is partly tied to her reputation as a writer. Women writing: this is a far more realistic power than those wielded by other women characters in romance—Morgan's sorcery, Cecropia's brutality, or Britomart's disguising as a knight—and one with a far greater potential for subversion of the established order.

Pamphilia speaks socially and politically, as well. In fact, it is remarkable that she has achieved such a reputation for discretion, given her willingness to express strong opinions. Her very first words in the romance are saucy ones in response to Amphilanthus' praise of Antissia's beauty: essentially what she says is that some people might admire the type. Her message is clear to the prince, who teases her about her sharp and envious tongue. Later, when the young men decide to free Meriana and reclaim Macedonia before making a major assault on Albania, Pamphilia participates as a tactician in changing the battle plans. She talks her father out of marrying her to Leandrus, but spends even more time and wit persuading Leandrus himself that a woman has no need for a man's protection. So cogent is her argument for feminine autonomy that, although we must presume it would not apply if Amphilanthus were the suitor, it seems to be spoken from deep personal conviction. Finally, even when her beloved cousin's unfaithfulness has brought her to despondency, she does not become a bad ruler, but keeps her subjects' love and admiration through her wise counsel and judgements.

Pamphilia also uses the power of words to blow smokescreens in the eyes of those who would know her too closely. Adroit at deflecting direct personal questions, she manages to evade admitting first that she loves, then whom, for quite some time. In daily contact with such self-possession, the passionate Antissia comes to believe that two such excellences as Pamphilia and Amphilanthus cannot exist in the same space without falling in love with each other. In an agony of theoretical jealousy, Antissia sees Rosindy, Pamphilia's younger brother, visit secretly in his sister's private garden, and mistakes him for his cousin. Respecting Rosindy's desire for secrecy, Pamphilia denies quite truthfully that he is Amphilanthus, but her not telling the whole truth drives Antissia wild. Pamphilia engages in such doublespeak quite often, but this particular instance obtains for her, whether she intended it or not, an underhanded revenge on the woman who had once held Amphilanthus' heart. Later, when another companion, Dorilena, presses her to share her personal poetry, Pamphilia puts her off by talking instead about the sad experiences of a woman called Lindamira. Dorilena's response to this tantalizing story is that it is "some thing more exactly related then a fixion", but she is too well brought up to press Pamphilia farther. For all her reputation for ladylike reticence, Pamphilia is a skilled wielder of words.

Obedience in the direct patriarchal sense is not much required of the young queen. Her father is gentle and indulgent; her uncle left her his kingdom of Pamphilia with no strings attached, and she has neither husband nor acknowledged lover who might claim the right to curb her behavior. She does, however, set limits on herself in keeping with what she feels is generally expected of her. Although she is the governing Queen of Pamphilia, she doesn't linger much in her own country, located simply in "Asia," but spends most of her time in her father's household in Morea. One reason for this is that the company is liveliest here, but Pamphilia's asking her parents' permission to leave home and visit her own kingdom also reflects proper behavior in an unmarried daughter. She is recalled to sociability by her cousin the Princess Urania even when her heart is breaking most from Amphilanthus' inconstancy, because she accepts and obeys what is considered gracious behavior in a female member of a royal household. All in all, she puts high value on her reputation for the judgement and discretion that is said to be appropriate to her sex even as it is also praised as unusual.

Her strictest adherence of all, however, is to her own fierce standard of constancy. Nothing, not even his chilliest shunning, his most careless greetings, or his most deliberate mistreatment of her, can make her untrue to her love for her royal cousin. Just as she uses the patriarchal admonition to be chaste to such extremes that she challenges the "traffic in women" which is said to anchor the patriarchy's power, she carries obedience to her chosen ideal of constancy to such lengths that her independence is assured.

Queen Pamphilia, obedient to social expectations and to her own high standards, chaste beyond all ordinary ex-

pectations, and reputed to be discreet if not entirely silent at the same time that she displays enormous power over language, has pride enough to refuse unwanted suitors, but cannot break with social limits and speak first to the man she herself desires. Scornful of what she sees as excessive vanity in women, she cannot quite acknowledge that she deserves what she wants most, or that she has the right to seek it. When men importune reluctant women, as both Steriamus and Leandrus do her, she does not scorn them for presumption, because it is natural that men should want the best and try for it. She simply tries to make them see that she cannot return their love, no matter how deserving they might be. But when a woman demonstrates the self-confidence to claim a man before he speaks, Pamphilia is disturbed, and from the evidence of the fate of such women and from the narrator's comments on them, so is her creator.

And yet the *Urania* is rife with such women: unchaste, outspoken, disobedient, full of the confidence conferred by self-esteem. Although some are evil and none is to be admired as a perfectly virtuous lady by the standards of Wroth's society, they emerge as believable, energetic, and at least partially successful in the projects that they dare to undertake. One in particular deserves close attention, since onto her may well be displaced whatever impulses Mary Wroth might have given her heroine overtly to assert herself and openly to disobey social limits.

Woven into the many admonitory and ambiguous love stories of Book Two and Three are the adventures of Nereana, Princess of Stalamina. The first part of Nereana's story is told by Amphilanthus to his sister Urania and his cousin Pamphilia. It is thus through the eyes of exemplary masculinity that the reader first sees her, and the great prince is not impressed. He tells how he and his companion Steriamus, heir to the Albanian throne, happened onto the island of Stalamina. Here they found the ruler to be a woman, "the most ignorantly proud that euer mine eyes saw." Amphilanthus' illustration of her pride is the story of her pursuit of Steriamus, himself in an agony of love for Pamphilia. Insensitive to Steriamus' desire to be left alone—just as he had been to Pamphilia's similar desire—Nereana woos him with a conventionally masculine argument: that he ought to feel honored to be loved by a princess descended from the kings of Romania who is absolute ruler of this island. When he scorns her boldness and tells her "Twere more credit he was sure for her, to be more sparingly, and silently modest, then with so much boldnesse to proclaime affection to any stranger," she simply calls him a fool "to refuse the profferd loue of a Princesse." To be sure, this argument is more often presented by a suitor to his lady's father than to the lady herself, but in the bargains between men, it is usually effective. Steriamus next attempts to silence her by extolling Pamphilia and declaring that Nereana is not worthy to kiss her feet; saying that Pamphilia is the "perfectest" woman and Nereana is her contrary. Nereana's response to this is to continue to pursue him with attention until he flees, and then, taking a vow of love, to pursue him literally to Morea, where she also wants to have a look at her rival.

All this is narrated by Amphilanthus, whose tone is as scornful as the words he repeats. Pamphilia says that she shrinks from the idea of meeting this woman who hates her so much, but Urania is as fascinated as she would be by any freak of nature: "I wish she were here (said Urania), since it is a rare thing surely to see so amorous a Lady." The story resumes when Nereana does arrive at the Morean court. She finds Steriamus not there, but she explains herself without embarrassment to the king and all assembled, then publicly addresses her rival. Pamphilia's response to Nereana show none of the timidity she had earlier expressed to Amphilanthus; instead it shows an interesting ambivalence. She begins by reflecting the view of both her cousins that this is a prodigy:

> In truth I a[m] sorry, that such a Lady should take so great and painfull a voyage, to so fond an end, being the first that euer I heard of, who took so Kingth-like a search in hand; men being us'd to follow scornefull Ladies, but you to wander after a passionate, or disdainfull Prince, it is great pitie for you.

But then she goes on to express not pity but an ambiguity of encouragement and scorn:

> Yet Madam, so much I praise you for it, as I would incourage you to proceede, since neuer feare of winning him, when so many excellencies may speake for you: as great beauty, high birth, rich possessions, absolute command, and what is most, matchless loue, and loyaltie . . .

Pamphilia assures Nereana that to her knowledge Steriamus "loues not mee," which is rather a polite lie, and that "I affect not him," which is certainly true. "Thus are you secure, that after some more labour you may gaine, what I will not accept, if offered me, so much do I esteeme of your affectionate search."

Nereana is not sure how to react: the words are faultless, but the tone may not quite match them. And no wonder: the list of excellencies Pamphilia acknowledges in Nereana mirror her own qualities, the qualities that she would have Amphilanthus love, but which, because she is the discreetest of women, she cannot parade before him. Nereana, who has no way of knowing Pamphilia's heart, acknowledges the young queen's excellent mind, brushes off the mix of admonitory comments and compliments from the king, and single-mindedly pursues her quest into the surrounding wilderness, where she is soon lost by her attendants.

Although Pamphilia dissociates herself from this astonishing woman, what happens next to Nereana continues to be a weird mirror of Pamphilia's situation. At first, no two women's lives could seem more different: Nereana in open pusuit of a man, Pamphilia determined to conceal the identity of the one she loves; Nereana battered by a storm at sea, Pamphilia enclosed and protected by architecture and ceremony; Nereana wandering alone in wild woods; Pamphilia also alone but in her private garden writing formal verse. But Nereana has a protection that Pamphilia cannot quite match. Although both women have a strong sense of self-worth, Nereana's is virtually unshakable, while Pamphilia's depends on her perception of what others, especially Amphilanthus, think of her.

Still, a wild wood holds dangers that require more than ego strength to withstand. As she wanders and rails, and as her servants search for her in vain, Nereana is captured. Her captor is Allanus, a lover gone mad. Mistaking her for his cruel Liana (whose side of this story Urania will tell later), Allanus tries to embrace her, begging her pardon, offering his, in a chaos of words very like her own railings. Angry and scornful, she does her best to deny that she is his mistress; to his "O pity me" she responds "I hate thee," and these dread words send him into a further fit, from which he emerges no longer believing that she is Liana. Now she must be the goddess of those woods, whether she wants to or not, and to make sure of it, he ties her to a tree. At this point she is so furious, "with rage growing almost as madd as he," she has no power to dissuade or resist his treatment:

> hee vndress'd her, pulling her haire down to the full length; cloathes hee left her none, saue onely one little petticoate of carnation tafatie; her green silke stockin[g]s hee turn'd, or rowld a little downe, making them serue for buskins; garlands hee put on her head, and armes, tucking vp her smock-sleeues to the elbowes, her necke bare, and a wreath of fine flowers he hung crosse from one shoulder vnder the other arme, like a belt, to hang her quiuer in: a white sticke, which he had newly whittled, he put into her hand, instead of a boare speare: then setting her at liberty he kneeled downe, and admired her . . .

It is a brilliant parody of five centuries of woman-worship and fetish-creation, a marvellous cartoon of courtly love's inevitable results, horrid for men and women alike. Creating safe distance from all the dangers of real affection by placing women on pedestals and demanding that they stay there, men create new dangers for themselves: for instance, that such treatment, paralyzing to natural sexual responses in women, will cause a hypertrophy of pride, and that some men will take the fiction of female supremacy so literally that they find themselves relegated to an eternal chaste and passionate adoration, and truly go mad. On the other hand, in an effort to avoid such absurd and dehumanizing treatment, some women harden themselves against even the possibility of reciprocal partnership: Nereana's grotesque adventure mirrors the vulnerability against which Pamphilia would protect herself.

Once she is untied, Nereana takes flight. In the morning, hearing the voice of a knight who has sheltered nearby, she believes she will be rescued, but her own arrogance prevents it. The errant knight, who is Pamphilia's youngest brother Philarchos, at first only teases her because her antic and immodest dress makes him believe her to be insane; when his treatment angers her she insults both him and his sister, and he simply leaves her there. In order to rescue ladies in distress, knights must first recognize them by their humility.

This is illustrated when, after seventy intervening pages of text, she is discovered, still wandering, by Prince Perissus on his way to the siege of Albania. At first, ashamed of her dishevelled state, she hides from him, but because her instincts do run to self-preservation, soon she approaches him humbly. What he sees in her then is "more then ordenary behauior, and a countenance that might carry greatnes with it, and had in it, though shadowed vnder pouerty." When she declared her nobility to Philarchos, he thought she was mad; when she convinced Allanus of it, he left her to it. Now Perissus, an exemplary knight, finds nobility in her humbleness and is pleased by it, enjoying the masculine prerogative of discovering and recreating a fair lady out of this pitiable creature, "carrying her to the Towne, where that night she was to lye, in his owne Charriot which was led spare, she rid thither, where he cloathed her according to her dignity."

Although in telling Perissus her story she had admitted that she owed her situation to her behavior in pursuing Steriamus and scorning Pamphilia only to condemn it, as soon as she is restored to the accoutrements of royalty she regains her more than royal self-esteem. Her rationalizations are absurd: that fortune cast her down only for the honor of raising one so deserving as she, that the adoration of a madman validated her, that Steriamus is now beneath her and King Perissus (in fact married and devoted to his queen) is obviously her slave, suffering because she cannot requite him. "Alas, I faine would helpe it if I could, but constancy (though a foolish vertue) gouerns me." Since at this point she has dismissed Steriamus, saying to herself, "Soare like the Hobby, and scorne to stoop to so poore a prey as Steriamus, who now looks before mine eyes, like a Dorr to a Faulcon; my mind preserued for height, goes vpward, none but the best shall haue liberty to ioyne with me, none Master me," her constancy can only be to her conception of her own self-worth.

But her pride is dealt another harsh blow when she returns to Stalamina only to find that her subjects, tired of both her arrogance and her year-long absence, have replaced her with her younger sister. In earlier years she had imprisoned and threatened her sister; now the new queen and the nobles imprison her, excusing the break in succession by telling the people that she is mad. Her subjects, the narrator tells us, "had suffiecient cause to belieue it, seeing her passions, which though naturall to her, yet appeared to their capacities meere lunatick actions." Here she remains at the end of Book Two. She will appear in the text one more time, near the end of Book Three (the Book in which many, though not all, loose ends are tied), again chastened by deprivation, restored to her throne by a conservative council, "and she deserud their due restoring her proouing an excellent Gouerness, and braue Lady, being able to ouerrule her old passions, & by the[m] to iudge how to fauour, licence, and curb others, & this experience, though late, is most profitable to Princes." As no further mention is made of her former desire for Steriamus, it can be assumed that love is among the passions successfully overruled. Nereana is just one of many examples of the way in which women in Wroth's world have to choose between a kingdom and a man and, by not far-fetched analogy, between love and independence. With no husband to indulge her or curb her, she ends up without love, but she becomes a responsible ruler for her people with a firm hold on her rightful throne. If she has been tamed by misfortune, she is still autonomous. Although her author could not approve of her, she could imagine her and let her live.

Nereana's resilient if often absurd self-confidence puts Pamphilia's wavering self-image into vivid relief. This is not to say that the young queen is without self-esteem: she is proud of her reputation as the discreetest of princesses, of her ability to control her own behavior, of her talent for writing. But this pride, appropriate to her noble nature, has a soft middle. Because story after story in the first two Books, many of which she hears or even observes unfold, show the dangers to women of letting their passions be publicly known, it is not surprising that she is slow to let anyone, even Amphilanthus himself, find out how she feels about him. But when she finally does, and he betrays her with Musalina, even though her passion is still far from a public matter she is devastated. It is not a matter of public shame, but of private self-doubt. Her cure for this is a hypertrophy of virtue.

Alone, she pours out her heart in chaotic contradiction, blaming him, blaming herself, blaming fortune. But every time she turns her anger outward to the man who is causing her pain, she quickly draws it in again, even if no one is listening. If another is sounding her, she is even more guarded, dissembling to his mother, the Queen of Naples, "because her spirit disdained to say she was lost, but most because she could not say so, but the saying blemished his worth." This motif reappears in a more extreme form when Meriana's innocent gossip about Amphilanthus' many love affairs tears at Pamphilia's heart. The young queen thinks to herself, "I could almost be brought to tell her [about her secret heartache] my selfe, and would, were it not to discouer his forgetfulnes and cruelty; but rather than my lips shall giue the least way to discouer any fault in him, I wil conceale all though they breake my heart; and if I only could be saued by accusing him, I sooner would be secret and so dye." Finally, when Urania is urging reason on her, saying she should openly scorn any man who truly mistreated her, and would say so "though I knew it were mine owne brother had caused this mischiefe," Pamphilia's response is that as his sister Urania ought "to hide, or couer his imperfections" if he were faulty, which she does not admit.

In her own chaotic thoughts, she does often accuse him, but each time she does she offers instant retraction, usually in the form of self-blame. At first this is urgent: tell me what I've done! Was it because I went to sea? I only did it at the urging of others. He is perfect, she believes, therefore his defection must be her fault. But she knows she has done nothing wrong, so she must simply be deficient. News of his glorious coronation comes from Germany: "nothing did she see or heare, but still of his glory and his loue. This was once, said shee, belonging vnto me, but I was not worthy of them, sure else he had-not alter'd." On and on this goes:

> Did I reiect the firme, and spotles loue of that excellent Prince Steriamus, the humble suites of all the greatest subiects and neighbor Princes, slighted the earnestnesse of the noble Prince Leandrus, refused all, and made myselfe a Vassall in affection to him, that weighes neither mee, nor these expressions of loue? I haue done all this, and I yet haue not done enough; for, O how worthy is he?

"I will truly and religiously confess, I am not worthy of you," she says a little later to an imaginary Amphilanthus, first cursing the self-confidence that led her to think she was, then assuring him that she would be worthy if she could, but that she does not wish the glory of such worthiness for herself, but only for his sake, so he could have someone to love who truly deserves him. She goes on to suggest that perhaps her constant and passionate suffering has made her worthy, then cries that he has done her no offence, "for I am yours, and may not you dispose of yours, as best doth like your selfe?" She ends this confessional with the thought that if he hears she has died, "your matchlesse heart may be content to let a sad thought hold you for a while, and if so, too too much for mee, who still do wish your blessednesse." It seems she must maintain Amphilanthus' worth to insure the worthiness of her declared obsession at the same time that she must use his special flaw to insure her own martyrdom, the saintly suffering that validates and excuses her unfeminine authonomy.

Urania, Pamphilia's cousin, Amphilanthus' sister and contented wife to be of Steriamus, has a simpler response. Sympathizing with Pamphilia's suffering and scorning her brother's bad behavior, she desires for Pamphilia the same clearheaded and deep but lighthearted love she herself has found, and tries to talk her out of this heart's prison. But Pamphilia is adamant; if she is unworthy of Amphilanthus in every other way, at least she outdoes him in constancy. To this she clings, an *idee fixe,* because without it there can be no Pamphilia. Twice Urania tries, twice her cousin answers her in much the same way, first asking her not to make her more unhappy, which, she says, "I shall bee, if I let in that worthless humour change, which I can neuer doe till I can change my selfe, and haue new creation and another soule; for this is true and loyall." In their second encounter, Pamphilia again claims that if she fails in her constancy, she will not be herself, but the context is more complex. Urania accuses Pamphilia of idolatry, saying she is worshipping love as a god when he is really nothing but a presumptuous child, charming if well-used and handled sensibly. Pamphilia replies by proving Urania to be correct, but her language is ambiguous. Almost from the start of this reply, "he" is not "loue" but Amphilanthus, then becomes "loue" and Amphilanthus at once, confirming Urania's accusation:

> Alasse my friend said she, how sorry am I your excelle[n]t counsell is bestowed on one so little deseruing it, as not being able to right it by following it, which I am not able to doe, but some answere I must make to you, I am so wholy his as it is past mistaking, the wound being giuen mee deeply by his vnkindnes which martyrs mee. . . . To leaue him for being false, would shew my loue was not for his sake, but mine owne, that because he loued me, I therefore loued him, but when hee leaues, I can doe soe to. O noe deere Cousen, I loued him for him selfe, and would haue loued him had hee not loued mee, and will loue though he dispise me; this is true loue. . . . Pamphilia must be of a new composition before she can let such thoughts fall into her constant breast, which is a Sanctuary of zealous affection, and so well hath loue instructed me, as I can neuer leaue my master nor his precepts, but still maintaine a vertuous constancy.

During their previous encounter, Urania had said to her cousin, "Change . . . deserues no honour; but discretion may make you discerne when you should bee constant and when discreete, and then you doe not change but continue, iudiciall as alwayes you haue beene"; in the second, in the midst of a much longer lecture, Urania asks, "Where is that iudgement, and discreet govern'd spirit, for which this and all other places happy with the knowledge of your name, hath made you famous? . . . Call your powers together, you that haue been admired for a Masculine spirit, will you descend below the poorest Femenine in loue?" This is reasonable, but it does no good. Pamphilia is not in search of easy pleasure. Preferring the self-esteem she has conjured out of constancy, she has tossed out both Urania's notion of discretion and Amphilanthus himself. Her love for him has been the way she represented a desire to be his acknowledged equal and, if not that, to overgo him through exercise of the one virtue he does not have.

Thus she remains, though not in the sense Urania understands it, discrete. If she cannot be one with the matchless prince by annexing him and putting on his power, she will at least be self-defined in her monomania, a woman writer all alone making sonnets of her sorrow and the matchless constancy she has declared synonymous with her being. Furthermore, her story is told by yet another woman writer for whom the relations between men and women are not a patriarchal given—as they are in the medieval romances where the best knight wins the most beautiful lady as his rightful prize, even if she is married to his liege or his uncle—but matter for detailed examination. Inventing some women characters like Nereana who are overtly unchaste, foolishly outspoken, and clumsily disobedient, she punishes them in varying degrees, but in Pamphilia she invents a subversive, suffering rebel who gets away with an autonomy she can blame on male "perfection." Censored by courtiers made uncomfortable by stories "more exactly related then a fixion," Mary Wroth invents a heroine whose chastity is so fierce and so artfully defined as constancy that the two great transgressions she shares with her creator, daring to write and refusing to wed (Wroth, widowed at 27, never remarries), have a chance of slipping by unremarked. The *Urania* is most innovative in its focus on the psychology of women, on their mixed responses to a society that both represses them and offers them unprecedented possibilities for secular self-expression.

Barbara K. Lewalski (essay date 1991)

SOURCE: "Mary Wroth's *Love's Victory* and Pastoral Tragicomedy," in *Reading Mary Wroth: Representing Alternatives in Early Modern England,* edited by Naomi J. Miller and Gary Waller, The University of Tennessee Press, 1991, pp. 88-109.

[*Lewalski provides a brief history of the pastoral tragicomedy and discusses the influence of this tradition in Wroth's* Love's Victory.]

Mary Wroth's pastoral tragicomedy, *Love's Victory,* has recently been published for the first and only time; it was unknown except to a small contemporary coterie, and is still virtually unread. Only one complete manuscript is extant, at Penshurst; the Huntington Library has a partial manuscript. Both are holograph. The date of composition is uncertain: Wroth's editors, Josephine Roberts and Michael J. Brennan, suggest the 1620s on the strength of a few parallels to an early section of the unpublished second part of Wroth's *Urania,* extant only in one manuscript at the Newberry Livrary. We know more about Wroth than about most women writers of the Elizabethan and Jacobean era . . . but we know next to nothing about this drama. It might have been written for performance at private theatricals at the Wroths' country estate at Durrants in Enfield but there is no record of such performance. Nor are there other contemporary records to supply context, nor any contemporary, or subsequent criticism of the work. As with much other Renaissance women's writing now being uncovered, we are made to encounter here the thing itself, the bare, unaccommodated text.

Margaret McLaren's useful essay ["An Unknown Contient," in *English Literary Renaissance,* 19, 1989] (based only on the incomplete Huntington manuscript) focuses on the intersection and at times conflict of several discourses: courtly Petrarchanism and Neoplatonism, comedic satire, myth and ritual, and what she calls "a special language of avoidance" papering over the increasing powerlessness of women at James's court. Carolyn Swift, using both manuscripts, reads the drama as a dream of female empowerment and autonomy compensating for Wroth's own frustrations in love, and makes the plausible (though I think too restrictive) argument that it rewrites the Philip Sidney—Penelope Rich relationship with a happy ending. I mean to examine here the evidence of deliberate genre transformation to suggest a bolder thesis: that Wroth's drama encodes an implicit feminist politics emphasizing the values of female agency, egalitarianism, female friendship, and community, a politics which subverts both the norms of the genre and of Jacobean society.

Happily, genre affords a useful entrée for Wroth's drama, since this work is carefully positioned within the complex genre systems and codes of the Renaissance literary institution. The few parallels between *Love's Victory* and the manuscript continuation of *Urania* highlight the difference in genre. Both have a band of shepherds smitten with Love, but in the romance they are royalty and nobility in shepherd guise, led by a brother and sister famed for poetry; in the drama they are true shepherds who share alike in poetry and leadership. There are a few parallel characters—Rustick, Dalinea/Magdalaine, Arcas—though Arcas is a faithful knight in the romance and in the drama a mean-spirited slander-mongering shepherd. *Love's Victory* is much more usefully contextualized in relation to pastoral tragicomedy, a mixed genre especially popular at the Renaissance courts of Italy, France, and England. Comparison with these texts allows us to inspect the literary and political choices Wroth's drama incorporates.

The label itself—pastoral tragicomedy—points up the multiplicity and complexity of the generic codes which can intersect in a given Renaissance text. This new, mixed kind was usually seen as a development from pastoral eclogue. These brief dialogic poems were usually classified as "dramatic" in systems deriving from Plato's and Aristotle's three kinds of imitation or representation. In schemes deriving from the Alexandrian *Canons,* Horace, Cicero and Quintilian, pastoral was classed with epic because written in hexameter, providing a basis for Renaissance claims that it can include or covertly treat great persons and events; the canonical pastoral writers were Theocritus and Virgil. This influential system reinforced the central importance of model texts and authors to Renaissance conceptions of genre.

Pastoral eclogues held an anomalous position in Renaissance systems that identify many particular historical genres (or *kinds,* the Renaissance term) by formal and thematic elements, *topoi,* and conventions. In Puttenham's highly politicized system [described in his *The Arte of English Poesie*] these kinds were arranged hierarchically according to nobility of subjects and persons treated, and height of style; pastoral eclogues (though not the most ancient kind of poetry) are associated with the life and first literary activities of the lowly, presenting

> in base and humble stile by maner of Dialogue . . . the private and familiar talke of the meanest sort of men, as shepheards, heywards, and such like . . . the first familiar conversation, and their babble and talk under bushes and shadie trees, the first disputation and contentious reasoning . . . the first idle wooings and their songs made to their mates or paramours, either upon sorrow or jolity of courage, the first amorous musicks, sometime also they sang and played on their pipes for wagers . . . no doubt the shepheards life was the first example of honest fellowship, their trade the first art of lawful acquisition or purchase. (sigs Eiiv)

Yet he also described eclogue as the creation of sophisticated poets, who often used it for moral teaching (Mantuan) or for covert political commentary (Virgil):

> The Poet devised the *Eclogue* . . . not of purpose to counterfait or represent the rusticall manner of loves and communication: but under the vaile of homely persons, and in rude speeches to insinuate and glaunce at greater matters, and such as perchance had not bene safe to have been disclosed in any other sort, which may be perceived by the Eclogues of *Virgill* in which

are treated by figure matters of greater importance than the loves of *Titirus* and *Corydon*. (Fiiiv-Fiv)

In the Renaissance, pastoral became a mode, interpenetrating works or parts of works in several genres. We find not only pastoral eclogues but also pastoral songs, pastoral dramas of various kinds, pastoral funeral elegies, pastoral entertainments and masques, pastoral romances, pastoral episodes in epics (as in Tasso's *Gerusalemme Liberata* and especially Spenser's *Faerie Queene* VI). Sidney evidently thought of it as a mode participating in several genres (eclogue, tale, romance) and emphasized the uses of pastoral for moral teaching and for covert political commentary, instancing Virgil's First Eclogue [in his *The Defense of Poesie*]:

> Is the poore pipe disdained, which sometimes out of *Moelibeus* mouth can shewe the miserie of people, under hard Lords and ravening souldiers? And again by *Titerus,* what blessednesse is derived, to them that lie lowest, from the goodness of them that sit highest? Sometimes under the prettie tales of Woolves and sheepe, can enclude the whole considerations of wrong doing and patience.

The politics of pastoral has been much studied recently— by Louis Montrose as a vehicle for Elizabethan courtiership; by Stephen Orgel [in his *The Illusion of Power*] as a *locus amoenus* myth for the Stuart court; and by Annabel Patterson as a means to negotiate multiple and complex stances toward ideology, especially through Virgil's First Eclogue [*Pastoral and Ideology: Virgil to Valery*]. I suggest that in *Love's Victory* pastoral is adapted to the concerns of a feminist politics.

In the mixture that is pastoral tragicomedy, pastoral is the mode, carrying multiple associations from the long history of pastoral in western literature. The genre, tragicomedy, is a new Renaissance kind, whose emergence into prominence with Tasso's *Aminta* (1580) and Guarini's *Il Pastor Fido* (1590) touched off a storm of controversy. Italian critics complained that the mix of comedy and tragedy violated artistic unity, that the mixture of clowns and kings violated artistic decorum, and that stories of rude shepherds could not instruct sophisticated city dwellers. Guarini, the chief defender and analyst of the new form, declared it to be natural (since nature is full of mixture); defined its specific purpose (to purge melancholy by pleasure); found some warrant for it in antiquity in Aristotle's double plot and in Plautus's *Amphitryo;* praised its comprehensiveness in portraying gods, kings, and shepherds of several ranks and classes; and even proclaimed it the highest kind, best suited to the refined modern age, in that it included all the good features and rejected the excesses of both tragedy and comedy. Denying it to be a crude mixture of comedy and tragedy, he pronounced it a unified and perfect "third thing" using only those elements of comedy and tragedy that can blend together:

> He who composes tragicomedy takes from tragedy its great persons but not its great action, its verisimilar

plot but not its true one, its movement of the feelings but not its disturbance of them, its pleasure but not its sadness, its danger but not its death; from comedy it takes laughter that is not excessive, modest amusement, feigned difficulty, happy reversal, and above all the comic order.... [Yet] it is still not impossible for the plot to have more of one quality than of another, according to the wish of him who composes it.

In England, Sidney repeated the Italian critics' charges against "mongrell Tragicomedie" that mixes Kings and Clowns, "horne Pipes and Funeralls," though his target seems to be the use of comic scenes in tragedy rather than the new mixed kinds, which he explicitly allowed: "some *Poesies* have coupled togither two or three kindes, as the *Tragicall* and *Comicall,* whereupon is risen the *Tragicomicall* . . . if severed they be good, the coniunction cannot be hurtfull" (sigs. Iv, E3v). In 1610 [John] Fletcher [in Florena Kirk's *The Faithful Shepherdess by John Fletcher: A Critical Edium*] provided a much simplified definition of the kind: "it wants deaths, which is inough to make it no tragedie, yet brings some neere it, which is inough to make it no comedie."

When Lady Mary Wroth wrote **Love's Victory** she may have had only a general awareness of these definitions and controversies. But she certainly looked to the canon of the new kind—Tasso, Guarini, Daniel, Fletcher—to provide what Hans Robert Jauss terms "the horizon of generic expectations" [in *New Literary History* 2, 1970-71] and to suggest a range of generic possibilities and identifying topics, made more obvious as each text responded to its predecessors. All have a five-act structure. Except for Daniel's *The Queen's Arcadia,* all contain lyrical songs and choruses. All contain stock characters: a shepherdess sworn to chastity, a lustful satyr, a libertine or worldly-wise nymph. All use the device of a narrator to describe miraculous escapes from death and the final reunion of lovers. And all present an Arcadia that has declined some distance (small or great) from its Golden Age perfection and that has been infiltrated by characters and values from City and Court.

The chief canonical text was Tasso's *Aminta,* produced for the court at Ferrara in 1573-74, first published in 1580, and instantly popular throughout Europe. If Wroth didn't know it in Italian, an English translation was readily accessible in *The Countess of Pembroke's Ivychurch* (1591) by her aunt's client, Abraham Fraunce. Tasso's style is lyrical throughout, heightened by songs, poignant love complaints, and choruses, the most famous of them extolling the lost Golden Age when love was free and unhampered by notions of chastity and honor. Here the source of trouble is the psyche of the nymph Silvia, whose dedication to chastity and the chase leads her to scorn the devoted and honorable love of the hero, Aminta, who refuses all persuasions (by the libertine Nymph Daphne and the cynic Thyrsis) to take her by force. Saved by Aminta from rape by a lustful satyr, Silvia is reported killed by wolves, prompting Aminta to cast himself off a cliff; but he miraculously survives, Silvia repents, and the lovers are at last united. Cupid in prologue claims his agency in these affairs, undertaken to conquer Silvia's cold chastity; and an epilogue by Venus describes her errant son's power over humankind. There is some local allegory in allusions to personages at the Ferrari court, with Tasso himself shadowed in Thyrsis.

Guarini's *Il Pastor Fido* (1590) was designed for court occasions in Turin and Mantua. By 1602 twenty Italian editions had appeared, as well as an anonymous English translation set forth with commendatory verses by Samuel Daniel, who may well have introduced Guarini's drama to Wroth. Guarini offers a darker alternative for tragicomedy, an Arcadia which has declined much further than Tasso's from the Golden Age, as his parallel "Golden Age" chorus indicates. Only the subplot reprises the *Aminta* plot and tone—in comic reversal: a shepherd (Silvio) is devoted to chastity and the chase, his lover disguises herself as a wolf to be near him, Silvio shoots her by mistake, then repents, loves her, and cures her wound with herbs. The main plot is much more complex than Tasso's, proliferating violence and threats of death from many sources—the gods, society, human evil. Guarini's perverse characters are worse than Tasso's: a lustful satyr who attempts not only rape but murder, a libertine nymph, Corisca, who will stop at nothing to satisfy her ever-changing desires. A curse by the goddess Diana requires the yearly sacrifice of an unfaithful maiden or wife, or volunteer substitute; it will be lifted only when two descendants of the gods wed, occasioning the forced betrothal of Silvio and Amarillis and thereby threatening the true and mutual love of Amarillis and the titular hero, Mirtillo. Corisca and the lustful satyr trap these lovers together in a cave and slander them as adulterers, the priests prepare to sacrifice Amarillis, and Mirtillo offers himself as a substitute; then come reports of Corisca's confession and Mirtillo's newly discovered divine descent, permitting the reprieve and union of the lovers.

Wroth may have read or even seen Samuel *The Queen's Arcadia* (1606), which was presented to Queen Anne and her ladies by the University of Oxford in August 1605, the year Wroth danced with the queen in Jonson's *Masque of Blackness*. Daniel further darkens Guarini's vision, with an Arcadia marred by manifold evils from many sources and lacking the usual songs or choruses that signify pastoral *otium*. Daniel's dedicatory verses to the queen deny any references to matters of state, but so strenuously as in fact to intimate parallels between the great changes the choral figures Ergastus and Meliboeus find when they return to Arcadia and the new mores of King James's court. A licentious traveler, Colax, imports the mores of foreign lands and courts, seducing some nymphs away from their true lovers and slandering others, while his female associate unsettles the nymphs with city fashions, styles, cosmetics, and wanton attitudes. Besides, there is a lawyer who promotes litigation, a doctor who promotes illness, and a religious imposter who undermines established rites and customs. The heroine, Chloris, denies love and her true lover, Amyntas, not from devotion to chastity but from doubt that faithful love can exist. In a version of Guarini's cave trick, Colax attempts to rape and seduce her, and Amyntas, believing her wanton, takes

poison; Chloris then admits her love for him and Urania cures him with herbs. In final scenes, Ergastus and Meliboeus reveal all the evils, banish the corrupt foreigners, and urge Arcadians to return to their old ways.

Wroth may or may not have known Fletcher's *Faithful Shepherdess* (c. 1610); this effort to translate a court genre to the private stage (probably Blackfriars) was a disaster. The title and several episodes signal a response to Guarini, lighter in tone but with more overt violence, due to unrestrained passions. Perigot and the titular heroine, Amoret, are faithful, mutual lovers; Amarillis (who also desires Perigot) takes on Amoret's semblance by magic and behaves wantonly; deceived, Perigot stabs Amoret on two occasions, but she responds with unquestioning fidelity and forgiveness. Comic variants of the genre's stock figures include a satyr who is noble and chaste and who rescues nymphs in danger of rape; a libertine shepherdess whose promiscuous solicitations never succeed; and a swain who loves a chaste nymph only for her chastity and is cured when she pretends love to him. The restoration of Arcadia begins as the permanently chaste shepherdess, Clorin, uses her powers to cure both physical wounds and unchaste desires for all the lovers (except for the incurably wicked Sullen Shepherd), and joins them in virtuous love.

Daniel's pastoral drama, *Hymen's Triumph* (1615), was presented at the queen's court in the Strand. As befits a wedding entertainment, it is closer in tone to Tasso than Guarini, incorporating many songs and comic mischances arising from cross-dressing and gender confusion. The prologue identifies the allegorical passions of Envy, Avarice, and Jealousy as enemies of Hymen. The chief source of trouble is paternal avarice, which leads Silvia's father to promise her to a wealthy swain instead of to her true love, Thirsis. Captured and held by pirates for two years and presumed dead, Silvia preserves her chastity, escapes, and returns in male disguise (as Clorindo) to wait out her betrothed's wedding day; betimes, Viola-like, she woos her lover for her mistress, Cloris, and attracts the misguided love of Phillis. A jealous forester who loves Phillis stabs Clarindo and reveals Silvia, Thirsis collapses with grief, both are cured by Lamia, and Silvia's father repents and blesses the union which the chorus celebrates as an ornament to Arcadia.

Wroth's **Love's Victory** appears to draw upon and respond to this entire tradition. In tone it is closest to Tasso, but even more lyrical, with songs and choruses resounding throughout; on Guarini's scale, it stands much closer to comedy than tragedy. Wroth's Arcadia is also closer than Tasso's to the Golden Age. Here, troubles arise chiefly from love's natural anxieties—jealousy, misapprehensions, suspicions, and fears rather than treacherous plots and violence: no near-rapes or near-murders in this work. Moreover, Wroth's drama portrays (beyond anything in this genre) an extended egalitarian community, without gender or class hierarchy, bound together by friendships strong enough to survive even rivalries in love—a community in which friends aid, console, and even sacrifice themselves for each other.

There are four pairs of lovers. Philisses loves Musella but believes she loves his friend Lissius and so prepares to relinquish her and die of grief; he is restored when Musella confesses her love to him. Lissius begins as a scorner of women and love but soon comes to love Simeana (Philisses's sister); their love is threatened by Arcas's slander and Simeana's jealousy, but they are reunited by Musella's good counsel. Silvesta loves Philisses but devotes herself to a life of chastity when she realizes that he loves her friend Musella; accordingly she rejects (until the end) the Forester's faithful love for her—although their names of course predict their final union. In the final act the fickle but not unchaste coquette Dalina is matched with the boorish Rustick—both of them seeking comfort and convenience, not passion or ideal unions. Others exemplify misguided or unrequited love: the foreigner Climeana who is (by Arcadian standards) too bold in wooing Lissius, Fillis who loves Philisses faithfully but hopelessly, and Lacon who so loves Musella. Finally, there is the lone villain, Arcas, who claims to have been rejected by Musella and who takes malicious delight in crossing true love by slander.

In the fifth act Arcas sets in train Guarini-like complications but the expected marvelous escapes are contrived by human wit and natural means. Musella's mother, for "bace gaine" (V.14 [according to Michael J. Brennan's edition of the play]), arranges her daughter's immediate marriage to Rustick, spurred on by Arcas's slanders about her wanton pursuit of Philisses. Philisses and Musella go to the Temple of Love to pray; they are about to stab themselves in a mutual suicide pact when Silvesta persuades them to die by poison instead of knives and offers them a potion which (apparently) causes their death. Simenea and Silvesta report all this to the rest of the troop, who then repair to Love's Temple, where Venus's priests condemn Silvesta to be burned at the stake. But the Forester offers himself in her stead and (as in Guarini) this substitution must be accepted. Rustick then formally disclaims all right in Musella, and her mother repents the hasty wedding arrangements. At this point the potion wears off, the seeming dead are called forth by Venus and her priests, Silvesta promises to love the Forester (whether other than chastely is left unclear), Rustick matches with the fickle Dalina, and Arcas is punished by public shame.

Love's Victory is marked by conceptual and structural innovations which register an implicit feminist politics. As Richard Cody observes, [in his *The Landscape of the Mind*] the genre usually expresses a very different ethos: "The pastoral is as much a man's world as the heroic. Nymph and shepherdess are not personalities but images of women." Wroth, however, emphasizes female agency throughout. In the supernatural realm, Venus, not Cupid, is the dominant presence. Tasso's prologue has Cupid (escaped from Venus) claiming credit for the love complications, whereas in Wroth Venus masterminds the entire enterprise. In the prologue she sends Cupid to foment trials and troubles so as to subject all these lovers more completely to love's power and he agrees to serve "your will and minde" (I.31). At the end of Act I she complains that he still spares half the lovers—"I wowld have all to

waile, and all to weepe" (387)—and he promises to effect that, and thereby to do her honor. At the end of Act II, Venus and Cupid appear together in glory, as in a Triumph. At the end of Act III, Cupid brags of his conquests, but Venus is still unsatisfied—"Tis pretty, butt tis nott enough; some are / To slightly wounded" (355-56)—and Cupid promises to cause the lovers still more grief. At the end of Act IV Venus pities the now-humble lovers and (with her priests) urges Cupid to cease the torments. But now Cupid resists, determined to inflict more pain on some before saving them. It is probably significant that when Cupid departs from the sway of Venus's wishes the Guarini-like complications come into play: Arcas's treachery, the apparent suicide, the threat of a burning at the stake.

At the end of Act V Venus again takes firm charge, managing the entire resolution. She accepts the Forester's offer to die for Silvesta; she claims that the "resurrection" of the lovers was "my deed, / Who could nott suffer your deere harts to bleed"; she terms Silvesta "my instrument ordain'd / To kill, and save her friends" (V.487-88); and she directs her priests to celebrate these events with joyful songs. At the very end Cupid asks her to pass judgment on Arcas and she does so, imposing what he sees as a sentence worse than death—to live on in this society bearing the marks of shame, infamy, and a gnawing conscience.

The emphasis on female agency is also evident in the human sphere. As Musella's father is dead her mother is the familial authority who decides when to enforce the marriage arrangement with Rustick. Moreover, it is chiefly the women who act to resolve problems and to foster friendships and community. To be sure, most of the Arcadian shepherds, male and female, do the offices of friendship for each other—proffering aid and good advice in the tribulations of love, generously giving way to others' better love claims, maintaining friendship despite rivalries in love. They are committed to the principle Philisses enunciates: "Yett when the paine is greatest, 'tis some ease / To lett a friend partake his freind's disease" (I.295-96). Only a few are excluded from this noble ethos: the villain Arcas, and to a lesser degree the insensitive farmer Rustick and the foreigner Climeana, who boldly pursues Lissius despite the better claims of her friend Simeana. Nevertheless, the women's actions and values are dominant and decisive. They are so also in the *Urania* where, as Naomi Miller has shown, values of community and human relationships are central and are promoted chiefly by women [*Studies in English Literature* 29, 1989].

Male friendship is important in *Love's Victory,* but is somewhat more exclusive in its objects and more limited in its scope than female friendship. Philisses and Lissius are a typical pair of male friends, rather like Pyrocles and Musidorus in the *Arcadia*. Believing that his beloved Musella loves Lissius, Philisses tries to hide the cause of his pain from his friend and relinquish his own claims. Lissius at length prevails in his repeated appeals to their bond of friendship (II.251-310) and their shared confidences result in mutual help: Lissius reveals his newfound love for Philisses's sister Simeana and encourages Philisses to declare his love openly to Musella; Philisses in turn pledges his good offices with his sister. But other male friendships are less profound. Lissius listens to the Forester's complaint that his beloved Silvesta has withdrawn to the woods after being rejected by Philisses, but these friends are so at odds about love philosophy that their exchange of advice is unhelpful. Lissius—as yet untouched by and scornful of love and women—urges the pursuit of sexual pleasure; the Forester is as yet a strict Neoplatonist who desires to love Silvesta "in truest kind" (I.261), simply in the chaste beholding of her. Rustick also invites but cannot gain love confidences from Philisses, because of the wide abyss in sensibility between them.

The principal female characters are more nearly agreed on the nature and claims of love, more unstinting in the offices of friendship to both women and men, and more active in problem-solving for themselves and each other. Silvesta is the most eminent exemplar of all these traits. Conquering her unrequited love for Philisses by embracing a life devoted to chastity and the chase, she rejoices in her new freedom and independence; she also remains a true friend to both Philisses and Musella. When Musella at length confides her love for Philisses and his failure to declare himself to her, Silvesta finds a solution, hiding Musella where she will hear Philisses's plaints and can respond, reassuring him of her love. Later, Silvesta puts herself at risk of death to rescue them. When she hears of the impending marriage to Rustick, she immediately declares, "It showld nott bee, nor shall bee; noe, noe, / III rescue her, or for her sake will dy" (V.176-78). When she offers them the supposed poison draft Philisses praises her as the embodiment of noble friendship:

> Freindship, what greater blessing then thou art,
> Can once desend into a mortall hart.
> Silvesta, freind and priest doth now apeere,
> And as our loves, lett this thy deed shine cleere.
> 　　　　　　　　　　(V.250-53)

Venus grants "immortall fame" (V.493) to her deed of friendship, and Musella declares, "in you only was true freindship found" (V.506). At the end, when the Forester matches Silvesta's self-sacrifice by his own offer to die in her stead, she recognizes him as her true soul-mate and offers him her chaste love. Though Venus used her as instrument, Silvesta herself produced the happy resolution—not by magical or supernatural powers (like Fletcher's chaste shepherdess, Clorin), but by her wit, her skill in potions, and her high ideal of friendship.

The other women are also active in their own and their friends' troubles. The coquette Dalina is Simeana's first confidante, advising her not to be won too soon by lovers' protestations. But when they overhear Lissius complain of his love miseries, she counsels pity and a trial of his affections—advice Simeana promptly acts on. Musella is friend and confidante to men and women alike—Lissius, Fillis, Simeana, even Rustick—and is always ready with good sense, warm sympathy, and useful advice. Her most notable accomplishment is the reuniting of Lissius and Simeana, parted by Arcas's slanderous tales about Lissius's infidelity. She first extracts Lissius's story of Simeana's unaccountable scorn and unjust accusations; then she answers all Simeana's jealous charges with cool reason, urging her to overcome "this vild humour of bace jealousie, / Which breedeth nothing butt self misery" (IV.262-63), and to ask pardon of Lissius. At length the ecstatic, reunited lovers praise her as "sole restorer of this joy" (IV.330).

Acting in her own affairs Musella is not always so wise, and she has need of her friends' help. She was arguably too discreet in hiding her love for Philisses, and she clearly misjudged his feelings for her. But she insists on taking responsibility for her choices and actions, despite the power of social constraints and the tyranny of Cupid. Distraught at the news that she must marry Rustick at once, Musella is aided by Simeana's counsels of patience to think through her duties and her options. She sees herself bound by the will of her father who arranged the marriage, and by her mother's commands, "beeing in her hands" (V.45). At length, however, she identifies as the principal bond her own formal consent to that contract, given when she despaired of Philisses's love. Accepting this responsibility empowers her to act: she immediately proposes a visit to the Temple of Venus, where the lovers will either find some means for their union, or die together.

Wroth's representation of a tight-knit, non-hierarchical community linked by bonds of friendship and love is aided by certain structural innovations, the most important of which reaches back to the origins of the genre in pastoral eclogue. Each of the first four acts has at its structural center an eclogue-like game or contest which several members of the community (sometimes called the "troop," or the "flock") play when they withdraw at noon into a shady grove. Even here, female agency is underscored, as in each case Dalina initiates the discussion about game-playing. Each exercise comments on the nature and circumstances of the participants, thereby highlighting thematic and plot issues as well as enhancing the drama's lyrical quality.

In Act I, the game is that most eclogic of activities, a singing match in which the characters sing of their own love experiences. Climeana breaks through the initial impasse over choice of game by singing a love complaint of her wandering eyes and heart; Philisses and Musella propose themselves as judges since they do not have glad hearts for song; Rustick sings a comic blazon of Musella, comparing her parts to farmyard animals and crops; and Lacon sings of initiation into love by Cupid's dart and beauty's sight.

The game in Act II (proposed by Arcas) is fortune-telling: and the characters' chosen fortunes closely anticipate their own futures. Rustick extends the book of fortunes first to Musella, hinting his claim on her: "What shalbee you need nott feare, / Rustick doth thy fortune beare" (II.150-51). Her fortune, read out by Philisses, affirms that though her patience will be much tried, "Fortune can nott cross your will" (161). Philisses's fortune, read out by Dalina, promises that he will suffer much but then obtain his bliss (179). Dalina's lot predicts that her choices in love have and will conform to her nature: "Fickle people, fickly chuse, / Slightly like, and soe refuse" (II.194-95).

In Act III the game, played only by women, is confessions of past loves and passions. Dalina recounts her former coquetry: many lovers wooed her, but she was too fickle to choose any of them, so all at length abandoned her; she now terms that behavior youthful folly and determines to accept the next man who offers. Simeana, without identifying the man, tells of her constancy despite rejection, and her tentative hopes. Fillis follows with her tale of unrequited love for Philisses. Finally, Climeana tells of leaving home and country for a lover who then rejected her; and of her new love for Lissius. A love-debate follows, in which Simeana challenges Climeana's claims and charges her with inconstancy and folly but accepts the love contest with good grace: "But take your course, and win him if you can" (245).

The game in Act IV is riddles, which the characters decide not to expound: in each case they allude to the nature and circumstances of the speaker. Musella begins with a riddle about shunning what is easy but does not please (Rustick) and desiring what can only be gained without pain (Philisses). Dalina's riddle is about seeking what she cannot find in herself (constancy). Philisses riddles about a star whose light he thought to be his own (Musella) and which though clouded is still visible. Rustick betrays his bluntness by repudiating the pastoral wit game altogether and insisting on the superiority of his low georgic interests and talents:

> Truly, I can nott ridle, I 'was not taught
> Thes tricks of witt; my thoughts ne're higher
>   wrought
> Then how to marck a beast, or drive a cowe
> To feed, or els with art to hold a plowe,
> Which if you knew, you surely soone would find
> A matter of more worth then thes od things,
> Which never profitt, butt some laughter brings.
> Thes others bee of body, and of mind.
>
> (IV.391-98)

Lissius follows with a riddle alluding to a fog (jealousy) and an unwanted light (Climeana), then two suns (himself and Simeana) who "without envy hold each deere" (424). Fillis's riddle alludes to her disappointment (over Philisses's love) in spring, summer, and autumn.

In Act V the communal dimension is heightened by another structural change. Generic convention calls for the final resolutions—the wonderful escapes of the lovers from danger and their reunion—to be narrated, in the classical manner, rather than represented. Wroth partly follows this convention as the narratives of Simeana and Silvesta report Musella's impending marriage, the suicide attempt in the Temple, Sylvesta's potion, and the lovers' "death." But she adds to this a more dramatic resolution scene

with all the company assembled in the Temple of Venus—a scene which opens out to a Kommos-like finale. Here in sight of all, the supposedly dead lovers arise, all pairs of lovers are properly matched, true friendship is honored, and villainy is punished by public shame.

Seen in its generic context Wroth's drama is conceptually and structurally innovative, and often stylistically charming, especially when we imagine (as I think we should) a performance in which the pervasive songs and choruses are set to music. The dialogue, rendered in heroic couplets whose rhymes are neither forced nor obvious, is usually natural and easy. It also manages nice distinctions—as in the following exchange which catches the accents of Lissius's early cynicism:

> Musella: Lissius, I hope this sight doth somthing
>   move
>   In you to pitty soe much constant
>   love.
> Lissius: Yes, thus itt moves, that man showld
>   bee soe fond,
>   As to bee tide t'a woman's faithles
>   bond.
>   For wee showld women love butt as
>   owr sheep
>   Who beeing kind and gentle gives us
>   ease,
>   But cross, or strying, stuborne, and
>   unmeeke,
>   Shun'd as the wulf, which most owr
>   flocks disease. (II.63-70)

Or this exchange, which reflects Rustick's lowness of mind in his low diction, and the power of Philisses's passion in his high rhetoric:

> Philisses: Rustick, faith tell mee, hast thou ever
>   lov'd?
> Rustick: What call you love? I'have bin to
>   trouble mov'd
>   As when my best cloke hath by chance
>   bin torne.
>   I have liv'd wishing till itt mended
>   were
>   And butt soe lovers doe; nor cowld
>   forbeare
>   To cry if I my bag, or bottle lost,
>   As lovers doe who by theyr loves are
>   crost,
>   And grieve as much for thes, as they
>   for scorne.
> Philisses: Call you this love? Why love is noe
>   such thing,
>   Love is a paine which yett doth
>   pleasure bring
>   A passion which alone in harts doe
>   move
>   And they that feele nott this they
>   cannott love.
>   'Twill make one joyfull, merry,
> pleasant, sad,

Cry, weepe, sigh, fast, mourne, nay
somtims stark mad. (II.85-98)

Woven into the texture of the heroic couplet dialogue are
several generic set-pieces, often with their own distinctive metrical patterns. The hymns of Venus's priests
(II.311-42), the prayers of Musella and Philisses to Venus
and Cupid (V.188-225), the chant-like fortunes and riddles of Acts II and IV, Philisses's song celebrating Reason guiding Love (II.213-24), and Lacon's love complaint
(I.358-74) are all in ocosyllabic couplets. Other set-pieces
include the little autobiographical narratives of Act III
followed by the love debate between Simeana and Climeana. Scattered throughout are also several kinds of love
songs in many different stanzaic patterns: Philisses's love
complaint (I.38-62); Lissius's spring song (I.75-80, 85-
90); the Forester's complaint-sonnet (I.185-98); Climeana's love complaint (I.311-22); Rustick's comic blazon of
Musella (I.335-52); Lissius's song defying Cupid (II.79-
85); the paragone of Chastity and Love spoken by Silvesta and Musella (III.1-24); the spring/winter duet of Lissius and Simeana (IV.153-58). This variety is somewhat
reminiscent of Mary Sidney's stanzaic experimentation in
her Psalm versions, and seems clearly meant to display
Wroth's technical skill. We can sample this variety in the
following three extracts:

1. CLIMEANA'S LOVE LAMENT

O mine eyes, why doe you lead
My poore hart thus forth to rang
From the wounted course, to strange
Unknowne ways, and pathes to tread?
Lett itt home returne againe,
Free, untouch'd of gadding thought,
And your forces back bee brought
To the ridding of my paine.
Butt mine eyes if you deny
This small favor to my hart,
And will force my thoughts to fly
Know yett you governe butt your part
(I.311-22)

2. THE SILVESTA-MUSELLA PARAGONE
OF CHASTITY AND LOVE

Silvesta: Silent Woods with desart's shade
Giving peace
Where all pleasures first ar made
To increase.
Give you favor to my mone
Now my loving time is gone.
Chastity my pleasure is.
Folly fled
From hence, now I seeke my blis.
Cross love dead,
In your shadowes I repose
You then love I rather chose.

Musella: Choice ill made were better left,
Being cross.
Of such choice to bee bereft

Were no loss.
Chastitie, you thus commend,
Doth proceed butt from love's end.
And if Love the fountaine was
Of your fire,
Love must chastitie surpass
In desire.
Love lost bred your chastest thought,
Chastitie by love is wrought (III.1-24)

3. THE LISSIUS/SIMEANA DUET

Love's beginning like the spring,
Gives delight in sweetnes flowing.
Ever pleasant flourishing,
Pride in her brave colors showing.
But love ending is att last
Like the storms of winter's blast (IV.153-59).

What of the political resonance of this pastoral tragicomedy? Wroth's drama may well allude to particular
court personages (as does her *Urania*); it probably does
figure in some way her own relations with Sir Robert
Wroth and Pembroke (and possibly alludes to Philip
Sidney and Penelope Rich); but that must be explored in
future research. Some connection between Rustick and
Sir Robert Wroth is strengthened by Jonson's verse epistle ["To Sir Robert Wroth" in *The Forest*] which characterizes him as wholly devoted to country affairs (hunting, hawking, husbandry, sheep, rude country festivals),
repudiating such court activities as feasting, masquing,
arms, and office-seeking. That portrait is encomiastic,
but Jonson later (1619) uses [in his *Conversations with
Drummond*] the common pun on Wroth/worth to intimate that his nature is somehow base: "My lord Lisle's
daughter, my Lady Wroth, is unworthily married on a
jealous husband." Through the portrait of Rustick, Mary
Wroth aligns herself firmly with the myth and some of
the values of Stuart court pastoral (love, leisure, harmonious community, wit, artful play) in opposition to the
plain "country" values often invoked to criticize court
extravagance and license.

More importantly, however, Wroth's pastoral drama subverts the patriarchal ideology of the Jacobean court. Her
generic alterations evidence a sophisticated knowledge
of literary tradition and appear to be used deliberately,
to develop an implicit feminist politics which emphasizes a non-hierarchical community, female and cross-gen-
der friendships, and especially female agency in the roles
of Venus, Silvesta, Musella, and even Dalina. This female agency is pervasive and positive, not diluted by
gestures of containment or critique, a clear challenge to
both generic and cultural norms.

Attention to genre affords us some access both to the
literary values and the political resonances of this newly
discovered and obviously un-canonical work. It invites
further speculation about the attraction of pastoral for
women writers and readers. And it exemplifies the usefulness of contextualizing such "new" women's texts in
literary as well as historical terms.

Nona Fienberg (essay date 1991)

SOURCE: "Mary Wroth and the Invention of Female Poetic Subjectivity," in *Reading Mary Wroth: Representing Alternatives in Early Modern England,* edited by Naomi J. Miller and Gary Waller, The University of Tennessee Press, 1991, pp. 175-90.

[In the following excerpt, Feinberg explores Wroth's innovative use of a female perspective in Pamphilia to Amphilanthus *and her evocation of "a fictional audience of women readers and writers."]*

The nature of women's writing was clearly at issue early in the seventeenth century. Remember Rosalind's response to Phoebe's verses: "I say she never did invent this letter, / This is a man's invention and his hand" ([William Shakespeare, *As You Like It,*] IV.ii.28-29). She insists that "women's gentle brain / Could not drop forth such giant-rude invention" (IV.iii.34-35). While Rosalind as Ganymede speculates about how a woman's writing might sound, the work of feminist scholars confirms the range of women writers. Yet as scholars have reexamined the writings of Vittoria Colonna, Veronica Gambara, Marguerite de Navarre, and Margaret More Roper, they have reconstructed a history of the invention of female subjectivity that Renaissance women writers themselves worked to recover. When Mary Wroth writes *Pamphilia to Amphilanthus* (1621), the first sonnet sequence in English written from the point of view of a woman, she demonstrates her poetic invention. [. . .], Wroth situates her texts in the line of her aunt, Mary Sidney, Countess of Pembroke, by interweaving references to Sidney's literary reputation and her poetry. In addition, Wroth creates a fictional audience of women readers and writers. This female community testifies to the mythological, allegorical, and historical traditions of women in the making of culture, while it is also generative of that creativity.

In sonnet 38 of *Pamphilia to Amphilanthus,* Wroth's speaker describes a woman's marginal relationship to the dominant culture. But her question also suggests the need for an audience to confirm her contributions to poetic invention: "What pleasure can a bannish'd creature have / In all the pastimes that invented arr / By witt or learning." The "pastimes" of "witt or learning" as the court culture would define them have been "invented" by men. While her question expresses the pain of her banishment, earlier in the sequence sonnet 23 provides an alternative perspective on her social isolation. In sonnet 23, Wroth's speaker engages in the process of inventing herself:

> When every one to pleasing pastime hies
> Some hunt, some hauke, some play, while some delight
> In sweet discourse, and musique showes joys might
> Yett I my thoughts doe farre above thes prise.
>   . . .
> When others hunt, my thoughts I have in chase;
> If hauke, my minde att wished end doth fly,
> Discourse, I with my spiritt tauke, and cry

> While others, musique choose as greatest grace.
> O God, say I, can thes fond pleasure move?
> Or musique bee butt in sweet thoughts of love?

Not the pastimes of the court "invented" by men, but her own invention, the pleasures of her inward self, shape her sonnet. In the third quatrain, the speaker redefines terms that allow her to create her own subjectivity. Instead of the courtly hunt, she will chase her thoughts. Instead of accepting the court's definition of hawking, discourse, and music, the speaker appropriates those terms into her interior landscape. Instead of praising the beloved, she praises and values her own "thoughts." Such a re-evaluation of courtly values offers liberation. Instead of being the object seen or spoken of, she declares herself "free from eyes" and discoursing with "my spiritt." Still, the couplet's turn to questions and to the authority of God in her struggle marks the extent to which the speaker's internalizing of courtly values undermines the apparent confidence of the quatrains' assertions.

Surely the speaker's retreat from the public court world into an inward, private world is familiar. Derived from Petrarch's self-making in his *Canzoniere,* the turn inward becomes part of the sonnet tradition in the line of Wyatt, Sidney, Spenser, Shakespeare, and perhaps Donne. Yet the female authorship of *Pamphilia to Amphilanthus* marks the work's difference and its danger. Since Petrarch's songs and sonnets, the poet's turn to an interior self had been valorized by the humanist tradition. By means of his learning, the poet as humanist justified his preoccupation with himself as subject. Through Virgil and Ovid, through rediscovery of the classics, male poets created voices of authority in poetry. In Petrarch's love poetry, however, the male poetic corpus is substantiated at the cost of the dismemberment of Laura, his beloved. As Thomas Greene [in *The Yale Journal of Criticism* Spring, 1989] argues in demonstrating Donne's self-discovery in his elegies, "for males at any rate the habit of transforming the object of desire, and especially her body, into a symbol seems virtually irresistible." To Greene's speculation that the love poetry of a female poet might escape this process, Wroth's poetry provides one clear answer: no blazons scattering the parts of her beloved, no fetishizing of a veil, a foot, an eyebrow, and thus no self-creation out of the scattered parts of the beloved. But if the women of the English Renaissance won only limited access to the classical learning through which the humanist poets validated their self-exploration, and if Wroth rejected reification of the beloved, then what are the materials out of which she invented female poetic subjectivity? In articulating the process of transforming herself from object to subject, Wroth speaks of the pleasures of the self.

Wroth's authorship and 1621 publication of *The Countess of Mountgomeries Urania* offers a partial answer. By writing a secular text and by publishing the fine folio volume of her romance with its accompanying songs and sonnets, Wroth transgresses the boundaries of sacred writings that had largely contained women writers in

English. Her collection violates the courtly codes of co-terie transmission of aristocratic poetry and disrupts male conversation with female discourses. Wroth knows, I believe, the danger of "dismemberment," exclusion from membership in her community, that her writing and pub-lication challenge. She knows the codes of her courtly world. In writing her poetry she negotiates between the violation she risks and the work she values.

Wroth gives that danger narrative form in the dynamic exchange between the theatrical spectacles of the Jaco-bean court masques, tilts, and barriers, and the secret cabinets where the women of the court keep their portrait miniatures, their love sonnets, and their intimate writings. In the past, the public life and heroic action in a chivalric sense attested to worth in the court world. In the early decades of the seventeenth century in England, a new definition of value in interiority begins to emerge, to which Drayton ironically attests [(in *Poly-Olbion*, 1613, quoted by Wendy Wall in *Studies in English Literature*, Winter, 1989)], "nothing is esteemed in this lunatic age but what is kept in cabinets." Although the authorities in Wroth's court society came to view the increasing emphasis on the private world strictly in terms of conspiracy and cabal, Wroth places new value on female subjectivity and in-vites her readers to contemplate the consequences.

While the disparity between public shows and private secrets could inform Ben Jonson's gossip that "my lady Wroth is unworthily married on a jealous husband," his play upon Wroth's name becomes—for Wroth herself, in *Pamphilia to Amphilanthus*—a means of creating female poetic subjectivity. Wroth thematizes the danger of writ-ing and publishing in her social position through serious play upon her name. The contemporary regulation of women's lives in marriage sought to preclude the value of female subjectivity, but Wroth asserts her "worth" in her writing. Her name holds both a public standing and a private, interior measure of value. Each time she writes her own name, it is also her husband's. She doubts her "worth," questions her "work," and detaches herself from what she has "wrought." So Wroth's praise of her "true worth" in sonnet 13 may also encode the financial indebt-edness in which her husband's death left her (P15). The name bespeaks her husband's family, but neither her lit-erary ancestry nor her love. In writing about cultural conditions which would impose female silence, Wroth both risks punishment and challenges those conditions. Our cultural work, to recover the female subjectivity she in-vents, begins with Wroth's inscribing of Pamphilia as a reader and writer of her self.

Reading and writing serve as critical moves in the cre-ation of female subjectivity in the central moment of *Urania*. A crucial act of reading and self-invention lies at the heart of the romance. Even as Pamphilia and Am-philanthus struggle to declare their love, Wroth's heroine retreats into her private chambers to read a romance which recounts "the affection of a Lady to a brave Gentleman." Although they "equally loved," his manhood demands that he "exceed a woman in all things," including his "incon-stancie," and so "hee left her for a new" (264). Pamphilia

is reading a book very like *Urania* itself, the story of her constant love for the inconstant Amphilanthus. To read, and to recognize in her reading the story of her self, is Pamphilia's occasion for self-discovery.

The moment recalls analogous events of self-discovery in the creation of male subjectivity, like Augustine's reading of the pertinent Bible passage at the conver-sion scene in the *Confessions,* or Petrarch's reading of Augustine when he recalls himself to interiority on the peak of Mount Ventoux. But the differences in Wroth's interior world help to mark her position in cultural history as an inventor of female subjectivity. Pamphilia is reading neither the Bible nor the confessions of a Church father. The value of her subjectivity is not measured by the judgment of spiritual authority. Her reading is not prompted by a voice of admonition, ei-ther external as when Augustine hears a voice call "take it and read," or internal as in Petrarch's guilt in his pleasures in the view from the mountain. Instead, we may imagine Pamphilia reading the very text in which Mary Wroth has inscribed her as a character. Pamphil-ia's turn inward is, thus, validated by a woman writer, whose plots of women's self-discovery turn not on admonitions from male authorities but on the women reading, speaking, and writing stories of themselves.

This scene of Pamphilia as a reader of her self is fol-lowed immediately by a scene which marks the social danger of her writing. When Amphilanthus returns from his adventures to Pamphilia's side, he asks for her vers-es. She admits him to the privacy of "her Cabinet." Step by step, Amphilanthus appropriates Pamphilia's private, inward places:

> When they were there, she tooke a deske, wherein her papers lay, and kissing them, delivered all shee had saved from the fire, being in her owne hand unto him, yet blushing told him, she was ashamed, so much of her folly should present her selfe unto his eyes.

Amphilanthus wonders at the emotion she reveals "in her owne hand," in her own poetry. She blushes and he kisses her. In the same box Amphilanthus discovers Pamphilia's picture, "drawne by the best hand of the time." With increasing physical intimacy, Pamphilia al-lows Amphilanthus to enter her private cabinet, then to read her own verses, then to kiss her, then to handle her portrait miniature, and finally to claim it as a love token. Amphilanthus's discovery of Pamphilia's phys-ical self depends upon her own self-discovery as a subject, first through reading her own story, and then through her writing. But the cabinet, the box, the vers-es, and the miniature which had been Pamphilia's in-ward places have become a site of appropriation, even violation. Amphilanthus's intrusion into her secret cab-inets is architectural, but it is also somatic. Her body responds not in fear, but in embarrassment. Pamphilia adopts Amphilanthus's evaluation of her verses in her blushes and in her shame. She has become the work, the artifact he now claims as an object for his pleasure.

In the romance the intimate encounter between the two lovers has greater narrative value than Pamphilia's loss. Thus, although the text of *Urania* has unfolded many lyrics written by female characters, in this encounter readers are not privy to Pamphilia's poems. Once Amphilanthus has opened Pamphilia's desk, her poetry, like her body, becomes an object of his speculation. The poetry disappears into Amphilanthus's eyes. But the songs and sonnets which follow *Urania* suggest a different measure of value. When Pamphilia's poetry is finally revealed to the readers of *Urania,* Amphilanthus's shocking transgression mediates the intrusion of Pamphilia's female discourses into the world of print.

Wroth's *Urania* establishes a female subjectivity which finds its center in reading and in writing. But the romance pressure toward adventure turns outward, where the sonnets turn inward, toward invention. Also, unlike *Urania,* where women's participation in the material world is given such concrete form as Pamphilia's embroidering of a waistcoat, *Pamphilia to Amphilanthus* banishes the signs of women's material culture. In the songs and sonnets there is no needlework, no housecleaning, no childrearing, no supervising of servants, no cookery, preserving, surgery, physic, tailoring, and no hospitality. Wroth's avoidance of such signs of women's culture proves politically telling. King James sought to enforce the power of his state machinery through policing material culture. In the year of Wroth's publication of *Urania* he instructed the clergy to "inveigh vehemently against the insolencies of our women, and their wearing of broad brimmed hats, pointed doublets, their hair cut short or shorne, and some of them stilletoes or poniards." James's attempts to enforce the boundaries of dress in the formation of gender roles constitute part of the fiction of a state where only men are producers. Wroth, however, asserts her value as a producer through the writing of her own hand.

Thus, in *Pamphilia to Amphilanthus* the work wrought by a woman's hand is the poetic lines themselves. Like the interior world the portrait miniature creates, Wroth's poetry creates a world of interiority, where everyday life is deferred and excluded. Instead of the pull of adventure of public life, Wroth finds freedom in the imaginative sanctuary of reading and writing. But she also writes of the dangers of oppression and pain posed both by that retreat and by the public world. For all her efforts to banish those signs of her contingent being, subject to the enforcement of the state, the absolutist court powers compel her to withdraw her book from circulation. Those Jacobean attempts to suppress female authorship are reinscribed in some contemporary formulations of the history of consciousness.

Since Wroth's invention of female poetic subjectivity in *Pamphilia to Amphilanthus* contributes to our understanding of self-fashioning in the Renaissance, it is important to distinguish her materials from those Stephen Greenblatt has described in his use of the term. In *Renaissance Self-Fashioning,* Greenblatt posits a theatrical sense of selfhood and self-making that proves compelling in his discussion of the participants in a court dominated by

men. He demonstrates that self-fashioning takes place in language, that the self is fashioned in relation both to the sources of authority and to those defined as alien to a culture, and that achieved identity is always vulnerable to subversion or loss. Nevertheless, questions remain about the adequacy of Greenblatt's work as a model for female expressiveness. Not only does his model exclude women from participation in a masculinist stage-play world, it also appropriates women's own discourse as a product of the dominant culture. Remember Amphilanthus's appropriation of Pamphilia's verse. How, then, does a woman, who has been ascribed the roles of object of vision and of speech, write herself as the subject who sees and who speaks?

In her poetry, Wroth invents a different authority of origin from that the court validates. Wroth's speaker declares herself as a subject not in a theatrical sense, but in a private accounting like that which might take place in devotional or financial secret cabinets. For example, in sonnet 42, the metaphor of "this stage of woe / wher sad disasters have theyr open showe" (12-13) contrasts with the contemplative manner of the octave:

> If ever love had force in humaine brest?
> > If ever hee could move in pensive hart?
> > Or if that hee such powre could butt impart
> > To breed those flames whose heart brings joys unrest.
> Then looke on mee: I am to thes adrest,
> I, ame the soule that feeles the greatest smart;
> I, ame that hartles trunk of harts depart
> And I, that one, by love, and griefe oprest.

In summoning the eyes of the beloved to look on "mee," the "I" of the speaker calls upon an inward self that "this stage of woe" with its "open showe" cannot reveal. The subjunctive verbs of the opening quatrain lead the reader to an inward, imagined state of possibility, which reveals the speaker's "I." In contrast, the "o" sound of the rhymes in the final four lines reject "this stage of woe" as hollow:

> For had hee seene, hee must have pitty show'd;
> I should nott have bin made this stage of woe
> > Wher sad disasters have theyr open showe
> > O noe, more pitty he had sure beestow'd.

The stage of woe becomes a site of violation, and of exposure to misreading. The subjunctive inwardness of the opening quatrain offers an alternative derived from the secret cabinet of spiritual or economic accounting, but translated into the making of the female "I."

How does Wroth's invention of female poetic subjectivity differ from what Joel Fineman has described [in *Shakespeare's Perjured Eye: The Invention of Poetic Subjectivity in the Sonnets*] as the invention of poetic subjectivity in Shakespeare's sonnets? The "perjured eye" of Shakespeare's sonnets praises a subject about whose shattered image he must lie. In sonnet 59, when he is "laboring for invention," Shakespeare's speaker must "beare amisse /

The second burthen of a former child." Only so monstrous a birth remains possible to the speaker, so exhausted is the rhetoric of praise. Wroth too acknowledges the exhaustion of epideictic poetics in sonnet 7 in the second half of her sequence. Her opening quatrain asserts:

> An end fond jealousie alas I know
>> Thy hidenest and thy most secrett art
>> Thou canst noe new invention frame but part
> I have allreddy seene, and felt with woe.

Like Shakespeare's speaker, Wroth's identifies the problematics of poetic invention. She knows her "eye" to have been "perjured" by "fained show." But Wroth rejects that tired subject for invention: "thy flattery, and thy skill, / Which idly made mee to observe thy will; / Thus is my learning by my bondage bought." Instead of paying obeisance to the male "will" which impels Shakespeare's speaker, Wroth subverts that observation. Wroth's speaker finds the words that Petrarch's Laura, Sidney's Stella, and Shakespeare's Dark Lady had been denied. In declaring "Thus is my learning by my bondage bought." she is, through the poetics of the Petrarchan tradition, asserting her freedom to rewrite that tradition.

Wroth thematizes her resistance in her most physically and politically explicit sonnet. In sonnet 35, Wroth creates in the shape of the sonnet a body which unlike both the body politic and her own body does not betray her. Male appropriation of birth to provide metaphors for poetic creation, like Shakespeare's monstrous birth and Sidney's comical "great with child to speak and helpless in my throes," constitutes a poetic commonplace. For a woman to write a poem about birth, however, as Wroth does in sonnet 35, is to reclaim her body as her own. In this poem about miscarriage, Wroth gives a new and natural meaning to a wrenched and overused convention:

> Faulce hope which feeds but to destroy, and spill
>> What itt first breeds; unaturall to the birth
>> Of thine owne wombe; conceaving butt to
>> kill,
> And plenty gives to make the greater dearth.

Only late in her marriage to Robert Wroth and the year before his death did she bear their one child, a son, James, who may have, had he lived, spared his mother the financial difficulties of her later years. She may, perhaps, be writing from the pain of her body's betrayal. The opening quatrain carries a powerful conviction of an internal deception. When Wroth moves from her natural body to the body politic in the second quatrain, she broaches dangerously political territory:

> Soe Tirants doe who faulsly ruling earth
>> Outwardly grace them, and with profitts fill
>> Advance those who appointed are to death
> To make theyr greater falle to please theyr
> will.

By the third quatrain, she explicates the analogy between the "faire showes" tyrants employ to deceive those they would kill and the hopes that delude those who rely on appearances. Not love, but physical and political betrayal, and biological and social oppression impel this sonnet. Just as a woman's body may betray itself, so does the body politic betray those it contains. But the tyrant's "will" places him in control. In contrast, in the most interior places, "thine owne wombe," the speaker acknowledges that she is not in control. That involuntary self-hood is privileged in the closing sestet:

> Thus shadow they theyr wicked vile intent
>> Coulering evill with a show of good
>> While in faire showes theyr malice soe is
>> spent;
>> Hope kills the hart, and tirants shed the blood.
> For hope deluding brings us to the pride
> Of our desires the farder downe to slide.

The "faire showes" of tyrants reveal "the pride / Of our desires." The speaker, on the other hand, contains secrets beyond mere human will, with the power implicit in such secrets.

While Wroth's rewriting of Petrarchan poetics accounts for her debt to her uncle, Sir Philip Sidney, her aunt, Mary Sidney, Countess of Pembroke, helps her to claim female origins for her poetic authority. In Mary Sidney's work, Wroth might well have found an alternative Petrarchan tradition more suited to her poetics. Wroth announces her debt to the visionary Petrarch of the *Trionfi* in the liminal sonnet of the sequence. In so doing, she places herself in a line of women writers that extends from Queen Elizabeth through the Countess of Pembroke, for whom the *Triumphs* provide an invitation to female poetics. Queen Elizabeth's translation of *The Triumph of Eternity* is eclipsed in importance to Wroth, however, by her aunt's translation of *The Triumph of Death*. Wroth found, in that vision where Laura at last declares her love for Petrarch, the familial and female precedent for her poetry's open declaration of female desire. While Wroth's debt is not a verbal one, in the opening vision of her sequence she speaks as a woman who loves, like Laura in *The Triumph of Death*. The sonnet translates both the visionary Petrarch and the visionary Dante of the *Vita Nuova* into the making of her poetic subject:

> When nights black mantle could most darkness
>> prove,
>> And sleepe deaths Image did my sences hiere
>> From knowledge of my self, then thoughts did
>> move
> Swifter then those most swiftnes need require:
> In sleepe, a Chariot drawne by wing'd desire
>> I sawe: wher sate bright Venus Queene of
>> love,
>> And att her feete her sonne, still adding fire
>> To burning hearts which she did hold above,
> Butt one hart flaming more then all the rest
>> The goddess held, and putt itt to my brest,
>> Deare sonne, now shutt sayd she: thus must
>> wee winn;

Hee her obay'd, and martir'd my poore hart,
  I, waking hop'd as dreames it would depart
Yett since: O mee: a lover I have binn.

In this, the first of the 103 poems of *Pamphilia to Amphilanthus,* Wroth announces her poetic intentions. The danger of her enterprise is suggested by the 558-page prose and poetry "preface" to the sequence. By envisioning her opening sonnet in implicit response to the opening visionary sonnet of Dante's *Vita Nuova,* Wroth is challenging the Italianist world. Where Dante saw a man feeding Dante's own burning heart to his beloved lady, Wroth sees a flaming heart held by Venus, then shut within the visionary speaker's breast. The vision which makes a lover and a poet of Dante constitutes a similarly metamorphic moment for Wroth: "Yett since: O mee: a lover I have binn." Like the poetry of Dante and Petrarch, Wroth's poetry investigates her origins as a poet. But her answers are complicated by the male legacy of female silencing. How can she create a language for female desire?

This liminal sonnet both poses the problems she must engage and begins to suggest her solutions. Her vision responds on the one hand to Dante's and Petrarch's. But on the other hand, by enclosing the flaming heart within her breast, the speaker lays claim to her own body. Moreover, the vision of woman's desire is generated through a female community, including Mary Sidney, the translator of Laura's declaration of female desire in *The Triumph of Death.*

This opening poem of the sequence also rewrites Wroth's own text. Self-referential in two ways, Wroth announces herself as a reader and writer of her own work. First, the frontispiece of the published volume frames with a classical triumphal arch an expansive landscape with, at its center, a statue of Venus holding a flaming heart. Then, in Urania's early wanderings, she comes upon a Palace on a Hill, on which stands a white marble statue of Venus "in her left hand holding a flaming Heart" (39). Venus's statue directs the spectators' attention to the figure of "*Constancy,* holding in her hand the Keyes of the Pallace." From allegorical engraved frontispiece, through prose and poetry in the romance, to the opening sonnet, Wroth leads readers on a journey inward.

Analogously, Wroth creates an inwardness out of Mary Sidney's public legacy of writing. Much as Wroth's rewriting of the male invention of subjectivity depends upon her reclamation of her name, similarly her use of the traditions of female writing reclaims the ideology of the name. Wroth's romance heroine's name, Urania, alludes to Edmund Spenser's praise in "Colin Clout's Come Home Again" of Mary Sidney, Countess of Pembroke. He calls her: "Urania, sister to *Astrofell,* / In whose brave mynd, as in a golden cofer, / All heavenly gifts and riches locked are."

For Wroth, that "golden cofer," like Pamphilia's locked cabinet, contains verses in a woman's own hand: Mary Sidney's poetry. In weaving Mary Sidney's verses from her elegy, "The Dolefull Lay of Clorinda," into her own text in song 2 of *Pamphilia to Amphilanthus,* Wroth reveals a female origin for herself as a reader and writer. Mary Sidney distances her lament for her brother's death through the pastoral voice of the shepherdess, Clorinda, who begins: "Ay mee, to who shall I my case complaine? / That may compassion my impatient griefe?" Sidney's sighs, "Ay mee," and her questioning effort to find an audience for her complaint are echoed in Wroth's song 2:

All night I weepe, all day I cry, Ay mee;
I still doe wish though yett deny, Ay mee;
I sigh, I mourne, I say that still
I only ame the store for ill, Ay mee; . . .
Whether (alass) then shall I goe Ay mee;
When as dispaire all hopes outgoe Ay mee;
Iff to the Forest, Cupid hyes,
And my poore soule to his lawe ties Ay mee.

Sidney's opening sigh, "Ay mee," has become Wroth's insistent refrain. Instead of Mary Sidney's iambic pentameter lines and six-line stanza, Wroth invents an exploded ballad form. That is, she extends the ballad's four-line stanzas of tetrameter verse in lines 1, 2, and 4 by an additional foot, with her "Ay mee" refrain. If, at first, the refrain sounds a note of defeat, as the song goes on, the "I" both in the refrain and in the repeated "i" rhyme (cry, deny, hy, ly) becomes an assertion, an "Aye," and a declaration of the life of an "I." Wroth's challenge to the ballad form, disrupting it by the bold repetition of the refrain, asserts a new, unashamed voice, ready to retell the story of Petrarchism. Because of the more salient mediation of Mary Sidney's poem, the Petrarchan signature antitheses seem remote indeed. The sigh, "Ay mee," is the breath that takes us inside.

Mary Sidney's and Wroth's poems share the subject of the loss of a loved one. While Sidney's poem asks where she should "enfold" her "inward paine," Wroth's asks where she shall "goe." In Sidney's initially inner-directed approach, she asks, "To heavens?" and "To men?," rejecting both in favor of her "selfe." By the fourth stanza, she seems to have resolved her grief in inward resources. But the elegy's closing stanzas assume a more public role, celebrating the eternal glory of Astrophel, as "Joy of the world, and shepheards pride." Wroth's six-stanza song again echoes Clorinda's questions, asking if she should run "To the Court?" to relieve her distress. Like Clorinda, the speaker of Wroth's song rejects the outward resources her culture provides. But Wroth's briefer poem stops with its repose in "quiett rest." Neither the court nor the forest serve as refuge for this lover: "All places ar alike to love Ay mee." Addressing herself, the speaker empowers herself through the truth of her love: "Your true love all truth discovers." Wroth, then, does not provide a resolution of loss through apotheosizing the beloved, but celebrates an examination of a new subject, the female "I."

Wroth addresses the issue of female authorship in her thematics of writing. In sonnet 22, for example, she compares the requisite hiding of her verses, "the marke" she makes to express Cupid's power, with open sacrificial rites of Indians (P25). Just as the sun abuses with sunburn those Indians who worship it, so the speaker's worship of her beloved leads only to "hopes undunn." But the sestet suggests that the Indian's relationship to the sun may indeed be more rewarding than hers to her beloved:

> Beesids theyr sacrifies receav'ds in sight
>   Of theyr chose sainte: Mine hid as worthles
>   rite;
> Grant mee to see where I my offrings give,
> Then lett mee weare the marke of Cupids might
>   In hart as they in skin of Phoebus light
>   Nott ceasing offrings to love while I Live.

At least the Indians' sacrifice can be shown; hers must be "hid as worthles rite." Wroth's intricate puns on her name, "worth/wroth," and on her writing, "rite/write," encode the intimate entanglement of the activity of writing and the creation of female subjectivity. When the poem at its close turns inward to her "hart," it is not in despair but in determination that she will continue making her "marke," her "offrings to love while I Live." However devalued her "rite" may be in a public forum, she attests to its "worth" in the sonnet. Wroth takes her metaphor of the Indians from Ben Jonson and Inigo Jones's *Masque of Blackness* (1605) in which she had appeared as Baryte, one of the Daughters of the Niger. In that Jacobean court masque, she had participated in one of those "pleasing pastimes" invented by men. Returning in this sonnet to rewrite the experience, she reclaims it as her own.

Part of Wroth's work in reclaiming poetic invention for women occurs in **Urania,** where she imagines communities of women who read, support, and generate each others' writing. In the lyrics, Venus, Night, Time, Fortune, Folly, and Philomela speak with the voices of female authority from mythology, allegory, and philosphy. The song series following the corona in *Pamphilia to Amphilanthus* develops this female community. In song 2, Silvia and her nymphs hide in the woods, viewing Cupid's solipsistic play:

> All naked playing with his wings
>   Within a mirtle tree
> Which sight a soddaine laughter brings
>   His godhead soe to see;
> And fondly they beegan to jest,
>   With scoffing and delight,
> Nott knowing hee did breed unrest,
>   And that his will's his right.

Instead of a comic encounter, Cupid turns the incident into a violent assault on the nymphs when he shoots his "murdring dart." The poem explains such a turn through the punning assertion, "his will's his right." But Wroth replaces "powrfull Cupids name" in her next song with the powerful Ovidian name of Philomela, "Philomeale in this arbour / Makes now her loving harbour." By providing Philomela with a song, Wroth returns a voice to that violated heroine. Further, the female community of Silvia and her nymphs generates the creation of Philomela's song.

Similarly, Wroth revises the misogynist representation of Lady Fortune, for example, in sonnet 31. In the interior drama of that sonnet, Fortune offers warmth, comfort, and resolve to the speaker:

> Till, rise, sayd she, Reward to thee doth send
>   By mee the servants of true lovers, joy:
>   Bannish all clowds of doubt, all feares
>   destroy,
>   And now on Fortune, and on Love depend.

The speaker withdraws into an interior realm where the once indifferent or hostile figure of Fortune becomes instead a friend. The peace Fortune brings is reiterated in the closing sonnet of *Pamphilia to Amphilanthus*. There, the speaker first acknowledges her muse in a farewell:

> My muse now happy lay thyself to rest,
>   Sleepe in the quiett of faithfull love,
>   Write you no more, but lett thes phant'sies
>   move
>   Some other harts, wake not to new unrest.

In contrast to Sir Philip Sidney's chiding muse, who opens his sequence with her summons, "Fool . . . look in thy heart and write," Wroth's muse has been an assumed partner, not absent, but a tacit collaborator.

Wroth's community of women recalls Christine de Pisan's *Book of the City of Ladies,* where, to undo the damage misogynist texts have wrought, allegorical figures of Reason, Rectitude, and Justice appear to the author. These worthy women lead Christine de Pisan to rewrite history, mythology, and religion. In a similar way, the female population of Wroth's lyrics pays silent, but no less eloquent, tribute to the origins of female subjectivity in reading and writing: the twelfth-century letters of Heloise, the fables and lays of Marie de France, the allegories of Christine de Pisan, *The Book of Margery Kempe,* and the lyrics of Louise Labé and Gaspara Stampa. They, too, should be numbered in Wroth's company, in the invention of female poetic subjectivity.

Gary Waller (essay date 1993)

SOURCE: " 'Watch, gaze, and marke': The Poetry of Mary Wroth," in *The Sidney Family Romance: Mary Wroth, William Herbert, and the Early Modern Construction of Gender,* Wayne State University Press, 1993, pp. 190-219.

[*In this essay, Waller presents an overview of the traditions, influences, and seventeenth-century gender roles that shaped Wroth's poetry.*]

Despite their apparent obviousness, the words we use to describe gender assignments are sites of continual struggle. "Man" and "woman" are sliding, not stable, signifiers. Nor are the material practices that embody our lived sexual roles adequately descibed by the tragic limitations of such binarism. New forms of gender assignment emerge; new patterns of what we persist in calling "masculinity" and "femininity" are engendered. Representations never fully correspond to lived experiences, yet experiences are given form only by means of their representations. No literary text attempting to articulate gendered experiences is, therefore, ever "merely" literary; inevitably part of the history of ideologies, it opens political, religious, racial, class, and gender related questions—and perhaps the more intensely so when it is situated on the margins of the dominant literary forms of its society, where it is a reminder that any moment in history is constituted by a multiplicity of material practices and that what appears to be dominant depends, in part, for its power on what has been, at least for the moment, marginalized.

Mary Wroth's poems constitute a major document in tracing the ways both assigned and lived gender roles were under pressure in the early seventeenth century. The first collection of Petrarchan love poetry in English by a woman, *Pamphilia to Amphilanthus* was published in 1621, appended to Wroth's prose romance, *The Countesse of Mountgomeries Urania*. The date is important: even in the time it was written, it was a culturally marginal work. 1621 is some thirty years after the main vogue of sonneteering in England (and twelve years after even Shakespeare's belated and probably pirated collection appeared). In the previous decade Wroth had been mentioned by family members, a few friends, and dependents in a predictably adulatory manner as an inheritor of the Sidney poetic genius, but the actual publication of *Pamphilia to Amphilanthus* received virtually no notice. Nevertheless, along with the poems she inserted into *Urania* itself, *Pamphilia to Amphilanthus* is a major document at the end of the dominant tradition of Renaissance love poetry and a focal point in the long struggle to challenge the assumptions and practices of that tradition. It is a prime source for our attempting to read, today, what it was to be gendered as a woman in early modern England, and to try to write within and against the structures of desire determined by that gender assignment.

Vilified when they appeared in print, Wroth's writings were virtually unknown, except as curiosities, until the mid-1970s. After over three centuries of neglect, they are currently receiving an increasing amount of attention: since 1977 there have been three editions of her writings (with a further one, the complete *Urania,* awaited), a monograph, a collection of critical essays, and a number of articles and chapters of books on her. Much of the (very sparse) earlier attention she received was because she was a member of the Sidney family, but today it is largely because of the seriousness and power of her writing. Wroth is certainly the most important woman writer in English before Aphra Behn: we are not dealing as we are with Pembroke, with an undeniably minor writer for whom poetry was just a spasmodic pastime. Simply in terms of the amount of poetry she wrote, Wroth deserves careful attention. There are over two hundred of her poems extant: 103 in the 1621 version of *Pamphilia to Amphilanthus;* another nineteen in *Urania* itself (some of which had been in an earlier manuscript version of *Pamphilia to Amphilanthus,* now in the Folger, which also contains an additional six poems that were excluded from the 1621 edition); another fifty-six in the published *Urania* and a further eighteen in the unpublished second part that were excluded from both versions of *Pamphilia to Amphilanthus;* and, finally, nine separate lyrics-in her verse play, *Love's Victory*. It is possible that there are still more unidentified in manuscripts. So far as dating is concerned, from some internal references at least a few were probably written in the first decade of James I's reign—the period for which we have the most detailed documentary evidence for the liaison between Wroth and Pembroke—and some may have been circulating by 1613, when Johnson refers to Wroth's poems making him both a better lover and a better poet. There is no way of saying definitely which poems Jonson saw; if the poems he praises were indeed part of what became *Pamphilia to Amphilanthus,* they were no doubt revised in subsequent years, even as late as 1618-21, when Wroth was probably composing *Urania* and deciding which poems should be inserted into the romance. The years 1614-21, after her husband's death—when she was sexually and socially independent, when she bore her two illegitimate children, and when she wrote *Urania*—was most likely a period of great insecurity, but, quite possibly, unexpected satisfaction to her. Even if it originated earlier, *Pamphilia to Amphilanthus* was almost certainly revised in these years, and records more directly than her other writings her struggles against the constraints of being a woman. Much of the power of her poetry lies in the record of those struggles.

In writing in the Petrarchan mode, Mary Wroth was following paths that were (to put it mildly) heavily trodden. Not only are her poems among the last recognizably Petrarchan poetry in English, but they are doubly "belated," to use Harold Bloom's term, in relation to her own family. The commitment to the poetic vocation and to the details of craft that all three of the first generation Sidney poets—Philip, Mary, and Robert—showed is evident in her poems, but no doubt being a Sidney was itself a provocation to write, even for a woman. That she took her writing seriously can be documented from the extensive changes she made over perhaps a decade to the poems. The holograph copy in the Folger contains corrections which were later included in the revised text appended to *Urania,* and many of the poems were moved back and forth between the main body of the prose romance and the appended sequence. The Folger manuscript is perhaps rather like the manuscript of Greville's *Caelica,* essentially a private, cumulative collection designed primarily or even exclusively for the author herself.

Even though they are far less frustrating than Pembroke's, Wroth's poems still present any modern editor with a dilemma in reconstructing their history. If the 1621 printing is used as the copytext, then the editor needs to either ignore or find a way of sorting through printer's accidentals, and then must somehow fit in or append those poems found only in the Folger copy. If the Folger manuscript is used as copytext, then an undatable ordering, even though with authorial accidentals, becomes the basis for the edition, and the reordering, additions and omissions of 1621 are obscured. In my edition of *Pamphilia to Amphilanthus* (1977), I chose the former course; in her edition of the complete poems (1983), Roberts followed the Folger text, but used the ordering of 1621. Neither is entirely satisfactory, and that in large part is because of the nature of the collection. As with most Petrarchan sequences, even as it was being written it was being reread and rewritten by its author. Adapting Deleuze and Guattari's terms, Roger Kuin [in the *Sidney Newsletter* 9.1, 1988] has suggested that we should view the Petrarchan text as a desiring machine, combining the "power of the continuum" with "rupture in direction" in its "capacity for an unlimited number of connections." *Pamphilia to Amphilanthus* might be best seen as a continuous text, unravelling as it is put together, never resting in a final form, in which a variety of discoveries, demands, and changing occasions clash and contradict.

As with Pembroke's poems, we are clearly in the familiar world of belated Petrarchism—plaint and paradox, sophisticated but general emotions, rhetorical smoothness and lyric grace frequently counterpointed by the disruptiveness of question or cry, and beneath all the Petrarchan stock-in-trade of juxtaposed despair and joy. If Pembroke's poems are often more "Cavalier" than "Petrarchan," Wroth's poems often read as if they would be at home in the collections of poems that had been fashionable twenty and more years before. But the cousins share the central Petrarchan inheritance: as with his, it is easy to construct from her poems a miscellany of such Petrarchan clichés, almost three hundred years old by the time she is writing. Love is "truth, and doth delight," and yet makes the lover "true slave to Fortune's spite"; it is at once the "hottest beames of zeale" and shows a "coldenesse" which "can but my despaires descry." The lover's spirit is "cloyd with griefe and paine," captive and yet free; the joys of love are rapturous and yet "heape disdaine" on the lover; the spring which the lovers see around them reflects back on the "sad sowrs / Which from mine eyes doe flow" inside the lover's minds, which exist in the delicious agony of frustration and indecision: "Restlesse I live, consulting what to doe, / And more I study, more I still undoe." Such conventional paradoxes and complaints are frequently dressed in stylized in neoplatonic garb, thus bringing Wroth closer to some of the poetic fashions of the Jacobean and Caroline court lyric. At times, in some of her less felicitous moments, her verse can sound like the drabbest of poets thirty years earlier, at others like a Jacobean court wit. Overall, her preferred style is closer to the direct voice of a Jonson than the elaborate wit of a Donne. Jonson may well have admired those many poems with direct and uncluttered metaphors:

> Sleepe fy possess mee nott, nor doe nott fright
>   Mee with thy heavy, and thy deathlike might
>   For counterfetting vilder then deaths sight,
>   And such deluding more my thought doe
>   spite.
>
>   (*Poems*)

Around 1610, perhaps about the same time as she was starting to write what became *Pamphilia to Amphilanthus,* Lord Dudley North dedicated a treatise on poetry to her, which contains a strong attack on what was to become known as "Metaphysical" poetry and a defence of the plain Jonsonian style. Predictably setting his argument in terms of the prestige of the Sidney family, he claims that "the admirable inventions and matter of your unimitable Uncles extant works flourish in applause of all"; further, he praises such features as "the well wrought and exquisite harmony of their Cadence," their "round, cogent cleare and gracefull delivery," and asserts (again in accord with Jonson) that "the best eloquence is to make our selves clearly understood." It may well be that Wroth herself was starting to write with such notions in mind about the time that North was writing. Her poetry can therefore be placed in a transitional position between Elizabethan "drab" verse and the Jonsonian style which grew from it. Wroth's poems rarely catch the lyric qualities of Elizabethan song: in the terms I used to speak of Pembroke's poems, even the "songs" in *Pamphilia to Amphilanthus* are brooding and melancholy, "declamatory" rather than songlike. But the most significant aspect of her writing arises from the contradictions between the predominantly masculinist rhetoric of the Petrarchan sonnet and her sense of her own gendered position as a woman, lover, reader, and writer. What was it for a woman to write a blazon? To gaze at a woman's beauties, her "ruby lips, pearl teeth, damask cheeks, face, neck, chin, formed of purest snow" (*Newberry 1*, fol. 24) may seem a "natural" default position for a male writer. But what happens when the passive object of such "devotion" wants to write in the same mode? To what extent is she aware of being a multiply split subject? The conventional answer is that she should not notice: that the form itself dictates the response. But that is to assume that the "neutral" reading position is not gendered, while in fact it institutionalizes a wholesale gagging of women readers and writers. In 1630 the courtesy book writer Robert Cleaver voiced the whole culture's proscription of women's language when he recommended [in his *A Godly Form of Household Government*] that "as the echo answereth but one word for many, which are spoken to her, so a woman's answer should be in a word." A very condition of Wroth's permission to write poetry meant that she had to locate herself within a tradition that largely denied her, as a woman, a place from which to speak.

Pamphilia to Amphilanthus is more various than most collections of Petrarchan sonnets, and not surprisingly, critics intent on finding a "unity" to the whole—quite apart from the textual problem discussed above—have perceived quite different structural organizations. Jeff Masten argues [in *Reading Mary Wroth*] that we should see *Pamphilia to Amphilanthus* not as a single collection, but as several sequences of poems copied into a single manuscript. This, he argues, accounts for the unusual numbering, which starts at #1 at several places and has blank pages between groups of poems. McLaren sees the 1621 order as divided into two, the title sequence and an unfinished **"Crowne of Sonnets"**; May Pauliessen [in *The Love Sounds of Lady Mary Wroth: A Critical Introduction*] sees four sequences: the opening one courtly, witty, and frequently flirtatious; the second, more erotic, "occult, more debauched"; third, the **"Crowne"**; and then a concluding group focusing on spiritual love. Roberts agrees on a four-fold structure, but sees the focus differently: an opening section of fifty-five sonnets and songs focusing on Pamphilia's struggle for love; a second on the darker side of love; the crowne of sonnets in which different versions of love are debated; and a final section in which unpredictability, pain, and loss are all acknowledged as an inevitable part of love. Roberts's reading is a pleasurable and comfortable (in Barthes's sense) narrativization, but, as we read any sustained collection of Petrarchan lyrics, inevitably we discover that what holds it together is less (or not only) the "story" but the arbitrariness of desire, the surges of discontinuity and surprise. It is as if the self that writes is continually being rewritten by the experiences it seeks to enclose and comprehend. . . .

[The] Petrarchan poem centers on its fragile and self-obsessed "I." It is a device, at once rhetorical and psychological, that functions to provide an impression of stability and continuity to the experience the poem tries to encode, but so often what the poem records (and evokes) is a disturbing instability. Part of the power of Petrarchism had traditionally been that it encouraged its readers (including the poet) to acknowledge that the self that writes feels not harmony but continual dissatisfaction. Except under the most stringent ideological constraints the Petrarchan "I" is always under attack, always liable to be surprised by change, dislocated by the pull of impossible futures and indelible pasts. In Wroth's case this painful discovery is all the more threatening because of the way the poems highlight the dilemmas of her gender assignment.

Petrarchism involves the encoding of a set of recurrent, perhaps even inherent, male strategies for dealing with desire. I say "perhaps even inherent": a more optimistic reading suggests that they are typical of a society that rigidly hierarchizes gender differences along the line of domination and submission. In this chapter I want to ask what variations and distortions occur when a woman, traditionally occupying the place of the ostensible object of the poet's devotion, the focus of the "I"'s gaze, takes up the subject position itself? Necessarily caught up in the enormously powerful discourses of an authoritarian patriarchy that went far beyond poetry, what opportunities did a woman poet at this time have to discover a voice that she herself owned, if not "individually," at least as a woman voicing the shared subjectivity of other women? In a poetic tradition where male formulations of desire were so dominant, could she settle for (or even envisage) anything more than fragmentation? Would it be the "same" fragmentation as that articulated on behalf of the male subject position? While these questions are fundamental to our understanding of Wroth, and all will recur in my discussion, rather than treating her as a "woman poet"— as if that were a self-explanatory category determined by a fixed gender role—I want to raise questions about how her options and possibilities as a writer were affected by her gender assignment. . . . I want to show how that

process works out in a particular discursive form, the Petrarchan sonnet collection, which had traditionally been as rigidly coded "male" as the society that had engendered it.

There is no doubt that Wroth's poems, far more than those of her cousin, ring with a distinctive voice, one that speaks powerfully to her age and beyond. It is a rhetorically confrontational voice, something which derives only in part from the insistent sense of audience in the Petrarchan tradition. It typically makes demands on its audience for attention that seems, on occasion, defensive to the point of petulance:

> Bee you all pleas'd? your pleasures grieve nott
>   mee:
> Doe you delight? I envy nott your joy:
> Have you content? contentment with you bee:
> Hope you for bliss? hope still, and still injoye:
>   (*Poems*)

Frequently, it is a voice that seemingly resents speaking at all, at least so as to be overheard. Yet while reluctantly acknowledging the presence of listeners, the poems nonetheless convey a sense of active dialogue and dissension: conversations rather than monologues emerge through the poems. This is a paradoxial effect arising from the encoded situation of a woman writer: desiring to write, she finds herself unauthorized to do so by the very form she chooses in which to write. She resents being overheard trespassing on ground already occupied, but it is ground that she must nonetheless step firmly upon. Wroth is uncommonly effective at setting up multiple voices within the poem that belong to the speaker herself, brooding alone, giving herself advice:

> Yett is ther hope: Then Love butt play thy part
> Remember well thy self, and think on mee;
> Shine in those eyes which conquer'd have my
>   hart;
> And see if mine bee slack to answere thee.
>   (*Poems*)

As in her uncle Philip's *Astrophil and Stella* or many of her father's lyrics (even some of her aunt's sometimes intensely dramatic psalm metaphrases), Wroth's poems stage the process of internalization by which both women and men alike were positioned by contradictory erotic and social demands. And sometimes, like those of her male relations, Wroth's poems show her heroine trying to withdraw from public responsibilities, even from public view, in order to deal with the internal dialogue of her desires. As in her father's and her uncle's poems, public or ideological contradictions are internalized as private debates. But in *Pamphilia to Amphilanthus,* most of these psychological divisions arise specifically from a woman's gender assignment:

> Why should wee nott loves purblind charmes
>   resist?
> Must wee bee servile, doing what hee list?
> Noe, seeke some hoste to harbour thee: I fly

Thy babish trickes, and freedome doe profess;
  Butt O my hurt, makes my lost hart confess
  I love, and must: So farwell liberty.

  (*Poems*)

To what extent are these poems autobiographical? Can
we trace any consistent (or significantly inconsistent) relations between the "I" of the poems and their author? Or
are we dealing, as we were with Pembroke, with the apparent anonymity of coterie verse? Unlike her cousin's
poems, Wroth's include a tissue of narratives taken from
her own life, the most obvious of which refers to her
relationship with her cousin. Kristeva [in her *Tales of
Love*] speaks of poetry enabling us to "play around that
exquisite border where the 'true' trips over into the 'make-
believe',", and, especially in the early sonnets of *Pamphilia to Amphilanthus,* there are a number of references
to the relationship between the two cousins that seem to
hover titillatingly between personal revelation and fantasy, perhaps in the way that Philip's "Rich" sonnets do.
Pamphilia claims that "many Poets write as well by imitation, as by sence of passion" (*Urania*). The names attached to the sequence's hero and heroine—the names
also of the main characters of *Urania*—mean, respectively, "all-loving" and "lover of two." That they are in part
a projection of Wroth's wishfulfillment fantasies about
her relationship with Pembroke, what she conceived as
her own fidelity and his lack of commitment, seems undeniable. The two lovers in both the poems and romance
are first cousins, whose love, we are told, though for no
explicable reason, must be kept secret. It is clear, moreover, that while he gains from such secrecy, she suffers
privately from lack of public recognition of her love. In
Urania this insistent secrecy lasts even after the two have
concluded a public vow of commitment . . . it is as if
they both are and are not committed to each other, just as
their love both is and is not secret. In the poems, although
likewise no reason is provided, secrecy is also a given:
"thy chiefe paine is that I must itt hide / From all save
only one who showld itt see." Like the romance, too, the
poems give clear signals about the "real" identity of the
protagonists. There are recurring puns on the name "will,"
conventional enough in themselves, but too many to be
coincidental. Such references include, from the sixth poem:
"Long have I suffer'd, and esteem'd itt deere / Since such
thy will; yett grew my paine more neere"; or, two poems
later:

But now, itt seemes, thou would'st I should thee
  love;
  I doe confess, t'was thy will made mee chuse;
  And thy faire showes made mee a lover prove
  When I my freedome did, for paine refuse.

  (*Poems*)

In a song late in the collection, Wroth puns on both her
cousin's name and her own, asserting that "your chiefe
honors bee in this / By worth what wunn is, nott to leave,"
and admonishing him that "if worthles to bee priz'd /
Why att first will you itt move, / And if worthy, why
dispis'd?" Merging the figure of Cupid with the male
lover, she acknowledges that instead of falling in love

with the "wanton boy" who shot her, she has found herself in love with "Will," who is the object of her poetry,
and who is therefore even more dangerous than Cupid
himself: "When love came blindfold, and did chaleng mee
/ Indeed I lov'd butt wanton boy not hee." In a poem in
the Folger MS, the poem's speaker identifies "Will" with
her own will, and begs him not to seek freedom from the
bonds of love. As Pauliessen suggests, the enigma or riddle of the poem is that, despite the poem's admonition to
do so, "Wee will not seeke to free will." In another sonnet where she puns on her cousin's name in the opening
line, "Deare cherish this, and with itt my soules will," the
second part of the poem reads like "a coy letter of a
proposal of love" to Will, suggesting that his heart will
not be abused in the exchange: "Butt if you will bee kind,
and just indeed, / Send mee your hart which in minds
place shall feed." One poem in particular makes the biographical reference extremely clear:

How like a fire both love increase in mee,
  The longer that itt lasts, the stronger still,
  The greater, purer, brighter, and doth fill
  Noe eye with wunder more, then hopes still
    bee

Bred in my brest, when fires of love are free
  To use that part to theyr best pleasing will,
  And now impossible itt is to kill
  The heat soe great wher Love his strength doth
    see.

My eyes can scarce sustain the flames my hart
  Doth trust in them my passions to impart,
  And languishingly strive to show my love;

My breath nott able is to breathe least part
  Of that increasing fuell of my smart;
  Yet love I will till I butt ashes prove.

  (*Poems*)

As Roberts notes [in *Poems*], this is "one of the very few
places in which the identification of Amphilanthus is made
explicit." The poem marks the end of the first section of
sonnets and is signed "Pamphilia."

There are enough such references that if these poems were
circulated among Wroth's family and close friends, the
autobiographical level would surely have been recognized.
J. B. Broadbent [in his *Poetic Love*] speaks of the "air of
public intimacy" of such verse, with its tone of a friendly
correspondence that we are invited to overhear. Unfortunately, none of Wroth's poems seem to be "answer" poems like those Pembroke wrote with Rudyerd, so the
connections between the two cousins' poems are generic
rather than specific. What they share is the ubiquitous
Petrarchan paraphernalia: metaphors of lovers stealing
glances; the contradictions of love, its magnetizing disdain and compulsive misery. Stretching matters somewhat,
we could put Pembroke's "If her disdaine" alongside some
of Wroth's sonnets and see it replying to a number of
hers. But if we are, as Pauliessen argues [in her *Love
Sonnets*], in the middle of a coterie, it is a coterie of all

Petrarchist poets, a ubiquitous rather than a private lexicon, with only occasional specific references to note.

So far as a narrative is concerned, only the opening sequence of forty-eight sonnets and six songs seems to have any plausible internal coherence, and that at such a general level that no precise sequence of biographical references could be constructed. It seems likely, indeed, that this group of poems was organized into a sequence. It starts out with two sonnets dealing with the opening of a love affair. The speaker feels, not entirely happily, that she has been picked out by love (1); this victimization has occurred in an encounter within the court (2); she thus finds herself in the conventional Petrarchan state of oscillation between misery and hope (3-5). This opening group of six sonnets culminates in an assertion in which she indicates that the source of her joyful grief lies in the desires of another: "Long I have suffer'd, and esteem'd itt deare / Since such thy will" (6). (I will not, at this point, pause over the gender politics of that subservience to another's desire, but will return to it and like sentiments later.) A song is placed after each group of six sonnets, except the last: in song 1, Pamphilia bewails the contrast between the spring outside and her internal winter, and vows that if she is not happy, she will at least make poetry from her miseries. The second group (sonnets 7-12, song 2) resumes the bewailing of her fate: the pun on "will" is again in evidence. She writes poetry to contain her misery (8), and asserts that she is married not to her beloved but to sorrow (9). Her lover arrives, a weary traveler (10), causing her increasing torments, especially as she lies awake at night (11, 12). The second song, concluding the second group of sonnets, depicts her weeping, alone, at night. The third group (sonnets 13-18, song 3) again starts with a sonnet begging that she, "one, who att your will, yeelds to the grave," will be spared destruction (13), even though she cannot resist him (14). This is followed by four sonnets (15-18) and a song on sleeplessness.

The next group (sonnets 19-24, song 4) continues the concern with sleeplessness and brooding alone. Pamphilia considers her plight while her beloved is outside hunting (23), and warns herself against jealousy (24). The following group (sonnets 25-30, song 5) focuses on her absence from the beloved. A light, courtly song (song 4) announces the theme, and then the following sonnet (25) pleads with him to return from his journey. The next sonnet once again points to the identity of the beloved, begging him for an exchange of hearts (26), especially as he produces only hopelessness and grief in his absence (27-30). The fifth song is, appropriately, a complaint against time. The sixth group (sonnets 31-36, song 6) opens with Pamphilia lying down, asking Fortune for comfort: she regrets that love has to be snatched from time (31), thus producing increasing frustration. She describes herself as a hive of love (32), is aware of and even glorifies in being watched in public (33, 34), even though she feels her love is hopeless (35) and must be hidden from all except one (36). The song that concludes the sequence concerns eyes, the means by which she is watched. The seventh group (sonnets 37-42, song 7) opens with poems on night (37) and

banishment (38), followed by an expression of the inadequacy of her poetry, even when it is admired (39). The group concludes with two sonnets on emphasizing that true love is an inner state (40, 41) and one affirming that her great love is also her great woe (42), while the concluding song of the group also dwells on sorrow. The final group (sonnets 43-47) starts by imagining her lover as a light shining everywhere except where she is: "But now alas, your sight is heare forbid, / And darkness must these poore lost rooms posesse." Again, her state is contrasted with the burgeoning spring (44), as she bewails her lover's absence (45). Once again punning on "will" (46), she acknowledges she has engaged in a forbidden love and that, therefore, her devotion is hopeless (47). Then, in the final sonnet, signed "Pamphilia" in the Folger manuscript, she simply acknowledges that however unfulfillable it may be, she cannot help the increase of her love, and once again, in this culminating sonnet of the sequence, explicitly acknowledges the commitment to "Will": "Yett love I will till I but ashes prove."

In this way, one can, then, construct a coherent reading of the main sequence of *Pamphilia to Amphilanthus*. But what does such a reading give us beyond some extremely general narrative coherence and some scattered if undeniable biographical reference? When we have "identified" the beloved as a fantasy projection of Pembroke, what have we gained? More important than tracking down biographical references, I suggest, are the ways in which Wroth's poems are written by broader discursive structures, and therefore, [. . .] I turn to the poems as articulations of cultural, not merely individual, narratives.

Far more self-consciously and with more evident effort than a male poet working within the Petrarchan tradition, Wroth has to struggle to define her own voice in her poems against overwhelming gender stereotypes. How does a woman poet write within such an overwhelmingly male discourse? What emerges through her poetry is a variety of moods, only some of which she shares with male poets in the tradition. They range from passive uneasiness to outright anger at the treatment that she, as a woman, receives. Some of these feelings are common to male protagonists of Petrarchan poems, but others seem to grow more directly from becoming conscious of what it is to be assigned the "woman's part" in a relationship. And some are directed towards the very structures that have brought her poetry and, more broadly, her very sense of being a woman, into existence. Like a kleptomaniac, she must steal what has hitherto been the prerogative of the male. Drawing on both case studies and theoretical work by Otto Fenichel and Gregorio Kohon, Kaplan explains [in *Female Perversions*] how in a society where power rests largely in the hands of a few superior males, the kleptomaniac may feel both revenge and erotic excitement. Cautioning that how "the theft relates to her childhood deprivations and humiliations can be understood only by a reading of her unique unconscious script," Kaplan nonetheless notes that there are some prototypical kleptomania scripts. In the clinical literature, some relate specifically to modern commodity fetishism, with consumption as an outlet for anxiety and emptiness; others more readily grow from pre-capitalist society where the power possessed by men and desired by women also included language, movement, autonomy of many kinds. Kaplan sees Joan of Arc as a historical prototype: as Denny's reaction to the publication of **Urania** shows, men can be content when a woman's ambitions are held within approved limits, but should she "openly declare her ambitions in territories that have been defined as masculine," then she may have to "awaken the infantile fantasy that [her] intelligence is a stolen trophy," and often she must "run for cover" in her "masquerades of womanliness." Historically, Kaplan notes, when women have expressed themselves in politics or writing, males have commonly reacted by constructing the image of the virago," convinced that the castrated ones are out to castrate the phallic ones." Denny's virulent reaction to Mary Wroth's leaving the approved confinement of pious translator and "stealing" the roles of erotic poet and romance writer is the classic reaction, even to the point of his anger being articulated as sexual abuse. Her reaction to withdraw the work and retire from public exposure is likewise the classic reaction of the abused victim of the patriarchal system.

We do, however, have the spoils of her thefts. In **Pamphilia to Amphilanthus,** Wroth explores a series of situations in which her protagonist searches for the causes of her restlessness. In some poems she focuses on the very institution that from early in her life had complemented her family as the institutional reinforcer of her gender assignment, the court. Often her suspicion of the court is conventional, emerging in the commonplace *otium* of the pastoral:

> Love as well can make abiding
>   In a faythfull shepheards brest
> As in Princese whose thoughts sliding
>   Like swift rivers never rest.
>
> (*Poems*)

Less conventional, however, is the insistence that becomes repeated, even obsessional, as the collection moves along: that the court should be left "to faulscest lovers" (*Poems*). Such rejection characteristically suggests that the true lover may find his or her happiness in the country, since there too infidelity and, especially in her case, imprisonment and frustration are found. Love is fundamentally deceptive, whether in the court or the fields. A woman is happy only when alone, in some rare private space—which may be only inside her head—where she can be silent with her memories. Even there, in the supposedly comforting stability of her mind, however, she discovers she cannot escape. The intense melancholy of the sequence is more focused than the usual betrayal of the Petrarchan plaint. It is rooted in a woman's alienation from the court and from the continual pressure to occupy the disempowering roles which the court and the wider patriarchal society it represents have constructed for her. Her innermost thoughts, "stolen" from the public world in which she must perform demeaning roles, are hers when she is alone. The poems thus present a fascinating gendered variation of a common Petrarchan paradox: she is trapped yet free. **Pamphilia to Amphilanthus,** then, enacts a distinctively

gendered fantasy of autonomy. Pamphilia's speaking, even to herself, is like Wroth's writing itself, an act of self-assertion. But it is never an easy achievement: the more agency is affirmed, the more she finds that, because she is a woman, she must struggle in what the poems repeatedly term a "labyrinth." Both Wroth and Pamphilia are unavoidably caught up in discursive positions that they occupy only at the cost of self-violation. In psychoanalytic terms, a turn to writing—like any act of agency—is to turn from the mother to the father, to choose assertion, activity, possession of the phallus over passivity, castration, and masochism. Nowhere would such moves be a greater breach with the gender assignment of a woman than in a noble family in early modern England. Yet once presented to her—in the form of sexual possibilities or the encouragement to write—the choice is one that must be taken. This is a recurring pattern in Wroth's work: in **Urania** women seem inevitably to be punished for making sexual choices, yet they insist on making them since, however dimly, it is through such choices that they are offered the possibility of emulating or stealing for themselves the autonomy apparently enjoyed by men.

[. . .] Pembroke's poetry, in common with the Petrarchan tradition, articulates a range of characteristically male perversions. Wroth's poems, I suggest, illustrate the classic kleptomaniac tendencies of the woman living in a repressive society and wanting to affirm herself. But, like Pembroke's, her poems display a broad range of what Kaplan terms characteristic "female" perversions. Most especially, they betray a masochism born of frustrated wishes to emulate the apparent freedom of men and a desire for a mutual relationship that the masochistic, self-destructive desires in which she finds herself caught continually deny her. "Molestation" [. . .] is a recurring metaphor for her situation. Kaplan writes of how we use our fantasy lives to work over the "ordinary, expected traumas of childhood," but if these traumas are reinforced by society as the child grows up, then the mind may be crippled not only from them but by the very survival mechanisms she has "to enlist to continue to think and feel." Behind the term "molestation," then, may be historically specific physical realities and powerful myths. Molestation is thus closely related to what Clark terms [in *Women's Silence*] an "extension of the social construction of male sexuality as active, dominant and aggressive." Once a woman starts to resent being regarded as the property of a man, she might well regard the traditional proprietal sexual actions of a patriarchal husband as invasive and "molesting" in a direct physical sense. Part of a sense of agency is the right to say no; to have that no taken as rebellion, or as in fact saying yes, is part of "molestation." Wroth is evoking part of the cultural unconscious, the fears built into being a woman in a society in which gender relations are structured by an ideology of bipolar authoritarianism.

Within **Pamphilia to Amphilanthus**'s rewriting of the Petrarchan scheme, these contradictions of a woman's gender assignments often emerge as a discontented passivity and are given a distinctively masochistic edge. The conventional emphasis in Petrarchism on love as an invasion of a (supposedly) more powerful beloved encourages a stance of helpless passivity by the lover. The conventional masculine response is to look for relief or rescue not directly to the beloved but to a fetishized token for her absent presence, even to a higher love, perhaps to God for whom she is, at least in his rhetoric, a privileged though imperfect substitute. Wroth associates the lover's anguish not just with conventional postures of pain or martyrdom—Cupid "still adding fire / to burning hearts," or the feeling that one is kept in a cage, or the recurring metaphor of a labyrinth in which the love suffers (*Poems,* pp. 85, 121, 127)—but, more characteristically, with the emotional and physical retreat, even regression, into the roles that have been assigned to her as a woman.

But such a move may be tactical, not merely reactive: in which case it might be seen as an attempted act of agency. As Benjamin comments, "the masochist's wish to be reached, penetrated, found, released—a wish that can be expressed in the metaphor of violence as well as in metaphors of redemption—is the other side of the sadist's wish to discover the other." The masochist's desire to experience her "authentic, inner reality in the company of another parallels the sadist's wish to get outside the self into a shared reality." Pamphilia describes herself as desiring isolation and silence—desiring, that is, precisely what the dominant ideology prescribes for women: to have her organs of self-assertion, her mouth (for speech), her genitals (for sexual self-assertion), and the door or gate of her room, house, or garden closed or locked. She knows that by voicing her miseries, pursuing love, or going abroad, she could overcome her victimization, but instead she accepts her assignment of silence, isolation, and frigidity. Her posture is frequently described as sleeping, or near sleep, or lying down in a small space, and addressing the shadows around her as comforting, even if confusing. In one poem she broods:

> How oft in you I have laine heere opprest,
>   And have my miseries in woefull cries
>   Deliver'd forth, mounting up to the skies
> Yett helples back returnd to wound my brest.
>   (*Poems*)

In the next sonnet, she states that "lay'd downe to ease my paine," she still is trapped and can rise only by the aid of "Fortune," who is interestingly described as a fellow woman lover, who "in her bless'd arms did mee inchaine." As she rises, she acknowledges that even with another woman, she is responding rather than initiating: "I, her obay'd, and rising felt that love / Indeed was best, when I did least itt move" (*Poems*). Discussing what he believed to be the inherently masochistic situation of being a woman, Freud claimed [in "Three Essays on Sexuality", in the *Standard Edition* VII] that it consisted of neurotic passivity, whether shown in ordinary timidity or the "extreme instance" of sexual satisfaction being "conditional upon suffering physical or mental pain at the hands of the sexual object." Either way, he saw it as an individual aberration, and one inherent in being a woman. But the construction of female (or for that matter, male) masochism in our cultural history is far more complex than Freud's

account. The unconscious is not a given, biological "place"; it is rather a metaphor for those assumptions and practices whereby the contradictions of a society's ideology are repressed, transferred, and reproduced. The passivity that Pamphilia sometimes displays—and I choose that exhibitionist term deliberately—is more a cultural construct than the "individual" neurosis of which Freud speaks. "Female masochism" is not, as Freud thought, biological: even though biological factors enter into its being women's most characteristic preversion; it is predominantly the result of women's socialization and gender assignments in patriarchal society.

In the Petrarchan scheme the lover typically asserts that he becomes the victim of the power of the beloved. From such a systematization of the dynamics of desire, it seems that only two possible gender positions are possible, "one of rapacious domination, the other of docile submission." Yet though the (male) lover may assert that he is trapped or paralyzed by the power of the (female) beloved, he is inevitably the active participant: he pursues, is called to public duties as courtier or soldier; he speaks out, hunts, fights, complains. A man has the independence to move, to be restless, unfaithful, or simply assume the freedom to move through the world; a woman remains at home, constant, reassuring, mothering. Wroth's emphasis on Pamphilia's constancy never removes her from this male fantasy in which a man assumes he may move, travel, or choose, and a woman stays at home. The woman's role is to be the focus for his self-division and his physical and emotional restlessness. Moreover, her absence or coldness, while a matter for complaint, and the cause of his insecurity, is often the necessary stimulus for his being able to feel that self-division and to write about it. If she were present, which he desires, he would not write, which he also desires. She is therefore required to be absent so he can desire her presence, a paradox that Greville grimly deconstructs in *Caelica* 45, when he insists that absence, far from being the ideal state of love, the "glorious bright" of absence is in fact, pain:

> But thoughts be not so brave,
>   With absent joy;
> For you with that you have
>   Yourself destroy:
> The absence which you glory
> Is that which makes you sorry
>   And burn in vain:
> For thought is not the weapon,
> Wherewith thought's ease men cheapen,
>   Absence is pain.

Greville's is a rare, unqualified demystification of the Petrarchan pose by a male poet. Wroth's critique is more detailed and more interesting because it is written by and on behalf of a woman.

The role of Petrarchan mistress in which Pamphilia finds herself is primarily, then, a passive one. Her desire is defined and licensed by her lover's "will." She is positioned by forces, reified as "love," that are, she assumes, outside her control, and the range of feelings she is permitted consists almost entirely of the largely negative ones of entrapment, loss, and bondage. Unlike her male lover, she has no recourse to other activities by which to develop a sense of autonomy. She accepts that she must wait upon his initiative: the female "complement to the male refusal to recognize the other is woman's own acceptance of her lack of subjectivity, her willingness to offer recognition without expecting it in return." She makes herself available to her lover when he choose to visit her. Her satisfactions are those of the master/slave relationship, finding satisfaction in submission, humbling herself not out of fear but because she has been socialized, in the family and beyond, to find self-recognition in service. Moreover, she feels, in part, that she is a willing accomplice in her own victimization, as if the "molestation" she experiences is not merely a consequence of her being a woman but in some sense her own fault. A woman is more helpless than a man before love's deceptiveness because she does not have the male assumption of agency in love—represented by his ability to move, change, accept or even revel in unpredictability. She cannot claim any autonomy, it seems, without submitting to further pain and disillusion. In waiting and being hurt by him, she feels that she is at least being reached: her pain gives her authentication. As Masud Khan noted [In his *Alienation in perversion*] it is important to find a witness for one's psychic pain, the audience allowing for the achievement, however temporary, of a deeper sense of achievement. "Molestation" may thus be the alternative to psychic breakdown.

The dominant code by which women have historically been made available for male pleasure rather than their own (or even for mutual) pleasure, is based on this reification of what had tradionally been praised as a woman's constancy. Donne's poem of that name dramatizes, albeit amusingly, the male nervousness before the threat embodied (literally) in women that they will be untrue, unavailable, beyond possession. The reassuring mother must always be, if not present, at least available when need calls. Elaine Beilin [in *Redeeming Eve*] has argued that "constancy," which is particularly intensely apostrophized in the final sonnet of *Pamphilia to Amphilanthus,* has a "fundamental importance" in Wroth's scheme, and that "separated from Amphilanthus . . . Pamphilia is wholly dedicated to the love of virtue." But repeatedly in Wroth's poems, constancy seems to be a role forced upon a woman in a dangerous environment, a defensive posture at best, an assigned and unavoidable role within an aggressively patriarchal situation at worst—and far more typically. In her constancy, Pamphilia has internalized the residual female role of possessing a "faith untouch'd, pure thoughts . . . wher constancy bears sway." In one of the later sonnets she acknowledges that "No time, noe roome, no thought, or writing" can give her "loving hart" quiet, and yet she is powerless to give up her love:

> Yett would I nott (deere love) thou shouldst
> depart
> Butt lett my passions as they first began
> Rule, wounde, and please, itt is thy choysest
> art

To give disquiett which seemes ease to man.

The erotic Cupid can give only "disquiett"; by contrast, the divine offers "glory," presented as a relief from the perpetual disease of erotic desire:

> When all alone, I think upon thy paine
> How thou doest traveile owr best selves to
> gaine;
>
> Then howerly thy lessons I doe learne,
> Think on thy glory which shall still assend
> Untill the world come to a finall end,
> And then shall wee thy lasting powre deserne.
>
> (*Poems*)

Constancy, then, is hardly the virtue it seems. Indeed, *Pamphilia to Amphilanthus* is a remarkable demystification of the ideal of constancy as, in effect, a device of patriarchy to keep women under control and available whenever the needs of their struggles for individuation become unbearable: women need to be in a state of unchanging constancy so as to relieve men of some anxieties. Amphilanthus' own sister Urania points out to Pamphilia that "tis pittie . . . that ever that fruitlesse thing Constancy was taught you as a vertue" (*Urania*). Men are not required to be constant. Why then should women? This is a theme on which *Urania* dwells incessantly. . . . Whereas a courtier, like Amphilanthus, has a sense of assigned agency, the autonomy of continual adventure and innumerable mistresses, Pamphilia must wait, resigned and insecure, threatened by her love and by her own faithfulness:

> Love grown proud with victory,
>   Seekes by sleights to conquer me,
>   Painted showes he thinkes can bind
>   His commands in womens mind,
> Love but glories in fond loving,
> I most joy in not removing.
>
> (*Urania*)

The "painted showes" of the court—including the masques and celebrations that had won Wroth herself some momentary "glories"—are here taken as a metonymy for the seductive attractions by which the court lady is assigned her passive, decorative role. Love, like the court itself, is characterized by superficiality and insecurity. And the speaker? Do we read the last line as "most" or "must"? If as "most," then the passive, masochistic, self-punishing role has been accepted; if "must," then the reluctance to accept such a role is inevitable but still resented. Either way, constancy, with its idealized tone of willing devotion and dedication, is proved to be deceiving, a construct designed by men to keep women in subjection.

Perhaps the idealization of constancy throughout the sequence can be read as a clear, if singularly depressing, indication of how a dominant masculinist ideology has been internalized by a woman. Seen in that light, it acts to conceal the contradictions of Pamphilia's assigned roles. The ninth sonnet records a protracted degree of bitterness at such an assignment, as it caustically describes the lover married only to sorrow in a socially constructed world where faithfulness, although imposed as a duty and a sign of belonging to a male lover, seems nonetheless an imposition:

> Bee you all pleas'd? your pleasures grieve nott
>   mee:
>   Do you delight? I envy nott your joy:
>   Have you content? contentment with you bee:
>   Hope you for bliss? hope still, and still injoye:
>
> Lett sad misfortune, haples me destroy,
>   Leave crosses to rule mee, and still rule free,
>   While all delights theyr contrairies imploy
>   To keepe good backe, and I butt torments see.
>
> Joyes are beereav'd, harmes doe only tarry,
>   Dispaire takes place, disdaine hath gott the
>   hand:
>   Yett firme love holds my sences in such band
>   As since dispis'ed, I with sorrow marry;
>   Then if with griefe I now must coupled bee
>   Sorrow I'le wed: Dispaire thus governs mee.
>
>   (*Poems*)

The poem is racked by a deep helplessness. Demands are made upon the speaker that are seemingly irresistible; petulant defiance seems the most positive alternative to helpless acquiescence. Although one of the more extreme of the sonnets, it is typical in that love is presented not only as deceptive and disruptive, as it is so often to a male Petrarchan lover, but as enforcing helplessness and passivity. A woman is a "stage of woe" (*Poems*) on which others' desires rather than her own are acted out. Her constancy, the virtue with which she is most praised (and thereby by what she is imprisoned), may be opening her to further victimization. Writing on "mourning and melancholia," Freud speaks of the melancholic's sense of loss involving "painful dejection, cessation of the interest in the outside world, loss of the capacity to love, inhibition of all activity and a lowering of the self-regarding feelings to a degree that finds utterance in self-reproaches and self-revilings" ["Mourning and melancholia" in *Standard Edition XIV*; "Three Essays on Sexuality" in *Standard Edition VII*]. Many sonnets show Pamphilia withdrawn to her bed, both night and day, brooding over her misery and her lover's absence. But where Freud insisted that narcissistic melancholia was an "individual" neurosis, Wroth's poems show how thoroughly it is socially constructed. It is as if the need for secrecy, the sense of non-fulfillment and above all the awareness that the beloved is an active agent elsewhere—hunting, traveling, moving through more complex social worlds—provides a contrast that is at once humiliating and yet inescapable. Pamphilia's withdrawal is an attempt to restore some sense of an acceptable self-representation. She needs the sense of her own loss and pain to buttress any feelings she retains of having a coherent sense of self.

One of the recurring metaphors of male Petrarchism is the controlling power of the male gaze. It is built upon an assumption so deeply rooted in our history's dominant ideologies of perception and knowledge production that it has overwhelmingly seemed unassailably true. Men gaze at women; women are gazed at and, as Kaplan puts it [in *Female Perversions*], "the man's excited responses to her body reassure the woman that she actually exists." What response could a female protagonist have to such a situation? Was it possible to construct an alternative to the dominance of the gaze? Part of Pamphilia's enforced (or chosen) passivity—her acknowledgement that love "indeed was best, when I did least it move"—is the awareness that she is being both watched by others for signs of her love and thereby in a sense given an identity by their gazes.

Within recent feminist theory, the psychosocial dynamics of the gaze have been much debated. A standard viewpoint, represented by the work of Tania Modleski and Laura Mulvey, has focused on the male gaze as the normal subject position for the viewer of classic cinema, and the need to develop an alternative point of view, especially for women viewers. More recently, Gaylyn Studlar has argued that, on the contrary, many films interpellate a male viewing position not simply based on the desire to over-see and dominate, but rather on a masochistic fear/ desire of being dominated and absorbed themselves by women. Both analyses, of course, may be pointing to the variety of ways by which the dominance of the male subject position has been reinforced. Either way it is clearly rooted in the way our history has constructed our dominant gender assignments. But perhaps it is possible to discuss the confounding of such situations by the woman's own active participation in the gaze. As Constance Penley puts it, if the gaze in traditional art is "an inscription of the look on the body of the mother, we must now begin to consider the possibilities of the mother returning the look" [quoted by Stephen Heath in *Screen*, Vol. 19, 1978)]. What happens, in short, if "she" looks back at "him"? Or even actively watches herself being watched and instead of feeling positioned as an object, and assumes "gazing back" is a viable subject position? If vision connotes aggression and control, can a woman—even while she knows she is the object of the gaze—appropriate its power? Wroth's poems explore a number of these possible subject positions. At times Pamphilia is "molested" by her role as an object of the desiring gaze; at others she tries to escape the gaze of lover and other people's, in loneliness, isolation, or sleep. Such reactions are attempts to avoid the repetitive constructing of sexual relations by patterns of male desire and domination and female submission. In such relationships the values of the patriarchal male predominate: they emerge as the urge to overwhelm, penetrate, defeat, and triumph over.

[An] analysis of the gender politics of Petrarchism suggests that this, one of the dominant discourses of desire in the western world, has been overwhelmingly destructive for at the very least half of those human subjects caught up in it: the traditional Petrarchan situation against which *Pamphilia to Amphilanthus* is written is part of a historical pattern of "normal" sexuality as defined by Western society, in which, as Stoller puts it [in *Perversions*], "an essential purpose is for one to be superior to, harmful to, triumphant over another." The seeming neutrality of "one" in Stoller's remark covers the preponderant historical identification of assumed control with the male. Beneath the language of sexual dependence, idealized admiration, even (occasionally) sexual reciprocity to which the Petrarchan lover lays claim, there is a predominantly one-sided emphasis on domination and submission. One of the poems in Wroth's opening sequence in ***Pamphilia to Amphilanthus*** is a remarkable critique of this whole tradition. It attempts to subvert the dominant male subject position by appropriating not only the gaze, but its pleasure:

> Take heed mine eyes, how you your lookes do
>   cast
> Least they beetray my harts most secrett
>   thought;
> Bee true unto your selves for nothings bought
> More deere then doubt which brings a lovers
>   fast.
>
> Catch you all waching eyes, ere they bee past,
>   Or take yours fixt wher your best love hath
>   sought
> The pride of your desires; lett them bee taught
> Theyr faults for shame, they could noe truer l
>   last;
>
> Then looke, and looke with joye for conquest
>   wunn
> Of those that search'd your hurt in double
>   kinde;
> Soe you kept safe, lett them themselves looke
>   blinde
> Watch, gaze, and marke till they to madnes
>   runn,
>
> While you, mine eyes injoye full sight of love
> Contented that such happinesses move.
>
> *(Poems)*

The poem opens with a warning against indiscretion, but the tone is unusually paranoid, as if guarding not just against betrayal of a secret with which the woman has been entrusted, but of the multiple "selves" in which she lives. The tactics of the poem, indeed, become not the passive slipping into the role of a secret lover or of the modest object of another's forbidden desire, but the more aggressive one of "catching" or trapping and defeating "all waching eyes." It is a matter of self-identity, not merely of love—primarily a matter of acknowledging how the self is constructed. Given that identity consists in being assigned a multiplicity of roles, that very multiplicity and its contradictory assigned positions will, she determines, become her basis for action. Her fantasy of female agency becomes based on her returning the gaze, on reminding herself to "looke with joye for conquest wunn," and acknowledging that it is her own active desire—accepting her construction by the contradictory gazes and returning them—that affords her power. Stoller remarks—as so often, irritatingly essentializing but nonetheless pointing

to a seemingly fixed aspect of Western patriarchy—on the little boy's assumed "right to sexual looking and a little girl's training that she is not to permit that looking." Placed within the history of gender assignment, Wroth's Pamphilia marks an attempt, however spasmodic and isolated, to break with such a pattern. She is not merely fixed by the gaze, but turns it to an active and defiant exhibitionism. She has started to reappropriate herself as a subject, distancing herself from the narcissism of self-involvement and starting to see herself as a man might see her. But because she appropriates both the traditional gender roles and so sees with both the eyes of a woman and the gaze of a man, by involvement and reflection, she acquires a secret authority unknown to the men who gaze on her and think they control her. It is the clearest expression of the fantasy of emulation, what Kaplan terms "a retribution scenario, a vengeance on those who have been assigned to abandonment and mutilation." Or, more optimistically put, she has asserted her right to gaze back, just as her poems assert the right to talk back.

This poem also reflects upon another part of the Petrarchist situation, the interpellation of the reader (him) self as a voyeur. The gaze of the (male) reader is a part of the male display built into Petrarchism: Sidney's poems, for instance, typically look out to their audiences, often with a wink or an invitation to laugh, inviting his reader's amusement as well as disapproval of or sympathy with his dilemmas. *Astrophil and Stella* is typical of the mode: it is what [Roland Barthos in *Untying the Text*] terms a playful text, one that depends strongly on an audience, inviting our participation, asking us to watch, identify, judge, laugh, and learn. But it assumes a "universal" gaze that in fact is that of the dominant male, and the sympathy it asks for is for the suffering lover, wanting separation from and yet desiring the presence of, the woman. What we are asked to watch and assume to be "natural" is the textual/sexual spectacle of another human displaying him- or herself according to gender-specific stereotypes—or refusing to, which in its effect on the viewer amounts to the same thing. Women display for men; men display for themselves, and then are authorized to display, in writing, their accounts of the experience. What happens when such a situation is complicated by having a woman protagonist/poet? By a woman who displays herself, not merely sexually but textually as well, in her act of writing? The reader's trajectory of desire makes his (or her) complicity more complex. Where the male reader/spectator can see his own gendered roles in harmony with those valorized by the poems, the gaze can appear neutral. When the gaze is complicated by gender, either by a woman reader or, in the way that operates in Wroth's poems, by a woman writer, then the male power over objects in the Petrarchan scheme is called into question.

At this point, . . . reading theory and a discussion of the place of gender in reading acquires some immediacy. Wroth's poems, parading the gender of both their author and protagonist, catch us in a reading situation where the shifts in subject position call into question any "natural" order of gender. We are not simply observing the woman's acceptance of the conventional role of cruel beauty and perpetual tease, produced to both generate a man's desire and overcome his fears of that desire. However fitfully it is occurring, we can observe the slow and contradictory emergence of alternative subject positions for women and, implicitly, for men. As [Catherine] Belsey, Francis Barker, and others have argued, before the development of the humanist subject in the seventeenth century, women were afforded places within the period's dominant ideology only by being incorporated into structures and discourses which assigned them subsidiary roles, as objects of others' desires, not as subjects of their own. There is, in the early modern period—in *Hamlet,* most forcefully—the emergence of a new sense of subjectivity, a claim for a unique and "essential interiority, which, even if it is never fully articulated and is therefore historically "premature," nonetheless anticipates the emergent claims of a bourgeois subjectivity that will emerge in the next century or more. Wroth's poems record the stirrings—against enormous odds, it needs to be stressed—to establish an equivalent female subject position. Her poems' struggle to find an authentic voice for a woman are related to the frustrations of gender assignment. The dominant gendered subject positions of early modern England did not permit such autonomy to a woman writer or protagonist—any more than they did, as Dollimore has argued, to gays. But we can note, across the range of constructed gender roles, points of strain and contradiction where alternatives are struggling to emerge.

The dominant gender politics of Petrarchism are constructed so that the male lover-poet can fulfill his desires even if his beloved is absent. If she is present, he is fulfilled as a lover; if absent, as a poet. He therefore plays, according to his own rules, an elaborate version of the *fort-da* game Freud so famously described [in "Beyond the Pleasure Principle" in *Standard Edition XXIV*], moving her at his will back and forth, from presence to absence. Within the Petrarchan framework, however much a man may protest, he has the autonomy to love or leave, to write or be silent. But a woman? If she is not accorded her own desire, what role can she claim? What starts to emerge in *Pamphilia to Amphilanthus,* taking on even greater significance in the stories in *Urania,* is a counter-discourse of indignation and envy of men's autonomy and movement, what are termed their "adventures." Pamphilia also yearns for her own "adventures." Even if they are denied her, over and over she struggles to find them and, through them, a sense of an individuated self that seemingly is "natural" to a man. So if the residual oppression of "constancy" is, in the end, part of the patriarchal entrapment of women, producing at worst a subordinated passivity and at best anger and envy, against it must be set surges of defiance and claims of autonomy. The two areas that stand out within the poetry are those which, as I have suggested, we can observe struggling within Wroth's life as a whole—her writing and her sexuality.

Writing is an act shared by Pamphilia with her creator. So far as Wroth's writing is concerned, we should not underemphasize its importance as an act of self-affirmation, even a defiance of patriarchy, despite the encouragement afforded by being a member of the Sidney family. Mary

E. Hazard has noted [in *Texas Studies in Language and Literature* 29, 1987] that, typically, a Petrarchan poet fashions for (him)self a fictive role (which may at times be close to that claimed by the poet outside the poems). The one constructed in *Pamphilia to Amphilanthus* for both writer and character is more varied than most. It certainly includes, as we have noted, passivity, "constancy." But it also includes a measure of defiance and self-assertion that echoes something of the desires of the author herself. Even though her family probably encouraged her to see herself as a writer, Wroth took that permission far more daringly than, say, her aunt, the countess of Pembroke, had. To write a prose romance, a pastoral play, and, perhaps above all, a collection of Petrarchan love poems, was to go well beyond what the family might have seen fit—and it is significant that it was in part because she exceeded what were felt to be the decorous precedents of translation and devotional works set by her pious aunt that Wroth was bitterly attacked by Denny upon the publication of *Urania*. Even, as Masten suggests, the seemingly mundane acts of arrangement, revision, and circulation of her poems—or, he insists, not to be underestimated as an act of choice, the refusal to circulate them—were acts of defiance. Within the poems, too, writing is depicted as a way of giving a woman not merely reactive roles to male desires but multiple and changing voices of her own. Like the male Petrarchan lover, Pamphilia determines to "seeke for some small ease by lines," only to realize that "greife is nott cur'd by art." Poetry "tires" her mind, yet the "debate" it produces in her makes her realize that it is her thinking, brooding mind that is carving out an area of autonomy—even through her pain—which affords her not only comfort but power (*Poems,* pp. 90, 91, 92). While others, men in particular, may be subject to the whims of the king, or to some "pleasing past time" required by their roles at court, she has, she claims, a small but autonomous space to explore:

> When every one to pleasing pastime hies
>   Some hunt, some hauke, some play, while some delight
>   In sweet discourse, and musique showes joys might
>   Yett I my thoughts doe farr above thes prise.
>   (*Poems*)

Masten's argument [in *Reading Many Wroth*] that the poems "encode" a desire for "withdrawal from circulation" has some force here. Refusing to voice one's love and doing so in anguished public language is, of course, a conventional trick of the Petrarchan poet—"they love indeed, who quake to say they love" as her uncle Philip's volubly silent Astrophil put it in *Astrophil and Stella* 54. But *Pamphilia to Amphilanthus* is not trying to carve out a space for a dominant male subject who can be assured of his audience even (and perhaps especially) when they are eloquently told not to listen to his inner and supposedly private revelations. The space Wroth is trying to establish is for a female subject, one who necessarily has to absorb and neutralize metaphors that have been encultured by dominant male practice: "When others hunt, my thought I have in chase." Masten points up the paradox that Wroth "is writing in Petrarchan discourse to write against it," but there are broader cultural issues at stake: in so doing she is contradicting on more than the level of conceit the encoded subject position of the male speaker of Petrarchan poetry. She claims withdrawal as a tactic of self-affirmation for a woman's subjectivity.

If writing is an act—or at least an enacted fantasy—of agency, what of desire itself? If, as Marx put it, praxis— meaning sensuous human activity, the practices of the body—is the basis of real power, what space is *Pamphilia to Amphilanthus* trying to carve out not only for its protagonist but also for its author, and for the language and praxis of women's desire? As I have suggested, much of Pamphilia's desire emerges as pain, deprivation, mo- lestation, by which sexuality is experienced as harm, shame, self-obliteration. Wroth overwhelmingly offers us a distinctively privileged perspective on the negative eros produced by male domination and female masochism. This perspective allows us to see the relative paucity of love "objects" to which a woman had access in the early modern period. Freud noted frequently that repressed objects of desire are represented by a series of unsatisfying substi- tutes: Pamphilia's growing self-awareness, her "waking" as a lover, brings her the realization of the distinctive kind of cruelty Cupid affords women. He is responsible for love's "wounding . . . delights," the producer of dis- plays, for male delectation, of "endless torments" upon "this stage of woe," ending in self-immolation, even death. Repeatedly the lover is "in chaines" or trapped in a "lab- yrinth." The recurring labyrinth metaphor is the night- mare underside of a woman's private space. The extreme- ly popular mazes in Elizabethan and Jacobean gardens reflect an obsessive concern with what Wotton termed a "very wilde Regularitie," a special place designed to trans- gress the restrictions of the house and its regime of har- mony and control. But such a view is from the perspec- tive of the proprietor of the house or the architect. For someone lost in the labyrinth, the point of view may be very different. The private chamber is an area of orderli- ness and control, however compromised by its surround- ings; the labyrinth consists of potentially infinite attempts to find an escape: it constructs a series of "tense" blind spaces that produce incessant, frustrated, "restless' move- ments to escape. Petrarch had used the labyrinth as an image of the cognitive and emotional confusion in love, and there were a number of commonplace analogies be- tween the labyrinth and the sonnet itself.

The **"crowne of Sonetts dedicated to Love,"** which are grouped together towards the end of *Pamphilia to Am- philanthus,* explore some of these difficulties from the viewpoint of the woman lover trapped within, certainly not a designer of, labyrinths. The "crowne" consists of fourteen sonnets, the last lines of each constituting the first line of the next. [In *Poems of Lady Mary Wroth*] Roberts speaks of the "universalized concept of love" in the Crowne and Beilin of its "catalogues of love's divin- ity," [in *Redeeming Eve*] but the Crowne sonnets are more distinctive for their demarcation of contradictions than in its acceptance of some kind of transcendent resignation.

The labyrinth is, despite its emphasis on puzzlement and entrapment, a metaphor of action: one enters a labyrinth and tries to find one's way out, or to its heart, or both. Pamphilia, surrounded by alternatives, nonetheless insits that contradiction and difficulty offer her more fulfilling choices:

> In this strang labourinth how shall I turne?
> Wayes are on all sids while the way I misse:
> If to the right hand, ther, in love I burne;
> Lett mee goe forward, therin danger is,
>
> *(Poems)*

Her determination is to "take the thread of love," to be constant to her growing sense of self, to "feele the weight of true desire," and to produce a mutual, united love. Such agency within contradiction allows each lover to open him(or her)self to previously unsensed possibilities: "Itt doth inrich the witts, and make you see / That in your self, which you knew nott before." Yet even in such a fantasy of love, stasis—what she terms "constancy"—is never the end. The final poem points to the self-explora- tion that love has opened up, not to achieve a final goal so much as to begin a never-ending search: "Soe though in Love I fervently doe burne, / in this strange labourinth how shall I turne?"

So far I have read Wroth's poems in terms of their strug- gle, fitful but not entirely accidental, to assert some sus- tained, even momentary, agency for women. They artic- ulate one of the dominant fantasies of the woman's fam- ily romance, to achieve the same sense of agency that has been promised, as he emerges from childhood, to the boy: becoming a man, he will, like his father, assume indepen- dence, autonomy, power over others, especially over women. There are, however, signs in *Pamphilia to Am- philanthus* of another counter-discourse taking shape. There is, for instance, the acknowledgement that the vic- timization of women is not Pamphilia's alone: other wom- en share her helplessness or anger. The poems frequently address other women, sometimes an unnamed friend and sometimes, as Naomi Miller points out, those women who have been described in the lines of men's poems. In the sonnet just quoted, for instance, Fortune is described as Pamphilia's supporter. Fortune is, conventionally, female and a consoler of the suffering male; but because the poem is spoken and written by a woman, Fortune takes on a less conventional role. She becomes a fellow female sufferer, helping Pamphilia face the anguish of being a mistress whose desires are controlled by her lover. The community of "oprest" women lovers in the poems in- cludes Night, Reclining, and other personifications of the assigned female passive role, providing, as Miller puts it, [in an unpublished paper, "Ancient Fictions and in True Forms"] a "litany of parallels" with Pamphilia's grief, which in some of the poems often deepens into anger at being pressured by overwhelming social forces into ac- cepting the roles society thrusts upon them because they are women. As Lamb notes in her splendid analysis of anger in *Urania* [entitled *Gender and Authorship*], "the Renaissance offered women few healthy models for en- couraging the expression of justified rage or for acknowledging the heroism of their ordinary lives." It offered even fewer models for an alternative fantasy of genuinely mutual constancy.

The experience of most women in the early modern period—that they were not possessors of their own bodies, that they did not have a sense of choice and deliberation in their gender assignments—causes, as [Erik H.] Erikson noted in his classic studies of life stages [entitled *Life History and the Historical Moment*], "the most pervasive anger." How can a fantasy of mutual constancy be generated from such a situation? We are used today to women's relations to their own bodies being, no less than for men, a source of power, vulnerability, betrayal, a space of agency as much as of restriction. Such a spectrum of relations with a sense of self was only barely becoming possible in the early modern period. Wroth's poems are a kind of dream space, in which only dimly graspable subject positions are being tentatively and partly unconsciously explored, interacting with more powerful discourses of restriction. *Pamphilia to Amphilanthus* is a dream of a still to be found autonomy that will lead not to dominance but to mutuality.

FURTHER READING

Biography

Paulissen, May Nelson. "The Life and Milieu of Lady Mary Wroth." In *The Love Sonnets of Lady Mary Wroth: A Critical Introduction,* edited by Dr. James Hogg, pp. 1-77. Austria: Institut für Anglistik und Amerikanistik Universität Salzburg, 1982.

Roberts, Josephine A. "The Biographical Problem of *Pamphilia to Amphilanthus." Tulsa Studies in Women's Literature,* Vol. 1, No. 1, Spring, 1982, pp. 43-53.

Provides a biography of Wroth and comments on the autobiographical nature of *Pamphilia to Amphilanthus.*

———. "The Life of Lady Mary Wroth." In *The Poems of Lady Mary Wroth,* edited by Josephine A. Roberts, pp. 3-40. Baton Rouge: Louisiana State University Press, 1983.

A comprehensive history of Wroth's life, including her relationship with the poet Ben Jonson and the biographical sources of the *Urania.*

Criticism

Beilin, Elaine V. " 'The Onely Perfect Vertue': Constancy in Mary Wroth's *Pamphilia to Amphilanthus."* In *Spenser Studies: A Renaissance Poetry Annual,* Vol. II, edited by Patrick Cullen and Thomas P. Roche, Jr., pp. 229-45. Pittsburgh: University of Pittsburgh Press, 1981.

Studies Wroth's presentation of gender roles and attributes from the point of view of the female sonneteer Pamphilia.

———. "Heroic Virtue: Mary Wroth's *Urania* and *Pamphilia to Amphilanthus."* In *Redeeming Eve: Women Writers of the English Renaissance,* pp. 208-43. Princeton: Princeton University Press, 1987.

Provides biographical overview and describes Wroth's successful adaptation of exclusively male literary forms to a female perspective in the *Urania* and *Pamphilia to Amphilanthus.*

Hannay, Margaret Patterson. "Lady Wroth, Mary Sidney." In *Women Writers of the Renaissance and Reformation,* edited by Katharina M. Wilson, pp. 548-65. Athens: The University of Georgia Press, 1987.

Presents biographical overview, textual and historical information on the *Urania,* and selected poems from *Pamphilia to Amphilanthus.*

Jones, Ann Rosalind. "Feminine Pastoral as Heroic Martyrdom: Gaspara Stampa and Mary Wroth." In *The Currency of Eros: Women's Love Lyric in Europe, 1540-1620,* pp. 118-54. Bloomington: Indiana University Press, 1990.

Studies the use of the pastoral genre to define feminine strengths and virtues in the poetry of Wroth and Gaspara Stampa.

Lamb, Mary Ellen. "The Heroics of Constancy in Mary Wroth's *Countess of Montgomery's Urania."* In *Gender and Authorship in the Sidney Circle,* pp. 142-93. Madison: The University of Wisconsin Press, 1990.

Discusses the structure and themes of the *Urania,* with emphasis on the autobiographical elements present in the text.

Miller, Naomi J. "Rewriting Lyric Fictions: The Role of the Lady in Lady Mary Wroth's *Pamphilia to Amphilanthus."* In *The Renaissance Englishwoman in Print: Counterbalancing the Canon,* pp. 295-310. Amherst: The University of Massachusetts Press, 1990.

Examines Wroth's restructuring of the traditional sonnet form to reverse gender roles and convey a feminine perspective on love.

Paulissen, May Nelson. "The Structural Character of Lady Mary Wroth's Sonnets." In *The Love Sonnets of Lady Mary Wroth: A Critical Introduction,* edited by Dr. James Hogg, pp. 174-209. Austria: Institut für Anglistik und Amerikanistik Universität Salzburg, 1982.

Structural analysis of Wroth's sonnets in *Pamphilia to Amphilanthus.*

Quilligan, Maureen. "Lady Mary Wroth: Female Authority and the Family Romance." In *Unfolded Tales: Essays on Renaissance Romance,* edited by George M. Logan and Gordon Teskey, pp. 257-280. Ithaca: Cornell University Press, 1989.

Explores family relationships in the *Urania* and women's roles in these relationships.

Salzman, Paul. "*Urania* and the Tyranny of Love." In *English Prose Fiction 1558-1700: A Critical History,* pp. 138-44. Oxford: Clarendon Press, 1985.

Provides an overview of scandal surrounding publication of the *Urania*, and discusses the role of love and magic as plot devices.

Shapiro, Michael. "Lady Mary Wroth Describes a 'Boy Actress'." In *Medieval & Renaissance Drama in England,* Vol. IV, edited by Leeds Barroll and Paul Werstine, pp. 187-94. New York: AMS Press, 1989.

Discusses Wroth's simile in the *Urania* between deceitful women and the impersonation of female stage roles by boy actors in the Jacobean period.

Waller, Gary F. " 'Some thing more exactly related than a fixion': *The Countesse of Mountgomeries Urania.*" In *The Sidney Family Romance: Mary Wroth, William Herbert, and the Early Modern Construction of Gender,* pp. 246-81. Detroit: Wayne State University Press, 1993.

Comprehensive overview of the plot and publication history of the *Urania*. Studies major themes and motifs.

Literature Criticism from 1400 to 1800

Cumulative Indexes

How to Use This Index

The main references

Calvino, Italo
1923-1985.....CLC 5, 8, 11, 22, 33, 39,
73; SSC 3

list all author entries in the following Gale Literary Criticism series:

BLC = *Black Literature Criticism*
CLC = *Contemporary Literary Criticism*
CLR = *Children's Literature Review*
CMLC = *Classical and Medieval Literature Criticism*
DA = *DISCovering Authors*
DC = *Drama Criticism*
HLC = *Hispanic Literature Criticism*
LC = *Literature Criticism from 1400 to 1800*
NCLC = *Nineteenth-Century Literature Criticism*
PC = *Poetry Criticism*
SSC = *Short Story Criticism*
TCLC = *Twentieth-Century Literary Criticism*
WLC = *World Literature Criticism, 1500 to the Present*

The cross-references

See also CANR 23; CA 85-88;
obituary CA 116

list all author entries in the following Gale biographical and literary sources:

AAYA = *Authors & Artists for Young Adults*
AITN = *Authors in the News*
BEST = *Bestsellers*
BW = *Black Writers*
CA = *Contemporary Authors*
CAAS = *Contemporary Authors Autobiography Series*
CABS = *Contemporary Authors Bibliographical Series*
CANR = *Contemporary Authors New Revision Series*
CAP = *Contemporary Authors Permanent Series*
CDALB = *Concise Dictionary of American Literary Biography*
CDBLB = *Concise Dictionary of British Literary Biography*
DLB = *Dictionary of Literary Biography*
DLBD = *Dictionary of Literary Biography Documentary Series*
DLBY = *Dictionary of Literary Biography Yearbook*
HW = *Hispanic Writers*
JRDA = *Junior DISCovering Authors*
MAICYA = *Major Authors and Illustrators for Children and Young Adults*
MTCW = *Major 20th-Century Writers*
NNAL = *Native North American Literature*
SAAS = *Something about the Author Autobiography Series*
SATA = *Something about the Author*
YABC = *Yesterday's Authors of Books for Children*

Literary Criticism Series
Cumulative Author Index

A. E. . . . . TCLC 3, 10
See also Russell, George William

Abasiyanik, Sait Faik 1906-1954
See Sait Faik
See also CA 123

Abbey, Edward 1927-1989 . . . . . . CLC 36, 59
See also CA 45-48; 128; CANR 2, 41

Abbott, Lee K(ittredge) 1947- . . . . . . CLC 48
See also CA 124; DLB 130

Abe, Kobo 1924-1993 . . . . . CLC 8, 22, 53, 81
See also CA 65-68; 140; CANR 24; MTCW

Abelard, Peter c. 1079-c. 1142 . . . CMLC 11
See also DLB 115

Abell, Kjeld 1901-1961 . . . . CLC 15
See also CA 111

Abish, Walter 1931- . . . . CLC 22
See also CA 101; CANR 37; DLB 130

Abrahams, Peter (Henry) 1919- . . . . . CLC 4
See also BW 1; CA 57-60; CANR 26;
DLB 117; MTCW

Abrams, M(eyer) H(oward) 1912-. . . CLC 24
See also CA 57-60; CANR 13, 33; DLB 67

Abse, Dannie 1923-. . . . . CLC 7, 29
See also CA 53-56; CAAS 1; CANR 4, 46;
DLB 27

Achebe, (Albert) Chinua(lumogu)
1930- . . . . . CLC 1, 3, 5, 7, 11, 26, 51, 75;
BLC; DA; WLC
See also BW 2; CA 1-4R; CANR 6, 26, 47;
CLR 20; DLB 117; MAICYA; MTCW;
SATA 40; SATA-Brief 38

Acker, Kathy 1948- . . . . CLC 45
See also CA 117; 122

Ackroyd, Peter 1949-. . . . . CLC 34, 52
See also CA 123; 127

Acorn, Milton 1923-. . . . . CLC 15
See also CA 103; DLB 53

Adamov, Arthur 1908-1970 . . . . . . CLC 4, 25
See also CA 17-18; 25-28R; CAP 2; MTCW

Adams, Alice (Boyd) 1926- . . . CLC 6, 13, 46
See also CA 81-84; CANR 26; DLBY 86;
MTCW

Adams, Andy 1859-1935. . . . . TCLC 56
See also YABC 1

Adams, Douglas (Noel) 1952- . . . CLC 27, 60
See also AAYA 4; BEST 89:3; CA 106;
CANR 34; DLBY 83; JRDA

Adams, Francis 1862-1893 . . . . NCLC 33

Adams, Henry (Brooks)
1838-1918 . . . . TCLC 4, 52; DA
See also CA 104; 133; DLB 12, 47

Adams, Richard (George)
1920- . . . . CLC 4, 5, 18
See also AITN 1, 2; CA 49-52; CANR 3,
35; CLR 20; JRDA; MAICYA; MTCW;
SATA 7, 69

Adamson, Joy(-Friederike Victoria)
1910-1980 . . . . CLC 17
See also CA 69-72; 93-96; CANR 22;
MTCW; SATA 11; SATA-Obit 22

Adcock, Fleur 1934-. . . . . CLC 41
See also CA 25-28R; CANR 11, 34;
DLB 40

Addams, Charles (Samuel)
1912-1988 . . . . CLC 30
See also CA 61-64; 126; CANR 12

Addison, Joseph 1672-1719 . . . . LC 18
See also CDBLB 1660-1789; DLB 101

Adler, C(arole) S(chwerdtfeger)
1932- . . . . CLC 35
See also AAYA 4; CA 89-92; CANR 19,
40; JRDA; MAICYA; SAAS 15;
SATA 26, 63

Adler, Renata 1938-. . . . . CLC 8, 31
See also CA 49-52; CANR 5, 22; MTCW

Ady, Endre 1877-1919 . . . . TCLC 11
See also CA 107

Aeschylus
525B.C.-456B.C. . . . . CMLC 11; DA

Afton, Effie
See Harper, Frances Ellen Watkins

Agapida, Fray Antonio
See Irving, Washington

Agee, James (Rufus)
1909-1955 . . . . TCLC 1, 19
See also AITN 1; CA 108;
CDALB 1941-1968; DLB 2, 26, 152

Aghill, Gordon
See Silverberg, Robert

Agnon, S(hmuel) Y(osef Halevi)
1888-1970 . . . . CLC 4, 8, 14
See also CA 17-18; 25-28R; CAP 2; MTCW

Agrippa von Nettesheim, Henry Cornelius
1486-1535 . . . . LC 27

Aherne, Owen
See Cassill, R(onald) V(erlin)

Ai 1947-. . . . . CLC 4, 14, 69
See also CA 85-88; CAAS 13; DLB 120

Aickman, Robert (Fordyce)
1914-1981 . . . . CLC 57
See also CA 5-8R; CANR 3

Aiken, Conrad (Potter)
1889-1973 . . . CLC 1, 3, 5, 10, 52; SSC 9
See also CA 5-8R; 45-48; CANR 4;
CDALB 1929-1941; DLB 9, 45, 102;
MTCW; SATA 3, 30

Aiken, Joan (Delano) 1924-. . . . . CLC 35
See also AAYA 1; CA 9-12R; CANR 4, 23,
34; CLR 1, 19; JRDA; MAICYA;
MTCW; SAAS 1; SATA 2, 30, 73

Ainsworth, William Harrison
1805-1882 . . . . NCLC 13
See also DLB 21; SATA 24

Aitmatov, Chingiz (Torekulovich)
1928- . . . . CLC 71
See also CA 103; CANR 38; MTCW;
SATA 56

Akers, Floyd
See Baum, L(yman) Frank

Akhmadulina, Bella Akhatovna
1937-. . . . . CLC 53
See also CA 65-68

Akhmatova, Anna
1888-1966 . . . . CLC 11, 25, 64; PC 2
See also CA 19-20; 25-28R; CANR 35;
CAP 1; MTCW

Aksakov, Sergei Timofeyvich
1791-1859 . . . . NCLC 2

Aksenov, Vassily
See Aksyonov, Vassily (Pavlovich)

Aksyonov, Vassily (Pavlovich)
1932- . . . . CLC 22, 37
See also CA 53-56; CANR 12, 48

Akutagawa Ryunosuke
1892-1927 . . . . TCLC 16
See also CA 117

Alain 1868-1951 . . . . TCLC 41

Alain-Fournier . . . . TCLC 6
See also Fournier, Henri Alban
See also DLB 65

Alarcon, Pedro Antonio de
1833-1891 . . . . NCLC 1

Alas (y Urena), Leopoldo (Enrique Garcia)
1852-1901 . . . . TCLC 29
See also CA 113; 131; HW

Albee, Edward (Franklin III)
1928- . . . . . . CLC 1, 2, 3, 5, 9, 11, 13, 25,
53, 86; DA; WLC
See also AITN 1; CA 5-8R; CABS 3;
CANR 8; CDALB 1941-1968; DLB 7;
MTCW

Alberti, Rafael 1902-. . . . . CLC 7
See also CA 85-88; DLB 108

Alcala-Galiano, Juan Valera y
See Valera y Alcala-Galiano, Juan

Alcott, Amos Bronson 1799-1888 . . NCLC 1
See also DLB 1

Alcott, Louisa May
1832-1888 . . . . NCLC 6; DA; WLC
See also CDALB 1865-1917; CLR 1, 38;
DLB 1, 42, 79; JRDA; MAICYA;
YABC 1

Aldanov, M. A.
See Aldanov, Mark (Alexandrovich)

Aldanov, Mark (Alexandrovich)
1886(?)-1957 . . . . TCLC 23
See also CA 118

Aldington, Richard 1892-1962. . . . . CLC 49
See also CA 85-88; CANR 45; DLB 20, 36,
100, 149

Aldiss, Brian W(ilson)
1925- . . . . CLC 5, 14, 40
See also CA 5-8R; CAAS 2; CANR 5, 28;
DLB 14; MTCW; SATA 34

Alegria, Claribel 1924- . . . . CLC 75
See also CA 131; CAAS 15; DLB 145; HW

Alegria, Fernando 1918- . . . . CLC 57
See also CA 9-12R; CANR 5, 32; HW

Aleichem, Sholom . . . . TCLC 1, 35
See also Rabinovitch, Sholem

Aleixandre, Vicente 1898-1984 . . . CLC 9, 36
See also CA 85-88; 114; CANR 26;
DLB 108; HW; MTCW

Alepoudelis, Odysseus
See Elytis, Odysseus

Aleshkovsky, Joseph 1929-
See Aleshkovsky, Yuz
See also CA 121; 128

Aleshkovsky, Yuz . . . . CLC 44
See also Aleshkovsky, Joseph

Alexander, Lloyd (Chudley) 1924- . . CLC 35
See also AAYA 1; CA 1-4R; CANR 1, 24,
38; CLR 1, 5; DLB 52; JRDA; MAICYA;
MTCW; SAAS 19; SATA 3, 49, 81

Alfau, Felipe 1902- . . . . CLC 66
See also CA 137

Alger, Horatio, Jr. 1832-1899 . . . . . NCLC 8
See also DLB 42; SATA 16

Algren, Nelson 1909-1981 . . . . CLC 4, 10, 33
See also CA 13-16R; 103; CANR 20;
CDALB 1941-1968; DLB 9; DLBY 81,
82; MTCW

Ali, Ahmed 1910- . . . . CLC 69
See also CA 25-28R; CANR 15, 34

Alighieri, Dante 1265-1321 . . . . CMLC 3

Allan, John B.
See Westlake, Donald E(dwin)

Allen, Edward 1948- . . . . CLC 59

Allen, Paula Gunn 1939- . . . . CLC 84
See also CA 112; 143; NNAL

Allen, Roland
See Ayckbourn, Alan

Allen, Sarah A.
See Hopkins, Pauline Elizabeth

Allen, Woody 1935- . . . . CLC 16, 52
See also AAYA 10; CA 33-36R; CANR 27,
38; DLB 44; MTCW

Allende, Isabel 1942- . . . . CLC 39, 57; HLC
See also CA 125; 130; DLB 145; HW;
MTCW

Alleyn, Ellen
See Rossetti, Christina (Georgina)

Allingham, Margery (Louise)
1904-1966 . . . . CLC 19
See also CA 5-8R; 25-28R; CANR 4;
DLB 77; MTCW

Allingham, William 1824-1889 . . . NCLC 25
See also DLB 35

Allison, Dorothy E. 1949- . . . . CLC 78
See also CA 140

Allston, Washington 1779-1843 . . . . NCLC 2
See also DLB 1

Almedingen, E. M. . . . . CLC 12
See also Almedingen, Martha Edith von
See also SATA 3

Almedingen, Martha Edith von 1898-1971
See Almedingen, E. M.
See also CA 1-4R; CANR 1

Almqvist, Carl Jonas Love
1793-1866 . . . . NCLC 42

Alonso, Damaso 1898-1990 . . . . CLC 14
See also CA 110; 131; 130; DLB 108; HW

Alov
See Gogol, Nikolai (Vasilyevich)

Alta 1942- . . . . CLC 19
See also CA 57-60

Alter, Robert B(ernard) 1935- . . . . . . CLC 34
See also CA 49-52; CANR 1, 47

Alther, Lisa 1944- . . . . CLC 7, 41
See also CA 65-68; CANR 12, 30; MTCW

Altman, Robert 1925- . . . . CLC 16
See also CA 73-76; CANR 43

Alvarez, A(lfred) 1929- . . . . CLC 5, 13
See also CA 1-4R; CANR 3, 33; DLB 14,
40

Alvarez, Alejandro Rodriguez 1903-1965
See Casona, Alejandro
See also CA 131; 93-96; HW

Alvaro, Corrado 1896-1956 . . . . TCLC 60

Amado, Jorge 1912- . . . . . CLC 13, 40; HLC
See also CA 77-80; CANR 35; DLB 113;
MTCW

Ambler, Eric 1909- . . . . CLC 4, 6, 9
See also CA 9-12R; CANR 7, 38; DLB 77;
MTCW

Amichai, Yehuda 1924- . . . . . . CLC 9, 22, 57
See also CA 85-88; CANR 46; MTCW

Amiel, Henri Frederic 1821-1881 . . NCLC 4

Amis, Kingsley (William)
1922- . . CLC 1, 2, 3, 5, 8, 13, 40, 44; DA
See also AITN 2; CA 9-12R; CANR 8, 28;
CDBLB 1945-1960; DLB 15, 27, 100, 139;
MTCW

Amis, Martin (Louis)
1949- . . . . CLC 4, 9, 38, 62
See also BEST 90:3; CA 65-68; CANR 8,
27; DLB 14

Ammons, A(rchie) R(andolph)
1926- . . . . CLC 2, 3, 5, 8, 9, 25, 57
See also AITN 1; CA 9-12R; CANR 6, 36;
DLB 5; MTCW

Amo, Tauraatua i
See Adams, Henry (Brooks)

Anand, Mulk Raj 1905- . . . . CLC 23
See also CA 65-68; CANR 32; MTCW

Anatol
See Schnitzler, Arthur

Anaya, Rudolfo A(lfonso)
1937- . . . . CLC 23; HLC
See also CA 45-48; CAAS 4; CANR 1, 32;
DLB 82; HW 1; MTCW

Andersen, Hans Christian
1805-1875 . . NCLC 7; DA; SSC 6; WLC
See also CLR 6; MAICYA; YABC 1

Anderson, C. Farley
See Mencken, H(enry) L(ouis); Nathan,
George Jean

Anderson, Jessica (Margaret) Queale
. . . . CLC 37
See also CA 9-12R; CANR 4

Anderson, Jon (Victor) 1940- . . . . CLC 9
See also CA 25-28R; CANR 20

Anderson, Lindsay (Gordon)
1923-1994 . . . . CLC 20
See also CA 125; 128; 146

Anderson, Maxwell 1888-1959 . . . . . TCLC 2
See also CA 105; DLB 7

Anderson, Poul (William) 1926- . . . . CLC 15
See also AAYA 5; CA 1-4R; CAAS 2;
CANR 2, 15, 34; DLB 8; MTCW;
SATA-Brief 39

Anderson, Robert (Woodruff)
1917- . . . . CLC 23
See also AITN 1; CA 21-24R; CANR 32;
DLB 7

Anderson, Sherwood
1876-1941 . . . . TCLC 1, 10, 24; DA;
SSC 1; WLC
See also CA 104; 121; CDALB 1917-1929;
DLB 4, 9, 86; DLBD 1; MTCW

Andouard
See Giraudoux, (Hippolyte) Jean

Andrade, Carlos Drummond de . . . . . . CLC 18
See also Drummond de Andrade, Carlos

Andrade, Mario de 1893-1945 . . . . . TCLC 43

Andreas-Salome, Lou 1861-1937 . . . TCLC 56
See also DLB 66

Andrewes, Lancelot 1555-1626 . . . . LC 5
See also DLB 151

Andrews, Cicily Fairfield
See West, Rebecca

Andrews, Elton V.
See Pohl, Frederik

Andreyev, Leonid (Nikolaevich)
1871-1919 . . . . TCLC 3
See also CA 104

Andric, Ivo 1892-1975 . . . . CLC 8
See also CA 81-84; 57-60; CANR 43;
DLB 147; MTCW

Angelique, Pierre
See Bataille, Georges

Angell, Roger 1920- . . . . CLC 26
See also CA 57-60; CANR 13, 44

Angelou, Maya
1928- . . . . CLC 12, 35, 64, 77; BLC; DA
See also AAYA 7; BW 2; CA 65-68;
CANR 19, 42; DLB 38; MTCW;
SATA 49

Annensky, Innokenty Fyodorovich
1856-1909 . . . . TCLC 14
See also CA 110

Anon, Charles Robert
See Pessoa, Fernando (Antonio Nogueira)

Anouilh, Jean (Marie Lucien Pierre)
1910-1987 . . . . . . CLC 1, 3, 8, 13, 40, 50
See also CA 17-20R; 123; CANR 32;
MTCW

Anthony, Florence
See Ai

Anthony, John
See Ciardi, John (Anthony)

Anthony, Peter
See Shaffer, Anthony (Joshua); Shaffer, Peter (Levin)

Anthony, Piers 1934- .... **CLC 35**
See also AAYA 11; CA 21-24R; CANR 28; DLB 8; MTCW

Antoine, Marc
See Proust, (Valentin-Louis-George-Eugene-) Marcel

Antoninus, Brother
See Everson, William (Oliver)

Antonioni, Michelangelo 1912- ..... **CLC 20**
See also CA 73-76; CANR 45

Antschel, Paul 1920-1970
See Celan, Paul
See also CA 85-88; CANR 33; MTCW

Anwar, Chairil 1922-1949 .... **TCLC 22**
See also CA 121

Apollinaire, Guillaume .. **TCLC 3, 8, 51; PC 7**
See also Kostrowitzki, Wilhelm Apollinaris de

Appelfeld, Aharon 1932- .... **CLC 23, 47**
See also CA 112; 133

Apple, Max (Isaac) 1941- .... **CLC 9, 33**
See also CA 81-84; CANR 19; DLB 130

Appleman, Philip (Dean) 1926- ..... **CLC 51**
See also CA 13-16R; CAAS 18; CANR 6, 29

Appleton, Lawrence
See Lovecraft, H(oward) P(hillips)

Apteryx
See Eliot, T(homas) S(tearns)

Apuleius, (Lucius Madaurensis)
125(?)-175(?) .... **CMLC 1**

Aquin, Hubert 1929-1977.......... **CLC 15**
See also CA 105; DLB 53

Aragon, Louis 1897-1982........ **CLC 3, 22**
See also CA 69-72; 108; CANR 28; DLB 72; MTCW

Arany, Janos 1817-1882........ **NCLC 34**

Arbuthnot, John 1667-1735.......... **LC 1**
See also DLB 101

Archer, Herbert Winslow
See Mencken, H(enry) L(ouis)

Archer, Jeffrey (Howard) 1940- .... **CLC 28**
See also BEST 89:3; CA 77-80; CANR 22

Archer, Jules 1915- .... **CLC 12**
See also CA 9-12R; CANR 6; SAAS 5; SATA 4

Archer, Lee
See Ellison, Harlan (Jay)

Arden, John 1930- .... **CLC 6, 13, 15**
See also CA 13-16R; CAAS 4; CANR 31; DLB 13; MTCW

Arenas, Reinaldo
1943-1990 .... **CLC 41; HLC**
See also CA 124; 128; 133; DLB 145; HW

Arendt, Hannah 1906-1975 .... **CLC 66**
See also CA 17-20R; 61-64; CANR 26; MTCW

Aretino, Pietro 1492-1556 .... **LC 12**

Arghezi, Tudor.................... **CLC 80**
See also Theodorescu, Ion N.

Arguedas, Jose Maria
1911-1969 .... **CLC 10, 18**
See also CA 89-92; DLB 113; HW

Argueta, Manlio 1936-............ **CLC 31**
See also CA 131; DLB 145; HW

Ariosto, Ludovico 1474-1533........ **LC 6**

Aristides
See Epstein, Joseph

Aristophanes
450B.C.-385B.C.... **CMLC 4; DA; DC 2**

Arlt, Roberto (Godofredo Christophersen)
1900-1942 .... **TCLC 29; HLC**
See also CA 123; 131; HW

Armah, Ayi Kwei 1939-.... **CLC 5, 33; BLC**
See also BW 1; CA 61-64; CANR 21; DLB 117; MTCW

Armatrading, Joan 1950-.......... **CLC 17**
See also CA 114

Arnette, Robert
See Silverberg, Robert

Arnim, Achim von (Ludwig Joachim von Arnim) 1781-1831 .... **NCLC 5**
See also DLB 90

Arnim, Bettina von 1785-1859.... **NCLC 38**
See also DLB 90

Arnold, Matthew
1822-1888 ..... **NCLC 6, 29; DA; PC 5; WLC**
See also A. E.
See also CDBLB 1832-1890; DLB 32, 57

Arnold, Thomas 1795-1842 ...... **NCLC 18**
See also DLB 55

Arnow, Harriette (Louisa) Simpson
1908-1986 .... **CLC 2, 7, 18**
See also CA 9-12R; 118; CANR 14; DLB 6; MTCW; SATA 42; SATA-Obit 47

Arp, Hans
See Arp, Jean

Arp, Jean 1887-1966.............. **CLC 5**
See also CA 81-84; 25-28R; CANR 42

Arrabal
See Arrabal, Fernando

Arrabal, Fernando 1932-... **CLC 2, 9, 18, 58**
See also CA 9-12R; CANR 15

Arrick, Fran...................... **CLC 30**
See also Gaberman, Judie Angell

Artaud, Antonin 1896-1948 ..... **TCLC 3, 36**
See also CA 104

Arthur, Ruth M(abel) 1905-1979.... **CLC 12**
See also CA 9-12R; 85-88; CANR 4; SATA 7, 26

Artsybashev, Mikhail (Petrovich)
1878-1927 .... **TCLC 31**

Arundel, Honor (Morfydd)
1919-1973 .... **CLC 17**
See also CA 21-22; 41-44R; CAP 2; CLR 35; SATA 4; SATA-Obit 24

Asch, Sholem 1880-1957 .... **TCLC 3**
See also CA 105

Ash, Shalom
See Asch, Sholem

Ashbery, John (Lawrence)
1927- ...... **CLC 2, 3, 4, 6, 9, 13, 15, 25, 41, 77**
See also CA 5-8R; CANR 9, 37; DLB 5; DLBY 81; MTCW

Ashdown, Clifford
See Freeman, R(ichard) Austin

Ashe, Gordon
See Creasey, John

Ashton-Warner, Sylvia (Constance)
1908-1984 .... **CLC 19**
See also CA 69-72; 112; CANR 29; MTCW

Asimov, Isaac
1920-1992 ...... **CLC 1, 3, 9, 19, 26, 76**
See also AAYA 13; BEST 90:2; CA 1-4R; 137; CANR 2, 19, 36; CLR 12; DLB 8; DLBY 92; JRDA; MAICYA; MTCW; SATA 1, 26, 74

Astley, Thea (Beatrice May)
1925- .... **CLC 41**
See also CA 65-68; CANR 11, 43

Aston, James
See White, T(erence) H(anbury)

Asturias, Miguel Angel
1899-1974 .... **CLC 3, 8, 13; HLC**
See also CA 25-28; 49-52; CANR 32; CAP 2; DLB 113; HW; MTCW

Atares, Carlos Saura
See Saura (Atares), Carlos

Atheling, William
See Pound, Ezra (Weston Loomis)

Atheling, William, Jr.
See Blish, James (Benjamin)

Atherton, Gertrude (Franklin Horn)
1857-1948 .... **TCLC 2**
See also CA 104; DLB 9, 78

Atherton, Lucius
See Masters, Edgar Lee

Atkins, Jack
See Harris, Mark

Atticus
See Fleming, Ian (Lancaster)

Atwood, Margaret (Eleanor)
1939- ..... **CLC 2, 3, 4, 8, 13, 15, 25, 44, 84; DA; PC 8; SSC 2; WLC**
See also AAYA 12; BEST 89:2; CA 49-52; CANR 3, 24, 33; DLB 53; MTCW; SATA 50

Aubigny, Pierre d'
See Mencken, H(enry) L(ouis)

Aubin, Penelope 1685-1731(?)........ **LC 9**
See also DLB 39

Auchincloss, Louis (Stanton)
1917- .... **CLC 4, 6, 9, 18, 45**
See also CA 1-4R; CANR 6, 29; DLB 2; DLBY 80; MTCW

Auden, W(ystan) H(ugh)
1907-1973 ...... **CLC 1, 2, 3, 4, 6, 9, 11, 14, 43; DA; PC 1; WLC**
See also CA 9-12R; 45-48; CANR 5; CDBLB 1914-1945; DLB 10, 20; MTCW

Audiberti, Jacques 1900-1965 ...... **CLC 38**
See also CA 25-28R

Audubon, John James
1785-1851 .... **NCLC 47**

Auel, Jean M(arie) 1936-......... **CLC 31**
See also AAYA 7; BEST 90:4; CA 103;
CANR 21

Auerbach, Erich 1892-1957...... **TCLC 43**
See also CA 118

Augier, Emile 1820-1889....... **NCLC 31**

August, John
See De Voto, Bernard (Augustine)

Augustine, St. 354-430.......... **CMLC 6**

Aurelius
See Bourne, Randolph S(illiman)

Austen, Jane
  1775-1817..... **NCLC 1, 13, 19, 33, 51;**
                                    DA; WLC
See also CDBLB 1789-1832; DLB 116

Auster, Paul 1947-............... **CLC 47**
See also CA 69-72; CANR 23

Austin, Frank
See Faust, Frederick (Schiller)

Austin, Mary (Hunter)
  1868-1934.................. **TCLC 25**
See also CA 109; DLB 9, 78

Autran Dourado, Waldomiro
See Dourado, (Waldomiro Freitas) Autran

Averroes 1126-1198............. **CMLC 7**
See also DLB 115

Avison, Margaret 1918-.......... **CLC 2, 4**
See also CA 17-20R; DLB 53; MTCW

Axton, David
See Koontz, Dean R(ay)

Ayckbourn, Alan
  1939-............ **CLC 5, 8, 18, 33, 74**
See also CA 21-24R; CANR 31; DLB 13;
MTCW

Aydy, Catherine
See Tennant, Emma (Christina)

Ayme, Marcel (Andre) 1902-1967... **CLC 11**
See also CA 89-92; CLR 25; DLB 72

Ayrton, Michael 1921-1975........ **CLC 7**
See also CA 5-8R; 61-64; CANR 9, 21

Azorin........................ **CLC 11**
See also Martinez Ruiz, Jose

Azuela, Mariano
  1873-1952............. **TCLC 3; HLC**
See also CA 104; 131; HW; MTCW

Baastad, Babbis Friis
See Friis-Baastad, Babbis Ellinor

Bab
See Gilbert, W(illiam) S(chwenck)

Babbis, Eleanor
See Friis-Baastad, Babbis Ellinor

Babel, Isaak (Emmanuilovich)
  1894-1941(?)...... **TCLC 2, 13; SSC 16**
See also CA 104

Babits, Mihaly 1883-1941....... **TCLC 14**
See also CA 114

Babur 1483-1530.................. **LC 18**

Bacchelli, Riccardo 1891-1985..... **CLC 19**
See also CA 29-32R; 117

Bach, Richard (David) 1936-....... **CLC 14**
See also AITN 1; BEST 89:2; CA 9-12R;
CANR 18; MTCW; SATA 13

Bachman, Richard
See King, Stephen (Edwin)

Bachmann, Ingeborg 1926-1973..... **CLC 69**
See also CA 93-96; 45-48; DLB 85

Bacon, Francis 1561-1626.......... **LC 18**
See also CDBLB Before 1660; DLB 151

Bacon, Roger 1214(?)-1292...... **CMLC 14**
See also DLB 115

Bacovia, George.................. **TCLC 24**
See also Vasiliu, Gheorghe

Badanes, Jerome 1937-........... **CLC 59**

Bagehot, Walter 1826-1877...... **NCLC 10**
See also DLB 55

Bagnold, Enid 1889-1981.......... **CLC 25**
See also CA 5-8R; 103; CANR 5, 40;
DLB 13; MAICYA; SATA 1, 25

Bagritsky, Eduard 1895-1934..... **TCLC 60**

Bagrjana, Elisaveta
See Belcheva, Elisaveta

Bagryana, Elisaveta.............. **CLC 10**
See also Belcheva, Elisaveta
See also DLB 147

Bailey, Paul 1937-............... **CLC 45**
See also CA 21-24R; CANR 16; DLB 14

Baillie, Joanna 1762-1851........ **NCLC 2**
See also DLB 93

Bainbridge, Beryl (Margaret)
  1933-.... **CLC 4, 5, 8, 10, 14, 18, 22, 62**
See also CA 21-24R; CANR 24; DLB 14;
MTCW

Baker, Elliott 1922-............... **CLC 8**
See also CA 45-48; CANR 2

Baker, Nicholson 1957-........... **CLC 61**
See also CA 135

Baker, Ray Stannard 1870-1946... **TCLC 47**
See also CA 118

Baker, Russell (Wayne) 1925-...... **CLC 31**
See also BEST 89:4; CA 57-60; CANR 11,
41; MTCW

Bakhtin, M.
See Bakhtin, Mikhail Mikhailovich

Bakhtin, M. M.
See Bakhtin, Mikhail Mikhailovich

Bakhtin, Mikhail
See Bakhtin, Mikhail Mikhailovich

Bakhtin, Mikhail Mikhailovich
  1895-1975.................. **CLC 83**
See also CA 128; 113

Bakshi, Ralph 1938(?)-............ **CLC 26**
See also CA 112; 138

Bakunin, Mikhail (Alexandrovich)
  1814-1876................. **NCLC 25**

Baldwin, James (Arthur)
  1924-1987...... **CLC 1, 2, 3, 4, 5, 8, 13,**
      15, 17, 42, 50, 67; BLC; DA; DC 1;
                              SSC 10; WLC
See also AAYA 4; BW 1; CA 1-4R; 124;
CABS 1; CANR 3, 24;
CDALB 1941-1968; DLB 2, 7, 33;
DLBY 87; MTCW; SATA 9;
SATA-Obit 54

Ballard, J(ames) G(raham)
  1930-......... **CLC 3, 6, 14, 36; SSC 1**
See also AAYA 3; CA 5-8R; CANR 15, 39;
DLB 14; MTCW

Balmont, Konstantin (Dmitriyevich)
  1867-1943.................. **TCLC 11**
See also CA 109

Balzac, Honore de
  1799-1850.... **NCLC 5, 35; DA; SSC 5;**
                                        WLC
See also DLB 119

Bambara, Toni Cade
  1939-........... **CLC 19, 88; BLC; DA**
See also AAYA 5; BW 2; CA 29-32R;
CANR 24; DLB 38; MTCW

Bamdad, A.
See Shamlu, Ahmad

Banat, D. R.
See Bradbury, Ray (Douglas)

Bancroft, Laura
See Baum, L(yman) Frank

Banim, John 1798-1842......... **NCLC 13**
See also DLB 116

Banim, Michael 1796-1874...... **NCLC 13**

Banks, Iain
See Banks, Iain M(enzies)

Banks, Iain M(enzies) 1954-....... **CLC 34**
See also CA 123; 128

Banks, Lynne Reid................ **CLC 23**
See also Reid Banks, Lynne
See also AAYA 6

Banks, Russell 1940-.......... **CLC 37, 72**
See also CA 65-68; CAAS 15; CANR 19;
DLB 130

Banville, John 1945-.............. **CLC 46**
See also CA 117; 128; DLB 14

Banville, Theodore (Faullain) de
  1832-1891.................. **NCLC 9**

Baraka, Amiri
  1934-........ **CLC 1, 2, 3, 5, 10, 14, 33;**
                                  BLC; DA; PC 4
See also Jones, LeRoi
See also BW 2; CA 21-24R; CABS 3;
CANR 27, 38; CDALB 1941-1968;
DLB 5, 7, 16, 38; DLBD 8; MTCW

Barbauld, Anna Laetitia
  1743-1825................ **NCLC 50**

Barbellion, W. N. P............... **TCLC 24**
See also Cummings, Bruce F(rederick)

Barbera, Jack (Vincent) 1945-...... **CLC 44**
See also CA 110; CANR 45

Barbey d'Aurevilly, Jules Amedee
  1808-1889........... **NCLC 1; SSC 17**
See also DLB 119

Barbusse, Henri 1873-1935........ **TCLC 5**
See also CA 105; DLB 65

Barclay, Bill
See Moorcock, Michael (John)

Barclay, William Ewert
See Moorcock, Michael (John)

Barea, Arturo 1897-1957........ **TCLC 14**
See also CA 111

Barfoot, Joan 1946-............. **CLC 18**
See also CA 105

Baring, Maurice 1874-1945 . . . . **TCLC 8**
See also CA 105; DLB 34

Barker, Clive 1952- . . . . **CLC 52**
See also AAYA 10; BEST 90:3; CA 121;
129; MTCW

Barker, George Granville
1913-1991 . . . . **CLC 8, 48**
See also CA 9-12R; 135; CANR 7, 38;
DLB 20; MTCW

Barker, Harley Granville
See Granville-Barker, Harley
See also DLB 10

Barker, Howard 1946- . . . . **CLC 37**
See also CA 102; DLB 13

Barker, Pat 1943- . . . . **CLC 32**
See also CA 117; 122

Barlow, Joel 1754-1812 . . . . **NCLC 23**
See also DLB 37

Barnard, Mary (Ethel) 1909- . . . . **CLC 48**
See also CA 21-22; CAP 2

Barnes, Djuna
1892-1982 . . . **CLC 3, 4, 8, 11, 29; SSC 3**
See also CA 9-12R; 107; CANR 16; DLB 4,
9, 45; MTCW

Barnes, Julian 1946- . . . . **CLC 42**
See also CA 102; CANR 19; DLBY 93

Barnes, Peter 1931- . . . . **CLC 5, 56**
See also CA 65-68; CAAS 12; CANR 33,
34; DLB 13; MTCW

Baroja (y Nessi), Pio
1872-1956 . . . . **TCLC 8; HLC**
See also CA 104

Baron, David
See Pinter, Harold

Baron Corvo
See Rolfe, Frederick (William Serafino
Austin Lewis Mary)

Barondess, Sue K(aufman)
1926-1977 . . . . **CLC 8**
See Kaufman, Sue
See also CA 1-4R; 69-72; CANR 1

Baron de Teive
See Pessoa, Fernando (Antonio Nogueira)

Barres, Maurice 1862-1923 . . . . **TCLC 47**
See also DLB 123

Barreto, Afonso Henrique de Lima
See Lima Barreto, Afonso Henrique de

Barrett, (Roger) Syd 1946- . . . . **CLC 35**

Barrett, William (Christopher)
1913-1992 . . . . **CLC 27**
See also CA 13-16R; 139; CANR 11

Barrie, J(ames) M(atthew)
1860-1937 . . . . **TCLC 2**
See also CA 104; 136; CDBLB 1890-1914;
CLR 16; DLB 10, 141; MAICYA;
YABC 1

Barrington, Michael
See Moorcock, Michael (John)

Barrol, Grady
See Bograd, Larry

Barry, Mike
See Malzberg, Barry N(athaniel)

Barry, Philip 1896-1949 . . . . **TCLC 11**
See also CA 109; DLB 7

Bart, Andre Schwarz
See Schwarz-Bart, Andre

Barth, John (Simmons)
1930- . . . . . . **CLC 1, 2, 3, 5, 7, 9, 10, 14,
27, 51, 89; SSC 10**
See also AITN 1, 2; CA 1-4R; CABS 1;
CANR 5, 23; DLB 2; MTCW

Barthelme, Donald
1931-1989 . . . . . **CLC 1, 2, 3, 5, 6, 8, 13,
23, 46, 59; SSC 2**
See also CA 21-24R; 129; CANR 20;
DLB 2; DLBY 80, 89; MTCW; SATA 7;
SATA-Obit 62

Barthelme, Frederick 1943- . . . . **CLC 36**
See also CA 114; 122; DLBY 85

Barthes, Roland (Gerard)
1915-1980 . . . . **CLC 24, 83**
See also CA 130; 97-100; MTCW

Barzun, Jacques (Martin) 1907- . . . . **CLC 51**
See also CA 61-64; CANR 22

Bashevis, Isaac
See Singer, Isaac Bashevis

Bashkirtseff, Marie 1859-1884 . . . **NCLC 27**

Basho
See Matsuo Basho

Bass, Kingsley B., Jr.
See Bullins, Ed

Bass, Rick 1958- . . . . **CLC 79**
See also CA 126

Bassani, Giorgio 1916- . . . . **CLC 9**
See also CA 65-68; CANR 33; DLB 128;
MTCW

Bastos, Augusto (Antonio) Roa
See Roa Bastos, Augusto (Antonio)

Bataille, Georges 1897-1962 . . . . **CLC 29**
See also CA 101; 89-92

Bates, H(erbert) E(rnest)
1905-1974 . . . . **CLC 46; SSC 10**
See also CA 93-96; 45-48; CANR 34;
MTCW

Bauchart
See Camus, Albert

Baudelaire, Charles
1821-1867 . . . . . **NCLC 6, 29; DA; PC 1;
SSC 18; WLC**

Baudrillard, Jean 1929- . . . . **CLC 60**

Baum, L(yman) Frank 1856-1919 . . . **TCLC 7**
See also CA 108; 133; CLR 15; DLB 22;
JRDA; MAICYA; MTCW; SATA 18

Baum, Louis F.
See Baum, L(yman) Frank

Baumbach, Jonathan 1933- . . . . . . **CLC 6, 23**
See also CA 13-16R; CAAS 5; CANR 12;
DLBY 80; MTCW

Bausch, Richard (Carl) 1945- . . . . . . **CLC 51**
See also CA 101; CAAS 14; CANR 43;
DLB 130

Baxter, Charles 1947- . . . . **CLC 45, 78**
See also CA 57-60; CANR 40; DLB 130

Baxter, George Owen
See Faust, Frederick (Schiller)

Baxter, James K(eir) 1926-1972 . . . . **CLC 14**
See also CA 77-80

Baxter, John
See Hunt, E(verette) Howard, (Jr.)

Bayer, Sylvia
See Glassco, John

Baynton, Barbara 1857-1929 . . . . . **TCLC 57**

Beagle, Peter S(oyer) 1939- . . . . **CLC 7**
See also CA 9-12R; CANR 4; DLBY 80;
SATA 60

Bean, Normal
See Burroughs, Edgar Rice

Beard, Charles A(ustin)
1874-1948 . . . . **TCLC 15**
See also CA 115; DLB 17; SATA 18

Beardsley, Aubrey 1872-1898 . . . . . **NCLC 6**

Beattie, Ann
1947- . . . . **CLC 8, 13, 18, 40, 63; SSC 11**
See also BEST 90:2; CA 81-84; DLBY 82;
MTCW

Beattie, James 1735-1803 . . . . **NCLC 25**
See also DLB 109

Beauchamp, Kathleen Mansfield 1888-1923
See Mansfield, Katherine
See also CA 104; 134; DA

Beaumarchais, Pierre-Augustin Caron de
1732-1799 . . . . **DC 4**

**Beauvoir, Simone (Lucie Ernestine Marie
Bertrand) de**
1908-1986 . . . . **CLC 1, 2, 4, 8, 14, 31, 44,
50, 71; DA; WLC**
See also CA 9-12R; 118; CANR 28;
DLB 72; DLBY 86; MTCW

Becker, Jurek 1937- . . . . **CLC 7, 19**
See also CA 85-88; DLB 75

Becker, Walter 1950- . . . . **CLC 26**

Beckett, Samuel (Barclay)
1906-1989 . . . . . . **CLC 1, 2, 3, 4, 6, 9, 10,
11, 14, 18, 29, 57, 59, 83; DA; SSC 16;
WLC**
See also CA 5-8R; 130; CANR 33;
CDBLB 1945-1960; DLB 13, 15;
DLBY 90; MTCW

Beckford, William 1760-1844 . . . . **NCLC 16**
See also DLB 39

Beckman, Gunnel 1910- . . . . **CLC 26**
See also CA 33-36R; CANR 15; CLR 25;
MAICYA; SAAS 9; SATA 6

Becque, Henri 1837-1899 . . . . **NCLC 3**

Beddoes, Thomas Lovell
1803-1849 . . . . **NCLC 3**
See also DLB 96

Bedford, Donald F.
See Fearing, Kenneth (Flexner)

Beecher, Catharine Esther
1800-1878 . . . . **NCLC 30**
See also DLB 1

Beecher, John 1904-1980 . . . . **CLC 6**
See also AITN 1; CA 5-8R; 105; CANR 8

Beer, Johann 1655-1700 . . . . **LC 5**

Beer, Patricia 1924- . . . . **CLC 58**
See also CA 61-64; CANR 13, 46; DLB 40

Beerbohm, Henry Maximilian
1872-1956 . . . . **TCLC 1, 24**
See also CA 104; DLB 34, 100

Beerbohm, Max
See Beerbohm, Henry Maximilian

Beer-Hofmann, Richard
1866-1945 .... TCLC 60
See also DLB 81

Begiebing, Robert J(ohn) 1946-..... CLC 70
See also CA 122; CANR 40

Behan, Brendan
1923-1964 .... CLC 1, 8, 11, 15, 79
See also CA 73-76; CANR 33;
CDBLB 1945-1960; DLB 13; MTCW

Behn, Aphra
1640(?)-1689 ...... LC 1, 30; DA; DC 4;
PC 12; WLC
See also DLB 39, 80, 131

Behrman, S(amuel) N(athaniel)
1893-1973 .... CLC 40
See also CA 13-16; 45-48; CAP 1; DLB 7,
44

Belasco, David 1853-1931 .... TCLC 3
See also CA 104; DLB 7

Belcheva, Elisaveta 1893- .... CLC 10
See also Bagryana, Elisaveta

Beldone, Phil "Cheech"
See Ellison, Harlan (Jay)

Beleno
See Azuela, Mariano

Belinski, Vissarion Grigoryevich
1811-1848 .... NCLC 5

Belitt, Ben 1911-................. CLC 22
See also CA 13-16R; CAAS 4; CANR 7;
DLB 5

Bell, James Madison
1826-1902 .... TCLC 43; BLC
See also BW 1; CA 122; 124; DLB 50

Bell, Madison (Smartt) 1957- ...... CLC 41
See also CA 111; CANR 28

Bell, Marvin (Hartley) 1937-..... CLC 8, 31
See also CA 21-24R; CAAS 14; DLB 5;
MTCW

Bell, W. L. D.
See Mencken, H(enry) L(ouis)

Bellamy, Atwood C.
See Mencken, H(enry) L(ouis)

Bellamy, Edward 1850-1898 ...... NCLC 4
See also DLB 12

Bellin, Edward J.
See Kuttner, Henry

Belloc, (Joseph) Hilaire (Pierre)
1870-1953 .... TCLC 7, 18
See also CA 106; DLB 19, 100, 141;
YABC 1

Belloc, Joseph Peter Rene Hilaire
See Belloc, (Joseph) Hilaire (Pierre)

Belloc, Joseph Pierre Hilaire
See Belloc, (Joseph) Hilaire (Pierre)

Belloc, M. A.
See Lowndes, Marie Adelaide (Belloc)

Bellow, Saul
1915- ...... CLC 1, 2, 3, 6, 8, 10, 13, 15,
25, 33, 34, 63, 79; DA; SSC 14; WLC
See also AITN 2; BEST 89:3; CA 5-8R;
CABS 1; CANR 29; CDALB 1941-1968;
DLB 2, 28; DLBD 3; DLBY 82; MTCW

Belser, Reimond Karel Maria de
See Ruyslinck, Ward

Bely, Andrey .... TCLC 7; PC 11
See also Bugayev, Boris Nikolayevich

Benary, Margot
See Benary-Isbert, Margot

Benary-Isbert, Margot 1889-1979... CLC 12
See also CA 5-8R; 89-92; CANR 4;
CLR 12; MAICYA; SATA 2;
SATA-Obit 21

Benavente (y Martinez), Jacinto
1866-1954 .... TCLC 3
See also CA 106; 131; HW; MTCW

Benchley, Peter (Bradford)
1940- .... CLC 4, 8
See also AAYA 14; AITN 2; CA 17-20R;
CANR 12, 35; MTCW; SATA 3

Benchley, Robert (Charles)
1889-1945 .... TCLC 1, 55
See also CA 105; DLB 11

Benda, Julien 1867-1956 .... TCLC 60
See also CA 120

Benedict, Ruth 1887-1948 .... TCLC 60

Benedikt, Michael 1935- .... CLC 4, 14
See also CA 13-16R; CANR 7; DLB 5

Benet, Juan 1927-................ CLC 28
See also CA 143

Benet, Stephen Vincent
1898-1943 .... TCLC 7; SSC 10
See also CA 104; DLB 4, 48, 102; YABC 1

Benet, William Rose 1886-1950 ... TCLC 28
See also CA 118; DLB 45

Benford, Gregory (Albert) 1941-.... CLC 52
See also CA 69-72; CANR 12, 24;
DLBY 82

Bengtsson, Frans (Gunnar)
1894-1954 .... TCLC 48

Benjamin, David
See Slavitt, David R(ytman)

Benjamin, Lois
See Gould, Lois

Benjamin, Walter 1892-1940 ...... TCLC 39

Benn, Gottfried 1886-1956........ TCLC 3
See also CA 106; DLB 56

Bennett, Alan 1934-........... CLC 45, 77
See also CA 103; CANR 35; MTCW

Bennett, (Enoch) Arnold
1867-1931 .... TCLC 5, 20
See also CA 106; CDBLB 1890-1914;
DLB 10, 34, 98, 135

Bennett, Elizabeth
See Mitchell, Margaret (Munnerlyn)

Bennett, George Harold 1930-
See Bennett, Hal
See also BW 1; CA 97-100

Bennett, Hal .... CLC 5
See also Bennett, George Harold
See also DLB 33

Bennett, Jay 1912-.............. CLC 35
See also AAYA 10; CA 69-72; CANR 11,
42; JRDA; SAAS 4; SATA 41;
SATA-Brief 27

Bennett, Louise (Simone)
1919- .... CLC 28; BLC
See also BW 2; DLB 117

Benson, E(dward) F(rederic)
1867-1940 .... TCLC 27
See also CA 114; DLB 135, 153

Benson, Jackson J. 1930-........... CLC 34
See also CA 25-28R; DLB 111

Benson, Sally 1900-1972 .... CLC 17
See also CA 19-20; 37-40R; CAP 1;
SATA 1, 35; SATA-Obit 27

Benson, Stella 1892-1933........ TCLC 17
See also CA 117; DLB 36

Bentham, Jeremy 1748-1832 ..... NCLC 38
See also DLB 107

Bentley, E(dmund) C(lerihew)
1875-1956 .... TCLC 12
See also CA 108; DLB 70

Bentley, Eric (Russell) 1916-....... CLC 24
See also CA 5-8R; CANR 6

Beranger, Pierre Jean de
1780-1857 .... NCLC 34

Berendt, John (Lawrence) 1939-.... CLC 86
See also CA 146

Berger, Colonel
See Malraux, (Georges-)Andre

Berger, John (Peter) 1926- ...... CLC 2, 19
See also CA 81-84; DLB 14

Berger, Melvin H. 1927-........... CLC 12
See also CA 5-8R; CANR 4; CLR 32;
SAAS 2; SATA 5

Berger, Thomas (Louis)
1924- .... CLC 3, 5, 8, 11, 18, 38
See also CA 1-4R; CANR 5, 28; DLB 2;
DLBY 80; MTCW

Bergman, (Ernst) Ingmar
1918- .... CLC 16, 72
See also CA 81-84; CANR 33

Bergson, Henri 1859-1941........ TCLC 32

Bergstein, Eleanor 1938-........... CLC 4
See also CA 53-56; CANR 5

Berkoff, Steven 1937-............. CLC 56
See also CA 104

Bermant, Chaim (Icyk) 1929- ...... CLC 40
See also CA 57-60; CANR 6, 31

Bern, Victoria
See Fisher, M(ary) F(rances) K(ennedy)

Bernanos, (Paul Louis) Georges
1888-1948 .... TCLC 3
See also CA 104; 130; DLB 72

Bernard, April 1956- .... CLC 59
See also CA 131

Berne, Victoria
See Fisher, M(ary) F(rances) K(ennedy)

Bernhard, Thomas
1931-1989 .... CLC 3, 32, 61
See also CA 85-88; 127; CANR 32;
DLB 85, 124; MTCW

Berriault, Gina 1926-............. CLC 54
See also CA 116; 129; DLB 130

Berrigan, Daniel 1921-............. CLC 4
See also CA 33-36R; CAAS 1; CANR 11,
43; DLB 5

Berrigan, Edmund Joseph Michael, Jr.
1934-1983
See Berrigan, Ted
See also CA 61-64; 110; CANR 14

Berrigan, Ted. . . . . **CLC 37**
See also Berrigan, Edmund Joseph Michael,
Jr.
See also DLB 5

Berry, Charles Edward Anderson   1931-
See Berry, Chuck
See also CA 115

Berry, Chuck. . . . . **CLC 17**
See also Berry, Charles Edward Anderson

Berry, Jonas
See Ashbery, John (Lawrence)

Berry, Wendell (Erdman)
1934- . . . . **CLC 4, 6, 8, 27, 46**
See also AITN 1; CA 73-76; DLB 5, 6

Berryman, John
1914-1972 . . . . . . **CLC 1, 2, 3, 4, 6, 8, 10,**
13, 25, 62
See also CA 13-16; 33-36R; CABS 2;
CANR 35; CAP 1; CDALB 1941-1968;
DLB 48; MTCW

Bertolucci, Bernardo   1940- . . . . **CLC 16**
See also CA 106

Bertrand, Aloysius   1807-1841 . . . . **NCLC 31**

Bertran de Born   c. 1140-1215 . . . . . **CMLC 5**

Besant, Annie (Wood)   1847-1933 . . . **TCLC 9**
See also CA 105

Bessie, Alvah   1904-1985. . . . . **CLC 23**
See also CA 5-8R; 116; CANR 2; DLB 26

Bethlen, T. D.
See Silverberg, Robert

Beti, Mongo. . . . . **CLC 27; BLC**
See also Biyidi, Alexandre

Betjeman, John
1906-1984 . . . . **CLC 2, 6, 10, 34, 43**
See also CA 9-12R; 112; CANR 33;
CDBLB 1945-1960; DLB 20; DLBY 84;
MTCW

Bettelheim, Bruno   1903-1990 . . . . . . **CLC 79**
See also CA 81-84; 131; CANR 23; MTCW

Betti, Ugo   1892-1953 . . . . **TCLC 5**
See also CA 104

Betts, Doris (Waugh)   1932- . . . . **CLC 3, 6, 28**
See also CA 13-16R; CANR 9; DLBY 82

Bevan, Alistair
See Roberts, Keith (John Kingston)

Bialik, Chaim Nachman
1873-1934 . . . . **TCLC 25**

Bickerstaff, Isaac
See Swift, Jonathan

Bidart, Frank   1939- . . . . **CLC 33**
See also CA 140

Bienek, Horst   1930- . . . . **CLC 7, 11**
See also CA 73-76; DLB 75

Bierce, Ambrose (Gwinett)
1842-1914(?) . . . . **TCLC 1, 7, 44; DA;**
SSC 9; WLC
See also CA 104; 139; CDALB 1865-1917;
DLB 11, 12, 23, 71, 74

Billings, Josh
See Shaw, Henry Wheeler

Billington, (Lady) Rachel (Mary)
1942- . . . . **CLC 43**
See also AITN 2; CA 33-36R; CANR 44

Binyon, T(imothy) J(ohn)   1936- . . . . **CLC 34**
See also CA 111; CANR 28

Bioy Casares, Adolfo
1914- . . . **CLC 4, 8, 13, 88; HLC; SSC 17**
See also CA 29-32R; CANR 19, 43;
DLB 113; HW; MTCW

Bird, Cordwainer
See Ellison, Harlan (Jay)

Bird, Robert Montgomery
1806-1854 . . . . **NCLC 1**

Birney, (Alfred) Earle
1904- . . . . **CLC 1, 4, 6, 11**
See also CA 1-4R; CANR 5, 20; DLB 88;
MTCW

Bishop, Elizabeth
1911-1979 . . . . . . **CLC 1, 4, 9, 13, 15, 32;**
DA; PC 3
See also CA 5-8R; 89-92; CABS 2;
CANR 26; CDALB 1968-1988; DLB 5;
MTCW; SATA-Obit 24

Bishop, John   1935- . . . . **CLC 10**
See also CA 105

Bissett, Bill   1939- . . . . **CLC 18**
See also CA 69-72; CAAS 19; CANR 15;
DLB 53; MTCW

Bitov, Andrei (Georgievich)   1937- . . . **CLC 57**
See also CA 142

Biyidi, Alexandre   1932-
See Beti, Mongo
See also BW 1; CA 114; 124; MTCW

Bjarme, Brynjolf
See Ibsen, Henrik (Johan)

Bjornson, Bjornstjerne (Martinius)
1832-1910 . . . . **TCLC 7, 37**
See also CA 104

Black, Robert
See Holdstock, Robert P.

Blackburn, Paul   1926-1971 . . . . . . **CLC 9, 43**
See also CA 81-84; 33-36R; CANR 34;
DLB 16; DLBY 81

Black Elk   1863-1950 . . . . **TCLC 33**
See also CA 144; NNAL

Black Hobart
See Sanders, (James) Ed(ward)

Blacklin, Malcolm
See Chambers, Aidan

Blackmore, R(ichard) D(oddridge)
1825-1900 . . . . **TCLC 27**
See also CA 120; DLB 18

Blackmur, R(ichard) P(almer)
1904-1965 . . . . **CLC 2, 24**
See also CA 11-12; 25-28R; CAP 1; DLB 63

Black Tarantula, The
See Acker, Kathy

Blackwood, Algernon (Henry)
1869-1951 . . . . **TCLC 5**
See also CA 105; DLB 153

Blackwood, Caroline   1931- . . . . **CLC 6, 9**
See also CA 85-88; CANR 32; DLB 14;
MTCW

Blade, Alexander
See Hamilton, Edmond; Silverberg, Robert

Blaga, Lucian   1895-1961 . . . . **CLC 75**

Blair, Eric (Arthur)   1903-1950
See Orwell, George
See also CA 104; 132; DA; MTCW;
SATA 29

Blais, Marie-Claire
1939- . . . . **CLC 2, 4, 6, 13, 22**
See also CA 21-24R; CAAS 4; CANR 38;
DLB 53; MTCW

Blaise, Clark   1940- . . . . **CLC 29**
See also AITN 2; CA 53-56; CAAS 3;
CANR 5; DLB 53

Blake, Nicholas
See Day Lewis, C(ecil)
See also DLB 77

Blake, William
1757-1827 . . . . **NCLC 13, 37; DA;**
PC 12; WLC
See also CDBLB 1789-1832; DLB 93;
MAICYA; SATA 30

Blasco Ibanez, Vicente
1867-1928 . . . . **TCLC 12**
See also CA 110; 131; HW; MTCW

Blatty, William Peter   1928- . . . . **CLC 2**
See also CA 5-8R; CANR 9

Bleeck, Oliver
See Thomas, Ross (Elmore)

Blessing, Lee   1949- . . . . **CLC 54**

Blish, James (Benjamin)
1921-1975 . . . . **CLC 14**
See also CA 1-4R; 57-60; CANR 3; DLB 8;
MTCW; SATA 66

Bliss, Reginald
See Wells, H(erbert) G(eorge)

Blixen, Karen (Christentze Dinesen)
1885-1962
See Dinesen, Isak
See also CA 25-28; CANR 22; CAP 2;
MTCW; SATA 44

Bloch, Robert (Albert)   1917-1994 . . . **CLC 33**
See also CA 5-8R; 146; CAAS 20; CANR 5;
DLB 44; SATA 12

Blok, Alexander (Alexandrovich)
1880-1921 . . . . **TCLC 5**
See also CA 104

Blom, Jan
See Breytenbach, Breyten

Bloom, Harold   1930- . . . . **CLC 24**
See also CA 13-16R; CANR 39; DLB 67

Bloomfield, Aurelius
See Bourne, Randolph S(illiman)

Blount, Roy (Alton), Jr.   1941- . . . . . **CLC 38**
See also CA 53-56; CANR 10, 28; MTCW

Bloy, Leon   1846-1917. . . . . **TCLC 22**
See also CA 121; DLB 123

Blume, Judy (Sussman)   1938- . . . **CLC 12, 30**
See also AAYA 3; CA 29-32R; CANR 13,
37; CLR 2, 15; DLB 52; JRDA;
MAICYA; MTCW; SATA 2, 31, 79

Blunden, Edmund (Charles)
1896-1974 . . . . **CLC 2, 56**
See also CA 17-18; 45-48; CAP 2; DLB 20,
100; MTCW

Bly, Robert (Elwood)
1926- ..... **CLC 1, 2, 5, 10, 15, 38**
See also CA 5-8R; CANR 41; DLB 5;
MTCW

Boas, Franz 1858-1942 ..... **TCLC 56**
See also CA 115

Bobette
See Simenon, Georges (Jacques Christian)

Boccaccio, Giovanni
1313-1375 ..... **CMLC 13; SSC 10**

Bochco, Steven 1943- ..... **CLC 35**
See also AAYA 11; CA 124; 138

Bodenheim, Maxwell 1892-1954 ... **TCLC 44**
See also CA 110; DLB 9, 45

Bodker, Cecil 1927- ..... **CLC 21**
See also CA 73-76; CANR 13, 44; CLR 23;
MAICYA; SATA 14

Boell, Heinrich (Theodor)
1917-1985 .... **CLC 2, 3, 6, 9, 11, 15, 27,
32, 72; DA; WLC**
See also CA 21-24R; 116; CANR 24;
DLB 69; DLBY 85; MTCW

Boerne, Alfred
See Doeblin, Alfred

Boethius 480(?)-524(?) ..... **CMLC 15**
See also DLB 115

Bogan, Louise
1897-1970 ..... **CLC 4, 39, 46; PC 12**
See also CA 73-76; 25-28R; CANR 33;
DLB 45; MTCW

Bogarde, Dirk ..... **CLC 19**
See also Van Den Bogarde, Derek Jules
Gaspard Ulric Niven
See also DLB 14

Bogosian, Eric 1953- ..... **CLC 45**
See also CA 138

Bograd, Larry 1953- ..... **CLC 35**
See also CA 93-96; SATA 33

Boiardo, Matteo Maria 1441-1494 .... **LC 6**

Boileau-Despreaux, Nicolas
1636-1711 ..... **LC 3**

Boland, Eavan (Aisling) 1944- ... **CLC 40, 67**
See also CA 143; DLB 40

Bolt, Lee
See Faust, Frederick (Schiller)

Bolt, Robert (Oxton) 1924-1995 .... **CLC 14**
See also CA 17-20R; 147; CANR 35;
DLB 13; MTCW

Bombet, Louis-Alexandre-Cesar
See Stendhal

Bomkauf
See Kaufman, Bob (Garnell)

Bonaventura ..... **NCLC 35**
See also DLB 90

Bond, Edward 1934- ..... **CLC 4, 6, 13, 23**
See also CA 25-28R; CANR 38; DLB 13;
MTCW

Bonham, Frank 1914-1989 ..... **CLC 12**
See also AAYA 1; CA 9-12R; CANR 4, 36;
JRDA; MAICYA; SAAS 3; SATA 1, 49;
SATA-Obit 62

Bonnefoy, Yves 1923- ..... **CLC 9, 15, 58**
See also CA 85-88; CANR 33; MTCW

Bontemps, Arna(ud Wendell)
1902-1973 ..... **CLC 1, 18; BLC**
See also BW 1; CA 1-4R; 41-44R; CANR 4,
35; CLR 6; DLB 48, 51; JRDA;
MAICYA; MTCW; SATA 2, 44;
SATA-Obit 24

Booth, Martin 1944- ..... **CLC 13**
See also CA 93-96; CAAS 2

Booth, Philip 1925- ..... **CLC 23**
See also CA 5-8R; CANR 5; DLBY 82

Booth, Wayne C(layson) 1921- ..... **CLC 24**
See also CA 1-4R; CAAS 5; CANR 3, 43;
DLB 67

Borchert, Wolfgang 1921-1947 ..... **TCLC 5**
See also CA 104; DLB 69, 124

Borel, Petrus 1809-1859 ..... **NCLC 41**

Borges, Jorge Luis
1899-1986 ... **CLC 1, 2, 3, 4, 6, 8, 9, 10,
13, 19, 44, 48, 83; DA; HLC; SSC 4;
WLC**
See also CA 21-24R; CANR 19, 33;
DLB 113; DLBY 86; HW; MTCW

Borowski, Tadeusz 1922-1951 ..... **TCLC 9**
See also CA 106

Borrow, George (Henry)
1803-1881 ..... **NCLC 9**
See also DLB 21, 55

Bosman, Herman Charles
1905-1951 ..... **TCLC 49**

Bosschere, Jean de 1878(?)-1953 ... **TCLC 19**
See also CA 115

Boswell, James
1740-1795 ..... **LC 4; DA; WLC**
See also CDBLB 1660-1789; DLB 104, 142

Bottoms, David 1949- ..... **CLC 53**
See also CA 105; CANR 22; DLB 120;
DLBY 83

Boucicault, Dion 1820-1890 ..... **NCLC 41**

Boucolon, Maryse 1937-
See Conde, Maryse
See also CA 110; CANR 30

Bourget, Paul (Charles Joseph)
1852-1935 ..... **TCLC 12**
See also CA 107; DLB 123

Bourjaily, Vance (Nye) 1922- .... **CLC 8, 62**
See also CA 1-4R; CAAS 1; CANR 2;
DLB 2, 143

Bourne, Randolph S(illiman)
1886-1918 ..... **TCLC 16**
See also CA 117; DLB 63

Bova, Ben(jamin William) 1932- .... **CLC 45**
See also CA 5-8R; CAAS 18; CANR 11;
CLR 3; DLBY 81; MAICYA; MTCW;
SATA 6, 68

Bowen, Elizabeth (Dorothea Cole)
1899-1973 ..... **CLC 1, 3, 6, 11, 15, 22;
SSC 3**
See also CA 17-18; 41-44R; CANR 35;
CAP 2; CDBLB 1945-1960; DLB 15;
MTCW

Bowering, George 1935- ..... **CLC 15, 47**
See also CA 21-24R; CAAS 16; CANR 10;
DLB 53

Bowering, Marilyn R(uthe) 1949- ... **CLC 32**
See also CA 101

Bowers, Edgar 1924- ..... **CLC 9**
See also CA 5-8R; CANR 24; DLB 5

Bowie, David ..... **CLC 17**
See also Jones, David Robert

Bowles, Jane (Sydney)
1917-1973 ..... **CLC 3, 68**
See also CA 19-20; 41-44R; CAP 2

Bowles, Paul (Frederick)
1910- ..... **CLC 1, 2, 19, 53; SSC 3**
See also CA 1-4R; CAAS 1; CANR 1, 19;
DLB 5, 6; MTCW

Box, Edgar
See Vidal, Gore

Boyd, Nancy
See Millay, Edna St. Vincent

Boyd, William 1952- ..... **CLC 28, 53, 70**
See also CA 114; 120

Boyle, Kay
1902-1992 ..... **CLC 1, 5, 19, 58; SSC 5**
See also CA 13-16R; 140; CAAS 1;
CANR 29; DLB 4, 9, 48, 86; DLBY 93;
MTCW

Boyle, Mark
See Kienzle, William X(avier)

Boyle, Patrick 1905-1982 ..... **CLC 19**
See also CA 127

Boyle, T. C.
See Boyle, T(homas) Coraghessan

Boyle, T(homas) Coraghessan
1948- ..... **CLC 36, 55; SSC 16**
See also BEST 90:4; CA 120; CANR 44;
DLBY 86

Boz
See Dickens, Charles (John Huffam)

Brackenridge, Hugh Henry
1748-1816 ..... **NCLC 7**
See also DLB 11, 37

Bradbury, Edward P.
See Moorcock, Michael (John)

Bradbury, Malcolm (Stanley)
1932- ..... **CLC 32, 61**
See also CA 1-4R; CANR 1, 33; DLB 14;
MTCW

Bradbury, Ray (Douglas)
1920- ... **CLC 1, 3, 10, 15, 42; DA; WLC**
See also AITN 1, 2; CA 1-4R; CANR 2, 30;
CDALB 1968-1988; DLB 2, 8; MTCW;
SATA 11, 64

Bradford, Gamaliel 1863-1932 ..... **TCLC 36**
See also DLB 17

Bradley, David (Henry, Jr.)
1950- ..... **CLC 23; BLC**
See also BW 1; CA 104; CANR 26; DLB 33

Bradley, John Ed(mund, Jr.)
1958- ..... **CLC 55**
See also CA 139

Bradley, Marion Zimmer 1930- ..... **CLC 30**
See also AAYA 9; CA 57-60; CAAS 10;
CANR 7, 31; DLB 8; MTCW

Bradstreet, Anne
1612(?)-1672 ..... **LC 4, 30; DA; PC 10**
See also CDALB 1640-1865; DLB 24

Brady, Joan 1939- ..... **CLC 86**
See also CA 141

Bragg, Melvyn 1939- .... **CLC 10**
See also BEST 89:3; CA 57-60; CANR 10, 48; DLB 14

Braine, John (Gerard)
1922-1986 .... **CLC 1, 3, 41**
See also CA 1-4R; 120; CANR 1, 33; CDBLB 1945-1960; DLB 15; DLBY 86; MTCW

Brammer, William 1930(?)-1978 .... **CLC 31**
See also CA 77-80

Brancati, Vitaliano 1907-1954 ..... **TCLC 12**
See also CA 109

Brancato, Robin F(idler) 1936- ..... **CLC 35**
See also AAYA 9; CA 69-72; CANR 11, 45; CLR 32; JRDA; SAAS 9; SATA 23

Brand, Max
See Faust, Frederick (Schiller)

Brand, Millen 1906-1980 .... **CLC 7**
See also CA 21-24R; 97-100

Branden, Barbara .... **CLC 44**

Brandes, Georg (Morris Cohen)
1842-1927 .... **TCLC 10**
See also CA 105

Brandys, Kazimierz 1916- .... **CLC 62**

Branley, Franklyn M(ansfield)
1915- .... **CLC 21**
See also CA 33-36R; CANR 14, 39; CLR 13; MAICYA; SAAS 16; SATA 4, 68

Brathwaite, Edward Kamau 1930-... **CLC 11**
See also BW 2; CA 25-28R; CANR 11, 26, 47; DLB 125

Brautigan, Richard (Gary)
1935-1984 .... **CLC 1, 3, 5, 9, 12, 34, 42**
See also CA 53-56; 113; CANR 34; DLB 2, 5; DLBY 80, 84; MTCW; SATA 56

Braverman, Kate 1950- .... **CLC 67**
See also CA 89-92

Brecht, Bertolt
1898-1956 ...... **TCLC 1, 6, 13, 35; DA; DC 3; WLC**
See also CA 104; 133; DLB 56, 124; MTCW

Brecht, Eugen Berthold Friedrich
See Brecht, Bertolt

Bremer, Fredrika 1801-1865 ..... **NCLC 11**

Brennan, Christopher John
1870-1932 .... **TCLC 17**
See also CA 117

Brennan, Maeve 1917- .... **CLC 5**
See also CA 81-84

Brentano, Clemens (Maria)
1778-1842 .... **NCLC 1**
See also DLB 90

Brent of Bin Bin
See Franklin, (Stella Maraia Sarah) Miles

Brenton, Howard 1942- .... **CLC 31**
See also CA 69-72; CANR 33; DLB 13; MTCW

Breslin, James 1930-
See Breslin, Jimmy
See also CA 73-76; CANR 31; MTCW

Breslin, Jimmy .... **CLC 4, 43**
See also Breslin, James
See also AITN 1

Bresson, Robert 1901- .... **CLC 16**
See also CA 110

Breton, Andre 1896-1966 ... **CLC 2, 9, 15, 54**
See also CA 19-20; 25-28R; CANR 40; CAP 2; DLB 65; MTCW

Breytenbach, Breyten 1939(?)- .. **CLC 23, 37**
See also CA 113; 129

Bridgers, Sue Ellen 1942- .... **CLC 26**
See also AAYA 8; CA 65-68; CANR 11, 36; CLR 18; DLB 52; JRDA; MAICYA; SAAS 1; SATA 22

Bridges, Robert (Seymour)
1844-1930 .... **TCLC 1**
See also CA 104; CDBLB 1890-1914; DLB 19, 98

Bridie, James. .... **TCLC 3**
See also Mavor, Osborne Henry
See also DLB 10

Brin, David 1950- .... **CLC 34**
See also CA 102; CANR 24; SATA 65

Brink, Andre (Philippus)
1935- .... **CLC 18, 36**
See also CA 104; CANR 39; MTCW

Brinsmead, H(esba) F(ay) 1922- .... **CLC 21**
See also CA 21-24R; CANR 10; MAICYA; SAAS 5; SATA 18, 78

Brittain, Vera (Mary)
1893(?)-1970 .... **CLC 23**
See also CA 13-16; 25-28R; CAP 1; MTCW

Broch, Hermann 1886-1951 ...... **TCLC 20**
See also CA 117; DLB 85, 124

Brock, Rose
See Hansen, Joseph

Brodkey, Harold 1930- .... **CLC 56**
See also CA 111; DLB 130

Brodsky, Iosif Alexandrovich 1940-
See Brodsky, Joseph
See also AITN 1; CA 41-44R; CANR 37; MTCW

Brodsky, Joseph .. **CLC 4, 6, 13, 36, 50; PC 9**
See also Brodsky, Iosif Alexandrovich

Brodsky, Michael Mark 1948- ..... **CLC 19**
See also CA 102; CANR 18, 41

Bromell, Henry 1947- .... **CLC 5**
See also CA 53-56; CANR 9

Bromfield, Louis (Brucker)
1896-1956 .... **TCLC 11**
See also CA 107; DLB 4, 9, 86

Broner, E(sther) M(asserman)
1930- .... **CLC 19**
See also CA 17-20R; CANR 8, 25; DLB 28

Bronk, William 1918- .... **CLC 10**
See also CA 89-92; CANR 23

Bronstein, Lev Davidovich
See Trotsky, Leon

Bronte, Anne 1820-1849 .... **NCLC 4**
See also DLB 21

Bronte, Charlotte
1816-1855 ... **NCLC 3, 8, 33; DA; WLC**
See also CDBLB 1832-1890; DLB 21

Bronte, (Jane) Emily
1818-1848 .... **NCLC 16, 35; DA; PC 8; WLC**
See also CDBLB 1832-1890; DLB 21, 32

Brooke, Frances 1724-1789 .... **LC 6**
See also DLB 39, 99

Brooke, Henry 1703(?)-1783 .... **LC 1**
See also DLB 39

Brooke, Rupert (Chawner)
1887-1915 .... **TCLC 2, 7; DA; WLC**
See also CA 104; 132; CDBLB 1914-1945; DLB 19; MTCW

Brooke-Haven, P.
See Wodehouse, P(elham) G(renville)

Brooke-Rose, Christine 1926- ...... **CLC 40**
See also CA 13-16R; DLB 14

Brookner, Anita 1928- ...... **CLC 32, 34, 51**
See also CA 114; 120; CANR 37; DLBY 87; MTCW

Brooks, Cleanth 1906-1994 ..... **CLC 24, 86**
See also CA 17-20R; 145; CANR 33, 35; DLB 63; DLBY 94; MTCW

Brooks, George
See Baum, L(yman) Frank

Brooks, Gwendolyn
1917- ...... **CLC 1, 2, 4, 5, 15, 49; BLC; DA; PC 7; WLC**
See also AITN 1; BW 2; CA 1-4R; CANR 1, 27; CDALB 1941-1968; CLR 27; DLB 5, 76; MTCW; SATA 6

Brooks, Mel. .... **CLC 12**
See also Kaminsky, Melvin
See also AAYA 13; DLB 26

Brooks, Peter 1938- .... **CLC 34**
See also CA 45-48; CANR 1

Brooks, Van Wyck 1886-1963 ...... **CLC 29**
See also CA 1-4R; CANR 6; DLB 45, 63, 103

Brophy, Brigid (Antonia)
1929- .... **CLC 6, 11, 29**
See also CA 5-8R; CAAS 4; CANR 25; DLB 14; MTCW

Brosman, Catharine Savage 1934-.... **CLC 9**
See also CA 61-64; CANR 21, 46

Brother Antoninus
See Everson, William (Oliver)

Broughton, T(homas) Alan 1936- ... **CLC 19**
See also CA 45-48; CANR 2, 23, 48

Broumas, Olga 1949- .... **CLC 10, 73**
See also CA 85-88; CANR 20

Brown, Charles Brockden
1771-1810 .... **NCLC 22**
See also CDALB 1640-1865; DLB 37, 59, 73

Brown, Christy 1932-1981 .... **CLC 63**
See also CA 105; 104; DLB 14

Brown, Claude 1937- .... **CLC 30; BLC**
See also AAYA 7; BW 1; CA 73-76

Brown, Dee (Alexander) 1908- .. **CLC 18, 47**
See also CA 13-16R; CAAS 6; CANR 11, 45; DLBY 80; MTCW; SATA 5

Brown, George
See Wertmueller, Lina

Brown, George Douglas
1869-1902 .... **TCLC 28**

Brown, George Mackay 1921-.... **CLC 5, 48**
See also CA 21-24R; CAAS 6; CANR 12, 37; DLB 14, 27, 139; MTCW; SATA 35

Brown, (William) Larry 1951-...... **CLC 73**
See also CA 130; 134

Brown, Moses
See Barrett, William (Christopher)

Brown, Rita Mae 1944-..... **CLC 18, 43, 79**
See also CA 45-48; CANR 2, 11, 35;
MTCW

Brown, Roderick (Langmere) Haig-
See Haig-Brown, Roderick (Langmere)

Brown, Rosellen 1939-............ **CLC 32**
See also CA 77-80; CAAS 10; CANR 14, 44

Brown, Sterling Allen
1901-1989 .... **CLC 1, 23, 59; BLC**
See also BW 1; CA 85-88; 127; CANR 26;
DLB 48, 51, 63; MTCW

Brown, Will
See Ainsworth, William Harrison

Brown, William Wells
1813-1884 ...... **NCLC 2; BLC; DC 1**
See also DLB 3, 50

Browne, (Clyde) Jackson 1948(?)-... **CLC 21**
See also CA 120

Browning, Elizabeth Barrett
1806-1861 ..... **NCLC 1, 16; DA; PC 6;**
WLC
See also CDBLB 1832-1890; DLB 32

Browning, Robert
1812-1889 .... **NCLC 19; DA; PC 2**
See also CDBLB 1832-1890; DLB 32;
YABC 1

Browning, Tod 1882-1962 .... **CLC 16**
See also CA 141; 117

Brownson, Orestes (Augustus)
1803-1876 .... **NCLC 50**

Bruccoli, Matthew J(oseph) 1931-.. **CLC 34**
See also CA 9-12R; CANR 7; DLB 103

Bruce, Lenny.................... **CLC 21**
See also Schneider, Leonard Alfred

Bruin, John
See Brutus, Dennis

Brulard, Henri
See Stendhal

Brulls, Christian
See Simenon, Georges (Jacques Christian)

Brunner, John (Kilian Houston)
1934-..................... **CLC 8, 10**
See also CA 1-4R; CAAS 8; CANR 2, 37;
MTCW

Bruno, Giordano 1548-1600........ **LC 27**

Brutus, Dennis 1924-........ **CLC 43; BLC**
See also BW 2; CA 49-52; CAAS 14;
CANR 2, 27, 42; DLB 117

Bryan, C(ourtlandt) D(ixon) B(arnes)
1936-...................... **CLC 29**
See also CA 73-76; CANR 13

Bryan, Michael
See Moore, Brian

Bryant, William Cullen
1794-1878 .... **NCLC 6, 46; DA**
See also CDALB 1640-1865; DLB 3, 43, 59

Bryusov, Valery Yakovlevich
1873-1924 .... **TCLC 10**
See also CA 107

Buchan, John 1875-1940 .... **TCLC 41**
See also CA 108; 145; DLB 34, 70; YABC 2

Buchanan, George 1506-1582 .... **LC 4**

Buchheim, Lothar-Guenther 1918-... **CLC 6**
See also CA 85-88

Buchner, (Karl) Georg
1813-1837 .... **NCLC 26**

Buchwald, Art(hur) 1925-.......... **CLC 33**
See also AITN 1; CA 5-8R; CANR 21;
MTCW; SATA 10

Buck, Pearl S(ydenstricker)
1892-1973 ....**CLC 7, 11, 18; DA**
See also AITN 1; CA 1-4R; 41-44R;
CANR 1, 34; DLB 9, 102; MTCW;
SATA 1, 25

Buckler, Ernest 1908-1984........ **CLC 13**
See also CA 11-12; 114; CAP 1; DLB 68;
SATA 47

Buckley, Vincent (Thomas)
1925-1988 .... **CLC 57**
See also CA 101

Buckley, William F(rank), Jr.
1925- .... **CLC 7, 18, 37**
See also AITN 1; CA 1-4R; CANR 1, 24;
DLB 137; DLBY 80; MTCW

Buechner, (Carl) Frederick
1926-.................**CLC 2, 4, 6, 9**
See also CA 13-16R; CANR 11, 39;
DLBY 80; MTCW

Buell, John (Edward) 1927-........ **CLC 10**
See also CA 1-4R; DLB 53

Buero Vallejo, Antonio 1916-... **CLC 15, 46**
See also CA 106; CANR 24; HW; MTCW

Bufalino, Gesualdo 1920(?)-........ **CLC 74**

Bugayev, Boris Nikolayevich 1880-1934
See Bely, Andrey
See also CA 104

Bukowski, Charles
1920-1994 .... **CLC 2, 5, 9, 41, 82**
See also CA 17-20R; 144; CANR 40;
DLB 5, 130; MTCW

Bulgakov, Mikhail (Afanas'evich)
1891-1940 .... **TCLC 2, 16; SSC 18**
See also CA 105

Bulgya, Alexander Alexandrovich
1901-1956 .... **TCLC 53**
See also Fadeyev, Alexander
See also CA 117

Bullins, Ed 1935- .... **CLC 1, 5, 7; BLC**
See also BW 2; CA 49-52; CAAS 16;
CANR 24, 46; DLB 7, 38; MTCW

Bulwer-Lytton, Edward (George Earle Lytton)
1803-1873 .... **NCLC 1, 45**
See also DLB 21

Bunin, Ivan Alexeyevich
1870-1953 .... **TCLC 6; SSC 5**
See also CA 104

Bunting, Basil 1900-1985.... **CLC 10, 39, 47**
See also CA 53-56; 115; CANR 7; DLB 20

Bunuel, Luis 1900-1983 .. **CLC 16, 80; HLC**
See also CA 101; 110; CANR 32; HW

Bunyan, John 1628-1688 .. **LC 4; DA; WLC**
See also CDBLB 1660-1789; DLB 39

Burckhardt, Jacob (Christoph)
1818-1897 .... **NCLC 49**

Burford, Eleanor
See Hibbert, Eleanor Alice Burford

Burgess, Anthony
CLC 1, 2, 4, 5, 8, 10, 13, 15, 22, 40, 62,
81
See also Wilson, John (Anthony) Burgess
See also AITN 1; CDBLB 1960 to Present;
DLB 14

Burke, Edmund
1729(?)-1797 .... **LC 7; DA; WLC**
See also DLB 104

Burke, Kenneth (Duva)
1897-1993 .... **CLC 2, 24**
See also CA 5-8R; 143; CANR 39; DLB 45,
63; MTCW

Burke, Leda
See Garnett, David

Burke, Ralph
See Silverberg, Robert

Burney, Fanny 1752-1840 .... **NCLC 12**
See also DLB 39

Burns, Robert 1759-1796............ **PC 6**
See also CDBLB 1789-1832; DA; DLB 109;
WLC

Burns, Tex
See L'Amour, Louis (Dearborn)

Burnshaw, Stanley 1906-..... **CLC 3, 13, 44**
See also CA 9-12R; DLB 48

Burr, Anne 1937-.................. **CLC 6**
See also CA 25-28R

Burroughs, Edgar Rice
1875-1950 .... **TCLC 2, 32**
See also AAYA 11; CA 104; 132; DLB 8;
MTCW; SATA 41

Burroughs, William S(eward)
1914- .... **CLC 1, 2, 5, 15, 22, 42, 75;**
DA; WLC
See also AITN 2; CA 9-12R; CANR 20;
DLB 2, 8, 16, 152; DLBY 81; MTCW

Burton, Richard F. 1821-1890.... **NCLC 42**
See also DLB 55

Busch, Frederick 1941-... **CLC 7, 10, 18, 47**
See also CA 33-36R; CAAS 1; CANR 45;
DLB 6

Bush, Ronald 1946- .... **CLC 34**
See also CA 136

Bustos, F(rancisco)
See Borges, Jorge Luis

Bustos Domecq, H(onorio)
See Bioy Casares, Adolfo; Borges, Jorge
Luis

Butler, Octavia E(stelle) 1947-..... **CLC 38**
See also BW 2; CA 73-76; CANR 12, 24,
38; DLB 33; MTCW

Butler, Robert Olen (Jr.) 1945-..... **CLC 81**
See also CA 112

Butler, Samuel 1612-1680 .... **LC 16**
See also DLB 101, 126

Butler, Samuel
1835-1902 ...... **TCLC 1, 33; DA; WLC**
See also CA 143; CDBLB 1890-1914;
DLB 18, 57

Butler, Walter C.
See Faust, Frederick (Schiller)

Butor, Michel (Marie Francois)
    1926- . . . . CLC **1, 3, 8, 11, 15**
    See also CA 9-12R; CANR 33; DLB 83;
    MTCW

Buzo, Alexander (John) 1944- . . . . . . CLC **61**
    See also CA 97-100; CANR 17, 39

Buzzati, Dino 1906-1972 . . . . CLC **36**
    See also CA 33-36R

Byars, Betsy (Cromer) 1928- . . . . CLC **35**
    See also CA 33-36R; CANR 18, 36; CLR 1,
    16; DLB 52; JRDA; MAICYA; MTCW;
    SAAS 1; SATA 4, 46, 80

Byatt, A(ntonia) S(usan Drabble)
    1936- . . . . CLC **19, 65**
    See also CA 13-16R; CANR 13, 33;
    DLB 14; MTCW

Byrne, David 1952- . . . . CLC **26**
    See also CA 127

Byrne, John Keyes 1926-
    See Leonard, Hugh
    See also CA 102

Byron, George Gordon (Noel)
    1788-1824 . . . . . . NCLC **2, 12;** DA; WLC
    See also CDBLB 1789-1832; DLB 96, 110

C. 3. 3.
    See Wilde, Oscar (Fingal O'Flahertie Wills)

Caballero, Fernan 1796-1877 . . . . . NCLC **10**

Cabell, James Branch 1879-1958 . . . TCLC **6**
    See also CA 105; DLB 9, 78

Cable, George Washington
    1844-1925 . . . . TCLC **4;** SSC **4**
    See also CA 104; DLB 12, 74

Cabral de Melo Neto, Joao 1920- . . . CLC **76**

Cabrera Infante, G(uillermo)
    1929- . . . . CLC **5, 25, 45;** HLC
    See also CA 85-88; CANR 29; DLB 113;
    HW; MTCW

Cade, Toni
    See Bambara, Toni Cade

Cadmus and Harmonia
    See Buchan, John

Caedmon fl. 658-680 . . . . CMLC **7**
    See also DLB 146

Caeiro, Alberto
    See Pessoa, Fernando (Antonio Nogueira)

Cage, John (Milton, Jr.) 1912- . . . . . CLC **41**
    See also CA 13-16R; CANR 9

Cain, G.
    See Cabrera Infante, G(uillermo)

Cain, Guillermo
    See Cabrera Infante, G(uillermo)

Cain, James M(allahan)
    1892-1977 . . . . CLC **3, 11, 28**
    See also AITN 1; CA 17-20R; 73-76;
    CANR 8, 34; MTCW

Caine, Mark
    See Raphael, Frederic (Michael)

Calasso, Roberto 1941- . . . . CLC **81**
    See also CA 143

Calderon de la Barca, Pedro
    1600-1681 . . . . LC **23;** DC **3**

Caldwell, Erskine (Preston)
    1903-1987 . . . . CLC **1, 8, 14, 50, 60;**
                                            SSC **19**
    See also AITN 1; CA 1-4R; 121; CAAS 1;
    CANR 2, 33; DLB 9, 86; MTCW

Caldwell, (Janet Miriam) Taylor (Holland)
    1900-1985 . . . . CLC **2, 28, 39**
    See also CA 5-8R; 116; CANR 5

Calhoun, John Caldwell
    1782-1850 . . . . NCLC **15**
    See also DLB 3

Calisher, Hortense
    1911- . . . . CLC **2, 4, 8, 38;** SSC **15**
    See also CA 1-4R; CANR 1, 22; DLB 2;
    MTCW

Callaghan, Morley Edward
    1903-1990 . . . . CLC **3, 14, 41, 65**
    See also CA 9-12R; 132; CANR 33;
    DLB 68; MTCW

Calvino, Italo
    1923-1985 . . . . . CLC **5, 8, 11, 22, 33, 39,
                                    73;** SSC **3**
    See also CA 85-88; 116; CANR 23; MTCW

Cameron, Carey 1952- . . . . CLC **59**
    See also CA 135

Cameron, Peter 1959- . . . . CLC **44**
    See also CA 125

Campana, Dino 1885-1932 . . . . TCLC **20**
    See also CA 117; DLB 114

Campbell, John W(ood, Jr.)
    1910-1971 . . . . CLC **32**
    See also CA 21-22; 29-32R; CANR 34;
    CAP 2; DLB 8; MTCW

Campbell, Joseph 1904-1987 . . . . CLC **69**
    See also AAYA 3; BEST 89:2; CA 1-4R;
    124; CANR 3, 28; MTCW

Campbell, Maria 1940- . . . . CLC **85**
    See also CA 102; NNAL

Campbell, (John) Ramsey
    1946- . . . . CLC **42;** SSC **19**
    See also CA 57-60; CANR 7

Campbell, (Ignatius) Roy (Dunnachie)
    1901-1957 . . . . TCLC **5**
    See also CA 104; DLB 20

Campbell, Thomas 1777-1844 . . . . NCLC **19**
    See also DLB 93; 144

Campbell, Wilfred . . . . TCLC **9**
    See also Campbell, William

Campbell, William 1858(?)-1918
    See Campbell, Wilfred
    See also CA 106; DLB 92

Campos, Alvaro de
    See Pessoa, Fernando (Antonio Nogueira)

Camus, Albert
    1913-1960 . . . . CLC **1, 2, 4, 9, 11, 14, 32,
                                63, 69;** DA; DC **2;** SSC **9;** WLC
    See also CA 89-92; DLB 72; MTCW

Canby, Vincent 1924- . . . . CLC **13**
    See also CA 81-84

Cancale
    See Desnos, Robert

Canetti, Elias
    1905-1994 . . . . CLC **3, 14, 25, 75, 86**
    See also CA 21-24R; 146; CANR 23;
    DLB 85, 124; MTCW

Canin, Ethan 1960- . . . . CLC **55**
    See also CA 131; 135

Cannon, Curt
    See Hunter, Evan

Cape, Judith
    See Page, P(atricia) K(athleen)

Capek, Karel
    1890-1938 . . . . . TCLC **6, 37;** DA; DC **1;**
                                            WLC
    See also CA 104; 140

Capote, Truman
    1924-1984 . . . . . . CLC **1, 3, 8, 13, 19, 34,
                            38, 58;** DA; SSC **2;** WLC
    See also CA 5-8R; 113; CANR 18;
    CDALB 1941-1968; DLB 2; DLBY 80,
    84; MTCW

Capra, Frank 1897-1991 . . . . CLC **16**
    See also CA 61-64; 135

Caputo, Philip 1941- . . . . CLC **32**
    See also CA 73-76; CANR 40

Card, Orson Scott 1951- . . . . CLC **44, 47, 50**
    See also AAYA 11; CA 102; CANR 27, 47;
    MTCW

Cardenal (Martinez), Ernesto
    1925- . . . . CLC **31;** HLC
    See also CA 49-52; CANR 2, 32; HW;
    MTCW

Carducci, Giosue 1835-1907 . . . . TCLC **32**

Carew, Thomas 1595(?)-1640 . . . . LC **13**
    See also DLB 126

Carey, Ernestine Gilbreth 1908- . . . . CLC **17**
    See also CA 5-8R; SATA 2

Carey, Peter 1943- . . . . CLC **40, 55**
    See also CA 123; 127; MTCW

Carleton, William 1794-1869 . . . . . . NCLC **3**

Carlisle, Henry (Coffin) 1926- . . . . . . CLC **33**
    See also CA 13-16R; CANR 15

Carlsen, Chris
    See Holdstock, Robert P.

Carlson, Ron(ald F.) 1947- . . . . CLC **54**
    See also CA 105; CANR 27

Carlyle, Thomas 1795-1881 . . NCLC **22;** DA
    See also CDBLB 1789-1832; DLB 55; 144

Carman, (William) Bliss
    1861-1929 . . . . TCLC **7**
    See also CA 104; DLB 92

Carnegie, Dale 1888-1955 . . . . TCLC **53**

Carossa, Hans 1878-1956 . . . . TCLC **48**
    See also DLB 66

Carpenter, Don(ald Richard)
    1931- . . . . CLC **41**
    See also CA 45-48; CANR 1

Carpentier (y Valmont), Alejo
    1904-1980 . . . . CLC **8, 11, 38;** HLC
    See also CA 65-68; 97-100; CANR 11;
    DLB 113; HW

Carr, Caleb 1955(?)- . . . . CLC **86**
    See also CA 147

Carr, Emily 1871-1945 . . . . TCLC **32**
    See also DLB 68

Carr, John Dickson 1906-1977 . . . . . . CLC **3**
    See also CA 49-52; 69-72; CANR 3, 33;
    MTCW

Carr, Philippa
See Hibbert, Eleanor Alice Burford

Carr, Virginia Spencer 1929-....... **CLC 34**
See also CA 61-64; DLB 111

Carrere, Emmanuel 1957- .... **CLC 89**

Carrier, Roch 1937-.......... **CLC 13, 78**
See also CA 130; DLB 53

Carroll, James P. 1943(?)-......... **CLC 38**
See also CA 81-84

Carroll, Jim 1951- .... **CLC 35**
See also CA 45-48; CANR 42

Carroll, Lewis .... **NCLC 2; WLC**
See also Dodgson, Charles Lutwidge
See also CDBLB 1832-1890; CLR 2, 18;
DLB 18; JRDA

Carroll, Paul Vincent 1900-1968.... **CLC 10**
See also CA 9-12R; 25-28R; DLB 10

Carruth, Hayden
1921- ...... **CLC 4, 7, 10, 18, 84; PC 10**
See also CA 9-12R; CANR 4, 38; DLB 5;
MTCW; SATA 47

Carson, Rachel Louise 1907-1964... **CLC 71**
See also CA 77-80; CANR 35; MTCW;
SATA 23

Carter, Angela (Olive)
1940-1992 ...... **CLC 5, 41, 76; SSC 13**
See also CA 53-56; 136; CANR 12, 36;
DLB 14; MTCW; SATA 66;
SATA-Obit 70

Carter, Nick
See Smith, Martin Cruz

Carver, Raymond
1938-1988 ... **CLC 22, 36, 53, 55; SSC 8**
See also CA 33-36R; 126; CANR 17, 34;
DLB 130; DLBY 84, 88; MTCW

Cary, Elizabeth 1585-1639 .... **LC 30**

Cary, (Arthur) Joyce (Lunel)
1888-1957 .... **TCLC 1, 29**
See also CA 104; CDBLB 1914-1945;
DLB 15, 100

Casanova de Seingalt, Giovanni Jacopo
1725-1798 .... **LC 13**

Casares, Adolfo Bioy
See Bioy Casares, Adolfo

Casely-Hayford, J(oseph) E(phraim)
1866-1930 .... **TCLC 24; BLC**
See also BW 2; CA 123

Casey, John (Dudley) 1939-........ **CLC 59**
See also BEST 90:2; CA 69-72; CANR 23

Casey, Michael 1947-.............. **CLC 2**
See also CA 65-68; DLB 5

Casey, Patrick
See Thurman, Wallace (Henry)

Casey, Warren (Peter) 1935-1988 ... **CLC 12**
See also CA 101; 127

Casona, Alejandro................ **CLC 49**
See also Alvarez, Alejandro Rodriguez

Cassavetes, John 1929-1989........ **CLC 20**
See also CA 85-88; 127

Cassill, R(onald) V(erlin) 1919-... **CLC 4, 23**
See also CA 9-12R; CAAS 1; CANR 7, 45;
DLB 6

Cassity, (Allen) Turner 1929- .... **CLC 6, 42**
See also CA 17-20R; CAAS 8; CANR ,11;
DLB 105

Castaneda, Carlos 1931(?)-......... **CLC 12**
See also CA 25-28R; CANR 32; HW;
MTCW

Castedo, Elena 1937- .... **CLC 65**
See also CA 132

Castedo-Ellerman, Elena
See Castedo, Elena

Castellanos, Rosario
1925-1974 .... **CLC 66; HLC**
See also CA 131; 53-56; DLB 113; HW

Castelvetro, Lodovico 1505-1571..... **LC 12**

Castiglione, Baldassare 1478-1529 ... **LC 12**

Castle, Robert
See Hamilton, Edmond

Castro, Guillen de 1569-1631........ **LC 19**

Castro, Rosalia de 1837-1885 ..... **NCLC 3**

Cather, Willa
See Cather, Willa Sibert

Cather, Willa Sibert
1873-1947 .... **TCLC 1, 11, 31; DA;**
SSC 2; WLC
See also CA 104; 128; CDALB 1865-1917;
DLB 9, 54, 78; DLBD 1; MTCW;
SATA 30

Catton, (Charles) Bruce
1899-1978 .... **CLC 35**
See also AITN 1; CA 5-8R; 81-84;
CANR 7; DLB 17; SATA 2;
SATA-Obit 24

Cauldwell, Frank
See King, Francis (Henry)

Caunitz, William J. 1933-......... **CLC 34**
See also BEST 89:3; CA 125; 130

Causley, Charles (Stanley) 1917-..... **CLC 7**
See also CA 9-12R; CANR 5, 35; CLR 30;
DLB 27; MTCW; SATA 3, 66

Caute, David 1936-............... **CLC 29**
See also CA 1-4R; CAAS 4; CANR 1, 33;
DLB 14

Cavafy, C(onstantine) P(eter)...... **TCLC 2, 7**
See also Kavafis, Konstantinos Petrou

Cavallo, Evelyn
See Spark, Muriel (Sarah)

Cavanna, Betty .... **CLC 12**
See also Harrison, Elizabeth Cavanna
See also JRDA; MAICYA; SAAS 4;
SATA 1, 30

Cavendish, Margaret Lucas
1623-1673 .... **LC 30**
See also DLB 131

Caxton, William 1421(?)-1491(?)..... **LC 17**

Cayrol, Jean 1911-............... **CLC 11**
See also CA 89-92; DLB 83

Cela, Camilo Jose
1916- .... **CLC 4, 13, 59; HLC**
See also BEST 90:2; CA 21-24R; CAAS 10;
CANR 21, 32; DLBY 89; HW; MTCW

Celan, Paul ...... **CLC 10, 19, 53, 82; PC 10**
See also Antschel, Paul
See also DLB 69

Celine, Louis-Ferdinand
.... **CLC 1, 3, 4, 7, 9, 15, 47**
See also Destouches, Louis-Ferdinand
See also DLB 72

Cellini, Benvenuto 1500-1571 .... **LC 7**

Cendrars, Blaise .... **CLC 18**
See also Sauser-Hall, Frederic

Cernuda (y Bidon), Luis
1902-1963 .... **CLC 54**
See also CA 131; 89-92; DLB 134; HW

Cervantes (Saavedra), Miguel de
1547-1616 ...... **LC 6, 23; DA; SSC 12;**
WLC

Cesaire, Aime (Fernand)
1913- .... **CLC 19, 32; BLC**
See also BW 2; CA 65-68; CANR 24, 43;
MTCW

Chabon, Michael 1965(?)- .... **CLC 55**
See also CA 139

Chabrol, Claude 1930- .... **CLC 16**
See also CA 110

Challans, Mary 1905-1983
See Renault, Mary
See also CA 81-84; 111; SATA 23;
SATA-Obit 36

Challis, George
See Faust, Frederick (Schiller)

Chambers, Aidan 1934- .... **CLC 35**
See also CA 25-28R; CANR 12, 31; JRDA;
MAICYA; SAAS 12; SATA 1, 69

Chambers, James 1948-
See Cliff, Jimmy
See also CA 124

Chambers, Jessie
See Lawrence, D(avid) H(erbert Richards)

Chambers, Robert W. 1865-1933... **TCLC 41**

Chandler, Raymond (Thornton)
1888-1959 .... **TCLC 1, 7**
See also CA 104; 129; CDALB 1929-1941;
DLBD 6; MTCW

Chang, Jung 1952- .... **CLC 71**
See also CA 142

Channing, William Ellery
1780-1842 .... **NCLC 17**
See also DLB 1, 59

Chaplin, Charles Spencer
1889-1977 .... **CLC 16**
See also Chaplin, Charlie
See also CA 81-84; 73-76

Chaplin, Charlie
See Chaplin, Charles Spencer
See also DLB 44

Chapman, George 1559(?)-1634...... **LC 22**
See also DLB 62, 121

Chapman, Graham 1941-1989 ...... **CLC 21**
See also Monty Python
See also CA 116; 129; CANR 35

Chapman, John Jay 1862-1933 ..... **TCLC 7**
See also CA 104

Chapman, Walker
See Silverberg, Robert

Chappell, Fred (Davis) 1936-.... **CLC 40, 78**
See also CA 5-8R; CAAS 4; CANR 8, 33;
DLB 6, 105

Author Index

Char, Rene(-Emile)
1907-1988 . . . . **CLC 9, 11, 14, 55**
See also CA 13-16R; 124; CANR 32;
MTCW

Charby, Jay
See Ellison, Harlan (Jay)

Chardin, Pierre Teilhard de
See Teilhard de Chardin, (Marie Joseph)
Pierre

Charles I 1600-1649 . . . . **LC 13**

Charyn, Jerome 1937- . . . . **CLC 5, 8, 18**
See also CA 5-8R; CAAS 1; CANR 7;
DLBY 83; MTCW

Chase, Mary (Coyle) 1907-1981 . . . . . . **DC 1**
See also CA 77-80; 105; SATA 17;
SATA-Obit 29

Chase, Mary Ellen 1887-1973 . . . . **CLC 2**
See also CA 13-16; 41-44R; CAP 1;
SATA 10

Chase, Nicholas
See Hyde, Anthony

Chateaubriand, Francois Rene de
1768-1848 . . . . **NCLC 3**
See also DLB 119

Chatterje, Sarat Chandra 1876-1936(?)
See Chatterji, Saratchandra
See also CA 109

Chatterji, Bankim Chandra
1838-1894 . . . . **NCLC 19**

Chatterji, Saratchandra . . . . **TCLC 13**
See also Chatterje, Sarat Chandra

Chatterton, Thomas 1752-1770 . . . . **LC 3**
See also DLB 109

Chatwin, (Charles) Bruce
1940-1989 . . . . **CLC 28, 57, 59**
See also AAYA 4; BEST 90:1; CA 85-88;
127

Chaucer, Daniel
See Ford, Ford Madox

Chaucer, Geoffrey
1340(?)-1400 . . . . **LC 17; DA**
See also CDBLB Before 1660; DLB 146

Chaviaras, Strates 1935-
See Haviaras, Stratis
See also CA 105

Chayefsky, Paddy . . . . **CLC 23**
See also Chayefsky, Sidney
See also DLB 7, 44; DLBY 81

Chayefsky, Sidney 1923-1981
See Chayefsky, Paddy
See also CA 9-12R; 104; CANR 18

Chedid, Andree 1920- . . . . **CLC 47**
See also CA 145

Cheever, John
1912-1982 . . . . . . **CLC 3, 7, 8, 11, 15, 25,**
64; DA; SSC 1; WLC
See also CA 5-8R; 106; CABS 1; CANR 5,
27; CDALB 1941-1968; DLB 2, 102;
DLBY 80, 82; MTCW

Cheever, Susan 1943- . . . . **CLC 18, 48**
See also CA 103; CANR 27; DLBY 82

Chekhonte, Antosha
See Chekhov, Anton (Pavlovich)

Chekhov, Anton (Pavlovich)
1860-1904 . . . . . **TCLC 3, 10, 31, 55; DA;**
SSC 2; WLC
See also CA 104; 124

Chernyshevsky, Nikolay Gavrilovich
1828-1889 . . . . **NCLC 1**

Cherry, Carolyn Janice 1942-
See Cherryh, C. J.
See also CA 65-68; CANR 10

Cherryh, C. J. . . . . **CLC 35**
See also Cherry, Carolyn Janice
See also DLBY 80

Chesnutt, Charles W(addell)
1858-1932 . . . . **TCLC 5, 39; BLC; SSC 7**
See also BW 1; CA 106; 125; DLB 12, 50,
78; MTCW

Chester, Alfred 1929(?)-1971 . . . . **CLC 49**
See also CA 33-36R; DLB 130

Chesterton, G(ilbert) K(eith)
1874-1936 . . . . **TCLC 1, 6; SSC 1**
See also CA 104; 132; CDBLB 1914-1945;
DLB 10, 19, 34, 70, 98, 149; MTCW;
SATA 27

Chiang Pin-chin 1904-1986
See Ding Ling
See also CA 118

Ch'ien Chung-shu 1910- . . . . **CLC 22**
See also CA 130; MTCW

Child, L. Maria
See Child, Lydia Maria

Child, Lydia Maria 1802-1880 . . . . **NCLC 6**
See also DLB 1, 74; SATA 67

Child, Mrs.
See Child, Lydia Maria

Child, Philip 1898-1978 . . . . **CLC 19, 68**
See also CA 13-14; CAP 1; SATA 47

Childress, Alice
1920-1994 . . **CLC 12, 15, 86; BLC; DC 4**
See also AAYA 8; BW 2; CA 45-48; 146;
CANR 3, 27; CLR 14; DLB 7, 38; JRDA;
MAICYA; MTCW; SATA 7, 48, 81

Chislett, (Margaret) Anne 1943- . . . . **CLC 34**

Chitty, Thomas Willes 1926- . . . . **CLC 11**
See also Hinde, Thomas
See also CA 5-8R

Chivers, Thomas Holley
1809-1858 . . . . **NCLC 49**
See also DLB 3

Chomette, Rene Lucien 1898-1981
See Clair, Rene
See also CA 103

Chopin, Kate . . . . . . **TCLC 5, 14; DA; SSC 8**
See also Chopin, Katherine
See also CDALB 1865-1917; DLB 12, 78

Chopin, Katherine 1851-1904
See Chopin, Kate
See also CA 104; 122

Chretien de Troyes
c. 12th cent. - . . . . **CMLC 10**

Christie
See Ichikawa, Kon

Christie, Agatha (Mary Clarissa)
1890-1976 . . . . . . **CLC 1, 6, 8, 12, 39, 48**
See also AAYA 9; AITN 1, 2; CA 17-20R;
61-64; CANR 10, 37; CDBLB 1914-1945;
DLB 13, 77; MTCW; SATA 36

Christie, (Ann) Philippa
See Pearce, Philippa
See also CA 5-8R; CANR 4

Christine de Pizan 1365(?)-1431(?) . . . . **LC 9**

Chubb, Elmer
See Masters, Edgar Lee

Chulkov, Mikhail Dmitrievich
1743-1792 . . . . **LC 2**
See also DLB 150

Churchill, Caryl 1938- . . . **CLC 31, 55; DC 5**
See also CA 102; CANR 22, 46; DLB 13;
MTCW

Churchill, Charles 1731-1764 . . . . **LC 3**
See also DLB 109

Chute, Carolyn 1947- . . . . **CLC 39**
See also CA 123

Ciardi, John (Anthony)
1916-1986 . . . . **CLC 10, 40, 44**
See also CA 5-8R; 118; CAAS 2; CANR 5,
33; CLR 19; DLB 5; DLBY 86;
MAICYA; MTCW; SATA 1, 65;
SATA-Obit 46

Cicero, Marcus Tullius
106B.C.-43B.C. . . . . **CMLC 3**

Cimino, Michael 1943- . . . . **CLC 16**
See also CA 105

Cioran, E(mil) M. 1911- . . . . **CLC 64**
See also CA 25-28R

Cisneros, Sandra 1954- . . . . . . **CLC 69; HLC**
See also AAYA 9; CA 131; DLB 122, 152;
HW

Clair, Rene . . . . **CLC 20**
See also Chomette, Rene Lucien

Clampitt, Amy 1920-1994 . . . . **CLC 32**
See also CA 110; 146; CANR 29; DLB 105

Clancy, Thomas L., Jr. 1947-
See Clancy, Tom
See also CA 125; 131; MTCW

Clancy, Tom . . . . **CLC 45**
See also Clancy, Thomas L., Jr.
See also AAYA 9; BEST 89:1, 90:1

Clare, John 1793-1864 . . . . **NCLC 9**
See also DLB 55, 96

Clarin
See Alas (y Urena), Leopoldo (Enrique
Garcia)

Clark, Al C.
See Goines, Donald

Clark, (Robert) Brian 1932- . . . . **CLC 29**
See also CA 41-44R

Clark, Curt
See Westlake, Donald E(dwin)

Clark, Eleanor 1913- . . . . **CLC 5, 19**
See also CA 9-12R; CANR 41; DLB 6

Clark, J. P.
See Clark, John Pepper
See also DLB 117

Clark, John Pepper
1935- .... **CLC 38; BLC; DC 5**
See also Clark, J. P.
See also BW 1; CA 65-68; CANR 16

Clark, M. R.
See Clark, Mavis Thorpe

Clark, Mavis Thorpe 1909- .... **CLC 12**
See also CA 57-60; CANR 8, 37; CLR 30;
MAICYA; SAAS 5; SATA 8, 74

Clark, Walter Van Tilburg
1909-1971 .... **CLC 28**
See also CA 9-12R; 33-36R; DLB 9;
SATA 8

Clarke, Arthur C(harles)
1917- ...... **CLC 1, 4, 13, 18, 35; SSC 3**
See also AAYA 4; CA 1-4R; CANR 2, 28;
JRDA; MAICYA; MTCW; SATA 13, 70

Clarke, Austin 1896-1974........ **CLC 6, 9**
See also CA 29-32; 49-52; CAP 2; DLB 10,
20

Clarke, Austin C(hesterfield)
1934- .... **CLC 8, 53; BLC**
See also BW 1; CA 25-28R; CAAS 16;
CANR 14, 32; DLB 53, 125

Clarke, Gillian 1937- .... **CLC 61**
See also CA 106; DLB 40

Clarke, Marcus (Andrew Hislop)
1846-1881 .... **NCLC 19**

Clarke, Shirley 1925-............. **CLC 16**

Clash, The
See Headon, (Nicky) Topper; Jones, Mick;
Simonon, Paul; Strummer, Joe

Claudel, Paul (Louis Charles Marie)
1868-1955 .... **TCLC 2, 10**
See also CA 104

Clavell, James (duMaresq)
1925-1994 .... **CLC 6, 25, 87**
See also CA 25-28R; 146; CANR 26, 48;
MTCW

Cleaver, (Leroy) Eldridge
1935- .... **CLC 30; BLC**
See also BW 1; CA 21-24R; CANR 16

Cleese, John (Marwood) 1939- ..... **CLC 21**
See also Monty Python
See also CA 112; 116; CANR 35; MTCW

Cleishbotham, Jebediah
See Scott, Walter

Cleland, John 1710-1789 .... **LC 2**
See also DLB 39

Clemens, Samuel Langhorne 1835-1910
See Twain, Mark
See also CA 104; 135; CDALB 1865-1917;
DA; DLB 11, 12, 23, 64, 74; JRDA;
MAICYA; YABC 2

Cleophil
See Congreve, William

Clerihew, E.
See Bentley, E(dmund) C(lerihew)

Clerk, N. W.
See Lewis, C(live) S(taples)

Cliff, Jimmy..................... **CLC 21**
See also Chambers, James

Clifton, (Thelma) Lucille
1936- .... **CLC 19, 66; BLC**
See also BW 2; CA 49-52; CANR 2, 24, 42;
CLR 5; DLB 5, 41; MAICYA; MTCW;
SATA 20, 69

Clinton, Dirk
See Silverberg, Robert

Clough, Arthur Hugh 1819-1861.. **NCLC 27**
See also DLB 32

Clutha, Janet Paterson Frame 1924-
See Frame, Janet
See also CA 1-4R; CANR 2, 36; MTCW

Clyne, Terence
See Blatty, William Peter

Cobalt, Martin
See Mayne, William (James Carter)

Cobbett, William 1763-1835 ..... **NCLC 49**
See also DLB 43, 107

Coburn, D(onald) L(ee) 1938- ...... **CLC 10**
See also CA 89-92

Cocteau, Jean (Maurice Eugene Clement)
1889-1963 .... **CLC 1, 8, 15, 16, 43; DA; WLC**
See also CA 25-28; CANR 40; CAP 2;
DLB 65; MTCW

Codrescu, Andrei 1946- .... **CLC 46**
See also CA 33-36R; CAAS 19; CANR 13,
34

Coe, Max
See Bourne, Randolph S(illiman)

Coe, Tucker
See Westlake, Donald E(dwin)

Coetzee, J(ohn) M(ichael)
1940- .... **CLC 23, 33, 66**
See also CA 77-80; CANR 41; MTCW

Coffey, Brian
See Koontz, Dean R(ay)

Cohan, George M. 1878-1942 ..... **TCLC 60**

Cohen, Arthur A(llen)
1928-1986 .... **CLC 7, 31**
See also CA 1-4R; 120; CANR 1, 17, 42;
DLB 28

Cohen, Leonard (Norman)
1934- .... **CLC 3, 38**
See also CA 21-24R; CANR 14; DLB 53;
MTCW

Cohen, Matt 1942-................ **CLC 19**
See also CA 61-64; CAAS 18; CANR 40;
DLB 53

Cohen-Solal, Annie 19(?)- .... **CLC 50**

Colegate, Isabel 1931- .... **CLC 36**
See also CA 17-20R; CANR 8, 22; DLB 14;
MTCW

Coleman, Emmett
See Reed, Ishmael

Coleridge, Samuel Taylor
1772-1834 .. **NCLC 9; DA; PC 11; WLC**
See also CDBLB 1789-1832; DLB 93, 107

Coleridge, Sara 1802-1852...... **NCLC 31**

Coles, Don 1928- .... **CLC 46**
See also CA 115; CANR 38

Colette, (Sidonie-Gabrielle)
1873-1954 ...... **TCLC 1, 5, 16; SSC 10**
See also CA 104; 131; DLB 65; MTCW

Collett, (Jacobine) Camilla (Wergeland)
1813-1895 .... **NCLC 22**

Collier, Christopher 1930-........ **CLC 30**
See also AAYA 13; CA 33-36R; CANR 13,
33; JRDA; MAICYA; SATA 16, 70

Collier, James L(incoln) 1928- ..... **CLC 30**
See also AAYA 13; CA 9-12R; CANR 4,
33; CLR 3; JRDA; MAICYA; SATA 8,
70

Collier, Jeremy 1650-1726.......... **LC 6**

Collier, John 1901-1980............. **SSC**
See also CA 65-68; 97-100; CANR 10;
DLB 77

Collins, Hunt
See Hunter, Evan

Collins, Linda 1931-.............. **CLC 44**
See also CA 125

Collins, (William) Wilkie
1824-1889 .... **NCLC 1, 18**
See also CDBLB 1832-1890; DLB 18, 70

Collins, William 1721-1759 .... **LC 4**
See also DLB 109

Colman, George
See Glassco, John

Colt, Winchester Remington
See Hubbard, L(afayette) Ron(ald)

Colter, Cyrus 1910- .... **CLC 58**
See also BW 1; CA 65-68; CANR 10;
DLB 33

Colton, James
See Hansen, Joseph

Colum, Padraic 1881-1972........ **CLC 28**
See also CA 73-76; 33-36R; CANR 35;
CLR 36; MAICYA; MTCW; SATA 15

Colvin, James
See Moorcock, Michael (John)

Colwin, Laurie (E.)
1944-1992 .... **CLC 5, 13, 23, 84**
See also CA 89-92; 139; CANR 20, 46;
DLBY 80; MTCW

Comfort, Alex(ander) 1920-........ **CLC 7**
See also CA 1-4R; CANR 1, 45

Comfort, Montgomery
See Campbell, (John) Ramsey

Compton-Burnett, I(vy)
1884(?)-1969 ...... **CLC 1, 3, 10, 15, 34**
See also CA 1-4R; 25-28R; CANR 4;
DLB 36; MTCW

Comstock, Anthony 1844-1915 .... **TCLC 13**
See also CA 110

Conan Doyle, Arthur
See Doyle, Arthur Conan

Conde, Maryse 1937-............. **CLC 52**
See also Boucolon, Maryse
See also BW 2

Condillac, Etienne Bonnot de
1714-1780 .... **LC 26**

Condon, Richard (Thomas)
1915- .... **CLC 4, 6, 8, 10, 45**
See also BEST 90:3; CA 1-4R; CAAS 1;
CANR 2, 23; MTCW

Congreve, William
1670-1729 ... **LC 5, 21; DA; DC 2; WLC**
See also CDBLB 1660-1789; DLB 39, 84

Connell, Evan S(helby), Jr.
1924- .... CLC **4, 6, 45**
See also AAYA 7; CA 1-4R; CAAS 2;
CANR 2, 39; DLB 2; DLBY 81; MTCW

Connelly, Marc(us Cook)
1890-1980 .... CLC **7**
See also CA 85-88; 102; CANR 30; DLB 7;
DLBY 80; SATA-Obit 25

Connor, Ralph .... TCLC **31**
See also Gordon, Charles William
See also DLB 92

Conrad, Joseph
1857-1924 .... TCLC **1, 6, 13, 25, 43, 57;**
DA; SSC **9**; WLC
See also CA 104; 131; CDBLB 1890-1914;
DLB 10, 34, 98; MTCW; SATA 27

Conrad, Robert Arnold
See Hart, Moss

Conroy, Pat 1945- .... CLC **30, 74**
See also AAYA 8; AITN 1; CA 85-88;
CANR 24; DLB 6; MTCW

Constant (de Rebecque), (Henri) Benjamin
1767-1830 .... NCLC **6**
See also DLB 119

Conybeare, Charles Augustus
See Eliot, T(homas) S(tearns)

Cook, Michael 1933- .... CLC **58**
See also CA 93-96; DLB 53

Cook, Robin 1940- .... CLC **14**
See also BEST 90:2; CA 108; 111;
CANR 41

Cook, Roy
See Silverberg, Robert

Cooke, Elizabeth 1948- .... CLC **55**
See also CA 129

Cooke, John Esten 1830-1886 ..... NCLC **5**
See also DLB 3

Cooke, John Estes
See Baum, L(yman) Frank

Cooke, M. E.
See Creasey, John

Cooke, Margaret
See Creasey, John

Cooney, Ray .... CLC **62**

Cooper, Douglas 1960- .... CLC **86**

Cooper, Henry St. John
See Creasey, John

Cooper, J. California .... CLC **56**
See also AAYA 12; BW 1; CA 125

Cooper, James Fenimore
1789-1851 .... NCLC **1, 27**
See also CDALB 1640-1865; DLB 3;
SATA 19

Coover, Robert (Lowell)
1932- .. CLC **3, 7, 15, 32, 46, 87**; SSC **15**
See also CA 45-48; CANR 3, 37; DLB 2;
DLBY 81; MTCW

Copeland, Stewart (Armstrong)
1952- .... CLC **26**

Coppard, A(lfred) E(dgar)
1878-1957 .... TCLC **5**
See also CA 114; YABC 1

Coppee, Francois 1842-1908 ...... TCLC **25**

Coppola, Francis Ford 1939- ...... CLC **16**
See also CA 77-80; CANR 40; DLB 44

Corbiere, Tristan 1845-1875 ..... NCLC **43**

Corcoran, Barbara 1911- .... CLC **17**
See also AAYA 14; CA 21-24R; CAAS 2;
CANR 11, 28, 48; DLB 52; JRDA;
SAAS 20; SATA 3, 77

Cordelier, Maurice
See Giraudoux, (Hippolyte) Jean

Corelli, Marie 1855-1924 .... TCLC **51**
See also Mackay, Mary
See also DLB 34

Corman, Cid .... CLC **9**
See also Corman, Sidney
See also CAAS 2; DLB 5

Corman, Sidney 1924-
See Corman, Cid
See also CA 85-88; CANR 44

Cormier, Robert (Edmund)
1925- .... CLC **12, 30; DA**
See also AAYA 3; CA 1-4R; CANR 5, 23;
CDALB 1968-1988; CLR 12; DLB 52;
JRDA; MAICYA; MTCW; SATA 10, 45

Corn, Alfred (DeWitt III) 1943- .... CLC **33**
See also CA 104; CANR 44; DLB 120;
DLBY 80

Corneille, Pierre 1606-1684 .... LC **28**

Cornwell, David (John Moore)
1931- .... CLC **9, 15**
See also le Carre, John
See also CA 5-8R; CANR 13, 33; MTCW

Corso, (Nunzio) Gregory 1930- ... CLC **1, 11**
See also CA 5-8R; CANR 41; DLB 5, 16;
MTCW

Cortazar, Julio
1914-1984 ...... CLC **2, 3, 5, 10, 13, 15,**
33, 34; HLC; SSC **7**
See also CA 21-24R; CANR 12, 32;
DLB 113; HW; MTCW

Corwin, Cecil
See Kornbluth, C(yril) M.

Cosic, Dobrica 1921- .... CLC **14**
See also CA 122; 138

Costain, Thomas B(ertram)
1885-1965 .... CLC **30**
See also CA 5-8R; 25-28R; DLB 9

Costantini, Humberto
1924(?)-1987 .... CLC **49**
See also CA 131; 122; HW

Costello, Elvis 1955- .... CLC **21**

Cotter, Joseph Seamon Sr.
1861-1949 .... TCLC **28**; BLC
See also BW 1; CA 124; DLB 50

Couch, Arthur Thomas Quiller
See Quiller-Couch, Arthur Thomas

Coulton, James
See Hansen, Joseph

Couperus, Louis (Marie Anne)
1863-1923 .... TCLC **15**
See also CA 115

Coupland, Douglas 1961- .... CLC **85**
See also CA 142

Court, Wesli
See Turco, Lewis (Putnam)

Courtenay, Bryce 1933- .... CLC **59**
See also CA 138

Courtney, Robert
See Ellison, Harlan (Jay)

Cousteau, Jacques-Yves 1910- ...... CLC **30**
See also CA 65-68; CANR 15; MTCW;
SATA 38

Coward, Noel (Peirce)
1899-1973 .... CLC **1, 9, 29, 51**
See also AITN 1; CA 17-18; 41-44R;
CANR 35; CAP 2; CDBLB 1914-1945;
DLB 10; MTCW

Cowley, Malcolm 1898-1989 .... CLC **39**
See also CA 5-8R; 128; CANR 3; DLB 4,
48; DLBY 81, 89; MTCW

Cowper, William 1731-1800 .... NCLC **8**
See also DLB 104, 109

Cox, William Trevor 1928- ... CLC **9, 14, 71**
See also Trevor, William
See also CA 9-12R; CANR 4, 37; DLB 14;
MTCW

Coyne, P. J.
See Masters, Hilary

Cozzens, James Gould
1903-1978 .... CLC **1, 4, 11**
See also CA 9-12R; 81-84; CANR 19;
CDALB 1941-1968; DLB 9; DLBD 2;
DLBY 84; MTCW

Crabbe, George 1754-1832 .... NCLC **26**
See also DLB 93

Craig, A. A.
See Anderson, Poul (William)

Craik, Dinah Maria (Mulock)
1826-1887 .... NCLC **38**
See also DLB 35; MAICYA; SATA 34

Cram, Ralph Adams 1863-1942 .... TCLC **45**

Crane, (Harold) Hart
1899-1932 .... TCLC **2, 5; DA; PC 3;**
WLC
See also CA 104; 127; CDALB 1917-1929;
DLB 4, 48; MTCW

Crane, R(onald) S(almon)
1886-1967 .... CLC **27**
See also CA 85-88; DLB 63

Crane, Stephen (Townley)
1871-1900 .... TCLC **11, 17, 32; DA;**
SSC **7**; WLC
See also CA 109; 140; CDALB 1865-1917;
DLB 12, 54, 78; YABC 2

Crase, Douglas 1944- .... CLC **58**
See also CA 106

Crashaw, Richard 1612(?)-1649 ...... LC **24**
See also DLB 126

Craven, Margaret 1901-1980 .... CLC **17**
See also CA 103

Crawford, F(rancis) Marion
1854-1909 .... TCLC **10**
See also CA 107; DLB 71

Crawford, Isabella Valancy
1850-1887 .... NCLC **12**
See also DLB 92

Crayon, Geoffrey
See Irving, Washington

Elkin, Stanley L(awrence)
1930- ... **CLC 4, 6, 9, 14, 27, 51; SSC 12**
See also CA 9-12R; CANR 8, 46; DLD 2,
28; DLBY 80; MTCW

Elledge, Scott .... **CLC 34**

Elliott, Don
See Silverberg, Robert

Elliott, George P(aul) 1918-1980 ..... **CLC 2**
See also CA 1-4R; 97-100; CANR 2

Elliott, Janice 1931- .... **CLC 47**
See also CA 13-16R; CANR 8, 29; DLB 14

Elliott, Sumner Locke 1917-1991 ... **CLC 38**
See also CA 5-8R; 134; CANR 2, 21

Elliott, William
See Bradbury, Ray (Douglas)

Ellis, A. E. .... **CLC 7**

Ellis, Alice Thomas .... **CLC 40**
See also Haycraft, Anna

Ellis, Bret Easton 1964- .... **CLC 39, 71**
See also AAYA 2; CA 118; 123

Ellis, (Henry) Havelock
1859-1939 .... **TCLC 14**
See also CA 109

Ellis, Landon
See Ellison, Harlan (Jay)

Ellis, Trey 1962- .... **CLC 55**
See also CA 146

Ellison, Harlan (Jay)
1934- .... **CLC 1, 13, 42; SSC 14**
See also CA 5-8R; CANR 5, 46; DLB 8;
MTCW

Ellison, Ralph (Waldo)
1914-1994 .... **CLC 1, 3, 11, 54, 86;
BLC; DA; WLC**
See also BW 1; CA 9-12R; 145; CANR 24;
CDALB 1941-1968; DLB 2, 76;
DLBY 94; MTCW

Ellmann, Lucy (Elizabeth) 1956- .... **CLC 61**
See also CA 128

Ellmann, Richard (David)
1918-1987 .... **CLC 50**
See also BEST 89:2; CA 1-4R; 122;
CANR 2, 28; DLB 103; DLBY 87;
MTCW

Elman, Richard 1934- .... **CLC 19**
See also CA 17-20R; CAAS 3; CANR 47

Elron
See Hubbard, L(afayette) Ron(ald)

Eluard, Paul .... **TCLC 7, 41**
See also Grindel, Eugene

Elyot, Sir Thomas 1490(?)-1546 ..... **LC 11**

Elytis, Odysseus 1911- .... **CLC 15, 49**
See also CA 102; MTCW

Emecheta, (Florence Onye) Buchi
1944- .... **CLC 14, 48; BLC**
See also BW 2; CA 81-84; CANR 27;
DLB 117; MTCW; SATA 66

Emerson, Ralph Waldo
1803-1882 ...... **NCLC 1, 38; DA; WLC**
See also CDALB 1640-1865; DLB 1, 59, 73

Eminescu, Mihail 1850-1889 ..... **NCLC 33**

Empson, William
1906-1984 .... **CLC 3, 8, 19, 33, 34**
See also CA 17-20R; 112; CANR 31;
DLB 20; MTCW

Enchi Fumiko (Ueda) 1905-1986 .... **CLC 31**
See also CA 129; 121

Ende, Michael (Andreas Helmuth)
1929- .... **CLC 31**
See also CA 118; 124; CANR 36; CLR 14;
DLB 75; MAICYA; SATA 61;
SATA-Brief 42

Endo, Shusaku 1923- ..... **CLC 7, 14, 19, 54**
See also CA 29-32R; CANR 21; MTCW

Engel, Marian 1933-1985 .... **CLC 36**
See also CA 25-28R; CANR 12; DLB 53

Engelhardt, Frederick
See Hubbard, L(afayette) Ron(ald)

Enright, D(ennis) J(oseph)
1920- .... **CLC 4, 8, 31**
See also CA 1-4R; CANR 1, 42; DLB 27;
SATA 25

Enzensberger, Hans Magnus
1929- .... **CLC 43**
See also CA 116; 119

Ephron, Nora 1941- .... **CLC 17, 31**
See also AITN 2; CA 65-68; CANR 12, 39

Epsilon
See Betjeman, John

Epstein, Daniel Mark 1948- .... **CLC 7**
See also CA 49-52; CANR 2

Epstein, Jacob 1956- .... **CLC 19**
See also CA 114

Epstein, Joseph 1937- .... **CLC 39**
See also CA 112; 119

Epstein, Leslie 1938- .... **CLC 27**
See also CA 73-76; CAAS 12; CANR 23

Equiano, Olaudah
1745(?)-1797 .... **LC 16; BLC**
See also DLB 37, 50

Erasmus, Desiderius 1469(?)-1536 .... **LC 16**

Erdman, Paul E(mil) 1932- .... **CLC 25**
See also AITN 1; CA 61-64; CANR 13, 43

Erdrich, Louise 1954- .... **CLC 39, 54**
See also AAYA 10; BEST 89:1; CA 114;
CANR 41; DLB 152; MTCW; NNAL

Erenburg, Ilya (Grigoryevich)
See Ehrenburg, Ilya (Grigoryevich)

Erickson, Stephen Michael 1950-
See Erickson, Steve
See also CA 129

Erickson, Steve .... **CLC 64**
See also Erickson, Stephen Michael

Ericson, Walter
See Fast, Howard (Melvin)

Eriksson, Buntel
See Bergman, (Ernst) Ingmar

Ernaux, Annie 1940- .... **CLC 88**
See also CA 147

Eschenbach, Wolfram von
See Wolfram von Eschenbach

Eseki, Bruno
See Mphahlele, Ezekiel

Esenin, Sergei (Alexandrovich)
1895-1925 .... **TCLC 4**
See also CA 104

Eshleman, Clayton 1935- .... **CLC 7**
See also CA 33-36R; CAAS 6; DLB 5

Espriella, Don Manuel Alvarez
See Southey, Robert

Espriu, Salvador 1913-1985 .... **CLC 9**
See also CA 115; DLB 134

Espronceda, Jose de 1808-1842 ... **NCLC 39**

Esse, James
See Stephens, James

Esterbrook, Tom
See Hubbard, L(afayette) Ron(ald)

Estleman, Loren D. 1952- .... **CLC 48**
See also CA 85-88; CANR 27; MTCW

Eugenides, Jeffrey 1960(?)- .... **CLC 81**
See also CA 144

Euripides c. 485B.C.-406B.C. .... **DC 4**
See also DA

Evan, Evin
See Faust, Frederick (Schiller)

Evans, Evan
See Faust, Frederick (Schiller)

Evans, Marian
See Eliot, George

Evans, Mary Ann
See Eliot, George

Evarts, Esther
See Benson, Sally

Everett, Percival L. 1956- .... **CLC 57**
See also BW 2; CA 129

Everson, R(onald) G(ilmour)
1903- .... **CLC 27**
See also CA 17-20R; DLB 88

Everson, William (Oliver)
1912-1994 .... **CLC 1, 5, 14**
See also CA 9-12R; 145; CANR 20; DLB 5,
16; MTCW

Evtushenko, Evgenii Aleksandrovich
See Yevtushenko, Yevgeny (Alexandrovich)

Ewart, Gavin (Buchanan)
1916- .... **CLC 13, 46**
See also CA 89-92; CANR 17, 46; DLB 40;
MTCW

Ewers, Hanns Heinz 1871-1943 ... **TCLC 12**
See also CA 109

Ewing, Frederick R.
See Sturgeon, Theodore (Hamilton)

Exley, Frederick (Earl)
1929-1992 .... **CLC 6, 11**
See also AITN 2; CA 81-84; 138; DLB 143;
DLBY 81

Eynhardt, Guillermo
See Quiroga, Horacio (Sylvestre)

Ezekiel, Nissim 1924- .... **CLC 61**
See also CA 61-64

Ezekiel, Tish O'Dowd 1943- ...... **CLC 34**
See also CA 129

Fadeyev, A.
See Bulgya, Alexander Alexandrovich

Fadeyev, Alexander .... **TCLC 53**
See also Bulgya, Alexander Alexandrovich

Fisher, Rudolph
1897-1934 . . . . **TCLC 11; BLC**
See also BW 1; CA 107; 124; DLB 51, 102

Fisher, Vardis (Alvero) 1895-1968. . . . **CLC 7**
See also CA 5-8R; 25-28R; DLB 9

Fiske, Tarleton
See Bloch, Robert (Albert)

Fitch, Clarke
See Sinclair, Upton (Beall)

Fitch, John IV
See Cormier, Robert (Edmund)

Fitzgerald, Captain Hugh
See Baum, L(yman) Frank

FitzGerald, Edward 1809-1883 . . . . **NCLC 9**
See also DLB 32

Fitzgerald, F(rancis) Scott (Key)
1896-1940 . . . . . . **TCLC 1, 6, 14, 28, 55;**
                                    DA; SSC 6; WLC
See also AITN 1; CA 110; 123;
CDALB 1917-1929; DLB 4, 9, 86;
DLBD 1; DLBY 81; MTCW

Fitzgerald, Penelope 1916-. . . **CLC 19, 51, 61**
See also CA 85-88; CAAS 10; DLB 14

Fitzgerald, Robert (Stuart)
1910-1985 . . . . **CLC 39**
See also CA 1-4R; 114; CANR 1; DLBY 80

FitzGerald, Robert D(avid)
1902-1987 . . . . **CLC 19**
See also CA 17-20R

Fitzgerald, Zelda (Sayre)
1900-1948 . . . . **TCLC 52**
See also CA 117, 126, DLBY 84

Flanagan, Thomas (James Bonner)
1923- . . . . **CLC 25, 52**
See also CA 108; DLBY 80; MTCW

Flaubert, Gustave
1821-1880 . . . . **NCLC 2, 10, 19; DA;**
                                         SSC 11; WLC
See also DLB 119

Flecker, (Herman) James Elroy
1884-1915 . . . . **TCLC 43**
See also CA 109; DLB 10, 19

Fleming, Ian (Lancaster)
1908-1964 . . . . **CLC 3, 30**
See also CA 5-8R; CDBLB 1945-1960;
DLB 87; MTCW; SATA 9

Fleming, Thomas (James) 1927- . . . . **CLC 37**
See also CA 5-8R; CANR 10; SATA 8

Fletcher, John Gould 1886-1950 . . . **TCLC 35**
See also CA 107; DLB 4, 45

Fleur, Paul
See Pohl, Frederik

Flooglebuckle, Al
See Spiegelman, Art

Flying Officer X
See Bates, H(erbert) E(rnest)

Fo, Dario 1926-. . . . . **CLC 32**
See also CA 116; 128; MTCW

Fogarty, Jonathan Titulescu Esq.
See Farrell, James T(homas)

Folke, Will
See Bloch, Robert (Albert)

Follett, Ken(neth Martin) 1949- . . . . **CLC 18**
See also AAYA 6; BEST 89:4; CA 81-84;
CANR 13, 33; DLB 87; DLBY 81;
MTCW

Fontane, Theodor 1819-1898 . . . . . **NCLC 26**
See also DLB 129

Foote, Horton 1916-. . . . . **CLC 51**
See also CA 73-76; CANR 34; DLB 26

Foote, Shelby 1916- . . . . **CLC 75**
See also CA 5-8R; CANR 3, 45; DLB 2, 17

Forbes, Esther 1891-1967. . . . . **CLC 12**
See also CA 13-14; 25-28R; CAP 1;
CLR 27; DLB 22; JRDA; MAICYA;
SATA 2

Forche, Carolyn (Louise)
1950- . . . . **CLC 25, 83, 86; PC 10**
See also CA 109; 117; DLB 5

Ford, Elbur
See Hibbert, Eleanor Alice Burford

Ford, Ford Madox
1873-1939 . . . . **TCLC 1, 15, 39, 57**
See also CA 104; 132; CDBLB 1914-1945;
DLB 34, 98; MTCW

Ford, John 1895-1973. . . . . **CLC 16**
See also CA 45-48

Ford, Richard 1944-. . . . . **CLC 46**
See also CA 69-72; CANR 11, 47

Ford, Webster
See Masters, Edgar Lee

Foreman, Richard 1937-. . . . . **CLC 50**
See also CA 65-68; CANR 32

Forester, C(ecil) S(cott)
1899-1966 . . . . **CLC 35**
See also CA 73-76; 25-28R; SATA 13

Forez
See Mauriac, Francois (Charles)

Forman, James Douglas 1932-. . . . . . **CLC 21**
See also CA 9-12R; CANR 4, 19, 42;
JRDA; MAICYA; SATA 8, 70

Fornes, Maria Irene 1930-. . . . . . **CLC 39, 61**
See also CA 25-28R; CANR 28; DLB 7;
HW; MTCW

Forrest, Leon 1937- . . . . **CLC 4**
See also BW 2; CA 89-92; CAAS 7;
CANR 25; DLB 33

Forster, E(dward) M(organ)
1879-1970 . . . . . **CLC 1, 2, 3, 4, 9, 10, 13,**
                              15, 22, 45, 77; DA; WLC
See also AAYA 2; CA 13-14; 25-28R;
CANR 45; CAP 1; CDBLB 1914-1945;
DLB 34, 98; DLBD 10; MTCW;
SATA 57

Forster, John 1812-1876 . . . . **NCLC 11**
See also DLB 144

Forsyth, Frederick 1938-. . . . . . **CLC 2, 5, 36**
See also BEST 89:4; CA 85-88; CANR 38;
DLB 87; MTCW

Forten, Charlotte L. . . . . **TCLC 16; BLC**
See also Grimke, Charlotte L(ottie) Forten
See also DLB 50

Foscolo, Ugo 1778-1827. . . . . **NCLC 8**

Fosse, Bob . . . . **CLC 20**
See also Fosse, Robert Louis

Fosse, Robert Louis 1927-1987
See Fosse, Bob
See also CA 110; 123

Foster, Stephen Collins
1826-1864 . . . . **NCLC 26**

Foucault, Michel
1926-1984 . . . . **CLC 31, 34, 69**
See also CA 105; 113; CANR 34; MTCW

Fouque, Friedrich (Heinrich Karl) de la Motte
1777-1843 . . . . **NCLC 2**
See also DLB 90

Fourier, Charles 1772-1837 . . . . . . **NCLC 51**

Fournier, Henri Alban 1886-1914
See Alain-Fournier
See also CA 104

Fournier, Pierre 1916-. . . . . **CLC 11**
See also Gascar, Pierre
See also CA 89-92; CANR 16, 40

Fowles, John
1926- . . . . . . **CLC 1, 2, 3, 4, 6, 9, 10, 15,**
                                                 33, 87
See also CA 5-8R; CANR 25; CDBLB 1960
to Present; DLB 14, 139; MTCW;
SATA 22

Fox, Paula 1923-. . . . . **CLC 2, 8**
See also AAYA 3; CA 73-76; CANR 20,
36; CLR 1; DLB 52; JRDA; MAICYA;
MTCW; SATA 17, 60

Fox, William Price (Jr.) 1926- . . . . . **CLC 22**
See also CA 17-20R; CAAS 19; CANR 11;
DLB 2; DLBY 81

Foxe, John 1516(?)-1587 . . . . **LC 14**

Frame, Janet . . . . . . **CLC 2, 3, 6, 22, 66**
See also Clutha, Janet Paterson Frame

France, Anatole . . . . **TCLC 9**
See also Thibault, Jacques Anatole Francois
See also DLB 123

Francis, Claude 19(?)- . . . . **CLC 50**

Francis, Dick 1920- . . . . **CLC 2, 22, 42**
See also AAYA 5; BEST 89:3; CA 5-8R;
CANR 9, 42; CDBLB 1960 to Present;
DLB 87; MTCW

Francis, Robert (Churchill)
1901-1987 . . . . **CLC 15**
See also CA 1-4R; 123; CANR 1

Frank, Anne(lies Marie)
1929-1945 . . . . **TCLC 17; DA; WLC**
See also AAYA 12; CA 113; 133; MTCW;
SATA-Brief 42

Frank, Elizabeth 1945-. . . . . **CLC 39**
See also CA 121; 126

Franklin, Benjamin
See Hasek, Jaroslav (Matej Frantisek)

Franklin, Benjamin 1706-1790. . . **LC 25; DA**
See also CDALB 1640-1865; DLB 24, 43,
73

Franklin, (Stella Maraia Sarah) Miles
1879-1954 . . . . **TCLC 7**
See also CA 104

Fraser, (Lady) Antonia (Pakenham)
1932- . . . . **CLC 32**
See also CA 85-88; CANR 44; MTCW;
SATA-Brief 32

Fraser, George MacDonald 1925-. . . . **CLC 7**
See also CA 45-48; CANR 2, 48

Fraser, Sylvia 1935-.............. CLC 64
See also CA 45-48; CANR 1, 16

Frayn, Michael 1933-...... CLC 3, 7, 31, 47
See also CA 5-8R; CANR 30; DLB 13, 14;
MTCW

Fraze, Candida (Merrill) 1945-..... CLC 50
See also CA 126

Frazer, J(ames) G(eorge)
1854-1941 .... TCLC 32
See also CA 118

Frazer, Robert Caine
See Creasey, John

Frazer, Sir James George
See Frazer, J(ames) G(eorge)

Frazier, Ian 1951-................ CLC 46
See also CA 130

Frederic, Harold 1856-1898...... NCLC 10
See also DLB 12, 23

Frederick, John
See Faust, Frederick (Schiller)

Frederick the Great 1712-1786...... LC 14

Fredro, Aleksander 1793-1876..... NCLC 8

Freeling, Nicolas 1927- .... CLC 38
See also CA 49-52; CAAS 12; CANR 1, 17;
DLB 87

Freeman, Douglas Southall
1886-1953 .... TCLC 11
See also CA 109; DLB 17

Freeman, Judith 1946-........... CLC 55

Freeman, Mary Eleanor Wilkins
1852-1930 .... TCLC 9; SSC 1
See also CA 106; DLB 12, 78

Freeman, R(ichard) Austin
1862-1943 .... TCLC 21
See also CA 113; DLB 70

French, Albert 1943- .... CLC 86

French, Marilyn 1929-...... CLC 10, 18, 60
See also CA 69-72; CANR 3, 31; MTCW

French, Paul
See Asimov, Isaac

Freneau, Philip Morin 1752-1832.. NCLC 1
See also DLB 37, 43

Freud, Sigmund 1856-1939 .... TCLC 52
See also CA 115; 133; MTCW

Friedan, Betty (Naomi) 1921-...... CLC 74
See also CA 65-68; CANR 18, 45; MTCW

Friedman, B(ernard) H(arper)
1926-....................... CLC 7
See also CA 1-4R; CANR 3, 48

Friedman, Bruce Jay 1930-.... CLC 3, 5, 56
See also CA 9-12R; CANR 25; DLB 2, 28

Friel, Brian 1929-........... CLC 5, 42, 59
See also CA 21-24R; CANR 33; DLB 13;
MTCW

Friis-Baastad, Babbis Ellinor
1921-1970 .... CLC 12
See also CA 17-20R; 134; SATA 7

Frisch, Max (Rudolf)
1911-1991 ..... CLC 3, 9, 14, 18, 32, 44
See also CA 85-88; 134; CANR 32;
DLB 69, 124; MTCW

Fromentin, Eugene (Samuel Auguste)
1820-1876 .... NCLC 10
See also DLB 123

Frost, Frederick
See Faust, Frederick (Schiller)

Frost, Robert (Lee)
1874-1963 .... CLC 1, 3, 4, 9, 10, 13, 15,
26, 34, 44; DA; PC 1; WLC
See also CA 89-92; CANR 33;
CDALB 1917-1929; DLB 54; DLBD 7;
MTCW; SATA 14

Froude, James Anthony
1818-1894 .... NCLC 43
See also DLB 18, 57, 144

Froy, Herald
See Waterhouse, Keith (Spencer)

Fry, Christopher 1907-....... CLC 2, 10, 14
See also CA 17-20R; CANR 9, 30; DLB 13;
MTCW; SATA 66

Frye, (Herman) Northrop
1912-1991 .... CLC 24, 70
See also CA 5-8R; 133; CANR 8, 37;
DLB 67, 68; MTCW

Fuchs, Daniel 1909-1993 .... CLC 8, 22
See also CA 81-84; 142; CAAS 5;
CANR 40; DLB 9, 26, 28; DLBY 93

Fuchs, Daniel 1934-.............. CLC 34
See also CA 37-40R; CANR 14, 48

Fuentes, Carlos
1928-...... CLC 3, 8, 10, 13, 22, 41, 60;
DA; HLC; WLC
See also AAYA 4; AITN 2; CA 69-72;
CANR 10, 32; DLB 113; HW; MTCW

Fuentes, Gregorio Lopez y
See Lopez y Fuentes, Gregorio

Fugard, (Harold) Athol
1932-.... CLC 5, 9, 14, 25, 40, 80; DC 3
See also CA 85-88; CANR 32; MTCW

Fugard, Sheila 1932- .... CLC 48
See also CA 125

Fuller, Charles (H., Jr.)
1939-.............. CLC 25; BLC; DC 1
See also BW 2; CA 108; 112; DLB 38;
MTCW

Fuller, John (Leopold) 1937-....... CLC 62
See also CA 21-24R; CANR 9, 44; DLB 40

Fuller, Margaret .... NCLC 5, 50
See also Ossoli, Sarah Margaret (Fuller
marchesa d')

Fuller, Roy (Broadbent)
1912-1991 .... CLC 4, 28
See also CA 5-8R; 135; CAAS 10; DLB 15,
20

Fulton, Alice 1952-................ CLC 52
See also CA 116

Furphy, Joseph 1843-1912........ TCLC 25

Fussell, Paul 1924-................ CLC 74
See also BEST 90:1; CA 17-20R; CANR 8,
21, 35; MTCW

Futabatei, Shimei 1864-1909...... TCLC 44

Futrelle, Jacques 1875-1912 ...... TCLC 19
See also CA 113

Gaboriau, Emile 1835-1873 ...... NCLC 14

Gadda, Carlo Emilio 1893-1973 .... CLC 11
See also CA 89-92

Gaddis, William
1922- ..... CLC 1, 3, 6, 8, 10, 19, 43, 86
See also CA 17-20R; CANR 21, 48; DLB 2;
MTCW

Gaines, Ernest J(ames)
1933-......... CLC 3, 11, 18, 86; BLC
See also AITN 1; BW 2; CA 9-12R;
CANR 6, 24, 42; CDALB 1968-1988;
DLB 2, 33, 152; DLBY 80; MTCW

Gaitskill, Mary 1954-............. CLC 69
See also CA 128

Galdos, Benito Perez
See Perez Galdos, Benito

Gale, Zona 1874-1938 .... TCLC 7
See also CA 105; DLB 9, 78

Galeano, Eduardo (Hughes) 1940-... CLC 72
See also CA 29-32R; CANR 13, 32; HW

Galiano, Juan Valera y Alcala
See Valera y Alcala-Galiano, Juan

Gallagher, Tess 1943-.... CLC 18, 63; PC 9
See also CA 106; DLB 120

Gallant, Mavis
1922-............ CLC 7, 18, 38; SSC 5
See also CA 69-72; CANR 29; DLB 53;
MTCW

Gallant, Roy A(rthur) 1924- .... CLC 17
See also CA 5-8R; CANR 4, 29; CLR 30;
MAICYA; SATA 4, 68

Gallico, Paul (William) 1897-1976 ... CLC 2
See also AITN 1; CA 5-8R; 69-72;
CANR 23; DLB 9; MAICYA; SATA 13

Gallup, Ralph
See Whitemore, Hugh (John)

Galsworthy, John
1867-1933 .... TCLC 1, 45; DA; WLC 2
See also CA 104; 141; CDBLB 1890-1914;
DLB 10, 34, 98

Galt, John 1779-1839............. NCLC 1
See also DLB 99, 116

Galvin, James 1951-.............. CLC 38
See also CA 108; CANR 26

Gamboa, Federico 1864-1939...... TCLC 36

Gandhi, M. K.
See Gandhi, Mohandas Karamchand

Gandhi, Mahatma
See Gandhi, Mohandas Karamchand

Gandhi, Mohandas Karamchand
1869-1948 .... TCLC 59
See also CA 121; 132; MTCW

Gann, Ernest Kellogg 1910-1991.... CLC 23
See also AITN 1; CA 1-4R; 136; CANR 1

Garcia, Cristina 1958- .... CLC 76
See also CA 141

Garcia Lorca, Federico
1898-1936 .... TCLC 1, 7, 49; DA;
DC 2; HLC; PC 3; WLC
See also CA 104; 131; DLB 108; HW;
MTCW

Garcia Marquez, Gabriel (Jose)
1928- .... CLC 2, 3, 8, 10, 15, 27, 47, 55,
68; DA; HLC; SSC 8; WLC
See also AAYA 3; BEST 89:1, 90:4;
CA 33-36R; CANR 10, 28; DLB 113;
HW; MTCW

Ginzburg, Natalia
1916-1991 .... **CLC 5, 11, 54, 70**
See also CA 85-88; 135; CANR 33; MTCW

Giono, Jean 1895-1970......... **CLC 4, 11**
See also CA 45-48; 29-32R; CANR 2, 35;
DLB 72; MTCW

Giovanni, Nikki
1943- ...... **CLC 2, 4, 19, 64; BLC; DA**
See also AITN 1; BW 2; CA 29-32R;
CAAS 6; CANR 18, 41; CLR 6; DLB 5,
41; MAICYA; MTCW; SATA 24

Giovene, Andrea 1904-............. **CLC 7**
See also CA 85-88

Gippius, Zinaida (Nikolayevna) 1869-1945
See Hippius, Zinaida
See also CA 106

Giraudoux, (Hippolyte) Jean
1882-1944 .... **TCLC 2, 7**
See also CA 104; DLB 65

Gironella, Jose Maria 1917- .... **CLC 11**
See also CA 101

Gissing, George (Robert)
1857-1903 .... **TCLC 3, 24, 47**
See also CA 105; DLB 18, 135

Giurlani, Aldo
See Palazzeschi, Aldo

Gladkov, Fyodor (Vasilyevich)
1883-1958 .... **TCLC 27**

Glanville, Brian (Lester) 1931- ...... **CLC 6**
See also CA 5-8R; CAAS 9; CANR 3;
DLB 15, 139; SATA 42

Glasgow, Ellen (Anderson Gholson)
1873(?)-1945 .... **TCLC 2, 7**
See also CA 104; DLB 9, 12

Glaspell, Susan (Keating)
1882(?)-1948 .... **TCLC 55**
See also CA 110; DLB 7, 9, 78; YABC 2

Glassco, John 1909-1981 .... **CLC 9**
See also CA 13-16R; 102; CANR 15;
DLB 68

Glasscock, Amnesia
See Steinbeck, John (Ernst)

Glasser, Ronald J. 1940(?)- .... **CLC 37**

Glassman, Joyce
See Johnson, Joyce

Glendinning, Victoria 1937-........ **CLC 50**
See also CA 120; 127

Glissant, Edouard 1928-........ **CLC 10, 68**

Gloag, Julian 1930- .... **CLC 40**
See also AITN 1; CA 65-68; CANR 10

Glowacki, Aleksander
See Prus, Boleslaw

Glueck, Louise (Elisabeth)
1943- .... **CLC 7, 22, 44, 81**
See also CA 33-36R; CANR 40; DLB 5

Gobineau, Joseph Arthur (Comte) de
1816-1882 .... **NCLC 17**
See also DLB 123

Godard, Jean-Luc 1930-........... **CLC 20**
See also CA 93-96

Godden, (Margaret) Rumer 1907-... **CLC 53**
See also AAYA 6; CA 5-8R; CANR 4, 27,
36; CLR 20; MAICYA; SAAS 12;
SATA 3, 36

Godoy Alcayaga, Lucila 1889-1957
See Mistral, Gabriela
See also BW 2; CA 104; 131; HW; MTCW

Godwin, Gail (Kathleen)
1937- .... **CLC 5, 8, 22, 31, 69**
See also CA 29-32R; CANR 15, 43; DLB 6;
MTCW

Godwin, William 1756-1836...... **NCLC 14**
See also CDBLB 1789-1832; DLB 39, 104,
142

Goethe, Johann Wolfgang von
1749-1832 .... **NCLC 4, 22, 34; DA;
PC 5; WLC 3**
See also DLB 94

Gogarty, Oliver St. John
1878-1957 .... **TCLC 15**
See also CA 109; DLB 15, 19

Gogol, Nikolai (Vasilyevich)
1809-1852 .... **NCLC 5, 15, 31; DA;
DC 1; SSC 4; WLC**

Goines, Donald
1937(?)-1974 .... **CLC 80; BLC**
See also AITN 1; BW 1; CA 124; 114;
DLB 33

Gold, Herbert 1924-....... **CLC 4, 7, 14, 42**
See also CA 9-12R; CANR 17, 45; DLB 2;
DLBY 81

Goldbarth, Albert 1948-......... **CLC 5, 38**
See also CA 53-56; CANR 6, 40; DLB 120

Goldberg, Anatol 1910-1982 .... **CLC 34**
See also CA 131; 117

Goldemberg, Isaac 1945-......... **CLC 52**
See also CA 69-72; CAAS 12; CANR 11,
32; HW

Golding, William (Gerald)
1911-1993 .... **CLC 1, 2, 3, 8, 10, 17, 27,
58, 81; DA; WLC**
See also AAYA 5; CA 5-8R; 141;
CANR 13, 33; CDBLB 1945-1960;
DLB 15, 100; MTCW

Goldman, Emma 1869-1940...... **TCLC 13**
See also CA 110

Goldman, Francisco 1955-......... **CLC 76**

Goldman, William (W.) 1931-.... **CLC 1, 48**
See also CA 9-12R; CANR 29; DLB 44

Goldmann, Lucien 1913-1970 ...... **CLC 24**
See also CA 25-28; CAP 2

Goldoni, Carlo 1707-1793 .... **LC 4**

Goldsberry, Steven 1949-......... **CLC 34**
See also CA 131

Goldsmith, Oliver
1728-1774 .... **LC 2; DA; WLC**
See also CDBLB 1660-1789; DLB 39, 89,
104, 109, 142; SATA 26

Goldsmith, Peter
See Priestley, J(ohn) B(oynton)

Gombrowicz, Witold
1904-1969 .... **CLC 4, 7, 11, 49**
See also CA 19-20; 25-28R; CAP 2

Gomez de la Serna, Ramon
1888-1963 .... **CLC 9**
See also CA 116; HW

Goncharov, Ivan Alexandrovich
1812-1891 .... **NCLC 1**

Goncourt, Edmond (Louis Antoine Huot) de
1822-1896 .... **NCLC 7**
See also DLB 123

Goncourt, Jules (Alfred Huot) de
1830-1870 .... **NCLC 7**
See also DLB 123

Gontier, Fernande 19(?)- .... **CLC 50**

Goodman, Paul 1911-1972.... **CLC 1, 2, 4, 7**
See also CA 19-20; 37-40R; CANR 34;
CAP 2; DLB 130; MTCW

Gordimer, Nadine
1923- .... **CLC 3, 5, 7, 10, 18, 33, 51, 70;
DA; SSC 17**
See also CA 5-8R; CANR 3, 28; MTCW

Gordon, Adam Lindsay
1833-1870 .... **NCLC 21**

Gordon, Caroline
1895-1981 ... **CLC 6, 13, 29, 83; SSC 15**
See also CA 11-12; 103; CANR 36; CAP 1;
DLB 4, 9, 102; DLBY 81; MTCW

Gordon, Charles William 1860-1937
See Connor, Ralph
See also CA 109

Gordon, Mary (Catherine)
1949- .... **CLC 13, 22**
See also CA 102; CANR 44; DLB 6;
DLBY 81; MTCW

Gordon, Sol 1923-................. **CLC 26**
See also CA 53-56; CANR 4; SATA 11

Gordone, Charles 1925-.......... **CLC 1, 4**
See also BW 1; CA 93-96; DLB 7; MTCW

Gorenko, Anna Andreevna
See Akhmatova, Anna

Gorky, Maxim.............. TCLC 8; WLC
See also Peshkov, Alexei Maximovich

Goryan, Sirak
See Saroyan, William

Gosse, Edmund (William)
1849-1928 .... **TCLC 28**
See also CA 117; DLB 57, 144

Gotlieb, Phyllis Fay (Bloom)
1926-.................... **CLC 18**
See also CA 13-16R; CANR 7; DLB 88

Gottesman, S. D.
See Kornbluth, C(yril) M.; Pohl, Frederik

Gottfried von Strassburg
fl. c. 1210-................. **CMLC 10**
See also DLB 138

Gould, Lois .... CLC 4, 10
See also CA 77-80; CANR 29; MTCW

Gourmont, Remy de 1858-1915.... **TCLC 17**
See also CA 109

Govier, Katherine 1948-.......... **CLC 51**
See also CA 101; CANR 18, 40

Goyen, (Charles) William
1915-1983 .... **CLC 5, 8, 14, 40**
See also AITN 2; CA 5-8R; 110; CANR 6;
DLB 2; DLBY 83

Goytisolo, Juan
1931-............ **CLC 5, 10, 23; HLC**
See also CA 85-88; CANR 32; HW; MTCW

Gozzano, Guido 1883-1916 .... **PC 10**
See also DLB 114

Gozzi, (Conte) Carlo 1720-1806 .. **NCLC 23**

Grabbe, Christian Dietrich
1801-1836 .... NCLC **2**
See also DLB 133

Grace, Patricia 1937-............ CLC **56**

Gracian y Morales, Baltasar
1601-1658 .... LC **15**

Gracq, Julien .... CLC **11, 48**
See also Poirier, Louis
See also DLB 83

Grade, Chaim 1910-1982 .... CLC **10**
See also CA 93-96; 107

Graduate of Oxford, A
See Ruskin, John

Graham, John
See Phillips, David Graham

Graham, Jorie 1951-............. CLC **48**
See also CA 111; DLB 120

Graham, R(obert) B(ontine) Cunninghame
See Cunninghame Graham, R(obert)
B(ontine)
See also DLB 98, 135

Graham, Robert
See Haldeman, Joe (William)

Graham, Tom
See Lewis, (Harry) Sinclair

Graham, W(illiam) S(ydney)
1918-1986 .... CLC **29**
See also CA 73-76; 118; DLB 20

Graham, Winston (Mawdsley)
1910- .... CLC **23**
See also CA 49-52; CANR 2, 22, 45;
DLB 77

Grant, Skeeter
See Spiegelman, Art

Granville-Barker, Harley
1877-1946 .... TCLC **2**
See also Barker, Harley Granville
See also CA 104

Grass, Guenter (Wilhelm)
1927- ..... CLC **1, 2, 4, 6, 11, 15, 22, 32,
49, 88; DA; WLC**
See also CA 13-16R; CANR 20; DLB 75,
124; MTCW

Gratton, Thomas
See Hulme, T(homas) E(rnest)

Grau, Shirley Ann
1929-.............. CLC **4, 9; SSC 15**
See also CA 89-92; CANR 22; DLB 2;
MTCW

Gravel, Fern
See Hall, James Norman

Graver, Elizabeth 1964-........... CLC **70**
See also CA 135

Graves, Richard Perceval 1945- .... CLC **44**
See also CA 65-68; CANR 9, 26

Graves, Robert (von Ranke)
1895-1985 ...... CLC **1, 2, 6, 11, 39, 44,
45; PC 6**
See also CA 5-8R; 117; CANR 5, 36;
CDBLB 1914-1945; DLB 20, 100;
DLBY 85; MTCW; SATA 45

Gray, Alasdair (James) 1934- ...... CLC **41**
See also CA 126; CANR 47; MTCW

Gray, Amlin 1946- .... CLC **29**
See also CA 138

Gray, Francine du Plessix 1930-.... CLC **22**
See also BEST 90:3; CA 61-64; CAAS 2;
CANR 11, 33; MTCW

Gray, John (Henry) 1866-1934 .... TCLC **19**
See also CA 119

Gray, Simon (James Holliday)
1936- .... CLC **9, 14, 36**
See also AITN 1; CA 21-24R; CAAS 3;
CANR 32; DLB 13; MTCW

Gray, Spalding 1941- .... CLC **49**
See also CA 128

Gray, Thomas
1716-1771 ...... LC **4; DA; PC 2; WLC**
See also CDBLB 1660-1789; DLB 109

Grayson, David
See Baker, Ray Stannard

Grayson, Richard (A.) 1951-....... CLC **38**
See also CA 85-88; CANR 14, 31

Greeley, Andrew M(oran) 1928-.... CLC **28**
See also CA 5-8R; CAAS 7; CANR 7, 43;
MTCW

Green, Brian
See Card, Orson Scott

Green, Hannah
See Greenberg, Joanne (Goldenberg)

Green, Hannah .... CLC **3**
See also CA 73-76

Green, Henry .... CLC **2, 13**
See also Yorke, Henry Vincent
See also DLB 15

Green, Julian (Hartridge) 1900-
See Green, Julien
See also CA 21-24R; CANR 33; DLB 4, 72;
MTCW

Green, Julien .... CLC **3, 11, 77**
See also Green, Julian (Hartridge)

Green, Paul (Eliot) 1894-1981...... CLC **25**
See also AITN 1; CA 5-8R; 103; CANR 3;
DLB 7, 9; DLBY 81

Greenberg, Ivan 1908-1973
See Rahv, Philip
See also CA 85-88

Greenberg, Joanne (Goldenberg)
1932- .... CLC **7, 30**
See also AAYA 12; CA 5-8R; CANR 14,
32; SATA 25

Greenberg, Richard 1959(?)-....... CLC **57**
See also CA 138

Greene, Bette 1934- .... CLC **30**
See also AAYA 7; CA 53-56; CANR 4;
CLR 2; JRDA; MAICYA; SAAS 16;
SATA 8

Greene, Gael .... CLC **8**
See also CA 13-16R; CANR 10

Greene, Graham
1904-1991 .... CLC **1, 3, 6, 9, 14, 18, 27,
37, 70, 72; DA; WLC**
See also AITN 2; CA 13-16R; 133;
CANR 35; CDBLB 1945-1960; DLB 13,
15, 77, 100; DLBY 91; MTCW; SATA 20

Greer, Richard
See Silverberg, Robert

Gregor, Arthur 1923-............. CLC **9**
See also CA 25-28R; CAAS 10; CANR 11;
SATA 36

Gregor, Lee
See Pohl, Frederik

Gregory, Isabella Augusta (Persse)
1852-1932 .... TCLC **1**
See also CA 104; DLB 10

Gregory, J. Dennis
See Williams, John A(lfred)

Grendon, Stephen
See Derleth, August (William)

Grenville, Kate 1950-............. CLC **61**
See also CA 118

Grenville, Pelham
See Wodehouse, P(elham) G(renville)

Greve, Felix Paul (Berthold Friedrich)
1879-1948
See Grove, Frederick Philip
See also CA 104; 141

Grey, Zane 1872-1939 .... TCLC **6**
See also CA 104; 132; DLB 9; MTCW

Grieg, (Johan) Nordahl (Brun)
1902-1943 .... TCLC **10**
See also CA 107

Grieve, C(hristopher) M(urray)
1892-1978 .... CLC **11, 19**
See also MacDiarmid, Hugh
See also CA 5-8R; 85-88; CANR 33;
MTCW

Griffin, Gerald 1803-1840 .... NCLC **7**

Griffin, John Howard 1920-1980.... CLC **68**
See also AITN 1; CA 1-4R; 101; CANR 2

Griffin, Peter 1942- .... CLC **39**
See also CA 136

Griffiths, Trevor 1935-.......... CLC **13, 52**
See also CA 97-100; CANR 45; DLB 13

Grigson, Geoffrey (Edward Harvey)
1905-1985 .... CLC **7, 39**
See also CA 25-28R; 118; CANR 20, 33;
DLB 27; MTCW

Grillparzer, Franz 1791-1872...... NCLC **1**
See also DLB 133

Grimble, Reverend Charles James
See Eliot, T(homas) S(tearns)

Grimke, Charlotte L(ottie) Forten
1837(?)-1914
See Forten, Charlotte L.
See also BW 1; CA 117; 124

Grimm, Jacob Ludwig Karl
1785-1863 .... NCLC **3**
See also DLB 90; MAICYA; SATA 22

Grimm, Wilhelm Karl 1786-1859 .. NCLC **3**
See also DLB 90; MAICYA; SATA 22

Grimmelshausen, Johann Jakob Christoffel
von 1621-1676 .... LC **6**

Grindel, Eugene 1895-1952
See Eluard, Paul
See also CA 104

Grisham, John 1955- .... CLC **84**
See also AAYA 14; CA 138; CANR 47

Grossman, David 1954-........... CLC **67**
See also CA 138

Grossman, Vasily (Semenovich)
1905-1964 .... CLC **41**
See also CA 124; 130; MTCW

Hammon, Jupiter
1711(?)-1800(?) . . . . **NCLC 5; BLC**
See also DLB 31, 50

Hammond, Keith
See Kuttner, Henry

Hamner, Earl (Henry), Jr. 1923- . . . **CLC 12**
See also AITN 2; CA 73-76; DLB 6

Hampton, Christopher (James)
1946- . . . . **CLC 4**
See also CA 25-28R; DLB 13; MTCW

Hamsun, Knut . . . . **TCLC 2, 14, 49**
See also Pedersen, Knut

Handke, Peter 1942- . . **CLC 5, 8, 10, 15, 38**
See also CA 77-80; CANR 33; DLB 85,
124; MTCW

Hanley, James 1901-1985 . . . **CLC 3, 5, 8, 13**
See also CA 73-76; 117; CANR 36; MTCW

Hannah, Barry 1942- . . . . **CLC 23, 38**
See also CA 108; 110; CANR 43; DLB 6;
MTCW

Hannon, Ezra
See Hunter, Evan

Hansberry, Lorraine (Vivian)
1930-1965 . . . . . . **CLC 17, 62; BLC; DA;
DC 2**
See also BW 1; CA 109; 25-28R; CABS 3;
CDALB 1941-1968; DLB 7, 38; MTCW

Hansen, Joseph 1923- . . . . **CLC 38**
See also CA 29-32R; CAAS 17; CANR 16,
44

Hansen, Martin A. 1909-1955 . . . . . **TCLC 32**

Hanson, Kenneth O(stlin) 1922- . . . . **CLC 13**
See also CA 53-56; CANR 7

Hardwick, Elizabeth 1916- . . . . **CLC 13**
See also CA 5-8R; CANR 3, 32; DLB 6;
MTCW

Hardy, Thomas
1840-1928 . . . . . . **TCLC 4, 10, 18, 32, 48,
53; DA; PC 8; SSC 2; WLC**
See also CA 104; 123; CDBLB 1890-1914;
DLB 18, 19, 135; MTCW

Hare, David 1947- . . . . **CLC 29, 58**
See also CA 97-100; CANR 39; DLB 13;
MTCW

Harford, Henry
See Hudson, W(illiam) H(enry)

Hargrave, Leonie
See Disch, Thomas M(ichael)

Harjo, Joy 1951- . . . . **CLC 83**
See also CA 114; CANR 35; DLB 120;
NNAL

Harlan, Louis R(udolph) 1922- . . . . . **CLC 34**
See also CA 21-24R; CANR 25

Harling, Robert 1951(?)- . . . . **CLC 53**
See also CA 147

Harmon, William (Ruth) 1938- . . . . . **CLC 38**
See also CA 33-36R; CANR 14, 32, 35;
SATA 65

Harper, F. E. W.
See Harper, Frances Ellen Watkins

Harper, Frances E. W.
See Harper, Frances Ellen Watkins

Harper, Frances E. Watkins
See Harper, Frances Ellen Watkins

Harper, Frances Ellen
See Harper, Frances Ellen Watkins

Harper, Frances Ellen Watkins
1825-1911 . . . . **TCLC 14; BLC**
See also BW 1; CA 111; 125; DLB 50

Harper, Michael S(teven) 1938- . . **CLC 7, 22**
See also BW 1; CA 33-36R; CANR 24;
DLB 41

Harper, Mrs. F. E. W.
See Harper, Frances Ellen Watkins

Harris, Christie (Lucy) Irwin
1907- . . . . **CLC 12**
See also CA 5-8R; CANR 6; DLB 88;
JRDA; MAICYA; SAAS 10; SATA 6, 74

Harris, Frank 1856(?)-1931 . . . . **TCLC 24**
See also CA 109

Harris, George Washington
1814-1869 . . . . **NCLC 23**
See also DLB 3, 11

Harris, Joel Chandler
1848-1908 . . . . **TCLC 2; SSC 19**
See also CA 104; 137; DLB 11, 23, 42, 78,
91; MAICYA; YABC 1

**Harris, John (Wyndham Parkes Lucas)
Beynon** 1903-1969
See Wyndham, John
See also CA 102; 89-92

Harris, MacDonald . . . . **CLC 9**
See also Heiney, Donald (William)

Harris, Mark 1922- . . . . **CLC 19**
See also CA 5-8R; CAAS 3; CANR 2;
DLB 2; DLBY 80

Harris, (Theodore) Wilson 1921- . . . . **CLC 25**
See also BW 2; CA 65-68; CAAS 16;
CANR 11, 27; DLB 117; MTCW

Harrison, Elizabeth Cavanna 1909-
See Cavanna, Betty
See also CA 9-12R; CANR 6, 27

Harrison, Harry (Max) 1925- . . . . . . **CLC 42**
See also CA 1-4R; CANR 5, 21; DLB 8;
SATA 4

Harrison, James (Thomas)
1937- . . . . **CLC 6, 14, 33, 66; SSC 19**
See also CA 13-16R; CANR 8; DLBY 82

Harrison, Jim
See Harrison, James (Thomas)

Harrison, Kathryn 1961- . . . . **CLC 70**
See also CA 144

Harrison, Tony 1937- . . . . **CLC 43**
See also CA 65-68; CANR 44; DLB 40;
MTCW

Harriss, Will(ard Irvin) 1922- . . . . . . **CLC 34**
See also CA 111

Harson, Sley
See Ellison, Harlan (Jay)

Hart, Ellis
See Ellison, Harlan (Jay)

Hart, Josephine 1942(?)- . . . . **CLC 70**
See also CA 138

Hart, Moss 1904-1961 . . . . **CLC 66**
See also CA 109; 89-92; DLB 7

Harte, (Francis) Bret(t)
1836(?)-1902 . . . . **TCLC 1, 25; DA;
SSC 8; WLC**
See also CA 104; 140; CDALB 1865-1917;
DLB 12, 64, 74, 79; SATA 26

Hartley, L(eslie) P(oles)
1895-1972 . . . . **CLC 2, 22**
See also CA 45-48; 37-40R; CANR 33;
DLB 15, 139; MTCW

Hartman, Geoffrey H. 1929- . . . . **CLC 27**
See also CA 117; 125; DLB 67

Hartmann von Aue
c. 1160-c. 1205 . . . . **CMLC 15**
See also DLB 138

Haruf, Kent 19(?)- . . . . **CLC 34**

Harwood, Ronald 1934- . . . . **CLC 32**
See also CA 1-4R; CANR 4; DLB 13

Hasek, Jaroslav (Matej Frantisek)
1883-1923 . . . . **TCLC 4**
See also CA 104; 129; MTCW

Hass, Robert 1941- . . . . **CLC 18, 39**
See also CA 111; CANR 30; DLB 105

Hastings, Hudson
See Kuttner, Henry

Hastings, Selina . . . . **CLC 44**

Hatteras, Amelia
See Mencken, H(enry) L(ouis)

Hatteras, Owen . . . . **TCLC 18**
See also Mencken, H(enry) L(ouis); Nathan,
George Jean

Hauptmann, Gerhart (Johann Robert)
1862-1946 . . . . **TCLC 4**
See also CA 104; DLB 66, 118

Havel, Vaclav 1936- . . . . **CLC 25, 58, 65**
See also CA 104; CANR 36; MTCW

Haviaras, Stratis . . . . **CLC 33**
See also Chaviaras, Strates

Hawes, Stephen 1475(?)-1523(?) . . . . . **LC 17**

Hawkes, John (Clendennin Burne, Jr.)
1925- . . . . . . **CLC 1, 2, 3, 4, 7, 9, 14, 15,
27, 49**
See also CA 1-4R; CANR 2, 47; DLB 2, 7;
DLBY 80; MTCW

Hawking, S. W.
See Hawking, Stephen W(illiam)

Hawking, Stephen W(illiam)
1942- . . . . **CLC 63**
See also AAYA 13; BEST 89:1; CA 126;
129; CANR 48

Hawthorne, Julian 1846-1934 . . . . . **TCLC 25**

Hawthorne, Nathaniel
1804-1864 . . . . . . **NCLC 39; DA; SSC 3;
WLC**
See also CDALB 1640-1865; DLB 1, 74;
YABC 2

Haxton, Josephine Ayres 1921-
See Douglas, Ellen
See also CA 115; CANR 41

Hayaseca y Eizaguirre, Jorge
See Echegaray (y Eizaguirre), Jose (Maria
Waldo)

Hayashi Fumiko 1904-1951 . . . . **TCLC 27**

Haycraft, Anna
See Ellis, Alice Thomas
See also CA 122

Hayden, Robert E(arl)
1913-1980 ..... **CLC 5, 9, 14, 37; BLC;**
                                    DA; PC 6
See also BW 1; CA 69-72; 97-100; CABS 2;
CANR 24; CDALB 1941-1968; DLB 5,
76; MTCW; SATA 19; SATA-Obit 26

Hayford, J(oseph) E(phraim) Casely
See Casely-Hayford, J(oseph) E(phraim)

Hayman, Ronald 1932-............ **CLC 44**
See also CA 25-28R; CANR 18

Haywood, Eliza (Fowler)
1693(?)-1756 .... **LC 1**

Hazlitt, William 1778-1830 ...... **NCLC 29**
See also DLB 110

Hazzard, Shirley 1931- .... **CLC 18**
See also CA 9-12R; CANR 4; DLBY 82;
MTCW

Head, Bessie 1937-1986... **CLC 25, 67; BLC**
See also BW 2; CA 29-32R; 119; CANR 25;
DLB 117; MTCW

Headon, (Nicky) Topper 1956(?)- ... **CLC 30**

Heaney, Seamus (Justin)
1939- .... **CLC 5, 7, 14, 25, 37, 74**
See also CA 85-88; CANR 25, 48;
CDBLB 1960 to Present; DLB 40;
MTCW

Hearn, (Patricio) Lafcadio (Tessima Carlos)
1850-1904 .... **TCLC 9**
See also CA 105; DLB 12, 78

Hearne, Vicki 1946-.............. **CLC 56**
See also CA 139

Hearon, Shelby 1931-............. **CLC 63**
See also AITN 2; CA 25-28R; CANR 18,
48

Heat-Moon, William Least.......... **CLC 29**
See also Trogdon, William (Lewis)
See also AAYA 9

Hebbel, Friedrich 1813-1863..... **NCLC 43**
See also DLB 129

Hebert, Anne 1916- .... **CLC 4, 13, 29**
See also CA 85-88; DLB 68; MTCW

Hecht, Anthony (Evan)
1923- .... **CLC 8, 13, 19**
See also CA 9-12R; CANR 6; DLB 5

Hecht, Ben 1894-1964 .... **CLC 8**
See also CA 85-88; DLB 7, 9, 25, 26, 28, 86

Hedayat, Sadeq 1903-1951........ **TCLC 21**
See also CA 120

Hegel, Georg Wilhelm Friedrich
1770-1831 .... **NCLC 46**
See also DLB 90

Heidegger, Martin 1889-1976 ...... **CLC 24**
See also CA 81-84; 65-68; CANR 34;
MTCW

Heidenstam, (Carl Gustaf) Verner von
1859-1940 .... **TCLC 5**
See also CA 104

Heifner, Jack 1946-.............. **CLC 11**
See also CA 105; CANR 47

Heijermans, Herman 1864-1924 ... **TCLC 24**
See also CA 123

Heilbrun, Carolyn G(old) 1926-..... **CLC 25**
See also CA 45-48; CANR 1, 28

Heine, Heinrich 1797-1856 .... **NCLC 4**
See also DLB 90

Heinemann, Larry (Curtiss) 1944- .. **CLC 50**
See also CA 110; CAAS 21; CANR 31;
DLBD 9

Heiney, Donald (William) 1921-1993
See Harris, MacDonald
See also CA 1-4R; 142; CANR 3

Heinlein, Robert A(nson)
1907-1988 ...... **CLC 1, 3, 8, 14, 26, 55**
See also CA 1-4R; 125; CANR 1, 20;
DLB 8; JRDA; MAICYA; MTCW;
SATA 9, 69; SATA-Obit 56

Helforth, John
See Doolittle, Hilda

Hellenhofferu, Vojtech Kapristian z
See Hasek, Jaroslav (Matej Frantisek)

Heller, Joseph
1923- .... **CLC 1, 3, 5, 8, 11, 36, 63; DA;**
                                      WLC
See also AITN 1; CA 5-8R; CABS 1;
CANR 8, 42; DLB 2, 28; DLBY 80;
MTCW

Hellman, Lillian (Florence)
1906-1984 ...... **CLC 2, 4, 8, 14, 18, 34,**
                                 44, 52; DC 1
See also AITN 1, 2; CA 13-16R; 112;
CANR 33; DLB 7; DLBY 84; MTCW

Helprin, Mark 1947- ..... **CLC 7, 10, 22, 32**
See also CA 81-84; CANR 47; DLBY 85;
MTCW

Helvetius, Claude-Adrien
1715-1771 .... **LC 26**

Helyar, Jane Penelope Josephine 1933-
See Poole, Josephine
See also CA 21-24R; CANR 10, 26

Hemans, Felicia 1793-1835 ...... **NCLC 29**
See also DLB 96

Hemingway, Ernest (Miller)
1899-1961 .... **CLC 1, 3, 6, 8, 10, 13, 19,**
30, 34, 39, 41, 44, 50, 61, 80; DA; SSC 1;
                                      WLC
See also CA 77-80; CANR 34;
CDALB 1917-1929; DLB 4, 9, 102;
DLBD 1; DLBY 81, 87; MTCW

Hempel, Amy 1951-.............. **CLC 39**
See also CA 118; 137

Henderson, F. C.
See Mencken, H(enry) L(ouis)

Henderson, Sylvia
See Ashton-Warner, Sylvia (Constance)

Henley, Beth .... **CLC 23**
See also Henley, Elizabeth Becker
See also CABS 3; DLBY 86

Henley, Elizabeth Becker 1952-
See Henley, Beth
See also CA 107; CANR 32; MTCW

Henley, William Ernest
1849-1903 .... **TCLC 8**
See also CA 105; DLB 19

Hennissart, Martha
See Lathen, Emma
See also CA 85-88

Henry, O......... **TCLC 1, 19; SSC 5; WLC**
See also Porter, William Sydney

Henry, Patrick 1736-1799 .... **LC 25**

Henryson, Robert 1430(?)-1506(?).... **LC 20**
See also DLB 146

Henry VIII 1491-1547............. **LC 10**

Henschke, Alfred
See Klabund

Hentoff, Nat(han Irving) 1925-..... **CLC 26**
See also AAYA 4; CA 1-4R; CAAS 6;
CANR 5, 25; CLR 1; JRDA; MAICYA;
SATA 42, 69; SATA-Brief 27

Heppenstall, (John) Rayner
1911-1981 .... **CLC 10**
See also CA 1-4R; 103; CANR 29

Herbert, Frank (Patrick)
1920-1986 ...... **CLC 12, 23, 35, 44, 85**
See also CA 53-56; 118; CANR 5, 43;
DLB 8; MTCW; SATA 9, 37;
SATA-Obit 47

Herbert, George 1593-1633 .... **LC 24; PC 4**
See also CDBLB Before 1660; DLB 126

Herbert, Zbigniew 1924-......... **CLC 9, 43**
See also CA 89-92; CANR 36; MTCW

Herbst, Josephine (Frey)
1897-1969 .... **CLC 34**
See also CA 5-8R; 25-28R; DLB 9

Hergesheimer, Joseph
1880-1954 .... **TCLC 11**
See also CA 109; DLB 102, 9

Herlihy, James Leo 1927-1993 ...... **CLC 6**
See also CA 1-4R; 143; CANR 2

Hermogenes fl. c. 175-........... **CMLC 6**

Hernandez, Jose 1834-1886...... **NCLC 17**

Herrick, Robert
1591-1674 .... **LC 13; DA; PC 9**
See also DLB 126

Herring, Guilles
See Somerville, Edith

Herriot, James 1916-1995 .... **CLC 12**
See also Wight, James Alfred
See also AAYA 1; CANR 40

Herrmann, Dorothy 1941-......... **CLC 44**
See also CA 107

Herrmann, Taffy
See Herrmann, Dorothy

Hersey, John (Richard)
1914-1993 .... **CLC 1, 2, 7, 9, 40, 81**
See also CA 17-20R; 140; CANR 33;
DLB 6; MTCW; SATA 25;
SATA-Obit 76

Herzen, Aleksandr Ivanovich
1812-1870 .... **NCLC 10**

Herzl, Theodor 1860-1904....... **TCLC 36**

Herzog, Werner 1942-............ **CLC 16**
See also CA 89-92

Hesiod c. 8th cent. B.C.-......... **CMLC 5**

Hesse, Hermann
1877-1962 .... **CLC 1, 2, 3, 6, 11, 17, 25,**
                             69; DA; SSC 9; WLC
See also CA 17-18; CAP 2; DLB 66;
MTCW; SATA 50

Hewes, Cady
See De Voto, Bernard (Augustine)

Heyen, William 1940- .... **CLC 13, 18**
See also CA 33-36R; CAAS 9; DLB 5

Heyerdahl, Thor 1914-............ **CLC 26**
See also CA 5-8R; CANR 5, 22; MTCW;
SATA 2, 52

Heym, Georg (Theodor Franz Arthur)
1887-1912 .... **TCLC 9**
See also CA 106

Heym, Stefan 1913-.............. **CLC 41**
See also CA 9-12R; CANR 4; DLB 69

Heyse, Paul (Johann Ludwig von)
1830-1914 .... **TCLC 8**
See also CA 104; DLB 129

Heyward, (Edwin) DuBose
1885-1940 .... **TCLC 59**
See also CA 108; DLB 7, 9, 45; SATA 21

Hibbert, Eleanor Alice Burford
1906-1993 .... **CLC 7**
See also BEST 90:4; CA 17-20R; 140;
CANR 9, 28; SATA 2; SATA-Obit 74

Higgins, George V(incent)
1939-............... **CLC 4, 7, 10, 18**
See also CA 77-80; CAAS 5; CANR 17;
DLB 2; DLBY 81; MTCW

Higginson, Thomas Wentworth
1823-1911 .... **TCLC 36**
See also DLB 1, 64

Highet, Helen
See MacInnes, Helen (Clark)

Highsmith, (Mary) Patricia
1921-1995 .... **CLC 2, 4, 14, 42**
See also CA 1-4R; 147; CANR 1, 20, 48;
MTCW

Highwater, Jamake (Mamake)
1942(?)-...................... **CLC 12**
See also AAYA 7; CA 65-68; CAAS 7;
CANR 10, 34; CLR 17; DLB 52;
DLBY 85; JRDA; MAICYA; SATA 32,
69; SATA-Brief 30

Higuchi, Ichiyo 1872-1896....... **NCLC 49**

Hijuelos, Oscar 1951- ...... **CLC 65; HLC**
See also BEST 90:1; CA 123; DLB 145; HW

Hikmet, Nazim 1902(?)-1963....... **CLC 40**
See also CA 141; 93-96

Hildesheimer, Wolfgang
1916-1991 .... **CLC 49**
See also CA 101; 135; DLB 69, 124

Hill, Geoffrey (William)
1932-................**CLC 5, 8, 18, 45**
See also CA 81-84; CANR 21;
CDBLB 1960 to Present; DLB 40;
MTCW

Hill, George Roy 1921-........... **CLC 26**
See also CA 110; 122

Hill, John
See Koontz, Dean R(ay)

Hill, Susan (Elizabeth) 1942- .... **CLC 4**
See also CA 33-36R; CANR 29; DLB 14,
139; MTCW

Hillerman, Tony 1925-............ **CLC 62**
See also AAYA 6; BEST 89:1; CA 29-32R;
CANR 21, 42; SATA 6

Hillesum, Etty 1914-1943 .... **TCLC 49**
See also CA 137

Hilliard, Noel (Harvey) 1929-...... **CLC 15**
See also CA 9-12R; CANR 7

Hillis, Rick 1956-................ **CLC 66**
See also CA 134

Hilton, James 1900-1954........ **TCLC 21**
See also CA 108; DLB 34, 77; SATA 34

Himes, Chester (Bomar)
1909-1984 .... **CLC 2, 4, 7, 18, 58; BLC**
See also BW 2; CA 25-28R; 114; CANR 22;
DLB 2, 76, 143; MTCW

Hinde, Thomas .... **CLC 6, 11**
See also Chitty, Thomas Willes

Hindin, Nathan
See Bloch, Robert (Albert)

Hine, (William) Daryl 1936-....... **CLC 15**
See also CA 1-4R; CAAS 15; CANR 1, 20;
DLB 60

Hinkson, Katharine Tynan
See Tynan, Katharine

Hinton, S(usan) E(loise)
1950-................... **CLC 30; DA**
See also AAYA 2; CA 81-84; CANR 32;
CLR 3, 23; JRDA; MAICYA; MTCW;
SATA 19, 58

Hippius, Zinaida .... **TCLC 9**
See also Gippius, Zinaida (Nikolayevna)

Hiraoka, Kimitake 1925-1970
See Mishima, Yukio
See also CA 97-100; 29-32R; MTCW

Hirsch, E(ric) D(onald), Jr. 1928-... **CLC 79**
See also CA 25-28R; CANR 27; DLB 67;
MTCW

Hirsch, Edward 1950- .... **CLC 31, 50**
See also CA 104; CANR 20, 42; DLB 120

Hitchcock, Alfred (Joseph)
1899-1980 .... **CLC 16**
See also CA 97-100; SATA 27;
SATA-Obit 24

Hitler, Adolf 1889-1945.......... **TCLC 53**
See also CA 117; 147

Hoagland, Edward 1932-.......... **CLC 28**
See also CA 1-4R; CANR 2, 31; DLB 6;
SATA 51

Hoban, Russell (Conwell) 1925- .. **CLC 7, 25**
See also CA 5-8R; CANR 23, 37; CLR 3;
DLB 52; MAICYA; MTCW; SATA 1,
40, 78

Hobbs, Perry
See Blackmur, R(ichard) P(almer)

Hobson, Laura Z(ametkin)
1900-1986 .... **CLC 7, 25**
See also CA 17-20R; 118; DLB 28;
SATA 52

Hochhuth, Rolf 1931-........ **CLC 4, 11, 18**
See also CA 5-8R; CANR 33; DLB 124;
MTCW

Hochman, Sandra 1936-.......... **CLC 3, 8**
See also CA 5-8R; DLB 5

Hochwaelder, Fritz 1911-1986...... **CLC 36**
See also CA 29-32R; 120; CANR 42;
MTCW

Hochwalder, Fritz
See Hochwaelder, Fritz

Hocking, Mary (Eunice) 1921- ..... **CLC 13**
See also CA 101; CANR 18, 40

Hodgins, Jack 1938-.............. **CLC 23**
See also CA 93-96; DLB 60

Hodgson, William Hope
1877(?)-1918 .... **TCLC 13**
See also CA 111; DLB 70, 153

Hoffman, Alice 1952-............. **CLC 51**
See also CA 77-80; CANR 34; MTCW

Hoffman, Daniel (Gerard)
1923-................. **CLC 6, 13, 23**
See also CA 1-4R; CANR 4; DLB 5

Hoffman, Stanley 1944-........... **CLC 5**
See also CA 77-80

Hoffman, William M(oses) 1939- ... **CLC 40**
See also CA 57-60; CANR 11

Hoffmann, E(rnst) T(heodor) A(madeus)
1776-1822 .... **NCLC 2; SSC 13**
See also DLB 90; SATA 27

Hofmann, Gert 1931-............. **CLC 54**
See also CA 128

Hofmannsthal, Hugo von
1874-1929 .... **TCLC 11; DC 4**
See also CA 106; DLB 81, 118

Hogan, Linda 1947- .... **CLC 73**
See also CA 120; CANR 45; NNAL

Hogarth, Charles
See Creasey, John

Hogg, James 1770-1835.......... **NCLC 4**
See also DLB 93, 116

Holbach, Paul Henri Thiry Baron
1723-1789 .... **LC 14**

Holberg, Ludvig 1684-1754........ **LC 6**

Holden, Ursula 1921-............. **CLC 18**
See also CA 101; CAAS 8; CANR 22

Holderlin, (Johann Christian) Friedrich
1770-1843 .... **NCLC 16; PC 4**

Holdstock, Robert
See Holdstock, Robert P.

Holdstock, Robert P. 1948-........ **CLC 39**
See also CA 131

Holland, Isabelle 1920- .... **CLC 21**
See also AAYA 11; CA 21-24R; CANR 10,
25, 47; JRDA; MAICYA; SATA 8, 70

Holland, Marcus
See Caldwell, (Janet Miriam) Taylor
(Holland)

Hollander, John 1929-...... **CLC 2, 5, 8, 14**
See also CA 1-4R; CANR 1; DLB 5;
SATA 13

Hollander, Paul
See Silverberg, Robert

Holleran, Andrew 1943(?)-......... **CLC 38**
See also CA 144

Hollinghurst, Alan 1954-.......... **CLC 55**
See also CA 114

Hollis, Jim
See Summers, Hollis (Spurgeon, Jr.)

Holmes, John
See Souster, (Holmes) Raymond

Holmes, John Clellon 1926-1988.... **CLC 56**
See also CA 9-12R; 125; CANR 4; DLB 16

Holmes, Oliver Wendell
1809-1894 . . . . NCLC 14
See also CDALB 1640-1865; DLB 1;
SATA 34

Holmes, Raymond
See Souster, (Holmes) Raymond

Holt, Victoria
See Hibbert, Eleanor Alice Burford

Holub, Miroslav 1923- . . . . CLC 4
See also CA 21-24R; CANR 10

Homer c. 8th cent. B.C.- . . . . . CMLC 1; DA

Honig, Edwin 1919- . . . . CLC 33
See also CA 5-8R; CAAS 8; CANR 4, 45;
DLB 5

Hood, Hugh (John Blagdon)
1928- . . . . CLC 15, 28
See also CA 49-52; CAAS 17; CANR 1, 33;
DLB 53

Hood, Thomas 1799-1845. . . . . . . NCLC 16
See also DLB 96

Hooker, (Peter) Jeremy 1941- . . . . . . CLC 43
See also CA 77-80; CANR 22; DLB 40

Hope, A(lec) D(erwent) 1907- . . . . CLC 3, 51
See also CA 21-24R; CANR 33; MTCW

Hope, Brian
See Creasey, John

Hope, Christopher (David Tully)
1944- . . . . CLC 52
See also CA 106; CANR 47; SATA 62

Hopkins, Gerard Manley
1844-1889 . . . . NCLC 17; DA; WLC
See also CDBLB 1890-1914; DLB 35, 57

Hopkins, John (Richard) 1931- . . . . . . CLC 4
See also CA 85-88

Hopkins, Pauline Elizabeth
1859-1930 . . . . TCLC 28; BLC
See also BW 2; CA 141; DLB 50

Hopkinson, Francis 1737-1791 . . . . . . LC 25
See also DLB 31

Hopley-Woolrich, Cornell George 1903-1968
See Woolrich, Cornell
See also CA 13-14; CAP 1

Horatio
See Proust, (Valentin-Louis-George-Eugene-)
Marcel

Horgan, Paul (George Vincent O'Shaughnessy)
1903-1995 . . . . CLC 9, 53
See also CA 13-16R; 147; CANR 9, 35;
DLB 102; DLBY 85; MTCW; SATA 13

Horn, Peter
See Kuttner, Henry

Hornem, Horace Esq.
See Byron, George Gordon (Noel)

Hornung, E(rnest) W(illiam)
1866-1921 . . . . TCLC 59
See also CA 108; DLB 70

Horovitz, Israel (Arthur) 1939- . . . . . CLC 56
See also CA 33-36R; CANR 46; DLB 7

Horvath, Odon von
See Horvath, Oedoen von
See also DLB 85, 124

Horvath, Oedoen von 1901-1938 . . . TCLC 45
See also Horvath, Odon von
See also CA 118

Horwitz, Julius 1920-1986 . . . . CLC 14
See also CA 9-12R; 119; CANR 12

Hospital, Janette Turner 1942- . . . . . CLC 42
See also CA 108; CANR 48

Hostos, E. M. de
See Hostos (y Bonilla), Eugenio Maria de

Hostos, Eugenio M. de
See Hostos (y Bonilla), Eugenio Maria de

Hostos, Eugenio Maria
See Hostos (y Bonilla), Eugenio Maria de

Hostos (y Bonilla), Eugenio Maria de
1839-1903 . . . . TCLC 24
See also CA 123; 131; HW

Houdini
See Lovecraft, H(oward) P(hillips)

Hougan, Carolyn 1943- . . . . CLC 34
See also CA 139

Household, Geoffrey (Edward West)
1900-1988 . . . . CLC 11
See also CA 77-80; 126; DLB 87; SATA 14;
SATA-Obit 59

Housman, A(lfred) E(dward)
1859-1936 . . . . . . TCLC 1, 10; DA; PC 2
See also CA 104; 125; DLB 19; MTCW

Housman, Laurence 1865-1959 . . . . . TCLC 7
See also CA 106; DLB 10; SATA 25

Howard, Elizabeth Jane 1923- . . . CLC 7, 29
See also CA 5-8R; CANR 8

Howard, Maureen 1930- . . . . . CLC 5, 14, 46
See also CA 53-56; CANR 31; DLBY 83;
MTCW

Howard, Richard 1929- . . . . . . CLC 7, 10, 47
See also AITN 1; CA 85-88; CANR 25;
DLB 5

Howard, Robert Ervin 1906-1936 . . . TCLC 8
See also CA 105

Howard, Warren F.
See Pohl, Frederik

Howe, Fanny 1940- . . . . CLC 47
See also CA 117; SATA-Brief 52

Howe, Irving 1920-1993 . . . . CLC 85
See also CA 9-12R; 141; CANR 21;
DLB 67; MTCW

Howe, Julia Ward 1819-1910 . . . . . TCLC 21
See also CA 117; DLB 1

Howe, Susan 1937- . . . . CLC 72
See also DLB 120

Howe, Tina 1937- . . . . CLC 48
See also CA 109

Howell, James 1594(?)-1666 . . . . LC 13
See also DLB 151

Howells, W. D.
See Howells, William Dean

Howells, William D.
See Howells, William Dean

Howells, William Dean
1837-1920 . . . . TCLC 7, 17, 41
See also CA 104; 134; CDALB 1865-1917;
DLB 12, 64, 74, 79

Howes, Barbara 1914- . . . . CLC 15
See also CA 9-12R; CAAS 3; SATA 5

Hrabal, Bohumil 1914- . . . . CLC 13, 67
See also CA 106; CAAS 12

Hsun, Lu . . . . TCLC 3; SSC 20
See also Shu-Jen, Chou

Hubbard, L(afayette) Ron(ald)
1911-1986 . . . . CLC 43
See also CA 77-80; 118; CANR 22

Huch, Ricarda (Octavia)
1864-1947 . . . . TCLC 13
See also CA 111; DLB 66

Huddle, David 1942- . . . . CLC 49
See also CA 57-60; CAAS 20; DLB 130

Hudson, Jeffrey
See Crichton, (John) Michael

Hudson, W(illiam) H(enry)
1841-1922 . . . . TCLC 29
See also CA 115; DLB 98, 153; SATA 35

Hueffer, Ford Madox
See Ford, Ford Madox

Hughart, Barry 1934- . . . . CLC 39
See also CA 137

Hughes, Colin
See Creasey, John

Hughes, David (John) 1930- . . . . CLC 48
See also CA 116; 129; DLB 14

Hughes, (James) Langston
1902-1967 . . . . . CLC 1, 5, 10, 15, 35, 44;
BLC; DA; DC 3; PC 1; SSC 6; WLC
See also AAYA 12; BW 1; CA 1-4R;
25-28R; CANR 1, 34; CDALB 1929-1941;
CLR 17; DLB 4, 7, 48, 51, 86; JRDA;
MAICYA; MTCW; SATA 4, 33

Hughes, Richard (Arthur Warren)
1900-1976 . . . . CLC 1, 11
See also CA 5-8R; 65-68; CANR 4;
DLB 15; MTCW; SATA 8;
SATA-Obit 25

Hughes, Ted
1930- . . . . CLC 2, 4, 9, 14, 37; PC 7
See also CA 1-4R; CANR 1, 33; CLR 3;
DLB 40; MAICYA; MTCW; SATA 49;
SATA-Brief 27

Hugo, Richard F(ranklin)
1923-1982 . . . . CLC 6, 18, 32
See also CA 49-52; 108; CANR 3; DLB 5

Hugo, Victor (Marie)
1802-1885 . . NCLC 3, 10, 21; DA; WLC
See also DLB 119; SATA 47

Huidobro, Vicente
See Huidobro Fernandez, Vicente Garcia

Huidobro Fernandez, Vicente Garcia
1893-1948 . . . . TCLC 31
See also CA 131; HW

Hulme, Keri 1947- . . . . CLC 39
See also CA 125

Hulme, T(homas) E(rnest)
1883-1917 . . . . TCLC 21
See also CA 117; DLB 19

Hume, David 1711-1776. . . . . LC 7
See also DLB 104

Humphrey, William 1924- . . . . CLC 45
See also CA 77-80; DLB 6

Humphreys, Emyr Owen 1919- . . . . . CLC 47
See also CA 5-8R; CANR 3, 24; DLB 15

Humphreys, Josephine 1945- . . . . CLC 34, 57
See also CA 121; 127

Hungerford, Pixie
See Brinsmead, H(esba) F(ay)

Hunt, E(verette) Howard, (Jr.)
1918- .... CLC 3
See also AITN 1; CA 45-48; CANR 2, 47

Hunt, Kyle
See Creasey, John

Hunt, (James Henry) Leigh
1784-1859 .... NCLC 1

Hunt, Marsha 1946- .... CLC 70
See also BW 2; CA 143

Hunt, Violet 1866-1942 .... TCLC 53

Hunter, E. Waldo
See Sturgeon, Theodore (Hamilton)

Hunter, Evan 1926- .... CLC 11, 31
See also CA 5-8R; CANR 5, 38; DLBY 82;
MTCW; SATA 25

Hunter, Kristin (Eggleston) 1931-... CLC 35
See also AITN 1; BW 1; CA 13-16R;
CANR 13; CLR 3; DLB 33; MAICYA;
SAAS 10; SATA 12

Hunter, Mollie 1922- .... CLC 21
See also McIlwraith, Maureen Mollie
Hunter
See also AAYA 13; CANR 37; CLR 25;
JRDA; MAICYA; SAAS 7; SATA 54

Hunter, Robert (?)-1734............. LC 7

Hurston, Zora Neale
1903-1960 .... CLC 7, 30, 61; BLC; DA;
SSC 4
See also BW 1; CA 85-88; DLB 51, 86;
MTCW

Huston, John (Marcellus)
1906-1987 .... CLC 20
See also CA 73-76; 123; CANR 34; DLB 26

Hustvedt, Siri 1955-............... CLC 76
See also CA 137

Hutten, Ulrich von 1488-1523....... LC 16

Huxley, Aldous (Leonard)
1894-1963 ..... CLC 1, 3, 4, 5, 8, 11, 18,
35, 79; DA; WLC
See also AAYA 11; CA 85-88; CANR 44;
CDBLB 1914-1945; DLB 36, 100;
MTCW; SATA 63

Huysmans, Charles Marie Georges
1848-1907
See Huysmans, Joris-Karl
See also CA 104

Huysmans, Joris-Karl.............. TCLC 7
See also Huysmans, Charles Marie Georges
See also DLB 123

Hwang, David Henry
1957- .... CLC 55; DC 4
See also CA 127; 132

Hyde, Anthony 1946-............. CLC 42
See also CA 136

Hyde, Margaret O(ldroyd) 1917- ... CLC 21
See also CA 1-4R; CANR 1, 36; CLR 23;
JRDA; MAICYA; SAAS 8; SATA 1, 42,
76

Hynes, James 1956(?)-............ CLC 65

Ian, Janis 1951- .... CLC 21
See also CA 105

Ibanez, Vicente Blasco
See Blasco Ibanez, Vicente

Ibarguengoitia, Jorge 1928-1983.... CLC 37
See also CA 124; 113; HW

Ibsen, Henrik (Johan)
1828-1906 .... TCLC 2, 8, 16, 37, 52;
DA; DC 2; WLC
See also CA 104; 141

Ibuse Masuji 1898-1993.......... CLC 22
See also CA 127; 141

Ichikawa, Kon 1915-............. CLC 20
See also CA 121

Idle, Eric 1943-................. CLC 21
See also Monty Python
See also CA 116; CANR 35

Ignatow, David 1914-....CLC 4, 7, 14, 40
See also CA 9-12R; CAAS 3; CANR 31;
DLB 5

Ihimaera, Witi 1944- .... CLC 46
See also CA 77-80

Ilf, Ilya........................TCLC 21
See also Fainzilberg, Ilya Arnoldovich

Immermann, Karl (Lebrecht)
1796-1840 .... NCLC 4, 49
See also DLB 133

Inclan, Ramon (Maria) del Valle
See Valle-Inclan, Ramon (Maria) del

Infante, G(uillermo) Cabrera
See Cabrera Infante, G(uillermo)

Ingalls, Rachel (Holmes) 1940-..... CLC 42
See also CA 123; 127

Ingamells, Rex 1913-1955 .... TCLC 35

Inge, William Motter
1913-1973 .... CLC 1, 8, 19
See also CA 9-12R; CDALB 1941-1968;
DLB 7; MTCW

Ingelow, Jean 1820-1897 .... NCLC 39
See also DLB 35, SATA 33

Ingram, Willis J.
See Harris, Mark

Innaurato, Albert (F.) 1948(?)- .. CLC 21, 60
See also CA 115, 122

Innes, Michael
See Stewart, J(ohn) I(nnes) M(ackintosh)

Ionesco, Eugene
1909-1994 .... CLC 1, 4, 6, 9, 11, 15, 41,
86; DA; WLC
See also CA 9-12R; 144; MTCW; SATA 7;
SATA-Obit 79

Iqbal, Muhammad 1873-1938 ..... TCLC 28

Ireland, Patrick
See O'Doherty, Brian

Iron, Ralph
See Schreiner, Olive (Emilie Albertina)

Irving, John (Winslow)
1942- .... CLC 13, 23, 38
See also AAYA 8; BEST 89:3; CA 25-28R;
CANR 28; DLB 6; DLBY 82; MTCW

Irving, Washington
1783-1859 .... NCLC 2, 19; DA; SSC 2;
WLC
See also CDALB 1640-1865; DLB 3, 11, 30,
59, 73, 74; YABC 2

Irwin, P. K.
See Page, P(atricia) K(athleen)

Isaacs, Susan 1943- .... CLC 32
See also BEST 89:1; CA 89-92; CANR 20,
41; MTCW

Isherwood, Christopher (William Bradshaw)
1904-1986 .... CLC 1, 9, 11, 14, 44
See also CA 13-16R; 117; CANR 35;
DLB 15; DLBY 86; MTCW

Ishiguro, Kazuo 1954- ...... CLC 27, 56, 59
See also BEST 90:2; CA 120; MTCW

Ishikawa Takuboku
1886(?)-1912 .... TCLC 15; PC 10
See also CA 113

Iskander, Fazil 1929-............. CLC 47
See also CA 102

Ivan IV 1530-1584 .... LC 17

Ivanov, Vyacheslav Ivanovich
1866-1949 .... TCLC 33
See also CA 122

Ivask, Ivar Vidrik 1927-1992....... CLC 14
See also CA 37-40R; 139; CANR 24

Jackson, Daniel
See Wingrove, David (John)

Jackson, Jesse 1908-1983 .... CLC 12
See also BW 1; CA 25-28R; 109; CANR 27;
CLR 28; MAICYA; SATA 2, 29;
SATA-Obit 48

Jackson, Laura (Riding) 1901-1991
See Riding, Laura
See also CA 65-68; 135; CANR 28; DLB 48

Jackson, Sam
See Trumbo, Dalton

Jackson, Sara
See Wingrove, David (John)

Jackson, Shirley
1919-1965 .... CLC 11, 60, 87; DA;
SSC 9; WLC
See also AAYA 9; CA 1-4R; 25-28R;
CANR 4; CDALB 1941-1968; DLB 6;
SATA 2

Jacob, (Cyprien-)Max 1876-1944 ... TCLC 6
See also CA 104

Jacobs, Jim 1942-................. CLC 12
See also CA 97-100

Jacobs, W(illiam) W(ymark)
1863-1943 ....TCLC 22
See also CA 121; DLB 135

Jacobsen, Jens Peter 1847-1885 .. NCLC 34

Jacobsen, Josephine 1908-......... CLC 48
See also CA 33-36R; CAAS 18; CANR 23,
48

Jacobson, Dan 1929- .... CLC 4, 14
See also CA 1-4R; CANR 2, 25; DLB 14;
MTCW

Jacqueline
See Carpentier (y Valmont), Alejo

Jagger, Mick 1944-............... CLC 17

Jakes, John (William) 1932-........ CLC 29
See also BEST 89:4; CA 57-60; CANR 10,
43; DLBY 83; MTCW; SATA 62

James, Andrew
See Kirkup, James

James, C(yril) L(ionel) R(obert)
1901-1989 . . . . **CLC 33**
See also BW 2; CA 117; 125; 128; DLB 125;
MTCW

James, Daniel (Lewis) 1911-1988
See Santiago, Danny
See also CA 125

James, Dynely
See Mayne, William (James Carter)

James, Henry
1843-1916 . . . . . . **TCLC 2, 11, 24, 40, 47;**
DA; SSC 8; WLC
See also CA 104; 132; CDALB 1865-1917;
DLB 12, 71, 74; MTCW

James, M. R.
See James, Montague (Rhodes)

James, Montague (Rhodes)
1862-1936 . . . . **TCLC 6; SSC 16**
See also CA 104

James, P. D. . . . . **CLC 18, 46**
See also White, Phyllis Dorothy James
See also BEST 90:2; CDBLB 1960 to
Present; DLB 87

James, Philip
See Moorcock, Michael (John)

James, William 1842-1910 . . . . . **TCLC 15, 32**
See also CA 109

James I 1394-1437 . . . . **LC 20**

Jameson, Anna 1794-1860 . . . . **NCLC 43**
See also DLB 99

Jami, Nur al-Din 'Abd al-Rahman
1414-1492 . . . . **LC 9**

Jandl, Ernst 1925- . . . . **CLC 34**

Janowitz, Tama 1957- . . . . **CLC 43**
See also CA 106

Jarrell, Randall
1914-1965 . . . . **CLC 1, 2, 6, 9, 13, 49**
See also CA 5-8R; 25-28R; CABS 2;
CANR 6, 34; CDALB 1941-1968; CLR 6;
DLB 48, 52; MAICYA; MTCW; SATA 7

Jarry, Alfred
1873-1907 . . . . **TCLC 2, 14; SSC 20**
See also CA 104

Jarvis, E. K.
See Bloch, Robert (Albert); Ellison, Harlan
(Jay); Silverberg, Robert

Jeake, Samuel, Jr.
See Aiken, Conrad (Potter)

Jean Paul 1763-1825 . . . . **NCLC 7**

Jefferies, (John) Richard
1848-1887 . . . . **NCLC 47**
See also DLB 98, 141; SATA 16

Jeffers, (John) Robinson
1887-1962 . . . . **CLC 2, 3, 11, 15, 54; DA;**
WLC
See also CA 85-88; CANR 35;
CDALB 1917-1929; DLB 45; MTCW

Jefferson, Janet
See Mencken, H(enry) L(ouis)

Jefferson, Thomas 1743-1826 . . . . **NCLC 11**
See also CDALB 1640-1865; DLB 31

Jeffrey, Francis 1773-1850 . . . . **NCLC 33**
See also DLB 107

Jelakowitch, Ivan
See Heijermans, Herman

Jellicoe, (Patricia) Ann 1927- . . . . . . **CLC 27**
See also CA 85-88; DLB 13

Jen, Gish . . . . **CLC 70**
See also Jen, Lillian

Jen, Lillian 1956(?)-
See Jen, Gish
See also CA 135

Jenkins, (John) Robin 1912- . . . . **CLC 52**
See also CA 1-4R; CANR 1; DLB 14

Jennings, Elizabeth (Joan)
1926- . . . . **CLC 5, 14**
See also CA 61-64; CAAS 5; CANR 8, 39;
DLB 27; MTCW; SATA 66

Jennings, Waylon 1937- . . . . **CLC 21**

Jensen, Johannes V. 1873-1950 . . . . **TCLC 41**

Jensen, Laura (Linnea) 1948- . . . . . . **CLC 37**
See also CA 103

Jerome, Jerome K(lapka)
1859-1927 . . . . **TCLC 23**
See also CA 119; DLB 10, 34, 135

Jerrold, Douglas William
1803-1857 . . . . **NCLC 2**

Jewett, (Theodora) Sarah Orne
1849-1909 . . . . **TCLC 1, 22; SSC 6**
See also CA 108; 127; DLB 12, 74;
SATA 15

Jewsbury, Geraldine (Endsor)
1812-1880 . . . . **NCLC 22**
See also DLB 21

Jhabvala, Ruth Prawer
1927- . . . . **CLC 4, 8, 29**
See also CA 1-4R; CANR 2, 29; DLB 139;
MTCW

Jiles, Paulette 1943- . . . . **CLC 13, 58**
See also CA 101

Jimenez (Mantecon), Juan Ramon
1881-1958 . . . . **TCLC 4; HLC; PC 7**
See also CA 104; 131; DLB 134; HW;
MTCW

Jimenez, Ramon
See Jimenez (Mantecon), Juan Ramon

Jimenez Mantecon, Juan
See Jimenez (Mantecon), Juan Ramon

Joel, Billy . . . . **CLC 26**
See also Joel, William Martin

Joel, William Martin 1949-
See Joel, Billy
See also CA 108

John of the Cross, St. 1542-1591 . . . . **LC 18**

Johnson, B(ryan) S(tanley William)
1933-1973 . . . . **CLC 6, 9**
See also CA 9-12R; 53-56; CANR 9;
DLB 14, 40

Johnson, Benj. F. of Boo
See Riley, James Whitcomb

Johnson, Benjamin F. of Boo
See Riley, James Whitcomb

Johnson, Charles (Richard)
1948- . . . . **CLC 7, 51, 65; BLC**
See also BW 2; CA 116; CAAS 18;
CANR 42; DLB 33

Johnson, Denis 1949- . . . . **CLC 52**
See also CA 117; 121; DLB 120

Johnson, Diane 1934- . . . . **CLC 5, 13, 48**
See also CA 41-44R; CANR 17, 40;
DLBY 80; MTCW

Johnson, Eyvind (Olof Verner)
1900-1976 . . . . **CLC 14**
See also CA 73-76; 69-72; CANR 34

Johnson, J. R.
See James, C(yril) L(ionel) R(obert)

Johnson, James Weldon
1871-1938 . . . . **TCLC 3, 19; BLC**
See also BW 1; CA 104; 125;
CDALB 1917-1929; CLR 32; DLB 51;
MTCW; SATA 31

Johnson, Joyce 1935- . . . . **CLC 58**
See also CA 125; 129

Johnson, Lionel (Pigot)
1867-1902 . . . . **TCLC 19**
See also CA 117; DLB 19

Johnson, Mel
See Malzberg, Barry N(athaniel)

Johnson, Pamela Hansford
1912-1981 . . . . **CLC 1, 7, 27**
See also CA 1-4R; 104; CANR 2, 28;
DLB 15; MTCW

Johnson, Samuel
1709-1784 . . . . **LC 15; DA; WLC**
See also CDBLB 1660-1789; DLB 39, 95,
104, 142

Johnson, Uwe
1934-1984 . . . . **CLC 5, 10, 15, 40**
See also CA 1-4R; 112; CANR 1, 39;
DLB 75; MTCW

Johnston, George (Benson) 1913- . . . **CLC 51**
See also CA 1-4R; CANR 5, 20; DLB 88

Johnston, Jennifer 1930- . . . . **CLC 7**
See also CA 85-88; DLB 14

Jolley, (Monica) Elizabeth
1923- . . . . **CLC 46; SSC 19**
See also CA 127; CAAS 13

Jones, Arthur Llewellyn 1863-1947
See Machen, Arthur
See also CA 104

Jones, D(ouglas) G(ordon) 1929- . . . . **CLC 10**
See also CA 29-32R; CANR 13; DLB 53

Jones, David (Michael)
1895-1974 . . . . **CLC 2, 4, 7, 13, 42**
See also CA 9-12R; 53-56; CANR 28;
CDBLB 1945-1960; DLB 20, 100; MTCW

Jones, David Robert 1947-
See Bowie, David
See also CA 103

Jones, Diana Wynne 1934- . . . . **CLC 26**
See also AAYA 12; CA 49-52; CANR 4,
26; CLR 23; JRDA; MAICYA; SAAS 7;
SATA 9, 70

Jones, Edward P. 1950- . . . . **CLC 76**
See also BW 2; CA 142

Jones, Gayl 1949- . . . . **CLC 6, 9; BLC**
See also BW 2; CA 77-80; CANR 27;
DLB 33; MTCW

Jones, James 1921-1977 . . . . **CLC 1, 3, 10, 39**
See also AITN 1, 2; CA 1-4R; 69-72;
CANR 6; DLB 2, 143; MTCW

Keene, Donald 1922- . . . . CLC 34
See also CA 1-4R; CANR 5

Keillor, Garrison . . . . CLC 40
See also Keillor, Gary (Edward)
See also AAYA 2; BEST 89:3; DLBY 87;
SATA 58

Keillor, Gary (Edward) 1942-
See Keillor, Garrison
See also CA 111; 117; CANR 36; MTCW

Keith, Michael
See Hubbard, L(afayette) Ron(ald)

Keller, Gottfried 1819-1890 . . . . . . NCLC 2
See also DLB 129

Kellerman, Jonathan 1949- . . . . CLC 44
See also BEST 90:1; CA 106; CANR 29

Kelley, William Melvin 1937- . . . . . . CLC 22
See also BW 1; CA 77-80; CANR 27;
DLB 33

Kellogg, Marjorie 1922- . . . . CLC 2
See also CA 81-84

Kellow, Kathleen
See Hibbert, Eleanor Alice Burford

Kelly, M(ilton) T(erry) 1947- . . . . . . CLC 55
See also CA 97-100; CANR 19, 43

Kelman, James 1946- . . . . CLC 58, 86

Kemal, Yashar 1923- . . . . CLC 14, 29
See also CA 89-92; CANR 44

Kemble, Fanny 1809-1893 . . . . NCLC 18
See also DLB 32

Kemelman, Harry 1908- . . . . CLC 2
See also AITN 1; CA 9-12R; CANR 6;
DLB 28

Kempe, Margery 1373(?)-1440(?) . . . . . LC 6
See also DLB 146

Kempis, Thomas a 1380-1471 . . . . LC 11

Kendall, Henry 1839-1882 . . . . . . NCLC 12

Keneally, Thomas (Michael)
1935- . . . . . . CLC 5, 8, 10, 14, 19, 27, 43
See also CA 85-88; CANR 10; MTCW

Kennedy, Adrienne (Lita)
1931- . . . . CLC 66; BLC; DC 5
See also BW 2; CA 103; CAAS 20; CABS 3;
CANR 26; DLB 38

Kennedy, John Pendleton
1795-1870 . . . . NCLC 2
See also DLB 3

Kennedy, Joseph Charles 1929-
See Kennedy, X. J.
See also CA 1-4R; CANR 4, 30, 40;
SATA 14

Kennedy, William 1928- . . . CLC 6, 28, 34, 53
See also AAYA 1; CA 85-88; CANR 14,
31; DLB 143; DLBY 85; MTCW;
SATA 57

Kennedy, X. J. . . . . CLC 8, 42
See also Kennedy, Joseph Charles
See also CAAS 9; CLR 27; DLB 5

Kenny, Maurice (Francis) 1929- . . . . CLC 87
See also CA 144; NNAL

Kent, Kelvin
See Kuttner, Henry

Kenton, Maxwell
See Southern, Terry

Kenyon, Robert O.
See Kuttner, Henry

Kerouac, Jack . . . . . CLC 1, 2, 3, 5, 14, 29, 61
See also Kerouac, Jean-Louis Lebris de
See also CDALB 1941-1968; DLB 2, 16;
DLBD 3

Kerouac, Jean-Louis Lebris de 1922-1969
See Kerouac, Jack
See also AITN 1; CA 5-8R; 25-28R;
CANR 26; DA; MTCW; WLC

Kerr, Jean 1923- . . . . CLC 22
See also CA 5-8R; CANR 7

Kerr, M. E. . . . . CLC 12, 35
See also Meaker, Marijane (Agnes)
See also AAYA 2; CLR 29; SAAS 1

Kerr, Robert . . . . CLC 55

Kerrigan, (Thomas) Anthony
1918- . . . . CLC 4, 6
See also CA 49-52; CAAS 11; CANR 4

Kerry, Lois
See Duncan, Lois

Kesey, Ken (Elton)
1935- . . . . . . CLC 1, 3, 6, 11, 46, 64; DA;
WLC
See also CA 1-4R; CANR 22, 38;
CDALB 1968-1988; DLB 2, 16; MTCW;
SATA 66

Kesselring, Joseph (Otto)
1902-1967 . . . . CLC 45

Kessler, Jascha (Frederick) 1929- . . . . CLC 4
See also CA 17-20R; CANR 8, 48

Kettelkamp, Larry (Dale) 1933- . . . . CLC 12
See also CA 29-32R; CANR 16; SAAS 3;
SATA 2

Keyber, Conny
See Fielding, Henry

Keyes, Daniel 1927- . . . . CLC 80; DA
See also CA 17-20R; CANR 10, 26;
SATA 37

Khanshendel, Chiron
See Rose, Wendy

Khayyam, Omar
1048-1131 . . . . CMLC 11; PC 8

Kherdian, David 1931- . . . . CLC 6, 9
See also CA 21-24R; CAAS 2; CANR 39;
CLR 24; JRDA; MAICYA; SATA 16, 74

Khlebnikov, Velimir . . . . TCLC 20
See also Khlebnikov, Viktor Vladimirovich

Khlebnikov, Viktor Vladimirovich 1885-1922
See Khlebnikov, Velimir
See also CA 117

Khodasevich, Vladislav (Felitsianovich)
1886-1939 . . . . TCLC 15
See also CA 115

Kielland, Alexander Lange
1849-1906 . . . . TCLC 5
See also CA 104

Kiely, Benedict 1919- . . . . CLC 23, 43
See also CA 1-4R; CANR 2; DLB 15

Kienzle, William X(avier) 1928- . . . . CLC 25
See also CA 93-96; CAAS 1; CANR 9, 31;
MTCW

Kierkegaard, Soren 1813-1855 . . . . NCLC 34

Killens, John Oliver 1916-1987 . . . . . CLC 10
See also BW 2; CA 77-80; 123; CAAS 2;
CANR 26; DLB 33

Killigrew, Anne 1660-1685 . . . . LC 4
See also DLB 131

Kim
See Simenon, Georges (Jacques Christian)

Kincaid, Jamaica 1949- . . . CLC 43, 68; BLC
See also AAYA 13; BW 2; CA 125;
CANR 47

King, Francis (Henry) 1923- . . . . . CLC 8, 53
See also CA 1-4R; CANR 1, 33; DLB 15,
139; MTCW

King, Martin Luther, Jr.
1929-1968 . . . . CLC 83; BLC; DA
See also BW 2; CA 25-28; CANR 27, 44;
CAP 2; MTCW; SATA 14

King, Stephen (Edwin)
1947- . . . . . . CLC 12, 26, 37, 61; SSC 17
See also AAYA 1; BEST 90:1; CA 61-64;
CANR 1, 30; DLB 143; DLBY 80;
JRDA; MTCW; SATA 9, 55

King, Steve
See King, Stephen (Edwin)

King, Thomas 1943- . . . . CLC 89
See also CA 144; NNAL

Kingman, Lee . . . . CLC 17
See also Natti, (Mary) Lee
See also SAAS 3; SATA 1, 67

Kingsley, Charles 1819-1875 . . . . . NCLC 35
See also DLB 21, 32; YABC 2

Kingsley, Sidney 1906-1995 . . . . CLC 44
See also CA 85-88; 147; DLB 7

Kingsolver, Barbara 1955- . . . . . . CLC 55, 81
See also CA 129; 134

Kingston, Maxine (Ting Ting) Hong
1940- . . . . CLC 12, 19, 58
See also AAYA 8; CA 69-72; CANR 13,
38; DLBY 80; MTCW; SATA 53

Kinnell, Galway
1927- . . . . CLC 1, 2, 3, 5, 13, 29
See also CA 9-12R; CANR 10, 34; DLB 5;
DLBY 87; MTCW

Kinsella, Thomas 1928- . . . . CLC 4, 19
See also CA 17-20R; CANR 15; DLB 27;
MTCW

Kinsella, W(illiam) P(atrick)
1935- . . . . CLC 27, 43
See also AAYA 7; CA 97-100; CAAS 7;
CANR 21, 35; MTCW

Kipling, (Joseph) Rudyard
1865-1936 . . . . . . TCLC 8, 17; DA; PC 3;
SSC 5; WLC
See also CA 105; 120; CANR 33;
CDBLB 1890-1914; DLB 19, 34, 141;
MAICYA; MTCW; YABC 2

Kirkup, James 1918- . . . . CLC 1
See also CA 1-4R; CAAS 4; CANR 2;
DLB 27; SATA 12

Kirkwood, James 1930(?)-1989 . . . . . . CLC 9
See also AITN 2; CA 1-4R; 128; CANR 6,
40

Kis, Danilo 1935-1989 . . . . CLC 57
See also CA 109; 118; 129; MTCW

Kivi, Aleksis 1834-1872 . . . . NCLC 30

Kizer, Carolyn (Ashley)
1925- .... CLC 15, 39, 80
See also CA 65-68; CAAS 5; CANR 24;
DLB 5

Klabund 1890-1928 .... TCLC 44
See also DLB 66

Klappert, Peter 1942- .... CLC 57
See also CA 33-36R; DLB 5

Klein, A(braham) M(oses)
1909-1972 .... CLC 19
See also CA 101; 37-40R; DLB 68

Klein, Norma 1938-1989 .... CLC 30
See also AAYA 2; CA 41-44R; 128;
CANR 15, 37; CLR 2, 19; JRDA;
MAICYA; SAAS 1; SATA 7, 57

Klein, T(heodore) E(ibon) D(onald)
1947- .... CLC 34
See also CA 119; CANR 44

Kleist, Heinrich von
1777-1811 .... NCLC 2, 37
See also DLB 90

Klima, Ivan 1931- .... CLC 56
See also CA 25-28R; CANR 17

Klimentov, Andrei Platonovich 1899-1951
See Platonov, Andrei
See also CA 108

Klinger, Friedrich Maximilian von
1752-1831 .... NCLC 1
See also DLB 94

Klopstock, Friedrich Gottlieb
1724-1803 .... NCLC 11
See also DLB 97

Knebel, Fletcher 1911-1993 .... CLC 14
See also AITN 1; CA 1-4R; 140; CAAS 3;
CANR 1, 36; SATA 36; SATA-Obit 75

Knickerbocker, Diedrich
See Irving, Washington

Knight, Etheridge
1931-1991 .... CLC 40; BLC
See also BW 1; CA 21-24R; 133; CANR 23;
DLB 41

Knight, Sarah Kemble 1666-1727 ..... LC 7
See also DLB 24

Knister, Raymond 1899-1932 ...... TCLC 56
See also DLB 68

Knowles, John
1926- .... CLC 1, 4, 10, 26; DA
See also AAYA 10; CA 17-20R; CANR 40;
CDALB 1968-1988; DLB 6; MTCW;
SATA 8

Knox, Calvin M.
See Silverberg, Robert

Knye, Cassandra
See Disch, Thomas M(ichael)

Koch, C(hristopher) J(ohn) 1932- ... CLC 42
See also CA 127

Koch, Christopher
See Koch, C(hristopher) J(ohn)

Koch, Kenneth 1925- .... CLC 5, 8, 44
See also CA 1-4R; CANR 6, 36; DLB 5;
SATA 65

Kochanowski, Jan 1530-1584 .... LC 10

Kock, Charles Paul de
1794-1871 .... NCLC 16

Koda Shigeyuki 1867-1947
See Rohan, Koda
See also CA 121

Koestler, Arthur
1905-1983 .... CLC 1, 3, 6, 8, 15, 33
See also CA 1-4R; 109; CANR 1, 33;
CDBLB 1945-1960; DLBY 83; MTCW

Kogawa, Joy Nozomi 1935- .... CLC 78
See also CA 101; CANR 19

Kohout, Pavel 1928- .... CLC 13
See also CA 45-48; CANR 3

Koizumi, Yakumo
See Hearn, (Patricio) Lafcadio (Tessima
Carlos)

Kolmar, Gertrud 1894-1943 ...... TCLC 40

Komunyakaa, Yusef 1947- .... CLC 86
See also CA 147; DLB 120

Konrad, George
See Konrad, Gyoergy

Konrad, Gyoergy 1933- ...... CLC 4, 10, 73
See also CA 85-88

Konwicki, Tadeusz 1926- ..... CLC 8, 28, 54
See also CA 101; CAAS 9; CANR 39;
MTCW

Koontz, Dean R(ay) 1945 .... CLC 78
See also AAYA 9; BEST 89:3, 90:2;
CA 108; CANR 19, 36; MTCW

Kopit, Arthur (Lee) 1937- .... CLC 1, 18, 33
See also AITN 1; CA 81-84; CABS 3;
DLB 7; MTCW

Kops, Bernard 1926- .... CLC 4
See also CA 5-8R; DLB 13

Kornbluth, C(yril) M. 1923-1958 .... TCLC 8
See also CA 105; DLB 8

Korolenko, V. G.
See Korolenko, Vladimir Galaktionovich

Korolenko, Vladimir
See Korolenko, Vladimir Galaktionovich

Korolenko, Vladimir G.
See Korolenko, Vladimir Galaktionovich

Korolenko, Vladimir Galaktionovich
1853-1921 .... TCLC 22
See also CA 121

Kosinski, Jerzy (Nikodem)
1933-1991 .... CLC 1, 2, 3, 6, 10, 15, 53,
70
See also CA 17-20R; 134; CANR 9, 46;
DLB 2; DLBY 82; MTCW

Kostelanetz, Richard (Cory) 1940- .. CLC 28
See also CA 13-16R; CAAS 8; CANR 38

Kostrowitzki, Wilhelm Apollinaris de
1880-1918
See Apollinaire, Guillaume
See also CA 104

Kotlowitz, Robert 1924- .... CLC 4
See also CA 33-36R; CANR 36

Kotzebue, August (Friedrich Ferdinand) von
1761-1819 .... NCLC 25
See also DLB 94

Kotzwinkle, William 1938- ... CLC 5, 14, 35
See also CA 45-48; CANR 3, 44; CLR 6;
MAICYA; SATA 24, 70

Kozol, Jonathan 1936- .... CLC 17
See also CA 61-64; CANR 16, 45

Kozoll, Michael 1940(?)- .... CLC 35

Kramer, Kathryn 19(?)- .... CLC 34

Kramer, Larry 1935- .... CLC 42
See also CA 124; 126

Krasicki, Ignacy 1735-1801 .... NCLC 8

Krasinski, Zygmunt 1812-1859 .... NCLC 4

Kraus, Karl 1874-1936 .... TCLC 5
See also CA 104; DLB 118

Kreve (Mickevicius), Vincas
1882-1954 .... TCLC 27

Kristeva, Julia 1941- .... CLC 77

Kristofferson, Kris 1936- .... CLC 26
See also CA 104

Krizanc, John 1956- .... CLC 57

Krleza, Miroslav 1893-1981 .... CLC 8
See also CA 97-100; 105; DLB 147

Kroetsch, Robert 1927- ...... CLC 5, 23, 57
See also CA 17-20R; CANR 8, 38; DLB 53;
MTCW

Kroetz, Franz
See Kroetz, Franz Xaver

Kroetz, Franz Xaver 1946- .... CLC 41
See also CA 130

Kroker, Arthur 1945- .... CLC 77

Kropotkin, Peter (Aleksieevich)
1842-1921 .... TCLC 36
See also CA 119

Krotkov, Yuri 1917- .... CLC 19
See also CA 102

Krumb
See Crumb, R(obert)

Krumgold, Joseph (Quincy)
1908-1980 .... CLC 12
See also CA 9-12R; 101; CANR 7;
MAICYA; SATA 1, 48; SATA-Obit 23

Krumwitz
See Crumb, R(obert)

Krutch, Joseph Wood 1893-1970 .... CLC 24
See also CA 1-4R; 25-28R; CANR 4;
DLB 63

Krutzch, Gus
See Eliot, T(homas) S(tearns)

Krylov, Ivan Andreevich
1768(?)-1844 .... NCLC 1
See also DLB 150

Kubin, Alfred 1877-1959 .... TCLC 23
See also CA 112; DLB 81

Kubrick, Stanley 1928- .... CLC 16
See also CA 81-84; CANR 33; DLB 26

Kumin, Maxine (Winokur)
1925- .... CLC 5, 13, 28
See also AITN 2; CA 1-4R; CAAS 8;
CANR 1, 21; DLB 5; MTCW; SATA 12

Kundera, Milan
1929- .... CLC 4, 9, 19, 32, 68
See also AAYA 2; CA 85-88; CANR 19;
MTCW

Kunene, Mazisi (Raymond) 1930- ... CLC 85
See also BW 1; CA 125; DLB 117

Kunitz, Stanley (Jasspon)
1905- .... CLC 6, 11, 14
See also CA 41-44R; CANR 26; DLB 48;
MTCW

Lavin, Mary 1912- ...... **CLC 4, 18; SSC 4**
See also CA 9-12R; CANR 33; DLB 15;
MTCW

Lavond, Paul Dennis
See Kornbluth, C(yril) M.; Pohl, Frederik

Lawler, Raymond Evenor 1922- .... **CLC 58**
See also CA 103

Lawrence, D(avid) H(erbert Richards)
1885-1930 .... **TCLC 2, 9, 16, 33, 48;**
DA; SSC 4, 19; WLC
See also CA 104; 121; CDBLB 1914-1945;
DLB 10, 19, 36, 98; MTCW

Lawrence, T(homas) E(dward)
1888-1935 .... **TCLC 18**
See also Dale, Colin
See also CA 115

Lawrence of Arabia
See Lawrence, T(homas) E(dward)

Lawson, Henry (Archibald Hertzberg)
1867-1922 .... **TCLC 27; SSC 18**
See also CA 120

Lawton, Dennis
See Faust, Frederick (Schiller)

Laxness, Halldor .... **CLC 25**
See also Gudjonsson, Halldor Kiljan

Layamon fl. c. 1200- .... **CMLC 10**
See also DLB 146

Laye, Camara 1928-1980 ... **CLC 4, 38; BLC**
See also BW 1; CA 85-88; 97-100;
CANR 25; MTCW

Layton, Irving (Peter) 1912- ..... **CLC 2, 15**
See also CA 1-4R; CANR 2, 33, 43;
DLB 88; MTCW

Lazarus, Emma 1849-1887 .... **NCLC 8**

Lazarus, Felix
See Cable, George Washington

Lazarus, Henry
See Slavitt, David R(ytman)

Lea, Joan
See Neufeld, John (Arthur)

Leacock, Stephen (Butler)
1869-1944 .... **TCLC 2**
See also CA 104; 141; DLB 92

Lear, Edward 1812-1888 .... **NCLC 3**
See also CLR 1; DLB 32; MAICYA;
SATA 18

Lear, Norman (Milton) 1922- ...... **CLC 12**
See also CA 73-76

Leavis, F(rank) R(aymond)
1895-1978 .... **CLC 24**
See also CA 21-24R; 77-80; CANR 44;
MTCW

Leavitt, David 1961- .... **CLC 34**
See also CA 116; 122; DLB 130

Leblanc, Maurice (Marie Emile)
1864-1941 .... **TCLC 49**
See also CA 110

Lebowitz, Fran(ces Ann)
1951(?)- .... **CLC 11, 36**
See also CA 81-84; CANR 14; MTCW

Lebrecht, Peter
See Tieck, (Johann) Ludwig

le Carre, John .... **CLC 3, 5, 9, 15, 28**
See also Cornwell, David (John Moore)
See also BEST 89:4; CDBLB 1960 to
Present; DLB 87

Le Clezio, J(ean) M(arie) G(ustave)
1940- .... **CLC 31**
See also CA 116; 128; DLB 83

Leconte de Lisle, Charles-Marie-Rene
1818-1894 .... **NCLC 29**

Le Coq, Monsieur
See Simenon, Georges (Jacques Christian)

Leduc, Violette 1907-1972 .... **CLC 22**
See also CA 13-14; 33-36R; CAP 1

Ledwidge, Francis 1887(?)-1917 ... **TCLC 23**
See also CA 123; DLB 20

Lee, Andrea 1953- .... **CLC 36; BLC**
See also BW 1; CA 125

Lee, Andrew
See Auchincloss, Louis (Stanton)

Lee, Don L. .... **CLC 2**
See also Madhubuti, Haki R.

Lee, George W(ashington)
1894-1976 .... **CLC 52; BLC**
See also BW 1; CA 125; DLB 51

Lee, (Nelle) Harper
1926- .... **CLC 12, 60; DA; WLC**
See also AAYA 13; CA 13-16R;
CDALB 1941-1968; DLB 6; MTCW;
SATA 11

Lee, Helen Elaine 1959(?)- .... **CLC 86**

Lee, Julian
See Latham, Jean Lee

Lee, Larry
See Lee, Lawrence

Lee, Lawrence 1941-1990 .... **CLC 34**
See also CA 131, CANR 43

Lee, Manfred B(ennington)
1905-1971 .... **CLC 11**
See also Queen, Ellery
See also CA 1-4R; 29-32R; CANR 2;
DLB 137

Lee, Stan 1922- .... **CLC 17**
See also AAYA 5; CA 108; 111

Lee, Tanith 1947- .... **CLC 46**
See also CA 37-40R; SATA 8

Lee, Vernon .... **TCLC 5**
See also Paget, Violet
See also DLB 57, 153

Lee, William
See Burroughs, William S(eward)

Lee, Willy
See Burroughs, William S(eward)

Lee-Hamilton, Eugene (Jacob)
1845-1907 .... **TCLC 22**
See also CA 117

Leet, Judith 1935- .... **CLC 11**

Le Fanu, Joseph Sheridan
1814-1873 .... **NCLC 9; SSC 14**
See also DLB 21, 70

Leffland, Ella 1931- .... **CLC 19**
See also CA 29-32R; CANR 35; DLBY 84;
SATA 65

Leger, Alexis
See Leger, (Marie-Rene Auguste) Alexis
Saint-Leger

Leger, (Marie-Rene Auguste) Alexis
Saint-Leger 1887-1975 .... **CLC 11**
See also Perse, St.-John
See also CA 13-16R; 61-64; CANR 43;
MTCW

Leger, Saintleger
See Leger, (Marie-Rene Auguste) Alexis
Saint-Leger

Le Guin, Ursula K(roeber)
1929- .... **CLC 8, 13, 22, 45, 71; SSC 12**
See also AAYA 9; AITN 1; CA 21-24R;
CANR 9, 32; CDALB 1968-1988; CLR 3,
28; DLB 8, 52; JRDA; MAICYA;
MTCW; SATA 4, 52

Lehmann, Rosamond (Nina)
1901-1990 .... **CLC 5**
See also CA 77-80; 131; CANR 8; DLB 15

Leiber, Fritz (Reuter, Jr.)
1910-1992 .... **CLC 25**
See also CA 45-48; 139; CANR 2, 40;
DLB 8; MTCW; SATA 45;
SATA-Obit 73

Leimbach, Martha 1963-
See Leimbach, Marti
See also CA 130

Leimbach, Marti .... **CLC 65**
See also Leimbach, Martha

Leino, Eino .... **TCLC 24**
See also Loennbohm, Armas Eino Leopold

Leiris, Michel (Julien) 1901-1990 ... **CLC 61**
See also CA 119; 128; 132

Leithauser, Brad 1953- .... **CLC 27**
See also CA 107; CANR 27; DLB 120

Lelchuk, Alan 1938- .... **CLC 5**
See also CA 45-48; CAAS 20; CANR 1

Lem, Stanislaw 1921- .... **CLC 8, 15, 40**
See also CA 105; CAAS 1; CANR 32;
MTCW

Lemann, Nancy 1956- .... **CLC 39**
See also CA 118; 136

Lemonnier, (Antoine Louis) Camille
1844-1913 .... **TCLC 22**
See also CA 121

Lenau, Nikolaus 1802-1850 ...... **NCLC 16**

L'Engle, Madeleine (Camp Franklin)
1918- .... **CLC 12**
See also AAYA 1; AITN 2; CA 1-4R;
CANR 3, 21, 39; CLR 1, 14; DLB 52;
JRDA; MAICYA; MTCW; SAAS 15;
SATA 1, 27, 75

Lengyel, Jozsef 1896-1975 .... **CLC 7**
See also CA 85-88; 57-60

Lennon, John (Ono)
1940-1980 .... **CLC 12, 35**
See also CA 102

Lennox, Charlotte Ramsay
1729(?)-1804 .... **NCLC 23**
See also DLB 39

Lentricchia, Frank (Jr.) 1940- ...... **CLC 34**
See also CA 25-28R; CANR 19

Lenz, Siegfried 1926- .... **CLC 27**
See also CA 89-92; DLB 75

Lynch Davis, B.
See Bioy Casares, Adolfo; Borges, Jorge
Luis

Lyndsay, Sir David 1490-1555 ...... **LC 20**

Lynn, Kenneth S(chuyler) 1923- .... **CLC 50**
See also CA 1-4R; CANR 3, 27

Lynx
See West, Rebecca

Lyons, Marcus
See Blish, James (Benjamin)

Lyre, Pinchbeck
See Sassoon, Siegfried (Lorraine)

Lytle, Andrew (Nelson) 1902- ...... **CLC 22**
See also CA 9-12R; DLB 6

Lyttelton, George 1709-1773 .... **LC 10**

Maas, Peter 1929- .... **CLC 29**
See also CA 93-96

Macaulay, Rose 1881-1958 ..... **TCLC 7, 44**
See also CA 104; DLB 36

Macaulay, Thomas Babington
1800-1859 .... **NCLC 42**
See also CDBLB 1832-1890; DLB 32, 55

MacBeth, George (Mann)
1932-1992 .... **CLC 2, 5, 9**
See also CA 25-28R; 136; DLB 40; MTCW;
SATA 4; SATA-Obit 70

MacCaig, Norman (Alexander)
1910- .... **CLC 36**
See also CA 9-12R; CANR 3, 34; DLB 27

MacCarthy, (Sir Charles Otto) Desmond
1877-1952 .... **TCLC 36**

MacDiarmid, Hugh
.... **CLC 2, 4, 11, 19, 63; PC 9**
See also Grieve, C(hristopher) M(urray)
See also CDBLB 1945-1960; DLB 20

MacDonald, Anson
See Heinlein, Robert A(nson)

Macdonald, Cynthia 1928- ...... **CLC 13, 19**
See also CA 49-52; CANR 4, 44; DLB 105

MacDonald, George 1824-1905 ..... **TCLC 9**
See also CA 106; 137; DLB 18; MAICYA;
SATA 33

Macdonald, John
See Millar, Kenneth

MacDonald, John D(ann)
1916-1986 .... **CLC 3, 27, 44**
See also CA 1-4R; 121; CANR 1, 19;
DLB 8; DLBY 86; MTCW

Macdonald, John Ross
See Millar, Kenneth

Macdonald, Ross ..... **CLC 1, 2, 3, 14, 34, 41**
See also Millar, Kenneth
See also DLBD 6

MacDougal, John
See Blish, James (Benjamin)

MacEwen, Gwendolyn (Margaret)
1941-1987 .... **CLC 13, 55**
See also CA 9-12R; 124; CANR 7, 22;
DLB 53; SATA 50; SATA-Obit 55

Macha, Karel Hynek 1810-1846 .. **NCLC 46**

Machado (y Ruiz), Antonio
1875-1939 .... **TCLC 3**
See also CA 104; DLB 108

Machado de Assis, Joaquim Maria
1839-1908 .... **TCLC 10; BLC**
See also CA 107

Machen, Arthur .... **TCLC 4; SSC 20**
See also Jones, Arthur Llewellyn
See also DLB 36

Machiavelli, Niccolo 1469-1527 .. **LC 8; DA**

MacInnes, Colin 1914-1976 ...... **CLC 4, 23**
See also CA 69-72; 65-68; CANR 21;
DLB 14; MTCW

MacInnes, Helen (Clark)
1907-1985 .... **CLC 27, 39**
See also CA 1-4R; 117; CANR 1, 28;
DLB 87; MTCW; SATA 22;
SATA-Obit 44

Mackay, Mary 1855-1924
See Corelli, Marie
See also CA 118

Mackenzie, Compton (Edward Montague)
1883-1972 .... **CLC 18**
See also CA 21-22; 37-40R; CAP 2;
DLB 34, 100

Mackenzie, Henry 1745-1831 .... **NCLC 41**
See also DLB 39

Mackintosh, Elizabeth 1896(?)-1952
See Tey, Josephine
See also CA 110

MacLaren, James
See Grieve, C(hristopher) M(urray)

Mac Laverty, Bernard 1942- .... **CLC 31**
See also CA 116; 118; CANR 43

MacLean, Alistair (Stuart)
1922-1987 .... **CLC 3, 13, 50, 63**
See also CA 57-60; 121; CANR 28; MTCW;
SATA 23; SATA-Obit 50

Maclean, Norman (Fitzroy)
1902-1990 .... **CLC 78; SSC 13**
See also CA 102; 132

MacLeish, Archibald
1892-1982 .... **CLC 3, 8, 14, 68**
See also CA 9-12R; 106; CANR 33; DLB 4,
7, 45; DLBY 82; MTCW

MacLennan, (John) Hugh
1907-1990 .... **CLC 2, 14**
See also CA 5-8R; 142; CANR 33; DLB 68;
MTCW

MacLeod, Alistair 1936- .... **CLC 56**
See also CA 123; DLB 60

MacNeice, (Frederick) Louis
1907-1963 .... **CLC 1, 4, 10, 53**
See also CA 85-88; DLB 10, 20; MTCW

MacNeill, Dand
See Fraser, George MacDonald

Macpherson, James 1736-1796 ...... **LC 29**
See also DLB 109

Macpherson, (Jean) Jay 1931- ...... **CLC 14**
See also CA 5-8R; DLB 53

MacShane, Frank 1927- .... **CLC 39**
See also CA 9-12R; CANR 3, 33; DLB 111

Macumber, Mari
See Sandoz, Mari(e Susette)

Madach, Imre 1823-1864 .... **NCLC 19**

Madden, (Jerry) David 1933- .... **CLC 5, 15**
See also CA 1-4R; CAAS 3; CANR 4, 45;
DLB 6; MTCW

Maddern, Al(an)
See Ellison, Harlan (Jay)

Madhubuti, Haki R.
1942- .... **CLC 6, 73; BLC; PC 5**
See also Lee, Don L.
See also BW 2; CA 73-76; CANR 24;
DLB 5, 41; DLBD 8

Maepenn, Hugh
See Kuttner, Henry

Maepenn, K. H.
See Kuttner, Henry

Maeterlinck, Maurice 1862-1949 ... **TCLC 3**
See also CA 104; 136; SATA 66

Maginn, William 1794-1842 ...... **NCLC 8**
See also DLB 110

Mahapatra, Jayanta 1928- .... **CLC 33**
See also CA 73-76; CAAS 9; CANR 15, 33

Mahfouz, Naguib (Abdel Aziz Al-Sabilgi)
1911(?)-
See Mahfuz, Najib
See also BEST 89:2; CA 128; MTCW

Mahfuz, Najib .... **CLC 52, 55**
See also Mahfouz, Naguib (Abdel Aziz
Al-Sabilgi)
See also DLBY 88

Mahon, Derek 1941- .... **CLC 27**
See also CA 113; 128; DLB 40

Mailer, Norman
1923- ...... **CLC 1, 2, 3, 4, 5, 8, 11, 14,
28, 39, 74; DA**
See also AITN 2; CA 9-12R; CABS 1;
CANR 28; CDALB 1968-1988; DLB 2,
16, 28; DLBD 3; DLBY 80, 83; MTCW

Maillet, Antonine 1929- .... **CLC 54**
See also CA 115; 120; CANR 46; DLB 60

Mais, Roger 1905-1955 .... **TCLC 8**
See also BW 1; CA 105; 124; DLB 125;
MTCW

Maistre, Joseph de 1753-1821 .... **NCLC 37**

Maitland, Sara (Louise) 1950- ...... **CLC 49**
See also CA 69-72; CANR 13

Major, Clarence
1936- .... **CLC 3, 19, 48; BLC**
See also BW 2; CA 21-24R; CAAS 6;
CANR 13, 25; DLB 33

Major, Kevin (Gerald) 1949- .... **CLC 26**
See also CA 97-100; CANR 21, 38;
CLR 11; DLB 60; JRDA; MAICYA;
SATA 32

Maki, James
See Ozu, Yasujiro

Malabaila, Damiano
See Levi, Primo

Malamud, Bernard
1914-1986 ...... **CLC 1, 2, 3, 5, 8, 9, 11,
18, 27, 44, 78, 85; DA; SSC 15; WLC**
See also CA 5-8R; 118; CABS 1; CANR 28;
CDALB 1941-1968; DLB 2, 28, 152;
DLBY 80, 86; MTCW

Malaparte, Curzio 1898-1957 ..... **TCLC 52**

Malcolm, Dan
See Silverberg, Robert

Malcolm X .... **CLC 82; BLC**
See also Little, Malcolm

Malherbe, Francois de 1555-1628 ..... **LC 5**

Martinez Sierra, Maria (de la O'LeJarraga)
1874-1974 . . . . TCLC 6
See also CA 115

Martinsen, Martin
See Follett, Ken(neth Martin)

Martinson, Harry (Edmund)
1904-1978 . . . . CLC 14
See also CA 77-80; CANR 34

Marut, Ret
See Traven, B.

Marut, Robert
See Traven, B.

Marvell, Andrew
1621-1678 . . . . . LC 4; DA; PC 10; WLC
See also CDBLB 1660-1789; DLB 131

Marx, Karl (Heinrich)
1818-1883 . . . . NCLC 17
See also DLB 129

Masaoka Shiki . . . . TCLC 18
See also Masaoka Tsunenori

Masaoka Tsunenori 1867-1902
See Masaoka Shiki
See also CA 117

Masefield, John (Edward)
1878-1967 . . . . CLC 11, 47
See also CA 19-20; 25-28R; CANR 33;
CAP 2; CDBLB 1890-1914; DLB 10, 19,
153; MTCW; SATA 19

Maso, Carole 19(?)- . . . . CLC 44

Mason, Bobbie Ann
1940- . . . . CLC 28, 43, 82; SSC 4
See also AAYA 5; CA 53-56; CANR 11,
31; DLBY 87; MTCW

Mason, Ernst
See Pohl, Frederik

Mason, Lee W.
See Malzberg, Barry N(athaniel)

Mason, Nick 1945- . . . . CLC 35

Mason, Tally
See Derleth, August (William)

Mass, William
See Gibson, William

Masters, Edgar Lee
1868-1950 . . . . . . TCLC 2, 25; DA; PC 1
See also CA 104; 133; CDALB 1865-1917;
DLB 54; MTCW

Masters, Hilary 1928- . . . . CLC 48
See also CA 25-28R; CANR 13, 47

Mastrosimone, William 19(?)- . . . . . . CLC 36

Mathe, Albert
See Camus, Albert

Matheson, Richard Burton 1926- . . . CLC 37
See also CA 97-100; DLB 8, 44

Mathews, Harry 1930- . . . . CLC 6, 52
See also CA 21-24R; CAAS 6; CANR 18,
40

Mathews, John Joseph 1894-1979. . . CLC 84
See also CA 19-20; 142; CANR 45; CAP 2;
NNAL

Mathias, Roland (Glyn) 1915- . . . . . . CLC 45
See also CA 97-100; CANR 19, 41; DLB 27

Matsuo Basho 1644-1694. . . . . PC 3

Mattheson, Rodney
See Creasey, John

Matthews, Greg 1949- . . . . CLC 45
See also CA 135

Matthews, William 1942- . . . . CLC 40
See also CA 29-32R; CAAS 18; CANR 12;
DLB 5

Matthias, John (Edward) 1941- . . . . . . CLC 9
See also CA 33-36R

Matthiessen, Peter
1927- . . . . CLC 5, 7, 11, 32, 64
See also AAYA 6; BEST 90:4; CA 9-12R;
CANR 21; DLB 6; MTCW; SATA 27

Maturin, Charles Robert
1780(?)-1824 . . . . NCLC 6

Matute (Ausejo), Ana Maria
1925- . . . . CLC 11
See also CA 89-92; MTCW

Maugham, W. S.
See Maugham, W(illiam) Somerset

Maugham, W(illiam) Somerset
1874-1965 . . . . . . CLC 1, 11, 15, 67; DA;
SSC 8; WLC
See also CA 5-8R; 25-28R; CANR 40;
CDBLB 1914-1945; DLB 10, 36, 77, 100;
MTCW; SATA 54

Maugham, William Somerset
See Maugham, W(illiam) Somerset

Maupassant, (Henri Rene Albert) Guy de
1850-1893 . . . . NCLC 1, 42; DA; SSC 1;
WLC
See also DLB 123

Maurhut, Richard
See Traven, B.

Mauriac, Claude 1914- . . . . CLC 9
See also CA 89-92; DLB 83

Mauriac, Francois (Charles)
1885-1970 . . . . CLC 4, 9, 56
See also CA 25-28; CAP 2; DLB 65;
MTCW

Mavor, Osborne Henry 1888-1951
See Bridie, James
See also CA 104

Maxwell, William (Keepers, Jr.)
1908- . . . . CLC 19
See also CA 93-96; DLBY 80

May, Elaine 1932- . . . . CLC 16
See also CA 124; 142; DLB 44

Mayakovski, Vladimir (Vladimirovich)
1893-1930 . . . . TCLC 4, 18
See also CA 104

Mayhew, Henry 1812-1887 . . . . . . NCLC 31
See also DLB 18, 55

Mayle, Peter 1939(?)- . . . . CLC 89
See also CA 139

Maynard, Joyce 1953- . . . . CLC 23
See also CA 111; 129

Mayne, William (James Carter)
1928- . . . . CLC 12
See also CA 9-12R; CANR 37; CLR 25;
JRDA; MAICYA; SAAS 11; SATA 6, 68

Mayo, Jim
See L'Amour, Louis (Dearborn)

Maysles, Albert 1926- . . . . CLC 16
See also CA 29-32R

Maysles, David 1932- . . . . CLC 16

Mazer, Norma Fox 1931- . . . . CLC 26
See also AAYA 5; CA 69-72; CANR 12,
32; CLR 23; JRDA; MAICYA; SAAS 1;
SATA 24, 67

Mazzini, Guiseppe 1805-1872 . . . . NCLC 34

McAuley, James Phillip
1917-1976 . . . . CLC 45
See also CA 97-100

McBain, Ed
See Hunter, Evan

McBrien, William Augustine
1930- . . . . CLC 44
See also CA 107

McCaffrey, Anne (Inez) 1926- . . . . . . CLC 17
See also AAYA 6; AITN 2; BEST 89:2;
CA 25-28R; CANR 15, 35; DLB 8;
JRDA; MAICYA; MTCW; SAAS 11;
SATA 8, 70

McCall, Nathan 1955(?)- . . . . CLC 86
See also CA 146

McCann, Arthur
See Campbell, John W(ood, Jr.)

McCann, Edson
See Pohl, Frederik

McCarthy, Charles, Jr. 1933-
See McCarthy, Cormac
See also CANR 42

McCarthy, Cormac 1933- . . . . . CLC 4, 57, 59
See also McCarthy, Charles, Jr.
See also DLB 6, 143

McCarthy, Mary (Therese)
1912-1989 . . . CLC 1, 3, 5, 14, 24, 39, 59
See also CA 5-8R; 129; CANR 16; DLB 2;
DLBY 81; MTCW

McCartney, (James) Paul
1942- . . . . CLC 12, 35
See also CA 146

McCauley, Stephen (D.) 1955- . . . . . CLC 50
See also CA 141

McClure, Michael (Thomas)
1932- . . . . CLC 6, 10
See also CA 21-24R; CANR 17, 46;
DLB 16

McCorkle, Jill (Collins) 1958- . . . . . . CLC 51
See also CA 121; DLBY 87

McCourt, James 1941- . . . . CLC 5
See also CA 57-60

McCoy, Horace (Stanley)
1897-1955 . . . . TCLC 28
See also CA 108; DLB 9

McCrae, John 1872-1918. . . . . TCLC 12
See also CA 109; DLB 92

McCreigh, James
See Pohl, Frederik

McCullers, (Lula) Carson (Smith)
1917-1967 . . . . CLC 1, 4, 10, 12, 48; DA;
SSC 9; WLC
See also CA 5-8R; 25-28R; CABS 1, 3;
CANR 18; CDALB 1941-1968; DLB 2, 7;
MTCW; SATA 27

McCulloch, John Tyler
See Burroughs, Edgar Rice

McCullough, Colleen 1938(?)- . . . . . . CLC 27
See also CA 81-84; CANR 17, 46; MTCW

McElroy, Joseph 1930- . . . . CLC 5, 47
See also CA 17-20R

McEwan, Ian (Russell) 1948- . . . CLC 13, 66
See also BEST 90:4; CA 61-64; CANR 14,
41; DLB 14; MTCW

McFadden, David 1940- . . . . CLC 48
See also CA 104; DLB 60

McFarland, Dennis 1950- . . . . CLC 65

McGahern, John
1934- . . . . CLC 5, 9, 48; SSC 17
See also CA 17-20R; CANR 29; DLB 14;
MTCW

McGinley, Patrick (Anthony)
1937- . . . . CLC 41
See also CA 120; 127

McGinley, Phyllis 1905-1978 . . . . . . CLC 14
See also CA 9-12R; 77-80; CANR 19;
DLB 11, 48; SATA 2, 44; SATA-Obit 24

McGinniss, Joe 1942- . . . . CLC 32
See also AITN 2; BEST 89:2; CA 25-28R;
CANR 26

McGivern, Maureen Daly
See Daly, Maureen

McGrath, Patrick 1950- . . . . CLC 55
See also CA 136

McGrath, Thomas (Matthew)
1916-1990 . . . . CLC 28, 59
See also CA 9-12R; 132; CANR 6, 33;
MTCW; SATA 41; SATA-Obit 66

McGuane, Thomas (Francis III)
1939- . . . . CLC 3, 7, 18, 45
See also AITN 2; CA 49-52; CANR 5, 24;
DLB 2; DLBY 80; MTCW

McGuckian, Medbh 1950- . . . . CLC 48
See also CA 143; DLB 40

McHale, Tom 1942(?)-1982 . . . . . . CLC 3, 5
See also AITN 1; CA 77-80; 106

McIlvanney, William 1936- . . . . CLC 42
See also CA 25-28R; DLB 14

McIlwraith, Maureen Mollie Hunter
See Hunter, Mollie
See also SATA 2

McInerney, Jay 1955- . . . . CLC 34
See also CA 116; 123; CANR 45

McIntyre, Vonda N(eel) 1948- . . . . . CLC 18
See also CA 81-84; CANR 17, 34; MTCW

McKay, Claude . . . . . TCLC 7, 41; BLC; PC 2
See also McKay, Festus Claudius
See also DLB 4, 45, 51, 117

McKay, Festus Claudius 1889-1948
See McKay, Claude
See also BW 1; CA 104; 124; DA; MTCW;
WLC

McKuen, Rod 1933- . . . . CLC 1, 3
See also AITN 1; CA 41-44R; CANR 40

McLoughlin, R. B.
See Mencken, H(enry) L(ouis)

McLuhan, (Herbert) Marshall
1911-1980 . . . . CLC 37, 83
See also CA 9-12R; 102; CANR 12, 34;
DLB 88; MTCW

McMillan, Terry (L.) 1951- . . . . . CLC 50, 61
See also BW 2; CA 140

McMurtry, Larry (Jeff)
1936- . . . . CLC 2, 3, 7, 11, 27, 44
See also AITN 2; BEST 89:2; CA 5-8R;
CANR 19, 43; CDALB 1968-1988;
DLB 2, 143; DLBY 80, 87; MTCW

McNally, T. M. 1961- . . . . CLC 82

McNally, Terrence 1939- . . . . . . CLC 4, 7, 41
See also CA 45-48; CANR 2; DLB 7

McNamer, Deirdre 1950- . . . . CLC 70

McNeile, Herman Cyril 1888-1937
See Sapper
See also DLB 77

McNickle, (William) D'Arcy
1904-1977 . . . . CLC 89
See also CA 9-12R; 85-88; CANR 5, 45;
NNAL; SATA-Obit 22

McPhee, John (Angus) 1931- . . . . . . CLC 36
See also BEST 90:1; CA 65-68; CANR 20,
46; MTCW

McPherson, James Alan
1943- . . . . CLC 19, 77
See also BW 1; CA 25-28R; CAAS 17;
CANR 24; DLB 38; MTCW

McPherson, William (Alexander)
1933- . . . . CLC 34
See also CA 69-72; CANR 28

Mead, Margaret 1901-1978 . . . . CLC 37
See also AITN 1; CA 1-4R; 81-84;
CANR 4; MTCW; SATA-Obit 20

Meaker, Marijane (Agnes) 1927-
See Kerr, M. E.
See also CA 107; CANR 37; JRDA;
MAICYA; MTCW; SATA 20, 61

Medoff, Mark (Howard) 1940- . . . CLC 6, 23
See also AITN 1; CA 53-56; CANR 5;
DLB 7

Medvedev, P. N.
See Bakhtin, Mikhail Mikhailovich

Meged, Aharon
See Megged, Aharon

Meged, Aron
See Megged, Aharon

Megged, Aharon 1920- . . . . CLC 9
See also CA 49-52; CAAS 13; CANR 1

Mehta, Ved (Parkash) 1934- . . . . CLC 37
See also CA 1-4R; CANR 2, 23; MTCW

Melanter
See Blackmore, R(ichard) D(oddridge)

Melikow, Loris
See Hofmannsthal, Hugo von

Melmoth, Sebastian
See Wilde, Oscar (Fingal O'Flahertie Wills)

Meltzer, Milton 1915- . . . . CLC 26
See also AAYA 8; CA 13-16R; CANR 38;
CLR 13; DLB 61; JRDA; MAICYA;
SAAS 1; SATA 1, 50, 80

Melville, Herman
1819-1891 . . . . . NCLC 3, 12, 29, 45, 49;
DA; SSC 1, 17; WLC
See also CDALB 1640-1865; DLB 3, 74;
SATA 59

Menander
c. 342B.C.-c. 292B.C. . . . . CMLC 9; DC 3

Mencken, H(enry) L(ouis)
1880-1956 . . . . TCLC 13
See also CA 105; 125; CDALB 1917-1929;
DLB 11, 29, 63, 137; MTCW

Mercer, David 1928-1980 . . . . CLC 5
See also CA 9-12R; 102; CANR 23;
DLB 13; MTCW

Merchant, Paul
See Ellison, Harlan (Jay)

Meredith, George 1828-1909 . . . TCLC 17, 43
See also CA 117; CDBLB 1832-1890;
DLB 18, 35, 57

Meredith, William (Morris)
1919- . . . . CLC 4, 13, 22, 55
See also CA 9-12R; CAAS 14; CANR 6, 40;
DLB 5

Merezhkovsky, Dmitry Sergeyevich
1865-1941 . . . . TCLC 29

Merimee, Prosper
1803-1870 . . . . NCLC 6; SSC 7
See also DLB 119

Merkin, Daphne 1954- . . . . CLC 44
See also CA 123

Merlin, Arthur
See Blish, James (Benjamin)

Merrill, James (Ingram)
1926-1995 . . . . CLC 2, 3, 6, 8, 13, 18, 34
See also CA 13-16R; 147; CANR 10;
DLB 5; DLBY 85; MTCW

Merriman, Alex
See Silverberg, Robert

Merritt, E. B.
See Waddington, Miriam

Merton, Thomas
1915-1968 . . CLC 1, 3, 11, 34, 83; PC 10
See also CA 5-8R; 25-28R; CANR 22;
DLB 48; DLBY 81; MTCW

Merwin, W(illiam) S(tanley)
1927- . . . CLC 1, 2, 3, 5, 8, 13, 18, 45, 88
See also CA 13-16R; CANR 15; DLB 5;
MTCW

Metcalf, John 1938- . . . . CLC 37
See also CA 113; DLB 60

Metcalf, Suzanne
See Baum, L(yman) Frank

Mew, Charlotte (Mary)
1870-1928 . . . . TCLC 8
See also CA 105; DLB 19, 135

Mewshaw, Michael 1943- . . . . CLC 9
See also CA 53-56; CANR 7, 47; DLBY 80

Meyer, June
See Jordan, June

Meyer, Lynn
See Slavitt, David R(ytman)

Meyer-Meyrink, Gustav 1868-1932
See Meyrink, Gustav
See also CA 117

Meyers, Jeffrey 1939- . . . . CLC 39
See also CA 73-76; DLB 111

Meynell, Alice (Christina Gertrude Thompson)
1847-1922 . . . . TCLC 6
See also CA 104; DLB 19, 98

Meyrink, Gustav . . . . TCLC 21
See also Meyer-Meyrink, Gustav
See also DLB 81

Michaels, Leonard
1933- . . . . **CLC 6, 25; SSC 16**
See also CA 61-64; CANR 21; DLB 130;
MTCW

Michaux, Henri 1899-1984 . . . . . . **CLC 8, 19**
See also CA 85-88; 114

Michelangelo 1475-1564. . . . . **LC 12**

Michelet, Jules 1798-1874 . . . . . . **NCLC 31**

Michener, James A(lbert)
1907(?)- . . . . **CLC 1, 5, 11, 29, 60**
See also AITN 1; BEST 90:1; CA 5-8R;
CANR 21, 45; DLB 6; MTCW

Mickiewicz, Adam 1798-1855 . . . . . **NCLC 3**

Middleton, Christopher 1926- . . . . . . **CLC 13**
See also CA 13-16R; CANR 29; DLB 40

Middleton, Richard (Barham)
1882-1911 . . . . **TCLC 56**

Middleton, Stanley 1919- . . . . **CLC 7, 38**
See also CA 25-28R; CANR 21, 46;
DLB 14

Middleton, Thomas 1580-1627. . . . . . . **DC 5**
See also DLB 58

Migueis, Jose Rodrigues 1901- . . . . . **CLC 10**

Mikszath, Kalman 1847-1910 . . . . . **TCLC 31**

Miles, Josephine
1911-1985 . . . . **CLC 1, 2, 14, 34, 39**
See also CA 1-4R; 116; CANR 2; DLB 48

Militant
See Sandburg, Carl (August)

Mill, John Stuart 1806-1873 . . . . . **NCLC 11**
See also CDBLB 1832-1890; DLB 55

Millar, Kenneth 1915-1983 . . . . **CLC 14**
See also Macdonald, Ross
See also CA 9-12R; 110; CANR 16; DLB 2;
DLBD 6; DLBY 83; MTCW

Millay, E. Vincent
See Millay, Edna St. Vincent

Millay, Edna St. Vincent
1892-1950 . . . . . . **TCLC 4, 49; DA; PC 6**
See also CA 104; 130; CDALB 1917-1929;
DLB 45; MTCW

Miller, Arthur
1915- . . . . **CLC 1, 2, 6, 10, 15, 26, 47, 78;
DA; DC 1; WLC**
See also AITN 1; CA 1-4R; CABS 3;
CANR 2, 30; CDALB 1941-1968; DLB 7;
MTCW

Miller, Henry (Valentine)
1891-1980 . . . . **CLC 1, 2, 4, 9, 14, 43, 84;
DA; WLC**
See also CA 9-12R; 97-100; CANR 33;
CDALB 1929-1941; DLB 4, 9; DLBY 80;
MTCW

Miller, Jason 1939(?)- . . . . **CLC 2**
See also AITN 1; CA 73-76; DLB 7

Miller, Sue 1943- . . . . **CLC 44**
See also BEST 90:3; CA 139; DLB 143

Miller, Walter M(ichael, Jr.)
1923- . . . . **CLC 4, 30**
See also CA 85-88; DLB 8

Millett, Kate 1934- . . . . **CLC 67**
See also AITN 1; CA 73-76; CANR 32;
MTCW

Millhauser, Steven 1943- . . . . **CLC 21, 54**
See also CA 110; 111; DLB 2

Millin, Sarah Gertrude 1889-1968 . . **CLC 49**
See also CA 102; 93-96

Milne, A(lan) A(lexander)
1882-1956 . . . . **TCLC 6**
See also CA 104; 133; CLR 1, 26; DLB 10,
77, 100; MAICYA; MTCW; YABC 1

Milner, Ron(ald) 1938- . . . . **CLC 56; BLC**
See also AITN 1; BW 1; CA 73-76;
CANR 24; DLB 38; MTCW

Milosz, Czeslaw
1911- . . . **CLC 5, 11, 22, 31, 56, 82; PC 8**
See also CA 81-84; CANR 23; MTCW

Milton, John 1608-1674 . . . **LC 9; DA; WLC**
See also CDBLB 1660-1789; DLB 131, 151

Min, Anchee 1957- . . . . **CLC 86**
See also CA 146

Minehaha, Cornelius
See Wedekind, (Benjamin) Frank(lin)

Miner, Valerie 1947- . . . . **CLC 40**
See also CA 97-100

Minimo, Duca
See D'Annunzio, Gabriele

Minot, Susan 1956- . . . . **CLC 44**
See also CA 134

Minus, Ed 1938- . . . . **CLC 39**

Miranda, Javier
See Bioy Casares, Adolfo

Mirbeau, Octave 1848-1917 . . . . . . **TCLC 55**
See also DLB 123

Miro (Ferrer), Gabriel (Francisco Victor)
1879-1930 . . . . **TCLC 5**
See also CA 104

Mishima, Yukio
. . . . . . **CLC 2, 4, 6, 9, 27; DC 1; SSC 4**
See also Hiraoka, Kimitake

Mistral, Frederic 1830-1914 . . . . . . **TCLC 51**
See also CA 122

Mistral, Gabriela. . . . . **TCLC 2; HLC**
See also Godoy Alcayaga, Lucila

Mistry, Rohinton 1952- . . . . **CLC 71**
See also CA 141

Mitchell, Clyde
See Ellison, Harlan (Jay); Silverberg, Robert

Mitchell, James Leslie 1901-1935
See Gibbon, Lewis Grassic
See also CA 104; DLB 15

Mitchell, Joni 1943- . . . . **CLC 12**
See also CA 112

Mitchell, Margaret (Munnerlyn)
1900-1949 . . . . **TCLC 11**
See also CA 109; 125; DLB 9; MTCW

Mitchell, Peggy
See Mitchell, Margaret (Munnerlyn)

Mitchell, S(ilas) Weir 1829-1914 . . **TCLC 36**

Mitchell, W(illiam) O(rmond)
1914- . . . . **CLC 25**
See also CA 77-80; CANR 15, 43; DLB 88

Mitford, Mary Russell 1787-1855. . **NCLC 4**
See also DLB 110, 116

Mitford, Nancy 1904-1973. . . . . **CLC 44**
See also CA 9-12R

Miyamoto, Yuriko 1899-1951 . . . . . **TCLC 37**

Mo, Timothy (Peter) 1950(?)- . . . . . . **CLC 46**
See also CA 117; MTCW

Modarressi, Taghi (M.) 1931- . . . . . . **CLC 44**
See also CA 121; 134

Modiano, Patrick (Jean) 1945- . . . . . **CLC 18**
See also CA 85-88; CANR 17, 40; DLB 83

Moerck, Paal
See Roelvaag, O(le) E(dvart)

Mofolo, Thomas (Mokopu)
1875(?)-1948 . . . . **TCLC 22; BLC**
See also CA 121

Mohr, Nicholasa 1935- . . . . . . **CLC 12; HLC**
See also AAYA 8; CA 49-52; CANR 1, 32;
CLR 22; DLB 145; HW; JRDA; SAAS 8;
SATA 8

Mojtabai, A(nn) G(race)
1938- . . . . **CLC 5, 9, 15, 29**
See also CA 85-88

Moliere 1622-1673 . . . . **LC 28; DA; WLC**

Molin, Charles
See Mayne, William (James Carter)

Molnar, Ferenc 1878-1952 . . . . **TCLC 20**
See also CA 109

Momaday, N(avarre) Scott
1934- . . . . **CLC 2, 19, 85; DA**
See also AAYA 11; CA 25-28R; CANR 14,
34; DLB 143; MTCW; NNAL; SATA 48;
SATA-Brief 30

Monette, Paul 1945-1995 . . . . **CLC 82**
See also CA 139; 147

Monroe, Harriet 1860-1936 . . . . . . **TCLC 12**
See also CA 109; DLB 54, 91

Monroe, Lyle
See Heinlein, Robert A(nson)

Montagu, Elizabeth 1917- . . . . **NCLC 7**
See also CA 9-12R

Montagu, Mary (Pierrepont) Wortley
1689-1762 . . . . **LC 9**
See also DLB 95, 101

Montagu, W. H.
See Coleridge, Samuel Taylor

Montague, John (Patrick)
1929- . . . . **CLC 13, 46**
See also CA 9-12R; CANR 9; DLB 40;
MTCW

Montaigne, Michel (Eyquem) de
1533-1592 . . . . **LC 8; DA; WLC**

Montale, Eugenio
1896-1981 . . . . **CLC 7, 9, 18; PC 12**
See also CA 17-20R; 104; CANR 30;
DLB 114; MTCW

Montesquieu, Charles-Louis de Secondat
1689-1755 . . . . **LC 7**

Montgomery, (Robert) Bruce 1921-1978
See Crispin, Edmund
See also CA 104

Montgomery, L(ucy) M(aud)
1874-1942 . . . . **TCLC 51**
See also AAYA 12; CA 108; 137; CLR 8;
DLB 92; JRDA; MAICYA; YABC 1

Montgomery, Marion H., Jr. 1925- . . **CLC 7**
See also AITN 1; CA 1-4R; CANR 3, 48;
DLB 6

Montgomery, Max
See Davenport, Guy (Mattison, Jr.)

Montherlant, Henry (Milon) de
1896-1972 . . . . CLC 8, 19
See also CA 85-88; 37-40R; DLB 72;
MTCW

Monty Python
See Chapman, Graham; Cleese, John
(Marwood); Gilliam, Terry (Vance); Idle,
Eric; Jones, Terence Graham Parry; Palin,
Michael (Edward)
See also AAYA 7

Moodie, Susanna (Strickland)
1803-1885 . . . . NCLC 14
See also DLB 99

Mooney, Edward 1951-
See Mooney, Ted
See also CA 130

Mooney, Ted . . . . CLC 25
See also Mooney, Edward

Moorcock, Michael (John)
1939- . . . . CLC 5, 27, 58
See also CA 45-48; CAAS 5; CANR 2, 17,
38; DLB 14; MTCW

Moore, Brian
1921- . . . . CLC 1, 3, 5, 7, 8, 19, 32
See also CA 1-4R; CANR 1, 25, 42; MTCW

Moore, Edward
See Muir, Edwin

Moore, George Augustus
1852-1933 . . . . TCLC 7; SSC 19
See also CA 104; DLB 10, 18, 57, 135

Moore, Lorrie . . . . CLC 39, 45, 68
See also Moore, Marie Lorena

Moore, Marianne (Craig)
1887-1972 . . . . CLC 1, 2, 4, 8, 10, 13, 19,
                                          47; DA; PC 4
See also CA 1-4R; 33-36R; CANR 3;
CDALB 1929-1941; DLB 45; DLBD 7;
MTCW; SATA 20

Moore, Marie Lorena 1957-
See Moore, Lorrie
See also CA 116; CANR 39

Moore, Thomas 1779-1852 . . . . NCLC 6
See also DLB 96, 144

Morand, Paul 1888-1976 . . . . CLC 41
See also CA 69-72; DLB 65

Morante, Elsa 1918-1985 . . . . CLC 8, 47
See also CA 85-88; 117; CANR 35; MTCW

Moravia, Alberto . . . . . . CLC 2, 7, 11, 27, 46
See also Pincherle, Alberto

More, Hannah 1745-1833 . . . . NCLC 27
See also DLB 107, 109, 116

More, Henry 1614-1687 . . . . LC 9
See also DLB 126

More, Sir Thomas 1478-1535 . . . . LC 10

Moreas, Jean . . . . TCLC 18
See also Papadiamantopoulos, Johannes

Morgan, Berry 1919- . . . . CLC 6
See also CA 49-52; DLB 6

Morgan, Claire
See Highsmith, (Mary) Patricia

Morgan, Edwin (George) 1920- . . . . . CLC 31
See also CA 5-8R; CANR 3, 43; DLB 27

Morgan, (George) Frederick
1922- . . . . CLC 23
See also CA 17-20R; CANR 21

Morgan, Harriet
See Mencken, H(enry) L(ouis)

Morgan, Jane
See Cooper, James Fenimore

Morgan, Janet 1945- . . . . CLC 39
See also CA 65-68

Morgan, Lady 1776(?)-1859 . . . . . . NCLC 29
See also DLB 116

Morgan, Robin 1941- . . . . CLC 2
See also CA 69-72; CANR 29; MTCW;
SATA 80

Morgan, Scott
See Kuttner, Henry

Morgan, Seth 1949(?)-1990 . . . . CLC 65
See also CA 132

Morgenstern, Christian
1871-1914 . . . . TCLC 8
See also CA 105

Morgenstern, S.
See Goldman, William (W.)

Moricz, Zsigmond 1879-1942 . . . . . TCLC 33

Morike, Eduard (Friedrich)
1804-1875 . . . . NCLC 10
See also DLB 133

Mori Ogai . . . . TCLC 14
See also Mori Rintaro

Mori Rintaro 1862-1922
See Mori Ogai
See also CA 110

Moritz, Karl Philipp 1756-1793 . . . . . . LC 2
See also DLB 94

Morland, Peter Henry
See Faust, Frederick (Schiller)

Morren, Theophil
See Hofmannsthal, Hugo von

Morris, Bill 1952- . . . . CLC 76

Morris, Julian
See West, Morris L(anglo)

Morris, Steveland Judkins 1950(?)-
See Wonder, Stevie
See also CA 111

Morris, William 1834-1896 . . . . NCLC 4
See also CDBLB 1832-1890; DLB 18, 35, 57

Morris, Wright 1910- . . . CLC 1, 3, 7, 18, 37
See also CA 9-12R; CANR 21; DLB 2;
DLBY 81; MTCW

Morrison, Chloe Anthony Wofford
See Morrison, Toni

Morrison, James Douglas 1943-1971
See Morrison, Jim
See also CA 73-76; CANR 40

Morrison, Jim . . . . CLC 17
See also Morrison, James Douglas

Morrison, Toni
1931- . . . . CLC 4, 10, 22, 55, 81, 87;
                                          BLC; DA
See also AAYA 1; BW 2; CA 29-32R;
CANR 27, 42; CDALB 1968-1988;
DLB 6, 33, 143; DLBY 81; MTCW;
SATA 57

Morrison, Van 1945- . . . . CLC 21
See also CA 116

Mortimer, John (Clifford)
1923- . . . . CLC 28, 43
See also CA 13-16R; CANR 21;
CDBLB 1960 to Present; DLB 13;
MTCW

Mortimer, Penelope (Ruth) 1918- . . . . CLC 5
See also CA 57-60; CANR 45

Morton, Anthony
See Creasey, John

Mosher, Howard Frank 1943- . . . . . . CLC 62
See also CA 139

Mosley, Nicholas 1923- . . . . CLC 43, 70
See also CA 69-72; CANR 41; DLB 14

Moss, Howard
1922-1987 . . . . CLC 7, 14, 45, 50
See also CA 1-4R; 123; CANR 1, 44;
DLB 5

Mossgiel, Rab
See Burns, Robert

Motion, Andrew (Peter) 1952- . . . . . . CLC 47
See also CA 146; DLB 40

Motley, Willard (Francis)
1909-1965 . . . . CLC 18
See also BW 1; CA 117; 106; DLB 76, 143

Motoori, Norinaga 1730-1801 . . . . NCLC 45

Mott, Michael (Charles Alston)
1930- . . . . CLC 15, 34
See also CA 5-8R; CAAS 7; CANR 7, 29

Moure, Erin 1955- . . . . CLC 88
See also CA 113; DLB 60

Mowat, Farley (McGill) 1921- . . . . . CLC 26
See also AAYA 1; CA 1-4R; CANR 4, 24,
42; CLR 20; DLB 68; JRDA; MAICYA;
MTCW; SATA 3, 55

Moyers, Bill 1934- . . . . CLC 74
See also AITN 2; CA 61-64; CANR 31

Mphahlele, Es'kia
See Mphahlele, Ezekiel
See also DLB 125

Mphahlele, Ezekiel 1919- . . . . . CLC 25; BLC
See also Mphahlele, Es'kia
See also BW 2; CA 81-84; CANR 26

Mqhayi, S(amuel) E(dward) K(rune Loliwe)
1875-1945 . . . . TCLC 25; BLC

Mr. Martin
See Burroughs, William S(eward)

Mrozek, Slawomir 1930- . . . . CLC 3, 13
See also CA 13-16R; CAAS 10; CANR 29;
MTCW

Mrs. Belloc-Lowndes
See Lowndes, Marie Adelaide (Belloc)

Mtwa, Percy (?)- . . . . CLC 47

Mueller, Lisel 1924- . . . . CLC 13, 51
See also CA 93-96; DLB 105

Muir, Edwin 1887-1959 . . . . TCLC 2
See also CA 104; DLB 20, 100

Muir, John 1838-1914 . . . . TCLC 28

Mujica Lainez, Manuel
1910-1984 . . . . CLC 31
See also Lainez, Manuel Mujica
See also CA 81-84; 112; CANR 32; HW

Mukherjee, Bharati 1940- .... **CLC 53**
See also BEST 89:2; CA 107; CANR 45;
DLB 60; MTCW

Muldoon, Paul 1951- .... **CLC 32, 72**
See also CA 113; 129; DLB 40

Mulisch, Harry 1927-............. **CLC 42**
See also CA 9-12R; CANR 6, 26

Mull, Martin 1943-.............. **CLC 17**
See also CA 105

Mulock, Dinah Maria
See Craik, Dinah Maria (Mulock)

Munford, Robert 1737(?)-1783 .... **LC 5**
See also DLB 31

Mungo, Raymond 1946-........... **CLC 72**
See also CA 49-52; CANR 2

Munro, Alice
1931- .... **CLC 6, 10, 19, 50; SSC 3**
See also AITN 2; CA 33-36R; CANR 33;
DLB 53; MTCW; SATA 29

Munro, H(ector) H(ugh) 1870-1916
See Saki
See also CA 104; 130; CDBLB 1890-1914;
DA; DLB 34; MTCW; WLC

Murasaki, Lady................. **CMLC 1**

Murdoch, (Jean) Iris
1919- ...... **CLC 1, 2, 3, 4, 6, 8, 11, 15,
22, 31, 51**
See also CA 13-16R; CANR 8, 43;
CDBLB 1960 to Present; DLB 14;
MTCW

Murnau, Friedrich Wilhelm
See Plumpe, Friedrich Wilhelm

Murphy, Richard 1927-........... **CLC 41**
See also CA 29-32R; DLB 40

Murphy, Sylvia 1937-............. **CLC 34**
See also CA 121

Murphy, Thomas (Bernard) 1935-... **CLC 51**
See also CA 101

Murray, Albert L. 1916- .... **CLC 73**
See also BW 2; CA 49-52; CANR 26;
DLB 38

Murray, Les(lie) A(llan) 1938- ..... **CLC 40**
See also CA 21-24R; CANR 11, 27

Murry, J. Middleton
See Murry, John Middleton

Murry, John Middleton
1889-1957 .... **TCLC 16**
See also CA 118; DLB 149

Musgrave, Susan 1951- .... **CLC 13, 54**
See also CA 69-72; CANR 45

Musil, Robert (Edler von)
1880-1942 .... **TCLC 12; SSC 18**
See also CA 109; DLB 81, 124

Musset, (Louis Charles) Alfred de
1810-1857 .... **NCLC 7**

My Brother's Brother
See Chekhov, Anton (Pavlovich)

Myers, L. H. 1881-1944......... **TCLC 59**
See also DLB 15

Myers, Walter Dean 1937- ... **CLC 35; BLC**
See also AAYA 4; BW 2; CA 33-36R;
CANR 20, 42; CLR 4, 16, 35; DLB 33;
JRDA; MAICYA; SAAS 2; SATA 41, 71;
SATA-Brief 27

Myers, Walter M.
See Myers, Walter Dean

Myles, Symon
See Follett, Ken(neth Martin)

Nabokov, Vladimir (Vladimirovich)
1899-1977 ..... **CLC 1, 2, 3, 6, 8, 11, 15,
23, 44, 46, 64; DA; SSC 11; WLC**
See also CA 5-8R; 69-72; CANR 20;
CDALB 1941-1968; DLB 2; DLBD 3;
DLBY 80, 91; MTCW

Nagai Kafu..................... **TCLC 51**
See also Nagai Sokichi

Nagai Sokichi 1879-1959
See Nagai Kafu
See also CA 117

Nagy, Laszlo 1925-1978............ **CLC 7**
See also CA 129; 112

Naipaul, Shiva(dhar Srinivasa)
1945-1985 .... **CLC 32, 39**
See also CA 110; 112; 116; CANR 33;
DLBY 85; MTCW

Naipaul, V(idiadhar) S(urajprasad)
1932- .... **CLC 4, 7, 9, 13, 18, 37**
See also CA 1-4R; CANR 1, 33;
CDBLB 1960 to Present; DLB 125;
DLBY 85; MTCW

Nakos, Lilika 1899(?)-............ **CLC 29**

Narayan, R(asipuram) K(rishnaswami)
1906- .... **CLC 7, 28, 47**
See also CA 81-84; CANR 33; MTCW;
SATA 62

Nash, (Frediric) Ogden 1902-1971 .. **CLC 23**
See also CA 13-14; 29-32R; CANR 34;
CAP 1; DLB 11; MAICYA; MTCW;
SATA 2, 46

Nathan, Daniel
See Dannay, Frederic

Nathan, George Jean 1882-1958 ... **TCLC 18**
See also Hatteras, Owen
See also CA 114; DLB 137

Natsume, Kinnosuke 1867-1916
See Natsume, Soseki
See also CA 104

Natsume, Soseki .... **TCLC 2, 10**
See also Natsume, Kinnosuke

Natti, (Mary) Lee 1919-
See Kingman, Lee
See also CA 5-8R; CANR 2

Naylor, Gloria
1950- .... **CLC 28, 52; BLC; DA**
See also AAYA 6; BW 2; CA 107;
CANR 27; MTCW

Neihardt, John Gneisenau
1881-1973 .... **CLC 32**
See also CA 13-14; CAP 1; DLB 9, 54

Nekrasov, Nikolai Alekseevich
1821-1878 .... **NCLC 11**

Nelligan, Emile 1879-1941....... **TCLC 14**
See also CA 114; DLB 92

Nelson, Willie 1933-.............. **CLC 17**
See also CA 107

Nemerov, Howard (Stanley)
1920-1991 .... **CLC 2, 6, 9, 36**
See also CA 1-4R; 134; CABS 2; CANR 1,
27; DLB 6; DLBY 83; MTCW

Neruda, Pablo
1904-1973 ..... **CLC 1, 2, 5, 7, 9, 28, 62;
DA; HLC; PC 4; WLC**
See also CA 19-20; 45-48; CAP 2; HW;
MTCW

Nerval, Gerard de
1808-1855 ..... **NCLC 1; PC 12; SSC 18**

Nervo, (Jose) Amado (Ruiz de)
1870-1919 .... **TCLC 11**
See also CA 109; 131; HW

Nessi, Pio Baroja y
See Baroja (y Nessi), Pio

Nestroy, Johann 1801-1862...... **NCLC 42**
See also DLB 133

Neufeld, John (Arthur) 1938- ...... **CLC 17**
See also AAYA 11; CA 25-28R; CANR 11,
37; MAICYA; SAAS 3; SATA 6, 81

Neville, Emily Cheney 1919-...... **CLC 12**
See also CA 5-8R; CANR 3, 37; JRDA;
MAICYA; SAAS 2; SATA 1

Newbound, Bernard Slade 1930-
See Slade, Bernard
See also CA 81-84

Newby, P(ercy) H(oward)
1918- .... **CLC 2, 13**
See also CA 5-8R; CANR 32; DLB 15;
MTCW

Newlove, Donald 1928- .... **CLC 6**
See also CA 29-32R; CANR 25

Newlove, John (Herbert) 1938-..... **CLC 14**
See also CA 21-24R; CANR 9, 25

Newman, Charles 1938-.......... **CLC 2, 8**
See also CA 21-24R

Newman, Edwin (Harold) 1919- .... **CLC 14**
See also AITN 1; CA 69-72; CANR 5

Newman, John Henry
1801-1890 .... **NCLC 38**
See also DLB 18, 32, 55

Newton, Suzanne 1936-........... **CLC 35**
See also CA 41-44R; CANR 14; JRDA;
SATA 5, 77

Nexo, Martin Andersen
1869-1954 .... **TCLC 43**

Nezval, Vitezslav 1900-1958 ...... **TCLC 44**
See also CA 123

Ng, Fae Myenne 1957(?)-.......... **CLC 81**
See also CA 146

Ngema, Mbongeni 1955- .... **CLC 57**
See also BW 2; CA 143

Ngugi, James T(hiong'o)........ **CLC 3, 7, 13**
See also Ngugi wa Thiong'o

Ngugi wa Thiong'o 1938-..... **CLC 36; BLC**
See also Ngugi, James T(hiong'o)
See also BW 2; CA 81-84; CANR 27;
DLB 125; MTCW

Nichol, B(arrie) P(hillip)
1944-1988 .... **CLC 18**
See also CA 53-56; DLB 53; SATA 66

Nichols, John (Treadwell) 1940-.... **CLC 38**
See also CA 9-12R; CAAS 2; CANR 6;
DLBY 82

Nichols, Leigh
See Koontz, Dean R(ay)

Nichols, Peter (Richard)
1927- .... CLC **5, 36, 65**
See also CA 104; CANR 33; DLB 13;
MTCW

Nicolas, F. R. E.
See Freeling, Nicolas

Niedecker, Lorine 1903-1970.... CLC **10, 42**
See also CA 25-28; CAP 2; DLB 48

Nietzsche, Friedrich (Wilhelm)
1844-1900 .... TCLC **10, 18, 55**
See also CA 107; 121; DLB 129

Nievo, Ippolito 1831-1861 .... NCLC **22**

Nightingale, Anne Redmon 1943-
See Redmon, Anne
See also CA 103

Nik. T. O.
See Annensky, Innokenty Fyodorovich

Nin, Anais
1903-1977 ...... CLC **1, 4, 8, 11, 14, 60;**
SSC **10**
See also AITN 2; CA 13-16R; 69-72;
CANR 22; DLB 2, 4, 152; MTCW

Nissenson, Hugh 1933-.......... CLC **4, 9**
See also CA 17-20R; CANR 27; DLB 28

Niven, Larry .... CLC **8**
See also Niven, Laurence Van Cott
See also DLB 8

Niven, Laurence Van Cott 1938-
See Niven, Larry
See also CA 21-24R; CAAS 12; CANR 14,
44; MTCW

Nixon, Agnes Eckhardt 1927-...... CLC **21**
See also CA 110

Nizan, Paul 1905-1940.......... TCLC **40**
See also DLB 72

Nkosi, Lewis 1936-......... CLC **45; BLC**
See also BW 1; CA 65-68; CANR 27

Nodier, (Jean) Charles (Emmanuel)
1780-1844 .... NCLC **19**
See also DLB 119

Nolan, Christopher 1965-......... CLC **58**
See also CA 111

Norden, Charles
See Durrell, Lawrence (George)

Nordhoff, Charles (Bernard)
1887-1947 .... TCLC **23**
See also CA 108; DLB 9; SATA 23

Norfolk, Lawrence 1963-........ CLC **76**
See also CA 144

Norman, Marsha 1947- .... CLC **28**
See also CA 105; CABS 3; CANR 41;
DLBY 84

Norris, Benjamin Franklin, Jr.
1870-1902 .... TCLC **24**
See also Norris, Frank
See also CA 110

Norris, Frank
See Norris, Benjamin Franklin, Jr.
See also CDALB 1865-1917; DLB 12, 71

Norris, Leslie 1921-............. CLC **14**
See also CA 11-12; CANR 14; CAP 1;
DLB 27

North, Andrew
See Norton, Andre

North, Anthony
See Koontz, Dean R(ay)

North, Captain George
See Stevenson, Robert Louis (Balfour)

North, Milou
See Erdrich, Louise

Northrup, B. A.
See Hubbard, L(afayette) Ron(ald)

North Staffs
See Hulme, T(homas) E(rnest)

Norton, Alice Mary
See Norton, Andre
See also MAICYA; SATA 1, 43

Norton, Andre 1912- .... CLC **12**
See also Norton, Alice Mary
See also AAYA 14; CA 1-4R; CANR 2, 31;
DLB 8, 52; JRDA; MTCW

Norton, Caroline 1808-1877...... NCLC **47**
See also DLB 21

Norway, Nevil Shute 1899-1960
See Shute, Nevil
See also CA 102; 93-96

Norwid, Cyprian Kamil
1821-1883 .... NCLC **17**

Nosille, Nabrah
See Ellison, Harlan (Jay)

Nossack, Hans Erich 1901-1978..... CLC **6**
See also CA 93-96; 85-88; DLB 69

Nostradamus 1503-1566........... LC **27**

Nosu, Chuji
See Ozu, Yasujiro

Notenburg, Eleanora (Genrikhovna) von
See Guro, Elena

Nova, Craig 1945-.............. CLC **7, 31**
See also CA 45-48; CANR 2

Novak, Joseph
See Kosinski, Jerzy (Nikodem)

Novalis 1772-1801 .... NCLC **13**
See also DLB 90

Nowlan, Alden (Albert) 1933-1983 .. CLC **15**
See also CA 9-12R; CANR 5; DLB 53

Noyes, Alfred 1880-1958 .... TCLC **7**
See also CA 104; DLB 20

Nunn, Kem 19(?)-................ CLC **34**

Nye, Robert 1939- .... CLC **13, 42**
See also CA 33-36R; CANR 29; DLB 14;
MTCW; SATA 6

Nyro, Laura 1947- .... CLC **17**

Oates, Joyce Carol
1938- ...... CLC **1, 2, 3, 6, 9, 11, 15, 19,**
33, 52; DA; SSC 6; WLC
See also AITN 1; BEST 89:2; CA 5-8R;
CANR 25, 45; CDALB 1968-1988;
DLB 2, 5, 130; DLBY 81; MTCW

O'Brien, Darcy 1939-............. CLC **11**
See also CA 21-24R; CANR 8

O'Brien, E. G.
See Clarke, Arthur C(harles)

O'Brien, Edna
1936- ... CLC **3, 5, 8, 13, 36, 65; SSC 10**
See also CA 1-4R; CANR 6, 41;
CDBLB 1960 to Present; DLB 14;
MTCW

O'Brien, Fitz-James 1828-1862... NCLC **21**
See also DLB 74

O'Brien, Flann........ CLC **1, 4, 5, 7, 10, 47**
See also O Nuallain, Brian

O'Brien, Richard 1942-.......... CLC **17**
See also CA 124

O'Brien, Tim 1946-.......... CLC **7, 19, 40**
See also CA 85-88; CANR 40; DLB 152;
DLBD 9; DLBY 80

Obstfelder, Sigbjoern 1866-1900... TCLC **23**
See also CA 123

O'Casey, Sean
1880-1964 ...... CLC **1, 5, 9, 11, 15, 88**
See also CA 89-92; CDBLB 1914-1945;
DLB 10; MTCW

O'Cathasaigh, Sean
See O'Casey, Sean

Ochs, Phil 1940-1976............. CLC **17**
See also CA 65-68

O'Connor, Edwin (Greene)
1918-1968 .... CLC **14**
See also CA 93-96; 25-28R

O'Connor, (Mary) Flannery
1925-1964 .... CLC **1, 2, 3, 6, 10, 13, 15,**
21, 66; DA; SSC 1; WLC
See also AAYA 7; CA 1-4R; CANR 3, 41;
CDALB 1941-1968; DLB 2, 152;
DLBD 12; DLBY 80; MTCW

O'Connor, Frank........... CLC **23; SSC 5**
See also O'Donovan, Michael John

O'Dell, Scott 1898-1989........... CLC **30**
See also AAYA 3; CA 61-64; 129;
CANR 12, 30; CLR 1, 16; DLB 52;
JRDA; MAICYA; SATA 12, 60

Odets, Clifford 1906-1963 .... CLC **2, 28**
See also CA 85-88; DLB 7, 26; MTCW

O'Doherty, Brian 1934-........... CLC **76**
See also CA 105

O'Donnell, K. M.
See Malzberg, Barry N(athaniel)

O'Donnell, Lawrence
See Kuttner, Henry

O'Donovan, Michael John
1903-1966 .... CLC **14**
See also O'Connor, Frank
See also CA 93-96

Oe, Kenzaburo
1935- .... CLC **10, 36, 86; SSC 20**
See also CA 97-100; CANR 36; MTCW

O'Faolain, Julia 1932-....... CLC **6, 19, 47**
See also CA 81-84; CAAS 2; CANR 12;
DLB 14; MTCW

O'Faolain, Sean
1900-1991 .... CLC **1, 7, 14, 32, 70;**
SSC **13**
See also CA 61-64; 134; CANR 12;
DLB 15; MTCW

O'Flaherty, Liam
1896-1984 .... CLC **5, 34; SSC 6**
See also CA 101; 113; CANR 35; DLB 36;
DLBY 84; MTCW

Ogilvy, Gavin
See Barrie, J(ames) M(atthew)

Pancake, Breece D'J. . . . . CLC 29
See also Pancake, Breece Dexter
See also DLB 130

Panko, Rudy
See Gogol, Nikolai (Vasilyevich)

Papadiamantis, Alexandros
1851-1911 . . . . TCLC 29

Papadiamantopoulos, Johannes 1856-1910
See Moreas, Jean
See also CA 117

Papini, Giovanni 1881-1956 . . . . . . TCLC 22
See also CA 121

Paracelsus 1493-1541 . . . . LC 14

Parasol, Peter
See Stevens, Wallace

Parfenie, Maria
See Codrescu, Andrei

Parini, Jay (Lee) 1948- . . . . CLC 54
See also CA 97-100; CAAS 16; CANR 32

Park, Jordan
See Kornbluth, C(yril) M.; Pohl, Frederik

Parker, Bert
See Ellison, Harlan (Jay)

Parker, Dorothy (Rothschild)
1893-1967 . . . . CLC 15, 68; SSC 2
See also CA 19-20; 25-28R; CAP 2;
DLB 11, 45, 86; MTCW

Parker, Robert B(rown) 1932- . . . . . . CLC 27
See also BEST 89:4; CA 49-52; CANR 1,
26; MTCW

Parkin, Frank 1940- . . . . CLC 43
See also CA 147

Parkman, Francis, Jr.
1823-1893 . . . . NCLC 12
See also DLB 1, 30

Parks, Gordon (Alexander Buchanan)
1912- . . . . CLC 1, 16; BLC
See also AITN 2; BW 2; CA 41-44R;
CANR 26; DLB 33; SATA 8

Parnell, Thomas 1679-1718 . . . . LC 3
See also DLB 94

Parra, Nicanor 1914- . . . . CLC 2; HLC
See also CA 85-88; CANR 32; HW; MTCW

Parrish, Mary Frances
See Fisher, M(ary) F(rances) K(ennedy)

Parson
See Coleridge, Samuel Taylor

Parson Lot
See Kingsley, Charles

Partridge, Anthony
See Oppenheim, E(dward) Phillips

Pascoli, Giovanni 1855-1912 . . . . . TCLC 45

Pasolini, Pier Paolo
1922-1975 . . . . CLC 20, 37
See also CA 93-96; 61-64; DLB 128;
MTCW

Pasquini
See Silone, Ignazio

Pastan, Linda (Olenik) 1932- . . . . . . CLC 27
See also CA 61-64; CANR 18, 40; DLB 5

Pasternak, Boris (Leonidovich)
1890-1960 . . . . . . CLC 7, 10, 18, 63; DA;
PC 6; WLC
See also CA 127; 116; MTCW

Patchen, Kenneth 1911-1972 . . . CLC 1, 2, 18
See also CA 1-4R; 33-36R; CANR 3, 35;
DLB 16, 48; MTCW

Pater, Walter (Horatio)
1839-1894 . . . . NCLC 7
See also CDBLB 1832-1890; DLB 57

Paterson, A(ndrew) B(arton)
1864-1941 . . . . TCLC 32

Paterson, Katherine (Womeldorf)
1932- . . . . CLC 12, 30
See also AAYA 1; CA 21-24R; CANR 28;
CLR 7; DLB 52; JRDA; MAICYA;
MTCW; SATA 13, 53

Patmore, Coventry Kersey Dighton
1823-1896 . . . . NCLC 9
See also DLB 35, 98

Paton, Alan (Stewart)
1903-1988 . . . . . . CLC 4, 10, 25, 55; DA;
WLC
See also CA 13-16; 125; CANR 22; CAP 1;
MTCW; SATA 11; SATA-Obit 56

Paton Walsh, Gillian 1937-
See Walsh, Jill Paton
See also CANR 38; JRDA; MAICYA;
SAAS 3; SATA 4, 72

Paulding, James Kirke 1778-1860 . . NCLC 2
See also DLB 3, 59, 74

Paulin, Thomas Neilson 1949-
See Paulin, Tom
See also CA 123; 128

Paulin, Tom . . . . CLC 37
See also Paulin, Thomas Neilson
See also DLB 40

Paustovsky, Konstantin (Georgievich)
1892-1968 . . . . CLC 40
See also CA 93-96; 25-28R

Pavese, Cesare
1908-1950 . . . . . TCLC 3; PC 12; SSC 19
See also CA 104; DLB 128

Pavic, Milorad 1929- . . . . CLC 60
See also CA 136

Payne, Alan
See Jakes, John (William)

Paz, Gil
See Lugones, Leopoldo

Paz, Octavio
1914- . . . . CLC 3, 4, 6, 10, 19, 51, 65;
DA; HLC; PC 1; WLC
See also CA 73-76; CANR 32; DLBY 90;
HW; MTCW

Peacock, Molly 1947- . . . . CLC 60
See also CA 103; CAAS 21; DLB 120

Peacock, Thomas Love
1785-1866 . . . . NCLC 22
See also DLB 96, 116

Peake, Mervyn 1911-1968 . . . . CLC 7, 54
See also CA 5-8R; 25-28R; CANR 3;
DLB 15; MTCW; SATA 23

Pearce, Philippa . . . . CLC 21
See also Christie, (Ann) Philippa
See also CLR 9; MAICYA; SATA 1, 67

Pearl, Eric
See Elman, Richard

Pearson, T(homas) R(eid) 1956- . . . . CLC 39
See also CA 120; 130

Peck, Dale 1968(?)- . . . . CLC 81

Peck, John 1941- . . . . CLC 3
See also CA 49-52; CANR 3

Peck, Richard (Wayne) 1934- . . . . . . CLC 21
See also AAYA 1; CA 85-88; CANR 19,
38; CLR 15; JRDA; MAICYA; SAAS 2;
SATA 18, 55

Peck, Robert Newton 1928- . . . . CLC 17; DA
See also AAYA 3; CA 81-84; CANR 31;
JRDA; MAICYA; SAAS 1; SATA 21, 62

Peckinpah, (David) Sam(uel)
1925-1984 . . . . CLC 20
See also CA 109; 114

Pedersen, Knut 1859-1952
See Hamsun, Knut
See also CA 104; 119; MTCW

Peeslake, Gaffer
See Durrell, Lawrence (George)

Peguy, Charles Pierre
1873-1914 . . . . TCLC 10
See also CA 107

Pena, Ramon del Valle y
See Valle-Inclan, Ramon (Maria) del

Pendennis, Arthur Esquir
See Thackeray, William Makepeace

Penn, William 1644-1718 . . . . LC 25
See also DLB 24

Pepys, Samuel
1633-1703 . . . . LC 11; DA; WLC
See also CDBLB 1660-1789; DLB 101

Percy, Walker
1916-1990 . . . . CLC 2, 3, 6, 8, 14, 18, 47,
65
See also CA 1-4R; 131; CANR 1, 23;
DLB 2; DLBY 80, 90; MTCW

Perec, Georges 1936-1982 . . . . CLC 56
See also CA 141; DLB 83

Pereda (y Sanchez de Porrua), Jose Maria de
1833-1906 . . . . TCLC 16
See also CA 117

Pereda y Porrua, Jose Maria de
See Pereda (y Sanchez de Porrua), Jose
Maria de

Peregoy, George Weems
See Mencken, H(enry) L(ouis)

Perelman, S(idney) J(oseph)
1904-1979 . . . CLC 3, 5, 9, 15, 23, 44, 49
See also AITN 1, 2; CA 73-76; 89-92;
CANR 18; DLB 11, 44; MTCW

Peret, Benjamin 1899-1959 . . . . TCLC 20
See also CA 117

Peretz, Isaac Loeb 1851(?)-1915 . . . TCLC 16
See also CA 109

Peretz, Yitzkhok Leibush
See Peretz, Isaac Loeb

Perez Galdos, Benito 1843-1920 . . . TCLC 27
See also CA 125; HW

Perrault, Charles 1628-1703 . . . . LC 2
See also MAICYA; SATA 25

Perry, Brighton
See Sherwood, Robert E(mmet)

Perse, St.-John . . . . CLC 4, 11, 46
See also Leger, (Marie-Rene Auguste) Alexis
Saint-Leger

Perutz, Leo 1882-1957 . . . . TCLC 60
  See also DLB 81

Peseenz, Tulio F.
  See Lopez y Fuentes, Gregorio

Pesetsky, Bette 1932- . . . . CLC 28
  See also CA 133; DLB 130

Peshkov, Alexei Maximovich 1868-1936
  See Gorky, Maxim
  See also CA 105; 141; DA

Pessoa, Fernando (Antonio Nogueira)
  1888-1935 . . . . TCLC 27; HLC
  See also CA 125

Peterkin, Julia Mood 1880-1961 . . . . CLC 31
  See also CA 102; DLB 9

Peters, Joan K. 1945- . . . . CLC 39

Peters, Robert L(ouis) 1924- . . . . CLC 7
  See also CA 13-16R; CAAS 8; DLB 105

Petofi, Sandor 1823-1849 . . . . NCLC 21

Petrakis, Harry Mark 1923- . . . . CLC 3
  See also CA 9-12R; CANR 4, 30

Petrarch 1304-1374 . . . . PC 8

Petrov, Evgeny . . . . TCLC 21
  See also Kataev, Evgeny Petrovich

Petry, Ann (Lane) 1908- . . . . . . CLC 1, 7, 18
  See also BW 1; CA 5-8R; CAAS 6;
  CANR 4, 46; CLR 12; DLB 76; JRDA;
  MAICYA; MTCW; SATA 5

Petursson, Halligrimur 1614-1674 . . . . LC 8

Philips, Katherine 1632-1664 . . . . LC 30
  See also DLB 131

Philipson, Morris H. 1926- . . . . CLC 53
  See also CA 1-4R; CANR 4

Phillips, David Graham
  1867-1911 . . . . TCLC 44
  See also CA 108; DLB 9, 12

Phillips, Jack
  See Sandburg, Carl (August)

Phillips, Jayne Anne
  1952- . . . . CLC 15, 33; SSC 16
  See also CA 101; CANR 24; DLBY 80;
  MTCW

Phillips, Richard
  See Dick, Philip K(indred)

Phillips, Robert (Schaeffer) 1938- . . . CLC 28
  See also CA 17-20R; CAAS 13; CANR 8;
  DLB 105

Phillips, Ward
  See Lovecraft, H(oward) P(hillips)

Piccolo, Lucio 1901-1969 . . . . CLC 13
  See also CA 97-100; DLB 114

Pickthall, Marjorie L(owry) C(hristie)
  1883-1922 . . . . TCLC 21
  See also CA 107; DLB 92

Pico della Mirandola, Giovanni
  1463-1494 . . . . LC 15

Piercy, Marge
  1936- . . . . CLC 3, 6, 14, 18, 27, 62
  See also CA 21-24R; CAAS 1; CANR 13,
  43; DLB 120; MTCW

Piers, Robert
  See Anthony, Piers

Pieyre de Mandiargues, Andre 1909-1991
  See Mandiargues, Andre Pieyre de
  See also CA 103; 136; CANR 22

Pilnyak, Boris . . . . TCLC 23
  See also Vogau, Boris Andreyevich

Pincherle, Alberto 1907-1990 . . . CLC 11, 18
  See also Moravia, Alberto
  See also CA 25-28R; 132; CANR 33;
  MTCW

Pinckney, Darryl 1953- . . . . CLC 76
  See also BW 2; CA 143

Pindar 518B.C.-446B.C. . . . . CMLC 12

Pineda, Cecile 1942- . . . . CLC 39
  See also CA 118

Pinero, Arthur Wing 1855-1934 . . . TCLC 32
  See also CA 110; DLB 10

Pinero, Miguel (Antonio Gomez)
  1946-1988 . . . . CLC 4, 55
  See also CA 61-64; 125; CANR 29; HW

Pinget, Robert 1919- . . . . CLC 7, 13, 37
  See also CA 85-88; DLB 83

Pink Floyd
  See Barrett, (Roger) Syd; Gilmour, David;
  Mason, Nick; Waters, Roger; Wright,
  Rick

Pinkney, Edward 1802-1828 . . . . . NCLC 31

Pinkwater, Daniel Manus 1941- . . . . CLC 35
  See also Pinkwater, Manus
  See also AAYA 1; CA 29-32R; CANR 12,
  38; CLR 4; JRDA; MAICYA; SAAS 3;
  SATA 46, 76

Pinkwater, Manus
  See Pinkwater, Daniel Manus
  See also SATA 8

Pinsky, Robert 1940- . . . . CLC 9, 19, 38
  See also CA 29-32R; CAAS 4; DLBY 82

Pinta, Harold
  See Pinter, Harold

Pinter, Harold
  1930- . . . . . CLC 1, 3, 6, 9, 11, 15, 27, 58,
                                    73; DA; WLC
  See also CA 5-8R; CANR 33; CDBLB 1960
  to Present; DLB 13; MTCW

Pirandello, Luigi
  1867-1936 . . . . . TCLC 4, 29; DA; DC 5;
                                          WLC
  See also CA 104

Pirsig, Robert M(aynard)
  1928- . . . . CLC 4, 6, 73
  See also CA 53-56; CANR 42; MTCW;
  SATA 39

Pisarev, Dmitry Ivanovich
  1840-1868 . . . . NCLC 25

Pix, Mary (Griffith) 1666-1709 . . . . . . LC 8
  See also DLB 80

Pixerecourt, Guilbert de
  1773-1844 . . . . NCLC 39

Plaidy, Jean
  See Hibbert, Eleanor Alice Burford

Planche, James Robinson
  1796-1880 . . . . NCLC 42

Plant, Robert 1948- . . . . CLC 12

Plante, David (Robert)
  1940- . . . . CLC 7, 23, 38
  See also CA 37-40R; CANR 12, 36;
  DLBY 83; MTCW

Plath, Sylvia
  1932-1963 . . . . . CLC 1, 2, 3, 5, 9, 11, 14,
                      17, 50, 51, 62; DA; PC 1; WLC
  See also AAYA 13; CA 19-20; CANR 34;
  CAP 2; CDALB 1941-1968; DLB 5, 6,
  152; MTCW

Plato 428(?)B.C.-348(?)B.C. . . . . CMLC 8; DA

Platonov, Andrei . . . . TCLC 14
  See also Klimentov, Andrei Platonovich

Platt, Kin 1911- . . . . CLC 26
  See also AAYA 11; CA 17-20R; CANR 11;
  JRDA; SAAS 17; SATA 21

Plick et Plock
  See Simenon, Georges (Jacques Christian)

Plimpton, George (Ames) 1927- . . . . . CLC 36
  See also AITN 1; CA 21-24R; CANR 32;
  MTCW; SATA 10

Plomer, William Charles Franklin
  1903-1973 . . . . CLC 4, 8
  See also CA 21-22; CANR 34; CAP 2;
  DLB 20; MTCW; SATA 24

Plowman, Piers
  See Kavanagh, Patrick (Joseph)

Plum, J.
  See Wodehouse, P(elham) G(renville)

Plumly, Stanley (Ross) 1939- . . . . . . CLC 33
  See also CA 108; 110; DLB 5

Plumpe, Friedrich Wilhelm
  1888-1931 . . . . TCLC 53
  See also CA 112

Poe, Edgar Allan
  1809-1849 . . . . . NCLC 1, 16; DA; PC 1;
                                      SSC 1; WLC
  See also AAYA 14; CDALB 1640-1865;
  DLB 3, 59, 73, 74; SATA 23

Poet of Titchfield Street, The
  See Pound, Ezra (Weston Loomis)

Pohl, Frederick 1919- . . . . CLC 18
  See also CA 61-64; CAAS 1; CANR 11, 37;
  DLB 8; MTCW; SATA 24

Poirier, Louis 1910-
  See Gracq, Julien
  See also CA 122; 126

Poitier, Sidney 1927- . . . . CLC 26
  See also BW 1; CA 117

Polanski, Roman 1933- . . . . CLC 16
  See also CA 77-80

Poliakoff, Stephen 1952- . . . . CLC 38
  See also CA 106; DLB 13

Police, The
  See Copeland, Stewart (Armstrong);
  Summers, Andrew James; Sumner,
  Gordon Matthew

Polidori, John William
  1795-1821 . . . . NCLC 51
  See also DLB 116

Pollitt, Katha 1949- . . . . CLC 28
  See also CA 120; 122; MTCW

Pollock, (Mary) Sharon 1936- . . . . . . CLC 50
  See also CA 141; DLB 60

Polo, Marco 1254-1324 . . . . CMLC 15

Pomerance, Bernard 1940-......... **CLC 13**
See also CA 101

Ponge, Francis (Jean Gaston Alfred)
1899-1988 .... **CLC 6, 18**
See also CA 85-88; 126; CANR 40

Pontoppidan, Henrik 1857-1943 ... **TCLC 29**

Poole, Josephine .... **CLC 17**
See also Helyar, Jane Penelope Josephine
See also SAAS 2; SATA 5

Popa, Vasko 1922-............... **CLC 19**
See also CA 112

Pope, Alexander
1688-1744 .... **LC 3; DA; WLC**
See also CDBLB 1660-1789; DLB 95, 101

Porter, Connie (Rose) 1959(?)-..... **CLC 70**
See also BW 2; CA 142; SATA 81

Porter, Gene(va Grace) Stratton
1863(?)-1924 .... **TCLC 21**
See also CA 112

Porter, Katherine Anne
1890-1980 ...... **CLC 1, 3, 7, 10, 13, 15,**
                      27; DA; SSC 4
See also AITN 2; CA 1-4R; 101; CANR 1;
DLB 4, 9, 102; DLBD 12; DLBY 80;
MTCW; SATA 39; SATA-Obit 23

Porter, Peter (Neville Frederick)
1929-.................. **CLC 5, 13, 33**
See also CA 85-88; DLB 40

Porter, William Sydney 1862-1910
See Henry, O.
See also CA 104; 131; CDALB 1865-1917;
DA; DLB 12, 78, 79; MTCW; YABC 2

Portillo (y Pacheco), Jose Lopez
See Lopez Portillo (y Pacheco), Jose

Post, Melville Davisson
1869-1930 .... **TCLC 39**
See also CA 110

Potok, Chaim 1929-....... **CLC 2, 7, 14, 26**
See also AITN 1, 2; CA 17-20R; CANR 19,
35; DLB 28, 152; MTCW; SATA 33

Potter, Beatrice
See Webb, (Martha) Beatrice (Potter)
See also MAICYA

Potter, Dennis (Christopher George)
1935-1994 .... **CLC 58, 86**
See also CA 107; 145; CANR 33; MTCW

Pound, Ezra (Weston Loomis)
1885-1972 ...... **CLC 1, 2, 3, 4, 5, 7, 10,**
            13, 18, 34, 48, 50; DA; PC 4; WLC
See also CA 5-8R; 37-40R; CANR 40;
CDALB 1917-1929; DLB 4, 45, 63;
MTCW

Povod, Reinaldo 1959-1994 .... **CLC 44**
See also CA 136; 146

Powell, Adam Clayton, Jr.
1908-1972 .... **CLC 89; BLC**
See also BW 1; CA 102; 33-36R

Powell, Anthony (Dymoke)
1905-........... **CLC 1, 3, 7, 9, 10, 31**
See also CA 1-4R; CANR 1, 32;
CDBLB 1945-1960; DLB 15; MTCW

Powell, Dawn 1897-1965 .... **CLC 66**
See also CA 5-8R

Powell, Padgett 1952-............. **CLC 34**
See also CA 126

Powers, J(ames) F(arl)
1917-.......... **CLC 1, 4, 8, 57; SSC 4**
See also CA 1-4R; CANR 2; DLB 130;
MTCW

Powers, John J(ames) 1945-
See Powers, John R.
See also CA 69-72

Powers, John R. .... **CLC 66**
See also Powers, John J(ames)

Pownall, David 1938-............. **CLC 10**
See also CA 89-92; CAAS 18; DLB 14

Powys, John Cowper
1872-1963 .... **CLC 7, 9, 15, 46**
See also CA 85-88; DLB 15; MTCW

Powys, T(heodore) F(rancis)
1875-1953 .... **TCLC 9**
See also CA 106; DLB 36

Prager, Emily 1952-............. **CLC 56**

Pratt, E(dwin) J(ohn)
1883(?)-1964 .... **CLC 19**
See also CA 141; 93-96; DLB 92

Premchand .... **TCLC 21**
See also Srivastava, Dhanpat Rai

Preussler, Otfried 1923-.......... **CLC 17**
See also CA 77-80; SATA 24

Prevert, Jacques (Henri Marie)
1900-1977 .... **CLC 15**
See also CA 77-80; 69-72; CANR 29;
MTCW; SATA-Obit 30

Prevost, Abbe (Antoine Francois)
1697-1763 .... **LC 1**

Price, (Edward) Reynolds
1933-..... **CLC 3, 6, 13, 43, 50, 63**
See also CA 1-4R; CANR 1, 37; DLB 2

Price, Richard 1949-........... **CLC 6, 12**
See also CA 49-52; CANR 3; DLBY 81

Prichard, Katharine Susannah
1883-1969 .... **CLC 46**
See also CA 11-12; CANR 33; CAP 1;
MTCW; SATA 66

Priestley, J(ohn) B(oynton)
1894-1984 .... **CLC 2, 5, 9, 34**
See also CA 9-12R; 113; CANR 33;
CDBLB 1914-1945; DLB 10, 34, 77, 100,
139; DLBY 84; MTCW

Prince 1958(?)-.................. **CLC 35**

Prince, F(rank) T(empleton) 1912-.. **CLC 22**
See also CA 101; CANR 43; DLB 20

Prince Kropotkin
See Kropotkin, Peter (Aleksieevich)

Prior, Matthew 1664-1721.......... **LC 4**
See also DLB 95

Pritchard, William H(arrison)
1932-...................... **CLC 34**
See also CA 65-68; CANR 23; DLB 111

Pritchett, V(ictor) S(awdon)
1900-....... **CLC 5, 13, 15, 41; SSC 14**
See also CA 61-64; CANR 31; DLB 15,
139; MTCW

Private 19022
See Manning, Frederic

Probst, Mark 1925-................ **CLC 59**
See also CA 130

Prokosch, Frederic 1908-1989.... **CLC 4, 48**
See also CA 73-76; 128; DLB 48

Prophet, The
See Dreiser, Theodore (Herman Albert)

Prose, Francine 1947-............. **CLC 45**
See also CA 109; 112; CANR 46

Proudhon
See Cunha, Euclides (Rodrigues Pimenta) da

Proulx, E. Annie 1935-........... **CLC 81**

Proust, (Valentin-Louis-George-Eugene-)
Marcel
1871-1922 ... **TCLC 7, 13, 33; DA; WLC**
See also CA 104; 120; DLB 65; MTCW

Prowler, Harley
See Masters, Edgar Lee

Prus, Boleslaw 1845-1912 .... **TCLC 48**

Pryor, Richard (Franklin Lenox Thomas)
1940-...................... **CLC 26**
See also CA 122

Przybyszewski, Stanislaw
1868-1927 .... **TCLC 36**
See also DLB 66

Pteleon
See Grieve, C(hristopher) M(urray)

Puckett, Lute
See Masters, Edgar Lee

Puig, Manuel
1932-1990 ... **CLC 3, 5, 10, 28, 65; HLC**
See also CA 45-48; CANR 2, 32; DLB 113;
HW; MTCW

Purdy, Al(fred Wellington)
1918-................ **CLC 3, 6, 14, 50**
See also CA 81-84; CAAS 17; CANR 42;
DLB 88

Purdy, James (Amos)
1923-............ **CLC 2, 4, 10, 28, 52**
See also CA 33-36R; CAAS 1; CANR 19;
DLB 2; MTCW

Pure, Simon
See Swinnerton, Frank Arthur

Pushkin, Alexander (Sergeyevich)
1799-1837 .... **NCLC 3, 27; DA; PC 10;**
                         WLC
See also SATA 61

P'u Sung-ling 1640-1715 .... **LC 3**

Putnam, Arthur Lee
See Alger, Horatio, Jr.

Puzo, Mario 1920-......... **CLC 1, 2, 6, 36**
See also CA 65-68; CANR 4, 42; DLB 6;
MTCW

Pym, Barbara (Mary Crampton)
1913-1980 .... **CLC 13, 19, 37**
See also CA 13-14; 97-100; CANR 13, 34;
CAP 1; DLB 14; DLBY 87; MTCW

Pynchon, Thomas (Ruggles, Jr.)
1937-..... **CLC 2, 3, 6, 9, 11, 18, 33, 62,**
                   72; DA; SSC 14; WLC
See also BEST 90:2; CA 17-20R; CANR 22,
46; DLB 2; MTCW

Qian Zhongshu
See Ch'ien Chung-shu

Qroll
See Dagerman, Stig (Halvard)

Quarrington, Paul (Lewis) 1953-.... CLC 65
See also CA 129

Quasimodo, Salvatore 1901-1968 ... CLC 10
See also CA 13-16; 25-28R; CAP 1;
DLB 114; MTCW

Queen, Ellery........................CLC 3, 11
See also Dannay, Frederic; Davidson,
Avram; Lee, Manfred B(ennington);
Sturgeon, Theodore (Hamilton); Vance,
John Holbrook

Queen, Ellery, Jr.
See Dannay, Frederic; Lee, Manfred
B(ennington)

Queneau, Raymond
1903-1976 .... CLC 2, 5, 10, 42
See also CA 77-80; 69-72; CANR 32;
DLB 72; MTCW

Quevedo, Francisco de 1580-1645.... LC 23

Quiller-Couch, Arthur Thomas
1863-1944 .... TCLC 53
See also CA 118; DLB 135, 153

Quin, Ann (Marie) 1936-1973....... CLC 6
See also CA 9-12R; 45-48; DLB 14

Quinn, Martin
See Smith, Martin Cruz

Quinn, Simon
See Smith, Martin Cruz

Quiroga, Horacio (Sylvestre)
1878-1937 .... TCLC 20; HLC
See also CA 117; 131; HW; MTCW

Quoirez, Francoise 1935-........... CLC 9
See also Sagan, Francoise
See also CA 49-52; CANR 6, 39; MTCW

Raabe, Wilhelm 1831-1910 .... TCLC 45
See also DLB 129

Rabe, David (William) 1940-... CLC 4, 8, 33
See also CA 85-88; CABS 3; DLB 7

Rabelais, Francois
1483-1553 .... LC 5; DA; WLC

Rabinovitch, Sholem 1859-1916
See Aleichem, Sholom
See also CA 104

Racine, Jean 1639-1699 .... LC 28

Radcliffe, Ann (Ward) 1764-1823 .. NCLC 6
See also DLB 39

Radiguet, Raymond 1903-1923 .... TCLC 29
See also DLB 65

Radnoti, Miklos 1909-1944 .... TCLC 16
See also CA 118

Rado, James 1939-................ CLC 17
See also CA 105

Radvanyi, Netty 1900-1983
See Seghers, Anna
See also CA 85-88; 110

Rae, Ben
See Griffiths, Trevor

Raeburn, John (Hay) 1941-........ CLC 34
See also CA 57-60

Ragni, Gerome 1942-1991 .... CLC 17
See also CA 105; 134

Rahv, Philip 1908-1973 .... CLC 24
See also Greenberg, Ivan
See also DLB 137

Raine, Craig 1944-................ CLC 32
See also CA 108; CANR 29; DLB 40

Raine, Kathleen (Jessie) 1908- ... CLC 7, 45
See also CA 85-88; CANR 46; DLB 20;
MTCW

Rainis, Janis 1865-1929 .... TCLC 29

Rakosi, Carl...................... CLC 47
See also Rawley, Callman
See also CAAS 5

Raleigh, Richard
See Lovecraft, H(oward) P(hillips)

Rallentando, H. P.
See Sayers, Dorothy L(eigh)

Ramal, Walter
See de la Mare, Walter (John)

Ramon, Juan
See Jimenez (Mantecon), Juan Ramon

Ramos, Graciliano 1892-1953 ..... TCLC 32

Rampersad, Arnold 1941-......... CLC 44
See also BW 2; CA 127; 133; DLB 111

Rampling, Anne
See Rice, Anne

Ramsay, Allan 1684(?)-1758 .... LC 29
See also DLB 95

Ramuz, Charles-Ferdinand
1878-1947 .... TCLC 33

Rand, Ayn
1905-1982 ...... CLC 3, 30, 44, 79; DA;
WLC
See also AAYA 10; CA 13-16R; 105;
CANR 27; MTCW

Randall, Dudley (Felker)
1914- .... CLC 1; BLC
See also BW 1; CA 25-28R; CANR 23;
DLB 41

Randall, Robert
See Silverberg, Robert

Ranger, Ken
See Creasey, John

Ransom, John Crowe
1888-1974 .... CLC 2, 4, 5, 11, 24
See also CA 5-8R; 49-52; CANR 6, 34;
DLB 45, 63; MTCW

Rao, Raja 1909- .... CLC 25, 56
See also CA 73-76; MTCW

Raphael, Frederic (Michael)
1931- .... CLC 2, 14
See also CA 1-4R; CANR 1; DLB 14

Ratcliffe, James P.
See Mencken, H(enry) L(ouis)

Rathbone, Julian 1935- .... CLC 41
See also CA 101; CANR 34

Rattigan, Terence (Mervyn)
1911-1977 .... CLC 7
See also CA 85-88; 73-76;
CDBLB 1945-1960; DLB 13; MTCW

Ratushinskaya, Irina 1954- .... CLC 54
See also CA 129

Raven, Simon (Arthur Noel)
1927- .... CLC 14
See also CA 81-84

Rawley, Callman 1903-
See Rakosi, Carl
See also CA 21-24R; CANR 12, 32

Rawlings, Marjorie Kinnan
1896-1953 .... TCLC 4
See also CA 104; 137; DLB 9, 22, 102;
JRDA; MAICYA; YABC 1

Ray, Satyajit 1921-1992........ CLC 16, 76
See also CA 114; 137

Read, Herbert Edward 1893-1968.... CLC 4
See also CA 85-88; 25-28R; DLB 20, 149

Read, Piers Paul 1941- ...... CLC 4, 10, 25
See also CA 21-24R; CANR 38; DLB 14;
SATA 21

Reade, Charles 1814-1884 .... NCLC 2
See also DLB 21

Reade, Hamish
See Gray, Simon (James Holliday)

Reading, Peter 1946- .... CLC 47
See also CA 103; CANR 46; DLB 40

Reaney, James 1926- .... CLC 13
See also CA 41-44R; CAAS 15; CANR 42;
DLB 68; SATA 43

Rebreanu, Liviu 1885-1944 .... TCLC 28

Rechy, John (Francisco)
1934- .... CLC 1, 7, 14, 18; HLC
See also CA 5-8R; CAAS 4; CANR 6, 32;
DLB 122; DLBY 82; HW

Redcam, Tom 1870-1933 .... TCLC 25

Reddin, Keith.................... CLC 67

Redgrove, Peter (William)
1932- .... CLC 6, 41
See also CA 1-4R; CANR 3, 39; DLB 40

Redmon, Anne.................... CLC 22
See also Nightingale, Anne Redmon
See also DLBY 86

Reed, Eliot
See Ambler, Eric

Reed, Ishmael
1938- ... CLC 2, 3, 5, 6, 13, 32, 60; BLC
See also BW 2; CA 21-24R; CANR 25, 48;
DLB 2, 5, 33; DLBD 8; MTCW

Reed, John (Silas) 1887-1920 ...... TCLC 9
See also CA 106

Reed, Lou........................ CLC 21
See also Firbank, Louis

Reeve, Clara 1729-1807 .... NCLC 19
See also DLB 39

Reich, Wilhelm 1897-1957........ TCLC 57

Reid, Christopher (John) 1949-..... CLC 33
See also CA 140; DLB 40

Reid, Desmond
See Moorcock, Michael (John)

Reid Banks, Lynne 1929-
See Banks, Lynne Reid
See also CA 1-4R; CANR 6, 22, 38;
CLR 24; JRDA; MAICYA; SATA 22, 75

Reilly, William K.
See Creasey, John

Reiner, Max
See Caldwell, (Janet Miriam) Taylor
(Holland)

Reis, Ricardo
See Pessoa, Fernando (Antonio Nogueira)

Roberts, Charles G(eorge) D(ouglas)
1860-1943 .... **TCLC 8**
See also CA 105; CLR 33; DLB 92;
SATA-Brief 29

Roberts, Kate 1891-1985 .... **CLC 15**
See also CA 107; 116

Roberts, Keith (John Kingston)
1935- .... **CLC 14**
See also CA 25-28R; CANR 46

Roberts, Kenneth (Lewis)
1885-1957 .... **TCLC 23**
See also CA 109; DLB 9

Roberts, Michele (B.) 1949-........ **CLC 48**
See also CA 115

Robertson, Ellis
See Ellison, Harlan (Jay); Silverberg, Robert

Robertson, Thomas William
1829-1871 .... **NCLC 35**

Robinson, Edwin Arlington
1869-1935 .... **TCLC 5; DA; PC 1**
See also CA 104; 133; CDALB 1865-1917;
DLB 54; MTCW

Robinson, Henry Crabb
1775-1867 .... **NCLC 15**
See also DLB 107

Robinson, Jill 1936- .... **CLC 10**
See also CA 102

Robinson, Kim Stanley 1952- ...... **CLC 34**
See also CA 126

Robinson, Lloyd
See Silverberg, Robert

Robinson, Marilynne 1944-........ **CLC 25**
See also CA 116

Robinson, Smokey................. **CLC 21**
See also Robinson, William, Jr.

Robinson, William, Jr. 1940-
See Robinson, Smokey
See also CA 116

Robison, Mary 1949- .... **CLC 42**
See also CA 113; 116; DLB 130

Rod, Edouard 1857-1910 .... **TCLC 52**

Roddenberry, Eugene Wesley 1921-1991
See Roddenberry, Gene
See also CA 110; 135; CANR 37; SATA 45;
SATA-Obit 69

Roddenberry, Gene .... **CLC 17**
See also Roddenberry, Eugene Wesley
See also AAYA 5; SATA-Obit 69

Rodgers, Mary 1931- .... **CLC 12**
See also CA 49-52; CANR 8; CLR 20;
JRDA; MAICYA; SATA 8

Rodgers, W(illiam) R(obert)
1909-1969 .... **CLC 7**
See also CA 85-88; DLB 20

Rodman, Eric
See Silverberg, Robert

Rodman, Howard 1920(?)-1985 ..... **CLC 65**
See also CA 118

Rodman, Maia
See Wojciechowska, Maia (Teresa)

Rodriguez, Claudio 1934-......... **CLC 10**
See also DLB 134

Roelvaag, O(le) E(dvart)
1876-1931 .... **TCLC 17**
See also CA 117; DLB 9

Roethke, Theodore (Huebner)
1908-1963 ...... **CLC 1, 3, 8, 11, 19, 46**
See also CA 81-84; CABS 2;
CDALB 1941-1968; DLB 5; MTCW

Rogers, Thomas Hunton 1927- ..... **CLC 57**
See also CA 89-92

Rogers, Will(iam Penn Adair)
1879-1935 .... **TCLC 8**
See also CA 105; 144; DLB 11; NNAL

Rogin, Gilbert 1929-.............. **CLC 18**
See also CA 65-68; CANR 15

Rohan, Koda .... **TCLC 22**
See also Koda Shigeyuki

Rohmer, Eric.................... **CLC 16**
See also Scherer, Jean-Marie Maurice

Rohmer, Sax .... **TCLC 28**
See also Ward, Arthur Henry Sarsfield
See also DLB 70

Roiphe, Anne (Richardson)
1935- .... **CLC 3, 9**
See also CA 89-92; CANR 45; DLBY 80

Rojas, Fernando de 1465-1541 ...... **LC 23**

**Rolfe, Frederick (William Serafino Austin
Lewis Mary)** 1860-1913...... **TCLC 12**
See also CA 107; DLB 34

Rolland, Romain 1866-1944...... **TCLC 23**
See also CA 118; DLB 65

Rolvaag, O(le) E(dvart)
See Roelvaag, O(le) E(dvart)

Romain Arnaud, Saint
See Aragon, Louis

Romains, Jules 1885-1972 .... **CLC 7**
See also CA 85-88; CANR 34; DLB 65;
MTCW

Romero, Jose Ruben 1890-1952 ... **TCLC 14**
See also CA 114; 131; HW

Ronsard, Pierre de
1524-1585 .... **LC 6; PC 11**

Rooke, Leon 1934-............. **CLC 25, 34**
See also CA 25-28R; CANR 23

Roper, William 1498-1578 .... **LC 10**

Roquelaure, A. N.
See Rice, Anne

Rosa, Joao Guimaraes 1908-1967 ... **CLC 23**
See also CA 89-92; DLB 113

Rose, Wendy 1948-......... **CLC 85; PC 12**
See also CA 53-56; CANR 5; NNAL;
SATA 12

Rosen, Richard (Dean) 1949-....... **CLC 39**
See also CA 77-80

Rosenberg, Isaac 1890-1918...... **TCLC 12**
See also CA 107; DLB 20

Rosenblatt, Joe .... **CLC 15**
See also Rosenblatt, Joseph

Rosenblatt, Joseph 1933-
See Rosenblatt, Joe
See also CA 89-92

Rosenfeld, Samuel 1896-1963
See Tzara, Tristan
See also CA 89-92

Rosenthal, M(acha) L(ouis) 1917-... **CLC 28**
See also CA 1-4R; CAAS 6; CANR 4;
DLB 5; SATA 59

Ross, Barnaby
See Dannay, Frederic

Ross, Bernard L.
See Follett, Ken(neth Martin)

Ross, J. H.
See Lawrence, T(homas) E(dward)

Ross, Martin
See Martin, Violet Florence
See also DLB 135

Ross, (James) Sinclair 1908-....... **CLC 13**
See also CA 73-76; DLB 88

Rossetti, Christina (Georgina)
1830-1894 ..... **NCLC 2, 50; DA; PC 7;
WLC**
See also DLB 35; MAICYA; SATA 20

Rossetti, Dante Gabriel
1828-1882 .... **NCLC 4; DA; WLC**
See also CDBLB 1832-1890; DLB 35

Rossner, Judith (Perelman)
1935- .... **CLC 6, 9, 29**
See also AITN 2; BEST 90:3; CA 17-20R;
CANR 18; DLB 6; MTCW

Rostand, Edmond (Eugene Alexis)
1868-1918 .... **TCLC 6, 37; DA**
See also CA 104; 126; MTCW

Roth, Henry 1906-........... **CLC 2, 6, 11**
See also CA 11-12; CANR 38; CAP 1;
DLB 28; MTCW

Roth, Joseph 1894-1939.......... **TCLC 33**
See also DLB 85

Roth, Philip (Milton)
1933- ...... **CLC 1, 2, 3, 4, 6, 9, 15, 22,
31, 47, 66, 86; DA; WLC**
See also BEST 90:3; CA 1-4R; CANR 1, 22,
36; CDALB 1968-1988; DLB 2, 28;
DLBY 82; MTCW

Rothenberg, Jerome 1931-........ **CLC 6, 57**
See also CA 45-48; CANR 1; DLB 5

Roumain, Jacques (Jean Baptiste)
1907-1944 .... **TCLC 19; BLC**
See also BW 1; CA 117; 125

Rourke, Constance (Mayfield)
1885-1941 .... **TCLC 12**
See also CA 107; YABC 1

Rousseau, Jean-Baptiste 1671-1741 ... **LC 9**

Rousseau, Jean-Jacques
1712-1778 .... **LC 14; DA; WLC**

Roussel, Raymond 1877-1933 ..... **TCLC 20**
See also CA 117

Rovit, Earl (Herbert) 1927-......... **CLC 7**
See also CA 5-8R; CANR 12

Rowe, Nicholas 1674-1718.......... **LC 8**
See also DLB 84

Rowley, Ames Dorrance
See Lovecraft, H(oward) P(hillips)

Rowson, Susanna Haswell
1762(?)-1824 .... **NCLC 5**
See also DLB 37

Roy, Gabrielle 1909-1983....... **CLC 10, 14**
See also CA 53-56; 110; CANR 5; DLB 68;
MTCW

Rozewicz, Tadeusz 1921-........ **CLC 9, 23**
See also CA 108; CANR 36; MTCW

Ruark, Gibbons 1941- .... **CLC 3**
See also CA 33-36R; CANR 14, 31;
DLB 120

Rubens, Bernice (Ruth) 1923-... **CLC 19, 31**
See also CA 25-28R; CANR 33; DLB 14;
MTCW

Rudkin, (James) David 1936- ...... **CLC 14**
See also CA 89-92; DLB 13

Rudnik, Raphael 1933-............. **CLC 7**
See also CA 29-32R

Ruffian, M.
See Hasek, Jaroslav (Matej Frantisek)

Ruiz, Jose Martinez .... **CLC 11**
See also Martinez Ruiz, Jose

Rukeyser, Muriel
1913-1980 .... **CLC 6, 10, 15, 27; PC 12**
See also CA 5-8R; 93-96; CANR 26;
DLB 48; MTCW; SATA-Obit 22

Rule, Jane (Vance) 1931-.......... **CLC 27**
See also CA 25-28R; CAAS 18; CANR 12;
DLB 60

Rulfo, Juan 1918-1986.... **CLC 8, 80; HLC**
See also CA 85-88; 118; CANR 26;
DLB 113; HW; MTCW

Runeberg, Johan 1804-1877...... **NCLC 41**

Runyon, (Alfred) Damon
1884(?)-1946 .... **TCLC 10**
See also CA 107; DLB 11, 86

Rush, Norman 1933-.............. **CLC 44**
See also CA 121; 126

Rushdie, (Ahmed) Salman
1947- .... **CLC 23, 31, 55**
See also BEST 89:3; CA 108; 111;
CANR 33; MTCW

Rushforth, Peter (Scott) 1945- ..... **CLC 19**
See also CA 101

Ruskin, John 1819-1900.......... **TCLC 20**
See also CA 114; 129; CDBLB 1832-1890;
DLB 55; SATA 24

Russ, Joanna 1937-.............. **CLC 15**
See also CA 25-28R; CANR 11, 31; DLB 8;
MTCW

Russell, George William 1867-1935
See A. E.
See also CA 104; CDBLB 1890-1914

Russell, (Henry) Ken(neth Alfred)
1927- .... **CLC 16**
See also CA 105

Russell, Willy 1947- .... **CLC 60**

Rutherford, Mark .... **TCLC 25**
See also White, William Hale
See also DLB 18

Ruyslinck, Ward 1929-............ **CLC 14**
See also Belser, Reimond Karel Maria de

Ryan, Cornelius (John) 1920-1974 ... **CLC 7**
See also CA 69-72; 53-56; CANR 38

Ryan, Michael 1946- .... **CLC 65**
See also CA 49-52; DLBY 82

Rybakov, Anatoli (Naumovich)
1911- .... **CLC 23, 53**
See also CA 126; 135; SATA 79

Ryder, Jonathan
See Ludlum, Robert

Ryga, George 1932-1987 .... **CLC 14**
See also CA 101; 124; CANR 43; DLB 60

S. S.
See Sassoon, Siegfried (Lorraine)

Saba, Umberto 1883-1957 .... **TCLC 33**
See also CA 144; DLB 114

Sabatini, Rafael 1875-1950 ...... **TCLC 47**

Sabato, Ernesto (R.)
1911- .... **CLC 10, 23; HLC**
See also CA 97-100; CANR 32; DLB 145;
HW; MTCW

Sacastru, Martin
See Bioy Casares, Adolfo

Sacher-Masoch, Leopold von
1836(?)-1895 .... **NCLC 31**

Sachs, Marilyn (Stickle) 1927- ..... **CLC 35**
See also AAYA 2; CA 17-20R; CANR 13,
47; CLR 2; JRDA; MAICYA; SAAS 2;
SATA 3, 68

Sachs, Nelly 1891-1970 .... **CLC 14**
See also CA 17-18; 25-28R; CAP 2

Sackler, Howard (Oliver)
1929-1982 .... **CLC 14**
See also CA 61-64; 108; CANR 30; DLB 7

Sacks, Oliver (Wolf) 1933- .... **CLC 67**
See also CA 53-56; CANR 28; MTCW

Sade, Donatien Alphonse Francois Comte
1740-1814 .... **NCLC 47**

Sadoff, Ira 1945-................. **CLC 9**
See also CA 53-56; CANR 5, 21; DLB 120

Saetone
See Camus, Albert

Safire, William 1929-............. **CLC 10**
See also CA 17-20R; CANR 31

Sagan, Carl (Edward) 1934-........ **CLC 30**
See also AAYA 2; CA 25-28R; CANR 11,
36; MTCW; SATA 58

Sagan, Francoise .... **CLC 3, 6, 9, 17, 36**
See also Quoirez, Francoise
See also DLB 83

Sahgal, Nayantara (Pandit) 1927-... **CLC 41**
See also CA 9-12R; CANR 11

Saint, H(arry) F. 1941- .... **CLC 50**
See also CA 127

St. Aubin de Teran, Lisa 1953-
See Teran, Lisa St. Aubin de
See also CA 118; 126

Sainte-Beuve, Charles Augustin
1804-1869 .... **NCLC 5**

**Saint-Exupery, Antoine (Jean Baptiste Marie
Roger) de**
1900-1944 .... **TCLC 2, 56; WLC**
See also CA 108; 132; CLR 10; DLB 72;
MAICYA; MTCW; SATA 20

St. John, David
See Hunt, E(verette) Howard, (Jr.)

Saint-John Perse
See Leger, (Marie-Rene Auguste) Alexis
Saint-Leger

Saintsbury, George (Edward Bateman)
1845-1933 .... **TCLC 31**
See also DLB 57, 149

Sait Faik .... **TCLC 23**
See also Abasiyanik, Sait Faik

Saki .... **TCLC 3; SSC 12**
See also Munro, H(ector) H(ugh)

Sala, George Augustus .... **NCLC 46**

Salama, Hannu 1936-............. **CLC 18**

Salamanca, J(ack) R(ichard)
1922- .... **CLC 4, 15**
See also CA 25-28R

Sale, J. Kirkpatrick
See Sale, Kirkpatrick

Sale, Kirkpatrick 1937- .... **CLC 68**
See also CA 13-16R; CANR 10

Salinas (y Serrano), Pedro
1891(?)-1951 .... **TCLC 17**
See also CA 117; DLB 134

Salinger, J(erome) D(avid)
1919- ...... **CLC 1, 3, 8, 12, 55, 56; DA;
SSC 2; WLC**
See also AAYA 2; CA 5-8R; CANR 39;
CDALB 1941-1968; CLR 18; DLB 2, 102;
MAICYA; MTCW; SATA 67

Salisbury, John
See Caute, David

Salter, James 1925- .... **CLC 7, 52, 59**
See also CA 73-76; DLB 130

Saltus, Edgar (Everton)
1855-1921 .... **TCLC 8**
See also CA 105

Saltykov, Mikhail Evgrafovich
1826-1889 .... **NCLC 16**

Samarakis, Antonis 1919- .... **CLC 5**
See also CA 25-28R; CAAS 16; CANR 36

Sanchez, Florencio 1875-1910..... **TCLC 37**
See also HW

Sanchez, Luis Rafael 1936-........ **CLC 23**
See also CA 128; DLB 145; HW

Sanchez, Sonia 1934-... **CLC 5; BLC; PC 9**
See also BW 2; CA 33-36R; CANR 24;
CLR 18; DLB 41; DLBD 8; MAICYA;
MTCW; SATA 22

Sand, George
1804-1876 ...... **NCLC 2, 42; DA; WLC**
See also DLB 119

Sandburg, Carl (August)
1878-1967 .... **CLC 1, 4, 10, 15, 35; DA;
PC 2; WLC**
See also CA 5-8R; 25-28R; CANR 35;
CDALB 1865-1917; DLB 17, 54;
MAICYA; MTCW; SATA 8

Sandburg, Charles
See Sandburg, Carl (August)

Sandburg, Charles A.
See Sandburg, Carl (August)

Sanders, (James) Ed(ward) 1939- ... **CLC 53**
See also CA 13-16R; CAAS 21; CANR 13,
44; DLB 16

Sanders, Lawrence 1920-.......... **CLC 41**
See also BEST 89:4; CA 81-84; CANR 33;
MTCW

Sanders, Noah
See Blount, Roy (Alton), Jr.

Sanders, Winston P.
See Anderson, Poul (William)

Sandoz, Mari(e Susette)
1896-1966 .... **CLC 28**
See also CA 1-4R; 25-28R; CANR 17;
DLB 9; MTCW; SATA 5

Saner, Reg(inald Anthony) 1931- .... **CLC 9**
See also CA 65-68

Sannazaro, Jacopo 1456(?)-1530 ...... **LC 8**

Sansom, William 1912-1976 ...... **CLC 2, 6**
See also CA 5-8R; 65-68; CANR 42;
DLB 139; MTCW

Santayana, George 1863-1952 ..... **TCLC 40**
See also CA 115; DLB 54, 71

Santiago, Danny .... **CLC 33**
See also James, Daniel (Lewis); James,
Daniel (Lewis)
See also DLB 122

Santmyer, Helen Hoover
1895-1986 .... **CLC 33**
See also CA 1-4R; 118; CANR 15, 33;
DLBY 84; MTCW

Santos, Bienvenido N(uqui) 1911- ... **CLC 22**
See also CA 101; CANR 19, 46

Sapper .... **TCLC 44**
See also McNeile, Herman Cyril

Sappho fl. 6th cent. B.C.- .... **CMLC 3; PC 5**

Sarduy, Severo 1937-1993 .... **CLC 6**
See also CA 89-92; 142; DLB 113; HW

Sargeson, Frank 1903-1982 .... **CLC 31**
See also CA 25-28R; 106; CANR 38

Sarmiento, Felix Ruben Garcia
See Dario, Ruben

Saroyan, William
1908-1981 ..... **CLC 1, 8, 10, 29, 34, 56;**
DA; WLC
See also CA 5-8R; 103; CANR 30; DLB 7,
9, 86; DLBY 81; MTCW; SATA 23;
SATA-Obit 24

Sarraute, Nathalie
1900- .... **CLC 1, 2, 4, 8, 10, 31, 80**
See also CA 9-12R; CANR 23; DLB 83;
MTCW

Sarton, (Eleanor) May
1912- .... **CLC 4, 14, 49**
See also CA 1-4R; CANR 1, 34; DLB 48;
DLBY 81; MTCW; SATA 36

Sartre, Jean-Paul
1905-1980 .... **CLC 1, 4, 7, 9, 13, 18, 24,**
44, 50, 52; DA; DC 3; WLC
See also CA 9-12R; 97-100; CANR 21;
DLB 72; MTCW

Sassoon, Siegfried (Lorraine)
1886-1967 .... **CLC 36; PC 12**
See also CA 104; 25-28R; CANR 36;
DLB 20; MTCW

Satterfield, Charles
See Pohl, Frederik

Saul, John (W. III) 1942- .... **CLC 46**
See also AAYA 10; BEST 90:4; CA 81-84;
CANR 16, 40

Saunders, Caleb
See Heinlein, Robert A(nson)

Saura (Atares), Carlos 1932- ...... **CLC 20**
See also CA 114; 131; HW

Sauser-Hall, Frederic 1887-1961 .... **CLC 18**
See also Cendrars, Blaise
See also CA 102; 93-96; CANR 36; MTCW

Saussure, Ferdinand de
1857-1913 .... **TCLC 49**

Savage, Catharine
See Brosman, Catharine Savage

Savage, Thomas 1915- .... **CLC 40**
See also CA 126; 132; CAAS 15

Savan, Glenn 19(?)- .... **CLC 50**

Sayers, Dorothy L(eigh)
1893-1957 .... **TCLC 2, 15**
See also CA 104; 119; CDBLB 1914-1945;
DLB 10, 36, 77, 100; MTCW

Sayers, Valerie 1952- .... **CLC 50**
See also CA 134

Sayles, John (Thomas)
1950- .... **CLC 7, 10, 14**
See also CA 57-60; CANR 41; DLB 44

Scammell, Michael .... **CLC 34**

Scannell, Vernon 1922- .... **CLC 49**
See also CA 5-8R; CANR 8, 24; DLB 27;
SATA 59

Scarlett, Susan
See Streatfeild, (Mary) Noel

Schaeffer, Susan Fromberg
1941- .... **CLC 6, 11, 22**
See also CA 49-52; CANR 18; DLB 28;
MTCW; SATA 22

Schary, Jill
See Robinson, Jill

Schell, Jonathan 1943- .... **CLC 35**
See also CA 73-76; CANR 12

Schelling, Friedrich Wilhelm Joseph von
1775-1854 .... **NCLC 30**
See also DLB 90

Schendel, Arthur van 1874-1946 ... **TCLC 56**

Scherer, Jean-Marie Maurice 1920-
See Rohmer, Eric
See also CA 110

Schevill, James (Erwin) 1920- .... **CLC 7**
See also CA 5-8R; CAAS 12

Schiller, Friedrich 1759-1805 .... **NCLC 39**
See also DLB 94

Schisgal, Murray (Joseph) 1926- ..... **CLC 6**
See also CA 21-24R; CANR 48

Schlee, Ann 1934- .... **CLC 35**
See also CA 101; CANR 29; SATA 44;
SATA-Brief 36

Schlegel, August Wilhelm von
1767-1845 .... **NCLC 15**
See also DLB 94

Schlegel, Friedrich 1772-1829 .... **NCLC 45**
See also DLB 90

Schlegel, Johann Elias (von)
1719(?)-1749 .... **LC 5**

Schlesinger, Arthur M(eier), Jr.
1917- .... **CLC 84**
See also AITN 1; CA 1-4R; CANR 1, 28;
DLB 17; MTCW; SATA 61

Schmidt, Arno (Otto) 1914-1979 .... **CLC 56**
See also CA 128; 109; DLB 69

Schmitz, Aron Hector 1861-1928
See Svevo, Italo
See also CA 104; 122; MTCW

Schnackenberg, Gjertrud 1953- ..... **CLC 40**
See also CA 116; DLB 120

Schneider, Leonard Alfred 1925-1966
See Bruce, Lenny
See also CA 89-92

Schnitzler, Arthur
1862-1931 .... **TCLC 4; SSC 15**
See also CA 104; DLB 81, 118

Schopenhauer, Arthur
1788-1860 .... **NCLC 51**
See also DLB 90

Schor, Sandra (M.) 1932(?)-1990 ... **CLC 65**
See also CA 132

Schorer, Mark 1908-1977 .... **CLC 9**
See also CA 5-8R; 73-76; CANR 7;
DLB 103

Schrader, Paul (Joseph) 1946- ..... **CLC 26**
See also CA 37-40R; CANR 41; DLB 44

Schreiner, Olive (Emilie Albertina)
1855-1920 .... **TCLC 9**
See also CA 105; DLB 18

Schulberg, Budd (Wilson)
1914- .... **CLC 7, 48**
See also CA 25-28R; CANR 19; DLB 6, 26,
28; DLBY 81

Schulz, Bruno
1892-1942 .... **TCLC 5, 51; SSC 13**
See also CA 115; 123

Schulz, Charles M(onroe) 1922- .... **CLC 12**
See also CA 9-12R; CANR 6; SATA 10

Schumacher, E(rnst) F(riedrich)
1911-1977 .... **CLC 80**
See also CA 81-84; 73-76; CANR 34

Schuyler, James Marcus
1923-1991 .... **CLC 5, 23**
See also CA 101; 134; DLB 5

Schwartz, Delmore (David)
1913-1966 ... **CLC 2, 4, 10, 45, 87; PC 8**
See also CA 17-18; 25-28R; CANR 35;
CAP 2; DLB 28, 48; MTCW

Schwartz, Ernst
See Ozu, Yasujiro

Schwartz, John Burnham 1965- .... **CLC 59**
See also CA 132

Schwartz, Lynne Sharon 1939- ..... **CLC 31**
See also CA 103; CANR 44

Schwartz, Muriel A.
See Eliot, T(homas) S(tearns)

Schwarz-Bart, Andre 1928- .... **CLC 2, 4**
See also CA 89-92

Schwarz-Bart, Simone 1938- .... **CLC 7**
See also BW 2; CA 97-100

Schwob, (Mayer Andre) Marcel
1867-1905 .... **TCLC 20**
See also CA 117; DLB 123

Sciascia, Leonardo
1921-1989 .... **CLC 8, 9, 41**
See also CA 85-88; 130; CANR 35; MTCW

Scoppettone, Sandra 1936- .... **CLC 26**
See also AAYA 11; CA 5-8R; CANR 41;
SATA 9

Shaw, Irwin 1913-1984...... **CLC 7, 23, 34**
See also AITN 1; CA 13-16R; 112;
CANR 21; CDALB 1941-1968; DLB 6,
102; DLBY 84; MTCW

Shaw, Robert 1927-1978 .... **CLC 5**
See also AITN 1; CA 1-4R; 81-84;
CANR 4; DLB 13, 14

Shaw, T. E.
See Lawrence, T(homas) E(dward)

Shawn, Wallace 1943- .... **CLC 41**
See also CA 112

Shea, Lisa 1953-................. **CLC 86**
See also CA 147

Sheed, Wilfrid (John Joseph)
1930-................ **CLC 2, 4, 10, 53**
See also CA 65-68; CANR 30; DLB 6;
MTCW

Sheldon, Alice Hastings Bradley
1915(?)-1987
See Tiptree, James, Jr.
See also CA 108; 122; CANR 34; MTCW

Sheldon, John
See Bloch, Robert (Albert)

Shelley, Mary Wollstonecraft (Godwin)
1797-1851 .... **NCLC 14; DA; WLC**
See also CDBLB 1789-1832; DLB 110, 116;
SATA 29

Shelley, Percy Bysshe
1792-1822 .... **NCLC 18; DA; WLC**
See also CDBLB 1789-1832; DLB 96, 110

Shepard, Jim 1956-................ **CLC 36**
See also CA 137

Shepard, Lucius 1947- .... **CLC 34**
See also CA 128; 141

Shepard, Sam
1943- .... **CLC 4, 6, 17, 34, 41, 44; DC 5**
See also AAYA 1; CA 69-72; CABS 3;
CANR 22; DLB 7; MTCW

Shepherd, Michael
See Ludlum, Robert

Sherburne, Zoa (Morin) 1912-...... **CLC 30**
See also AAYA 13; CA 1-4R; CANR 3, 37;
MAICYA; SAAS 18; SATA 3

Sheridan, Frances 1724-1766........ **LC 7**
See also DLB 39, 84

Sheridan, Richard Brinsley
1751-1816 ... **NCLC 5; DA; DC 1; WLC**
See also CDBLB 1660-1789; DLB 89

Sherman, Jonathan Marc........... **CLC 55**

Sherman, Martin 1941(?)- .... **CLC 19**
See also CA 116; 123

Sherwin, Judith Johnson 1936-... **CLC 7, 15**
See also CA 25-28R; CANR 34

Sherwood, Frances 1940-......... **CLC 81**

Sherwood, Robert E(mmet)
1896-1955 .... **TCLC 3**
See also CA 104; DLB 7, 26

Shestov, Lev 1866-1938 .... **TCLC 56**

Shiel, M(atthew) P(hipps)
1865-1947 .... **TCLC 8**
See also CA 106; DLB 153

Shiga, Naoya 1883-1971.......... **CLC 33**
See also CA 101; 33-36R

Shih, Su 1036-1101............. **CMLC 15**

Shilts, Randy 1951-1994 .... **CLC 85**
See also CA 115; 127; 144; CANR 45

Shimazaki Haruki 1872-1943
See Shimazaki Toson
See also CA 105; 134

Shimazaki Toson................. **TCLC 5**
See also Shimazaki Haruki

Sholokhov, Mikhail (Aleksandrovich)
1905-1984 .... **CLC 7, 15**
See also CA 101; 112; MTCW;
SATA-Obit 36

Shone, Patric
See Hanley, James

Shreve, Susan Richards 1939-...... **CLC 23**
See also CA 49-52; CAAS 5; CANR 5, 38;
MAICYA; SATA 46; SATA-Brief 41

Shue, Larry 1946-1985............ **CLC 52**
See also CA 145; 117

Shu-Jen, Chou 1881-1936
See Hsun, Lu
See also CA 104

Shulman, Alix Kates 1932- ...... **CLC 2, 10**
See also CA 29-32R; CANR 43; SATA 7

Shuster, Joe 1914- .... **CLC 21**

Shute, Nevil...................... **CLC 30**
See also Norway, Nevil Shute

Shuttle, Penelope (Diane) 1947- ..... **CLC 7**
See also CA 93-96; CANR 39; DLB 14, 40

Sidney, Mary 1561-1621 .... **LC 19**

Sidney, Sir Philip 1554-1586.... **LC 19; DA**
See also CDBLB Before 1660

Siegel, Jerome 1914- .... **CLC 21**
See also CA 116

Siegel, Jerry
See Siegel, Jerome

Sienkiewicz, Henryk (Adam Alexander Pius)
1846-1916 .... **TCLC 3**
See also CA 104; 134

Sierra, Gregorio Martinez
See Martinez Sierra, Gregorio

Sierra, Maria (de la O'LeJarraga) Martinez
See Martinez Sierra, Maria (de la
O'LeJarraga)

Sigal, Clancy 1926-................ **CLC 7**
See also CA 1-4R

Sigourney, Lydia Howard (Huntley)
1791-1865 .... **NCLC 21**
See also DLB 1, 42, 73

Siguenza y Gongora, Carlos de
1645-1700 .... **LC 8**

Sigurjonsson, Johann 1880-1919... **TCLC 27**

Sikelianos, Angelos 1884-1951 .... **TCLC 39**

Silkin, Jon 1930- .... **CLC 2, 6, 43**
See also CA 5-8R; CAAS 5; DLB 27

Silko, Leslie (Marmon)
1948- .... **CLC 23, 74; DA**
See also AAYA 14; CA 115; 122;
CANR 45; DLB 143; NNAL

Sillanpaa, Frans Eemil 1888-1964... **CLC 19**
See also CA 129; 93-96; MTCW

Sillitoe, Alan
1928- .... **CLC 1, 3, 6, 10, 19, 57**
See also AITN 1; CA 9-12R; CAAS 2;
CANR 8, 26; CDBLB 1960 to Present;
DLB 14, 139; MTCW; SATA 61

Silone, Ignazio 1900-1978 .... **CLC 4**
See also CA 25-28; 81-84; CANR 34;
CAP 2; MTCW

Silver, Joan Micklin 1935- .... **CLC 20**
See also CA 114; 121

Silver, Nicholas
See Faust, Frederick (Schiller)

Silverberg, Robert 1935- .... **CLC 7**
See also CA 1-4R; CAAS 3; CANR 1, 20,
36; DLB 8; MAICYA; MTCW; SATA 13

Silverstein, Alvin 1933- .... **CLC 17**
See also CA 49-52; CANR 2; CLR 25;
JRDA; MAICYA; SATA 8, 69

Silverstein, Virginia B(arbara Opshelor)
1937- .... **CLC 17**
See also CA 49-52; CANR 2; CLR 25;
JRDA; MAICYA; SATA 8, 69

Sim, Georges
See Simenon, Georges (Jacques Christian)

Simak, Clifford D(onald)
1904-1988 .... **CLC 1, 55**
See also CA 1-4R; 125; CANR 1, 35;
DLB 8; MTCW; SATA-Obit 56

Simenon, Georges (Jacques Christian)
1903-1989 .... **CLC 1, 2, 3, 8, 18, 47**
See also CA 85-88; 129; CANR 35;
DLB 72; DLBY 89; MTCW

Simic, Charles 1938-... **CLC 6, 9, 22, 49, 68**
See also CA 29-32R; CAAS 4; CANR 12,
33; DLB 105

Simmons, Charles (Paul) 1924-..... **CLC 57**
See also CA 89-92

Simmons, Dan 1948-.............. **CLC 44**
See also CA 138

Simmons, James (Stewart Alexander)
1933- .... **CLC 43**
See also CA 105; CAAS 21; DLB 40

Simms, William Gilmore
1806-1870 .... **NCLC 3**
See also DLB 3, 30, 59, 73

Simon, Carly 1945-.............. **CLC 26**
See also CA 105

Simon, Claude 1913-....... **CLC 4, 9, 15, 39**
See also CA 89-92; CANR 33; DLB 83;
MTCW

Simon, (Marvin) Neil
1927- .... **CLC 6, 11, 31, 39, 70**
See also AITN 1; CA 21-24R; CANR 26;
DLB 7; MTCW

Simon, Paul 1942(?)- .... **CLC 17**
See also CA 116

Simonon, Paul 1956(?)- .... **CLC 30**

Simpson, Harriette
See Arnow, Harriette (Louisa) Simpson

Simpson, Louis (Aston Marantz)
1923- .... **CLC 4, 7, 9, 32**
See also CA 1-4R; CAAS 4; CANR 1;
DLB 5; MTCW

Simpson, Mona (Elizabeth) 1957-... **CLC 44**
See also CA 122; 135

Simpson, N(orman) F(rederick)
1919- .... CLC 29
See also CA 13-16R; DLB 13

Sinclair, Andrew (Annandale)
1935- .... CLC 2, 14
See also CA 9-12R; CAAS 5; CANR 14, 38;
DLB 14; MTCW

Sinclair, Emil
See Hesse, Hermann

Sinclair, Iain 1943- .... CLC 76
See also CA 132

Sinclair, Iain MacGregor
See Sinclair, Iain

Sinclair, Mary Amelia St. Clair 1865(?)-1946
See Sinclair, May
See also CA 104

Sinclair, May .... TCLC 3, 11
See also Sinclair, Mary Amelia St. Clair
See also DLB 36, 135

Sinclair, Upton (Beall)
1878-1968 ...... CLC 1, 11, 15, 63; DA;
WLC
See also CA 5-8R; 25-28R; CANR 7;
CDALB 1929-1941; DLB 9; MTCW;
SATA 9

Singer, Isaac
See Singer, Isaac Bashevis

Singer, Isaac Bashevis
1904-1991 .... CLC 1, 3, 6, 9, 11, 15, 23,
38, 69; DA; SSC 3; WLC
See also AITN 1, 2; CA 1-4R; 134;
CANR 1, 39; CDALB 1941-1968; CLR 1;
DLB 6, 28, 52; DLBY 91; JRDA;
MAICYA; MTCW; SATA 3, 27;
SATA-Obit 68

Singer, Israel Joshua 1893-1944 ... TCLC 33

Singh, Khushwant 1915- .... CLC 11
See also CA 9-12R; CAAS 9; CANR 6

Sinjohn, John
See Galsworthy, John

Sinyavsky, Andrei (Donatevich)
1925- .... CLC 8
See also CA 85-88

Sirin, V.
See Nabokov, Vladimir (Vladimirovich)

Sissman, L(ouis) E(dward)
1928-1976 .... CLC 9, 18
See also CA 21-24R; 65-68; CANR 13;
DLB 5

Sisson, C(harles) H(ubert) 1914- ..... CLC 8
See also CA 1-4R; CAAS 3; CANR 3, 48;
DLB 27

Sitwell, Dame Edith
1887-1964 .... CLC 2, 9, 67; PC 3
See also CA 9-12R; CANR 35;
CDBLB 1945-1960; DLB 20; MTCW

Sjoewall, Maj 1935- .... CLC 7
See also CA 65-68

Sjowall, Maj
See Sjoewall, Maj

Skelton, Robin 1925- .... CLC 13
See also AITN 2; CA 5-8R; CAAS 5;
CANR 28; DLB 27, 53

Skolimowski, Jerzy 1938- .... CLC 20
See also CA 128

Skram, Amalie (Bertha)
1847-1905 .... TCLC 25

Skvorecky, Josef (Vaclav)
1924- .... CLC 15, 39, 69
See also CA 61-64; CAAS 1; CANR 10, 34;
MTCW

Slade, Bernard .... CLC 11, 46
See also Newbound, Bernard Slade
See also CAAS 9; DLB 53

Slaughter, Carolyn 1946- .... CLC 56
See also CA 85-88

Slaughter, Frank G(ill) 1908- ...... CLC 29
See also AITN 2; CA 5-8R; CANR 5

Slavitt, David R(ytman) 1935- .... CLC 5, 14
See also CA 21-24R; CAAS 3; CANR 41;
DLB 5, 6

Slesinger, Tess 1905-1945 .... TCLC 10
See also CA 107; DLB 102

Slessor, Kenneth 1901-1971 .... CLC 14
See also CA 102; 89-92

Slowacki, Juliusz 1809-1849 ..... NCLC 15

Smart, Christopher
1722-1771 .... LC 3; PC 12
See also DLB 109

Smart, Elizabeth 1913-1986 .... CLC 54
See also CA 81-84; 118; DLB 88

Smiley, Jane (Graves) 1949- .... CLC 53, 76
See also CA 104; CANR 30

Smith, A(rthur) J(ames) M(arshall)
1902-1980 .... CLC 15
See also CA 1-4R; 102; CANR 4; DLB 88

Smith, Anna Deavere 1950 .... CLC 86
See also CA 133

Smith, Betty (Wehner) 1896-1972 ... CLC 19
See also CA 5-8R; 33-36R; DLBY 82;
SATA 6

Smith, Charlotte (Turner)
1749-1806 .... NCLC 23
See also DLB 39, 109

Smith, Clark Ashton 1893-1961 .... CLC 43
See also CA 143

Smith, Dave .... CLC 22, 42
See also Smith, David (Jeddie)
See also CAAS 7; DLB 5

Smith, David (Jeddie) 1942-
See Smith, Dave
See also CA 49-52; CANR 1

Smith, Florence Margaret 1902-1971
See Smith, Stevie
See also CA 17-18; 29-32R; CANR 35;
CAP 2; MTCW

Smith, Iain Crichton 1928- .... CLC 64
See also CA 21-24R; DLB 40, 139

Smith, John 1580(?)-1631 .... LC 9

Smith, Johnston
See Crane, Stephen (Townley)

Smith, Lee 1944- .... CLC 25, 73
See also CA 114; 119; CANR 46; DLB 143;
DLBY 83

Smith, Martin
See Smith, Martin Cruz

Smith, Martin Cruz 1942- .... CLC 25
See also BEST 89:4; CA 85-88; CANR 6,
23, 43; NNAL

Smith, Mary-Ann Tirone 1944- ..... CLC 39
See also CA 118; 136

Smith, Patti 1946- .... CLC 12
See also CA 93-96

Smith, Pauline (Urmson)
1882-1959 .... TCLC 25

Smith, Rosamond
See Oates, Joyce Carol

Smith, Sheila Kaye
See Kaye-Smith, Sheila

Smith, Stevie .... CLC 3, 8, 25, 44; PC 12
See also Smith, Florence Margaret
See also DLB 20

Smith, Wilbur (Addison) 1933- ..... CLC 33
See also CA 13-16R; CANR 7, 46; MTCW

Smith, William Jay 1918- .... CLC 6
See also CA 5-8R; CANR 44; DLB 5;
MAICYA; SATA 2, 68

Smith, Woodrow Wilson
See Kuttner, Henry

Smolenskin, Peretz 1842-1885 .... NCLC 30

Smollett, Tobias (George) 1721-1771 .. LC 2
See also CDBLB 1660-1789; DLB 39, 104

Snodgrass, W(illiam) D(e Witt)
1926- .... CLC 2, 6, 10, 18, 68
See also CA 1-4R; CANR 6, 36; DLB 5;
MTCW

Snow, C(harles) P(ercy)
1905-1980 .... CLC 1, 4, 6, 9, 13, 19
See also CA 5-8R; 101; CANR 28;
CDBLB 1945-1960; DLB 15, 77; MTCW

Snow, Frances Compton
See Adams, Henry (Brooks)

Snyder, Gary (Sherman)
1930- .... CLC 1, 2, 5, 9, 32
See also CA 17-20R; CANR 30; DLB 5, 16

Snyder, Zilpha Keatley 1927- ...... CLC 17
See also CA 9-12R; CANR 38; CLR 31;
JRDA; MAICYA; SAAS 2; SATA 1, 28,
75

Soares, Bernardo
See Pessoa, Fernando (Antonio Nogueira)

Sobh, A.
See Shamlu, Ahmad

Sobol, Joshua .... CLC 60

Soderberg, Hjalmar 1869-1941 .... TCLC 39

Sodergran, Edith (Irene)
See Soedergran, Edith (Irene)

Soedergran, Edith (Irene)
1892-1923 .... TCLC 31

Softly, Edgar
See Lovecraft, H(oward) P(hillips)

Softly, Edward
See Lovecraft, H(oward) P(hillips)

Sokolov, Raymond 1941- .... CLC 7
See also CA 85-88

Solo, Jay
See Ellison, Harlan (Jay)

Sologub, Fyodor .... TCLC 9
See also Teternikov, Fyodor Kuzmich

Solomons, Ikey Esquir
See Thackeray, William Makepeace

Solomos, Dionysios 1798-1857 ... NCLC 15

Suarez Lynch, B.
See Bioy Casares, Adolfo; Borges, Jorge
Luis

Su Chien 1884-1918
See Su Man-shu
See also CA 123

Suckow, Ruth 1892-1960 . . . . SSC
See also CA 113; DLB 9, 102

Sudermann, Hermann 1857-1928 . . TCLC 15
See also CA 107; DLB 118

Sue, Eugene 1804-1857 . . . . NCLC 1
See also DLB 119

Sueskind, Patrick 1949- . . . . CLC 44
See also Suskind, Patrick

Sukenick, Ronald 1932- . . . . . CLC 3, 4, 6, 48
See also CA 25-28R; CAAS 8; CANR 32;
DLBY 81

Suknaski, Andrew 1942- . . . . CLC 19
See also CA 101; DLB 53

Sullivan, Vernon
See Vian, Boris

Sully Prudhomme 1839-1907 . . . . . TCLC 31

Su Man-shu . . . . TCLC 24
See also Su Chien

Summerforest, Ivy B.
See Kirkup, James

Summers, Andrew James 1942- . . . . . CLC 26

Summers, Andy
See Summers, Andrew James

Summers, Hollis (Spurgeon, Jr.)
1916- . . . . CLC 10
See also CA 5-8R; CANR 3; DLB 6

Summers, (Alphonsus Joseph-Mary Augustus)
Montague 1880-1948 . . . . TCLC 16
See also CA 118

Sumner, Gordon Matthew 1951- . . . . CLC 26

Surtees, Robert Smith
1803-1864 . . . . NCLC 14
See also DLB 21

Susann, Jacqueline 1921-1974 . . . . CLC 3
See also AITN 1; CA 65-68; 53-56; MTCW

Suskind, Patrick
See Sueskind, Patrick
See also CA 145

Sutcliff, Rosemary 1920-1992 . . . . . . CLC 26
See also AAYA 10; CA 5-8R; 139;
CANR 37; CLR 1, 37; JRDA; MAICYA;
SATA 6, 44, 78; SATA-Obit 73

Sutro, Alfred 1863-1933 . . . . TCLC 6
See also CA 105; DLB 10

Sutton, Henry
See Slavitt, David R(ytman)

Svevo, Italo . . . . TCLC 2, 35
See also Schmitz, Aron Hector

Swados, Elizabeth 1951- . . . . CLC 12
See also CA 97-100

Swados, Harvey 1920-1972 . . . . CLC 5
See also CA 5-8R; 37-40R; CANR 6;
DLB 2

Swan, Gladys 1934- . . . . CLC 69
See also CA 101; CANR 17, 39

Swarthout, Glendon (Fred)
1918-1992 . . . . CLC 35
See also CA 1-4R; 139; CANR 1, 47;
SATA 26

Sweet, Sarah C.
See Jewett, (Theodora) Sarah Orne

Swenson, May
1919-1989 . . . . CLC 4, 14, 61; DA
See also CA 5-8R; 130; CANR 36; DLB 5;
MTCW; SATA 15

Swift, Augustus
See Lovecraft, H(oward) P(hillips)

Swift, Graham (Colin) 1949- . . . . CLC 41, 88
See also CA 117; 122; CANR 46

Swift, Jonathan
1667-1745 . . . . . . LC 1; DA; PC 9; WLC
See also CDBLB 1660-1789; DLB 39, 95,
101; SATA 19

Swinburne, Algernon Charles
1837-1909 . . . . . . TCLC 8, 36; DA; WLC
See also CA 105; 140; CDBLB 1832-1890;
DLB 35, 57

Swinfen, Ann . . . . CLC 34

Swinnerton, Frank Arthur
1884-1982 . . . . CLC 31
See also CA 108; DLB 34

Swithen, John
See King, Stephen (Edwin)

Sylvia
See Ashton-Warner, Sylvia (Constance)

Symmes, Robert Edward
See Duncan, Robert (Edward)

Symonds, John Addington
1840-1893 . . . . NCLC 34
See also DLB 57, 144

Symons, Arthur 1865-1945 . . . . TCLC 11
See also CA 107; DLB 19, 57, 149

Symons, Julian (Gustave)
1912-1994 . . . . CLC 2, 14, 32
See also CA 49-52; 147; CAAS 3; CANR 3,
33; DLB 87; DLBY 92; MTCW

Synge, (Edmund) J(ohn) M(illington)
1871-1909 . . . . TCLC 6, 37; DC 2
See also CA 104; 141; CDBLB 1890-1914;
DLB 10, 19

Syruc, J.
See Milosz, Czeslaw

Szirtes, George 1948- . . . . CLC 46
See also CA 109; CANR 27

Tabori, George 1914- . . . . CLC 19
See also CA 49-52; CANR 4

Tagore, Rabindranath
1861-1941 . . . . TCLC 3, 53; PC 8
See also CA 104; 120; MTCW

Taine, Hippolyte Adolphe
1828-1893 . . . . NCLC 15

Talese, Gay 1932- . . . . CLC 37
See also AITN 1; CA 1-4R; CANR 9;
MTCW

Tallent, Elizabeth (Ann) 1954- . . . . . CLC 45
See also CA 117; DLB 130

Tally, Ted 1952- . . . . CLC 42
See also CA 120; 124

Tamayo y Baus, Manuel
1829-1898 . . . . NCLC 1

Tammsaare, A(nton) H(ansen)
1878-1940 . . . . TCLC 27

Tan, Amy 1952- . . . . CLC 59
See also AAYA 9; BEST 89:3; CA 136;
SATA 75

Tandem, Felix
See Spitteler, Carl (Friedrich Georg)

Tanizaki, Jun'ichiro
1886-1965 . . . . CLC 8, 14, 28
See also CA 93-96; 25-28R

Tanner, William
See Amis, Kingsley (William)

Tao Lao
See Storni, Alfonsina

Tarassoff, Lev
See Troyat, Henri

Tarbell, Ida M(inerva)
1857-1944 . . . . TCLC 40
See also CA 122; DLB 47

Tarkington, (Newton) Booth
1869-1946 . . . . TCLC 9
See also CA 110; 143; DLB 9, 102;
SATA 17

Tarkovsky, Andrei (Arsenyevich)
1932-1986 . . . . CLC 75
See also CA 127

Tartt, Donna 1964(?)- . . . . CLC 76
See also CA 142

Tasso, Torquato 1544-1595 . . . . LC 5

Tate, (John Orley) Allen
1899-1979 . . . . CLC 2, 4, 6, 9, 11, 14, 24
See also CA 5-8R; 85-88; CANR 32;
DLB 4, 45, 63; MTCW

Tate, Ellalice
See Hibbert, Eleanor Alice Burford

Tate, James (Vincent) 1943- . . . CLC 2, 6, 25
See also CA 21-24R; CANR 29; DLB 5

Tavel, Ronald 1940- . . . . CLC 6
See also CA 21-24R; CANR 33

Taylor, C(ecil) P(hilip) 1929-1981 . . . CLC 27
See also CA 25-28R; 105; CANR 47

Taylor, Edward 1642(?)-1729 . . . . LC 11; DA
See also DLB 24

Taylor, Eleanor Ross 1920- . . . . CLC 5
See also CA 81-84

Taylor, Elizabeth 1912-1975 . . . CLC 2, 4, 29
See also CA 13-16R; CANR 9; DLB 139;
MTCW; SATA 13

Taylor, Henry (Splawn) 1942- . . . . . . CLC 44
See also CA 33-36R; CAAS 7; CANR 31;
DLB 5

Taylor, Kamala (Purnaiya) 1924-
See Markandaya, Kamala
See also CA 77-80

Taylor, Mildred D. . . . . CLC 21
See also AAYA 10; BW 1; CA 85-88;
CANR 25; CLR 9; DLB 52; JRDA;
MAICYA; SAAS 5; SATA 15, 70

Author Index

Tolstoi, Aleksei Nikolaevich
See Tolstoy, Alexey Nikolaevich

Tolstoy, Alexey Nikolaevich
1882-1945 . . . . TCLC 18
See also CA 107

Tolstoy, Count Leo
See Tolstoy, Leo (Nikolaevich)

Tolstoy, Leo (Nikolaevich)
1828-1910 . . . . . TCLC 4, 11, 17, 28, 44;
DA; SSC 9; WLC
See also CA 104; 123; SATA 26

Tomasi di Lampedusa, Giuseppe 1896-1957
See Lampedusa, Giuseppe (Tomasi) di
See also CA 111

Tomlin, Lily . . . . CLC 17
See also Tomlin, Mary Jean

Tomlin, Mary Jean 1939(?)-
See Tomlin, Lily
See also CA 117

Tomlinson, (Alfred) Charles
1927- . . . . CLC 2, 4, 6, 13, 45
See also CA 5-8R; CANR 33; DLB 40

Tonson, Jacob
See Bennett, (Enoch) Arnold

Toole, John Kennedy
1937-1969 . . . . CLC 19, 64
See also CA 104; DLBY 81

Toomer, Jean
1894-1967 . . . . . CLC 1, 4, 13, 22; BLC;
PC 7; SSC 1
See also BW 1; CA 85-88;
CDALB 1917-1929; DLB 45, 51; MTCW

Torley, Luke
See Blish, James (Benjamin)

Tornimparte, Alessandra
See Ginzburg, Natalia

Torre, Raoul della
See Mencken, H(enry) L(ouis)

Torrey, E(dwin) Fuller 1937- . . . . CLC 34
See also CA 119

Torsvan, Ben Traven
See Traven, B.

Torsvan, Benno Traven
See Traven, B.

Torsvan, Berick Traven
See Traven, B.

Torsvan, Berwick Traven
See Traven, B.

Torsvan, Bruno Traven
See Traven, B.

Torsvan, Traven
See Traven, B.

Tournier, Michel (Edouard)
1924- . . . . CLC 6, 23, 36
See also CA 49-52; CANR 3, 36; DLB 83;
MTCW; SATA 23

Tournimparte, Alessandra
See Ginzburg, Natalia

Towers, Ivar
See Kornbluth, C(yril) M.

Towne, Robert (Burton) 1936(?)- . . . . CLC 87
See also CA 108; DLB 44

Townsend, Sue 1946- . . . . CLC 61
See also CA 119; 127; MTCW; SATA 55;
SATA-Brief 48

Townshend, Peter (Dennis Blandford)
1945- . . . . CLC 17, 42
See also CA 107

Tozzi, Federigo 1883-1920 . . . . TCLC 31

Traill, Catharine Parr
1802-1899 . . . . NCLC 31
See also DLB 99

Trakl, Georg 1887-1914 . . . . TCLC 5
See also CA 104

Transtroemer, Tomas (Goesta)
1931- . . . . CLC 52, 65
See also CA 117; 129; CAAS 17

Transtromer, Tomas Gosta
See Transtroemer, Tomas (Goesta)

Traven, B. (?)-1969 . . . . CLC 8, 11
See also CA 19-20; 25-28R; CAP 2; DLB 9,
56; MTCW

Treitel, Jonathan 1959- . . . . CLC 70

Tremain, Rose 1943- . . . . CLC 42
See also CA 97-100; CANR 44; DLB 14

Tremblay, Michel 1942- . . . . CLC 29
See also CA 116; 128; DLB 60; MTCW

Trevanian . . . . CLC 29
See also Whitaker, Rod(ney)

Trevor, Glen
See Hilton, James

Trevor, William
1928- . . . . CLC 7, 9, 14, 25, 71
See also Cox, William Trevor
See also DLB 14, 139

Trifonov, Yuri (Valentinovich)
1925-1981 . . . . CLC 45
See also CA 126; 103; MTCW

Trilling, Lionel 1905-1975 . . . . CLC 9, 11, 24
See also CA 9-12R; 61-64; CANR 10;
DLB 28, 63; MTCW

Trimball, W. H.
See Mencken, H(enry) L(ouis)

Tristan
See Gomez de la Serna, Ramon

Tristram
See Housman, A(lfred) E(dward)

Trogdon, William (Lewis) 1939-
See Heat-Moon, William Least
See also CA 115; 119; CANR 47

Trollope, Anthony
1815-1882 . . . . . . NCLC 6, 33; DA; WLC
See also CDBLB 1832-1890; DLB 21, 57;
SATA 22

Trollope, Frances 1779-1863 . . . . . NCLC 30
See also DLB 21

Trotsky, Leon 1879-1940 . . . . TCLC 22
See also CA 118

Trotter (Cockburn), Catharine
1679-1749 . . . . LC 8
See also DLB 84

Trout, Kilgore
See Farmer, Philip Jose

Trow, George W. S. 1943- . . . . CLC 52
See also CA 126

Troyat, Henri 1911- . . . . CLC 23
See also CA 45-48; CANR 2, 33; MTCW

Trudeau, G(arretson) B(eekman) 1948-
See Trudeau, Garry B.
See also CA 81-84; CANR 31; SATA 35

Trudeau, Garry B. . . . . CLC 12
See also Trudeau, G(arretson) B(eekman)
See also AAYA 10; AITN 2

Truffaut, Francois 1932-1984 . . . . . . CLC 20
See also CA 81-84; 113; CANR 34

Trumbo, Dalton 1905-1976 . . . . CLC 19
See also CA 21-24R; 69-72; CANR 10;
DLB 26

Trumbull, John 1750-1831 . . . . . . NCLC 30
See also DLB 31

Trundlett, Helen B.
See Eliot, T(homas) S(tearns)

Tryon, Thomas 1926-1991 . . . . CLC 3, 11
See also AITN 1; CA 29-32R; 135;
CANR 32; MTCW

Tryon, Tom
See Tryon, Thomas

Ts'ao Hsueh-ch'in 1715(?)-1763 . . . . . . LC 1

Tsushima, Shuji 1909-1948
See Dazai, Osamu
See also CA 107

Tsvetaeva (Efron), Marina (Ivanovna)
1892-1941 . . . . TCLC 7, 35
See also CA 104; 128; MTCW

Tuck, Lily 1938- . . . . CLC 70
See also CA 139

Tu Fu 712-770 . . . . PC 9

Tunis, John R(oberts) 1889-1975 . . . CLC 12
See also CA 61-64; DLB 22; JRDA;
MAICYA; SATA 37; SATA-Brief 30

Tuohy, Frank . . . . CLC 37
See also Tuohy, John Francis
See also DLB 14, 139

Tuohy, John Francis 1925-
See Tuohy, Frank
See also CA 5-8R; CANR 3, 47

Turco, Lewis (Putnam) 1934- . . . CLC 11, 63
See also CA 13-16R; CANR 24; DLBY 84

Turgenev, Ivan
1818-1883 . . . . . . NCLC 21; DA; SSC 7;
WLC

Turgot, Anne-Robert-Jacques
1727-1781 . . . . LC 26

Turner, Frederick 1943- . . . . CLC 48
See also CA 73-76; CAAS 10; CANR 12,
30; DLB 40

Tutu, Desmond M(pilo)
1931- . . . . CLC 80; BLC
See also BW 1; CA 125

Tutuola, Amos 1920- . . . CLC 5, 14, 29; BLC
See also BW 2; CA 9-12R; CANR 27;
DLB 125; MTCW

Twain, Mark
. . . . . TCLC 6, 12, 19, 36, 48, 59; SSC 6;
WLC
See also Clemens, Samuel Langhorne
See also DLB 11, 12, 23, 64, 74

Tyler, Anne
1941- . . . . CLC **7, 11, 18, 28, 44, 59**
See also BEST 89:1; CA 9-12R; CANR 11,
33; DLB 6, 143; DLBY 82; MTCW;
SATA 7

Tyler, Royall 1757-1826. . . . . NCLC **3**
See also DLB 37

Tynan, Katharine 1861-1931 . . . . TCLC **3**
See also CA 104; DLB 153

Tyutchev, Fyodor 1803-1873 . . . . . NCLC **34**

Tzara, Tristan . . . . CLC **47**
See also Rosenfeld, Samuel

Uhry, Alfred 1936- . . . . CLC **55**
See also CA 127; 133

Ulf, Haerved
See Strindberg, (Johan) August

Ulf, Harved
See Strindberg, (Johan) August

Ulibarri, Sabine R(eyes) 1919- . . . . . CLC **83**
See also CA 131; DLB 82; HW

Unamuno (y Jugo), Miguel de
1864-1936 . . . . TCLC **2, 9; HLC; SSC 11**
See also CA 104; 131; DLB 108; HW;
MTCW

Undercliffe, Errol
See Campbell, (John) Ramsey

Underwood, Miles
See Glassco, John

Undset, Sigrid
1882-1949 . . . . TCLC **3; DA; WLC**
See also CA 104; 129; MTCW

Ungaretti, Giuseppe
1888-1970 . . . . CLC **7, 11, 15**
See also CA 19-20; 25-28R; CAP 2;
DLB 114

Unger, Douglas 1952- . . . . CLC **34**
See also CA 130

Unsworth, Barry (Forster) 1930- . . . . CLC **76**
See also CA 25-28R; CANR 30

Updike, John (Hoyer)
1932- . . . . . . CLC **1, 2, 3, 5, 7, 9, 13, 15,
23, 34, 43, 70; DA; SSC 13; WLC**
See also CA 1-4R; CABS 1; CANR 4, 33;
CDALB 1968-1988; DLB 2, 5, 143;
DLBD 3; DLBY 80, 82; MTCW

Upshaw, Margaret Mitchell
See Mitchell, Margaret (Munnerlyn)

Upton, Mark
See Sanders, Lawrence

Urdang, Constance (Henriette)
1922- . . . . CLC **47**
See also CA 21-24R; CANR 9, 24

Uriel, Henry
See Faust, Frederick (Schiller)

Uris, Leon (Marcus) 1924- . . . . CLC **7, 32**
See also AITN 1, 2; BEST 89:2; CA 1-4R;
CANR 1, 40; MTCW; SATA 49

Urmuz
See Codrescu, Andrei

Ustinov, Peter (Alexander) 1921- . . . . CLC **1**
See also AITN 1; CA 13-16R; CANR 25;
DLB 13

Vaculik, Ludvik 1926- . . . . CLC **7**
See also CA 53-56

Valdez, Luis (Miguel)
1940- . . . . CLC **84; HLC**
See also CA 101; CANR 32; DLB 122; HW

Valenzuela, Luisa 1938- . . . CLC **31; SSC 14**
See also CA 101; CANR 32; DLB 113; HW

Valera y Alcala-Galiano, Juan
1824-1905 . . . . TCLC **10**
See also CA 106

Valery, (Ambroise) Paul (Toussaint Jules)
1871-1945 . . . . TCLC **4, 15; PC 9**
See also CA 104; 122; MTCW

Valle-Inclan, Ramon (Maria) del
1866-1936 . . . . TCLC **5; HLC**
See also CA 106; DLB 134

Vallejo, Antonio Buero
See Buero Vallejo, Antonio

Vallejo, Cesar (Abraham)
1892-1938 . . . . TCLC **3, 56; HLC**
See also CA 105; HW

Valle Y Pena, Ramon del
See Valle-Inclan, Ramon (Maria) del

Van Ash, Cay 1918- . . . . CLC **34**

Vanbrugh, Sir John 1664-1726 . . . . . . LC **21**
See also DLB 80

Van Campen, Karl
See Campbell, John W(ood, Jr.)

Vance, Gerald
See Silverberg, Robert

Vance, Jack . . . . CLC **35**
See also Vance, John Holbrook
See also DLB 8

Vance, John Holbrook 1916-
See Queen, Ellery; Vance, Jack
See also CA 29-32R; CANR 17; MTCW

**Van Den Bogarde, Derek Jules Gaspard Ulric
Niven** 1921-
See Bogarde, Dirk
See also CA 77-80

Vandenburgh, Jane . . . . CLC **59**

Vanderhaeghe, Guy 1951- . . . . CLC **41**
See also CA 113

van der Post, Laurens (Jan) 1906- . . . CLC **5**
See also CA 5-8R; CANR 35

van de Wetering, Janwillem 1931- . . CLC **47**
See also CA 49-52; CANR 4

Van Dine, S. S. . . . . TCLC **23**
See also Wright, Willard Huntington

Van Doren, Carl (Clinton)
1885-1950 . . . . TCLC **18**
See also CA 111

Van Doren, Mark 1894-1972 . . . . . CLC **6, 10**
See also CA 1-4R; 37-40R; CANR 3;
DLB 45; MTCW

Van Druten, John (William)
1901-1957 . . . . TCLC **2**
See also CA 104; DLB 10

Van Duyn, Mona (Jane)
1921- . . . . CLC **3, 7, 63**
See also CA 9-12R; CANR 7, 38; DLB 5

Van Dyne, Edith
See Baum, L(yman) Frank

van Itallie, Jean-Claude 1936- . . . . CLC **3**
See also CA 45-48; CAAS 2; CANR 1, 48;
DLB 7

van Ostaijen, Paul 1896-1928 . . . . . TCLC **33**

Van Peebles, Melvin 1932- . . . . . . CLC **2, 20**
See also BW 2; CA 85-88; CANR 27

Vansittart, Peter 1920- . . . . CLC **42**
See also CA 1-4R; CANR 3

Van Vechten, Carl 1880-1964 . . . . . . CLC **33**
See also CA 89-92; DLB 4, 9, 51

Van Vogt, A(lfred) E(lton) 1912- . . . . . CLC **1**
See also CA 21-24R; CANR 28; DLB 8;
SATA 14

Varda, Agnes 1928- . . . . CLC **16**
See also CA 116; 122

Vargas Llosa, (Jorge) Mario (Pedro)
1936- . . . . CLC **3, 6, 9, 10, 15, 31, 42, 85;
DA; HLC**
See also CA 73-76; CANR 18, 32, 42;
DLB 145; HW; MTCW

Vasiliu, Gheorghe 1881-1957
See Bacovia, George
See also CA 123

Vassa, Gustavus
See Equiano, Olaudah

Vassilikos, Vassilis 1933- . . . . CLC **4, 8**
See also CA 81-84

Vaughan, Henry 1621-1695 . . . . LC **27**
See also DLB 131

Vaughn, Stephanie . . . . CLC **62**

Vazov, Ivan (Minchov)
1850-1921 . . . . TCLC **25**
See also CA 121; DLB 147

Veblen, Thorstein (Bunde)
1857-1929 . . . . TCLC **31**
See also CA 115

Vega, Lope de 1562-1635 . . . . LC **23**

Venison, Alfred
See Pound, Ezra (Weston Loomis)

Verdi, Marie de
See Mencken, H(enry) L(ouis)

Verdu, Matilde
See Cela, Camilo Jose

Verga, Giovanni (Carmelo)
1840-1922 . . . . TCLC **3**
See also CA 104; 123

Vergil
70B.C.-19B.C. . . . . . CMLC **9; DA; PC 12**

Verhaeren, Emile (Adolphe Gustave)
1855-1916 . . . . TCLC **12**
See also CA 109

Verlaine, Paul (Marie)
1844-1896 . . . . NCLC **2, 51; PC 2**

Verne, Jules (Gabriel)
1828-1905 . . . . TCLC **6, 52**
See also CA 110; 131; DLB 123; JRDA;
MAICYA; SATA 21

Very, Jones 1813-1880 . . . . NCLC **9**
See also DLB 1

Vesaas, Tarjei 1897-1970 . . . . CLC **48**
See also CA 29-32R

Vialis, Gaston
See Simenon, Georges (Jacques Christian)

Vian, Boris 1920-1959 . . . . TCLC **9**
See also CA 106; DLB 72

Wilde, Oscar (Fingal O'Flahertie Wills)
1854(?)-1900 .... **TCLC 1, 8, 23, 41; DA;
SSC 11; WLC**
See also CA 104; 119; CDBLB 1890-1914;
DLB 10, 19, 34, 57, 141; SATA 24

Wilder, Billy .... **CLC 20**
See also Wilder, Samuel
See also DLB 26

Wilder, Samuel 1906-
See Wilder, Billy
See also CA 89-92

Wilder, Thornton (Niven)
1897-1975 ...... **CLC 1, 5, 6, 10, 15, 35,
82; DA; DC 1; WLC**
See also AITN 2; CA 13-16R; 61-64;
CANR 40; DLB 4, 7, 9; MTCW

Wilding, Michael 1942- .... **CLC 73**
See also CA 104; CANR 24

Wiley, Richard 1944- .... **CLC 44**
See also CA 121; 129

Wilhelm, Kate .... **CLC 7**
See also Wilhelm, Katie Gertrude
See also CAAS 5; DLB 8

Wilhelm, Katie Gertrude 1928-
See Wilhelm, Kate
See also CA 37-40R; CANR 17, 36; MTCW

Wilkins, Mary
See Freeman, Mary Eleanor Wilkins

Willard, Nancy 1936- .... **CLC 7, 37**
See also CA 89-92; CANR 10, 39; CLR 5;
DLB 5, 52; MAICYA; MTCW;
SATA 37, 71; SATA-Brief 30

Williams, C(harles) K(enneth)
1936- .... **CLC 33, 56**
See also CA 37-40R; DLB 5

Williams, Charles
See Collier, James L(incoln)

Williams, Charles (Walter Stansby)
1886-1945 .... **TCLC 1, 11**
See also CA 104; DLB 100, 153

Williams, (George) Emlyn
1905-1987 .... **CLC 15**
See also CA 104; 123; CANR 36; DLB 10,
77; MTCW

Williams, Hugo 1942- .... **CLC 42**
See also CA 17-20R; CANR 45; DLB 40

Williams, J. Walker
See Wodehouse, P(elham) G(renville)

Williams, John A(lfred)
1925- .... **CLC 5, 13; BLC**
See also BW 2; CA 53-56; CAAS 3;
CANR 6, 26; DLB 2, 33

Williams, Jonathan (Chamberlain)
1929- .... **CLC 13**
See also CA 9-12R; CAAS 12; CANR 8;
DLB 5

Williams, Joy 1944- .... **CLC 31**
See also CA 41-44R; CANR 22, 48

Williams, Norman 1952- .... **CLC 39**
See also CA 118

Williams, Sherley Anne
1944- .... **CLC 89; BLC**
See also BW 2; CA 73-76; CANR 25;
DLB 41; SATA 78

Williams, Shirley
See Williams, Sherley Anne

Williams, Tennessee
1911-1983 ..... **CLC 1, 2, 5, 7, 8, 11, 15,
19, 30, 39, 45, 71; DA; DC 4; WLC**
See also AITN 1, 2; CA 5-8R; 108;
CABS 3; CANR 31; CDALB 1941-1968;
DLB 7; DLBD 4; DLBY 83; MTCW

Williams, Thomas (Alonzo)
1926-1990 .... **CLC 14**
See also CA 1-4R; 132; CANR 2

Williams, William C.
See Williams, William Carlos

Williams, William Carlos
1883-1963 .... **CLC 1, 2, 5, 9, 13, 22, 42,
67; DA; PC 7**
See also CA 89-92; CANR 34;
CDALB 1917-1929; DLB 4, 16, 54, 86;
MTCW

Williamson, David (Keith) 1942- .... **CLC 56**
See also CA 103; CANR 41

Williamson, Ellen Douglas 1905-1984
See Douglas, Ellen
See also CA 17-20R; 114; CANR 39

Williamson, Jack .... **CLC 29**
See also Williamson, John Stewart
See also CAAS 8; DLB 8

Williamson, John Stewart 1908-
See Williamson, Jack
See also CA 17-20R; CANR 23

Willie, Frederick
See Lovecraft, H(oward) P(hillips)

Willingham, Calder (Baynard, Jr.)
1922-1995 .... **CLC 5, 51**
See also CA 5-8R; 147; CANR 3; DLB 2,
44; MTCW

Willis, Charles
See Clarke, Arthur C(harles)

Willy
See Colette, (Sidonie-Gabrielle)

Willy, Colette
See Colette, (Sidonie-Gabrielle)

Wilson, A(ndrew) N(orman) 1950- .. **CLC 33**
See also CA 112; 122; DLB 14

Wilson, Angus (Frank Johnstone)
1913-1991 .... **CLC 2, 3, 5, 25, 34**
See also CA 5-8R; 134; CANR 21; DLB 15,
139; MTCW

Wilson, August
1945- .. **CLC 39, 50, 63; BLC; DA; DC 2**
See also BW 2; CA 115; 122; CANR 42;
MTCW

Wilson, Brian 1942- .... **CLC 12**

Wilson, Colin 1931- .... **CLC 3, 14**
See also CA 1-4R; CAAS 5; CANR 1, 22,
33; DLB 14; MTCW

Wilson, Dirk
See Pohl, Frederik

Wilson, Edmund
1895-1972 .... **CLC 1, 2, 3, 8, 24**
See also CA 1-4R; 37-40R; CANR 1, 46;
DLB 63; MTCW

Wilson, Ethel Davis (Bryant)
1888(?)-1980 .... **CLC 13**
See also CA 102; DLB 68; MTCW

Wilson, John 1785-1854 .... **NCLC 5**

Wilson, John (Anthony) Burgess 1917-1993
See Burgess, Anthony
See also CA 1-4R; 143; CANR 2, 46;
MTCW

Wilson, Lanford 1937- .... **CLC 7, 14, 36**
See also CA 17-20R; CABS 3; CANR 45;
DLB 7

Wilson, Robert M. 1944- .... **CLC 7, 9**
See also CA 49-52; CANR 2, 41; MTCW

Wilson, Robert McLiam 1964- ..... **CLC 59**
See also CA 132

Wilson, Sloan 1920- .... **CLC 32**
See also CA 1-4R; CANR 1, 44

Wilson, Snoo 1948- .... **CLC 33**
See also CA 69-72

Wilson, William S(mith) 1932- ..... **CLC 49**
See also CA 81-84

Winchilsea, Anne (Kingsmill) Finch Counte
1661-1720 .... **LC 3**

Windham, Basil
See Wodehouse, P(elham) G(renville)

Wingrove, David (John) 1954- ...... **CLC 68**
See also CA 133

Winters, Janet Lewis .... **CLC 41**
See also Lewis, Janet
See also DLBY 87

Winters, (Arthur) Yvor
1900-1968 .... **CLC 4, 8, 32**
See also CA 11-12; 25-28R; CAP 1;
DLB 48, MTCW

Winterson, Jeanette 1959- .... **CLC 64**
See also CA 136

Wiseman, Frederick 1930- .... **CLC 20**

Wister, Owen 1860-1938 .... **TCLC 21**
See also CA 108; DLB 9, 78; SATA 62

Witkacy
See Witkiewicz, Stanislaw Ignacy

Witkiewicz, Stanislaw Ignacy
1885-1939 .... **TCLC 8**
See also CA 105

Wittgenstein, Ludwig (Josef Johann)
1889-1951 .... **TCLC 59**
See also CA 113

Wittig, Monique 1935(?)- .... **CLC 22**
See also CA 116; 135; DLB 83

Wittlin, Jozef 1896-1976 .... **CLC 25**
See also CA 49-52; 65-68; CANR 3

Wodehouse, P(elham) G(renville)
1881-1975 ... **CLC 1, 2, 5, 10, 22; SSC 2**
See also AITN 2; CA 45-48; 57-60;
CANR 3, 33; CDBLB 1914-1945;
DLB 34; MTCW; SATA 22

Woiwode, L.
See Woiwode, Larry (Alfred)

Woiwode, Larry (Alfred) 1941-... **CLC 6, 10**
See also CA 73-76; CANR 16; DLB 6

Wojciechowska, Maia (Teresa)
1927- .... **CLC 26**
See also AAYA 8; CA 9-12R; CANR 4, 41;
CLR 1; JRDA; MAICYA; SAAS 1;
SATA 1, 28

Yourcenar, Marguerite
1903-1987 . . . . CLC **19, 38, 50, 87**
See also CA 69-72; CANR 23; DLB 72;
DLBY 88; MTCW

Yurick, Sol 1925- . . . . CLC **6**
See also CA 13-16R; CANR 25

Zabolotskii, Nikolai Alekseevich
1903-1958 . . . . TCLC **52**
See also CA 116

Zamiatin, Yevgenii
See Zamyatin, Evgeny Ivanovich

Zamora, Bernice (B. Ortiz)
1938- . . . . CLC **89; HLC**
See also DLB 82; HW

Zamyatin, Evgeny Ivanovich
1884-1937 . . . . TCLC **8, 37**
See also CA 105

Zangwill, Israel 1864-1926. . . . . . . TCLC **16**
See also CA 109; DLB 10, 135

Zappa, Francis Vincent, Jr. 1940-1993
See Zappa, Frank
See also CA 108; 143

Zappa, Frank . . . . CLC **17**
See also Zappa, Francis Vincent, Jr.

Zaturenska, Marya 1902-1982. . . . CLC **6, 11**
See also CA 13-16R; 105; CANR 22

Zelazny, Roger (Joseph) 1937- . . . . . CLC **21**
See also AAYA 7; CA 21-24R; CANR 26;
DLB 8; MTCW; SATA 57;
SATA-Brief 39

Zhdanov, Andrei A(lexandrovich)
1896-1948 . . . . TCLC **18**
See also CA 117

Zhukovsky, Vasily 1783-1852 . . . . NCLC **35**

Ziegenhagen, Eric . . . . CLC **55**

Zimmer, Jill Schary
See Robinson, Jill

Zimmerman, Robert
See Dylan, Bob

Zindel, Paul 1936- . . . CLC **6, 26; DA; DC 5**
See also AAYA 2; CA 73-76; CANR 31;
CLR 3; DLB 7, 52; JRDA; MAICYA;
MTCW; SATA 16, 58

Zinov'Ev, A. A.
See Zinoviev, Alexander (Aleksandrovich)

Zinoviev, Alexander (Aleksandrovich)
1922- . . . . CLC **19**
See also CA 116; 133; CAAS 10

Zoilus
See Lovecraft, H(oward) P(hillips)

Zola, Emile (Edouard Charles Antoine)
1840-1902 . . . . . . TCLC **1, 6, 21, 41; DA;**
WLC
See also CA 104; 138; DLB 123

Zoline, Pamela 1941- . . . . CLC **62**

Zorrilla y Moral, Jose 1817-1893. . NCLC **6**

Zoshchenko, Mikhail (Mikhailovich)
1895-1958 . . . . TCLC **15; SSC 15**
See also CA 115

Zuckmayer, Carl 1896-1977. . . . . . . CLC **18**
See also CA 69-72; DLB 56, 124

Zuk, Georges
See Skelton, Robin

Zukofsky, Louis
1904-1978 . . . . CLC **1, 2, 4, 7, 11, 18;**
PC 11
See also CA 9-12R; 77-80; CANR 39;
DLB 5; MTCW

Zweig, Paul 1935-1984. . . . . CLC **34, 42**
See also CA 85-88; 113

Zweig, Stefan 1881-1942 . . . . TCLC **17**
See also CA 112; DLB 81, 118

Literary Criticism Series
Cumulative Topic Index

This index lists all topic entries in Gale's *Classical and Medieval Literature Criticism, Contemporary Literary Criticism, Literature Criticism from 1400 to 1800, Nineteenth-Century Literature Criticism,* and *Twentieth-Century Literary Criticism.*

LC Cumulative Nationality Index

LC Cumulative Title Index

The Art of Poetry (Boileau-Despreaux)
See *L'art poétique*
"The Art of Procuring Pleasant Dreams"
(Franklin) **25**:141
Art of Reasoning (Condillac)
See *Art de raisonner*
"The Art of Sinking in Poetry" (Pope)
See "Peri Bathous; or, The Art of Sinking in
Poetry"
"The Art of the Paper War" (Hopkinson)
25:271
Art of Thinking (Condillac)
See *Art de penser*
The Art of War (Machiavelli)
See *Libro della arte della guerra*
Art of Writing (Condillac)
See *Art d'écrire*
L'art poétique (*The Art of Poetry*) (Boileau-
Despreaux) **3**:16, 22, 25-35, 39
Art Poétique (Ronsard)
See *L'abbrégé de l'art poétique françois*
Arud risālesi (Babur) **18**:89-90
"A sa Muse" (Ronsard) **6**:430
"Ascension" (Donne) **24**:167
"Ascension Day" (Vaughan) **27**:323, 340, 383
"Ascension-Hymn" (Vaughan) **27**:323, 327
"The Ascension of Our Lord Jesus Christ"
(Smart) **3**:378
Ascent of Mount Carmel (John of the Cross)
See *Subida del Monte Carmelo*
"Asclepiads" (Sidney) **19**:326
Ash'i'atu 'l Lama'át (*Rays of the Flashes*)
(Jami) **9**:67
The Ash Wednesday Supper (Bruno)
See *La cena de le ceneri*
"L'asino d'oro" ("The Golden Ass")
(Machiavelli) **8**:128, 135, 178-79
"Ask me no more where Jove bestows"
(Carew) **13**:11, 20, 28-9, 58
"As Love and I, Late Harbour'd in One Inne"
(Drayton)
See "Sonnet LIX"
"A son ame" (Ronsard) **6**:436
"A son livre" (Ronsard) **6**:425-27, 433-34
"Aspiración" ("Aspiration") (Quevedo)
23:178
"Aspiration" (Quevedo)
See "Aspiración"
"The Ass" (Vaughan) **27**:300, 315, 338, 340
"Assaulted and Pursued Chastity" (Cavendish)
30:186, 188-189
*An assertion of the Seven Sacraments, against
Martin Luther* (Henry VIII)
See *Assertio septem sacramentorum adversus
Martinum Lutherum haeresiarchon*
*Assertio septem sacramentorum adversus
Martinum Lutherum haeresiarchon* (*An
assertion of the Seven Sacraments, against
Martin Luther; Defense of the Seven
Sacraments against Martin Luther*) (Henry
VIII) **10**:117-118, 120-22, 133-34, 138-39,
141-43, 146-47
The Assignation (Dryden) **3**:230
The Ass of Silenius (Bruno) **27**:96
"As Spring the Winter Doth Succeed"
(Bradstreet) **4**:99
"The Ass's Skin" (Perrault)
See "Peau d'ane"
"Astrea Redux. A Poem on the Happy
Restoration and Return of His Sacred
Majesty Charles the Second" (Dryden)
3:178, 223, 225-26; **21**:85

"Les Astres" ("Hymne des astres") (Ronsard)
6:410, 422, 429
"Astrologer" (Butler) **16**:55
*Astronomia magna, or the Whole Sagacious
Philosophy of the Great and Small World*
(Paracelsus) **14**:199
Astronomical Libra (Siguenza y Gongora)
See *Libra astronomica y philosophica*
Astrophel and Stella (Sidney) **19**:318-19, 329,
334, 345, 352, 354, 358, 360-61, 374-76, 391-
97, 406, 409, 413-15, 421-22, 424
"Astrophel: A Pastoral Elegy" (Spenser)
5:312, 314, 354
"As virtuous men pass mildly away" (Donne)
See "A Valediction: forbidding mourning"
"As Weary Pilgrim" ("A Pilgrim")
(Bradstreet) **4**:98, 102, 108
Athaliah (Racine)
See *Athalie*
Athalie (*Athaliah*) (Racine) **28**:295-97, 302,
305, 309, 311-13, 315-16, 344, 346, 349, 351-
53, 355-58, 365, 371, 374, 378-79, 381
Athalie (Voltaire) **14**:354
"A' the Airts" (Burns)
See "Of A' the Airts"
"The Atheist" (Donne) **10**:30
"The Atheist and the Acorn" (Winchilsea)
3:451
"At Roslin Inn" (Burns) **29**:59
Attila (Corneille) **28**:5, 16, 29, 33, 35, 37
"Attributes of the Supreme Being" (Smart)
3:399
"Au beuf qui tout le jour" (Ronsard) **6**:433-
34
Audiencias del rey Don Pedro (*The Royal
Hearings of King Pedro*) (Vega) **23**:402
"Au feu roi sur l'heureux succez du voyage de
Sedan" (Malherbe) **5**:184
De augmentis scientiarum (*De Dignitate et
Augmentis Scientiarum*) (Bacon) **18**:111,
117-18, 120, 126, 146, 152-53, 161-62, 168,
174, 178, 187, 193, 195
Aui maux raisonnables (Lesage) **28**:208
Aula (Hutten) **16**:239-41, 246
"The Auld Farmer's New Year Morning
Salutation" (Burns)
See "The Auld Farmer's New Year Morning
Salutation"
"The Auld Farmer's New Year's Day Address
to His Auld Mare Maggie" (Burns) **3**:57,
60, 64, 67, 87, 93; **29**:4-6, 29, 64
"Auld Lang Syne" (Burns) **3**:561, 62, 66, 78;
29:93
"Auld Lang Syne" (Ramsay) **29**:320
Auld Reikie (Fergusson) **29**:179, 181-84, 186-
87
"A une jeune veuve" (Rousseau)
See "A une veuve"
"A une veuve" ("A une jeune veuve")
(Rousseau) **9**:340, 344
*Aunswere to Frithes Letter agaynst the Blessed
Sacramen of the Aulter* (*Letter*) (More)
10:366, 398
"Au prince de Vendôme" (Rousseau) **9**:340
"Au prince Eugêne de Savoie, après la paix de
Passarowitz" (Rousseau) **9**:340, 344-45
Aureng-Zebe (Dryden) **3**:193, 222, 232-33;
21:72, 75, 88, 120
"Au roi de la Grande-Bretagne" (Rousseau)
9:344
"Au roi de Pologne" (Rousseau) **9**:344

La Aurora en Copacavana (Calderon de la
Barca) **23**:19, 22
Aussichten zu einer Experimentalseelenlehre
(Moritz) **2**:235-36
*The Austrian in Love; or, The Love and Life
Story of Sorona, Incomparable in Virtues and
Beauty* (Beer)
See *Der verliebte Österreicher*
"The Author" (Churchill) **3**:150-51, 155-56,
159-60, 163
*The Author's Apology for Heroic Poetry and
Poetic License* (*Apology for Heroic Poetry*)
(Dryden) **3**:197, 236, 238; **21**:66, 85
*The Authors Dreame to the Ladie Marie the
Countesse Dowager of Pembroke* (Lanyer)
30:251
*The Author's Farce and the Pleasures of the
Town* (Fielding) **1**:203, 219
"The Author's Life" (Fergusson) **29**:194
"Authors Motto" (Crashaw) **24**:75
"The Author to her Book" (Bradstreet)
4:107, 112; **30**:130-1, 140-1
"Author to His Book" (Beer) **5**:59
"The Author upon Himself" (Swift) **1**:482,
523
Autobiography (Cellini)
See *Vita di Benvenuto Cellini*
Autobiography (Fanshawe)
See *Memoirs of Lady Fanshawe*
*The Autobiography and Correspondence of
Mary Granville (Mrs. Delany)* (*Life and
Correspondence*) (Delany) **12**:135, 140, 143,
148-51, 154
The Autobiography of Benjamin Franklin
(Franklin) **25**:113, 117-24, 129-30, 132,
134, 138, 144-49, 151-53, 155, 157, 161-63,
166, 168-73, 175-76, 179-83, 185-86, 188-89
*The Autobiography of Venerable Marie of the
Incarnation* (Marie de l'Incarnation)
See *Relation autobiographique*
Aut regem aut fatuum (Erasmus) **16**:198
Autres baludes (Christine de Pizan) **9**:41
"Autumn" (Pope) **3**:334
Autumn (Thomson) **16**:363-64, 372-74, 380-
84, 395, 402-05, 411-13, 415, 419, 424-26,
432; **29**:378-79, 381, 384-85, 387, 393-94,
403, 415
"Aux princes chrétiens" (Rousseau) **9**:340,
344
"Aux Suisses" (Rousseau) **9**:344
*Les Avantages que l'établissement du
christianisme a procurÉs au genre humain*
(*The Advantages that the Establishment of
Christianity Has Conferred upon the Human
Race*) (Turgot) **26**:348, 370
"Avant-entrée" (Ronsard) **6**:431
L'avare (*The Miser*) (Moliere) **10**:268, 271,
280, 283-85, 287, 290-91, 293, 297, 313, 341,
343, 345-46; **28**:245, 255-56, 258-59, 261,
266, 270, 275
Aventure indienne (Voltaire) **14**:346
Les aventures de Monsieur Robert Chevalier
(*Adventures of the Chevalier de Beauchêne*)
(Lesage) **2**:176, 182; **28**:200, 203-07, 210-11
Avision (Christine de Pizan)
See *Lavision-Christine*
Le avventure della villeggiatura (Goldoni)
4:265-66
L'avvocato veneziano (Goldoni) **4**:262
"Away, away, my cares" (Juana Ines de la
Cruz)
See "Afuera, afuera, ansias mías"

Title Index

Title Index

Title Index

Title Index

Title Index

Title Index

Title Index

Title Index

Title Index

Title Index

"To the Countesse of Bedford. 'This twilight of'" (Donne) 10:9

"To the Countesse of Huntingdon. 'That unripe side'" (Donne) 10:36

"To the Countess of Anglesie upon the immoderately-by-her lamented death of her Husband" (Carew) 13:49-50

"To the Countess of Burlington" (Garrick) 15:97

"To the Countess of Roscommon" (Philips) 30:315

"To the De'il" (Burns)
See "Address to the De'il"

"To the doubtfull Reader" (Lanyer) 30:249

"To the Duchess of Ormond" (Dryden) 3:243; 21:87

"To the Earle of Portland, Lord Treasurer; on the marriage of his Sonne" (Davenant) 13:205

"To the Eccho" (Winchilsea) 3:454

"To the E. of D." (Donne) 24:169

"To the Excellent Mrs Anne Owen upon receiving the Name of Lucasia and Adoption into our Society December 28 1651" (Philips) 30:308

"To the Holy Bible" (Vaughan) 27:337, 389

"To the Honourable Charles Montague, Esq." (Prior) 4.461, 465

"To the Honour of Pimps and Pimping; dedicated to the Court; and written at a Time when such were most considerable there" (Wycherley) 21:348

"To the King" (Herrick) 13:395

"To the King" (Young) 3:488

"To the King at his entrance into Saxham" (Carew) 13:61

"To the King on New-yeares day 1630" (Davenant) 13:205

"TO THE KING, to cure the Evill" (Herrick) 13:395-96

"TO THE KING, upon His Comming with His Army into the West" (Herrick) 13:389

"To the Lady Castlemaine, upon Her Incouraging His First Play" (Dryden) 3:223

"To the Lady Crew, upon the Death of Her Child" ("To Lady Crew, upon the Death of Her Child") (Herrick) 13:353, 366

"To the Linden Tree" (Kochanowski)
See "Na lipe"

"To the little Spinners" (Herrick) 13:374

"To the Lord Cary of Lepington" (Davenant) 13:206

"To the Maids to walk abroad" (Herrick) 13:360

"To the Majestie of King James" (Drayton) 8:30

To the Memory of a Lady Lately Deceased: A Monody (*Monody*) (Lyttelton) 10:198-99, 201, 203, 207, 209-10, 215

"To the Memory of Master Newbery" (Smart) 3:374

"To the Memory of Mr. Congreve" ("A Poem to the Memory of Mr. Congreve") (Thomson) 16:428-29

"To the Memory of Mr. Oldham" (Dryden) 3:201

"To the Memory of My Beloved, the Author, Mr. William Shakespeare, and What He Hath Left Us" (Jonson) 6:348, 350

To the Memory of Sir Isaac Newton (Thomson)
See *A Poem Sacred to the Memory of Sir Isaac Newton*

"To the Mcmory of thc Right Honourable the Lord Talbot" (Thomson) 16:428

"To the morning" (Crashaw)
See "To the morning in satisfaction for sleep"

"To the morning in satisfaction for sleep" ("To the morning") (Crashaw) 24:9, 53

"To the Name Above Every Name" (Crashaw)
See "Hymn to the Name above every Name-the Name of Jesus"

"To the Name of Jesus" (Crashaw)
See "Hymn to the Name above every Name-the Name of Jesus"

"To the New Yeere" ("Ode on the New Year") (Drayton) 8:17, 27

"To the Nightengale" (Thomson) 16:427

"To the Nightingale" ("The Nightingale") (Winchilsea) 3:441-42, 444, 447, 451, 454

"To the Noble Palemon on His Incomparable Discourse of Friendship" (Philips) 30:281

"To the Painter" (Carew) 13:63

"To the Ph--an Ode" (Ramsay) 29:330, 337

"To the Pious Memory of C. W. Esquire" (Vaughan) 27:376

"To the Pious Memory of the Accomplisht Young Lady Mrs. Anne Killigrew" (Dryden) 3:186, 216, 223

"To the Principal and Professors of the University of St. andrews, on their superb treat to Dr. Samuel Johnson" (Fergusson) 29:189, 191, 194, 211, 216, 231

"To the Queen" (Carew) 13:59

"To the Queenes most Excellent Majestie" (Lanyer) 10:183

"To the Queen of inconstancie" (Philips) 30:309

"To the Queen's Majesty" (Crashaw) 24:38-9

"To the Queen's most excellent Majestic" (Lanyer) 30:245

"To the Reader of Master William Davenant's Play" (Carew) 13:67

"To the Reader of My Works" (Cavendish) 30:200-03, 225

"To the Reader of These Sonnets" (Drayton) 8:37

"To the Reverend Shade of his Religious Father" (Herrick) 13:350

"To the Rev John M'Math" (Burns) 29:32

"To the Right Honorable William, Earl of Dartmouth, His Majesty's Principal Secretary of State for North America" (Wheatley) 3:415, 423, 427, 429, 434

"To the River Isca" (Vaughan) 27:359

"To the River Lodon" (Warton) 15:435, 443

"To the Rose" (Herrick) 13:334

"To the Rose. Song" ("Song") (Herrick) 13:398

"To the Royal Academy" (Franklin)
See "Letter to the Royal Academy"

"To the Same (i.e., to Celia)" (Jonson) 6:349

"To the same Party Counsel concerning her choice" (Crashaw) 24:62

"To the Toothache" ("Address to the Toothache") (Burns) 3:67, 85

"To the Tron-Kirk Bell" (Fergusson) 29:169, 179, 189, 193, 205, 217, 225

"To the truly Noble Mrs Anne Owne on my first Approaches" (Philips) 30:300

"To the two Universities" (Cavendish) 30:200

"To the University of Cambridge, in New England" (Wheatley) 3:413, 415-16, 423, 427, 429

"To the Vertuous Reader" ("Epistle to the Vertuous Reader") (Lanyer) 10:181-82, 184, 190; 30:243-44, 249, 252, 260

"To the Virginian Voyage" ("Virginian Ode") (Drayton) 8:18, 25-7, 30, 42-5

"To the Virgins, to Make Much of Time" ("Gather Ye Rosebuds while Ye May") (Herrick) 13:319, 337, 354, 357, 361, 367

"To the Weaver's gin ye go" (Burns) 29:22, 54-5

"To the Woodlark" (Burns) 3:81

"The Tournament" (Chatterton) 3:124, 135

Tour of Corsica (Boswell)
See *An Account of Corsica, The Journal of a Tour to that Island; and the Memoirs of Pascal Paoli*

A Tour through the Whole Island of Great Britain (Defoe) 1:173-74

"To Violets" (Herrick) 13:337

"To William Simpson of Ochiltree, May 1785" (Burns)
See "Epistle to William Simpson of Ochiltree, May 1785"

"The Town and Country Contrasted. In an Epistle to a Friend" (Fergusson) 29:205

Town Eclogues (Montagu)
See *Court Poems*

The Town Fop; or, Sir Timothy Tawdrey (Behn) 1:33, 39, 46-7; 30:71-4, 81

Los trabajos de Persiles y Sigismunda (*Persiles y Sigismunda*) (Cervantes) 6:142-43, 151, 169-70, 174-76, 178, 180; 23:94-99, 111, 115, 120-21, 132-34, 143-44

Tractatus theologico-politicus continens dissertationes all quot, quibus ostenditur libertatem philosophandi non tantum salva pietate, & reipublicae (*Theological-Political Treatise*) (Spinoza) 9:393, 397-98, 402, 408-09, 418-19, 423-24, 431, 436, 438-40

"Tract on the Popery Laws" (Burke) 7:46

La tragedia por los celos (Castro) 19:7-8

The Tragedie of Mariam, Faire Queene of Jewry (*Mariam*) (Cary) 30:158-159, 162-64, 166-71

The Tragedie of Soliman and Perseda (*Hamlet*) (Kyd) 22:248, 254-55, 257, 259, 271

Tragedy (Pompey the Great; his faire Cornelias Tragedie; effected by her Father and Husbands downe-cast death and fortune; Solyman and Perseda) (Kyd) 22:246, 254

The Tragedy of Bussy D'Ambois (*Bussy D'Ambois; D'Ambois*) (Chapman) 22:3, 5, 7-8, 11, 15, 18-19, 20-2, 30-1, 34, 36-9, 40, 42, 44, 52, 54, 56, 57, 78-9, 80-1

The Tragedy of Caesar and Pompey (*Caesar and Pompey*) (Chapman) 22:7, 12-13, 15, 30, 34, 46-7, 54

Tragedy of Cato (Addison) 18:7, 10-11, 14-15, 17-19, 31-2, 46-7, 76-7

The Tragedy of Chabot, Admiral of France (*Chabot; Philip Chabot, Admiral of France*) (Chapman) 22:7, 13, 15, 45-6

The Tragedy of Cleopatra (*Cleopatra*) (Daniel) 24:85, 89, 98, 107, 112-15, 118, 122, 130-31, 134

The Tragedy of Dido, Queen of Carthage (*Dido, Queen of Carthage*) (Marlowe) 22:362

Title Index

ISBN 0-8103-9275-5